Environmental Law

Environmental Law
A0047089

Environmental Law

Stuart Bell

Eversheds Professor of Environmental Law,
Nottingham Law School, Nottingham Trent University

Donald McGillivray

Senior Lecturer in Law
University of Kent

OXFORD
UNIVERSITY PRESS

OXFORD
UNIVERSITY PRESS

Great Clarendon Street, Oxford OX2 6DP

Oxford University Press is a department of the University of Oxford.
It furthers the University's objective of excellence in research, scholarship,
and education by publishing worldwide in

Oxford New York

Auckland Cape Town Dar es Salaam Hong Kong Karachi
Kuala Lumpur Madrid Melbourne Mexico City Nairobi
New Delhi Shanghai Taipei Toronto

With offices in

Argentina Austria Brazil Chile Czech Republic France Greece
Guatemala Hungary Italy Japan Poland Portugal Singapore
South Korea Switzerland Thailand Turkey Ukraine Vietnam

Oxford is a registered trade mark of Oxford University Press
in the UK and in certain other countries

Published in the United States
by Oxford University Press Inc., New York

British Library Cataloguing in Publication Data
Data available

Library of Congress Cataloging in Publication Data
Data available

ISBN 0–19–926056–7   978–0–19–926056–0

10 9 8 7 6 5 4 3 2

Typeset by RefineCatch Limited, Bungay, Suffolk
Printed in Great Britain
on acid-free paper by
Ashford Colour Press Limited, Gosport, Hampshire

OUTLINE CONTENTS

DETAILED CONTENTS

The preface to the fifth edition of this book began with a lengthy plea in mitigation which was designed to explain the growth of the book from the original 15 chapters and 381 pages to its current gargantuan proportions. This plea consisted of five points. First, environmental law is becoming increasingly complex. Second, the breadth of sources of environmental law is increasing, with new approaches to environmental problems and burgeoning case law. Third, the maturing of the subject means that central principles such as sustainable development are much more coherent than they were in 1990. Fourth, there are a number of other shorter texts which are suitable if readers want a different approach. Finally and perhaps most importantly, the book reflects the personal choices and interests of its authors. These expand and change as new areas of the law develop.

All of these points remain equally valid for this edition. In terms of new legislation that has had to be taken account of, we have had, from the EC, a number of major pieces of legislation, including the Water Framework Directive and Directives on Environmental Liability, Strategic Environmental Assessment, and the setting up of an EC Emissions Trading Scheme; more producer responsibility directives (on End of Life Vehicles and on Waste Electrical and Electronic Equipment); revisions to the Large Combustion Plants Directive; new controls on emissions ceilings for air pollutants; measures on noise from products and on noise mapping; and directives giving effect to changes made to implement the seminal Aarhus Convention on public participation in environmental matters which came into force in 2001. Most of these have already been implemented through national regulations. At the international level the Stockholm Convention on Persistent Organic Pollutants and the Cartagena Biosafety Protocol have recently entered into force. The Kyoto Protocol has also come into force, albeit without Banquo at the feast. At national level we have had the Waste and Emissions Trading Act 2003 (which establishes trading systems for landfill capacity and atmospheric emissions); the Planning and Compulsory Purchase Act 2004 (which makes major changes to development planning); the Water Act 2003 (which makes amendments to many different aspects of water legislation); and the Household Waste Recycling Act 2003 (which deals with kerbside collection of waste for recycling).

In relation to the wider 'baggage' of environmental law, it goes without saying that this continues to evolve and expand. Important developments here include some key decisions from bodies like the World Trade Organization and arbitration tribunals which shed further light on the powers and duties of states seeking to protect the environment, and a continuing expansion in the number of judicial decisions at European and national level, particularly on things like the meaning of waste and waste management duties; duties under the Environmental Impact Assessment and Habitats Directives; the controls on statutory nuisances; and on environmental tort law. There have also been some important decisions on the role of the European Convention on Human Rights in relation to environmental protection, the main ones being the European Court of Human Rights' decision in the Heathrow Night Noise case (*Hatton v UK*) and the House of Lords' ruling in *Marcic v Thames Water Utilities*, both of which ended up with the higher court giving a more restrictive ruling on the scope of human rights to serve environmental protection purposes than the lower courts had done. In terms of developments to less formal sources of environmental law, notable developments include major revisions to the corpus of town and country planning policy and the continuing expansion of the Climate Change Programme.

There have also been some important institutional changes since the last edition. At departmental level, however, these have been driven less by a search for institutional coherence and more by the need to satisfy the power demands of authoritative figures within New Labour. Thus in 2001 the former Department of Environment, Transport and the Regions was split three ways, with a separate Transport Ministry returning to the fold, and the creation of the Department for the Environment, Food and Rural Affairs and the Office of the Deputy Prime Minister (which now deals with planning and environmental assessment matters). At the non-departmental level, there are to be changes, in England, to the main conservation and countryside bodies, with the creation of an Integrated Agency (now to be called Natural England) merging the functions of English Nature and the protective aspects of the Countryside Agency (in some ways taking us back to where we were before the NCC was divided in the early 1990s).

All of these developments present the usual challenges of trying to provide a useful overview and analysis of the present state of environmental law, as well as pointing to emerging trends. Our main aim in writing this sixth edition, however, has been threefold.

First, we have tried to strip out as much of the procedural detail as we reasonably can, especially from the later chapters, where we feel this would primarily be of interest to the practitioner rather than the student (to whom this book is primarily aimed). In an area like environmental law, however, where much of the law is essentially procedural, this is easier said than done. To give one example, the terms on which an environmental licence might be transferred to another operator might be regarded as mainly of commercial interest. However, if a licence can be transferred to a 'man of straw', or if continuing clean-up obligations could be avoided by such a transfer, then obviously these rules have environmental implications as much as they have a commercial focus. In addition, if too much procedural detail is stripped away, the overall shape of important areas of environmental law is distorted.

Second, we have tried to integrate better our general coverage of environmental law and policy in the first half of the book with the sectoral coverage in the latter chapters. Although, in our defence, we always thought that it was the job of students and teachers to do this, we have finally relented and have tried to give the reader more pointers, in particular about how the issues covered in the chapters in what is now Part III can be seen through some suggested frames introduced earlier in the book. We must stress, however, that these are just suggestions. As we try to explain in Chapter 1, there are different ways of writing a book on environmental law, and different kinds of connections (or disconnections) emerge whether one takes an approach based on the environmental media, the main threats to the environment, the different types of pollutants, or the things that are being protected. We hope that any attempt on our part to make connections does not result in any corresponding languor in the reader in making their own.

Third, and perhaps most importantly, we have made some changes to the general layout of the book, again aimed at making it more accessible to students of environmental law. Some of these (learning objectives, chapter summaries) are, by now, fairly common to student textbooks and require little comment, other than the usual caveat that we would hate to think that environmental law was ever actually taught in the mechanistic way that these pedagogic features might be used. Accordingly, we have not adopted the use of these features in a slavish fashion, preferring instead to try and break up text, distil detail, and highlight what we hope will be interesting aspects of topics which will contextualize matters. Weblinks are also increasingly common, and we have tried to give key links at the end of most of the chapters.

There is also an Online Resource Centre for this book. The idea behind this, which can be found at <www.oup.com/uk/booksites/law>, is that, on a chapter by chapter basis, it will contain links to the key documents that are referred to, as well as information on recent developments—such as summaries of important new cases or laws—which fall between editions of the book. The intention at this stage is not to establish a general environmental law portal through the Online Resource Centre—or to post model answers to the chapter-end questions that we pose—and there is some flexibility about how the web site develops over time.

The main pedagogic development that does deserve some comment is that we have moved away from a wholly linear text. Through boxed examples of varying kinds, each chapter tries to look in a little more depth at the leading cases, analyses of policy problems, institutional and legal developments, and so on. This gives the opportunity to highlight key issues and to make some of the connections mentioned above, but also in some cases to try to explore alternative interpretations of developments, or even 'the real story' behind a case (a particularly dispiriting feature of environmental law is that often the law may be progressed by legislation or by a case, but ultimately the environment still comes off second best).

A consequence of this change is that, even with using some tables and charts to condense the coverage (e.g. using timelines to chart historical developments) the overall length of the text has increased. The sheer size of the book may be daunting for some and we are aware that an increase in length may not be the best selling point. We know that few students, however, will read this book from cover to cover, and most will be directed towards particular chapters reflecting the nature of their study of environmental law, or will be drawn to issues that are of particular personal interest. Where, as with some of the coverage in Part III, the chapters remain lengthy, we trust that teachers will continue to take a sensible approach. For example, the chapter on water pollution and water quality continues to cover a lot of ground, including international water pollution conventions, EC water directives and their implementation, the development of national policy and legislation, criminal offences and the use of alternative regulatory instruments. Readers may find that they get more out of this material by seeing each of these as material that can be drawn upon when looking at wider issues such as EC environmental law or environmental crime (on which we have a new chapter) rather than ploughing through it comprehensively when 'doing water pollution'.

This is the first edition of the book that does not bear the name of Simon Ball. This is not to say that his influence on the work has diminished. The more that we rewrite this text, the more we appreciate just how incisive his work was in shaping this book (and environmental law as a whole) and introducing the subject to a generation of students, and just how enduring his legacy is. Again, we dedicate this to him. Any errors are, of course, ours.

Stuart would like to thank all those who have helped to flesh out any paucity of thought, sometimes without proper acknowledgement. Particular thanks go to Laurence Etherington who has had the good grace to participate freely and fully in sharing ideas and workloads. Thanks also to Bob Lee, Malcolm Forster, Stephen Tromans and Peter Kunzlik who have all offered useful insights and helpful suggestions. With a practitioner 'hat' on, thanks go to Paul Smith, Sarah Taylor, John De Belin and the many members of the Eversheds Regulatory team who illustrate the point that environmental law is best seen as law in action. The biggest and most heartfelt thanks are reserved for Philippa, Nicholas, Oliver, Andrew and Thomas. The large amount of time invested in this book over the years has meant much less time with them than they deserve and this debt will never truly be repaid.

Donald would like to thank, at Birkbeck, Patrick McAuslan, and at Kent, Bill Howarth, with whom it has been a great pleasure to teach and share ideas. Thanks also to the teaching teams at Birkbeck in Property Law, and at Kent in Tort Law and Property Law, which provided valuable tangential support, especially Tatiana Flessas, Andreas Philipopoulous-Mihaelopolous, John Wightman, Alan Thompson, Geoffrey Samuel, Kirsty Horsey, Nick Jackson, Anne Bottomley and Stuart Motha. Elsewhere, thanks to Chris Hilson, Ludwig Kramer, Maria Lee, Richard Macrory, Mike Purdue, Ray Purdy, Chris Rodgers, Andrea Ross-Robertson, Philippe Sands, Joanne Scott, Mark Stallworthy and Sharon Turner. Particular thanks to Mark Dean for technical support. Closer to home, the biggest debt is owed to Jane Holder, to Gus and Sam, and to Roddy and Ben, our new arrivals since the last edition. Jane in particular has worked tirelessly at keeping a home that is both functioning and intellectually stimulating, something that I fail to tell her as often or in as heartfelt a way as she deserves.

We have tried to state the law as at 1 February 2005, although certain important changes after that date have been added at proof stage. This means that we have not been able to incorporate substantive comment on, for example, the Clean Neighbourhoods and Environment Act 2005 which, amongst other things, makes a number of changes to the law on statutory nuisance, noise and waste (this will follow on the Online Resource Centre). We had hoped that this date might have been much sooner (some of the reasons why it was not are named above!). We are grateful for the faith that our publishers showed in, firstly, taking us into the OUP stable and, secondly, for their hard work and patience in seeing the book through to publication. Thanks in particular go to Christina White, Clare Brewer, Jasmin Naim, Sarah Hyland and Gabriella La Cava.

Stuart Bell
Donald McGillivray
August 2005

TABLE OF CASES

TABLE OF STATUTES

TABLE OF STATUTORY INSTRUMENTS

TABLE OF EUROPEAN LEGISLATION

Regulations

LIST OF BOXES

AEBC	Agriculture and Environment Biotechnology Commission
ACBE	Advisory Committee on Business and the Environment
ACEA	European Automobile Manufacturers Association
AONB	Area of Outstanding Natural Beauty
AQMA	Air Quality Management Area
AQS	air quality standard
ATF	authorized treatment facility
AWE	Atomic Weapons Establishment
BAT	best available techniques
BATNEEC	best available techniques not entailing excessive cost
BATRRT	best available treatment recovery and recycling techniques
BOD	biochemical oxygen demand
BPEO	best practicable environmental option
BPM	best practicable means
BREF	BAT Reference Document
BSE	Bovine spongiform encephalopathy
CAFE	Clean Air for Europe
CCL	Climate Change Levy
CERCLA	Comprehensive Environmental Response Compensation and Liability Act 1981
CFC	chlorofluorocarbon
CICS	Common Incident Classification Scheme
CITES	Convention on the International Trade in Endangered Species
COD	chemical oxygen demand
COPFS	Crown Office and Procurator Fiscal Service
COP	Conference of the Parties
CPRE	Campaign to Protect Rural England
CROWA	Countryside and Rights of Way Act
DEFRA	Department for Environment, Food and Rural Affairs
DETR	Department of the Environment, Transport, and the Regions
DLTR	Department of Local Government, Transport and the Regions
DOE	Department of the Environment
DTI	Department of Trade and Industry
EA	Environment Agency
EA	environmental assessment

EC	European Community
ECCP	European Climate Change Programme
ECHR	European Court of Human Rights
ECJ	European Court of Justice
ECSC	European Coal and Steel Commission
EEC	European Economic Community
EEZ	exclusive economic zone
EHS	Environmental and Heritage Service
EIA	Environmental Impact Assessment
ELV	End-of-Life Vehicle
EMAS	Eco-Management and Audit Scheme
EMEP	Programme for Monitoring and Evaluation of Long-Range Transmission of Air Pollutants in Europe
EMS	European Monetary System
EPAC	Environment Protection Advisory Committee
EPA	Environmental Protection Act
EPAQS	Expert Panel on Air Quality Standards
EPER	European Pollutant Emission Register
EQS	Environmental Quality Standard
ES	Environmental Statement
ESA	Environmentally Sensitive Area
EU	European Union
Euratom	European Atomic Energy Community
FOI	Freedom of Information
FTSE	Financial Times and the London Stock Exchange
GATS	General Agreement on Trade in Services
GATT	General Agreement on Tariffs and Trade
GBRs	General Binding Rules
GDPO	General Development Procedure Order
GEF	Global Environment Facility
GGI	Greening Government Initiative
GHI	Grant in Aid
GM	genetically modified
GMO	genetically modified organism
GQA	General Quality Assessment
HFC	hydrofluorocarbon
HMIP	Her Majesty's Inspectorate of Pollution
HMIPI	Her Majesty's Industrial Pollution Inspectorate
HSA	Hazardous substances authority

IAPI	Industrial Air Pollution Inspectorate
ICJ	International Court of Justice
ILC	International Law Commission
IMPEL	European Union Network for Implementation and Enforcement of Environmental Law
IPC	integrated pollution control
IPCC	Intergovernmental Panel on Climate Change
IPPC	integrated pollution prevention and control
ISO	International Organization for Standardization
ITLOS	International Tribunal on the Law of the Sea
IUCN	International Union for the Conservation of Nature
JNCC	Joint Nature Conservation Committee
JPL	Journal of Planning and Environment Law
LCPD	Large Combustion Plants Directive
LDD	Local Development Document
LDS	Local Development Scheme
LTP	Local Transport Plan
MARAD	The US Maritime administration
MARPOL	The International Convention for the Prevention of Pollution from Ships (1973)
MBC	Metropolitan Borough Council
MNR	Marine nature reserve
MOD	Ministry of Defence
MOX	Mixed Oxide Plant
MWDF	Minerals and Waste Development Framework
NDPB	Non-departmental public body
NGO	Non-governmental organization
NIMBY	Not in my back yard
NNR	National Nature Reserve
NPPG	National Planning Policy Guidance
NRA	National Rivers Authority
NVZ	Nitrate Vulnerable Zone
ODPM	Office of the Deputy Prime Minister
OFRs	Operating and Financial Reviews
Ofwat	Office of Water Services
OSPAR	The Convention for the Protection of the Marine Environment of the North-East Atlantic (1992)
PCP	pentachlorophenol
PCT	polychlorinated triphenyl
PFC	perfluorocarbon

POP   Persistent Organic Pollutant
PPC   Pollution Prevention and Control
PRN   packaging recovery note
PRTR   Pollutant Reference and Transfer Registry
PSA   Public Service Agreement
RCEP   Royal Commission on Environmental Pollution
RGP   Regional Planning Guidance
RPB   Regional Planning Body
RSPB   Royal Society for the Protection of Birds
RSPCA   Royal Society for the Prevention of Cruelty to Animals
RSS   Regional Spatial Strategy
SAC   special area of conservation
SARA   Superfund Amendments and Reauthorization Act 1980
SBT   Southern Bluefish Tuna Treaty
SEA   strategic environmental assessment
SEPA   Scottish Environment Protection Agency
SLF   substitute liquid fuel
SPA   special protection area
SPL   significant pollutant linkage
SPS   Agreement on the Application of Sanitary and Phytosanitary Measures
SPZ   simplified planning zone
SSSI   Site of Special Scientific Interest
TBT   Agreement on Technical Barriers to Trade

TED   turtle excluder device
THORP   Thermal Oxide Reprocessing Plant
TPO   Tree Preservation Order
TPR   Town Planning Review
UNECE   United Nations Economic Commission for Europe
UNEP   United Nations Environment Programme
USEPA   United States Environmental Protection Agency
VOC   volatile organic compound
WEEE   Waste Electrical and Electronic Equipment Directive
WHS   World Heritage Site
WMO   World Meteorological Organization
WSC   Water Supply Company
WTO   World Trade Organization
WWF   World Wide Fund for Nature

PART I

Introductory themes

1 What is environmental law? A brief introduction

 Overview

This introductory chapter deals with the difficult issue of defining environmental law for the purposes of this book. It covers the definition of certain key terms and provides an outline of some of the underlying themes which will be found in many chapters. It is designed to be used at the very beginning of a course of study to help establish a context for future study. The notes and questions at the end of the chapter are designed to provoke thought about the way in which law, policy, and rights might affect everyday environmental issues and problems.

After studying this chapter you should be able to:

✔ Understand basic definitions of 'the environment' and 'law'.
✔ Appreciate some of the difficulties of defining 'environmental law'.
✔ Understand the basic outline of some of the key themes of this book and the subject.
✔ Understand the basic interrelationship between environmental law and policy.
✔ Understand some of the different meanings of 'rights' within environmental law.

Why a book on environmental law?

Before we launch into a description of the subject it is perhaps pertinent to start with a few points of justification. Why have a book on environmental law? Without wanting to prejudge some of the matters which will be dealt with in other chapters we would like to propose some starting points, opinions which justify why we think the subject is important and why you should study it:

• The environment is important

There is a general recognition that the environment is important and that efforts should be made to protect it. It is clear that the general topic is one of the big issues, perhaps the biggest contemporary issue we face. Issues such as climate change and rising waste production require significant responses. Environmental considerations have become central to policy making and decision-making across a wide range of issues and it is increasingly perceived that environmental considerations are integral to all aspects of life.

• Protecting the environment presents a big challenge

It is a big challenge in political terms, since protection of the environment is high on most people's priorities in the 21st century. It is big in terms of the size of the problems faced and the solutions required; climate change, the destruction of the ozone layer, acid rain, deforestation and toxic waste are all global issues which require an appropriately global response. It is big in terms of the range of problems and issues—air pollution, water pollution, noise pollution, waste management, radioactivity, pesticides, countryside protection, conservation of wildlife—the list is virtually endless. Finally, it is big in terms of the knowledge and skills required to understand a particular issue. Law is only one element in what is a major cross-disciplinary topic. Lawyers need some understanding of the scientific, political, and economic processes involved in environmental degradation. Equally, all those whose activities and interests relate to the environment need to acquire an understanding of the structure and content of environmental law, since it has a large and increasing role to play in environmental protection.

• Law is central to the management of the environment

This remains the case despite the increasing use of voluntary approaches and market mechanisms such as taxes, subsidies, and instruments which affect the behaviour of consumers. To some extent the centrality of environmental law as a tool to manage the environment merely reflects the regrouping or re-categorization of matters that have always been there. Of course this depends on the tricky question of the exact scope and definition of 'environmental law' which the rest of this chapter seeks to answer.

• Environmental protection laws are vast in numbers and complexity

The last 10 or so years have seen a dramatic increase in the number and complexity of laws which seek to protect the environment. Numerous EC Directives have been agreed. There are major pieces of domestic legislation (such as the Environment Act 1995, the Water Resources Act 1991 and the Countryside and Rights of Way Act 2000); and there is a vast amount of secondary legislation and an even vaster amount of policy and guidance.

• Environmental disputes and cases with an environmental element are becoming more frequent

It is increasingly the case that the public views the results of 'environmental' decisions as unsatisfactory—in other words there is a perception that policies and decision-making procedures are failing the public and the environment. This has led to the increasing use of law by environmental groups as an alternative to direct action and to pressure on the planning system as local residents protect their own personal and property interests against unwelcome developments.

What is environmental law?

In identifying the subject matter of this book, it is first necessary to consider whether there is any identifiable subject which could be termed 'environmental law'. It might seem to be a defensive or unnecessary starting point but it could be argued that the boundaries of the subject are not particularly well defined[1] or that the subject is not necessarily distinctive. This potential lack of doctrinal certainty has, in the United Kingdom at least, led to a

1. See Z. Plater, (1999) 23 Harvard Environmental Law Review 359, and R. Lazarus, (1999) 23 Harvard Environmental Law Review 327.

number of attempts to 'justify' the existence of a coherent subject known as environmental law as a discrete legal subject area.[2] A major aim of this book is, therefore, to illustrate the proposition that there has developed such a thing as environmental law and whilst not seeking to straitjacket the boundaries of the subject, to provide an outline of a number of key components which form the substantive heart of the subject.

Most lawyers are brought up on the idea that there are a number of core, or basic, subjects which are essentially about techniques and in which a set of central organizing principles can be distilled from the law. Criminal law, constitutional law, public law, contract law, torts, equity and property law would be good examples. The traditional view would then be that, alongside those basic subjects, there are as many areas of law as there are areas of life, in each of which the techniques of the basic subjects are used; for example, the law relating to family relationships, the law relating to housing. But over a period of time, there is no doubt that these topic-related areas build up their own principles and reasoning processes (e.g. through the application and interpretation of subject specific laws and policy in decision making and through cases in the courts). A good example of this process would be the development of the principles of family law over the last 30 or 50 years.

We would argue that environmental law has its own conceptual apparatus, in the sense that there is a set of principles and concepts which can be said to exist across the range of subjects covered. Although there is a valid debate about the extent to which these principles have gained universal acceptance as principles with meaningful legal effect, there can be little doubt that environmental law has now matured into an identifiable discipline in its own right. Thus although principles such as the precautionary principle or the polluter pays principle have a status as principles/tools of good environmental management they may not necessarily have any agreed meaning. Clearly these principles provide a theoretical context in which to view the detail of environmental law and thus it is important to provide some explanation of what we think principles such as the 'precautionary principle' or the 'polluter pays' mean near the beginning of the book.

In a similar fashion we would argue that there is a core grouping of topics which might comprise substantive environmental laws. Whilst there may be people who disagree about the exact nature of the 'core' topics we would suggest that there is an inclusive definition which would include most of the topics included in this book. For example, most courses (or text books) on environmental law will consider different aspects of pollution control (air, water, land contamination). In addition there will be certain topics such as European environmental law or planning law which have a general application across different parts of the 'core'. These are so integral that they must form part of the core itself.

On the other hand there are other topics which could be said to lie on the periphery of the subject. That is not to say that such topics are unimportant, indeed, some of them are at the forefront of modern concerns about the environment. These include topics such as natural resource depletion, deforestation, international trade, transport, genetically modified organisms, agriculture, pesticides, and power generation. This list, which is by no means exhaustive, illustrates the fact that there are difficult decisions to make about drawing the boundaries of the subject. Clearly all of these topics raise environmental issues and all of them have a legal dimension to them in some respects. Nevertheless, there is a danger that in drawing the boundaries too wide the subject becomes 'The Environment and the Law'

---

2. See e.g. C. Reid, (1998) 4 Jur. Rev. 236.

rather than 'Environmental Law'. Whilst there is nothing inherently wrong in taking a broad definition of the subject, the lack of focus and precision can hinder the development of the law and the institutions which administer it. For example, the fact that the definition of environmental law was unclear was put forward as a potential reason for rejecting the idea of an Environmental Court.[3]

This discussion explains the division of the book into three parts, the first on the general themes of environmental law, the second dealing with those areas of law which apply in a general fashion across a range of environmental media and activities, and the third on the law relating to specific environmental issues. Much of this third part of the book deals with the laws and procedures relating to these individual issues or media. As such it can be fairly turgid going compared with the principled and themed aspects of the first two sections. This reflects one of the challenges of studying environmental law for those who are interested in how it operates in the real world. Much of the operational aspects of environmental law centre not around flexible general principles but detailed procedures of how and when to apply for licences and such like. It may not be the most attractive aspect of the subject but it forms its heart and needs to be covered.

The importance of definitions

Part of the uncertainty about the definition of environmental law is that many of the ideas which are central to the subject are contested—that is to say certain terms have no generally agreed objective definition. This may be a result of a clash between the subjective and objective or the distinction between 'facts' and values. As we shall see certain terms such as 'environment' and 'pollution' are often used to describe particular sets of 'facts' (e.g. to describe our surroundings in terms of environmental media). This should be distinguished from interpretations of such terms which reflect particular values or judgments. For example, what may be a wilderness environment worthy of protection from any human influence whatsoever to one person may be the source of natural resources worthy of exploitation to another or the home of indigenous peoples who have helped to sustain and manage biodiversity for many centuries to another. When defining things by reference to values, we automatically view things in the way we think they should be viewed. Of course, this influences our response to what we think should be done in terms of environmental policies and laws.

But we cannot ignore definitions as they mark out what is worthy of protection. In some cases a definition may be stretched and developed to accommodate new challenges. For example, there are Treaties protecting the Moon and other celestial bodies from 'harmful contamination' (Art. 7). Definitions also make a difference because as Dryzek puts it 'language matters . . . the way we construct, interpret, discuss and analyse environmental problems has all kinds of consequences'.[4] For good or bad environmental law provides us with part of the language to discuss and hopefully solve environmental problems.

Although there are many definitions which are contested, the challenge of defining the

---

3. See the speech of Lord Bach in the House of Lords at <http://www.publications.parliament.uk/pa/ld199900/ldhansrd/vo001009/text/01009-26.htm>.

4. John S. Dryzek, *The Politics of the Earth: Environmental Discourses* (Oxford: Oxford University Press, 1997).

boundaries of environmental law is fundamentally interlinked with the two central concepts of what we mean by 'the environment' and what we mean by 'law'. As we shall see, these two concepts are capable of many different meanings all of which have some substance, but which would be distinctive enough to lead to very different formulations of the boundaries of the subject (and this book).

Environment[al]

This is a difficult word to define. It is generally considered to be a phrase which has no singular definition as it is a relational concept.[5] Its normal meaning relates to 'surroundings', but obviously that is a concept that is relative to whatever object it is which is surrounded. Used in that sense, environmental law could include virtually anything; indeed, as Einstein is said to have remarked, 'The environment is everything that isn't me.'[6] However, certainly in the context of environmental *law*, 'the environment' can be given a rather more specific meaning, though still a very vague and general one, and may be treated as covering the physical surroundings that are common to all of us, including air, space, waters, land, plants, and wildlife (see Box 1.1). In this more specific sense, the idea of 'the environment' is relatively recent. Certainly in terms of policy and law-making, this concept of 'the environment' as something worthy of protection and enhancement through policies and law-making dates only to the 1960s.[7] Prior to this time, private law mechanisms such as the law of nuisance and trespass controlled activities which were environmentally harmful but only in the context of interferences with the rights of ownership of property. The idea of protecting something for its contribution to biodiversity is something that is linked to recent times.

The definition of 'the environment' is a central but problematic term in environmental law. It has no singular description or definition. Generally, it is defined by reference to the physical non-human environmental media including land, water, air, foral and fauna, and so on. In this context the environment is given some scientific significance. Some specific definitions are set out in Box 1.1.

BOX 1.1 Definitions of 'The Environment'

'all, or any, of the following media, namely, the air, water and land; and the medium of air includes the air within buildings and the air within other natural or man-made structures above or below ground.'

Environmental Protection Act 1990, s. 1

'surroundings in which an organisation operates, including air, water, land, natural resources, flora, fauna, humans and their interrelation. Surroundings in this context extend from within the organisation to the global system.'

Environmental Management Standard ISO 14001

---

5. J Barry, *Environment and Social Theory* (London: Routledge, 1999) 11–13.

6. Even this however doesn't present the full picture as Einstein himself and any individual is part of the 'Environment'.

7. Although previously legislation and policies were introduced to deal with aspects of society which might have involved aspects of environmental protection, see J Dryzek, *The Politics of the Earth* (Oxford: Oxford University Press, 1997) 4–5 and see below Chapter 2.

'the combination of elements whose complex interrelationships make up the settings, the surroundings and the conditions of life of the individual and of society, as they are or as they are felt.'

European Commission definition

These definitions are helpful in establishing the operating parameters for environmental law but only take us so far. In order to define the environment we must know the subject to which it relates. For example, there are different layers to the environment—international, European, national (English, Scottish, etc.), and local (e.g. Areas of Outstanding Natural Beauty, Sites of Special Scientific Interest) but these are legal constructs. Delineating the boundaries of 'the environment' in this way makes no sense to flora and fauna. Migrating birds do not choose to winter in 'England' or a particular Nature Reserve.

Social and cultural influences also play a part in defining the environment. Someone living in a mining town may consider large slag heaps as part of their environment. A city dweller will think about parks, open spaces, and buildings, whilst a country dweller may consider the environment to be stone walls, ploughed fields, and woodland. One final thought is that the environment also needs to be considered by reference to time. In thinking about the laws which protect our environment today we need to be aware that future generations' environment may also need to be considered.

Rather than offering a hostage to fortune by attempting to lay down some impossibly precise definition of the environment, we propose to avoid the issue by adopting a general description of the book's content. A more precise description can be given simply by stating what is and what is not covered by the book. We intend to concentrate on those laws and practices which relate primarily to the protection of the whole or part of the general surroundings, as opposed to those where the true objective is the protection of public health, or individual people such as workers or consumers.

Obviously, it is not possible to consign some areas of law with certainty to one category or another and, as a result, the exact dividing line between what is and what is not included is rather artificial. But a line has to be drawn somewhere. Accordingly, we cover the law and practice on the protection of air, water and land against pollution, laws relating to development and the conservation of biodiversity and landscape features, together with those ancillary issues which help to explain these areas, such as public participation, remedies, and procedures.

Such things as consumer protection laws, product liability laws, health and safety legislation, and animal protection laws are not covered, although they can often be relevant to solving environmental problems. There are also a number of areas of what is undeniably environmental law which are omitted on grounds of space. The growing package of legislation on the protection of the cultural heritage is omitted. Little will be said about radioactivity, where the law is very complex indeed and where there is a large overlap between the environmental and human protection parts of the law. The provisions in the EPA 1990 on the introduction of genetically modified organisms into the environment and on litter are also omitted.

Law

This book is not intended to be merely a description of the various rules and regulations, although obviously that is a part of any useful book on the law. Such a description would give little clue to what happens in practice. Whether, and how, the law is enforced is just as important as what the law is. Indeed, given the discretionary nature of many of the powers and duties imposed on environmental decision-makers, it is unreal to draw a hard and fast distinction between what the law is and how it is used. This book will therefore seek to emphasize policy as much as law, and practice as much as principle.

Law in practice is also affected by the values and culture of those who make the rules; set the standards by which those rules operate; implement and enforce the rules and standards; and those whose activities are controlled by those rules and standards. In environmental law and policy this extends to us all and the impact of these values can be stretched further to include non-human interests and the interests of future generations. The word 'values' covers the things which are important to us and the priority we give to them. There is therefore a direct connection between that which we consider to be a priority and the laws and policies which are introduced to control, promote or otherwise regulate the area concerned. We therefore cover the role that values play in environmental law and policy and the various perspectives on environmental issues or decisions.

The terms 'rules' and 'law' are often used interchangeably in many parts of the book. That is because environmental 'law' arguably comes from different sources, many of which would not necessarily fall within the definition of statutes or regulations. Thus there are guidance notes, circulars, official policy documents, codes of practice, even politicians' speeches which can have a marked effect upon the way in which the law operates in practice. For example, the Environment Agency or the Department of the Environment, Food and Rural Affairs may publish some guidance on the interpretation of a vague statutory phrase, such as the meaning of 'waste'. Although there may be arguments over whether the guidance is 'correct', it can only be overturned by a legal challenge. Unless a challenge is made, this interpretation may become the new rule for practical purposes. In other situations, the statutory scheme may require either policy or technical guidance to flesh out the general definitions. Thus decisions on whether to grant planning permission for out of town retail development are closely controlled by a series of rules dressed up as policy in Planning Policy Guidance Notes. In the area of pollution control, there are many technical guidance notes which set process or other standards which act as rules which guide decision-makers (or more properly, structure their discretion) in granting authorizations, consents or permissions. Understanding the role of these rules and in particular the legal effect which is created when such rules exist is crucial to any understanding of the way in which environmental law works in practice.

There are some other general limitations on the subject matter of the book in addition to the ones mentioned above. It is not about all those laws which 'relate to' the environment, since that too could cover virtually anything. Instead we intend to concentrate on those laws and practices which have as their object or effect the *protection* of the environment. Those things which merely have an indirect impact on the state of the environment, such as general tax levels, grants and incentives, are thus excluded from full coverage, although their relevance is referred to in passing and they may frequently be of crucial importance to the policy-maker.

As the understanding of the global nature of environmental impacts grows, there is an increasing recognition that principles and rules need to be agreed in the international arena if there is to be a concerted effort to address common issues. Thus the role played by international agreements and principles in influencing and moulding our domestic law is covered in outline. We do not, however, attempt to deal with truly international problems in any detail, leaving such coverage to specialized works which are referred to in the bibliography.

The crucial relevance of European Community (EC) law must be emphasized. We adopt the attitude that EC law *is* domestic law in the sense that it cannot be ignored even though it does not always give rise to enforceable obligations and remedies. Therefore EC controls are integrated into each part of the book where relevant. In addition, there is a separate chapter on the basic constitutional rules of the EC and on the history, philosophy, and current direction of its environmental policy. It is hard to overestimate the central importance of EC law and policy to British environmental law. This importance is often masked by the fact that in the environmental field, EC law tends to require some form of transposition and implementation in this country before it is formally recognized. Once implemented, the EC derivation of the rule is then frequently forgotten because the domestic law is cited as the applicable law.

Some themes of the book

This description of the scope of the book highlights a number of important themes. One is that there is a great deal of interaction between rules which have as their main objective the protection of the environment and those which aim to protect people. Just as in nature conservation it has become accepted in the last 30 years that there is no use in protecting individual animals or species unless you also protect their habitats, in all matters we now accept that protection of human beings involves protection of their environment. The converse is also true in that many rules originally aimed at protection of people end up protecting the environment. For example, standards in relation to radio-activity are often set with the protection of humans in mind, but have an important impact on environmental levels of radiation. Similarly, the presence or absence of laws on cruelty to animals has a significant impact on nature conservation even though that is not their primary motive.

A related theme is that rules are simply the tools of the trade of law-makers, environmental protection agencies and environmentalists. A rule which has as its objective one goal is frequently of enormous use in an entirely different way. For example, the law of private nuisance owes its existence and shape to the objective of protecting property rights, but it still has an important, though often unpredictable, part to play in regulating environmental standards in the interests of the community. This is one of the major themes of this book: that there is often more than one way of tackling a problem and that the environmental lawyer must be seen as a problem-solver who chooses the most appropriate tool for the particular problem encountered. Often this will involve using a combination of different tools. As an example, many rules of property law may be used to further environmental ends: the Royal Society for the Protection of Birds follows a policy of buying land for nature reserve purposes on the principle that the exercise of ownership rights will often provide a better method of protection than many statutory designations or protections. This is not to say that the whole of property law must somehow be annexed as a part of environmental law, but that environmental lawyers should make use of any piece of law which has a relevance to the problem in hand.

A further issue relates to the nature of law. It is often stated that law is not constructive; that it does not build houses or plant trees. We regard this as an inaccurate notion. There is no doubt that many laws do lay down straightforward negative rules restricting specified forms of behaviour. But many laws lay down rights as well as wrongs. Much of environmental law consists of setting out a framework for behaviour—who should make decisions, how they should make them, what procedures must be followed. In promoting good environmental decision-making, or in giving subsidies to clean technologies, such law is clearly not just negative. There is also the practical point that the regulatory agencies spend a far greater proportion of their time providing positive advice on how to reach the standards they set than on enforcing those standards through legal threats and remedies.

This distinction between negative and positive tools links to a division in the subject matter of environmental law. It is common to equate environmental protection with pollution control. However, whilst pollution control undoubtedly represents a major part of environmental law, there are many other issues, such as the conservation of biological diversity and landscape, which also make up the subject. These issues often require slightly different legal mechanisms. Indeed the evidence of a growing maturity of environmental law can be seen in the use of a more extensive range of these positive tools. The producer responsibility legislation which sets out targets for the recycling and recovery of specific waste streams (e.g. packaging and electrical equipment) along with take-back requirements for end of life products (with the implicit incentive to reduce the amount of waste produced) is a good example of the use of positive legal rules to bring about environmental improvement.

Another theme of the book is that it is a central function of environmental law to assist in dispute resolution. Disputes about the environment are distinctive although care must be taken here to differentiate what is different about environmental *issues* and what is different about environmental *disputes*. Many legal subjects involve the adjudication of disputes which are characterized as involving a relatively small number of parties (typically two) seeking answers to yes–no questions. Environmental disputes can involve many parties and are often multi-faceted or 'polycentric'. In these cases substantive legal control (as opposed to procedures which lay down a framework for the resolution of disputes) is of little use. Take for example a dispute about whether to build a wind farm. This could involve negative local impacts such as loss of amenity, detrimental impact on nature conservation or an increase in noise (there might also be positive impacts such as an increase in employment). There are other, broader issues which could be considered which have wider national and international impacts such as reducing the reliance on fossil fuels with consequent reductions in polluting emissions and gases which contribute to climate change. The determination of whether to build a wind farm involves the balancing of difficult policy questions. In this sense there is no 'right' answer and the interconnection of interests cannot be accommodated fully within the legal system or any dispute resolution mechanism. Typically, therefore, environmental decisions are made 'in the public interest' or 'on balance weighing various considerations'. Environmental law—or more accurately the decisions made within the procedural and substantive framework of environmental law—has to incorporate this notion of polycentricity as a fundamental element of the subject.

In addition, environmental disputes often have different causes. Take for example, the question of flooding from overflowing sewers. Is the problem caused by the Water Under-takers under investment in satisfactory infrastructure; or by the Water Regulator's refusal to allow water prices to rise to pay for the sewerage improvement; or by developers building houses where there is inadequate sewerage provision; or by planning authorities granting planning permission for hard impermeable surfaces such as car parks where rain water cannot be absorbed; or by the increase in rainfall brought about by climate change? Of course each of these explanations has multiple causes and so the complexity of the problem increases.

This last point raises a further feature of environmental disputes—their complexity. The facts are often in dispute which typically leads to complex scientific and economic arguments about what is 'safe' or whether the cost of doing something would outweigh the benefits. Furthermore, the issues often involve a complex interplay between public, private, and criminal law with parties desiring remedies across those different areas of law. For example, a house owner complaining about a waste storage site on land adjacent to their home sees the dispute in relatively simple terms—the cessation of the storage. However, the lawfulness of the activities on the site depends upon a large number of factors including whether there is a waste management licence and planning permission in relation to the activities, whether the site is causing a statutory or private nuisance and whether any criminal offences are being committed.

This links to the final and perhaps most important theme, which is that environmental law provides remedies. To many people, whether they are environmentalists or industrialists or lawyers giving advice, this is the most central aspect of law, since they need to know what they can do about a situation. One of the interesting developments of recent years has been the search for adequate remedies for environmental problems. Legal tools have been accepted as legitimate devices for helping to solve environmental problems. Law plays an often underrated but enormously important role, alongside scientific, technological, social, and economic solutions, in helping to combat environmental degradation. In this role, many novel legal concepts have been developed.

The shape of the book

Part I of the book looks at those general issues which cut across all issues of environmental protection, but which are in practice an essential part of any understanding of the law. The discussion in this part should also provide a form of vocabulary to help with an understanding of the context of the specific laws and practices which are dealt with in Parts II and III. Part I thus covers perspectives on the environment and how the law overlaps with environmental issues, the nature of the regulatory systems adopted for environmental protection, the sources of environmental law, the institutions and agencies involved in environmental protection, the process of setting environmental standards and the different types of standards that may be adopted and the role of the EC and international law.

In *Part II* we examine certain issues which also play a role in addressing environmental problems but which are impossible to explain in terms of environmental media, pollutants, or targets. The law on town and country planning is an example. It clearly has a central role in protecting against threats to amenity and is in other ways an important part of the law on environmental protection. For example, hazardous or undesirable developments can be prevented or controlled by the imposition of conditions making the need for planning permission an essential part of most systems of pollution control. But it also has a role in organizing economic development which is outside environmental law in its strict sense. We also look at the role of public participation in environmental law, the role of private law and environmental crime including the important question of how environmental laws are actually enforced.

In *Part III* the specific laws relating to particular environmental issues are treated on a chapter by chapter basis. However, there is a significant problem of organization here. Should the law be divided up according to the medium in which the environmental threat manifests itself (e.g. air, water, land, etc.)? Should it be divided according to the identity of the polluter (e.g. cars, factories, power stations, etc.)? Should it be divided according to the nature of the pollutant (e.g. radiation, chemicals, pesticides, CFCs, etc.)? Or should it even be divided according to the nature of the target which is being protected (e.g. people, animals, ecosystems, and the atmosphere)? There is no single answer. The laws are not designed on any one of these four axes, but on all four at once. The best that can be done is to select groupings of laws that more or less hang together in a way that makes sense to someone faced with a problem. It must then be remembered that in reality all these things interrelate, so that a problem on the disposal of waste to land cannot be considered without some consideration of the law on incineration, or discharges to water, or recycling.

Policy and environmental law

Environmental law is a political discipline. It is political in the narrow sense that major differences can be discerned between political parties as to the correct policy to apply. These differences do not normally relate to the ends to be achieved, but to the methods to be adopted in doing so, and the costs to be incurred. A clear example is the controversy provoked by the passage of the Wildlife and Countryside Act 1981 over whether voluntary or compulsory controls should be adopted in relation to the protection of important natural sites (see Chapter 21). A further example relates to the whole history of town and country planning in the 1980s, when the very dramatic changes to planning policy led to disagreement and dispute. These are clear examples of the application of 'Thatcherism' to the environment, as a Government with a deep suspicion of planning and regulation sought to grapple with a system based on coherent planning for the future. However, there are others which relate to such things as privatisation and deregulation. The Deregulation and Contracting Out Act 1994 showed that little has really changed since the 1980s and also emphasized the point that the whole context of environmental law can change when a different administration is elected.

Environmental law is also political in the wide sense that it involves the making of policy decisions about the best way to achieve certain objectives. This is emphasized in this book by looking at law as being about techniques or tools for solving problems. It is not just lawyers and environmentalists who have a choice of tools they may use to achieve a particular objective. Legislators and policy-makers also have a range of tools available to them. The law is one tool alongside such things as fiscal policy, education, research, and voluntary solutions. There are different types of legal mechanism that may be used, such as the setting of environmental quality objectives, or of strict limits on emissions, or controls attached to processes or products. These various possibilities are discussed in detail in Chapter 8, but it ought to be recognized that, in order to combat complex problems of pollution and environmental harm, a combination of methods is often required.

It is impossible to say that Britain always adopts one method rather than another, but it is clear that the tendency has been to adopt flexible mechanisms of control, where what is permitted is judged by reference to its effect on the receiving environment. As a result, the British approach to pollution control tends to be fairly pragmatic, and involves a great deal of discretion. This discretion is normally exercised by specialist regulatory agencies, although local authorities also have very significant environmental protection functions. An important point is that this discretion is exercised on grounds that are not restricted to environmental factors. There is a traditionally close connection in British environmental regulation between social, political, and economic factors and decisions on environmental protection.

This emphasis on taking into account a wide range of factors before making a decision links to a fundamental point about the way that 'pollution' and 'environmental harm' are defined. Once again, it is difficult to formulate precise definitions, but a general guide would be to say that they cover situations where there is an excess of something over what is desirable. There is no doubt that they are relative concepts; one person's waste is another's raw material. This relativity also applies to other forms of environmental harm. For example, a rock concert for some is a noise nuisance for others and what would be thought as intrusive development in one locality will blend in in another.

The level of pollution is also relative. For example, because of the self-cleansing properties of the environment, it may well be said to be less polluting to discharge into a large fast-flowing river than into a small sluggish one, and higher levels of pollution from industrial sources may be tolerated in one area than in another because of the corresponding advantages of the economic prosperity that the industries bring. It is nonsensical to talk of getting rid of pollution. Pollution and the harm caused thereby are to a certain extent necessary risks because they accompany activities which most of us are unwilling to do without. Certain polluting processes are beneficial to our existence, so to prohibit them entirely would arguably cause more harm than good. Reducing pollution comes at a price and the more levels are reduced the greater the cost. In addition, there are limits to what can be achieved through technological means and even if great reductions can be made there are questions about how activities would be monitored and enforced. Accordingly, it only makes sense to consider how to reduce pollution and the levels which are acceptable.

Everything depends on what is considered acceptable. This involves economic, political, social, and cultural criteria as well as scientific and environmental ones. It is therefore important to understand that, in implementing environmental protection policies, regulatory agencies are effectively carrying out a political balancing process. As Hawkins puts it in *Environment and Enforcement* (Oxford: Oxford University Press, 1984), 'The power to define and enforce consents is ultimately a power to put people out of business, to deter the introduction of new business or to drive away a going concern'.

Rights and environmental law

In recent years the language of 'rights' and environmental law has emerged as a potential counterpoint to the discretionary, flexible basis of much of environmental law and decision making. Many of the typical characteristics of domestic environmental law appear to be weak because of the inherent substantive flexibility and discretion and the reliance on the pragmatic approach of acceptability. One is left with an impression that there is little definite substance. Therefore the talk of 'rights' with its inherent certainty and enforceability appears to be much more attractive. If an individual or group of people have a 'right' to a 'clean' environment (whatever that might mean), that right can be relied upon as against a political decision to allow a development (e.g. a road) which interferes with those 'rights'. Accordingly, a decision made in the public interest where various factors are balanced such as economic and social considerations in order to determine what is 'acceptable' can be overridden by the right.[8]

As with many other of the key terms discussed in this chapter, the phrase 'rights' and its interpretation needs some explanation. The language of rights is very common—but what does the phrase mean in the context of environmental protection? The need for clarity comes from the manner in which the word is used. One might see reference to a 'right' to pollute or trade in pollution credits, a right to be heard at an inquiry, a right to bring a judicial review action, a right of access to environmental information, a right to a healthy environment, a right to clean air or water and a right to participate in environmental decision making. Clearly, all these things cannot possibly invoke the same right. Moral rights must be distinguished from legal rights, procedural rights from substantive rights, derivative rights from 'first order' rights and so on. The term 'rights' is used in a number of different context both in this book and more generally.

In general the term 'right' is used to convey something which is a permanent entitlement normally protected by objective rules. In this sense a legal right can be differentiated from a moral right which may be a claim for a right where the basis of the right is disputed but which proponents may argue is valid for its own sake (e.g. compare and contrast the rights of a child with animal rights). In practice, moral rights and legal rights may be mutually supportive (i.e. a right which is disputed may become valid because it is protected by rules (e.g. animal rights in the context of animal welfare legislation).

There are two broad strands of rights which might be used as a means of protecting the environment. The first is the concept of legal rights for the natural environment such as trees, rivers, animals, plants and geological features.[9] The basic argument for the creation of such rights is that this would be one of the natural consequences of human development. Historically we have recognized the role that law, through the granting of rights, has had to play in the granting of autonomy to people (e.g. women and children) and the control that

8 The phrase 'rights as trumps' conveys this overriding power. See, e.g., J. Rawls, *Political Liberalism* (New York: Columbia University Press, 1993) 6. For Dworkin's idea of rights as trumps, see his book *Taking Rights Seriously* (Cambridge, MA: Harvard University Press, 1978), ch. 4, and his article 'Rights as Trumps' in J. Waldron (ed.), *Theories of Rights* (Oxford: Oxford University Press, 1984) 153–167.

9 For a discussion of the creation of this sort of right and generally see, C. Stone, *Should Trees Have Standing?: and other essays on law, morals and the environment* (New York: Oceana Publishing, 1996) Ch. 1.

people have over things (e.g. rights of ownership of real property, ideas and even other people such as slaves). Given our understanding of the importance of and the need to protect the environment, it would be one way for law to recognize the significance of environmental protection for its own sake.

The notion that the environment should be granted rights of its own is not without objection. One of the main criticisms is that it is simply unnecessary to grant the environment rights because the questions involved in protecting animals, plants and geological features are essentially moral questions which cannot necessarily be addressed through the creation of new rights. For example we might agree that it would be wrong to take a hammer to the statue of the Venus de Milo but we would not consider that the best way of protecting the Venus de Milo would be to grant legal rights to all statues.[10] In the same way whilst we all may agree that we have a preference that biodiversity is protected or even enhanced it is not the same as saying that rare species should be granted rights. Thus, whilst the idea of this type of such 'environmental right' is the subject of philosophical debate, the concrete examples of the granting of such rights are few and far between.[11]

The second strand of 'rights' as a means of protecting the environment is more anthropocentric in nature i.e. used to protect human interests, although in many cases environmental protection can be 'derived' from the basic right. Thus a right to bring a nuisance action may help prevent pollution of the environment as well as protecting private property rights. In this book, the term 'rights' is typically used in this anthropocentric fashion. In general the term is used in three broad ways:

- *Private rights.* These tend to be based upon the protection of property interests such as the right to take action against nuisances to prevent unreasonable interference with the enjoyment of land or the right to prevent a trespass.

- *Public Law Rights.* These tend to be procedural in nature including the right to participate in decision making, the right to information, the right to be heard at an inquiry or the right to bring a judicial review action or a private prosecution.

- *Substantive legal rights.* These include the European Convention on Human Rights. These provide basic rights such as a right to life or a right to respect for private life.

Much of the recent activity surrounding 'rights' stems from this last category and the formal incorporation of certain, identified human rights into UK law (see further p. 357). These rights are mainly substantive in nature although there are examples of procedural rights such as the right to 'a fair and public hearing within a reasonable time by an independent and impartial tribunal established by law'. Some of the relevant substantive rights include the right to life, the right to respect for private life, home and correspondence and the right to property. The European Court of Human Rights has not generally taken an expansionist view of human rights as a tool for environmental protection, using the idea of a 'margin of appreciation' to apply their own balancing of political, environmental and economic considerations as against individual rights. Much of the Court's reticence to

---

10 See J. Merrills, 'Environmental Protection and Human Rights: Conceptual Aspects' in A. Boyle and M. Anderson (eds) *Human Rights Approaches to Environmental Protection* (Oxford: Clarendon Press, 1998), 34.

11 For arguments in relation to the creation of 'ecocentric' environmental rights from existing laws see C. Miller, *Environmental Rights* (London: Routledge, 1998) esp. Ch. 9.

develop the law in this way is linked to the difficult nature of environmental disputes (see p. 11).

CHAPTER SUMMARY

1   Environmental law is a significant subject because law is central to managing the environment which is considered to be an important and challenging issue.

2   The boundaries of environmental law are not very well defined although there are certain 'core' principles and topics which would form an inclusive definition that most people would probably agree to most of.

3   Defining certain key terms in environmental law is difficult because they can have a factual and value based meaning. Thus great care needs to be taken when using concepts such as 'environment' and 'pollution' in order to make this fact/value distinction.

4   Environmental law originates from a range of sources. Law in practice is different from law on the page. Such things as the way the law is enforced make a huge difference to its effectiveness.

5   There are various important underlying themes in this book. These are: laws are tools which can be used to protect the environment, selecting the right tool for the right task is critical; laws which protect humans can also be used to protect the environment; law is not only restrictive in nature it can be used as a positive tool to encourage environmental improvement; law assists in the resolution of complex environmental disputes; and environmental law provides remedies.

6   Environmental law is a political discipline as it involves the making of policy decisions about the best way to achieve acceptable environmental objectives.

7   Although the term 'rights' can have a number of meanings, in this book it is generally used to cover public law rights, private law rights, and substantive legal rights.

QUESTIONS

1   Consider the following examples. In each case, what interests are involved, what issues of policy arise, what rights (if any) are being infringed, and is there any issue about the conception of the environment?

   a   A proposal to ban people entering a National Park to prevent damage to sensitive ecosystems and landscapes.

   b   The use of a new chemical which is linked to harm to fish and to impacts on human fertility.

   c   Empty bottles of spring water left behind by students after a lecture.

   d   A non-native bird which, because of climate change, is now found in the south of England and is having a negative impact on (although not yet endangering) the robin.

   e   The transportation of waste from a wealthy part of the country to an incinerator sited in an area of relative poverty.

   f   Giving contraception to an expanding seal population that is having a detrimental impact upon fish stocks.

   g   Culling badgers living in a sett under Stonehenge. Would your answer differ if the damage was being done by rats.

   h   A proposal to develop a large off-shore wind farm, which may have an adverse effect on migratory birds. How would your answer differ if it was being built near to a successful sea-side resort?

i The UK has agreed to reduce its emissions to combat climate change; UK industry has increased its emissions in the last 10 years.

j The imposition of a tax of £100 on 'no-frills' airline tickets to counter the effects of air transport on climate change.

k An application to extend a waste landfill into a locally important nature conservation site where there is a risk that when the waste breaks down it will pollute nearby drinking water supplies within the next 100 years.

l Revoking a power station's licence to abstract water because of fears that low flows will damage an endangered mayfly's habitat.

2 How far should society go in conferring rights on the environment? Do groups have rights which are different from the rights of individuals who make up the group'?

3 Look at three websites of bodies operating in the environmental field; if you are stuck for suggestions, look at the websites of the Environment Agency, Friends of the Earth and the Chemical Industries Association). How would you characterise their concepts of the environment? To what extent do these groups seem to be pressing for changes to policy? Or to law? What role do environmental rights seem to play?

4 What would you include within your definition of environmental law? How might this differ in 10, 50, and 100 years time?

 FURTHER READING

Environmental law is quite a difficult subject to access for the complete beginner. You may want a gentle introduction and to read around the subject to get a feel for the language. Some of the best introductions can be found in Routledge's *Introductions to the Environment Series*, in particular the Environment and Society texts (eds D. Pepper and P. O'Keefe). These include D. Wilkinson *Environment and Law* (London: Routledge, 2002), J. Barry, *Environment and Social Theory* (London: Routledge 1999), and T. Doyle and D. McEachern, *Environment and Politics* (London: Routledge 2001). Another helpful introduction which helps 'set the scene' for later discussions is J. Dryzek, *The Politics of the Earth, Environmental Discourses* (Oxford: Oxford University Press, 1997).

On the difficult question of the definition of environmental law have a look at Z. Plater, 'Environmental law and three economies: navigating a sprawling field of study, practice, and societal governance in which everything is connected to everything else', (1999) 23 Harvard Environmental Law Review, 359 and R. Lazarus, 'Environmental scholarship and the Harvard difference', (1999) 23 Harvard Environmental Law Review, 327. For a British perspective see C. Reid, 'Environmental Law: Sifting Through the Rubbish', (1998) Jur. Rev. 236.

For a discussion on the creation of environmental rights see C. Stone, *'Should Trees Have Standing? And Other Essays on Law, Morals and the Environment'* (New York: Oceana Publishing, 1996), ch. 1. For a more general discussion on the role of human rights as a tool for environmental protection see J. Merrills, 'Environmental Protection and Human Rights: Conceptual Aspects' in a fine collection of essays on the topic, A. Boyle and M. Anderson (eds), *Human Rights Approaches to Environmental Protection* (Oxford: Clarendon Press, 1998), 34. For arguments in relation to the creation of 'ecocentric' environmental rights from existing laws see C. Miller, *Environmental Rights* (London: Routledge 1998), esp. ch. 9.

The best way to get an insight into what is happening in the 'real world' of environmental law is to visit the web pages of environmental organisations such as Greenpeace <www.greenpeace.org.uk> which tends to concentrate on global issues and Friends of the Earth <www.foe.org.uk> which is more local. These provide up to the minute information on the most significant (or media friendly, depending upon your viewpoint) topics of the moment. In recent years, there have been some interesting books attempting to counter what are seen by some as excessive 'green pessimism': three good examples of the genre are R. North, *Life on a Modern Planet: A Manifesto for Progress* (Manchester: Manchester University Press, 1995) or J. Simon, *Ultimate Resource 2* (Princeton: Princeton University Press, 1998) and B. Lomborg, *The Skeptical Environmentalist* (Cambridge: Cambridge University Press, 2001). A. Markham, *A Brief History of Pollution* (London: Earthscan, 1994) provides a good contextual introduction to the issue of what much of environmental law is seeking to control.

2 · History and challenges

→ Overview

What we now call environmental law has tended to develop incrementally (and often haphazardly) rather than by revolutionary leaps. This means that some of its shape and content is still influenced by what has gone before. But in regulating polluting industries and dealing with environmental problems, challenges have been thrown up, and (in theory) lessons learnt, which it is important to appreciate. This chapter builds on Chapter 1 by considering, through a broad lens, the origins and evolution of environmental law and policy. It then moves on to look at some of the key challenges for the future, and possible trends in environmental law and in the costs of complying (and not complying) with environmental law.

At the end of this chapter you will:

✔ Understand in outline the origins, development and main features of UK environmental law.
✔ Appreciate some of the main difficulties in making environmental laws that work.
✔ Appreciate possible future directions in environmental policy and some of the legal challenges these raise.

Lessons from the past

Not surprisingly for such a densely populated country, environmental controls have a long history, going back to medieval statutes on small-scale pollution and the development of private law principles to deal with threats to communal assets such as water. Of course, until recently, few would have thought of these laws as part of something called 'environmental law', since their main focus was on the protection of private and common property. The adequacy of the private law in particular fell far short of an effective protection regime, even for affected individuals (see Box 2.1).

BOX 2.1 **Royal Commission on the Pollution of Rivers, Third Report, *The Rivers Aire and Calder* (1867) Cmnd 3850, pp li–liii**

So far as river abuses affect only private rights, each individual is left to protect himself by putting the law in motion. An aggrieved individual has the option of bringing an action for damages . . . or an injunction. Either course is necessarily invidious, expensive and doubtful in its result. . . . The plaintiff may prove that he has suffered injury from the pollution of the river and that the defendant has polluted the river above him; but that is not enough. The plaintiff has also to prove that what he has suffered has been caused wholly or in part by the special act of the defendant, which is always difficult – often impossible. . . . Several instances have come before us where a manufacturer, sued for polluting running water, has brought the litigation to a close, not by ceasing to foul the river, but by simply removing the discharge into the river to a point below the works of the complainant. . . . In the neighbourhood of large towns it has come to be thought that a river foul with sewage is inevitable; inhabitants are reluctant to come forward as witnesses to denounce that to which they have become long familiar. . . . In the case of sewage pollution it is not usually difficult to trace the offender home. . . . For the principal offenders are the governing bodies of the large towns. These do not prosecute one another for the reason that each is guilty of the same offence towards his neighbour, and they are rarely prosecuted by private persons because few are willing to bear the expense and odium of acting as public prosecutors. . . . The expense of such litigation generally far exceeds the value of the personal interest of any individual in the stoppage of the nuisance. Accordingly, whatever the inconvenience to the public, the nuisance continues unabated. Rich and poor alike submit to it as a sort of destiny

Or, as a later Royal Commission put it:

In such centres the interests of the community are largely bound up with the interests of the manufacturer and that to demand from manufacturers costly schemes of purification might injure the community without any corresponding improvement in the character of the river which is already materially, if not hopelessly impaired (Cmnd 7819, 1914–16, 3).

Britain's position as the cradle of the Industrial Revolution led to the very early development of public controls specifically related to environmental protection. The most significant provisions were developed in response to public health problems such as typhoid and cholera in the mid-19th century, which were traced to the state of the urban environment and the drinking of contaminated water. Although the legal response was initially to give permissive powers to local bodies, mandatory duties on local sanitary authorities were eventually provided for in 1872, and the legislation consolidated in the landmark Public Health Act 1875.

Although the early public health laws were largely successful in removing sewage from the centres of industrial towns, this was often achieved by encouraging the dumping of untreated wastes into convenient watercourses. Water pollution controls were therefore needed, and followed in the Rivers Pollution Prevention Act 1876. This Act gives a flavour of the traditional approach to pollution control through the use of criminal offences and a practical reliance on the 'best practicable means' of pollution control. But it also shows a reluctance to use criminal law enforcement for environmental protection, or to allow individuals to enforce the law (see Box 2.2).

Britain also introduced some of the earliest provisions on town planning. The first legislation to cover this subject was the Housing, Town Planning etc. Act 1909, which again derived from public health pressures and which vested controls in local authorities, at this stage on a non-obligatory basis. Obligatory town and country planning controls were introduced on a nationwide scale in 1947—again early in world terms.

Most public health and environmental protection was therefore carried out at a local level by a vast array of local boards and, at a later stage, local authorities (although in the case of water pollution, a river catchment approach to regulation began with the River Boards Act 1948, which removed some of the incoherence caused by more than one local authority having responsibility for discharges to a river). Britain can, though, boast what is normally considered the world's first national public pollution control agency, the Alkali Inspectorate, which was established by the Alkali Act 1863 to control atmospheric emissions primarily from the caustic soda industry (see Box 2.3). But national, centralized control of problems (such as through the Alkali Inspectorate) was very much the exception in this period of development, and most of the early provisions reflected a tendency (which to a lesser extent is still apparent) to regulate only the most dangerous or sensitive matters at a central level.

BOX 2.2 **The Rivers Pollution Prevention Act 1876**

Under this Act, the first general water pollution prevention statute in the UK, all forms of river pollution were prohibited, but enforcement action against the manufacturing and mining sectors was only possible in very limited situations:

- only a sanitary authority could bring proceedings, and then only with the consent of the Local Government Board (LGB);

- in deciding whether to grant consent, the LGB was to have regard to 'the industrial interests involved in the case and to the circumstances and requirements of the locality';

- consent to prosecution was not to be granted where the district in question was 'the seat of any manufacturing industry', unless the LGB was satisfied 'after due enquiry' that there were reasonably practicable and available means for rendering the polluting liquid harmless *and* that proceedings would not inflict material injury on the interests of industry; and

- two months notice had to be given before proceedings were brought.

'The extraordinary character of these legislative provisions scarcely requires emphasis: there can hardly have been a more blatant attempt by Parliament to obstruct the enforcement of a law which by the same enactment it created' (Richardson, Ogus and Burrows, *Policing Pollution* (Oxford: Clarendon, 1983) p.41).

In addition to these public controls, the law of nuisance was developed (especially in the 19th century) as a means of providing private redress for environmental harm, although on a very selective basis (see Box 2.1 and, further, Chapter 11).

Britain also had some of the earliest voluntary bodies concerned with environmental protection. The National Smoke Abatement Society campaigned for higher fines for polluters under the Public Health Act, and a number of bodies were concerned in particular with the protection of nature. In the absence of laws protecting important wildlife habitats, these bodies began to use ordinary private property laws to acquire nature reserves. With the exception of miscellaneous Acts protecting sea birds from slaughter, and ancient hunting laws designed to maintain numbers of quarry species, there was little legislation in this area.

In these formative years, law-making tended to be ad hoc in the extreme. This is self-evident with case law, which by its very nature, as Box 2.1 above illustrates, must react to the facts of cases brought. But legislative changes were also reactive, piecemeal and shortsighted, with Parliament tending to legislate for problems on an individual basis, in isolation from other areas. The Alkali Act 1863 illustrates many of the difficulties (see Box 2.3).

BOX 2.3 **The Alkali Act 1863**

Although this Act controlled certain noxious fumes from alkali works, it did not prohibit the emission of smoke into the atmosphere, which brought about problems of lower-level pollution with the production of smog. Nor could the imposition of individualised emission standards for alkali works take into account the cumulative effect of a large concentration of such operations. As the Act had only set a reduction for acidic emissions in terms of a percentage for each plant, the overall concentration of such emissions rose as the number of factories increased. Finally, in an echo of the adverse consequences for the water environment of early public health legislation, one effect of the early Alkali Acts and the controls over atmospheric emissions is reputed to have been an immediate worsening of water quality as industries chose liquid discharge as a replacement method for the disposal of their wastes.

A century later, controls on smog introduced after the serious London smog in 1952 killed nearly 4000 people, led indirectly to the policy of dispersing emissions via taller chimney stacks. This reduced emissions nationally, but exported the problem of acid rain to Scandinavia.

These early pollution Acts also show clearly how the concern of the law was not with what we would now call pollution of 'the environment', but with the human consequences of, for example, poor air and water quality, or insanitary housing conditions. The objective of these early Acts was improvements to human health, and improving environmental quality was merely the means to this end.

The legacy of early controls

One effect of this long, and unplanned, history is that modern Britain has inherited a far less coherent system of pollution control than many other countries, with individual pieces of legislation dealing with what are perceived to be individual problems. The same historical factors also explain the relatively large number of agencies dealing with environmental matters, although changes in institutional responsibility have significantly improved matters in this respect (see below).

A further point to note here is the continuing relevance of what might seem to be some very dated legislative provisions. For example, although changes were made in the Environmental Protection Act 1990, we still have laws on statutory nuisances (which have also been adopted as a loose model for the regulation of historically contaminated land) which retain the essential shape they were given in the Public Health Act 1875, and key provisions of the Water Resources Act 1991 on water pollution offences use key terms which date from the Victorian era. The courts have been forced to consider the extent to which the continuing relevance of their historical context should prevail over the fact that these provisions are now contained in statutes which have environmental protection as their main aim.

The modern age of environmental law

As we have just seen, it is hard to differentiate sharply between consecutive phases or 'ages' of environmental law, because some of the features of very early controls remain today. Nevertheless, by the early 1970s it was clear that the developments begun in the late stages of the 19th century had gained momentum, and widespread recognition that the state had to take a more active role in the control of pollution and protection of the environment. A very clear measure of this was the creation in 1970 of the Department of the Environment (previously, environmental affairs had formed part of other ministerial portfolios, such as housing and town planning) 1970 was also the year of the first Earth Day, a recognition of increasing global environmental concerns.

There are a number of possible explanations for this shift. They stretch from the theoretical (e.g. that private law failed either to reflect the external costs of pollution or to protect the interests of future generations by conserving resources, and the changes in public consciousness emerging in a post-industrial era) to the pragmatic and political (e.g. impending membership of the European Community or the growth in environmental regulation in other developed countries which required some form of governmental response). Whatever the reason, the beginning of the modern age of environmental law was characterised by the passing of environmental 'laws' or statutory frameworks in relation to aspects of environmental protection. Typically, these environmental statutes were based upon a model which has become known as 'command and control' whereby centralized environmental standards are set and policed by a combination of government and regulatory agencies. This growth in the number of environmental laws over the last 30 years reflects the readiness with which the UK government adopted this type of environmental regulation.

Landmarks in the Modern History of Environmental Law and Policy (1962–2005)	
1962	Publication of Rachel Carson's *Silent Spring* (a book on the effect of pesticides on the natural environment) raises wide-reaching questions about human impact on the environment.
1968	Apollo 8 sends back first pictures of the Earth from space. Seen by many as showing both the Earth's beauty and fragility. Coincides with a period of growing concerns about possible human impacts on the environment. The late 1960s marks the start of a first wave of modern environmental concern.[1]
1969	Greenpeace and Friends of the Earth founded.
1970	UK Department of the Environment established. Earth Day celebrated globally—first mass global citizen action on environmental issues.
1972	UN (Stockholm) Conference on the Human Environment. First major global gathering to address environmental issues. Neo-Malthusian dimension to environmentalism seen in the publication of the Club of Rome's *Limits to Growth*.

1 For key developments in the US during the 1960s see 'Environmentalism 1960–1986' at <history.sandiego.edu/gen/nature/environ5.html>.

1973	As a direct result of the Stockholm Conference, the first EEC Environmental Action Programme is adopted, marking the emergence of what is now the European Union as an important actor in the development of environmental policy and a major source of environmental law.
1974	Control of Pollution Act enacted. First piece of legislation not simply targeted at single environmental media or industrial processes, but far short of integrated control. OECD reports into making the 'polluter pay'.
1985	Ozone Treaty agreed. Subsequent discovery of hole in ozone layer over Antarctica.
1987	The Brundtland Report (*Our Common Future*) is published by the UN. Seen as a seminal report on the linkages between developmental and environmental problems, and on the advancement of technological solutions, and popularises the term 'sustainable development'. The Single European Act formally embeds environmental policy within the EC.
1988	Intergovernmental Panel on Climate Change established. Mrs Thatcher's 'Green' speech stresses environmental stewardship.
1989	National Rivers Authority established as the first regulatory body in this area without conflicting operational duties. Marks a shift in attitudes generally towards environmental crime.
1990	The Environmental Protection Act establishes a system of integrated pollution control for the most polluting industrial processes.
1992	The (Rio) UN Conference on the Environment and Development marks the highpoint of this second wave of environmental concern. Major treaties on climate change and biodiversity signed.
1995	The Environment Act establishes (in England and Wales) a national Environment Agency, subject to sustainable development duties. The Agency becomes the largest of its kind in the world.
2001	Aarhus Convention comes into force, a key landmark in environmental citizenship establishing rights in relation to public participation, environmental information and access to justice.

There has also been a shift in the emphasis of the law to reflect newer environmental concerns. Many problems were simply not perceived as such in the 1960s, or were subordinated to other more pressing matters, such as the raising of living standards or the provision of full employment. The emphasis at that stage was on health and safety matters, a point well illustrated by the placing of the Alkali and Clean Air Inspectorate within the Health and Safety Executive when it was established in 1974. Land use was also emphasized; indeed, it could be argued that the very fact that Britain had (and still has) what is probably the world's most comprehensive system of land use planning led to the concentration of controls at that stage rather than to encouraging the development of adequate continuing pollution controls.

By comparison, the focus of the laws that have been enacted in the last 30 years or so has been on the control of pollution, with the environment increasingly being regarded as worthy of protection in its own right. This does not mean that the environment has been accorded 'rights' (as the definitions of 'pollution' and 'the environment' in the EPA 1990 illustrates, see p. 7), but it is undeniable that pollution control laws have moved on from narrow, public health-based concerns to encompass a much wider range of adverse changes to the natural environment. There has also been a growing concern, and legal responses, to global and transfrontier problems, the control of hazardous substances and processes, the minimisation and management of waste, the conservation of natural resources and the protection of ecosystems. In short, current concerns tend to reflect the need to control the almost inevitable by-products of the modern, technological, post-industrial information age.

Features of the modern age

Legislative consolidation and direction

The process of producing a coherent body of environmental law began with the Control of Pollution Act 1974. This put most of the law on water pollution and waste disposal in one place, but a measure of the sectoral approach of the time is that it had little to say about air pollution.

Although the Control of Pollution Act 1974 is now virtually fully replaced by later legislation in England and Wales, the emergence of a more coherent statute book has certainly moved forward some distance. In terms of legislation, the law is becoming more concentrated in a smaller number of Acts (see Box 2.4). One of the important features of this process is that the development and direction of the statutory controls is more planned than before. The main Acts referred to below are all government-sponsored Acts, illustrating an increasing tendency to plan and interlink legislation properly (The Government White Paper *This Common Inheritance* (Cm 1200, 1990) underlined this commitment to a planned development of environmental policy.) By contrast, many environmental measures in the past resulted from single issue campaigns, of from private members' bills.

BOX 2.4 **The main environmental statutes**

Environmental Protection Act 1990: contains the main bulk of provisions on air pollution from stationary sources, waste management and disposal, the integrated control of the most potentially polluting processes (but see below), litter, the environmental impact of genetically modified organisms, noise and statutory control of environmental nuisances.

Pollution Prevention and Control Act 1999: the provisions controlling industrial processes in an integrated way are being replaced by the permitting system provided for in this Act (but fleshed out in regulations).

Water Resources Act 1991: contains much of the law on water pollution and water resources (the latter significantly revised by the Water Act 2003).

Water Industry Act 1991: matters relating to water supply and sewerage, including economic regulation of the water and sewerage companies.

Wildlife and Countryside Act 1981: includes much of the relevant law on nature conservation in Parts I and II (significantly amended by the Countryside and Rights of Way Act 2000).

Environment Act 1995: introduced new legal provisions in relation to liability for contaminated land (as Part IIA of the EPA 1990). Also created the Environment Agency, which took over functions related to integrated pollution control, waste regulation, water pollution and water resources, and radioactive substances, although without any major changes in the substance of the law.

Town and Country Planning Act 1990: consolidated most of the relevant statutory law on town and country planning and tree protection (major changes to the planning of development have been made by the Planning and Compulsory Purchase Act 2004).

None of these Acts is a full code in relation to the relevant subject matter. There are numerous individual issues dealt with by separate pieces of legislation, such as on radioactivity, or on pesticides. There are other issues where the controls are still spread amongst a large number of Acts, such as in relation to landscape protection. It is also necessary to point out that much of the detailed law in any area is actually provided in statutory instruments and a wide range of other documents made under the relevant Acts. This is especially true of much of the vast body of law with its origins in EC environmental directives.

National strategies

Alongside this more planned approach has been, in recent years, the introduction of a more strategic approach to many environmental issues. In a response to the traditional reactive mode of policy and rule making, a wide array of national strategies have been adopted. This is partly because of the need to flesh out the policy framework in the sustainable development strategy; partly to indicate the manner of achieving certain goals or targets which have been set down either nationally or internationally; and partly because of the history of inadequate policy making in many areas of environmental policy. Thus we have (or in some cases will have) strategies on sustainable development, waste management, air quality, chemicals, climate change, soil protection, sustainable distribution and sustainable construction. Whilst these can provide a helpful framework for future action and specific targets which can be aimed at, there is a danger that the overuse of such strategies can be used to present mere 'aspirations' which can be manipulated or dropped if progress in meeting the targets is slow. On the other hand, recent legislation on strategic environmental assessment should give the public a greater say in the process by which some of these strategic plans are adopted.

Institutional coherence

There is also an increasing institutional coherence. Her Majesty's Inspectorate of Pollution was established in 1987 to bring together a number of sectoral Inspectorates. The National Rivers Authority was established in 1989 as a national body (in England and Wales) regulating water pollution and a number of other activities affecting water quality. In 1996, the creation of the Environment Agency brought the main pollution control functions (integrated pollution control, waste management and the regulation of water pollution) under one administrative body for the first time. (Specialist conservation agencies like the Nature Conservancy Council have historically remained separated from the pollution control authorities, although the extent to which nature and landscape conservation have been linked institutionally has tended to fluctuate.)

A different aspect of developments in relation to institutional responsibilities has been the policy of splitting production from regulation (or differentiating the 'poachers' from the 'gamekeepers'). As early as the Victorian period the reluctance of bodies which were themselves polluters to prosecute others for doing so was recognized (see Box 2.1). In more recent years this was achieved by the creation of the National Rivers Authority. Prior to that the regulation of water pollution was the responsibility of the regional water authorities which were also responsible for causing pollution from sewage works which they operated. Another example is the enforced separation of waste regulation functions from waste disposal functions in the EPA 1990, a process that was taken further in the Environment Act 1995 (see p. 586).

Integrative laws

The EPA 1990 gave Her Majesty's Inspectorate of Pollution integrated powers over the most hazardous industrial processes, meaning that for the first time discharges to air, water, and land were regulated in a unified way. This was intended to overcome some of problems of a sectoral approach (which have a long history—see Box 2.3). Central to this new approach to integrated pollution control was that the best available techniques not entailing excessive cost (BATNEEC) had to be used for controlling releases, and that these had to take the environment as a whole, having regard to the best practicable environmental option (BPEO) available in respect of the substances which may be released. This approach has been taken further under the Pollution Prevention and Control Act 1999—which takes integration a step further by looking at *inputs* such as energy consumption and resource use as well as polluting releases—but the vast majority of polluters remain subject to separate legal controls contained in separate statutes and regulations.

Administrative centralization

A final change, which may be seen from the examples referred to, is that environmental protection is becoming increasingly centralized (see further p. 253), both in terms of where standards are set and which bodies implement and enforce these. This must, however, be seen against the perspective that, as stated above, the system inherited from earlier years was particularly decentralized. There are many reasons for this centralization:

- the increasing complexity of environmental risks which create technological and scientific demands on regulators;
- years of central government antipathy towards local government;
- the growth in emphasis on uniform and integrated planning of solutions to problems;
- the increase in institutional coherence; and
- the impact of EC membership.

Changing styles of regulation

The development of regulatory approaches, and current policy, is considered in detail in Chapter 8. But we cover here some of the main developments that have taken place.

Command and control remains the central pillar of pollution control legislation, and more prescriptive approaches have also been introduced in other areas like the protection of important wildlife sites where the law previously took a more voluntaristic approach (see the changes to the Wildlife and Countryside Act made by the Countryside and Rights of Way Act 2000, p. 806). But other legal techniques have been used to try to influence decision-making and behaviour. These have ranged from procedural laws (such as those requiring that significant environmental impacts of certain major development projects are assessed before consent is given), and information-based provisions (rules opening up access to environmental information, or eco-labels), to the use of economic instruments (such as taxes on disposing of waste in landfills, and the Climate Change Levy).

This use of a broader range of instruments reflects a third phase in the growth of sources of environmental law: traditional public law 'command and control' legislation is combined with different regulatory approaches to secure the most effective forms of control over environmental pollution. This blend of instruments has been termed 'smart regulation.'[2] Underlying this search for the optimal mix of controls is the idea that regulation should work with the market wherever possible.

This search for flexibility in the selection of the instruments is illustrated by climate change policy:

BOX 2.5 **Flexibility and climate change**

Consultation papers on the Climate Change programme considered a range of instruments including voluntary agreements to reduce energy consumption, a direct tax on the use of energy, emissions trading schemes, growth in renewable energy and emission controls under the implementation of the Integrated Pollution Prevention and Control Directive.

In addition the Kyoto Protocol (which contains the latest agreed programme for reduction in emissions which contribute to climate change) has other innovative mechanisms for achieving compliance with cuts in emissions of greenhouse gases including: 'emissions trading' whereby an industrialised country can buy or sell emission 'credits' to or from other countries; or the use of the so-called 'clean development mechanism' whereby industrialised countries can earn cuts in their own targets by investing in greenhouse gas reduction projects in developing countries. These 'flexibility mechanisms' are not without criticism but they reflect an increasing concern that policies should be as adaptable as possible in order to meet the specified goals and targets.

The blending of different types of instruments means that if one mechanism is less effective, another mechanism may reduce the gap between aspiration and the achievement of the policy objective (see further Chapters 8 and 16).

Enforcement

Access to information is important in ensuring that there is adequate enforcement of environmental legislation. Leaving enforcement to specialized regulators has historically given rise to potential conflicts (see Box 2.2 and also p. 290), and there are good reasons why other actors such as environmental NGOs should be able to bring enforcement proceedings

---

2. See Gunningham and Grabosky, *Smart Regulation: Designing Environmental Policy* (Oxford: Clarendon Press, 1998).

or at the very least to bring potential breaches of the law to the notice of enforcement bodies such as the European Commission. (The costs of non-compliance are discussed in more detail at p. 41).

The rise of EC environmental law

A most important factor in all of these changes has been the influence of the European Community (EC). The EC has a well-developed environmental policy and has passed numerous pieces of environmental law in the past 30 years since it adopted its first Environmental Action Programme in 1973, some of which pre-date explicit reference to the environment in the EC Treaty which did not occur until the Single European Act 1987 (see p. 183). Some of these have been implemented through the framework of national statute law described above, while others have (or will be) given effect to by secondary legislation.

BOX 2.6 **Some Key EC Directives**

- Directives 75/442 and 91/156 (Waste Framework Directives).

- Directive 76/160 (Bathing Waters).

- Directive 2001/80 (Large Combustion Plants).

- Directives 79/409 (Wild Birds) and 92/43 (Habitats).

- Directive 85/337 (Environmental Impact Assessment).

- Directive 96/61 (Integrated Pollution Prevention and Control).

- Directive 2000/60 (Water Framework Directive).

At a general level, membership of the EC has led to the consideration and adoption of new methods of control and to the need to confront environmental issues in an organised way at central government level. More specifically, EC legislation and pressure has led to many actual and proposed changes in the law (often after British resistance), for example, on sulphur dioxide emissions, nature conservation, and reductions in emissions from vehicles. Some of these, such as the introduction of a ban on dumping sewage sludge at sea, also illustrate the way in which international law has played a part in the evolution of UK environmental law in the modern era (see Box 2.7). Because of concerns that it should not get too involved in the substance of individual decisions about things like development consents, the EC has played an important role in the rise of procedural environmental laws such as the Environmental Impact Assessment Directive, mentioned above.

BOX 2.7 **Marine disposal of sewage sludge**

1990: The Third International North Sea Conference (attended by the Environment Ministers of the eight North Sea states and the EC) reached a political agreement to phase out the disposal of sludge by dumping from ships, or discharge from pipelines, by the end of 1998. Such agreements are, in law, strictly non-binding.

1990: The provisions of the ban are repeated in Decision 90/1 of the Oslo and Paris Commissions (the predecessors of what is now the Commission of the OSPAR North Atlantic Convention); in theory, Decisions are 'binding' but there is no legal enforcement mechanism.

1991: The ban is provided for in Article 14 EC Urban Waste Water Treatment Directive.

1996/97: UK still dumping around one-quarter of its sewage sludge, 264,000 tonnes, at sea.

December 1998: Sludge ban under EC law effective. All UK dumping ceased.

Other changes have been more indirect; for example, the Wildlife and Countryside Act 1981 was necessary to comply with EC Directive 79/409 on Wild Birds, and the opportunity was taken to modify other areas of the law at the same time. Without the EC obligation there must be some doubt whether any legislation would have been brought forward at that time—and even greater doubt as to whether it would have been persevered with in the light of the widespread opposition to the Government's original proposals, which were significantly altered as the Bill passed through Parliament.

Internationalization

A feature of the modern age of environmental law has been the international dimension of many problems. High-profile issues, such as global warming, depletion of the ozone layer, and the global conservation of biological diversity, have galvanized interest in environmental issues, and an increasing amount of legislation gives effect to international obligations, either directly or via EC law. Major conferences at Stockholm in 1972 and at Rio de Janeiro in 1992 in particular played important roles in spurring the global community into action. There is little doubt that the future agenda will increasingly be set on the international stage.

Sustainable development and environmental integration

In the last 20 years or so a central concept has been 'sustainable development', an idea that was originally developed by the World Commission on Environment and Development (the Brundtland Commission) in its report, *Our Common Future*, in 1987. We can think of sustainable development as a bridge between the emergence and development of a body of environmental law, from the Victorian era onwards, to some of the future developments and challenges that are considered later in this chapter.

There are three key strands to *Our Common Future*. First, it defined sustainable development in general terms as 'development that meets the needs of the present without compromising the ability of future generations to meet their own needs', thus suggesting that global resources (including environmental resources) should be measured, with the objective of ensuring that they are not depleted over time. Clearly, this idea requires some further development itself, in particular in relation to how one goes about measuring intangible global assets and whether it is permissible to substitute one type of asset for another.

Secondly, its central concern was the increasing globalization of various crises (environmental, developmental, energy, etc.), and the connections between them, noting that 'They are all one.' It therefore went much further than the steps towards policy and legal integration of the kind that we have seen took place with the EPA 1990, because it stressed that real progress would only be made if the connections between, for example, environmental protection and energy consumption could be made.

Thirdly, although sustainable development represents a commitment to economic growth, growth can be positive if it is steered in the right direction. For example, since all pollution is a waste of something (energy, raw materials, etc.) to the polluter, then businesses ought to be able to reduce pollution and at the same time increase profits. In other words, environmental policy should work with the market and shift from simply penalizing polluters to trying to make them internalize the external costs of their pollution or simply spreading good advice on how to cut down on waste in its various forms. This is one aspect of what is known as ecological modernization (see p. 68).

As a matter of UK law, the term 'sustainable development' first appeared in the Environment Act 1995, which requires the Agency, in discharging its functions so to protect or enhance the environment, taken as a whole, as to make the contribution towards attaining the objective of achieving sustainable development required of it by Ministers (see further p. 176). It now appears across a wide range of Acts and policy guidance, and since the changes made by the 1997 Amsterdam Treaty is mentioned in the EC Treaty, which expressly links integrating environmental protection into all other EC policy areas with reference to sustainable development. The European Court of Justice has used this duty to justify some quite far reaching relaxations to the basic free movements laws in the interests of environmental protection (see pp. 215 and 217). And it also has legal status in international law, including international trade law (e.g. the preamble to the WTO Agreement refers to the 'optimal use [of resources] . . . in accordance with the objective of sustainable development').

BOX 2.8 Sustainable development—solution or sham?

The leading environmental lawyer Stephen Tromans has written that: 'The principle of "sustainability" has now become a totem to which all must bow, a debased currency appropriated by politicians more concerned with the next election result than any supposed long term consequences. Or it is seen as a useful profit line for advice by consultants, who then self-interestedly promote it. To doubt it has become heresy. A decision to expand Stansted airport can be justified as the "sustainable" option. . . . Ah, you may say, but "sustainability" is simply shorthand for the relevant criteria in each case, and everyone understands it as such. To some extent that may be a fair point, but the response is that it would be better to justify or repudiate a proposed course of action on the relevant explicit grounds rather than under the spurious rigour of portmanteau "sustainability" criteria' (UKELA e-journal (March 2004) 10).

Second generation environmental policy

In the light of EC membership and the pressure now brought to bear by the whole international community on environmental issues, it is difficult to disentangle British policies from global and regional ones. It is also difficult to predict the future accurately in this area because—as the US rejection of the Kyoto Protocol on climate change shows—environmental policy continues to be a highly political area.

That said, there is a clear shift of emphasis away from controlling the impact of pollution, towards in effect trying to design pollution (and other environmental harms like adverse consequences on nature) out of industrial and other processes. Put differently, there is a change of focus away from tackling the most apparent symptoms of environmental problems and on to their source. This evolution is often referred to as modern environmental policy entering its *second generation*. Some examples of this shift are as follows.

First generation	Second generation
Waste disposal and management	Waste minimization and elimination
Environmental quality standards	Eliminating hazardous substances
Controlling stationary, point source pollution (e.g. chimneys)	Controlling the effects of pollutants from diffuse and mobile sources (e.g. climate change)
Focus on polluting industries	Shared responsibility for environmental problems between government, producers and consumers.
Environmental regulation (top-down, mainly via command and control regulation)	Environmental governance (more diffuse, greater role for public participation in decision-making)

Preventing environmental harm

As we said the emphasis is shifting away from the more traditional reactive methods of solving environmental problems towards the prevention of harm. There are different aspects to this. For example, harm can be prevented by setting stringent discharge or emissions limits, including bans on certain substances entering the natural environment (an example of this is the Water Framework Directive which requires the 'cessation' of discharges of priority hazardous substances (see Box 18.1)). Although this looks like traditional command and control regulation, the innovation is the underlying assumption that no safe level can be set for certain dangerous substances in an environmental medium. In the case of these water pollutants, the main reason for seeking their elimination is that they bio-accumulate (i.e. they accumulate the higher up the marine food chain one goes) and are not dispersed in the environment in the way that some pollutants can be. But as a policy shift it is still quite a radical step.

Alternatively, harm can be prevented not just by looking at the production process but by trying to 'design out' various harms that such products might give rise to. This is the approach taken, for example, with old vehicles, the disposal of which gives rise to various environmental problems. Under a recent EC directive on so-called 'end of life vehicles', producers are required to set up collection systems and ensure that a minimum percentage of each vehicle is recycled and re-used. This puts the burden on lessening the wider impact of the product (and the associated costs) firmly on the producer, who is clearly best placed to know what materials etc have been used (see p. 615).

Looking at the whole life-cycle of products is also the approach that is now being taken to waste reduction more generally. For many years both law and policy have put waste minimization at the top of the hierarchy of controls without any noticeable impact (indeed, the amount of waste being generated has continued to rise). One way to tackle this is to shift the focus away from the question 'what should we do with waste?' to the prior question 'how can we generate less waste?' This approach, shifting attention towards the product and away from the waste it generates is at the heart of recent moves by the EC to introduce an integrated product policy (see p. 621).

Setting environmental targets

First generation environmental law and policy was, as we have said, often about curbing the worst excesses of industrialization as these affected humans (e.g. preventing the spread of disease or environmental blight), and only latterly encompassing other adverse changes. There are some signs that the new era will also judge the legality of activities against a notional environment free from human activity. Indeed, this is the approach taken in the 2000 EC Water Framework Directive. Although the main obligation is to aim to achieve 'good status' of water (meaning good chemical and ecological status), its higher aspiration is that high ecological status is established where (amongst other things):

there are no, or only very minor, anthropogenic alterations to the values of the physico-chemical and hydromorphological elements for the surface water body type from those normally associated with that type under undisturbed conditions.

Although not without its analytical difficulties, and strong doubts about how much effort will be expended to achieve high ecological status, this is a move from (negatively) controlling pollution to (positively) setting and achieving environmental quality objectives. Moreover, these objectives are not based on the environment being the conduit for any harm to humans; environmental quality is clearly being regarded as an end in itself.

Tackling diffuse pollution

There are various aspects to this. There may be no environmental gain if emissions from one factory are controlled but more factories are constructed (see Box 2.3). For example, laws making car engines quieter have barely kept pace with the rapid rise in the number of cars on the road. There are also problems in curbing pollution from diffuse sources rather than more readily identifiable sources such as factory chimneys or discharge pipes. The entry of nitrates causes water quality problems, but these tend to leach unseen from agricultural land or fall as deposits of nitric acid originating from vehicle exhausts. It is difficult to use traditional command and control techniques to tackle problems like this, which often stem from the aggregate of numerous activities which in themselves seem fairly innocuous, and more imaginative solutions need to be found.

Sharing responsibility

The EC has championed the notion of 'shared responsibility' meaning that responsibility for environmental problems is shared between government, producers and consumers. By suggesting that producers and consumers should be empowered to make decisions that have an impact on environmental performance, it heralds the development of a wider range of legal and policy responses to environmental problems.

There is another dimension to the idea of shared responsibility which is that important environmental policy issues are not only the concern of a remote group of individuals or companies with the label of 'polluters' (and whose changed behaviour would make everything all right), but that environmental protection is a matter for everyone and involves everyone making informed decisions about their own lifestyles.

Although some general pollution offences can be committed by anyone, traditionally the law has not always imposed the same responsibilities on individuals as it has on companies. For example, householders are generally exempt from waste management licensing (see p. 597). Or in practice, individuals may not feel the force of the law in the way that companies may, e.g. anyone pouring paint down a drain is unlikely to be prosecuted, either because the individual amount of the pollution loading is fairly minimal or, more likely, because the law is simply not designed to identify, regulate, and punish individuals in this situation. It is easier and more effective to regulate the solvent factory, but when the low hanging regulatory fruit has been picked and additional improvements are being sought then this might only be possible by regulating individual behaviour more closely (e.g. by-laws which provide offences for not separating domestic waste). The more that the law regulates individual behaviour rather than just trying to steer it, the more that conflicts will arise between environmental protection and other values like individual liberty.[3]

A final point here is that the law must strike the right balance between those whose behaviour might be changed to address an environmental problem. This is a longstanding concern. For example, Britain's ageing industrial base creates difficulties when new, improved controls and standards are introduced. Fairness requires that existing producers are given some time to adapt to new standards, yet there is at the same time a problem of unfairness if controls are introduced so as to produce an inequality between new and existing producers. The same essential problem can be seen in trying to introduce clean energy technologies. These will only make a difference if they are used. This might be done in part by requiring that new developers only use energy from sources such as on-site renewable electricity generation (but at the moment government guidance makes this unlawful because of the undue burden on developers). Another example is that all the new EC Member States have derogations which allow them to postpone the deadlines for complying with key environmental directives for several years (see Box 7.9).

Environmental governance

At a simple level, 'governance' is a term used to distinguish forms of decision-making which are less top-down than traditional approaches have been (where the legislature makes the rules with little public input; described by one commentator as the 'vote, shut up, and obey' approach).[4] Central to governance is widening public participation in decision-making. Involving a wider community of interest is said to provide for greater legitimation of the decision-making process (which is important when law enforcement is in the hands of specialist, unelected bodies such as the Environment Agency) and lead to a better quality of decision-making by involving key actors in the rule-making process and

---

3. D. Wilkinson, *Environment and Law* (London: Routledge, 2002), 262–3.
4. P. Selznick, *The Moral Commonwealth* (Berkeley: University of California Press), 314.

improving the feedback processes that allow regulators to improve on the existing ways of doing things.

Environmental law—reflections and future prospects

The uncertainties about how environmental policy will develop are magnified when it comes to forecasting the further evolution of environmental law. For example, the obligations entered into under the climate change treaty provided targets without identifying the specific legal (or otherwise) instruments that would have to be used. So even where the direction of policy is fairly clear, there is the added uncertainty of knowing which way (and to what extent) law will be used to reach these goals.

The starting point, however, is to repeat the proposition that environmental law has not been developed as a self-contained discipline, but has simply borrowed concepts from other areas of law. One result is undoubtedly a degree of incoherence, but another is that the objective of the protection of the environment is not always best served by the legal mechanisms available, because these other areas were not developed with the particular problems of environmental protection in mind. For example, the private law concentrates on the protection of private interests and has difficulties when it comes to protecting common or public interests in the unowned environment. No damages are payable for harm to the environment as such, and only those with personal or property rights may bring an action (thus excluding animals, trees, rivers, etc). No value is placed on the environment itself and environmental protection is simply an incidental by-product of the protection of other interests (see Case box 2.1). As Lord Scarman observed, 'for "environment" a traditional lawyer reads "property": English law reduces environmental problems to questions of property. . . . The judicial development of the law, vigorous and imaginative though it has been, has been found wanting' (*English Law—The New Dimension* (1974)).

CASE 2.1 *Cambridge Water Co. v Eastern Counties Leather plc* [1994] 2 AC 264

Over many years, solvents had been spilt at a tannery, ending up in an aquifer from which CWC had the right to abstract water. The contamination took the water below EC drinking water quality standards. The most cost-effective action for CWC was to sink another borehole at a cost of £1m. CWC eventually lost its case in the House of Lords (see p. 362). Even had it won, however, the groundwater would have remained contaminated. The legal interest at stake was the public law right to abstract the water; as a matter of common law principle, there were no property rights in the groundwater. So whether CWC won or lost, the aquifer would remain contaminated.

Note that the National Rivers Authority (now the Environment Agency) did in fact require the aquifer to be cleaned up—showing the reach of public regulation beyond private law disputes—which resulted in an indemnity dispute (*Eastern Counties Leather plc v Eastern Counties Leather Group Ltd* [2003] Env LR 13, see also p. 696).

There have been some steps to use private liability mechanisms to combat particular environmental problems—for example, liability funds to pay for the clean up after major oil spills, which can also be used to pay for restoration of the natural environment (at least where spending money would be more appropriate than simply letting nature restore itself over time; see p. 392). Recently there have also been some limited steps to use civil liability as a supporting mechanism to bolster other environmental regimes like those protecting important species and habitats, but again the response has been partial and we still remain some way from having general laws that would in effect allow bodies like environmental NGOs to sue for damages when some aspect of the unowned environment has been harmed (see p. 393).

Public law does recognize the public interest, but difficulties arise out of a lack of acceptance of the idea that the environment has some independent status or value, as distinct from rights conferred on individuals and communities. Even the criminal law struggles with environmental 'crimes', since it has often been pointed out in the courts that many of the offences created are not criminal in the 'true' sense (see the acceptance by the House of Lords in *Alphacell Ltd v Woodward* [1972] AC 824 that water pollution offences are in the category of 'acts which in the public interest are prohibited under a penalty).'[5] Finally, the structure of the judicial system (with its emphasis on adversarial and backward-looking two-party litigation and with its procedural rules which are not user-friendly to those wishing to bring environmental cases and which fail to give the public interest a separate voice)[6] is not particularly well-suited to consideration of most typical environmental disputes, for a variety of reasons (considered in more detail in Chapters 1 and 3):

- they have multiple causes;
- they give rise to complex scientific arguments;
- they involve a complex interplay between public, private and criminal law; and
- they require the balancing of difficult political or policy questions.

With these current defects in mind, the following thoughts can be put forward about the evolution of environmental law.

One criticism of 'command and control' laws has always been that the sanctions that may be imposed may be inappropriate. Consideration may,[7] therefore, be given to the 'decriminalization' of whole areas of environmental law, so that a distinction could be drawn between, on the one hand, infringements that are properly characterized as administrative in nature and, on the other, truly criminal breaches, such as blatant cases of environmental vandalism. One advantage of this may be to encourage stiffer penalties for those in the second category. In turn this is linked with the idea of improving the effectiveness of sentencing for environmental crimes. Although there have been attempts to introduce consistent sentencing principles which would encourage judges to impose higher

5. But note that one consequence of this is that the offences themselves are interpreted more strictly in favour of the prosecution than they would be if they were 'true crimes' where greater protections are given to the defendant. See further Box 3.3 and p. 281.

6. There now appears to be greater scope to bring amicus curiae (friend of the court) briefs—see the *Alconbury* case (*R v Secretary of State for the Environment, Transport and the Regions ex parte Holding and Barnes plc and others* [2001] UKHL 23)—but concern at how much court time is given to counsel to argue these.

7. And in some respects has, see Woods and Macrory, *Environmental Civil Penalties: A More Proportionate Response to Regulatory Breach* (London: UCL, 2003).

fines, particularly in relation to wealthy defendants, these will only magnify the problems associated with conflating true environmental crime with routine administrative breaches. Neither is acceptable but sentencing for the former should be based upon the need to sanction and deter whilst in the case of the latter it should be aimed at ensuring any environmental harm is rectified and prevented in future. Politically, 'decriminalization' may be difficult to sell, but in relation to new obligations there are already examples of the use of civil penalties (see, e.g., in relation to the renewable transport fuel obligation under the Energy Act 2004, s. 129).

There is, perhaps, a growing realization that the different areas of law—public law, private law, criminal law—merely provide, in the environmental context, a set of different tools to achieve a specified objective, in this case the protection of the environment. For example, in relation to contaminated land leading to groundwater contamination, someone has to 'pay' for the contamination, either by cleaning it up, or by living with the consequences (see Box 2.9). The interesting thing about the solution provided in the Environment Act 1995 is that it combines the various tools in quite a sophisticated fashion and produces a situation where the public interest is protected by a combination of mechanisms that borrow from public, private, and criminal law (see further Chapter 17).

BOX 2.9 **Paying for contaminated land**

There are essentially four possible parties who could 'pay' for historically contaminated land: the polluter could be made liable; the current owner or occupier could be liable; the state could pay (i.e. through some public clean-up mechanism)—this really means that the public pays through some form of taxation; or, finally, the loss could lie where it falls, meaning that the environment and the local community (e.g. fishery owners, water companies) effectively 'pay'. For a policy-maker the issue is how to come up with a solution that is effective, efficient and fair, whilst the tools that are available include, but are not limited to, legal mechanisms.

The above example raises the question of whether the development of the law is a matter for the courts or for Parliament. In *Cambridge Water Co. v Eastern Counties Leather plc* [1994] 2 AC 264 (see Case box 2.1), Lord Goff stated in respect of environmental protection:

given that so much well-informed and carefully structured legislation is now being put in place for this purpose, there is less need for the courts to develop a common law principle to achieve the same end, and indeed it may well be undesirable that they should do so.

This can be interpreted as a reflection of the fact that Parliament is able to create a coherent and structured system, rather than one developed on an ad hoc, case-by-case basis. But it also reflects the point that Parliament has a greater democratic legitimacy than the courts when it comes to allocating responsibility for environmental harm. In the same passage Lord Goff also stated:

As a general rule, it is more appropriate for strict liability in respect of operations of high risk to be imposed by Parliament, than by the courts.

This raises a different point about the *nature* of the liability that should be imposed. At present there is a clear division between those, such as the Government and most industrial organizations, who see the imposition of strict liability as unfair and punitive and therefore wish to retain a fault-based system as far as possible, and those, including the EC Commission, who see strict liability as the most efficient and effective method of allocating responsibility for environmental harm. This issue is likely to remain a controversial one for many years (see further pp. 393–5).

Notwithstanding the above points about the shortcomings of the courts system, there is a healthy debate as to whether there should be a separate court or tribunal dealing with environmental cases. Some tentative steps towards this goal have already been made with the amalgamation of administrative appeals within the Planning Inspectorate. The proponents of such a court argue that many of the procedural hurdles which are inherent in the current system could be bypassed with the creation of a new institutional framework for resolving environmental disputes (see p. 347). Although there is a strong connection between the inadequacies of the current system and certain procedural flaws (e.g. the rules on standing, delay, representative actions, funding and expert evidence), it must be borne in mind that there are many occasions where the substantive defects of the law would remain.

What does current experience tell us about the way in which the approach of British Courts may develop in future? Whilst acknowledging the dangers of generalization, it is possible to detect different approaches to different types of cases. In the civil or common law cases, the courts appear to be keen to restrict the extension of liability for environmental harm unless there are clearly identifiable parameters within which future decisions can be made. In *Cambridge Water Co. v Eastern Counties Leather plc* [1994] 2 AC 264 (see Case box 2.1) and *Hunter v Canary Wharf Ltd* [1997] 2 WLR 684, the House of Lords refused to extend common law principles to accommodate the concept of environmental damage or damage to those who did not have any property interests respectively. There may be some change to this to accommodate human rights concerns (see p. 366) but the basic point remains that the courts are always likely to defer to Parliament and decisions of specialist regulators when it comes to setting environmental standards.

Administrative challenges to environmental decisions have also been dealt with in a very narrow fashion by the courts. Although the courts have not rejected every challenge, it is uncommon for environmental decisions to be overturned. (In a recent study, in only 4 out of 55 environmental judicial review cases was the decision overturned.)[8] Although this often reflects the essentially discretionary nature of the decision-making process in many environmental matters, it also suggests that, in the main, the courts have been very cautious when it comes to developing new ideas on environmental protection.

In contrast, the cause of environmental protection has tended to fare rather better where administrative discretion is less at issue. This comes through most clearly from decisions on the balancing of freedom of trade and national measures restricting this for environmental reasons. When bodies like the European Court of Justice, and also the Appellate Body of the World Trade Organisation (in effect, the world trade court) have had to rule on this, the cause of environmental protection has tended to fare rather well.

---

8. *Modernising Environmental Justice: Regulation and the Role of an Environmental Tribunal* (London: UCL, 2003).

In relation to criminal cases, the courts have increasingly adopted a purposive approach to construing statutes. For example, in the case of water pollution offences, the extent to which successive courts have been willing to find that a party has 'caused' pollution has been very wide. This purposive approach appears to stem from the judicial desire to provide law that is effective in terms of environmental protection.

There is another area where the courts have proved active. In more recent years, there has been an increased willingness to develop judicial review mechanisms to provide for openness in decision-making and accountability to the public for decisions made in its name. For example, the courts now accept a very wide role for environmental and other public interest groups in litigation, and the value of meaningful public participation in decision-making has been recognized at the highest level (see p. 545). This can be seen as part of a wider process of recognizing the contested nature of environmental decision-making (see Box 2.10)

BOX 2.10 **Values and environmental standards**

'Setting environmental standards is an exercise in practical judgement. Judgement is reached by a process of deliberation which seeks ways of meeting a multiplicity of constraints and viewpoints ... Better ways need to be developed for articulating people's values and taking them into account from the earliest stage in what have been hitherto relatively technocratic procedures.'
(Royal Commission on Environmental Pollution, *Setting Environmental Standards*, 21st Report (1998) Cm 4053, paras 8.31 and 8.37.)

Despite the negative points that have emerged in the previous discussion, there will certainly be a continuing increase in environmental litigation. The increased formality of many areas of environmental policy increases the possibility of a successful public law challenge; practising lawyers are increasingly aware of the possibilities thrown up by legal action; environmental interest groups have learnt the usefulness of the legal process in making political points as well as in winning cases; and EC law and now the ECHR throw up a whole new area of litigation arising out of the doctrines of claims about EC rights and of Convention rights. All manner of legal claims are now being brought in areas—such as airport expansion, the dismantling of old ships, discharges from Sellafield, oil exploration, the redevelopment of football stadia, the import of mahogany from Brazil—where even a few years ago the likelihood that such claims would have been brought was very slim.

Finally, whatever happens in relation to these major issues, there will continue to be some fine-tuning of the mechanisms that already exist. One of the defects of the law has been its piecemeal development, and it is clear that measures that have proved successful in one area are likely to be adopted in others.

The costs of compliance

Whatever the exact direction that the law takes, one thing is clear about the future; the cost of compliance with the law is going to rise sharply, both for polluters and for society in general. This is mainly because regulatory standards are getting stricter and are being enforced more rigorously. But there are other factors, such as a heightened perception of the true environmental cost of many activities (which is further increased when explicit links are drawn with the introduction of environmental taxes) and the greatly increased pressure that is being brought to bear by the public, environmental groups and green consumers and investors. The cost of sewage disposal illustrates the point (see Box 2.11).

BOX 2.11 **The demise of 'Flush and Forget'**

Disposal to the sewers has traditionally been a fairly cheap and efficient way of disposing of wastes. But the introduction of integrated pollution control meant that increased controls have been applied to discharges of prescribed substances to the sewers. The costs of sewage treatment are also increasing because of changes relating to the disposal of their own wastes by sewage works. For example, the standards set for discharges to controlled waters are being tightened as the Environment Agency reviews existing consents, in the light of the need to meet the requirements of the Urban Waste Water Treatment Directive. The cost of disposal of sewage sludge is rising fast. Not only has the cheap option of dumping sewage sludge in the sea been phased out (see Box 2.6), but the cost of disposal on land has risen significantly. Incineration is another possibility for disposal of sludge, but that too is coming under increasingly tight regulation (not to mention public opposition). The privatized nature of the sewerage undertakers emphasizes the need to take these factors into account, and undertakers are imposing tighter conditions and levying higher charges on discharges. All of which is putting pressure back up the chain on producers to reduce the polluting nature of their effluent.

There are other aspects to the cost of compliance. It may be that in the future certain operators will be required to have insurance covering the costs of cleaning up and restoring the environment in the event of a damaging incident (much in the way that all drivers must have compulsory third party insurance). There is also the issue of environmental subsidies and other incentives which governments might give to promote things like clean technologies and zero-carbon energy generation. In a European, and increasingly globalized, context, these will come under scrutiny for the possible effects they may have on the freedom of trade. But it may be asked whether, without some form of subsidy, these will really be able to compete with technologies which may themselves have been heavily subsidized to begin with.

The costs of non-compliance

Apart from the direct cost to business of complying with stricter regulatory controls, the potential liabilities for non-compliance are also increasing. These liabilities fall into six general categories:

- *Criminal liabilities.* The number of criminal offences for non-compliance with environmental legislation is immense, and the regulatory agencies have shown an increased willingness to resort to prosecution. Private prosecution is also a possibility.

Fines will be the usual penalty, though in a number of cases sentences of imprisonment have been imposed (there is normally a potential personal liability for directors and senior managers). Maximum fine levels have risen as have actual levels of fines imposed.

- *Administrative sanctions.* In most regulatory systems there is a range of options available to the regulator, including variation, suspension or revocation of a licence. Since these steps may lead to the closure of a plant, they are obviously of great importance.

- *Other administrative penalties.* If Member States do not meet their obligations under EC environmental law they can be fined. In some areas individual local authorities can be penalized if they fail to make the appropriate contribution to meeting these obligations, e.g. targets for diverting waste from landfill. Ultimately it is therefore local residents who will pay for non-compliance, through higher council tax bills.

- *Clean-up costs.* In most environmental legislation there is a power to clean up after a pollution incident and recover the cost from the polluter or (in some cases) the occupier. These costs often exceed the levels of fine which can be imposed.

- *Civil liability.* There is growing interest in the 'toxic torts', although many of the actions have in fact been around for a long time. Many environmental actions rest upon strict liability. Although liability may often be difficult to establish, the size of claims may be very high indeed.

- *Adverse publicity.* In practice the publicity attracted as a result of infringements of the law may be as costly as any direct costs.

In the light of all these risks, not to mention the increased costs of waste disposal and of complying with stricter standards, some of the most significant recent developments in the environmental field relate to management issues. For example, there is an international standard for environmental management systems (ISO 14001). Although this scheme is voluntary in the sense that there is no compulsion to join, there are pressures from within industry (e.g. the supply chain) and outside (e.g. from the public, insurers, and financial institutions) which mean that, in practice, environmental management systems need to be adopted.

 CHAPTER SUMMARY

1 The history of environmental law is the history of the state using statutory law to address some of the weaknesses of private law controls.

2 The central failings of private law (such as nuisance law) were that it protected private property rights rather poorly, and largely failed altogether in furthering broader environmental protection interests.

3 Much of what we now call environmental law has its origins in statutory public health-based controls from the Victorian and Edwardian era. This legacy is important—public health control is an important dimension to many environmental statutes—but it provides a narrow, anthropo-centric basis for the emergence of modern environmental law.

4 Early legal controls, which were often ad hoc and lacking coherence, tended to be formulated in

a way that gave public bodies—which were usually local rather than centralized authorities—considerable discretion in enforcing them.

5   Modern environmental law (from the 1960s to the present) departs from this earlier body of law in several ways.

6   A key development is the rise both of the European Community and of international agreements in setting environmental standards and making environmental laws.

7   In part because of this, there is a trend towards environmental standards being set centrally as a matter of law rather than locally as an exercise of administrative discretion, and greater formalism and legalism generally. There is a greater resort to law to challenge environmental decisions (which is not to say that the courts are necessarily any more likely to find in favour of such challengers).

8   A national (and powerful) Environment Agency has been created to implement and enforce key statutes on water, waste, seriously contaminated land and industrial processes.

9   There have been moves towards regulating the more polluting processes on an integrated basis, and on a broader scale ever increasing attention is being given to integrating environmental concerns into other areas of policy making (e.g. agriculture, transport, energy).

10 In terms of policy development there is a shift beyond fighting some of the 'easier battles' of tackling pollution from identifiable sources towards trying to combat pollution from diffuse sources and trying to design waste and pollution out of industrial processes. This usually involves trying to find the right blend of legal and non-legal tools rather than any single solution.

11 Increasing attention is being paid to the contribution that individuals make to environmental problems, but also to their role in improving environmental decision-making. These can be taken together as a concern with the 'green citizen'.

12 The costs of complying with environmental law, and with not complying with it, are both likely to rise.

Q QUESTIONS

1   What should the objectives of environmental law be (e.g. how far should we go to try to recreate an undisturbed environment?)

2   Catalogue the steps that have been taken to integrate the environment into decision-making, and to consider the environment in an integrated way. Do these go far enough?

3   What are the main challenges that environmental law will have to face in the immediate future? What lessons from history can help in addressing these?

4   To what extent does English law recognise the *public* interest in environmental protection?

FURTHER READING

There are several good books on the history of environmental problems. A. Markham, *A Brief History of Pollution* (London: Earthscan, 1994) is a short volume which gives an engaging overview, while more comprehensively C. Ponting, *A Green History of the World* (London: Sinclair-Stevenson, 1991) contains what can seem an almost unremitting stream of salient historical evidence (and also reminds us that what we now call environmental problems did not begin with the Victorians). A. Wohl, *Endangered Lives: Public Health in Victorian Britain* (London: Metheun, 1984) is the definitive history in this field. C. Rose, *The Dirty Man of Europe: The Great British Pollution Scandal*

(London: Simon & Schuster, 1990) is written by a leading campaigner of the 1980s who coined the term 'The Dirty Man of Europe' to describe the UK (particularly because of its reticence to introduce controls on sulphur emissions). D. Vogel, *National Styles of Regulation* (Ithaca: Cornell University Press, 1986) stretches back to the 19th century to try to explain the (then) shape of UK environmental policy. Further reading on the history of controls can be found within, and at the end of, the chapters in Part III of the book, while the regulatory issues introduced in this chapter are explored in more depth in Chapter 8.

G. Winter, 'Perspectives for environmental law—entering the fourth phase' (1989) 1 Journal of Environmental Law 38 remains a thought-provoking contribution and charts what the author sees as the shift from use to exploitation to management to new solutions respecting environmental uncertainties. As it was written in the very first issue of the Journal of Environmental Law it is interesting to reflect on how far we have come since then, and in which direction. A good source for thinking about current challenges is D. Osborn, 'From pollution control to sustainable development: lucid law for fuzzy objectives' (1999) 1 Env L Rev 79 which argues that modern environmental laws must *tend towards* solutions that are integrative and that pursue sustainable development rather than try to tackle single environmental problems with single, simplistic, legal solutions, but that the role of law in doing so, and making sure that everyone plays by the book, is no less important for that.

@ WEB LINKS

See our Online Resource Centre for links to a range of relevant historical and contemporary documents.

Values, principles, and environmental law

3

 Overview

In this chapter we consider the interaction between values and environmental law; this involves some reflection on differing attitudes to the environment. We then examine some of the ways in which these values are translated into political principles such as the goal of sustainable development or the precautionary principle and the question of whether these principles are capable of being rules or law in the sense that they create legally enforceable rights and duties. Finally we consider the role of human rights and environmental protection.

At the end of this chapter you should be able to:

✔ Identify some of the different approaches to environmental decision-making and some of the considerations which are taken into account when making decisions.

✔ Understand in outline the interaction between values and law, and the way in which differing environmental perspectives have an impact upon decision-making and dispute resolution.

✔ Understand in outline some of the main environmental principles and their role, and their translation into legal principles.

✔ Understand in outline the role that rights, especially human rights, play in environmental law and policy.

Introduction

One of the defining characteristics of environmental problems is their complexity. They are complex in the sense that there are often many interconnected variable elements to the problem. For example, there are strong links between the burning of fossil fuels, emissions from transport, deforestation, depletion of the ozone layer and climate change. Trying to 'solve' environmental problems means addressing different aspects of the problem which in turn give rise to their own challenges. For example, a partial solution to climate change might be to reduce the amount of energy produced from fossil fuels. This could be done by increasing the use of wind or nuclear energy. Unfortunately, these solutions have their own connected problems including visual impact, interference with nature conservation interests, capacity (i.e. low energy output requiring huge wind farms), nuclear waste disposal and associated risks. Other solutions might involve the creation of more forests as 'carbon sinks' or reducing car use. These have corresponding disadvantages (e.g. loss of agricultural land and loss of individual autonomy).

This complexity of environmental problems has the consequence that there are many ways of looking at, thinking about, even talking about the same problem. Just as an optical illusion can look like two different things at the same time so perspectives on the same environmental problems can vary. To some wind farms are a sustainable alternative energy source[1] to others an 'ineffective source of electricity . . . an example of green tokenism, which does nothing to meet any environmental objectives'.[2] Whether or not these alternatives are more or less attractive depends largely upon the values anyone attaches to the different variables (see further Box 22.1).

Environmental law may provide some assistance in resolving these sorts of tensions through pollution control or planning legislation which sets down a framework for making decisions. There is, however, no necessary connection between this framework and the decisions on what pollutants to ban, at what level to set an acceptable legal emission standard or what to decide in relation to an individual application for planning permission or pollution control authorisation. This gap between the procedural framework and the substantive decision is where environmental values play a critical role.

Values and environmental law

What do we mean by values? In its 21st Report, the Royal Commission on Environmental Pollution suggested that values were 'beliefs, either individual or social, about what is important in life and thus about the ends or objectives which should govern and shape public policies'.[3] The Royal Commission went further and identified certain factors which may influence individuals' attitudes to the environment. These included such things as the environment as a vital resource for humans; the richness of biodiversity; and the cultural, historical or social significance of the environment (e.g. an industrial landscape may be an important part of the local environment, or such natural features as the 'seven oaks' of the eponymous Kent town).

Taking the broad definition adopted by the RCEP, we can characterize 'environmental values' as 'what people believe to be important about the environment and thus what should be the priorities for environmental policy and ultimately environmental law'. At the outset, however, it is important to distinguish between, on the one hand, 'opinions and attitudes' and on the other, the wider, deeper sort of values which are held by groups and sections of society as a whole. Individual 'values' can be sincerely held opinions that fluctuate or are mutually inconsistent; at their worst they are little more than consumer-type preferences for a favourite brand of chocolate bar or washing powder. Representative values held by groups and sections of society should be the product of debate, participation and where possible the attainment of consensus and therefore much more likely to be consistent and underpin rational rule- and decision-making.

The definition of values stated above, which is adopted for the purposes of this chapter, distinguishes 'environmental values' from a different categorization of environmental ethics. The latter is not covered in detail. Partly this is because the subject has been covered more than adequately elsewhere.[4] More importantly, perhaps, the aim of this chapter is to

---

1. <www.yes2wind.com> a site set up by Friends of the Earth, Greenpeace and WWF to advocate for more wind energy projects.
2. <www.countryguardians.net>.
3. *Setting Environmental Standards* (Cm 4053, 1998).
4. E.g. see J. Alder and D. Wilkinson, *Environmental Law and Ethics* (London: Macmillan Press, 1999).

place values as part of a matrix, which includes strongly held moral and ethical positions and environmental principles such as sustainable development and the precautionary principle. It also includes formal law and other rules and the values contained in these, which can be environmental values (e.g. the need to take into account the interests of future generations) or legal values (e.g. legal certainty and respect for the 'rule of law'). There is, therefore, no deep analysis of underlying ethical issues nor is there much detailed discussion of so-called normative ethics, that is the question of what is right and wrong or what the law should be (as opposed to what it is).

That is not to say that these normative questions are irrelevant or that these aspects of environmental ethics are unimportant. There is, however, no necessary connection between normative environmental ethics and the way people behave in practice (just as most murderers probably believe murder is wrong). There are many people who subscribe to the idea that environmental protection is important and that certain things are 'right' or 'wrong' but that view makes no impact on the way in which they live their lives. Alternatively, there are others who follow what we might term 'green' lifestyles (e.g. do not own a car and recycle their waste) but do not adopt this stance from an environmentalist perspective.

Also, the domestic courts appear not to be interested in the concept of normative environmental ethics. This is true of both administrative and public law but also in relation to judge-made law such as the common law tort of nuisance. Although many of the participants in the environmental disputes which end up in the courts are concerned with the fundamental issues of what is 'right' and 'wrong', the judiciary tend to refocus attention on legalistic interpretation of rules; deference to Parliament's capacity and authority to decide complicated questions of what is in the public interest; and the exercise of lawful administrative powers (for examples see Box 3.1). By contrast, values have had a limited impact upon the way the courts view, for example, environmental offences.

BOX 3.1 **Moral judgments and the courts**

In *R v Somerset CC, ex parte Fewings and others* [1995] 1 WLR 1037, the County Council, as land owners, banned hunting on its land. In doing so they relied upon a statutory power to manage land for the 'benefit of the area'. The applicants, members of the Quantock Hunt, sought to challenge the decision on the ground that the decision had been unlawfully based on the moral ground that deer hunting was cruel. The Court of Appeal quashed the ban holding (by a majority of 2–1) that the ban was unlawful because it was made on moral instead of administrative grounds. The alternative dissenting judgment from Simon Brown LJ was that cruelty could be a relevant consideration provided it was balanced against all other considerations.

The Case illustrates the Courts' reluctance to get involved in ethical issues. The Master of the Rolls, Sir Thomas Bingham, said:

'The court has no role whatever as an arbiter between those who condemn hunting as barbaric and cruel and those who support it as a traditional country sport . . . This is of course a question on which most people hold views one way or the other. But our personal views are wholly irrelevant to the drier and more technical question which the court is obliged to answer . . . In other words, were members entitled in reaching their decision to give effect to their acceptance of the cruelty argument?'

Even the dissenting judgment relied heavily on administrative notions of 'fairness' in placing ethical issues within the framework of relevant considerations. It is important to note that it is perfectly possible for a private land owner to prevent hunting on their own land. The issue here was that a public body such as a local authority can only act within the powers given to it by statute.

This was confirmed in a later decision based on the same power in which Sefton MBC lawfully cancelled a wildfowl shooting licence on its own land on the basis that it was for the 'benefit of the area' (see *R v Sefton MBC, ex parte British Association of Shooting and Conservation Ltd*, [2001] Env LR 10). The key distinction between the two cases was that Sefton MBC did not base its decision on the morality of the sport but on the wording of the statute. Of course it may have been the case that morality was a factor but if so, it was not explicit.

The interaction between values and law

Environmental values affect the way in which law is made and the way it operates on a practical level. Although there is no direct connection between the two, there are many ways in which values play a part in the operation of an environmental regulatory system.

(a) Triggering the formulation of new policy and law

The rules which make up environmental law are a consequence of the establishment of political aims and goals and the setting of scientific standards which form a framework for the law. The ignition of the policy 'fuse', however, can be brought about by shifts in environmental values, in the sense that new priorities are identified and action called for. These may be general shifts in public opinion or they may be generated by specific interest groups. Box 3.2 has a number of examples of legislative or policy changes brought about by changing values and a public outcry over particular events.

BOX 3.2 **Examples of changing values triggering new legislation**

The history of environmental law has a number of examples of legislation responding to public concern over a single issue or particular event.[5] The following examples reflect the way in which shifts in values can bring something to the forefront of environmental policy and consequently result in changes in environmental law.

Public Health Act 1848—triggered by the Chadwick report into Sanitary Living Conditions.

Sea Birds Preservation Act 1869—introduced a close season for hunting 33 species of bird in response to wholesale slaughter of sea birds whose feathers were used in hat making.

Clean Air Act 1956—followed a public outcry after smog descended on London caused by poor quality coal burnt in the capital's homes and power stations. It is estimated that 4,000 people lost their lives as a result of the pollution.

---

5. For more examples in the field of nature conservation see D. Evans, *A History of Nature Conservation in Britain* (London: Routledge, 1997).

Deposit of Poisonous Waste Act 1972—containers of cyanide waste were dumped at a derelict brick kiln near Nuneaton. A public outcry and newspaper articles outlining the dubious activities of 'cowboy' waste operators triggered legislative intervention. The severity of the outcry was reflected in the fact that the legislation only took a month to pass through Parliament.

Control of Pollution (Anglers' Lead Weights) Regulations 1986 and the *Environmental Protection (Restriction on Use of Lead Shot) (England) Regulations 1999*—banned the supply and import of lead weights used in angling because of a public concern over harm to wildlife caused by poisoning.

These shifts in values have tended to be narrowly focused and resulted in piecemeal, reactive legislation. For this reason, they should be distinguished from more fundamental changes in the way in which we view the environment. The general public is now much more aware of the need for environmental protection at an individual, local, regional, national and international level. This means that although issues-based values continue to be important (e.g. the controversy over GMOs or the disposal of the *Brent Spar* oil platform in the North Sea, see Box 3.4), there are shifts in the general way of looking at environmental issues, in particular, the future impacts of current pollution levels and the pursuit of the goal of sustainable development.

(b) Influencing the interpretation and enforcement of environmental laws

The day-to-day interpretation of environmental law shifts slowly to reflect changing public values. Judicial attitudes can reflect these shifts (see Box 3.3). Sometimes it is difficult to distinguish between causes and effects, particularly where new laws establish new rights or approaches. For example the influence of European law has had an impact upon the way in which domestic environmental law is interpreted. This in turn affects the way in which the public and the legal profession use law to protect the environment. We can take other more general examples such as the precautionary principle, bio-diversity damage, or sustainable development and can see how concepts which were unknown 30 or so years ago have had a significant impact on the way laws are inter-preted and made today.

BOX 3.3 **Changes in judicial attitudes to environmental protection**

If we take a relatively straightforward pollution control provision which is designed to protect water from pollution (now contained in the Water Resources Act 1991, s. 85(1)), we can compare and contrast judicial attitudes underlying the interpretation of similar provisions over a period of 30 years in which environmental values have shifted. The first quote reflects the notion that the nature of pollution control offences were seen to be 'technical' in nature with no moral blame:

'This Act is, in my opinion, one of those Acts . . . which . . . deals with acts which are not criminal in any real sense, but are acts which in the public interest are prohibited under a penalty.'

Viscount Dilhorne in *Alphacell Ltd v Woodward* [1972] 2 All ER 475.

Within 20 years the judicial view had shifted to considering water pollution as a clearly criminal activity. The breach of the analogous provision was considered clearly to be 'criminal' with greater emphasis being placed on the importance of environmental protection:

'The object of the relevant words of s. 85(1) and the crime created thereby is the keeping of streams free from pollution for the benefit of mankind generally and the world's flora and fauna.'

Morland J in *National Rivers Authority v Alfred McAlpine Homes East Ltd* [1994] 4 All ER 286.

More recently, this view has been reinforced:

'The environment in which we live is a precious heritage and it is incumbent on the present generation to preserve it for the future. Rivers and watercourses are an important part of the environment and there is an increasing awareness of the necessity to preserve them from pollution.'

Scott Baker LJ in *R v Anglian Water* [2004] Env LR 10.

Of course it is possible to read too much into quotes taken in isolation, particularly when the rhetoric in the latter two quotes was not necessarily matched by effective criminal sanctions (see p. 307) but these cases tend to illustrate a much wider picture of the way in which the courts reflect changing public attitudes to the environment. Other examples can be seen in the shifting judicial attitudes to public participation in the environmental assessment process and the purposive approaches which have been taken to waste management offences and nature conservation provisions (see p. 88 and p. 576 respectively).

(c) Influencing individual decision-making

The 'British approach' to environmental law is heavily dominated by discretionary decision-making based upon political factors (see further Chapter 8). It is possible to identify the impact that shifting values have upon the way in which new policies are given weight in the context of individual decision-making. As we shall see, the principle of sustainable development and the precautionary principle are particularly difficult to transform into legal rules. In the context of policy formulation and individual decision-making, however, the principles can be fleshed out and applied in a practical manner with practical consequences. For example, the policy of developing 'brownfield' sites and the consequent effect on planning applications for such developments reflects an understanding and acceptance of the need to use resources effectively and sustainably. We can also see the effect of the public perception of environmental risks and associated values in the sequence of planning cases which suggest that even where such perceptions of risk are 'unsubstantiated' they may still be taken into account when making development decisions (see p. 500).

(d) Influencing the regulated

Changing public values can affect those who are regulated. For example, regulated companies may change their behaviour in response to shifting consumer values even where their activities are officially sanctioned and supported at the highest level (see Box 3.4).

BOX 3.4 **Influencing the regulated—the *Brent Spar* saga**

One of the clearest examples of shifting values affecting the regulated was the *Brent Spar* saga.[6] Between 1991 and 1993 Shell considered various options for the disposal of the *Brent Spar*, one of its defunct storage and loading buoys, before finally deciding to sink the rig in deep Atlantic waters. In December 1994 the UK Government approved the disposal plan under the Petroleum Act 1987 and the Food and Environment Protection Act 1985. During 1995 Greenpeace encouraged direct action in the form of a boycott of Shell petrol stations across Europe. In the light of this protest and despite support from the UK Government, Shell abandoned its planned disposal route. Shell towed the *Brent Spar* to Norway to consider other disposal options. In 1999 the *Brent Spar* was dismantled and recycled as part of a new ferry terminal in Norway.

Although it is not unusual for public campaigns to be launched against companies on environmental issues, the *Brent Spar* saga is notable because it took place against a background of active government support within the existing framework of legislation and policy. In addition, there was reasonable evidence that the planned sea disposal was in fact the best practicable environmental option. Whilst this may have been true for the isolated example of the *Brent Spar*, there were serious misgivings about the knock on effects on future disposals of oil rigs, which led to the Greenpeace protests and shift in public opinion.

In 1998, the majority of European Countries (including the EC) agreed to ban all disposals of offshore installations, subject to certain derogations, under OSPAR Decision 98/3 (see p. 709).

Shifts in values can have a more general impact on the regulated. There is an increasing reliance upon self-regulatory or voluntary instruments in environmental regulation. These include such things as corporate environmental reporting or the introduction of accredited systems of environmental management (see further Chapter 8). There are various explanations for the growth of the 'privatization' of environmental regulation but at least part of the reason is that there has been a commercial recognition of the importance of environmental values as weighed against the accumulation of profit. It could be argued that certain unrelated factors such as the cost of environmental compliance (with a consequent need for cost reduction and risk minimization) and the maintenance of a competitive industrial advantage have been particularly influential. The impact of changing public perceptions of environmental values has, however, also been significant, leading to, amongst other things, the promotion of 'green advertising'.[7]

(e) Assisting with the legitimacy of environmental laws

Just as values provide a trigger for new environmental laws, they also ensure that laws are considered to be legitimate by those who are regulated and the general public. For example, one of the reasons for the many delays in the introduction of the contaminated land regime under Part IIA of the Environmental Protection Act 1990 was the perceived unfairness of a

---

6. For a more detailed analysis see G. Jordan (1998) 76 Public Administration 716.

7. See F. Jarvis, 'Save as you Spend: Consumer Protection of the Environment and Local Social Cohesion' in J. Holder, D. McGillivray (eds), *Locality and Identity: Environmental Issues in Law and Society* (Aldershot: Dartmouth, 1999).

system of law which introduced retrospective strict liability. Where environmental legislation does not reflect contemporary values it becomes difficult to police as the regulated feel justified in ignoring 'unfair' requirements.

Law and balancing environmental values

There is a general consensus that environmental protection is an important matter, indeed one of the justifications for introducing a system of comprehensive environmental regulation was that it was and is in the public interest to protect the environment. Thus, everyone from the judiciary to regulators to industrial interests stresses that environmental protection should be at the heart of our activities (or to put it another way it is very rare to hear the contrary view, i.e. that it is desirable to destroy the environment). This general consensus, however, masks fundamental differences in the choices which different people might make and the emphasis they might place upon the importance of the environment as weighed against other factors.

Environmental law is controversial and thus interesting because it deals with questions of changing values and therefore priorities. The key question is 'how does the law interact with the process of change?' If there is a spectrum of views on the importance of environmental protection, it might range from one end where environmental interests were paramount and all other considerations overridden, to the other end where environmental interests were inconsequential and did not play a part in any aspect of life. Of course simplistic views such as these tend to caricature the problems involved in regulating for environmental protection. For example, should the law make owners clean up contaminated land notwithstanding the fact that they were not responsible for the original pollution? What if the owners were a company and they had to make workers redundant to balance the books? What if they were to be made bankrupt? Should the law protect the habitat of a rare species? What if the destruction of the habitat was going to be of direct benefit to people living in a village on the basis that localized pollution from traffic congestion was to be transferred onto a new bypass? These are very specific questions, but there are other more general concerns such as how we should use resources today so that they can be used by future generations (we discuss 'resource' issues more in relation to 'strong' and 'weak' forms of sustainability below).

Each of these issues magnifies the problem of establishing a legal framework of rules which can assist in the balancing of competing interests. They also raise the question of whether the law should have anything to do with these issues at all. Some might argue that law is unsuited to dealing with political balancing acts where competing interests need to be 'traded off' with one another. We would argue that law promotes the consistency, transparency and accountability of decision-making and controls the discretion of the decision-maker (although there are other things that law could do, e.g. increase the legitimacy of some of the environmental principles which are discussed below).

Law and risk

One of the factors which is placed into the balance of environmental decision making is the nature and extent of risk to the environment and human health. In this context the term 'risk' covers the probability of an event causing harm to the environment or human health in relation to the magnitude of that event occurring. For example a 0.1 per cent chance of a methane gas explosion which will blow up a town may be considered to be 'riskier' than a 50 per cent chance of a discharge which may pollute an already contaminated watercourse.

One of the characteristics of many of the hottest debates about environmental issues has been the role of risk and the perception of that risk. If we think of the BSE crisis, the *Brent Spar* fiasco, or the controversy over the potential hazards posed by genetically modified crops and foods, we can see that the disagreement and doubts over the long-term implications of associated risks have only helped to obscure the decision-making process. The problem of risk is not, however, confined to individual issues, but permeates the whole of environmental regulation whether it be by way of analysing the costs and benefits of taking action against pollution as the Environment Agency is required by law to do (see p. 128), in assessing whether it is appropriate to clean up a contaminated site, or in determining the appropriate strategy to reduce the threat of climate change. It is hard enough to decide upon individual priorities or policy goals where the issues are clear without the additional complexity of factoring in short- or long-term risks which are the subject of scientific and non-scientific debate.

The problem of risk is often linked to the relationship between science and environmental law. Science plays a role in the identification and assessment of environmental risks. The science of environmental hazards is often uncertain (largely as a consequence of the complex nature of environmental problems) and therefore scientists have developed methods of risk assessment to bridge the gap between this scientific uncertainty and the need for an objective framework for decision making. Whilst there are quantitative methods for assessing risks (e.g. by ranking hazards in relation to the size of risk), the objectivity and reliability of these methods in providing *all* the answers is flawed for a number of reasons. First, certain assumptions are made when undertaking a scientific risk assessment. These may be in terms of the nature of the hazard, the aggregation of different events, the existence of alternatives or anticipating future trends as against present knowledge. These assumptions are often determined by reference to subjective and unscientific criteria. Secondly, as a consequence of the differing assumptions which underpin risk assessment, the final conclusions can be variable. For example, a risk assessment carried out on the potential effects of accidental releases of ammonia resulted in eleven different risk estimates ranging from 1 in 400 to 1 in 10 million.[8] Finally, a scientific risk assessment fails to take into account the public perception of risk which is not necessarily based upon objective criteria.

There are different ways of approaching the question of defining and assessing environmental risks (which are similar to the general perspectives on environmental issues discussed below). These approaches influence the way in which decisions are made about

8. S. Contini, et al, *Benchmark Exercise on Major Hazard Analysis*, 1991 EUR 13386 EN 1991.

regulating environmental risks (e.g. banning a pollutant) or making an individual decision where risks are involved (e.g. to grant permission for an incinerator). Thus the decision- or rule-maker may be influenced differently depending upon whether risk is measured economically (i.e. through balancing costs and benefits); scientifically (i.e. based around a statistical basis of probabilities based upon past experiences or by assessing the incidence of hazards across large numbers of people); or psychologically, (i.e. based around people's perception of the risk with, for example, voluntary risks such as those associated with smoking seen as more acceptable than imposed risks such as risks associated with the granting of planning permission for a landfill site in the locality).

Environmental risks can be addressed in a number of ways from increasing the accuracy and independence of 'expert' analysis (e.g. with the creation of a 'Risk Commission'), to improving public participation in rule-making and decision-making. Ultimately, however, the problem of how to deal with environmental risks is concerned with underlying issues such as priorities for regulatory action, the trade-off between environmental protection (including human health) as against other goals and the acceptance of priorities for action by the general public.

Perspectives on environmental issues

We have seen how values underpin many aspects of environmental law but values on their own can only progress matters so far. In the case of many of the difficulties that environmental law and policy seek to resolve, the underlying values may not be controversial. Collective or public values like the need to protect human health, the need to use our resources wisely or the need to provide food, warmth, and accommodation would not raise much debate. Problems arise, however, when competing values need to be prioritized.

When it comes to rule-making, for example, there may be benefits from banning a pollutant which has a causal link with disease or is degrading our environment. But what if the ban means the closure of factories in a number of depressed areas which puts people out of work, lowers the quality of life for many others, and has an overall detrimental effect on the national economy? What if scientists could 'prove' that the effects of the pollutant would only be revealed over a 250-year period or that it would only result in one death per 100,000 residents per year?

These practical problems highlight a number of theoretical issues. How do we compare costs and benefits which appear to be so different? What weight should we give to environmental interests over other considerations? How do we assess what we should forfeit today in order to do justice to future generations? What sort of information should assist in the decision as to whether or not regulatory intervention is required? Of course these issues are magnified when they are put into the context of individual decision-making such as planning applications. In these circumstances the subjectivity of the participants in the decision-making process makes the choices much starker (although there is often some confusion between individual attitudes and collective values perhaps best illustrated by the so-called 'NIMBY'—'not in my backyard'—argument).

These issues are complex without any obvious solution. In seeking some way out of the problem of making environmental rules and decisions we have to examine some of the different approaches which may be taken. In doing so, there is no suggestion that these perspectives are strictly drawn or exclusive. Indeed, people may adopt different perspectives in relation to different issues. There is, however, some value in trying to disassemble some of the justifications for making (or not making) rules or decisions. These perspectives provide some way of trying to balance competing values and explain how and why opposing arguments are put forward to support individual positions. By 'perspective', we imply an overview of values rather than a particular view on a particular issue. In general, when rules or decisions are made, they are often influenced by many different perspectives; the significance lies in the weight which is attached to each perspective or perhaps the perspective which can best justify the end result which the maker of the decision or rule desires.

(a) Environmental perspectives

An environmentalist perspective can be characterized as placing greatest weight (and at its extreme to the exclusion of other balancing factors) on the need to protect the environment and, where there is no conflict with such protection, human health. Thus, an 'environmentalist' would presume that environmental protection was paramount and outweighed considerations such as cost, or scientific arguments that any associated risks were small (although in the context of the examples quoted above where environmental protection is to be balanced against 'quality of life' issues and societal inequalities, this crude representation of views masks more sophisticated arguments).

There is a spectrum of views which might fall within the category of what we have termed 'environmentalist' perspectives. The spectrum can be linked to basic viewpoints associated with environmental ethics. The critical distinction between these viewpoints is the extent to which they give the environment moral worth in its own right (what we might term 'ecocentric') as opposed to placing it within the sphere of human interests (i.e. the environment has a value only within the context of its relationship to humans—what we might term 'anthropocentric').

(b) Economic perspectives

The economic perspective of environmental issues and values is concerned with making rational decisions on the basis of an analysis of the costs and benefits of individual options. In this sense some argue that it allows more representative forms of decision-making as there can be an acknowledgement of intensity of people's preferences (e.g. to what extent they value a habitat, not simply whether a development of that habitat should be allowed to go ahead). Accordingly, it would be concerned with only taking action where it is economically efficient, such that the benefits which accrued from the action outweighed the costs of doing so. Thus an economist aims to identify underlying measures of value including attaching worth to such intangibles as a human life and the environment. On a theoretical level, this sort of valuation is, however, fraught with difficulties. For the purposes of this discussion, however, economic techniques are simply one way of determining whether or not a particular decision will generate the maximum benefit to the most people (and therefore be a basis for decision- or rule-making).

Valuation of intangibles such as the environment can be based upon the preferences which people have (i.e. by examining people's behaviour and analysing the choices that they make). For example, the reduction in house prices of properties surrounding a polluted area or the increase in prices where the environment is desirable may form the basis of such a valuation (termed 'hedonistic pricing'). Even in the case of a human life, it is possible to determine, on an objective level at least (sometimes referred to as a 'statistical life'), what someone might be willing to pay to avoid the risk of death. For example someone might be willing to pay £1,000 to avoid a 1 in 10,000 chance of death. From the economic perspective this would make a statistical life worth £10,000,000.[9]

It is not possible to value everything on the basis of explicit preferences particularly in the case of things which are unrelated to human life or property (which typically includes the unowned environment). For example in the case of a remote wilderness, it is unlikely that there are any objective measures of what people would be willing to pay to preserve it. In these circumstances, economists use 'contingent values' by carrying out a survey of people, asking them the amount of money they would be willing to pay to conserve some environmental feature (or *be* paid to compensate them for its loss).

BOX 3.5 Costing the Earth

Some economists have attempted to estimate the value of the global ecosystem by reference to the 'services' that it provides.[10] Such services include the supply of raw materials (e.g. timber, fuel), food production, climate regulation, purification of air and water, mitigation of floods, pest control, and the generation of fertile soils. Such things as the value of intangibles such as recreational and cultural services (e.g. outdoor adventure holidays, eco-tourism, and artistic or spiritual uses of the environment) were included. In 1997, the average value of these services was estimated at $33 trillion.

The process of 'costing the earth' was controversial. The methodology was criticized for being too 'broad brush'. For example assumptions had been made about the uniformity of the value of ecosystems across the world (e.g. a hectare of grassland in the US providing the same services as a similar area in Africa). Some economists argued that it was not possible to place a value on aggregated resources on a 'willingness to pay' basis. Whilst it may be possible for people to put a price on a woodland or even a wilderness area, it was not credible to ask people to put a value on the loss of *every* eco-system.

In response to this and other criticisms it was argued that the justification for the valuation was as much political as economic. The claim was that the value of ecosystem services had been largely ignored. As the estimated value of the services was larger than global Gross National Product it was actually much more important to human welfare than had been previously assumed, and therefore the value of ecosystem services deserved much more attention than had been previously given. The failure to put a monetary value on these services had distorted global pricing mechanisms and that certain commodities which depended more on ecosystem services (e.g. water supply) would demand higher prices if the true value of ecosystems services was factored in. Although the valuation methodology may have been open to criticism, the exercise was important because it raised the general issue of how to take into account the value of ecosystem services both generally and in relation to individual projects.

---

9. See further F. Ackerman and L. Heinzerling, Priceless (New York: New Press, 2004).
10. See R. Costanza *et al* (1997) 387 Nature 253 and the summary of the response in Anon (1998) 395 Nature 430.

(c) Social and cultural perspectives

Taking social and cultural perspectives into account in decision-making has been relatively late in coming, but is gaining currency. In contrast to economic perspectives, this approach questions whether it makes sense, e.g. to ask people how much they are willing to pay for environmental assets. Instead, it argues that values are not static, in the sense of being beliefs that we argue *from*, but rather are things that we reason *towards*. Deliberative techniques involve stakeholder (in its widest sense including those from whom an interest in the environment is a 'stake'), consultation in order to arrive at a common understanding of the different factors which can lead to decisions which are acceptable to all. This is easier said than done but involves the construction of ways of decision-making that involve some form of collective deliberation about what things we value and why, rather than asking for individual preferences in surveys.

A socially and culturally informed perspective would also question attitudes to natural scientific assessments of risk. This might be for failing to take local attitudes or 'lay' knowledge seriously enough; for example, by having too much confidence that 'laboratory' assumptions apply to the real world in which regulation takes place. It might also be for the wider reason that, inevitably, risk is constructed culturally. That is, our attitudes to risk (and therefore also to precaution) are related, at an individual level, to how risk-seeking or risk-averse we are, and to broader issues about how much trust we place in regulators and in 'official' knowledge. Our attitudes to risk are also affected by wider public perceptions, formed by numerous factors, about how fragile the environment is.

From this perspective, therefore, cost–benefit and other economic approaches to habitat conservation will be rejected for wrongly equating natural resources with consumer goods. Instead, more discursive valuation techniques will be preferred. There are already some signs of this: the Environment Agency now requires the use of deliberative valuation techniques, involving small groups discussing which criteria they think are important, when drawing up Local Environment Agency Plans. A good illustration of how law may fail to take cultural importance seriously enough is provided by the Hedgerows Regulations 1997 which arguably take too narrow an approach to the local cultural importance of these landscape features (see p. 881).

(d) Scientific perspectives

Broadly, a scientific perspective (by which we mean here a natural science approach) embodies what we might call a 'technocratic' approach to environmental regulation. That is, it both suggests that a range of environmental issues and disputes can be resolved 'scientifically' and provides a means for reaching 'objective', conclusive opinions about such matters. Arguably, much UK pollution control law has, at least ostensibly, been framed along such lines, in particular standards relating to public health such as drinking water standards or air quality (see further Box 16.6). The approach has also been seen in something of an elitist 'we know best' attitude by regulators towards things like granting environmental licences. To operate successfully, such a 'top down' approach requires a considerable degree of public trust in science and in scientists acting for regulatory bodies and governments. Events such as the BSE crisis have led to something of a crisis of confidence here, and levels of public trust in scientific evidence, especially evidence produced by government, is low compared with the trust placed in research seen as being more 'independent', e.g. by respected environmental pressure groups. Faith in official science has also been one of the reasons behind the traditionally secretive nature of decision-making, since a technocratic approach has little reason for public involvement other than, perhaps, to rubber-stamp decisions already taken. On the other hand it must be recognized that those who are sceptical of the role of science in decision-making still tend to rely upon scientific evidence to *reveal* environmental problems. For example most of climate change policy is based upon scientific evidence of the causes and effects.

BOX 3.6 Different perspectives in practice

These differing perspectives can usefully be illustrated by thinking about how decisions would be reached about a local green space threatened with a mixed use development (housing, retail and light industrial uses).

Ecological/environmental perspective

An ecological perspective would view the destruction of the habitat in purely ecological terms. The ecocentrist would view the benefits of the provision of the new development as an irrelevant factor, indeed the status of the habitat (whether it was protected or 'special' in any way) would also be irrelevant. The guiding principle would be that humans did not have any right to interfere with nature. The anthropocentrist perspective might, however, involve different considerations. For example, although the habitat would be considered to be of great importance, there would be some justifications for its destruction where the overall contribution to human welfare was substantial (i.e. building a much needed hospital) or where the environmental importance of the site was limited (i.e. it was of little ecological significance).

Economic perspective

An economist would undertake a valuation of the development (after deducting construction costs). This represents what a buyer would be willing to pay for the development. There is an assumption that this valuation reflects, in the absence of any value which could be attached to the habitat, what the development is 'worth'. If the habitat had no direct connection to local people (i.e. it could not be valued by its use alone), an economist would undertake a survey to determine what an accurate contingent valuation might be. If that survey showed that local residents would be willing to pay (or be paid) more than the value of the development, the development should be refused. Of course much depends upon how widely the survey sample is drawn.

Cultural/social perspective

A social perspective would concentrate on 'capturing' the importance of the green space along with other considerations through stakeholder consultation and public participation. The site may be thought to be important because it is used for recreational purposes by local people (e.g. dog walking, children's play area); because it is the 'focal point' of the village; or because it has historical connections with a famous Civil War battle. Alternatively, the development might provide jobs and low cost housing for young families in the area who would otherwise be forced to move away. In cases of dispute, alternative dispute resolution (ADR) mechanisms would be used to rationalise differences and try and achieve a consensus (or the nearest to a consensus that could reasonably be achieved). A social or cultural approach would also hesitate before accepting any quantitative valuation of harm to a species or habitat. It would almost certainly find problematic the idea of 'translocating' habitat elsewhere, since the value of the habitat is not only its contribution to national or global biodiversity but also includes its meaning and importance for (usually local) people.

Scientific perspective

A scientific or technocratic approach would concentrate entirely upon the nature conservation interest of the site. This is exemplified in the approach to the designation of sites of special scientific interest under the Wildlife and Countryside Act 1981 (as amended by the Countryside and Rights of Way Act 2000), and to the designation of 'European Sites' under EC law, where only scientific criteria can be taken into account. This would be a matter for technical judgment which would not involve the public or political or economic considerations. Thus if the area is home to a number of rare species, designation may be made regardless of the benefits or otherwise of the development.

By contrast, the planning system that decides whether development will be permitted is more open to participation, and is less technocratic in the sense that decisions are taken at both local and national level by elected politicians. In contrast to other perspectives, therefore, a scientific or technocratic approach would only form part of the overall assessment of whether economic development could outweigh the nature conservation interests.

Environmental principles

As a response to some of the problems of approaching environmental law or decisions from any one particular perspective, attempts have been made to formulate general concepts and principles which can accommodate at least some of the features of these various perspectives. The difficulty in doing this is that there has to be flexibility in the manner in which the principle can be interpreted. This flexibility can create problems of certainty and precision. By their very nature such principles need to be applied across sweeping expanses of environmental law and policy and also beyond the environmental field. Thus, a dynamic relationship exists between these principles, which underpin environmental laws at all levels, both in relation to the formulation of the law and as to its implementation and enforcement.

The most common substantive principles associated with environmental law and policy are those relating to sustainable development, the precautionary principle, the preventative principle and the polluter pays principle. We focus here on sustainable development and the precautionary principle as these are the most developed as matters of law and policy within international, European and domestic law. The polluter pays principle is discussed on p. 265. Other general underpinning approaches, particularly of a procedural nature, also have an impact (see, e.g., the process of environmental impact assessment covered in Chapter 14). Finally there are certain subsidiary principles including the principles of proximity, self sufficiency, public participation, and substitution. Many of these are found as constituents of the overarching principle of sustainable development (and are found in the 1992 Rio Declaration on the Environment and Development) whereas others tend to be used in specific contexts (e.g. the proximity principle used in the context of waste management policies). As principles are general guides to action rather than detailed rules, there are different versions found in different legislation and policy. A definition of these principles can be found in Box 3.7.

Some care should be taken with these definitions as they are not the *only* definitions of these principles and they are often incomplete. For example, the polluter pays principle says nothing about the crucial definitions of the 'polluter' or what 'pollution' is? What is important is the background purpose of the principle. What is it trying to promote? Whether it promotes this background purpose or not is heavily dependent upon the weight which is attached to it as a guiding principle. In this sense principles do not operate in an all or nothing fashion, they indicate desired objectives but leave the fulfilment of those objectives to individual law and decision-makers.

One last point which can be made about the interrelationship of these principles is that they are not necessarily mutually supportive. For example, there may be a tension between the local management of environmental problems and what might be perceived to be the 'best' solution to the problem. Thus in the case of waste management, local disposal and management may bring home the costs of waste (which therefore links in with the polluter pays principle) and may meet the aims of the self-sufficiency and proximity principles. This may, however, be antagonistic towards what could be viewed as being the 'best' solution in terms of promoting sustainable development which might involve exporting the waste for re-use or recycling in developing countries.

BOX 3.7 **Environmental principles—a summary**

Sustainable Development

'development that meets the needs of the present without compromising the ability of future generations to meet their own needs'.

Report of the 1987 World Commission on Environment and Development
Our Common Future (The Brundtland Report).

Of all environmental principles sustainable development has the most contested definition, i.e. it means different things to different people. The focus of sustainable development under the Brundtland definition is on improving the quality of life for humans without increasing the use of natural resources beyond the capacity of the environment to supply them indefinitely.

Precautionary Principle

'Where there are threats of serious or irreversible damage, lack of full scientific certainty shall not be used as a reason for postponing cost-effective measures to prevent environmental degradation.'

Com (2000) 1 on the Precautionary Principle (European Commission, 2000).

The basis of the principle is that science cannot predict absolutely how, when or why adverse impacts will occur, or what their effect may be on humans or ecosystems. In the absence of proof there is often enough information to identify a serious risk that some impacts are likely to lead to unacceptably high costs, which should be avoided. Where reasonable evidence exists actions to avoid these impacts are necessary. In this sense the precautionary principle is about being 'safe rather than sorry'.

Polluter Pays Principle

'The Polluter should bear the expenses of carrying out . . . pollution prevention and control measures . . . to ensure that the environment is in an acceptable state. In other words, the cost of these measures should be reflected in the cost of goods and services which cause pollution in production and/or consumption.'

1974 OECD Recommendation on the Implementation of the Polluter-Pays Principle [C(74)223].

The basis of the Polluter-Pays Principle is that those responsible for pollution meet the costs of its consequences. This includes retrospective liability for historic pollution, for example, under the clean up provisions of Part IIA of the Environmental Protection Act (see Chapter 17). More recently, the principle has been extended to cover paying for pollution prevention measures and wider responsibility on the producers of waste (see Chapter 15).

Preventative Principle

'States have . . . the responsibility to ensure that activities within their jurisdiction or control do not cause damage to the environment of other States or of areas beyond the limits of national jurisdiction.'

1992 Rio Declaration on the Environment and Development, Principle 2.

The preventative principle is often linked to the precautionary principle. This principle promotes the prevention of environmental harm as an alternative to remedying harm already caused. A good example of the preventative principle is the use of the Best Available Techniques to prevent pollution under the integrated pollution prevention and control regime (see p. 781).

Principle of integration

'Environmental protection requirements must be integrated into the definition and implementation of [all areas of policy] in particular with a view to promoting sustainable development.'

EC Treaty, Article 6.

The integration principle seeks to apply environmental considerations across all policy areas. The aim is to avoid otherwise contradictory policy objectives which result from a failure fail to take into account environmental protection or resource conservation goals. An example would be the failure to consider the environmental consequences of liberalizing air travel or road building programmes which are designed to meet priority transport objectives. The integration principle is considered in more depth in Chapter 5.

Public Participation Principle

'Environmental issues are best handled with the participation of all concerned citizens, at the relevant level. At the national level, each individual shall have appropriate access to information concerning the environment that is held by public authorities, including information on hazardous materials and activities in their communities, and the opportunity to participate in decision-making processes. States shall facilitate and encourage public awareness and participation by making information widely available. Effective access to judicial and administrative proceedings, including redress and remedy, shall be provided.'

1992 Rio Declaration on the Environment and Development, Principle 10.

The participation principle seeks to encourage widespread and informed public participation in decision-making through the three 'pillars' of participation in decision making, access to information on the environment and access to justice. These are considered further in Chapter 10.

Substitution Principle

'Chemicals that are of concern should be substituted with safer chemicals, or with materials or safer technologies not entailing the use of such chemicals, especially where safer alternatives already exist, taking account of socio-economic aspects in the choice of the best substitute.'

Commission White Paper on Strategy for a New Chemicals Policy COM (2001) 88.

The Substitution principle is an emerging principle which encourages the replacement of dangerous substances or processes by other, less harmful substances or processes. The substitution principle lies at the heart of the European Chemicals Strategy. The principle is again an extension of the precautionary principle in the sense that it promotes technology driven changes instead of waiting for the proof of harm. A good example of the substitution principle would be the application of the 'best practicable environmental option' in selecting waste disposal options as described in the National Waste Strategy for England and Wales.[11]

Proximity Principle

'Waste should generally be managed as near as possible to its place of production, mainly because transporting waste has a significant environmental impact.'

PPG 10 Planning and Waste Management—Box 1.

This is linked very closely with the Self-Sufficiency Principle which requires that most waste should be treated or disposed of within the region in which it is produced.

Sustainable development

The concept of sustainable development is central to the recent and future development of environmental law and policy. The idea of 'sustainability' (indicating the state of something being sustainable in the long term) has always been considered as part of the system of land-use planning within the UK in the sense that the long-term implications of resource depletion and other environmental factors have always been material considerations when determining planning applications. The precise principle of 'sustainable development' which has gained credibility within international law is, however, both relatively new and uncertain although its all-pervasive characteristics can be found explicitly in many environmental policy documents in relation to different topic areas. The fullest discussion of the subject can be found in the White Paper, *A Better Quality of Life: A Strategy for Sustainable Development for the United Kingdom* (Cm 4345, 1999) and the subsequent annual reviews.

What is meant by the phrase 'sustainable development'? Although the idea can be traced back at least to 1972 and the United Nations Stockholm Conference on the Human Environment, the common definition which is used most often comes from the Brundtland Commission's 1987 Report, *Our Common Future*, in which it was suggested that the phrase covered:

'Development that meets the needs of the present without compromising the ability of future generations to meet their own needs.'

This definition is, however, vague, and requires further elaboration. First, the primary objective of the principle is to meet current and future *human* needs and aspirations (there

---

11. See para. 4.4, also see *R (on the application of Blewett) v Derbyshire CC* [2005] Env LR 15 discussed further at p. 572.

is a further issue in relation to what is meant by 'needs and aspirations'). Thus the emphasis is anthropocentric although under the Brundtland Commission's definition, the environment is considered to be an integral part of human well-being. Secondly, there is an underlying objective of fairness in the manner of development which applies as between different sectors of the current generation (e.g. 'poor' and 'rich' nations and classes of society) and future generations (i.e. inter-generational equity). Thus, future generations have the same rights to develop as we do and preventing such development would be unfair. Finally, there is an inherent assumption that we can identify the impact of current activity in terms of resource depletion and the ability of the environment to absorb pollution. Any doubts over the nature of the risks involved will inevitably cloud the decisions which need to be made to achieve the goal of sustainable development.

Although sustainable development is found in a number of legal instruments, the most coherent attempts to flesh out the bare bones of the Brundtland Commission's definition of sustainable development can be found in policy documents, although even here there is a great deal of 'woolliness' as befits the breadth of the matters covered under the principle. Most of the significant policy work is aimed at providing meaningful goals and objectives against which the pursuit of sustainable development can be benchmarked.

Sustainable development as a legal and policy instrument

The goal of sustainable development has been translated into some form of legal obligation in a number of international, European and domestic sources of law, although the nature of the legal effects of the obligation is the subject of some debate. The transposition of the goal of sustainable development into legal forms, perhaps a legal principle, is becoming increasingly common and is set to continue. The implementation of the principle is perhaps more problematic.

(a) International law

In international law, sustainable development as a *legal* concept has tended to be found mostly in 'soft law' documents, i.e. documents that are not directly binding and which have more of a policy feel to them. The most important document here is 'Agenda 21', signed at the 1992 Rio 'Earth Summit', which is essentially a lengthy blueprint for realizing sustainable development. This pays particular attention to action at the local level, and picks up many of the recommendations in the Brundtland Report about greater public involvement in decision-making through, e.g. access to environmental information. There are signs that at least some of the judges of the International Court of Justice are beginning to recognize the procedural dimension to issues of sustainable development, and recognize sustainable development as a *principle* rather than just a *concept*.

CASE 3.1 The *Gabčikovo-Nagymaros* case ('Danube Dam')

The principle of sustainable development was first recognized explicitly in a judgment of the International Court of Justice in a case concerning an International Treaty on the construction of a dam and associated development on the River Danube between Bratislava and Budapest, Hungary (see further p. 162). Some years after the development was commenced, Hungary suspended and later abandoned work in response to criticisms of the environmental impacts of the project. The issue that was brought before the International Court of Justice was whether Hungary was entitled to abandon the project. Amongst other points, Hungary argued that new 'environmental norms' such as the principle of sustainable development had emerged since the signing of the original treaty, which had radically transformed the nature of the obligations under the Treaty.

The ICJ rejected that argument finding that the developing 'environmental norms' were foreseeable at the time the Treaty was agreed. For the first time, the ICJ referred to the need to balance economic development and environmental protection. In a strong separate opinion Vice President Weeramantry discussed the role of sustainable development in international law in the context of legal instruments and the historical background, concluding that:

'The principle of sustainable development is ... a part of modern international law by reason not only of its inescapable logical necessity, but also by reason of its wide and general acceptance by the global community.'

In spite of clear recognition by the ICJ, and beyond agreement on basic procedural requirements of the kind referred to in the Rio Declaration (information, public participation, etc.), there is little sign yet of anything resembling an international legal consensus on what sustainable development might mean substantively. This lack of progress on the principle of sustainable development was characterized by the World Summit on Sustainable Development held in Johannesburg in 2002. In contrast to the Rio Conference no conventions or statements of principle were adopted and the Declaration on Sustainable Development issued at the conclusion of the conference was aspirational in intent rather than binding.

(b) European law and policy

Perhaps most significantly the principle has been made a fundamental *justification* for the existence of the EC with the incorporation of sustainable development into Article 2 of the EC Treaty which states that the Community 'shall have as [one of its tasks] ... to promote throughout the Community harmonious, balanced and sustainable development of economic activities'. This justification applies across all policy areas and legislation and is not necessarily restricted to environmental considerations, and is backed up by the principle explicitly requiring the integration of environmental protection requirements into other policy areas 'in particular with a view to promoting sustainable development' (Article 6 EC).

The ECJ has not explicitly interpreted or fleshed out the concept of sustainable development, although it is possible to identify judgments which implicitly incorporate some of the more important aspects of sustainable development, including the balancing of environmental considerations as against other issues (e.g. in relation to the irrelevance of economic considerations in determining have been judged to be irrelevant, see *R v Secretary of State for the Environment, ex parte RSPB* [1997] QB 206 and *R v Secretary of State for the Environment, Transport and the Regions, ex parte First Corporate Shipping* [2001] ECR I-9235 and further Case box 21.1 and Box 21.5 below).

European policy on sustainable development can be found in the Sixth Environmental Action Programme: *Environment 2010: Our Future, Our Choice* and the *EU Strategy for Sustainable Development* COM (2001) 264. Both the Action Programme and the Strategy are frameworks within which detailed objectives are to be set. The two documents set a number of priority areas for action including climate change, nature and biodiversity, public health, natural resources and waste management. Clearer objectives are set in several 'Thematic Strategies' which address the headline issues in more detail. These objectives, are, however, general and not intended to be legally binding (see Case C-142/95P *Associazone Agricoltori della Provincia di Rovigo and Others v Commission* [1996] ECR I-6669).

(c) UK law and policy

The transformation and integration of the principle of sustainable development into formal rules within the UK reflects the European experience in the sense that it is relatively recent and is taking place within an overarching administrative and institutional framework rather than through changes to substantive environmental laws. Although 'sustainable' was introduced in the Natural Heritage (Scotland) Act 1991 as something which Scottish Natural Heritage must have 'regard to the desirability of securing' (s. 1(1)), the initial step of incorporating sustainable development in UK law was taken with the introduction of the Environment Agency's principal aim under section 4 of the Environment Act 1995. This requires the Agency, in discharging its functions so to protect or enhance the environment, taken as a whole, as to make the contribution towards attaining the objective of achieving sustainable development (see further p. 126).

The 1999 White Paper on Sustainable Development contained a government commitment to consider incorporating the sustainable development principle as a legal goal for any newly created public body. There are various statutory obligations which address sustainable development (see Box 3.8).

BOX 3.8 **Examples of the application of sustainable development in UK legislation**

'Every local authority must prepare a strategy . . . for promoting or improving the economic, social and environmental well-being of their area and contributing to the achievement of sustainable development in the United Kingdom.'

Local Government Act 2000, s. 4.

'The [Welsh] Assembly shall make a scheme setting out how it proposes, in the exercise of its functions, to promote sustainable development.'

Government of Wales Act 1998, s. 121.

'A regional development agency shall . . . contribute to the achievement of sustainable development in the United Kingdom where it is relevant to its area to do so.'

Regional Development Agencies Act 1998, s. 4(e).

Other examples include section 3A of the Electricity Act 1989 which requires the Secretary of State to carry out his functions in a manner calculated to contribute to the achievement of sustainable development and section 39 of the Planning and Compulsory Purchase Act 2004, which requires planning authorities to exercise their functions in relation to regional spatial strategies with the objective of contributing to the achievement of sustainable development.

These legal instruments are of interest because they demonstrate a formal commitment to the sustainable development principle but there are a number of factors affecting the practical implementation of the legal duty. First, and perhaps most significantly, there is no specific definition of the phrase 'sustainable development'. Even if the Brundtland Commission definition were to be adopted as a suitable definition by default, there would still be a number of ambiguities which would make precise legal interpretation impossible. Secondly, the wording of the relevant sections is too wide to create a legally enforceable duty, even if a suitably consistent definition of the principle could be agreed. Thirdly, the content and objectives of the duty are, in some of the cases (e.g. RDAs and the Environment Agency) controlled centrally by way of a requirement to 'have regard to' guidance set by central government. Finally, the different Acts have slightly different impacts on the activities of the statutory bodies concerned. The wording of the different statutory provisions have different effects. Some impose specific obligations whereas others are much more flexible without any obvious legal effect. Whether there is any practical distinction in terms of the consequences for environmental law or decision-making is perhaps more difficult to anticipate.

Although there are a number of examples of statutory requirements to 'achieve' or 'contribute to' sustainable development, the principle is too loose a concept to be developed by the courts (fitting in nicely with the discretionary, policy based approach of other aspects of environmental decision-making). This is not to say that the principle will have no practical impact, as the aims and objectives of administrative bodies play an integral part in influencing the setting of policies and the making of individual decisions.

As in the case of legal instruments, domestic policy is following the same path as European measures (although unusually perhaps the use of specific measures of sustainable development is slightly more advanced). The 1999 White Paper, *A Better Quality of Life: A Strategy for Sustainable Development for the United Kingdom* set out four main objectives, i.e. social progress which recognizes the needs of everyone; the effective protection of the environment; the prudent use of natural resources; and the maintenance of high and stable levels of economic growth. These objectives provide some indication that economic, social and environmental factors have equal weight.

These objectives are fleshed out with the introduction of seven 'priorities for action' (e.g. reducing social exclusion; promoting energy efficiency and waste reduction; and improving the quality of life in cities and large towns). Finally, the White Paper offered 15 'headline indicators' (there are a further 150 indicators) which are to be used for assessing progress towards sustainable development: total economic output (GDP); expected years of healthy life; unfit accommodation; levels of crime; traffic levels; wild bird populations; and waste arisings. The stated policy aim is to 'move in the right direction over time, or where a satisfactory level has been reached, to prevent a reversal'. The White Paper did not set any specific targets, although in relation to some areas, such as waste arisings or greenhouse gas emissions, binding targets have been set in other legislation (see further p. 571 and p. 649 respectively). The lack of measurable targets in some areas (e.g. traffic reduction) means that in these areas, there is only a broad commitment to enhance the current state of affairs which does not necessarily coincide with the principle of sustainable development (in the sense that a shift from a terrible situation to a bad one might still be detrimental, by merely prolonging the reaching of a crisis point).

Although the White Paper sets out general domestic policy, it is only part of a broad incorporation of the sustainable development principle within all areas of administration. At a national level, the Sustainable Development Commission is responsible for monitoring progress on sustainable development and for building consensus on action to accelerate its achievement. In addition the 'Sustainable Development in Government' initiative is intended to monitor the achievement of sustainable development across all government activities (see further Box 5.2). At a regional and local level, the regional sustainable development frameworks are to be prepared for eight English regions, whilst Local Agenda 21 strategies are to be prepared by all local authorities; both the frameworks and the strategies should set policies which are closely linked to the 'headline indicators' set out in the White Paper.

Achieving sustainable development in practice

Anyone reading the above discussion of the burgeoning legal and policy instruments might consider that there has been a great deal of progress towards a practical, workable definition of sustainable development. This would, however, mask some of the fundamental problems underlying the principle. In particular, the feasibility of sustainable development is dependent on the manner in which some of these problems are addressed.

(a) 'Weak' v 'Strong' versions of sustainable development

Although not without criticism, a distinction is often made between 'strong' and 'weak' versions of sustainable development. The distinction is really about matters of emphasis as much as it relates to matters of principle. Thus, a 'strong' approach to sustainability emphasizes the extent to which natural assets are irreplaceable in the sense that their loss cannot be adequately replaced by compensatory benefits. In contrast, 'weak' sustainability would accept that natural assets may be consumed or sacrificed if the overall benefit is positive, that is if the total stock of resources passed on to future generations is not diminished. 'Resources' here, however, would include non-environmental resources such as human knowledge and creativity; this would mean that there should not be too much concern about losing any individual environmental resource so long as there is sufficient ingenuity (or sufficient investment to ensure that there will be sufficient ingenuity) to come up with something equivalent or better.

On one view, strong sustainability is morally abhorrent since it privileges environmental 'assets' above all others, suggesting that we should devote whatever it takes to save a species even if this means that individual humans starve.[12] Further, weak sustainability is seen as no different from the kinds of trade-offs that have been made for centuries in the interests of raising human standards of living, and in this sense is simply 'business as usual'. Many environmental economists and philosophers agree that, presented in these terms, weak sustainability is something of an empty concept. However, others stress, for example, that environmental and human resources are not completely interchangeable: no matter how skilful we become, we will still need a base of natural resources to live off. A difficulty is therefore knowing which resources future generations will need and value or rather maintaining a sufficient *diversity* of resources.

---

12. W. Beckerman, *A Poverty of Reason* (Oakland: The Independent Institute, 2002), 2.

(b) The definition of 'needs'

The 'needs' of future generations are central to the Brundtland definition of sustainable development. 'Needs' are distinguishable from preferences. Beyond those things which form the very minimum necessary for survival—food, clean air and water, shelter, a tolerable climate—there is considerable debate about what we really 'need', even amongst present generations.[13] Even thinking about some of these basic needs shows some of the problems involved. For example, humans are not dependent on any single food source in the way that giant pandas require bamboo shoots, nor do we need to make our homes out of any particular raw material. We cannot therefore say that the sources of even our most common foodstuffs must be conserved, even for present generations (although we might make an argument that a sufficient *diversity* of seeds, genetic material, etc. should be conserved to guard against the impacts of climate change and other unknowns). The problem is also compounded when we engage in judging what the needs of those several generations hence will be, since apart from the basics necessary for survival the things that have been valued over the centuries have of course changed. Even where things have been treasured as 'necessary' in the past and present, this is no guarantee that future generations will 'need' or even value them. While conceivably we might find agreement across the generations in relation to what humans need, it is difficult to say objectively that anything particular must be conserved or preserved to satisfy such needs. Indeed, it has been argued that in seeking to prioritise the unknown needs of future generations we ignore the known needs of the current generation.[14]

Ultimately, there is some connection between one's view of sustainability, in strong or weak terms, and the question of needs, since those with more optimistic views of human ingenuity to 'fix' environmentally related problems will be more sanguine about exploiting resources today in the confidence that future generations will be able to satisfy their needs through a lesser abundance of natural resources. There is also the thorny question of the 'right to develop' (central to the Rio Declaration), and thus the liberty of present generations to destroy the natural environment in the interests of development.

(c) The role of technology

Central to weak and strong sustainability, and to the question of needs, is the role of technology. There are various strands to this, including how much faith to place in technological progress as against the conservation of natural resources, and whether we can say that developing countries 'need' technology from the developed world to give practical effect to their right to develop. Central to the two Conventions signed at Rio, on Climate Change and on Biodiversity, is the idea that there should be a transfer of technology to developing countries; either 'clean technology' to reduce greenhouse gas emissions, or pharmaceutical-type technology to allow for the commercial exploitation, and thus, it is argued, sustainable use, of biological diversity.

This approach marks something of a shift from earlier 'waves' of environmentalism which have generally been sceptical of technical 'fixes' to what have been seen as deeper-seated problems with the structuring of societies and economies. However, the Brundtland Report stressed that it did not consider capitalism as necessarily destructive of the environ-

---

13. M. Redclift (1993) Environmental Values 3.
14. W. Beckerman and J. Pasek, *Justice, Posterity and the Environment* (Oxford: Oxford University Press, 2001).

ment and therefore advocated solutions from within the existing economic framework. In a climate where support for alternative models of organisation is practically non-existent, it is perhaps inevitable that there is growing backing for fine-tuning the current model, and reliance on more effective technology and its more efficient use are central to what has been termed[15] 'ecological modernization'. This is the idea that environmental resources can be more efficiently managed to produce the same or higher levels of goods and services, leading to so-called 'win–win' results where both the economy and the environment benefit. (Since social issues are generally included within sustainable development, however, we really need to find virtuous circles leading to 'win–win–win' solutions.) This has obvious relevance to issues such as waste management or climate change, and in some senses is obviously fur-thered by making polluters pay for the 'external' costs imposed on society caused by their activities (such as air pollution which does not infringe on private rights). But a 'more from less' approach could also mean more efficient use of space and therefore less pressure on land of conservation interest. A growing body of what we might call the 'literature of hope' therefore argues that there is a path to sustainability which does not involve adopting a strong environmentalist perspective (as defined above).

(d) The assessment of fairness and inter-generational equity

Finally, there are considerable difficulties in deciding what is 'fair' to future generations. As discussed above, the background to this question will include factors like faith in human creativity and what 'needs' are, which in practice tend to be highly subjective. There is also the problem that there will never be a consensus on values, even if values did not shift over time.

One influential attempt to guide decisions about future generations is given by Brown Weiss.[16] She argues for three principles to underpin inter-generational equity: 'conservation of options' (e.g. conserving biodiversity contributes to the robustness of ecosystems); 'conservation of quality' (i.e. handing on environmental quality, at local and global level, without worsening its state); and 'conservation of access' (equitable rights of access to what past generations have handed on, while keeping open equitable access for future genera-tions). A virtue of this approach is that it tries not to second-guess what future generations will want or value, e.g. conserving options does not require any particular species to be saved from extinction. But difficulties remain. For example, how is environmental quality to be measured? How are the trade-offs between the principles to be handled, e.g. if improving conservation of access within the present generation means that someone's environmental quality is necessarily reduced? And why should one generation not decide to sacrifice a measure of environmental quality in the interests of future generations? As issues like climate change testify, there are no easy answers to deciding who, within the current generation, should have to bear burdens for past greenhouse gas emissions, or whether these burdens (or at least changes) should be sufficient to allow developing countries to continue increasing their emissions to further their chosen development path.

15. See e.g., M. Hajer, *The Politics of Environmental Discourse: Ecological Modernisation and the Policy Process* (Oxford: Clarendon Press, 1996).

16. E. Brown Weiss, 'Intergenerational Equity: A Legal Framework for Global Environmental Change' in E. Brown Weiss (ed), *Environmental Change and International Law* (Tokyo: United Nations University, 1991) for an opposing view see W. Beckerman and J. Pasek, *Justice, Posterity and the Environment* (Oxford: Oxford University Press, 2001).

The precautionary principle

Although there are a number of different interpretations of the precautionary principle, it generally describes an approach to the protection of the environment or human health based around precaution even where there is no clear evidence of harm or risk of harm from an activity or substance. For example, the precautionary principle suggests that we should ban a pollutant suspected of causing serious harm even in circumstances where there is no conclusive scientific proof of a clear link between the substance and the harm. In other words, although scientific evidence is never final (in the sense that it is only conclusive to the extent that it is based on premises which have not yet been overturned), there comes a point where we have to rely upon 'instinct' and take action regardless.

The precautionary principle is often associated with areas of high public controversy and concern where there are unknown (or in some cases arguably unknowable) risks to the environment or human health. Obvious examples which have been mentioned elsewhere in this book include the BSE crisis, the planting of genetically modified crops or the link between diseases such as cancer and mobile phone masts. The precautionary principle is often used in the debates about such issues to support the notion that scientific analysis of risks should form the core of environmental rules and decisions notwithstanding the fact that such analysis may be uncertain. Alternatively, the principle could be used to support an argument that there are limits to the extent that science can inform the debate and that ultimately, rules and decisions have to be made having regard to other considerations such as the public perception of the risk and the potential for harm.

These mutually inconsistent views underline the fact that the principle is necessarily subject to interpretations of concepts such as the significance of risks, and the acceptability of scientific evidence as 'proof'. Ultimately, the use of the precautionary principle is subject to the same limitations, restricting the resolution of any debate about environmental values. In other words the precautionary principle provides a framework for any discussion about how to 'trade-off' the risk of environmental harm as against other considerations, but it does not necessarily provide any 'right' answer. In this sense, the principle is merely another ingredient which goes into the melting pot of environmental rule- and decision-making along with other relevant considerations such as the public perception of risk, the benefit of the proposed activity, the notion of the 'public interest' and protection of individual rights.

(a) The precautionary principle in international law

The formal origin of the precautionary principle can be traced back to Germany in the 1970s with the *vorsorgeprinzip*. Translated as the 'foresight' principle this broad principle is a philosophical approach to risk prevention involving concepts of good environmental management in taking protective measures against specific environmental hazards in order to avoid or reduce environmental risks.[17] This approach was subsequently adopted in various international agreements. For example, a number of North Sea Ministerial Conferences including the 1984 Bremen Declaration on the Protection of the North Sea were based on the precautionary principle (a similar approach has been taken in relation to

---

17. See S. Boehmer-Christiansen 'The Precautionary Principle in Germany—Enabling Government' in T. O'Riordan and J. Cameron (eds), *Interpreting the Precautionary Principle* (London: Earthscan, 1994).

the reductions of radioactive and other hazardous substances under the 1992 OSPAR Convention). In addition, the principle has been adopted in an increasing number of international conventions from the 1980s onwards.

BOX 3.9 Examples of the precautionary principle in international law

States . . . must not wait for proof of harmful effects before taking action . . .

1984 Bremen Ministerial Declaration of the International Conference on the Protection of the North Sea.

The Contracting Parties shall apply the precautionary principle, i.e., to take preventive measures when there is reason to assume that substances or energy introduced, directly or indirectly, into the marine environment may create hazards to human health, harm living resources and marine ecosystems, damage amenities or interfere with other legitimate uses of the sea even when there is no conclusive evidence of a causal relationship between inputs and their alleged effects.

1992 Helsinki Convention on the Protection of the Baltic Sea, Art. 3(2).

The Parties should take precautionary measures to anticipate, prevent or minimize the causes of climate change and mitigate its adverse effects. Where there are threats of serious or irreversible damage, lack of full scientific certainty should not be used as a reason for postponing such measures . . .

1992 Framework Convention on Climate Change, Art. 3(3).

. . . where there is a threat of significant reduction or loss of biological diversity, lack of full scientific certainty should not be used as a reason for postponing measures to avoid or minimize such a threat.

1992 Convention on Biological Diversity, Preamble.

Lack of scientific certainty due to insufficient relevant scientific information and knowledge regarding the extent of the potential adverse effects of a living modified organism on the conservation and sustainable use of biological diversity in the Party of import, taking also into account risks to human health, shall not prevent that Party from taking a decision, as appropriate, with regard to the import of that living modified organism intended for direct use as food or feed, or for processing, in order to avoid or minimise such potential adverse effects.

2000 Cartagena Protocol on Biosafety, Art. 11.

A number of important international conventions have incorporated the principle including the Conventions on Climate Change, and on Biological Diversity (and its associated Protocol on Biosafety which is concerned with the handling and use of genetically modified organisms). These are described in Box 3.9. As can be seen, however, each convention tends to contain a slightly different formulation of the principle, which makes it difficult to identify an interpretation with which all states can be said to agree implicitly as a matter of binding international law (see p. 154).

Like sustainable development, precaution has found only limited judicial support so far in international law, this despite many commentators arguing that it has reached the status of a principle of customary international law.[18] In a case challenging the right of France to carry out nuclear tests in the South Pacific (*New Zealand v France* [1995] ICJ Rep 288), Judge

---

18. See, e.g., O. McIntyre and T. Mosedale (1997) 9 JEL 221.

Weeramantry's opinion suggested that the precautionary principle—which was 'gaining increasing support as part of the international law of the environment'—should be used where there was insufficient material before the Court to justify action, even if this meant acting ahead of 'full scientific evidence'.

This opinion, however, was a dissent, and it is worth comparing more recent examples where the precautionary principle has featured in international disputes (see Box 3.10). Whilst both the International Tribunal for the Law of the Sea (ITLOS) and the World Trade Organization Appellate Body acknowledged the idea of the precautionary principle they rejected its use as a norm of customary international law and failed to arrive at any concrete conclusions about the application of the principle. Partly this is because as Box 3.9 illustrates there is no consistent application of the principle in international conventions (there are differing obligations and formulations of the principle) and partly because as a *principle* it is by nature incapable of being prescribed as anything other than a general guide to action. As the cases illustrate, the application of the principle depends largely on evidence about the nature of the risk and the correct 'trigger' point or standard at which the principle is invoked.

BOX 3.10 **The precautionary principle in international cases**

EC Measures Concerning Meat and Meat Products (Hormones) WT/DS26/AB/R and WT/DS48/AB/R, 16 January 1998

The US and Canada brought a dispute settlement case before the World Trade Organisation against the EC, which in 1989 had banned the import of beef fed with growth hormones on the grounds that it was not safe for human health to eat such meat. The EC argued that its import ban was justified in the light of the precautionary principle, which it presented as a binding rule of international customary law. The USA and Canada denied that the principle already had such a status. (Canada did admit that it was an emerging principle.) The WTO found that the EC import ban violated WTO law but in doing so found that the role of the precautionary principle in international law was uncertain. In spite of the judgment, the EC has continued to impose its ban and was forced by the WTO to compensate Canada and the US for lost trade.

Southern Bluefish Tuna Cases (New Zealand v Japan; Australia v Japan) 2001 ILR 148

Australia and New Zealand brought a claim against Japan for breaching obligations under the Southern Bluefish Tuna (SBT) Treaty. The Treaty had been agreed in order to address the decline in numbers of SBT brought about by over fishing. Japan had subsequently commenced an 'Experimental Fishing Programme' which was intended to assess the numbers of fish. This involved breaching the agreed fishing quotas under the Treaty. Australia and New Zealand sought a provisional measure that the parties to the Treaty 'act consistently with the precautionary principle' in fishing for the SBT. ITLOS ordered the parties to observe the fishing quotas and to 'act with prudence and caution to ensure that effective conservation measures are taken to prevent serious harm to the [SBT] stock'. Judge Laing's opinion, however, rejected the notion, on the basis of the arguments put to the Tribunal, that the precautionary principle was an established norm of customary international law. He was, however, keen to distinguish the precautionary *approach* taken by the Tribunal and the application of the precautionary *principle*. In doing so he stated that adopting an approach, rather than a principle, was more flexible and highlighted the problems of making 'premature pronouncements about desirable normative structures' in cases of risk and scientific uncertainty.

The MOX Plant Case (Ireland v United Kingdom) 41 ILM 405

Ireland sought to prevent continuing operations at the mixed oxide plant (MOX) plant at Sellafield in the UK. One of Ireland's arguments was that that the precautionary principle required the UK to demonstrate that no harm would arise from the operation of the plant. The UK countered that there was no evidence of serious harm and therefore the precautionary principle did not apply. The Tribunal did not agree with Ireland's arguments. Judge Wolfram's opinion stated that whether the precautionary principle was a part of international customary law was still 'a matter for discussion'. The only aspect of the principle upon which there was agreement was that it reversed the burden of proof so that that those undertaking a risky activity had to prove that it would not result in any harm. Judge Wolfram went further stating that even if the principle were a part of customary international law the matter should not be resolved by a Tribunal assessing 'provisional measures' (effectively an injunction hearing). In contrast to the *Southern Bluefin Tuna Cases* where there was agreement on the nature of the problem and the potential harm caused (i.e. low levels of fish and over-fishing), there was disagreement about the nature of the potential harm from the MOX Plant. This question could only be assessed against full evidence (see further Box 17.2).

(b) European law and the precautionary principle

The requirement to take account of the precautionary principle in European law and policy is now enshrined in Article 174(2) of the EC Treaty.

'Community policy on the environment shall . . . be based on the precautionary principle and on the principles that preventive action should be taken, that environmental damage should as a priority be rectified at source and that the polluter should pay.'

What is the practical effect of this provision? It was assumed that the general nature of the wording of Article 174(2) was such that the precautionary principles (and others) did not have binding legal effect.[19] The ECJ hinted that, in extreme cases, it might be prepared to find that EC legislation had not taken the precautionary principle into account, but this would probably require complete oversight or wilful disregard (see Case box 3.2).

CASE 3.2 Case C-341/95 *Bettati v Safety Hi-Tech Srl* [1998] ECR I-4355

The manufacturer of a HCFC sought to overturn the ban under Regulation 3093/94 on substances that deplete the ozone layer on the basis that the Regulation did not accord with (amongst others) the precautionary principle set out in Article 130R(2) of the Treaty (now Art. 174(2)). The ECJ was prepared to consider the compatibility of the Regulation with (amongst other principles) the precautionary principle. It considered that there was a need to strike a balance between certain objectives such as the precautionary principle and the complexity of

---

19. See, e.g., J. Holder, 'Safe Science? The Precautionary Principle in UK Environmental Law' in J. Holder (ed.), *The Impact of EC Environmental Law in the United Kingdom* (Chichester: Wiley, 1997).

actually implementing the objectives. Thus some discretion would be given to the Council of Ministers as law makers and the ECJ would only overturn laws in which the principles had clearly been ignored.[20]

Although the *Bettati* decision established the role of the principle in law-making it did little to define what the principle might mean in European law. The lack of clarity was highlighted in the Beef Hormones litigation (see Box 3.10) and in response, the first attempt at a detailed explanation of the precautionary principle came in the shape of a communication from the European Commission (COM (2000) 1) which set out the Commission's guidelines on using the precautionary principle. The document sets out the risk-based context of the precautionary principle, emphasizing the relationship between the principle and the management of risks which might impinge upon the environment, human, animal, or plant health. The communication also makes it clear that the precautionary principle is not to be invoked defensively (i.e. as a 'disguised form of protectionism') reflecting the fact that the principle has been invoked as a justification of what might more appropriately be called a 'trade ban' (e.g. in relation to the French and German ban on British beef, although this might be contrasted with the EC's own use of precaution in relation to beef hormones).

In particular, the policy makes it clear that identifying an 'acceptable' level of risk is an essentially political decision, which must take into account such things as proportionality (i.e. the steps taken must be in proportion to the risks involved), an analysis of the costs and benefits associated with the measure (involving non-economic considerations such as public acceptability of other options and their effectiveness), and consistency (in relation to the measures taken in similar areas). Some assistance with the 'fleshing out' of the precautionary principle has come with the ECJ's judgment in the *Pfizer* case which addressed, for the first time, the nature and application of the principle (see Box 3.7).

CASE 3.3 Case T-13/99 *Pfizer v European Commission* [2002] ECR II-3305

Following scientific advice given to the European Commission, EC Regulation 2821/98 banned the use of four antibiotics as additives in animal foodstuff on the grounds that there was a risk of increasing resistance to the antibiotics in animals and that resistance could be transmitted to humans through consumption. The sole manufacturer of one of the banned antibiotics, Pfizer, sought to challenge the Regulation primarily on the ground that there had been an unlawful application of the precautionary principle. Pfizer argued that a scientific assessment of risk was a condition precedent of the application of the precautionary principle and no proper assessment had been carried out. In the alternative, if a risk assessment had been carried out, Pfizer argued for a much higher standard of proof than had been accepted by the European Commission, i.e. before banning, any risks identified were probable rather than hypothetical.

The Court of First Instance disagreed with Pfizer's interpretation of the Precautionary Principle noting that the application of the precautionary principle could not be based purely on a hypothetical risk but was acceptable in situations where a risk existed even if the risk could not be fully

---

20. See further M. Doherty (1999) 11 JEL 378.

demonstrated completely. Accordingly, the Court found that the Commission and other Community institutions had acted lawfully when they had relied upon the scientific advice given to them.[21]

Whilst the decision in *Pfizer* was an important step towards defining the parameters of the application of the precautionary principle it leaves a lot of issues undetermined. In particular, there is the problem of the trigger point for the application of the principle. It is clear that the principle applies where there is more than 'zero' risk. What was not made clear in the judgment was the point at which uncertainty would demand a precautionary response.

In comparison with the principle of sustainable development, however, the precautionary principle is explicitly or implicitly incorporated into a number of different substantive European laws. For example, the Environmental Assessment Directive (85/337/EEC, as amended) makes express reference to the need to assess the environmental impact of development projects within the context of the precautionary principle (see Chapter 14). Another example would be the Nitrates Directive (91/676/EEC) which creates a system of nitrate vulnerable zones in which farming activities are restricted notwithstanding that pollution and the risk of environmental harm may have come from a different source (see p. 747). Thus, even where there is no evidence of pollution from individual farms, activities are restricted on those farms based upon the need to take precaution in areas which are vulnerable to nitrate pollution. A further example is provided by the establishment of various environmental quality standards implicitly adopting the precautionary approach where substances are liable or likely to cause harm (e.g. in relation to the Titanium Dioxide Waste Directive 78/109/EEC and the Pesticides Directive 91/414/EEC). As the dates of these directives show, precautionary measures were being taken before precaution found its way into the EC Treaty. The classic example of this is Directive 90/220/EEC, perhaps the most explicitly precautionary EC measure, which restricted the deliberate release of genetically modified organisms despite the complete lack of evidence then about possible harmful impacts (see now Directive 2001/18/EC).

(c) UK law and the precautionary principle

One of the first detailed references to the precautionary principle can be found in the 1990 White Paper, *This Common Inheritance*. This put forward a 'weak' form of the precautionary principle on the basis that there would be action taken against 'significant risks' even in cases of scientific uncertainty if the 'balance of costs and benefits' justified it. Although this was a firm policy commitment to the *idea* of the precautionary principle, the practical significance of this statement was little more than an acceptance of the growing international and European recognition of the principle. This approach was followed subsequently in the guidance to the Environment Agency under section 4 of the Environment Act 1995 and in weak policy responses to such episodes as the BSE Crisis, Brent Spar and the debate over GMOs.

Even this weak form of the precautionary principle has not been incorporated directly into domestic legislation. Thus there is no overarching statutory duty to achieve or aspiration to attain the precautionary principle (unlike sustainable development). There

---

21. See W. Th. Douma (2003) 15 JEL 372.

has, however, been a number of domestic cases which have discussed the application of the precautionary principle. The general thrust of these decisions is that whilst the precautionary principle may be an integral part of international, European and domestic law (see *R v Derbyshire CC ex parte Murray* [2001] Env LR 26), it has no legal force and should be viewed as a policy objective (see *R v Secretary of State for Trade and Industry ex parte Duddridge* (Case box 3.4). Even where the courts have been willing to consider the substantive application of the precautionary principle the lack of any settled, specific or identifiable mechanism of risk assessment as part of the principle, (in relation to pesticides) was fatal (see *R (Amvac Chemical UK Ltd) v Secretary of State for Environment, Food and Rural Affairs and Others* (2002) ACD 219).

CASE 3.4 *R v Secretary of State for Trade and Industry ex parte Duddridge* [1995] Env. LR 151

Three children living in close proximity to newly laid power lines sought a judicial review of the Secretary of State's failure to protect them from non-ionizing radiation emitted from the lines. The applicants argued that the Secretary of State was obliged, under the precautionary principle, to make regulations specifying maximum thresholds for such radiation. In dismissing the application, Smith LJ acknowledged the existence of the precautionary principle in EC and international law but concluded that there was no direct obligation to apply the principle within Member States, nor should the principle be applied as a matter of 'common sense'.

Although there are no explicit references to the precautionary principle in domestic law, there are other rules which involve aspects of the precautionary principle. For example, the Water Resources Act 1991, s. 92 gives the Secretary of State power to make regulations in order to take precautions against water pollution (a power which has been exercised in relation to precautions to be taken in the storage of oil and silage, see further p. 746). Other examples include the powers to serve works notices to prevent water pollution under section 161 of the Water Resources Act 1991 (see p. 744) and the concept of the 'best available techniques' process standard adopted under IPPC to prevent unacceptable environmental impacts (see p. 781).

The precautionary principle has had some impact on individual decision-making. There have been a number of decisions based around the need to take precaution, particularly in relation to drinking water supplies (e.g. the dismissal of a planning application for a landfill site in Hampshire).[22] In general terms, however, there is relatively scant mention of precaution in things like planning policy statements compared with the now ritual mention of sustainable development, although PPG 25 on Development and Flood Risk, to control development in the flood plain takes an overtly precautionary approach. Otherwise, at best we find modestly precautionary policies such as giving 'draft' sites for protection under EC habitat conservation law the same level of protection as fully designated areas (although it is somewhat difficult to say that the level of protection actually given to such sites is precautionary; see generally p. 828). And whether precaution is wholly compatible with moves to speed up things like planning decisions might be questioned.

---

22. See (1998) ENDS Report 280, 15.

Applying the precautionary principle in practice

The practical application of the precautionary principle is afflicted with similar issues as those besetting sustainable development. First, there is the problem of 'weak' and 'strong' versions of the principle. In the case of the former, the requirement to take precaution is modified by balancing the costs and benefits of taking action (mirroring current EC and UK approaches to the principle). At its extreme, the 'strong' version of the principle would prohibit any action, resulting in significant or irreversible environmental harm, regardless of the cost of doing so. Both versions of the principle raise theoretical concerns. Under the weak version, there are difficulties in assessing the costs and benefits of uncertain risks that may need to be extrapolated over a long period of time. On the other hand, a 'strong' interpretation of the principle can be criticized on the basis that there is no such thing as a zero risk activity and a strong interpretation of the precautionary principle could result in a prohibition on beneficial activities simply on the basis that the understanding of the risks was uncertain. This is impractical and stifles the development of progressive technologies. Moreover, a strong interpretation assumes that there is no cost in doing nothing. Thus, it is argued, in some circumstances *not* doing something may actually be more harmful than doing it.

The second problem with the practical application of the precautionary principle is the reliance upon 'sound science' in the assessment of risks.[23] Of course there can never be 'certain' or 'exact' science, but it does suggest a privileging of science over other forms of knowledge or constructions of belief, and therefore a certain rationality and unresponsiveness to shifts in public opinion. The *Pfizer* decision emphasises that it is the wider scientific process that is important, as much as the end result. However, it also continues the approach to decision-making which assumes that assessing risks and then agreeing responses to risk (either legally or politically) are completely separate. Many now question whether this can ever be the case. As Jasanoff observes:

Studies of scientific advising leave in tatters the notion that it is possible, in practice, to restrict the advisory process to technical issues or that the subjective values of scientists are irrelevant to decision-making. The negotiated and constructed model of scientific knowledge, which closely captures the realities of regulatory science, rules out the possibility of drawing sharp boundaries between facts and values or claims and context.[24]

The third problem with the precautionary principle is that it does not determine what kinds of standards should be used. Inserting precaution into the EC Treaty, for example, has not resolved the tension between environmental quality standards and process controls (see further p. 249), even if resolving this were desirable. Indeed for countries like Germany, precaution implied the use of the best pollution abatement techniques (i.e. process controls), while the UK response was to emphasize 'sound science' and costs and benefits, on which the traditional 'British' preference for quality standards was based.

Finally, and perhaps most importantly, the precautionary principle does not fit easily into the institutional and administrative framework which so happily accommodates the

23. See, e.g., DEFRA's Sustainable Development Strategy, *Foundations for our Future* (DEFRA, 2002).
24. S. Jasanoff, *The Fifth Branch: Science Advisers as Policymakers* (Cambridge MA: Harvard UP, 1990), 231.

principle of sustainable development. Precaution is not an aspiration which cuts across departmental boundaries and which can be the subject of 'indicators' and fleshed out policy documents. Rather, many see it as a response to the public mistrust of scientific 'objectivity' and a recognition that there will be circumstances where there is a policy gap between what a decision-maker 'knows' about a risk (or can be told by science) and what the public are concerned about. Thus the precautionary principle fills that gap and provides the decision-maker with a flexible principle which assists with the balance or trade-off between different options involving environmental risks which may be little more than a further justification for decisions which would have been reached anyway. At its worst, by suggesting a clear divide between the certain and uncertain, the precautionary principle may, paradoxically, give strength to the idea of certainty in some situations.

Human rights and environmental values

It may seem surprising to conclude a chapter on environmental *values* and environmental *law* with discussion of something that might not appear directly concerned with either. But, as we have said, environmental regulation does not take place in a vacuum, but within its own 'matrix' of values, practices and moral standpoints relating to our interaction with the natural environment. Beyond this, however, environmental law also exists in a wider context of generally held values that underpin modern liberal-democratic societies. These include things like respect for individual rights and for private property, for procedural fairness in decision-making and respect for the 'rule of law', which generally fall under the rubric of human rights law. We outline some of the more important provisions of human rights law and its case law elsewhere (see especially pp. 357–9), and generally touch on relevant human rights issues throughout this book. The purpose of this section is therefore to consider the impact that the increasing attention given to human rights will have, and how the various perspectives described above are furthered or constrained when human rights enter the equation.

The idea that individuals *should* enjoy various general rights and freedoms has a long heritage, but only relatively recently have these values been laid down in binding legal texts. In a European context, the most important is the 1950 European Convention on Human Rights and Fundamental Freedoms. This was a response both to the aftermath of the Second World War and to the onset of the Cold War, and sought to embed a number of civil rights and freedoms in law. The Convention provides for various degrees of protection for the interests it covers; for example, while freedom from torture is protected absolutely, with most other interests the state has a 'margin of appreciation' to decide whether a stated exception should apply (e.g. the right to privacy and the protection of home life can be outweighed by economic interests, so long as these are 'necessary in a democratic society'). Under the Human Rights Act 1998, UK courts and public bodies are bound to act in accordance with the Convention. There is one exception to this, which is that the Convention right to an individual remedy is not transposed. Instead, there are in effect 'collective' remedies, in the sense that legislation can be declared incompatible with the Convention and fast-tracked through Parliament for reform (in practice this has meant that there are certain individual remedies). The ECJ has already accepted that the European

Convention on Human Rights provides one of the general principles of law it must uphold.

(a) The European Convention on Human Rights and the environment

In broad terms, European human rights law operates at three levels in relation to the environment. At a general level, it clearly gives great symbolic weight to the idea that human rights are deserving of protection, and that they are actually protected (there is considerable debate on this latter point). Alongside trade freedom, human rights are one of the major 'narratives' of our times. For the vast majority of people, human rights will tend to outweigh environmental rights or interests.

Secondly, as we discuss elsewhere (see p. 358), the European Court of Human Rights has interpreted some civil and political rights to protect against environmental harms. For example, the Court has, in fairly extreme cases, creatively interpreted the right to respect for home life (in Article 8) to provide a remedy against extreme pollution (although it is also notable that those who have suffered more serious injury, unconnected with property, have been less successful; see e.g. *LCB v UK* (1999) 27 EHRR 212).

Thirdly, human rights law may have a more indirect impact in the environmental sphere. For example, the Convention provides for various qualified freedoms such as the freedom of expression (Art. 10) and the right to assemble peacefully (Art. 11). To the extent that changes to environmental law or policy are argued for through public protest rather than lobbying, depending on various factors human rights law may justify such protest or, conversely, it may be restricted by the use of one of the exceptions which the Convention allows governments to rely on.

(b) 'Pros' and 'cons' of environmental rights

Because the European Convention on Human Rights mostly protects civil and political freedoms, it is rather light on protections for other interests. In particular, the Convention, and human rights law generally, has yet to protect or further genuinely collective rights such as rights relating to environmental quality or resources. One reason for this is the extent to which broad questions of public interest, and often a complex balancing of various factors, are involved. Alternatively, as with European law, a rights-based approach to environmental law has been shunned in the EC Treaty in favour of integrating environmental protection into other policy sectors and reference to 'protecting the quality of the environment' (Arts 6 and 174(1) EC). Although the European Court of Justice sometimes speaks the language of 'rights', what is really at stake is compliance by the Member States with specific, existing, legal obligations (see Chapter 7).

The 1992 Rio Declaration consciously avoids reference to environmental rights, although it does speak of national 'rights' to exploit the environment, and the right to develop. Elsewhere in international law, however, we can see a gradual coming together of various 'strands' including sustainable development and human rights, indicating the extent to which rights *within* generations, or *intra-generational rights*, are seen as indivisible from the pursuit of sustainability. For example, Article 4 of the IUCN's Draft International Covenant on Environment and Development from 1995 provides that: 'Peace, development, environmental protection and respect for human rights and fundamental freedoms are interdependent'.

On the other hand, it is notable that most modern constitutions make some reference to environmental rights, usually by enshrining a very general right to a 'clean' or 'decent' environment.[25] Although often this gives little hard legal edge to the right, attempts to flesh out a human 'right to environment' have been made. This is the approach taken in parts of the 'Ksentini' Report, a report by the UN Special Rapporteur on Human Rights and the Environment from 1994 (see further Chapter 6). This report identifies various substantive rights and freedoms, such as freedom from pollution and environmental degradation, and the right to the highest attainable standard of health free from environmental harm, qualified by exceptions similar to those found in the European Convention on Human Rights. From what has been said above, however, it should be apparent that whether these are anything more than policy aspirations or symbolic gestures is questionable. While they may guide decision-makers in a general sense, Courts are reluctant to require potentially vast sums of money to be spent on environmental improvement works to uphold such rights, not least because this might involve protecting the 'first right to get to court' at the expense of other, perhaps more worthy, improvement schemes.[26]

CHAPTER SUMMARY

1 The complexity and interconnectedness of environmental problems mean that it is possible to take different perspectives on how they should be addressed.

2 Environmental law does not necessarily resolve these different perspectives but it does set down a framework for making decisions. Law also promotes the consistency, transparency and accountability of decision-making and controls the discretion of the decision-maker.

4 There is, however, a gap between the procedural framework about how to make law and decisions and the substantive decisions themselves (i.e. what laws and decisions to make). Part of this gap is 'filled in' by collective values which are held about the environment.

5 Environmental values can be defined as 'what people believe to be important about the environment and thus what should be the priorities for environmental policy and ultimately environmental law'.

6 Environmental values affect environmental law in a number of ways including acting as a trigger for new policy and laws, promoting new interpretation of existing laws, influencing those who are regulated by environmental laws and reinforcing the legitimacy of environmental law.

7 Problems arise, however, when competing values need to be prioritized. Different perspectives on environmental problems provide some way of trying to balance competing values and explain how and why opposing arguments are put forward to support individual positions. Thus competing values can be prioritized by reference to environmental, economic, social, and scientific criteria.

8 Another way of addressing the problem of prioritising environmental values is through the use of environmental principles such as the polluter pays principle, precautionary principle and preventative principle.

9 Environmental principles are guides to action rather than rules and although they have been

25. See generally, A. Boyle and M. Anderson (eds), *Human Rights Approaches to Environmental Protection* (Oxford: Clarendon Press, 1996).
26. See, e.g., W. Howarth (2003) 14(5) Journal of Water Law 235.

incorporated to a greater or lesser extent in law at all levels, the courts have generally declined to elaborate on this general guiding role.

10   The sustainable development principle is overarching in the sense that it includes many aspects of other environmental principles. It is referred to in many legal and policy documents although its meaning is contested and its application is largely aspirational.

11   The precautionary principle attempts to fill the gap between states of certainty and uncertainty—where a threat of environmental harm can be ascertained but the possibility of the occurrence of the risk of that harm remains uncertain. It has been incorporated into laws at international and European levels. Although its meaning is contested, the European Court of Justice has attempted to flesh out its practical meaning.

12   Human rights law can also underpin decision-making on environmental matters. The European Court of Human Rights has interpreted some of the civil and political rights in the European Convention on Human Rights to protect against environmental harms.

Q QUESTIONS

1   How do different values and perspectives on environmental issues contribute to environmental decision-making?

2   In what ways do you think a truly ecocentric approach would affect environmental law and policy in the UK? What are the barriers to such an approach?

3   What are the arguments for and against putting a value on the environment?

4   How do environmental principles play a role in environmental law and decision-making? What are the problems of using the principles in practice? How could environmental principles be made more effective?

5   Look at the latest sustainable development policy adopted by the UK Government (accessible from <www.sustainable-development.gov.uk/performance/performance.htm>). In what ways has the UK Government established benchmark indicators of sustainable development? How accurate and helpful do you think these indicators are?

6   How are risk and precaution addressed in environmental law and decision-making? Why do you think the Courts are so reluctant to 'flesh out' the precautionary principle?

7   Consider the different issues in question 5 at the end of Chapter 1 on p. 17. How might the different perspectives and environmental principles outlined in this chapter affect your consideration of those issues?

 FURTHER READING

This chapter has ranged across a number of topics which stray into other areas of environmental ethics, economics, politics and social theory. Bear in mind therefore, that this list is very selective.

General

J. Alder and D. Wilkinson, *Environmental Law and Ethics* (London: Macmillan Press, 1999) is an outstanding text which covers environmental ethics within the legal and policy context of environmental law. An extremely interesting portrayal of different ways of looking at environmental issues can be found in J. Ruhl, 'The Case of the Speluncean Polluters—Six Themes of Environmental Law,

Policy, and Ethics' (1997) 27 Environmental Law 343, which takes a mythical case before a Supreme Court and presents different judicial perspectives in a manner which is immediately accessible without being simplistic—highly recommended for raising the interest of the disinterested and uninterested student! Another great introduction to the idea of different perspectives on the environment can be found in J. Dryzek, *The Politics of the Earth: Environmental Discourses* (Oxford: Oxford University Press, 1997) which contains a fuller and deeper analysis of the range of perspectives (or discourses) than we have covered here (e.g. the administrative/bureaucratic perspective).

Environmental Perspectives

For a consideration of some of the issues surrounding the environmentalist perspective have a look at C. Stone, *Should Trees Have Standing? And Other Essays on Law, Morals and the Environment* (New York: Oceana Publications, 1996), D. Wilkinson, 'Using Environmental Ethics to Create Ecological Law' in J. Holder and D. McGillivray (eds), *Locality and Identity: Environmental Issues in Law and Society*, and J. Holder, 'New Age: Rediscovering Natural Law' (2000) *Current Legal Problems* vol. 53, 151–79, particularly 165–71. These all contain good ways of rethinking law in a more ecocentric fashion.

Economic Perspectives

A classic critique of the economic perspective can be found in M. Sagoff, *The Economy of the Earth* (Cambridge: Cambridge University Press, 1988). His thesis is forcefully presented in a clear and readable fashion. In similar vein (although with different conclusions) D. Farber, *Eco Pragmatism* (Chicago: University of Chicago Press, 1999), and L. Tribe 'Ways Not to Think About Plastic Trees: New Foundations for Environmental Law' (1974) 83 Yale Law Journal 1315 consider the rights and wrongs of valuing nature. In particular, C. Sunstein, *Risk and Reason* (Cambridge: Cambridge University Press, 2002) argues for the 'cost benefit state' and claims that environmental laws have the capacity of killing more people then they protect. This last text prompts one word of warning, most of these originate from the US and therefore come from a tradition where formal cost–benefit analysis is much more developed than here in the UK. For further reading on how decisions about conservation and development might be framed, we recommend F. Ackerman and L. Heinzerling, *Priceless* (New York: New Press, 2004), P. Macnaghten and J. Urry, *Contested Natures* (London: Sage, 1998) and C. Harrison, J. Burgess, and J. Clark, 'Capturing Values for Nature' in J. Holder and D. McGillivray (eds), *Locality and Identity: Environmental Issues in Law and Society* (Aldershot: Ashgate, 1999) as good counterpoints to the economic approaches referred to above. There is also a specialist journal—*Environmental Values* (quarterly, White Horse Press)—where much of the debate on values and sustainability is conducted.

Participatory Approaches

The idea that participatory approaches are the best way of resolving different perspectives on the environment is gathering pace. For a discussion of the main themes see M. Lee and C. Abbot, 'The Usual Suspects? Public Participation Under the Aarhus Convention' (2003) 66 Modern Law Review 80 and J. Steele 'Participation and deliberation in environmental law: Exploring a problem-solving approach' (2001) 21 Oxford Journal of Legal Studies 415. Further reading on this issue will be found at the end of Chapter 10.

Scientific perspectives

There is a plethora of material dealing with the perception of risk (including environmental risk). For an entertaining and illuminating examination of the topic see Adams, *Risk* (London: UCL Press, 1994) complete with idiosyncratic diagrams of angels and fish. A more difficult book (but one which is definitive in the area) is U. Beck, *Risk Society* (London: Sage, 1992) which suggests that environmental impacts and the associated risks are part of a fundamental shift in society. Also have a look at J. Steele, *Risks and Legal Theory* (Oxford: Hart Publishing, 2004) esp. Part III on environmental risk generally. Whilst not necessarily an easy read it is thought provoking and well considered.

Environmental Principles

Comprehensive coverage of the form and function of environmental principles can be found in N. De Sadeleer, *Environmental Principles: From Political Slogans to Legal Rules* (Oxford: Oxford University Press, 2002). This is a heavyweight work which covers not only the substantive issues but also a deeper analysis of the role of principles in the shift from rules based 'modernist' law to principles based 'post-modernist' law. Another (shorter) general introduction to the area can be found in M. Doherty, 'The Status of the Principles of EC Environmental Law' (1999) 11 JEL 379.

Sustainable Development

For those wanting a general introduction to sustainable development, A. Dobson, *Green Political Thought* (London: Routledge, 2000) gives a clear overview. For more detail see A. Dobson, *Fairness and Futurity: Essays on Environmental Sustainability and Social Justice* (Oxford: Oxford University Press, 1999). On the relationship between law and sustainable development see M. Jacobs, 'Sustainable development as a contested concept' in A. Dobson (ed) *Fairness and Futurity: Essays on Environmental Sustainability and Social Justice*. For an up-to-date critique see A. Ross-Robertson, 'Is the environment getting squeezed out of sustainable development? [2003] Public Law 249. One of the best-known critics of sustainable development is Wilfred Beckerman a former member of the RCEP. As an introduction to his work see, 'Sustainable development: Is it a Useful Concept?' (1994) 3 Environmental Values 191; and a response H. E. Daly, 'On Wilfred Beckerman's Critique of Sustainable Development' (1995) 4 Environmental Values 49. A more comprehensive critique of sustainable development and the precautionary principle can be found in W. Beckerman's *A Poverty of Reason: Sustainable Development & Economic Growth* (Oakland: Independent Institute, 2002), well worth reading if only for a balanced counterpoint to the mainstream support for sustainable development. A. Boyle and D. Freestone (eds), *International Law and Sustainable Development* (Oxford: Oxford University Press, 2001) covers the main legal developments of sustainable development in international law.

Precautionary Principle

Huge amounts of literature on this topic. As a starting point try P. Harremoës et al. (eds), *The Precautionary Principle in the 20th Century: Late Lessons from Early Warnings* (London: Earthscan, 2001). This presents 14 detailed accounts of the application of the precautionary principle in relation to various hazards. It also reflects on the lessons learned and how they might inform the development of the principle. For an alternative view see J. Morris (ed.), *'Rethinking Risk and the Precautionary Principle'* (London: Butterworth Heinemann, 2000): a collection of essays which are highly critical of the precautionary principle as a 'meaningless soundbite that can be used to justify just about any policy, including quite contradictory policies'.

You will have no problem identifying any number of good books and articles on law and the precautionary principle. Try any of: R. Harding and E. Fisher (eds), *Perspectives on the Precautionary Principle* (Sydney Federation Press, 1999), T. O'Riordan and J. Cameron (eds), *Reinterpreting the Precautionary Principle* (London: Cameron May, 2000); and (D. Freestone and E. Hey (eds), *The*

Precautionary Principle and International Law: The Challenge of Implementation (The Hague: Kluwer, 1995). All three of these provide comprehensive collections of essays on different aspects of the precautionary principle. Shorter articles on the topic include: O. McIntyre and T. Mosedale, 'The Precautionary Principle as a Norm of Customary International Law' (1997) 9 JEL 221, M-C. Cordonnier Segger and M. Gehring, 'The WTO and Precuation: Sustainable Development Implications of the WTO Asbestos Dispute' (2003) 15(3) JEL 289 and E. Fisher 'Is the Precautionary Principle Justiciable?' (2001) 13 JEL 315.

Rights

On rights issues, an excellent introduction is C. Miller, *Environmental Rights: Critical Perspectives* (London: Routledge, 1998), which critically probes the value of thinking about environmental protection (both generally and in particular areas like air quality or nature conservation) through rights. Equally good as a way in, although with much more of an international and comparative perspective, is A. Boyle and M. Anderson (eds), *Human Rights Approaches to Environmental Protection* (Oxford: Oxford University Press, 1996), the opening chapter of which neatly locates environmental rights in the context of the evolution of rights more generally.

4 Sources of environmental law

 Overview

In this chapter we consider the main sources of environmental law. The range and nature of environmental problems means that environmental law emerges at international, European and national levels. This is partly because the complex interconnected nature of environmental problems requires a range of solutions at international, regional and national levels but it is also because each source of law can fulfil different purposes. The general focus of this Chapter is national law but we also introduce international and European sources. Thus we concentrate on UK environmental statutes as they continue to represent the majority of the 'tools of the trade' for the environmental lawyer. We also examine some of the key characteristics of environmental laws which help to explain both the form and function of UK environmental law.

There is a large degree of overlap between this chapter and others in this book. You might find it useful to read the sections on law-making in the chapters on International and European law and to reflect on the role of private law in environmental protection as covered in Chapter 11. When considering the Courts as a source of law you may want to refer to the material on the calls for an Environmental Court in Chapter 10 which deals with Public Participation. We also consider briefly the role of overarching principles and rules which play a part in environmental protection. Further coverage of these can be found in Chapters 1 and 3.

At the end of this Chapter you should be able to:

✔ Understand where environmental law comes from (internationally, regionally, nationally).
✔ Appreciate some of the interrelationships between different sources of environmental law.
✔ Identify some of the basic characteristics of different sources of environmental law.
✔ Identify some of the key features of environmental legislation.
✔ Appreciate the status and force of different forms of law for decision-makers.

Introduction

Environmental law is made at international, European, and national levels. Each source possesses its own characteristics and functions. For example, international environmental law often functions as a way of negotiating and achieving international consensus in relation to the nature and response to global environmental problems. European law is more specific in nature and has a harmonizing function aimed at having common standards and approaches to environmental problems amongst Member States but often leaving the exact nature of implementation and enforcement to be determined at a national level. National law has to fulfil a number of functions including the need to comply with obligations which have been agreed at an international and European level.

Rights and principles

Although this chapter is largely about sources of environmental law, certain rights and principles also play a part in addressing environmental problems. Indeed, the language of rights and principles overarch environmental laws at every level. Law may form the basis of legal rights and obligations which are used to protect the environment but they are maintained, expanded, and reinforced by rights, principles, objectives, and policies.

The existence and role of rights in environmental law has already been discussed at pp. 15 and 78. Rights grant a permanent entitlement which is normally protected by objective rules. There are, however, examples of rights whose origin and existence are independent from legal rules. Those who argue for environmental rights often take the position that the environment holds rights simply by virtue of it being worthy of protection for its own sake. In this way, rights can be independent of law although law is often the most effective way of giving substance to the right. What is critical is whether there is an effective remedy for infringement of the right and for guaranteeing that it is acknowledged.

Principles, on the other hand, possess different characteristics based around the notion of values. Principles are rooted in concepts of morality, justice, or equity. As such they are distinguishable from laws in that they act as a guide, i.e. they must be taken into account when making decisions but they do not necessarily have to be obeyed. For example the polluter pays principle is based upon notions that it would be unfair to transfer the environmental cost of pollution onto people other than those who are responsible for the pollution in the first place. This does not necessarily answer the question as to how the principle should work in practice as a determination has to be made as to the identity of the polluter.

Such rights and principles may or may not constitute binding rules but they are used by judges, decision-makers and law-makers to guide actions and decisions. Whilst it is true to say that the use of rights and principles has been more prominent at the international and European level, the UK Parliament and Courts have had to consider rights in the context of the incorporation of the European Convention on Human Rights and it is likely that the growth of the use of principles at the international level will see a greater acceptance of their value in the domestic context over time.

International law

International law governs relations between states and international *environmental* law seeks to address environmental concerns applicable across different states or of general global application. By definition such problems are likely to be complex and difficult to solve. Thus international environmental law is characterized by negotiation and the need to gain a consensus from across a large number of countries as possible. International environmental law is often aspirational in nature, laying down broad frameworks for action. Unlike EC law, it has no direct effect on domestic law or on individuals. However, it will often have an indirect effect, for example by publicizing a particular issue, by laying down generally accepted standards, or by imposing political pressure on states to change their laws or practices. Thus the Climate Change Convention and the Kyoto Protocol have had an important impact on British law and policy in relation to greenhouse gas emissions. Many pieces of legislation include powers for the government to introduce changes into domestic law in order to comply with international obligations. For example, the Pollution Prevention and Control Act 1999, s. 2 and sch. 1, para. 3 enables the Secretary of State to make regulations for the purpose of implementing EC or international obligations.

For the most part, international environmental law consists of broad Conventions agreed by signatory states, such as the Ramsar Convention on Wetlands of International Importance, or the Vienna Convention for the Protection of the Ozone Layer. Conventions can be precise and specific in terms of the obligations they create. For example the Convention on International Trade in Endangered Species lists certain categories of protected species (e.g. species in danger of becoming extinct are listed in Annex I) and corresponding obligations in relation to each category.

More typically, however, Conventions are developed in an incremental way. There may be an initial agreement over a framework which will promote an understanding of a particular environmental problem through general obligations to exchange information, share research and take 'appropriate measures' to address the problem. The Convention is then fleshed out by further, more specific obligations under further agreements called Protocols. The important point is that however precise the obligation, such law is not ultimately binding, except in a political sense, because of the lack of sanctions available for non-compliance.

This approach reflects the pragmatic nature of much of international environmental law. The negotiation process lets States begin to thrash out a controversial problem even before there is full agreement on the exact nature of the problem or indeed if there is a problem in the first place. Such an approach can accommodate countries who are unconvinced of the need for action because it is better to participate and influence the shape of the agreement than being 'on the outside'. High levels of participation lend legitimacy to the issue, and this in turn can lead to pressure to take the subject seriously by participating in a convention or risk international isolation.

European Community (EC) law

The European Community is a very important source of environmental law. Post enlargement, the European Community includes 25 Member States working jointly through common institutions (i.e. the European Parliament, the European Commission, the Council of Ministers, the Court of Justice, etc.) The EC is often referred to as the European Union (or EU). Strictly speaking, the European Union includes not only the European Community but also the other two European pillars of the European integration process, namely the Justice and Home Affairs Policy and the Common Foreign and Security Policy. In practice the two are synonymous.

EC environmental law is often purposive in character although the purposes are combined with very specific standards in relation to environmental quality and emission levels. This purposive approach is the product of the influence of civil law countries. In such countries the law is found in Codes which lay down general principles. These principles are given effect by the national courts which take a purposive approach in trying to apply the law. This is reflected in the extensive recitals which accompany EC legislation which explain the basis for the Directives. Another reason for the purposive approach is that clarity is needed when drafting in many different languages. There is often a danger that misunderstandings will arise unless the differences can be smoothed out by reference to the general purposes of the legislation. The wording of the substantive provisions of environmental directives may be unclear. Certain key phrases will be open to interpretation (e.g. the definition of 'project' for the purposes of the environmental assessment Directive see p. 520). The purposive approach in EC law suggests that the recitals help to define the statutory provisions. This is in contrast to the British approach which has traditionally been based upon a literal approach to the plain meaning of words (see Box 4.1).

BOX 4.1 Purposive and literal interpretations of Environmental law

---

The distinction between the literal and purposive approaches has been noted particularly in relation to the interpretation of the Environmental Assessment Directive 85/337 (as amended from 1999 by Directive 97/11). The contrast is greatest when comparing cases decided in the early 1990s when the European case law in the area was relatively under-developed, with cases from the mid-1990s when the ECJ took a strong purposive line in interpreting some key provisions of the Directive.

In 1993, Alder argued that English law was 'inadequate to secure the aims' of the EIA Directive and that English legal culture was hostile to purposive regulation. In relation to literalism he commented:

'A ... characteristic of English legal culture is a semantic and literalistic approach to drafting and interpreting legal rules. It would be an oversimplification to contrast this automatically with a purposive approach because some approaches may well be advanced by semantic techniques. However in the context of European law the semantic approach is especially likely to clash with the policies of the European Community because their policies are implemented by draftsmen schooled in the more open textured and purposive methods used by continental lawyers.'[1]

Although this was true in the early 1990s, the position has changed somewhat given the weight of purposive case law which has emanated from the ECJ, particularly in relation to the interpretation of the EIA Directive. Examples of this shift in judicial approach can be seen in relation to many different aspects of EIA from the definition of 'consent' (see *R v North Yorkshire CC, ex parte Brown* [1998] Env LR 623 and Box 14.6) to the question of whether a project should be subject to EIA at all. In the latter situation the English courts originally treated the question as a matter of fact and degree for the planning authority to determine (see the much criticised decision in *R v Swale BC ex parte RSPB* [1991] 1 PLR 6). Subsequently, the ECJ took a purposive approach to this question. In Case C-72/95 *Aanemersbedriff P K Kraaijeveld BV v Gedeputeerde*

---

1 J. Alder (1993) 5 JEL 217.

Staten van Zuid-Holland [1996] ECR I-5403, the ECJ held that the 'wide scope and broad purpose of the Directive' should not be undermined by granting unlimited discretion to Member States to determine whether all projects of a certain type would or would not have 'significant effects' (see p. 526). This purposive approach was then adopted in subsequent cases in England, notably by the House of Lords in *Berkeley v Secretary of State for the Environment, Transport & The Regions and Fulham Football Club* [2001] Env LR 16 (see Box 14.2).

Purposive approaches have also been adopted in relation to substantive issues such as the definition of waste (see p. 576). In particular the semantic difficulties of agreeing on a consistent definition of the word 'discard' across different Member States and different situations has seen both the ECJ and the domestic courts relying on the overall purposes of the Waste Framework Directive in determining whether or not something is waste. The case law on the subject illustrates the advantages and disadvantages of taking a purposive approach. On the positive side the test is coherent and easily stated as the preamble to the Directive spells out the underlying purposes of the legislation. On the negative side, the purposes of the legislation may themselves be vague and difficult to pin down when applied to specific situations.

Membership of the EC has clearly involved a distinct loss of sovereignty for Member States, and in this country this is given constitutional force by the European Communities Act 1972. Section 2(1) provides that EC legislation is recognized as law in Britain, although by no means all EC environmental legislation is directly effective in the sense that it can be relied upon by individuals before it is implemented by domestic measures. For example, although EC Regulations are effective as law without any further intervention/action on the part of the Member States, EC Directives are only 'binding as to the result to be achieved' in the sense that they lay down objectives but leave the Member States with some discretion as to how to achieve it. Thus a distinction is drawn between the requirement to transpose a Directive (i.e. translate it into national law) and the fulfilment of the obligations created. The amount of discretion varies greatly. Problems arise when Member States exceed the discretion by failing to implement EC law. This might arise from a failure to implement certain substantive or procedural provisions of a directive.

In addition to the concept of EC law as British law, there are rules and principles which can be applied to the institutions of the EC (i.e. EC law as it affects internal bodies). Thus such things as the precautionary principle and the need to integrate environmental considerations into all areas of EC policy apply to the Commission when it is formulating legislative proposals and the European Parliament and Council of Ministers when they are debating and making European environmental laws. EC law is explained in greater detail in Chapter 7 but an important point to establish here is that, as with the position in domestic law, EC environmental law consists of far more than legal rules. It is as necessary to understand the policies, principles and future direction of EC law as it is to understand its current legal content.

Layers of law

Although international law, EC law and domestic law are described as separate sources of law, they are increasingly interdependent. Obligations under international environmental law are often implemented by domestic or EC legislation. The relationship is not only 'top-down' as the EC plays an important part in negotiating international agreements on behalf of its Member States and the UK plays an important part in setting the agenda on certain environmental issues in the EC. A good example of the latter point is the way in which the UK was a leader in the development of the Integrated Prevention Pollution and Control Directive, based largely on experience with integrated pollution control introduced under the Environmental Protection Act 1990 (see p. 771).

The interaction of domestic, European and international sources of environmental law produces a 'layering' effect which sees laws which address particular problems overlapping. To illustrate this Box 4.2 sets out the layering of various sources of law on air pollution. It illustrates the division between Conventions and Protocols in International law; Framework and Daughter Directives in EC law; and primary statutes and secondary legislation in national law. This is only schematic and is not a comprehensive description of all relevant laws on air pollution. For example, it could have a further layer below the UK which described laws in the devolved countries or it could have described technical or policy documents at all levels. It does, however, highlight a number of points. First, there are layers within layers, namely broad frameworks which have the details fleshed out in other legislation. Secondly, not all topics will be layered in the same way. Although the law on any particular environmental issue can come from a variety of sources, there are certain issues such as transboundary pollution which require international solutions. Other areas are more appropriately dealt with at regional or national levels. Finally, there is no 'conveyor belt' system where environmental law is transferred from one layer to another. Because international and European obligations are often framed in very broad terms, a range of measures may be adopted at a national level. They may not be directly linked to any European or international measures even though they have the function of meeting the obligations laid down elsewhere.

National law

In the UK the term 'environmental law' is commonly used to mean that branch of public law containing statutes which cover pollution control and wider environmental issues. This only provides part of the picture, however, as there are other mechanisms which control or influence activities which cause environmental harm which are not governed by statute. These could be voluntary in nature or based upon the use of the market. As the nature of environmental issues becomes more complex and the diversity of ways of addressing them increases, so the sources of environmental law expand and the traditional boundaries and divisions of legal mechanisms blur (as to the development of environmental laws see p. 20). As examples of this diversity there are:

• Instruments which are hybrids of the public and private law (e.g. environmental

BOX 4.2 **Layers of law—air pollution**

International

1979 Geneva Convention on Long Range Transboundary Pollution

| 1984 Monitoring and Evaluation Protocol | 1985 Helsinki Protocol on Reductions of Sulphur Emissions | 1988 Sofia Protocol on Nitrogen Oxides | 1991 Geneva Protocol on Volatile Organic Compounds | 1994 Oslo Protocol on Further Reduction of Sulphur Emissions | 1998 Aarhus Protocol on Persistent Organic Pollutants (POPs) | 1998 Aarhus Protocol on Heavy Metals | 1999 Gothenburg Protocol to Abate Acidification, Eutrophication and Ground-level Ozone |

EC

Framework Directive 1996/62 on ambient air quality assessment and management

| Directive 1999/30 on limits for NOx, SO2, PM10, Pb | Directive 2000/69 on limits for Benzene and Carbon Monoxide | Directive 2002/3/EC on limits for ozone | Directive 1996/61 EC on IPPC | Directive 1999/13/EC on volatile organic compounds | Directive 2000/76/EC on the incineration of waste | Directive 2001/80/EC on large combustion plants | Directive 2001/81/EC on national emission ceilings |

UK

| Air Quality Limit Values Regulations 2003 | National Emissions Ceiling Regulations 2002 | Air Quality (England) Regulations 2000 | National Air Quality Strategy | Environment Act 1995 | European Communities Act 1972 | Pollution Prevention and Control Act 1999 | Pollution Prevention and Control (England and Wales) Regulations 2000 | Technical Guidance Documents |

agreements made under statutory powers by public bodies with private individuals or groups. These would include such things as planning contributions under the Planning and Compulsory Purchase Act 2004, s. 46 or management agreements in nature conservation).

- Instruments which impose self-regulatory requirements. An example of this would be the existence of compliance schemes under the producer responsibility legislation for the recovery and recycling of packaging waste. The regulations exempt all companies who would otherwise have had to comply with the producer responsibility obligations if they are members of a compliance scheme which is registered for the purposes of the regulations. The compliance scheme takes on collective responsibility for meeting its members' obligations under the legislation. Thus the regulation of the activities is delegated to a small number of self-regulated organizations.

- Instruments based upon increasing public information about polluting activities. These include not only rights of access to information on specific emissions and activities regulated under licences which are held on public registers, but also more sophisticated information such as inventories of general and aggregated pollution levels, product labelling and possible requirements to include environmental information in companies' annual reports.

- Economic instruments which can cover a range of measures from the direct taxation of polluting substances (e.g. the landfill tax) and the creation of a market in the pollution credits (e.g. the emissions trading scheme) to fees and charges for licences which reflect the level of environmental risk or harm which an authorised activity causes.

This use of a broader range of instruments reflects a growth of sources of environmental law: where traditional public law 'command and control' legislation is combined with different regulatory approaches to secure the most effective forms of control over environmental pollution.[2]

Categories of environmental legislation

Although the boundaries between different types of legislation and rules are often blurred in practice, the source of domestic environmental legislation can be broken down into three main categories.

(a) Primary legislation

Acts of Parliament (also known as statutes or enactments) provide the basic framework for most domestic environmental law. Although they are subject to full Parliamentary scrutiny, their general nature means that there is often little controversy concerning the substantive provisions of environmental statutes as they do not contain anything of sufficient certainty to give rise to party political disputes (although there are notable exceptions to this; the primary example being the Wildlife and Countryside Act 1981). Another notable feature

---

2. N. Gunningham and P. Grabosky, *Smart Regulation: Designing Environmental Policy*, (Oxford: Clarendon Press, 1998).

of environmental statutes is that legislation on single environmental issues is often promoted in the form of Private Members' Bills, reflecting the individual interests of MPs and the effective lobbying of non-governmental organisations (NGOs). Examples of Private Members' Bills on environmental issues which have reached the statute book in recent years include the Waste Minimisation Act 1998 and the Household Waste Recycling Act 2003.

There is little direct public participation (e.g. by way of public consultation) in the creation of environmental statutes. The main justification for this is that Parliament has representative accountability through the electorate and is therefore presumed to pass laws on behalf of everyone. In addition, both Houses of Parliament scrutinize new legislation in standing committees and debates. In reality, this scrutiny is often no more than passing consideration because of pressure on Parliamentary time and commonly the numerical strength of the incumbent government.

Although there has been a consolidation of the administration of environmental protection over recent years, environmental legislation still extends over a relatively large area. The main environmental legislation is outlined in Box 2.4. This is by no means a comprehensive list. It is increasingly common to have narrower statutes which focus on perhaps one or two main issues rather than the broad coverage of these Acts.

There is another more general statute which could be said to be a primary source of environmental law. The European Communities Act 1972, s. 2(2) gives powers for the passing of secondary legislation which is necessary to comply with EC law. One of the main disadvantages of this power is that it only permits bare implementation measures (i.e. secondary legislation must accord exactly with the European obligations, no more and no less). Many important pieces of environmental legislation have been passed under the powers of the European Communities Act including the Town and Country Planning (Assessment of Environmental Effects) (England and Wales) Regulations 1999 and the Conservation (Natural Habitats etc.) Regulations 1994. This power has been supplemented with a wider power to transpose and modify environmental obligations under EC law under the Pollution Prevention and Control Act 1999, sch. 1, para. 20.

(b) Secondary legislation

The second main source of environmental law stems from the first. Beneath the tier of primary legislation there is a range of detailed secondary legislation which is used to flesh out much of the detail of environmental law. Regulations are commonly made by the appropriate Secretary of State under the delegated authority of Parliament. Typically, they are known as regulations or statutory instruments although in relation to environmental laws, there are other types of secondary legislation (e.g. the Use Classes Order). This tier of legislation is entirely dependent upon the powers which have been granted within the primary statute. In environmental law, there has been some controversy about the breadth of some of the powers which have been granted by primary statutes. There appears to have been a desire to broaden the scope of the power to make secondary legislation in order to give more and more flexibility to the rule makers. The Pollution Prevention and Control Bill featured a particularly wide power allowing the Secretary of State to pass regulations in respect of a series of statutory purposes relating to environmental pollution. This would have given a virtually unlimited scope to control any activity which gave rise to pollution without any Parliamentary scrutiny. This power was subsequently amended after objections were lodged in the House of Lords.

This controversy illustrates some of the concerns about using secondary legislation for many of the elements of environmental laws. Unlike primary legislation, there is little Parliamentary scrutiny of detailed secondary legislation. Many environmental regulations are passed under a negative resolution procedure which, in practice, consists of laying the statutory instrument before both Houses of Parliament for a specified period before it comes into force. Some more controversial aspects of secondary legislation are subject to the alternative affirmative procedure which ensures that there are debates in both Houses before the legislation is passed.

One of the main reasons for the lack of Parliamentary scrutiny is that environmental secondary legislation tends to be highly technical and the lack of any sufficient expertise would make Parliamentary scrutiny less than effective. Secondly, environmental secondary legislation is commonly sent out for public consultation which enables a broad range of technical views to be taken into account prior to finalising the details. In these circumstances, the lower levels of Parliamentary scrutiny can be justified as there is a broader public scrutiny which is involved in the law-making process.

It is impossible to provide any comprehensive list of environmental secondary legislation but there are certain categories which can be identified.

• *Procedural.* Certain aspects of environmental regulation are too detailed and complex to be placed in primary legislation. Procedures for applications for licences and for appealing against refusals or enforcement action can often be found in secondary legislation. In addition, provisions on other procedural matters such as registers of information on emissions are left to delegated powers. For examples see the Contaminated Land (England) Regulations 2000 (SI 2000/227) and the Statutory Nuisance (Appeals) Regulations 1995 (SI 1995/2644).

• *Detailed categories.* Primary legislation may set down general definitions which can be more properly defined in technical secondary legislation. Thus categories of installations controlled under IPPC (see Pollution Prevention and Control (England and Wales) Regulations 2000 (SI 2000/1973)), exemptions from the need for planning permission (e.g. see the Town and Country Planning Use Classes Order 1987, (SI 1987/764)) or categories of waste which qualify for the lower rate of Landfill Tax (see the Landfill Tax (Qualifying Materials) Order 1996 (SI 1996/1528)) are all to be found in secondary legislation.

• *Standards.* It is common for the many different types of standards which play an important role in environmental regulation to be set out in secondary legislation (see further p. 243). Examples include the Air Quality Limit Values Regulations 2003 (SI 2000/928) and the Urban Waste Water Treatment (England and Wales) Regulations 1994 (SI 1994/2841).

• *Transposing European obligations.* Certain European obligations have been transposed directly into secondary legislation. The justification for using secondary legislation is that there should be little political controversy over the transposition of measures which have been agreed at a European level. Thus these regulations are direct translations of the corresponding European measures and examples include the Conservation (Natural Habitats etc.) Regulations 1994 (SI 1994/2716) (transposing the Habitats Directive (92/43)), and the Waste Management Licensing Regulations 1994 (SI 1994/1056) (transposing the Framework Directive on Waste (91/271)).

(c) Tertiary legislation, guidance and other 'rules'

Although secondary legislation provides the bulk of the technical details of environmental law, it is still not particularly user-friendly nor does it set out a comprehensive set of definitions. There is an increasing reliance on other rules and guidance to explain the practical workings of environmental laws and to provide a structure for statutory discretion. There are so many different types of this source of law that it is impossible to identify any meaningful classification other than looking at the purpose behind the guidance or rule. These rules can have a number of purposes.

- *As an aid to the interpretation of statutory provisions.* As the main statutory provisions in primary and secondary legislation can be complex and technical, there is often a need to flesh out definitions and provide an interpretation of such provisions in non-legalistic language. An example is the definition of waste which is defined in the primary statute in a few lines, fleshed out in different ways in the Waste Management Licensing Regulations 1994 (SI 1994/1056) but is explained in simpler terms in the Department of the Environment Circular 11/94.

- *As a more flexible form of informal guidance or rule.* There are some areas which do not lend themselves to the traditional sources of environmental law. These include matters which cannot easily be reduced to simple rules as there is a need for a little more flexibility and less legal rigidity in the use of language. An example is the code of practice on the duty of care which provides detailed guidance on the type of conduct which might be considered to be reasonable when handling materials throughout the waste management chain. Another example is the statutory guidance in the contaminated land regime. Both of these examples set out principles and rules in a prose style which enables a wider range of issues to be discussed and balanced than would be the case if they were set out in formal legislation. In addition, broad strategic documents are more easily framed in informal documents than in formal legislation as they set out general policies, strategies and programmes which are to be used in meeting statutory or non-statutory environmental quality targets. Examples include the national strategies on waste and air quality.

- *As statements of regulatory agency policy and practice.* Regulatory agencies will often publish policy documents which set out their aims and policies on particular areas. The EA has policy and practice documents in a number of areas including the protection of groundwater and of floodplains. These documents are used in liaison with other agencies (primarily the planning authorities) in carrying out overlapping functions and in exercising decision-making powers such as determining planning applications.

- *As a way of structuring discretion and promoting consistency and transparency in decision-making.* Where environmental agencies implement and enforce wide discretionary statutory powers there is often guidance which aims to direct them in the exercise of those powers. Documents such as the Environment Agency's Enforcement and Prosecution Policy set out objective principles which guide individual officers as to when and how enforcement action should be taken when environmental laws are breached. This should ensure that there is a degree of consistency and uniformity in enforcement practices across the country and thereby increases the transparency and fairness of the otherwise unstructured use of enforcement powers.

- *As rules and guidance on procedure or other technical matters.* Although secondary legislation often sets out the formal legislative requirements for procedural or other technical matters, it does not deal with many of the practical issues which can arise on a day-to-day basis. Thus there is a need to provide information and practical guidance in non-legalistic language. Examples of this can be found in general guidance issued by the Secretary of State and the Environment Agency in relation to the BAT process standard under Pollution Prevention and Control legislation.

These types of tertiary rules and guidance have become a common method of supplementing formal primary and secondary legislation as a source of environmental law. In areas of policy rather than law, the use of circulars and other guidance documents is relatively well established. Whilst there is a very significant degree of overlap between law and policy, the range of tertiary rules in modern environmental law goes much further than mere policy documents providing assistance with decision-making. The use of technical guidance and documents which interpret general statutory concepts is one of the ways in which environmental laws operate in the real world. The use of such documents is not, however, without its own set of difficulties. The level of formality of such rules differs. Some, such as the code of practice on the duty of care or the statutory guidance on contaminated land, have their origins in primary or secondary legislation (and which could be referred to as sub-delegated legislation). Others appear somewhat spontaneously and do not have any formal basis.

The key problem with the use of tertiary rules is, however, that there is a great deal of uncertainty and confusion about the extent to which such rules have legal effect. For example, if an interpretive guidance document sets out a detailed interpretation of a general statutory definition (such as the government's interpretation of the definition of waste in Circular 11/94 or the EA's view on the definition of packaging), does that interpretation have any legal force? Theoretically, at least, such interpretations or rules do not have any determinative status as law (indeed, it is common for such guidance documents to make it clear that the individual interpretation is no substitute for a court's view). This theory unfortunately ignores the fact that in practice the interpretation often supplants the general definition in the minds of the regulator and the regulated. Moreover, if the interpretation is ever challenged in court, there is a great temptation for a judge to 'adopt' the official interpretation over any other.

Generally speaking, tertiary rules will have a persuasive status, either as material considerations (e.g. in the case of planning circulars) which cannot be ignored but are not prescriptive, or as presumptive starting points for a decision-maker or regulatory agency (e.g. in the case of guidance notes in relation to IPPC where the process standard set out is presumed to represent BAT but other circumstances could give rise to alternatives). The one exception to this general rule is in the case of the National Waste Strategy which has been held to carry special weight in the decision-making process (see p. 571 and Case box 15.1).

Characteristics of UK environmental legislation

Environmental legislation covers a wide range of areas which means that the substance of the legislation is often very different. There are, however, some characteristics which could be said to be common to all.

(a) Complex tiers of rules

Much of the detail of environmental statutes is left to be worked out in various forms of delegated legislation. This is particularly true of some of the main pieces of legislation in environmental law—the Environmental Protection Act 1990, the Water Resources Act 1991, the Environment Act 1995, the Town and Country Planning Act 1990, and the Pollution Prevention and Control Act 1999. In each case, the statute only provides a limited description of what the law is. For example, in the Town and Country Planning Act 1990, the central definition of what requires planning permission owes just as much to statutory instruments—the General Permitted Development Order and the Use Classes Order—as to the general definition laid down in section 55 of the Act. There is no typical type of delegated legislation within UK environmental law and detailed laws come under names such as regulations, rules, orders and schemes.

As this detailed type of delegated legislation is often technical and complex, there is a further layer of rules which form what we might term 'tertiary' or 'quasi' legislation. There is no set pattern to this type of rule but it is made up of different forms of guidance, circulars and other technical advice. As environmental regulation becomes more multifaceted, this type of rule-making is becoming more popular as it provides a simple, flexible and efficient way of expanding upon basic statutory concepts.

The upshot of all of these different types of legislation and other rules is that it is often difficult to find out about the law on a particular issue in anything other than a very general manner. For example, if one wanted to find out about the rules which governed an application for a pollution prevention and control permit, the basic information about application procedures would have to be supplemented with technical guidance on specific industrial sectors and general guidance on such things as monitoring requirements. The complexity and interaction of these many tiers of rules can obscure the effects of the law in that the informal rules and guidance can have greater practical significance than the primary or secondary legislation.

(b) Delayed commencement

Legislation often requires implementation by statutory instrument before it comes into force. The Control of Pollution Act was enacted in 1974, yet Part II relating to water pollution was not brought into force until 1986, and then only in a piecemeal and gradual manner. Some parts of the Act were never brought into force (e.g. s. 46(1)–(3) on the powers of water authorities to vary consents after an act of pollution). Apart from the suspicion that such delays are used for political purposes, this gradualist approach obscures what the law is and brings it into disrepute by creating uncertainty for the public, regulatory bodies and industry alike.

The EPA 1990 included a provision for most of it to be brought into force by commencement order. This led to the provisions on waste management licensing not being brought into force until May 1994. Other key provisions on Contaminated Land Registers (s. 143) and closed landfill sites (s. 61) were repealed before they ever came into force. It seems contrary to the rule of law that the decision on whether, and how far, to implement enacted legislation should be left entirely to the discretion of the Secretary of State. However, that is the position and the same approach is adopted in most major pieces of environmental legislation.

(c) Definitions

Definitions are often left unclear in the legislation. Normally this is to preserve flexibility in the application of the law. For example, until the enactment of the EPA 1990, the central concept in the law on air pollution was that of 'best practicable means' (BPM). This phrase was never statutorily defined. Instead, it was explained in relation to different processes in BPM Notes published by Her Majesty's Inspectorate of Pollution (HMIP) and its predecessors. Even these were not comprehensive, since an important feature of BPM was that it allowed flexibility to cater for local and individual circumstances. Interestingly, the BPM Notes were often drawn up in consultation with interested parties, including representatives of the industry concerned.

A similar process can be seen in the Town and Country Planning Act 1990, where fundamental concepts such as development and material change of use have deliberately been left as open as possible in the legislation. In this case, they have been further defined by the courts in numerous cases, but the original flexibility has been retained by the courts' insistence that the application of the law to the facts of any individual case is a matter for the relevant decision-maker (the so-called 'fact and degree' test). If anything, this approach is becoming more common. Under the contaminated land regime in Part IIA of the EPA 1990 (brought in by the Environment Act 1995), the fundamental question of whether land is 'contaminated' owes as much to guidance issued by the Secretary of State which local authorities must follow, as it does to the partial definition set out in the Act. What should be determined as a matter of law is thus relegated to a matter of administrative discretion. An even more remarkable example is provided by the Deregulation and Contracting Out Act 1994, which included a general power for any Minister to amend or repeal existing legislation by means of a statutory instrument if it appeared that the measure imposed a burden on any trade, business, or profession, and that the amendment or repeal would reduce that burden. These examples illustrate a clear shift in power away from Parliament and the courts to the executive government.

(d) Purposive and listing approaches

One of the consequences of having to balance such wide definitions against the technical nature of much of environmental law is that there are two typical approaches to drafting legislative concepts. First, and probably the most common, is the approach outlined above where the rule maker balances flexibility and certainty by creating complex tiers of rules. Characteristically, this will involve having a broad definition within primary legislation followed by lists of a more technical nature in secondary regulations. Examples of this can be found in the formation of exemptions from the legislative system in many areas of environmental legislation (e.g. from the need for planning permission or waste management licences). The primary statute empowers the rule maker to create classes of exempt activities and these are set down in detailed secondary legislation. The main alternative to this approach is to set down a purposive definition which stands alone without any need for further clarification. The purpose of the definition is self-explanatory. An example of this can be found in Water Resources Act 1991, s. 85, which makes it an offence to cause the entry of 'polluting' matter into controlled waters. The key phrase 'polluting' is not defined in the Act (see Box 18.3). Some environmental laws combine both of these approaches. For example, the definition of waste relies both on a general purposive definition ('substances or objects which have been discarded'), general descriptions of categories of wastes, recovery, and disposal operations found in Annexes to the Waste Management Licensing Regulations 1994 and extremely detailed classifications of waste found in the European Waste Catalogue (see the List of Wastes (England) Regulations 2005 (SI 2005/895)).

Interestingly in this context, European law sets out the specific purposes of legislation in recitals which form part of directives. Since more and more European law is being transposed into domestic law by means of straight translation (also referred to as 'copy out'), and the doctrine of indirect effects (that national laws should be interpreted so as to comply with EC law), this means that courts are interpreting national environmental laws in accordance with the underlying purposes.

(e) Discretions

Wide discretions are frequently given in the legislation. This is a particularly clear feature of British environmental law. There are many examples, ranging from the discretion given to the Secretary of State on the form of delegated legislation, through discretion as to whether an area should be designated for special protection, discretion on the setting of standards (e.g. in the permitted level of a pollutant discharged or emitted), to discretion over the enforcement of the law. In all areas of environmental law it is hard to get away from discretionary decision-making.

However, two important trends must be pointed out at this stage. These are the increases in both the structuring of discretion and the role played by central government. In the past, it has been normal for environmental legislation to grant regulatory agencies and bodies a large amount of discretion, often in the form of a subjective power which is then controlled by the courts. More recently, the agencies have themselves structured the exercise of their discretion through such things as internal agency guidelines and strategies, and have thus made the whole system more formalized (an example is the adoption by the Environment Agency of a formal policy on prosecution and other enforcement action). This gives the courts a greater potential role in environmental decisions. However, the effect is arguably limited by the other trend which, as pointed out above, is that ever greater powers are being given to central government to dictate the sorts of considerations that must be taken into account in any exercise of a discretion. This process is seen very clearly in the Environment Act 1995. As a specific example, section 39 imposes a requirement that the EA take into account the likely costs and benefits before making decisions; but, more generally, the whole way in which the EA operates is effectively decided by guidance and directions issued by central government.

These features of environmental legislation help to explain some of the essential characteristics of the 'British approach' to environmental protection, such as flexibility and pragmatism. The width of the discretions given also militates against uniformity in either the definition or the application of the law.

Environmental laws in practice

As much of the above discussion illustrates, the reading of environmental statutes may provide us with a source of environmental law but it does not necessarily represent how such laws work in the real world. One of the key characteristics of environmental law is that it is (or rather should be) law in action rather than law for lawyers. It involves the solving of practical problems, so everything which is likely to have an impact on the solution of a problem should be understood including tertiary rules such as guidance and evidence of practice. The sources of environmental law are forward-looking in the sense that they often provide frameworks for future action (e.g. the structured implementation of the integrated pollution prevention and control (IPPC) legislation). Thus, it is often desirable to know what the law is going to be as well as what it is. Finally, it may also be argued that the sources of law should include the actual practice of agencies with responsibilities in the environmental field; an argument which is at its strongest when dealing with enforcement. This makes it desirable that as much as possible about the practice and policy actually relied upon by decision-makers is published officially, an aim which is still not yet met in practice.

Thus there is often a gap between published law and policy and what actually happens in the real world. This gap illustrates that making environmental law is not the end of the process. The manner in which laws are transformed from the legislative page into effective action depends upon how they are implemented and enforced. Inadequate implementation leads to regulatory failure. There are many factors which may influence how laws are implemented. Legislation may be too vague or complex to be put into practice. It may be unrealistic in terms of timescale for compliance or the requirements that it imposes on the regulated. Even in cases where legislation is clear, simple and not excessively onerous there is no guarantee that the rules or standards will be imposed in practice. Administrative arrangements may mean that different regulatory bodies find it difficult to coordinate and cooperate on implementation or may adopt different approaches on overlapping issues. Financial or resource constraints may mean that there are not enough suitably qualified regulators to issue licences or to supervise regulated activities. Scientific limitations may mean that it is difficult to monitor some emissions accurately or there may be alternative measurement methods which produce inconsistent results.

The inadequate implementation of environmental regulation can be contrasted with another aspect of the gap between sources of law and effective environmental regulation, namely the proper enforcement of those laws. Whilst there may be an overlap in these issues (e.g. lack of sufficient regulators) the enforcement of environmental law is more influenced by the exercise of discretion by regulators in taking a cooperative stance with those who are in breach. There are a variety of reasons why such an approach is adopted which are covered more fully in Chapter 9.

Case law

In the UK most of the formal sources of environmental law are statutory. Compared with subjects such as contract or tort there is very little judge made law, and most of what there is consists of the interpretation of statutory provisions. Having said that, case law, that is the decisions made by judges in the courts, forms a growing source of law. On a very general level, substantive environmental cases come before the courts in three main ways. First, where there is a dispute about a statutory definition in primary or secondary legislation, a court can be asked to interpret the statutory phrase. In these cases, the court's interpretation of the definition becomes the law (in this context it is also important to note the role and influence of the European Court of Justice which is discussed further in Chapter 7). Secondly, there are common law disputes which have an environmental flavour. These include actions in nuisance, negligence, and trespass. In these cases, the courts are developing principles which have a long history in order to address modern environmental disputes. Finally, as most of the sources of environmental law are statutory, cases arise where the powers granted to government and regulatory agencies are used unlawfully or statutory procedures ignored and the courts are asked to judicially review the exercise of the power.

In addition to the domestic cases, the decisions of the European Court of Justice exert an increasing influence over the interpretation of domestic law. Theoretically this was always the case, as domestic courts are bound to not only accept the authority of European Court of Justice on the interpretation of European law (European Communities Act 1972, ss. 2(4), 3(1)) but also to ensure that the objectives of directives are to be achieved under the indirect effects doctrine. In practice, however, the courts have struggled to move away from a discretionary based approach to the implementation of European law.

Administrative appeals and decision-making

In addition to judicial decisions, there is a range of quasi-judicial decisions which can provide a source of law in its widest sense (in the same way that tertiary rules form a source of law). In a subject which is heavily dominated by policy, it is clear that the Secretary of State (which we use loosely to cover the relevant decision-makers in Scotland, Wales and Northern Ireland), in his role as ultimate arbiter on questions of policy in the system of administrative appeals, can set precedents in terms of the manner in which central rules or guidance are to be interpreted both generally and on a case-by-case basis. Although such administrative decisions are not binding upon other decision-makers (i.e. not in the way that judicial pronouncements bind lower courts), they can effectively dictate the decision-making processes of the regulatory agencies to whom such powers have been devolved. An example of this can be found in the way in which decisions in planning appeals were used to reinforce deregulatory planning policies in the 1980s.

The system of environmental appeals addresses questions of law (e.g. whether or not something is 'development' within the meaning of the Town and Country Planning Act 1990), fact (e.g. whether a planning use was commenced more than 10 years ago), policy (e.g. whether a particular development should be situated outside a town centre in contravention of central government guidance), scientific and technical issues (e.g. whether a particular process option represents BAT) or any combination of these. In this way, such appeals are concerned with the substantive (as opposed to procedural) 'rights and wrongs' of environmental decision-making with all of the consequential impact that this has on public participation; provision of adequate and objective evidence; and clarity and transparency of the decision itself.

In many ways, the 'battleground' of environmental decision-making lies within the context of the administrative appeals system. Although the courts have supervisory powers under the judicial review process this is not concerned with the substantive decision but the manner in which the decision was made (see p. 347). One of the main problems with this approach is that there can be a tendency for administrative appeals to be viewed by the public as being more concerned with going through the correct procedures than with debating and adjudicating on the substantive issues at hand, as the appeal process is primarily concerned with applying central policy within an individual set of facts rather than debating whether that policy is in itself acceptable (e.g. whether an incinerator is acceptable at a particular location, rather than whether we should be using waste minimisation techniques to ensure that there is no need for further incinerators).

CHAPTER SUMMARY

1   Certain rights and principles overarch all sources of law in the sense that they are either general guides for decision makers at all levels (e.g. the precautionary principle or the polluter pays principle) or rights which overlap with sources of environmental law (e.g. human rights).

2   International law generally consists of agreements between countries on the approach to be taken in relation to international environmental problems. By nature it is broad in application and general in terms of the obligations imposed.

3   EC law is a very significant source of environmental law. Many areas of British environmental law have their origins in EC law particularly in relation to environmental quality and emission standards. Although EC Regulations do not need transposing into national law, there is a requirement to transpose and implement the obligations in the case of Directives.

4   Different sources of law are interrelated to one another through the 'layering' of different obligations. Thus international obligations may be transposed through European and/or domestic legislation. The relationship is not only 'top down' as the EC plays an important part in negotiating international agreements on behalf of its Member States and the UK plays an important part in setting the agenda on certain environmental issues in the EC.

5   Modern environmental law is characterized by the development of a mixed regulation approach whereby a range of different instruments are used to address environmental problems including economic instruments such as taxes, greater access to environmental information, public participation and voluntary agreements.

6   Primary legislation in British environmental law is dominated by broad framework acts which need fleshing out in detailed secondary legislation and technical and policy guidance.

7   British environmental law can be characterized as having many tiers, delayed commencement and wide discretionary definitions which promotes flexibility and pragmatism.

8   Although rules and decision-making may be clear, there is no guarantee that these standards

are imposed in practice. There is a gap between the sources of law and what happens in the real world. This gap is caused by inadequacies in implementation and enforcement.

9 Compared to other subjects such as contract or tort, environmental law has relatively little judge made law. What there is consists mostly of statutory interpretation of environmental legislation.

10 Historically the British judiciary has been conservative in its interpretation of environmental statutes preferring to take a non-interventionist approach to largely discretionary decisions made by regulatory bodies. In recent years the decisions of the European Court of Justice and a greater understanding of the purposive approach of European law has seen a shift in emphasis.

11 Decisions which are determined by regulators and on administrative appeal can take into account a range of factors including issues of fact, law and policy. The British judicial tradition is that the courts should not intervene in policy decisions unless it is so extreme as to be irrational or where procedural injustices have occurred.

Q QUESTIONS

1 Look at the following:
   (a) Kyoto Protocol: Article 17 available at <unfccc.int/resource/docs/convkp/kpeng.html>.
   (b) EC Directive 2003/87/EC on Greenhouse Gas Emissions Trading available at <europa.e-u.int/comm/environment/climat/emission/implementation_en.htm>.
   (c) The Waste and Emissions Trading Act 2003 ss. 38 and 39 available at <http://www.opsi.gov.uk/acts/acts2003/20030033.htm>.
   (d) The Greenhouse Gas Emissions Trading Scheme Regulations 2003 (SI 2003/3311) available at <www.opsi.gov.uk/si/si2003/20033311.htm>.
   (e) Rules for the UK Emissions Trading Scheme available at <www.defra.gov.uk/environment/climatechange/trading/uk/pdf/trading-rules_rev2.pdf>.
   (f) The Climate Change Programme, Ch. 4 paras 29–38 <www.defra.gov.uk>.

   Try and classify each document as a 'source of law'. What, if any, relationship does each of these documents have with each other? What does this tell you about the 'layering' of environmental law?

2 What factors affect the level from which environmental law originates? What justifications are there for legislating at the international, European and national levels?

3 Compare and contrast the decisions in *Wychavon District Council v Secretary of State for the Environment* [1994] Env LR 239 and *Berkeley v Secretary of State for the Environment* [2001] Env LR 303. How may these two judgments show how the judiciary has changed its attitude to the interpretation of European environmental legislation?

FURTHER READING

Much of the specific reading on the different sources of law will be found at the end of the relevant chapters dealing with European law, International law and the Regulation of Environment Protection. For a general introduction and a historical account of different sources of law have a look at D. Robinson, 'Regulatory Evolution in Pollution Control' in T. Jewell and J. Steele (eds) *Law in Environmental Decision Making* (Oxford: Clarendon Press 1998). This gives a clear picture of the development of new types of law. The relationship between EC and UK sources of law is explored in chapter 3 of C. Hilson, *Regulating Pollution—a UK and EC Perspective* (Oxford: Hart Publishing, 2000). It provides a good overview of the justifications for legislating at different levels both generally in Federal/devolved countries and more particularly in the UK and EC. A. Gouldson and J. Murphy, *Regulatory Realities* (London: Earthscan, 1998) provides an interesting comparative study of the implementation of industrial environmental regulation. In particular chapter 1 examines the role of implementation and some of the barriers which prevent perfect implementation.

Two articles which give some historical perspective on the way English Courts used to approach questions of European Law, particularly in relation to environmental assessment are J. Alder, 'Environmental Impact Assessment—The Inadequacies of English Law' (1993) 5 JEL 203 and A. Ward 'The Right to an Effective Remedy in European Community Law and Environmental Protection: A Case Study of United Kingdom Judicial Decisions Concerning the Environmental Assessment Directive' (1993) 5 JEL 221. For a more up-to-date perspective have a look at W. Upton, 'The EIA Process and the Directly Enforceable Rights of Citizens' (2001) 13 JEL 98.

5 The administration of environmental law and policy

 Overview

This chapter covers those institutions that are involved in the administration of environmental law and policy. As such it links in with many other different chapters in this book. Most obviously it links in with the chapters in Part III which deal with specific sectoral topics in the sense that it explains who is responsible for what in terms of the day-to-day running of different regulatory systems. We will concentrate almost exclusively on British structures and institutions as European and international administrative arrangements are considered elsewhere. In addition, the position and powers of local authorities are considered in detail in Chapter 12. An underlying theme of this Chapter is the way in which administrative structures are used to encourage the integration of environmental law and policy both internally (e.g. through the creation of the Environment Agency as a single regulatory agency) and externally (e.g. through various methods of scrutinising environmental policy across Government departments).

At the end of this chapter you should be able to:

✔ Identify and understand the role of the main regulatory bodies involved in environmental protection in the UK
✔ Understand the general functions of these bodies
✔ Identify and understand some of the general statutory aims and objectives of these bodies
✔ Appreciate the role played by a range of different bodies (governmental, non-governmental and judicial) in the process of making decisions, law and policy in relation to environmental protection
✔ Appreciate the main similarities and differences in the institutional structures in the devolved administrations

Introduction

The administration of environmental law and policy is carried out by a diversity of bodies. By administration primarily we mean responsibilities for making, implementing and enforcing environmental law and policy. This includes central government departments, regulatory agencies such as the Environment Agency and a range of quasi-governmental bodies. Their functions range from rule- and policy-making through implementation (e.g. by way of decision-making) to enforcement and the imposition of sanctions. In addition, there are many non-governmental organizations (NGOs) which play a role in environmental administration in various ways such as influencing policy through direct and indirect means (e.g. lobbying or public campaigns to raise issues). Finally, the Courts have a partial role to play in the enforcement of environmental law and also in supervising the actions of other administrative bodies.

Why are institutional arrangements important? The establishment of any effective system of environmental regulation is largely dependent upon the administrative structures and institutions which are responsible for implementing and enforcing the laws. By this we mean that whatever the substance of the laws which are brought in to deal with particular environmental problems, the practical impact of those laws depends upon the actions of various agencies and government departments within pre-existing administrative structures. Moreover, there is a direct link between the way in which environmental bodies are structured or organized and the type of laws which are introduced and the way in which they operate. The history of environmental law has demonstrated that typical changes in environmental law have been incremental rather than dramatic (see Chapter 2). Part of the reason for this is that historical institutional arrangements constrain the range of policies and laws which can be adopted. The law making process becomes 'path dependent' whereby alternative solutions to environmental problems are reduced because of the pre-existing administrative arrangements. As North puts it:

At every step along the way there are choices—political and economic—that provide . . . real alternatives. Path dependence is a way to narrow conceptually the choice set and link decision-making through time.[1]

As such, institutional change can be locked into a particular path of development and that in turn can influence the range and types of solutions which are proposed. For example, the historical development of the water industry proposals for a single body to regulate pollution control matters were originally suggested by the RCEP in 1974,[2] part of the reluctance to implement change can be explained by institutional inertia and path dependency.

Any attempt to identify who does what in environmental law and policy runs into the same definitional problems we faced in Chapter 1. The large number of bodies with responsibilities, duties and powers in relation to the protection of the environment reflects some of the difficulties in drawing up boundaries for a subject which could cover every aspect of political, social, economic, and legal life. Coordinating diverse policy areas such as transport, energy, agriculture and trade and industry which all have direct links to environmental protection presents very real difficulties. There is an increasing understanding that the decisions and actions of many bodies which do not necessarily have any direct interest in the environment can have an indirect environmental consequence and one distinctive feature of environmental problems is their interdependence. Governments have to address ideas and concerns that do not necessarily fit neatly into nicely delineated administrative structures. Even within areas with a clear link to the environment there has been a tendency to consider pollution as a series of discrete problems requiring fragmented responses, typically involving separate regulatory systems with different administrative arrangements.

---

1. D. North, *Institutions, Institutional Change and Economic Performance* (Cambridge: Cambridge University Press, 1990), 99.

2. Royal Commission on Environmental Pollution: Fifth Report, *Air Pollution Control: an Integrated Approach*, Cmnd 6371, 1976.

In recent years the integration of environmental law and policy has been offered as a solution to this problem. Integration here is used in two senses,[3] to reflect external and internal changes. External integration addresses the problem of coordination across different Departments by promoting the consideration of environmental issues across all policy areas.[4] Internal integration addresses the problem of fragmentation amongst diverse regulatory agencies by drawing together regulatory responsibilities for different environmental emissions and impacts within one single authority (see further Chapters 20 on IPPC and 14 on environmental impact assessment). Both of these topics are considered in further detail below.

Scotland, Northern Ireland, Wales, and the regions

As there are separate legal systems in Scotland and Northern Ireland, there have always been slightly different administrative and regulatory arrangements in these two countries (although it should be pointed out the private law mechanisms in Scotland are much more distinctive). These differences, in so far as the system of environmental regulation is concerned, are more structural and procedural than substantive (reflecting the fact that many new laws are the result of EC or international influences which apply to the United Kingdom as a whole), although some minor differences do occur. Devolution has, however, shifted responsibility for most matters of environmental protection to the national assemblies. This has had some impact upon the administration of environmental protection in the United Kingdom. It is, however, important to note that there is not a wide diversity in environmental laws across the different countries for a number of reasons:

- The devolution of primary law-making powers is not comprehensive. Whilst the Scottish and Northern Ireland assemblies have the powers to pass primary legislation in certain areas including the environment,[5] Wales only has the power to pass secondary legislation.

- The power to pass any new environmental legislation is constrained by the need to comply with EC law or international obligations.[6] As the United Kingdom is a Member State of a EC, it has the responsibility to ensure that there is overall compliance with any obligations imposed in each country (historically, this has led to problems of non-implementation and non-transposition of directives particularly in the case of Northern Ireland). There are powers available to UK authorities where there has been any failure to give effect to EC law in each country, whether it be the country passing incompatible legislation or failing to transpose EC measures.[7]

- The need to comply with European/international obligations raises another issue. As the

3. Integration can be used in other ways, see J. Steele and T. Jewell, 'Law in Environmental Decision Making' in T. Jewell and J. Steele (eds), *Law in Environmental Decision Making* (Oxford: Clarendon Press, 1998), 3.
4. The integration of environmental issues at the European level is discussed in A. Weale and A. Williams (1992) 1(4) Environmental Politics 45–64.
5. E.g. Scotland Act 1998, ss. 28–30.
6. Ibid, s. 29.
7. Ibid, s. 35.

obligations fall upon the United Kingdom as a whole, they are negotiated on behalf of the UK and none of the devolved assemblies has a formal say in the formation of those laws or policies.[8] Thus the uniformity of obligations as between different countries of the UK will continue. It should be noted, however, that EC law and policy is becoming more sensitive to regional environmental differences which could mean that in future, the nature of the obligations may vary in emphasis.

• Control over certain aspects of law-making have not been devolved (although in practice there is some political involvement).[9] For example, most aspects of revenue raising by way of taxes or duties do not fall under the control of the new assemblies. Thus any economic instruments such as the landfill tax could not be introduced or altered. Other areas including transport, energy and consumer protection have been transferred to a greater or lesser extent.

In the light of the above restrictions, these constitutional changes brought about by devolution mean that the opportunity for wholesale amendments to environmental law in each country is limited. That is not to say, however, that different styles of environmental regulation could not be adopted. In particular, there is an opportunity (within the constraints mentioned above) to construct and scrutinize environmental legislation from the very different cultural perspectives of each country. There is also scope to alter the terms of secondary legislation to take into account national concerns. For example, such things as statutory exemptions from pollution control licensing vary from country to country (see Box 5.1 below). Over time, the aggregation of these minor differences could result in distinct bodies of law with national characteristics. Indeed, in relation to Scotland and Northern Ireland at least, there are sufficient substantive differences already to warrant individual text books on national environmental law which are referred to in the Further Reading at the end of the Chapter.

BOX 5.1 Scotland and waste exemptions

A good example of the impact that regionalized and local issues can have on post devolution law making can be seen in the case of the outcry over the land-spreading of waste in the small village of Blairingone in Kinrosshire in Scotland in 1997. The practice of spreading certain wastes on agricultural land has been exempt from waste management controls where the spreading is for the purpose of 'agricultural benefit', land reclamation and construction (see Box 15.12). In Blairingone, sewage, blood, and guts from abattoirs were spread on fields for a number of years despite protests from local communities who experienced certain health problems including increased incidences of throat infections and blisters among young children. A local action group petitioned the Scottish Parliament, a procedure which enables the public to petition elected representatives over matters of public concern.[10] The Scottish Parliament is the only assembly in the UK with such a procedure. Following a highly critical public report[11] on the matter the

---

8. G. Little, (2000) 12 JEL 155, 171.
9. Ibid 158–165.
10. <www.scottish.parliament.uk/petitions/public/pdfs/pe327.pdf>.
11. <www.scottish.parliament.uk/S1/official_report/cttee/trans–02/trr02–04–02.htm#2>.

Parliament introduced Regulations which introduced a system of registration for previously exempt spreading operations coupled with increased monitoring and enforcement powers.[12] By contrast, in England and Wales, the land spreading of industrial wastes was heavily criticized by the RCEP in 1996[13] but despite promises and various consultation exercises no similar regulations have been introduced.

Although the differences which devolution will make to new environmental legislation may take some time to gain real significance in the UK context, it is perhaps more likely that individual policy areas in the devolved countries will provide an interesting contrast. It is quite clear that each country has its own priorities and problems in relation to environmental issues. For example, nature conservation sites cover a greater proportion of land in Scotland than in England and Wales and different policy approaches to the management of such sites are already being pursued. In addition, rural issues such as the environmental impact of agriculture and forestry will have a greater significance than, for example, pressure to release green belt land for housing or economic development.

This raises questions of uniformity and consistency in the application and implementation of national and international obligations in the UK. The dangers of inconsistency of application can be seen in the debate over the separation of nature conservation responsibilities under the EPA 1990. It is not inconceivable that an increase in distinct national approaches to other environmental issues could give rise to inequalities across the United Kingdom (although it could be argued that these existed under arrangements where policy- and rule-making were more centralized).

The changes in law-making powers are part of a wider attempt to decentralize certain aspects of government and can be viewed in tandem with other attempts to regionalize facets of environmental policy-making. The Regional Development Agencies Act 1998 created English Regional Development Agencies to match similar agencies in Scotland (Scottish Enterprise) and Wales (Welsh Development Agency). Whilst these bodies are not directly concerned with environmental protection policies, they have a remit to consider economic and social issues in a regional setting which will have inevitable consequences for the pursuit of sustainable development (see s. 4(c)of the 1998 Act). More recently, the role of regional planning has been elevated by the emergence of Regional Spatial Strategies under Part I of the Planning and Compulsory Purchase Act 2004 (see further p. 456).

The substantive and procedural differences are such that trying to accommodate coverage of each jurisdiction in a book of this type is impossible. There are some brief details of the administrative arrangements below but the majority of this book will cover the law and administration of environmental protection in England.

12. Waste Management Licensing (Amendment)(Scotland) Regulations 2003 SSI 2003/171.
13. RCEP, 19th Report, *Sustainable Use of Soil* (Cm 3165 HMSO 1996).

Central government

The main policy- and rule-making powers in environmental matters lie with central government. The Table below sets out the main central government departments and their areas of responsibility. Central government plays a part in environmental matters in many ways. Historically, the responsibility for many important environmental functions such as pollution control and planning lay with one major department. There has been a Department of the Environment since 1970, although prior to that other Departments such as Housing and Local Government had dealt with relevant areas such as Town and Country Planning. Since that time the responsibility for the Environment has been shared with a number of additional responsibilities which have included policy areas such as local government and transport. Currently, the Department of the Environment, Food and Rural Affairs (DEFRA), created in June 2001, is responsible for many environmental policy areas. As the name suggests it is also responsible for food safety, fisheries and rural affairs such as agricultural policy. There are some substantial environmental policy areas which fall outside DEFRA's remit. Perhaps most significantly, the Office of the Deputy Prime Minister (ODPM) has responsibility for all town and country planning law and policy including environmental assessment. This separation of planning and environmental matters originally took place in June 2001 with the creation of the Department of Local Government, Transport and the Regions (DLTR). This was the first time that planning had been taken out of the 'Environment' Department for 30 years.

As noted above, one of the characteristics of central government is the fragmentation of responsibilities which have environmental implications across a number of departments. Government departments such as the Department of Trade and Industry (DTI), Transport and the Treasury all have key responsibilities for activities and issues which have tremendous environmental implications from new power stations to the building of new roads, airports and other major infrastructure projects. Other departments have responsibilities for residual matters (e.g. the Home Office is responsible for neighbourhood nuisances and licensing, the Foreign Office plays an important role in the negotiation of environmental treaties). All of these departments exercise enormous influence in their own fields. In some areas (e.g. Producer Responsibility) coordination is facilitated through joint Departmental responsibility with a 'Lead Department' being responsible for legislation and issuing policy. As discussed above, the Executive bodies in Scotland, Wales and Northern Ireland exercise an increasing control within their own geographical areas.

Government Department	Main areas of responsibility for environmental matters	Other areas of responsibility
Environment, Food and Rural Affairs	• Access to environmental information • Agriculture • Climate Change Programme • Contaminated Land • Forestry	• Animal Health and Welfare • Farming • Fisheries Policy • Food and Drink • Horticulture (Plants and Seeds including GM crops)

Government Department	Main areas of responsibility for environmental matters	Other areas of responsibility

	• Landscape Protection (including National Parks)
	• Nature Conservation
	• Noise
	• Pollution Control
	  – Air Quality and Pollution
	  – Water Quality and Pollution
	   – Water Supply
	   – Water Resources
	   – Drinking Water
	   – Sewerage
	   – Coastal and Marine Environment
	  – Integrated Pollution Prevention and Control
	  – Waste Management
	• Radioactivity
	  – Licensing
	  – Radioactive waste management
	• Sustainable Development
		• Rural Affairs (including Hunting)
		• Zoos

Office of the Deputy Prime Minister	• Town and Country Planning • Environmental Assessment	• Devolution • Housing • Local Government and the Regions • Regeneration • Urban Policy

Trade and Industry	• Waste Management
	  – Producer Responsibility
	   – Packaging Waste
	   – Waste Electrical and Electronic Equipment
	   – Restriction on Hazardous Substances
	   – End of Life Vehicles
	   – Batteries
	   – Waste Tyres
	• Energy production and transmission including renewable energy
		• Company Law (including Corporate Social Responsibility)
		• Competition (including World Trade)
		• Consumer Protection Policy (including Product Labelling)
		• Oil and Gas Industries

Transport	• Transport including infrastructure projects including road building, new airports and ports	• Local Transport (including Buses, Taxis and Cycle provision) • Motor Vehicles (including emissions and other product standards) • Railways • Roads (including road safety and traffic management) • Vehicles

Government Department	Main areas of responsibility for environmental matters	Other areas of responsibility
Treasury	• Environmental taxes such as the Landfill Tax, Climate Change Levy and Aggregates Levy • Provides central funding for certain environmental regulators	• Overseas Debt Relief

This fragmentation of responsibilities has significant consequences in terms of the potential for integrated solutions across different departmental areas. For example, an integrated transport policy will have implications for localised air quality, climate change (road traffic is a significant source of greenhouse gases), planning policy (in terms of areas for new development, traffic generation and demand), nature conservation, public health, and resource depletion.

This wide diversity of departments raises difficult questions of coordination and how environmental considerations are taken into account in practice. For some departments it is clear that there will be direct or indirect conflict between the main responsibility and the need to give weight to environmental considerations. In other circumstances departments may not consider the environmental implications of new policies or decisions because they are not immediately obvious. For example a programme to build prisons or hospitals may meet a clear need for new facilities but the aggregated environmental consequences may not have been taken into account.

Accordingly the idea of external integration promotes the incorporation of environmental considerations across all policy areas. This can be through legal means[14] but in the UK a looser policy approach has been taken under what was initially called the 'Greening Government Initiative' (GGI). The GGI was originally launched in 1990 when a Minister in each government department was made responsible for considering the environmental implications of its policies and programmes and for the introduction of some form of wider environmental appraisal of policies.[15] In 2001, the Greening Government Initiative was 'rebranded' as 'Sustainable Development in Government', reflecting the shift from considerations of environmental impacts to broader issues such as economic and social impacts (see Box 5.2).

BOX 5.2 **Sustainable Development in Government**

'Sustainable Development in Government' is a collective phrase for a number of bodies and initiatives.

The *Cabinet Committee on the Energy and the Environment* (abbreviated to EE) replaced the Cabinet Committee on the Environment and Sustainable Development (ENV) in a reorganisation of the Cabinet Committee structure in May 2005. The Committee provides a high level, inter-departmental strategic forum for the discussion of energy and environmental policies, to monitor the impact on sustainable development of the Government's policies, and to consider issues of

---

14. E.g. Art. 6 of the EC Treaty explicitly requires external integration; see further p. 201.
15. HM Government *This Common Inheritance*, Cm. 1200 (HMSO,1990).

climate change, security of supply and affordability of energy. This inclusion of energy issues within the Committee's remit reflects the significance placed upon the UK's climate change programme and the difficulty of co-ordinating these policies acrooss many different areas.

The *Ministerial Sub-Committee on Sustainable Development in Government* (EE(SD)) is a sub-committee of EE. It replaced the Green Ministers Committee (often referred to as ENV(G)). It has a dual role in the sense that it considers the operational impacts of different Government departments as well as considering cross-departmental sustainable development issues. The scope of the operational side of the Committee's work is largely shaped by the *Framework for Sustainable Development on the Government Estate* which sets targets for environmental improvement in areas such as waste production, energy consumption and transport.

The *House of Commons Environmental Audit Select Committee* acts as a 'watchdog' over Central Government departments and their attempts to broaden the base of environmental appraisal, in the same way as the Parliamentary Accounts Committee checks public spending. The committee produces regular reports covering such things as annual reviews of progress, the Budget and the Climate Change Programme. The Audit Committee has drawn unfavourable comparisons between the relative unimportance of this initiative as compared with other cross-departmental policy measures.

Is 'Sustainable Development in Government' an effective method of external integration? The Environmental Audit Select Committee identified ENV as being poor at providing adequate leadership on many cross-departmental environmental issues.[16] The complexity of external integration should not be underestimated, however, and cross departmental initiatives at least provide some form of institutional structure which should enable environmental issues to be integrated into the wider policy arena over time. Perhaps most importantly, the Environmental Audit Committee is pursuing departments and policies which are not obviously environmental but which have a clear environmental impact, whilst providing accountability and transparency for 'Sustainable Development in Government' as a whole.[17]

Department of the Environment, Food, and Rural Affairs (DEFRA)

A significant proportion of control of environmental matters falls to the Department created in June 2001. As the name suggests, the department is also responsible for food policy and certain countryside issues. Control is mainly manifested at the level of policy, but since environmental law is essentially about the taking of discretionary, political decisions, this means that DEFRA has an enormous impact, even if this is not always apparent from a bare statement of the law. However, a number of important qualifications must be made about the role of DEFRA.

First, it could be argued that DEFRA is not a particularly strong department within

---

16. House of Commons Environmental Audit Select Committee, *The Greening Government Initiative 1999*, Sixth Report, 1998–9 Session and see A. Ross (2000) 12 JEL 175.

17. Ibid.

central government. The direct predecessor of DEFRA, the Department of the Environment, Transport and the Regions, had a much more significant portfolio of responsibilities incorporating town and country planning, transport and regional policy. The separation of these functions from environmental protection could hardly be argued to have been a progressive step.[18] Indeed, the incorporation of one of the weakest Governmental departments, the Ministry of Agriculture, Fisheries and Food, into DEFRA has been argued to be a downgrading of the political significance of environmental responsibilities.[19] Even in relation to environmental matters, DEFRA is not necessarily strong. For example, as certain controversies have shown (such as the climate change effects from aviation, see Box 5.3), other Government departments often carry greater weight in inter-departmental disputes. Secondly, DEFRA has few operational powers relating to environmental protection. Those that it does have are often delegated to others. For example, although certain classes of environmental appeals are made to the Secretary of State, in the majority of cases they are decided by members of the Planning Inspectorate, which is an executive agency of the ODPM. These include appeals concerning waste management licences, water pollution discharge consents and local air pollution control authorisations. Thirdly, DEFRA has a very wide portfolio and is not concerned simply with environmental *protection*. Some of these areas (e.g. the regulation of the economic and competition aspects of the water industry) not only take priority over environmental protection but are often in direct conflict with environmental aims.

BOX 5.3 **How government works—air travel and the environment**

The diffusion of responsibilities with environmental implications across different Government Departments can lead to a lack of coordination on important issues. In some cases, environmental policies can be overridden by other, arguably stronger, departments' policy initiatives in related areas.

When the Department of Transport was amalgamated with the department of the Environment in 1997 to form the Department of the Environment, Transport and the Regions, it was taken as a sign of the importance of the integration of these two policy areas. The subsequent 'divorce' of these two departments in 2001 has seen an increasing divergence of views on such issues as the impact of future transport policies on agreed reduction targets for greenhouse gases. This should not, however, be viewed as a simple row between two Government Departments. Following a recommendation from the RCEP, the 2003 Energy White Paper (produced by the DTI) contained an aim to reduce Greenhouse Gas emissions by some 60 per cent by 2050.[20] This was to be achieved through a variety of mechanisms but largely through reductions in greenhouse gas emissions across different industry sectors under pollution control regulation.

The Department of Transport then published proposals to liberalize and expand provision for air travel. These proposals suggested that the aviation sector would increase greenhouse gas

---

18. 'Restructure in haste, repent at leisure' and 'Whitehall restructuring sidelines environment' (2001) ENDS Report 317 2–4.

19. Environment, Food and Rural Affairs Select Committee, *The Role of DEFRA* Session 2001–2002, Tenth Report: paras 9–10.

20. Department of Trade and Industry: *Our Energy Future: Creating a Low Carbon Economy* (2003).

emissions by a factor of three during the period up to 2050.[21] In order to meet the general reduction target the increase from aviation sources would mean that other industrial sectors would have to reduce emissions by more than 50 per cent.

The Department of Transport's aviation policy was heavily criticized by a number of independent environmental bodies including the Royal Commission on Environmental Pollution,[22] the Sustainable Development Commission[23] and the House of Commons Environmental Audit Committee[24] on the grounds that it made it unlikely that the significant environmental policy aim of long-term greenhouse gas reduction would be achieved.

The Secretary of State has very wide legislative and quasi-legislative powers which stem from the framework nature of the main environmental protection legislation, and also from the need to update legislation in the light of EC requirements. Other very wide discretionary powers are also granted; for example, the decision to give the Environment Agency a specific or general 'direction' to do something is virtually an unfettered discretion given to the Secretary of State. In relation to individual functions they include:

- directions requiring the inclusion of specific conditions in IPC or waste management licences (see EPA 1990, ss. 7(3) and 35(7));

- directions requiring the Agency to take specific enforcement action in relation to IPC and waste management licences (EPA 1990, ss. 12–14, 37, 38, and 42);

- directions requiring the Agency (amongst other things) to carry out surveys of waste arisings in relation to the national waste strategy (s. 44A);

- directions made in the interests of national security or mitigating the effects of a civil emergency (Water Resources Act 1991, s. 207).

Section 40 of the Environment Act 1995 gives the Secretary of State a further general power to issue any directions of a specific or general character. This power is exercisable under the Secretary of State's discretion and represents a formidable tool to centralize certain aspects of the Agency's activities.

There are also very wide powers in relation to appeals against decisions made by the regulatory bodies. This is most obvious in the planning area, but an appeal to the Secretary of State is a common feature of many of the regulatory systems covered in this book. This reflects the political (i.e. policy-based) nature of much of this area of law. For example, it is significant that the Planning Inspectorate has always been kept within the ODPM (and its predecessors) which is responsible for planning policy, rather than being moved to the Department of Constitutional Affairs (and its predecessor, the Lord Chancellor's Office) which is responsible for the Tribunals and Courts. This reflects the fact that the important

21. Department of Transport: *The Future of Air Transport* (2004).

22. RCEP, 22nd Report: *Energy—The Changing Climate* (2000); and RCEP, Special Report: *The Environmental Effects of Civil Aircraft in Flight* (2002).

23. Sustainable Development Commission: *Missed Opportunity: Summary Critique of the Air Transport White Paper* (2004).

24. House of Commons Environmental Audit Committee: 9th Report, Session 2002–3, *Budget Report and Aviation* and House of Commons Environmental Audit Committee: 3rd Report, Session 2003–4, *Pre-Budget Report: Aviation Follow-Up.*

feature of its decisions is that they are based on policy rather than on any notion of judicial fairness, despite the increasing formality of planning procedures.

DEFRA may impose its policies in a number of ways. One is by changing the law (a feature of the British administrative system is that the government is rarely defeated in Parliament). Another is through exercising powers granted under the legislation. This may include the making of directions, the power to approve actions of regulatory bodies, the power to make appointments to the various regulatory bodies, or the power to hear appeals. Interference has been at its clearest in town planning, where there is the greatest opportunity to disagree over matters of policy. A third method is by the manipulation of available resources. DEFRA and the Treasury have complete responsibility for the budgets of a number of the regulatory agencies (e.g. the Countryside Agency and the Nature Conservancy Councils). One avenue for future development here is the way that regulatory agencies are being encouraged to acquire some financial independence by charging for parts of their work. This theme has been developed strongly in the Environment Act 1995, with a range of revenue-raising measures (see p. 129). Given the importance of independent regulatory agencies in environmental law, it is also significant that DEFRA is the channel through which Parliamentary accountability of a number of these agencies, such as the Environment Agency and the Countryside Agency, is provided.

General environmental duties

There are further areas where Central Government plays a part in environmental matters. There are bodies which are bound to take into account environmental considerations in relation to the exercise of their functions. This can apply to Executive Bodies (e.g. The Welsh Assembly, see Government of Wales Act 1998, s. 121), Government Ministers and Departments, Local Authorities, regulators and operational bodies such as utility companies. For example, a number of pieces of legislation now include general requirements to take the environment into account either through the pursuit of the general goal of sustainable development (see further p. 65) or more specific requirements to have regard to the desirability of conserving and enhancing such things as biodiversity (e.g. CROWA 2000, s. 74) or landscape (e.g. CROWA 2000, s. 85). In the utilities sector, the Secretary of State is under an obligation to provide environmental guidance to regulators (e.g. Utilities Act 2000, s. 10 (Gas), s. 14 (Electricity) and the Water Act 2003, s. 40) with the aim of trying to ensure that in fulfilling the primary statutory duties such as promoting competition and protecting consumers, utilities operators are also obliged to take into account the environmental costs of operations. Although these general duties can be so vague as to be meaningless (other than in cases where the duty has been completely ignored), they do provide certain formal requirements which can have a positive longer term effect upon the policy- and rule-making process. They also provide a benchmark against which policies, decisions and performance can be measured.

Scrutiny of central government—Parliamentary Select Committees

Given the wide discretion to make law and policy which is given to Central Government Departments, there is a need to have some accountability mechanisms for the day-to-day activities of Government Departments. Parliamentary Select Committees may be said to perform these functions. In the area of environmental law and policy the Select Committee plays an important role in helping to inform the public debate outside Parliament and therefore increasing the accountability of and accessibility to the policy and rule makers in DEFRA and elsewhere (particularly in otherwise unaccountable regulatory agencies such as the Environment Agency). In the House of Lords, the European Communities sub-committee has been especially important in analysing the potential impact of proposed EC legislation. In the House of Commons, the select committees are organized so as to mirror government departments. Thus, there is a House of Commons Select Committee on the Environment, Food and Rural Affairs. This body has had a large impact on the direction of environmental policy in the recent past, arguably constituting the loudest Parliamentary voice for a greater role for environmental regulation. The issues considered by the Environment Select Committee reflect the remit of the government department and therefore include areas outside the traditional boundaries of environmental protection (including such things as local government, housing and transport). The range of topics covered by the Select Committees includes most of the main areas of environmental policy and administration. Along with the evidence given to the Committee, they make interesting reading and give a good introduction to many of the practical issues surrounding controversial topics. Most Reports contain recommendations for changes in law, policy and practice. The Government responds to each of these in a Special Report. Recent topics include the work of the Environment Agency (2000), the role of DEFRA (2002), the Future of Waste Management (2003), and the Water Framework Directive (2003).

As the Select Committee structure generally mirrors Government departments, there are other Select Committees which have reported on environmental issues. Naturally, these vary according to the different departmental responsibilities but the ODPM Select Committee,[25] Trade and Industry Select Committee,[26] and Transport Select Committee all regularly consider important issues with environmental significance. As mentioned above (see Box 5.2), the House of Commons Environmental Audit Committee, launched as part of the Greening Government Initiative, has played an active role in scrutinising various environmental issues. The primary responsibility of the Environmental Audit Committee is to oversee the implementation of the external integration of environmental policies. Thus it is concerned not so much with the performance of DEFRA and associated legislation and policies, but in the manner in which environmental policies are taken into account across other Government Departments. Over time, there has been an increasing amount of overlap between the DEFRA Select Committee and the Environmental Audit Committee with a number of Reports on similar topics.[27]

25. ODPM Select Committee, Planning, Competitiveness and Productivity, Session 2003/04 4th Report.
26. DTI Select Committee, End of Life Vehicles Directive, Session 2001/01, 1st Report.
27. E.g. Environmental Audit Committee, Waste: An Audit, 2002/3 Session, 4th Report and EFRA Select Committee, The Future of Waste Management, 2002/3 Session, 9th Report.

There is little doubt that the reports of these inquiries, all of which have been unanimous on a cross-party basis, have an influence on government policy and legislation. The Committee is not, however, necessarily expert in any of the areas upon which it reports. It relies heavily on expert advisors and the witnesses who give evidence (normally representatives of interested parties such as DEFRA, the Environment Agency, NGOs and relevant industry sectors). Accordingly, the Committee's views are shaped by what is a relatively select group of witnesses. This can have two consequences. First, there is little attempt to elicit wider views or public values which would promote greater public participation. Secondly, some of the conclusions can be based on erroneous or incomplete information. Having said this, however, the Committee has acted as the 'ignition point' for many changes in environmental law, policy and practice over the last 20 or so years. For example, the introduction of the controls over the clean up of historically contaminated land in the Environment Act 1995 owes a lot to the Select Committee's inquiry and report (see p. 674).

Royal Commission on Environmental Pollution (RCEP)

This is a rather rare beast, an independent standing Royal Commission with its own secretariat. It was established in 1970 with a wide remit to advise Government on 'matters concerning the pollution of the environment'. It is a multi-disciplinary body made up of individual experts from various fields who consider the legal, economic, technical, and social aspects of environmental issues. Beyond this very general framework, the Commission is not restricted in its choice of topics to study. The Commission takes a leading role in the development of environmental law and policy by providing a forum for discussion on controversial or emerging issues. The RCEP process in producing Reports is much more deliberative than the Select Committee process. It can take up to two years to investigate a particular issue and the Commission seeks a wide range of views through oral and written evidence and by holding public meetings and site visits. At the end of 2002, the Commission published its first Special Report. These Special Reports have had a much narrower focus than the general reports. As such, they are compiled over a shorter period and normally address a particular short term need for policy advice and recommendation. For example, the First Special Report on Aviation was compiled quickly prior to the publication of the White Paper on Air Transport (see Box 5.3).

The RCEP's reports have enormous authority in relation to the subject matter discussed and exert a significant influence on the direction of future policy, although by no means all the recommendations of the Royal Commission are implemented. The Royal Commission has been a particularly strong supporter of public participation in environmental decision-making including the widening of access to environmental information and the investigation of the public's perception of environmental risk. It has also been at the forefront of promoting a number of fundamental concepts in environmental law and policy and can claim to have popularised such ideas as 'Best Practicable Environmental Option' and the integration of pollution controls (see below).

Number, title, and year of report	Subject matter covered
1st Report (Cmnd 4585), 1971.	A 'scene setting' report looking at the nature of the challenges to the environment. Included a contemporary state of the environment review with priorities for future action to tackle pollution.
2nd Report, *Three Issues in Industrial Pollution* (Cmnd. 4894), 1972.	The 'three issues' were secrecy (which was to become a recurring theme), hazardous chemicals and controls over industrial waste disposal. The latter predated the introduction of the first controls over waste disposal in the Deposit of Poisonous Waste Act 1972 and the Control of Pollution Act 1974.
4th Report, *Pollution Control: Progress and Problems* (Cmnd 5780), 1974.	An overview of the substance and administrative structures of environmental law and policy in the UK. Along with the Government's response *Pollution Paper No 4*, represents a historical picture of many aspects of the 'British Approach' to pollution control.
5th Report, *Air Pollution Control: an Integrated Approach* (Cmnd 6371), 1976.	Introduced the concept of 'best practicable environmental option' (BPEO) as a means of integrating pollution controls.
The 9th Report, *Lead in the Environment* (Cmnd 8852), 1983.	Indicated that the lead levels in blood were too high. One of the key recommendations led to the introduction of unleaded petrol.
The 10th Report, *Tackling Pollution— Experience and Prospects* (Cmnd 9149), 1984.	Published to mark the 10-year anniversary of the 4th Report. Featured a wide ranging review of environmental law and policy. Focused on the impact of European environmental law and policy. Further coverage of access to environmental information and BPEO.
The 11th Report, *Managing Waste: The Duty of Care* (Cmnd. 9675), 1985	Damning critique of the problems involved in the chain from the production of waste to its final disposal. Introduced the concept of the Duty of Care now found in s. 34, EPA 1990.
The 12th Report, *Best Practicable Environmental Option* (Cm 310), 1988.	Further development of the concept of BPEO first covered in the 5th, 10th, and 11th Reports. Influential in the setting up of the system of integrated pollution control found in Part I of the Environmental Protection Act 1990.
The 21st Report, *Setting Environmental Standards* (Cm 4053), 1998.	Broad-ranging discussion of environmental standards and the role that values and the public and its perception of risk have to play in the setting of standards.
The 23rd Report, *Environmental Planning* (Cm 5459), 2002.	Discusses the role of town and country planning in environmental protection. Revisits the enhancement of public participation methods in decision-making and policy-making. Discussed the idea of Spatial Strategies now found in Part I of the Planning and Compulsory Purchase Act 2004.

Other advisory bodies

In addition to the RCEP, central government has established a number of other non-departmental public bodies (NDPBs) with various roles. They play an increasingly important role in the implementation of environmental law and policy. There are over 50 NDPBs listed on the DEFRA web-pages ranging from the Advisory Committee on Business and the Environment (ACBE) to the Pesticides Residue Committee and the Zoos Forum. They are non-statutory in the sense that they are set up by Government without explicit statutory authority. In most cases they are 'sponsored' by a Government Department who select members, provide staff and funding. These bodies provide assistance to the Government on a wide range of technical matters, providing expert advice on scientific matters (e.g. Expert Panel on Air Quality Standards), or other areas (e.g. Advisory Committee on Packaging), a forum for the exchange of views (e.g. The Hazardous Waste Forum) or a conduit for best practice (e.g. Advisory Committee on Business and the Environment).

Regulatory agencies

The day-to-day implementation and enforcement of environmental law and policy lies in the hands of a variety of regulatory bodies. The main bodies and their duties are outlined below.

Who Does What in Environmental Law and Policy?			
England and Wales			
Agency	**Primary Responsibilities**	**Key Legislation**	**Other Comments**
Environment Agency	• Pollution Control • Industrial Regulation (IPPC—Part A Installations) • Water Resource Management (abstraction licensing) • Waste Management (including the National Waste Strategy) • Producer Responsibility (Packaging Waste, ELV, WEEE) • Historically contaminated land (Special Sites)	• Environment Act 1995 Pollution, • Prevention and Control Act 1999 • Water Resources Act 1991 • Environmental Protection Act 1990	Other general water related functions include: the supervision and administration of flood defences; fisheries regulation; and navigation, harbour and conservancy duties.

Agency	Primary Responsibilities	Key Legislation	Other Comments
English Nature	• Nature Conservation • Species and Habitats Protection • Protection of Geological Features	• National Parks and Access to the Countryside Act 1949 • Countryside Act 1968 • Wildlife and Countryside Act 1981 • Conservation (Natural Habitats, etc.) Regulations 1994 • Countryside and Rights of Way Act 2000	Haskins Review has proposed a merger with the Countryside Agency.
Water and Sewerage Undertakers	• Water Supply • Sewers • Regulation of Trade Effluent discharges	• Water Resources Act 1991 • Water Industry Act 1991 • Water Act 2003	Private companies created subject to regulation on economic issues, water pricing and competition from Ofwat
Local Authorities	• Town and Country Planning • Air Quality and Management • Historically contaminated land (Non Special Sites) • Statutory Nuisance • Noise Control	• Town and Country Planning Act 1990 • Environmental Protection Act 1990 • Environment Act 1995	
Marine Coastguard Agency	• Marine Pollution from ships and Off-shore installations	• The Merchant Shipping Act 1995	There is an overlap with the Environment Agency in cases of estuarine oil pollution
Countryside Agency	• Landscape Protection and Rural Affairs	• Countryside Act 1968 • Countryside and Rights of Way Act 2000	Haskins Review has proposed a merger with English Nature. Countryside Council for Wales is the equivalent in Wales.
Drinking Water Inspectorate	• Monitoring and enforcing drinking water quality	• Water Industry Act 1991	Enforces standards under the Water Supply (Water Quality) Regulations 2000
Nuclear Installations Inspectorate	• Licensing nuclear sites • Storage and accumulation of radioactive waste at licensed nuclear sites	• Radioactive Substances Act 1993	

Scotland			
Agency	**Primary Responsibilities**	**Key Legislation**	**Other Comments**
Scottish Environment Protection Agency	• Pollution Control	• Environment Act 1995 • Environmental Protection Act 1990 • Control of Pollution Act 1974	
Scottish Water	• Water Supply • Treatment of sewage and trade effluent	• Water Industry (Scotland) Act 2002	Performs the functions of the water and sewerage undertakers in England and Wales
Scottish Natural Heritage	• Conservation and enhancement of habitats, species, and landscapes.	• Natural Heritage (Scotland) Act 1991 • Nature Conservation (Scotland) Act 2004	Broadly SNH combines the roles of English Nature and the Countryside Agency in Scotland
Drinking Water Quality Regulator	• Monitors and enforces drinking water quality	• Water (Scotland) Act 1980 • Water Industry (Scotland) Act 2002	

In England and Wales, primary control over pollution is carried out by a single body, the Environment Agency, although, as explained below, the administrative arrangements are far from simple and there is a degree of overlap in institutional responsibilities. Indeed, even within the Agency itself, there are different sections carrying out separate functions and the true integration of the pollution control functions is perhaps clearer in theory than in practice.

For many years prior to the creation of the Environment Agency, the number of different agencies involved in environmental protection reflected the fragmented nature of policy and law enforcement in this area. The creation of the Agency, in April 1996, saw the amalgamation of three of the four main regulatory agencies at the time: the National Rivers Authority in relation to water quality and other operational functions; the Waste Regulation Authorities in relation to the regulation of waste management; and Her Majesty's Inspectorate of Pollution primarily in relation to controls over emissions from industrial processes. The creation of the Agency was accompanied by a recentralization of many regulatory powers, certainly within England and Wales, for example with national strategies on waste and air quality and centralized guidance on such things as IPPC and contaminated land. Whilst individual decisions continue to be made on a case-by-case basis, reflecting individual conditions, there has been a shift away from local control probably on the basis of improving the quality and consistency of decision-making. A side-effect of this recentralization is the consequential loss of accountability. A distinction needs to be drawn between those bodies with and without electoral accountability. The Environment Agency is a creature of statute with no direct public accountability. In the light of the wide discretionary powers which the agency exercises and the policy and rules which it is responsible for, this remains a central issue.

As mentioned above, the institutional arrangements in Northern Ireland and Scotland are different from England and Wales. During the Parliamentary debates on the Environment Bill there were strong arguments put forward in favour of creating separate agencies for England and Wales. This was rejected on the basis that there were geographical (e.g. river catchments) and institutional (e.g. the National Rivers Agency's personnel) overlaps which suggested that integrated management across national boundaries was to be preferred. Provisions were made, however, to ensure that the Welsh national interest was furthered by creating one place on the Environment Agency Board for Welsh interests and setting up an Advisory Committee for Wales (Environment Act 1995, s. 11).

(a) Regulatory agencies—Scotland

The Environment Act 1995 introduced a unified agency for Scotland known as the Scottish Environment Protection Agency (SEPA). The range of powers, functions, aims, and duties applicable to SEPA broadly reflect the position of the Environmental Agency (as to which, see below). There is, however, a narrower regulatory focus on fundamental pollution control matters without the wider issues of water resource management which were transferred from the National Rivers Authority (NRA) to the Environment Agency. This focus is reflected in the title of the agency (with the significant omission of the word 'protection' from the Anglo-Welsh agency) and the fact that there are some minor variations in the legislative provisions which could become more significant with the passage of time (e.g. SEPA does not have a 'principal aim' as specified under section 4 of the 1995 Act for the Environment Agency (see below)).

There are two major differences in the scope of the powers of the two agencies. First, SEPA has control over all industrial regulation under the IPPC system, whereas in England and Wales control remains partially divided between the Environment Agency and the local authorities. Secondly, as mentioned above, SEPA has none of the non-pollution-related water management functions. The majority of these remain with the unitary local authorities created by the Local Government etc. (Scotland) Act 1994. The position of the water and sewerage undertakers is also different in Scotland. Unlike England and Wales, which has privatized water companies, Scotland has a public, non-departmental water authority, Scottish Water.

(b) Regulatory agencies—Northern Ireland

The current administrative set-up in Northern Ireland is somewhat different from the rest of the UK reflecting the fact that, in many ways, the institutional arrangements could be said to be about ten years behind the other countries. For example, operational functions for water and sewerage matters fall within the same department as the regulatory functions in relation to water pollution (a position which was altered in 1989 in England and Wales under the Water Act 1989). In other ways, however, the administrative arrangements are much more integrated than elsewhere in the UK with a broader range of environmental issues brought within the control of one body (although each area of control is theoretically autonomous within the department).

Under existing arrangements, regulatory controls for many environmental matters fall under the control of an executive agency of the Department of the Environment for Northern Ireland, namely the Environment and Heritage Service. This body has similar responsibilities to SEPA and the Environment Agency, including the general pollution control matters (e.g. the regulation and protection of water quality, air quality, radioactivity, and waste management). It also has control over nature conservation matters and wider countryside issues. The provision of sewage treatment and control over drinking water quality is undertaken by the water service of the department. These administrative arrangements have been the subject of criticism with calls for an independent regulator and a change in the structure and culture of environmental law within Northern Ireland.[28]

The Environment Agency

The history of the Environment Agency (EA) is long and tortuous. In 1989 the House of Commons Select Committee on the Environment, in its Report on Toxic Waste, recommended that an Environmental Protection Commission should be established with responsibility for the whole range of pollution control matters. This recommendation was rejected by the government of the time, a stance that was reiterated in the White Paper, *This Common Inheritance* (Cm 1200, 1990). One reason given was that there had been many changes in relation to environmental protection in recent years, and that such a major change might have to wait until things had settled down. The White Paper did suggest, however, that consideration would be given to the establishment of an umbrella body overseeing the work of HMIP and the NRA. It also proposed that HMIP should become a separate executive agency within the government (i.e. a 'Next Steps' agency) 'as soon as possible', although it would still remain part of the (then) DoE. This mechanism was popular with the Conservative Government as a means of providing regulatory agencies with a degree of independence, whilst at the same time injecting some basic management principles and subjecting the agencies to some of the rigours of the marketplace.

However, in an important reversal of policy, in July 1991 it was announced that it was the Government's intention to create a unified environmental protection agency, a move that had already gained the support of all other political parties. Details of what was intended gradually emerged. There were two main points of argument which led to a significant period of delay. One was whether the waste regulation duties of the local authorities should be included within the agency's ambit—to do so would create a uniformity of practice that was lacking, but would obviously reduce local accountability. The other was whether the NRA should be brought within the agency *en bloc*, or whether only its pollution control functions properly belonged there. The then Minister of Agriculture argued strongly for the NRA's non-pollution control functions to be devolved to the Ministry of Agriculture, Fisheries and Food, but that was strongly opposed by environmentalists and the NRA itself, which argued that the need to retain integrated catchment management was at the heart of everything that the NRA did. After some discussion and consultation the Government accepted that the EA would take over all the powers and functions of HMIP and the NRA, together with the waste regulation duties of the local authorities.

---

28. UKELA, *Environmental Regulation in Northern Ireland: An Agenda for Reform* (2004) at <www.ukela.org.uk> and R. Macrory, *Transparency and Trust: Reshaping Environmental Governance in Northern Ireland* (UCL 2004), at <www.ucl.ac.uk/laws/environment/docs/NI_report.pdf>.

(a) Structure of the agency

The EA is an independent corporate body (Environment Act 1995, s. 1(1)) and does not have Crown immunity, although partial immunity can be granted where the Agency exercises its functions under an agreement to carry out a Ministerial function (s. 38). In order to assist with the carrying out of its functions, the Agency is under a duty to establish an Environment Protection Advisory Committee (EPAC), made up of people with a 'significant interest' in the Agency's functions. An EPAC is established for each Agency region. Once established, the Agency is under a duty to consult the committee and consider any representations made by it.

(b) Role and functions

The name of the Agency is misleading. It does not have control over all environmental regulation. The Drinking Water Inspectorate is not included; nor are any direct functions relating to nature conservation or landscape protection (although there are a number of general duties relating to sites which are of nature conservation interest). These omissions (when coupled with the areas of environmental regulation which remain with local authorities) mean the EA is effectively a pollution control authority with a large number of water-related functions such as land drainage and flood defence (with the interesting side effect that the number of staff in these areas outnumber those in pollution control). Having said that the EA is one of the largest environmental regulators in the world and its responsibilities range from issuing fishing licences to regulating the disposal of hazardous waste. It was formed from over 80 predecessor bodies with different styles and roles. This broad diversity of functions can create some tension between those responsibilities which could be considered to be mutually antagonistic (conserving salmon fisheries and issuing rod licences) or potentially harmful to biodiversity or the environment (constructing sea and flood defences). These tensions raise questions about the nature and role of the Agency.

In order to provide some coherence to these differing functions, the Agency is subject to a complicated framework of aims, duties and objectives. These aims and duties are also designed to underpin the policy decisions of the Agency, but do not fetter that discretion unduly. The duties are expressed in a variety of ways (see below), with the Agency being required to 'have regard to' some duties whereas others have to be 'taken into account'. When it comes to individual decision-making, the Agency has a wide discretion and the weight which attaches to each duty will be variable. Therefore, it would be difficult to challenge legally any decision made by the Agency on the basis that it had failed to carry out the duty unless the Agency had acted unreasonably in the *Wednesbury* sense.

It is important to bear in mind that the aim, objectives, and duties are not framed in a statutory vacuum. In addition to the general matters set out in the Environment Act 1995 there is an increasing range of specific statutory objectives which are set out in relation to individual functions of the Agency. Many of these have been imposed as a result of the need to meet EC legislation which favours the use of such specific targets. For example, the Agency must seek to achieve water or air quality objectives when exercising its functions in determining authorizations and consents and in doing so it must place those objectives above the general aims and duties.

(c) The principal aim, other duties and objectives

Section 4 of the Environment Act 1995 defines the principal aim for the Agency (Box 5.4). This is a broad obligation and its legal significance is somewhat uncertain. A number of factors, set out in s. 4, are designed to influence the implementation of the duty in practice.

BOX 5.4 Principal aim and objectives of the Environment Agency

---

Section 4(1) of the Environment Act 1995 provides:

It shall be the principal aim of the Agency (subject to and in accordance with the provisions of this Act or any other enactment and taking into account any likely costs) in discharging its functions so to protect or enhance the environment, taken as a whole, as to make the contribution towards attaining the objective of achieving sustainable development . . .

First, the Agency must take into account the likely costs of achieving the principal aim. This ensures that environmental considerations are not paramount when pursuing the aim of sustainable development, and the cost of the pursuit of the principal aim is to be taken into account. This emphasises the fact that protecting the environment is not the same as seeking sustainable development. The former puts the environment as a central and singular pursuit which takes precedence over other considerations. The latter involves balancing a range of factors including costs.

Secondly, the principal aim is to be pursued in relation to the conservation and enhancement of the environment 'taken as a whole'. This ensures that policy and decision-making is not overburdened by detailed consideration of impacts on individual environmental media.

Thirdly, the principal aim has to be viewed in relation to all of the other objectives which apply to the Agency (surprisingly there are no other statutory 'aims'—which rather begs the question over the use of the word 'principal'). The 'principal' aim will only take precedence over other statutory objectives where there is a direct conflict between the two. Thus in situations where the Agency is making a decision to act and it cannot meet both objectives, the principal aim would take precedence. Confusingly, however, the aim is stated to be 'subject to' other provisions of the Act, which would include the other objectives. This confusion over the hierachy of the principal aim and the other statutory objectives under-lines the difficulty of introducing a principal aim which does not actually create any legally enforceable rights. It rather defeats the purpose of a 'principal aim' when it is subject to the myriad of other statutory objectives and functions. Finally, the Agency must have regard to guidance issued by the Secretary of State when discharging its functions (s. 4(3)).[29]

In addition to the principal aim of the EA, a range of other duties and objectives is set out in sections 5–9 of the Environment Act 1995. Section 5 provides that the EA's pollution control powers shall be exercised for the purpose of preventing, minimizing, remedying, or mitigating the effects of pollution of the environment. Section 6 places the EA under a duty generally to promote the conservation and enhancement of the amenities of inland and

---

29. Department of the Environment, MAFF, *The Environment Agency and Sustainable Development* (1996) and see p. 127.

coastal waters, the use of such waters for recreational purposes and the conservation of water dependent flora and fauna. This duty is not particularly onerous, requiring action only when the Agency considers that it is desirable to do so. Section 7 provides that the Agency (and the relevant Secretaries of State), when formulating or considering any proposals, is to *have regard to* the desirability of conserving and enhancing natural beauty and the conservation of flora, fauna and geological or physiographical features (s. 7(1)(b)). In relation to non-pollution control powers and functions this duty is raised so that the Agency is required to *further* conservation etc. (s. 7(1)(a)). This distinction reflects the fact that the Agency cannot be said to be furthering environmental conservation when it is issuing consents, authorizations or licences for activities which by definition will be polluting. The meaning of 'proposals' is undefined and therefore would appear to apply to any context from individual determinations for discharge consents to general matters such as river basin management plans or general policy formulation. In addition the Agency must have regard to a range of matters including the desirability of protecting heritage sites or public access to areas of natural beauty, the effect of proposals on the beauty of any area and the effect on the economic and social well-being of rural communities (s. 7(1), (2)).

There are specific duties in relation to notification and consultation in the case of any land of a special conservation interest which may be affected by any works carried out by the Agency or by any authorization which it is considering. Where land of special interest has been previously notified to the EA by English Nature or CCW, the EA is under a duty to consult with either of those bodies before carrying out or authorizing works, operations or activities which are likely to destroy or damage the features of special interest or importance (s. 8(1)–(4)) (see further in relation to duties under CROWA 2000 Chapter 21).

The Secretary of State has the power to issue codes of practice under section 9 of the Environment Act 1995 to assist the EA in carrying out any of the duties referred to above. This power has been exercised in the issue of the Water and Sewerage (Conservation, Access and Recreation) (Code of Practice) Order 2000 (SI 2000/477) and the *Code of Practice on Conservation, Access and Recreation* which gives practical guidance to the Agency (and water and sewerage undertakers) relating to their environmental and recreational duties. Another example is the *Code of Practice on Environmental Procedures for Flood Defence Operating Authorities*. Contravention of a Code does not give rise to any criminal offence or civil right of action, but will be taken into account by relevant bodies in deciding whether to use any powers available to them.

BOX 5.5 **The practical significance of the Environment Agency's duties**

All of these different duties and obligations can be confusing. On any analysis (legal, philosophical or even semantic), the complexities of the principal aim and the other duties obscure the nature of the legal obligations which are created. Do they actually make any difference in practice? It is difficult to identify the impact of these duties in relation to individual decision-making as they are all factors which will be thrown into the balance. It is more helpful to consider how the duties would have affected past decisions and actions where environmental damage has been caused by regulatory agencies carrying out operational functions which are now undertaken by the EA.

Consider the situation where a land owner wants to drain some land in order to mitigate the effects of sea-flooding. The site is designated as a Site of Special Scientific Interest (SSSI) for its ecological importance. The land owner enters into an agreement with the EA to undertake land drainage works. Regardless of other statutory controls (including the need for planning permission, environmental assessment or other procedures) which may or may not apply, the Agency would be under an obligation to consult with English Nature prior to undertaking the works. In addition, the *Code of Practice on Environmental Procedures for Flood Defence Operating Authorities* emphasizes the importance of the minimization of environmental impacts and the need to avoid damage to sensitive wildlife features. These practical steps are underpinned by the general duties to further the conservation of flora and fauna when undertaking operational functions (see further p. 821).

Whilst none of these safeguards guarantee that the works would not be undertaken, they mean that it would be much more difficult to carry out without due regard to the consequences and the anticipation of mitigation of severe environmental effects. In *Southern Water Authority v Nature Conservancy Council* (see further p. 814), land drainage works were carried out by a water authority on a Site of Special Scientific Interest. Southern Water were aware of the site's ecological importance as it owned land in a different part of the SSSI. The works which would now be undertaken by the EA, were described as 'ecological vandalism' by the House of Lords. Such vandalism should now be unthinkable.

Thus although there is a great deal of uncertainty over the nature of the legal obligation created by the aims and duties, they are still of importance in internal decision-making within the Agency, as political levers for environmentally sensitive decisions and for shaping and developing the culture of the Environment Agency.

(d) The cost–benefit duty

In addition to these general duties and obligations there is an explicit duty upon the EA to take into account the costs and benefits of exercising its powers (s. 39). 'Costs' are defined as environmental as well as personal costs (s. 56(1)) and although 'benefits' are surprisingly (given the mutual relationship between the phrases) not defined, the term would arguably include environmental benefits in addition to any personal benefits.

There are two important restrictions on the application of the duty. First, it does not apply if it would be unreasonable in the circumstances of a particular case. The clearest example of this would be where emergency action was required by the Agency. Secondly, the duty does not affect the exercise of other mandatory obligations such as complying with environmental quality objectives. In such circumstances, the decision-making discretion of the Agency is constrained within the pursuit of the specific objective and the costs and the benefits become less relevant.

The general cost–benefit duty does, however, apply where the Agency can select from a range of potential options when seeking to achieve these objectives and the costs and benefits of each of those options can be considered when selecting which is the most appropriate. Thus, taking account of costs and benefits does not necessarily mean that the Agency has to demonstrate that the costs outweigh the benefits (or vice versa) or even that, once it has carried out such an appraisal, it must act in accordance with the conclusions. A requirement to take account of costs and benefits arguably does no more than raise an evidential presumption that they will be considered. In classic administrative fashion it does not prescribe the weight which should be attached to such costs or benefits and therefore any decision based on such an analysis will be difficult to challenge.

The Secretary of State has issued non-statutory guidance on the cost–benefit duty as part of the explanatory document which accompanies the statutory guidance on the principal aim of the Agency.[30] The guidance emphasises the importance of carrying out environmental appraisals before exercising decision-making powers. In addition, the guidance points out the difficulties in quantifying environmental costs, benefits, and places, and sets out a number of factors which may be relevant in reaching a decision. Arguably the most important section of the guidance stresses the fact that in many situations, the application of the duty will require the exercise of judgement by the Agency—a judgment which is likely to be unchallengeable in the courts.

In addition to this general duty under section 39, the Agency has to consider the costs associated with other duties. Thus there is a duty to consider 'any likely costs' when seeking to achieve its principal aim under section 4 (see above) and the Agency must set out the costs and benefits for exercising its options under the pollution control functions in section 5.

(e) Financial arrangements

The EA derives its funding from three main sources. A good proportion is grant-in-aid received direct from DEFRA. This emphasizes the difficult nature of the EA's relationship with its primary funder. Whilst it is not part of Central Government it does rely upon DEFRA to fund key resources such as staffing and research and development. A second income stream funding operational flood defence schemes comes from levies raised on local authorities. The final significant proportion of funding is recovered through operating receipts, i.e. monies generated from charging schemes and licence fees related to pollution control systems. Sections 41 and 42 of the Environment Act 1995 provide the power to introduce charging schemes for all forms of environmental licensing. The Agency can exercise this power itself, unlike some of the previous powers to raise fees and charges which were exercisable by the Secretary of State (e.g. waste regulation and IPC under the EPA 1990). To ensure that the schemes are subject to proper scrutiny, each must be published in draft and approved by the Secretary of State and the Treasury before it can come into operation. Furthermore, the scheme must be made by statutory instrument and can be annulled by either House of Parliament. At present, all charges are levied on a fixed basis with variations for certain classes of licences, although in theory there are no restrictions on the amount which can be charged nor on any differentials in charging to reflect the administrative burden of each individual application.

In addition to this specific power, the Agency has general powers to charge for any services provided in connection with environmental licences under section 37(7) and (8) (there are further incidental powers under section 43). This would cover any advice or assistance

---

30. Department of the Environment, MAFF, and WO, *The Environment Agency and Sustainable Development* (1996). There is also an EA Policy Note, *Sustainable Development: Taking Accounts of Costs and Benefits* (1999).

provided to applicants when preparing applications. The use of this power would enable the Agency to introduce charging rates which more accurately reflect the administrative burden without necessarily complicating the existing charging schemes.

Other regulatory agencies

Although the EA has primary responsibility for the majority of powers in relation to pollution control, there are still a number of other bodies with direct responsibility for specific aspects of pollution control and wider areas of environmental protection. In particular, local authorities play an important role in regulating the clean up of historically contaminated land, statutory nuisances, noise, air quality (including smoke control and other atmospheric emissions), and planning. In addition, the privatized water companies act as sewerage undertakers, controlling discharges to sewers. There is a good deal of overlap in these areas which covers both substantive law and administration. An outline of these overlaps is given in each of the relevant chapters in Part II.

(a) Sewerage undertakers

In relation to discharges to sewers, the licensing body is the privatized sewerage undertaker, which grants what are called 'trade effluent consents'. This is an unusual example of a private body undertaking an environmental regulation function, although it is arguable that a sewerage undertaker is in reality doing little different from a private waste disposal contractor in providing a method of waste disposal through privately owned facilities. Appeals against trade effluent consent decisions are heard by Ofwat whose main functions relate to the regulatory control of the privatised water industry. For a further explanation of the water industry and trade effluent consenting see Chapter 19.

(b) Countryside bodies

One of the positive aspects of the creation of DEFRA was the integration of rural affairs into a department which deals with wider environmental concerns. DEFRA deals with agricultural policy and other related matters. There are, however, other independent agencies within the government responsible for specific matters. In England, English Nature and the Countryside Agency have responsibilities for nature conservation and for recreation, landscape and amenity respectively. This division of responsibility reflects a split in functions decided upon as long ago as 1949 and some reasons behind this are explained in Chapter 21. The Nature Conservancy Council was organized on a Great Britain basis until 1 April 1991 when, for largely political reasons, it was split into three separate national bodies by the EPA 1990. In Wales, the nature conservation functions were amalgamated with the amenity functions in a new Countryside Council for Wales. In Scotland, a similar body called Scottish Natural Heritage was established under the Natural Heritage (Scotland) Act 1991, which also combines the two functions.

The Haskins Review on rural affairs has proposed major changes to the administration of countryside matters. One of the Report's key recommendations was that there should be an integrated agency to promote sustainable use of land and the natural environment. This would be achieved through a merger of English Nature, the Countryside Agency and parts of DEFRA's Rural Development Service. The draft Natural Environment and Rural Communities Bill is intended to implement key aspects of the review.

Local authorities

There has been a great deal of restructuring in local authorities in England over recent years. In 1986, the abolition of the metropolitan county councils led to the creation of two separate structures for local government in England (with slight variations in the case of London). As a result of further local government reorganization under the Local Government Act 1992, there are now three main types of local authority:

- *Single-tier London boroughs and metropolitan districts.* In metropolitan areas, there is a one-tier system, the metropolitan district councils. These obviously have responsibility for all matters, although some functions (police, fire, and transport) are run by joint boards of the councils.

- *Non-metropolitan areas.* In non-metropolitan areas, there is a two-tier system of county and district councils. In constitutional terms these two tiers are equal, but they have differing responsibilities. County councils have responsibility for the police, fire services, personal social services, transport, highways, education, libraries, and development control in certain prescribed 'county matters' including waste disposal and minerals development. District councils have responsibility for housing, general development control, recreation, environmental and public health. This split causes problems for the public which often finds it difficult to identify which tier is responsible for any particular matter. The problem is particularly acute in the environmental sphere because of the overlapping powers of the two tiers (e.g. in town planning). This confusion was cited as one of the factors which led to the reorganisation of local government and the introduction of unitary authorities.

- *Unitary authorities.* This third class of local authority was created after a review of local government considered a large number of proposals to introduce more single-tier authorities to replicate the powers of the metropolitan district councils.

All local authorities undertake a wide variety of tasks in relation to environmental protection. These are considered in detail in Chapter 12. In outline, there are six main areas to consider:

(a) Town and country planning

The local authority is normally the local planning authority. This means that it is responsible for the making of development plans and for the control of development. The powers also incorporate responsibility for related matters, such as tree preservation orders, listed building protection, conservation areas, hazardous substances consents, the control of derelict land, and the protection of the countryside. As explained above, planning functions are split between county and district councils, with county councils being responsible for minerals and waste disposal matters, whilst district councils have responsibility for other development control decisions and smaller scale development planning in local plans. In

National Parks the planning function is undertaken by special planning authorities with representation from the various local authorities whose area falls within the National Park (see further p. 861).

(b) Public health matters

Local authorities have always had responsibility for a very wide range of matters under the Public Health Acts. In particular, this involves duties in relation to the control of statutory nuisances, the law on which was remodelled in the EPA 1990, Part III. Authorities also have responsibilities for monitoring the quality of private water supplies.

(c) The control of noise

Local authorities have primary responsibility for the control of noise from premises. In the past these provisions had been separate from those relating to statutory nuisance, but in the EPA 1990 the two sets of powers were treated together.

(d) Air pollution

Local authorities have long had responsibility for the control of smoke, dust, grit, and fumes under the Clean Air Acts and related legislation. In the EPA 1990, Part I, they were given more complete powers to control air pollution from plants which are not the responsibility of the EA under integrated pollution control. This general split was maintained under the IPPC system under the Pollution Prevention and Control Act 1999. In addition to these specific controls over emissions, the Environment Act 1995 gave local authorities greater responsibilities for establishing strategic control over air quality matters. This includes a duty to review air quality in an area in order to assess compliance with air quality standards, a duty to designate air quality management areas where those standards are not being met and a duty to prepare an action plan to address the problems of air quality.

(e) Waste collection and disposal

Responsibilities for waste collection and the arrangements for the disposal of waste remain with local authorities under the waste collection and waste disposal authorities. Local authorities also play an important role in ensuring that waste reduction (they are responsible for meeting landfill reduction quotas) and recycling targets can be achieved as they control a large proportion of the waste arising at the place of production.

(f) Contaminated land

Under Part IIA, EPA 1990, local authorities are responsible for the inspection and identification of land within their area for the existence of contaminated land and to take action against the person responsible for the contamination or the owner/occupier of the land. These responsibilities are shared (in some respects) with the EA which is given corresponding powers and duties in respect of sites which are more heavily contaminated (known as 'Special Sites').

(g) General duties and sustainable development

In addition to these areas, it is clear that local and regional policies on such things as transport provision, recreation and strategic planning specifically and all of an authority's functions generally all have a part to play in the protection of the environment and the pursuit of sustainability. Section 4 of the Local Government Act 2000 places on all local authorities (including county and district councils) a duty to prepare 'community strategies', for promoting or improving the economic, social and environmental well-being of their areas, and contributing to the achievement of sustainable development in the UK. It also gives authorities broad new powers to improve and promote local well-being as a means of helping them to implement those strategies. Section 4 of the Act also requires local authorities in England to have regard to any guidance issued by the Secretary of State in preparing their community strategies.[31]

Non-governmental organizations

'NGO' is a convenient label for a wide diversity of bodies ranging from huge membership groups with an international agenda such as Greenpeace and Friends of the Earth, to national groups like the National Trust and the Royal Society for the Protection of Birds as well as smaller groups such as the National Federation of Badger Groups or the local Wildlife Trusts. The defining characteristic of these groups is that the group exists to promote an environmental cause which is not only linked to the interest of its members. Thus the term 'public interest groups' has been used to distinguish these organizations from groups with a specified local agenda—often to stop local development proposals—which have been characterized as NIMBY groups.

Britain has a long tradition of non-governmental organizations (NGOs) being involved in different aspects of environmental law and policy. A number of NGOs have their origin in the 19th Century. In the early stages there were three main groupings with nature conservation (the RSPB in 1889), countryside (Commons, Open Spaces and Footpaths Preservation Society in 1865) and animal welfare (the RSPCA in 1824) all having groups formed in the 19th Century. An increase in the interest in environmental issues has been reflected by the dramatic growth in membership of environmental NGOs since the 1970s with membership of some groups such as the RSPB and Friends of the Earth increasing by a factor of 10. The Table below sets out a few of the main environmental NGOs in the UK along with the main areas of interest.

NGO	Comments
Campaign to Protect Rural England	Founded in 1926. Focus on rural aspects of town and country planning, agriculture and transport. Membership approx. 59,000.
Earth First!	Not a group as such but a 'convenient banner for people who share similar philosophies to work under.' Uses radical direct action including occupation and sabotage (see e.g. Box 21.4). Particularly active in relation to protests against road building.
Friends of the Earth	Founded in 1969. Largest international environmental NGO. Campaigns across a wide range of environmental issues. Particularly effective at securing changes in law.

---

31. ODPM, *Preparing Community Strategies: Government Guidance to Local Authorities* (2001).

NGO	Comments
Greenpeace	Founded in 1971. 221,000 members in the UK as part of 2.8 million members worldwide. Runs campaigns on GMOs, nuclear power, ancient forests, chemicals, climate change, and whaling.
National Society for Clean Air and Environmental Protection	Founded in 1899 as the Coal Smoke Abatement Society. Largely responsible for the introduction of the Clean Air Acts in the 1950s. Particular interest in air quality and noise. Membership includes public and private sector organizations and companies. Focus on training and education.
National Trust	Founded in 1895 with over 3 million members. Owns 250,000 hectares of land and around 650 miles of protected coastline. It is an incorporated body governed by powers in various National Trusts Act from 1907 to 1971.
Royal Society for the Protection of Birds	Founded in 1889. Over 1 million members. As its name suggests primary aim is to protect bird species and habitats. Owns or manages over 180 nature reserves which provide homes to 80 per cent of the UK's rarest birds. Plays a prominent role in investigating wildlife crime. Responsible for the introduction of many pieces of legislation including the Protection of Birds Act 1954.
Royal Society of Wildlife Trusts	Previously known as the Royal Society of Nature Conservation. Founded in 1912 to protect wild animals and their habitat across the UK. Owns or manages 2,560 nature reserves. Made up of 47 independent local Wildlife Trusts. Membership more than 560,000.
The Open Spaces Society	Founded in 1865. Oldest conservation group. Its aim is to create and conserve common land, village greens, open spaces and rights of public access, in town and country, in England and Wales.
Transport 2000	Lobbies and briefs Government on issues relating to transport and the environment. Representative sits on the Commission for Integrated Transport.
Wildlife and Countryside Link	Founded in 1980. Represents a coordinating body for many wildlife organizations. Members include the RSPB, Wildlife Trusts, the Ramblers Association, Greenpeace and Friends of the Earth. Influential in shaping the Wildlife and Countryside and Act 1981 and the Countryside and Rights of Way Act 2000.
WWF-UK	Founded in 1961 to promote the conservation of rare and endangered species. Over 330,000 members. In addition to campaigning internationally also involved in the enforcement of international wildlife laws (see Box 6.4).

Environmental NGOs play a variety of roles in the administration of environmental law and policy. For many groups there is a direct role as owners or stewards of land which is protected. For example, local Wildlife Trusts own or manage over 2,500 nature reserves. The primary role of NGOs is, however, to undertake activities which are designed to influence decision-makers and to secure favourable changes to environmental law and policy. They do this through a variety of mechanisms. At a local level such groups may participate in the Development Plan Process or as consultees on planning applications. Nationally they participate in the policy making process through such things as giving evidence to Select Committees and the RCEP and lobbying Government Departments and relevant agencies.

NGOs also seek to have a direct influence on environmental law by campaigning for new legislation. The Government has a large degree of control over the Parliamentary timetable and therefore any NGO which wants to introduce new legislation must either persuade the Government to adopt their ideas or use the Private Members Bill procedure. This procedure allocates time for Parliamentary debate for Bills introduced by MPs. The places are decided by a ballot with only 20 successful places allocated annually. Large numbers of MPs apply for places in the ballot without any specific Bill in mind. If allocated a high place in the Ballot, they will be targeted by NGOs with suggestions for Bills and draft clauses. The procedure can only be used for relatively uncontroversial proposals as the Government effectively has a veto over any Bill by controlling the amount of Parliamentary time available. As a consequence, the success rate for Environmental Bills is not particularly high although some do get passed. A recent example of a successful Private Members Bill on the Environment was the Household Waste Recycling Act 2003 which was drafted and promoted by Friends of the Earth and steered through Parliament by Joan Ruddock MP (see p. 589).

NGOs also play a role in the implementation and enforcement of environmental law. This could be through the setting of environmental standards (e.g. the role NGOs play in the IPPC Information Exchange (see p. Box 20.4)) or through the use of private prosecutions. NGOs have also developed a leading role in challenging government and regulatory agencies through the use of judicial review actions. In doing so they have clarified the rules on those who are able to bring such actions (the law on standing, see p. 341) and brought about changes to the law in such areas as the incorrect implementation of the Habitats Directive in relation to marine habitats (see *R v DTI ex parte Greenpeace* [2000] Env LR 221) and the unlawful shooting of protected birds (see *RSPB and The Wildfowl and Wetlands Trust v Secretary of State for Scotland* [2001] Env LR 19).

The courts

Although traditionally seen as separate from Parliament and therefore unconcerned with questions of policy, do the Courts play a role in the administration of environmental law? The High Court supervises the exercise of statutory powers and duties by many of the other regulatory bodies in this Chapter through the adjudication of judicial review actions (see further on this p. 340). In exercising this supervisory function the Courts have often emphasized that they are not concerned with the merits of any decision made as a result of exercising a particular power or fulfilling a duty but whether the proper procedures have been complied with. Thus where a regulatory body such as a local planning authority is determining whether to grant planning permission based upon different policy considerations (e.g. job creation as against environmental damage) a Court will intervene where the procedures for environmental assessment have not been followed but not on the ground that it was wrong to give greater weight to employment over the environment (see *Berkeley v*

Secretary of State for the Environment, Transport and the Regions [2001] Env LR 303 and Box 14.12). A court is also reluctant to intervene in cases where a regulatory agency has exercised its powers to make an expert determination. For example a court would not interfere with English Nature's determination that land was of special scientific interest unless it could be shown that it had ignored some statutory procedural requirement (see *Fisher v English Nature* [2004] EWCA Civ 663).

The Courts also fulfil an appellate function (e.g. Magistrates Courts hear appeals in relation to statutory nuisance abatement notices and some contaminated land remediation notices), determine civil disputes with an environmental flavour (e.g. in relation to environmental nuisances) and try cases involving environmental crimes. The effectiveness of the Courts' role in environmental cases has been the subject of a number of criticisms and proposals over recent years. The background to the calls for a separate form of Environmental Tribunal is covered further in Chapter 10. In terms of the administration of environmental law and policy, some of the general criticisms reflect some of the problems outlined above in relation to internal and external integration of environmental considerations across different areas of decision making and Government depart-ments. There are convincing arguments put forward that the courts are not necessarily effective when dealing with environmental disputes and a new structure and set of procedures probably involving some sort of environmental tribunal or court could address these issues.

The courts and environmental cases

Although the courts have been at the forefront of the development of some of the key issues in environmental law such as the definition of waste, the fulfilment of the idea of environ-mental assessment and the identity of the 'polluter' in relation to water pollution, some judges have questioned whether the development of the law is a matter for the courts or for Parliament. The House of Lords has made it clear that as more and more new legislation is addressing environmental problems in a structured fashion it is unnecessary and perhaps even undesirable for the Courts to develop private law principles to address the same issues (see *Cambridge Water Co. v Eastern Counties Leather plc* [1994] 2 AC 264 and further Case box 11.4). For example, the House of Lords deferred to a statutory scheme of compensation for damage from overflowing sewers rather than developing the law of nuisance (see *Marcic v Thames Water* [2004] Env LR 25 and Case box 11.8). This can be interpreted as a reflection of the fact that Parliament is able to create a coherent and structured system, rather than one developed on an ad hoc, case-by-case basis; but it also reflects the point that Parliament has a greater democratic legitimacy than the courts when it comes to allocating responsibility for environmental harm in particular when it comes to questions of the allocation of resources such as expenditure on environmental improvements.[32]

---

32. R. Lee [2005] Journal of Law and Society 111 and W. Howarth (2002) 14 JEL 353 makes the same point in a critical comment on the Court of Appeal's judgment.

CHAPTER SUMMARY

1 There are numerous bodies which are responsible for the administration of environmental law and policy. One of the major challenges of recent years has been to integrate environmental considerations across those different bodies.

2 Integration can be achieved externally by promoting the consideration of environmental issues across all policy areas or internally by drawing together regulatory responsibilities for different environmental emissions within one single authority.

3 Devolution has shifted responsibility for much of environmental law and policy to the national executives in Scotland, Wales and Northern Ireland. Although there are distinctive environmental laws in each country, the general framework of environmental law is the same because European and International law is so influential.

4 Within Central Government, the Department of the Environment, Food and Rural Affairs is responsible for many, but not all, environmental issues. Other departments with significant environmental responsibilities include the Office of the Deputy Prime Minister, the Department of Trade and Industry, and the Department of Transport.

5 Various bodies such as Parliamentary Select Committees play an important role in scrutinizing the activities of central government departments and regulatory agencies. They and the Royal Commission on Environmental Pollution are also catalysts for the creation of new laws and policies.

6 The Environment Agency is the primary environmental regulator in England and Wales. It is effectively a pollution control authority with a large number of water-related functions such as land drainage and flood defence. The Agency is subject to a complicated framework of aims, duties and objectives which underpin all its activities. The Agency provides a good example of the internal integration of environmental law as it is responsible for many different pollution control functions which had previously been regulated by different agencies.

7 In Scotland the Scottish Environment Protection Agency mirrors many of the Environment Agency's responsibilities. In Northern Ireland similar functions are carried out by the Environment and Heritage Service.

8 Other main environmental regulators include nature conservation and countryside bodies (English Nature, Scottish Natural Heritage, and Countryside Council for Wales) the private Water and Sewerage Industry (the public body Scottish Water in Scotland), and the Local Authorities (main responsibilities include: town and country planning, statutory nuisances and contaminated land).

9 Non-governmental organizations play an important role in the administration of environmental law through participation in law and policy making, implementation, and enforcement.

10 The Courts play an important role in the enforcement of environmental law. They supervise the exercise of administrative powers through judicial review, sanction offenders for pollution offences and adjudicate on environmental disputes. The Courts tend to be conservative and have been reluctant to expand their role in developing law as a mechanism for environmental protection.

Q QUESTIONS

1 In what ways has the administration of environmental law become more integrated over the last 10 years? In what ways has it become more fragmented?

2 What are the advantages and disadvantages of devolution in terms of the administration of environmental law and policy in the United Kingdom?

3 What responsibilities does the Environment Agency have? How does the Environment Act 1995 seek to balance some of the competing responsibilities?

4 What role do NGOs play in the administration of environmental law and policy?

FURTHER READING

The idea of administrative integration and the creation of the Environment Agency is covered in some depth in J. Steele and T. Jewell, 'Law in Environmental Decision Making' found in T. Jewell and J. Steele (eds), *Law in Environmental Decision Making* (Oxford: Clarendon Press, 1998). These themes are further developed in an article by the same authors, T. Jewell and J. Steele, 'UK Regulatory Reform and the Pursuit of "Sustainable Development": The Environment Act 1995' [1996] 8 JEL 283 which also gives a deeper analysis of the duties and powers of the Agency under the Environment Act 1995. There is an interesting analysis of the work of the Environment Agency and the criticisms of its role and performance in D. Bell and T. Gray, 'The Ambiguous Role of the Environment Agency in England and Wales' (2002) 11(3) Environmental Politics 76.

A good overview of the issues raised by devolution can be found in a collection of essays from the 1999 UKELA Conference on Devolution and the Environment in N. Farris and S. Turner (eds), *Public Law and the Environment: New Directions* (1997). Another introduction to the topic can be found in R. Macrory, 'The Environment and Constitutional Change' in R. Hazell (ed.) *Constitutional Futures: A History of the Next Ten Years* (Oxford: Oxford University Press, 1999). More detail on specific countries can be found in general texts. Northern Ireland is covered in S. Turner and K. Morrow, *Northern Ireland Environmental Law* (Dublin: Gill & Macmillan, 1997), K. Morrow and S. Turner, 'The Impact of EC Law on the Environmental Law of Northern Ireland' in J. Holder (ed.), *The Impact of EC Environmental Law in the United Kingdom* (Chichester: Wiley, 1997) 69 and Turner and Morrow, 'The More Things Change, the More They Stay the Same: Environmental Law, Policy & Funding In Northern Ireland' (1998) 10 JEL 41. Scotland is dealt with in C. Reid, *Environmental Law in Scoland*, (2nd edn Edinburgh: W. Green, 1997), G. Little, 'Scottish Devolution and Environmental Law' (2000) 12 JEL 155 and C. Reid, 'The Impact of EC Law in Scotland' (1997) Juridical Review 355.

The role of the Environmental Audit Committee and the general approach to scrutinizing Government activities is covered in A. Ross, 'Greening Government—Tales From the New Sustainability Watchdog' (2000) 12 JEL 175, and K. Hollingsworth, 'Environmental Monitoring of Government—the case for an environmental auditor' (2000) 20 LS 241.

NGOs

There are some general texts dealing with environmental NGOs although the best are a little dated. These are P. Lowe and J. Goyder, *Environmental Groups in Politics*, (London: Allen & Unwin, 1983), and G. Jordan and W. Maloney, *The Protest Business*, (Manchester: Manchester University Press, 1997). The long history of nature conservation NGOs and the significant impact that they have had on law and policy is chronicled in D. Evans, *A History of Nature Conservation in Britain* (2nd edn, London: Routledge, 1997).

@ WEB LINKS

Most of the web links for this chapter are self explanatory and can be sourced from the central government web portal <www.open.gov.uk>. The DEFRA web page <www.defra.gov.uk> is also a good link to many other related sites including the various executive and non departmental public bodies. A degree of perseverance and patience is needed with the Environment Agency's web-pages <www.environment-agency.gov.uk> and the judicious use of the search facility is the best way of navigating around. The Select Committees' pages of the Houses of Parliament web site <www.parliament.uk> gives access to the Evidence, Reports and any Government response on many areas of environmental law and policy. Details of the RCEP's work can be accessed at <www.rcep.org.uk>. Unfortunately there is only full access to the text of the most recent Reports.

PART II

Integrated themes

6 International law and environmental protection

Overview

International law, and hence international environmental law, is rather different from the other areas of law discussed in this book. Perhaps the most important difference is the absence of a single body with the power to make and enforce law effectively. The absence of such a body, and of coercive powers over states, companies and individuals, has often resulted in international 'law' being regarded as something rather closer to international relations. This positivistic view is receding, but its essence both pervades the subject and poses a challenge for the effective regulation of environmental affairs at the international level. Nevertheless, this feature of international law arguably means that the gap between law and policy is not so great here as in national or EC law.

Another key feature of international law is that, in the UK, it does not have a direct impact on domestic law or on individuals. Treaties need to be given effect to through national legislation, and—with some notable exceptions like the law on war crimes—are concerned with the action of states, not individuals within states. In this sense, international law is quite different from national law and, to the extent that it confers individual rights, EC law.

This chapter describes the development, scope and application of international environmental law, which has expanded significantly since the late 1960s. The focus is on international treaties relating to environmental protection, though fuller discussion of how the key international environmental treaties work is left to Part III.

In general, this chapter is restricted to discussing public rather than private international law, that is, the law between states rather than the conflict of legal systems. The latter is, of course, relevant in environmental law, e.g. which court should hear pollution-related claims against transnational corporations. Such cases raise the issue of whether different standards can be employed by such companies working in developing countries (which covers similar ground to wider questions about international environmental law and sustainable development), but are not directly addressed here.

At the end of this chapter you should be able to:

✔ Understand what international environmental law is, and how it is made.
✔ Appreciate the interaction between international law, EC law and UK national law.
✔ Assess the development of international environmental law and policy, especially in the last 30 years.
✔ Understand the potential conflicts between environmental standards and the rules of international free trade, and appreciate how these are currently resolved.
✔ Form a view on likely developments in international environmental law.

Why is international law important for environmental protection?

International law is important for environmental protection, and for the issues covered in the rest of this book, in the following central ways:

- Transboundary and global problems require international (or at the very least, bilateral) solutions, and international legal regulation of some kind will be either necessary or desirable.

- International agreements may generate standards which are adopted in national law, or by regional groupings like the European Community, or which guide decision-making in areas like the interface between international trade and the environment.

- The international arena is of some importance for the development of principles of environmental law, such as sustainable development or the precautionary principle (see further Chapter 3). Indeed, such principles often develop precisely because their origins are in agreements that are not legally binding.

- Because of its nature, recent developments in international law have focused on how an attention to procedures, and on positive inducements to comply rather than negative 'command and control' style enforcement mechanisms, can be used to secure compliance. Although borne of necessity, there is again much for national and EC law to learn from this experience.

- Perhaps negatively, the development of environmental law at all levels may be subject to restrictions originating in international law, for example import restrictions which are deemed to be incompatible with the rules regulating international trade.

International law and the UK

The relationship between international law and the UK has two dimensions. The first is the extent to which international law affects rights and duties and policy-making at national level. The second is the contribution of the UK to developments in international environmental law and policy.

(a) Direct application of international environmental law

In the UK, international agreements only become part of national law once they are given effect to by Parliament, usually through legislation. Moreover, both the making of treaties (*Blackburn v Attorney-General* [1971] 1 WLR 1037) and their implementation (*ex parte Molyneaux* [1986] 1 WLR 331) are seen by the courts as a matter solely for government: 'Treaties . . . are not self-executing. Quite simply, a treaty is not part of English law unless and until it has been incorporated into the law by legislation' (*Maclaine Watson v Department of Trade and Industry* [1989] 3 All ER 523 per Lord Oliver at 545). This is the case even where the treaty has been ratified, because in the UK ratification is a matter for central government, not Parliament. Following devolution, the power to ratify treaties remains with the UK government, being a matter of foreign affairs.

All of this means that international agreements have what might be called 'high-level' rather than 'low-level' effect: they create obligations that bind the UK in its international relations, rather than obligations of the kind on which individuals can rely or have duties under. There are exceptions—e.g. the direct application of human rights law—but international environmental law is mainly concerned with getting states to take action to influence non-state actors, rather than imposing burdens directly on polluters themselves. In the UK, international agreements cannot be used as the basis for an action by groups or individuals against the state or a public body (in the way that EC directives may be), nor are they in themselves a direct source of rights and duties in legal actions between individuals.

(b) Indirect application of international environmental law

Even if a treaty is not 'self-executing', courts will prefer interpretations of statutes which conform with international treaties to which the UK is a party to those which do not. This does not necessarily mean that in all cases of discretion, there is a presumption in favour of the convention (*R v Secretary of State for the Home Department, ex parte Brind* [1991] 1 AC 696). But where national legislation is introduced to give effect to a treaty or treaty obligation, then the treaty *can* be used as an aide to interpreting the national law and it is presumed that Parliament did not intend to legislate contrary to the UK's international commitments. In *R v Secretary of State for Trade and Industry, ex parte Greenpeace (No. 2)* [2000] Env LR 221 the High Court held that the Habitats Directive should have been applied beyond territorial waters. Although in this case it was EC legislation that was being interpreted, the court looked for an interpretation of the directive that seemed most consistent not just with other provisions of EC law but also with a range of international agreements on marine conservation (see also p. 828).

In some cases, the relationship between the treaty and implementing legislation will be spelt out more precisely. For example, the Human Rights Act 1998, which 'incorporates' the European Convention on Human Rights, makes it clear that the English courts must take account of previous decisions of the European Court of Human Rights when interpreting the Act. This is important because of the limited steps that the European Court of Human Rights has already taken to interpret the Convention in a creative way to give incidental protection to the environment (see p. 78). Rights under the Convention may also challenge some of the traditional common law rules on environmental protection. An example of this is *McKenna v British Aluminium* [2002] Env LR 30, where the High Court thought that the rules of who can bring a private law action in nuisance might need to be modified so that their human rights were adequately protected (see p. 366).

(c) Impact on policy

Developments in international law are often reflected in policy developments at national level. *Sustainable Development: The UK Strategy* (Cm 2426, 1994) was a response to Agenda 21, the soft law document agreed at the 1992 UN Conference on Environment and Development (the 'Rio Earth Summit'), and national policy in many areas reflects commitments originally made at Rio. These agreements, however, tend to contain general principles which give a considerable degree of latitude to governments in their implementation. The

UK government has arguably used this latitude to translate soft international law into soft policy commitments, for example in relation to improving access to environmental justice (and only with the legally binding 1998 Aarhus Convention which specifically covers this and related areas have there been moves to put this on a firmer international law footing; see Chapter 10). There has been a longstanding, pragmatic reluctance to sign up to international treaty obligations that appear incapable of being met in practice (for an example, the 1995 Fourth North Sea Declaration contained agreement on reducing hazardous substances in the marine environment, but a footnote stated that 'The UK shares the ideal of these aims, but does not accept that they are currently practicable').

(d) The UK and the development of international environmental law

As far as the role of the UK in developing international law is concerned, the record has tended to be patchy at best[1] and it is difficult to identify key environmental treaties where the UK has taken a lead in the negotiations. However, very often it is now the EC as a bloc which negotiates, which makes it difficult to assess the particular stance taken by the UK (though it appears to one of the more progressive Member States in relation to climate change). Its role often appears to be negative, attempting to weaken the wording of commitments, although there are of course examples the other way. For example, although the UK was initially sceptical of the Cartagena Protocol to the Convention on Biological Diversity, which regulates the international movement of living modified organisms, it eventually came to be one of the Member States within the EU pushing most strongly for it. Where the UK has shown most leadership has tended to be in relation to treaties like the 1946 Whaling Convention, an area where the UK no longer has any economic interests. In recent years, however, the attitude of the UK towards the making of international environmental agreements appears to have softened somewhat, although there is often a certain dragging of heels when it comes to the details, such as with radioactive discharges at sea (see further Box 6.5).

International law and the EC

In some cases, treaties may be open to signature by 'regional economic integration organizations', a term covering the EC, which has signed all the most recent multilateral environmental agreements. The basic procedure is that the Commission does the negotiating, but the Council signs any treaty: a unanimous vote in the Council may be needed if the treaty deals with issues which require unanimity within the EC (on voting procedures in relation to the EC adopting international environmental agreements see p. 202).

This should not hide the often hotly contested division of competence between the EC and the Member States as regards external matters. International trade and marine fisheries conservation are areas of exclusive Community competence, which means that it is the Community which negotiates any agreements in these areas (such as the GATT/WTO

---

1. See R. Churchill, 'International Environmental Law and the UK' in R. Churchill, L. Warren and J. Gibson (eds), *Law, Policy and the Environment* (Oxford: Blackwell, 1991).

Agreement). Where the EC is a party to a convention in an area of its exclusive competence then it may take cases, or be taken, before the relevant international court or tribunal For example, in *Chile/EC (Swordfish)* 40 ILM 475 (2001) Chile and the EC agreed to submit a dispute about conserving swordfish stocks to the International Tribunal for the Law of the Sea, and see also Boxes 6.7 and 6.9. Beyond these fields there is a considerable amount of scope for disagreement about the proper balance of competence in the environmental field. At a time when there are pulls both towards globalization and devolution, we might any way question what 'exclusive competence', either for the EC or for the Member States, actually means.

Where both the EC and the Member States are parties to a treaty, there needs to be some way of deciding on voting rights under the treaty and on coordinating their obligations. On the former the normal position is that the EC votes as a block, so if unanimity is required and this cannot be achieved then the EC may have to abstain. There are concerns that this means that the will of states forming a majority within the EC on a particular issue may not be counted. One example is the Convention on the International Trade in Endangered Species (CITES), where trade in ivory by certain countries was blocked where the EC was united but allowed where it could not agree a unanimous position. (There are obvious transparency problems here as well, if the position of the EC is left to last-minute, behind closed doors, negotiations.) On coordinating obligations a unique example of how this is done is under the 1997 Kyoto Climate Change Protocol. Both the UK and the EC are parties to this, which requires specified reductions of emissions. Under Article 4 of the Protocol, the Member States can 'bubble' their reductions, so that the EC decides which states take heavier and lighter loads depending on things like their state of economic development (see Box 16.3).

Although EC environmental law is said to flow from developments in international law, specifically the Stockholm Conference (see p. 156), the unique nature of the EC has made it a testing ground for international environmental cooperation. For example, the balancing of trade and environmental concerns in the EC is often held up as a model for integration. Also, the insertion of environmental policy principles in the EC Treaty (now contained in Art. 174(2)) means that their legal status can be explored within the EC, but also contributes to the development of similar principles in international environmental law. In this way there is a clear synergy between EC and international law and policy.

Nation states and global commons

Because international law is the law of nation states, different considerations apply depending on whether we are concerned with activities:

- taking place within a state and affecting only the environment of that state (such as most contamination of land, or harm to non-migratory species). Although other states could claim to be injured by non-compliance, in practice claims are not brought unless there is some direct cross-border problem;

- having an impact as between states, neighbouring or otherwise (e.g. transboundary air pollution, or pollution of an international river by an upstream state; for some examples see the *Trail Smelter* arbitration (Case box 6.3) and the *Gabčíkovo* (Case box 6.4) and MOX (Box 6.5) cases); or

- which affect the 'global commons' (that is, all natural resources beyond the territory of any individual state).

The global commons includes things like the atmosphere and the ozone layer. It also includes the oceans and deep seabed beyond the 200 nautical mile limit of states' 'exclusive economic zones' (although this does not apply to a state's continental shelf if it goes beyond this limit) and space.

The global commons should not be confused with resources that might be said to form a global 'common heritage'. The vast majority of known species, for example, live within or between national borders, which helps explain why the 1992 Biodiversity Convention refers only to the conservation of biodiversity (by definition, a global resource) as a matter of 'common concern' and makes explicit reference to principles of national sovereignty over natural resources. The concept of 'common heritage' developed, from the 1960s onwards, alongside demands for a new international economic order, and focused on the equitable sharing of benefits arising from the use of resources such as the Moon, the Antarctic and the deep seabed. Aside from these examples, however, such calls have largely gone unanswered, and there is a preference for other ways of dealing with global interest in environmental matters, e.g. through 'fair' sharing of the costs of clean technology and differentiated responsibilities on the developed and developing world for addressing problems like climate change (see p. 638).

Finally, the idea of nations owing obligations to all members of the international community (obligations said to be owed '*erga omnes*') is especially relevant to international environmental law.

BOX 6.1 **The first *Nuclear Tests* cases**

In 1974 Australia and New Zealand tried to stop French atmospheric nuclear testing in the South Pacific. An unsuccessful attempt was made in the International Court of Justice to argue that they could bring the claim because France owed a general obligation to all states to be free from nuclear tests generally or that France was in violation of the freedom of the high seas (*Australia v France* ICJ Rep (1974) 253; *New Zealand v France* ICJ Rep (1974), 457). Nevertheless, there were judges in the minority prepared to accept that the right to bring an action of behalf of the international community (an '*actio popularis*') might exist, and who linked the right to bring such an action with the substantive nature of such '*erga omnes*' obligations.

Although a matter of dispute, there are those who would argue for the right of a state to bring such an action in relation not just to the global commons, but also to matters of common concern. But as the example of international trade law shows (see p. 168), the difficulty is for states to avoid unilaterally imposing national standards beyond their borders, and to try to identify appropriate rules of international law that might apply. In treaty law, however, there are now examples of any state being able to enforce a treaty obligation without having to show it has suffered material damage from the alleged failure. The non-compliance and dispute-settlement mechanisms under the 1987 Montreal Protocol on Ozone Depletion, discussed below, are an example.

A tragedy of the commons?

A frequent justification for environmental regulation is to prevent damage to areas that are beyond effective individual control (i.e. where traditional property rights apply (the idea of environmental 'externalities' is discussed in more depth on p. 260)). This is a particular problem in international law, especially for the 'global commons'. Of course, there are some examples from international relations where it is always in all countries' interests to co-operate: e.g. it makes no sense for one state to go it alone when it comes to running international postal services. However, in environmental regulation there may be one-off situations where individual states have an incentive not to cooperate, even though mutual cooperation would ultimately benefit the state concerned (the so-called 'prisoner's dilemma'). This can be seen, for example, in the difficulties in reaching effective agreement about climate change, or over-fishing.

A variant of this argument is Hardin's infamous 'Tragedy of the Commons' thesis ((1968) 162 Science 1243). Hardin's main argument is that common or open access resources will always be prone to over-exploitation. His preferred solution is to 'privatize' common resources wherever possible. Failing this, regulation—'mutual coercion, mutually agreed upon'—is required. The former solution can be seen in, for example, the 1982 Law of the Sea Convention which extended the exclusive economic zone (EEZ) to 200 nautical miles, effectively 'privatizing' as much as 90 per cent of the known living resources of the seas.

As the failure to stem the decline in world fisheries demonstrates, however, such moves may not be enough in themselves to counter unsustainable resource use and, at a national level, the thesis is subject to various theoretical and empirical criticisms, principally that individuals and groups do not always (or necessarily) act in possessively individualistic ways. Whether states always act as rational individual actors at the international level is also subject to debate, but various factors appear to influence the extent to which states come together to reach international agreements (discussed in more detail at p. 165). Hardin's thesis does, however, point to a role for law and legal institutions in providing the necessary framework for states to have confidence that all parties are honouring the agreements into which they enter.

The global commons is only one area requiring international environmental regulation. Resources shared between states may also be subject to 'commons'-type problems, as evidenced by the use of the North Sea as little more than an international dumping ground for its riparian states, not least the UK. Shared resources, however, also include things like migratory species, some of which were the subject of early international 'conservation' law (e.g. the 1902 Convention for the Protection of Birds Useful to Agriculture) and which now receive a measure of protection for less directly economic reasons (1979 Bonn Convention on the Conservation of Migratory Species of Wild Animals). Finally, activities in one state may impact negatively on another state, for example through transboundary pollution (see the *Trail Smelter* case, discussed at p. 156).[2]

2. For a fuller discussion see C. Stone, *The Gnat is Older than Man* (Princeton: Princeton UP, 1993), chs 2–4.

What is becoming discernible, however, is the way that the linkages between globalization and continued economic development, and the natural environment on which that development depends, are becoming better understood. Notably, the emergence of truly global issues requiring regulation is perhaps the most important development of recent years. These include issues which affect everyone and which require common solutions (global warming, ozone layer protection, etc.). But they also include the range of concerns about the linkage between the global economy and environmental degradation that lie at the heart of theories of sustainable development (see p. 31). These include both the 'environmental shadow' cast by developed economies on less developed regions, and the relationship between poverty and environmental damage.

Sources of international law—'hard law'

The sources of international law are generally divided into 'hard' and 'soft' law. 'Hard law', which takes the various forms listed below (and is recognized by Article 38 of the ICJ Statute), is binding in the sense that any legal rule or principle binds a state only in its relations with *other states*. It is not necessarily of any relevance in deciding legal disputes between individuals and the state, such as a judicial review action, or as between individuals such as in nuisance law. By way of example, the 1992 Convention for the Protection of the Marine Environment of the North East Atlantic (the 'OSPAR' Convention) requires states to take 'all possible steps to prevent and eliminate pollution' and, in doing so, to apply the polluter pays principle. These provisions matter, if at all, only as between the parties to the Convention. They do not create general obligations of the kind that individuals can rely on. Nor can they be used as the basis for an action against the state or a public body, in the way that EC directives can sometimes be.

The same can be said of any rules of customary international environmental law. If it were decided that the UK was bound by the precautionary principle as customary law, this would not directly assist an individual in bringing a legal argument based on precaution, although it might add weight generally to precautionary arguments or be helpful in reaching a precautionary interpretation of an ambiguous legal text.

(a) Treaties (or 'conventions' or 'agreements')

These are the pre-eminent form of international law. The basic rules are laid down in the Vienna Convention on the Law of Treaties 1969. The fundamental principle is that states may only be bound with their consent, which is only fully given once the convention has been ratified. The various terms, 'treaties', 'conventions', and 'agreements', all mean the same thing. A 'protocol' also has the same legal force, although it is a sub-agreement to a treaty, generally used to flesh out or amend the treaty.

In 2001 it was estimated that there were over 500 international agreements related to the environment. Important international agreements, especially those that are referred to in this chapter and elsewhere in this book, have been made in the following areas. We use the shorter, common name of a treaty (e.g. the 1971 Ramsar Wetlands Convention) rather than the lengthier, formal name (Convention on Wetlands of International Importance especially as Waterfowl Habitat). As this example shows, often a convention is known by the name of the place where it was agreed. Where a common acronym or abbreviation is used, this is also given.

- Nature conservation (1971 Ramsar Wetlands Convention); 1973 Convention on International Trade in Endangered Species ('CITES'); 1979 Berne Convention on the Conservation of European Wildlife and Natural Habitats; 1979 Bonn Convention on Migratory Species of Wild Animals).
- Biodiversity conservation (1992 Convention on Biological Diversity; 2000 Cartagena Biosafety Protocol).
- Natural and cultural heritage (1972 UNESCO World Heritage Convention).
- Climate change (1992 Framework Convention on Climate Change; 1997 Kyoto Protocol).
- Protecting the ozone layer (1985 Vienna Convention for the Protection of the Ozone Layer; 1987 Montreal Protocol; 1990 Montreal Amendments).
- Air pollution (1979 Convention on Long-Range Transboundary Air Pollution ('LRTAP') and a number of protocols made under this on emissions of sulphur dioxide (1994), nitrous oxides (1988), volatile organic compounds (1991), persistent organic pollutants (1998) and heavy metals (1998).
- Waste shipments (1989 Basle Transboundary Waste Convention).
- The global marine environment (1982 UN Convention on the Law of the Sea ('UNCLOS').
- Regional seas (e.g. 1992 'OSPAR' Marine Environment Convention).
- Pollution from shipping (1973 'MARPOL' Convention).
- Landscape (2000 European Landscape Convention).

Most of these treaties contain provisions both about environmental standards (of varying degrees of strictness) and about the main mechanisms used to reach them. Other treaties, of varying importance, focus more on procedural aspects or seek to provide a general underpinning to international environmental law, e.g. conventions on:

- Environmental assessment (1991 Espoo Transboundary EIA Convention; 2004 Kiev Strategic Environmental Assessment Protocol);
- The rights of civil society (1998 Aarhus Convention on Access to Information, Public Participation and Decision-Making and Access to Justice in Environmental Matters);
- Environmental civil liability (1992 Civil Liability Convention and 1992 Oil Pollution Fund Convention, and Liability and Compensation for Hazardous and Noxious Substances at Sea Convention 1996 (adopted under MARPOL); 1993 Lugano Environmental Civil Liability Convention; 1999 Liability and Compensation Protocol to the Basle Hazardous Waste Convention);
- Environmental criminal liability (1998 Convention on the Protection of the Environment Through Criminal Law).

Treaties generally come into force a specified number of days after a certain number of states have ratified, although sometimes a formula is used to ensure that enough key states have ratified (see the example of the climate change regime, below). There are several factors which determine how quickly a treaty comes into force, most importantly the strictness and clarity of the obligations under it. Thus, the 1992 Convention on Biological Diversity entered into force within 18 months, in part because of the generality of its provisions. On the other hand, the 1982 United Nations Law of the Sea Convention took 12 years to come into force, largely because details about mining the resources of the deep sea bed were not satisfactorily agreed until the end of this period. Some treaties never come into force.

Ratification usually requires the approval of the legislature. This can delay treaties from coming into force, or from binding key states: the lobbying of the genetic and pharmaceutical industries has meant that the US has yet to ratify the Convention on Biological Diversity. But it does mean that treaties will only bind a state once the body responsible for enacting legislation to make the treaty work gives its approval. This is an important consideration in practice where (as in the US) the executive and legislature may be controlled by different groupings. But it may also be relevant where a convention is agreed by a government which then loses power in an election.

Of course, the success of a treaty will usually depend on whether key states are parties and have ratified (see Box 6.2).

BOX 6.2 Bringing the Kyoto Protocol into force

The 1997 Kyoto Protocol to the 1992 UN Climate Change Convention specifies a formula designed to ensure that a core of carbon-emitting developed world states have agreed to its provisions. For the Protocol to come into force, at least 55 parties to the Convention must ratify it *and* these 55 parties must include 'Annex I' parties (all OECD states, and certain states from the former Soviet Bloc) which accounted for at least 55 per cent of the total carbon dioxide emissions of Annex I parties in 1990. By July 2004, 124 Parties had ratified or acceded to the Protocol, including the EC. But the Protocol had not entered into force because these states only account for just over 44 per cent of emissions and key polluting states including Russia and the US had yet to ratify. In late 2004, seemingly as part of a deal to allow it entry to the WTO, the former ratified, which brought the Protocol into force in February 2005. However, in the US the Bush Administration has made it clear that it will not sign. Nevertheless, the parties to the Protocol have taken steps to bring the Protocol to life even in the absence of the world's major greenhouse gas emitter (see further p. 638).

There are some treaties, however, which may extend in practice to non-parties (see discussion of CITES in Box 6.6).

(b) Custom

Customary international law is created by implicit rather than explicit agreement, and needs both the practice of states and their conviction that what is done is done not because of usage but because of some felt legal obligation. There are problems in ascertaining exactly what a state does, and problems of identifying customs in the wider global community. However, custom does offer the potential for flexibility by its uncertainty, and scope for creative argument to develop principles of customary international environmental law.

In this sense, flexibility here offers possibilities for the development of principles in a way that vagueness elsewhere cannot (e.g. in more developed areas of law and policy). Many commentators, for example, assert that a number of the central principles of environmental law (including the precautionary and preventive principles and the polluter pays principle) are now established international customary law, at least for those states that are a party to a sufficient number of the many texts that now make reference to them. However, the precise scope and content of, for example, the precautionary principles laid down in various treaties and 'soft law' documents is rarely duplicated, which leads to the problem of identifying what it is *exactly* that states can be said to have implicitly agreed to, e.g. the degree of risk needed to trigger the principle's application (see the WTO *Beef Hormones* case p. 172 and also Box 3.10).

(c) Generally recognized principles of law

These are of limited scope, and used where no treaty provision or custom can be utilised. They are mostly used to identify basic principles of procedure on which to decide particular issues, (e.g. evidence that is admissible). They should not be confused with the 'principles' of international environmental law which are contained either in treaties or which may be distilled from treaties, or principles inferable from customary international law (see above).

(d) Judicial decisions and the work of international jurists

Judicial decisions include not just decisions of the International Court of Justice (ICJ) and the various international tribunals that exist but also those of regional bodies (e.g. the European Court of Justice) and national courts. Previous decisions of the ICJ are binding only between the parties, and only as to the case under consideration (Article 59, ICJ Statute), hence their subsidiary nature. They do not create precedents, although in practice they function in a not too dissimilar way. The dearth of previous case law may help explain why academic writing is often referred to in international law, although this also reflects a closer relationship between legal academics and the ICJ. The work of jurists is often referred to where relatively new ground is being covered. A good example of this is the *Nuclear Tests II* case (*New Zealand v France* [1995] ICJ Rep 288) where academic opinion about the requirements of the sustainable development principle was referred to in the dissenting opinion of Judge Weeramantry.

Sources of international law—'soft law'

'Soft law' is not binding in form, is often neither clear nor specific in content, and is not readily enforceable in character. Examples include:

(a) Declarations

Two key documents in international environmental law are the 1992 Rio Declaration on Environment and Development and its Stockholm predecessor of 1972 (see p. 156). Such declarations perform a number of functions: they consolidate and restate what are already rules of customary international law (e.g. national sovereignty over natural resources); they contribute towards moving principles forward to the status of custom; and they reflect the agreed aspirations of the international community. The five Declarations of the North Sea Conferences, which fall into this last-mentioned category, have had a marked impact on EC and UK policy on, for example, stopping the dumping of industrial waste and sewage sludge at sea.

(b) Principles

In addition to hard, binding obligations (however vaguely expressed), treaties may also contain what are essentially principles. Examples include Article 3 of the 1992 Framework Convention on Climate Change, which sets out a list of principles intended to guide the parties in implementing the treaty. These include principles relating to duties owed to future generations, and to the 'common but differentiated responsibilities and respective capabilities' of the parties (see further p. 166). The elaboration of specific principles in the treaty itself, as opposed to the preamble, is increasingly common.

(c) Recommendations

Towards the 'softer' end of the spectrum, recommendations may embody the germs of principles or even treaties. Good examples are the many Recommendations of the OECD which relate directly to the development of environmental policy, e.g. on the Polluter Pays Principle (1974) and on the Use of Economic Instruments in Environmental Policy (1991).

(d) Standards

International standards can be a useful way to encourage environmentally beneficial changes in behaviour, and have varying degrees of legal force: (1) binding standards may in practice be based on international standards, e.g. EC drinking water quality standards are influenced by World Health Organization standards; (2) some non-legislative international standards provide the benchmark against which international trade restrictions are judged, for example the *Codex Alimentarius* in relation to certain food standards under the WTO agreements; (3) some international standards may be accorded the status of binding law. The EC Regulation on Environmental Management and Auditing Systems, for example, allows for participation through compliance with specified national, European and international standards, such as ISO14001 (see p. 268).

An example of the use of international standards in the English courts is the *Glacier Metal* case (Case box 6.1).

CASE 6.1 *Murdoch v Glacier Metal Co. Ltd* [1998] Env LR 732

The claimants brought a civil action arguing that they were exposed to noise levels which exceeded World Health Organization standards. Although these are numeric, they are still 'soft law' standards. Standards like these can play a part in deciding whether there is an actionable nuisance. Here, however, the mere fact that noise exceeded WHO levels was not sufficient to found a claim of nuisance; in all the circumstances the noise from the metal company was judged to be reasonable. A crucial factor was that the complainants lived on a noisy road, i.e. the locality of the area was already noisy. Indeed, it is worth noting here that the majority of the UK population live in areas that exceed WHO noise guidelines (see the Noise Incidence Study/Noise Attitude Study). See also Case box 8.1.

The adoption of soft law over binding treaty law has several theoretical advantages: domestic treaty ratification processes can be avoided; it provides an autonomous form of law-making for international organizations; it is more easily amended or replaced than treaties; it provides immediate evidence of consensus; and it is easier to reach agreement on its content *because* of its non-binding character. Soft law instruments may codify existing law; interpret/amplify treaties and other existing legal rules; act as a step in the process of concluding binding agreements; and serve as evidence of the obligations states feel they are under. They are an important part of the repetition and interplay with multilateral treaties and state practice. There is some work however which questions some of these basic assumptions. For example, in his study of the North Sea Declarations,[3] Pallemaerts argues that soft law has been mainly used not as a precursor and supplement to hard law, but as a substitute for it, satisfying symbolic needs rather than effecting real change in an instrumental way. Obviously if commitments are too soft they may be virtually meaningless. Arguably the 1992 Non-Binding Authoritative Statement of Principles on Forests (see p. 157) serves only to highlight the absence of any measure of consensus in this area at the time.

International law and policy development

The development of international environmental law can be traced back at least to the 19th century and the adoption of a number of bilateral treaties concerning fishing stocks. Thereafter, other bilateral and regional treaties were adopted, but tended to cover things like species conservation. Although some bilateral treaties sought to regulate transboundary pollution, on the whole developments in treaty law were, as Sands notes, 'ad hoc, sporadic and limited in scope'.[4] Enforcement issues, in particular, received scant attention, and many conventions were little more than 'sleeping treaties', existing only on paper because of the absence of any effective institutional and enforcement arrangements (see p. 161). There was little development of customary international environmental law.

The approach of international law generally to environmental problems is well illustrated by two international arbitrations (see Case boxes 6.2 and 6.3).

CASE 6.2 *Behring Fur Seals Arbitration* (1898) 1 Moore's Int Arbitration Awards 755

Fur seals were born on US territory but then migrated beyond the (then) three nautical mile limit of US territorial waters where they were killed by Britain sealing ships. The US alleged that the seals were being over-exploited. The panel found that the US had no right of 'protection or property' in the seals, despite the importance of their conservation for local US citizens and the threat of their extinction. The radical argument that the US was acting 'for the benefit of mankind', i.e. an 'erga omnes' or perhaps even 'common heritage' argument, was also rejected. However, the outcome of the dispute was a series of provisions, binding on the two parties, to regulate seal fishing in the area, displaying many of the features of modern conservation treaties: closed seasons, limited means of killing or taking, etc. But the decision did not bind the other states sealing in the area, who continued unrestricted until a treaty binding all relevant states was agreed in 1911.

---

3. M. Pallemaerts, *Toxics and Transnational Law* (Oxford: Hart Publishing 2003).
4. P. Sands, *Principles of International Environmental Law*, (2nd edn Cambridge: Cambridge University Press, 2003), 27.

The second decision of note was in the *Trail Smelter* arbitration.

CASE 6.3 *US v Canada* ('Trail Smelter') 3 RIAA 1907 (1941)

Sulphur emissions from a factory in Canada damaged crops, trees and pastures in the US State of Washington. The issue was not the right to exploit natural resources on Canadian territory, but rather whether the manner of doing so was limited because of neighbouring states' interests. The tribunal held that:

No state has the right to use or permit the use of its territory in such a manner as to cause injury by fumes in or to the territory of another of the properties or persons therein, when the case is of serious consequence and the injury is established by clear and convincing evidence.

For further comment on this dispute see Case box 16.1.

From these beginnings an extensive body of international treaty law has emerged, together with the more tentative emergence of new norms of customary international environmental law. Three key landmarks—the Stockholm Conference, the Brundtland Report, and the Rio Conference—deserve special mention.

The Stockholm Conference

The United Nations Conference on the Human Environment (Stockholm, 1972) was the first occasion at which the international community of states united to discuss international environmental issues more generally and more coherently. Although no treaty was signed, the conference adopted an Action Plan of 109 Recommendations and a Declaration of 26 Principles. It also adopted a resolution on institutional and financial arrangements that led, amongst other things, to the establishment of the United Nations Environment Programme (UNEP) (see p. 160).

For some, the Stockholm Declaration is the foundation of modern international environmental law. Its principles, however, are largely aspirational rather than mandatory— 'should' rather than 'shall'—and few impose clear duties on states. The key principles in the Declaration are:

- the sovereign right [of States] to exploit their own resources pursuant to their own environmental policies, and the responsibility to ensure that activities within their jurisdiction or control do not cause damage to the environment of other States or of areas beyond the limits of national jurisdiction (Principle 21);

- a requirement (though not a duty) for international cooperation to 'effectively control, prevent, reduce and eliminate adverse environmental effects resulting from activities conducted in all spheres, in such a way that due account is taken of the sovereignty and interests of all States' (Principle 24).

Perhaps more importantly, the Stockholm Conference marked the beginning of a rapid increase in the number of international environmental agreements concluded. Sixty per cent of all international environmental agreements post-date Stockholm. It has been said that the development of EC environmental law is the Conference's most tangible outcome.

The Brundtland Report

Although a strictly non-legal text, the report of the World Commission on Environment and Development (*Our Common Future*, 1987: the 'Brundtland Report') was pivotal in changing the direction of international environmental law. Its central concern was the increasing globalization of various crises (environmental, developmental, energy, etc.), and the connections between them. As it memorably summarized this: 'They are all one.' The report is a landmark in respect of modern thinking about environmental problems, and gives prominence to the language of sustainable development, defined as 'development that meets the needs of the present without compromising the ability of future generations to meet their own needs' (see further Chapter 3). However, the report provided little solid guidance on the exact components of what such a duty to future generations might entail.

What was perhaps most important was the attention it gave to the linkages between economic and environmental considerations. Amongst other things it advocated greater use of international financing of environmentally beneficial projects, and arrangements under which the debts of developing countries might be traded for commitments to conserve their biodiversity. It is not at all clear, however, that the developing world should continue to bear the burden of debts often incurred by former regimes, and although there are some examples of so-called 'debt-for-nature swaps', their use has not been extensive.

The Rio Conference

The UN Conference on Environment and Development (Rio, 1992) provided a platform for putting flesh on the bones of sustainable development in international law and to address the concern, noted in the Brundtland report, of the 'sectoral' and 'piecemeal' nature of international environmental law. Although the legal texts to emerge from Rio marked an important stage in the development of international environmental law, it can be argued that they fell some way short of providing the radical change in direction some had envisaged. The legal texts to emerge were:

(a) the Rio Declaration (see below);

(b) the Convention on Biological Diversity (see Chapter 21, especially p. 848);

(c) the Framework Convention on Climate Change (see p. 638);

(d) Agenda 21 (an 800-page global action plan on development and the environment); and

(e) (in the absence of agreement on a Global Forest Convention) a 'non-legally binding authoritative statement' of principles in this area.

In terms of the general development of customary international environmental law, however, the Rio Declaration is central. Agreed to by all 176 states attending, it is a key soft law document, and an important text as regards the consolidation of a number of principles of customary international environmental law (see Box 6.3)

BOX 6.3	**Key regulatory principles in the Rio Declaration**
Principle 7	Common but differentiated responsibilities
Principle 10	Fostering public awareness and participation in environmental decision-making
Principle 15	Precautionary approach
Principle 16	Polluter pays principle
Principle 17	Environmental impact assessment
Principles 18 and 19	Risk communication

Although the preamble states that it is reaffirming and building upon the Stockholm Declaration, important principles are conspicuously modified (Principle 21, Stockholm) or even weakened. Thus Principle 1 of Stockholm, which refers to the 'fundamental right to . . . an environment of a quality that permits a life of dignity and well-being' becomes, in Principle 1 of Rio: 'Human beings are at the centre of concerns for sustainable development. They are entitled to a healthy and productive life in harmony with nature.' Interestingly, the Brundtland Commission had mandated an expert group, from North and South, to elaborate a set of general principles which could be submitted to the UN General Assembly with a view to their forming the basis of a universal declaration.[5] Ultimately, the Commission failed to give its endorsement to this work, which might have underpinned a more ecological 'Earth Charter' akin to the Universal Declaration of Human Rights, as advocated by some states.

The effect of the Rio Declaration, therefore, was something of a mixed bag as regards the development of international environmental law and legal principles. Specifically, the double-edged quality of the explicit incorporation of developmental concerns (see Principles 2 and 3) might be seen either as an important accommodation of developing world interests or as allowing generally for 'business as usual'. Similarly, the lack of development of common heritage concepts might be viewed differently according to whether the focus is the global commons or biodiversity, and depending on whether one adopts a 'northern' or 'southern' perspective.

Post-Rio

Developments up to and beyond Rio suggest a maturing of international environmental law, although numerous problems remain. As regards treaty law, many issues continued to be dealt with sectorally, e.g. ozone depletion and biodiversity conservation. Elsewhere, specific processes or products have come under international regulation, e.g. the agreement of a 1998 Protocol on Persistent Organic Pollutants to the 1979 Convention on Long Range Transboundary Air Pollution. A range of different types of agreements are now found, from

---

5. See R. Munro and J. Lammers (eds.), *Environmental Protection and Sustainable Development: Legal Principles and Recommendations* (London: Graham and Trotman, 1987).

bilateral, sub-regional and regional agreements to global conventions, and there has been no let-up in the number of agreements reached.

Sadly, sudden shocks rather than creeping crises—Chernobyl or the 'Ozone Hole' discovery, rather than global warming forecasts and concerns about biodiversity—tend to help secure agreement. This illustrates the continuing nature of international law as, in general, reactive rather than proactive. But the Biosafety Protocol, negotiated under the Convention on Biological Diversity, can be seen as the first example of a truly precautionary international environmental agreement, since it deals with threats to biodiversity—relating to the import and export of living modified organisms—where the nature of the threat is at best theoretical (and see Box 3.9).

As with developments in the EC, there has been a perceptible shift in recent years from just promulgating substantive new agreements to putting effort into making existing agreements more effective and achieving higher levels of compliance (see, e.g., Part I of the *Programme for the Development and Periodic Review of Environmental Law for the First Decade of the Twenty First Century*, adopted by the UNEP Governing Council in 2001). Particular mention should be made in this context of the 1998 UN/ECE Convention on Access to Information, Public Participation and Decision-Making and Access to Justice in Environmental Matters (the Aarhus Convention). This Convention has not only led to a strengthening of EC law, but it has also proved to be a catalyst for giving wider civil society participatory rights in other conventions, e.g. the Biosafety Protocol. Implementation and compliance issues, and other future developments, are discussed in more depth below.

Finally, mention should be made of the Johannesburg summit—the World Summit on Sustainable Development—in 2002. This was a 10-year follow up to the Rio Conference, but the main focus of the summit was on the alleviation of poverty. No statement of principles or conventions were adopted, and the Johannesburg Declaration on Sustainable Development did not propose any specific action. A Plan of Implementation was adopted, and this does contain certain targets and timetables. As with Agenda 21, however, which it confirms and, to a limited extent, takes a step further, the commitments are generally soft, mostly only requiring states to 'encourage', 'aim' and 'promote' certain objectives.

Institutional organizations and other actors

A feature of international environmental law is the wide range of bodies involved either in the development of treaties or their enforcement. This is because, unlike international trade law, for example, there is no main or 'umbrella' convention governing the area like the General Agreement on Tariffs and Trade (GATT) regulates these aspects of international trade. Nor is there a body similar to the World Trade Organization (WTO) when it comes to compliance (international trade and the environment is discussed more fully below).

The key players in international law remain individual states (including within this definition the EC, which may speak for all 25 Member States, see p. 146). Treaties are often advocated by individual states keen to see regulation in an area of particular importance to them, or conversely opposed by states, usually for economic reasons, and of course there can be no international law without the agreement of states.

A slightly less reactive and piecemeal approach to treaty-making ought to be a responsibility of the United Nations Environment Programme (UNEP), which was established following the Stockholm Conference (see p. 156). Based in Nairobi, UNEP is now the only UN body charged exclusively with international environmental matters, and has played an important role in the development of international environmental law, not least through its promotion of numerous regional seas treaties, the 1985 Vienna 'Ozone' Convention and the 1992 Biodiversity Convention. But in general terms UNEP has been a weak institution, somewhat under-funded and of relatively low visibility.

Although not a specialist environmental body, the International Law Commission (ILC) plays an important role in the drafting of treaties and the development of customary international law and general principles, although its work is not specific to the environmental area.

An institution that deserves special mention is the International Union for the Conservation of Nature (IUCN), established in 1948, which has a unique mix of governmental and non-governmental members and a quasi-institutional status. The IUCN was an influential force behind the Convention on the International Trade in Endangered Species (CITES) treaty, and the driving force behind the influential 1982 World Charter for Nature, both of which have played an important role in bringing nature conservation to international legal attention.

Increasingly, non-governmental organizations (NGOs) representing environmental and other interests are also involved in the negotiating of international agreements. Usually this is at the fringes, although some conventions have started life as texts drafted by NGOs. A notable development was that NGOs were formally involved in the negotiation of the 1998 Aarhus Convention, not just as observers (on this convention see p. 317) and, perhaps because of its subject matter, have important rights under it, including the right to nominate candidates for election to the Convention's implementation committee. Unquestionably, environmental NGOs have played an important role in shaping the general political climate that has spawned increased activity in this area in the last 30 years.

Like negotiation, enforcement is usually handled on a treaty-by-treaty basis, and treaties tend to establish their own 'executive' organizations like the CITES Secretariat or the OSPAR Commission. Some soft law documents also do this: the UN Commission on Sustainable Development is charged with implementing Agenda 21 (see p. 157). This proliferation of organizations (and of treaties) may frustrate attempts to establish policy coherence in this area, as well as making policy and legal integration more difficult.

Environmental NGOs also have an increasingly important role in relation to compliance. Formerly, this tended to be limited to their 'observer status' at the meetings of parties to conventions such as CITES and the 1946 Whaling Convention, with some scope for bringing implementation problems to wider attention. In some cases, their role now extends more directly to enforcement matters (see Box 6.4).

BOX 6.4 **TRAFFIC and the CITES convention**

TRAFFIC is the arm of WWF (Formerly the World Wildlife Fund) which monitors wildlife trade. Over time it has moved from an informal monitoring role to a point where it now has a formal role in policing the international trade in certain elephant species under the CITES convention. Its compliance function is helped by being an international organization not tied to any particular state, which has allowed it to take an ecoregional approach. Whether rich, northern states would be equally comfortable with formal NGO involvement in monitoring compliance with treaty obligations falling mainly on them might be questioned.

In the *Shrimp/Turtle* case (see p. 170), it was notable that environmental NGOs were allowed (as a matter of discretion rather than as of right) to make unsolicited representations to the WTO. This might be seen as a first step towards their greater involvement in world trade rule-making, although this whole issue is highly controversial.[6]

Finally, the role of bodies with primarily economic remits should not be overlooked. This is seen below in relation to the role of the WTO, but other bodies are also important. The lending policy of the World Bank, for example is crucial in relation to a wide range of development projects (we discuss this in relation to the Bank's internal requirements relating to environmental impact assessment at p. 510), and the OECD has played a significant role, e.g. in promoting the use of economic instruments and in advancing the polluter pays principle (the latter being largely promoted in the interests of trade harmonization rather than environmental protection). The integration of environmental objectives into economic and other policy areas is likely to increase the number of bodies which pursue (or ought to pursue) environmental issues, especially if, institutionally, international environmental law remains as fragmented as it is.

Dispute settlement and dispute settlement bodies

There are a number of reasons why resolving disputes before international courts and tribunals is problematic:

- Generally only states may be parties (but see below).
- Both states must accept the jurisdiction of the court or tribunal; even then, taking a case is often seen as politically unfriendly, and international diplomacy is usually preferred.
- Diplomatic solutions, e.g. mediation or negotiation, are less risky, since the likelihood of accepting a politically unacceptable decision is reduced.
- Very few disputes are exclusively, or even primarily, legal disputes. For the more powerful states, the temptation is not to submit to rules which mean that their advantages, and non-legal issues, are left at the door of the court or tribunal and not exploited politically.

All of this means that non-legal routes are generally preferred, but where international disputes need to be resolved formally, they will tend to be settled by arbitration. That said, some commentators have perceived a greater role for adjudication since the mid-1990s: 'the adjudicative function has assumed increasing importance in interpreting and applying— and even developing—the rules of international law in the field of the environment.'[7] This is

6. For an analysis see R. Howse (2003) 9 European Law Journal 496.

7. P. Sands, *Principles of International Environmental Law* (Cambridge: Cambridge University Press, 2nd ed., 2003), 13.

more a reflection on how little 'environmental jurisprudence' there has been until recent years, however, than a comment on any vast expansion in environmentally related disputes being decided by courts and tribunals.

It is also worth noting that, increasingly, consultation provisions are built into treaties where other states may be affected by actual or risky activities beyond their boundaries (see generally paragraph 39.10 of Agenda 21), i.e. a preventive approach to dispute resolution is increasingly been adopted.

(a) The International Court of Justice

Very little resort is made to the ICJ, a UN body consisting of 15 judges elected by the General Assembly and the Security Council, and less than one-third of UN members have accepted its compulsory jurisdiction (although the UK has). The ICJ's case load has not been substantial, amounting to roughly three decisions per year. In addition to hearing disputes between states, however, the Court can also be asked to deliver Advisory Opinions by specialist UN agencies. A notable example was the request by the UN General Assembly in relation to the *Legality of the Threat or Use of Nuclear Weapons* 35 ILM 809 and 1343 (1996) where states' responsibilities not to cause environmental damage beyond their territories or to the global commons were explicitly recognized by the ICJ:

The existence of the general obligations of States to ensure that activities within their jurisdictions and control respect the environment of other States or of areas beyond national control is now part of the corpus of international law relating to the environment.

Although an Environmental Chamber of the ICJ was established in 1993, it has yet to hear any cases, and the full ICJ has only ever heard one contested environmental 'case' (the *Gabčíkovo-Nagymaros* case, see Case box 6.4). Because the mechanisms available in international law have been under-utilized in the environmental sphere, the extent to which they are appropriate for resolving international environmental disputes remains, perhaps at best, unclear.

CASE 6.4 The *Gabčikovo-Nagymaros* case ('Danube Dam') 37 ILM (1998) 162

In 1977 Hungary and Czechoslovakia agreed, by treaty, to dam a section of the River Danube to facilitate economic development. This meant that, over a significant stretch of the river, most of the Danube would be diverted into a vast artificial waterway. The treaty contained some very rudimentary provisions to protect the environment. Following concerns about the projects' environmental impact, Hungary abandoned construction work in 1989. In 1991 the Czechoslovak government proceeded to a provisional solution involving construction work entirely on Slovak territory, and in 1992 the Danube was diverted, leading to considerable environmental damage. Hungary then terminated the treaty. The two countries eventually agreed to take their dispute to the ICJ (see *Case concerning the Gabčíkovo-Nagymaros Project (Hungary/Slovakia)* 37 ILM (1998) 162).

The central question was whether the situation was sufficiently serious to justify Hungary's actions. As a matter of the rules on treaties, the Court accepted that concerns about its natural environment could justify this, but then found that the environmental damage was not sufficiently serious or immediate. The ICJ also found that the Czechoslovak action in 1991 was disproportionate, violating the principle that shared watercourses should be utilized 'equitably'. But nor, finally, could Hungary lawfully terminate as it had done, since the 1977 Treaty provided, in theory, a means to adjust the obligations of the parties to new conditions.

The Court therefore emphasized the extent to which relations between the two countries continued to be governed primarily through terms agreed to between the parties. However, the Court did decide that, in implementing the treaty, the parties had to give effect to new norms of international environmental law, not just to new activities but also retrospectively, and in the light of sustainable development to 'look afresh' at the environmental consequences of the project with a view to reconciling economic development and environmental protection. The Court did not elaborate further on how this was to be done (perhaps because the Court lacked a specialist knowledge of the available techniques), although the separate opinion of Vice-President Weeramantry argued for a duty of 'continuous' environmental impact assessment, i.e. one which requires continual assessment of environmental impact in the light of modern knowledge. The Court also held that the parties had to find a 'satisfactory solution' to the volume of water being released into the old bed of the Danube, a strong reading of which suggests that the obligation on the parties is not just procedural.

In some ways the judgment is unsatisfactory; for example, it did not discuss the principles that should be used when calculating environmental damage. And, taking a wider perspective, it is not clear that the problem was limited to the two parties (the area affected is Europe's last inland delta, and arguably of much wider importance).[8] However, it is clear that the Court sees some legal substance to the concept of sustainable development, even if this is couched in terms of requiring states to ask the correct questions about whether environmental protection is being integrated in decision-making, and how this is being done (e.g. by ensuring that there are processes in place, like impact assessment, to do so).

It is worth considering, since both states now belong to the European Union, whether the ICJ has any continuing jurisdiction over this case (see the discussion in Box 6.5).

A telling example of the limits of the ICJ's jurisdiction is the *Fisheries Jurisdiction Case* (Case box 6.5).

CASE 6.5 *Fisheries Jurisdiction (Spain v Canada)* (1998) ICJ Reports 432

This case was brought after Canada had used force to stop a Spanish trawler (the 'Estai') fishing in an area important for Canadian fisheries interests, but which lay beyond the 200-mile limit of its exclusive economic zone. In 1994 Canada amended its coastal fisheries law to allow it to board such vessels if they were violating a law which was ostensibly aimed to prevent over-fishing. Canada was aware of the possible inconsistencies of this national law with the international law of the sea. Hence, two days before its coastal fisheries law was amended, Canada effectively refused to let the ICJ hear cases involving Canadian fisheries conservation matters like the one at stake. This was sufficient for the ICJ to decide that it had no right to hear the complaint, even though Canada's actions were at best of dubious legality otherwise.

---

8. A useful consideration here is the role that *amicus* briefs might play; for example, the Appellate Body of the WTO has given itself a discretion to accept these, not just from NGOs but also from other states not directly affected (see, e.g. *EC/Sardines* (2002), and see p. 161).

(b) Other international courts and tribunals

In addition to the International Court of Justice there are other international courts and tribunals that may hear environmental cases. These include the Appellate Body of the World Trade Organization (see p. 168) and the International Tribunal for the Law of the Sea. As with cases that might be decided by the ICJ, however, in general it is the interests of nation states, rather than individuals, that are at stake, and there are few opportunities for individuals to raise actions in these international fora. However, the right for individuals to take cases to the European Court of Human Rights is a notable exception (see p. 78) and, as a matter of private international law, arbitration tribunals can of course decide cases involving companies where the dispute is based on international law.

Some problems of litigating international environmental disputes, especially in a European context, emerge clearly from the dispute between Ireland and the UK over the MOX plant at Sellafield (see Box 6.5).

BOX 6.5 **The Sellafield dispute**

There is an ongoing dispute between Ireland and the UK about the operation of a mixed oxide (MOX) plant at Sellafield. There are concerns about discharges into the Irish Sea, and about the movement of nuclear materials to and from the plant. This has led to distinct legal disputes involving Ireland and the UK.[9] Together they illustrate how international law might be relied on in an inter-state environmental dispute, and how international environmental law intersects with other 'layers' of law like European Community law.

First, Ireland took a case under the UN Law of the Sea Convention, on the basis, amongst other things, that the UK had not carried out a proper environmental impact assessment before the plant was authorised. In November 2001 provisional measures were sought, essentially requesting something similar to a pre-emptive injunction to stop the plant commencing operation. The Law of the Sea Tribunal decided that the situation was not sufficiently serious for this, but did require the parties to cooperate by exchanging information, monitoring risks and preventing pollution. There was, though, disagreement amongst the judges on the importance of the environmental impact assessment in deciding how risky the operation of the plant would be.

Ireland also took a case against the UK under the OSPAR treaty over access to information about the economic justification for the plant. Ultimately the arbitration tribunal decided in favour of the UK, although it did decide that the obligation on states under OSPAR to make information available was not just an obligation on competent authorities within each party to do so. This is important because it shows how international environmental law can create both obligations within and between states.

Finally, which body has jurisdiction to hear these disputes? Both Ireland and the UK are parties to the OSPAR Convention, and Member States of the EC and Euratom Treaties. For matters covered by the latter, Member States must resolve any disputes through European law. The Tribunal decided that it had jurisdiction, but in 2003 proceedings in the subsequent arbitration tribunal were suspended pending clarification on jurisdictional issues relating to EC competence

---

9. See also the domestic challenge that the plant was not 'justified' under EURATOM law: *R (Friends of the Earth) v Secretary of State for the Environment, Food and Rural Affairs* [2002] Env LR 24.

(this is being decided in Case C-459/03 *Commission v Ireland*, the eventual outcome of which will have consequences for the balance between international, EC and national law). There is a deference to the European Court of Justice to decide the balance of competence between the EC and its Member States in areas of mixed competence like marine pollution. But if the European Court of Justice decides that this is an area where the EC has competence then this means that it will in effect have to apply international law as if it were EC law. It is not clear that all the Member States would welcome this (and if it decides that the EC has exclusive competence where does this leave the OSPAR tribunal decision?).

This range of tribunals raises concerns about their ability to decide cases with an environmental dimension, and the equally important question of which body is most appropriate to decide any particular dispute. This has implications for the development of a coherent body of international environmental law, although in practice problems have not yet arisen. Indeed, there is some evidence that competition between these various tribunals may stimulate useful reforms. For example, the ICJ has finally decided that its pre-judgment provisional measure orders create binding obligations on the parties (*Germany v USA (LaGrand)* (2001) ICJ Rep 516), which could be important where there is the threat of serious irreversible environmental harm (in this sense, the very essence of provisional measures can be seen as precautionary), and it may have been that this decision was reached because bodies like the Law of the Sea Tribunal already have this power. There is also an argument that specialist tribunals like the Law of the Sea Tribunal will have greater confidence to take a purposive approach to deciding disputes, which might lead to a more responsive body of case law (a similar line of reasoning is put forward for the establishment of environmental courts in the UK, see p. 349).

Making agreements more effective

As noted above, international law cannot be 'enforced' in the same way as domestic law or even EC law. The limited role for the courts in resolving international environmental disputes is also clear. This has meant a focus, particularly in the post-Rio period, on other means of securing compliance with international agreements, especially positive inducements rather than negative sanctions. It is also important to bear in mind that few states ever have individual incentives to initiate action for non-compliance. On the other hand, states are often reluctant to delegate enforcement matters to bodies like treaty secretariats. The following conclusions may be drawn as to what makes for a more 'successful' treaty (and see also Box 6.6).

(a) Who is a party?

Attention should be paid to which states will be party to any treaty or any agreements made under treaties. A good, and perhaps unique, example is the 1979 Bonn Convention on Migratory Species, which provides for AGREEMENTS (*sic*) open to accession by all states across whose borders species migrate regardless of whether they are parties to the convention (see, e.g., the 1995 AGREEMENT on the Conservation of African-Eurasian Migratory

Waterbirds). These 'sub-treaties' allow states to benefit from positive conservation measures without signing up to the negative restrictions imposed in relation to species which the convention lists as endangered.

(b) Implementation and monitoring

Increasing attention is now paid to implementation and monitoring provisions, both at an institutional level and in relation to procedures. For example, the establishment of an active treaty secretariat, regular meetings of the parties, and sometimes provision for NGO involvement are now common. NGOs have built up considerable adeptness in gathering information about non-compliance with treaties, and passing this on either to secretariats and/or to other sympathetic states.

More generally, success is likely to correlate with the extent to which information about compliance and non-compliance is collected and disseminated to the actors concerned; this task may be given to a specialist body such as the Subsidiary Body for Implementation established under the Climate Change Convention. Adverse reports about implementation may in themselves be sufficient to edge a party into compliance. Although information is usually gathered by the parties, there are examples of the possibility of on-site monitoring responsibilities. The 1971 Ramsar Wetlands Convention, e.g. allows for monitoring at the request of the host state authorities, which may prevent allegations of 'free-riding'. The functions of the Commission established under the 1992 'OSPAR' Convention on the North Sea include requiring the assessment of compliance, and where appropriate enable it to call for necessary compliance measures. Nevertheless, there is still a general problem of ensuring adequate monitoring, even where there are treaty arrangements under which developed countries pay for monitoring in developing countries.

(c) Positive assistance

Effectively designed institutions are also better able to administer the financial aspects of treaties, which in this context mean things like financing, technology-transfer and so on. Unlike the EC, where the basic starting point is that the cost of implementing environmental policy should be borne by the Member States and that the polluter should pay (subject to certain relaxations of this principle to alleviate particular national difficulties, see p. 202) there is no such starting point in international law. Giving positive assistance is therefore an acceptable, pragmatic and increasingly central aspect of environmental treaties.

The use of positive assistance for developing states began with the London amendments (1990) to the Montreal Protocol to the 1985 Vienna Ozone Treaty, establishing the Global Environment Facility (GEF), which is also used for the 1992 Climate Change Convention, the 1992 Biodiversity Convention and the 2001 Persistent Organic Pollutants Convention. Financial aid has been given for the agreed incremental costs of compliance with control measures (1990 London Amendments) and the agreed full costs of compliance with reporting and full incremental costs to secure compliance (e.g. Climate Change Convention and the POP Convention). Multilateral development banks such as the World Bank now acknowledge the need to incorporate environmental considerations into their lending policy (see Box 14.2).

In this context the increasing attention to taking the 'common but differentiated responsibilities' of parties seriously should be noted. An example of this is the Climate

Change Convention under which no new commitments are to be imposed on developing countries. Some would see the 'flexible implementation' provisions of the 1997 Kyoto Protocol (such as the Clean Development Mechanism, which allows industrialized parties which invest in emissions reduction projects in developing country parties to use accruing reductions to offset a part of their emissions reduction commitments; see p. 640) as also falling within this general principle. Technical assistance and education provisions are also found in some treaties.

(d) Cross-checking non-compliance

One possible approach is to design agreements that reduce the practical possibilities for non-compliance. For example, the requirements in the 1973 International Convention for the Prevention of Pollution from Ships (the 'MARPOL' treaty) to install pollution-prevention equipment would have to be violated by several parties (builders, classifiers, insurers, port authorities) for the rules to be evaded. Similarly, by requiring both import and export permits for species deemed most endangered, the CITES treaty reduces the scope for individual parties to evade their obligations.

(e) Involving non-state actors

In light of the considerable difficulties of interstate actions, increasing attention is being paid to the possibility of enforcement-type measures by non-state actors: governmental and non-governmental organizations and individual legal persons (for an example see Box 6.4). As far as individual and group rights are concerned, however, even the limited mechanisms provided for in EC law (see p. 222) have yet to be replicated in international environmental treaty law more generally, although there are signs that non-state bodies will enjoy greater access to international environmental justice in the future.

BOX 6.6 **Securing compliance—the Ozone, CITES and Biological Diversity treaties compared**

Comparing these three treaties illustrates some general points about reaching effective international environmental agreements. The relative success of the Ozone treaty regime is usually said to be because of the very small number of parties (those states producing ozone-depleting chemicals) from which to get agreement; a scientific consensus over the causes of the problem; the fact that no one state could be sure that they might lose if they did not cooperate (as some states might think is the case in relation to global warming); and the relatively low costs involved in addressing the problem (including the non-availability of alternatives). The initial use in 1985 of a framework convention, fleshed out by later protocols, also helped facilitate compliance (as it has with the Climate Change Convention, which has allowed the parties to move from 'soft' standards to more binding targets for emissions reductions under the 1997 Kyoto Protocol, though even with the use of independent international scientific assessment (the IPCC) there is arguably less agreement on the underlying science, and by contrast with the Ozone treaty a relative lack of interest from industry in tackling the problem).

CITES is also widely regarded as one of the more successful treaties. Despite a large membership, the Convention pays close attention to procedural issues, establishing a funded and

effective secretariat, and requiring (and in practice, helping) states to establish national management and scientific authorities. And the import-permitting requirement applies even to parties outside the Convention which must comply with this provision on export, providing less
incentive for non-participation.

By contrast, the 1992 Biological Diversity Convention is something of a qualified disappoint-
ment. The vagueness of the language used in many of its central provisions, often hedged with
phrases such as 'as far as possible and as appropriate', testifies to the considerable difficulties in
trying to reconcile North–South tensions between environmental and development goals. Moreover, the Convention is essentially based on the route to biodiversity conservation being through
realising the commercial value of biodiversity (e.g. for pharmaceuticals), which may be optimistic.
However, it has spawned a protocol on the movement of living modified organisms, the
Cartagena Biosafety Protocol, which sets out specific rules on their import.

It seems likely that, for the short term, the emphasis will be on the implementation of
existing treaties and improving compliance, especially with framework conventions like
those on climate change and biodiversity, rather than on the negotiation of new treaties. In
this context the developing of procedural rights under international law is an important
development (see p. 175).

International trade and the environment

A potent mechanism for making international agreements effective is the prospect of trade
restrictions being imposed against non-compliant states, and some treaties (as discussed
below) provide for this. However, trade controls are often used by one state against another
when the import of goods is banned or restricted, often on ostensibly environmental
grounds. This may happen either where there is an absence of agreed international rules, or
where the importing state goes beyond the restrictions allowed for under existing international rules.

National measures may hinder free international trade in one of two main ways:

• by regulating the quality of the commodities themselves (product standards); or
• by imposing restrictions on the manner in which commodities are produced (process and
  production methods).

Process controls may be concerned with the polluting impact on a neighbouring state, or the
way in which a national or global resource is exploited. Thus, restrictions may be enacted to
protect the environment of the importing state, the exporting state or the global commons.
Regulating the extent to which measures enacted for environmental protection reasons may
unlawfully hinder international trade is therefore of central importance to environmental
law at all levels (international, EC and national) and to sustainable development.

The regulation of international trade rests primarily with bodies connected to the World
Trade Organization (WTO). The WTO has a Committee on Trade and the Environment
which is mandated to 'identify the relationship between trade measures and environmental
measures in order to promote sustainable development' and make appropriate recom-

mendations. To date, however, it has been singularly unsuccessful in doing so. This is partly because of concerns of the developing world about trade protectionism on environmental grounds, but there are also ever greater differences of opinion within the developed world, most notably between the US and the EU on the application of the precautionary principle. As a result, rule-making has in effect been left to the Appellate Body of the WTO which is effectively becoming an international court of sustainable development, since it is taking the lead in deciding, under the WTO regime, where the balance between global free trade and environmental protection lies. This has raised understandable concerns amongst environ- mentalists and others, and is in contrast to the position in the EC, for example, where the European Court of Justice decides both trade and environment cases, and cases combining both issues (although the Appellate Body has indicated that trade rules ought to defer to the rules laid down in environmental treaties; see the *Shrimp/Turtle* case below).

This section focuses on three leading cases, one decided before and two after the GATT 1994 and the WTO agreement which governs this area, the preamble to which now qualifies emphasis on the 'full use of the resources of the world' with their:

optimal use . . . in accordance with the objective of sustainable development, seeking both to protect and preserve the environment and to enhance the means for doing so in a manner consistent with the respective needs and concerns at different levels of economic development.

BOX 6.7 *'Tuna/Dolphin'*

The *Tuna/Dolphin* dispute (1992) 30 ILM 1598 centred around import restrictions imposed by the US because of concerns about the incidental effect on dolphin populations of Mexican (and other) tuna-fishing methods. The panel upheld the complaint of Mexico that this violated the GATT's 'national treatment' provision (Article III) which requires that all 'like products' receive similar treatment in international trade law, regardless of how they are produced: imported and domestic tuna had to be compared as *products*.

The issue was then whether the US action amounted to a 'quantitative restriction' under Article XI of GATT 1994, i.e. an obstacle in practice to a level playing field for international trade. This had to be determined in light of various exceptions in Article XX. This provides that so long as measures do not unjustly or arbitrarily discriminate between countries where the same condi- tions apply, or act as a disguised restriction on international trade, parties to the GATT may adopt measures including those:

(a) necessary to protect human, animal, or plant life or health (Art. XX(b)); or which

(b) [relate] to the conservation of exhaustible natural resources if such measures are made effective in conjunction with restrictions on domestic production or consumption (Art. XX(g)).

The panel held that these exceptions only applied to activities within the national jurisdiction of the country adopting the measure. By impacting on activities in international waters, the US action was unlawful. The objective of the GATT—reducing trade restrictions and barriers—would be 'eviscerated' if the US could dictate conservation measures to Mexico as a condition of Mexican access to US markets. Even if the US could take action beyond its borders, it had not shown that doing so would be necessary. There were other means by which the US might pursue its conservation objectives, e.g. through financial incentives or through negotiating international agreements.

In a further, related dispute, brought by the EC against the US (*Tuna/Dolphin II* (1994) 33 ILM 839), a GATT panel again found that US action, adopted following the initial dispute, fell foul of the GATT. But, less restrictively, it did hold that there could be circumstances where a country could employ trade restrictions to influence environmental policies beyond its territory where this was necessary to protect a global resource pursuant to an international environmental agreement and where there was a direct causal connection between the measure and the environmental objective pursued.

As a footnote, in 1992 the US, Mexico and eight other nations, responsible for 99 per cent of the tuna catch in the disputed area, did in fact sign an international accord to phase out, by 1994, the use of 'dolphin-unfriendly' nets. This reduced incidental dolphin mortalities such that the US embargo was lifted, something that it was not as a matter of law required to do because Mexico did not ask the GATT Council to adopt the panel report. Would this have happened without the unlawful unilateral action of the US to begin with? In this context note that the US had been trying for 20 years to reach an international agreement on this issue.

Being pre-WTO, *Tuna/Dolphin* is now of historic interest legally. However, the disputes raised important questions about the interplay between trade freedom and environmental protection. For example, should it be unlawful unilaterally to block the import of products because they have been produced through relatively high energy use, contributing to global warming? How does the distinction between product and process restrictions allow for the polluter pays principle to be given effect to?

To understand current WTO law on trade and the environment, two key post-1994 disputes are examined (Boxes 6.8 and 6.9).

BOX 6.8 'Shrimp/Turtle'

The US required any state exporting shrimp to the US to show that its harvesting methods did not endanger sea turtles, or were at least regulated and no less damaging to sea turtle conservation than standards actually achieved in the US. *US—Import Prohibition of Certain Shrimp and Shrimp Products* (1999) 38 ILM 121 (*Shrimp/Turtle*) confirms that a two stage test will be used in relation to Article XX of GATT 1994: first, provisional justification if the measure correctly comes within one of the exceptions; secondly, further appraisal of these measures under the introductory clauses of Article XX.

On the first point, the US measures were acceptable under Article XX(g). The view of a previous panel, that 'exhaustible natural resources' were not to be limited to non-renewable resources such as minerals but extended to any finite resource and therefore covered living resources, was reaffirmed. But it appears that the turtle species in question were 'exhaustible' because of their recognized endangered status, not because action was required to prevent endangering them. (In *US—Gasoline* (1996) 35 ILM 603 clean air was held to be an exhaustible natural resource.) Nevertheless, the remaining requirements to come within Article XX(g) were fulfilled: the measure 'related to conservation' in light of an assessment of its primary aim, having regard both to its purpose and effect, and because it was sufficiently 'even-handed' as between imported and domestic shrimp. Because it satisfied Article XX(g), the Appellate Body did not need to consider also whether it was 'necessary' under Article XX(b).

The US measures were therefore substantively acceptable. However, they were an 'arbitrary or unjustified discrimination between countries where the same conditions prevail'. As to unjustified discrimination, four points were central. First, in practice the US rules forced importing states to adopt US policy without any flexibility of approach, i.e. the US only looked to see whether importing states required the fitting of 'turtle excluder devices' (TEDs), as required in the US, rather than authorizing comparable measures. (Using its own inspectors to certify was hardly helpful, and raises the question of whether something closer to 'mutual recognition' would have been preferable.) Secondly, the US also banned the import of shrimp caught by boats using TEDs if they did so in the waters of otherwise non-compliant states. Thirdly, the US had failed to engage the importing states in serious negotiations for an international treaty on sea turtle conservation before imposing trade sanctions. This was in violation of several important statements emphasizing multilateralism, including Principle 12 of the Rio Declaration. Finally, the US had provided different levels of support through technology transfer to different countries, affecting the ability of all states to comply on equal terms. The measures were also 'arbitrary' because of their informality, lack of transparency and absence of procedural protections, e.g. the absence of appeal or review rights.

What comes through clearly from *Shrimp/Turtle* is the evident tension between the interests of nation states and a 'common heritage' approach. 'Go it alone' approaches are strongly rejected, the Appellate Body encouraging the negotiation of multilateral agreements in the interests of opening up international decision-making to those affected.[10] (This is consistent with what the WTO calls its preference for a 'rules-based' approach to free trade; see below.) This does not mean, though, that international agreements must in fact be concluded. This was one of the arguments put forward by Malaysia in a subsequent challenge to the legality of Revised Guidelines issued by the US relating to its national conservation laws, which required importing states—if they did not use TEDs—to enforce the use of 'comparably effective' regulatory programmes. In *Shrimp/Turtle II* (2001), the Appellate Body thought this would go too far, because in practice it would give a veto to individual states, and found that the US had been engaged in sufficiently, and comparably, good faith efforts to negotiate international agreements with the countries concerned. The second challenge raised by Malaysia was that the Guidelines were insufficiently flexible, and still unilaterally imposed US standards on exporters. This claim was also rejected, because on their face the Guidelines did allow other countries' sea turtle conservation programmes to be considered when certification was being sought. This part of the judgment is seen as aimed at relieving importing states of the burden of having to consider the conditions in all exporting states before imposing a trade restriction (a concern that had arisen following the first decision in *Shrimp/Turtle*).

---

10. The dispute also deals rather unconvincingly with the question of jurisdictional limits to nation states' legitimate interests, doing little more than stating on the basis of flimsy reference to 'sustainable development', rather than positively arguing towards, the connection in law between the turtle populations involved and the US (though comparing the approach here with *Tuna/Dolphin* suggests a relaxation of the 'territorial nexus' issue).

Trade-environment disputes are not just covered by the GATT 1994. Also worth mentioning are the General Agreement on Trade in Services (GATS) which might be relevant to the greening of the financial services market, and two codes dating from 1994: the Agreement on Technical Barriers to Trade (the TBT Agreement) and the Agreement on the Application of Sanitary and Phytosanitary Measures (the SPS Agreement). The latter relates to additives, toxins etc. in food, drinks, and animal feed and is less relevant to environmental protection as discussed in this book although, subject to the Cartagena Biosafety Protocol, it is relevant to disputes about trade in products containing genetically modified organisms. It is also worth noting that disputes involving the SPS Agreement may shed light on some of the principles of environmental law, as the *Beef Hormones* (1997) case did when it rejected the precautionary principle as a general principle of international law but accepted that it could be an interpretive principle in risk assessment e.g. by allowing states to be guided not just by majority scientific opinion but also by the views of qualified scientists reaching different conclusions, an approach subsequently taken as regards the GATT in the *Asbestos* case below. (On *Beef Hormones* see further p. 72.) The TBT Agreement is perhaps of more direct relevance to trade-environment disputes, because it applies to product standards and process and production methods, and includes, for example, packaging rules, eco-labels and other regulatory controls. However, there is as yet no 'case law' from the WTO on this code.

The *Asbestos* case (Box 6.9) raises important issues about the interpretation of the GATT and its relationship with the TBT Agreement. Although for technical reasons it did not have to decide on the latter it seems that both agreements operate concurrently to any dispute. This means that even where the TBT Agreement is involved, the general GATT rules will still have a role to play (further discussion of the TBT Agreement is outside the scope of this analysis).

BOX 6.9 *'EC Asbestos'*

Asbestos is a known carcinogen. France banned the import of asbestos, and construction products containing asbestos, because of health concerns. Canada challenged the French law. In *EC— Measures Affecting Asbestos and Asbestos-Containing Products* (2001) 40 ILM 497 the Appellate Body upheld the import ban.

On whether, for the purposes of Article III(4) of the GATT, the banned asbestos products were 'like' alternative construction products, the Appellate Body essentially noted that because the two products were physically different, Canada had a higher hurdle to overcome in showing that they were 'like' because they were competing for the same share of the market. However, because of the health risks from the products containing asbestos fibres, this burden had not been discharged. This is an important development, because it shows a certain sensitivity to the *effect* of products when judging whether one product is 'like' another. (In deciding that products such as asbestos that are known killers are 'like' those that are not, the earlier Panel reached what many would consider an outrageous decision.) The Appellate Body also went on to note that, even if two products were 'like' each other, this does not mean that they must be treated the same by national regulations. There must still be some form of 'less favourable treatment', i.e. trade protectionism, as between domestic and imported products. This might be used to argue that differences in process and production methods could be relied upon as a ground for restricting imports—contrary to the *Tuna/Dolphin* decision—so long as imported products are not treated any less favourably than domestic ones.

As to Article XX, if there is a scientifically proven risk to health then 'WTO members have the right to determine the level of protection of health that they consider appropriate.' They can do this either because of the degree of seriousness of the risk (which can be a qualitative judgement about what is acceptable in the importing country) or the likelihood of it occurring. In effect, the greater the product of these two factors—quality and quantity—the more that the importing state's actions will be 'necessary' for the purposes of Article XX(b). The Appellate Body therefore took a less restrictive view of what this test requires than it had previously done, and by weighing the harm against the impact of the trade restriction took an approach which is similar to the approach of the European Court of Justice to trade/environment cases where the proportionality of the restrictions is an important factor (see p. 214). A measure will be necessary if no GATT-consistent alternative is reasonably available and provided it entails the least degree of inconsistency with other GATT provisions.

The *Asbestos* decision clearly shifts the emphasis of the Appellate Body away from a very pro-trade position, and it might be seen in part as a response to criticisms of the WTO system which flared up into riots at Seattle in 1999. It is therefore seen in broadly positive terms from an environmental perspective. (Indeed, note that in *Shrimp/Turtle* the US made no attempt to argue that shrimp caught with or without TEDs were not 'like products'.) But some care needs to be taken in assessing just how far-reaching the decision is. In accepting that health concerns could mean that products with the same end use were not 'like products', the Appellate Body emphasized that they would not be seen as alike by *consumers* of the products. This is some way from saying that *any* different effect that a product has will justify treating it as not 'like' a product that has the same end use, and in particular it does not necessarily mean that if harm to the environment is caused by making a product in one country but not another, that the latter will be able to block its import. The Appellate Body is still picking its way carefully and cautiously through issues of high political sensitivity. Or, as one commentator has put it: 'The case does not clarify; it restrains the strongest form of free trade impulse, in favour of ambiguity and political peace' (S. Dillon, *International Trade and Economic Law and the EU* (Oxford, Hart Publishing, 2002), 157).

Trade and environment—assessment and future developments

Given the number of important multilateral environmental agreements there are now, a key issue is where the balance will be struck between these and the GATT/WTO. Some, for example, would like to see the GATT amended to insert a defence that action was taken pursuant to treaties like CITES, the Basle Convention on Hazardous Wastes, the Montreal Ozone Protocol, or the Kyoto Protocol, all of which provide for enforcement through trade restrictions. The basic rule of international law, however, is that the treaty that is later in time prevails, and all of those just mentioned pre-date the 1994 GATT/WTO. There is a practical answer to this, which is that it is unlikely that two parties to such an agreement will raise a dispute over GATT-incompatibility. From a legal perspective, however, it is clear from cases like *Shrimp/Turtle* that the Appellate Body is keen that states seek to resolve their differences through genuine multilateral agreements, which suggests that it would look favourably at a specialist environmental treaty over the general provisions of the GATT. There appears to be some acceptance of this as a matter of political reality. For example, the

Cartagena Biosafety Protocol expressly takes precedence over the rules of international trade, even though the pro-GMO-trade 'Miami' group of states resisted this.

From the *Asbestos* case it is clear that the resolution of trade-environment disputes is in a state of flux, and many key questions remain undecided. For example, it is not clear how the increasing use of packaging and labelling requirements will be viewed.[11] And future disputes about what are 'like' products can be expected.

What does seem clear is that global trade rules have a much greater real-world impact than environmental treaties do. As the Executive Director of UNEP has said:

International governance structures, and the rules that flow from them, must have the capacity to shape national policy. While international trade policy is rather effective in this regard, the impact of international environmental agreements is often less evident.[12]

Indeed, although the details of GATT law are important, as Vogel points out the debate 'reflects a more profound clash of culture and world views between the trade community and environmentalists'.[13] This clash is based in part upon competing views of whether security through free trade, or environmental security, is the more fragile. But it is also based on disagreement over the extent to which unilateral action contributes either to the progressive ratcheting up of international standards or to a deregulatory 'race to the bottom', raising difficult questions concerning sustainable development. It should be noted that in *Tuna/Dolphin*, however, the greatest reduction in dolphin deaths occurred before the import ban, by which time there was no evidence that the dolphin populations affected were endangered. Trade restrictions may serve only to depress the commercial value of natural resources in other states, driving up the number of units (of tropical hardwood trees, of endangered species) that must be sold to maintain revenues, and driving down the incentives of national governments to invest in measures (e.g. anti-poaching measures or habitat conservation) to conserve the resource.

Whatever the *actual* rules and resolution of disputes, however, there is a general feeling that international trade law has a 'chilling effect' on the setting of environmental and other standards both within the EC and within individual nation states. There is perhaps an understandable caution about adopting laws on the basis of how the Appellate Body might be likely, in the future, to decide the issue, and a focus instead on how it would be decided according to a cautious reading of the present, limited, body of 'case law'. On the other hand, it may also suit some rule-makers to be able to point to international trade rules as a reason for regulatory inaction in tackling a problem.

For the immediate future, however, states are likely to prefer the speed and certainty provided by the WTO over dispute resolution under multilateral environmental agreements, which typically lack these features.[14] This has important implications for the development of customary principles of international law, which may become biased towards free trade concerns until such time as there is a greater shift in thinking in the WTO

---

11. Which throw up their own problems; see H. Ward (1997) 6 RECIEL 139.

12. UN Doc E/CN.17/2002/PC.2/7 (19 Dec. 2001), para. 153.

13. D. Vogel, *Trading Up: Consumer and Environmental Regulation in a Global Economy* (Harvard: Harvard University Press, 1995), 134.

14. See J. Cameron, 'Dispute Settlement and Conflicting Trade and Environment Regimes', in A. Fijalkowski and J. Cameron (eds), *Trade and the Environment: Bridging the Gap* (London: Earthscan, 1998).

towards realizing the effective integration of environmental protection into global trade rules.[15]

Future directions in international environmental law and policy

In addition to greater attention to matters of compliance, it is arguable that a mix of approaches will colour the future of international environmental law. Increased attention is likely to be paid to individuals and to organizations, rather than the traditional 'state-centric', intergovernmental approach of international law, although not necessarily through granting substantive individual environmental rights.

(a) Rights-based approaches: substantive rights

Although clearly rejected at Rio (see p. 158) there have been some attempts to advance a substantive environmental human right, most notably in a report by a UN Sub-Commission on Prevention of Discrimination and Protection of Minorities on the relationship between human rights and the environment.[16] Finding that over 60 national constitutions contained some form of environmental rights protection, the report concluded that there had been 'a shift from environmental law to the right to a healthy and decent environment', comprising substantive rights to life, health, and development. This, it claimed, was rather more than a 'greening' of international human rights law, and the report proposed the adoption of Principles of Human Rights and the Environment which would be enforceable by human rights organizations. There is little willingness within the international community to sign up to a rights-based approach, however, and the Principles are making no progress in the UN system. There are probably several reasons for this, including the large number of international environmental treaties that now exist and the general turn away from substantive to procedural rights. There is a similar lack of enthusiasm for granting specific rights to future generations (e.g. enforceable by a global trustee).

This vacuum might be filled by other means. Although an individual right to sustainable development is unlikely to emerge, with a preference for operationalizing sustainable development in procedural ways, it is possible that existing rights—such as the right to life—might be reinterpreted creatively. This is the approach taken in the Ksentini Report, and has been taken most notably by the Indian courts.[17]

(b) Procedural rights

There is a definite shift towards establishing and protecting procedural rights in international environmental law. This can be seen in, for example, Principle 10 of the Rio

---

15. An excellent analysis of how the de-regulatory WTO might nevertheless accommodate environmental protection norms in the way that the EC has done is contained in J. Scott (2004) European Journal of International Law 307.

16. F. Z. Ksentini, *Human Rights and the Environment*, UN Doc. E/CN.4/Sub.2/1994/9, 6 July 1994.

17. For an excellent summary see M. Anderson, 'Environmental Protection in India', in A. Boyle and M. Anderson (eds), *Human Rights Approaches to Environmental Protection* (Oxford: Clarendon Press, 1996).

Declaration. This notes that environmental problems are best handled with the participation of all concerned citizens, at the relevant level. Specifically, at national level individuals should have access to publicly held environmental information and the opportunity to participate in decision-making processes, while states should foster public awareness and participation by making information widely available, and provide effective access to judicial and administrative proceedings. More specific elaboration of procedural rights is contained in the 1998 UN/ECE Aarhus Convention on Access to Information, Public Participation in Decision-making and Access to Justice in Environmental Matters (discussed in more detail at p. 317). References there to 'the public concerned' includes references to non-governmental organizations promoting environmental protection, which are deemed to have a sufficient interest in environmental decision-making.

This leads to a slightly different point about procedural rights, which is that as individuals and companies increasingly become the subject of international environmental law then pressure may build to accommodate their interests at all levels of law-making and dispute resolution (see, for existing accommodation, the acceptance of amicus briefs by the WTO, at p. 161). As Sands notes of the emissions trading regimes established under the 1992 Climate Change Convention (see p. 638), 'If these instruments create rights and obligations for the private sector, then why should they be content to be excluded from the legislative process or subject to traditional intergovernmental dispute settlement processes?'[18]

(c) Liability rules

There are existing examples of international treaties providing for liability rules in the event of damage to the environment. The best-known examples, relied on most often in practice, are the conventions agreed under the MARPOL Treaty on marine pollution which provide for strict liability and compensation funds—financed by shippers—for the movement of oil (see p. 392). Principle 13 of the Rio Declaration requires states to cooperate in agreeing further liability rules, and more recently liability provisions have been agreed for the marine movement of other hazardous and noxious substances, and the transboundary movement of hazardous wastes (although the latter have been criticised because a compensation fund is not established). There is also the prospect of liability and compensation rules being agreed in other specialist areas (the parties to the 2000 Biosafety Protocol have essentially agreed to try to negotiate liability rules by 2005).

There is some enthusiasm for internationally agreed liability rules, although at the moment their application tends to be limited to particularly hazardous activities where compensation funds are seen as necessary to alleviate public fears. From an international law point of view, what is interesting is that they shift the focus away from the liability of the state and on to individual operators and (in the case of compensation funds) industrial sectors. There is therefore a role for state responsibility only where private parties are not liable (e.g. if liability is fault-based and they have not been at fault) or where the amount of damage exceeds the amount payable under the compensation fund. They can therefore be seen as a mechanism for promoting compliance with international agreements.

18. P. Sands (2001) 33 NYU J Int'l L & Pol 527.

(d) Duty-centred approaches

A range of duty-centred approaches now exists. In national law, many constitutions include provisions requiring either individuals or the state (or both) to protect the environment. The Spanish Constitution, for example, provides that: 'Everyone has the right to enjoy an environment suitable for the development of the person as well as the duty to preserve it' (1978, Article 45), while some texts also require states or citizens to 'improve' the environment (e.g. Turkish Constitution 1982, Art. 56). Perhaps the starkest example of legislating for individual responsibility is contained in the 1998 Rome Statute of the International Criminal Court, Article 8 of which provides for an international war crime against the environment.

(e) Institutional reform

The creation of some kind of global environmental agency has been mooted since before the Stockholm Conference. There is an argument that the present diversity of environmental treaty regimes, and of global institutions, is problematic. As Charnovitz has said, 'If an organization chart of world environmental governance existed, its incoherence would be exhibit A for reformers.'[19] Various reforms have been suggested to tackle this, including grouping treaties under general 'umbrellas' e.g. the marine environment, or biodiversity, in order to streamline some of the administration and make negotiating amendments and new treaties easier. On the other hand, the development of environmental treaties, and treaty law generally, has probably been helped rather than hindered by being negotiated on an issue by issue basis, and there is little enthusiasm for a global body to deal with all environmental treaties in the way that the WTO deals with the main trade conventions.

⇄ CHAPTER SUMMARY

1   Many environmental problems cannot be resolved at national level and require some form of regulation at the transboundary, regional or global level.

2   International environmental law is comprised mainly of treaties and customary law, but other sources such as the work of legal writers are also called upon. Although few international disputes ever reach courts or tribunals, the judgments in these also make up international law. Taking these sources together, international law often has an emergent quality, which can make it difficult to state with certainty what it requires.

3   Public international law is mainly about the rights and duties of states and—in the environmental sphere at least—has not been greatly concerned with the rights of individuals within states. However, the limits to this approach are beginning to appear, not least because some international law obligations now effectively 'bite' on individuals and companies.

4   In the UK, international treaties only have direct legal force once an Act of Parliament gives effect to them, though they can also be used to interpret other legislation.

5   The main tension in international environmental law is between the sovereign right of states to use their own natural resources and choose their own levels of environmental protection and development objectives, and their duties not to cause harm to other states or to the global commons.

---

19. 'A World Environment Organization' (2002), 27 Columbia Journal of Environmental Law 323 at 340.

6 There are hundreds of international environmental agreements; enforcing them is difficult because there is not usually an enforcement body with the power to impose effective sanctions. This means that a range of other methods are often used to try to induce compliance.

7 Most states belong to the World Trade Organisation and the rules of international trade can affect how the UK or the EC regulates for environmental protection. The central concern in this area is striking an appropriate balance between the interests of states to trade freely and to maintain control over questions of environmental and natural resource protection.

Q QUESTIONS

1 How sovereign are nation states when it comes to actions that *will* be harmful to the environment? That *may* be harmful to the environment?

2 How are environmental interests (as you define these) represented in international law?

3 What application does the polluter pays principle have in international environmental law?

4 Should environmentalists be concerned about international trade law? Consider, for example, the following:

   a State A imposes a product-based energy tax to imported products.

   b State B imposes a process-based energy tax to imported products.

   c State C imposes a tax based on the recycled content of bottles.

   d State D imposes a ban on fur from animals caught in the wild, but allows the import and marketing of fur from animals reared in fur farms.

   e State E requires all natural products circulating in its market to be labelled with information about the impact on biodiversity of their production.

   What further information would you need?

5 You are instructed by an NGO to draft an international treaty on conserving ancient woodlands. Prepare a short paper on the main legal and policy issues that will need to be addressed.

FURTHER READING

There are two excellent texts on international environmental law: P. Birnie and A. Boyle, *International Law and the Environment* (2nd edn, Oxford: Oxford University Press, 2002) and P. Sands, *Principles of International Environmental Law* (2nd edn, Cambridge: Cambridge University Press, 2003). The former is a little more doctrinal, while the latter is slightly more comprehensive, especially on the tools of international environmental law, and contains very useful bibliographic sources (in much more depth than we can provide here); it has also a more up to date companion volume containing the main treaties (P. Sands and P. Galizzi, *Documents in International Environmental Law* (Cambridge: Cambridge University Press, 2004)). A rather more forthright approach is taken in V. Nanda and G. Pring, *International Environmental Law and Policy for the 21st Century* (Ardsley: New York Transnational, 2003). Primary jurisprudential materials are contained in C. Robb (ed.) *International Environmental Law Reports*, the three published volumes of which cover 'Early Decisions' (1999), 'Trade and Environment' (2001), and 'Human Rights and Environment' (2001), with further volumes in the pipeline.

Valuable collections of essays are A. Boyle and D. Freestone (eds), *International Law and Sustainable Development* (Oxford: Oxford University Press, 1999) and R. Hurrell and D. Kingsbury (eds), *The International Politics of the Environment* (Oxford: Clarendon Press, 1992) (placing international law in its wider context) and, on compliance, J. Cameron, J. Werksman and P. Roderick (eds), *Improving Compliance with International Environmental Law* (London: Earthscan, 1996) (which combines general discussion and examples, many about climate change) and J. Werksman (ed.), *Greening International Institutions* (London: Earthscan, 1996).

J. Vogler, *The Global Commons: A Regime Analysis* (Chichester: Wiley, 1995) is a good account of this particular aspect to international law, and contains a very clear summary of the argument surrounding the 'tragedy of the commons' thesis. D. French 'A reappraisal of sovereignty in the light of global environmental concerns' (2001) 21 Legal Studies 376 examines the tension between the control of states over their own resources and their obligations not to cause environmental harm.

On the work of the ICJ, there is a symposium on the *Gabčíkovo-Nagymaros* case in (1997) *Yearbook of International Environmental Law*. R. Clark and M. Sann (eds), *The Case Against the Bomb* (Rutgers University School of Law at Camden, 1996) provides a first hand account of the ICJ's 'Nuclear Weapons' Advisory Opinion, and is an excellent way in to understanding the working of the ICJ. The role of national courts in implementation is researched in a 12-country study (including the UK), the results of which are published as M. Anderson and P. Galizzi (eds), *International Environmental Law in National Courts* (London: BIICL, 2002).

For keeping up-to-date, the *Review of European Community and International Environmental Law (RECIEL)* and *Environmental Policy and Law* are regular and informative; the former has themed issues, of which vol. 11(2) (2002) is a 10-year on follow up to Rio and has issues on climate change, biodiversity and trade, while vol. 12(1) considers the consequences of the Johannesburg Summit. The *Yearbook of International Environmental Law* contains both sectoral and country reports (including the implementation of international environmental law), recent primary materials and a useful bibliography, as well as lengthy articles. *International Legal Materials* (ILM) provides most of the major treaties and decisions although the internet is now the main way of keeping up-to-date.

@ WEB LINKS

There is, as yet, no single portal for international environmental law, though the *Electronic Information System for International Law*, produced by the American Society of International Law, contains links to most of the key conventions and many of the secretariats <www.eisil.org>. Every international organization, and most international agreements, have their own web sites. These are an invaluable way of becoming familiar with how international law regimes (treaties and soft law and the relevant institutions) operate. The fastest way to access these is via general search engines like google. The internet is also the primary way of accessing judicial material, such as judgments of the ICJ <www.icj-cij.org>, the International Tribunal for the Law of the Sea <www.itlos.org> and WTO decisions <www.wto.org>, and see also <www.worldtradelaw.net>. Finally, <www.wcl.american.edu/environment/iel> contains a neat set of links to accompany D. Hunter, J. Salzman, and D. Zaelke, *International Environmental Law and Policy* (2nd edn, Foundation Press, 2002), which is also recommended.

7 The European Community and the environment

 Overview

Notwithstanding its economic basis, the EC has long been a major source of British environmental protection law. It also has a central and profound influence on the direction of environmental policy, both at a Community level and within each Member State. As a result, every subject covered by this book is affected, either directly or indirectly, by the activities of the EC.

After a brief overview of how the EC shapes British environmental law and policy, the structure of this chapter is as follows. We start by providing an introductory guide to EC law, outlining the key institutions of the EC, the different sources of EC law and how EC law is made. We then look at the more substantive elements of EC law as they affect environmental protection, beginning with the policy and constitutional bases for EC environmental law and giving a flavour of the scope of EC environmental legislation before considering the scope for national standards to exceed those set at EC level or to disrupt free trade between the Member States. We then look at the key issue of trying to ensure that EC environmental law is actually complied with in the real world, while we conclude by offering some thoughts on the impact of the EC on British environmental law, policy and practice.

Alongside this chapter you may also find it useful to read those sections of Chapter 8 which outline some of the key historical differences of approach between the UK and other prominent Member States to environmental regulation, and to have access to key Articles of the EC Treaty (these can be found via the Web Links given at the end of this chapter). Most of the environmental laws mentioned in this chapter are covered in much greater depth in the relevant chapters of this book.

At the end of this chapter you should be able to:

✔ Understand how the EC is organized and the roles of the main institutions.
✔ Identify the main sources of EC environmental law, and assess the legal bases and policy justifications for EC environmental law.
✔ Appreciate the range of EC environmental legislation, and the degree of flexibility given to Member States in setting standards.
✔ Assess the extent to which the Member States may set standards above those in EC environmental laws, or which potentially hinder other objectives of the EC such as trade freedom.
✔ Evaluate the particular challenges of securing compliance with EC environmental laws, including the role of the European Court of Justice.

✔ Appreciate the impact of the EC on national environmental law and policy, and assess the role played by national courts.

Key developments in EC environmental law and policy

What might be considered the defining moments in the development of EC environmental law and policy are given in the following Table.

1957	European Economic Community (Treaty of Rome). No mention of the environment.
1967	First 'environmental' common market directive (on labelling dangerous products).
1972	UN Stockholm Conference. Seen as the catalyst for...
1973	First Environmental Action Programme. UK joins the EEC.
1973–86	Expansion of EC environmental law in water, waste and, latterly, air pollution.
1980	Common market measures can lawfully pursue environmental objectives (ECJ).
1985	Environmental protection is 'one of the Community's essential objectives' (ECJ).
1987	Single European Act. Environmental Title into EC Treaty. Increased emphasis on implementation following the high-profile 'Seveso' incident.
1987–93	Rapid expansion of environmental legislation, mostly to complete the single market.
1988	Environmental protection is a 'mandatory requirement' of the EC (ECJ).
1989	Separate Environment Directorate-General in the EC Commission.
1990	European Environment Agency agreed to (begins work in 1993).
1992	Seminal Fifth Environmental Action Programme, stressing 'shared responsibility' and greater flexibility in rule-making.
1993	Maastricht Treaty adds the precautionary principle to the Environmental Title.
1996	Expanded scope for individual enforcement of directives in national courts (ECJ).
1997	Amsterdam Treaty. Promoting sustainable development becomes an objective of the EC. EC Treaty also requires environmental protection to be integrated across other policies.
1998	'Cardiff process' begins, furthering environmental policy integration.
2001	EC Sustainable Development Strategy.
2004	Enlargement. Political agreement on an EU Constitution.
2005	Popular rejection of EU Constitution in French and Dutch referenda.

The EC and British environmental law and policy

There are four main ways in which the EC plays a role in shaping British environmental law and policy:

- Some pieces of EC legislation lay down rules and standards that are directly enforceable in Member States without any need for further implementation. In these cases EC law is British law.

- Other pieces of EC legislation are addressed to Member States and require changes in British law or administrative practice. This is normally the situation in relation to environmental legislation, because of the predominant use of directives, which are not necessarily directly effective within Member States. British law is therefore not the same as EC law until the EC law has been implemented. In such cases the precise role of the EC in initiating the change is often forgotten, since the domestic legislation resulting from the EC requirements will constitute the law which is applied in practice. An important point to note is that EC law and British law often differ in such circumstances, because EC law frequently consists of aims and goals and procedural frameworks rather than precise legal rules, and allows for discretion in the Member States as to how and (sometimes) when to implement it.

- The third role is somewhat wider and rests upon the constitutional position that the UK occupies as a Member State of the EC. The EC not only passes environmental laws, it has an environmental policy. This policy and the general economic and environmental principles which underpin it exert an important influence on British policy-making and on British attitudes towards environmental law and its enforcement. The direction in which environmental protection will go therefore depends as much on wider European attitudes (and the changing nature of the EC itself as new Member States join) as it does on ingrained British ideas, although of course British ideas will in turn help to mould the general EC view and to affect the attitudes of the other Member States (see Box 7.1).

BOX 7.1 The impact of EC environmental law and policy on UK law

Comparing the two most wide-ranging pollution control statutes enacted in the last 30 years illustrates the expanding influence of the EC on British environmental law. The Control of Pollution Act 1974 was driven entirely by British concerns and priorities, whereas the Environmental Protection Act 1990 was heavily influenced, and in some places driven, by EC law; several sections specifically implemented EC environmental directives (e.g. on GMOs) or were drafted with current or proposed EC laws in mind (e.g. on waste) and much of the Act was drafted to take full account of directives on e.g. air and water pollution. This was the case, for example, with integrated pollution control (IPC), which the 1990 Act introduced as a specifically national measure. But the case of IPC also shows how British environmental law and policy may in turn shape EC law; in 1996 the EC adopted a directive on Integrated Pollution Prevention and Control which drew heavily on the UK's IPC law for its inspiration. This is just one example of how the UK has become less a 'taker' and more a 'shaper' of EC environmental policy and law (see also p. 90 and, on IPPC, ch. 20).

• Finally, the economic policies of the EC have a profound effect on the direction of both EC and domestic environmental law. Environmental protection cannot be isolated from economic policy and the substantial completion of the single internal market by the end of 1992 had significant spin-off effects—none of which were formally assessed before, and most of which were negative—on the environment. Indeed, many 'green' commentators would argue that the economic policies of the EC, which continue to emphasise economic growth and economies of scale in industrial and agricultural production, remain antithetical to the achievement of the aims of a clean environment and conservation of natural resources.

An introductory guide to EC law

The nature of the EC

The EC is more than just a free trade agreement between (now) 25 European States. It has institutions and law-making powers of its own, making it a form of supranational state in which the Member States have restricted their sovereign rights, albeit within limited fields (although for political reasons the extent of this is often denied).

The activities over which the EC has powers are set out in the Treaties that establish the EC, which are effectively the EC's constitution. In the past there have been three Treaties and three linked Communities, the European Economic Community (EEC), the European Coal and Steel Community (ECSC) and the European Atomic Energy Community (Euratom). It has been the EEC, established by the Treaty of Rome 1957, which has been the central Community and to which environmental policy relates.[1] The Treaty of Rome was amended by the Single European Act 1986, which first introduced references to the environment. All the Treaties were further amended by the 1992 'Maastricht' Treaty on European Union, which came into force on 1 November 1993 and altered the name of the EEC Treaty to the EC Treaty. In this book all references to Treaty Articles are to the EC Treaty, as amended. Only aspects relating to the EC, which (together with foreign and defence matters, and justice and home affairs) forms one of three 'pillars' of the European Union (EU) are considered here, so references are to the EC rather than the EU.

Further amendments to the EC Treaty were made under the Treaty of Amsterdam which came into force on 1 May 1999. The Amsterdam Treaty renumbered the EC Treaty. References below are generally to the new articles, even where what we are referring to is pre-1999 (these are given in the form 'Article 6 EC', meaning Article 6 of the EC Treaty, and so on). As the Treaty has generally been added to over time, rather than re-written, this should not be too misleading. The Treaty of Nice put in place many of the necessary changes to allow for the accession of 10 new Member States in 2004 (known as 'enlargement'), but did not make any significant changes to the Treaty Articles relating to the environment.

At the time of writing, political agreement on a new European Constitution has been reached, but the Constitution has yet to come into force. We have tried to make reference to

---

1. The Euratom Treaty does not have an environmental title or policy, and so formally at least remains directed at promoting nuclear energy rather than dealing with issues like the disposal of hazardous nuclear waste.

any significant changes that may be made by the Constitution (and, conversely, problem areas left unaltered by the Constitution) in footnotes at the appropriate place, but it must be noted that there is no guarantee that the Constitution will be ratified in its present form (or even come into force at all).

The institutions of the EC

The four main EC institutions[2] are the Commission, the Council of Ministers, the Parliament, and the European Court of Justice. Each has powers and duties specified in the Treaty and an obligation to further the aims of the EC.

(a) The Commission

The Commission is the executive of the EC. It consists of 25 independent members appointed by the Member States (one from each Member State), serviced by officials.[3] The Commission has responsibility for implementing EC policies, including responsibility for enforcing EC law, in which role it has certain investigatory powers (although nothing like the powers of the Commission in areas like competition policy).

It is the Commission which draws up the environmental action programmes and drafts proposed EC legislation. (Commission documents are given a reference in the form of COM(date)(number), and on occasion we use this as a shorthand for a legislative proposal or Commission report.) By means of information agreements with the Member States, the Commission is informed of proposals for domestic legislation and these often give rise to a Commission proposal for a common policy across the EC. There are also some situations where the Commission makes substantive decisions; an example is its role in deciding whether damaging development may go ahead on very important wildlife sites (see p. 832).

The ambivalent nature of the Commission must be appreciated. On the one hand it is often the driving force behind new environmental policies: on the other it is responsible for enforcing the economic aims of the EC (see its position in the *Danish Bottles* case, p. 214, and the *Concordia Bus Finland* case, p. 217)).

Internally the Commission is divided into a number of Directorates-General. Environmental matters are mainly dealt with by the Environment Directorate-General (which became a separate directorate in 1989), but because environmental policies should form a component of the EC's other policies, there are Commission officials in other Directorates such as energy and transport that also deal with environmental issues.

(b) The Council of Ministers

The Council of Ministers ('the Council') is a political body made up of one representative of each Member State. The identity of this representative alters according to the nature of the business. Thus, environment ministers normally agree environmental measures, transport ministers normally agree transport measures, and so on.[4] As a body it has a duty to ensure

2. Other institutions, of less significance here, include the Court of Auditors (which has occasionally produced quite critical reports on how environmental damage is in effect subsidised by the EC), and the Committee of the Regions and the Economic and Social Council, which in relation to the environment have both played limited advisory roles.

3. In the draft Constitution this remains the case, but with provision to reduce the number after five years.

4. In the draft Constitution a General Affairs Council is provided for, which might weaken some of the coherence provided by the current approach.

the attainment of the Treaty objectives, but clearly national interests play a central role in the Council's decisions.

As a result the Council's voting procedures are crucial. There are some differences in the procedures to be adopted for different matters. Some pieces of legislation have to be passed unanimously by the Council, acting on a proposal from the Commission, and after consultation with Parliament and the Economic and Social Committee. But most environmental legislation can now be passed by a qualified majority of the Council—a system of weighted voting in which Member States can be outvoted; see p. 198—though in practice there is often unanimity.

(c) The European Parliament

The European Parliament, which began life as an unelected consultative Assembly, now has a much greater role in the making of new legislation (see below). The Parliament has also been a significant mouthpiece of concern over environmental issues and for many years had a vigorous Committee on the Environment, Public Health and Consumer Protection subjecting proposals to quite searching scrutiny. The Parliament has played a key role in making EC decision-making more transparent; has never considered a Commission proposal to be too environmentally protective; and has generally opposed the use of 'soft law' rules of environmental law. But in terms of its ability to affect the content of environmental legislation its powers have tended to be limited.

(d) The European Court of Justice

The European Court of Justice consists of judges appointed by common agreement of the Member States. It is assisted by Advocates-General, one of whom makes reasoned submissions to the Court in each case. It has supreme authority on matters of EC law. This means that it has ultimate power to interpret the meaning of the Treaties and of any legislation made by the other institutions. The Court can thus, if asked, review the legitimacy of the actions of the other institutions, provide answers on matters of EC law to Member States' courts and declare whether Member States are implementing EC law properly (and if they are not, impose penalty payments).

The ECJ is widely considered a force for good when it comes to environmental law; it tends to interpret EC environmental directives purposively, as much according to the spirit of their environmental objectives as to the letter of the law, and is particularly vigilant (and creative) in striving to ensure that EC law is properly implemented in the Member States.[5] It has generally been sympathetic on issues such as the extent to which environmental protection measures unlawfully limit the free movement of goods, and active in developing and applying key principles of environmental law and policy such as the integration and precautionary principles.

Article 234 EC plays a major role here. Under Article 234, any court or tribunal in a Member State can refer any matter of EC law to the European Court of Justice for its interpretation of the law. This procedure aims to ensure uniformity between Member States in their application of the law. It also provides a method of obtaining an authoritative ruling. Since the Court is the ultimate arbiter of any law having an EC input, Article 234 references should be made where there is any doubt as to the meaning of EC law, or the compatibility

5. See Box 4.1. One exception to this has been the Court's interpretation of Art. 230(4) EC, see Box 7.6.

of domestic law with it. However, many contentious issues of the interpretation of EC environmental law have often been resolved, without a reference, by national judges, who have often taken a less purposive interpretation than the ECJ has eventually taken (see Box 7.2).

BOX 7.2 Referring environmental cases to the European Court of Justice

In practice, national courts effectively have a discretion whether to make a reference. This is because they can deem an issue of European law to be sufficiently clear that a reference is not needed. In this sense, the Court of Justice is not a top court to which litigants have a right to appeal (like the European Court of Human Rights, which exists to uphold and interpret the European Convention on Human Rights and which the ECJ should not be confused with). So whether the ECJ gets to rule on a contested area of EC environmental law depends in part on the willingness of national judges to refer cases.

In the past, UK courts have seemed reluctant to refer environmental law cases (see p. 230). A clear example is the Court of Appeal's decision in the *Lappel Bank* case where, although the judges were fundamentally split on whether economic factors could be taken into account in designating important bird habitats under Directive 79/409 on Wild Birds, they declined to make a reference, although the House of Lords later rectified this absurdity by referring the case (*R v Secretary of State for the Environment, ex p RSPB* [1997] JEL 168 (CA) and [1997] Env LR 431 (HL), and see p. 825 below). While there have been a small number of references in recent years, there is still a reluctance to refer cases. Whether this is because of a general lack of familiarity with EC law, an undue confidence in the judges' ability to determine tricky points of EC law, or a hostility to procedural measures which go against the grain of national decision-making procedures, is hard to tell. But whether a reference will be made, and from which court, remains something of a lottery.

Regardless, if the aim is to have an environmental law issue ruled on by the ECJ, the best way is probably to bring the matter to the attention of the Commission, which can take a case against the Member State to the ECJ (see p. 219). In practice, environmental campaigning organizations will often use a twin-track approach, bringing a case in the national courts and notifying the Commission.

The Court gives one agreed judgment. These are often very brief and formal and for the full reasoning the opinion of the Advocate-General must be read, although on rare occasions the Court and the Advocate-General do not agree.[6]

(e) The European Environment Agency

Although not formally an EC 'institution', the European Environment Agency, provided for in Regulation 1210/90 and established in October 1993, plays an important role. Based in Copenhagen, the Agency has the role of gathering information and data on the state of the European environment. A report on the state of the environment must be published every three years and the three reports published in 1995, 1998, and 2003 provide a valuable account of pressures on the European environment (see p. 324). A recent development is

---

6. Notable examples of disagreement in cases with environmental implications are the *Danish Bottles* case (p. 214), where the Advocate-General considered both schemes to breach Art. 28, and the *UPA* case (see p. 193).

the European Pollutant Emission Register <www.eper.cec.eu.int>, based on monitoring of the Integrated Pollution Prevention and Control Directive (96/61).

The Agency has not been given any enforcement or policing powers in relation to environmental legislation. Despite determined efforts by the European Parliament in the 1990s to see this happen, it is unlikely that such a role will emerge because of the enormity and complexity of the task, and the political unpopularity it would probably generate. Instead, bodies like IMPEL (an Implementation Network set up by the Commission, consisting of representatives from the Member States) are developing best practice and benchmarking standards for monitoring implementation (on which see the Parliament and Council Recommendation on Minimum Criteria for Environmental Inspections (2001/331)). Hence, alongside greater enforcement by the Commission (see p. 219) the EC is trying to improve compliance within the Member States rather than create an EC body to police environmental legislation on the ground.

Sources of EC environmental law

EC environmental law is contained in:

- the Treaties;
- legislation passed by the institutions (regulations, directives);
- international treaties to which the EC is a party; and
- the judgments and principles of the European Court of Justice.

To understand the relevance of these sources, an explanation of the concept of the supremacy of EC law is required. The doctrine of the supremacy of EC law is that, where there is a conflict between EC law and national law, EC law prevails, even if the national law is later in time; national courts should thus apply EC law rather than national law which does not comply with EC law. This is, however, intimately linked with the related notions of 'direct effect' and 'useful effect'.

A law has direct effect if it gives rise to rights and obligations which can be enforced by individuals and companies before national courts. If an EC law is directly effective, the doctrine of supremacy means that the non-conforming national law can simply be ignored. Not all EC law is directly effective in this sense. For any provision to be directly effective it must be sufficiently clear and precise to form a cause of action. It must also be unconditional and must not require further definition at the discretion of the Member State. There are also limitations on direct effect related to the source of the EC law. Treaty Articles and regulations are capable of having direct effect, as long as they fulfil the above tests. For directives, the Treaty suggested that they would not be capable of having direct effect. However, the European Court of Justice has indulged in some significant judicial creativity and has decided that directives may have direct effect if the action is against the state or an emanation of the state, but not if against a private body (see p. 222).

In recent years there has been a greater focus by the Court of Justice on the concept of 'useful effect'. This has also been driven by the Court's concern that EC law should not be a 'dead letter' but the focus is more on ensuring that Member States should not avoid their obligations under EC law than on protecting individual rights (and as a result it is a particularly important development when it comes to environmental directives, which often do not set out to grant individuals rights but seek to improve environmental quality generally). Even if a directive is not directly effective, therefore, there are legal limits on how Member States exercise their discretion in implementing them, and an individual may be able to bring a case arguing that this discretion has been exceeded. An example of this is given in Box 7.4. Again, this is discussed in more detail below (see p. 222).

(a) Treaty provisions

The provisions of the EC Treaty lay down the objectives of the EC, the powers of its institutions and the procedures for decision-making as well as laying down certain substantive legal requirements. They are of enormous importance in actions before the ECJ relating to the legality of EC actions. The Treaty is the source of the environmental principles and provides the basic default rules on, e.g., where the balance between the free movement of goods and the environment should be struck. Some Treaty provisions are directly effective (e.g. Article 141 on equal pay), but this is not the case for the Articles concerned with the environment because of their policy orientation.

(b) Regulations

Regulations are legislative acts of general application.[7] They are normally directly effective, as long as they are sufficiently precise. However, there are few regulations in the environmental sphere, except those relating to the process of giving effect to international treaties (e.g. on reducing ozone-depleting substances), agricultural policy, administrative matters (such as setting up the European Environment Agency) and the eco-auditing and eco-labelling schemes.

(c) Directives

Directives are addressed to Member States and are 'binding as to the result to be achieved'.[8] This is discussed in more detail at p. 217 but a brief overview of what is required to comply with directives is given here.

Member States' duty to implement EC environmental directives is clearly central to their importance and enforceability. In the EC's early years, however, it was often thought that directives imposed little more on Member States than to make honest efforts to give effect to them. This was partly because in the late 1970s and early 1980s the Commission's attention tended to be focused more on adopting new legislation than on its implementation. In the UK, a further explanatory factor was probably the degree to which environmental laws generally tended to be seen as a framework for discretionary enforcement action rather than binding standards. However, the Court of Justice has given directives greater weight (see Box 7.3).

BOX 7.3 **Complying with environmental quality standards**

The Court of Justice has made it clear that 'binding as to the result to be achieved' means what it says. A leading environmental case is the first *UK Drinking Water* case (Case C-337/89 *Commission*

---

7. In the draft Constitution these are termed 'European laws'.
8. In the draft Constitution these are termed 'European framework laws'.

v UK [1992] ECR I-6103; see also p. 714). This involved alleged breaches of the 1980 Drinking Water Directive by exceeding the maximum allowable concentration of nitrate in drinking water in various areas. In its defence the UK argued that it was sufficient to take all practicable steps to achieve the water quality requirements, but the Court of Justice rejected this and held that practical compliance is an absolute obligation. The only get-out for the UK would have been if it had fallen within one of the specific derogations contained in the Directive (which in this case it did not). The same approach was taken in Case C-56/90 *Commission v UK* [1993] ECR I-4109, a case concerning the quality of bathing waters at Blackpool and Southport beaches. The ECJ held that it was not enough for the UK to take all necessary steps to achieve compliance; what was required was compliance with the quality standards in the Directive. Because it did not fall within any of the recognized exceptions in the Directive, the UK was in breach of its obligations. The strength of the compliance duty in the latter case is undoubtedly more onerous, because the state has far less control over the factors that influence bathing water quality. Both of these cases show how the UK government was trying to maintain its traditionally pragmatic approach to environmental policy, at a time by when the legal outcome of these cases was, as a matter of law, not really in doubt.

EC environmental law (which has numerous directives laying down practical compliance targets) would be of little value if the Court of Justice did not take this strict approach. But to avoid unnecessary and unexpected costs on the Member States one consequence is that environmental directives often lack detail, contain vague commitments, and may contain quite wider-ranging derogations aimed at softening the impact on Member States that might be particularly hard hit. Environmental directives are in essence often framework directives, and the less specific a directive, the more difficult it is in practice to say that a Member State has not complied with it. The leading case on these more general obligations is the *San Rocco Valley* case (Box 7.4).

BOX 7.4 **Complying with general pollution reduction obligations**

In the San Rocco valley area of Italy there had been a failure over many years to tackle unlawful waste tipping, which led to human health risks and damage to a watercourse. Under Article 4 of the Waste Framework Directive, Member States must take the necessary measures to ensure that waste is disposed of without endangering human health and without harming the environment. This is a general obligation rather than a specific emission control or environmental quality standard, and while not every situation which was inconsistent with Article 4 would be a breach of the Directive, the factors here—a persistent breach resulting in significant environmental damage without any remedial intervention by the authorities—meant that Italy had exceeded the limits of its discretion (see Case C-365/97 *Commission v Italy* [2003] Env LR 1). This judgment opens up to judicial scrutiny some of the more general duties on Member States, but it seems to suggest that with such provisions it is not the severity of the resulting harm but rather the inadequacy of the response which is central in determining whether the directive has been properly implemented. For an interesting comparison see the view of the ECtHR; see Case box 11.1.) This makes it very difficult to argue that such a directive has not been properly complied with at the stage when, for example, an environmental licence is being applied for.

Directives are well-suited to environmental measures, since they leave the choice of how to implement them to the Member States, which will each have different methods for setting environmental laws. Most EC environmental legislation is in the form of directives. In this book we refer to directives by their common names (e.g. the 'Habitats Directive') rather than the often lengthy titles they are given formally ('Council Directive 92/43/EEC of 21 May 1992 on the conservation of natural habitats and of wild fauna and flora').

Implementation is required within a specified time period (often two years). This will be done by the Member State changing its domestic law and it will be in breach if it has not *fully and correctly* implemented the directive within the time limit. In Britain, once the Directive is transposed the domestic rule will constitute the relevant law, unless there has been partial or incomplete transposition.

A distinction must be drawn here between formal and actual compliance. Changing the law to comply with EC law constitutes formal compliance. However, this is no guarantee that the law is complied with in practice since, for example, a regulatory agency may exercise its discretion not to enforce the law. In enforcing environmental directives generally, however, the Commission's lack of an inspection function and lack of resources for monitoring developments in the Member States and bringing actions before the Court of Justice is a significant constraint.

(d) Decisions, recommendations and opinions

Decisions are binding on the individual or group to whom they are addressed, and may also be directly effective. They are rare in environmental law, being limited mainly to matters of monitoring and information gathering, but precautionary steps in relation to CFCs were taken in the 1980s by means of decisions and there is a Council Framework Decision on Environmental Protection through Criminal Law (2003/80) (see p. 218). The institutions may also issue recommendations and opinions. These are not binding and only have a persuasive effect and are seldom used in the environmental area (though a recent example can be seen in relation to the controversial issue of minimum criteria for environmental inspection, p. 187 above). Historically, they have made little impact.

(e) Court decisions

The decisions of the European Court of Justice give rise to law and this has been a particularly fertile area. The Court has borrowed and developed general principles of law from the jurisprudence of the Member States, such as the principles of natural justice, proportionality, certainty, equality and the protection of legitimate expectations and fundamental rights. In particular, proportionality is also a general standard against which all EC law is to be judged (see Box 7.5).

In practice, however, Member States often tend to be forced to act by judgment in a Commission action against them, or a reference from their national courts. Decisions involving other Member States often take much longer to influence decision-making.

BOX 7.5 **Proportionality and EC environmental law**

Proportionality is a central concept in EC law. It entails that laws must be appropriate and not go beyond what is necessary to achieve the desired objectives, and must take the least trade restrictive form. At national level it is one of the key criteria against which proposals for new regulation, and their enforcement, are to be judged (see pp. 260 and 302), but only at the level of policy. Proportionality is also central to deciding whether certain human rights have been breached e.g. the right to property (see p. 820).

In relation to EC environmental law proportionality is used by the Court of Justice in:

- judging the validity of EC legislation (although EC lawmakers are given a wide discretion where areas of social policy like environmental regulation are concerned, see the *Standley* case, p. 748);

- balancing trade freedom and environmental protection (as applied in the *Danish Bottles* case, p. 214);

- assessing whether a Member State may maintain or introduce national legislation providing stricter environmental protection than under an EC environmental directive (see p. 207).

Assessing proportionality tends to be a matter of judgement, but the court in Case T-13/99 *Pfizer Animal Health SA v Council* [2002] ECR II-3305 (a case about the validity of a precautionary ban on antibiotics in animal feed, see p. 74) held that 'a cost/benefit analysis is a particular expression of the principle of proportionality in cases involving risk management'. It is not clear, however, how far the European courts will go in specifying the assessment methods that decision-makers must use, but cases like *Pfizer* indicate that the courts will give in-depth scrutiny to the basis of any scientific decisions.

Proportionality also plays a role in enforcing EC environmental law. Although the Court has not allowed proportionality to be used when it comes to the implementation of directives it has accepted that proportionality is relevant to any fine payable by a Member State under Article 228 EC. These propositions can be seen, respectively, in the first *Spanish Bathing Water* case (Case 92/96), discussed at p. 715, and the second *Spanish Bathing Water* case (Case 278/01), p. 219). Finally, a national implementing law can be challenged if it does not specify sanctions that are proportionate (see p. 218).

Making EC environmental law

The making of EC environmental legislation involves either unanimity or, more usually, qualified majority voting, subject to some form of involvement of the Parliament.

(a) The role of the Council and the Parliament

Following the Amsterdam Treaty, the 'co-decision procedure' is now used for legislation adopted under both Articles 95 and 175, the main bases in the EC Treaty for environmental legislation (see p. 198). The procedure is contained in Article 251.

The co-decision procedure gives a strengthened role in the legislative process to the Parliament, although this is still quite negative in character. For example, as mentioned above the Parliament still has no right to initiate new proposals. One feature of this procedure is the resolution of disputes, on matters of detail, by a Conciliation Committee made up of representatives of the Parliament and Council. This conciliation procedure has been invoked on a number of occasions in the environmental area, e.g. in relation to the first 'Auto-Oil' Directive (98/69) and the Water Framework Directive (2000/60). One important consequence of the greater involvement of the Parliament is that decision-making is rather more open than it used to be, which goes some way towards tackling problems of secrecy and lack of democratic accountability inherent in EC legislative procedures (see p. 185), although by their nature Conciliation Committees involve last-minute deals and lack transparency.

(b) Unanimity or majority voting?

The other key development in this area has been the extension of qualified majority voting, the system whereby the number of votes in the Council are weighted roughly according to population (from 1 November 2004, the UK has 29 votes in the Council out of 321).[9] This has restricted the number of areas where unanimity amongst all the Member States is needed, and therefore the scope for one unsupportive Member State to veto a proposal.

For example, the UK government was outvoted on the EC list of hazardous wastes adopted pursuant to Directive 91/689 on Hazardous Waste. The UK also opposed the ban on leaded fuel as from 2000 which was nevertheless contained in Directive 98/70 relating to the quality of petrol and diesel fuels. However, another reason is that the system encourages the Member States to reach a compromise position within the Council. The combined effect may enable some proposed directives to avoid the fate of, for example, Directives 88/609 on Emissions from Large Combustion Plants (which deals with the causes of acid rain) and 85/337 on Environmental Impact Assessment, both of which were delayed for many years by the opposition of one or two Member States. However, this does not mean that directives will always be agreed swiftly, even with qualified majority voting, because there are also complex political considerations to take into account, although less-developed Member States may now be bought off by concessions based on Article 175(5) (see p. 203). The increasing involvement of the European Parliament is also relevant to whether a compromise position can be reached.

Since the Maastricht Treaty, most environmental legislation is subject to qualified majority voting. The only exceptions, where unanimity is still required, are those primarily of a fiscal nature (note here that the Energy Tax Directive 2003/96 was adopted under Article 93 EC), measures relating to town and country planning or land use (unless they are concerned with waste management), measures concerning the quantitative management of water resources,[10] and measures affecting national policies on energy supply (e.g. any proposal restricting the use of coal on environmental grounds).

Challenging EC legislation

The validity of regulations, directives and decisions can be challenged within two months under Article 230. This Article sets out grounds which are slightly wider than the English *ultra vires* rules. As a judicial review action it also requires the applicant to have standing.

9. In the draft European Constitution, a qualified majority will normally comprise at least 55 per cent of the members of the Council, comprising at least 15 of them and representing Member States comprising at least 65 per cent of the population of the Union (Art. I-25). To block legislation, the minority must include at least four Member States. The present system of giving a certain number of votes to a Member State will therefore no longer apply.

10. 'Quantitative' was inserted by the Treaty of Nice, but this merely clarifies the interpretation given in Case C-36/98 *Spain v Council* [2001] ECR I-779.

Member States, the Commission, the Council and Parliament have it, but a private litigant must show direct and individual concern. Such a requirement virtually restricts individuals to challenging decisions addressed to them specifically, making challenges to environment measures highly problematic (see Box 7.6).

BOX 7.6 Article 230 EC and environmental protection challenges

In Case C-321/95P *Stichting Greenpeace Council and others v Commission* [1998] ECR I-1651 a decision by the Commission to allocate regional development funding to Spain for the construction of two power stations in the Canary Islands was challenged by Greenpeace as well as concerned local residents individually. The Court of Justice held that none of the applicants was individually concerned for the purposes of Article 230, and was unmoved by the argument that in areas such as environmental protection, where interests are often common and shared, there will never be a closed class of applicants satisfying the test of individual concern. In Case C-50/00P *Unión de Pequeños Agricultores v Council* [2002] ECR I-6677 Advocate-General Jacobs saw no particular reason why 'individual concern' should be interpreted as requiring applicants to differentiate themselves from all other parties subject to the measure being challenged, and favoured an approach which would look at whether the measure has, or is liable to have, a substantial adverse effect on the applicant's interests, an approach which would, he said, remove the anomaly (seen in environmental cases like *Greenpeace*) that the greater the number of persons affected the less likely it is that effective judicial review is available. The Court of Justice, however, took a more conservative approach, and restated the orthodox interpretation of individual concern, ruling that any change to this approach would have to be made by amending the EC Treaty. Why a test relating to differential impact rather than the degree of impact should be the only legally correct interpretation of individual concern is debatable.

Finally, note that the Advocate General's harm-based test would have given standing to environmental organizations to challenge legislation,[11] whereas the test proposed by the Court of First Instance in Case T-177/01 *Jégo-Quéré & Cie SA v Commission* [2002] ECR II-2365, another reformist case decided just prior to the Court of Justice's ruling in the *UPA* case, was based on there being adverse *legal* effects (and while environmental interest groups serve a valuable role their *legal* interests are unlikely to be affected by EC environmental law). However, the Court of Justice also overturned this decision (Case C-263/02P [2004] 2 CMLR 12), again restating the orthodox position.

One way to get round this is to challenge the validity of EC law in national litigation. If the challenge has merit then it may be (see p. 186) that the matter will be referred to the Court of Justice under Article 234 EC, and the Court will then rule on the question of validity. An example of this is the *Standley* case (Case C-293/97 *R v Secretary of State for the Environment and Minister of Agriculture, Fisheries and Food, ex parte Standley* [1999] ECR I-2603) where, in the English courts, farmers challenged certain provisions of the 1991 Agricultural Nitrates Directive as being incompatible with various principles of EC environmental policy. The High Court referred the case to the Court of Justice, which

11. See the discussion of contrasting approaches to judicial review at national level, p. 340.

ultimately upheld the directive against the challenge, amongst other things, that it unfairly discriminated against farmers (who are not the only contributors to this particularly challenging environmental problem). In the *Greenpeace, UPA* and *Jégo Quéré* cases, the availability of an Article 234 reference was stressed by the Court of Justice in reaching its restrictive interpretation of Article 230, but relying on this way to challenge EC law is subject to the vagaries of national court's referring cases to the Court of Justice. The Court's ruling that, together, Articles 230 and 234 provide a complete system of legal remedies for challenging, directly and indirectly, the legality of EC action seems unduly optimistic.[12] It may be that this will be considered again in relation to the EC's implementation of the Aarhus Convention.

EC environmental law and policy

The rationale for EC environmental law and policy—the common market

The fundamental basis of the EC has always been economic. The primary aims were originally set out in Articles 2 and 3 of the Treaty of Rome, which established the EEC in 1957. These are the creation of a 'common market' (i.e. a fully integrated single internal market within the boundaries of the Member States) in 'goods, persons, services and capital', together with the progressive harmonisation of the economic policies of the Member States. In order to achieve these primary aims, internal barriers to trade and competition need to be dismantled, so that there are no internal frontiers to hamper the free movement of goods, persons, services and capital, and no discrimination between people or firms on the grounds of nationality. This policy may be referred to as the provision of an economic level playing field across the EC. In which respects the playing field should be level, however, is controversial (see Box 7.7).

BOX 7.7 **Economic 'level playing fields' and beyond**

In Case 91/79 *Commission v Italy* [1980] ECR 1099, the Court was clear that environmental matters could fall within Article 94 (i.e. within trade harmonization directives):

Provisions which are made necessary by considerations relating to the environment and health may be a burden on the undertakings to which they apply, and if there is no harmonisation of national provisions on the matter, competition may be appreciably distorted.

But which provisions, exactly, are necessary in an EC context? Minimum standards for products that circulate in the internal market are more easily justified than similar standards relating to how such products are manufactured. If production processes do not give rise to adverse environmental effects in another Member State why should they be regulated under EC environmental law? Indeed it is only *because* there are various differences in market conditions—relating to

---

12. The draft Constitution requires only direct rather than individual concern to challenge a 'regulatory act' which does not entail implementing measures (i.e. where no reference from a national court would be possible). This was the position in *Jégo Quéré*, where a fisheries regulation was being challenged.

things like climate, the availability of natural resources, infrastructure, and social and fiscal regimes—that there is any trade between states. So why should the EC try to level the economic playing field for manufacturers etc, whose products do not lead to negative environmental effects (negative externalities, or spillovers) beyond their borders? One answer is that not doing so would lead to negative *economic* spillovers between Member States; these might make the EC as a whole less productive (and, insofar as environmental protection must be paid for, make regulating national environments that much harder economically).[13] Another explanation is that in reality the long-term effects of certain pollutants are not easily confined within national borders, and that there is a danger in underestimating these physical spillovers (this is especially true of the more persistent, bioaccumulative pollutants). For example, the former British policy of discharging sewage effluent into coastal waters was justified on the grounds that the pollution would be diluted but it has now been shown that many of the more polluting substances remain in the marine environment and give rise to problems for neighbouring states. Perhaps the best explanation, however, is that the EC has never just been a free trade area; the common market always had a political objective—a peaceful and integrated Europe—and even in its early years the notion of a common market was being stretched, by EC legislation and by the European Court of Justice, to accommodate this agenda in a range of policy areas including the environment.

It is clear that there is a fundamental conflict between some of the economic aims of the EC and the protection of the environment. This problem has been tackled by the creation of an environmental policy.

The EC's environmental policy

There was no mention of the environment in the original Treaty of Rome. To some extent this was because the primary aims of the EEC were, as explained above, economic, but it was mainly because the potential environmental impact of the expansionist, growth-related economic policies adopted at the time was not perceived. By the early 1970s, however, the need for some form of policy on the protection of the environment was accepted. There were two reasons for this. One was the acceptance of the interrelationship between economic growth and environmental degradation. The other was that the environment was then emerging as a significant political issue. Environmental protection thus fits into the activities of the EC in two overlapping ways: first as an adjunct to economic policy, and secondly as a positive end in itself.

In October 1972, declaring that 'economic expansion is not an end in itself', the heads of state of the Member States accordingly requested the Commission to draw up an EC environmental policy. The Commission responded by formulating the first Action Programme on the Environment. (This has been followed by further Action Programmes in 1977, 1982, 1987, 1992, and 2002.) This was the effective beginning of what is now a very wide-ranging environmental strategy. But it was not the beginning of EC involvement in environmental matters. As long ago as 1967, Directive 67/548 provided specifically for

---

13. See, J. Scott, *EC Environmental Law* (London: Longman, 1998), 12–15 for a good general discussion of this issue.

the classification, packaging and labelling of dangerous substances. This was justified as necessary to achieve the common market, but environmental protection considerations were also influential.[14] Over 200 items of new environmental legislation (and the same number of amending laws) have now been agreed as part of this policy—both as an adjunct to the EC's economic and other policies but also as primarily environmental measures—and these range across the whole spectrum of matters covered by this book.

Taking the story of the development of EC environmental policy up to date, in 2001 an EU Sustainable Development Strategy was adopted. As with the Cardiff process begun in 1998 (see below) the Strategy emphasized the importance of integrating environmental protection requirements into other areas of EU policy, effectively placing the promotion of environmental protection alongside economic growth and social cohesion (by decoupling economic growth from negative environmental impacts) as the key aims of the EU. Opinion differs on whether this marks a genuine shift in attitudes, perhaps elevating sustainable development (and with it environmental protection) as an underpinning rationale for the legitimacy of the EU, or whether it is merely window-dressing, aiming for a degree of environmental integration for which, in key policy areas of the EU like industry, transport, and agriculture, there is still insufficient political will.

The constitutional basis of EC environmental policy and law

The constitutional basis for environmental law and policy must be considered in two distinct phases: before and after the Single European Act 1986. The history of the development of the EC's environmental policy will be considered first, because it is a good illustration of the way that the institutions have in practice widened the scope of what the EC deals with by a generous reading of the Treaty.

(a) Before the Single European Act 1986

Before 1986 the legal justification for the policy was not entirely clear. In practice, two Articles of the Treaty, Articles 94 and 308 (the former relating to the harmonization of national laws in order to further the establishment of the common market, the latter relating to the EC's general and residual powers), were used as justification. The majority of directives, especially those relating to pollution control and common standards, tended to be justified on the basis of Article 94, whilst those where the content was almost purely environmental, such as Directive 79/409 on Wild Birds, were justified on the basis of Article 308. It was not unusual for both Articles to be cited, just in case of a challenge.

In cases that did come to the European Court of Justice, the environmental policy was supported, which is not surprising since it had been formulated with the agreement of all the Member States (see e.g Case 91/79 *Commission v Italy* [1980] ECR 1099, p. 194 above). Most notably, in Case 240/83 *Procureur de la République v Association de Défense des Brûleurs d'Huiles Usagées* [1985] ECR 531, on the legitimacy of Directive 75/439 on Waste Oils, the European Court of Justice stated that environmental protection was 'one of the Community's essential objectives', and as such it justified some restrictions on the operation of

---

14. Arguably it was not until the 6th amendment to this directive in 1979, which provided for pre-market control of hazardous chemicals, that a *primarily* environmental objective to this regime emerged.

the common market. In a sense this amounted to a rewriting of the Treaty by the European Court of Justice as a matter of political reality.

(b) Single European Act 1986

In 1986, the Single European Act (SEA) went some way towards reflecting the reality of the situation by amending the Treaty to add a whole new title relating to the protection of the environment. By adding what are now Articles 174, 175, and 176, the SEA introduced explicit law-making powers in relation to environmental matters making reliance on Article 308 redundant. In addition, it added Article 95, which has been of great importance for the development of environmental policy, even though it is primarily aimed at speeding up the completion of the single internal market. To some extent these changes regularized the existing *de facto* position, but they also established some clearer constitutional rules than there had been in the past on the extent of the law-making powers and on how decisions were to be made. These required, for example, that differing environmental conditions across the Community, and potential costs and benefits of action or inaction, should be taken into account, but policy principles such as the 'polluter pays' principle and that damage should be prevented and rectified at source were also added by the SEA.

For some, however, the insertion of an environmental title was more about structuring and perhaps even *restricting* the competence of the Community, through procedural pro-visions such as requiring available scientific and technical data to be taken account of, than about regularising and strengthening the role of the Community in the field of the environment by giving it an explicit legal base.[15] Regardless, they failed to check the rapid growth in environmental legislation following the SEA.

(c) Treaty on European Union ('Maastricht Treaty') 1992

The Maastricht Treaty continued the process of integrating environmental matters into the heart of the EC's activities by making further amendments to the Articles mentioned above. It also recognized for the first time that the development of 'a policy in the sphere of the environment' is one of the EC's main activities (see Art. 3), and replaced Article 2, which sets out the objectives of the EC, with a new version that included the tasks of promoting throughout the Community 'a harmonious and balanced development of economic activities' and 'sustainable and non-inflationary growth respecting the environment'. The Treaty thus acknowledged that there is a balance to be struck between economic and environmental factors, though the balance remained firmly with the former.

(d) Treaty of Amsterdam 1997

Further amendments to the Treaty came into force in 1999 which continued the develop-ment of European environmental policy. A new main goal of 'promoting a harmonious and balanced and sustainable development of economic activities', together with 'a high level of protection and improvement of the quality of the environment' was included in Article 2, and therefore applies to all policies and all institutions, not just to Commission initiatives. These goals are reinforced by Article 6 which provides that 'environmental protection requirements must be integrated into the definition and implementation of Community

---

15. The main proponent of this view is J. Golub (1996) 44 Political Studies 686.

policies and activities . . . in particular with a view to promoting sustainable development'. Although a version of this objective previously appeared in the environmental title, its elevation to the start of the Treaty is of considerable symbolic, legal and policy importance (for examples of the Court of Justice using Article 6 see pp. 215 and 217). It has led, under what is known as the 'Cardiff Process', to publication by the Commission of a number of policy documents exploring the integration of the environment into Community policy generally or in specific sectors like energy and agriculture but, as yet, little radically integrative legislation (for a review see COM(2004)394)). It is notable that neither Article 2 nor Article 6 seek to define sustainable development.

(e) The draft Constitution

In 2004 political agreement was reached on a draft EU Constitution. This is unlikely to come into force before 2006, and indeed may never do so because its ratification is subject to difficult political hurdles (e.g. the referendum promised for the UK). In many ways the Constitution either restates existing provisions of the EC Treaty, such as the provisions on internal market harmonization in Article 95 and environmental harmonization in Articles 174–6, or clarifies issues that have long been accepted (e.g. that the EU and the Member States share law-making powers in relation to environmental policy). In the early stages of negotiating the Constitution it seemed that the environment was either completely off the radar screen or was being consciously downgraded (e.g. there were moves to begin with to define sustainable development as being primarily about economic growth and social justice, and excluding mention of environmental protection). In broad terms, however, the final outcome is fairly neutral. The environmental provisions of Article 2 EC remain essentially unchanged, and although the environmental integration principle in Article 6 EC has been moved to a position further back in the draft Constitution its legal status is probably unaffected. From a purely environmental perspective therefore the draft Constitution is most notable for being the first Treaty revision where the remit of the EU has not been expanded (the enlargement-focussed Nice Treaty excluded).

Which article?

It is clear from the above that EC law must have an explicit treaty basis (this is known as 'attribution'—any legislation must be attributed to one or more articles of the Treaty). If there is no legal basis for an EC environmental regulation or directive, or if the incorrect basis has been given, then the Court of Justice can annul the law. In deciding which article of the Treaty to base legislation on, the following factors may be at issue:

(a) Which law-making process to use.

(b) Whether the EC has competence to adopt the legislation.

(c) Whether higher national standards can be used.

(a) Voting procedure

Historically, differences in the procedures used to adopt EC legislation in different areas meant that the Article used in adopting a directive was often of considerable importance. This was because the Single European Act introduced qualified majority voting for measures adopted under Article 95 but made no change to measures adopted under the new environmental provisions in the Treaty, so legislation adopted under Article 175 still required the unanimous agreement of all the Member States (see p. 192). This encouraged the Commission to introduce proposals under Article 95, to speed their process into legislation. However, different voting procedures meant that the Parliament had a greater legislative role in 'internal market' legislation than in proposals introduced under the environmental title.

In Case C-300/89 *Commission v Council* [1991] ECR I-2867, the Court of Justice held that Directive 89/428 on the Titanium Dioxide Industry could be adopted under Article 95—the argument of the Commission—because where environmental measures also contributed to the establishment of the internal market they fell within Article 95. This suggested that most environmental directives could be based on Article 95. It also suggested that, where there was a choice between alternative Articles, Article 95 should be chosen because it allowed greater input from Parliament through the cooperation procedure, a conclusion difficult to square with its view that only 'objective factors . . . amenable to judicial review' counted. This decision opened the way at the time for the wider use of qualified majority voting on environmental matters (and is a nice example of the Commission's greater enthusiasm for European integration and expansion into new policy areas as the environment then was).

However, in a later case concerning the correct legal basis of the amending Waste Framework Directive (91/156) (Case C-155/91 *Commission v Council* [1993] ECR I-939), the Court of Justice altered its view and adopted instead a test based on the centre of gravity of the Directive. In this case it decided that the principal objective of the Directive—the protection of the environment—was the crucial factor, and not any ancillary effect on the functioning of the internal market. Directive 91/156 could thus be distinguished from Directive 89/428. It is notable that this decision followed the conclusion of the Maastricht negotiations which sanctioned the general use of qualified majority voting under Article 175 (see also Case C-187/93 *Parliament v Council* [1994] ECR I-2857 concerning transboundary waste movement).

These cases suggest that most environmental directives should now be based on Article 175, although it remains possible to adopt harmonization directives having some environmental elements under Article 95, as product-related directives tend to be (see below). Instead, we may be more likely to see disputes where measures in other fields have an environmental component to them, something which should be ever more frequent now that the Treaty requires the integration of environmental protection requirements when legislative proposals are made in *all* other areas. For example, in Cases C-164 and 165/97 *Parliament v Council* [1999] ECR I-1139, the Parliament challenged the validity of regulations protecting forests from air pollution and from fire. The regulations had been adopted by the Council under Article 37 which relates to agriculture, under which the Parliament only needs to be consulted, the very weakest form of Parliament involvement in decision-making. The regulations were annulled because the measures were primarily intended to protect forest ecosystems and forests were not agricultural products as the Council, rather weakly, argued. While this was a fairly straightforward decision to reach, more difficult cases will doubtless emerge.

(b) Competence

In Opinion 2/00 *Cartagena Protocol on Biosafety* [2001] ECR I-9713 the Court of Justice was asked to rule on the correct legal base for adopting the Protocol (a subsidiary agreement made under the 1992 UN Convention on Biological Diversity). The Commission sought a dual legal base in Article 174(4) and Article 133 regarding the EC's external trade policy (where the EC has exclusive competence and negotiates on behalf of all the Member States), whereas the Council sought a single legal basis in the Environmental Title, the environment being a matter of shared competence between the EC and the Member States. Voting procedure was not at stake, since both bases required qualified majority voting. The Court held that the Protocol was primarily an environmental protection measure (e.g. it governed the interstate movement of living modified organisms even where this was not for commercial reasons), and so the view of the Council was upheld.

An example going the other way is Case C-281/01 *Commission v Council* [2002] ECR I-12049. This case concerned the EC's 'buying into' the US of the 'Energy Star' energy-saving labelling on office equipment like computer monitors. Since the programme is voluntary and does not itself require greater energy efficiency, the Court held it was primarily related to external trade and therefore should be based on the EC's common commercial policy (where the Community's competence is exclusive) rather than on Article 175 (a conclusion premised on voluntary labelling provisions being a trade barrier, see also p. 173).

(c) Higher national standards

The rules allowing Member States to adopt national standards going beyond those contained in EC environmental directives is another reason why legal base may be important. A good illustration of this is the adoption, under Article 175, of Directive 2002/96 on Waste Electrical and Electronic Equipment, and the simultaneous adoption, under Article 95, of Directive 2002/95, which restricts the use of certain hazardous substances in electrical and electronic equipment. These two directives were originally contained in a single legislative proposal based on Article 175, but they were split so that it would be more difficult for Member States to maintain further bans or restrictions of dangerous substances in electrical and electronic equipment going beyond Directive 2002/95 except under the stricter conditions of Article 95(4) and (5) (see further p. 616).

The scope of EC environmental law

(a) Harmonizing legislation

Article 94 enables directives to be made that seek to harmonize laws and administrative practices of Member States which directly affect the establishment or functioning of the common market. The normal methods of achieving this are to lay down uniform, common standards or to outlaw specified discriminatory practices.

The relationship with the environment here is that a unified internal market depends upon trade and competition not being distorted by Member States applying different rules and standards. The EC has therefore tried to harmonize laws in all the Member States so that a producer in one country does not have an unfair advantage over one in another. Initially used to harmonize *product* standards, this soon extended to *process* standards (see Box 7.7).

By inserting Article 95, the Single European Act introduced qualified majority voting for many proposals of this nature. However, as a safeguard, it also required as an objective that, if action is taken under Article 95 concerning health, safety, environmental or consumer protection, a high level of protection should be taken for those standards. In addition,

Member States may derogate from the common standards in certain limited ways (Article 95(4) and (5)—see p. 207—and Article 95(10)).

(b) 'Environmental' legislation—objectives, principles, policy

Articles 174–6, on the other hand, provide a specific justification for environmental protection laws, even where there is no direct link to the economic aims of the EC. Article 175 provides the mechanics by setting out the voting procedures in the Council (see below). In contrast with Articles 94 and 95, either directives or regulations are possible, although few environmental regulations have been made. A further contrast is that, whilst Article 95 generally requires uniform baseline standards (subject to the scope for Member States to derogate from these under Articles 95(4) and (5)), under these Articles that is not always required, since the motivating force behind them is the improvement of environmental standards rather than realising the internal market. Accordingly, Article 176 specifically allows Member States to employ stricter measures than those agreed under Article 175, as long as they are compatible with the rest of the Treaty (see further p. 209).

Article 174(1) includes as *objectives* of the EC's environmental activities the preservation, protection, and improvement of the quality of the environment, the protection of human health, and the prudent and rational utilization of resources. Article 174(2) uniquely sets out the central *principles* of EC environmental policy, which should be taken into account when framing policy and legislation (on principles generally see pp. 59 et seq):

(a) preventative action should be preferred to remedial measures;

(b) environmental damage should be rectified at source;

(c) the 'polluter pays' principle; and

(d) policy should be based on the precautionary principle.

A high level of environmental protection must also be aimed at, while the principle that environmental policies should form a component of the EC's other policies is now a general principle of the EC Treaty (Art. 6 EC).

The principles are essentially policy principles, the purpose of which is to guide the form and content of EC environmental legislation. As noted, they must be taken into account; at best, this means that if legislation has been adopted which completely fails to have regard to a principle, it might be annulled. This was the approach of the Court of Justice when asked to review the compatibility of the Ozone Regulation 3093/94 with the precautionary principle (Case C-341/95 *Bettati v Safety Hi-Tech Srl* [1998] ECR I-4435, and see case box 3.2). Where environmental principles have been cited, the Court has tended to use them to justify a decision reached—or at least reachable—on other grounds.[16] A good example is Case C-2/90 *Commission v Belgium* [1992] ECR I-4431, where the Court of Justice used the rectification at source principle to justify upholding a ban on waste imports into the Walloon region of Belgium in the face of arguments that this infringed the right (see p. 214). There have been some recent cases, however, where the environmental integration principle in Article 6 EC has been invoked in a way that suggests a re-ordering of the relative importance of trade and environmental interests within the Community (see the *PreussenElektra* and *Concordia Bus Finland* cases, at pp. 215 and 217).

16. M. Doherty (2000) Env L Rev 251.

A difficulty, however, is that the meaning of the principles is far from settled. It was not clear whether the approach of the ECJ in the *Safety Hi-Tech* case was to avoid difficulties by deciding that only if the principle has not been considered will legislation be reviewable, or whether it also allows arguments based on fundamental misconceptions of the principles. However, later cases like *Pfizer Animal Health* (see p. 74) show that the Court has been prepared to engage with the interpretation of environmental principles (in that case, the degree of risk needed to trigger the precautionary principle needing to be more than just a hypothetical risk).[17]

It is important to note that the principles are not directly enforceable obligations. That is, they cannot be relied on in the abstract by an individual claiming that a polluter has not 'paid' for some aspect of pollution (e.g. by a claimant in a private nuisance case arguing that a polluter should pay for environmental pollution where there is no national law remedy) or that all regulatory action should be precautionary (see *R v Secretary of State for Trade and Industry, ex parte Duddridge* [1995] Env LR 151, discussed further on p. 76). It can only be said with any certainty that they can be used to uphold or challenge EC law or, as in exceptional cases like *Walloon Waste*, justify national measures.[18] Case C-293/97 *R v Secretary of State for Environment & Others ex parte Standley & Metson* [1999] ECR I-2603 (discussed at p. 748) provides a good example of how the Court of Justice deals with challenges to EC environmental law based on alleged breach of environmental principles (in that case, the polluter pays principle).

Under Article 174(3) of the Treaty, the EC institutions are required to *take account of* available scientific and technical data, environmental conditions in the various regions of the EC, and the balanced development of those regions when preparing any proposals. In addition, some form of cost-benefit analysis should be performed before environmental measures are agreed. These requirements are in accord with the 'British approach' to pollution (see p. 252), and the UK Government lobbied for their inclusion.

The international dimension is covered by Article 174(4). Many pollution, conservation and environmental matters, such as acid rain, the protection of migratory species, or pollution of the North Sea, are international in scope. A supranational body such as the EC is well-placed to tackle them by having a common internal environmental policy with agreed standards. It may also act by putting forward a common platform in dealings with the rest of the world.[19] Article 174(4) specifically permits the negotiation and conclusion of international agreements, a power which justifies the EC's independent involvement in international treaties and dealings with Eastern Europe (though it appears from the *Cartagena Biosafety Protocol Opinion* that, notwithstanding Article 174(4), Article 175(1) is the correct legal basis for any measures imposing obligations on the Community). Promoting international cooperation is also an objective of the EC (Art. 174(1)).

The basic principle is that the Member States bear the costs of implementing EC

---

17. A decision which is consistent with, and perhaps influenced by, the jurisprudence of the World Trade Organization, see J. Scott (2003) Columbia Journal of European Law 213, 228.

18. On their ambiguous status vis-à-vis the Member States see J. Scott and E. Vos, 'The Juridification of Uncertainty' in C. Joerges and R. Dehousse (eds), *Good Governance in Europe's Integrated Market* (Oxford: Oxford University Press, 2002).

19. In the draft Constitution, fostering global sustainable development becomes an explicit objective of the EU's external policies.

environmental laws (Art. 175(4)). However Article 175(5) provides that if a measure agreed under Article 175 involves disproportionate costs for a particular Member State, the Council may allow for temporary derogations and/or for financial support to meet those costs out of the special Cohesion Fund. This provision was inserted at Maastricht to buy off complaints from a number of the less-developed Member States that the burden of EC environmental policy fell unfairly on them since it hindered their industrial and economic development. They perceived this to be unfair because the other Member States have arguably reached their current level of development only by taking advantage of the absence in the past of the standards now imposed by modern environmental laws. (On derogations under Article 175(5) see further p. 211.)

(c) Environmental Action Programmes

The scope of the future content of EC environmental policy can also be seen from the six environmental Action Programmes. The first two Action Programmes were reactive in nature and concentrated on pollution control and on remedial measures. This fitted in with the economic justification of environmental policy under Article 94, but was also designed to tackle the most obvious and pressing problems first. The Third and Fourth Action Programmes emphasized preventive measures at the same time as continuing the work on pollution control. For example, a number of directives were agreed on product standards and on the design of industrial plant and processes. They also stressed the need to integrate environmental protection into other EC policies. However, perhaps the most significant feature of the third and fourth Action Programmes was that attention was increasingly paid to structural, or 'horizontal', measures that laid down procedures or ancillary administrative matters. For example, legislation was passed on the assessment of the environmental impact of major projects, eco-labelling, freedom of access to environmental information held by public bodies, and eco-management and audit.

There is no doubt that the amendments made by the Single European Act aided this shift in emphasis by encouraging more wide-ranging measures. For example, because of Danish objections to the use of Article 308, it was accepted after the passage of the Wild Birds Directive 79/409 that no further legislation would be passed on wildlife unless it related to trade. Such a limitation is now clearly removed, as the passage of the Habitats Directive 92/43 illustrated. As a further example, the 1990 Environment Information Directive was made under Article 175 and there is little doubt that it would have been difficult to justify as a market harmonization measure.

The Fifth Action Programme, entitled *Towards Sustainability*, covered the period 1993 to 2000 and has perhaps been the most influential in shaping and redirecting policy. It reflected in part the agreements adopted at the Rio 'Earth Summit' earlier that year (see p. 157) and stressed the sustainable management of natural resources and provided a more wide-ranging environmental policy than before. It further switched the emphasis away from grouping environmental controls by reference to environmental media, such as air, water, or land, to looking horizontally at all the environmental implications of various sectors of the economy, especially industry, transport, agriculture, energy, and tourism. The legal counterpart of this has been Article 6 EC, added by the Amsterdam Treaty, which made environmental integration a fundamental objective of the EC (though there is still pessimism about what real changes this has made).

A central concept in the scheme of the Fifth Action Programme was that of 'shared responsibility'. This is the idea that responsibility for solving environmental problems is shared between government, industry, and consumers. A good example has been addressing waste management problems by requiring waste reduction and recycling (e.g. Directive 94/62 on Packaging and Packaging Waste, Directive 2000/53 on End of Life Vehicles and Directive 2002/96 on Waste Electronic and Electrical Equipment). This so-called producer responsibility legislation recognises that the polluter is as much the manufacturer of the good as the user. The programme also heralded a movement away from using legislation and regulation to solve problems towards a greater use of financial and other market mechanisms. It also suggested a more inventive use of legal instruments, including civil liability and voluntary mechanisms, the provision of more information on the state of the environment, a greater role for NGOs, and scrutiny of the financial sector's contribution towards sustainable development (see generally Chapter 8).

The Sixth Action Programme was approved in 2002. In many ways it continued the general approach taken in the previous Action Programme, emphasizing that environmental laws should work with the market, use a range of regulatory tools, and be better enforced. It identifies four priority environmental areas that need to be tackled: climate change, nature and biodiversity, environment and health and quality of life, and natural resources and waste. Continuing the emphasis on integration, it also envisages thematic strategies, seen as a way to tackle key environmental issues requiring a holistic approach because of their complexity, the diversity of actors concerned and because no singular or traditional approach to regulation will be effective. Thematic strategies are to be developed for soil protection; the marine environment; pesticides; air pollution; the urban environment; the sustainable use and management of resources; and waste recycling. In effect, these strategies are mini-environmental action programmes.

Although not a themed area for action, the period of the Sixth Action Programme is likely to see further 'post-regulatory', procedural law emphasized, and measures adopted which give effect to the provisions of the Aarhus Convention, e.g. on access to justice in environmental matters. It may also see further emphasis both on the rights of individuals and groups and, deepening the notion of shared responsibility, the responsibilities owed by these actors. Economic instruments are again stressed. However, as the Commission itself recognized in 1999, developments in this area at EC level have been stifled in large part by the need for unanimity amongst the Member States when environmental measures of a fiscal nature are agreed (see Article 175(2) EC). This has so far proved fatal to proposals for carbon taxes, not least because of UK hostility (though see now Directive 2003/96). Even where unanimity is not required, however, progress has been slow; attempts to adopt an EC-wide civil liability regime dragged on for many years before finally being adopted in 2004 (see p. 393). Examples of 'working with the market' include the recently adopted EC greenhouse gas emissions trading scheme, and tradable permit schemes may be explored further (though there seems little enthusiasm for them). Securing better compliance with EC environmental law, an enduring theme of recent action programmes, is said to be a 'strategic priority'.

It must be stressed that Action Programmes are guides to policy development and that EC environmental laws have been adopted which have not been heralded by such Programmes (and similarly that some measures which are suggested have not been adopted).

The range of environmental directives

It is neither possible (nor terribly helpful) in the space available to list all EC directives that relate to the environment. What follows is a selective list intended to illustrate the major areas of EC involvement, together with some indication of legislation in the pipeline. Greater detail on individual directives is given in the relevant chapters of Part 3 of this book and in Haigh, *Manual of Environmental Policy: the EC and Britain* (Longman, looseleaf), which explains each directive, and its implementation, in turn.

Important EC directives have been made in relation to the following (only directives currently in force are mentioned; some of these replace earlier directives). In some cases, such as in relation to the use and production of CFCs or emissions from vehicles, no number is given simply because the amount of legislation is very great.

- setting quality standards for water (e.g. Drinking Water 80/778; Bathing Waters 76/160; Freshwater Fish Waters 78/659; Shellfish Waters 79/923; Nitrates 91/676);

- setting emission standards for discharges to water (e.g. Dangerous Substances in Water 76/464; Groundwater 80/68);

- holistic management of the water environment, including quality and emission standards (Water Framework Directive 2000/60);

- setting quality standards for air (Ambient Air Quality Assessment and Management 96/62, and its daughter directives covering limit values for sulphur dioxide, nitrogen dioxide, particulate matter and lead (1999/30); benzene and carbon monoxide (2000/69) and ozone (2002/3);

- setting emission standards for emissions to the atmosphere (e.g. various Directives on Emissions from Vehicles such as 70/220, 88/76, 89/548 and 91/441; Emissions from Industrial Plants 84/360; Emissions from Large Combustion Plants 2001/80; Waste Incineration 2000/76; Volatile Organic Compounds 94/63 and 99/13);

- setting noise standards (e.g. Noise in the Workplace 86/188; Noise from Outdoor Equipment (2000/14)) and monitoring and mapping noise (2002/49);

- controlling emissions of dangerous pollutants (e.g. Dangerous Substances in Water 76/464; Toxic Waste 78/319 as amended by 91/689; Mercury 84/156; Lindane 84/491; Cadmium 83/513; Disposal of PCBs 76/403 and various Directives and Regulations on ozone depleting substances, Lead and Pesticides);

- controlling the disposal, management and reduction of waste (e.g. Framework Directive on Waste 75/442 as amended by 91/156; Toxic Waste 78/319 as amended by 91/689; Sewage Sludge 86/278; Urban Waste Water Treatment 91/271; Landfill 99/31);

- setting product standards (e.g. Noise from Outdoor Equipment 2000/14; Emissions from Vehicles; Classification, Packaging and Labelling of Dangerous Substances 79/831); Content of Petrol and Diesel Fuels 98/70; Hazardous Substances in Electrical and Electronic Equipment 2002/95; Phasing out Ozone-Depleting Substances Regulation 2037/2000);

- promoting waste reduction amongst producers (Packaging and Packaging Waste 94/62; End of Life Vehicles 2000/53; Waste Electronic and Electrical Equipment 2002/96);

- controlling the storage and use of hazardous materials (e.g. Major Accident Hazards 82/501 and 96/82 (the 'Seveso' I and II Directives); Asbestos 87/217);

- controlling dangerous activities (e.g. Transfrontier Shipment of Toxic Waste Regulation 259/93);

- setting standards for the operation of certain industries (e.g. Emissions from Industrial Plants 84/360; Titanium Dioxide Industry 78/176 and 89/428; Emissions from Large Combustion Plants 2001/80; Integrated Pollution Prevention and Control 96/61);

- procedures for the planning of development (e.g. Environmental Impact Assessment 85/337; Strategic Environmental Assessment 2001/42);

- protecting wildlife (e.g. Wild Birds 79/409; Habitats 92/43; Trade in Endangered Species Regulation 338/97);

- protecting the countryside (e.g. the Rural Development Regulation 1257/99);

- the contained use (90/219), deliberate release (2001/18) and transboundary movement (Regulation 1946/2003) of genetically modified organisms;

- promoting energy efficiency and combating climate change (Promoting Electricity from Renewable Energy Sources 2001/77; Energy Performance of Buildings 2002/91; Establishing a Greenhouse Gas Emissions Trading Scheme 2003/87; Taxation of Energy Products and Electricity 2003/96; Promoting Biofuels 2003/30).

There are also important directives and regulations on an ever-widening range of ancillary matters. Regulation 1210/90 established the European Environment Agency (see p. 186). Directive 2003/4 on Freedom of Access to Information on the Environment, and Directive 2003/35 on Public Participation in Relation to Plans and Programmes required under the EIA and IPPC Directives both form part of the essential process of sharing responsibility for environmental improvement between regulators, industry and the public. The Environmental Liability Directive (2004/35) and Council Framework Decision on Environmental Protection through Criminal Law (2003/80) are measures designed to improve compliance with existing laws. Regulation 880/92 on Eco-Labelling and Regulation 1836/93 on Eco-Management and Audit further emphasise the role that voluntary initiatives by business will play in future policy. Lastly, there is the Financial Instrument for the Environment (LIFE), originally contained within Regulation 1973/92, which provides financial support for environmental matters, especially on the promotion of sustainable development and nature conservation.

There are, of course, many areas of environmental policy where there has been little or no legislation from the EC. Examples relevant to this book include the use of energy and other taxes; town and country planning; and landscape conservation. There are various reasons for this inaction. Using the examples just mentioned, with energy taxes there has been strong opposition by certain Member States, especially the UK, to taxes set at EC level (where unanimity is required); and measures aimed directly at spatial planning or conserving landscape features solely on aesthetic grounds would probably be seen as in conflict with the principle of subsidiarity.

Environmental law—towards uniformity or flexibility?

As explained above, there is now a considerable body of EC environmental law, some of which has its origins in economic integration and some which has been adopted as more explicitly 'environmental' measures (under Art. 308 or Art. 175). In one sense, all of this legislation aims at harmonizing practice across the Community, although the desirability of setting uniform standards is somewhat greater when it comes to measures passed to complete the internal market (i.e. under Art. 95), especially product standards. Nevertheless, all of this legislation is essentially *minimum harmonization* legislation—it sets baseline standards which should not be breached. With both types of legislation, however, Member States have some scope to set stricter standards at national level.

Three issues arise:

- how far a Member State may go beyond EC environmental standards (the answer to which depends on whether the EC measure relates primarily to the internal market or to the environment);
- more generally, whether directives tend towards uniform standards or impose different standards on different Member States (i.e. how much flexibility there is *in the directive itself*);
- what the future holds.

Before considering these issues, however, it is worth noting that the *context* within which an environmental directive operates is important. A good example can be seen in relation to directives that regulate sound levels from motor vehicles under Directive 70/157, as amended. Member States may not refuse to grant EC or national type-approval to vehicles or exhaust systems, or restrict their free movement, if the requirements of this directive are met. But in *R v London Boroughs Transport Committee, ex parte Freight Transport Association Ltd* [1991] 1 WLR 828, the House of Lords held that a distinction was to be made between controlling the free circulation of vehicles manufactured in accordance with the directive, and legitimate traffic control measures, and allowed the latter (see also *R v London Borough of Greenwich* (1996) 255 ENDS Report 49). These cases illustrate that the *type* of harmonization has to be considered; a directive which fully harmonizes one area of control may not do so in other related areas.

(a) Higher national standards

Internal market legislation

For 'internal market' legislation, under Article 95(4), national provisions may be stricter than the directive if the national provision is justified by the need to protect the environment. This exception was intended to cover the situation where a directive[20] was agreed under Article 95 despite the opposition of a Member State (and for this reason is called the 'environmental guarantee'). It was central to the political balance agreed in the Single European Act because it provided a palliative to qualified majority voting. Following the Amsterdam Treaty, the Treaty now explicitly differentiates between national rules which are

20. The derogation provision also applies to harmonization measures emanating from the Commission through the comitology (committee) procedure, e.g. various scientific committees.

maintained (Art. 95(4)) and those which are subsequently *introduced* (Art. 95(5)). In both cases, whether a Member State voted against the harmonizing measure is irrelevant.

In both cases, the Commission must decide whether to approve or reject the national provisions having verified whether or not they are a means of arbitrary discrimination or a disguised restriction on internal trade or an obstacle to the internal market (Art. 95(6)). Because any national measures, existing or new, will potentially have some effect on the internal market, the Commission must in effect judge whether the derogation is *proportionate* to the aim of protecting the environment. If it does not do so within six months the national measures are deemed to be approved, which avoids problems which arose before 1999 when decisions from the Commission were sometimes delayed for many years; for an example see Case C-319/97 *Kortas* [1999] ECR I-3143.

The Court of Justice has held that a Member State may maintain stricter national provisions if its risk assessment differs from that of the Commission and the area in question is one where divergent assessments of risk can be made because of levels of scientific uncertainty, and where it can show that its national measures do in fact lead to greater protection and are not disproportionate. Although it gave this ruling in a case about food additives (Case C-3/00 *Denmark v Commission* [2003] ECR I-2643) it would seem equally applicable to many areas of environmental regulation, though in the *Denmark* case the Commission's risk assessment was in fact held to be flawed (which might suggest that in cases where there are divergent views about the conclusions to be drawn from competing risk assessments that gave due weight to all relevant information the Court might not be so generous towards the Member State).

Because national laws introduced after a harmonization measure are potentially more disruptive to harmonization, however, under Article 95(5) a Member State may *introduce* further national provisions only in the light of new scientific evidence relating specifically to a problem arising in that Member State after the harmonizing law was passed and which is notified to the Commission. It is not yet clear what would amount to a problem specific to a Member State. Prior to 1999 the Commission interpreted this as meaning a country's specific objective needs, e.g. relating to its geography or demography, although it did so fairly generously. In Case C-3/00 *Denmark v Commission* [2003] ECR I-2643, the Court held that under Article 95(4) there did not have to be a problem related to a particular Member State, or new scientific evidence, although these would be relevant when the Commission made its decision whether or not to allow the derogation (though in fact Denmark was able to derogate without showing that either of these applied). These factors, then, go to deciding whether the Member State's actions are proportionate under Article 95(4), though as the Advocate General cautioned in the *Denmark* case, the fact that no specific problem relating to a Member State needs to be proven when national provisions are being *maintained* has the potential effect of allowing Member States a permanent opt-out of harmonizing measures. Since 1999, Member States have increasingly resorted to derogations from harmonization measures. In Case C-512/99 *Germany v Commission* [2003] ECR I-845, Germany argued both that its high consumption of mineral wool, and its traditionally strict environmental policy, justified the introduction of more stringent labelling rules for mineral wool than required under a decision made under Directive 67/548. The Court did not have to rule on these arguments because Germany had not provided any scientific evidence to the Commission which post-dated the decision, but it is submitted that the former might provide a stronger basis for relying on Article 95(5) than the latter.

Environmental legislation

Stricter protective measures may be maintained *or* introduced under Article 176, so long as they are notified to the Commission and 'compatible with the Treaty' (which seems to mean that they should not give rise to unlawful trade distortions). This provision dates back to the SEA, and was included to allay fears from, in particular, Germany and Denmark (states traditionally seen as environmental 'leaders') at the possible impact of the enlargement of the EC, at that time, to include Spain and Portugal (states which did not have strong environmental protection regimes). Member States therefore have much greater freedom to go beyond the minimum standards laid down in environmental legislation, and arguably a 'two-speed environmental Europe' has already emerged.[21]

(b) Subsidiarity, proportionality and flexibility

What does the Treaty require when it comes to agreeing the content of directives? The starting point is the general principle of subsidiarity, first introduced specifically to the environmental title by the SEA 1986 and now contained in Article 5. This states that:

> In areas which do not fall within its exclusive competence, the Community shall take action, in accordance with the principle of subsidiarity, only if and in so far as the objectives of the proposed action cannot be sufficiently achieved by the Member States and can therefore, by reason of the scale or effects of the proposed action, be better achieved by the Community. Any action by the Community shall not go beyond what is necessary to achieve the objectives of this Treaty.

In part this is a competency clause, but it also relates to the amount of discretion given to Member States in EC environmental legislation. Following the Maastricht negotiations, the concept was much discussed. The Edinburgh Summit in December 1992, for example, resolved that the Community should only legislate to the extent necessary, that framework directives should be preferred (see below), and voluntary codes used where appropriate. The threat posed by subsidiarity was shown by the UK Government's action in bringing forward a list of directives it wished to see amended and a further list of proposals it wished to see discontinued. The first category included the various directives on air quality standards, drinking water, bathing waters, and hazardous waste, whilst the second included the proposed directives on landfill, packaging waste, and ecological quality of water, as well as proposals for strategic environmental assessment. This pressure has largely been resisted although not without some drift towards more flexible legislation. A good illustration is the Water Framework Directive (2000/60), considered at p. 717.

Alongside subsidiarity must be considered the concept of proportionality. This relates to the intensity of EC legislation ('scale or effects'), although the concepts of subsidiarity and proportionality are closely linked (and are the joint subject of a Protocol to the Amsterdam Treaty).[22]

Internal market legislation

As noted above, directives adopted under Article 95 aim to secure the functioning of the internal market subject to the important exceptions provided by the 'environmental

---

21. M. Soverski (2004), 13 RECIEL 127 at 133.
22. In the draft Constitution there is a revised Protocol on these concepts (Protocol 2).

guarantee'. Generally this means that directives will apply uniformly to all the Member States. Invariably this is the case with directives that govern the use of harmful substances in products (e.g. Directive 2002/95 restricting the use of certain hazardous substances in electrical and electronic equipment) but there are examples of directives, agreed under Article 95, which have not been concerned with the make-up of products and where a more flexible approach has been taken. The Packaging Waste Directive (94/62), for example, requires Member States to establish national systems to provide for the collection and recovery of packaging. It then provides for recovery and recycling targets, though Member States may set higher targets if they wish. In addition, three Member States (Portugal, Greece, and Ireland) were allowed to meet lower targets, so long as they eventually came into line by 2005. It is clear that these differences were agreed as a political expedient, but it is hard to see how this fits in with the normal requirements of uniformity under Article 95 (unless one is pragmatic about the legal base for the directive, which if it were adopted now would probably be split between those aspects relating to packaging and those relating to packaging waste; see the example of Directives 2002/95 and 2002/96 at p. 616).

Partly this is because Article 95(10) enables harmonizing legislation to include *provisional* safeguarding measures where, for example, these are needed to deal with exceptional threats of limited duration. Examples include Article 23 of Directive 2001/18/EC on the deliberate release into the environment of genetically modified organisms[23] under which a Member State may suspend or terminate the placing on the market of a product containing a GMO, if this is done because of new or additional scientific information about risk to health or the environment. However, the time periods for such temporary derogations, and their justification, can in practice be rather generous (see Box 7.8)

BOX 7.8 **Derogations and internal market environmental legislation**

Directive 99/51 on PCPs amended an earlier Directive from 1991; the revised Directive allows five Member States including the UK to continue to apply the less strict provisions of the 1991 Directive until 2008, on the grounds that as 'oceanic maritime Member States' there are technical reasons why they need to make certain uses of PCPs. As Krämer remarks, this is odd because of strong evidence in 1999 of less dangerous alternatives to PCPs, and because other Member States *not* granted the derogation, like Greece, are clearly maritime nations. But most forcefully, he questions why a national measure seeking more protective environmental provisions needs to be taken over the procedural hurdles of Article 95, while a derogation from a strict Community standard which allows less stringent standards to be applied nationally 'may be explained in three or four words.'[24]

Environmental legislation

The background to this, especially the various policy principles, has been described above (see p. 201). In particular Article 174 provides that Community policy should be based on

---

23. Adopted under Art. 95 EC. The use of this legal base might be questioned.

24. L. Krämer, *Casebook on EU Environmental Law* (Oxford: Hart Publishing 2002), 42, noting the differing standards when it comes to the duty to give reasons for adopting EC legislation (Art. 253 EC).

the principle that environmental damage should, as a priority, be rectified at source. But it also provides that, in preparing its environmental policy, the Community must take account of environmental conditions in, and balanced development of, the various regions of the Community. Arguably, the former points to a preference for emission standards, while the latter suggests a preference for target standards.

In general terms, the EC appears to be resolving this contradiction by a subtle mixture of approaches which may require 'best available techniques' and similar types of standards to be used for things like industrial emissions, but then tempering this by requiring these standards to be set having regard to regional differences. A good example of this is the Integrated Pollution Prevention and Control Directive (96/61) under which emissions must be controlled with regard to firms' 'geographic location and local environmental conditions'. Thus, while all regulated firms have to use the best available techniques to minimize pollution, regional differences will play a part in determining what is 'best' for any installation (see p. 781). A slightly different example of taking regional differences into account is the 'bubbling' of the EC's greenhouse gas emission reduction targets. Thus, the Community's target of reducing its emissions by 8 per cent by 2008–12 (compared to 1990 levels) is imposed unequally on Member States, so that some states must reduce emissions (e.g. the UK must make a 12.5 per cent cut) while others can increase their emissions (e.g. Greece is allowed a 25 per cent increase), a good illustration, in EC law, of the international law concept of 'common but differentiated responsibilities' (see also p. 639).

Aside from this substantive differentiation, the other feature of environmental legislation has been an increasing use of procedural and reflexive techniques. This has taken two forms. One is that Member States are increasingly required to adhere to specific procedures when implementing environmental directives (an example of this is Directive 96/61, which sets out quite detailed procedures for determining what the best available techniques for any particular sector will be, see p. 782). The other is the use of directives which either comprise essentially procedural obligations (such as the Directives on Environmental Impact Assessment (85/337) and Strategic Environmental Assessment (2001/42)) or which try to stimulate improved environmental performance within the Member States without specifically laying down binding targets (an example of the latter being the Renewable Energy Sources Directive 2001/77, which lays down non-binding 'indicative' targets for the proportion of electricity generated from renewables, and requires Member States to publish reports on their performance).

In contrast to internal market laws, Article 175(5) allows disproportionate costs to be alleviated by temporary derogations and/or financial support from the Cohesion Fund. It is worth noting that there is a move away from resorting to reliance on derogations (which must generally be granted by the Commission) towards setting out different targets in directives (see, for example, the different national targets effectively provided for in the Landfill Directive 99/31, and further below). The latter may be preferable politically, since the Member States can exercise more influence on the Council than on the Commission. However, temporary derogations are still used; a recent example is the Waste Electronic and Electrical Equipment Directive (2002/96) which sets specific collection and recovery targets but under which Greece and Ireland have been granted derogations for up to two years because of, positively, the low level of consumption of this kind of equipment and, negatively, their poor recycling facilities. Derogations have been used in particular to facilitate enlarging the EC eastwards (see Box 7.9).

BOX 7.9 Enlargement and the future of environmental law and policy

---

Even in an EC of 15 Member States environmental laws had to be sufficiently flexible to take geographic differences, and sometimes pragmatic abilities to comply, into account. From 2004, enlargement brought 10 new Member States into the EC (with the prospect of more countries joining in the future), diversifying further both the European environment, the strength of its national economies and its institutional capacity to secure environmental protection. The 2003 Accession Treaty requires that all legislation applies fully to the new Member States. However, as with previous enlargements, derogations regarding practical compliance have been given for specific directives. These are normally time-limited, but there are differing degrees of deroga-tions. For example, every accession country has been granted an extension—in some cases up to a decade—to comply with key provisions of the Urban Waste Water Treatment Directive (91/271), and derogations in relation to the Large Combustion Plants Directive (2001/80) are quite widespread, reflecting the difficulties that the new Member States have in improving emission controls at existing power stations. In some cases, however, derogations have been granted which merely require 'all efforts' to be made (e.g. Estonia in relation to certain sulphur dioxide emissions, because of its use of oil shale for burning).

What is perhaps most notable about this is not that quite lengthy, and in some cases seemingly unenforceable, derogations have been agreed, but that there are so few.[25] It is highly unlikely that they mark the full extent to which the accession countries were complying with existing EC environmental law when they joined the EC; all existing Member States are normally breaching one or more directives at any given time. The reality is that it will take several years before the Commission can seek meaningful sanctions against the new Member States—penalty payments imposed by the Court of Justice—because the institutional apparatus to monitor practical non-compliance is under-developed. This period of delay will in practice serve as a form of derogation, and the Accession Treaty mainly protects only against very long-tail, or very expensive, economic risks.

(c) New directions

For some time the Community has been moving away from a model of regulation based on adopting legislation laying down binding legal obligations which try to harmonize laws across the Community. This has been a general trend, but it is particularly important for environmental protection law. Partly this has been because of perceived shortcomings in old-style 'command and control' legislation, because this is neither flexible enough nor responsive enough to the complex demands of environmental regulation (and will become ever more difficult as the EU expands). But it has also been in response to some of the problems which the EC has faced in terms of its legitimacy, that is the perception that EC rule-making is too remote from those it affects and does not sufficiently engage with key stakeholders and the wider public (which in an area like environmental law with a wide array of private and public interests is a particular problem). For these reasons there has

---

25. The Council can grant new Member States temporary derogations from legislation adopted between November 2002 and April 2003, the date of the Accession Treaty, and all the new States have been granted derogations from the Directive on Waste Electrical Equipment adopted during this period.

been a shift of focus towards environmental *governance*. There are three related features to this development (which, it must be stressed, is already taking shape).

The first is a move away from exclusively 'top-down' environmental law-making to encompass decision-making processes which try to involve both state and non-state actors. In the environmental field, an existing example is the 'Auto-Oil' initiative, which brought together the Commission, vehicle manufacturers and the oil industry in trying to tackle a problem (air pollution) which could not be addressed coherently without, in effect, the problem being 'shared' by these two sectors (though it is notable that this initiative resulted in traditional regulatory standards being adopted, see p. 643). The second is a consequence of moving away from a focus on harmonization (especially substantive harmonization), and can be seen from the approach of the Court of Justice in the *Standley* case, where the Member States were given a considerable degree of discretion in how to implement the Agricultural Nitrates Directive (91/676) when it came to designating areas for protection (see p. 747). The third is that there is an emphasis on using different regulatory techniques which seem to fit better with this approach. Thus, in place of binding standards set at EC level there is much greater emphasis on trying to stimulate improved environmental performance within the Member States. This is through such learning strategies as benchmarking and sharing best practice, but there is likely to be some legal force behind this approach, for example, legislation will set out, procedurally, the terms by which information is generated and require that reports are published and reviewed by the Commission. The Renewable Energy Sources Directive 2001/77 (p. 643) illustrates how this approach is already taken.

In short, therefore, there are various pressures to move away from legislative harmonization (and even, as in the case of the environment, away from minimum harmonization). At the level of policy, the 'Cardiff process' can be seen as a far-reaching example of this approach (see p. 198). But it is possible that this new approach will also be adopted in place of relying on traditional legal approaches like the use of the standard-setting directives which have tended to predominate in environmental law, especially in those areas where issues about subsidiarity are more keenly felt.

There are, however, contrasting views on what is going on here. One view sees these developments in generally positive terms, emphasizing the need to give Member States— and key actors—greater freedom to pursue environmental protection in ways that they consider to be the most appropriate, albeit against a backdrop of transparency and structured evaluation and coordination. Another view, however, sees these developments in a more negative light, since substantive legal standards can at least in principle be enforced either through traditional legal means or, indirectly, by pressure groups raising awareness of non-compliance. On this view, headlines reporting that a Member State has breached EC law by failing to submit an evaluative report on how it is combating pollution simply carry less force than similar publicity that the Member State is polluting.

Free trade and environmental protection

The tensions between uniformity and flexibility, or between harmonization and national interests, are also seen in the extent to which, in the absence of the EC having adopted legislation under Articles 95 or 175, environmental considerations may override the free movement of goods within the EC. Thus Article 30 permits national laws effectively to restrict imports under Article 28 (or exports, under Art. 29) if there is a genuine need to protect, amongst other things, human, plant, or animal health, or national treasures. ('Animal health' has been defined to include wider biodiversity conservation concerns, an important extension from its narrower agricultural origins (Case C-67/97 *Bluhme* [1998] ECR I-8033)). The very important decision of the European Court of Justice in the *Danish Bottles* case amplifies this point into a more general rule (Case box 7.1).

CASE 7.1 Case 302/86 *Commission v Denmark* [1988] ECR 4607 ('*Danish Bottles*')

This case arose from a Commission challenge to Danish laws that required beer and soft drink containers to be returnable. The Commission argued they were a form of disguised discrimination against foreign manufacturers and hence an impediment to free trade under Article 28. The European Court of Justice held in clear terms that it was permissible to use environmental protection to justify such discrimination. This was because the protection of the environment is one of the EC's so-called 'mandatory requirements'. As such it can justify an interference with the operation of the common market (even though environmental protection is not mentioned in Art. 30).

However, it went on to hold that such a derogation from the internal market must be proportionate to the end to be achieved. Since a returnability requirement was clearly more environment-friendly than a recycling one, this requirement was acceptable. But a further licensing requirement, whereby only a limited number of container shapes was permitted, was disproportionate and thus illegal in EC law. Denmark argued that this limitation was needed to make facilities for cleaning bottles etc less complex and therefore more efficient, but these shapes coincided with the shapes of bottles used by Danish producers.

This decision has an obvious impact on the ability of Member States to pass environmental legislation that is stricter than in other Member States and which thus interferes with the common market. But it also has an impact on the attitude of the Commission, since in order to re-establish the single internal market, it will seek to lay down common standards by proposing EC legislation. There is an incentive to move towards common standards based on the stricter environmental protection legislation of the non-conforming state, using Article 95(3) as a justification. Indeed, to some extent the Community has done this with the Packaging and Packaging Waste Directive (94/62).[26]

Some extension of the *Danish Bottles* principle can be seen in the *Walloon Waste* case (Case Box 7.2).

CASE 7.2 Case C-2/90 *Commission v Belgium* [1992] ECR I-4431 ('*Walloon Waste*')

This case concerned what was effectively a ban on waste imports imposed by the Walloon Regional Executive. The European Court of Justice decided that waste constituted goods for the purposes of the Treaty and thus there was a clear infringement of the provisions on free movement of goods.

---

26. In Case C-246/99 *Commission v Denmark* the Commission challenged the Danish drinks packaging regime (which included a ban on metal packaging), but the national law was repealed and the case was therefore dropped before reaching the Court of Justice. Some indication of the trade, environment and harmonization issues involved, however, is given in the Advocate General's opinion (which broadly favoured the Commission).

However, it decided that the ban was justified on environmental grounds. In so doing, it held that wastes are goods of a special character. Accordingly, the general principle set out in Article 174(2), that pollution should be rectified at source, was called into play to suggest that wastes should be disposed of as close to their place of origin as possible. This enabled the Court to avoid the otherwise inevitable conclusion that the ban was discriminatory and is an important example of how these general principles can be used so as to have an impact on the development of the law. A further interesting feature of the case was the rather bizarre (but logical) result that the ban was legal as far as it applied to ordinary wastes, but not as far as hazardous wastes were concerned, because Directive 84/631 had already laid down an exhaustive system for the transfrontier shipment of hazardous waste. Therefore, the ban on hazardous waste was illegal because it contravened the provisions of the Directive (which Belgium had obviously agreed to).

Some attempt to formalize these decisions was made by the Maastricht Treaty, which added a new paragraph to Article 174(2). This allows directives seeking to harmonize EC laws to include a safeguard clause permitting a Member State to take *provisional* measures for environmental reasons. This does not appear to alter anything decided by *Danish Bottles*, but the Article does add a further requirement that such measures are subject to inspection by the Commission.

A further important factor is whether, in the interests of environmental protection, laws may directly discriminate in favour of a country's own nationals but nevertheless be lawful if the restrictions are for environmental protection reasons. In the *Walloon Waste* case the Court clearly tried to avoid having to answer this, but later cases make it fairly clear that this can be justified (see Case box 7.3).

CASE 7.3 Case C-379/98 *PreussenElektra AG v Schleswag AG* [2001] ECR I-2159

PreussenElektra operated a large number of conventional and nuclear power stations and an electricity grid, and Schleswag was the regional electricity distributor. Under German law, electricity suppliers must purchase electricity from renewables if this has been put on the German market. The price is determined by a complex formula intended to make renewables competitive, but the end result is that the supplier may have to pay more overall for its electricity. Above a certain threshold, the supplier can pass on the extra costs to the grid operator. Because of a vast increase in wind energy, PreussenElektra was faced with monthly costs of DM 10 million. The European Court of Justice decided that these rules did not contravene the rules on the free movement of goods (even though they clearly favoured green energy generated within Germany and therefore discriminated against green energy supplied by importers). This is not a case like *Danish Bottles*, because the Court decided that there was no impediment to free trade, i.e. there was no breach of Article 28 EC (so the Court did not approach this case as one where a barrier to free trade had to be justified under Article 30 using the 'mandatory requirement' of environmental protection). This was because of the environmental aims of the laws—which included meeting the EC's climate change obligations—as well as the specific characteristics of the EC electricity market (this had not been fully liberalized, so producers and suppliers did not operate in a completely free market). The Court accepted that, as things stood, once electricity was put into the grid it was impossible to trace its origin and this was a reason for favouring German producers by a guaranteed price. The Court also referred to Article 6 EC to emphasize the need for an 'environmentally conscious' internal market.

Together with a number of disputes which have been settled without resort to the Court—which also shed light on how the balance between trade and environmental protection is being struck[27]—the case law indicates that a Member State may adopt measures which disrupt the free movement of goods if such action

- is not already covered by EC legislation which fully regulates the area in question (as seen as in *Walloon Waste* case, but for a more recent leading case see Case C-473/98, *Kemikalieinspektionen v Toolex Alpha AB* [2000] ECR I-5681, which in essence held that a framework directive does not fully regulate an area where, for example, an environmentally harmful substance is not yet the subject of a daughter directive);

- does not arbitrarily discriminate between national producers and traders and those in other Member States (although note that in the *Danish Bottles* case, the Court implicitly accepted that the returnability requirement did not discriminate against importers, even though the cost either of transporting glass to and from Denmark, or setting up a deposit-and-return scheme there, would have been high);

- is proportional (see *Danish Bottles*, and see Box 7.5).

Other aspects of the market beyond the free circulation of goods are also becoming more responsive to environmental interests, and national environmental protection requirements are spreading to areas like state aids (see *British Aggregates Association and others v HM Treasury* [2002] CMLR 51, an unsuccessful challenge to the aggregates levy as being in breach of EC rules on, amongst other things, state aids) and taxes (Case C-213/96 *Outokumpu* [1998] ECR I-1777). The Court of Justice's decisions in relation to the 'greening' of public procurement contracts are indicative of a generally sympathetic approach (see Box 7.10).

BOX 7.10 **EC public procurement law and the environment**

Public procurement rules promote effective competition for things like public works contracts. The size of the EU public procurement market—around 11 per cent of the EU's gross domestic product—means that steering it towards environmentally preferable goods, services or works can make a direct and major contribution to environmental protection, and indirectly facilitate the development of greener products generally. EC public procurement rules aim at ensuring that tendering processes do not discriminate in favour of domestic contractors. So contracts must be awarded on the basis of the lowest price, or on the basis of what is 'economically most advantageous'. As with the tension between the free movement of goods and environmental protection, there is a balance to be struck between allowing Member State's to favour environmentally preferable products and the risk that they will use this to pursue a protectionist purchasing policy. 'Economically most advantageous' can include things like running costs, and can therefore include criteria like energy efficiency. But can it relate to factors which are aimed primarily at environmental protection?

---

27. The best overview is L. Krämer, *EC Environmental Law* (London: Sweat and Maxwell, 2003), 96–111.

In Case C-513/99 *Concordia Bus Finland* [2002] ECR I-7213 the issue was the legality of Helsinki's system of awarding points to tenderers whose bus fleets met specified air and noise pollution levels. On a restrictive interpretation of the rules (interestingly, supported by the Commission) there would not be any 'economic advantage'. But the Court of Justice gave a generous interpretation to this phrase, ruling that it could include factors which were not purely economic, so long as there were certain safeguards, e.g. that the criteria were transparent and linked to the subject-matter of the contract. They must also be objectively quantifiable, so a tender which, without elaboration, favours bids which are 'environmentally friendly' or which 'promote sustainable development' is unlikely to be lawful (see further P. Kunzlik (2003) 15 JEL 175). It also seems that criteria protecting not just the immediate locality but also the global environment would also be permissible, e.g. a requirement that electricity is supplied from renewable energy sources (Case C-448/01 *EVN Ag and Wienstrom Gmbh v Austria/Stadtwerke Klagenfurt Ag* [2004] 1 CMLR 22). The *Concordia Bus Finland* case is also notable for invoking Article 6 EC concerning environmental integration to support its conclusion.

Compliance by Member States with EC law

Articles 249 and 10 of the EC Treaty make clear that abiding by EC law entails a positive and a negative obligation: implementation of relevant directives, and not doing anything contrary to EC law. Since environmental law consists mainly of directives, compliance will be discussed in terms of them.

'A directive shall be binding, as to the result to be achieved, upon each Member State to which it is addressed, but shall leave to the national authorities the choice of form and method' (Art. 249 EC).

'Member States must 'take all appropriate measures, whether general or particular, to ensure fulfilment of the obligations arising out of this Treaty or resulting from action taken by institutions of the Community . . . [and] abstain from any measure which could jeopardise the attainment of the objectives of the Treaty' (Art. 10 EC).

In order to comply with a directive, a Member State must implement it fully and within the time limit. Any incompatible law must be repealed. It is irrelevant whether other states have also failed to comply.

It thus appears that there are a number of ways in which there may be non-compliance with a directive:

- a failure to transpose any or all of the directive within the time allowed ('the communication duty')—the case law is clear that there is no real excuse for this, since the Member State will have agreed the time limit in the first place;

- implementing by adopting an incorrect interpretation of the directive ('the conformity duty')—the European Court of Justice being the ultimate arbiter of this point;

- inadequate implementation in practice ('the application duty').

A key issue is how much discretion Member States have in selecting the method of implementing a directive. The Court of Justice has made it clear that mere changes in administrative practices are not sufficient, since they do not provide binding guarantees that the legal requirements of the directive will be complied with (thus forcing a change of approach by the UK which in the early years of EC environmental law relied heavily on this approach). This is particularly relevant to broadening the range of tools away from traditional forms of regulation such as licensing and criminal penalties and towards the use of economic instruments (key themes of the 5th and 6th Action Programmes). For example, a Member State may not use agreements to implement a directive, because an agreement is usually only enforceable by either of the contracting parties and does not therefore sufficiently guarantee the protection of rights (although there is an exception to this rule if the directive expressly provides for this, as with certain provisions of the End of Life Vehicles Directive (2000/53) and the Waste Electrical and Electronic Equipment Directive (2002/96)).

In this context note that determining the penalties for breaching laws which implement EC environmental directives is generally a matter for the discretion of the Member States. Indeed, the Court of Justice does not require criminal sanctions to be used, so long as the sanction is effective, proportionate and dissuasive (though interestingly the Greenhouse Gas Emissions Trading Directive (2003/87) prescribes fixed sanctions that the Member States have to impose where certain emission limits are breached). This generally deferential approach is also contained in the Framework Decision on Environmental Criminal Law (2003/80) which also requires criminal offences for intentional or seriously negligent conduct which causes substantial environment damage (though not necessarily to the exclusion of administrative controls).

The last type of non-compliance arises where a Member State has passed all the legislation required to implement a directive, but there is no compliance in fact. For example, it could arise where a Member State fails to enforce the provisions of a law, where standards laid down in a directive are not adhered to in practice, or where there is a failure to establish a protected area. As noted above, in the first *UK Drinking Water* case the European Court of Justice effectively equated non-compliance in fact with non-compliance in law (see p. 188).

This is not to say, however, that a breach of a directive will always be easy to identify. For example, many directives require Member States to designate protected areas for nature conservation or pollution control reasons. A complaint might be lodged with the Commission that a particular area has not been designated, and that this is in breach of a directive. In practice, though, the Commission rarely pursues infringement actions unless the failure to designate the area is a fairly clear-cut breach, or if it forms part of a failure to designate sufficient areas more generally (i.e. as with many areas of law, it is not always clear, in marginal cases, whether the law has not been implemented).

A further point is that a directive may set an environmental objective (e.g. an environmental quality standard or a limit value) but may also require Member States to implement pollution reduction programmes (see Box 7.11)

BOX 7.11 Compliance and pollution reduction programmes

The Court of Justice has held that even if a Member State complies with the environmental objective this does not relieve it from the need to implement programmes like these (Case C-184/97 *Commission v Germany* [1999] ECR I-7837). This case, which concerned the implementation of the Dangerous Substances in Water Directive (76/464) also raised the interesting issue of whether, being a directive, the Member State has any obligations beyond the obligation of result mentioned in Article 249 EC. This was raised by Germany but rejected by the Court, which in effect found that establishing the pollution reduction programmes was also 'the result to be achieved', i.e. both the substantive and procedural aspects of the directive had to be complied with. This makes practical sense, since the latter are presumably intended to ensure continuing compliance with the former. It is also worth noting here that the Court of Justice has held that where pollution reduction programmes are required they must be 'comprehensive and coherent'; neither general reduction programmes, nor ad hoc measures, will do (see, e.g. Case C-207/97 *Commission v Belgium* [1999] ECR I-275).

In an increasingly decentralized country like the UK one issue is that the national government may not necessarily be the body that was actually responsible for non-compliance and, indeed, may not, in some cases, be in a very strong position to rectify matters. Nevertheless, the national government will be held responsible as a matter of EC law. In practice, if it gets to the stage of the Member State being fined for non-compliance, it will almost certainly recoup the penalty from the budget of the region responsible, as is the stated policy in the UK. Indeed, an example of where this is automatically provided for is Part I of the Waste and Emissions Trading Act 2003 which deals with waste sent to landfills. If a waste disposal authority exceeds its landfill allowance, then a penalty is payable to the Secretary of State (and a higher penalty is payable if the waste disposal authority's actions mean that a target date for staged compliance under the directive is missed, or there is slippage from a target already met).

Non-compliance—enforcement by the Commission

If a Member State does not implement a Directive properly, or maintains in force a law which is contrary to EC law, there are only a limited number of options. The main responsibility for ensuring compliance rests with the Commission, which has a discretion to start infringement proceedings. Its current policy is to start these automatically in cases where any failure to comply is alleged. Although its stated policy is to focus on formal non-compliance, in practice the Commission tends to pursue more cases where non-compliance in practice is at stake,[28] doubtless because these tend to be the higher profile cases and the kinds of cases which are brought to their attention by aggrieved individuals and pressure groups.

These infringement proceedings have various stages. The Commission will write to the state informally, asking it to explain its position. If a satisfactory answer is not received, a formal letter will be sent, and the state's observations will be formally required. If the Commission is still not satisfied that the matter can be settled, it will issue a Reasoned Opinion, explaining what it thinks are the main features of the non-compliance. Most cases are resolved at these preliminary stages, and there are obvious parallels with the graded procedures adopted in practice by most regulatory agencies when dealing with breaches of domestic environmental law.

28. See E Hatton (2003) 15(3) JEL 273.

Under Article 226, the Commission is generally thought to have an absolute discretion to bring the Member State before the European Court of Justice. Another Member State may join in Article 226 proceedings as a third party to argue for one side or the other (e.g. Britain did this to support the Commission in the *Danish Bottles* case). An individual has no standing to bring infringement proceedings, or to compel the Commission to do so, but is limited to drawing an alleged non-compliance to the attention of the Commission. While the Community has been pursuing non-implementation of EC environmental law with greater rigour than previously, there is strong evidence pointing to a continuing culture, at least within the upper echelons of the Commission, that remains hostile to what is deemed to be over zealous enforcement (see the example of the restructuring of the waste and nature sections of DG Environment, motivated it is alleged by such concerns.)

The European Court of Justice is the ultimate arbiter of whether there has been compliance in law, and will give a decision on whether the state is in breach of EC law, but in the past it simply had declaratory powers. Nevertheless, states normally comply as a matter of political necessity. Otherwise the Commission or another Member State can reinstitute the infringement proceedings (again this is rare).

Penalty payments

The Maastricht Treaty changed matters considerably. Under Article 228, the Commission may now issue a Reasoned Opinion if it considers that a Member State has not complied with a judgment of the Court. If the Member State then continues to fail to comply, the Commission can bring the case back before the Court, which may impose a fine. The level of financial penalty will depend upon the seriousness and duration of the violation and the need for a 'dissuasive' effect. In addition to these factors, there is a degree of weighting which is applied taking into account the Member State's ability to pay. If all of these factors resulted in the maximum daily penalty it could lead to significant fines, upwards of £500,000 in some cases, which could be a serious deterrent. For example, in the late 1990s the Commission sought a fine of £106,800 per day against the UK for non-compliance with the judgment in the first *UK Bathing Water* case (Case C-56/90 *Commission v UK* [1993] ECR I-4109), though in fact the penalty payment case never reached the Court because the limit values in the Directive were finally complied with.

The Commission began seeking fines in environmental cases in 1997 and the first such cases involving Article 228 are now coming before the ECJ. The first decided case involved non-compliance by Greece with two waste directives

---

CASE 7.4 Case C-387/97 *Commission v Hellenic Republic* [2000] ECR I-3823 ('*Chania Waste*')

In this case the ECJ imposed a daily fine of £20,000 against Greece, judging the failure to implement management plans for toxic waste in an area of Crete as serious a breach as actual unlawful disposal of non-toxic waste. The Commission closed the case, i.e. the penalty payments were no longer payable, when the unauthorized landfill was fenced off and another temporary landfill began operation, and after Greece had paid about £5 million. However, it was not clear that the breach had in fact been remedied by then. The illegally disposed of waste had not been removed, and a better view may be that it would only be at the point when the environmental impairment ceases that the breach has been remedied (for support see Case C-365/97 *Commission v Italy* [1999] ECR I-7773).

The second Article 228 penalty imposed, also for a breach of an environmental directive, provides a good illustration of how the various factors are applied (see Case box 7.5).

CASE 7.5 Case 278/01 *Commission v Spain* [2004] Env LR D3 ('*Spanish Bathing Water*')

In 1998 Spain was found to have breached the Bathing Waters Directive in relation to the quality of various inshore waters (Case C-92/96 *Commission v Spain* [1998] ECR I-505, discussed at p. 715). The Court of Justice subsequently found that Spain was liable to a penalty under Article 228 EC. Because compliance with the directive was assessed annually, however, the penalty payment also had to be determined on this basis (otherwise a penalty might be paid for a compliant period). Also, because the penalty had to be proportionate to the seriousness of the breach, the fine would be based on the percentage of bathing areas not complying with the directive's mandatory values. This would reduce the penalty the closer that Spain got to full practical compliance. The duration co-efficient was also reduced because, under EC law (see p. 216), the works needed to remedy the breach (e.g. new treatment plant) had to be properly tendered for. In assessing the seriousness of the breach the Court took into account the directive's objectives of protecting public health and the environment but also the improvements that Spain had made to the waters. Ability to pay was reflected by a coefficient based on Spain's GDP and votes in the Council (the latter can also be said to be a proxy for the influence of the Member State over the legislation, though here the directive had had to be adopted unanimously). Multiplying the various coefficients together with the base unit for penalties (£500) gave £625,140 for every 1 per cent non-compliance per year.

The first penalty payment was based on just under 80 per cent compliance. Whether Spain will have to continue making penalty payments until there is 100 per cent compliance, however, is most unlikely. Nearly 20 years after the implementation date, no Member State has fully complied, and it would be invidious to continue to fine one Member State if its compliance levels are exceeding those of other Member States. At some point, therefore, the Commission will close the case and, following its case law on Article 226, the Court of Justice is unlikely to permit any legal challenge to the exercise of this discretion.

It is still too early to say what effect the Article 228 procedure is having in practice. There have certainly been cases where the threat of a fine has had the desired effect of bringing a Member State into compliance. However, the time taken to impose a penalty payment is lengthy (even in the *Spanish Bathing Water* case, where Spain argued that the Commission was too hasty in seeking a fine, five years had elapsed). The Commission has also explored the possibility of withholding EC funds provided for environmental matters in the event of non-compliance, and there is some evidence that this form of cross compliance may be effective. For example, compliance with the 1991 Agricultural Nitrates Directive is now a precondition for granting aid under the EC's agri-environmental programmes, and the Commission appears to be enthusiastic about the effectiveness of this approach.[29] It should also be stressed that EC environmental law is chronically under-enforced, which tempers the strictness of the duty to comply in practice.

29. HC Select Committee on Environment, Food and Rural Affairs, *The Water Framework Directive*, Fourth Report, Session 2002–03(evidence from DG Environment).

Non-compliance—individual remedies

In addition to these formal infringement procedures, the Court of Justice has used the concept of the supremacy of Community law to develop various strands of case law which relate to the question of compliance with EC law. Two of these—the doctrine of direct effect and the concept of useful effect—have already been mentioned above (p. 187). But it is worth looking at these, and other types of remedies, in more detail because, when these judicial developments are all taken together, they ensure that a lot of pressure can be exerted on Member States to implement directives properly and in full.

(a) Direct effect

The doctrine of direct effect is of great importance, since directly effective EC laws can be relied upon in the courts of Member States without the need for implementation: any incompatible national law can simply be ignored. If a national court is unwilling to accept that a directive is directly effective, the applicant may ask it to refer the question to the European Court of Justice under the Article 234 procedure. However, the doctrine has its limitations. Because the obligations must be sufficiently clear and precise, there are difficulties with directives that seem to impose more general obligations to achieve results. For example, in Case C-236/92 *Comitato di Coordinamento per la Difesa della Cava v Regione Lombardia* [1994] ECR I-483, the European Court of Justice found that Article 4 of the Waste Framework Directive (75/442) did not have direct effect. This was because the Court held that it only laid down a general objective to be pursued, and general measures to do so, rather than anything more concrete and binding (but see the *San Rocco valley* case below).

(b) Useful effect

By contrast with direct effect, the concept of useful effect means that a provision of a directive could be imprecise, but nevertheless it could be clear that in implementing it a Member State has gone beyond the bounds of its discretion. It is therefore the legality of the state's actions that are increasingly the focus; Member States have *duties* to give proper effect to directives within their legal systems, and these must be capable of being enforced through the courts. This approach has been developed by the Court of Justice in particular in cases relating to the Environmental Impact Assessment Directive (85/337) and how much discretion Member States have not to require impact assessment. The landmark case here is Case C-72/96 *Aanemersbedriff PK Kraaijeveld BV v Gedeputeerde Staaten van Zuid-Holland* [1996] ECR I-5403 but the approach has been fully confirmed most recently in Case C-287/98 *Luxembourg v Linster* [2000] ECR I-6917 (see further p. 534).

(c) Direct effect and useful effect compared

It is clear that direct effect and useful effect are related in so far as they both derive from a concern of the Court of Justice that Member States should not be able to evade the implementation of EC law. The main difference can be stated as follows. With direct effect the *degree* to which a Member State has not properly implemented a directive is irrelevant, whereas it is central to the useful effect approach (as the *San Rocco Valley* case (Box 7.4) illustrates).

A related point is that the 'useful effect' route can be used where the obligations in a directive are vague, which is not the case with direct effect which requires that the obligation is sufficiently clear and precise. For example, under the Water Framework Directive the main obligation relating to ecological water quality is 'good status' which the Member State must 'aim to achieve'. There is a lack of precision about both what is being required and whether it amounts to a binding legal standard (see p. 717) but if a body like the Environment Agency was clearly exceeding its discretion by giving too lenient an interpretation to 'good status' and making no efforts to achieve this then their actions could be reviewable.

A further point is that, unlike state liability claims (see below), it is still not clear whether individual rights need to be breached for a directive to have direct effect. There is a line of authority which suggests that they do but much of this comes out of actions brought by the Commission for non-compliance e.g. Case C-131/88 *Commission v Germany* [1991] ECR I-825, and does not address the question directly. That said, most directives setting standards can be interpreted as conferring implied rights on individuals. It is clear, however, that individual rights play little role when it comes to considering the useful effect of a directive (since it is based much more on the duties of the Member States).

(d) Vertical and horizontal effect

A potential drawback of direct effect and useful effect is that it only applies 'vertically' against central government or other 'emanations of the state', such as public bodies like the Environment Agency or local planning authorities, and not against another private body or person (this is known as 'horizontal effect'). The reason for this distinction is that the state itself cannot plead a failure to implement the directive properly as a defence—a form of the estoppel principle. An 'emanation of the state' is to be decided according to the function that a body performs, and not its precise legal ownership and structure. Hence, bodies which the state gives a public function to—such as the privatized water and sewerage companies—will be treated as emanations of the state, at least as far as their 'public' functions are concerned. In *Griffin v South West Water Services Ltd* [1995] IRLR 15, it was decided, in the context of employment law, that a privatized water company is an emanation of the state.

It has always been an area of some uncertainty whether a challenge by one individual effectively alleging breach of a directive by another private party (e.g. a company) would fall foul of the rule prohibiting directives having horizontal effect. This issue came before the UK courts in a case involving a challenge by a local resident to the grant of a planning permission for quarrying by a private company which had been given without an environmental impact assessment under Directive 85/337 (*R v Durham CC, Sherburn Stone Company Ltd & Secretary of State for Environment, Transport and the Regions, ex parte Huddleston* [2000] JPL 409). Although the case was brought as a review of the local planning authority's decision, the developer argued that the effect would be to impose obligations on it, including possible criminal liabilities for mining the site without permission. The Court of Appeal, however, rejected this line of argument, and held that there was a distinction between effectively imposing legal obligations as between individuals, and imposing conditions upon an individual's right to secure a benefit from the state. Sherburn's situation, it said, fell into the latter category. In a forceful judgment, Sedley LJ held that an individual could not be prevented from enforcing a directive against the state just because of its impact on other individuals.

This approach has been confirmed by the Court of Justice. In Case C-201/02 *R (Wells) v Secretary of State for Transport, Local Government and the Regions* [2004] Env LR 27, a subsequent reference in another case from the English High Court about the Environmental Impact Assessment Directive and quarrying, the Secretary of State tried, unsuccessfully, to have this approach to incidental direct effect overturned. However, the European Court of Justice held that the obligation to carry out an impact assessment did not amount to 'inverse direct effect', even though a consequence of challenging the permission that had been granted was that mining operations had to be halted. 'Adverse repercussions' on individuals could be tolerated, and the motive for the challenge—as here, to deprive an individual of the benefit of a planning decision—was irrelevant.

Related to this is the question whether direct effect is a doctrine that can be relied on by another public body. In *R (Mayor and Citizens of the City of Westminster, Preece and Adamson) v The Mayor of London* [2002] EWHC 2440, although the issue did not need to be decided, the High Court held that a local authority could not challenge an allegedly wrongful implementation of the Environmental Impact Assessment Directive in relation to the London Congestion Charge, because direct effect is a remedy that is only available to individuals. This is somewhat restrictive since the local authority could reasonably claim to be acting on behalf of its residents (and paying the costs of doing so), although there are obviously cases where a public body will not be acting in a directly representative capacity e.g. where a public body like the Environment Agency is trying to argue that the unimplemented terms of a directive should apply against another public authority such as a local planning authority.

(e) State liability

The decision of the European Court of Justice in Cases C-6 and 9/90 *Francovich and Boniface v Italy* [1991] ECR I-5357 developed a judicial damages remedy for certain breaches of EC law by Member States. As developed in later cases the state liability principle applies where:

(i) the rule of law is intended to confer rights on the individuals concerned;

(ii) the breach is sufficiently serious; and

(iii) there is a direct causal link between the breach of the obligation resting on the state and the damage sustained by the injured parties.

The development in the case law has come in relation to the second criteria. While *Francovich* was a case of failure to implement a directive, in later cases the Court has held that there may be liability for incorrect transposition where the Member State has 'manifestly and gravely disregarded' the limits of its discretion (effectively a fault-based standard). What will constitute this includes, for example, persisting with a breach in the face of a contrary ECJ ruling or other settled case law. It will also depend on the breadth of discretion given to the state. (In this respect, contrast the very prescriptive Drinking Water Directive with, for example, the Waste Framework Directive.) Complete failure to implement a directive, or failure to take any measures to achieve the objectives of the directive, will always be a serious breach. In the case of environmental directives, it is interesting to consider what degree of non-implementation in practice (e.g. through non-enforcement of the law) would amount to a sufficiently serious breach.

Requirements (i) and (iii) also raise difficulties in an environmental context. While it is clear that directives such as the Drinking Water Directive or the Environmental Information

Directive give rights to individuals, in many cases the directive is primarily directed towards protection of the environment. However, as noted above most directives laying down standards can be interpreted as conferring implied rights on individuals. In addition, economic harmonisation directives may confer individual rights. This was the view of the Court of Appeal in *Bowden v South West Water Services Ltd* [1999] Env LR 438, which held that it was at least arguable that a shellfisherman had a state liability claim where his economic interests were harmed following alleged failures in the implementation of the Shellfish Waters Directive. However, similar claims made under the Bathing Water Directive and Urban Waste Water Treatment Directive were struck out, because the claims were for losses of income from the claimant's business. The Court did, though, keep the door open to a potential claim under the other directives by holding merely that the claimant was not directly affected as a bather or by waste water. The causation issue is also tricky, since in most situations the harm will be caused by an operational failure rather than by the government's faulty implementation.

In its favour the action is against the state, and the liability of individual polluters need not be shown. But the absence to date of any successful environmental actions under *Francovich* suggest that it is of limited practical importance.

A final point is that the Court of Justice has held that in some situations there is an obligation owed between *individuals* to compensate for breaches of EC law. The Court has been careful to limit this so far to breaches of competition law (Case C-435/99 *Courage Ltd v Crehan* [2001] ECR I-6297) but whether it will remain restricted in this way remains to be seen.[30]

(f) National Procedural Rules and Remedies

The final area worth mentioning is the extent to which national procedural rules (such as the rules on standing, the time within legal challenges must be brought to the courts, or the remedies available to the courts) must be set aside to give effect to EC law. The basic principle is that procedural matters are for the Member States to decide, and will not be interfered with so long as they do not make it impossible or excessively difficult in practice to obtain a remedy (Case C-188/95 *Fantask* [1998] All ER (EC) 1). However, there is something of a balance to be struck here between making EC law effective and respecting very different national procedural rules. This is particularly problematic where discretionary remedies are being sought, which is the case with judicial review applications. As noted below (p. 231) the House of Lords suggested in the *Berkeley* case that, where EC obligations are concerned, the courts have little room for discretion, but later cases have stressed that there may be reasons why an applicant for judicial review should not succeed if this would place too great a burden on, say, a developer whose planning permission is challenged several years after it was granted. The important point is that even if the breach of EC law is clear, this does not necessarily mean that an applicant must succeed.

The *Wells* case, however, places an important restriction on the Member State's discretion in cases of non-compliance. In making good any harm caused by the failure to carry out its legal obligations, the national courts have to determine whether it is possible under domestic law to remedy the breach administratively (e.g. by revoking or suspending a

---

30. Expanding private liability in the environmental field would require the Court to go beyond the specific, though highly restrained, steps taken politically regarding environmental (civil) liability, see p. 393.

planning permission if an environmental assessment has not been conducted). It is clear that, before *Wells*, the UK courts did not seriously consider, in cases of non-compliance, revoking environmental licences like planning permissions (where compensation must be paid) and certainly did not consider that they had an obligation to do so. In addition, however, the Court of Justice went on to say that the national courts had to consider 'alternatively, if the individual so agreed, whether it was possible for the latter to claim compensation for the harm suffered'.

It is not exactly clear what the Court means by this, but it may have had in mind a situation where a development or industrial installation has been constructed (or construction has already begun) and where, from an economic point of view, the efficient solution is to compensate the person bringing the legal challenge and not require demolition. Potentially this accommodates both the rights of the applicant and the wider public interest. Quite how compensation to an environmental group challenging a decision should be calculated, however, remains obscure. Also, any compensation would be paid by the public authority responsible for authorizing the development and not the developer, since requiring the latter to pay would clearly violate the basic rules of direct effect about horizontality, and there seems to be no mechanism for clawing back the compensation from the party who stands to gain from receiving a benefit which, as a matter of law, they may not be entitled to. Another difficulty is knowing what the Court means when it says that the remedy must be agreed to by the applicant. Presumably whether an applicant agrees to be compensated depends on whether the court is minded to revoke the authorisation, which suggests that courts should first ask the applicant whether they would be satisfied with compensation.

These various developments set in motion by the ECJ to improve compliance with EC law give rise to a range of propositions. For example, if a consumer were to become ill as a result of drinking water from the public supply that did not comply with the standards laid down in the Drinking Water Directive, it would seem that there is a claim either directly in tort, relying on the direct effect of the Directive, or under the *Francovich* doctrine (as a breach of statutory duty), even if the water did comply with national standards. A more far-reaching example might be where an environmental group wished to challenge the non-implementation of a directive (or even a failure to enforce it, since the two are arguably the same thing in practice). In addition to making a complaint to the Commission, it could seek a declaration claiming that directly effective standards were not being enforced, or that a national authority had exceeded the limits of its discretion, and argue that any obstructive rules on delay should not be used to deny it access to the courts. It might even carry out a clean-up operation and claim its expenses under *Francovich*, even though such a claim would be bound to fail if only national laws were used.

Non-compliance—new approaches and future prospects

The need to improve the enforcement of existing legislation has been an aim of the Commission for several years. Currently around 500 complaints are made to the Commission every year and it is remarkable that over a third of all complaints received and infringement cases taken by the Commission relate to environmental legislation. Moreover this is probably the tip of the iceberg as only the most serious cases will be reported to the

Commission and these will not involve the thorny question of under-enforcement (i.e. where there has been formal compliance in terms of the transposing legislation but no implementation in practice). Improving compliance with existing EC environmental law is, as noted above, a 'strategic priority' in the 6th Environmental Action Programme and several points may be made about how this is being addressed and what the future may hold.

First, the Commission's work on implementation has led to a wider focus on the nature of the whole 'regulatory chain': 'the whole process through which legislation is designed, conceived, drafted, adopted, implemented and enforced until its effectiveness is assessed'. This has led to a greater concern with trying to 'design in' implementation, before problems arise.

Secondly, there is a desire to use new tools, and bring in more actors. For example, in addition to traditional infringement actions and the greater use of cross-compliance mechanisms the Commission has suggested using 'naming, shaming and praising', while various steps are being taken to improve access to justice in environmental matters (through implementing this 'pillar' of the Aarhus Convention; see COM(2003)624).

Thirdly, and perhaps running contrary to the last-mentioned point, there is the wider issue of how the search for 'new forms of governance' will impact on implementation and enforcement. If environmental policy and law becomes more concerned with ensuring active cooperation between the Member States and resorts less on traditional regulation through setting environmental standards, then it may be more difficult to determine whether there has been non-compliance. This may again put an onus on the courts to devise novel approaches to ensuring this new style legislation is effective bearing in mind the interests it is ultimately trying to protect.

EC environmental law and Britain

There is little doubt that the EC's environmental policy and the various directives and regulations adopted in pursuance of it have had an important influence on British environmental law. They have led directly to new legislation, new standards being adopted, significant changes in government policy, and also a general reassessment of the whole British approach to pollution control. It is not practical to provide an exhaustive list, but the following examples should give a flavour of the impact of EC environmental law. Further examples are covered at relevant places elsewhere in the book.

(a) Legislation
- New domestic legislation has been passed in relation to: environmental assessment (see the Town and Country Planning (Environmental Impact Assessment) (England and Wales) Regulations 1999 (SI 1999/293)); drinking water quality (see the Water Supply (Water Quality) Regulations 1989 (SI 1989/1147)); the protection of important natural habitats (see the Conservation (Natural Habitats etc.) Regulations 1994 (SI 1994/2716)); the definition of 'waste' (see the Waste Management Licensing Regulations 1994 (SI 1994/1056), sch. 4); the recovery and recycling of packaging waste (see the Producer Responsibility Obligations (Packaging Waste) Regulations 1997 (SI 1997/648); and access to environmental information (see the Environmental Information Regulations 1992 (SI 1992/3240), now see p. 328).

- New standards have been adopted for such things as air quality (see the Air Quality Standards Regulations 1989 (SI 1989/317)), emissions from cars (e.g. in relation to lead and carbon dioxide) and bathing waters (in order to reflect the standards laid down in Directive 76/160). In addition, consents for discharges to controlled waters incorporate standards laid down in EC directives, as do the water quality objectives which underpin many decisions on the control of water pollution.

- In the making of legislation, the move away from unanimous voting to qualified majority voting has undoubtedly forced the UK to agree to some measures it might not otherwise have done, although probably less than might be expected. Although the influence has not all been in one direction, it is notable that nearly all of the measures which the UK objected to in the early 1990s on subsidiarity grounds (e.g. on landfill) have now been adopted. One explanation for this, of course, is that EC environmental legislation is becoming more flexible in the style of the characteristically 'British approach'. Important examples include the Directives on IPPC and the Water Framework Directive.

- There has been far less direct impact in relation to establishing environmental principles as *legislative* principles. The environmental principles in the EC Treaty are essentially policy principles, and not directly enforceable, and while they may be having an indirect effect on national policy formulation, there is little sign that they are yet crystallizing into legislative principles of the kind that have direct application in the national courts. The classic example of this remains *R v Secretary of State for Trade and Industry, ex parte Duddridge* [1995] Env LR 151, where the Divisional Court refused to apply the precautionary principle, listed in Article 175 of the Treaty, as a matter of English law. The Court held that the principle did not impose any immediate obligations on Member States. While this was not surprising, the fact that the court also described the proposition that the principle should be adopted as 'startling' does, perhaps, illustrate that British judges may struggle when it comes to developing principles of environmental law and policy to cope with the peculiarities of environmental litigation and good administration.

(b) Policy

The impact on policy can be seen clearly in the case of the privatization of the water industry. The then government originally intended to privatise the whole industry, including the regulatory aspects, but was forced to create a public regulatory agency (in the form of the National Rivers Authority) because a private regulator would not fulfil the requirement for a 'competent authority' to have responsibility for overseeing the directives on water pollution. A different example is that Directives 91/271 on Urban Waste Water Treatment and 76/160 on Bathing Waters in particular have led to important changes in capital spending programmes in the water industry (the full extent of which would almost certainly never have been undertaken as a purely national measure). It is also arguable that the partial shift in British policy from basing controls on the impact on the receiving environment to using concepts based on best available techniques has been strongly influenced by the EC.

The existence of formal EC standards has also been of great importance for environmental groups, who have something with which to compare British practice when publicising alleged deficiencies in environmental performance.[31] These lobbying groups have also been able to influence the development of environmental policy at the EC level directly as well as at national level, which is an important aspect of the system of multi-level governance which now characterises the EU, though balanced against this it is important to mention that national governments can act as 'gatekeepers' in protecting national interests, and maintaining national policy styles, in the face of European-level developments.

A good illustration of the impact of EC environmental law can be seen in the national experience of implementing the Drinking Water Directive (Box 7.12).

BOX 7.12 **The UK drinking water litigation**

In the *First UK Drinking Water* case (Case C-337/89 *Commission v UK* [1992] ECR I-6103), the European Court of Justice decided that there had been a failure to implement the Drinking Water Directive (80/778) by, amongst other things, failing to comply with the maximum admissible concentration of nitrate in some supply zones. As noted above (p. 186) this part of the decision held the duty to comply with maximum admissible concentrations to be an absolute one, thus effectively treating non-compliance in practice in the same way as formal non-compliance and opening the way for future infringement proceedings based on a failure to enforce EC standards properly in practice. In Britain this is important because of the way that much of the practical implementation of the law is delegated to independent agencies and quangos.

When it later transpired that certain water companies were supplying water that was in breach of the pesticide standards set out in the Directive, the Secretary of State had accepted undertakings from them about their plans to remedy the situation, rather than making an enforcement order. This was challenged in *R v Secretary of State for the Environment, ex parte Friends of the Earth* [1995] Env LR 11, but the Court of Appeal accepted that, whilst the *primary* duty imposed by the Directive on the government was absolute, this then gave rise to a *secondary* duty to comply with the judgment. This secondary duty, said the Court, is not absolute in the same way, but is capable of being qualified by practical considerations.

Subsequently, the Commission took further infringement proceedings against the UK, alleging that the use of these undertakings (which in practice are drafted by the water companies and then agreed with government) breached the Directive. The UK Government argued that the undertakings were a reasonable and legitimate response to remedying the problem after it was recognized that the deadline for complying with the Directive had been breached. But in the *Second UK Drinking Water* case the Court of Justice supported the Commission (Case C-340/96 *Commission v UK* [1999] ECR I-2023). This decision was not really surprising, since the Water Industry Act 1991, under which the undertakings are made, does not specify the kinds of things to be covered in the compliance programme, nor indeed the speed with which compliance should be attained. But it does show the rather different approaches taken by the European Court of Justice and the national courts. For the latter, in the *ex parte Friends of the Earth* case, there was an obvious reluctance to interfere with the undertakings that had been accepted by government. For the ECJ, however, the undertakings were clearly incompatible with its established case law on implementation and the need for effective EC legislation.

---

31. For a deeper analysis of the impact on policy see A. Jordan, *The Europeanisation of British Environmental Policy* (London: Palgrave, 2002).

As a postscript, following the second infringement case the Drinking Water (Undertakings) (England and Wales) Regulations 2000 (SI 2000/1297) were enacted. These are an explicit response to the ECJ's judgment, and in effect require undertakings to be entered into only for the shortest possible period and only if no reasonable alternatives exist. It is unlikely that they really bring national law into compliance with EC law, but they are probably the least worse option politically (and seem to have headed off any action by the Commission under Art. 228); at any event they are a further example of formalism in response to EC law.

(c) Transposing directives

Two related issues arise in relation to transposing directives into national law. First, in response to worries about the formal transposition of directives into British legislation, the tendency nowadays is for implementing regulations to repeat the wording of the relevant directive and to make little attempt to 'translate' what are often unclear terms into the sort of precise language that is normal in British legislation. (So-called 'gold-plating' enacting implementing measures that go beyond the minimum required by a directive, is expressly contrary to government policy unless there are exceptional reasons.)'[32] The regulations implementing the Habitats Directive (92/43) illustrate this point perfectly (see p. 835). The result is that the meaning of the regulations remains unclear and fuller enlightenment must await either administrative guidance (which gives undesirably wide powers to the administration and is, in any case, not conclusive), or a decision by the courts (normally this would involve a judicial review action, with all the difficulties and expense that entails, or a ruling from the ECJ in infringement proceedings against a Member State). Such a roundabout method of discovering the scope of the law is most undesirable.

The second issue is that regulations to transpose directives are usually enacted under the European Communities Act 1972, which means that matters not covered by the directive cannot be legislated on at the same time (see, e.g., the environmental assessment of projects not covered under Directive 85/337, discussed at p. 516). Given the limitations on Parliamentary time, this may have the practical effect of restricting the passage of environmental legislation in some situations. One way to avoid this difficulty is to enact framework statutes which allow for both EC and national measures to be passed. This is the case with the Pollution Prevention and Control Act 1999 which, although criticized for the width it gives the Minister to make regulations, allows for regulations to be made that go beyond simply transposing the IPPC Directive (96/61).

(d) The approach of the courts

In the past, this book was critical of the British courts' negative attitude towards EC environmental law. This was for a variety of reasons: a tendency to interpret directives and implementing legislation restrictively, a phobia of referring cases to the Court of Justice under Article 234 EC, and a tendency to find some procedural reason why, even if, for example, a directive was found to be directly effective, the applicant should not succeed. All of these are nicely illustrated by the attitude of the courts to the Environmental Assessment Directive (85/337), discussed in more detail in Chapter 14. By contrast, the Court of Justice

---

32. Regulatory Impact Unit, *Better Policy Making: A Guide to Regulatory Impact Assessment* (Cabinet Office, 2003).

has been willing on a number of occasions to interpret the somewhat vague provisions of environmental directives as laying down clear objective criteria to ensure that their provisions are given effect to in the Member States. For example, in Case C-56/90 *Commission v United Kingdom* [1993] ECR I-4109 the Court stated that the criteria for designation as a traditional bathing water were objectively clear from Directive 76/160, despite the rather vague language used in the Directive. The drinking water litigation mentioned above is a good example of the extent to which the performance of the British courts in interpreting EC environmental law tended to compare unfavourably with the more robust approach to interpretation of the law taken by the ECJ.

There have of course been examples of the courts taking a purposive approach to interpreting EC environmental law and its implementing legislation. An excellent example is *R v Secretary of State for the Environment ex parte Kingston upon Hull City Council* [1996] Env LR 248 where two local authorities successfully challenged the Secretary of State's unduly restrictive decisions as to the designation of zones for reduced levels of sewage treatment under the Urban Waste Water Treatment Directive 91/271. The High Court rejected the Secretary of State's contention that the cost of designation was a material factor in determining what an 'estuary' was, because this could frustrate the underlying purpose of the Directive. This case was also notable because the court looked to giving effect to the directive and no challenge appears to have been made to the action on the grounds that individual rights were not affected.

In the light of some significant recent cases, a re-evaluation of the general approach of the national courts towards environmental law seems appropriate. Three cases illustrate a change in attitudes. In *R v Secretary of State for Trade and Industry, ex parte Greenpeace (No. 2)* [2000] Env LR 221 the High Court held that the Habitats Directive should have been applied beyond territorial waters, and that any delay in bringing the proceedings was outweighed by the environmental public interest at stake, a decision which was clearly unwelcome to the government because of possible constraints on the expansion of UK oil exploration (see p. 828). In *R (Murray) v Derbyshire County Council* [2002] Env LR 28 the Court of Appeal held that the waste management objectives in Article 4 of the Waste Framework Directive could not be reduced to mere 'material considerations' in deciding whether to grant planning permission, since this would mean that a decision-maker could give them no weight (see p. 573). Finally, in *Berkeley v Secretary of State for the Environment, Transport and the Regions* [2001] Env LR 16 the House of Lords held that for the purposes of the Environmental Assessment Directive, the failure of the developer to prepare a proper environmental statement (instead of a 'paper chase') was fatal to planning permission being granted (see Box 14.12).

Berkeley is perhaps the most important of these cases. It gave a highly purposive interpretation to the Directive, emphasising the rights of the public to be involved in the decision-making process in a meaningful way. But the House of Lords also said that when it came to errors of EC law, the courts had little room for discretion. This seemed to suggest that rules of EC environmental law should not be avoided either because of some procedural obstacle or because of any adverse impact on other important social and legal interests (such as the rights of developers to develop their land and to do so with relative certainty about what the relevant rules are).

However, later cases have emphasized that these remarks were made in a case where, by the time it reached the House of Lords, the developer no longer had an interest in developing the site, and that the courts must take factors such as the public interest in the development and possible losses to developers into account when deciding whether, as a matter of their discretion, to grant relief (*Bown v Secretary of State for Transport* [2004] Env LR 26). For this reason, it may be that the *Berkeley* case will turn out to be a false dawn in relation to the discretion that the courts have to give effect to directives where economic interests are at stake.

Q QUESTIONS

1 The EC has passed legislation on:
   (i)   wild bird conservation
   (ii) the quality of bathing waters
   (iii) lawnmower noise
   As a matter of law and of policy, do you think it should have?

2 Developing the issues raised in question 1 and applying them to issues of contemporary salience, consider the arguments for and against the EC having competence to adopt laws on the energy efficiency of:
   (i)   products
   (ii) industrial processes
   (iii) buildings.
   If so, how should it act? (i.e. consider the appropriate legal base, and the issues of subsidiarity and flexibility). As a follow up, you could take a critical look at what legislation has in fact been adopted in these areas so far: see WebLinks for sources.

3 The EC Treaty does not prohibit pollution (whereas it does prohibit, with exceptions, things like unlawful barriers to trade). Do you agree with the proposal that, to mirror the Treaty's basic provisions on trade, 'Subject to imperative reasons of overriding public interest, significantly impairing the environment or human health shall be prohibited'? Could the integration principle in Article 6 achieve the same objective?

4 Is making EC environmental law more responsive to different national circumstances consistent with its greater integration? What are the challenges?

5 Denmark introduces a national law prohibiting the operation of wind turbines that create noise levels above 50 decibels (50dB). Wind turbines are manufactured in France which make 60dB of noise (an increase of 10dB is the equivalent of a doubling in loudness). There is no EC directive on noise levels from wind turbines. Is this an unlawful barrier to the free movement of goods in the EC? Would it make a difference if there was a directive on wind turbines which required that they could only be sold with a noise-rating label?

6 What are the advantages and disadvantages of relying on the Commission to enforce EC environmental law? Is individual redress through the national courts a better option?

FURTHER READING

EC Environmental Law

A very thoughtful introduction is J. Scott, *EC Environmental Law* (London: Longmans, 1998) a text which is especially engaging on arguments for and against EC intervention. D. Gillies, *A Guide to EC Environmental Law* (London: Earthscan, 1999) is more of a user's guide, setting out clearly the decision-making processes as they effect environmental law, and also giving helpful guidance on how to bring complaints. More comprehensive coverage is given in J. Jans, *European Environmental Law* (Gronigen: 2nd edn Europa, 2000) and in L. Krämer, *EC Environmental Law* (London: 5th edn Sweet & Maxwell, 2003). Many of the leading articles, capturing the development of EC environmental law up to the Millennium, are gathered together in one volume, L. Krämer (ed.), *European Environmental Law* (London: Ashgate, 2003). This might usefully be supplemented by articles on the two key developments since then, the draft constitution and enlargement. At the time of writing, J. Jans and J. Scott (2003) 15 JEL 323 and P. Beyer et al (2004) EELR 216 provide commentary on the former (but not on the final version) while on the latter M. Soverski (2004) 13 RECIEL 127 is an excellent analysis, linking enlargement with changing trends in policy approaches. L. Krämer, *Casebook on EC Environmental Law* (Oxford: Hart Publishing, 2002), analyses 50 recent leading cases and sets them in context, and is highly recommended. J. Holder (ed.), *The Implementation of EC Environmental Law in the UK* (Chichester: Wiley, 1997) remains the only work to date with this focus. Students who like a challenge should read D. Chalmers, 'Inhabitants in the Field of EC Environmental Law', in P. Craig and G. de Burca (eds), *The Evolution of EC Law* (Oxford: Oxford University Press, 1999), a close read of which will, we promise, pay dividends. D. McGillivray and J. Holder, 'Locating EC Environmental Law' (2001) 20 Yearbook of European Law 139, tries to take a thematic approach to recent developments. C. Hilson, 'Legality Review of Member State Discretion Under Directives', in T. Tridimas and P. Nebbia (eds.), *European Union Law for the Twenty-First Century: Volume 1* (Oxford: Hart Publishing, 2004) uses a number of examples from environmental directives to question the limits of Member States' discretion in implementation, perhaps the thorniest legal problem.

EC Environmental Policy

The best introductory text is J. McCormick, *Environmental Policy in the European Union* (London: Palgrave, 2001), though P. Barnes and I. Barnes, *Environmental Policy in the European Union* (Cheltenham: Edward Elgar, 1999) is also useful. For a single chapter overview, J. Connolly and G. Smith, *Politics and the Environment* (London: 2nd edn, Routledge, 2003) can be recommended. A. Jordan (ed.), *Environmental Policy in the European Union* (London: Earthscan, 2002) gathers together the leading journal articles (especially recommended is the editor's article on 'The implementation of EU environmental policy: a policy problem without a political solution?, also found in (1999) 17 Environment and Planning C: Government and Policy 69, a comprehensive overview of implementation problems in their political context). W. Grant, D. Matthews, and P. Newell, *The Effectiveness of European Union Environmental Policy* (London: Macmillian, 2000) considers this issue in detail, with detailed case studies on air and water pollution and climate change. An excellent introduction to how national policy style has evolved in response to EC membership is P. Lowe and S. Ward (eds), *British Environmental Policy and Europe* (London: Routledge, 1998). As well as thematic coverage, there are sectoral chapters which might usefully be read alongside the chapters in Part 3 of this book.

Keeping up to date, N. Haigh, *Manual of Environmental Policy: The EC and Britain* (Leeds: Money Publishing, looseleaf updated), is an expensive work but updated fairly regularly (and now available on-line). It spans law and policy and analyses the history and scope of most environmental directives, and how they are implemented at national level. Other ways of keeping up to date are obviously through specialist journals: the *European Environmental Law Review* (monthly, The Hague: Kluwer) combines news and articles, as does the *Review of EC and International Environmental Law* (tri-annually, Oxford: Blackwell) which has excellent coverage of case law. The *Yearbook of European Environmental Law* (Oxford: Oxford University Press) also has a useful annual survey, but its real strength is the quality of its articles.

@ WEB LINKS

Some aspects of EC decision-making are still comparatively secretive, but there is now much greater access to accessible information. Much of this can be found on the central web site of the EU <www.europa.eu.int/eur-lex/en/index.html>, which links to legislation, case law, and preparatory documents. The *Official Journal*, the definitive source for legislative material, is now also available online. A better starting point for further information and research, however, is the website of DG Environment <europa.eu.int/comm/environment/index_en.htm> which groups information by sectors and also includes the 6th Environmental Action Programme and the annual survey on implementation and enforcement. A site which combines official information—treaties, legislation, case law, and other documents—as well as helpful dossiers and extensive links is the European Environmental Law Homepage <www.eel.nl>.

8 The regulation of environmental protection

Overview

This chapter provides an introduction to the system of environmental regulation by building upon Chapter 4 in which sources of environmental law were examined. In practice environmental law is made up of more than mere rules which forbid pollution. The process of environmental regulation begins before laws are made with establishment of policies which can be translated into laws. Once in place, laws have to be given practical effect through the establishment of environmental standards, systems of administrative decision-making and enforcement. Thus, the system of environmental regulation involves many different aspects including the setting, application, enforcement and on-going review of environmental standards. This means that this chapter is merely an introductory, but nonetheless significant, building block. Many of the ideas explored will be returned to in different contexts in later chapters and you may find yourself re-reading different elements, e.g. in relation to environmental standards and the way they are used in the system of Integrated Pollution Prevention and Control. In addition, bear in mind that some material in later chapters including environmental crime and public participation supplement this one. Finally, parts of this chapter cover themes which underscore many of the remaining chapters and environmental law as a whole (e.g. the impacts of discretion and gradualism) and should be reflected on within many different contexts. Before reading this chapter it might be helpful to have considered the material on the history and challenges of environmental law (Chapter 2) and European environmental law (Chapter 7).

At the end of this chapter you should be able to:

- ✔ Identify and understand in outline the system for addressing environmental problems by controlling activities through regulation by public bodies.
- ✔ Identify and understand the main types of environmental standards used in environmental regulation.
- ✔ Appreciate the different types of environmental standards and how they relate to one another.
- ✔ Identify the characteristics which might be classed as the 'British' approach to environmental regulation.
- ✔ Compare and contrast the 'British' approach to other, notably European, approaches.
- ✔ Understand in outline the idea of addressing environmental problems through the use of economic or market mechanisms and other means such as self regulation.

Introduction

In Chapter 4 it was argued that there are many different sources of environmental law. Indeed, the diversification of regulatory 'tools' has increased dramatically over the last 30 years, reflecting not only the growth in the complexity of laws and regulatory systems generally but also the continuing development of the understanding of how to address environmental problems through legal means. In addition to the diversity of domestic sources of law, there is an increasing 'layering' of laws with different instruments having differing legal effects at international, European and national and even regional levels.

Despite this proliferation of legal mechanisms and in particular the current vogue for suggesting economic or fiscal mechanisms for combating environmental problems, the system of regulation by public bodies remains the prime tool for environmental protection in this country. There has been a spate of environmental taxes which have been either introduced (e.g. on waste going to landfill, the use of energy and the production of aggregates) or proposed (e.g. on such things as pesticides and the discharge of effluent) but whatever the political rhetoric, the use of taxation and subsidies will always be secondary to regulation in its widest sense.

What does regulation mean in this sense? At one level all the word means is the use of rules to control activities. This could be through mandatory regulation, often referred, in very broad terms, as 'command and control' regulation, characterized by the imperative 'you must' and the prohibitive 'you must not'. Under this definition these could include criminal law rules, civil law rules or private non-legal rules operated by a body such as a trade association, or maybe even the 'rules' of the market. In Chapter 4 there was some discussion of the wide range of environmental rules which might fall within this definition. In this book, however, the word 'regulation' is generally used as shorthand for administrative or bureaucratic regulation (i.e. the application of rules and procedures by public bodies so as to achieve a measure of control over activities carried on by individuals and firms). This definition does not, however, encompass all aspects of environmental regulation. For example, European regulatory systems and self regulatory mechanisms are not included.[1] Other means of controlling activities, such as criminal law or civil law and the use of the market, will be considered later in this chapter, but since these are often subsidiary to administrative regulation, this will be explained first.

Administrative regulation

Administrative regulation is far more than just the setting of rules on what can and cannot be done. It denotes a coherent *system* of control in which the regulating body sets a framework for activities on an ongoing basis, with a view to conditioning and policing behaviour as well as laying down straight rules. The advantages of such a system include the ability to

---

1. See further, C. Hilson, *Regulating Pollution: A UK and EC Perspective* (Oxford: Hart Publishing, 2000), 1–2, A. Ogus, *Regulation: Legal Form and Economic Theory* (Oxford: Clarendon Press, 1994), 1.

provide uniformity, rationality, and fairness between those who are regulated. Some form of public accountability is also produced by having a public body responsible for regulation. In particular, one advantage over the criminal law is that a coherent link can be made with other policies, so as to balance all relevant factors. This is often seen as an important part of the 'British' approach to regulation: that it involves an explicit balancing of environmental factors with such things as economic and social considerations.

British regulatory systems can be said to exhibit a pragmatic and flexible approach: the same mechanism is not used for each situation. In some cases the reason for this is simply that it is recognised that a control mechanism that works for one problem is unlikely to work for a different one. This is a good illustration of the use of law as a tool or a technique to help to solve particular problems. In other cases, there are historical reasons, since one of the features of having a long history of environmental control is that the administrative structures have built up piecemeal and in response to problems as they arise (see Chapter 2). For example, many controls have in the past been given to local authorities purely because they happened to be dealing with similar matters already, or because there was no other relevant body around at the time.

The processes of regulatory decision-making

Before looking at the main features of regulation in this country, it is necessary to summarise the main processes or stages in regulatory decision-making. These are set out in Box 8.1:

BOX 8.1 **The regulatory process—a summary**

The main stages of the environmental regulatory system include:

- Establishing general policies on the environment.
- Setting standards or specific policies in relation to the environmental issue concerned.
- Applying these standards and policies to individual situations normally through some sort of licensing system.
- Enforcing standards and permissions through administrative and criminal sanctions.
- Providing information about the environment and the regulatory process itself.
- Using mechanisms to monitor and improve the regulatory system.

(a) The establishment of general policies

The decision about *which* environmental problems to regulate and *how* to do so is determined within the process of environmental policy making. This process has been characterised as having three stages.[2] The first is the 'ignition stage' where Governments are

---

2. E. Ashby, *Reconciling Man with the Environment*, (Oxford: Oxford University Press, 1978).

stimulated to address a problem either through public opinion or particular events or environmental conditions.[3] Although shifts in environmental values play a part (see Box 3.2), it is not easy to identify any common trigger for the policy making process although there has been a shift from the historical reaction to particular events or catastrophes to a broader awareness of environmental issues from Government, environmental groups and the general public. Secondly, the examination of the problem and an assessment of the issues and risks involved and potential solutions. Finally, decisions have to be made about *whether* to regulate and these are essentially subjective decisions made on the basis of information gathered during the second stage. It is only at this third stage that the manner of regulation is considered in any depth.

The process of establishing general policies is not really part of the regulatory system, but a necessary precondition for any system of environmental control. Having said that, one of the most obvious features of the British political system is the absence of a formal national 'policy for the environment'.[4] Even where there are local or sectoral plans, there is often no national plan, or, if there is, it is made up of somewhat imprecise and flexible policies laid down in a variety of documents. A good illustration of the flexible nature of policy-making in Britain is provided by the town and country planning system, where the 'national plan' is to be found scattered amongst numerous Circulars, Planning Policy Statements, Ministerial decisions, White Papers and other assorted policy statements. There is some evidence that the position is altering with moves towards National Sectoral Strategies in waste and air quality. EC law has been the trigger for many of these changes with a number of Directives requiring coherent 'plans and programmes' for addressing certain environmental problems (e.g. the Waste Framework Directive, 75/442, Art. 7).

Given the essentially political nature of much of environmental law, the general tenor of the policies tends to be decided by central government. The presumption in favour of development in town planning is one example, but general decisions on energy and transport policy, such as the favouring of road transport over rail, or the expansion of the wind energy programme, are others. Certain political philosophies may also be imposed by central government; good examples are the principle of voluntariness in relation to controlling agricultural activities, or the policy of privatization. However, because of the decentralized nature of much of pollution control, some general policies are effectively decided by bodies other than the elected central government. Other policies stem from general assumptions about the nature of the regulatory system itself—which we later refer to as the 'British approach' to environmental regulation.

A final factor is that the shape of many policies is now decided, or at least affected, by the EC. Arguably some of the most significant impacts on the environment in the next few years will follow from the process of integrating environmental policy into other, more general areas of EC policy (under Art. 6 of the EC Treaty).

---

3. Royal Commission on Environmental Pollution: 21st Report: *Setting Environmental Standards* Cm 4053, 1998, paras 1.33–1.34.

4. R. Garner, *Environmental Politics: Britain Europe and the Global Environment* (2nd edn, London: MacMillan Press, 2000), 152, S. Young, *The Politics of the Environment* (Manchester: Baseline Books, 1993) 65.

(b) The setting of standards or specific policies in relation to the environmental issue concerned

The implementation of regulation requires more than just rules telling people what shall or shall not happen. Any system of control must have some objectives or standards that are set for it, otherwise it runs the risk of ceasing to be rational, uniform or fair. These may be fairly explicit objectives, such as air quality standards with specific maximum concentrations for a range of pollutants, or they may be far more vague, such as a water quality objective to the effect that a river should be capable of supporting fish. These standards ensure that those that are regulated understand what they need to do to comply with regulation but more importantly they guide those who regulate in determining how to achieve the overall objectives of the regulation and enforce the rules effectively.

In the past reliance has usually been placed on rather vague standards, such as the test of nuisance at common law (see p. 359), or the idea that best practicable means should be used to reduce gaseous emissions to the atmosphere. In addition, standards were often set in an informal manner, as used to happen with non-statutory water quality objectives. More specific and more formal standards are becoming the norm rather than the exception, a good example being the use of the BAT (Best Available Techniques) standard to prevent pollution from industrial installations controlled under Integrated Pollution Prevention and Control which is fleshed out with technical guidance on the manner in which to achieve the standard. In the development control system, policies of this type are set out in development plans and in Planning Policy Statements. There is often overlap between this stage and stage (a) above because in determining the policy to adopt in relation to a particular environmental problem it is often necessary to consider what specific standard should be adopted and/or what objectives should be set.

(c) The application of these standards and policies to individual situations

This is often seen as the central part of the regulatory process. There are numerous examples where a permission, authorization, consent, or licence is required from a public body. Different pieces of legislation use different words but they all mean essentially the same thing. Whether one is granted, and the nature of any conditions attached, will normally be a discretionary decision, but one that is made by reference to the general standards established at stage (b). The application of standards may also be seen in such processes as court actions for nuisance and the specific application of whether best practicable means or best available techniques are being used. The application of standards and policies is essentially a discretionary decision made by the expert regulator which is difficult to challenge in the courts unless there has been a procedural error.

(d) The enforcement of standards and permissions

In practice, one of the most important areas of environmental law is whether the legal instruments that are available are used, since there is often considerable discretion given to the regulatory body. 'Enforcement' covers a far wider range of matters than the single question whether to prosecute for breaches of the law. In any regulatory system, there is normally a whole range of administrative and other remedies available in addition to prosecution. The question of which remedy to use is also tied up with how the regulator should proceed. There is a wealth of evidence to show that informal methods of enforcement are often preferred, and that regulators normally adopt a 'compliance strategy' towards enforcement, rather than a 'sanctioning strategy' (see Chapter 9). Questions of inspection and monitoring also arise as part of the enforcement process.[5]

(e) The provision of information about the environment and the regulatory process

A theme which runs through the regulatory process concerns the openness of the system. This includes such questions as the production of official information on the state of the environment, the availability of public registers, and the publication of information about how the regulatory system itself works. Britain's traditionally secretive administrative processes have become more open and the emphasis has shifted in recent years to ensuring that the use of information is effective in encouraging public participation in the regulatory process. This is most obvious in relation to stage (c), but is also apparent in other stages of the regulatory process, enabling participation in the policy formulation and standard setting stage through increased consultation and the availability of more environmental information for enforcement purposes.

(f) The use of feedback mechanisms to monitor and improve decision-making

The final stage of the regulatory process links back into the first. An efficient regulatory system needs to be responsive to practical operational experience and changes in scientific and public opinion. Thus, monitoring and the review of the operation of existing regulation is now an integral part of many environmental laws. These iterative mechanisms work both generally in terms of pieces of legislation, particularly European directives (e.g. IPPC Directive 96/6, Art. 16(3) and the Packaging and Packaging Waste Directive 94/62, Art. 17) and in relation to specific requirements to keep up to date with advances in pollution abatement technologies under IPPC legislation or to supervise and vary pollution control permits/authorizations at certain periods (e.g. the supervision and monitoring of waste management licences under EPA 1990, s. 35) or in response to newly identified problems (e.g. variation of discharge consents to meet new environmental quality requirements). Finally, there are other methods of monitoring the operation of environmental laws through informal mechanisms (e.g. the Parliamentary Select Committees and organisations such as the RECP have a role to play in the monitoring of the effectiveness of environmental law and policy, see p. 117).

Anticipatory and continuing controls

Regulatory mechanisms may be divided into two general types, anticipatory controls and continuing controls.

(a) Anticipatory controls

These are measures in which controls are imposed on an activity at its commencement in order to forestall potential environmental problems. Usually the objective is to prevent the activity unless certain requirements or conditions are met. The category includes a wide

---

5. W. Howarth (1997) MLR 200.

range of licensing-type controls, where permission of some sort is required before an activity may be started or carried on. These are normally complemented by a combination of criminal and administrative sanctions if the activity starts without permission, or if the permission is contravened.

BOX 8.2 The range of anticipatory controls

The range of possible anticipatory controls is quite wide. It includes:

- An outright ban (e.g. the ban on the use of CFCs in products, or the ban on the dumping of tyres in landfills). Of course, there is no *necessity* for a public regulatory body to be involved here, but someone will need to police the ban.

- A prohibition on an activity unless a particular body is notified in advance.

- A prohibition on an activity unless it is registered, registration being something that cannot normally be refused by the registering body (e.g. there is a requirement that carriers of controlled waste register with the Environment Agency).

- A prohibition on an activity until a licence, permission, authorization, or consent is obtained, where the granting of the permission is at the discretion of the regulating body.

There are two distinct categories of permission or consent. Some are one-off permissions which, once granted, create what are in effect permanent rights because it is difficult to vary or revoke them. A good example is the granting of planning permission, where revocation entails the payment of compensation. Others provide for variation or revocation in the light of future circumstances. Most pollution control consents fall into this category, examples being the requirement to obtain an authorization/permit from the Environment Agency for carrying on a prescribed process, or a consent for a discharge to controlled waters.

(b) Continuing controls

These are measures where the carrying out of an activity is controlled on a continuing basis. Typically they relate to the way an activity is carried on, so another way of referring to them would be as *operational* controls. An obvious example is the ongoing duty to comply with the terms of a consent, licence, authorization, or permission granted by a pollution control authority, which will normally be combined with a range of other regulatory controls relating to monitoring and enforcement. The distinction between anticipatory controls and continuing controls is thus that one relates to *whether* an activity should be carried on in the first place, whilst the other relates to *how* it is carried on once it has started.

Of course, anticipatory and continuing controls are mutually supportive and most regulatory systems combine the two types of mechanism. Anticipatory controls still require some monitoring to ensure that the prohibited activity is not being carried on. Conversely, most continuing controls rest on the need for some initial permission before an activity may be started; indeed, the threat of withdrawal of the initial permission may well constitute the strongest inducement to comply with continuing regulatory requirements. For example, planning permission is required before a new activity is started, but that permission will often include conditions that require some adherence to defined standards over a period of time, such as permitted working hours or noise limits. Similarly, consents, authorizations and licences obtained from pollution control authorities normally combine the initial need for a consent with an ability to vary the requirements as the situation changes. This mutually supportive position is reinforced by the fact that many activities are subject to the requirements of more than one regulatory system.

Planning and prevention

The town and country planning system is the major system of anticipatory control in environmental law. To a large extent this stems from the very nature of planning control. It involves the preparation of plans, which may then guide future behaviour. The controls are necessarily imposed at the outset, whilst most pollution control mechanisms basically assume a continuing activity. Planning also mainly concerns land use, siting and locational issues that logically pre-date the operational controls.

A further reason results from practice. In these other systems, it is rare for the initial consent to be refused or revoked (although this power does remain as a threat for those who contravene the continuing controls). For example, it appears that no instance was ever recorded of a certificate of registration being refused under the Alkali Acts, either at the outset or on renewal.[5] In other areas of pollution control, the record may be slightly different, but there are still few examples of a consent from a pollution control authority actually being refused where there is already a planning permission.

One result is that the main burden of deciding whether a particular plant should go ahead normally falls upon the local planning authority. By way of example, a new factory will require planning permission as well as consents for emissions from the EA, local authority (in its capacity as regulator of air pollution) and the sewerage undertaker as well. It will be the local planning authority that decides whether to have the factory in that particular place. The pollution control authorities tend to see their task as setting limits on what is acceptable in terms of pollution from the site proposed rather than as stopping the development going ahead at all. Traditionally, these authorities have had little scope for saying, 'this development would be better somewhere else', though that is a matter they could raise when consulted by the local planning authority over the development proposal. (For an analysis of the relationship between the systems of planning and pollution control, see *Gateshead Metropolitan Borough Council v Secretary of State for the Environment* [1995] JPL 432 discussed at p. 790).

This is perhaps inevitable given the differences in nature between local planning authorities and other regulatory bodies. A local planning authority has a specific remit under the Town and Country Planning Act 1990, s. 70 to consider *all* material factors relating to a development, whilst other bodies often have a more limited range of relevant factors to consider in making their decision (factors which should relate to pollution control issues alone, i.e. not economic, spatial, or social). It is also an elected body, where ultimate

6. C. Wood, *Planning Pollution Prevention* (London: Butterworths, 1989).

power resides with elected members, and therefore has greater legitimacy in terms of making a balanced policy decision to refuse a development.

Standards in environmental law

Most environmental controls rely on some form of measurable standard. This standard may be used as a guideline (i.e. an objective) or it may be used as a means of defining what an individual or firm may do. Indeed, one of the distinctive features of environmental regulation is that the regulatory body often has responsibility for defining the standard as well as enforcing its application.

There are a number of different types of standards, but a crude division can be made into those which are set by reference to the *target* which is being protected and those which are set by reference to the *source* of the pollution. Source-related standards may be further divided into emission standards, process standards, and product standards. There are other factors that have a significant impact on the nature of a standard, such as whether it is centrally or locally set, uniform or flexible, precise or imprecise.

The following summary is not intended to be an exhaustive list of the various types of standard (from the list of variables above obviously the number of potential types is very great), but is an attempt to introduce a basic vocabulary of terms. It also aims to illustrate some of the more common methods used, together with some thoughts on their relative strengths and weaknesses. In a sense, these are the tools available to the legislator in deciding how a regulatory system is to work.

(a) Environmental quality standards

Some standards (known as target standards, environmental quality standards or ambient environmental standards) concentrate on the effect on a particular target. In many cases, the protected target may be human beings and the standard is accordingly set by reference to the effect on them (e.g. the control of noise levels from machinery). However, since this is a book about environmental protection, it will mainly concentrate on situations where the protected target is the environment, or part of it. The controls over noise covered in Chapter 12 is the main exception as they are mainly directed at humans. The phrases 'target standards' and 'environmental quality standards' will therefore be treated as interchangeable.

The effect on the target may be measured in different ways. It may relate to a biological effect, thus channelling all information directly into a consideration of the actual impact of a pollutant (e.g. a standard requiring that a discharge to water is not harmful to fish or aquatic animals). Alternatively, it may relate to the exposure of the target, from which certain biological or other effects may be presumed. In the environmental field, however, it will more usually relate simply to some measurable quality of the receiving environment, such as the level of a particular pollutant.

An environmental quality standard can therefore be defined as a standard where conformity is measured by reference to the effect of a pollutant on the receiving environment. It is unusual for the selected target to be the whole environment. More commonly a particular medium will be chosen as the reference point, such as air or water. In order to retain flexibility, there will frequently also be a geographical limitation: the standard may thus be set by reference to a particular river or area (e.g. in relation to Water Protection Zones, see p. 746), or may be even more specific, such as where air quality or noise levels are fixed within factories or any other enclosed area.

BOX 8.3 Examples of environmental quality standards

- Air quality standards for the maximum or minimum concentration of any specified substance in air; e.g. the Air Quality (England) Regulations 2000 (SI 2000/928) set mandatory standards for sulphur dioxide, nitrogen dioxide, lead, carbon monoxide, benzene, 1.3 butadiene and small particles (PM_{10}).

- The sharing out of percentage reduction of greenhouse gas emissions under the Kyoto Protocol and amongst Member States under EC Decision 2002/358/EC.

- Water quality standards for the concentration of specified pollutants in water e.g. see Water Supply (Water Quality) Regulations 2000 (SI 2000/3184) which set quality parameters for water supplied in England for drinking, washing, cooking and food preparation and production.

- The nuisance test at common law, under which property owners are entitled to the enjoyment of their property without unreasonable interference from neighbours.

It will be clear that these standards may be set by reference to any number of parameters. For example, a water quality standard could be set specifically for the maximum concentration of a specific substance, or a whole range of parameters may be used, as is the case for drinking water and water supply under the Water Supply (Water Quality) Regulations 2000 (SI 2000/3184) and associated regulations which specify various criteria to assess whether water is 'wholesome'. It will also be clear that the standard can be precise or imprecise—the nuisance standard is a good example of an imprecise standard.

CASE 8.1 Imprecise and Precise Standards—*Murdoch v Glacier Metals* [1998] Env LR 732

Different types of environmental quality standards can overlap. In the case of *Murdoch v Glacier Metals* the imprecise standard of nuisance law overlapped with precise standards found in international guidelines on acceptable noise levels. In this case the claimants argued that noise from a local factory was a nuisance. They brought evidence to show that measured noise levels breached the maximum noise levels for night time recommended by the World Health Organization. The Court held that notwithstanding the breach of WHO guidelines, the noise was not a nuisance because the interference was not unreasonable. The claimants lived on a noisy road and none of the neighbours had complained.

Imprecise standards have the advantage of being able to be applied variably taking into account different situations. Thus in another situation it might be the case that noise levels below the WHO recommended standard would be an actionable nuisance, because for example background noise levels were very low or because the characteristics of the noise were unreasonable (e.g. low humming or sudden unexpected noises (see Case box 6.1)).

(b) Emission standards

An emission standard (sometimes referred to as emission limit value) can be defined as a standard where conformity is measured by reference to what is emitted rather than the effect on the receiving environment. Emission standards thus tend to concentrate on wastes produced. Emissions standards can be specified in terms of specified levels, concentration, mass of substances, or percentage reduction requirements.

BOX 8.4 Examples of emission standards

- The maximum content of a particular substance in a liquid discharge from a pipe to a sewer or 'controlled waters.
- The noise level measured as it emanates from a piece of machinery.
- The maximum content of a particular substance in an emission from a chimney or exhaust pipe.

(c) Process standards

Process standards (sometimes also referred to as technical prescriptions, performance standards, or specification standards) may be imposed on a process either by stipulating precisely the process which must be carried on, or by setting performance requirements that the process must reach. In the second case there would be a choice as to how to reach these requirements. These standards may relate to the whole of the process or, alternatively, to a part of it, such as the way that a product is made or the way effluent is treated. They may include requirements about the technology that is used, the raw materials, or operational factors such as whether the process is being carried out properly.

BOX 8.5 Examples of process standards

- A requirement that a particular pre-treatment plant for effluent be used; e.g. a requirement for secondary treatment of urban waste water under the Urban Waste Water Treatment Directive 91/271/EEC.
- A stipulation on the height of a factory chimney; e.g. under the Clean Air (Height of Chimneys) Regulations 1969.
- A requirement that the 'best available techniques' are used to prevent environmental harm (although the general requirement is often translated into a set of emission standards in practice; e.g. under the IPPC Directive 96/61/EC).
- Conditions attached to the operation of a landfill site; e.g. in relation to operational conditions on landfill sites found in the Landfill (England and Wales) Regulations 2002.

It is clear that current practice is to emphasise the use of process standards, and this is illustrated by their use in the pollution prevention and control legislation. They are a good means of preventing harm to the environment arising in the first place.

(d) Product standards

Product standards may be defined as where the characteristics of an item that is being produced are controlled. This may be done with the aim of protecting against damage the product may cause whilst it is being used, or when it is disposed of, or even during its manufacture.

BOX 8.6 Examples of product standards

- A requirement that a class of products are designed and constructed so that they may be recovered and recycled at the point of disposal; e.g. in relation to motor vehicles, see the End of Life Vehicles Directive 2000/53/EC and in relation to electrical equipment see the Waste Electronic and Electrical Equipment Directive 2002/96/EC.

- A requirement that products meet energy efficiency levels; e.g. the energy efficiency of boilers, see Directive 78/170/EEC.

- It may even be thought that requirements on the labelling of goods are a type of product standard; e.g. see under the Eco-labelling scheme, Regulation 1980/2000/EC.

(e) Use standards

Another form of standard which is closely related to product standards is a standard which relates to the use of a product. As the name suggests, whilst product standards are primarily concerned with characteristics or concentrations, use standards relate to the marketing or use of the product. Examples include the restrictions on the use and marketing of new chemical substances, pesticides, veterinary medicines and, most controversially, genetically modified organisms. These standards are concerned with the measurement of any risk associated with the consequences of the use of such products rather than any restrictions on the product itself.

Interrelationship of standards

Of course, these five types of standards are not exclusive of each other. An emission standard will often be set so as to achieve an environmental quality standard. Product standards for a car will include many matters relating to the emissions from it, such as lead, carbon dioxide or noise. A process standard may be set by reference to the meeting of certain emissions standards or environmental quality standards. In addition, the cumulative effect of these emissions will have an impact on the attainment or otherwise of any environmental quality standard.

BOX 8.7 An example of different types of standard—lead in the environment

Taking one particular toxic pollutant, lead, environmental concentrations may be controlled in a number of ways:

- Environmental quality standards may be set, stating that levels of lead should not rise above a certain level in the air, in water, or in the soil.

- Emissions of lead may be controlled, so that any emission, whether into air or water or on to land, should not include more than a specified concentration of lead, to be set in some form of permission or consent.

- Processes may be regulated to reduce the use of lead, or to reduce by good design possible emissions and escapes of lead into the environment.

- Products likely to include lead may be regulated, either to ban its use (e.g. lead fishing weights) or to limit the use of lead (e.g. setting maximum amounts of lead in drinking water or in petrol).

Other characteristics of standards

As stated earlier, a number of other matters are also important in relation to the nature of a standard. The standard may be a precise one, such as one set by reference to a quantifiable maximum or minimum—often a numerical value. Alternatively, it may be an imprecise one, such as a requirement that 'best practicable means' (BPM) or 'best available techniques' (BAT) are used, or one applying the common law test of nuisance.

The standard may be a uniform one across the country (or the EC), or it may vary from area to area. Indeed, it may be set on an individual basis. Certain matters demand uniform standards. For example, uniformity is normally desirable for emissions from mobile sources such as cars, otherwise problems are caused at boundaries. For similar reasons, most product standards are set on a uniform basis. It is strongly argued by some that uniformity creates equality, a particularly important consideration in the context of the EC and the single internal market. Limit values, as used by the EC in a number of directives, create a special form of uniformity. They require that a certain standard is reached, but allow Member States to impose more stringent standards if circumstances require.

The standard may be set centrally or locally. This distinction tends to reflect the same division as that between uniform and individualized standards, since centrally set standards will usually be uniform whilst locally set ones will vary with the discretion given to the decision-maker. In this context, it must be remembered that historically, few standards in Britain were set by legislation. In recent years this has changed to some extent with statutory standards set in relation to air, water and technical requirements for the landfill of waste.

Strengths and weaknesses of different types of standards

Obviously it is not possible to cover all types of standards, but it is possible to see the relative strengths and weaknesses of the more commonly used examples.

Environmental quality standards, by concentrating on what it is that requires protection, are able to deal with inputs to the environment from all sources and via all potential pathways, whilst the other mechanisms, used on their own, tend to permit cumulation of any particular pollutant. For the same reason, environmental quality standards can also cater for potentially harmful combinations of substances on the environment. They can thus enable a policy-maker to identify areas where work is needed, and channel resources effectively. They can also be tailored for particular circumstances, for example by being more stringent in sensitive areas than in others.

However, there are a number of limitations to environmental quality standards. They require constant monitoring of the environment, which may prove to be impractical or expensive. Enforcement poses difficulties, since failure to reach a standard may alert us to the existence of a problem, but does not necessarily tell us the cause or how to remedy it. For example, in order to clean up a river which is chronically contaminated with organic wastes, a regulator would first have to identify the causes of the pollution and then find some method of restricting inputs that was fair and enforceable. A further problem of environmental quality standards is that they may give no incentive to polluters to improve their performance in areas where the standard is already being met. Finally, environmental quality standards are difficult to use for very large areas of the environment (e.g. oceans) in part because of uncertainties over what the 'right' standard should be and in part because of the problems of monitoring compliance with such a standard over a large area.

The very nature of environmental quality standards is that they tend to be set as *objectives* rather than as legal requirements, except in those situations where there is a limited number of sources and targets, such as enclosed work environments. This use as objectives makes them useful at the strategic and planning stages of the regulatory process. For example, development plans often set environmental quality standards, even if they are frequently very imprecise, such as a policy that developments liable to cause a nuisance should not be permitted in a defined area.

By contrast, the strength of *emission standards* is that they are relatively easy to control and monitor by sampling at the point of emission. Enforcement is also easier because of the simplicity of the causation requirements where there is a point of discharge. In addition, an emission standard may be tightened progressively to encourage a discharger to improve the process, whilst still retaining choice as to how this is done.

A main drawback of emission standards relates to the difficulty of controlling diffuse (or non-point) emissions, such as fertiliser or pesticide run-off, by these means. There is also the difficulty (shared with process standards and product standards) of organising a system that can cope with an accumulation of similar emissions in one area, such as car exhausts within cities or similar industrial concerns in one water catchment area. This second difficulty is not an insoluble problem, however. It may be tackled by setting very strict local emission standards, by linking them explicitly to an environmental quality standard, or by applying the 'bubble' approach. Under the bubble approach all emissions in a particular region/country/area are aggregated and a total amount of emissions for that area is specified. This aggregated amount is then usually shared out amongst different countries/sources. A good example of this approach can be found in the allocation of the EU's apportionment of greenhouse gas reductions under the Kyoto Protocol (see further p. 642).

Process standards are obviously limited to where there is a process to control and thus tend to apply mainly to the manufacturing industry. Their main strength is that they may be set so as to prevent a problem arising in the first place. They may also help to pool resources for research at a central level. There is a potential disincentive for producers to find more effective ways of reducing pollution, unless the standards are made progressively stricter, or are periodically altered, or are set at levels that force the producer to develop the technology so as to reach the standard (so-called 'technology forcing' rules).

Product standards are similarly limited to where there is a product and have similar strengths and weaknesses as process standards. As stated above, both categories also have difficulty in catering for the cumulative effect of pollutants on their own. Increasingly, however, product standards are being used to make producers responsible for the whole life cycle of a product from 'cradle to grave'. This has two advantages: first, it brings home the full environmental cost of the product; secondly, by requiring the use of the non-hazardous and recyclable materials it reduces overall environmental impacts caused by the use and disposal of (mostly) consumer products. On the other hand product standards do nothing in relation to the *use* of a product. For example, the ELV Directive may address the design of cars and the way in which they should be recovered or recycled but it does not seek to control fuel consumption, which probably causes greater environmental harm than product inputs or unsuitability for recycling.

Locally set and centrally set standards—Britain versus the EC

It has often been noted that Britain and the rest of the EC do not seem to see eye to eye on pollution control.[7] This is sometimes translated into a conflict between a British preference for locally set and variable (i.e. non-uniform) emission standards, set by reference to local environmental quality, and an EC preference for centrally set uniform emission standards.[8] These two types of standards provide an excellent opportunity for a case study on their relative strengths and weaknesses.

(a) Locally set and variable emission standards set by reference to local environmental quality

Each of the features of this combination of ideas merits some mention. Referring everything to environmental quality can be said to target controls where they are needed—at the protection of the environment. In this way, the impact of non-point emissions and background levels of pollution may be taken into account, as well as discharges from pipes and chimneys. The fact that neither the emission standards nor the environmental quality standards are uniform provides flexibility. This enables more sensitive areas to be protected more strictly, or polluters who are seen as more useful to the community to be treated more leniently. In all cases, a great deal of discretion is granted to decision-makers. It is also argued that, since standards can be varied to take account of local circumstances, the mechanism is economically efficient. For example, greater pollutant loads could be permitted in remote, unpopulated areas or where the self-cleansing properties of the local environment are greater.

(b) Centrally set uniform emission standards

These have obvious advantages. Uniform standards are easily imposed, easily implemented, and easily monitored. They are fair between polluters since all are treated the same, and they avoid difficult problems about allocating the right to pollute amongst different polluters. As a result they may be relatively cheap for the regulator to operate, because they involve less

---

7. G. Lubbe-Wolff (2001) 13 JEL 79.

8. It has been argued that these differences have been exaggerated, see N. Haigh, *EEC Environmental Policy and Britain* (2nd edn, London: Longman 1990) and further below.

administrative discretion than variable standards. They also fit in well with the economic principles of the EC's single market.

On the other hand, they can be said not to allow local conditions to be taken into account, because there is no flexibility (although this can be provided at the enforcement stage). They are meant to be unable to deal with the situation where there is a number of polluters in one area, since there is no jurisdiction to reduce the emission standard to fit local conditions. They are also sometimes said to lead to the possibility of a uniformly polluted country if there is one relevant discharge in every area. These last two criticisms are rather too general, since good use of preventive controls would help in both cases.

Do Britain and the EC still differ?

It is not difficult to think of reasons why Britain may differ from other Member States within the EC. As an island, mainland Britain has no frontiers. Thus, the argument about fairness has never had the impact that it has in France and Germany, which share the Rhine as a border, and where the inequality of one factory being allowed to discharge more than another on the other bank is obvious. Other factors stem from the 'British approach' to pollution control, such as that Britain has a tradition of discretionary, local decision-making and a system based on pragmatism, in which the effects on the environment are balanced with social, economic and political factors.

But the main argument for the British position probably stems from self-interest. With its rainy climate, fast-running streams, ample coastline, and relative remoteness, Britain can claim a comparative advantage when it comes to pollution. Put very crudely, the same discharge is supposed to cause less pollution in Britain than in other countries, because of its lesser effect on the environment. When it comes to setting standards, some people in Britain do not see why stringent uniform standards should apply across the EC if they have no justification in terms of environmental protection in the British context, even if they provide that protection elsewhere.

These differences have been exaggerated. Even discounting the influence of EC legislation, there are many examples of uniform emission standards applying in Britain, although this is sometimes hidden by being the product of administrative practice rather than legislative action. This is especially the case in relation to dangerous substances, where no amount of discretionary balancing with other factors will make them safe. Also the differences set out above relate mainly to water pollution, which is, arguably, the area where Britain has the greatest comparative advantage. The debate about uniform emission standards versus individually determined process standards has also taken place in the context of the nature of the requirement to meet the BAT requirement under the IPPC Directive with the outcome appearing to be an uneasy compromise between the two (see further p. 771).

Even in relation to water pollution, the differences mainly surfaced over one particular directive—the framework Directive 76/464 on Dangerous Substances in Water. It was in relation to this directive that Britain's position led to alternative regimes being adopted for the control of dangerous substances (see p. 713). But, as Haigh points out, it seems that what the other EC Member States saw as cause for concern was not the use of environmental quality objectives to define the context for the setting of variable discharge consents, but the fact that these quality standards were, at the time, informal, unpublished, and set by regional authorities.[9] It is not hard to imagine that other Member States thought they were being told that the British approach to controlling dangerous substances was that 'it all depends on the circumstances'. In addition, it should be observed that in any case Directive 76/464 did *not* lay down uniform emission standards. It laid down limit values, and many of the arguments against uniform emission standards do not apply to these, because there is the flexibility to have a stricter standard if desirable.

As a final point, it is interesting to note how these sorts of arguments have been addressed in more recent European legislation. For example, the Water Framework Directive 2000/60/EC takes a 'combined approach' to standard setting which requires both emissions standards to control emissions from individual point sources along with broad overriding requirements to achieve 'good' water quality status to limit the cumulative impact of such emissions. The IPPC Directive relies largely upon application of broad process standards imposed in the light of local circumstances rather than specifying emission limit values. In this sense the more flexible approach promoted by the UK is winning the day. There is a degree of scepticism from some countries—notably Germany—as to whether such an approach will result in consistency of environmental improvement. It is also worth noting that although the trend may be towards flexibility, there are some significant examples of the imposition of centrally set, prescriptive, uniform standards such as those found in the Landfill Directive in relation to operation and technical requirements at landfill sites (see further p. 607).

In summary, therefore, although there are identifiable differences in approach to pollution control standards across different European countries,[10] these cannot be characterised as a simple Europe versus Britain dispute in terms of environmental regulation at the European level. The British influence over Directives is evidenced both by the final form of Directive 76/464 and more recently, the adoption of flexible standards over more specific emission limits in both the Water Framework Directive and the IPPC Directive.[11] These reflect a seemingly growing preference for the flexibility and individualized approach which is consistent with British styles of environmental regulation.

In another example deregulation has become increasingly common in the European context particularly in recent years through the doctrine of subsidiarity and consolidating framework legislation.[12] The idea that the detailed setting of standards should be delegated from the European level to Member States can be seen clearly in a number of recent Directives including the IPPC Directive and the Water Framework Directive where flexibility and the tailoring of regulatory solutions to individual circumstances at Member State level are at the heart of the regulatory system. The imposition of uniform European wide standards are only to be used as a fall back position; in cases where market distortions are present; or for persistent, bio-accumulative pollutants where an ambient approach is inappropriate.

9. N. Haigh, *EEC Environmental Policy and Britain* (2nd edn, London: Longman 1990).

10. G. Lubbe-Wolff (2001) 13 JEL 79.

11. M. Doppelhammer [2000] EELR 199.

12. Deregulation can also be applied in the context of removing market barriers to allow free movement of goods such as waste and recycled bottles see further C. Hilson, *Regulating Pollution: A UK and EC Perspective* (Oxford: Hart Publishing, 2000) 22–6.

Regulatory approaches and tools

Having considered the different types of standards we now turn to consider the next stage of the regulatory process, the practical application of those standards in individual circumstances. There are certain characteristics which dominate British environmental regulation and these all help to explain the way in which environmental law operates on a practical level.

(a) The 'British approach' to regulation

Since administrative regulation can take many forms, it is important to establish the distinctive features of the British style or approach. In other words, what types of rules and standards are employed? How are they set and by whom? How are they enforced and by whom? What role does the public play in these processes?

In 1986, Vogel identified a number of characteristics of the British style. He found that Britain's regulatory style to be characterised by flexibility and informality, and summarised the system as involving:

An absence of statutory standards, minimal use of prosecution, a flexible enforcement strategy, considerable administrative discretion, decentralised implementation, close co-operation between regulators and the regulated, and restrictions on the ability of non-industry constituents to participate in the regulatory process.[13]

At the risk of producing an unmanageable list, to these points could be added others, such as delegation of decision-making to autonomous quasi-governmental and non-governmental bodies, extensive use of industrial self-regulation, a limited availability of legislative and judicial scrutiny of regulators, a gradualist approach to change, reliance on scientific knowledge for decision-making, and habitual reference to economic factors before decisions are made.

Vogel compared this approach with that of the USA, which he characterized as rule-oriented, normally employing rigid and uniform standards, and making little use of industrial self-regulation. In addition, less use is made there of administrative discretion, prosecution is much more common, there is great executive and judicial scrutiny of regulators and technology-forcing rules are favoured. All of these features lead to conflict between regulator and regulated and to an adversary mentality.

Of course many of these differences are not unique to environmental regulation in the two countries, but are a matter of general political culture. They probably stem from different attitudes towards regulation engendered by different population densities and degrees of cultural homogeneity. In Britain the need for a balancing process is all too clear, whilst in the USA the 'frontier mentality' is understandably more prevalent.

At this point a warning should be given. Since the 1960s the situation in the USA has changed dramatically, and what Vogel describes in the 1980s is quite different from what happened before.[14] Similarly, the British approach has been undergoing a process of change

---

13. D. Vogel, *National Styles of Regulation* (Ithaca: Cornell University Press, 1986).
14. For an updated view see R. Kagan, *Adversarial Legalism: The American Way of Law* (Cambridge: Harvard University Press, 2001).

over the last 20 years. The informal and flexible basis remains, but the approach has undoubtedly got more open, more centralized, more legalistic and more contentious, especially in the last 10 years or so. The changes in legislation have been substantial, but there have also been more disguised internal changes of practice by regulators. As a result, Vogel's analysis is now somewhat outdated.

One crucial factor in this change is the attitude of the EC. The British approach has tended to conflict with that adopted by other Member States and has had to be modified to fit in with that. This is, however, a 'two-way street' and other Member States have also had to modify their own approaches in transposing and implementing Directives which reflect British modes of regulation.[15] At the same time, the increased profile of environmental issues, particularly international ones requiring common responses, has led to some changes of style out of political necessity. A further factor which has influenced the change away from the traditional British approach has been the changing political landscape within a period of radical change in the regulation of environmental protection. This commenced with the Conservative government in the early 1980s and has been adopted (to a greater or lesser extent) by the Labour Administrations of recent years. The major policy features during this time included the rejection of long-term planning in favour of market forces, deregulation of unnecessary bureaucratic controls, privatization of public services, imposition of strict spending controls on public bodies, the general weakening of local authority power, and the use of voluntary controls allowing choice wherever possible.

The following sections will explore some of the manifestations and implications of the British approach, and will seek to illustrate just how it is changing and in what direction. However, it must be stressed that this is only a general approach. No one would suggest that all these symptoms are displayed by each of the various regulatory processes in the country, merely that these are recognizable general features.

The implications of the British approach also vary at the different stages identified earlier, with the result that, for example, general policy-making remains mainly a central function, rather than being particularly decentralized (although many of these general policies are now in practice agreed at international or EC level). Nevertheless, the general features of the regulatory system can be illustrated by considering a number of key issues.

(b) Decentralization and centralization

Decision-making is decentralized in three ways: by being given to a wide range of bodies, by significant use of delegation, and by geographical decentralization.

A range of bodies exercise environmental responsibilities (see Chapter 5). Although the creation of the Environment Agency unified a variety of pollution control functions, Britain still has a large number of autonomous or semi-autonomous environmental agencies, such as the Nature Conservancy Councils and the Health and Safety Executive. Local authorities also have wide-ranging environmental protection powers in relation to such things as air pollution, contaminated land, noise control, town and country planning, and environmental health (see Chapter 12). Traditionally, there has also been decentralization within central government. For many years the nominal responsibility for environmental policy has been located with the Department of the Environment (and its variants). This has obscured the fact that many decisions and policies which have important environmental effects have been

---

15. See further, J. Zottl (2000) 12 JEL 281, G. Lubbe-Wolff (2001) 13 JEL 79, and J. Simila (2002) 14 JEL 143.

made by other Departments including Trade and Industry (e.g. on energy projects such as power stations and transmission lines), Transport (e.g. on emissions from vehicles and the routes of new roads) and Agriculture (e.g. on agricultural support schemes). At various times some of these areas have been considered within the same Department, e.g. the Department of the Environment, Transport and the Regions (DETR) but generally the responsibilities for environmental matters has been spread widely. This diversity was compounded by the tendency to have separate bodies in Wales and Scotland which has been increased with the re-emphasis of regional policy-making and devolution. It is also important to bear in mind the role of the Treasury as the decision-maker in terms of budgets for many of the environmental agencies. Various attempts have been made to integrate environmental considerations into all Government Departments through initiatives such as the introduction of the Environmental Audit Committee (see further p. 112). Even within single Government Departments which deal with environmental matters, decision-making is often delegated. For example, appeals against refusals of planning permission are normally dealt with by the Planning Inspectorate Executive Agency, although this remains formally part of the Office of the Deputy Prime Minister.

Over the years this decentralization of power has tended to result in a rather incoherent environmental policy, with very little uniformity across the country. Even such a central function as the monitoring of the environment has tended to be done in an uncoordinated way but there have been a number of changes which have altered matters. For example, the regulation of water pollution was organized on a regional basis until 1989, when the NRA was established as a national body covering England and Wales. HMIP was created in 1987 to draw together a number of inspectorates at that time operating separately within the Department of the Environment and the Health and Safety Executive. Both these institutional changes clearly fostered uniformity in decision-making. The Environment Act 1995 created the Environment Agency for England and Wales and the Scottish Environment Protection Agency for Scotland, thus continuing the process of producing a more coherent and uniform institutional structure.

Decisions are also commonly made locally. Local authorities have the wide powers referred to above, whilst many of the inspectorates and other agencies operate on a regional basis, granting some discretion to local decision-makers. There is a philosophy underpinning this, of course. The British approach is geared pragmatically towards the protection of the receiving environment, so it is sensible that decisions are taken by people or bodies with a knowledge of local conditions, whether environmental, social, or economic.

An important change has been the centralization of policy decisions in recent years. This has been most marked in relation to matters where there is conflict between central and local government. For example, in the town and country planning system, increased intervention in local decisions by central government was the major issue of the 1980s. It was manifested mainly through hard-hitting and directory Circulars, which were applied on appeal so as to alter the policy context of most planning decisions, though there were also changes to the law and in institutional structure designed to reduce local control, through such creations as urban development corporations. However, centralization is also a reality in relation to pollution control. For example, local authorities have lost a significant amount of discretion in relation to air pollution in addition to a reduction of the numbers of installations controlled as a result of the implementation of the Pollution Prevention and

Control system, whilst the EA has taken over the waste regulation functions previously carried out by local authorities. Even in an area where local authorities have been given new powers, such as in the regulation of historic contamination under Part IIA of the EPA 1990, they are obliged to act in accordance with central guidance or are subject to technical advice from the EA.

Centralization may also be seen at work in the control of public spending. Local authorities have been severely limited for many years in their ability to make capital expenditure decisions. For bodies such as the Nature Conservancy Councils which rely almost entirely on government grant, the position is even clearer.

Finally, there is a very significant element of centralization involved in the relationship between Britain and the EC. Not only is EC decision-making essentially secret, but there is little formal input to it by local or regional bodies in Britain. However, the crucial point is that EC law is binding on Member States. The requirement to conform with it, coupled with the policy goal of harmonization throughout the EC, means that power can be taken away from local and non-governmental bodies and given to central bodies.[16] This is clearly true in relation to the first two stages of the regulatory processes identified earlier (the policy-making and objective-setting stages), and it can be true for the third stage (the operational stage of setting individual consents) as well.

(c) Discretion

The amount of discretion is great at all the stages of regulatory decision-making. Parliament rarely sets firm policies and standards in legislation, allowing for these to be defined in delegated legislation or through administrative guidance. For example, in the town and country planning system the nature of central guidance is nowhere dictated in the legislation, but is set out in government Circulars and Planning Policy Statements, which may be altered at any time.

At the standard-setting and consent-setting levels the discretion is usually given to the relevant regulatory body. As examples, local planning authorities have the ability to grant or refuse planning permission as they think fit (subject mainly to the Secretary of State's control over policy on appeal and the provisions of the Development Plan—which normally contain general objectives set by the planning authorities themselves) and the Environment Agency has discretion over the setting of standards for discharges to water and in the definition of 'best available techniques' (BAT) in relation to Pollution Prevention and Control.

A similar wide discretion can be seen at the enforcement stage. There are few statutes which lay down duties to enforce the legislation, or which set out statutory factors to take into account, and usually the decision whether to take action is taken by the regulatory body on the basis of practical and political factors which are not mentioned in the legislation. Since many of the most important remedies are administrative remedies which are unavailable to individuals, this discretion is of enormous practical importance.

Judicial interference is frequently limited by the width of discretions given in legislation. This is best illustrated in the town and country planning legislation, where there is a clear

16. In this context, the principle of subsidiarity has a centralising nature when circumstances dictate that it is needed, see J. Golub (1996) Political Studies 686.

policy of judicial non-intervention in decisions about the weight to be attached to material considerations. An example of this policy was shown in *London Residuary Body v Lambeth London Borough Council* [1990] 1 WLR 744, where the Secretary of State's decision to grant planning permission for office development in London County Hall was held to be unchallengeable by the House of Lords. This was so even though he had accorded overriding weight to the presumption in favour of development where there was nothing else in favour of the development and some grounds against (see further Case box 13.1 on the *Tesco* case). As a result of all these factors, and also the general British preference for variable rather than uniform standards, the British system of environmental control has become characterised by flexibility and lack of uniformity.

Although there is a wide discretion granted to decision-makers, this is not completely unfettered and the courts have intervened in cases which demonstrate that the exercise of discretion can be challenged over and above the level of individual decisions. Thus, there have been a number of cases where both the European Court of Justice and the High Court have rejected discretionary decisions which have been based upon incorrect criteria. In particular, this has been the case when dealing with the relative importance of economic considerations over environmental factors (see e.g. Case box 8.2).

CASE 8.2 *R v Secretary of State for the Environment, ex parte Kingston upon Hull City Council* [1996] Env LR 248

The Secretary of State established the outer limits of the Humber and Severn estuaries for the purposes of the EC Urban Waste Water Directive. In doing so he relied upon the extra cost of treating waste waters within the designated area. The Court held that although Member States had a discretion in deciding how to establish limits, the cost of treatment was not a relevant consideration. What was required was a genuine and rational assessment of what constituted the estuary having regard to the purpose of the Directive and all other relevant considerations.

The *Kingston upon Hull* decision can be contrasted with the decision in *R v National Rivers Authority, ex parte Moreton* [1996] Env LR 234 in which it was held that the NRA was entitled to take into account economic considerations (i.e. the investment budget of the water company) in addition to the achievement of water quality standards when deciding whether or not to grant a discharge consent (perhaps illustrating the distinction between the exercise of general discretion in *Hull CC* compared to individual decision-making discretion in *Moreton*). Other examples of the limits of discretion in relation to establishing boundaries can be seen in various nature conservation cases (e.g. *R v Secretary of State for the Environment, ex parte RSPB* [1997] QB 206 and further Case box 21.1).

(d) Gradualism and reliance on scientific evidence

The place of these ideas as two of the key tenets of British pollution control is emphasised in Department of the Environment Pollution Paper No. 11, *Environmental Standards—The UK Practice*. This very readable document was published in 1975 and is now out of date, but it has great significance in terms of explaining the British approach to pollution control, since it is effectively a justification of that approach in the face of alternatives being put forward within the EC.

'The philosophy of gradualism is that pollution controls should be strengthened gradually as economic circumstances, the goodwill of producers and scientific abilities allow. This links very strongly with the related idea that decisions should be taken on the basis of a reliable scientific base, although it should be recognised that science does not necessarily produce facts in the environmental sphere, but estimates of risks or probabilities. There is accordingly always a political factor involved in whether to accept a risk or not.'

One major effect of these two ideas has been that environmental controls have tended to be reactive rather than anticipatory (see further p. 23). They have rarely been concerned with laying down a framework in advance, leading to the fragmentation of the system and to its lack of uniformity. A more specific effect is that time is normally given for changes to be made in order to give industry time to adjust capital programmes and work methods. In relation to the requirement that best practicable means be used, it was normal practice to allow any process to continue for its operational life (often 10 years) before declaring it in contravention of the requirement, even though it may have been superseded before then. Similar approaches have been taken in relation to both integrated pollution control and integrated pollution prevention and control.

The extended time scale for implementing the EPA 1990 (full implementation did not take place until 1996), apart from being a comment on the complexity of the new requirements, is a further example of the gradualist approach. Interestingly, the timetable for the introduction of Part I of the Act was laid down after an undertaking was given in Parliament to do so, thus attempting to avoid a re-run of the non-implementation of parts of the Control of Pollution Act 1974. At the EC level, this approach is also reflected in the time scale allowed for implementation of directives, which is normally at least two years, and often five years. A final example is that the British have frequently rejected the use of 'technology-forcing' rules. These represent the setting of a rule which is stricter than currently achievable, though with a time scale for its achievement. The theory is that producers will thus be forced to adapt their current technology to meet the requirements. This concept is much used in the USA, but in Britain the potential cost to industry, and benchmarking against best practice at national or international level, is more frequently used to argue for a gradual change.

(e) The importance of context

In establishing environmental controls, importance is nearly always attached to economic and other factors. As Pollution Paper No. 11 put it:

'The tendency in setting standards in the UK is less to seek an absolute scientific base than to use scientific principles and all relevant and reliable evidence, then to try and progressively reduce emissions in a way that is consistent with economic and technological feasibility and with what at any one time is thought to be an acceptable ultimate objective.'

It is difficult to separate the reasons for this policy from its effects. One reason is undoubtedly the historical influence that the town and country planning system, with its explicit requirement to balance all material considerations, has had on the development of the law, but a major reason must relate to the definition of pollution and the objectives of environmental controls (see p. 14).

Pollution has been defined as a relative concept, in the sense that there is no absolute rule about what amounts to pollution. The same applies to other forms of environmental change, such as urban or agricultural development. It is not possible to eradicate pollution, merely to reduce it. It follows that, at some stage, a choice has to be made about what is, and what is not, permissible. This is ultimately a political question, and involves a balancing of various factors. However, there are two possible objectives of pollution control. One is to aim to reduce pollution to 'acceptable' levels. An alternative is to aim to reduce pollution as far as possible. In Britain the first approach is implicitly adopted in relation to most substances. This explains the inevitability of a political balancing process, and also the preference for variable environmental quality standards. The second approach tends to lead to a reduction in discretion and to greater reliance on uniform standards, because if one producer can reduce to a particular level others should be able to do so as well.

Taking a contextual approach means that there is always going to be a trade-off between environmental protection and other factors, such as cost. This is fundamental to most British environmental controls. For example the use of 'best available techniques' within the IPPC Directive is balanced by the idea of proportionality which means that costs to the operator are balanced against the benefits to the environment when determining what process should be adopted.

This philosophy of balancing environmental protection with material welfare is apparent in most areas of the law. It explains the wide discretions given to decision-makers, the emphasis on decisions being taken by reference to local factors, and the practice of defining some concepts after consultation with the industry involved. The emphasis on balance also explains such fundamental features of British law as the preference for flexible environmental standards rather than uniform ones, and the flexible and cooperative enforcement strategies that are employed by regulatory agencies.

(f) Are things changing?

As the previous section suggests, a number of things appear to be changing in relation to the traditional British approach to regulation. In particular, there is an increasing tendency for standards to be set centrally (which often goes hand in hand with more uniform standards), and a further tendency for them to be set out more explicitly in legislative instruments or formal policy documents.

A number of examples could be used to illustrate the point. Perhaps the clearest relates to the way that EC standards are imposed through directives, thus effectively replacing local discretion with central prescription, but there are also examples from domestic legislation. In relation to air pollution, there has been a major change over recent years with the setting of statutory air quality objectives by the Secretary of State (under the Air Quality Limit Values Regulations 2003). Under the Air Quality (England) Regulations 2000, local authorities are under a duty to undertake an assessment of air quality in their areas and to take action where the statutory objectives are not being met (see p. 655). This covers, amongst other things, powers in relation to setting pollution control conditions and clearly entails the whole process becoming more open and predictable. It should be noted that this shift towards centralism and formalism does not necessarily imply that local air quality management areas will be set uniformly nor that individual pollution control conditions will be set in a blanket fashion. There will continue to be a considerable measure of local differentiation and local input in the setting of emission limits. It is, however, the *shift* from secretive, flexible, subjective and individualistic approaches, to more open, formal, objective, and collective forms of decision-making which is significant. A similar process can be seen at work in the town planning requirement (in the Planning and Compulsory Purchase Act 2004, s. 38(6)) that decisions are to be made in accordance with the provisions of the development plan, unless material considerations indicate otherwise.

As well as centralizing decisions and reducing discretions, this new formalism also increases the potential role of the courts. It has already been noted how the courts have played a lesser role in the development of environmental policy in this country than in, for example, Germany or the USA (see p. 135). This is probably because of the wider discretions provided in the legislation, which are often unchallengeable. However, the development of more explicit standards, coupled with clear operational duties imposed on the regulatory agencies, means that a greater number of decisions may potentially be challenged through judicial review. An example is the duty imposed on local authorities to manage air quality in their areas referred to above: it is quite possible that this could be used in the future to compel an authority to adopt a certain course of action. The likelihood of the courts playing an increasing role in the development of environmental law is further increased by developments in relation to judicial review and EC law. For example, the concept of the supremacy of EC law has been used to develop various doctrines with the aim of ensuring not only that legislation is passed to implement EC directives, but also that the laws that are passed are implemented and enforced in practice (see p. 222).

Of course, much of this discussion is only of real relevance to regulatory systems. If, as may be the case in the future, market mechanisms are preferred to regulation, they may represent a force moving in the opposite direction. One of the potential results of deregulation and a shift towards the use of market mechanisms is a decentralization of decisions from government to consumers and industry.

There is another general change that can be identified, which is that there is a discernible shift away from reliance on flexible standards based on the impact on the receiving environment towards standards based on the use of the best available techniques. This is seen at its clearest in relation to systems of pollution prevention and control, where the conditions attached to permits are set by reference to BAT, but it is also an inevitable by-product of a more centralized and formal system. It also follows from the increased involvement of lenders, insurers and other stakeholders in decisions on environmental management, since they are likely to insist on the use of the best available techniques as a protection against liability or loss of their stake.[17]

(g) Deregulation

In the context of the 'British' approach to regulation, this term appears to carry three separate, but overlapping, meanings.[18] One refers to the so-called 'war on red tape': in other words that excessively bureaucratic procedures and practices should be removed and simplified. A second meaning relates to the general disinclination to use regulatory mechanisms unless they are necessary, which often translates into favouring voluntary and

---

17. See L. Bergkamp (2003) 12 (3) RECIEL 269 and J. Lipton (1998) 6(6) Int ILR 198.

18. In the context of European legislation deregulation can have different meanings in terms of correcting market distortions and subsidiarity, see C. Hilson, *Regulating Pollution: A UK and EC Perspective* (Oxford: Hart Publishing, 2000), 22.

market-style mechanisms. A third meaning can be discerned in terms of a policy not to interfere with the operations of business.

The origins of the deregulation initiative can be traced back to the Conservative Government and in particular a formal programme which was commenced in 1993 which resulted in the active search for examples of perceived over-regulation by government departments. More recently, the concept has been adapted by the present administration and rebranded as a 'better regulation' initiative with the production of the White Paper, *Modernising Government* (Cm 4310, 1999) and the setting up of bodies such as the Better Regulation Task Force (with a remit to reduce unnecessary regulation, reflecting the first definition) and the Cabinet Office's Regulatory Impact Unit (with a role in overseeing new domestic and European proposals).

The main statutory basis for the deregulatory push is the Deregulation and Contracting Out Act 1994 (as amended by the Regulatory Reform Act 1997). It includes a general power for any Minister to amend or repeal legislation by means of a statutory instrument if they are of the opinion that the measure imposes a burden on any trade, business or profession, and that the amendment or repeal will reduce that burden. There are some limited consultation and procedural requirements that temper this very wide power, but it is clear that it could be used to reduce the impact of environmental protection legislation. In addition, section 5 of the 1994 Act empowers Ministers to 'improve' various enforcement procedures (a term which includes such things as revocation and variation of a licence, as well as criminal prosecution) by statutory instrument. Changes to environmental regulation brought about by the initiative include amendments to the Water Resources Act 1991, made by the Environment Act 1995, which: removed the requirement for tripartite sampling (paradoxically making life easier for the EA when bringing prosecutions); reduced public participation in setting discharge consents; and extended the period for varying discharge consents from two to four years. The real justification behind most amendments made under the 1994 Act appears to be in accordance with the third meaning discussed above: i.e. to minimize the interference with the operations of business.

Market mechanisms or the use of economic tools

These rather general phrases are meant to encompass all approaches which seek to use prices or economic incentives and deterrents to achieve environmental objectives. The production of goods and services involves not only costs to the producer (e.g. production costs) but also so-called social costs which are 'allocated' to society as a whole. These include the costs of pollution and the depletion of natural resources. Regulatory instruments seek to control activities in order to minimize social costs. Economic instruments seek to identify these social costs and include them in the prices of goods and services so that the market has a more accurate idea of the full cost of the product or service. For example, pricing systems might signal the true environmental costs of products to consumers, thereby making 'environment-friendly' items cheaper than those that pollute or waste natural resources. The general characteristic of all economic instruments is that they function through their impact on market signals. Economic instruments are often contrasted with 'command and control' regulation but in truth, command and control and economic instruments supplement and complement each other, often through the implementation of statutory objectives. For example, the Climate Change programme requires the reduction of greenhouse gas emissions. Some of these reductions can be met through regulation—by means of tightening conditions of pollution control permits—and by market-oriented approaches through the use of tradable quotas to allocate the emissions which are allowed in the most economically efficient manner.

In a sense, therefore, these economic tools or instruments are the exact opposite of using the free market, since they normally involve an interference or intervention in the free market for the purpose of environmental protection. However, they do involve the use of the market in the sense that they are normally designed to allow consumers and industry to make choices about their actions. By way of contrast, many people would argue that most, though certainly not all, regulatory systems tend to operate so as to remove choice. There is thus a potential confusion in referring simply to 'using the market' for environmental protection ends, since that runs together the policy of allowing an unrestricted free market to allocate resources on the assumption that that is somehow more efficient, and the separate policy of intervention in the market for protective purposes.

The OECD has identified five general categories of economic instrument used in environmental protection, namely: charges, subsidies, deposit or refund schemes, the creation of a market in pollution credits, and enforcement incentives.[19] These are expanded upon in Annex A of the White Paper, *This Common Inheritance* (Cm 1200, 1990). There are other classes of instrument which have been categorized as economic including property-rights, liability instruments and performance bonds. The use of economic instruments in Britain is increasing having been developed from a basic system of using charging mechanisms and subsidies to the adoption of more complex and sophisticated measures such as trading schemes. It also becomes clear that some of the mechanisms are self-standing whilst others, such as most charging schemes, require a regulatory framework and proper policing, so they must be seen as additional to, rather than separate from, regulatory systems.

A selection of economic tools or instruments is considered below.

(a) Charges for the administrative cost of operating the regulatory system

This now goes under the title of 'cost recovery charging' and has been adopted in relation to a number of regulatory activities. The idea is to recover the regulatory costs that are incurred in granting applications or consents, or in such things as inspecting, monitoring or policing those consents. The current policy is not to charge for the general costs of operating the whole regulatory system, but to limit the charge to the amount which can be referable to each consent or discharge. In the interests of administrative simplicity, the charges are normally arranged in bands, rather than being worked out individually. For example, in relation to water pollution there is a scheme of charging for applications for consent. This is intended to recoup the costs of administering the application procedures for discharge consents. There are also annual charges to recover the cost to the Environment Agency of policing any discharges to controlled waters. These are set so as to recoup the costs associated with inspecting and monitoring discharges, not the full cost of monitoring water quality, which will still be paid for by the taxpayer. Similar schemes operate in relation to

19. *Taxation and the Environment: Complementary Policies*, OECD, 1993.

applications and installation permits under Integrated Pollution Prevention and Control and waste management licences. Cost recovery charging systems may be progressive and thus have a beneficial environmental effect. For example, the charging schemes referred to involve higher charges for discharges which cost more to monitor, and these are often those which cause more pollution.

There has always been a rather different system of charging for discharges to sewers.[20] This involves a rate for domestic consumers which is normally linked to property value, and a variable rate for trade dischargers linked to the volume and strength of the discharge as measured by Chemical Oxygen Demand. This produces a relatively unsophisticated method of charging for the cost of sewage treatment according to the demands made upon the system by the discharge. An incidental effect of concentrating on volume is, however, to reduce the level of water used and the level of waste, and thus to encourage both conservation of resources and recycling.

(b) Charges reflecting the full environmental cost of an activity

The system of charging for sewage discharges shows the potential for use of charging systems which aim to charge for the full environmental cost of an activity. Such systems may be seen as true environmental or pollution taxes. Whilst such taxes are a relatively simple way in which to reflect the environmental cost of an activity or discharge, there are distinct problems with the idea. One is obtaining sufficient information about the discharge or process to make the taxes work properly. This would seem to demand a strong regulatory structure to police the system, although self-monitoring methods may have a large part to play in this respect. Another is the problem of obtaining accurate information about environmental effects on which to base the tax levels. In reality, the levels which are set often indicate that taxes are more aimed at raising revenue than at reflecting the full environmental cost of an activity.[21]

(c) Charges to finance environmental or pollution control measures

Some economic instruments work within a regulatory system by directly linking costs to the prevention, abatement or clean-up of pollution. A number of examples may be given here. Under section 161 of the Water Resources Act 1991. The EA may pass costs incurred in preventing or remedying water pollution back to the person who caused it. The EA may also recover costs incurred in cleaning up unlawful deposits of waste from the occupier or the person who made the deposit (EPA 1990, s. 59). In relation to statutory nuisances, there are similar abatement and cost-recovery powers available to local authorities (s. 81, EPA 1990).

Fines levied in court for offences may also be seen as a form of environmental charge. Indeed, given the nature of environmental offences and the limited moral blame often attached to them, many people treat fines as administrative penalties rather than as true criminal sanctions.[22] The typically low level of fines means that their economic effect is

20. Charges are either levied through the Trade Effluent Consent system or under private trade effluent agreement, see further p. 759 and W. Howarth and D. McGillivray, *Water Pollution and Water Quality Law* (Crayford: Shaw & Sons, 2001), 660

21. N. Gunningham and P. Grabosky, *Smart Regulation: Designing Environmental Policy* (Oxford: Clarendon Press, 1998), 76.

22. See further p. 302 and A. Ogus and C. Abbot (2002) 14 JEL 283 and P. De Prez (2000) 12 JEL 65.

limited, though levels are rising steadily. There is, however, no direct connection between the penalty and the environmental damage caused (primarily because there is no way of ensuring that fines are actually used for environmental benefit). One interesting development in this respect is the decision in *Herbert v Lambeth London Borough Council* (1991) 90 LGR 310, that a compensation order may be made under the Powers of Criminal Courts Act 1973, s. 35, where damage has been caused by a statutory nuisance, although there is a statutory limit of £5,000 on the sum which may be awarded.

Civil law remedies may also be seen as achieving the same objectives. Many statutes now include civil liability for damage to people or their property, and the creation of a remedy of breach of statutory duty may act as a potent method of reallocating costs. For example the 1992 Oil Pollution Compensation Fund provides for the payment of reasonable costs towards environmental reinstatement (though sometimes the most reasonable and cost effective response to oil pollution incidents is to let nature restore itself rather than spending excessive sums to try and remove all traces of oil pollution from the sea). The drawback at present is that there are few civil actions that recognise fully the costs involved in environmental damage. The law has never developed any concept of 'environmental rights', with the result that the only possible civil law claimants are people with private rights (see p. 15). Put more simply, animals, birds and plants do not yet have civil law rights although the Directive on Environmental Liability (2004/35/EC) may have a limited impact here (see p. 393).

(d) Charges levied on polluting materials or processes

Instead of a charge being levied on the results of pollution, it could be levied on a process or a product. The best example is the landfill tax whereby a tax is levied on every tonne of waste disposed of in landfill sites (with lower rates and exemptions for certain classes of waste) (see p. 613). It is interesting to note that landfill operators are able to obtain rebates from the tax by setting up environmental trusts which promote sustainable waste management practices. This use of tax income is somewhat of a breakthrough since, although it has been appreciated for some time that taxes could be used to combat pollution and contamination problems, little has been achieved. However, the Treasury has always vigorously opposed any attempt to earmark taxes and charges for specific spending purposes (a process known as 'hypothecation') and, without that, a subsidiary aim of environmental taxes, which is that they should be linked directly to environmental spending, will not be achieved. For example, the proceeds from the landfill tax could be used to fund the clean-up of 'orphaned' closed landfill sites (i.e. those where the original operator cannot be found or does not have the resources to afford the clean-up), although the environmental trust funds may also be used in the same way. An alternative is that a charge may be reduced for relatively environment-friendly activities. The most obvious example was the reduced tax payable on unleaded petrol compared with leaded petrol, which lead to a significant rise in the use of unleaded petrol. A further example is the use of waste recycling credits for authorities or others who retain waste for the purpose of recycling it so that a recycler of waste may receive a credit equivalent to the savings made by a waste collection authority from not having to dispose of the waste (EPA 1990, s. 52; see p. 588).

(e) Subsidies and grants

These are commonly used for environmental ends, although their use within the EC is restricted by the rules on illegal state aids. For example, subsidies are available for the construction of facilities for the improvement of the treatment of agricultural water and silage effluent—both particularly potent, and common, causes of pollution. Care has to be taken that the subsidies achieve the result intended. Some subsidies on forestry and agriculture, for example, have been accused of having detrimental environmental effects because of their inability to select between beneficial and non-beneficial projects.[23]

Compensation payments for environmentally sensitive activities may also be seen in this category. The prevailing policy in relation to countryside protection has tended to be one of voluntariness, whereby farmers and landowners are compensated for agreeing to forgo certain advantages in the interests of the environment. Sometimes this is through the payment of direct compensation and sometimes through the negotiation of management agreements. For example, management agreements or schemes may be agreed in relation to the protection of national nature reserves or sites of special scientific interest (see p. 816).

(f) The creation of a market in pollution credits

A further instrument is the use of tradable quotas, or emissions trading. These are methods of creating a market in the right to pollute. For example, a total for emissions of a specified substance may be set for a particular area. Firms may then bid for the right to take up a part of that total. Prospective or new polluters would have to buy the rights of existing holders if there was no spare capacity. By restricting the available emissions, prices would be driven up, providing an incentive to reduce emissions or to develop alternatives.

The idea is most developed in the USA,[24] but the groundwork for its use in Britain is laid in the EPA 1990, s. 3(5), which allows the Secretary of State to establish total emissions of any substance either nationally or for a limited area, and to allocate quotas, with power progressively to reduce the total allowed. This provision has been supplemented with a power to introduce emissions trading schemes under the Pollution Prevention and Control Act 1999 and the Waste and Emissions Trading Act 2003. This power can cover all emissions (including release to water and land) although the first target has been carbon dioxide emissions in order to meet internationally agreed reduction targets which have been set to combat climate change (see p. 649).

(g) Deposit and refund schemes

Although deposit and refund schemes are clearly severe interferences with a free market, it is also clear that they may have an enormous impact on the amount of waste produced. Traditionally, in Britain, voluntary mechanisms have been preferred over instruments imposed by law. By way of example, the UK Government intervened in the *Danish Bottles* case in the European Court of Justice, supporting the EC Commission's argument that a Danish law requiring drinks containers to be returnable was contrary to the free market principles of the EC. The Court of Justice upheld most of the Danish scheme despite its clear

---

23. C. Reid (1996) 8 Environmental Law & Management 59.

24. See generally R. Kosobud (ed.), *Emissions Trading: Environmental Policy's New Approach* (New York: Wiley, 2000).

anti-competitive effect, on the grounds that the aim of environmental protection justified some interference with the operation of the single market within the EC.[25]

Future uses of economic instruments

The above summary is not intended to be an exhaustive list of those mechanisms which might be tried, or even of those which are already in use, but to give an idea of the type of instrument that may be available (other examples include the use of performance bonds which require a deposit which is refunded on completion of a task such as the clean up of a contaminated site or the maintenance of aftercare conditions). As stated before, there is little doubt that market-related instruments will increasingly be used in the future. Indeed, they could currently be said to be the 'hottest growth industry in environmental law'.[26]

One reason for this is that market mechanisms have a degree of political acceptability which crosses party political ideological boundaries. There is a strong link with the principle of choice, the idea that people should be given a choice of how to act, as long as their actions do not breach some generally accepted limits. This idea is seen most strongly in the realm of town and country planning where the importance attached to market forces is made explicit in much of central government policy advice. The principle is also seen in relation to such things as the preference for voluntary methods of protection in the countryside and pollution control systems which set objectives whilst leaving producers to work out for themselves how to achieve them. For example, the adoption of the BAT standard in IPPC theoretically allows operators to minimize pollution by using the most economically efficient method (see p. 781). There is also a strong link with the related policy of deregulation discussed above. Amongst other things, this policy amounts to a rejection of imposed restrictions in favour of agreed ones and a removal of unnecessary state powers.

Within the EC, the Commission has also suggested a shift in EC environmental policy towards the greater use of economic instruments rather than the administrative regulation approach.[27] Although the Commission's proposals have seen little positive action, it is clear that European initiatives are likely to become more prevalent in the coming years with the introduction of the EC emissions trading system, and full cost-recovery charging for water use (though not pollution) under the Water Framework Directive.

The Polluter Pays Principle

The EC can claim another important contribution to the development of economic instruments; its environmental policy has always included the adoption of the 'Polluter Pays' Principle, although it was probably the OECD which first popularized the idea in the

25. Case 302/86 *Commission v Denmark* [1988] ECR 4607 and see further p. 214.

26. W. Orts (1995) 89 Northwestern University Law Review, 1227.

27. See, e.g., European Commission, 5th Action Environmental Action Programme, *Towards Sustainability* and COM 97 (9) on *Environmental Taxes and Charges in the Single Market*.

early 1970s.[28] The principle basically means that the producer of goods or other items should be responsible for the costs of preventing or dealing with any pollution which the process causes. This includes environmental costs as well as direct costs to people or property. It also covers costs incurred in avoiding pollution, and not just those related to remedying any damage. There is a very strong link between the principle and the idea that prevention is better than cure. It will also be clear from the foregoing discussion that these costs should include the full environmental costs, not just those which are immediately tangible.

The relevance of this principle to the discussion of economic instruments is obvious, since a producer will have to pass on any costs in the price of goods to the ultimate consumer. However, this is only a principle, it has no legal force and there is no agreed definition that has anything approaching the precision of a statute. On the contrary, there has frequently been dispute over its exact scope, especially over the limits on payments for damage caused. Even when the question of payment is relatively settled, there is a further issue as to the identity of the polluter. There are many examples of the difficulty of identifying the 'polluter' including the Contaminated Land Regime in EPA 1990, Part IIA (see further Box 17.10) and under the Nitrates Directive (*R v Secretary of State for the Environment and Minister of Agriculture, Fisheries and Food, ex parte Standley* [1999] Env LR 801; see p. 748). In any case where certain polluters are targeted or excluded for administrative or other purposes, the principle is watered down to 'some polluters pay' which weakens the legitimacy and application of the general principle. Like other environmental principles it is essentially a guide to desirable courses of action, but it is fairly clear that it has rarely been fully satisfied in either EC or British environmental legislation.

As a result the principle has sometimes seemed to be all things to all people, and has even been used to justify views with which it has little connection, for example the suggestion that producers may pollute as long as they pay for it. That is a complete misunderstanding of the principle's true meaning, and the potential abuse of such an imprecise phrase should be appreciated.

Self-regulation as a tool for environmental protection

One of the consequences of the deregulatory move away from direct methods of regulation has been the upsurge in interest in developing effective mechanisms based upon voluntary action. Such action can be termed 'self-regulation'.[29] Although this term can have more precise definitions (e.g. where a group is responsible for the action of its members without any form of governmental or regulatory supervision), for the purposes of this discussion the common identifying factor is that self-regulatory mechanisms are underpinned by voluntary action rather than compulsion. The triggers for such action may be diverse, including the threat of compulsory action, commercial benefit (e.g. through cost savings or green marketing initiatives), or even a shift in values which attaches greater importance to environmental protection (see Box 3.4).

---

28. OECD, *Environment and Economics: Guiding Principles Concerning International Economic Aspects of Environmental Policies*, 1972 and OECD, *The Implementation of the Polluter-Pays Principle*, 1974.

29. See further, S. Gaines and C. Kimber (2001) 13(2) JEL, 157.

These examples indicate that there are factors other than legal factors which can be influential in changing behaviour. Thus, economic benefits which accrue from increasing sales of so-called 'environmentally friendly' goods or the social benefits (e.g. employee satisfaction or enhanced public image) which result from environmental improvement can act as regulatory controls. Moreover, these triggers suggest that there are very few occasions where actions are purely 'voluntary'. Indeed, there is a broad spectrum of mechanisms which can fall within this definition of self-regulation, ranging from the purely voluntary (i.e. no form of compulsion at all) through to mechanisms which use a mixture of direct regulation and self-regulation (see e.g. the position of compliance schemes in relation to the producer responsibility legislation or the relationship between the links in the waste management chain under the duty of care).

The strengths of self-regulatory mechanisms are clear, in that they are quick, flexible, non-interventionist and therefore more acceptable to the companies which are regulated. Perhaps most importantly, they encourage a sense of environmental responsibility within the regulated companies which should promote environmental improvement not as a reaction to legislation but as part of corporate development generally. The disadvantages are that the voluntary nature of the mechanisms often means that there are no explicit enforcement mechanisms; there are problems of so-called 'free-riders', i.e. companies which do not adopt self-regulation and therefore possibly gain an advantage over competitors whilst employing lower environmental standards; there is a lack of transparency and accountability; and there is the problem of setting standards which are at the lower end of what is achievable rather than setting goals which might not be attained.[30]

Given that the range of mechanisms is wide and the suggested definition of self-regulation imprecise, it is possible to set out a selection of self-regulatory mechanisms below.

(a) Management standards

Theoretically, management standards could have been included in the list of environmental standards which were discussed earlier in this chapter, or within the discussion of economic instruments above as they can have a direct economic impact. It is, however, arguably most appropriate to consider such standards within the context of self-regulatory tools as they are voluntary and there are no specific legal sanctions for either failing to adopt the standards or comply with them once adopted. At its widest, the term 'environmental management standards' can be said to cover such things as the technical competence and financial security of a regulated operator. This would include the test of 'fit and proper person' in relation to waste management, (EPA 1990, s. 74 and see p. 592). The more common use of management standards, however, relates generally to the use of systems of management which measure environmental performance and provide benchmarks against which the improvement of a company can be measured.

The systems are backed by a certification procedure which provides a method of formal and objective verification for the system. The first EMS was introduced as a British standard, BS7750, in 1994, and the general requirements of this standard have provided the

---

30. See N. Gunningham and P. Grabosky, *Smart Regulation: Designing Environmental Policy* (Oxford: Clarendon Press, 1998), 50.

framework for others which have been adopted more widely. BS7750 was to influence the establishment of other EMSs including an international standard ISO 14001 (which triggered the withdrawal of BS7750 in 1997) and the EC Eco-Management and Audit Scheme (EMAS) under EC Regulation 1836/93.

These standards are based on a quality management approach with the result that no specific levels of environmental performance are stipulated in the EMS itself other than a general commitment to comply with all applicable environmental legislation. The setting of environmental objectives is a subjective matter for the company itself. These objectives are measured against a publicly produced environmental policy which includes the minimum commitment of compliance with all legal standards whilst improving environmental performance. This commitment required the company to understand the environmental effects created by the business; to set both broad and detailed goals for environmental performance with specific targets; to set up an active programme for managing the environmental performance which was designed to achieve these goals and targets; and a system for auditing the EMS. Adherence to the requirements of the EMS is verified on an annual basis by accredited independent verifiers. The ISO standard commits companies to a goal of 'pollution prevention' rather than environmental improvement whilst the EMAS scheme also requires companies to establish procedures to protect the environment and to commit themselves to continuous environmental improvement.

The most significant difference between EMAS and ISO 14001 is that EMAS requires a company to publish a report setting out its environmental performance every three years and to have that report verified by an independent body which has been accredited for that purpose. The aim of such a report is to enable stakeholders such as members of the public to assess whether the company is meeting the requirements of the EMAS standard.

The uptake of the standards has been steady rather than spectacular with an emphasis on those industries which have come under contractual pressures from customers, particularly in the global marketplace. Although the standards for the measurement of environmental performance can ensure that there is a degree of transparency (and objectivity) of assessment, it could be argued that the use of EMSs as a trigger for environmental improvement has been less successful. One of the main defects in the system is the subjective nature of the setting of improvement goals. It is perfectly possible for a company which achieves compliance with legal requirements to set very low targets and still achieve certification. On this level, an EMS is little more than an objective statement of keeping within the law. This, coupled with general antipathy towards the adoption of the standards, means that the use and effectiveness of EMS is still in some doubt.[31]

(b) Information based mechanisms

Although there are legal requirements to make certain environmental information available to the public through the systems of pollution control registers there are other voluntary mechanisms whereby environmental information is made available to the public on wider issues. Companies have, for example, incorporated environmental information into annual reports.[32] Corporate environmental reporting has been patchily adopted by UK

---

31. See (2000) ENDS Report 311, 27–9 and (2002) ENDS Report 327, 31–3.

32. See N. Gunningham and P. Grabosky, *Smart Regulation: Designing Environmental Policy* (Oxford: Clarendon Press, 1998) 62.

companies with a wide variety of both quality and quantity of information and an emphasis on industrial sectors which carry out particularly sensitive environmental operations (e.g. mining and energy).[33] Another interesting use of information is through the Environment Agency's 'name and shame' strategy whereby information on environmental performance (more typically environmental failings) are disseminated publicly through annual reports which identify the worst polluters by reference to industry sectors and numbers of pollution offences. This is made available not only to the general public but also to institutional investors and other commercially interested parties (e.g. insurers and trade customers) (see Box 9.15).

Other information-based mechanisms include eco-labelling or certification processes which give consumers information about the environmental impacts of goods and products. There is an EC regulation on the subject which set up the EC eco-labelling scheme (see EC Regulation 880/92 as revised and extended by Regulation 1980/00).[34] This scheme has had only limited success as it has proved to be administratively cumbersome with the consequence that relatively small numbers of products have been considered and the market credibility of the scheme has been undermined. Criteria are developed by the European Commission to enable the environmental impact of a product to be analysed by taking into account the whole of its life-cycle. Product groups which have been covered under the scheme include light bulbs, paints, personal computers, footwear, textiles, and washing machines. The regulation was originally implemented in Britain through the establishment of an Eco-Labelling Board in November 1992. This Board was, however, abolished in 1999 as part of a move towards an integrated products policy which places eco-labelling in a curtailed role in reducing the environmental impacts of consumer products (see p. 335). Although the European wide system continues to operate, the prospects for a national eco-labelling scheme appear to diminish. There is likely to be greater emphasis placed upon the top of the supply chain, i.e. the manufacturers of products providing information on the environmental impacts rather than the provision of general labelling criteria.

(c) Private agreements

The use of private agreements in environmental regulation ranges from the formal statutory mechanisms found in planning legislation (Planning and Compulsory Purchase Act 2004, s. 46) and nature conservation legislation (Countryside Act 1968, s. 15) to the more informal agreements which have been negotiated between government or the regulator and individual companies or industry sectors (see Box 16.4). Although the uptake of these more informal agreements has traditionally been more prevalent in other countries (particularly the US and the Netherlands), the UK has started to adopt this mechanism with an increasing frequency (e.g. in relation to the Climate Change Levy whereby energy intensive sectors have been offered tax reductions on the basis that they enter into voluntary agreements to improve energy efficiency agreements, see p. 647) The nature of these agreements differs widely and is dependent upon the parties to the agreement (e.g. the European Commission, national governments, regional bodies or regulatory agencies on the one side and industry sectors or individual operators on the other) and what is required (e.g. general or specific

33. (2002) ENDS Report 327, 28–30.
34. See L. Krämer (2000) YEEL 123.

targets for reducing pollution). At a European level, the European Commission has produced guidelines on the use of such agreements between public authorities and industry (see COM(96)561 final).

There are many criticisms of such voluntary agreements. Many of these reflect the criticisms of self-regulatory mechanisms generally (e.g. lack of transparency or accountability, no public participation, lack of satisfactory enforcement mechanisms), but most of these stem from the fact that the status of many of these agreements is uncertain given that they are neither private contracts nor agreements made under statutory powers. It would appear that the role of these agreements is to provide a further mechanism which is complementary to direct regulation. They allow government or regulators to set targets and goals which go beyond that which could be required under the legislative scheme. Whether private agreements are actually used in this way is a matter of debate. Experience has shown that such agreements have been used to set targets which at best are the same as would have been imposed under direct regulation (see Box 16.4 on voluntary agreements and the car sector).

The role of criminal and civil law

This chapter has provided an outline of the main regulatory techniques used to address environmental problems. As such most of the techniques used are administered or policed by public bodies. This is by no means a comprehensive list both in terms of the types of regulatory instruments used nor the range of *legal* techniques used as a part of or subsidiary to the regulatory system. As far as the latter is concerned both the criminal and civil (or private) law have a role to play as legal techniques to be used for environmental protection.

The criminal law can be used either to provide direct criminal sanctions for environmental harm, or in a subsidiary and complementary role within a regulatory system. It tends to be of greater use in the second way. This is because the main purpose of the criminal law is to punish clearly identified wrongs. Yet, in relation to many environmental matters, it is often impossible to identify wrong without reference to other factors. For example, it is clearly desirable to have industry and many other activities which may cause pollution. The question is not a simple one of whether to have them, but a more difficult one of how much pollution is acceptable. That requires a balancing of the various factors involved against what is reasonable—a discretionary, political process, for which the regulatory system is well-suited. The criminal law is rather inadequate for such a balancing process, and thus tends to be used mainly to deal either with clear acts of environmental vandalism, or to support the regulatory system once it has decided what is and what is not acceptable.

Many criminal offences consist not of committing a direct act of pollution or environmental damage, but instead of ignoring the dictates of the regulatory body. For example, in relation to town and country planning, the offence consists not of breaching planning control but of ignoring an enforcement notice. This makes the criminal offence truly subsidiary to the regulatory process, since only the local planning authority may issue an enforcement notice, thus taking the possibility of enforcement away from the public. All of these matters have an effect in decriminalizing the law. The offence is not directly linked to the environmental harm, but to an administrative process. Enforcement is normally by an administrative body and often for breach of an administrative requirement. The message that is given is that these things are truly related to administrative processes rather than the criminal law (see Box 9.1 and further Chapter 9).

As pointed out in the section on charges, the civil law can be seen as a form of market mechanism, so it is worth making a few general comments about civil liability in this chapter. There is little doubt that the last few years have seen a great increase in interest in the use that can be made of civil law mechanisms—by policy-makers as well as by lawyers.[35] This interest has been heightened by the development of an EC wide system of civil liability which was the subject of intense negotiations for over 10 years, beginning in 1993. The long delay and relative weakness of the final version of the Directive on Environmental Liability (2004/35) reflect the fundamental controversies surrounding rules which attempt to merge different approaches to environmental liability across Member States (see p. 393).

The imposition of civil liability has other effects as well as simply sorting out the question of liability for specific incidents. It acts as an incentive to act in a particular way, because of the high possible risks. In so doing, it fulfils the precautionary principle and fits in well with the current EC emphasis on shared responsibility, since producers will act so as to reduce and manage risks themselves. It thus acts as a stimulus to integrate risk management principles into all levels of business decision-making, as there is little doubt that the threat of civil action is a potent one, especially in an age when insurance against such risks is hard to obtain.

Optimal environmental regulation

In concluding this chapter it should be pointed out that no one regulatory instrument will be successful on its own. Historically, the means of addressing environmental problems was through the use of legal regulation, typically a system of consents/permits backed by criminal sanctions for breach. As our understanding of the complexity of the environment and the causes of pollution and degradation has increased so the range of regulatory instruments or tools has broadened. Traditional 'command and control' has its supporters[36] but regulation cannot properly address every issue.[37] The same could be said of other types of regulatory instrument. For example economic instruments have been criticized for failing to address moral concerns.[38] Other instruments are palpably inefficient or ineffective on their own. The key to using the 'tools' in the environmental lawyer's 'tool box' is to combine different instruments so that the strength of certain types of 'tool' complements the weaknesses of others (and vice versa). This is not to say that all instruments must be used in every situation. Indeed, this 'kitchen sink' or 'smorgasbordism' approach to selecting regulatory instruments and environmental standards has been argued to be 'seriously sub-optimal' and inefficient.[39] Optimal environmental regulation depends largely on combining those

---

35. E.g. see the collection of essays in J. Lowry and R. Edmunds (eds), *Environmental Protection and the Common Law* (Oxford: Hart Publishing, 2000).
36. E.g. see H. Latin (1985) 37 Stanford Law Review, 1267.
37. A. Alm (1992) EPA Journal 18 May 1992.
38. M. Sagoff, *The Economy of the Earth* (Cambridge: Cambridge University Press, 1988), esp. ch. 9.
39. See R. Hahn (1993) 102 Yale Law Journal 1719 and N. Gunningham and P. Grabosky, *Smart Regulation: Designing Environmental Policy* (Oxford: Clarendon Press, 1998), 389.

instruments which work well together to address particular environmental problems. This is a much broader question than a simple 'which tool/s will work best?' It involves understanding what the problem is, what standards to apply, who will be affected, which institutions will administer any new controls and what hurdles might prevent the efficient and effective implementation of any regulatory system which is finally adopted.

CHAPTER SUMMARY

1 Administrative regulation is the most common method of addressing environmental problems in Britain. Administrative regulation is the application of rules and procedures by public bodies so as to achieve a measure of control over activities carried on by individuals and firms.

2 The system of making regulations to address environmental problems involves a number of stages such as deciding what policies to adopt, what standards should apply, applying those standards through some form of consent, enforcing those standards, providing public information about the system and monitoring and improving the system in the light of experience.

3 There are different types of standard which are used in environmental regulation. Generally, these can be divided into those that apply to the receiving environment (target standards) and those that apply to emissions (source standards).

4 Other standards can be used including process, product and use standards. Each standard has advantages and disadvantages.

5 Traditionally, Britain has used target standards although European Directives based upon emissions standards have meant that different approaches have been adopted in recent years.

6 British regulatory systems can be said to exhibit a pragmatic and flexible approach involving an explicit balancing of environmental factors with such things as economic and social considerations.

7 Other characteristics which can be used to describe the British approach to environmental regulation include the use of discretion to set and enforce standards, gradualism and reliance on scientific evidence, and the decentralization of much decision-making.

8 There is an increasing use of instruments other than administrative regulation. These include the use of economic instruments and self-regulation. The challenge is to find the correct blend of instruments which will provide the most effective results.

QUESTIONS

1 What types of standard are used in environmental regulation?

2 Compare and contrast the different types of environmental standard in terms of the following:
   a Enforceability.
   b Cost.
   c Administrative simplicity.
   d Fairness.
   e Effectiveness.

3   What are the advantages and disadvantages of different methods of regulating environmental problems?

4   A new chemical substance terranium has been developed by a private company. It is thought to be harmful to humans, plants and animals at certain concentrations. How might an environmental regulatory system operate in order to control the risks associated with terranium? What standards might be applied and what regulatory instruments used? What further information about terranium would you want to know?

5   In what circumstances might voluntary mechanisms be more effective than compulsory regulation?

6   Give some examples of the use of economic instruments in British environmental regulation. What role do economic instruments play in conjunction with other regulatory instruments? Are they effective?

FURTHER READING

As the range of reading on regulation generally and environmental regulation is vast, the selection of further reading depends largely upon the nature of any further research. An excellent starting point for any deeper reading is N. Gunningham and P. Grabosky, *Smart Regulation: Designing Environmental Policy* (Oxford: Clarendon Press, 1998). For a historical perspective see J. McLoughlin and E. Bellinger, *Environmental Pollution Control: An Introduction to Principles and Practice of Administration* (London: Graham & Trotman, 1993) which is a very readable (if a little dated) account which combines legal and administrative insights and D. Robinson, 'Regulatory Evolution in Pollution Control' in T. Jewell and J. Steele (eds), *Law in Environmental Decision Making* (Oxford: Clarendon Press, 1998) which traces the different phases of regulatory evolution with an analysis of the reasons for those changes.

On the specific issue of the various types of standard that are available (and much more on environmental decision-making in general) see the RECP's 21st Report, *Setting Environmental Standards* (Cm 4053, 1998). R. Macrory, 'Regulating in a Risky Environment' (2001) Current Legal Problems 619 provides an analysis of command and control regulation in comparison to newer forms of regulatory instrument. A study of the different types of regulatory techniques with a comparison in terms of specific benchmarks such as accountability, efficiency and effectiveness can be found in C. Hilson, *Regulating Pollution: A UK and EC Perspective* (Oxford: Hart Publishing, 2000).

The nature and role of environmental standards are discussed in G. Lubbe-Wolff, 'Efficient Environmental Legislation—On Different Philosophies Of Pollution Control in Europe' (2001) 13 JEL 79 and there is an analysis of the true nature of the apparent conflict between Britain and Europe in relation to the use of standards in N. Haigh, *EEC Environmental Policy and Britain* (2nd edn, London: Longman 1990). A broader examination of the political background to the changing relationship between Britain and Europe can be found in P. Lowe and S. Ward (eds), *Britain Environmental Policy and Europe: Politics and Policy in Transition* (London: Routledge, 1998).

On the 'British approach' to pollution control, see D. Vogel, *National Styles of Regulation* (Ithaca:- Cornell University Press, 1986), which despite its age still provides a thought provoking comparison between British and American approaches. This book claims to be 'an examination of British environmental policy as seen through the eyes of a student of American politics', and consists of a comparison of approaches to environmental regulation in Britain and the USA. More recent coverage can be found in R. Kagan and L. Axelrad (eds), *Regulatory Encounters* (Berkeley: University of California Press, 2000). In particular Part I of this book contains comparative studies of the regulatory styles in the US, Britain and other countries by examining the different approaches to waste and contaminated land regulation.

A good introduction to various aspects of self regulation can be found in S. Gaines and C. Kimber, 'Redirecting Self-Regulation' (2001) 13 JEL 157 which argues for a redirecting of self regulation within the context of the private as opposed to public law contexts. A more theoretical (and perhaps more difficult) article on the fundamentals of self regulation can be found in E. Orts, 'Reflexive Environmental Law' (1995) 89(4) Northwestern University Law Review 1227. The use of environmental agreements are covered in E. Orts and K. Deketelaere, *Environmental Contracts: Comparative Approaches to Regulatory Innovation in the United States and Europe* (The Hague: Kluwer Law International, 2000), J. Verschuuren, 'EC Environmental Law and Self-Regulation in the Member States: In Search of a Legislative Framework' (2000) 1 Yearbook of European Environmental Law 103 and A. Ross and J. Rowan-Robinson, 'Behind Closed Doors: The Use of Agreements in the UK to Protect the Environment' (1999) Environmental Law Review 82. There is an interesting study of the implementation and effect of the use of Environmental Management Systems which can be found in A. Gouldson and J. Murphy, *Regulatory Realities* (London: Earthscan, 1998), particularly ch. 4.

An interested reader would find many illuminating parallels with other areas of regulation which are described in general texts on regulatory theory, of which the most accessible and relevant include: R. Baldwin and M. Cave, *Understanding Regulation* (Oxford: Oxford University Press, 1999) which has excellent chapters on standard setting, regulating risks and regulatory enforcement; R. Baldwin, C. Scott, and C. Hood (eds), *A Reader on Regulation* (Oxford: Oxford University Press, 1999); and A. Ogus, *Regulation: Legal Form and Economic Theory* (Oxford: Oxford University Press, 1994). The latter provides clear description of the use of different types of standard and is a nice bridge into other texts which examine the relationship between economics and environmental law. Although there are many such texts, the starting point should be D. Pearce, A. Markandya, and E. Barbier, *Blueprint for a Green Economy* (London: Earthscan, 1989) which has a number of sequels, the latest of which is D. Pearce and E. Barbier, *Blueprint for a Sustainable Economy* (London: Earthscan, 2000). These provide an interesting study in how economic theory has developed over the last 10 or so years. Another useful study is T. O'Riordan, *Eco-Taxation* (London: Earthscan, 1996). For a justification of economic instruments over 'command and control' regulation, see B. Ackerman and R. Stewart, 'Reforming Environmental Law, the Democratic Case for Market Incentives' (1988) Columbia Journal of Environmental Law 171. Finally B. Richardson (ed), *Environmental Regulation Through Financial Organisations* (The Hague: Kluwer, 2002) goes beyond the range of economic instruments discussed here.

@ WEB LINKS

There are not very many good web sites which capture the general nature of the fundamentals of environmental regulation. For an examination of regulatory approaches in context have a look at the Government's Better Regulation Task Force's report on Producer Responsibility at <www.brtf.gov.uk>. This Report looks at the regulatory process in relation to End of Life Vehicles and Waste Electronic and Electrical Equipment. For the latest thinking on regulatory tools at the European level the 6th Environmental Action Programme is available at <www.europa.eu.int/comm/environment/newprg/>. The OECD has a number of interesting resources. The organization has been a leading advocate for the role of economic instruments as well as regulatory reform. There is a lot of material of a specific environmental nature as well as more general information which can be found at <www.oecd.org>. Domestically, the Royal Commission on Environmental Pollution is one of the best sources of information on environmental regulation and can be found at <www.rcep.org.uk>. In addition to the excellent introduction to environmental standards found in the 21st Report, the other reports are an excellent way of looking at many different contemporary environmental challenges and with discussion and assessment of the various possible regulatory responses. The main weakness of the site is that the majority of Reports are summarized with only the most recent to be found in full.

9 Environmental crime

 Overview

This chapter is concerned with environmental crime and the enforcement of environmental law. The chapter starts with some consideration of the difficult definition of environmental crime including the distinction between moral and legal meanings of the term. We then consider some of the basic framework of environmental crime which helps to explain some of the approaches to the enforcement of environmental regulation. For example, the fact that many environmental crimes are strict liability offences explains why the rate of successful prosecutions is high (at around 95 per cent), but it may also provide an explanation as to why the sanctions which are imposed by the Courts are considered by some to be too low. The largest part of this chapter describes the enforcement practices adopted by regulatory agencies in the UK. There is a vast discrepancy between the number of potential offences committed and the number of prosecutions which is explained by the 'cooperative approach' adopted by enforcement agencies. The reasons for this approach are discussed along with alternative approaches. As the majority of environmental crime is policed by the Environment Agency there is greater emphasis placed upon the laws, policies and practices which relate to the Agency's activities as opposed to other environmental regulators such as English Nature, local authorities or HM Customs and Excise (in relation to the landfill tax).

At the end of this chapter you should be able to:

✔ Appreciate some of the difficulties in defining environmental crime.
✔ Appreciate a basic outline of the legal characteristics of environmental crimes including the nature of, justification for and consequences of strict liability.
✔ Identify and understand the law on corporate and individual liability for environmental offences.
✔ Identify the main regulatory agencies with responsibilities for enforcing environmental crime and understand the main factors which influence the way in which they operate.
✔ Appreciate the main issues involved in enforcing environmental law including the characteristics which underpin the 'British' approach to enforcement.
✔ Identify and distinguish the different approaches which could be taken when enforcing environmental law.
✔ Identify in outline the main sanctions for environmental crimes.
✔ Appreciate and evaluate the current dissatisfaction with the existing structures, processes and outcomes of the enforcement of environmental regulation.

What is environmental crime?

Various writers have attempted to define what is meant by an environmental crime (see Box 9.1). As with other key terms in environmental law these definitions tend to reflect different perspectives. Some writers consider that environmental crime should cover activities which may be lawful or licensed but which cause significant environmental harm.[1] For example, activities such as peat extraction at nationally important nature conservation sites under the benefit of long-standing planning permissions might be considered to be 'criminal' in the eyes of many conservationists (see Box 21.4). Other influential perspectives could be spatial (e.g. international environmental crime as compared to more localized amenity offences), race or social justice (e.g. in relation to inequalities of the causes and effects of environmental harm as between the developed and developing world and between rich corporations and poorer sections of society).[2] These general notions of environmental crime convey a sense of judgment about what is 'wrong' about certain activities but take us no further.

The definitions set out in Box 9.1 reflect different perspectives on environmental crime, from moral and philosophical to legal and local amenity-led perspectives. Each of these perspectives characterize environmental crime differently from a broad interpretation incorporating the notion of environmental harm which may be lawful as a crime to more legalistic definitions which place law at the centre of defining what is 'right' and 'wrong'.

BOX 9.1 Definitions of environmental crime

1 'An environmental crime is an act committed with the intent to harm or with a potential to cause harm to ecological and/or biological systems and for the purpose of securing business or personal advantage.'[3]

2 'An environmental crime is an unauthorised act or omission that violates the law and is therefore subject to criminal prosecution and criminal sanction. This offence harms or endangers people's physical safety or health as well as the environment itself. It serves the interests of either organizations—typically corporations—or individuals.'[4]

3 'Environmental crime includes littering, abandoned vehicles, graffiti, fly posting, dog fouling, fly-tipping, dumped business waste, vandalism, abandoned shopping trolleys and noise nuisance.'[5]

4 'Environmental crime includes all offences either created by statute or developed under the common law that relate to the environment.'[6]

---

1. See M. Halsey (1997) Current Issues in Criminology 217.

2. See, e.g., in relation to the literature on environmental justice, R. Bullard, (1993) Yale Journal of International Law 319.

3. M. Clifford, *Environmental Crime: Enforcement, Policy and Social Responsibility* (Gaithersburg: Aspen, 1998), 26.

4. Y. Situ and D. Emmons, *Environmental Crime: The Criminal Justice System's Role in Protecting the Environment* (Thousand Oaks: Sage, 2000), 3

5. *'Tackling Environmental Crime Together'* initiative at <www.together.gov.uk>.

6. Environmental Audit Committee: Session 2003–4, Sixth Report, *Environmental Crime.*

The definition of environmental crime matters because it helps to frame many of the key aspects of criminal liability for environmental harm. Whether an activity is viewed as a technical regulatory breach or a 'crime against the environment'; whether liability for environmental crime should be strict and if so what the justification is for doing so; the extent to which offenders should be viewed as truly criminal; the attitudes that should be taken towards enforcing the law; and the sanctions which should be imposed for breach.

(a) Legal approaches to defining 'environmental crime'

The most obvious way for lawyers to define environmental crime is to only include those actions or omissions which directly or indirectly damage the environment and which are prohibited by law. This has the advantage of being value free and objective. This approach includes both direct polluting acts (e.g. depositing waste without a licence) and indirect omissions (e.g. failing to pay landfill tax). But taking a legalistic, positivist approach to defining environmental crime still leaves a number of issues.

First, the problematic and uncertain definition of environmental law raises questions of where the outer boundaries of environmental crime are located. For example, compare and contrast the third and fourth definitions in Box 9.1. The fourth definition relies on a common understanding of what statutes 'relate to the environment'. Whereas this might not be an issue in relation to core topics such as pollution control and wildlife crime, there are other areas where there is uncertainty. The third definition refers to the local environment and includes such things as vandalism and graffiti which might otherwise be classified as 'criminal damage'. Whilst the definitions in Box 9.1 are not mutually exclusive, they illustrate that a legal approach can illicit broad and narrow definitions of 'environmental crime'.

Secondly, and following on from the first problem, a legal definition of environmental crime is uncertain because there is such a wide range of activities and offenders to which the phrase could be applied. Under a broad definition environmental crimes can be committed by the careless driver, the fly tipping 'man in a white van', organized criminal gangs, the egg collector and the global corporation. As we can see from the definitions in Box 9.1, typical offences could include littering, anti-social behaviour (e.g. noise nuisances), trade in endangered species and major incidents of oil pollution. Thus whilst it may be possible to characterise particular groups of offences by reference to particular criteria these would not necessarily be applicable across all possible environmental offences. For example the typical characteristics of pollution control offences may not be the equivalent of typical 'wildlife crimes' or landfill tax evasion.[7]

Thirdly, taking a legalistic approach to defining environmental crime has jurisdictional and geographical limitations. Whilst there are some international agreements which require signatories to impose standard criminal sanctions,[8] there is no guarantee that an environmental crime in one country will be a crime in another. This is particularly the case in civil law countries where the distinction between administrative offences and truly criminal offences is significant.[9]

---

7. For examples of typical characteristics of pollution control offences see P. De Prez (2000) 12 JEL 65 at 66.
8. Examples include illegal waste transport and trade in endangered species.
9. H-U. Paeffgen (1991) 13 JEL 247.

BOX 9.2 **Typical environmental crimes** [10]

Subject of offence	Nature of offence	Statutory provisions	Enforcement body
Air Pollution	Emissions of dark smoke	Clean Air Act 1993, Part I	Local Authorities
Contaminated land	Failing to comply with a remediation notice	Environmental Protection Act 1990, s. 78M	Environment Agency and Local Authority
Drinking water quality	Supplying water unfit for human consumption	Water Industry Act 1991, s. 70	Secretary of State Drinking Water Inspectorate
Environmental taxes	Avoiding landfill tax Avoiding Climate Change Levy	Finance Act 1996, Part III Finance Act 2000, Part II and Schedule 6	HM Customs and Excise
Forestry	Illegal felling of trees	Forestry Act 1967, s. 17	Forestry Commission
Genetically modified organisms	Unauthorized release of GMOs	Environmental Protection Act 1990, Part IV	Secretary of State Health and Safety Executive
Hazardous substances and major accident hazard sites	Offences relating to the storage, notification and emergency planning at major accident hazards	Control of Major Accident Hazards Regulations 1999	Health and Safety Executive and Environment Agency
Industrial pollution control	IPC/LAPC/PPC Pollution control licensing (e.g. operating without required permit)	Environmental Protection Act 1990, s. 6 Pollution Prevention and Control (England and Wales) Regulations 2000 (reg. 9)	Environment Agency and Local Authorities
Pesticides	Misuse of pesticides	Control of Pesticides Regulations 1986	DEFRA
Statutory nuisances	Failing to comply with an abatement notice	Environmental Protection Act 1990, s. 80(4)	Local Authorities
Waste management	Illegal waste disposal/ treatment	Environmental Protection Act 1990, s. 33	Environment Agency
Water abstraction	Abstracting water without a licence	Water Resources Act 1991, s. 24	Environment Agency
Water pollution	Causing, knowingly permitting entry of polluting matter into controlled waters	Water Resources Act 1991, s. 85	Environment Agency

10. Adapted from C. DuPont and P. Zakkow, *Trends in Environmental Sentencing in England and Wales*, DEFRA, 2003 ('Du Pont and Zakkow').

Subject of offence	Nature of offence	Statutory provisions	Enforcement body
Wildlife crime	Controls on trade and possession of wild animals and plants	Wildlife and Countryside Act 1981, Part I	Police
	Protection of habitats	Wildlife and Countryside Act 1981, Part IV	English Nature Police
	Trade in endangered species	EC Regulation 338/97 Control of Trade in Endangered Species (Enforcement) Regulations 1997	Secretary of State HM Customs and Excise Police

For the purposes of this chapter we adopt a fairly broad legal definition of 'environmental crime' based around the offences set out in the main environmental statutes outlined in Chapter 2. Box 9.2 sets out some of the main classes of environmental crime. Some are straightforward offences in and of themselves (e.g. supplying unwholesome drinking water). In other cases these could be general acts such as causing the entry of polluting matter in controlled waters (Water Resources Act 1991, s. 85) or they could be specified activities which require a permit or authorisation before being undertaken. In many of these latter offences acting in accordance with a regulatory permit or licence will normally act as a defence.

Box 9.2 only covers the main groupings of environmental offences but conveys the breadth of topics which might be considered to be mainstream environmental offences. There are many other environmental regulatory offences (e.g. under planning legislation or in relation to radioactive materials) as well as other non-regulatory criminal offences (e.g. public nuisance is a common law offence as well as a tort and the uprooting of wild plants for sale or commercial purposes can be theft under section 4(3) of the Theft Act 1968).

The lack of uniformity of environmental crime

The development of environmental criminal law has been fragmented and inconsistent.[11] One of the consequences of this is that there are many disparities between the laws which seek to address different types of environmental crime. This can be seen in the many different ways in which environmental crime is constructed within statutes. Slight differences between the strictness of liability or defences can be detected between different offences (e.g. the absence of a due diligence defence in water pollution see p. 284). These differences are not insignificant. For example, one of the historic weaknesses of nature conservation legislation has been the relative narrowness of both the rules and enforcement options (see Chapter 21). On the other hand, the offence of causing the pollution of controlled waters under the Water Resources Act 1991, s. 85 is comparatively wide covering a broad range of potential polluters. Moreover, there is a range of other enforcement mechanisms which can be selected to try to deal with any water pollution which has been caused (e.g. an enforcement notice under s. 191A or a works notice

11. W. Wilson, *Making Environmental Laws Work* (Oxford: Hart Publishing, 1998), 110.

under Water Resources Act 1991, s. 161A would be available). These examples illustrate how, at one extreme, an officer working for English Nature has relatively few enforcement options available to deal with damage to a SSSI (indeed they might not be able to do anything at all), whereas the Environment Agency officer has the ability to select from an assortment of formal enforcement powers and possibly even from a list of potential polluters.

The moral dimension of environmental crime

Perhaps the fundamental problem in defining environmental crime by reference to legal criteria is that relatively few activities which harm the environment are crimes in and of themselves. Clearly any definition which characterized environmental crime as being 'activities which caused harm to the environment' would ignore the fact that many such activities would be considered perfectly lawful (e.g. driving a car). Criminal law is normally reserved for the punishment of socially unacceptable behaviour. Harm to the environment is, in many situations, considered to be acceptable (for example in certain circumstances we are prepared to allow such pollution under licence or authorisation) because it is an inherent consequence of many industrial activities which provide significant benefits. This is the rationale for having a system of regulation which defines the framework for determining whether such benefits outweigh the harm caused. The criminal law is not suited to such a balancing process, and thus is mainly used to address clearly unacceptable behaviour or to reinforce the regulatory system.

The nature and extent of the environmental harm caused by these various crimes may be contested. There are many types of activities which cause harm to the environment but would not necessarily be classed as an *environmental* crime. Take for example the offence of driving a car with exhaust emissions that exceed the legal limit. The emissions may cause harm when aggregated with many other vehicles but should it be classified as an environmental crime? Whether this is an environmental crime depends largely upon whether a broad or narrow definition of the term is adopted.

This uncertainty contributes to the moral ambivalence surrounding regulatory offences in general and certain aspects of environmental crime in particular. The central question is whether environmental crime should be distinguished from 'real' crimes such as murder or theft. These latter offences are viewed as being acts which are 'evil in themselves' (*mala in se*) whereas environmental crime is not thought to be inherently immoral (indeed it is considered to be acceptable in some circumstances) but is made unlawful only by statute (*mala prohibita*). This is not merely a theoretical consideration. The extent to which pollution or other environmental harm is viewed as a 'crime' by operators, regulators and the general public is a factor which influences such things as whether to enforce and how to sanction or punish offenders. Thus, the moral opprobrium which attaches to environmental crime influences the exercise of discretion in taking enforcement action (i.e. which power to exercise or whether to prosecute), and sanctioning pollution (i.e. by taking into account mitigating factors when sentencing).

Historically, the commission of environmental crimes by industrial operators was viewed as purely regulatory in nature and therefore 'not criminal in any real sense' (see *Sherras v De Rutzen* [1895] 1 QB 918). It was thought that pollution was a natural consequence of industrial activity and the operators made a positive contribution to the local and regional economy. Arguably, attitudes to environmental harm generally and environmental crime more specifically have shifted over the years (see Box 3.3). This has led to calls to distinguish between routine cases of environmental harm which result from general activities and environmental crimes which have been wilfully committed with a view to personal or business advantage. In the former case it has been argued that civil penalties administered through civil or administrative means (such as standardised 'fines' for breaches of licence conditions) would be more appropriate leaving criminal sanctions only for the worst type of offences.[12]

Other factors have played a part in the ambiguous nature of the moral dimension of environmental crime. Traditionally, those who have polluted have been of high status in society and those affected by pollution of low status. Pollution was more commonplace in working-class areas of high industrial activity. For example, one of the reasons that the 'west end' of cities tends to be more affluent than the 'east end' is partly connected to the historical transmission of pollutants from the west to the east either by prevailing winds or via rivers. Many of those living in the area were working in the factory which was polluting the area. The pollution was often seen as a way of life rather than a matter for complaint.[13]

The changes in fundamental attitudes to the environment have started to have an impact upon attitudes to environmental crime. Underlying these changes is a basic shift in the way that environmental problems are perceived, not only by the public but also by the enforcement agencies and even the general category of 'polluters'. The acknowledgement that environmental protection is important in its own right has undermined previous assumptions about the benefits of activities which cause environmental harm.

As environmental issues have become more important in the public eye, there is a desire to ensure that environmental standards are maintained and environmental damage minimized. Moreover, when public interest in the environment and the understanding of the consequences of environmental harm increases, there is an equivalent escalation in the amount of moral opprobrium which attaches to environmental offences. The publicity which is given to pollution incidents and other notorious examples of environmental damage (even ironically where such damage might be lawful, e.g. the extraction of peat in South Yorkshire, see Box 21.4) tends to amplify the view that such harm and pollution is caused by something more than mere administrative difficulties and should be dealt with severely. Given this increase in the public perception of the importance of environmental interests, it is not inevitable that environmental crime will always be viewed as being somehow a 'lesser' offence than 'real' crimes such as burglary or assault. Indeed some writers have argued the idea that environmental crimes could 'swap places' with traditional crimes in the criminal justice system.[14]

---

12. M. Woods and R. Macrory, *Environmental Civil Penalties—A More Proportionate Response to Regulatory Breach* (London: UCL, 2003).

13. See J. Brenner (1974) OJLS and J. Mclaren (1983) OJLS 155.

14. See D. Nelken (1990) MLR 834.

Strict liability

Many of the common environmental offences impose strict liability. Thus to establish an offence, the only thing which needs to be proved is the act or omission which forms part of the offence and there is no need to prove any negligence or fault on the part of the defendant/operator. There is a link between the moral dimension of environmental crime and the imposition of strict liability. The moral foundation of 'real' criminal law is that a crime requires both an unlawful act and the requisite mental responsibility or fault. The use of strict liability can be justified by reference to both trivial offences (through ease of prosecution) *and* serious offences (by acting as a deterrent and through the polluter pays principle).

As a precursor to the following discussion of the arguments for the use of strict liability for environmental crimes it is important to inject a note of realism. Although the absence of fault is irrelevant to the commission of many environment crimes, in practice fault and blame are considered throughout the criminal process. First, enforcing authorities exercise a discretion when deciding whether and how to enforce and they are often reluctant to use the ultimate sanction of prosecution unless moral blame is towards the top end of the scale, i.e. in cases of criminal negligence or actual intent on behalf of the offender. Secondly, evidence of fault and blame is gathered and presented by enforcing authorities in order to establish the blameworthiness of defendants so that Courts can exercise sentencing discretion properly.

There are thought to be four main arguments for the use of strict liability.

The imposition of strict liability:

- promotes the public interest goal inherent in environmental legislation;
- acts as a deterrent which improves the quality of environmental risk prevention measures;
- increases the ease of prosecution which increases the deterrent effect;
- accords with the polluter pays principle.

(a) The public interest goal

Environmental regulation is primarily aimed at preventing environmental harm on the basis that this is in the public interest. Imposing strict liability for environmental crime ensures that this public interest goal is achieved by divorcing questions of blame or fault from the consequences of actions which cause environmental harm. Thus the emphasis is upon the prevention and minimization of harm rather than the motivation of a particular offender. The Courts have implicitly emphasized the public interest goal inherent in environmental legislation by interpreting criminal liability for environmental crime in a broad fashion (e.g. the broad interpretation of 'causing' in relation to water pollution offences, see p. 736).

(b) Deterrence and risk management

Strict liability encourages those to whom the law applies to be extra-cautious in their attempts to comply with environmental regulation. The imposition of strict liability acts as a deterrent which ensures that a broad approach is taken to environmental risk avoidance. The

Courts have emphasized this in adopting a expansive interpretation of criminal conduct in environmental cases. This can be found in cases such as *Alphacell v Woodward* [1972] AC 824 in which the House of Lords emphasized the need to do 'everything possible' to prevent pollution (as opposed to merely taking reasonable steps) (see Case box 18.4). More recently this approach has included imposing criminal liability for failing to conduct an assessment of the risks associated with *other people's* conduct (see Case box 9.1). In such circumstances it is clear that there will be an incentive to conduct operations going far beyond what is reasonable, to taking extreme steps to prevent pollution.

CASE 9.1 *Express Dairies v Environment Agency* [2005] Env LR 7

The defendant, ED owned a dairy depot at which it allowed one of its customers to take delivery of cream from an outside supplier. During the transfer, the cream escaped into the surface drains and consequently into the nearby river. ED was found guilty of an offence under section 217(3) of the Water Resources Act 1991 in that its customer had caused the entry of polluting matter into controlled waters and the offence was committed due to ED's default. The alleged default was that ED had failed to undertake an assessment of the risks associated with transferring cream in the yard. ED appealed against the conviction arguing that there was no statutory requirement to undertake such a risk assessment. The High Court held that in order to establish criminal liability under these provisions all that had to be shown was that the offence committed by ED's customer was due to an act or default of ED. Land owners like ED who allowed risky operations on their land were under an obligation to carry out a risk assessment and address the matters raised in that assessment. Only in those circumstances could they then argue that they were not in default.

The counter to this argument is that instead of acting as a deterrent, it actually undermines the moral force of identifying and distinguishing environmental crimes as serious offences. There are some cases where the defendant's conduct can hardly be said to be criminal in any true sense of the word (see e.g. the *CPC* case in Case box 9.2). Branding such actions as 'crimes' devalues the use of criminal law to address serious cases of environmental harm. According to this argument criminal sanctions should only be used to address the worst examples of environmental harm. In prosecuting and punishing seemingly trivial breaches of the law, regulatory agencies may discourage people from taking a stringent approach to compliance on the basis that they might as well be 'hung for a sheep as a lamb'. The *CPC* case also illustrates nicely that although fault is often taken into account when deciding whether to prosecute there will be cases where no significant fault can be found but where the environmental harm caused is so significant that prosecutions will still be brought. During the passage of the Environment Act 1995 various efforts were made to try and address the apparent harshness of strict liability in cases such as the *CPC* case. In particular amendments were proposed which would have introduced a 'due diligence' defence into water pollution legislation in a similar fashion as waste legislation (see Box 15.14). These were rejected on the ground that such a defence would have made it more difficult for regulators to enforce the law.[15]

---

15. W. Wilson, *Making Environmental Laws Work* (Oxford: Hart Publishing, 1998), 109.

CASE 9.2 *CPC (UK) v NRA* [1995] Env LR 131

Piping at the defendant's factory had fractured causing cleaning liquid to enter the drainage system and be discharged into the nearby river. The fracturing of the pipe had been caused by a failure to stick two sections together properly. This work had been undertaken by a sub-contractor before the defendant had purchased the factory. It was accepted that the defendant could not have known or foreseen the crack in the pipe work. The defendant was found to have 'caused' the pollution. The Court of Appeal upheld the conviction finding that the fact that the defect was latent and that the defendant could not have foreseen the problem was irrelevant as liability was strict.

A general counter to the deterrence argument in favour of strict liability is that given the relatively long history of criminal regulation of environmental harm, there is no objective evidence to suggest that imposing strict liability makes any difference to compliance rates. There may be a number of reasons for this including low sentences or the low rate of prosecution, but these are inextricably linked to the imposition of strict liability in the first place. Thus we have a 'chicken and egg' argument—is it strict liability or the responses to the harshness of strict liability (i.e. low sentences and prosecution rates) which leads to ineffective deterrence?

(c) Efficiency and ease of prosecution

A third reason for imposing strict liability presents a different aspect of this deterrence factor. The imposition of strict liability makes it easier for prosecutors to prove their case.[16] All that is needed is to establish the criminal act and the added complication of fault or blame can be ignored. Thus when prosecutions are brought they rarely fail. This 'freedom to prosecute' acts as a deterrent in various ways to those who would otherwise wish to fight cases on the basis that an offence had been accidental or that reasonable steps had been taken to avoid the commission of the offence. The imposition of strict liability also promotes flexibility in enforcement in the sense that enforcement agencies are able to target particular offences or classes of offenders where non-compliance may be a problem in order to emphasise the deterrence factor. Of course this also raises the question of whether this selective approach would be a fair or efficient approach to environmental enforcement.

(d) The Polluter Pays Principle

The final argument in favour of imposing strict liability is that it accords with one interpretation of the Polluter Pays Principle in the sense that the punishments imposed by criminal courts for environmental crime, represent a 'payment', sometimes in the shape of a fine, in other situations through compensation or even non-monetary sanctions such as imprisonment (see further p. 265).

---

16. C. Abbot (2004) ELM 16(2) 67.

Defences

Although there are many arguments in favour of imposing strict liability for environmental crimes there is still a basic objection that criminalisation of innocent or accidental actions is somewhat problematic. The true position is that there are very few environmental crimes which impose absolute strict liability (i.e. there are no defences) as most offences balance the potential unfairness of such liability with certain statutory defences. The courts have tended to construe these defences narrowly in order to protect the underlying aims of environmental legislation. For example, in *Durham CC v Peter O'Connor Industrial Services* [1993] Env LR 197, the Court specifically rejected the notion that taking 'reasonable care' to avoid the commission of an offence would amount to 'due diligence' as this would negate the strictness of criminal liability for environmental crime. In that case the Court suggested that for due diligence to be established, all that could be done to ensure compliance should be done even if that involved checking every transfer of waste from a site. Examples of typical defences include:

- *Acting in accordance with a statutory consent.* Typically this will include complying with the conditions of such things as discharge consents (see e.g. the Water Resources Act 1991, s. 88). Breaching conditions of a consent/authorisation is generally an additional/ alternative offence (e.g. WRA 1991, s. 85(6)).

- *Emergency situations.* This defence is normally subject to a requirement to minimize harm and to report to the enforcement agency within a reasonable period (see e.g. in relation to waste EPA 1990, s. 33(7); nature conservation Wildlife and Countryside Act 1981, s. 28(8)(b); and water pollution, Water Resources Act 1991, s. 89). Environmental harm caused in response to an emergency situation (e.g. water pollution from fire-fighting run-off) can still amount to an offence as the emergency does not necessarily break the chain of causation (unless the emergency arises in extraordinary conditions, see *Express Ltd (t/a Express Dairies Distribution) v Environment Agency* [2003] Env LR 29).

- *Exercising due diligence in carrying out operations.* This would include explicit defences (e.g. EPA 1990, s. 33(7) in relation to waste management) and implicit due diligence requirements in relation to the use of 'best practicable means' or the 'best available techniques'. Whether or not the due diligence defence can be made out is a question of fact in every case. The question arises whether due diligence applies to actions taken by a company or by the employee. For example, would it fulfil the requirement to exercise due diligence if a very large company in delegating responsibility to individual sites provides rigorous training and supervision on the steps to take to prevent pollution but an individual employee ignores these steps? The *Durham CC* case suggests that it will be the company which will be held responsible for the failures of its employees. Thus it would be harder to prove that a large undertaking has exercised sufficient due diligence to amount to a defence because higher standards will be expected. Greater resources are expected to be available to maintain standards in a large company. The 'due diligence' must relate to conduct aimed at preventing the offence, not putting matters right afterwards. The burden of proving due diligence is on the defendant.

- *Having a 'reasonable excuse'.* The test of whether something is a reasonable excuse is normally objective i.e. would a reasonable person consider that the excuse was consistent with a reasonable standard of conduct. Examples of the reasonable excuse defence can be found in nature conservation legislation (see e.g. the Wildlife and Countryside Act 1981, s. 28(7)) and in relation to statutory nuisances (e.g. EPA 1990, s. 80(4)).

Individual and corporate offenders

The activities which lead to breaches of environmental law are carried out by a diverse range of individuals and corporate bodies from solo fly-tippers to huge multi-national corporations. The most significant acts of environmental harm through breaches of pollution control legislation tend to be caused by companies simply because of the scale of the industrial operations. There are, however, important exceptions to this general rule in areas such as wildlife crime, pollution from agricultural sources and fly-tipping waste. Indeed, figures suggest that individuals are responsible for the majority of environmental crimes as a whole (see Box 9.3).[17] These figures are slightly misleading as they exclude local authority prosecutions but include a significant proportion of individual wildlife offences (e.g. egg collecting and animal cruelty) and from some sectors where individual offenders are far more prevalent (e.g. agriculture).

BOX 9.3 **Individual vs Corporate Offenders** [18]

	Year			
Offender type	**1999**	**2000**	**2001**	**2002**
Corporate	359	625	732	880
Individual	487	965	1020	922
Total	846	1590	1752	1802

This distinction between individual and corporate offenders raises a number of issues. First, it is often much easier to classify environmental offences as 'white collar' or business crimes, and therefore as being morally neutral, where the defendant is a major corporation. On the other hand, in circumstances where there is an individual who is responsible for the commission of an offence, there is likely to be criminal intent or negligence. Thus where individuals are found to have committed an environmental crime it will normally be easier for prosecutors to establish blameworthiness which would lead to a prosecution. On the other hand the number of prosecutions of corporate offenders does not correlate with corporate non-compliance with environmental law. In other words although there may be fewer corporate defendants, the offences they are being prosecuted for will tend to be at the

---

17. Also see, Environment Agency evidence to House of Commons Audit Committee on *Corporate Crime*, 2004 HC 1135-i where it was estimated that the 38–40 per cent of all prosecutions were brought against registered companies.
18. Adapted from DuPont and Zakkow, op. cit., n. 10.

serious end of the spectrum of environmental harm and there will be many more companies who are in breach but not prosecuted. Secondly, the structure of large companies means that it is often difficult to identify the root cause of many pollution incidents. Arguably this has the effect of obscuring the blameworthiness of offending companies as they seek to 'trivialize' their conduct by reference to factors outside their control.[19] This, however, obscures the fact that in large organizations, management deficiencies are often to blame and truly innocent offenders are rare. Finally, the prosecution of corporate offenders can be justified by the existence of the deterrence factor of the bad publicity associated with the prosecution for environmental crimes and the development of a 'name and shame' policy for such offenders (see Box 9.15). This justification does not exist to the same extent for individual offenders.

Corporate liability

The nature of liability of companies for environmental crime is not necessarily straightforward. Some offences apply directly to companies, e.g. where offences relate to the breach of licence conditions and the licence is held in the name of the company. In other situations, however, it is the acts or omissions of individual employees which will incur criminal liability. This raises the central question of corporate criminal liability, namely, in what circumstances can companies be held to account for the acts of its employees? It had been thought that such corporate liability would only be established where the employees responsible were of sufficient seniority to act as the 'controlling mind' of the company. The problem is that many pollution incidents are the responsibility of operational staff who are far removed from the 'controlling mind'. The Courts have held that the actions of employees will create corporate criminal liability where it is clear that the relevant statutory purposes would be defeated if a company could not be prosecuted for the acts of its employees.

Case 9.3 *National Rivers Authority v Alfred McAlpine Homes East Ltd* [1994] Env LR 198

The defendant ('AMHE') caused water pollution during construction works. At the trial, AMHE was acquitted on the basis that the prosecution had failed to demonstrate that the employees that had caused the pollution were of sufficiently senior standing within the company to bind the company by their actions. On appeal the Court found AMHE to be liable. In particular, Morland J. expanded on the purposive approach to vicarious liability, namely that the offence under s. 85 of the Water Resources Act 1991 was designed to prevent water pollution. In order to make the legislation effective there was a necessary implication that companies should be liable for the acts or omissions of *all* of their employees as opposed to simply the senior employees who were 'controlling minds'. Morland J. reinforced this by referring to the idea that companies were in fact best placed to control activities of even very junior employees through such things as training and supervision.

---

19. P. DePrez (2000) 12 JEL 11.

Case 9.4 *Shanks and McEwan (Teesside) Ltd v Environment Agency* [1997] Env LR 305

In this case the defendant waste company ('SM') was prosecuted for 'knowingly causing' the deposit of waste in breach of licence conditions. The relevant facts were that the supervisor of a landfill site, whilst complying with the requirements of the waste management licence on the delivery of some waste, had failed to complete a necessary waste disposal form when he re-directed it to a containment bund rather than the anticipated storage tank. At the trial, SM argued that it did not have the requisite knowledge of the deposit as it had only been in the knowledge of the supervisor. SM was convicted on the basis that the site supervisor was part of the 'controlling mind' of the company. On appeal, the Court held that the only knowledge which was required was general knowledge that waste was deposited as opposed to specific knowledge of the breach of condition. On this basis either the supervisor's knowledge could be attributed to the company or the company had the general knowledge of waste deposits at the site because it was a landfill site. Thus, the purposes of this particular waste offence—to prevent the unlawful disposal of waste—could be met either by saying that the 'controlling minds' of the company knew that waste was deposited at its landfill sites or that the supervisor's knowledge of specific deposits could be attributed to the company.

To underline the flexibility of the purposive approach these decisions can be contrasted with the approach to corporate liability taken in other areas where a company can only be held criminally liable for the acts of those who possess the 'controlling mind' of the company (see, e.g., *Tesco Supermarkets Ltd v Nattrass* [1972] AC 153).

Directors' liability

Generally in Britain, where companies commit environmental offences, prosecutions are brought against that company rather than any one individual who might have responsibility within that company. This is in contrast to many civil law countries where the doctrine of corporate liability is not particularly well developed and where it is far more common for individual managers of companies to be prosecuted.[20] The British approach is not, however, restricted by law. Under many environmental statutes directors and managers can be prosecuted individually in certain circumstances. For example, in 2003 eleven company directors were fined for environmental offences.[21]

Any director, manager, secretary, or other similar officer of a corporate body can be prosecuted personally if the offence is committed with their consent or connivance, or is attributable to their neglect (see, e.g., EPA 1990, s. 157, Water Resources Act 1991, s. 217, Town and Country Planning Act 1990, s. 331). Note these sections do not apply where the allegation is against an individual as principal in their own right. To establish personal liability for directors, there must be:

• an offence committed by the company; and

• consent, connivance, or neglect by the individual.

---

20. C. Wells, *Corporations and Criminal Responsibility* (2nd edn, Oxford: Oxford University Press, 2001), 138–40.
21. Environment Agency, *Spotlight on Business Environmental Performance in 2003.*

The liability applies primarily but not exclusively to 'directors' although the name is not critical. Section 741 of the Companies Act 1985 defines the term which covers 'shadow directors' and de facto directors i.e. those who do not take the title 'Director' but effectively run the business. As for the other categories, the case law suggests that what matters is whether the individual has sufficient responsibilities to amount to the 'controlling mind' of the organization (see Box 9.4).

BOX 9.4 Directors' liability—who is a manager?

The use of the term 'manager' is not particularly illuminating as the phrase can cover everyone from people acting in a Chief Executive role down to a lowly 'trainee Manager' who may have been in the job for a day. In *Woodhouse v Walsall MBC* [1994] Env LR 30, the general manager of a waste disposal site (along with his employers) was convicted of the illegal storage of waste at a waste disposal site. At the trial the Magistrates found the general manager guilty on the basis that he was in a position of 'real authority'. The manager appealed and the High Court was asked to determine whether the defendant was of sufficient status to be personally liable under EPA 1990, s. 157. The court held that what was important was not just the existence of authority but the *scope* of the authority. The correct test was to determine whether a defendant was in a position to control and guide the company in terms of policy and strategy. This is, of course, a question of fact and degree in every case.

Enforcement agencies

(a) Historical background—'Poachers and Gamekeepers'

Historically there were many overlaps between the operational and regulatory functions carried out by environmental agencies. The two main examples of this dual role were in the control of water pollution under the regional water authorities and the control of the disposal of waste to land through the county-wide waste disposal authorities under COPA 1974 (see Chapter 2). Both of these authorities carried out activities which had to be policed by themselves. The failure to separate these two contradictory roles created great problems. Often the greatest breaches of environmental laws were caused by the operational arms of the regulatory bodies. This, in turn, led the private sector to argue that it was inequitable for the enforcement agencies to enforce against private companies when their own operations were also in breach. In addition, it influenced attitudes towards the regulated. Many officers within enforcement agencies empathised with those in the private sector and therefore were happy to pursue other options other than prosecution. Where officers had experienced the discomfort of striving but failing to comply with environmental laws they were much more ready to be sympathetic as an educator and advisor rather than a policeman (see the compliance approach to enforcement, p. 296).

The creation of the National Rivers Authority under the Water Act 1989 and the formation of the system of regulation in the waste disposal industry under Part II of the EPA 1990 allowed the new and separate enforcement agencies to adopt an arm's length relationship with operators. This in turn allowed, for example, the NRA to employ a more aggressive attitude towards the enforcement of environmental crime. This was evidenced by an increase in the incidence of prosecution with figures suggesting that water pollution prosecutions rose at least 25 per cent each year in the initial years of the NRA's life.[22] The creation of the Environment Agency in April 1996 further redefined the relationship between enforcers and operators with the integration of the enforcement functions in relation to various pollution control responsibilities. Other steps have been taken to increase the distance between regulator and regulated including the adoption of transparent policies on enforcement and greater third party involvement in the setting of standards and drawing up of guidance. This is not to say that there is a complete separation of operational and regulatory powers. For example, the Environment Agency has a number of operational duties in relation to flood defence management.

(b) Regulatory agencies

Box 9.2 above identifies some of the main environmental enforcement bodies who have responsibility for prosecuting environmental crimes and other enforcement action in England and Wales. Research suggests that over 90 per cent of all non-local authority prosecutions for environmental crime are brought by the Environment Agency.[23]

BOX 9.5 **Prosecutions for environmental crime**[24]

	Number of prosecutions brought (per year)			
Regulatory Agency	**1999**	**2000**	**2001**	**2002**
Environment Agency	768	1478	1620	1713
Crown Prosecution Service	54	74	101	74
Forestry Commission	No data	12	18	3
Customs and Excise	No data	1	1	6
Health and Safety Executive	–	4	3	3
RSPCA	22	25	19	7
DEFRA	2	–	–	–

Along with the major environmental regulators such as the Environment Agency, the nature conservation bodies and local authorities, other groups such as the Drinking Water Inspectorate and the Police play an enforcement role in relation to certain offences (e.g. in relation to wildlife crime, see Box 9.6).

22. W. Howarth and D. McGillivray, *Water Pollution and Water Quality Law* (Crayford: Shaw, 2001), 105.
23. DuPont and Zakkow, op. cit., n. 10.
24. Adapted from DuPont and Zakkow. Note that these figures include some offenders who will have been prosecuted for more than one offence.

BOX 9.6 **Responsibility for wildlife crime**

The policing and enforcement of wildlife crime is undertaken by a mixture of statutory agencies, the police and non-governmental organizations. English Nature play a significant part in policing the protection of habitats but the Police have primary responsibility for investigating offences which relate to species. Appointed Police Wildlife Liaison Officers coordinate the response to wildlife crimes. They are assisted in relation to the illegal international trade in endangered species by HM Customs and Excise and NGOs such as the RSPB and WWF. Domestic groups such as the RSPB, RSPCA and others assist in the detection of domestic wildlife crimes. Although some of these groups bring private prosecutions the general trend is to encourage prosecution through public authorities. For example, the RSPB has not taken a private prosecution since 1992. The Partnership for Action Against Wildlife Crime was created in 1995 to co-ordinate these various groups' actions to address wildlife crimes. This group promotes cooperation between the different bodies and supports the police and HM Customs and Excise.

(c) Resources

The allocation of resources of enforcement agencies in terms of personnel and funding plays an important role in the policing of environmental crime. Historically, environmental enforcement bodies have had to cope with cuts in funding and understaffing. Partly this has been connected to the source of funding from central government (e.g. by way of grant in aid), and the restrictions on raising extra revenue. The funding limits imposed on local government are well documented and similar issues arise with other centrally funded agencies such as English Nature. These problems have a knock-on effect in terms of enforcement and inspection. For example, the Environment Agency has a mixed approach to funding with part coming in revenue from charges and a declining part from central grant. Funding for enforcement is paid solely from the central Grant in Aid (GIA) budget over which the Agency has no control (as opposed to the income from charges). As GIA decreases in real terms the proportion of money available to monitor and enforce against environmental crime also decreases. There has been a steady decline in the number of inspections carried out by the Agency with inspections of industrial sites and waste sites dropping by 50 per cent and 30 per cent over a five-year period respectively.[26] These cuts in inspection when coupled with an increase in the use of self-monitoring requirements as an automatic condition of pollution control licences calls into question the role of the Agency in this important aspect of enforcement. This has seen a move towards so-called risk-based regulation whereby resources are focused on areas where environmental risks are thought to be greatest. Whilst this might be seen as a means of promoting regulatory efficiency there is a danger that it is just a way of disguising the overall reduction in monitoring, inspection, and enforcement activity.

(d) Inspection, entry, and enforcement powers

As the main environmental regulator, the EA has a wide range of inspection and enforcement powers. These powers are exercised for the purpose of: determining whether any environ-

25. (2003) ENDS Report 346, 9–10.

mental legislation is being complied with; exercising or performing any of the agency's pollution control functions; and determining whether or how a pollution control function should be exercised (EA 1995, s. 108(1)). Section 108 of the Act provides that an officer appointed by the Agency can, when there is no emergency:

- enter premises at any reasonable time (s. 108(4)(a));
- be accompanied on to premises by a police constable should the officer apprehend that they will be obstructed in their duty (s. 108(4)(b));
- make any investigation as necessary including: measurements, taking samples, photographs and questioning individuals (answers given to such questions will not be admissible in any prosecution brought against *that person* although they can be, and in practice are used against another person, e.g. an employer) (s. 108(4));
- carry out experimental borings and install and maintain monitoring equipment (with at least seven days' notice) (s. 108(8)).

Where occupants are likely to refuse entry, the officer can seek a warrant prior to entry onto premises. Documents which are subject to legal professional privilege are exempt from the above requirements (s. 108(13)). In cases of emergency entry can be gained at any time, with force if necessary (s. 108(4)(a)). In such circumstances no prior notification is required when setting up monitoring equipment or carrying out experimental borings (s. 108(5)). Under section 110 it is an offence to obstruct intentionally an authorised officer in the exercise of his or her duties. There are specific offences in relation to the intentional obstruction and of failing to comply with requirements of authorised persons exercising these powers of entry (s. 108(4)).

In addition, there are specific powers to requisition information in writing in relation to individual functions (e.g. EPA 1990, s. 71, in relation to waste management offences). The answers to such requisitions are not subject to the rule against self-incrimination (referred to in s. 108), as the section impliedly excludes this protection on the basis that the purpose of the legislation would be defeated if a person could refuse to answer written requisitions (see *R v Hertfordshire County Council, ex parte Green Environmental Industries* [2000] 2 WLR 373). In exercising these powers, the EA cannot go on a 'fishing expedition', i.e. they must have some evidence which justifies them seeking written answers (see *JB & M Haulage Ltd v London Waste Regulation Authority* [1993] Env LR 247).

Although these powers are extensive, the EA do not have a total freedom to investigate breaches of environmental law. Unlike the police, EA officers have no right of arrest or to require the names and addresses of suspects, nor is there any general right to stop and search vehicles (e.g. in relation to the illegal transportation of waste).[26] Although the power to secure written answers is wide, there is no requirement for suspects to take part in interviews.[27] In non-emergency cases, the EA are also unable to gain entry to residential premises or take heavy equipment on to any premises without seven days' notice and either the consent of the occupier or a warrant (s. 108(6)).

26. Although there are limited rights to stop vehicles off road and to search and seize, see Control of Pollution (Amendment) Act 1989, ss. 5–6 and Control of Pollution (Amendment) Regulations 1991, regs 20–25.

27. Environmental Justice Project, *Environmental Justice* (2004) 70 (EJP Report).

(e) Private prosecutions

The power to prosecute some environmental crimes does not only rest with the statutory enforcement agencies. The general right to bring a private prosecution for any offence is preserved in section 6(1) of the Prosecution of Offenders Act 1985. Indeed there are specific powers to bring private prosecutions for statutory nuisances (see EPA 1990, s. 80). This general right is, however, restricted in certain statutes (e.g. in relation to water abstraction and related offences, see Water Resources Act 1991, s. 216). Private prosecutions are relatively rare, although not unknown. Groups such as the RSPCA and local Badger Groups utilize private prosecutions in relation to wildlife crime and animal cruelty offences. Indeed, the RSPCA has been formally recognized by DEFRA as an 'approved prosecutor' in relation to certain animal welfare offences under the Protection of Animals (Amendment) Act 2000.[28] This is very much the exception rather than the rule.

There are many factors which discourage private groups or individuals from taking action including funding and costs issues; the need to gather and present expert evidence; and the fear of the technical aspects of preparing and presenting a criminal case. In addition, many of the factors which influence the regulatory bodies in taking enforcement action, such as the relatively low penalties imposed by the courts, shape private attitudes to prosecution.

BOX 9.7 **Examples of private prosecutions**

Although private prosecutions are uncommon, they are still important. For example, a member of the public brought a private prosecution against Anglian Water for gross water pollution which resulted in a fine of £200,000, (later reduced to £60,000 on appeal, see *R v Anglian Water Services Ltd* [2004] Env LR 10, see further Case box 18.6 and below). It was notable in that case that the Court of Appeal appeared to discourage the bringing of private prosecutions in such cases. Scott Baker LJ took the view that it was 'unfortunate' that the private prosecutor had not allowed the Environment Agency to take over the proceedings. There appeared to be nothing to indicate why this should have been the case and the appeal had been brought against sentence rather than conviction which would seem to indicate that the prosecution had been brought meritoriously. In a number of other cases, the *threat* of private prosecution by groups such as Friends of the Earth and Greenpeace has acted as a trigger for action by the regulatory bodies. For example, in the case of the *Sea Empress* pollution incident, the threat of private prosecution by Friends of the Earth brought pressure to bear upon the Environment Agency which appeared to be reluctant to prosecute. The eventual successful prosecution by the Agency resulted in one of the largest ever fines for water pollution.

The enforcement of environmental law

The focus on the prosecution of environmental crime is only part of the picture. The use of powers of prosecution and consequent criminal sanctions are only a small element of a

---

28. *Guidance on Approved Prosecutors under the Protection of Animals (Amendment) Act 2000* at <www.defra.gov.uk>.

varied approach to the enforcement mechanisms. Pollution control legislation typically provides for licences, authorizations, etc. to be varied or revoked and for activities to be prohibited or enforced against without any reference to the criminal courts. Although the use of these powers does not impose any formal penalty in the same way as criminal penalties, there are other sanctions which are either explicit (e.g. the cessation or restriction of previously authorized activities) or implicit (e.g. they are steps which can lead to a prosecution). For example, the service of a statutory nuisance abatement notice or a notice for the requisition of ownership details under the Town and Country Planning Act 1990 are enforcement steps which can lead to prosecution although there is no element of direct punishment in taking such an action when taken in isolation.

Beyond these formal enforcement mechanisms there are other informal and more subtle practices which can be used to influence behaviour. These might include educating and advising the ignorant operator; imposing deadlines for the improvement of environmental performance; increased monitoring or inspection visits; or issuing verbal and written 'last warnings' prior to more formal enforcement action. As we shall see, these informal mechanisms play a central role in the enforcement practices of Britain's environmental regulatory agencies. On an even wider interpretation, the 'enforcement' of environmental law could include *any* mechanism which could be used to secure compliance with a legal obligation which afforded environmental protection. This might involve the enforcement of private obligations (e.g. English Nature enforcing the terms of a management agreement to compel an owner to manage a SSSI either by injunction or by an action for breach of contract; or a property owner bringing an action in nuisance to prohibit the operations of a nearby factory); the use of information by regulators or third parties (e.g. the 'naming and shaming' of polluters in the national press (see below); or even the threats of action or prosecution from the Secretary of State or regulator.

(a) Understanding enforcement practices

Why do we need to understand the enforcement practices of environmental agencies? When the figures for formal enforcement action are considered it is clear that although there are significant numbers of breaches of environmental legislation, the proportion of prosecutions or other enforcement action is very low. This is the case for different environmental enforcement agencies including local authorities (e.g. only 16 authorities brought prosecutions for local authority air pollution control (LAPC) offences in an eight-year period[29] and Clean Air Act 1993 prosecutions form less than 1 per cent of the total number of statutory breaches);[30] and English Nature (e.g. 15 cases of 'formal enforcement' in 1997 with one prosecution). In the case of the Environment Agency the figures including administrative enforcement (e.g. enforcement and revocation notices) are just as stark. For example, in 2002 there were just 36 formal enforcement actions taken against breaches of IPC legislation, of which three were prosecutions.[31] On average there have been around 25,000+ pollution incidents per year since the late 1990s. With most, if not all of these incidents being potential strict liability crimes, it is clear that there are still significant numbers of

---

29. *Local Authority Progress in Implementing the LAAPC Regime* (DETR, 1998).
30. Chartered Institute of Environmental Health, *Environmental Health Report* (1997/8).
31. EJP Report, 113 op. cit, n. 27.

breaches of environmental legislation of all types which are not enforced against in any formal sense.[32]

(b) Styles of enforcement

In trying to understand why there is such a disparity between the number of potential breaches of environmental law and the formal enforcement action which is taken, we must explore the purposes of enforcing environmental law and the different styles of enforcement which might be employed to meet those purposes. The central aim of the enforcement of environmental regulation is to *prevent* harm to the environment or human health rather than to detect and then punish those who cause such harm (although this is obviously one closely connected aim). Environmental enforcement is not, therefore, only concerned with punishment for breach of environmental laws but also with preventing those breaches occurring and assisting those who are regulated in doing so. These two elements of an enforcement strategy are linked with two different styles of enforcement; the compliance approach where there is an emphasis on all mechanisms other than prosecution in order to promote compliance with environmental laws; and the 'sanctioning' approach which prefers strict punitive measures, notably prosecutions to deter operators from future non-compliance.[33]

Cooperative

The cooperative (or conciliatory or compliance) approach is typically characterized in environmental enforcement by the development of a continuing relationship between enforcement agency and 'polluter'. At one extreme this might involve a patient, persuasive, educative role for the enforcer almost acting as an external advisor. In this case, mutual respect and trust can develop which can be used to ensure compliance with laws or standards (e.g. environmental quality standards). At the other extreme, the relationship might be more detached with the regulator seeking compliance within strict time limits (e.g. installing pollution abatement equipment or applying for a requisite licence).

Sanctioning

The sanctioning (or confrontational) approach punishes those who are responsible for causing environmental harm. At an extreme level, such an approach would result in the punishment of every breach of environmental laws. At first glance, this would not appear to meet the central aim of any enforcement strategy, namely preventing harm to the environment. Compliance is, however, achieved through the desire to prevent future breaches and thereby avoid any further enforcement action.

Responsive regulation

If deterrence and compliance styles are seen as two ends of an enforcement spectrum, a third approach has been identified as a 'pick and mix' blend of different enforcement mechanisms with officers varying strategies in response to whether the regulated are complying with their obligations.[34] Under 'responsive regulation' officers will use mechanisms of increasing

---

32. See further A. Ogus and C. Abbot (2002) 14 JEL 286–8.

33. See generally, G. Richardson et al, *Policing Pollution: A Study of Regulation and Enforcement* (Oxford: Clarendon Press, 1982), K. Hawkins, *Environment and Enforcement: Regulations and the Social Definition of Pollution* (Oxford: Clarendon Press, 1984).

34. I. Ayres and J. Braithwaite, *Responsive Regulation* (Oxford: Oxford University Press, 1992).

formality and impact as the regulated fail to meet their legal obligations. Thus the process of responsive regulation is described as forming an Enforcement Pyramid (see Figure 9.1 below).[35] For the majority of operators persuasion and education will secure compliance. Smaller numbers of operators may need more formal mechanisms such as warning letters or enforcement notices to bring them into compliance. At the upper end of the spectrum prosecution and even prohibition or revocation notices may be used on the very small minority of trenchant recalcitrants. The other side of this approach is that there will be more informal mechanisms used when the regulated come within compliance. The essence of responsive regulation is that an enforcement officer will use the minimum amount of formal regulation as possible in order to achieve compliance.[36]

(c) Using different enforcement styles

These different enforcement styles have been identified as distinctive for the purposes of explanation. In practice, however, the boundaries between the styles are much more imprecise. Regulators will adopt different styles with different people. The compliance style of enforcement is largely based upon the continuing relationship which exists between regulators and the regulated. Research has shown that where there were problems with trade effluent discharges, offenders were far more likely to be subjected to formal enforcement

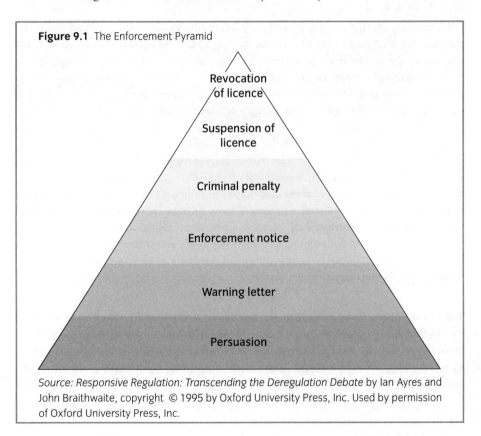

Figure 9.1 The Enforcement Pyramid

Revocation
of licence

Suspension of
licence

Criminal penalty

Enforcement notice

Warning letter

Persuasion

Source: Responsive Regulation: Transcending the Deregulation Debate by Ian Ayres and John Braithwaite, copyright © 1995 by Oxford University Press, Inc. Used by permission of Oxford University Press, Inc.

35. Ibid, see 35–8. The Pyramid has been adapted slightly to be more relevant to UK enforcement.
36. A more sophisticated analysis of optimal compliance can be found in A. Ogus and C. Abbot (2002) 14 JEL 283.

action and prosecution if the relationship was threatened or made more difficult as a result of the actions of the regulated.[37] The reverse was also true; if the offender had a good relationship with the regulator then the prospect of formal enforcement action was reduced.

The type of relationship was strongly influenced by the attitude taken by officers to individual operators. Certain offenders would be viewed as putting profit or their own interests before the environment and disobeying the law when it suited their interests to do so. In these circumstances, the enforcement agencies would adopt a strong deterrence style of enforcement. Another group of offenders would be viewed as breaching the law because the imposition of environmental controls were considered to be unreasonable in terms of the financial or technical burden. A further identifiable group would be viewed as well meaning but organizationally incompetent. In this latter situation, the regulators would adopt a compliance style of enforcement, in particular relying upon advice and education to overcome incompetence.[38] The idea of responsive regulation reflects this variable approach by concentrating on the most effective method of securing compliance at the least level of regulatory interference. This will often depend upon the nature of the relationship between the regulator and the regulated.

(d) Capture theory

It has been argued that the closeness of the relationship between 'polluters' and regulatory agencies can lead to the 'capture' of the agency, where the agency concentrates on the interests of the regulated to the exclusion of the public interest. A good example of the potential effects of 'capture theory' can be seen in the attitude of the Alkali Inspectorate to the disclosure of pollution information where the Inspectorate favoured the protection of private companies (through the maintenance of a secrecy policy) over public disclosure of information on pollution. There have been various explanations as to why 'capture' occurs, including: the political influence which major industrial or other interest groups (e.g. the farming community) hold over the rule makers and the regulators;[39] the distinction between the class of the regulator/regulated companies (tending to be middle/professional class) and those affected by pollution (working class); and the common interests which can be found in both regulators and regulated (e.g. some Environment Agency officers have worked for the industries which they regulate).

The British approach to environmental enforcement

The British approach to environmental enforcement as exercised by administrative regulatory bodies is strongly underscored by the themes which dominate Parts I and II of this book. These include: the flexibility in the setting of individualized emission and process standards; wide definitions found in key statutory provisions; informal guidance on the interpretation of statutory rules; reliance on self regulation and voluntary compliance; and the use of discretionary powers rather than mandatory duties.

---

37. K. Hawkins, op cit. n. 33.
38. E.g. see in relation to IPC A. Mehta and K. Hawkins (1998) 10 JEL 69, and C. Lovat (2004) 16 JEL 49, 52–61.
39. See P. Lowe et al, *Moralizing the Environment* (London: UCL Press 1997).

BOX 9.8 Enforcement in Scotland and Northern Ireland

Although the general characteristics of enforcement practices can be classified as a 'British' approach,[40] there are variations certainly in relation to the Scottish approach and arguably in relation to the Northern Irish approach to enforcement. Mostly, these variations are associated with institutional differences. These differences mean that although the general approach to the enforcement of environmental law is similar to across Britain (i.e. the adoption of a cooperative approach) the increase in the use of prosecution is much less marked outside England and Wales.[41] For example, in Scotland all prosecutions are brought by the Crown Office and Procurator Fiscal Service (COPFS), which has lacked expertise in relation to the enforcement of environmental offences.[42] Thus, unlike England and Wales where enforcement and prosecution are undertaken by the Environment Agency, the right to prosecute in Scotland is effectively held solely by COPFS and the final decision to prosecute is determined outside SEPA.[43] This separation of enforcement and prosecution and in particular the lack of specialist environmental expertise within COPFS explains why the number of prosecutions for environmental crimes is much lower in Scotland than in England. For example in Scotland there were 38 and 31 prosecutions in 2001–2 and 2002–3 respectively. This is about 2.5 per cent of the number of prosecutions brought by the Environment Agency over the same period. Attempts have been made to address this imbalance with the introduction of trained environmental prosecutors within COPFS to liaise with SEPA and coordinate enforcement and prosecutions.[44]

There has been criticism of the enforcement of environmental law in Northern Ireland.[45] Partly this is because of the low priority given historically to environmental issues and the inadequacies of the institutional framework for enforcement bodies. The body with responsibility for enforcing environmental law in Northern Ireland is the Environment and Heritage Service (EHS) which is an Executive Agency of the Department of the Environment. As the provision of water and sewage services remains a public sector function in Northern Ireland, this raises the sort of 'poacher–gamekeeper' issues referred to above. In addition the poor performance of the EHS in enforcing environmental law has been the subject of criticism both within and outside Government.

Other factors which have contributed to poor levels of enforcement in Northern Ireland include the lack of detailed policy guidance in the form of an enforcement and prosecutions policy and insufficient resources.[46] There is however the more fundamental issue of the late implementation of European directives and the consequent disparity between Northern Irish environmental legislation and the rest of the United Kingdom which often meant that actions which would have been considered to be an offence in, say, England were not illegal in Northern Ireland. Proposals for reform including the establishment of an enforcement agency which is separate from Government are intended to address these inadequacies.

---

40. The findings of Scottish research into enforcement practices broadly reflect the above studies, see P. Watchman, C. Barker, and J. Rowan-Robinson [1988] JPL 764.

41. E.g. see C. Lovat (2004) 16 JEL 49 for a study of IPC regulation in Scotland.

42. SEPA Board Paper 97/00 *Environmental Prosecutions in Scotland and Levels of Fine*, available at <www.sepa.org>.

43. C. Smith, N. Collar, and M. Poustie, *Pollution Control: The Law in Scotland* (Edinburgh: T&T Clark, 1997), 40–1 and A. Brown [1995] 47 SPEL 4.

44. (2004) ENDS Report 349, 10.

45. See geneally R. Macrory, *Transparency and Trust: Reshaping Environmental Governance in Northern Ireland* (London: UCL, 2004).

46. Northern Ireland Audit Office, *Control of River Pollution in Northern Ireland*, HC 693 Session 1997/8.

All of these factors (along with others) have a role to play in the style of enforcement adopted by the variety of environmental agencies. Whilst it is not possible to generalise across all agencies (indeed there will be variations of style between individual officers within the same agency), the British approach to environmental regulation facilitates the development of a flexible relationship between the regulator and regulated which is characteristic of the compliance style of enforcement. The amount of discretion given in setting the standards and in using enforcement powers means that enforcement officers can use the informal problem solving approach to breaches of environmental regulation rather than being forced to resort to formal sanctions such as prosecution.

There have been a number of empirical studies of the activities of environmental enforcement bodies in England in relation to the enforcement practices of the old style water authorities;[47] and in relation to local environmental health officers.[48] Each of these studies tended to confirm the adoption of a 'compliance' style of enforcement, with officers often walking a tightrope between a cooperative approach and the effective enforcement of pollution control rules. In other areas of environmental regulation, such as nature conservation, where the emphasis has traditionally been on voluntary measures, the cooperative approach is even more important.[49]

These studies indicated that a hierarchy of enforcement mechanisms was utilized in order to maintain good relationships between the regulator and the regulated. The first stage of the enforcement process primarily focused on advice and education about the mutual 'problem' which was connected with the breach. If this was not successful in gaining compliance, further warnings both informal and formal were given with prosecution only an option where the offence was serious or the offender culpable. The development of an ongoing relationship was central to the enforcement style. The work of environmental agencies was technically and scientifically based rather than founded on concepts of rules, sanctions and other penalties. Thus, education and advice were perceived as being more important than prosecution or other formal enforcement mechanisms. The continuing relationship with the operator/offender was designed to prevent harm and promote environmental protection and this could be achieved more effectively by cooperating with polluters rather than confronting them by adopting a 'sanctioning' style.

BOX 9.9 **Enforcement styles in practice**

The use of a cooperative approach to enforcement can have practical significance, particularly in circumstances where cooperation fails and more formal action is required. In *Environment Agency v Stanford* [1999] Env LR 286 a scrap metal dealer ('S') notified the Environment Agency that his activities were exempt from the need for a waste management licence. An Agency officer

---

47. K. Hawkins, *Environment and Enforcement* (Oxford: Clarendon Press, 1984) and G. Richardson et al, *Policing Pollution* (Oxford: Clarendon Press, 1988).

48. B. Hutter, *The Reasonable Arm of the Law* (Oxford: Clarendon Press, 1983).

49. This approach appears to continue notwithstanding the introduction of greater enforcement powers under CROWA, see p. 814. For a historical account see D. Withrington and W. Jones, 'The Enforcement of Nature Conservation Legislation: The Protection of SSSIs' in W. Howarth and C. Rodgers (eds), *Agriculture, Conservation and Land Use* (Aberystwyth: University of Wales Press, 1992).

visited the site and informed S that the activities were, in fact, unlawful and that he was committing an offence. Instead of prosecuting, the officer gave advice on the various steps which were required to make the activities exempt. On subsequent site visits Agency officers gave the impression that no prosecution would be commenced if the works were carried out within a specified time period. The works were not carried out and the Agency prosecuted. S tried to argue that the prosecution was an abuse of process and should be dismissed because of the promises which had been made by the various officers. The argument was dismissed on the ground that the Agency had never promised not to prosecute; indeed it was clear that they had always stated that the conduct was unlawful. This decision implicitly supports the idea of the cooperative approach to enforcement by ensuring that regulatory agencies are not estopped from taking formal enforcement action when they permit offenders some time to bring operations into compliance.[50] On the other hand there may be circumstances where there is such a clear promise or representation that no criminal proceedings would be brought that any subsequent prosecution would be an abuse of process (see *R v Croydon Justices ex parte Dean* [1993] QB 769). Thus agencies have to balance the need to secure compliance with the need to be fair to those who are regulated whilst not fettering their enforcement discretion.

Prosecution and enforcement policies

One of the findings of the different research projects carried out in the 1980s was that there were differing levels of enforcement in different geographical locations.[51] For example, it was shown that in a three-year period, one water authority brought 48 prosecutions for the contraventions of trade effluent consents (with 90 per cent coming from one area) whereas another did not bring any prosecutions during that time. There could be a number of explanations for regional variations in enforcement figures (e.g. a particular area might have a disproportionate number of breaches or 'difficult' operators), but it is primarily characteristic of the lack of uniformity created by a wide discretion. The research found that different officers were disturbed by this lack of consistency in enforcement practices. They favoured a more explicit policy applicable throughout different divisions. They were evidently anxious to ensure procedural reasonableness and the application of predetermined rules to guide the exercise of discretion.

The creation of new environmental agencies in the late 1980s saw the development of specific policies on enforcement which were designed to structure discretion and improve the consistency of enforcement style. During its lifetime, the NRA had an enforcement policy which used prosecution as an active component and this approach has been adopted by the Environment Agency which has a published *Enforcement and Prosecution Policy*. The Policy consists of a statement of the Agency's policies on enforcement and prosecution.[52] A summary of the general principles is set out in Box 9.10)

---

50. A similar example in relation to the interpretation of statutory exemptions can be found in *Environment Agency v Newcomb* discussed in Case box 15.6.
51. G. Richardson et al, op cit. n. 47.
52. Environment Agency, *Enforcement and Prosecution Policy* (1998).

BOX 9.10 **Enforcement policy and principles**

The Policy sets out four principles of enforcement:

* proportionality in the application of law and in securing compliance;
* consistency of approach;
* transparency about how the Agency operates;
* the targeting of enforcement action at activities which give rise to the most serious environmental damage or where the hazards are least well controlled.

In determining whether to *prosecute*, the Agency also considers the *Code for Crown Prosecutors* which sets down a two stage test. First, is there sufficient available evidence to raise a realistic prospect of conviction? Secondly, is it in the public interest to bring the prosecution? The former question is made much simpler in cases of strict liability (see above). The latter question is answered by reference to criteria set out in the *Enforcement and Prosecution Policy* which are summarized in Box 9.11.

BOX 9.11 **Factors taken into account when deciding to prosecute**

Prosecutions will 'normally' be taken in relation to:

* incidents or breaches with significant environmental consequences;
* operating without the required licence, consent or authorization; persistent or excessive breaches of statutory requirements;
* failure to comply with formal requirements to remedy environmental harm;
* 'reckless disregard' of environmental management or quality standards;
* obstructing Agency staff in the gathering of information.

Other influential factors are whether an incident was foreseeable, the intent of the offender, previous offences, and the deterrent effect of prosecuting.

In addition to the general policy on enforcement and prosecution, there are internal guidelines relating to particular offences and breaches.[53] These guidelines are comprehensive, dealing with every aspect of the Agency's functions and set out the 'Common Incident Classification Scheme' (CICS) which is a national system for recording and categorizing pollution incidents and assessing the appropriate level of enforcement response. The CICS classifies incidents in four categories from Category 1 (a major actual or potential environmental impact) to Category 4 (no actual or potential environmental impact). This general approach to categorizing incidents is supplemented by different methods of enforcement in relation to each of the Agency's functions (i.e. environmental protection, water resources,

53. Environment Agency, *Enforcement and Prosecution Policy: Functional Guidelines* (Version 7, 2004).

fisheries, flood defence, and navigation). Each individual section includes details of: the purpose of enforcement for that function; the enforcement powers available; the factors determining enforcement action; enforcement for non-criminal non-compliance; and the various criminal offences and enforcement options.

Although these policies attempt to introduce some consistency to enforcement across the Agency, it is arguable that all they actually do is to formalise policies which had been used on an informal basis over a number of years. The policies are worded in such a way as not to restrict the Agency's enforcement discretion and it is doubtful whether any enforceable legal rights are created which can be relied upon by the regulated (e.g. a legitimate expectation that the Policy will be followed). This continuing discretion is reflected in the fact that there are still identifiable discrepancies in the numbers of prosecutions in different Environment Agency regions although this may be connected to the different ways in which a 'prosecution' is recorded in each region (which in turn makes the figures difficult to interpret because of inconsistencies in charging practices across the regions).[54]

The courts have made it clear that, in general terms, the decision to prosecute (or not, as the case may be) is essentially within the discretion of the regulatory authority and cannot be subject to challenge on anything other than on the ground of *Wednesbury* unreasonableness (see e.g. in relation to the decision to prosecute in general criminal offences, *R v Metropolitan Police Commissioner, ex parte Blackburn (No 3)* [1973] 1 QB 241), although there is the potential for a challenge in circumstances where a regulator such as the Environment Agency fails to follow an unambiguous enforcement or prosecution policy (e.g. *R v DPP, ex parte C* (1995) 1 Cr App 136). The published *Enforcement and Prosecution Policy* adopted by the Agency is worded in such a way as to leave considerable discretion in determining whether to prosecute. The width of that discretion would be sufficient to ward off claims that the policy was unambiguous enough to found a successful challenge to any decision to prosecute or not.[55]

In the light of the detailed nature of the internal and external enforcement policies of the Environment Agency, it is perhaps surprising to find that other bodies with environmental regulatory functions are not covered by such guidance. For example, local authority enforcement of the air pollution control system has been criticized as being inconsistent and 'ad hoc'.[56] The Cabinet Office, through its Better Regulation initiative, has published an 'Enforcement Concordat' which local authorities have been urged to adopt.[57] In the absence of more prescriptive guidance, however, it is likely that inconsistency and lack of transparency will continue.

The Enforcement Concordat is the latest stage of the development of deregulatory initiatives as an influence over enforcement policy. The move towards more complex environmental rules has led industry to argue that legislation is becoming too complex and compliance entails excessive expenditure in comparison with the environmental benefits which are produced. The introduction of the Deregulation and Contracting Out Act 1994 was considered to be an initial response to this alleged problem and the deregulatory thrust

---

54. In addition, limited empirical research also indicates that enforcement policies do not play a major part in the decision of whether to prosecute, see C. Lovat. op cit, n. 40 at 63.

55. See further C. Hilson, *Regulating Pollution* (Oxford: Hart Publishing, 2000), 163–166.

56. See DETR, *Local Authority Progress in Implementing the LAPC Regime*, (October 1998).

57. Over 96 per cent of local authorities have adopted the concordat: see Cabinet Office and Local Government Association *Enforcement Concordat* (1998) available at <www.cabinetoffice.gov.uk>.

was continued into the Environment Act 1995 with general restrictions on enforcement such as the duty to consider the costs and benefits of taking enforcement action (s. 39) and other similar provisions (see p. 259).[58] Ironically, the deregulation initiative which started out as a 'war on red tape' has now produced numerous administrative tests and policies which the Environment Agency is under a duty to consider before commencing enforcement action.

Sanctions for environmental crime

(a) Administrative sanctions

The final element of the process of addressing environmental crime is the variety of sanctions imposed upon those who breach the law. As mentioned above some administrative enforcement mechanisms can be imposed under administrative mechanisms, i.e. through the use of enforcement, suspension, and revocation of environmental licences, etc. Such notices can be used irrespective of whether a crime has been committed (although in most cases the need for some form of administrative notice would indicate breaches or potential future breaches of licence conditions which could amount to a criminal offence).

As the 'enforcement pyramid' in Figure 9.1 demonstrates some of these administrative sanctions are, in effect, more serious than criminal penalties. Revocation, suspension and prohibition notices all have the effect of preventing a holder of a licence from carrying on otherwise lawful activities, which in the case of companies is the most serious sanction available and the equivalent of imprisonment for an individual.[59] In practice, however, these extreme administrative powers are used very sparingly. For example, there were 37 revocations of waste management licences from 1996 to 2003 and amongst these cases there were some revocations where the licence holder had ceased to exist or failed to pay fees.[60] Given the draconian consequences of these types of sanctions, it is perhaps unsurprising that they are used very infrequently. One of the consequences of this, however, is that the deterrent effect of such mechanisms and any threats to use them is weakened. On the other hand if such sanctions were going to be used more widely, there are dangers that the substantive and procedural protections offered by the criminal process could be bypassed. For example, although there is the right of appeal against such notices in many cases the effect of the notice is not suspended pending the appeal—effectively reversing any presumption of innocence (e.g. EPA 1990, s. 43 in relation to the suspension of waste management licences) and the final decision may be swayed by policy factors which would be assessed by a non-judicial inspector or the Secretary of State.[61]

(b) Criminal sanctions

Sanctions can also be imposed through the criminal process, e.g. fines, imprisonment, or community sentences following a successful prosecution for an environmental offence. In recent years there has been a growing sense of dissatisfaction with the sanctions imposed

---

58. See also C. Hilson, op cit n. 57 26–8.
59. A. Ogus and C. Abbot (2002) 14 JEL 288.
60. (2003) ENDS Report 347, 15.
61. A. Ogus and C. Abbot op cit n. 60, 296.

upon those who commit environmental crime. Various critics, including the Environment Agency itself, have questioned the extent to which the sanctions imposed are sufficient to act as a punishment and deterrent.[62] In response to these concerns, DEFRA commissioned research to establish an accurate picture of sentencing for environmental crime in England and Wales in the years 1999–2002.[63] The key findings are summarized in Box 9.12. The overall conclusions were that the vast majority of environmental offences are dealt with at a low level and are punished with relatively small fines which do not appear to be an effective sanction when compared with the profits which can be generated from activities which cause environmental damage.

BOX 9.12 **Key data on sentencing for environmental crime**

• Over 90 per cent of all environmental crimes are dealt with in the Magistrates' Court.

• Fines are the most common sanctions for environmental offences (68 per cent of all offences) with the vast majority of corporate environmental offenders (over 80 per cent) being punished in this manner.

• In the Magistrates' Courts the average fines for environmental offences rose over a three-year period from £1,979 to £2,730.

• All other types of sentence, e.g. community service order, conditional/absolute discharge, compensation, etc. are used in less than 10 per cent of cases.

• Custodial sentences are passed in relation to approximately 1 per cent of all environmental offences.

The low levels of fines which have been imposed by the judiciary can be attributed to a number of factors including the lack of judicial experience in dealing with environmental offences (which is closely connected to a paucity of prosecutions);[64] some of the conceptual difficulties in punishing strict liability offences referred to above; and the technical nature of some of the consequences of pollution which form the basis of the defendant's culpability.[65]

These low levels of fines have a knock-on effect in the sense that they tend to reinforce the view that environmental offences are morally neutral in the eyes of the judiciary. In the 1990s, the maximum level of fines in the magistrates' court was raised to take into account the need for the lower court to have wider powers to reflect the seriousness of the offences which do not merit being heard in the Crown Court. The EPA 1990 increased the level of fines for a number of pollution control offences from £2,000 to £20,000 although it was not until much later that the maximum fine for damage to SSSIs was raised from a derisory

---

62. E.g. see, Environment Agency, *Spotlight on Business Performance 2003*, 5. The details of others can be found in the further reading, at the end of the chapter.

63. C. DuPont and P. Zakkow, *Trends in Environmental Sentencing in England and Wales*, (DEFRA, 2003).

64. Ibid 44.

65. Which has been characterized as part of the 'trivialization' of environmental prosecutions, see P. De Prez (2000) JEL 65.

£2,500 to £20,000 under the Countryside and Rights of Way Act 2000, s. 28P(1). This trend has been further developed in Scotland, where the maximum for many common pollution control and nature conservation offences is £40,000 (see Anti-Social Behaviour (Scotland, Act 2004, s. 66 and Nature Conservation (Scotland) Act 2004, s. 19 respectively).

Although many environmental offences are triable either in the magistrates' court or the Crown Court, the option to try a matter in the Crown Court, with the opportunity to seek an unlimited fine and even imprisonment in the case of individual offenders has not often been taken. It is, however, becoming slightly more common for matters to be committed to the Crown Court for sentencing. Two significant examples are the cases of the prosecution of Shell (UK) in February 1990 and Milford Haven Port Authority in relation to its role in the *Sea Empress* disaster, both for water pollution offences under section 85 of the Water Resources Act 1991.

There are other powers of sentencing available to the courts in serious cases with individual defendants (as opposed to companies). These include community service orders and custodial sentences in the severest cases. These have been used sparingly in the past, though in keeping with other sentencing trends there has been an increase of these types of sentences, certainly in relation to imprisonment (e.g. see Box 9.13).

BOX 9.13 Custodial sentences for environmental crime

The Courts' approach to custodial offences for environmental crime was considered in *R v O'Brien and Enkel* (2000) Env LR 156. In that case the defendants had pleaded guilty to an offence of illegally storing 2,000 waste tyres at an unlicensed site and had been sentenced to 8 months' imprisonment. The defendants appealed arguing that the sentence was excessive. In quashing the sentence, the Court of Appeal identified certain factors which were relevant in deciding whether to send a offender to prison for an environmental crime. These included:

- repeated or blatant offences

- offences committed in a public place

- in circumstances where the public had been exposed to hazardous substances

In relation to the particular circumstances of the case, the fact that the tyres presented no long term risk to the environment, that this was the first environmental offence and that the defendants had pleaded guilty were all thought to indicate that a sentence of imprisonment was unjustified.

In contrast to pollution control offences, there is a growing recognition of the serious nature of wildlife crime and this is reflected in the proportion of significant custodial sentences for such crimes. For example, one of the longest prison sentences for environmental crime was passed in 2000 for the illegal importation of some of the world's rarest species of birds. At trial, the defendant Harry Sissen, a famous Parrot breeder was imprisoned for 30 months for illegally importing three Lear's Macaws and six Blue-Headed Macaws into the UK. On appeal, the Court of Appeal reduced the sentence to 18 months after taking into account, amongst other things, the age of the defendant (61), his financial position and his albeit misguided motives for breeding the birds in order to try to maintain the species. Ouseley J. emphasized the seriousness of such offences when he said:

> The law is clear as to where the interests of conservation lie. These are serious offences. An immediate custodial sentence is usually appropriate to mark their gravity and the need for deterrence. There is nothing wrong in principle with a sentence of 30 months for an offence such as this.

Other reported examples of custodial penalties include a sentence of 18 months' imprisonment passed for a waste management offence, although this was reduced to 12 months on appeal (see *R v Garrett* [1998] Env LR D2). It is interesting to note that in terms of pollution control offences the vast majority of sentences of imprisonment are passed in relation to waste management offences whereas in other areas (e.g. water pollution and IPC) the prevalent punishment is financial (i.e. a fine). The reason for this is closely connected to the identity of the polluter, with typical prosecutions for water and IPC offences involving major companies (with consequent restrictions on the nature of the sentence which can be passed) and a significant proportion of serious waste management offences being committed by single 'cowboy' operators.

(c) Sentencing guidelines

The general concern about the levels of sentence for environmental offences led, in 1999, to the then newly formed Sentencing Advisory Panel to issue proposals to the Court of Appeal to frame sentencing guidelines for environmental offences. On two separate occasions, however, the Court of Appeal rejected the guidelines in favour of a case-by-case approach based upon certain general principles (see Box 9.14).

BOX 9.14 **Sentencing principles for environmental crime**

The Court of Appeal has consistently rejected the idea of a tariff for environmental offences notwithstanding the Sentencing Advisory Panel's Advice on the matter. In a number of cases, the Court of Appeal have stressed the need to consider each case on its own facts. In the two main cases *R v Yorkshire Water Services Ltd* [2002] Env LR 18 and *R v Anglian Water Services Ltd* [2004] Env LR 10 (see Case box 18.6), the Court considered the following factors to be relevant:

- The degree of culpability involved in the commission of an offence of strict but not absolute liability. In *Anglian Water*, the Court of Appeal made it clear that notwithstanding relatively low culpability, a major industrial operator such as Anglian Water was under a greater obligation to minimize the chance of environmental harm. Presumably this would also apply to *any* significant industrial operation such as the waste management industry or IPPC installations where the risk of pollution was relatively high and the consequences of pollution potentially significant. When assessing the appropriate sentence in such circumstances less weight should be given to the relative lack of culpability.

- The damage done in physical and economic terms.

- The defendant's previous record including any failure to heed specific warnings.

- The defendant's attitude and performance after the event including any guilty plea (and presumably any clean up operation).

- An analysis of the costs and benefits of promoting environmental benefits as against the costs of doing so. There is a need to assess potential risks to the environment in addition to the extent and nature of the harm if the risk was realised. In situations where the risk of harm was low but the nature of the potential harm was significant, serious steps would need to be taken to ensure that the risk did not materialize and that if it did further steps could be taken to minimize any consequential impacts.

- The financial impact on the defendant. Any imposition of a financial penalty must be an effective sanction when viewed against the resources of the defendant. In the words of Scott Baker LJ in *Anglian Water*:

  the fine must be at a level to make some impact on the company and overcome any suggestion that it is cheaper to pay the fines than undertake the work that is necessary to prevent the offence in the first place

On the other hand, the fine should not be so high so as to threaten the viability of the company itself.

Notwithstanding the situation in the higher courts the Magistrates' Association has produced sentencing guidance for the lower courts. The *Fining of Companies for Environmental Health and Safety Offences* was endorsed by the Court of Appeal in *Anglian Water* as 'helpful advice'.

One final area of note is the use of compensation and confiscation orders in environmental cases. Under section 35 of the Powers of Criminal Courts Act 1973, the courts have the power to award compensation to anyone who has directly suffered as a result of an environmental offence. These powers have rarely been used. The Sentencing Advisory Panel suggested that where there is a specific victim (e.g. an owner who has had to pay to clean up after an incident or to re-stock after a fish kill), a court should always consider a compensation order although not before imposing a fine. The significance of the use of compensation orders is, however, reduced as a result of the existence of many statutory powers of clean up and cost recovery available to regulatory agencies in defined situations (e.g. EPA 1990, s. 59 or Water Resources Act 1991, s. 161A) and the fact that there is currently a limit of £5,000 for each order.

(d) Alternative sanctions

Another consequence of the dissatisfaction with existing criminal sanctions has been the development of alternatives to the traditional penalties (e.g. fines). One of the earliest forms of alternative sanction was the 'naming and shaming' of corporate polluters by the Environment Agency (see Box 9.15).

BOX 9.15 'Naming and shaming' of polluters

In 1999, the Environment Agency published a 'league table' of the worst corporate offenders who had committed environmental crimes in the previous year.[66] This policy of 'naming and shaming' companies was the first real attempt to increase the effect of prosecuting environmental crimes by publicising those companies who were not performing to the required standard. This first edition was relatively simplistic in its aims and was inadequate in that it failed to address issues of general environmental compliance, such as the numbers of administrative actions taken against individual companies. Nor did it seek to identify those companies who had improved compliance rates and made significant progress in, for example, pollution abatement. A year later these issues were addressed with the publication of a more comprehensive *Spotlight on Business Environmental Performance—2000* which sought to identify those who had reduced pollution alongside the notorious 'league table'. These reports have been published on an annual basis since 2000. In addition to the obvious effect of publicising poor environmental performance and the media interest that brings, the league table has other direct impacts. For example, the water regulator has considered environmental compliance as an issue when determining water pricing. In addition, others such as institutional investors, insurance companies and even customers and consumers are influenced by a poor criminal record in comparison with industry sector competitors. This last point raises one of the main criticisms of the whole process of 'naming and shaming' and that is the comparative nature of the rankings. The tables have little to say about overall performance and the worst performers could arguably be seen as the 'tip of the iceberg' with the best being the 'best of a bad bunch'.

More recently, DEFRA commissioned a study to examine the greater use of civil penalties as a sanction used against breaches of environmental law.[67] One of the most developed proposals involves the differentiation between those offences which are 'regulatory' in nature (i.e. those where criminal intent or negligence is the cause), and cases involving serious harm to the environment or human health. Other jurisdictions such as the US use a greater selection of administrative or civil penalties including fixed fines to punish relatively minor breaches of the law. These have the advantage of freeing enforcement resources to concentrate on truly criminal activity. Although there are disadvantages which can be identified (e.g. giving the impression that environmental harm is 'routine' or allowing wealthy operators the right to pollute), these can be minimised by using cumulative penalties (e.g. the points system in motoring offences) and ensuring that when true environmental crimes come before the courts there are adequate powers to punish offenders.

In addition in the US there is a much wider range of sentences which can and have been imposed. Some of these are outlined in Box 9.16. As the move towards innovative sanctioning for environmental crime develops, some or all of these ideas could be considered in Britain.

66. See further P. De Prez (2000) Env L Rev 11.
67. M. Woods and R. Macrory op cit. n. 13

BOX 9.16   **Possible future alternative sanctions** [68]

The range of possible alternative sanctions act as a punishment and deterrent in different ways. Most could be imposed by way of Court Order. Failure to comply with any of these orders within a given time frame would mean that the Company could be sentenced for the original offence.

Compliance through Probation Programmes

A Court Order specifying certain actions which were required to be undertaken in order to 'rehabilitate' the offending company. This might include environmental awareness training or developing environmental management systems or rectification of environmental damage. Supervision of compliance could be undertaken by the regulator or a representative could be placed on the company's Board.

Community Projects

A Court Order requiring the completion of an environmental improvement project and/or community education programmes at a cost of a specified sum equal to the benefit obtained by an offender or the environmental harm caused by the offending activities.

Share issues

A Court Order requiring a corporate offender to issue shares up to a specified sum related to the costs avoided or benefits obtained by an offender. Such an order would decrease the value of other shareholders interests, thus focussing investors' minds on the consequences of environmental offending and the need for greater efforts to comply.

Adverse publicity orders

A Court Order requiring the placing of an advert in the national media explaining the circumstances surrounding an offence along with an apology and an outline of the steps taken to address the causes of the offence. Further statements could be required to be placed in the corporate offender's annual report.

Environmental trusts

A Court Order requiring money to be placed into a Trust or Court Account which would be frozen, but activated to address any environmental harm arising in a specified period after sentence. This would address the problem of the offender who is at risk of going into insolvency.

Optimal enforcement

Most of the research on the enforcement of environmental crime referred to above dates back to the 1970s and early 1980s. Just as there has been a move away from flexible,

---

68. For a discussion of these see the supplementary memo from the Environment Agency to the EAC's Report into Environmental Crime op cit. n. 6.

discretionary styles of environmental regulation (see Chapter 8), there has also been a discernible shift away from the informal, cooperative approach to enforcement (e.g. notwithstanding the low percentages, there has been a rise in the total number of prosecutions for pollution control offences). Although this shift can just about be perceived in the empirical data, this does not necessarily mean that a 'deterrence' style of enforcement has been adopted across the board. The subtle blend of influencing factors means that a decision about when and how to enforce against breaches of environmental law is becoming much more complex. Any list of the factors which influence enforcement could never be comprehensive as each individual case will have peculiar circumstances which shape the exercise of an enforcement agency's discretion.

Although decisions to prosecute or take other formal enforcement action are still made on a discretionary basis, there is much more public scrutiny of individual incidents and enforcement policy suggests that moral culpability is only one factor in determining whether to take action against an offender. It would be easy to overstate any shift in emphasis in enforcement style. The true picture is that cooperation between regulator and regulated has not broken down and in some cases, particularly where a voluntary approach is relied upon such as nature conservation, it is probably the case that the continuing relationship is vital to the effectiveness of the rules which are being enforced.

It is likely that the future styles of enforcement will be eclectic with different approaches being taken in relation to different offenders. With more reliance on self-monitoring and inspection and voluntary performance indicators, such as accredited environmental management standards (e.g. ISO 14001), there will inevitably be a greater targeting of those who might be labelled 'free-riders' (i.e. allowing others to comply with legislative requirements whilst they evade responsibility). For example, the enforcement of packaging waste legislation initially concentrated on those companies who failed to register rather than monitoring those who have already registered.

This approach reflects the fact that the interpretation of enforcement and sanctioning practices is becoming more sophisticated. For the sake of simplicity, enforcement is often considered as a linear process whereby regulatory agencies seek compliance from the regulated. In fact enforcement is much more of a two-way process, where things can be learnt on both 'sides' of the regulator/regulated relationship. This means, for example, that where the Environment Agency identifies a problem with compliance rates in a particular area, it can target that area until such time as compliance rates rise. Once this happens, there is less need to undertake enforcement and other areas of non-compliance can be targeted. A more general form of this two-way process involves the review of the reasons for non-compliance and the ineffectiveness of environmental regulation in the light of experience of the regulatory agencies and the regulated.

All of the above points raise the issue of optimal enforcement. Just as optimality in regulation aims to use the right blend of instruments (see p. 271), so enforcement agencies and the criminal courts must keep in mind the right blend of enforcement and criminal sanctions in relation to environmental crime. Optimal enforcement is concerned with securing compliance with the least amount of interference and optimal punishment should be designed to 'press the right buttons' in relation to individual offenders. Thus the importance of developing alternatives to traditional sanctions is that in seeking to secure future compliance, different offenders will respond to different penalties. For example, in cases of incompetence or technical inadequacy it would arguably be more efficient to supervise upgrading of plant and equipment and proper training rather than paying a fine.[69]

Whatever style of enforcement and punishment is adopted in future, it is worth noting that there will continue to be incidents which cause significant pollution where no formal enforcement action is taken. The aftermath of the *Braer* oil pollution incident off the Shetland Islands is a good example of an event which caused significant environmental damage where no prosecution resulted. Perhaps this illustration is a postscript to the problems of enforcing environmental law in the real world: that there is no simplistic connection between criminal activity, environmental pollution and the imposition of appropriate enforcement mechanisms or sanctions.

CHAPTER SUMMARY

1   It is difficult to define an 'environmental crime' with any degree of certainty, primarily because there are relatively few activities which harm the environment which are crimes in and of themselves. The criminal law is mainly used to address clearly unacceptable behaviour and to underpin a system of environmental regulation.

2   Generally, environmental crimes are not 'evil in themselves' but are made so under regulatory systems and there is no necessary connection between pollution and environmental crime as many polluting acts are lawful.

3   Most environmental crimes impose strict liability, that is to say that there is no requirement of fault.

4   The justifications for imposing strict liability for environmental crimes include: it is in the public interest to do so; it acts as a deterrent so that those who have to comply with the law don't take risks; and it makes it easier for regulators to enforce and prosecute environmental offences.

5   The potential unfairness of strict liability is balanced by the existence of certain statutory defences, selective enforcement and the nature of any sanction (e.g. nominal fine).

6   Although environmental crimes are committed by individuals (particularly in relation to wildlife crimes) and corporations, the most significant crimes are committed by companies because of the scale of their operations.

7   Companies will be liable for the criminal acts of employees where the purposes of environmental legislation would be defeated if the company could not be prosecuted.

8   Senior managers of companies can be prosecuted in their capacity as managers for many environmental crimes where an offence is committed with their consent or connivance, or is attributable to their neglect.

9   The Environment Agency is responsible for the enforcing of the vast majority of breaches of environmental law and approximately 80–90 per cent of all prosecutions for environmental crime. Other regulatory bodies such as HM Customs and Excise and English Nature play a subsidiary role in certain areas.

---

69. Although it could be argued that such steps might not go beyond what a regulator could require through administrative means.

10   There is a general right to bring a private prosecution in relation to many environmental offences although this is seldom used in practice.

11   Prosecution rates for environmental crime are very low in relation to the number of breaches of environmental law. This is partly explained by the development of a cooperational style of enforcement but other reasons include a lack of resources to detect crimes.

12   There are alternative enforcement styles which are based around sanctioning breaches (deterrence) and responsive regulation which uses the minimum amount of formal regulation as possible to achieve compliance.

13   The Environment Agency has policies which guide the exercise of discretion over whether and how to enforce or prosecute. These polices are worded in such a way as to make it very unlikely that a challenge to a decision to take, or not to take, any particular enforcement decision would be successful.

14   There is a marked dissatisfaction with the low sentences which courts impose for environmental offences, particularly in relation to fines. Attempts to introduce sentencing tariffs have been rejected by the Court of Appeal in favour of a case-by-case approach.

15   In routine cases of environmental harm which result from general activities it has been argued that civil or administrative penalties would be appropriate leaving criminal sanctions only for crimes which have been wilfully committed with a view to personal or business advantage.

16   Securing compliance with environmental law is strongly connected with optimal enforcement. This involves selecting the right style of enforcement for individual operators and having a broader, more flexible range of sanctions.

Q QUESTIONS

1   Why is the definition of 'environmental crime' problematic? How do values and environmental perspectives play a part in establishing any definition of an environmental crime?

2   What are the arguments for and against strict liability for environmental offences? How do regulators and the Courts deal with cases where the imposition of strict liability might be unfair?

3   What is meant by 'enforcement styles' in relation to the enforcement of environmental law?

4   What single change in environmental law, procedure or enforcement practice would you introduce in order to reduce the number of environmental crimes?

FURTHER READING

There are no recommended general texts on environmental crime. Two US books, M. Clifford, *Environmental Crime: Enforcement, Policy and Social Responsibility* (Gaithersburg: Aspen, 1998) and Y. Situ and D. Emmons, *Environmental Crime: The Criminal Justice System's Role in Protecting the Environment* (Thousand Oaks: Sage, 2000) provide a general introduction. There is an interesting comparative perspective of US and UK approaches to environmental crime in W. Wilson, *Making Environmental Laws Work* (Oxford: Hart Publishing, 1998). In particular, Chapters 6 and 7 focus on the use of the criminal law and civil and administrative law enforcement. We do not consider the European aspect of environmental crime in this chapter. Partly this is for reasons of space. Also the idea is relatively underdeveloped in comparison with other areas of environmental law. For an overview of the issues have a look at F. Comte, 'Criminal Environmental Law and Community Competence' [2003] EELR 147, M Faure, 'European Environmental Criminal Law: Do We Really Need It?' [2004] EELR 18 and the collection of essays in F. Comte and L. Kramer (eds), *Environmental Crime in Europe; Rules of Sanctions* (Groningen: Europa Law Publishing, 2004).

On a practical level the House of Commons Environment Audit Committee's *'Environmental Crime and the Courts* (6th Report of Session 2003–4) provides the context for many of the issues in the chapter. The Report examines some of the contemporary problems of enforcing and sanctioning environmental crime and comes up with some interesting suggestions and solutions for addressing them. Finally, for an empirical survey of environmental crime and related opinions see the Environment Justice Project's Report on *Environmental Justice* especially Part III (2004) (see web links below).

There is not a huge amount of literature on the definitional aspects of environmental crime. There have been some attempts to develop 'green' criminology, or a theory of environmental crime. M. Lynch and P. Stretsky, 'The Meaning of Green: Contrasting Criminological Perspectives' (2003) Theor Crim 7(2) 217, and R. White, 'Environmental issues and the criminological imagination' (2003) Theor Crim 7(4) 483 form a two-part series on the definition and goals of environmental criminal law. In addition, a special issue of the Journal *Theoretical Criminology* focused on the different perspectives on environmental crime, see 'For a Green Criminology' (1998) Theor Crim 2(2). Readers may also find P. Lowe et al, *Moralizing the Environment* (London: UCL Press, 1997) an interesting study of the way in which shifts in the perception of the harm caused by agricultural pollution brought about tighter regulation and enforcement.

Anyone looking for some wider reading material on the enforcement of environmental law will find a number of good works and there are additional texts which cover regulatory enforcement generally but can be extremely useful when considering the theory of enforcement. In the former category there is G. Richardson, A. Ogus, and P. Burrows, *Policing Pollution—A Study of Regulation and Enforcement* (Oxford: Clarendon Press, 1982); K. Hawkins, *Environment and Enforcement: Regulation and the Social Definition of Pollution* (Oxford: Clarendon Press, 1984); and B. Hutter, *The Reasonable Arm of the Law* (Oxford: Clarendon Press, 1988) all of which provide an examination of environmental enforcement officers' experience of enforcing the law in the real world. In the latter category, there is K. Hawkins: *Law as a Last Resort: Prosecution Decision Making in a Regulatory Agency* (Oxford: Oxford University Press, 2002) which examines the process of prosecutions brought by the Health and Safety Executive and I. Ayres and J. Braithwaite, *Responsive Regulation* (Oxford: Oxford University Press, 1992) which, as the main text explains, provided an alternative view of regulatory enforcement (we hesitate to call it the 'third way'). Other relevant material includes J. Rowan-Robinson and A. Ross, 'The enforcement of environmental regulation in Britain' [1994] JPL 200. There are two articles which examine the practices and opinions of industrial pollution control enforcement officers. A. Mehta and K. Hawkins, 'IPC and its Impact: Perspectives from Industry' (1998) 10 JEL 61 and C. Lovat, 'Regulating IPC in Scotland: A Study of Enforcement Practice' (2004) 16 JEL 49.

There has been an upsurge of interest in the different sanctions for environmental crime. The weight of opinion and evidence suggests that current criminal penalties (largely fines) are too low and an inadequate response to environmental offences. The best aggregated data source can be found in C. DuPont and P. Zakkow, *Trends in Environmental Sentencing in England and Wales*, (DEFRA, 2003). The Environmental Justice Project's Report referred to above also has some empirical data. For an general introduction to the *issues* read A. Ogus and C. Abbot, 'Sanctions for Pollution: Do We have the Right Regime? (2002) 14 JEL 283 and the short response from top prosecutors in the Environment Agency, R. Navarro and D. Stott, 'A Brief Comment: Sanctions for Pollution' (2002) 14 JEL

299. Different solutions have been proposed. The most common theme is the introduction of civil penalties. The idea has been around for some time although the most comprehensive treatment can be found in M. Woods and R. Macrory, 'Environmental Civil Penalties—A More Proportionate Response to Breach? (London: UCL, 2003). Other useful articles on this topic include, M. Grekos, 'Environmental Fines—All Small Change' [2004] JPL 1330; R. Malcolm, 'Prosecuting for Environmental Crime: Does Crime Pay?' (2002) ELM 14(5) 289. Another approach is the 'Name and Shame' policy adopted by the Environment Agency. A discussion of this can be found in P. De Prez, 'Beyond Judicial Sanctions: The Negative Impact of Conviction for Environmental Offences' (2000) Env L. Rev. 2(1) 11. Finally, P. de Prez, 'Excuses, Excuses: The Ritual Trivialisation of Environmental Prosecutions' (2000) 12 JEL 65 provides a real world view of the ways in which companies address environmental crime and the mitigation they put before a court when sentencing. It is perhaps unsurprising to learn that companies play down their culpability.

@ WEB LINKS

Many of the reports which are referred to in this chapter can be accessed through DEFRA's environmental justice web page at <www.defra.gov.uk/environment/justice>. The Reports available from this site include the UCL report, the Environmental Justice report and the ERM Report all referred to above. The Partnership For Action Against Wildlife Crime's web page provides a database of wildlife prosecutions and can be found at <www.defra.gov.uk/paw/prosecutions>. The Centre for Corporate Accountability at <www.corporateaccountability.org> is aimed largely at Health and Safety legislation but is a good source of information of corporate liability. Any study of the enforcement of environmental law must keep abreast of current developments and figures which can be found in the most recent editions of the Environment Agency's *Enforcement and Prosecution Policy* and its Annual Report (both available from <www.environment-agency.gov.uk>).

10 Public participation

 Overview

This chapter deals with public participation in environmental law and policy. Over recent years there have been significant moves towards increasing both the quantity and quality of public participation in many different areas of environmental decision making. The exact nature of public participation can take many forms but this chapter concentrates on access to information on the environment, public participation in environmental decision making and access to justice in environmental matters. In Chapter 8 we made the point that the provision of information about the environment and the regulatory process was an integral element of the regulation of environmental protection. We explore this idea in greater detail, looking at some of the reasons for giving greater access to environmental information; the types of environmental information which are available; the use of environmental information as a regulatory instrument; international and European initiatives; and past, present and future approaches to access to environmental information in Britain. We also take a brief overview of various examples of public participation in environmental decision-making. This is in overview as many of the detailed provisions on participation in relation to particular regimes (e.g. EIA) are to be found in later chapters. Finally, we examine access to justice in relation to environmental law through the judicial review of administrative decisions and actions. In environmental regulation this involves some consideration of the question of the standing of individuals and groups to bring such actions and of the effectiveness of the procedure. Closely linked to these issues is the debate about whether there should be an environmental court. We conclude the chapter by examining some of the arguments for such a court.

At the end of this chapter you should be able to:

- ✔ Understand and distinguish between different types of participation in environmental law and decision-making.
- ✔ Appreciate the basic arguments for and against open access to environmental information.
- ✔ Understand the historical development of law and policy on access to environmental information.
- ✔ Identify and understand the law on access to environmental information.
- ✔ Appreciate the different types of environmental information which are available.
- ✔ Appreciate in outline the main methods of public participation in environmental decision-making.
- ✔ Understand the particular relevance of judicial review in relation to environmental disputes.
- ✔ Analyse the effectiveness of judicial review as a remedy in environmental cases.
- ✔ Appreciate the arguments for an Environmental Court.

Introduction

The general public is involved in environmental law and decision making in a number of different ways. These include democratic accountability through the election of politicians who make environmental law and policy to more direct participation such as local consultation on individual planning or pollution control applications or the availability of judicial review remedies for people with a 'sufficient interest'. In recent years there have been moves towards encouraging more public participation in environmental law and improving the quality of that participation.

The importance of public participation is recognised in Principle 10 of the Rio Declaration:

Environmental issues are best handled with the participation of all concerned citizens, at the relevant level. At the national level, each individual shall have access to information concerning the environment that is held by public authorities . . . and the opportunity to participate in decision-making processes. States shall facilitate and encourage public awareness and participation by making information widely available. Effective access to judicial and administrative proceedings, including redress and remedy shall be provided.

This basic principle has been developed at an international level as evidenced by the Aarhus Convention which was signed in 1998 and came into force on 30 October 2001. At its heart the Convention consists of three 'pillars' of promoting public participation, namely access to environmental information, public participation in environmental decision-making and access to justice in environmental matters. The EC and UK have signed the Convention and became full parties in early 2005. The shape of the Convention is reflected in the matters covered in this chapter. The first pillar of the Convention promotes access to environmental information by the public. This includes both the reactive supply of information—where public authorities supply certain information on request within certain time limits—as well as active dissemination of environmental information as a positive obligation. The aim is to ensure that information about the environment is freely available so as to enhance the public's role in decision-making in relation to environmental matters on an informed basis. Secondly, the Convention promotes increased public participation in environmental decision-making by requiring the establishment of a transparent and fair framework for decisions, within which the public will participate in the preparation of plans and programmes relating to the environment. Thirdly, the Convention promotes access to justice on environmental matters by giving the public the right to challenge decisions by means of an independent review by a court of law or other independent body. In order to implement the provisions of the Convention there have been significant changes of law at both EC and domestic level.

The arguments for greater public participation in environmental matters are relatively uncontested. First, the development of our understanding of environmental problems means that the increasing complexity of legislation is outstripping the ability of the basic administrative structures to address all of the environmental issues we face. Thus there is a growing reliance upon alternative mechanisms to secure environmental improvements (e.g. economic instruments, voluntary agreements). In many cases these require a greater degree of public understanding of the implications of different measures to function efficiently. Secondly, there is the challenge of implementation deficit (see further p. 100). That the easiest problems have been tackled means that we are now facing more fundamental concerns which can only be addressed through concerted effort by the different stakeholders including the general public. The emphasis on 'shared responsibility' as a means of addressing environmental problems reflects this view. For example, the shift from waste disposal regulation to waste reduction targets is primarily a shift from controlling industry to promoting shared responsibility. Thirdly, much has been made of the development of the 'Risk Society', with its reduced role for scientific experts and the breakdown of trust in the technocratic basis of decision-making (see p. 53). One of the ways of solving environmental problems in the Risk Society is through the development of deliberative and participative techniques. Fourthly, sustainable development with its focus on fairness and justice has public participation at its heart (see p. 62). A summary of these and other benefits which are brought about through increased public participation can be found in Box 10.1.

BOX 10.1 The benefits of public participation

Lee and Abbot identify a number of the potential benefits of promoting public participation:[1]

Improving the quality of decisions

The preamble to the Aarhus Convention emphasizes the role that public participation has to play in improving environmental decisions. It states that 'improved access and public participation in decision-making enhance the quality and the implementation of decisions. . . .' This can be done through such things as the input of specific expertise held by members of the public or through the elicitation of social and cultural values.

Environmental problem solving

One of the ways in which competing values can be resolved is through techniques of deliberation, i.e. 'bottom-up' discussions in which all sides of an issue are debated in an attempt to reach a consensus on an issue.

Promoting environmental citizenship

Environmental citizenship is loosely based upon the notion that individuals should take some responsibility for their own interaction with the environment. In promoting such citizenship, participation in environmental matters is critical. Engaging the public to play an active role in environmental policy-making and raising awareness of environmental issues are central to promoting environmental citizenship.

Improving procedural legitimacy

Increased involvement in decisions, access to good quality environmental information and ex post review mechanisms through such things as judicial review increases the accountability of the decision-maker and makes the process more legitimate in the eyes of the public.

---

1. M. Lee and C. Abbot (2003) 66 MLR 80.

Eliciting values

In Chapter 3 we discussed the role that different values play in the environmental decision-making process. Promoting public participation in decision-making and widening access to environmental information is the best way of eliciting such values.

Access to environmental information

There has been a steady increase in openness and access to environmental information over recent years. The reasons for this growing emphasis on access are many and varied, with European legislation and international initiatives playing a significant part in the process. In addition there has been a relaxation of secrecy in relation to all information held by public bodies. This has been formalised in the Freedom of Information Act 2000 (FOI) which promotes a general right of access to information held by public bodies. This is supplemented by greater powers of access in relation to environmental information in the Environmental Information Regulations 2004 ('the 2004 Regulations').

This legislation reflects a deeper understanding of the advantages that greater access to information, in particular information about the environment, brings. One of the basic features of environmental law is that, on a theoretical level at least, everyone has a 'stake' in the interests which the regulatory system is designed to protect (i.e. the environment). Whilst it is possible to take a narrow view that the 'stake' might be restricted to a proprietary interest (e.g. in the land a person 'owns'), a broader view would suggest that the interest is a general one held by everyone, both for themselves and on behalf of future generations. This stake in the environment competes with other interests such as industrial operations. In these circumstances, every attempt should be made to balance out conflicting interests by, for example, allowing access to information on the consequences of industrial activities, so that all relevant factors are taken into account. This has led the RCEP to talk of a general public 'right' to environmental information:

the public must be considered to have a right, analogous to a beneficial interest, in the condition of the air and water and to be able to obtain information on how far they are being degraded.[2]

In addition, there is a clear link here between the provision of environmental information and the achievement of the goal of sustainable development. This link is made in two places. First, the provision of environmental information can influence the behaviour and decisions of private individuals or companies. Making information available on a wider scale can be the catalyst in changes in behaviour or can increase the effectiveness of other instruments. For example, publishing information on energy efficiency and associated environmental benefits can be used in conjunction with grants and subsidies to encourage people to reduce their consumption of energy (e.g. by installing energy efficient boilers or by turning the heating down). Secondly, information can help us to understand the consequences of our current actions in terms of the legacy which is being passed on to future generations. Other justifications for widening access to information are summarized in Box 10.2.

---

2. RCEP, 10th Report *Tackling Pollution—Experience and Prospects* (Cmnd 9149, 1984).

BOX 10.2 **Rationales for access to environmental information**

Monitoring the effectiveness of regulation

One of the ways in which the effectiveness of a regulatory system can be monitored is to produce 'benchmarks' for performance (e.g. to gather and publish data on waste going to landfill and recycling rates). This legitimizes the introduction of new laws, ensures that existing laws are actually achieving the aims they were designed to meet and ensures that ineffective laws are replaced.

Improving the enforcement of environmental law

Without adequate information, public rights to enforce environmental laws have little value. This includes basic information on the identity of polluters, where they are polluting and how much is being emitted. To assess levels of compliance, either generally or in relation to an individual authorisation, the public require access not only to information concerning the details of an authorisation/consent but also to monitoring data.

Environmental information as a self-standing regulatory instrument

Environmental information can be used as a stand alone mechanism to regulate behaviour and to complement other regulatory instruments. The use of eco-labelling to provide consumers with information which enables them to make informed purchasing decisions is an example of this.

Informing the public about environmental risks

A lack of information can increase the perception of risks associated with an activity (whether in relation to human health or the environment). Greater disclosure of information enables informed debate about environmental risks and the manner in which they might be addressed by allowing the widest possible range of interpretations of raw data as opposed to relying upon assertions and interpretations of interested parties (although in reality, greater access merely enables the views of different interested parties to be placed in the balance).[3]

Although there are many arguments in favour of greater access to environmental information, the development of the legislation which has brought about this access was the subject of a vigorous debate, with opposition coming mainly from those to whom the information relates, namely industry and governmental organizations. These objections are reflected in some of the exemptions from disclosure which are found in the FOI Act and the 2004 Regulations.

One of the main objections to full public disclosure of environmental information has traditionally been that such disclosure would detrimentally affect the viability of business by breaching commercial confidentiality. Concern stemmed from the belief that industrial competitors would be able to use the data released to gain access to commercially confidential information. In rejecting these objections the RCEP suggested that industry's refusal to disclose information on the basis of commercial confidentiality was often a 'reflex action' which did not reflect the commercial risk involved and that the emphasis which was

3. See P. Wald 'Negotiations of Environmental Disputes: A New Role for the Courts' (1985) 10 Col. Jo. of Env. Law 1.

given to such confidentiality was 'disproportionate and misconceived'.[4] Notwithstanding this rejection of the argument against greater disclosure, most legislative schemes which promote greater access to environmental information have provisions which exclude commercially confidential information.

Another objection to greater disclosure was that openness would lead to mischief-making and an unacceptable level of interference by activists. In 1984, the industry organisation, the CBI, referred to the access to information provisions of the Control of Pollution Act 1974 as a 'busybody's charter'.[5] Other predicted consequences of greater disclosure put forward by MPs included the disappearance of the chemicals industry from Britain and 'an endless stream of prosecutions'.[6] During the passage of the Environmental Protection Bill through Parliament, one MP alleged that greater access to information and broader rights of prosecution would 'allow the "green nutters" to get on parade and have a field day of litigation against industry on entirely inconsequential grounds'.[7] With hindsight, these predictions appear to have been unduly alarmist. Although the information has been used by environmental interest groups (see e.g. Friends of the Earth's 'Factory Watch' web site at <www.foe.co.uk/factorywatch/index.html>), this has not been for the purpose of taking unreasonable enforcement action against industry.

The history of access to environmental information

An outline of the history of secrecy and access to environmental information is set out in Box 10.3. The roots of environmental secrecy can be traced back to the mid-19th century and the age of industrialization when the Alkali Inspectorate adopted a policy of keeping any information secret unless publication was demanded by a particular statute or was permitted by the owner/operator of the process to which the information related.

BOX 10.3 **Access to environmental information—timeline**

Year	Key Events
1864	Alkali Inspectorate created. Takes a general approach to secrecy by adopting a policy that 'all information regarding any work must be considered private unless publication is demanded by the Act or permitted by the owner'.
1911	Official Secrets Act, s. 2 provided that unauthorised disclosure of information (including environmental information) held by central government was an offence.
1956	Clean Air Acts 1956 and 1968 give Local Authorities a discretionary power to set up public registers containing details of non-domestic atmospheric emissions. Only five local authorities used the power and only eight premises were publicized. Procedural hurdles included the creation of a committee to discuss the proposals for disclosure and an appeal mechanism for operators affected by disclosure and the lack of resources to assist with the implementation of the system.

---

4. See RCEP 7th Report *Agriculture and Pollution* (Cmnd 7644, 1979) and 10th Report, op. cit., n. 2.
5. See RCEP 10th Report, op. cit., n. 2.
6. See a Parliamentary question from T. Devlin MP, 171 H.C. Debate, 30 April 1990, Col. 761.
7. See Hansard Debates, 2 May 1990.

Year	Key Events
1961	Rivers (Prevention of Pollution) Act restricts the public right of access to information concerning applications, discharge consents or effluent samples taken by the enforcing authority, unless the person/company making the discharge permitted its disclosure or there was a further statutory requirement to disclose.
1974	Alkali Inspectorate's unofficial policy was transposed into legislation in the Health and Safety at Work etc. Act 1974, s. 28, which prohibited the disclosure of any information relating to recordings or measurements taken during the exercise of the Inspectorate's duties.
	The Control of Pollution Act 1974 makes provision for pollution control registers although implementation was delayed until 1984 as a result of industry pressure to delay disclosure even further.
	The RCEP concluded in its Second Report that it was in the public interest to make environmental information more widely available to anyone who would use it to improve the environment.
1984	RCEP 10th Report sets out a proposed 'guiding principle' which suggested that there should be a presumption in favour of unrestricted access to information which the pollution control authorities obtain or receive by virtue of their statutory powers, with protection for secrecy only in those circumstances where a genuine case could be substantiated.
1985	Local Government (Access to Information) Act provides access to the reports and documents considered by local authorities. This includes planning and environmental health committees.
1989	Official Secrets Act 1989 reforms the 1911 Act with the effect of narrowly protecting only certain limited classes of central information, excluding environmental matters.
1990	The Environmental Protection Act 1990 creates pollution control registers for the waste management and integrated pollution control regime.
	First comprehensive system of access to environmental information created under Directive 90/313/EC which provides for general access subject to certain classes of exemption.
1992	The Environmental Information Regulations 1992 transpose the requirements of Directive 90/313/EC.
1997	The publication of the White Paper, *Your Right to Know*, foreshadows the introduction of a broad right of access to all information.
1998	The details of the Aarhus Convention are agreed. The EC and the UK are signatories, paving the way for changes to the Directive and domestic Regulations.
2000	The Freedom of Information Act 2000 (which fully came into force in 2005) introduces a general right of access to all information held by 'public authorities'. Environmental Information is excluded as a special regime.
2003	Directive 2003/4/EC on Access to Environmental Information repeals the 1990 Directive, addressing many of the defects in the old Directive and effectively transposing the requirements of the Aarhus Convention.

Year	Key Events
2004	Kiev Protocol on Pollutant Release and Transfer Registers represents international agreement on the dissemination of aggregated pollution data. The Environmental Information Regulations 2004 replace the 1992 Regulations, implementing the 2003 Directive.

International approaches to access to information

The importance of a right of access to environmental information at all levels is emphasized by the weight which greater disclosure is given in international law. In particular, the role of information in meeting the goal of sustainable development is acknowledged in Agenda 21, the policy blueprint agreed at the 1992 Rio Earth Summit, which stresses the importance of ensuring that all stakeholders in the environment have access to relevant environmental information relating to products or activities which have an environmental impact. This general commitment to greater access is specifically implemented in various international conventions including the Climate Change Convention (see Art. 6) where the exchange of public information on climate change is considered to be a pre-condition to the successful implementation of the other substantive provisions of the Convention.

The need to ensure greater consistency and transparency of public access to environmental information within international law is evidenced by the inclusion of access to information provisions in the Aarhus Convention. The relevant provisions of the Convention are now largely mirrored in current EC and domestic legislation (see below). The Kiev Protocol on Pollutant Release and Transfer Registers was signed in 2003 and makes provision for aggregated pollutant inventories which again are found in European and domestic legislation.

One other matter which should be considered within the international context is the effect of the incorporation of the European Convention of Human Rights into domestic legislation by way of the Human Rights Act 1998. In particular, the European Court of Human Rights has interpreted certain articles of the Convention (in particular, the right to privacy, home and family life under Art. 8) in a way which should mean that statutory provisions on access to information (including any Freedom of Information Act) might have a much wider application than has been the case previously.

For example, in *Guerra v Italy* (1998) 26 EHRR 357, the Court held that public authorities were under an obligation to supply information about the risks involved in living in close proximity to an environmentally sensitive use. The Court considered that the local authority was under a positive obligation to supply information which enabled the residents to assess the risks from the factory. On a broad interpretation it would not be possible for an authority to reject a request on the basis that it did not have the information (see also *McGinley and Egan v UK* (1999) 27 EHRR 1 and *Lopez Ostra v Spain* (1995) 20 EHRR 277).

Access to information held by European institutions

A distinction needs to be made between access to environmental information at Member State level and access to information about the decision-making process operated by European bodies, and in particular the European Commission and Council. Historically, the processes of decision-making within the European Commission and the Council were shrouded in secrecy. For example, documents relating to infringement proceedings such as letters of formal notice and reasoned opinions issued by the European Commission against Member States were secret. This meant that important information about possible breaches of European law were kept from the general public. Moves towards greater openness were formalized with a Code of Conduct on Public Access to Commission and Council Documents (see Decision 94/90). Article 255 of the EC Treaty (inserted following the Amsterdam amendments) gave a constitutional right to documents held by the European Parliament, Council, and Commission.[8]

This general right was fleshed out by Regulation 1049/2001 on Public Access to European Parliament, Council and Commission Documents (sometimes referred to as the 'Transparency Regulation'). This Regulation provides access to all information held by the main (but by no means all) European institutions.[9] The Regulation provides a general right of access to information for EU citizens (including corporate entities) (Art. 2(1)).[10] There are certain exceptions, in particular where disclosure would undermine commercial interests or the public interest (e.g. in relation to public security or defence matters). Any information relating to 'third parties' (e.g. Member States and other non-Community bodies) is subject to a duty to consult to determine whether an exception applies, unless it is 'clear' that the information is or is not exempt.

One final source of European information comes from the European Environment Agency. One of the reasons for the setting up of the Agency was to provide Member States and the European public with objective and reliable information on the state of the environment within the EC. The Agency has adopted the Transparency Regulation in relation to its own documents (see Regulation 1641/2003) and it produces periodic reports on the state of the European environment which are available from its web page <www.eea.eu.int>. The Agency is closely involved with the European Environment Information and Observation Network (EIONET) which connects national environmental information organizations within Member States and includes some countries outside the EC and other organizations such as the European Free Trade Association.

---

8. See also Art. 207 EC covering access to documents held by the Council which relate to law making activities.

9. Bodies not covered include the European Central Bank and the European Investment Bank.

10. The European Ombudsman has a policing role in relation to access to information and can make orders relating to specific documents; see the draft recommendation made in relation to a complaint from Friends of the Earth at <www.euro-ombudsman.eu.int/recommen/en/000271.htm>

European legislation on access to environmental information

The disclosure of environmental information at member state level has been a significant part of EC environmental policy since the drawing up of the First Environmental Action Programme in 1973. Although a wide range of environmental directives had provisions for access to individual elements of environmental information, the first general legislative measure was adopted during the Fourth Action Programme. Directive 90/313 on the Freedom of Access to Information on the Environment was a broad framework measure which was intended to facilitate general access rights but did not impose any requirements in terms of practical arrangements for access, leaving that to the discretion of the Member States. The Directive was interpreted in a broad manner with the ECJ taking a purposive approach to its provisions. In *Mecklenburg v Kreis Pinneberg—Der Landrat* [1998] ECR I-3809 a member of the public asked his local authority for a copy of a document which set out the countryside protection authority's views on a local road project. The authority refused on the basis that the information fell outside the terms of the Directive in that it was not 'information relating to the environment'. The ECJ held that the concept of 'information relating to the environment' was broad and included documents which could be influential in determining the outcome of the decision-making process in relation to the road project. On the question of whether the information was exempt, the ECJ took the view that exemptions should be viewed narrowly and in accordance with the aims of the Directive.

Notwithstanding this purposive interpretation, the Directive was defective in a number of aspects (see Box 10.4). In the light of these defects and the need to implement the Aarhus Convention, the 1990 Directive was replaced in 2003.

BOX 10.4 **The defects of Directive 90/313**[11]

Scope of application

The Directive applied to information held by public bodies with 'responsibilities for the environment'. This vague definition led to disputes about whether the provisions of the Directive applied to bodies such as the privatised utilities (e.g. energy and transport companies) whose primary functions were arguably neither public nor environmental.

Definition of 'Environmental Information'

Although the definition of environmental information in the Directive was broad, it was unclear in relation to certain categories of information. This included information relating to impacts upon human health or economic data used to justify the viability for a particular project.

---

11. See further COM (2000) 400 Final and R. Hallo (ed), *The Implementation and Implications of Directive 90/313* (The Hague: Kluwer, 1996).

Broad exemptions

The general right of access was tempered by wide categories of exempt information with discretionary rights of refusal. In determining whether to grant access there was no weight to be given to the public interest. These broad exemptions made it too easy for authorities to reject applications for disclosure even where there were no adverse impacts on legitimate interests protected under the exemptions.

Ineffective right to challenge decisions

Where applications for information had been rejected, the Directive only provided for challenge by way of judicial or administrative review. In many Member States, including the UK, this was a cumbersome and expensive route of challenge.

Excessive charges

In practice, many public authorities demanded unreasonably high charges for supplying information. In some cases people were charged and subsequently told that they were not entitled to the information.

Long time limits

The Directive required authorities to 'respond' to requests for access within two months. This led to delays as some authorities simply replied to the request within the time limit without actually making the information available within the two month period.

Reactive nature of the general scheme of access

The Directive was far too reactive in nature, imposing obligations to grant access to information purely on request. There was no general requirement to disseminate information, nor to provide aggregated information in the shape of reports on the state of the environment.

Directive 2003/4/EC on public access to environmental information was designed to address many of the defects of the 1990 Directive. In addition, it formed one of the key instruments which would enable the ratification of the Aarhus Convention. In many ways the revised Directive was developed in parallel with the access to information provisions of the Convention which were drafted in light of the experience with the 1990 Directive. Thus there is a marked similarity in the two regimes.

The Directive applies to 'environmental information' held by any 'public authority'. Environmental information is defined very broadly to include not only the state of the environment, releases to the environment and policies and plans relating to the environment, but also cost–benefit analyses and the state of human health and safety 'inasmuch as they are affected by the state of the environment' (Art. 1). The definition of 'Public Authority' has also been extended to include those bodies performing 'public administrative functions', 'specific duties, activities or services' in relation to the environment (Art. 2). Thus private companies with public duties are clearly covered.

The obligation to provide environmental information must be met as soon as possible or within one month (Art. 3). In cases of complex information the period can be extended to two months. There are general exemptions where a request is vague or otherwise unreasonable (Art. 4(1)). In addition, there is a list of exempt categories including information which is: commercially confidential; concerned with national defence or security matters, concerned with the 'course of justice'; or where information was supplied voluntarily. In these cases, the authorities are obliged to consider whether disclosure would 'adversely affect' the protected interest in question (Art. 4(2)). In all cases, there is a general 'public interest' test whereby the authority is obliged to consider whether it would be in the public interest to disclose the information. Any charges imposed for access have to be 'reasonable' and contained in a published schedule (Art. 5). In cases of refusal, an applicant should have access to an 'expeditious' appeals procedure which must be free or inexpensive (Art. 6). Finally, the Directive provides a positive obligation upon Member States to disseminate environmental information including: legislation at international, national and local levels, policies plans and programmes, and 'state of the environment' reports (Art. 7).

Access to environmental information in Britain

Britain's approach to access to environmental information can be characterized as having three identifiable phases (see Box 10.3). The first, up until about 1974, was based upon a presumption against disclosure. Examples can be found in many different statutes from the Rivers (Prevention of Pollution) Act 1961 and the Health and Safety at Work Act 1974, s. 28. The second phase lasted from the 1980s until the early 1990s and can be characterized as the time when pollution control registers were introduced. These related to discharges to water (under COPA 1974), waste management operations and industrial activities (under EPA 1990) as well as better access to planning information under the Local Government (Access to Information) Act 1985. Under the third phase there have been moves towards the broadening of the classes of available information subject only to restricted classes of exemptions in the Freedom of Information Act 2000 and the Environmental Information Regulations 2004. The basic practical distinction between these last two approaches is in the nature of the access. In the case of public registers, the information is held by public authorities specifically for the purpose of public access. In the case of broader access, the information is disclosed only where a request is made (although the provision of information on registers is included within this). Although these approaches characterize the approach to disclosure of pollution control information, there are other more sophisticated information instruments which are discussed further below.

The Freedom of Information Act 2000

The two main statutory schemes under the FOI and the 2004 Regulations operate in a complementary fashion with the minimum of overlaps. The Freedom of Information Act 2000 provides a general right to access information from public authorities subject only to a list of exempt information. Environmental information is one of the two exceptions to the universal application of the FOI (the other being in relation to information on individuals under data protection legislation). Environmental information is exempt from the Act (s. 39) and any access is governed by the Environmental Information Regulations 2004.

Subject to the exemptions in the Act, any person who makes a request to a public authority for information must be informed whether the public authority holds that infor-mation and, if so, be given access to the information. The request for information must be in writing with the name and address of the person seeking the information along with a description of the information required (s. 8). The Act applies to all 'public authorities'. Unlike previous legislation, the Act provides a comprehensive list of bodies to whom the duty to facilitate access applies (Sch. 1). It covers central and local Government bodies, regulators, and privatized utilities.

There are 23 exemptions to the general right of access under FOI (ss. 21–44). Most of the exemptions have to be considered in two stages. First, there must be a decision on whether any exemption applies to all or part of the information requested. If it does, the second consideration is whether the public interest in maintaining the exemption outweighs the public interest in disclosing the information. These are known as the *qualified* exemptions. There are also a number of *absolute* exemptions to which the public interest test does not apply. The exemption for environmental information under section 39 is qualified. Thus, there is a residual role for the FOI in relation to environmental information where it is exempt from disclosure under the 2004 Regulations and the public interest in disclosing the information is not outweighed by the public interest in maintaining the exemption under section 39 of the Act. It has been suggested that the circumstances where disclosure would be granted under the FOI where it had been refused under the 2004 Regulations would be few and far between.[12] The other potential application of the FOI is to information which may not fall completely within the definition of 'environmental information' for the purposes of the 2004 Regulations. In such circumstances, information can be sought under both regimes.

The application of the Act is governed by two Codes of Practice relating to Access and the Management of Records (ss. 45–46). Enforcement of the Act lies with the Information Commissioner who has powers to instruct public authorities to disclose information (ss. 50–56). There is also a right of appeal to the Information Tribunal (ss. 57–61).

The Environmental Information Regulations 2004

The Environmental Information Regulations 2004 transpose and implement the provisions of Directive 2003/4 and accordingly pave the way for the ratification of the information provisions of the Aarhus Convention. Under the 2004 regulations, 'public authorities' are under a duty to make 'environmental information' available to every person who requests it. The phrase 'environmental information' is defined widely in accordance with the directive definition (see Box 10.5).

BOX 10.5 **'Environmental Information'**

This includes (see Reg. 1, 2004 Regs):

(a) the state of the elements of the environment, such as air and atmosphere, water, soil, land, landscape and natural sites including wetlands, coastal and marine areas, biological

---

12. P. Coppel [2005] JPL 14.

diversity and its components, including genetically modified organisms, and the inter-action among these elements;

(b) factors, such as substances, energy, noise, radiation or waste, including radioactive waste, emissions, discharges and other releases into the environment, affecting or likely to affect the elements of the environment referred to in (a);

(c) measures (including administrative measures), such as policies, legislation, plans, programmes, environmental agreements, and activities affecting or likely to affect the elements and factors referred to in (a) and (b) as well as measures or activities designed to protect those elements;

(d) reports on the implementation of environmental legislation;

(e) cost–benefit and other economic analyses and assumptions used within the framework of the measures and activities referred to in (c);

(f) the state of human health and safety, including the contamination of the food chain, where relevant, conditions of human life, cultural sites and built structures inasmuch as they are or may be affected by the state of the elements of the environment referred to in (a) or, through those elements, by any of the matters referred to in (b) and (c);

The regulations apply to all 'public authorities'. Broadly speaking these are the same as the authorities listed in Schedule 1 of the FOI. The definition is extended slightly to cover the requirements of the Directive to include bodies with specific duties in relation to the environment. Authorities such as the Department of the Environment, Food and Rural Affairs, local authorities and the Environment Agency are clearly covered as are a broad range of other regulatory agencies such as English Nature. The definition has, however, extended the requirements of disclosure to privatized utilities. It is also notable that the classes of public authority covered under FOI and the 2004 Regulations has been extended on a number of occasions since 2000.[13]

When a request for information is made it must be answered within 20 working days of receipt of the request, which can be extended to a maximum 40 working days if the request is 'complex and voluminous'. There are no formal requirements and requests can be verbal or written, electronic or hardcopy. Any response, however, must be in writing (Regs 5–7). Public authorities have a responsibility to provide 'advice and assistance' to applicants (Reg. 9). Thus, if a request is considered to be 'too general' an authority would be obliged to contact an applicant as soon as possible to try to determine specifically the exact nature of the information required.

In cases where the public authority refuses to disclose all or part of the information requested, it must issue a refusal notice in writing stating the exception the information falls under with reasons for any decision that the exception should be applied (Reg. 14). In cases where the confirmation of the mere existence of certain sensitive information may prejudice one of the protected exceptions, the authority may issue a decision which neither denies nor confirms that the requested information is held (Reg. 12(6)).

13. See, e.g., the Freedom of Information (Additional Public Authorities) Order 2002 (SI 2002/2623).

There are various exceptions to the duty to disclose. The first is where the request is vague, manifestly unreasonable or not held by the authority. The second is where the information relates to personal data, internal communications or is incomplete. A good example of this type of information was seen in *Maile v Wigan MBC* (see Case box 10.1).

CASE 10.1 Incomplete information—*Maile v Wigan BC* [2001] Env LR 11

The Applicant lived in Wigan and made a request to his local authority to see a database detailing potentially contaminated sites which was being prepared in the light of the implementation of the contaminated land regime under Part IIA of the EPA 1990. The local authority refused, saying that the information was incomplete. The Court held that there was no requirement to disclose. Although under the predecessor regulations to the 2004 Regulations local authorities were under a general duty to disclose environmental information to those persons requesting it, this duty did not apply where the information was still in the course of completion or was otherwise exempt as confidential. The database was considered to be 'speculative' and disclosure would cause 'unnecessary alarm' and 'despondency among local citizens'.

Thirdly, disclosure may be exempt where it would adversely affect one of the identified categories of protected information (see Box 10.6). Where information falls within one of these categories it must also be shown that in all of the circumstances of the case the public interest in maintaining the exception outweighs the public interest in disclosing the information.

BOX 10.6 **Classes of exempt information**

A public authority may refuse to disclose information where its disclosure would adversely affect:

- international relations, defence, national security or public safety;[14]
- the course of justice, the ability of a person to receive a fair trial or the ability of a public authority to conduct an inquiry of a criminal or disciplinary nature;
- intellectual property rights;
- the confidentiality of the proceedings of that or any other public authority where such confidentiality is provided by law;
- commercially confidential information where such confidentiality is provided by law to protect a legitimate economic interest;[15]
- voluntarily supplied information;
- the protection of the environment to which the information relates.

---

14. See, e.g., *R v British Coal Corporation, ex parte Ibstock Building Products Ltd* [1995] Env LR 277.

15. See, e.g., *R v Secretary of State for the Environment, Transport and the Regions, ex parte Alliance against Birmingham Northern Relief Road (No. 1)* [1999] Env LR 447.

The authority is obliged to tell the applicant of the right to appeal the decision, first to the authority and, if not satisfied, to the Information Commissioner.

Where the application for information is refused, an applicant has various rights of appeal. First, there is a right to ask the public authority itself to reconsider its decision (Reg. 11). Following that there are consequent rights to appeal to the Information Commissioner (Reg. 18), the Information Tribunal (FOI, s. 58(1)) and to the High Court on a question of law (FOI, s. 59).

Public registers

Although the general right of access to environmental information under the 2004 Regulations represents a significant development in Britain, the traditional format of disclosure of pollution control information is through the system of statutory public registers. Although the statutory provisions vary depending upon the area of concern, there are common features in most of the pollution control registers. In these cases the common features include the following.

- *Availability of information.* Generally, information must be available at all reasonable times for inspection by the public free of charge. Copies of any document can be taken on payment of a reasonable charge. The registers are held at the principal offices of the relevant local authority or the regional office of the Environment Agency (in relation to the location of the operation which is the subject of the authorization or permissions).

- *Nature of the information.* The information on registers covers applications; details of permissions, authorizations, etc. including the name and address of the operator; particulars of any enforcement action or criminal actions; appeals; and information provided by the operator in order to comply with conditions (this normally includes self-monitoring data and spot samples of environmental releases). Records can generally be kept in any form (e.g. electronically).

- *Exemptions.* There are exemptions for certain classes of information where disclosure would affect national security or commercial confidentiality. Commercial confidentiality is defined by reference to whether disclosure would prejudice to an unreasonable degree the commercial interests of the person concerned (see, e.g., Environmental Protection Act 1990, ss. 22(11), 66(11), and 78T(10) in relation to IPC registers, waste management registers and contaminated land respectively and Water Resources Act 1991, s. 191B(11)). Where information is excluded from the register on the ground of commercial confidentiality, there is a statement in the register which indicates the existence of the information.

- *Rights of appeal.* The preliminary determination of whether a particular piece of information is commercially confidential lies with the regulatory body (usually the Environment Agency). There is a right of appeal against that determination to the Secretary of State within 21 days of provisional notification and until the appeal is finally decided the information is kept off the register.

The range of registers in environmental law is very large. Some of the most common can be found in Box 10.7.

BOX 10.7 The main environmental registers

Subject matter of register	Type of information	Relevant legislation	Agency responsible for keeping Information
Contaminated land	Notices identifying land as contaminated, remediation notices, appeals, remediation statements	EPA 1990, s. 78R The Contaminated Land (England) Regs 2000	EA (in relation to Special Sites); Local Authorities
GMOs	Particulars of environmental impact assessments, applications, prohibitions, consents granted	EPA 1990, s. 122 Genetically Modified Organisms (Deliberate Release) Regulations 2002	DEFRA
Industrial processes	Installations subject to IPPC	Pollution Prevention and Control Act 1999, Sch. 1 Pollution Prevention and Control (England and Wales) Regs 2000	EA Local Authorities
Planning	Environmental statements, planning applications, planning permissions, enforcement applications for planning permission	Town and Country Planning Act 1990, s. 69 Planning and Compulsory Purchase Act 2004 The Town and Country Planning (General Development) Order 1995	Local Authorities
Trade effluent	Consents for discharges of liquid waste to sewerage works, directions for discharges, agreements, notices	Water Industry Act 1991, s. 196	Sewerage Undertaker
Waste management	Details of waste management licences including enforcement and conditions	EPA 1990, s. 64 Waste Management Licensing Regulations 1994	EA
Water resources abstraction licenses	Abstraction licences and enforcement	Water Resources Act 1991, s. 189 Water Resources (Licences) Regulations 1965	EA

Subject matter of register	Type of information	Relevant legislation	Agency responsible for keeping Information
Water resources— discharge consents	Details of consents, compliance with conditions and enforcement	WRA 1991, ss.190, 191 The Control of Pollution (Applications, Appeals and Registers) Regs 1996	EA

Different classes of environmental information

There is an increasing recognition that the use of information can be an integral part of an environmental regulatory system in more sophisticated ways than through the provision of pollution data on public registers. There are, therefore, a number of broad, overlapping instruments which could be classified as 'information based'. Although such classifications are crude in the sense that they tend to be 'soft' and ill defined (often as a consequence of their voluntary nature) they paint a picture of how information can slot in to various aspects of the regulatory system.

Environmental reporting

In addition to mandatory disclosure of information in the form of statutory public regis-ters, many companies have developed a system of voluntary disclosure of environmental information through the provision of annual corporate environmental reports. Research indicates that 89 per cent of the FTSE All Share Index (570 companies) publish some environmental information as part of their annual reporting process.[16] Significantly, how-ever, many of these are criticized as lacking any depth or objective value with only 24 per cent of companies reporting quantitative data. One of the fundamental difficulties with corporate reporting is that there is no standard format for disclosure and the quality of the information can vary. The reports range from little more than one line references to the environment to detailed assessments of environmental impacts. Elements of a report could include a discussion of the environmental issues which are relevant to the business; legislative compliance and the result of any environmental audits of the business; informa-tion on releases to the environment (whether or not they are included on a public regis-ter); energy efficiency and other resource conservation issues; local issues; the setting of key performance indicators and targets for future environmental performance; a compara-tive analysis of performance within the relevant industrial sector; and the achievement of sustainable development targets. Many of these issues are covered in a rudimentary man-ner with more sophisticated analysis being dependent upon the development of environ-mental accounting which could place some of the matters covered into a corporate and financial context (e.g. by allocating a financial cost to the environmental impacts disclosed).

Environmental reporting has developed apace since the early 1990s. Part of the reason for this development has been external pressure from stakeholders (e.g. investors, environmental

16. Environment Agency, *Environmental Disclosures* (2004).

interest groups, and the general public) although it should be emphasized that internal corporate environmental responsibility and the competitive advantage to be gained from demonstrating environmental compliance and improvement (in relation to corporate clients) have also had a part to play. There are moves to formalize both the content of and the requirement to report. The International Standards Organization has published guidance on developing indicators of environmental performance (see ISO 14031). The first statutory requirement to report environmental impacts is found in proposals for the preparation and publication of Operating and Financial Reviews (OFRs).[17]

Real benefits can result from the process of voluntary disclosure. The most obvious benefit is that the public and other stakeholders have access to information about a company's operations which might not otherwise be disclosed. This might involve previously undisclosed qualitative (e.g. types of waste arisings) and quantitative (e.g. aggregated waste arisings) environmental information. In addition, the information will generally be in a format which can be easily communicated to and accessed by the public (e.g. via the internet). The second main benefit is internal to the company compiling the report. The preparation of an environmental report means that a company must be aware of and address the environmental impacts which it creates. This preparatory work can assist the company in identifying areas where environmental performance can be improved and/or cost savings made. The third benefit is that the publication of reports can set standards within an industry sector which others must follow. This could be on a simplistic level (e.g. the 'name and shame' policy adopted by government to isolate those companies which are not preparing environmental reports) or it could be more sophisticated in the sense that the presentation of comparative environmental performance indicators could set the standard within the industry sector.

In addition to this voluntary form of corporate environmental reporting there is a more formalized system of disclosing the environmental impacts of a business through the environmental management standard adopted under EC Regulation (1836/93) on Eco-management and Audit Scheme (known as EMAS). As part of the accreditation process, a business must publish a publicly available document outlining its environmental policy and targets for improvement. This written statement is subject to external and independent verification but there are potential weaknesses as a source of dependable environmental information (see further p. 267).

Environmental information to the consumer

Environmental information on products can assist consumer choice by facilitating a better assessment of the environmental impacts or costs which are involved in their production and thereby, on a theoretical level at least, internalize some of the external environmental costs (although there is a legitimate debate about the extent to which the consumption of consumer goods can 'benefit' the environment). The disclosure of information can, in conjunction with other instruments (e.g. product standards or economic instruments such as taxes or subsidies), help with the process of 'market transformation' whereby there is an

---

17. Under the draft Companies Act 1985 (Operating and Financial Review and Directors' Report etc.) Regulations 2005.

increase in the proportion of products which have lower environmental impacts whilst decreasing the proportion of products which bring about greater environmental harm.[18]

For example, a label could indicate the energy consumption of domestic central heating boilers. Secondly, there could be a ban on boilers with an energy efficiency rating below a certain standard. Finally, a financial grant could be made available to assist people who wanted to replace any boiler over 10 years old with a new boiler that came with a designated eco-label which indicated high levels of energy efficiency. The effect of these combined measures (the first and last of which are information instruments) would be to ensure that more energy efficient boilers were placed on the market.

The nature of this information can range from informal advertising information (often referred to as 'green claims') through more formal sectoral product certification schemes (e.g. timber products manufactured from sustainable managed timber certified by the Forest Stewardship Council, or the Marine Stewardship Council certifying sustainable fisheries) to official national eco-labelling schemes regulated by national authorities across a range of products with specific criteria for each product grouping (see below). Other matters which could be covered include information on the safe use, re-use, recycling, and disposal of products.

(a) Green claims

Once manufacturers recognized that environmental issues were a factor in purchasing decisions, they developed a range of green claims for their products which included meaningless and objectively immeasurable claims ('environmentally friendly') or statements which expressed a truism ('CFC free' in products after the implementation of the ban on CFCs). These sort of claims undermine the primary purpose of disclosure of this type of information to consumers (i.e. to differentiate objectively between different products). Although there are some safeguards against claims which are factually incorrect (under the Trade Descriptions Act 1968, s. 1 this would be a criminal offence), statements which are empty of meaning or axiomatic fall outside existing statutory control. The governmental response to this problem has been to rely on self-regulation by producing the *Green Claims Code*, a voluntary code of practice with all of the weaknesses that such self-regulatory systems possess.[19]

(b) Eco-labelling

One way of addressing some of the weaknesses of these green claims is to ensure that there is a consistent, objective, and identifiable symbol which can indicate to the consumer that a product has been assessed and approved against a set of approved criteria. The European eco-labelling scheme (originally under Regulation 880/92 which was replaced in 2000 with Regulations 980/2000) was designed to provide such a label in the shape of a characteristic blue and green flower. The scheme was launched across Member States in July 1993 and applied first in the UK to eco-labels on dishwashers and washing machines later that year.

The system of approval can be divided into three distinct phases. First, the European Commission classifies a product group after consulting and negotiating with interested parties (e.g. consumer groups, environmental interest groups and industry). Once the group

---

18. See DETR Consultation Paper, *Consumer Products and the Environment*, Oct. 1998.
19. The Code takes into account the international standard on environmental claims, ISO 14021.

is classified the criteria for the award are established (once again after consultation with stakeholders). The criteria for approval vary depending upon product groups but are generally associated with such things as raw materials consumption (e.g. water and detergent) in addition to a broader life cycle assessment.

The second phase sees the manufacturer applying to the national competent body for approval. In the UK, DEFRA deals with these applications. The third and final phase of the eco-labelling process is the revision of the product group criteria which, once again, is carried out by the European Commission.

The eco-labelling scheme has not been an overwhelming success either in terms of the quantity of the product groups which have been classified or the level of consumer or market interest. The scheme is perceived to be over-complicated, prescriptive in its criteria and too rigid.[20]

(c) Other forms of product certification

There are other product certification schemes which have had greater levels of acceptance and success than the eco-label. For example, at the European level, there is an 'energy label' under Directive 92/75 with subsequent daughter directives for particular appliances (see e.g. washing machines under Directive 95/12). At national level there are a number of sectoral labels such as the ones in the timber and fishing industries referred to above or a scheme designed to show the Volatile Organic Compound (VOC) content in paints promoted by the British Coating Federation. The main problem with this proliferation of schemes is that they tend to undermine the credibility and power of centralised labelling schemes with the inevitable consequences for the process of 'market transformation'.

Access to environmental information in Britain—an assessment

The broadening of access to environmental information over the last 20 or so years has not been without its criticisms.[21] Many of the problems encountered with the 1992 Regulations have been addressed through the clarifications found in the 2003 Directive and the transposing Regulations. The refining of certain definitions and extension of the scope and application of the Regulations in the light of experience should facilitate greater access. Much depends upon the interpretation of certain key matters by the Information Commissioner. In addition, the provision of information when requested is only part of the justification for more liberal access to information regimes. In many cases the information will require technical interpretation or may be presented in a way that presents data in a more favourable slant.[22]

Similarly, although the system of public registers provides an easy source of information about polluting activities, empirical evidence suggests that they are under-utilized by members of the general public.[23] There are a number of potential reasons for this which are primarily connected to the accessibility of the registers themselves and the quality and comprehensiveness of the information found on the registers. For example, raw monitoring

---

20. See, e.g., the consultation responses to *Consumer Products and the Environment*, DETR, Aug. 1999.
21. See, e.g., H. Jenn (1993) Water Law 163.
22. M. Lee and C. Abbot (2003) 66 MLR 93.
23. See, e.g., T. Burton (1989) 1 JEL 192 and J. Rowan-Robinson et al. (1996) 8 JEL 19.

data, of the sort which is found in the registers, often shows the results of single samples without providing 'non-experts' with a clear picture of overall levels of compliance. In most cases, there is no information relating to general environmental quality standards or the cumulative effects of releases into the environment.

The provisions within the regulations which are designed to promote the wider active dissemination of environmental information may assist in this regard. There have been a number of attempts to make pollution control information more accessible and user friendly specifically via the internet (in particular the Environment Agency's 'What's in your backyard?' web site <www.environment-agency.gov.uk> which sets out environmental data in a national, regional and local context) and general aggregated sources (see below). The greater availability of general information about the environment is part of a general shift away from the mere production of environmental data on pollution to a broader communication of the implications of activities in terms that people can understand. This is reflected in the moves towards active dissemination of information and the development of aggregated pollutant inventories (see Box 20.5).

Although access to such information can communicate on a much wider basis, it still has its limitations in the sense that it does little to capture the social or cultural aspects of environmental values (see further p. 57). For example, aggregated indicators may suggest that the loss of natural habitats has fallen on a year by year basis, but this might conceal the fact that in one village, a particularly important green space which has cultural significance has been lost to development. This example merely illustrates that there will be some aspects of environmental protection which only gain significance when viewed within the local context and as such, are difficult to capture as general information.

Public participation in environmental decision-making

There is a long history of public involvement in environmental decision-making. Typically, participation in the planning system through local consultation on planning applications and more general participation in development planning provided plenty of opportunities for the public to comment on development proposals and more strategic issues. Somewhat paradoxically, however, it has been argued that notwithstanding this long history of public involvement in the planning system, environmental regulation has been 'closed to public influence'.[24] This is because, in stark contrast to the planning system, most pollution control regimes had rudimentary notification and consultation processes and nature conservation decisions were almost entirely determined by experts without recourse to the general public. The reasons for this are largely concerned with the technical nature of such decisions. Other factors included the close relationship between industry and the regulators (see p. 296), the lack of transparency in decision-making and the large degree of discretion to set environmental standards (see p. 255).

This process of change has been relatively swift with increased participation in pollution control regimes and planning through the introduction of formal environmental impact

24. J. Steele (2001) OJLS 418.

assessment and the need to implement the requirements of the Aarhus Convention (see Arts. 6–9). This has led to the EC adopting Directive 2003/35/EC on public participation in certain environmental plans and programmes. The Directive provides for the public to have 'early and effective opportunities' to participate in the preparation and review of plans and programmes made under six existing EC Directives dealing with nitrates, waste, hazardous waste, packaging, batteries, and air-quality management. The Directive did not require wholesale changes to UK law although certain amendments to participation rights in respect of certain programmes have been added. For example, the Air Quality Limit Values (Amendment) (England) Regulations 2004 amended the requirement to consult on local air quality plans. Previously the local authority had had a discretion as to whether to consult the public on such plans with a duty only to consult business interests and statutory consultees. Under the regulations, there are formal requirements to inform the public about such plans, to take account of the results of public consultations, and to explain the decisions taken.

The increased emphasis upon participation in decision-making was taken up by the RCEP in its 21st Report, *Setting Environment Standards*,[25] which called for 'a more rigorous and wide-ranging exploration of people's values' at the 'earliest stage' in what had been 'hitherto relatively technocratic procedures' (see para 9). The RCEP called for more deliberative techniques in which the public played a significant role in setting strategies rather than being consulted on already drafted proposals (para. 7.22).

Types of public participation

On a very general level public participation consists of attempts to influence law, policies, and individual decisions made by Governmental or regulatory bodies. This involves many different things but it includes being able to have access to, understand, evaluate, formulate and comment upon proposals, plans and programmes. It can take the form of:

- Pluralistic participation where representative bodies such as NGOs or industry associations speak on behalf of individuals.
- Stakeholder participation where proposals which have already been formulated are transmitted to interested parties to comment upon and refine.
- Deliberative participation which consists of 'agreeing the ground rules', i.e. involving the public in determining what general policies and strategies should be adopted before moving to the stage of specific proposals.

In addition participation can have differing degrees of legal force. For example in environmental impact assessment, public participation is a mandatory substantive requirement which is a pre-condition of the grant of planning permission (see below). In many other situations participation is facilitated through a procedural 'right' to be consulted or heard at an inquiry. In other circumstances consultation takes place voluntarily in an attempt to use 'best practice' or to elicit values to settle issues of environmental risk (see Box 10.8).

25. Cm 4053 (1998).

BOX 10.8 **Participation and environmental risk—the Agriculture and Biotechnology Commission**

In 1999, in response to the growing public uncertainty about genetically modified crops and foods, the Government reviewed the advisory and regulatory framework for biotechnology. The conclusions were that opinions on the topic were deeply divided and that more effort was needed to involve the public in the debate about what should be done. Consequently the Agriculture and Biotechnology Commission (ABEC) was formed. The Commission's membership was deliberately taken from people with a wide range of views on the topic with a view to seeking expert opinion from all sides of the debate. It includes industry representatives, green activists, media personalities and a philosopher. Its role is to advise the Government on how to address the issues associated with GM crops and foods and in doing so it is obliged to consider ethical and social issues in addition to the more usual scientific considerations. The Commission has produced three reports but its main role in promoting public participation was the national debate on GM foods run in the Summer of 2003. Entitled *GM Nation?* this involved a series of workshops to frame the debate followed by over 600 meetings held across the country involving thousands of people. The headline results of the exercise were:

- People are generally uneasy about GM.
- The more people engage in GM issues, the harder their attitudes and more intense their concerns.
- There is little support for early commercialization of GM.
- There is widespread mistrust of government and multi-national companies.
- There is a broad desire to know more and for further research to be done.
- Developing countries have special interests.
- The debate was welcomed and valued.

That such efforts were expended upon seeking to elicit views from the wider public and the extent to which the evidence was put in an objective and comprehensive manner was unique in environmental regulation. Perhaps the results were unsurprising but the process was remarkable.

One of the central challenges of public participation is seeking to ensure that the *quality* of the participation is sufficient to actively engage the public and that proper opportunity is given to respond to any consultation exercise. In particular the importance of public participation as a fundamental rationale for undertaking an environmental impact assessment was consistently ignored by the judiciary (see p. 547). A number of early cases tended to view public participation as the 'icing on the cake' of what was merely an information gathering exercise. Thus in *R v Poole Borough Council, ex p. Beebee* [1991] JPL 643, the absence of an environmental statement and any public participation which would have produced it was considered to be superfluous as the necessary information was already before the planning authority (see p. 544).

This approach seemed to fly in the face of the original EIA Directive which was to provide a procedural framework so as to guarantee that the environmental impact of a project was a part of the public debate and informed the resulting decisions. In *Berkeley v Secretary of*

State for the Environment [2001] Env LR 16 ('*Berkeley (No. 1)*'), the House of Lords considered the role of public participation in the EIA process. The Lords emphasized that an important part of the environmental assessment procedure was to provide the public with all of the relevant information in a rational and digestible form, then facilitating public comment on that information. Thus it was the *process* of consultation which was important even if the result was informed by the public's 'misguided or wrongheaded views'. The *process* was designed to give the public an opportunity to express its opinion.

Access to environmental justice

The final aspect of facilitating public participation in environmental law is ensuring that there is adequate access to a means of enforcing environmental law or in seeking redress in resolving environmental disputes. This can have different aspects including the right to bring private prosecutions (see p. 294) or to bring private law actions with an environmental element (see Chapter 11). Under the Aarhus Convention this is referred to as access to justice in environmental matters.[26] Article 9(2) of the Convention provides that anyone who has a 'sufficient interest' shall be able to 'challenge the substantive or procedural legality of any decision, act or omission'. In the absence of third party rights to appeal in relation to administrative appeals the main 'right' to challenge the legality of administrative decisions in the UK courts comes through the mechanism of judicial review (see p. 475).

Thus, the focus of this section is mainly on procedural matters (e.g. a right to bring a judicial review) and structural issues (e.g. the establishment of an environmental court) as opposed to the quality of substantive decisions provided by the legal system. In this context it should be noted that 'justice' is probably not the most appropriate word to describe the objective of environmental law. Arguably, at least, that objective should be more accurately characterized as ensuring that the environment is properly protected. Whether environmental law meets that objective is a substantive question which should be addressed separately from whether procedures and structures function efficiently.

Judicial review

The process of judicial review is one way of making public bodies accountable to the courts and ensuring that they only act within the powers given to them by Parliament. Accordingly, judicial review addresses the legality and not the merits of a decision. The legality of a decision comprises two different aspects. Procedural legality ensures that people have a right to a fair hearing and that there should be no bias (or perception of bias) in a decision-making process. In circumstances where there is procedural illegality a court will overturn the decision but send the issue back to the original decision-maker to be redetermined.

On the other hand, where there is substantive illegality, courts overturn decisions made which are illegal either because they are unfair, unreasonable, or unlawful. The exact grounds of judicial review are not necessarily clearly defined. For example the edges between

---

26. See, in the EC context, the proposal for an implementing Directive COM(2003) 624.

unreasonableness, irrelevancy, and disproportionality are blurred. A right to challenge an illegal decision in this sense should not be confused with any statutory right of appeal, which may give rise to a reconsideration of the merits of a case, rather than consideration of questions of law. Indeed, theoretically, a court exercising its power of judicial review is not entitled to substitute its own decision for that of the administrative body. This general right to challenge administrative decisions is supplemented in certain cases by specific statutory rights to challenge decisions. For example, section 288 of the Town and Country Planning Act 1990 makes provision for High Court challenges to decisions of the Secretary of State on points of law. Although there are procedural distinctions between the two types of challenge (in particular there are often much stricter time limits), the substantive issues remain broadly the same. It is important to note, however, that the statutory challenge is often an exclusive power which prevents any further challenge under general judicial review proceedings.

There is also the increasingly important issue of the overlap of judicial review with the right to seek a remedy under the Human Rights Act 1998. Human Rights arguments have merged with arguments over illegality in judicial review actions.[27] Concepts such as proportionality have also emerged, taken from European law to further extend notions of illegality. These points merely emphasize the fluid nature of judicial review and the extent to which grounds of challenge emerge over time.

In examining judicial review as a tool for enhancing access to justice in environmental matters there are a number of factors which must be taken into account. There are certain legal hurdles which must be overcome before bringing a claim. (These are in addition to the hurdle of cost, which can deter otherwise meritous claims although it is notable that the Legal Services Commission appears to recognize the general public interest of environmental judicial review.) In order to bring a judicial review a claimant must have:

* standing (i.e. a 'sufficient interest' in the subject matter of the decision being challenged);
* commenced proceeding promptly;
* no other avenue of redress.

Standing

In order to bring a claim for judicial review, an applicant must show a 'sufficient interest' in the decision or power to which the application relates (Supreme Court Act 1981, s. 31(3)). In many cases a sufficient interest is created directly through the holding of a relevant pollution control licence or authorisation to which the application relates.

The basis of the law on standing is contained in *Inland Revenue Commissioners v National Federation of Self Employed and Small Businesses Ltd* [1982] AC 617, where Lord Wilberforce said that the decision as to who had a 'sufficient interest' under the Supreme Court Act 1981, s. 31 had to be considered with the known merits of a case:

It will be necessary to consider the powers or the duties of those against whom the relief is asked, the position of the applicant in relation to those powers or duties, and to the breach of those

---

27. It has been found that human rights arguments are invoked in almost 50% of all judicial review cases, see Public Law Project *The impact of the Human Rights Act on judicial review: An empirical Research Study* (London: Public Law Project, 2003).

duties said to have been committed. In other words, the question of sufficient interest cannot, in such cases, be considered in the abstract, or as an isolated point: it must be taken together with the legal and factual context.

More generally, it is clear that somebody with a private interest in land affected by an administrative decision would have 'sufficient interest' or standing. This can be expanded to include those who are living in proximity to an area which is affected by a decision although there would appear to be some limitations (see Box 10.9).

BOX 10.9 **Proximity and standing**

In *R (Edwards) v Environment Agency* [2004] Env LR 43, the claimant had lived in Rugby all of his life although he was temporarily homeless. He sought to challenge the grant of an IPPC permit by the Environment Agency to a local cement company. The claimant had played no part in the consultation process although he had attended meetings of a local campaign group. The Agency argued that as he was not an active participant in the consultation process he did not have a 'sufficient interest' in the application. In addition, it was argued that he had been put forward as the claimant purely on the ground that he could secure funding from the Legal Services Commission to bring the action. The Court held that the claimant had standing even if he was temporarily homeless, because as an inhabitant of Rugby he would be affected by any adverse impact on the environment from the cement works. The arguments about funding were also rejected.

In contrast, in *R v North West Leicestershire District Council ex parte Moses* [2000] JPL 733, an applicant sought to challenge various decisions to extend the runway at East Midlands International Airport. At the time of the decision and when she had applied for judicial review she had lived close to the end of the runway. Since that time she had moved some six miles away from the airport. The Court held that since moving the applicant no longer had a 'sufficient interest' in the proceedings. The Court considered that had she lived six miles away at the time of the decision she would have had no more interest in the decision than if she had lived in the 'Orkney or Shetland Islands'. This decision reflects a relatively limited view of the nature of the possible environmental impacts from the extension of a runway. It could equally be argued that a resident six miles away could be affected by indirect impacts such as an increase in noise or road transport associated with an expanding airport. It should be noted that on appeal to the Court of Appeal, the decision was made on different grounds.

It is, however, more difficult to show that a person has the necessary standing by virtue of an interest in the environment as a whole, as it is not generally accepted that there are 'environmental rights' available to the public at large. This raises the question of representational or public interest standing. In the planning system many actions have been brought by local interest groups where sufficient interest can be demonstrated by objecting to proposals or giving evidence at a local inquiry and an analogy can be drawn in relation to groups bringing challenges in connection with local environmental issues (e.g. waste management licences, statutory nuisances, or local air pollution). The position of general environmental interest groups (e.g. Friends of the Earth or Greenpeace) is more problematic as there is no necessary geographic connection with the matter being challenged. As Box

10.10 illustrates a significant number of judicial review actions are brought by representative bodies with a good percentage being brought by environmental NGOs.

BOX 10.10 **Estimated number of public interest court cases brought by environmental NGOs, citizen groupings or individuals: 1995–2001** [28]

Category of applicant	Total number of cases
Established environmental NGOs (e.g. Greenpeace, FoE)	25
Ad hoc identifiable grouping (e.g. the Crystal Palace Campaign)	20
Ad hoc collection of individuals (e.g. representing village residents)	21
Individual applicants reflecting a community concern (e.g. parents)	34
Individual applicants defending public interests (e.g. on radio masts)	8
Other (e.g. complaints engaging public environmental interest)	2

The Courts have taken an increasingly liberal approach to standing for representational bodies (see Box 10.11).

BOX 10.11 **Representational standing**

In *R v Secretary of State for the Environment ex parte Rose Theatre Trust* [1990] 1 All ER 754 a group of objectors to the redevelopment of the Rose Theatre banded together to form a Trust Company to challenge the decision not to list the site of the Theatre as protected under the Ancient Monuments and Archaeological Areas Act 1979. The Court rejected the application for judicial review on the basis that the Trust did not have standing to bring the action. Schiemann J. found that the mere assertion of an interest was not, in itself, sufficient to demonstrate sufficient interest even if made by 'thousands of people'. He stated:

it would be absurd if two people, neither of whom had standing could, by an appropriately worded memorandum, incorporate themselves into a company which thereby obtained standing.

This low point on representational standing was doubted in *R v Inspectorate of Pollution, ex parte Greenpeace Ltd (No. 2)* [1994] 4 All ER 329, in which Greenpeace challenged the decision to allow the thermal oxide reprocessing plant at Sellafield (THORP) to commence operations. Pointing to Greenpeace's genuine interest in the issues raised and to its expertise and resources, Otton J decided that the group had sufficient interest, although he did note that it also had many members in the region who might be affected. In *R v Secretary of State for Foreign and Commonwealth Affairs, ex parte World Development Movement Ltd* [1995] 1 WLR 386 (the *Pergau Dam* case), the court, if anything, went even further in allowing a pure public interest claim to proceed, since there were clearly no local residents involved. In particular, it was emphasised that if the applicants were not granted standing then a clear illegality would not be sub ject to challenge.

28. M. Sheridan, United Kingdom Report in N. de Sadeleer, G. Roller and M. Dross (eds) *Access to Justice in Environmental Matters and the Role of NGOs; Empirical Findings and Legal Appraisal* (Groeningen: Europa Law Publishing, 2005).

Although general environmental interest groups have become increasingly accepted as having standing in judicial review actions, there is still a degree of uncertainty and there have been cases where the courts have required a special interest in the subject matter of the challenge (e.g. see *R v North Somerset District Council, ex parte Garnett* [1998] Env LR 91). In *R v Somerset County Council, ex parte Dixon* [1998] Env LR 111, however, the decision in *Pergau Dam* was reaffirmed and the law on standing continued to be liberalised. In that case, the answer to the question of who had sufficient interest in the subject matter of the challenge was wide enough to include anyone who was not a busybody or a troublemaker. Public law challenges were concerned with the abuse of power, not the protection of private rights and therefore the classes of those who sought to draw attention to those abuses must include anyone who had a genuine interest in the subject matter of the challenge irrespective of any private law interest. There is a degree of contradiction in the cases of *Garnett* and *Dixon*. The two cases were strikingly similar in their facts with very different results. Whilst these differences emphasize the discretionary nature of judicial review proceedings, they also illustrate that there is little precedent value in previous decisions.

Challenges brought under the Human Rights Act 1998 are slightly different. As an assertion of rights is linked to the individual it is only a person who is a 'victim' of the rights abuse who can claim standing. A person who cannot show that he or she is personally affected by the law to a greater extent than any other person may not claim to be a victim. Thus there are no rights to bring a representative action for human rights breaches. For example, in *Adams v Advocate General for Scotland* (2002) UKHRR 1189, the Countryside Alliance and the Masters of the Foxhounds association sought to challenge the ban on foxhunting under the Protection of Wild Mammals (Scotland) Act 2002. The Court held that as representative bodies they did not have sufficient standing because some of the members of the group who lived outside Scotland would not have been affected by the ban. Similarly in *R v Mayor of London ex parte Westminster City Council* [2002] EWHC 2440, a challenge to the London congestion charge on the grounds of an inadequate environmental impact assessment and breaches of human rights failed because Westminster City Council did not fall within the definition of a 'victim' for the purposes of the Human Rights Act (on the EIA aspects, see p. 520).

It should be noted that there is one exception to all of this. The Attorney-General, as guardian of the public interest, always has standing. An applicant without 'sufficient interest' could therefore ask the Attorney-General to bring an action on their behalf. This is called a 'relator' action. The shadow applicant pays the costs but manages to side-step the rules on standing. However, the Attorney-General has an unchallengeable discretion whether to bring an action in this manner.

Delay

The second procedural hurdle for any application for judicial review is that the application must be made 'promptly'. Under Order 53, r. 4(1) and the Supreme Court Act 1981, s. 31(6), a court must refuse an application for permission or grant any relief where there has been a lack of promptness, unless there are good reasons for extending the time or it is unlikely that the persons affected by the grant of the relief would suffer hardship or prejudice.

There are three aspects to the issue of delay. The first relates to the time limit which is laid down for particular applications to be made. For example, challenges to planning decisions made by the Secretary of State must be brought within six weeks from the Secretary of State's decision (Town and Country Planning Act 1990, s. 288) whereas Order 53 applications must be brought within three months of the decision which is being challenged. The overlap between these two time limits was recognized by the courts by the adoption of an informal rule that applications should be made within the six-week period if they were to be considered 'prompt' (see *R v Ceredigion County Council, ex parte McKeown* (1998) 2 PLR 1). Thus applications which have not been made 'promptly' but fall within the longer three month time period can be dismissed (see *R v Swale BC, ex parte RSPB* [1991] 1 PLR 6 where an application for leave was made 10 weeks after the decision but was dismissed for lack of 'promptness') and applications made outside the period can be permitted where there are good reasons to do so. This practice was criticized by the House of Lords in *Burkett* in which the Lords emphasized the need to consider the three-month time limit and all the circumstances of the case (see Box 10.12).

BOX 10.12 **Time limits and delay**

In *R v Hammersmith LBC ex parte Burkett* [2003] Env LR 6, the applicant sought a judicial review of a decision to grant planning permission for a mixed use development of Imperial Wharf in London. The local planning authority had resolved to grant the permission, subject to a call-in by the Secretary of State. The Secretary of State declined to call in the application, and so outline permission was granted some eight months after the original resolution to grant permission. B had applied for judicial review, over a month before the final grant of permission, on the grounds that the Environmental Impact Assessment carried out had been inadequate. The application was refused at first instance and at the Court of Appeal on the grounds of delay. Time was taken to run from the date of the resolution to grant permission if the grounds for objection to the application had not changed. The House of Lords, however, rejected the idea that there was a six-week time limit for challenges to planning decisions, stating that this could not be displaced by a 'judicial policy decision'. The Lords also clarified the point that time only started to run when the planning permission was granted and not at the time of the resolution to grant. The rationale for the Lords decision appears to have been a desire to ensure a clear, definable time limit that potential claimants can rely upon when determining whether and when to challenge a decision. This ties in with the need to ensure compatibility with Article 6 of the European Convention on Human Rights. A settled time limit is much more likely to result in a fair trial rather than relying upon potentially uncertain discretionary judgments. In addition, there are added practical advantages in a specific time limit including giving flexibility to promote negotiated settlements prior to the deadline rather than applicants being forced to issue proceedings in order to avoid arguments about delay.

The second aspect of delay is the issue of when the time for challenge starts to run. Clearly, the decision-making process can have a number of stages from informal resolution to conditional and full permission. In addition, it may become clear, early on in the decision-making process, that an error of law has been made (e.g. taking into account an irrelevant consideration). Order 53, r. 4(2) makes it clear that time starts to run from the date on which grounds for the application first rose which is not necessarily the same as the date on which any final decision is made. If an application is made too early, there is a risk that it will be premature, too late and it will not have been made promptly. A lot of the uncertainty in relation to planning cases was removed by the decision of the House of Lords in *Burkett* where the Lords held that the trigger date was the grant of planning permission (see Box 10.12). In other areas the question is not necessarily as clear cut. A good example can be found in *R v Secretary of State for Trade and Industry, ex parte Greenpeace Limited* [1998] Env LR 413, where Greenpeace sought to challenge the grant of licences to explore for North Sea oil, on the ground that the decision-making process was contrary to the requirements of the Habitats Directive (some of the areas subject to the licences were the habitat of a protected species under the Directive). Greenpeace sought to challenge the decision to grant licences which was made in April 1997. The court dismissed the application on the basis that any application should have been made much earlier (i.e. before November 1995) when it was probable that licences would be granted in breach of the Directive.

The third aspect of delay is the question of extending the time for bringing an application beyond the need for 'promptness'. Generally, the courts have taken a strict line over the question of delay in environmental cases. The speed or otherwise of an application would appear to depend largely upon whether an affected third party would have suffered prejudice. This might include such things as spending large sums of money after being granted permission or a licence to do something (see e.g. *R v Secretary of State for Trade and Industry, ex parte Greenpeace Limited* [1998] Env LR 413 and *Mass Energy Limited v Birmingham CC* [1994] Env LR 298), or doing other things in reliance on the grant of permission (e.g. commencing development). The extent of this prejudice can be minimized by the applicant putting the affected third party on notice of potential proceedings.

Notwithstanding the decision of the House of Lords in *Burkett*, the ground of delay still allows the courts some discretion to determine applications for judicial review in accordance with general principles such as fairness, good administration, and prejudice. This discretion can, however, also be used to override any unfairness, where it is in the public interest to do so (e.g. where there have been clear and serious breaches of European legislation). In *R v Secretary of State for Trade and Industry, ex parte Greenpeace (No. 2)* [2000] Env LR 221, in which Greenpeace brought a second challenge to the grant of oil exploration licences, Maurice Kay J considered that the application for judicial review had not been made 'promptly' (thus mirroring the first challenge discussed above). He went on, however, to find that the implementation of the Habitats Directive had been incomplete within UK law (in particular in relation to offshore habitats) and that the failure to implement the Directive was more important than any prejudice which would have been caused by the delay in making the application.

Judicial review and other avenues of challenge

Although judicial review remains as one way of challenging a decision which has been made unlawfully, there are, in some cases, alternative remedies for aggrieved parties by way of a statutory right to administrative appeal. When considering the appropriate avenue of challenge, the courts have established two tests. First, would the statutory appeal process afford an adequate alternative remedy? If so, any application for permission to seek a judicial review would be refused. The adequacy of the statutory right of appeal as an alternative remedy is dependent upon a number of variables, including comparative speed, expense, and finality of the alternative procedure; the need and scope for fact finding; the desirability of an authoritative ruling on any point of law arising; and the apparent strength of the applicant's challenge (see *R v Falmouth & Truro Port Health Authority, ex parte South West Water Limited* [2000] NPC 36 and see also *R v Environment Agency, ex parte Petrus Oils Ltd* [1999] Env LR 732, where the court found that there was an adequate alternative remedy available to challenge the service of a revocation notice under Part I of the EPA 1990).

In the third situation, where a collateral challenge is brought (i.e. as an incidental challenge to the main proceedings) the courts have dismissed such challenges as being an abuse of process where the decision which is being challenged was made many years before and the period for statutory challenge had passed (see *R v Ettrick Trout Company Limited* [1994] Env LR 165).

The usefulness of judicial review

How useful is judicial review as a mechanism for promoting public participation and controlling the activities and decision-making of environmental bodies? As seen above, there are various procedural hurdles which must be overcome before an application for permission to bring a judicial review action will be granted, such as having standing, bringing any application 'promptly' and ensuring that there are no alternative adequate remedies available. The main problem here is not with the hurdles themselves but that the determination of whether an applicant succeeds in 'jumping the hurdles' is largely discretionary and rests with the particular judge hearing the case. Although the basic principles of standing and delay are laid down, the manner in which these principles are applied within the factual context of an individual application can vary depending upon the way in which a judge views the purposes of the procedural hurdles. Different judges can approach similar issues in entirely different ways. This discretion naturally leads to a degree of uncertainty as to whether an applicant might succeed, which in turn reduces the likelihood that an action will be taken.

In addition to these procedural hurdles, there is the difficult question of funding the cost of a judicial review action. As most environmental actions tend to be brought on a representative basis (either from local groups or interested parties), there is little direct financial interest in the outcome of an application (although there is a notable exception in the planning arena where commercial developers feature largely). The costs of going to litigation can be high particularly when considering that legal aid is seldom available in judicial review cases (see *R v Legal Aid Area No. 8 (Northern), ex parte Sendall* [1993] Env LR 167, although there are notable exceptions including cases where children have been selected as applicants in particular cases, see, for example, *R v Secretary of State for Trade and Industry, ex parte Duddridge* [1995] Env LR 151).

An extra pressure upon applicants is the fact that costs in judicial review proceedings normally follow the event, meaning that where an applicant loses (either at the full hearing or at the stage of seeking permission) they are normally obliged to pay the costs of the other side (again there are notable exceptions to this rule, in particular see *R v Secretary of State for the Environment, ex parte Greenpeace Limited* [1994] Env LR 401 where there was no award of costs against the applicant as the application was considered to be brought 'in the public interest').

Although the procedural issues and the costs of taking action represent significant factors in deciding whether to pursue a judicial review action, other factors also play a part in reducing the effectiveness of judicial review. For many individuals or interest groups a three-month time limit represents a very short period in which to receive notice of any decision, understand the implications, take legal advice, raise funds and possibly negotiate with the body making the decision. In many circumstances a potentially valid claim will not be brought because the uncertainties of bringing a claim may be unresolved within the three-month period. Secondly, the remedies which are available may be unsatisfactory or unsuitable. For example any attempt to prevent an unlawful operation taking place would need to be dealt with by way of interim injunction which prevents any further action until a full hearing. Such an injunction must be supported by an applicant giving an undertaking in damages which would mean that if the applicant was unsuccessful at the full hearing they would be obliged to pay for any loss of profit resulting from the halting of the activity in question. In.the case of certain projects this can amount to considerable sums of money.

Thirdly, when an application for judicial review is heard, there is no consideration of the merits of a case. Thus, when a decision is quashed or a duty is enforced, it does not necessarily mean that the final decision of the administrative body will be to the liking of the person seeking judicial review. A good example of this is in the case of the judicial review of planning decisions. If an inspector, on appeal, makes a decision which is contrary to the Inquiries Procedure Rules (for instance by not taking into account written representations from objectors), the resulting decision may be challenged. The inspector's decision in those circumstances could be overturned by the High Court, but the final decision would be referred back to a fresh inspector, who could very well arrive at the same decision as the first inspector, even though taking into account the representations made.

Furthermore, where individuals with 'sufficient interest' apply for judicial review of a decision they have to be able to show that they have suffered prejudice. Therefore, although the court is not entitled to make a judgment on the merits of the individual case, it may be that the substance of the point raised by the interested party shows an unlawful act, but, on the facts of the individual case, the applicant did not suffer any prejudice from the decision itself. Thus, where an interested party was not entitled to put its views across at a planning inquiry, there may well be a breach of the right to a fair hearing. However, where it could be shown that other people had put over a similar case, a judicial review remedy may be refused.

The Ombudsman

There may be instances where, although there is no abuse of the statutory power which would render a decision reviewable, there is some maladministration which could give rise to a public complaint. In such cases a complaint can be made to the Ombudsman in control of those activities. In the case of central government activities (e.g. DEFRA) the investigating Ombudsman is the Parliamentary Commissioner for Administration, whereas in the case of complaints against a local authority (e.g. in relation to planning, waste collection or air pollution matters), the matter is dealt with by the Commissioner for Local Administration. The governing factor in such complaints is whether or not the authority concerned has acted within appropriate standards of administrative conduct, rather than whether or not it has acted lawfully.

Complaints to the Ombudsman normally go through either a local councillor or an MP (depending upon the level of authority concerned), although they need not do so in all cases. The nature of the Ombudsman remedy is both singular and advisory. Therefore, an aggrieved party who has other rights of action, whether under the common law or by means of judicial review, must pursue that particular avenue, as long as it is realistic to do so. Secondly, an Ombudsman has no statutory power to impose an award of damages, or to alter the legal position (e.g. by quashing a decision). Normally, the Ombudsman will make a recommendation for compensation which, although having no statutory backing, is accepted by the statutory body concerned in over 95 per cent of cases. The role of the Ombudsman should not be underestimated. The incidence of complaints to the Ombudsman has risen in recent years because it is a quick, cheap, and often effective mechanism for channelling complaints about public authorities. It is a mechanism which the public are happy to utilise because of its informal nature and simple procedure. It is perhaps worthwhile to point out that the stages of a complaint are relatively straightforward and provide an adequate opportunity for the proper presentation of grievances. It is also important that the Ombudsman has significant investigatory powers: these will have an impact on the practices of the public bodies over which jurisdiction is exercised.

Other complaints mechanisms

In the case of the privatized utilities, the regulators (e.g. Ofwat) act as a controlling influence through various means such as the amendment of undertakers' licences and more informal mechanisms (such as threats of action in the case of continuous underperformance). The effectiveness of the Ombudsman in dealing with maladministration in central and local government and the alternative avenues of redress in relation to the utilities can be contrasted with the gaping accountability hole in relation to other important bodies with environmental responsibilities such as the Environment Agency, English Nature and the Regional Development Agencies. In cases of public bodies such as these, incompetence, unfairness or otherwise unsatisfactory performance can only be dealt with by way of internal complaints procedures.

An Environmental Court

There is a relatively long history of criticism of the existing arrangements for access to justice in environmental matters in the UK. A number of commentators including senior judges and academics have led the call to establish a specialist environmental court or tribunal. A specialist court would not be unique by any means since such courts have existed in Australia for many years.[29] New South Wales has a Land and Environment Court which was

29. Environmental courts in other jurisdictions are outlined in M. Grant, *Environmental Court Project: Final Report* (DETR, 2000).

established as long ago as 1980 as a Court of Record.[30] This court consists of judges and technical assessors and deals with criminal prosecutions, civil enforcement, appeals, and judicial reviews in relation to a range of planning and environmental legislation.[31] Proceedings are open to *any* person and there is great flexibility in terms of procedures and remedies. Similarly, South Australia has an Environmental Resources and Development Court which effectively started work in 1994. This is also a Court of Record, chaired by a judge and sitting with two lay members, whose qualifications will vary according to the nature of the case. It deals with criminal prosecutions and civil enforcement as well as appeals under a range of planning and environmental legislation. The procedures and powers are very flexible and include a mandatory pre-trial conference and that decisions are made to equitably reflecting the the substantial merits of the case.[32]

Returning to the UK, the first main proponent of a specialist Court was Sir Harry Woolf (who was to become the country's most senior judge) who suggested the creation of a special tribunal with general responsibility for overseeing and enforcing environmental law. It was to be a 'one-stop shop', combining services carried out by courts, tribunals and inspectors. He suggested an environmental division of the High Court rather than changing basic pre-existing structures. His proposals are outlined in Box 10.13.

BOX 10.13 **Woolf's proposals**[33]

Woolf suggested that a specialist tribunal should have:

- Discretion to determine its own simple and user friendly procedures.
- Power to appoint specialist members.
- Inquisitorial-type fact finding powers (similar to the current inquiry system).
- An informal and multi-disciplinary approach.
- Power to make ancillary enforcement decisions, e.g. on compensation, punishment, and public law remedies.
- Discretion to determine issues about standing, representation, and costs.
- An appeal structure with an appeal on a point of law to the Court of Appeal.

Another soon-to-be High Court Judge Robert Carnwath pursued these arguments, proposing an Environmental Division of the High Court probably supplemented by a second-tier tribunal or court operating at a lower level. Alternatively he suggested a unified tribunal answering to the 'needs of customers' to which the adjudicatory and sanctioning roles of planning and environmental law could be entrusted. He suggested combining the

---

30. Under the Land and Environment Court Act 1979 see P. Stein, 'A Specialist Environmental Court: An Australian Experience' in D. Robinson and J. Dunkley (eds), *Public Interest Perspectives in Environmental Law* (Chichester: Wiley Chancery, 1994) and see P. Stein, 'Specialist environmental courts: the Land and Environmental Court of New South Wales, Australia' (2002) Env L Rev 5.

31. For an up-to-date summary see P. Ryan (2002) 14 JEL 301.

32. W. Upton (1994) 1 Env Law 12.

33. See Sir Harry Woolf (1992) 3 JEL 1.

Planning Inspectorate with a High Court Environment Division, with a two-tier structure for appeals and review.[34]

Both Woolf and Carnwath point out the advantage such a tribunal would have in ensuring the consistent development of principles in a manner that is often incapable of achievement in the courts as presently constituted because environmental issues come before too many different courts and judges in too many different forms. Carnwath also added that a specialist court could have an important impact on the development of EC and international environmental law. Both Woolf and Carnwath put a high value on any suggested court being allowed to develop in an evolutionary manner and proposed leaving a number of matters to be developed by the court itself.

Taking a slightly different tack, McAuslan proposed an Environmental Court or tribunal which would 'help us forward into the new era of a more conscious and deliberate balancing of development and environmental protection, and a more knowledgeable weighing of risks, liabilities, and rights'.[35] On the surface, his court would be similar in structure to Woolf's. In substance, however, McAuslan proposed a model which went beyond traditional adjudicatory or dispute resolution types of court to one which was 'investigative' taking a 'pro-active role' and serving as an advisory body to all other courts on scientific and technical matters.[36]

The debate moved on in 1999 with official recognition of the need to examine the role of an environmental Court. The then DETR commissioned a report from Professor Malcolm Grant in which he identified both a number of fundamental characteristics of an environmental court or tribunal and a number of alternative models for an environmental court in England and Wales. He too favoured a two-tier judicial model with the lower tier dealing with merit based decisions which were reviewable by the second tier on questions of law.[37]

These proposals were considered but rejected by the Government in the House of Lords.[38] More modest proposals for reform have been made subsequently by the Royal Commission on Environment Pollution and in a Report commissioned by DEFRA.[39] These consist of extending the current tribunal system to deal with a wide range of environmental matters including such things as statutory nuisance and contaminated land appeals, currently dealt with by the Magistrates Court.[40]

All of these different proposals represent two different perspectives on the structural problems associated with access to justice in environmental matters. The vast majority of commentators (Woolf, Carnwath, Grant, RCEP, and UCL) see the issue as primarily a practical/professional problem, where the central dilemma is how to provide properly for cases that have an environmental element in the light of the perception that the significant features of environmental cases mean that they often sit uneasily in current legal structures. The uncharitable view is that this could be characterised as starting from the understanding that the system does not work from the practising lawyer's point of view. More charitably, it could be said that the system does not work properly from the claimant's point of view.

---

34. R. Carnwath (1992) 4 JPL 799.   35. P. McAuslan (1991) JEL 195.

36. Adopting the suggestions of Trubatch [1985] 10 Col Jo of Env Law 255.

37. M. Grant, *Environmental Court Project: Final Report* (DETR, 2000).

38. 617, H.L. Debate, 9 Oct. 2000, cols 86–100.

39. See RCEP 23rd Report, *Environmental Planning* (Cm 5459, 2002) and R. Macrory and M. Woods, *Modernising Environmental Justice: Regulation and the Role of an Environmental Tribunal* (London: UCL, 2003).

40. In relation to Contaminated Land appeals, the current Clean Neighbourhood and Environment Act 2005 transfers these powers to the Secretary of State.

McAuslan sees the issue as being more concerned with participation and deliberation. An Environmental Court should be concerned with taking complex policy decisions and therefore his proposal reflects the need for principled decision making for decisions with an environmental element. This is what enables him to move beyond the traditional models of adjudication and dispute resolution to one which involves the Court seeking different views in arriving at decisions on how to manage the environment.

Experience with the Land and Environment Court in Australia suggest that there have been 'unrealistic expectations'; 'misunderstanding about the Court's role'; 'unmet expectations' concerning how different interests would be balanced, and 'perceptions of Court bias' in favour of developers.[41] Largely this is because the adequacy of any specialist court may be judged by some in terms of its ability to enhance environmental protection. These reactions reflect the fact that a specialist environmental court is not the same thing as an ecocentric (or even anthropocentric) environmental court. McAuslan gets the closest to such a model but his underlying principles reflect the need to have principled and rational decision-making and not environmental concerns. The difficulty is that any court which makes 'environmental' decisions runs the risk of breaching the borderline between judicial and political functions.

At first sight, it is quite easy to establish a case that the current legal system does not work too well when confronted by environmental disputes and that a new structure and set of procedures, probably involving some sort of environmental court or tribunal would work better. Existing proposals reflect the views of professional lawyers concerned with the efficient operation of the legal system and therefore fail to capture either the need to facilitate true public participation (as opposed to the public represented by professional lawyers) or to address the question of whether environmental law is effective (in terms of protecting the environment). Ultimately, however, if the question is addressed from an environmental perspective, it becomes clear that the substance of the law is the problem, not the procedures or structure, although of course the two are related. This raises a paradoxical question. If the substance of environmental law was more effective in protecting the environment would there be any need to have a separate environmental court?

CHAPTER SUMMARY

1 Public participation in environmental law takes a number of different forms. It generally consists of access to information about the environment, participation in environmental decisions and the making of plans and programmes, and access to justice in environmental matters.

2 Public participation in environmental law has increased in importance over the last 20 years. This is evidenced by the agreement of the Aarhus Convention and the European and National legislation which implements the provisions of the Directive.

3 The arguments in favour of public participation are relatively uncontroversial. It brings many benefits including the improvement of environmental decisions, helping to resolve difficult environmental disputes, improving procedural legitimacy and promoting environmental citizenship.

41. See P. Ryan (2002) 14 JEL 301.

4   Access to environmental information has been widened in recent years through the adoption of a general right to such information under the Environmental Information Regulation 2004. These Regulations provide a general right to access 'environmental information' held by public bodies.

5   In addition to a general right of access to environmental information, there are a number of public pollution control registers which contain information on releases to the environment and other important licensing information.

6   Other types of environmental information are available and these include information to the consumer under such things as the eco-labelling scheme, and company information released in annual reports.

7   Public participation in environmental decision making takes many forms. The general trend is to improve both the quantity and quality of public participation and the use of deliberative systems to do so has been used in controversial areas such as GM food and crops.

8   The courts have emphasized the importance of ensuring that the quality of public participation is safeguarded through the use of procedural mechanisms such as environmental impact assessment.

9   The public has a right of access to justice in relation to environmental matters primarily through the route of judicial review.

10 In order to bring a judicial review action an applicant must show that they: have standing, have commenced the application promptly, and have no other avenue of redress.

11 The question of who has standing has been interpreted fairly liberally by the courts. This includes groups who represent particular environmental interests.

12 Applications have to be made within three months of the date when the grounds for the application first arose. In many but not all cases this will be the grant of permission or authorisation.

13 The effectiveness of judicial review is reduced by the uncertainly surounding the rules on standing, delay and costs.

14 The current court structure in the UK has been criticised as inadequate by many commentators. Various proposals have been made to replace the current system. Early proposals were mostly based around a two tier division of the High Court. Later reform proposals have focused on replacing magistrates' powers with a specialist tribunal.

 FURTHER READING

General reading

The best starting point is M. Lee and C. Abbot, 'The Usual Suspects? Public Participation Under the Aarhus Convention' (2003) 66 Modern Law Review 80 which gives a first rate overview of the issues both from a practical and theoretical viewpoint. J. Steele 'Participation and Deliberation in Environmental Law: Exploring a Problem-Solving Approach' (2001) 21 Oxford Journal of Legal Studies 415 is more theoretical but thought provoking (and argues that participation does make for better decisions). In similar vein, K. Getliffe, 'Proceduralisation and the Aarhus Convention—Does Increased Participation In the Decision-Making Process lead to More Effective EU Environmental Law?' [2002]

Env L Rev 101 considers the basic rationales for increasing public participation. The impact of Aarhus on European institutions is considered in V. Rodenhoff 'The Aarhus Convention and its implications for the "Institution" of the European Community' (2002) RECIEL 343.

Access to environmental information

If you are interested in the topic of access to information generally have a look at H. Brooke, *Your Right to Know: How to Use the Freedom of Information Act and Other Access Laws* (London: Pluto Press, 2004) which is a great guide to using the new Act to get hold of information that you want. It is also backed up by a good web page (see below). For a more 'legal' guide to the area see P. Coppel, 'Environmental Information: The New Regime' [2005] JPL 12 which provides a comprehensive guide to the operative provisions of the Regulations and the related role of the Freedom of Information Act 2000. The Royal Commission on Environmental Pollution has long campaigned for free access to environmental information. See in particular *Air Pollution Control: An Integrated Approach* (5th Report, Cmnd 6371, 1975) and *Tackling Pollution: Experience and Prospects* (10th Report, Cmnd 9149, 1984). The latter gives a good introductory account of the arguments for and against disclosure. A general discussion of the issues can be found in C. Kimber, 'Understanding Access to Environmental Information: the European Experience' in T. Jewell and J. Steele (eds), *Law in Environmental Decision Making* (Oxford: Oxford University Press, 1998). For an empirical study on the effectiveness of access to information see, J. Rowan-Robinson et al., 'Public Access to Environmental Information: A Means to What End?' [1996] 8 JEL 19. Consumer-based information is considered in R. Gertz 'Access to Environmental Information and the German Blue Angel—Lessons to be Learned' (2004) EELR 268.

Public participation

The starting point for any discussion of public participation in environmental law should be P. McAuslan, 'The Ideologies of Planning Law' (Oxford: Pergamon Press, 1980). The general thrust of the book is that planning law is a product of the tension between three competing 'ideologies' aimed at promoting private property, the public interest and public participation. Although way out of date, it provides a good background and historical introduction to many of the issues. Deliberative theory is discussed in J. Bohman and W. Rehg, 'Deliberative Democracy: Essays on Reason and Politics' (Cambridge: M.I.T. Press, 1997). The impact of Aarhus on planning is considered in P. Stookes and J. Razzaque, 'Community Participation: UK Planning Reforms and international obligations' (2002) JPL 786 and J. Thompson, 'Involving people, changing lives: Community Participation in the Development Process' (2004) JPL Occ Pap 32, 58.

An environmental court

Interesting to read (if you can get hold of a copy) is M. Grant (ed.), *Environmental Litigation: Towards an Environmental Court?* (London: UKELA, 1993) which far from being a historic document demonstrates that although the arguments may have become more sophisticated, the principles of the debate have moved on little over the last decade. Other articles include Sir Harry Woolf 'Are the Judiciary Environmentally Myopic?' (1992) 4 JEL 1, R. Carnwath, 'Environmental Enforcement: The Need for a Specialist Court' [1992] JPL 799, P. McAuslan, 'The Role of Courts and Other Judicial Type Bodies in Environmental Management' (1991) 2 JEL 195, G. McLeod, 'Do We Need an Environmental Court in Britain?' in D. Robinson and J. Dunkley (eds), *Public Interest Perspectives in Environmental Law*, M. Grant, *Environmental Court Project: Final Report*, (DETR, 2000), R. Macrory and M. Woods, *Modernising Environmental Justice: Regulation and the Role of an Environmental Tribunal*, (London: UCL,

2003), The Environmental Justice Project, *Environmental Justice* (2004) and the Royal Commission on Environmental Pollution, 23rd Report, *Environmental Planning* (Cm 5459, 2002).

QUESTIONS

1   What is meant by public participation in environmental law? Why are there moves to increase public participation? What problems might exist with involving the public more in environmental decision-making?

2   What types of environmental information exist and how might they be accessed?

3   Consider whether a request for information would have to be acceded to in relation to each of the following:

   (a) The details of a trade effluent agreement between a water company and its customer (see p. 762).

   (b) The exact location of the nesting sites of Corncrakes in Scotland.

   (c) The details of discussions between the UK Government and other countries in relation to the processing and disposal of nuclear waste, some of which comes from military sources.

4   Bert comes to see you wanting to challenge a decision of the Environment Agency to grant a waste management licence for a landfill site. What would you need to know before advising him whether he had a chance of challenging the decision? Would it make any difference if it was a national campaigning group who was asking the same question?

5   What are the arguments for and against the establishment of a specialist environmental court?

WEB LINKS

Comprehensive coverage of the Aarhus Convention can be found at <www.unece.org/env/pp/>. This includes the text of the Convention as well as subsequent developments in its implementation. On a European level <europa.eu.int/comm/environment/aarhus/> contains the texts of the relevant Directives and other literature relating to the three 'pillars' of public participation. The starting point for internet sources on freedom of information is the Information Commissioner's office at <www.informationcommissioner.gov.uk/>. www.landecon.cam.ac.uk/env_court.htm has a wide-ranging set of links to Environmental Courts across the world in addition to various reports and other documents relating to the debate in the UK.

11

Private law and environmental protection

 Overview

The development of environmental law is not solely governed by the realm of public and administrative law. Although the spread of regulatory control has accelerated within the last 60 years, traditionally, at first glance anyway, private law has attempted to serve a similar function in controlling environmental damage. As we describe below, however, the similarity is often superficial: the essential characteristic of private law is to regulate relationships between individuals (as opposed to the public law which governs the activities of public bodies like the EA and regulates the relationship between the state and individuals) by the balancing of individual interests, such as competing uses of land, rather than environmental protection.

In this chapter we look in more detail at the torts—or civil wrongs—traditionally relied on in environmental litigation: private and public nuisance, trespass, negligence and the 'rule in *Rylands and Fletcher*', as well as various instances of statutory civil liability. We preface this with some introductory remarks about the functions of civil liability as a tool for environmental protection. Alongside this chapter you may find it useful to revisit the remarks in Chapter 2 about the role of the courts in developing environmental law, and in particular the outline discussion there of the potential for civil liability to act as an environmental protection mechanism.

At the end of this chapter you will:

✔ Know about the main ways in which private litigation might be used to further environmental protection, and the available remedies.

✔ Appreciate the relationship between these claims and public regulation.

✔ Be able to evaluate the main strengths and weakness of private law compared to public environmental regulation.

✔ Appreciate in outline the relationship between tort law and human rights law, and be able to form a view of the impact of human rights law in this area.

Private law and environmental liability

In looking at each of the various private law liability provisions considered below, it is useful to have in mind the range of overlapping (and sometimes competing) functions that they could serve:

• to *compensate* for harm suffered (and whether this should be to people and their property, or more widely to compensate 'the environment' in some way);

• to *prevent* harm (to people, property or the environment);

- to internalize costs to producers (liability as a *market mechanism*);
- to provide an *incentive* to improve environmental performance;
- to express *social condemnation* of environmentally harmful behaviour;
- to raise awareness of environmental problems (an *Ombudsman* function).

Related to these are three further issues. The first is concerned with who has the right to bring any claim—who can sue? Should claims be restricted to where individual rights have been affected, or should claims also be allowed for damage to public goods or to the unowned environment? The second issue is about the strictness of liability. For example, is strict liability (liability without having to prove fault) used? Does it matter whether the defendant could have foreseen that harm would be caused? Does it matter whether the defendant had the resources to prevent the harm occurring?

Thirdly, how is a value to be placed on the environment? In the interests of certainty the defendant (or pollution fund) must know what they are liable for, and how much this may cost them. There are various possibilities, and valuation of damages could be based on:

- the effect on the market price of the environmental asset (e.g. the drop in value of land which has been polluted);
- the cost of *full* environmental restoration/remediation;
- the cost of providing for the *reasonable costs* of restoration/remediation.

An important aspect of how the environment is to be valued, therefore, is how wide we cast the net when calculating damage, e.g. how we quantify things like the loss of ecological services.

Human rights law

Before looking at the individual torts, we must consider the role that the Human Rights Act 1998 plays in relation to private law claims. This puts the cart before the horse historically, but it is important that potential breaches of human rights law are not thought of just as separate legal actions that might be taken on top of tort claims; human rights law can also influence the substance of tort law claims, i.e. what can be sued for and by whom.

This is because, while tort law is about relationships between legal persons (individuals, companies, etc), the courts are public bodies under the Human Rights Act 1998 (s. 6). They are therefore bound to act in a way which is compatible with the rights protected by the European Convention on Human Rights. The judges therefore ought to develop the common law in a way which is consistent with, or at least avoids clashing with, Convention rights. Indeed, we could go further and say that the common law torts must develop in a way that, as a *minimum*, protects human rights; the Human Rights Act provides a floor of protection rather than a ceiling.

This matters because the European Court of Human Rights has held that forms of environmental pollution may fall within the scope of the right to respect for private life and the home provided for in Article 8 of the Convention. For example, in *Powell and Rayner v United Kingdom* (1990) 12 EHRR 355, a case about noise from Heathrow airport, the court held that the rights of Mr Rayner, who owned land just over a mile away from a major runway, were clearly at stake because of the noise levels (although the Court ultimately found that running the airport was a modern economic necessity which justified the breach). In *López Ostra v Spain* (1995) 20 EHRR 277, however, a claim under Article 8 succeeded in relation to exceptionally severe pollution coming from a factory 12 metres away from the applicant's home.

The current tensions within the European Court of Human Rights about human rights based on poor levels of environmental protection can be seen in *Hatton v UK* (see Case box 11.1).

CASE 11.1 *Hatton v UK* (2003) 37 EHRR 28

Residents living near to Heathrow Airport brought an action before the European Court of Human Rights, alleging that noise from aircraft landing at night significantly disturbed their sleep, and that this violated their rights under Article 8 of the Convention to respect for their home life. Under a statute, private law claims in the national courts had not been possible (see further p. 366).[1] Initially the claim—which was different from that in *Powell and Rayner* because it focused on a limited number of night flights rather than noise generally—was successful, and modest damages were awarded (though the cost of compensating everyone similarly affected was estimated at around £2 billion). The UK Government appealed. The Grand Chamber held while there may have been a breach of Article 8, this was justified because of the economic necessity of the flights. Although in extreme cases, environmental pollution could be in breach of the Convention, here the degree of harm suffered was not severe and the Court deferred to the UK's assessment of the economic importance of the flights. Unlike in *López Ostra*, here there was no suggestion of any 'domestic irregularity' in the sense that Mrs López Ostra had clearly been let down by a culpable failure on the part of the regulatory authorities.[2] A strong dissenting judgment thought this approach to be too conservative, and argued that the rights in the Convention should be interpreted in a way that would expand protection in environmental pollution cases.

It is also worth mentioning that the majority were fairly unsympathetic to the applicants' situations, and this probably played a part in the decision that was reached.[3] Expanding on this point, it is hard to believe that the applicants in *Hatton* were the persons most affected by noise from Heathrow, but it is often the nature of litigation like this to be brought by those most willing and able to voice their concerns. This also raises more general issues as

---

1. Though public law actions had been taken to the regulatory decisions authorising increases in night noise, see *R v Secretary of State for Transport, ex parte Richmond upon Thames London Borough* [1994] 1 WLR 74; *(No. 2)* [1995] 7 ELM 52; *(No. 3)* [1995] 7 ELM 127; *(No. 4)* [1996] 8 ELM 77.

2. This moves environmental human rights claims away from in effect being based on strict liability—where the central question is simply whether rights have been violated—towards one which uses a notion of fault. For a comparable approach in national law to upholding private rights where there has been regulatory tardiness, see *Wheeler v JJ Saunders*, [1996] Ch 19, p. 387.

3. In *Khatun v UK*, see p. 390, the applicants' case was weakened because they did not suffer health problems from the dust and the interference was for a limited time only.

to whether individual litigation is able to pursue what are often, by their nature, collective interests (see further p. 382).

Under the Human Rights Act 1998, the courts must have regard to judgments and opinions of the European Court of Human Rights or the Commission respectively. Therefore, what has been a rather limited approach by these bodies so far to the use of human rights law for environmental protection may in fact hinder the national use of Convention rights for this purpose. The 1998 Act does not provide for a new tort of 'breach of the Convention' which one individual can rely on against another. But the courts must consider whether, e.g., a claimant receives 'just satisfaction' if their human rights have been breached. If national law does not provide a sufficient remedy then additional remedies may have to be given for the breach of Convention rights. There is no reason, however, why these must be remedies in tort law (see p. 366).

The law of tort and environmental protection

This book does not attempt to give a comprehensive account of the law of tort which is more than adequately covered in specialist texts. However, the various torts and their general principles are outlined below, and illustrations given as to their usefulness in protecting environmental interests.

Private nuisance

The law of nuisance is concerned with the unlawful interference with a person's use or enjoyment of land, or of some right over or in connection with it. This definition illustrates one of the primary distinctions between nuisance and other torts in that the protection afforded is directed towards protecting proprietary interests rather than the control of an individual's conduct. The generality of the definition also means that private nuisance can take an infinite variety of forms (unlike statutory nuisance, which is restricted to quite a narrow range of nuisances; see Chapter 12).

The protection of proprietary rights can have the incidental effect of providing a general benefit to the wider community by achieving improvements in environmental quality. But there have been occasions where the effect upon the community has been a negative one. In *Bellew v Cement Ltd* [1948] IR 61, an interim injunction was granted to restrain the noisy blasting at a quarry. This remained effective for several months. The effect of this stoppage upon the supply of cement in Ireland was devastating as 80 per cent of the cement used in Ireland was created by materials from the quarry and there was then a national housing shortage. Thus the court upheld the protection of the private right involved at the expense of employment and construction. Whether such strict protection would be given if a similar case arose today may, however, be doubted, as Case box 11.2 shows.

CASE 11.2 *Dennis v Ministry of Defence* [2003] Env LR 34

The claimants lived in a mansion on a large estate located near to RAF Wittering, a base used for the training of RAF Harrier jets. Noise levels from the aircraft were found to be 'particularly fearsome', making dogs cower and in some cases reducing visiting children to tears. The claimants brought a case in private nuisance, alleging significant economic losses because of their inability to use their estate for commercial purposes like hosting conferences, as well as losses because of damage to their enjoyment of their land. The MOD argued that the national interest at stake meant that no nuisance arose, but the High Court rejected this approach and held that there was an actionable nuisance. However, the Court refused to grant an injunction and awarded significant damages instead.

The basis for a claim in nuisance is founded upon a balancing exercise centred around the question of reasonableness. As was stated in *Sanders Clark v Grosvenor Mansions Co. Ltd* [1900] 2 Ch 373:

the court must consider whether the defendant is using his property reasonably or not. If he is using it reasonably, there is nothing which at law can be considered a nuisance; but if he is not using it reasonably . . . then the [claimant] is entitled to relief.

Thus, in attempting to assess liability in a nuisance claim, a balance is made between the reasonableness of the defendant's activity and its impact upon the claimant's proprietary rights. Some disturbances, however, would seem to be incapable of being a nuisance. Things like the everyday sounds of domestic life travelling between thin walls separating neighbours cannot amount to a nuisance, since both parties would be committing a nuisance (*Baxter v Camden (No. 2)* [2000] Env LR 112).

(a) Balancing factors in private nuisance

In assessing where to strike the balance, a court will take into account a number of specific factors including the locality of the nuisance, the nature, duration and extent of the nuisance, the use the claimant makes of her land, and the defendant's conduct. However, any public benefit accruing from the defendant's actions is unlikely to be taken into account in deciding whether there is a nuisance.

(i) The locality doctrine

The locality doctrine is usually traced to the decision in *St Helen's Smelting Co. v Tipping* (1865) 11 HL Cas 642. In the mid-19th century, St Helens was the centre of the alkali industry. The average life expectancy was well under 25 and it had built up a reputation as one of the dirtiest towns in Britain. The physical impact of the works had left most vegetation in the area dead and adversely affected the health of cattle. Mr Tipping brought a claim in private nuisance. The court drew the distinction between actual physical damage to property and a nuisance which would only cause 'personal discomfort'. In the latter situation, the locality of the nuisance would be a material factor in assessing the balancing exercise. In a famous quote in the case of *Sturges v Bridgman* (1879) 11 ChD 852, Thesiger LJ stated, 'What would be a nuisance in Belgrave Square would not necessarily be so in Bermondsey'. Or, as one commentator put it, 'Those who suffer most from the ravages of pollution are the least worthy of protection.'[4]

---

4. J. McLaren (1972) 10 Osgoode Hall LJ 505.

Although there is a distinction drawn between actual damage done to property and interference with the enjoyment of property, in practice there is often an overlap. It has been alleged that the economic effect of nuisance can be just as detrimental as physical damage to an interest in land. If, for instance, a house is situated by a pig farm, the smells emanating from that may well make the house less attractive to potential buyers, but under the locality doctrine it could be argued that in an agricultural area an owner has to expect such farm-yard smells.[5]

However, even in the most heavily industrialised areas, there is not an absolute freedom to produce polluting materials. An illustration was given in *Rushmer v Polsue and Alfieri Ltd* [1906] 1 Ch 234, where Cozens-Hardy LJ said:

It does not follow that because I live, say, in the manufacturing part of Sheffield I cannot complain if a steam-hammer is introduced next door, and so worked as to render sleep at night almost impossible, although previously to its introduction my house was a reasonably comfortable abode, having regard to the local standard; and it would be no answer to say that the steam-hammer is of the most modern approved pattern and is reasonably worked. In short, if a substantial addition is found as a fact in any particular case, it is no answer to say that the neighbourhood is noisy, and that the defendant's machinery is of first-class character.

In that case, an injunction was granted against a printing press being operated in Fleet Street, even though there were many other printing presses in the area and others also operated at night. The same approach can be seen with the noise disturbance from RAF aircraft in *Dennis v MOD* (see Case box 11.2). There, the judge noted in passing that if the next generation of fighter plane, projected to be twice as noisy, were to operate from the base, then this would be analogous to the steam hammer in *Rushmer*, i.e. even in an already noisy environment it could form the basis of a new claim in nuisance.

An important issue is what, precisely, judges do in locality cases. In some cases, e.g. difficult questions may arise about the boundaries of the locality or the intensity of the activities carried on there. What judges may end up doing, therefore, may be as much about prescribing what activities can reasonably take place in any location as it is about reaching an objective judgment about the state of the area.

Finally, it may be that the locality rule is incompatible with human rights law. Under Article 14 of the Convention, other Convention rights must be enjoyed without discrimination. This may mean that judging the reasonableness of a polluting activity differentially according to whether it interferes with a 'run down' or 'high class' location will be discriminatory. That said, the justification tests still have to be applied, as does the judicially constructed test of 'domestic irregularity', and the circumstances where amenity damage will be so excessive as to be a human rights violation requiring an action in tort will be rare.

(ii) The nature, duration, and intensity of the nuisance

Not every interference with property will be actionable in nuisance (contrast trespass, discussed below). There must be some appreciable harm, even in cases of property damage. This rule applies more generally to all nuisance claims, and the courts will look among other things to the nature, duration, and intensity (or seriousness) of the activity complained of.

---

5. See, however, *Wheeler v J.J. Saunders Ltd* [1996] Ch 19, see p. 389.

For a nuisance to be actionable it must be something which is more than temporary. Isolated incidents can give rise to a nuisance only where the use which gives rise to the risk of that isolated nuisance is of itself a continuing use. For example, a factory which produces fumes does not necessarily have to produce those fumes continuously over a period of years for there to be a nuisance. However, where there are isolated incidents occurring regularly then the use of the land for that purpose is of itself a nuisance. The more isolated the occurrence, however, the less the likelihood that the use being carried out is a nuisance, as Case box 11.3 illustrates.

CASE 11.3 *Harrison v Southwark and Vauxhall Water Co.* [1891] 2 Ch 409

The defendant water company had dug a shaft to pump water from land adjacent to the claimants. As the shaft was being sunk the pumps that were being used created a continuous noise. Mr Harrison brought a claim in nuisance to stop the noise. In finding against Mr Harrison the court held that the works were not actionable because they were temporary and that such temporary works would only be actionable if unreasonable methods were used, unless physical damage was caused. Vaughan Williams J said:

For instance, a man who pulls down his house for the purpose of building a new one no doubt causes considerable inconvenience to his next door neighbours during the process of demolition; but he is not responsible as for a nuisance if he uses all reasonable skill and care to avoid annoyance to his neighbour by the works of demolition. Nor is he liable to [a claim], even though the noise and dust and the consequent annoyance be such as would constitute a nuisance if the same . . . had been created in sheer wantonness, or in the execution of works for a purpose involving a permanent continuance of the noise and dust.

Again, judicial thinking seems to have been affected by taking a realistic balance of the number and type of occurrences as against the utility involved in the operation itself. Factors like the duration of a nuisance may also be relevant to deciding which remedy is to be awarded if a nuisance is established.[6]

It is unlikely that the view that a nuisance must be capable of being sensed would now be upheld. In cases relating to the meaning of 'damage' it was once the law that damage could not be established by scientific evidence alone.[7] But this Victorian view was really aimed at filtering out trivial claims, and is of doubtful authority today[8] when, e.g. alterations to the genetic make-up of crops by GM contamination might be regarded as property damage.

(iii) The claimant's use of their land

The test for assessing a nuisance has two elements. Not only must the use of land which is complained of be unreasonable, but also the use of the land to which the nuisance applies must be a reasonable use. If a potential claimant is particularly sensitive to one type of nuisance then it will not be actionable unless that nuisance would have affected a 'reasonable' person.[9]

---

6. See discussion of *Dennis v MOD* in Case box 11.2.

7. *Salvin v North Brancepath Coal Co.* (1874) 9 Ch App 705.

8. Support for this shift can be seen in *Blue Circle Industries v Ministry of Defence* [1998] 3 All ER 385, a case on radiation contamination, see p. 391.

9. *Robinson v Kilvert* (1889) 41 ChD 88.

The effect of this rule is perhaps not as wide as first imagined. The principle only applies when the unreasonableness of the conduct is specifically the result of the hypersensitivity of the claimant. If there is an independent claim brought because of the inherent unreasonableness of the nuisance, then action can still be taken. In the Canadian case of *McKinnon Industries Ltd v Walker* [1951] 3 DLR 577, the defendants operated a motor car plant which emitted poisonous gases. The claimant grew orchids for sale and the gases killed off his stock. He brought an action in nuisance. The defendants argued that the growing of orchids was a hypersensitive activity and therefore any damage suffered was not as a result of the unreasonable use of land. The court disagreed and held that the nuisance was independent of the special sensitivity of the claimant.

Thus, in pollution cases, there will be very few occasions where this particular factor will be taken into account. Normally, the type of pollution complained of will be itself a cause of action which can cancel out any arguments put forward about hypersensitivity. There are signs, however, that the courts are moving away from assessing hypersensitivity and subsuming this into the more general question of whether the relationship between the claimant and the defendant gives rise to reasonably foreseeable losses, considered in the next section (see the judgment of Buxton LJ in *Network Rail Infrastructure Limited v CJ Morris (t/a Soundstar Studio)* [2004] Env LR 41). If this approach is followed, then, for example, in the case of possible contamination of organic crops by genetically modified pollen the issue would not be whether organic crops are unduly sensitive to particular kinds of contamination (which the judge in *R v Secretary of State for the Environment and Ministry of Agriculture, Fisheries and Food, ex parte Watson* [1999] Env LR 310 suggested might be the case), but whether the GM farmer could reasonably foresee that harm might be caused (and in the case of things like crops grown to published standards this may not be too heavy a burden).

However, doing away entirely with the hypersensitive claimant poses some problems of its own. To take the example of a large-scale noise disturbance, it might be reasonably foreseeable that, over a wide area, there will be complaints. The device of the hypersensitive claimant allows unmeritous claims to be weeded out,[10] especially where the claimant is not the person most affected by the noise (there are clear echoes of this influencing the judgment in the *Hatton* case, above).

(iv) Fault

The defendant's conduct will be a relevant consideration in those nuisance cases where the activity complained of has ceased. (Questions of fault, of course, do not arise in cases where the activity complained of is ongoing, and an injunction is being sought.) There are various factors that go to make up fault, including the foreseeability of the damage caused and the cost of taking preventive action. However, the view that liability in nuisance is 'strict', if it were ever true, receded with the decision of the House of Lords in the *Cambridge Water Co.* case.

---

10. In *Gaunt v Fynney* (1872) 8 LR 8 Lord Selborne LC said that 'a nervous or anxious or prepossessed listener hears sounds which would otherwise have passed unnoticed, and exaggerates into some new significance, originating within himself, sounds which at other times have been passively heard and not regarded'.

CASE 11.4 *Cambridge Water Co. v Eastern Counties Leather plc* [1994] 2 AC 264

Eastern Counties Leather had for several years used particular solvents. Until 1976, the way that the solvent was delivered meant that there were often spillages. The solvent eventually found its way into underground strata and then into an aquifer from which the Cambridge Water Company abstracted water. In 1982 the water company began testing for the solvent in the water, because new EC drinking water standards, which included parameters for the solvent, were to come into force in 1985. The tests found high levels of solvent, traceable back to the leather works. The cheapest option for the water company was to close down the borehole and open a new source of supply. The water company sued the leather works in nuisance (and also negligence and *Rylands v Fletcher*, discussed below).

The House of Lords held that liability depended on the foreseeability of the relevant type of damage occurring (i.e. the pollution of groundwater above the levels laid down in the Directive). In the only full judgment, Lord Goff argued that as regards foreseeability it would be unjust if liability for property damage under nuisance was stricter than liability for personal injury under negligence, at least in relation to the remoteness of damages. Liability is still 'strict' in the sense that there is no need to prove that the defendant has been careless.[11] The water company's claim in nuisance was therefore unsuccessful. The costs incurred by the water company only arose because of the changes to the drinking water quality regulations, and the spillages had ceased before these came into force. (An interesting issue to consider is the fact that the Directive is based on World Health Organization standards which date from 1970.)

For comment see C. Shelbourn [1994] JPL 703; D. Wilkinson (1994) MLR 799 and G. Cross (1995) LQR 445.

It would seem that both the particular type of damage and the 'pollution pathway' must be foreseeable, although Lord Goff's reference to what the 'reasonable supervisor' and the actual staff at the leather company knew at the time seems to take an unduly subjective, and restrictive, approach as to what it is that reasonable foreseeability requires. While the costs of preventing such a spill will not be a relevant factor—and to that extent also liability remains strict—investing in 'state of the art' pollution prevention technology and management systems may mean that liability is avoided because either the type of environmental damage caused or the way in which it is caused is unforeseen at the time. In this sense, adherence to current regulatory standards (e.g. an industrial process using BAT) are likely to be directly relevant to whether there is liability in private law. In cases where the damage and its cause might be revealed not because of regulatory controls but if voluntary measures were followed—e.g. where a firm is seeking accreditation under the Eco-Management and Audit Scheme (see p. 267)—the position is less clear and seems inevitably to slide into questions of whether it would be reasonable for any particular industrial activity not to take such steps.

(v) Public benefit

Because nuisance is said to be about reasonable 'give and take' as between neighbours, this might be thought to imply that the greater the public benefit deriving from the

---

11. See also *Jan de Nul (UK) Ltd v Royale Belge* [2000] 2 Lloyd's Rep 790 (liability even though those responsible 'had taken all reasonable precautions to avoid such damage').

neighbouring land use the less likely that this will be an actionable nuisance (on the grounds that the affected neighbour, being a part of the general public, also benefits). However, in the absence of explicit statutory authority for doing so, the courts have been reluctant to allow private rights to be trumped by the public interest. In *Bamford v Turnley* (1862) 122 ER 27, a case about what would now be called local air pollution from brick burning, Bramwell B said that 'whenever a thing is for the public benefit, properly understood, the loss to the individuals of the public who lose will bear compensation out of the gains of those who gain'.

More recently, in *Dennis v MOD* (see Case box 11.2) Buckley J noted that the greater the public interests involved, the greater the interference may be (something which in *Dennis* itself was clear). Hence, there was an obvious danger if the public interest was considered when deciding whether a nuisance exists, since in the case of serious nuisances caused by activities of great public importance the sheer weight of the public benefit would, in effect, make it impossible to find in favour of the claimant. The judge therefore concluded, in a strong echo of *Bamford v Turnley*, 'that public interest should be considered and that selected individuals should not bear the cost of the public benefit'. Notably, Buckley J thought this approach had to be taken 'if the common law in this area is to be consistent with the developing jurisprudence of human rights'.

(b) Who can sue (and be sued) in private nuisance?

Anyone who, by their use of land,[12] creates a nuisance, or anyone who occupies land from which a nuisance emanates and who continues or adopts the nuisance, may be liable. Occupiers will be responsible for the acts of their employees and even for acts of trespassers, and (although the basic rule is that tenants are responsible for their own nuisances) land-lords may be liable in a number of situations. Importantly, a polluter may be sued even though they are only one of many contributing to the pollution. In *Graham and Graham v Re-Chem International Ltd* [1996] Env LR 158, although the claimants were ultimately unsuccessful, it was accepted that the defendant's dioxin emissions only had to amount to a 'material contribution' (a concept from the law of negligence, see below) to the damage to the claimant's cattle complained of.

The problem that has troubled the courts in recent years is who can bring a nuisance action. The issue was settled by the decision of the House of Lords in *Hunter v Canary Wharf Ltd* (see Case box 11.5).

CASE 11.5 *Hunter v Canary Wharf Ltd* [1997] 2 WLR 684

In two separate actions, over 500 residents in London's Docklands brought actions against the developers of Canary Wharf and the London Docklands Development Corporation for nuisance arising out of interference with television signals from Canary Wharf Tower and damage from dust emissions from road construction respectively. The Court of Appeal had held that nuisance did not just protect property rights but anyone with a 'substantial link' with the enjoyment of the property as a home. This reflected the view that the old ideas of nuisance did not adequately protect those without legal interests in land, such as the specific interests of children or

---

12. In *Southport Corp v Esso Petroleum* [1954] 2 QB 182, obiter remarks in the CA and HL supported both views, but see now *Lippiatt v South Gloucestershire Council* [2000] QB 51 (CA).

spouses.[13] But the House of Lords (by 4–1) rejected this approach, calculating the potential damages according to damage to the property interests. Damages, had they been awarded, would not have been dependent on the number of residents affected. (See further discussion at p. 381.) In doing so, the House of Lords strongly restated the view that the right to sue in private nuisance can only be exercised by those with rights to the land affected, usually freehold owners or tenants in possession. In nailing down nuisance as an adjunct to property rights, the opportunity to develop it in a way that might offer greater protection of wider environmental interests was possibly lost.

Whether this approach provides sufficient protection of the human rights of those, like children, who do not have rights in the land, may need to be reconsidered in the light of the Human Rights Act 1998. Some of the claimants in *Hunter v Canary Wharf* took their case to the European Commission of Human Rights. In *Khatun v UK* (1 July 1998, unreported) the alleged breach of Article 8 was ultimately unsuccessful (see p. 388). But the Commission did find that the right protected under Article 8 applied to *all* the applicants whether they were property owners or merely occupiers. This got round one of the major obstacles to the claim re-erected by the House of Lords.

In the more recent case of *McKenna v British Aluminium* [2002] Env LR 30, the High Court refused to strike out, as unarguable, an action brought amongst others by a number of children about alleged emissions and noise from the defendant's factory. The judge held that doing so would be inappropriate since there was a 'real possibility' that a court might modify the common law rule about who can sue in private nuisance in order to make the common law comply with Article 8 of the ECHR (though it is worth pointing out that, because the obligations of the Convention fall on the state, it is really up to the state to decide how it provides 'just satisfaction' to human rights victims; this might be by awarding them damages in claims against other private individuals, but it might be by tightening the criminal law, or an administrative licensing procedure).

Notably, though, the ECHR does use a 'victim' test—meaning that there must be some legal person affected—and the Strasbourg Court has rejected claims based just on protecting general ecological interests; there is no 'right to nature' (*X and Y v Federal Republic of Germany* (1976) 5 Eur Com HR Dec & Rep). So the ECHR is a long way from granting, say, an environmental pressure group a legal right to sue for damage to a natural habitat.

(c) Defences to a claim for nuisance

There are a number of defences which attempt to restrict the scope of the law of nuisance. However, in practice, they are either so difficult to prove as to be useless, or of dubious merit.

(i) The defence of prescription

Although it is possible in principle to acquire a right to pollute as an easement through 20 years continuous use, there are so many caveats that the practical use of the defence is very restricted. For the defence to apply, the right to pollute must be exercised openly, continuously and not with any specific permission of the person against whom it is so

---

13. *Khorasandjian v Bush* [1993] QB 727.

acquired. It must also be the result of a lawful act, so a discharge in breach of a consent would not suffice. For example, in the case of *Sturges v Bridgman* (1879) 11 ChD 852, the defendant, a confectioner, had used a noisy pestle and mortar in his premises in Wimpole Street for more than 20 years. There had not been any complaints over that period but a doctor residing at the back of the site built a new consulting room close to the defendant's operational area. Consequently, the noise became a problem. The Court of Appeal held that the defendant in this case had not acquired a right to pollute by prescription. The nuisance had commenced only after the consulting room had been constructed, because previously the activities complained of did not give rise to any interference. When the consulting room was occupied, however, such interference began. Thus, the period of 20 years did not start to run until the construction of the consulting rooms.

Prescription was also raised in *Dennis v MOD* (Case box 11.2) since the Harrier jets had been flying from the RAF base since 1969. However, the claim was rejected on the grounds, first, that the noise levels fluctuated too much and therefore any prescriptive claim would be too imprecise and also that Mr Dennis's repeated complaints over the years meant that he had not signalled his permission to the noise.

(ii) No defence to say that the claimant came to the nuisance

In *Bliss v Hall* (1838) 4 Bing NC 183, the defendant operated a business as a tallow chandler. This business had been operated for at least three years when the claimant moved in nearby. Unfortunately, the defendant's business created highly toxic fumes which were blown over the claimant's land. The defendant argued that, as he had been on the site before the claimant, the claimant should have realised the state of the premises nearby and should therefore not be able to bring a claim in nuisance. Tindal CJ said:

The [claimant] came to the house he occupies with all the rights which the common law affords, and one of them is the right to wholesome air. Unless the Defendant shows a prescriptive right to carry on his business in the particular area the [claimant] is entitled to judgment.

When this principle is combined with the principle contained in *Sturges v Bridgman*, it is clear that whenever an individual moves into an area there could be the creation of a new 'nuisance history' which negates the prescriptive rights principle because of the need to allow a further 20 years before a prescriptive right attaches. This might happen if there is a new development, or change to an existing use.

In practical terms, the principle that it is no defence for a defendant to allege that the claimant has come to the nuisance is very important. For example, many factories and sewage works initially built on the outskirts of towns are now surrounded by housing. These potentially antagonistic uses can give rise to conflict. Industrialists may feel aggrieved that they have been carrying out polluting activities for a large number of years without complaint and anyone who moved into the area would fully know of any problems. This principle may once have played an important role in facilitating the expansion of towns and cities which would otherwise have been hindered by factories without any legal reason to curb their pollution. This has led some to suggest that the advent of modern environmental regulation should kill the principle off.[14]

---

14. T. Weir, *Tort Law* (Oxford: Oxford University Press, 2002), 151.

(iii) Statutory authority

There may be occasions where nuisances are caused by statutory or non-statutory bodies under express statutory authority. Where a body can point to such authority then this will amount to a defence if an action is brought against them for any reasonably consequential nuisance.[15] This was the reason that there was no litigation in relation to noise disturbance from Heathrow, since private law claims relating to noise from civil aviation flying at a reasonable height are excluded by statute.[16]

Although most statutory obligations are expressly contained within the body of the statute itself, it is also clear that a defendant could claim the defence of statutory authority where there is a clear implication that such activities have been authorised by an Act.

CASE 11.6 *Allen v Gulf Oil Refining Ltd* [1981] AC 1001

The Gulf Oil Refining Act 1965 (a private Act of Parliament) gave the defendants power to acquire land for an oil refinery at Milford Haven. The oil refinery emitted smells, noise and vibration and a local resident brought a claim against Gulf Oil in nuisance. The claimant argued in that case that although the Act gave the defendant the power to acquire land for constructing the refinery, it did not give any guidelines about the refinery's operation. Therefore, when the defendant tried to rely on the defence of statutory authority it was argued that, as the Act did not specifically allow for the operating of the plant in a manner which gave rise to a nuisance, the defence was unavailable. The House of Lords held that the statute implicitly gave the defendant an immunity to every act inevitably flowing from the construction of the refinery. The only possible exception to this would be where the nuisance complained of was of a greater degree than was necessary or where such activities were carried out in a negligent manner.

It should be pointed out that, where private rights are interfered with, it is often the case that statutes themselves provide for compensation. For example, where a new road is being built, statutory compensation is payable where there is injurious affection to the enjoyment of property which is the direct result of the works carried out. There are, however, situations where the interference with private rights is not compensated, or where, as in *Marcic*, statute provides for what might be considered an unsatisfactory enforcement mechanism (see Case box 11.8).

Also, the statutory authority defence can be traced back to an era when nuisance liability was stricter (in terms of the foreseeability test) than it now is. When this is coupled with the *Dennis* case and the possibility of taking public interest expressly into account, this may have knock-on consequences in terms of the courts approaching statutory authority arguments less favourably to defendants.

More general issues relating to where private rights clash with public interests are discussed at p. 388.

---

15. B. Pontin [2001] 13 ELM 305 notes that, under s. 6(2) of the Human Rights Act 1998, there is a duty to respect the will of Parliament, meaning that there will be no national remedy, only the possibility of success in the Strasbourg Court.

16. Section 76(1), Civil Aviation Act 1982. See comment on *Hatton v UK* Case box 11.1.

Public nuisance

Although seemingly a close relative of private nuisance, the law relating to public nuisances contains some similar elements but as many distinguishing features. Public nuisance is primarily a crime involving nuisance affecting a section of the general public, although the law developed over time so that anyone suffering 'special damage' beyond that suffered by the public generally has a claim in tort. This need only be a different degree, rather than type, of harm, and may include purely economic losses. But in those environmental cases where all suffer equally, there would appear to be no remedy in tort under public nuisance. Injunctions can be sought either by the Attorney-General or by local authorities, although individuals can take a claim with the Attorney-General's permission (a 'relator' action).

Attorney-General v PYA Quarries Ltd [1957] 2 QB 169 shows the width of the class of persons that must be affected. The defendants operated a quarry. During operations they carried out various blasting activities. These caused vibration and noise over a wide area. In attempting to lay down guidelines, Denning LJ declined to specify what numbers would be required to show that a particular nuisance was public rather than private. But he did say (at p. 191):

I prefer to look to the reason of the thing and to say that a public nuisance is a nuisance which is so widespread in its range or so indiscriminate in its effect that it would not be reasonable to expect one person to take proceedings . . . to put a stop to it, but that it should be taken on the responsibility of the community at large.

If the need to show an effect over a section of the public is set aside, there is a good degree of overlap with the factors that are taken into account when deciding whether or not there is a private nuisance, although one important difference is that public nuisance is, in principle, capable of protecting interests other than land rights[17] and it appears, as well, that the defendant's actions need not take place on land.[18] An example of a claim in public nuisance is *Gillingham Borough Council v Medway (Chatham) Dock Co. Ltd* [1993] QB 343 (see p. 388). Some would argue that nowadays public nuisance is something of an incongruous hybrid, relied on only in those cases where the deficiencies of other torts have been exposed. For others, its strength lies in its potential elasticity and it may represent the basis for developing an environmental tort action unconnected to land and capable of protecting wider community interests.[19]

Trespass

Trespass is the direct interference with personal or proprietary rights without lawful excuse. Trespass is actionable per se (*Entick v Carrington* (1765) 19 St Tr 1029, 1066), that is, it does not require proof of damage. This is well illustrated in the use of trespass law by the League Against Cruel Sports to hamper deer hunting in *League Against Cruel Sports v Scott* [1985] 2 All ER 489. The League, which bought parcels of land on Exmoor, was successful in its action even though the hunt was not deliberately directed across its land. Simply walking

17. Although the situations where it is typically pleaded tend to involve land interests.
18. *Overseas Tankship (UK) Ltd v Miller Steamship Co (Wagon Mound No. 2)* [1967] 1 AC 617.
19. J. Wightman (1998) MLR 870; in a similar vein see D. Cooper (2003) 11 Social and Legal Studies 5.

over another's land without permission is sufficient basis under trespass for an injunction, even though no damage to property has been caused. By contrast, nuisance requires something consequential to the act complained of. For example, depositing waste on someone else's land will be a trespass, even if the waste can be removed without contaminating the soil or causing injury or disease. But if the waste is on other land but causing loss of amenity because of smells or is spreading disease, then the most likely private law remedy will be an action in nuisance, since the harm is a consequence of the deposit, not the deposit itself. Trespass and private nuisance actions are mutually exclusive (the same harm cannot be both direct and indirect).

The need to show direct interference has been a problem in environmental disputes, as two cases illustrate. In *Esso Petroleum v Southport Corporation* [1956] AC 218 an oil tanker stranded in an estuary jettisoned oil to lighten the ship and to try to refloat. The oil drifted ashore and polluted the claimants' foreshore. The claimants (the Corporation) claimed for the costs of cleaning up the beach. Although trespass was not argued, two judges in the House of Lords thought that it would have failed since the pollution was not inevitable.[20] This might be compared with a case like *Jones v Llanrwst UDC* [1911] 1 Ch 393, where the court did find that there was trespass when sewage was accidentally released and polluted the banks of a river downstream. In this case the interference was held to be direct, because of the natural flow of the river. By contrast, in the *Esso Petroleum* case, there was no inevitability about the deposit of oil on the foreshore, which depended on the action of the wind, waves and tide. Because of the requirement of directness, trespass to the *person* has not been properly developed in pollution cases, although in theory making someone inhale toxic fumes could give rise to an action.

If this requirement of directness is followed, it will be almost impossible to bring an action in trespass for air-borne pollution unless the pollutant is deposited directly over the claimant's property. In the Canadian case of *Kerr et al v Revelstoke Building Materials Ltd* (1976) 71 DLR (3d) 134 (Alta SC), for example, the claimants could claim for damages to them and their livestock because the offending cropduster had passed directly over their farm. Had the plane only sprayed over its own property, and the chemicals been blown over onto the claimants' land, there would be no action in trespass, although arguably a nuisance action could be taken. For these reasons, a tort law challenge to the spread of pollen from genetically modified crops would probably have to be taken under nuisance law, either where the pollen was blown in the wind or, most likely, if it was brought on to the claimant's land by bees.

Trespass must also be intentional or negligent. *McDonald v Associated Fuels Ltd* [1954] 3 DLR 775 illustrates the distinction well. Sawdust fuel was being supplied to the claimant's house. To deliver it, the defendants parked their truck and blew the sawdust into a bin inside the house by means of a blower unit. Unfortunately, the intake mechanism for the sawdust was too close to the truck's exhaust system, and both the sawdust and carbon monoxide fumes blew into the house. The occupants were overcome, one breaking a hip on collapsing. It is clear here that the trespass itself (i.e. the entrance of the carbon monoxide directly into the house) was not intentional, but the act which caused the trespass was.

---

20. But the matter is not clear-cut. In the Court of Appeal, Denning LJ also thought it was consequential, but Morris LJ treated it as direct.

Further points can be made about trespass law. Both illustrate the point that, unlike the other torts considered here, trespass cases can be initiated in order to *frustrate* action intended to further environmental protection. Two points can be seen in the following case:

CASE 11.7 *Monsanto v Tilly* [2000] Env LR 313

Members of the campaigning group genetiX snowball took direct action to destroy genetically modified crops at trial farm sites. One issue was whether Monsanto, by entering into an agreement with the farmer but not actually owning or occupying the site, had sufficient interest to bring a trespass claim. The Court of Appeal held that it did (although in another case it has held that a developer which just had a right of access on to land to carry out surveys did not have a right of possession to maintain a trespass claim against a protester; see *Countryside Residential (North Thames) Ltd v Tugwell (The Times*, 4 April 2000)).[21] A second issue was whether the trespass was necessary because, so the protesters alleged, destroying the crops was to protect third parties or the general public from harm. This line of defence is always difficult to rely on, and the Court of Appeal took a rather dim view of this, deciding that the protesters were really after publicity (they had arranged in advance for the press to be there, and in the event pulled up very few plants). In any event central government had responsibility for ensuring that the trials were carried out safely, so it would be difficult to justify third party intervention of this kind.

This case, and the wider protest it was part of, is discussed in F. Donson, *Legal Intimidation* (London: Free Association Press, 2000), which looks at how business may resort to law, and in particular to tort law (especially defamation, but also torts like nuisance), to restrict protest and free speech. The book illustrates how tort can also be used against those who campaign on things like the environment.

In similar vein, environmental protestors' have on a number of recent occasions unsuccessfully tried to defend possession proceedings in trespass actions on the grounds that their action has been justified in some way as upholding environmental law.[22] Examples include efforts to require, as a matter of EC law, environmental impact assessment of the Newbury bypass[23] and the conservation of a protected species found on the site.[24]

Negligence

The law of negligence is a particularly large area of tort law, and this book does not try to outline any more than its rudimentary features. The degree of coverage is also related to the general lack of utility of the law of negligence in environmental protection.

The three main principles of negligence are that the claimant must establish that (a) a duty of care is owed by the defendant to the claimant; (b) that the defendant has breached that duty; and (c) there has been foreseeable damage to the claimant resulting from the breach. There is no need to show a property interest, and so anyone who suffers damage

---

21. See also *Manchester Airport plc v Dutton* [2000] QB 133 (CA).

22. S. Tromans and J. Thomann [2003] JPL 1367.

23. *Secretary of State for Transport v Haughian* [1997] Env LR 59 (CA); for another failed case regarding the EIA Directive see *Mayor and Burgesses of the London Borough of Bromley v Susanna* [1998] Env LR D13 (CA).

24. *Secretary of State for Transport v Fillingham* [1997] Env LR 73.

from an act of negligence can bring a claim. Damage here, however, means actual damage to property or physical injury (though this might include the costs of assessing whether there has been damage; see *Jan de Nul (UK) Ltd v AXA Royale Belge SA* [2002] EWCA Civ 209, p. 381 below), so in relation to claims for distress, annoyance, inconvenience and physical symptoms short of personal injury—as might be the case, for example, with noise pollution—the torts of nuisance and *Rylands v Fletcher* would have to be used (insofar as the damage can be tied to a sufficient interest in land).[25]

A key drawback of negligence is that it is a fault-based system; to succeed, there has to be some fault of the defendant. Compared with nuisance, for example, what is at issue is not the reasonableness of the use of the land but the reasonableness of the defendant's actions (i.e. has the defendant acted carelessly?). In nuisance, as *Graham and Graham v Re-Chem* (see p. 365) shows, it is no defence to argue that state of the art technology is being used. But in negligence this is likely to be a critical factor, and compliance with current regulatory standards will be sufficient to avoid liability. Negligence therefore tends to be relied on only where other common law remedies are not available. It is also necessary to foresee the type of harm that will result from an activity. In the *Cambridge Water Co.* case (see Case box 11.4), therefore, the claim in negligence was dismissed at first instance because at the time of the spillages the reasonable supervisor could not have foreseen the changes to the drinking water regulations (and possibly also the pollution pathway). The House of Lords confirmed that it would not be sufficient to show that 'pollution' could have been foreseen, as that is too wide a category of damages.

But compared with trespass, for example, negligence (as with nuisance) requires proof that the defendant has caused damage to the claimant. Particularly in the so-called 'toxic tort' cases, this may be difficult, time-consuming and expensive. *Graham and Graham* and the Sellafield leukaemia litigation[26] are both prime examples of the evidential and technical difficulties involved in proving a case, the latter a salutary reminder of the problems of relying on epidemiological evidence.[27] Claimants may also be in a quandary because of the rules on the time limits for bringing cases. Waiting for certain proof of actual damage runs the risk that the court may say that the damage actually began beyond the limitation period.

Despite the frequent use of negligence in everyday legal life, it is perhaps surprising to find just how little it has been used to try to control environmental pollution. This appears to be changing slightly, perhaps in part because of the actions of a number of campaigning lawyers prepared to take on toxic tort cases. An example of a successful negligence action in the environmental field is *Tutton v A D Walker Ltd* [1986] QB 61. Farmers had been advised by the manufacturers and by central government that using a particular insecticide when oilseed rape was flowering could lead to the death of insects such as bees. Furthermore, they were told that the insecticide was most effectively used after the flowering period. But the

---

25. *McKenna v British Aluminium* [2002] Env LR 30.

26. *Reay and Hope v BNFL* [1994] 5 Med LR 1, discussed in J. Holder (1994) 47 Current Legal Problems 287. On causation and foreseeability see also J. Steele and N. Wikeley [1997] Modern Law Review 265.

27. The recent decision In *Fairchild v Glenhaven Funeral Services Ltd* [2002] UKHL 22 makes 'environmental' negligence actions slightly easier to bring, since in cases such as those relating to exposure to asbestos, for example, where it may be impossible to identify when the fatal inhalation took place (e.g. where an employee has worked for a number of different employers over the years) the House of Lords has now held that damages can be apportioned between defendants, essentially according to the likelihood that the disease was contracted when the employee worked for them.

defendant sprayed his crop whilst the rape was in flower and a number of bees owned by the claimant were killed. The farmer was held liable for negligent use of the insecticide.[28]

There are also cases where a failure to warn about environmental damage has been found to be negligent. In *Barnes v Irwell Valley Water Board* [1930] 1 KB 21 there was held to be a common law duty of care on a water company to warn consumers of potentially unwholesome water and damages in negligence were recoverable. The application of this principle in relation to regulatory authorities can be seen in *Scott-Whitehead v National Coal Board* (1987) P&CR 263. The defendants discharged a chlorine solution into a river. Because the river was in drought there was insufficient water to dilute the strength of the pollutant. The claimant farmer abstracted water downstream, causing damage to his crops. The second defendant, the regional water authority, was held liable for failing to warn the farmer of the potential danger from the condition of the water it knew was being abstracted. Extending the principle in this case, it would be possible to bring an action against an environmental regulator in negligence if it could be shown that a failure to warn materially contributed to damage. However, there appear to be no reported decisions where this has happened, and any such argument would now have to overcome the general judicial reluctance to impose private law duties on public bodies, or find that these bodies have been at fault, especially where they are exercising their discretion and there are resource implications of imposing such a duty. In a fairly extreme case, the failure to warn of an environmental risk has been held to be a violation of the human right to home life.[29]

Natural nuisances

Nuisances can arise other than by the clash of everyday uses of land. First, a deliberate act by one landowner, bringing a hazardous substance onto his land, may lead to damage if there is an escape (considered in the following section). Secondly, there are situations where a hazard arises *naturally* but which, if it goes unchecked, might damage neighbouring land. As we will see, the main difference between how nuisance law applies at these two ends of the spectrum relates to the degree of fault, i.e. negligence, that must be shown before the landowner is liable.

In *Leakey v National Trust* [1980] QB 485, a case involving a landslip, the general principle was established that:

Ownership of land carries with it a duty to do whatever is reasonable in all the circumstances to prevents hazards on the land, however they may arise, from causing damage to a neighbour.

In cases like this, where the hazard comes about without direct human intervention,[30] landowners have what is referred to a 'measured duty of care' imposed on them. The essence of this is that, although any claim will be similar to an ordinary private nuisance action, what it is 'reasonable' to expect a landowner to do will depend on whether they (a) knew of the risk, (b) had the means to prevent it happening, and (c) failed to do so in a reasonable time (*Goldman v Hargrave* [1967] AC 645). In this sense, it is like nuisance but with a strong

---

28. For another example, see *Jan de Nul (UK) Ltd v Royale Belge* [2000] 2 Lloyd's Rep 790, see p. 379.

29. *Guerra v Italy* (1998) 26 EHRR 357, see p. 323.

30. Lord Wilberforce in *Goldman v Hargrave* [1967] 1 AC 645 refers to hazards 'whether natural or man-made', but subsequent cases have all been about the former.

twist of negligence in that there must be a pre-existing duty to take care, and the courts look to whether the defendant failed to meet the standard of care appropriate to the circumstances. Whether they can be said to be careless will therefore depend, in part, on the resources of the defendant. In this sense, therefore, any claim is different from a private nuisance action because in private nuisance it is immaterial whether the defendant was careless and the resources of the defendant are not a relevant factor.[31] This concession reflects both the fact that the defendant has not consciously created something which is potentially harmful, and that the impact on neighbours of a naturally occurring hazard may be beyond the means of the defendant to prevent.

Liability under this principle has been established in several recent cases, including damage caused by pigeons fouling the road—and pedestrians—beneath a railway bridge in London,[32] and it has also been held to apply to naturally occurring flooding.[33] One important limitation to this principle, however, emerged in *Marcic v Thames Water Utilities plc.*, a case which is also important on human rights grounds.

CASE 11.8 *Marcic v Thames Water Utilities plc* [2004] Env LR 25

Mr Marcic suffered from repeated incidents of sewage flooding. The sewage flooded his garden and lapped at his back step but never flooded his house. Thames, the sewerage undertaker, prioritized renovation work to combat internal flooding. The cause of the flooding was the overloading of the sewer network which, although originally adequate, now had too many properties discharging into it. (Under statute, new properties are essentially given a right to connect to the existing sewerage network.) Following water privatization, a statutory scheme applies under which companies submit investment plans to the industry's economic regulator, who determines which projects to finance.[34] The claimant sued in nuisance, and for a breach of human rights under Article 8 of the Convention.

Overturning the Court of Appeal, the House of Lords rejected both claims. Although Thames had a natural hazard—sewage generated in the local area—on its land, it had not acted unreasonably. Because of its funding formula, it was a special kind of occupier of land whose ability to prevent or minimise the flooding had to be recognized. The statutory scheme under which it operated was also fatal to the human rights claim, because the Lords considered that Parliament had provided a statutory remedy, through enforcement orders, which the economic regulator can serve on sewerage companies where he feels that they should do more to protect the interests of their customers from things like sewage flooding. So, the issue was whether this *statutory* scheme was human rights compliant, and the Lords held that it did strike the right balance between the different interests involved (i.e. as between the interests of those affected by flooding and all customers who ultimately pay for improvements through their bills). Had the House of Lords found in favour of Mr Marcic, it was estimated that the cost to Thames alone would have been in the region of £1 billion (three times its gross annual profits).

---

31. Note that judges may find ways of taking them into account as, for example, when assessing the extent to which environmental damage was foreseeable, see *Cambridge Water*, Case box 11.4.

32. *Wandsworth London Borough Council v Railtrack plc* [2001] Env LR 441.

33. *Green v Somerleton* [2003] EWCA Civ 198.

34. See further p. 720.

Unnatural nuisances: the rule in *Rylands v Fletcher*

The principle known as 'the rule in *Rylands v Fletcher*' was first established in the case of that name ((1868) LR 3 HL 330). The defendant constructed a reservoir on his land, but the contractors failed to detect and block off mine shafts so that, when the reservoir filled up, water entered the shafts and flooded the claimant's mine. The problem was that there could be no action in negligence as the law then stood (there was no relationship between the contractor and the mine-owner) and, because it was an isolated escape, a nuisance action was thought to be precluded. In the lower court, Blackburn J first expounded the principle:

that the person who for his own purposes brings onto his land and collects and keeps there anything likely to do mischief if it escapes, must keep it at his peril, and, if he does not do so, is prima facie answerable for all the damage which is the natural consequence of its escape.

(a) Non-natural use/extraordinary use

In the House of Lords, however, the qualification was added that there would only be an action where there was a 'non-natural use' being made of the defendant's land. Originally this may have meant that there would have been no liability if the water (in *Rylands*) had been a natural lake or naturally flooded area rather than an artificial reservoir. But in time it came to mean that the use had to be 'some special use bringing with it increased danger to others and must not merely be the ordinary use of land or such a use as is proper for the general benefit of the community' (*Rickards v Lothian* [1913] AC 263). Over the years this was applied to numerous activities, so that 'natural' became synonymous with anything for the general public benefit, no matter how *un*natural. The high point was perhaps reached in *Read v Lyons* [1947] AC 156, where the manufacture of high explosive shells was held by the House of Lords not to be a dangerous operation imposing on the manufacturer an absolute liability.

This decision may well have been influenced by the ongoing war effort at the time of the accident. But what is more important is that the House of Lords explicitly refused to extend the doctrine into a general theory of strict liability for ultra-hazardous activities which, of course, would have had profound implications for the development of environmentally hazardous technologies. The House of Lords again took this approach in *Cambridge Water Co. v Eastern Counties Leather* (see Case box 11.4), and have done so again in *Transco v Stockport Metropolitan Borough Council* (see Case box 11.9).

CASE 11.9 *Transco v Stockport Metropolitan Borough Council* [2003] UKHL 61

Water was supplied to a block of flats owned by the council. Due to an undetected leak, a large volume of water collected under the flats, from where it leaked into an old railway embankment. The embankment collapsed leaving a gas pipe in the embankment exposed and unsupported, and the gas supplier incurred costs making the pipe (which seems not to have been damaged itself) safe. The supplier sued under the rule in *Rylands v Fletcher*. The House of Lords thought that the rule in Rylands had a continuing justification, but rejected the claim, essentially because it held that there was nothing extraordinarily risky about the council's use of its land. Although, as *Rylands* itself showed, large volumes of water can give rise to extraordinary risks, the water here, although contained in a larger than normal pipe, was not deliberately accumulated but piped into the block under normal mains pressure.

In *Transco*, then, what the House of Lords seems[35] to stress (whether they chose to call it 'non-natural use' or not) was that the defendant's use must, in the circumstances, be an extraordinary use of land giving rise to some extraordinary degree of risk. Whether something is extraordinary will depend on the time and place. But it is clear that, in the words of Lord Hoffmann, there is a 'high threshold for a claimant to surmount'. They also played down, contrary to parts of Lord Goff's speech in *Cambridge Water*, any relationship between 'natural use' and the 'reasonable user' test in nuisance. Industrial activities can be out of the ordinary but not 'unreasonable', for example because they operate properly under regulation (as, e.g., the Eastern Counties Leather tannery did).

The issue of the 'naturalness' of the activity is not unrelated to its dangerousness, i.e. whether it will do 'mischief' if it escapes. Over the years the rule has been applied in relation to water, fire, gases, electricity, oil, chemicals, colliery spoil, and poisonous vegetation. In *Transco*, differing approaches were taken in the House of Lords as to whether the 'mischief' test was a test to be applied separately, or rolled into the 'non-natural use of land' test. Given that the focus is on the degree of risk it probably makes little difference; if something creates an extraordinary risk if it escapes then the thing that escapes is likely to be dangerous (even if it is only dangerous because of the volume in which it escapes, as with water).

(b) Other features of the use of the rule

It is now clear, following Transco, that the claimant must have an interest in land to invoke the rule. This really just confirms a point that was fairly clear following the decisions of the House of Lords in *Cambridge Water*, which held that the rule in Rylands is really just an aspect of nuisance law, and in *Hunter v Canary Wharf* which restricted the right to sue in nuisance in this way. It also means that the rule cannot be used to claim for personal injury.[36] So, as with nuisance, there must be something which passes—or in the case of *Rylands*, escapes—from the defendant's land to the claimant's land.

Two further, related, points can be made here. The first relates to whether there has been 'an escape'. This might not always be clear cut. Indeed, in *Transco* there was disagreement between the judges on this point (Lord Hoffmann thought there was, because damage to the land supporting the pipe was analogous to damage to the pipe itself; Lord Scott held that there was not because the actual damage had been to the council's land, and the gas pipe had not actually been damaged). Secondly, while the effect of the escape must be felt beyond the

---

35. Five full judgments were given, each taking a slightly different approach.

36. Which sits uneasily with reference in some of the judgments in *Transco* to justifying the retention of the rule in *Rylands* because of the need for a rule to cover the consequences of disastrous escapes from land like those at Aberfan and Flixborough. In these disasters, dozens of people were killed, but the effect of *Transco* is that the rule in *Rylands* might compensate for their property losses but not for their loss of life. This is an inevitable, though potentially appalling, consequence of tying *Rylands* to interests in land, and one which is in tension with the notion—expressed most clearly In Lord Hoffmann's opinion—that the rule in *Rylands* is primarily about allocating the costs of dangerous activities (hence the irrelevance of whether the escape was reasonably foreseeable).

defendant's land, it need not be the substance accumulated which escapes. This can be seen in *Rainham Chemical Works Ltd v Belvedere Fish Guano Co.* [1921] 2 AC 465, where a munitions factory exploded. The claim did not fail just because it was the bits of the factory, rather than the dangerous substance stored, that escaped. What is clear is that the balancing act between relaxing 'non-natural use' and now stipulating the reasonable fore-seeability of the damage allows the courts to continue to pay attention to the costs of preventing damage arising.

(c) Defences

There are a number of defences to an action brought under the *Rylands* rule. As with nuisance, the defence of statutory authority may be argued. It may also be argued that the escape was an 'Act of God' or of a third party such as a vandal,[37] a further limitation on seeing the rule in *Rylands* as a strict liability tort, although in the nature of especially risky activities it must be the case that greater foresight and consideration is required than other situations where this defence can be argued. (If it were not covered by specific legislation, nuclear installations would be a prime example.). In *Transco*, Lord Hoffmann, in noting the emergence of various statutory liability regimes for things like pollution from waste and by radioactive matter (see p. 391) left open the question whether these kinds of statutory provisions create an exhaustive code of liability which would exclude the rule in *Rylands*, and was also wary of applying the rule in situations where liability might be excluded, by statute, for more risky activities (in a case like *Transco*, if the escape had been from the water company's high pressure main, liability would have been excluded under statute; see s. 209(3)(b), Water Industry Act 1991).

A final point here is that Lord Bingham's opinion in *Transco* casts doubt on whether there is any longer a defence of 'common benefit' or 'public benefit', as had been suggested in *Dunne v North Western Gas Board* [1963] 3 All ER 916. Any such defence would, in practice, extend the principle from one of risk-sharing to risk-imposing. Whether any benefit to the particular claimant from the harmful activity provides a defence, however, remains unclear, although in the past where gas, electricity or water supplies have caused damage to the claimant's property, no liability has been imposed on the basis that the potential claimant has in effect consented to the risk.[38]

The protection of riparian rights

There is a separate action for interference with the rights of owners of riparian land. Although this action has some similarities with private nuisance, it is in practice used far more frequently owing to the strength of riparian owners' natural rights to water. For further explanation see p. 752.

Breach of statutory duty

Where there is a breach of a statutory provision, so that a claimant suffers a loss, there may be a remedy in damages. Although there does not have to be any finding of negligence by the

---

37. In contrast to the position with criminal liability for causing pollution, see p. 283.
38. See *Attorney-General v Cory Brothers & Co.* [1921] 1 AC 521.

defendant, the tort is little used because the courts have held that a claim will succeed only if it can be shown that Parliament intended the claimant to have a civil remedy. Sometimes it is clear that Parliament specifically *excludes* this possibility, as is the case under the Water Resources Act 1991 (see s. 100(b)). Otherwise, if this is not spelt out in the statute, then it must be inferred, and if the statute involves general public law duties, then the broader the exercise of discretion involved the less likely will be a right of claim for breach of statutory duty).[39] Also, the statute must give rights to a limited class of persons rather than to the general public, which makes its application in relation to general pollution control legislation difficult. It is used most frequently in relation to industrial safety legislation, but one example of its use in an environmental context was following the incident at Camelford in 1988 when 20 tonnes of aluminium sulphate wrongly ended up in the public water supply. The water authority eventually ended up settling the case out of court on the basis of a breach of its statutory water supply duties.[40] (The Camelford incident is one reason why there is now a specific offence of supplying water that is unfit for human consumption under the Water Industry Act 1991, s. 70, see p. 722.)

The common view is that if the statute provides for criminal enforcement then this rules out civil claims. This is said to be because the criminal sanctions show that the interests of those affected are being taken seriously, although this would also support the view that this is precisely why civil claims for damages should also be available. Breach of statutory duty was argued before the High Court in *Bowden v South West Water Services Ltd* [1998] Env LR 445 and rejected, because the judge thought that the three EC water directives concerned were all too general in their application. However, the overturning of this decision in relation to the Directive on Shellfish Waters for the purposes of a state liability claim under the *Francovich* principle—because the directive was for the direct benefit of a limited class of shellfishermen—might suggest that a similar view could be taken in relation to breach of statutory duty (see the Court of Appeal decision at [1999] Env LR 438). Ultimately, however, the point remains that legislation intended to protect general environmental interests and which gives public authorities some discretion in implementation (such as in determining a licence), is unlikely to lead to a successful claim for breach of statutory duty.

Other private law mechanisms

Although the most common application of private law remedies as used for environmental protection is that of the law of tort, there are other private law mechanisms that may be useful in this context. Centrally, the law relating to property ownership shows both advantages and disadvantages for environmental protection. Using property law to exclude others from encroaching or trespassing on land has often been relied on by voluntary organizations like the Royal Society for the Protection of Birds to protect habitats, or by bodies like the National Trust to protect cherished landscape features. However, the reverse

---

39. *X (Minors) v Bedfordshire County Council* [1995] 2 AC 633.
40. See also *Read v Croydon Corporation* [1938] 4 All ER 631, discussed at p. 722.

of this is that, as a matter of property law, owners are in principle allowed to interfere with their land in any way they wish. So, as a matter of private law, wild plants can be uprooted and land contaminated so long as neighbouring landowners are not affected. Similarly, restrictive covenants may regulate future land development (see *Tulk v Moxhay* (1848) 41 ER 1143). This may help prevent damaging development, but preservation and 'doing nothing' are not always compatible with enlightened environmental protection and, in any case, their use is ultimately subject to statutory control.

Another example are planning obligations (see p. 486) which, unlike freehold covenants, can provide both for negative restrictions or for positive environmental benefits. Although such obligations are the creation of statute, developers and local planning authorities are given considerable width to enter into them. When they do so, they are contacts between the developer and the planning authority, and agreements entered into after the Contracts (Rights of Third Parties) Act 1999 came into force might be enforceable by local residents for whose benefits the agreements are undoubtedly made.

More recognizably, contractual agreements are also used in the form of management agreements such as those made under section 95, Water Resources Act 1991. These are essentially contracts between the Ministry of Agriculture, Fisheries and Food and individuals to restrict the use of certain agricultural activities to reduce water pollution by nitrates so that the nitrates used in farming will not pollute the waters in the areas (see p. 747). The agreements may be entered into voluntarily, and compensation is payable under them for any restrictions. These types of management agreements are not as wide-ranging as freehold or leasehold covenants as they are not necessarily binding on third parties (unless of course statute makes them so). There is some use of private agreements between industrial organisations (like the Chemical Industries Association) and government, but so far these are limited. Contracts will have to be used where, under an environmental management system, for example, the whole of the supply chain must operate to certain standards.

Civil law remedies

The use of the common law as a mechanism for environmental protection would be useless unless there were effective remedies once a cause of claim had been established. The two main types of remedies that can be sought are preventive and compensatory remedies. An injunction allows for actions creating environmental problems to be stopped by order of the court. Monetary damages act as compensation for any damage suffered but can also pay for any clean up costs involved in rectifying the damage.

Common law remedies have both positive and negative features when it comes to protecting the environment. On the positive side, the courts tend to treat remedies as following directly from the right that has been infringed. That is, they do not engage in a further balancing exercise between the claimant's rights and the defendant's (or wider social) interests. This is seen most clearly in relation to the preference for granting injunctions rather than awarding damages. Negatively, remedies are available to benefit claimants' rights not environmental interests. So, for example, damages need not be spent on restoring the environment.

(a) Injunctions

The granting of an injunction is a discretionary remedy that can either prohibit or restrict a defendant from carrying on an environmentally damaging activity. Normally, either the activity complained of has to be continuing at the date of claim, or there has to be a threat that the activity will continue. Even where the activity has ceased at the time of trial, an injunction can still be sought if it existed when the claim was brought. Although injunctions are discretionary, however, the general principle in the two torts where continuing damage is likely—nuisance and trespass—is that claimants can expect to obtain an injunction unless the activity complained of is not of sufficient gravity or duration to justify stopping the defendant's actions. Turner LJ in *Goldsmith v Tunbridge Wells Improvement Commission* (1866) LR 1 Ch App 349 said:

> It is not in every case of nuisance that this Court should interfere. I think that it ought not to do so in cases in which the injury is merely temporary or trifling; but I think that it ought to do so in cases in which the injury is permanent and serious; and in determining whether the injury is serious or not, regard must be had to all the consequences which may flow from it.

This principle was affirmed in *Kennaway v Thompson* [1981] QB 88, a complaint about noise from powerboat racing. The Court of Appeal decided to award the claimant an injunction restricting the times the boats raced and the noise they made, notwithstanding the public interest in the sport. The importance of this decision is that it confirms that a party which causes a nuisance or trespass cannot simply 'buy off' the rights of those affected by paying an award of damages.

In *Dennis v MOD* however (see Case box 11.2), the exceptional public necessity in training RAF fighter pilots was held to justify an award of damages rather than an injunction.[41] The judge also thought it was relevant that the Harrier jets had been flying at the base for over 30 years and the probability that most jet fighter training at the site would (partly because of the increased noise generated by the next generation of jets) cease after about a further nine years. This indicates that even nuisances which will continue many years into the future may not be stopped if, looking at the wider picture, this would be unduly harsh.

This and other cases illustrate a possible trend which plays down the right to an injunction, while at the same time stressing the importance that those who suffer harm to their land interests should be compensated. In other words, the less that a court feels it must award an injunction, the more likely it may be to hold that there has been a nuisance, and then compensate for the loss this causes. In the case of multi-party claims, of course, it is debatable whether courts could ever properly assess the right amount of damages payable if damages were ever to be preferred to injunctions on economic efficiency grounds.

There are situations where it is possible to obtain an injunction before the occurrence of the event causing injury or damage. Such anticipatory injunctions do not require proof of environmental damage at all. However, there must be sufficient proof of imminent damage and it must be demonstrated that if the activity were to continue the damage accruing would be significant enough to make it difficult to rectify. Such injunctions are seldom granted.

---

41. Strictly, in *Dennis* a declaration against the MOD was sought rather than an injunction (because of issues peculiar to seeking injunctions against the Crown), but the MOD agreed that it would 'act appropriately in the face of such a declaration.'

Injunctions are rarely specific in nature; the court merely sets the standard for the defendant to meet and this standard can be achieved in any way possible. For example, it may be met either by closing down a particular plant which is causing environmental difficulties or by fitting new arrestment equipment. To give defendants time to make such changes, injunctions are often 'suspended' for a certain period before being enforceable.[42]

(b) Damages

Unlike an injunction, a claimant can *demand* that the court award damages. The aim of such damages is to place the claimant as far as possible in the position they would have been in had the wrongful act not occurred. This could be calculated in two ways; on the cost of clean-up operations necessary to restore the property to its previous state, or the difference between the value of the property as it was after the pollution had affected it, and before. The approach of the courts now, however, is to calculate damages according to the latter method. So, where there has not been physical damage, damages will be based on lost capital values, usually the difference in possible rental value during the period of the nuisance (see *Hunter v Canary Wharf*). This means that damages will not depend on the number of people affected, in line with the idea that nuisance is a *land* tort. That said, damages can also be awarded for loss of amenity (i.e. interference with the enjoyment of the use of land) on top of capital losses, though the courts try to restrict such awards to relatively modest sums.[43] This type of loss is similarly calculated on the (somewhat artificial) basis of loss of amenity to the land, rather than people living on the land. This approach would seem to be capable of absorbing the impact of the Human Rights Act (see *Dennis v MOD*, para. 91).

However, if there is actual damage this will have to be compensated. An example of this is *Marquis of Granby v Bakewell UDC* (1923) 87 JP 105. The defendant operated a gas works which discharged poisonous effluent into a river over which the claimant had fishing rights, killing numerous fish. The claimant received compensation equalling the costs of restocking the river in addition to the loss of a large amount of the food supply for other stocks. The court also took into account the effects of the pollution on higher quality areas of the river and considered that the damages would be higher where environmental pollution was greater. But in some cases compensatory damages must have regard to what is fair both to the claimant and the plaintiff. For example, in *Scutt v Lomax* (2000) 79 P&CR D31 the claimant's land had been wrongly bulldozed, and a number of mature trees were lost. The claimant was awarded damages which were less than the cost of replanting replacement trees of the same maturity, together with a modest award of damages reflecting the loss of amenity for the years until they reached the maturity of the lost trees. There is clearly a practical problem here; the more mature a tree the higher the replacement cost, but beyond a certain point replacement will not be possible (a 200-year-old oak tree cannot be replaced, like for like). But even where reinstatement costs can be claimed, the *ecological* value of e.g. mature trees over saplings is absent.

A positive development in the area of damages comes from *Jan de Nul (UK) Ltd v AXA Royale Belge SA* [2002] EWCA Civ 209. A wildlife trust was awarded £100,000 of costs incurred in conducting surveys to assess whether, following dredging operations, silt had

---

42. An example is *Pride of Derby and Derbyshire Angling Association Ltd v British Celanese* [1953] Ch 149, see p. 754.

43. *Farley v Skinner* [2001] UKHL 49, a case about aircraft noise; for an example of an award outside these guidelines, because of the exceptional level of interference, see *Dennis v MOD* (Case box 11.2).

caused any long-term damage to a nature reserve that it owned. This was notwithstanding that the survey did not find any such damage. It was important, however, that there had actually been physical interference with the land, and that any clean-up would have cost more, which allowed the court to decide that the survey was a reasonable response. This case should not therefore be taken as deciding that any precautionary expenditure can be claimed when, in fact, no damage has been caused. For example, it is doubtful whether the costs of a private medical examination would be a reasonable response from someone who had been living in the vicinity of a release of hazardous substances into the air.

Damages for all *future* loss are only available in lieu of an injunction. This remedy is used only sparingly because of the ready availability of the more usual injunction procedure.

Lastly, exemplary or punitive damages can be awarded in specific instances. The basis of such an award is to deter the defendant and others from committing torts which may result in financial benefit to the person responsible. The scope for these damages is, however, limited to cases where there has been oppressive, arbitrary or unconstitutional action by servants of the government, or where the defendant's conduct was calculated to make a profit which would exceed the damages payable (*Rookes v Barnard* [1964] AC 1129). Thus a claim for exemplary damages in public nuisance after the public water supply at Camelford was polluted was rejected on the ground that public nuisance fell outside the above categories.[44] And in *Scutt v Lomax* an initial award of exemplary damages was overturned because the cavalier attitude of the defendant in thinking that the plot of land had been abandoned was not enough to show that its activities were motivated by a sufficient disregard for the claimant's rights.

The utility of private law for environmental protection

As the brief analysis above of the various private law mechanisms makes clear, there are a number of general limitations on the use of private law (especially tort law) to protect environmental interests. There is also the key issue of the affordability of private law claims and other practical difficulties in its use.[45]

(a) Private law acts only as a protector of private interests

Both the land torts and the contractual mechanisms considered above aim to protect private interests rather than the more nebulous concept of environmental 'rights' or 'interests'. This has two important consequences. First, the level of environmental protection that flows from these mechanisms will be determined according to private rather than public interests. *Cambridge Water Co. v Eastern Counties Leather* (see Case box 11.4) is a paradigm example, where the damages sought by the water company would, had it been successful, have paid for the relocation of its borehole to an unpolluted site. Whichever way the case was decided, the land and groundwater remained contaminated. Private law will only lead to the remediation of such sites if this is the most reasonable (which usually means the cheapest) way for the

---

44. *A.B. v South West Water Services Ltd* [1993] QB 507. For criticism, see P. Cane (1993) 5 JEL 149.

45. For detailed criticism from a broadly law-and-economics perspective of most of the following points, see D. Howarth, (2002) Washburn Law Journal 469.

claimant to be compensated. A similar point can be seen in *Hatton v UK* (see Case box 11.1) where the Strasbourg Court held that it was reasonable to take into account the affected individuals ability to leave the area without undue hardship. Again, any indirect environmental benefit from litigation is absent.[46]

Another negative example is the possibility that an easement to pollute a river might be acquired. It is arguable whether such a claim could ever be in the interests of the environment.

Secondly, the right to bring a claim is generally restricted in some way. For example, private nuisance claims are restricted in this way. On the other hand, under the Contracts (Rights of Third Parties) Act 1999, a third party can now sue on a contract and this means that local residents might conceivably be able to enforce agreements entered into between planning authorities and developers (see further p. 486). Although there are narrow rights for groups to take action in public nuisance, private law mechanisms serve narrowly drawn private interests, essentially interests relating to the ownership or possession of land. Even where a private right can be argued, the substance of the right may do little to improve the environment of those who would stand to benefit the most from such improvements, as the operation of the locality rule in private nuisance shows.

In both cases, effective environmental protection requires wider public interests to be taken into account, including both wider ecological interests and the interests of non-land owners and perhaps also of future generations. It is true, of course, that the exercise of private rights may coincide with the protection of wider ecological interests. But English private law seems a long way off accepting the idea that, for example, there should be scope to bring a claim on behalf of wild plants and animals rather as children bring claims through a guardian in family law proceedings.

(b) Private rights are based on imprecise or unduly absolute standards

As we have seen in Chapter 8, environmental regulation increasingly involves the setting both of specific target standards and then specifically worded licences to try to meet these standards. Often, both of these will be expressed as quantitative limits. One advantage of these is that they make enforcement easier as the detection of breaches can be accurately monitored and proper assessments made of any discharge. There are, of course, a range of more qualitative standards that are used. The BAT standard in IPPC permits is perhaps the best example, but even with BAT there is quite detailed guidance given to operators as to what standards will be required. The effective regulation of many industrial processes can only be dealt with through quantitative standards and scientific monitoring.

Private law mechanisms meet neither criteria. Generally the common law is based upon standards which are either unduly tightly drawn or necessarily imprecise. Both have their drawbacks. For example, trespass law does not require any proof of damage, and therefore provides a fairly absolute protection of property rights. While this level of protection does have its environmental advantages (e.g. in conserving nature conservation sites) the more general problem is that trespass law does not allow for the kind of balancing which might be needed in other contexts and arguably over-regulates in some situations, which may not be in the wider public interest. It also has the drawback that the absolute protection afforded to landowners' interests might be judged by some to prevent a wider experience of nature

---

46. Another illustration of this is *Ashworth and others v UK*, ECtHR, 20 Jan. 2004.

(although to some extent this has been rectified by the Countryside and Rights of Way Act 2000 which establishes a limited 'right to roam').

In the case of imprecise standards, as we see clearly in nuisance law, the law tries to balance competing private interests, looking to the reasonableness of the activities rather than restricting conduct to specified levels. What is reasonable depends on the circumstances of each case. While this may be necessary in order to deal with disputes over matters as subjective as some noise nuisances, it makes the outcome of a nuisance claim highly uncertain, especially where it involves amenity damage. Although the context-specificness of nuisance law is admired by theoretical economists—who point to its advantages over generalised rules which may over- or under-regulate—inevitably this uncertainty discourages arguable cases from being brought by private litigants.[47]

(c) Problems of proof

Environmental regulation typically involves the setting of standards which, if exceeded, lead to a punishable breach. Standards may either be breached without damage to the environment (this may happen with 'technical' breaches of process standards), or they are breached because some quantitative standard has not been met. The key point is that there will usually be some monitoring on the site recording the breach; only rarely does the regulator have to take samples from the environment and try to establish where the pollutant came from. This, however, is often what has to be done in environmental tort claims. For instance, it is the nature of airborne deposits that they could have originated from a site many miles from the area of the damage. Seeking to show that the damage emanates from a particular site in these circumstances is particularly difficult. In heavily industrialized areas the problem is even more acute.

The common law does go some way towards solving this problem. As we have seen, it will be enough in negligence and nuisance to show that the defendant 'materially contributed' to the damage caused, even where his or her own contribution was insignificant if viewed in isolation (see p. 364). This is an important rule, especially in those situations where it would be impossible to pin down the exact contribution of any one polluter, as with nitrate run-off. Nevertheless, it has its limits. First, it is not enough to show that the damage is of the kind generally associated with operators like the defendant, as *Cambridge Water Co v Eastern Counties Leather* illustrates. Secondly, there are practical and evidential limits: there must be evidence linking the defendant's operations with the damage caused, and proving causation is often technically difficult and very costly. Thirdly, and rather obviously, the rule is of no practical use where environmental damage has a vast number of small contributors (e.g. low level ozone pollution from motor vehicles). All of these problems arise, therefore, not because it may be difficult to show that an activity is genuinely causing harm—a problem common to private and public environmental law controls—but because in private law the nature of the burden of proving causation is individualised. In contrast, statutory regulation can shift the focus on to a polluting sector, and lead to improvements by imposing tighter controls across the board, e.g. on a particularly polluting sector of industry.

---

47. Uncertainty of outcome is a barrier to most litigation, see H. Genn, *Paths to Justice* (Oxford: Hart Publishing, 1999).

(d) Private law as a fault-based system

Although trespass gives rise to strict liability, in other circumstances the bringing of a claim under common law either requires some carelessness on behalf of the person creating the damage (negligence), or at least foreseeability of the damage caused (nuisance). But most pollution loading, and isolated pollution spills, does not occur because of deliberate actions by careless and unthinking individuals. Most pollution incidents arise because of a number of circumstances that would not normally be foreseeable but which give rise to damage. In the interests of doing justice to defendants, the common law does not always seek to redress any damage caused by such accidents, and corrective justice becomes a secondary consideration. Clearly, this is contrary to the general thrust of the polluter pays principle.

(e) Reactive controls

Private law controls are generally reactive[48] and compensatory rather than preventive. It is only very rarely that private law can be used to prevent environmental damage, although it is possible in limited situations to seek anticipatory injunctions. While the general priority given to injunctions over damages in nuisance law is beneficial, private law does not offer continuing controls which might gradually improve standards over time. Nor does it provide an appropriate mechanism for dealing with uncertain risks, since tort law does not really have the capacity to impose safety margins. Putting all these points somewhat differently, we doubt whether the prospect of being sued in nuisance ever really influences the behaviour of polluting industries in the way that meeting an environmental regulator does.

(f) An environmental injustice?

Despite many negative features, the common law torts contain a range of general principles that ought in theory to have gone much further in protecting both human and wider environmental interests. Instead, the need for environmental regulation was recognised at a relatively early stage of industrialisation. In large part this was because of an under-utilization of the common law, for a number of connected social, political and economic reasons.

Resort to the law in the 19th century was always a rich person's prerogative. Taking a claim to law was both lengthy and ultimately outside the reach of the vast majority of the population. Until 1875 a claim in nuisance seeking an injunction needed two claims to be taken, one through the common law and one through the Court of Chancery. Lack of access to technical knowledge and resources followed inevitably from poverty, and made monitoring almost impossible. Even today the costs of private litigation are prohibitive for many potential claimants, and present the biggest hurdle in bringing environmental law claims.[49]

Also, as we have seen, bringing a claim in nuisance required a proprietary interest. In the mid-19th century it has been estimated that only around 15 per cent of the population were owner/occupiers. Thus, the vast majority of the population would have had great difficulty

---

48. Even public regulation, of course, is often reactive In the sense of being a political or administrative response to perceived problems; see Chapter 2.

49. Genn, *Paths to Justice; Environmental Justice?* (WWF, ELF, and Leigh Day and Co., 2004).

in even founding a claim. When coupled with the level of damages, notoriously low for interference with the enjoyment of land, there were considerable obstacles to taking legal action.

Moreover, what has subsequently been identified as a complex system of power relationships ensured that in the social context there was tremendous pressure not to 'cause trouble'. Few workers would wish to proceed against their bosses and it was clear that there was a certain degree of class solidarity amongst the industrialists themselves. The perceived economic benefits to the local community were inevitably to the fore in the minds of the local authorities, which were most reluctant to use their powers to prosecute for public nuisances, and indeed were often responsible for much pollution themselves. Moreover, many factory owners bought up large areas of land surrounding their own sites and constructed low cost, high density housing for their workers. This, coupled with the impact of industry on surrounding land prices, effectively meant that a factory owner could purchase the right to pollute the surrounding area very cheaply. (Of course, the landowner would be most likely to have lived upwind of the prevailing westerly winds, one factor behind the association of affluence with the 'West End'.)

Furthermore, the relative expense of bringing private law actions is well illustrated by the Third Report of the Royal Commission on the Pollution of Rivers in 1867:

[Bringing a common law claim] is an expensive remedy. For the same money which is spent over a hard fought litigation against a single manufacturer, a Conservancy Board armed with proper powers, might for years keep safe from all abuse, a long extensive river with hundreds of manufacturers situated on its banks.

St Helens Smelting Co. v Tipping (see p. 360) illustrates some of these points well. Mr. Tipping was a rich cotton magnate who owned 1300 acres of land. He could afford to risk the backlash of industrialists because of the well-documented conflict between the cotton and chemical industries.[50] The damages received in his case and also in other nuisance cases were appallingly low. In one case (*Halsey v Esso Petroleum* [1961] 2 All ER 145) the claimant received only £200 damages following five years of noise, dirt and commotion from the neighbouring oil storage depot. This raises another problem with nuisance claims, namely that the effect of the locality rule means that any damages that are awarded may be small, reducing the incentive to complain.

The future of private law as an environmental protection mechanism

Following *Cambridge Water Co. v Eastern Counties Leather*, *Hunter v Canary Wharf*, and now *Transco v Stockport MBC*, it is clear that the House of Lords, at least, is reluctant to see significant development of the common law as a mechanism for environmental protection. In *Cambridge Water* they stated explicitly that the rule in *Rylands* should not be developed further into a more specific strict liability common law rule about the control of hazardous

---

50. *Dennis v MOD* (Case box 11.2) is a more recent example of 'rich claimant/deep pocket defendant'.

substances.[51] But this was wrapped up in more general language about private law and environmental regulation:

given that so much well-informed and carefully structured legislation is now being put in place for [the escape of hazardous substances], there is less need for the courts to develop a common law principle to achieve the same end, and indeed it may well be undesirable that they do so.

The approach taken by the House of Lords in *Hunter*, putting private nuisance law back to its original position of protecting only property rights holders, shows a similar cautiousness. As Lord Hoffmann said:

the development of the common law should be rational and coherent. It should not distort its principles and create anomalies as an expedient to fill a gap.

The distinction which the House of Lords in *Hunter* was eager to make—between damage to land and damage to persons—can however be conceived of too simply. Take, for example, interference with the use of a public footpath across private land. There may be no reason for the landowner to litigate to prevent or remedy any damage to the right of way if there is no damage to his agricultural interests. But those who use the footpath are left without a private law remedy. This calls into question the 'privateness' of private law.[52] There may therefore be an argument that the connection between nuisance and property rights is justified in so far as the holder of the right acts in his or her own interests. But if this feature is absent, and the litigant (perhaps an environmental organisation or conservation trust) acts in a custodial manner in pursuit of wider 'public' interests, the justification for the strict nexus with land loses force.

The more general point, however, is whether the judges should take such a conservative approach to the development of the common law as they have done recently. It is no answer to say that regulation is to be preferred, whether this is through contaminated land legislation at national or EC level (*Cambridge Water*) or town and country planning law (*Hunter*, discussed more fully below). Indeed, it is trite to say so, and the general advantages of regulation over private law mechanisms have been explored above. It is, however, worth reflecting on the extent to which, when Parliament acts, it does not always do so in a way that enhances the protection of individual rights or environmental interests. For example, the scheme for making enforcement orders under the Water Industry Act 1991 might be said to unduly insulate water and sewerage companies—not known for having difficulties in generating considerable profits—from compensating those who, like Mr Marcic (Case box 11.8), suffered because of their inaction. A second issue here is the extent to which public law controls are actually used by public regulators, for example the enforcement orders under the Water Industry Act 1991, so relied on by the House of Lords in *Marcic*, have never been used by the regulator.

The key point is that both private and public law controls must co-exist, even if this is through either (a) principles of private law that make statutory authority a defence to a claim in private nuisance, trespass or (most probably) the rule in *Rylands*; or (b) statutory rules which determine the extent to which compliance with an environmental licence may

---

51. See also Lord Bingham in *Transco v Stockport MBC* [2003] UKHL 61, adopting this reasoning.
52. J. Wightman (1998) MLR 870.

be a defence to a common law claim.)[53] If private law is to maintain the position that most commentators claim for it, that of a subsidiary control when considered alongside public regulation, then it must, at a minimum, be sustained in this function. The obvious danger that we have seen in this chapter is that, although there have been some important 'victories' in recent years (*Dennis* being one), the conservative orientation of the higher courts is frustrating the ability of the common law to keep pace, *even in its subsidiary role*, with developments in public regulation. Human rights law may force through some welcome developments, e.g. in relation to the rights to bring nuisance actions, but in other respects there appears to be a degree of ossification. One example that looks particularly outmoded is the right to claim in public nuisance where no particularized damage has been suffered; having to defer to public authorities to mount such actions has rightly been criticised as looking out of place alongside developments in the law of standing to bring public law challenges in environmental cases.[54]

Private law, public regulation, and 'the public interest'

There is often a conflict between private law and public regulation, in the sense that an activity may be lawful under one regime but not the other. Private law rights can clash with many regulatory controls, although most of the case law has been about planning law. Many uses of land that give rise to nuisances, for example, have the benefit of planning permission. In granting a planning application it must be assumed that the local planning authority has balanced the impact of the development upon private interests (e.g. neighbours) with any competing public interests and concluded that the public interests in allowing the development to proceed should prevail. But two problems remain. First, what weight do planning authorities have to give to private rights in the decision-making process? Secondly, how does the grant of the planning permission—or other environmental licence—affect such private rights?

On the first point, a planning permission can be granted which makes a nuisance action by the new owner/occupiers likely (*R v Exeter City Council, ex parte JL Thomas and Co. Ltd* [1991] 1 QB 471; see also p. 481). A public law challenge to such a planning permission will have to do something more than simply argue that private rights will be interfered with. Although environmental impact relating to land use will be a 'material consideration' to which the planning authority is to have regard, the courts have given considerable discretion to planning authorities to decide how much weight to give such considerations (including no weight at all).

In relation to the impact of the grant of planning permission, recent case law has now confined the scope of the controversial ruling in *Gillingham Borough Council v Medway (Chatham) Dock Co. Ltd* [1993] QB 343. The local authority granted planning permission for dock development, but later took a public nuisance action following complaints about noise and vibration caused by lorries going to and from the port, especially at night. There were two readings of Buckley J's judgment refusing to grant an injunction restricting lorry movements at night. A broad reading was that planning permission was equivalent to the

---

53. See, e.g., s. 100(b), Water Resources Act 1991, discussed at p. 752.

54. K. Stanton and C. Willmore, in J. Lowry and R. Edmunds (eds) *Environmental Protection and the Common Law* (Oxford: Hart, 2000).

defence of statutory authority. This raised concerns that any activities engaged in under a planning permission could not lead to liability in nuisance, meaning that private rights would be extinguished without any redress or compensation contrary to established principles of English law.

But it is the narrow reading of the judgment that has prevailed. On this view, planning permission does not act as a *defence* to a claim in nuisance. Instead, Buckley J's decision went to the heart of the *definition* of a nuisance and the locality doctrine in particular. The question was whether the planning permission had so changed the nature of the area that the locality became a commercial area, making the lorry movements a reasonable user of the locality. This narrower view was upheld by the Court of Appeal in *Wheeler v J.J. Saunders Ltd* [1996] Ch 19. There, planning permission was granted for pig-weaning units to be built close to the claimant's land. The claimant successfully complained of smell nuisance that followed once the development was implemented. The Court essentially laid down three rules. First, the *Gillingham* case only decided that 'strategic' planning decisions, affected by considerations of public interest, could legalise certain nuisances by changing the nature of the locality. This might have been the case with the major port development at the Chatham Dockyard, but it was not the case with lesser developments like pig units. (Quite where the dividing line is was not elaborated upon.) Secondly, the *Gillingham* decision is restricted to those situations where the effects of the development make a specific change in the nature of the locality. Building pig units in the countryside is not such a radical change.[55] Finally, the Court clarified that it is *actual* development, rather than development plans, which matters. This was sensible, not least because many developments earmarked in plans never materialize.

The basic approach taken in *Wheeler* was later upheld by the Court of Appeal in *Hunter*, and approved of in some of the speeches in the House of Lords in that case. What is perhaps most important about the law in this area is the way that it highlights a certain amount of unease amongst the judiciary about the overlap between the exercise of rights conferred by public law powers, and private law remedies. As Gibson LJ said in *Wheeler*:

The Court should be slow to acquiesce in the extinction of private rights without compensation as a result of administrative decisions which cannot be appealed and are difficult to challenge.

Certainly, traditional compensation concepts apply rather uneasily in relation to concepts like environmental harm. The value of keeping open the private law claim may therefore lie more with the way in which its existence may influence decision-making by public bodies, providing a means of keeping regulatory systems open and accountable. Indeed, this appears to have influenced the judges in *Wheeler*, who clearly were troubled by what they thought to be an injudicious grant of planning consent, seemingly obtained on the basis of inaccurate and incomplete information and with little or no regard to the claimant's interests. On this line of thinking, protecting private rights furthers, rather than restricts, public interests.

The relationship between private law and public regulation is not confined to questions involving planning permissions, and can arise in relation to other environmental licences, e.g. in *Blackburn v ARC Ltd* [1998] Env LR 469 a waste management licence was held not to change the locality surrounding a landfill site. In *Budden and Albery v BP Oil* [1980] JPL 586

---

55. Nor, it would seem, did operating the RAF base in *Dennis* change the location, which remained 'essentially rural' (see Case box 11.2).

a claim in negligence was brought against two oil companies based on their use of lead in petrol, even though the companies had adhered to regulatory standards. For the court, allowing the claim would mean that valid regulations prescribing the lead content in petrol would effectively be replaced by a lower, judicially determined standard. The case illustrates the way that, especially in negligence cases, statutory standards may dictate common law standards. But the 'balancing act' quality to nuisance law provides for rather more flexibility. Thus in *Murdoch v Glacier Metal Co. Ltd* [1998] Env LR 732 claim about noise levels exceeding World Health Organisation standards failed, in part because of the already noisy area—alongside a main road—in which the claimants lived (see also p. 244).

As to the impact of the Human Rights Act here, in cases where legislation is involved (such as under the Nuclear Installations Act 1965, or where a private law right comes up against a public law authorization like a planning permission or environmental licence) the courts must 'read and give effect to' this legislation to make it compatible with the Convention if it is at all possible to do so. This might mean, for example, some relaxations to the strict approach to statutory authority authorising a nuisance taken in *Allen v Gulf Oil*, (see Case box 11.6) although it is likely that the limits which the courts have already placed on such rights so that those rights cannot be used to authorise any interference which is more than necessary or which is negligent, will go a long way to showing that a proper balance has been struck.

It is also worth mentioning that in *Khatun v UK* (the follow up to *Hunter v Canary Wharf*) the European Commission on Human Rights ultimately rejected the claim that Article 8 had been breached because of the regard that must be had to the fair balance to be struck between the competing interests of the individual and of the community as a whole. In this context, the UK had shown that the development was 'necessary', i.e. that the interference corresponded to a pressing social need and was proportionate to the aim pursued, namely economic redevelopment. In a sense, the economic justification for the development legitimised what the planning permission alone could not do. A final point is that, as noted above (p. 358), the *Hatton* case suggests that there must be some sort of regulatory failure before there can be a breach of Article 8. This might suggest that any development e.g. with planning permission, cannot breach Article 8 rights. It is questionable whether the logic of this conclusion should, or will, be followed through (or it may be that, in cases similar to *Wheeler v Saunders* there will be much more scrutiny of the decision-making process).

The way ahead? Civil liability in statutes and EC developments

One of the obvious limitations of private law controls such as nuisance law is that they are essentially aimed at protecting individual rights, or rights relating to property. As cases like *Cambridge Water* and *Hunter* show, many judges are clearly reluctant to develop these mechanisms so that they are *directly* concerned with environmental protection. However, there are already some statutory regimes which try to overcome the inadequacies of ordinary private law in relation to problematic areas like pollution from international oil spills.

What links many of these statutory regimes (and any environmental liability directive that the EC might adopt) is the extent to which they might be directly concerned with environmental protection or remediation, and not just the protection of property. In this sense, these regimes can be said to follow on from measures such as those contained in Part IIA of the EPA 1990 relating to contaminated land, or the Water Resources Act 1991, s. 161 which allows for the clean-up of polluted water. Although in practice both might *indirectly* benefit other property owners (who will avoid having to pay for the cost of clean up), and directly affect the person paying for the cost of clean up in a way which, for them, is probably indistinguishable from compensating another private party (the person whose brownfield site is cleaned up benefits from the other party by seeing an increase in the value of his or her land). However, their central concern is with the quality of the environment in its own right, which can be cleaned up, for example, so that ecosystems are restored.

The purpose of the following sections is to explore the possibilities of statutory civil liability regimes, which would obviously meet the objection made by Lord Goff in the *Cambridge Water* case that it is not for the courts to develop the common law in areas where rule- and decision-making is complex and involves many stakeholders. Readers are invited to draw their own conclusions as to the merits of statutory civil liability as against, for example, regulatory clean-up regimes.

(a) Statutory civil liability

In addition to the common law, there are a number of statutes that impose liability by means of private law remedies, rather than the more usual public law methods.

(i) Nuclear Installations Act 1965

The individual problems of nuclear installations are not adequately dealt with by the law of tort. As the Chernobyl incident demonstrated, the damage caused by nuclear actions can be widespread and not confined to a specific period of time. There are also difficulties of proving a causal link between the injury caused and exposure to radiation. Many diseases that are caused by radiation also occur naturally, and trying to establish whether or not there is an epidemiological link is frequently fraught with difficulties. To avoid these difficulties, the Nuclear Installations Act 1965 introduced absolute civil liability for all damage caused from certain occurrences (ss. 7–10). Not all loss from nuclear damage is covered under the Act. Economic loss can only be recovered where there is specific physical harm caused to the land. Thus in *Merlin v British Nuclear Fuels plc* [1990] 2 QB 557 a claim for loss in value of a house in the area of the Sellafield nuclear installation resulting from radioactive contamination was refused because the 'contamination' had not given rise to physical harm. The presence of raised radioactivity levels in the house was not sufficient to amount to such harm.

The decision in *Merlin v British Nuclear Fuels plc* was considered in *Blue Circle Industries v Ministry of Defence* [1998] 3 All ER 385, in which a claim arose out of the contamination of land (owned by Blue Circle) neighbouring the Atomic Weapons Establishment (AWE) at Aldermaston. Although the MOD carried out remediation works on Blue Circle's land which effectively removed the radioactive material, sale of the land fell through due to blight resulting from the contamination. Blue Circle brought a claim to recover £5 million in damages arising out of the diminution in value of the estate. The court distinguished the damage in *Merlin* from the contamination at the AWE by linking the economic loss in Blue

Circle's case to the actual physical harm caused by the radioactive contamination. In *Merlin* it was thought that there was no physical harm and the nature of the loss was purely economic and non-actionable. The distinction, it must be said, is unconvincing and it is probably better to see *Blue Circle* as simple taking a less restrictive approach to damage (or, has been suggested, as the courts protecting business interests more than those of house-holders).[56] In finding in favour of Blue Circle the court also found that the 1965 Act imposed liability where there was *any* injury or damage, irrespective of the contamination levels.

(ii) Merchant Shipping Act 1995

In the wake of numerous oil disasters in the mid to late 1960s, international concern led to the introduction of legislation to compensate for damage from oil. This is now consolidated in the Merchant Shipping Act 1995,[57] which applies to spills both from tankers and other ships. The Act imposes strict liability on owners of ships in relation to physical damage to property and personal injury from oil pollution (ss. 153 and 154). The financing of the majority of losses stemming from the Act is covered by a compulsory insurance scheme, although there is a further international fund for compensation which pays out when the ship-owner cannot afford to. This fund paid out compensation following both the *Braer* (1993) and *Sea Empress* (1996) oil spills.

BOX 11.1 **Marine oil pollution compensation**

The basic principle for accidental or intentional oil spillages from ships is that if oil is discharged or escapes from a tanker, the registered owner is liable for:

(a) 'any damage caused . . . by *contamination* resulting from the discharge or escape' and

(b) the cost of any reasonable pollution prevention or reduction measures taken.

Claims for preventing marine contamination may also be made. However, the Act limits claims for environmental impairment to *reasonable reinstatement costs*, that is it rules out general claims about loss of environmental services or amenity unless reasonable costs have been incurred in making the situation better. This avoids having to calculate, in money terms, the 'damage' suffered by the environment. So, following the *Braer* spill in 1993, claims relating to health risks, general anxiety suffered by the affected community and for environmental amenity were rejected. In relation to pure environmental damage the Fund will only pay out, as it did following the *Sea Empress* spill in 1996, where, for example, charities have incurred the cost of cleaning oiled birds, or bodies like the Environment Agency have incurred costs.

Because reinstatement costs must be reasonable, compensation might be payable following a minor spill, but not after a major spill with devastating ecological consequences (since in the latter case reinstatement may just be impossible, or the cost of reinstating may be disproportionately expensive). Unlike some areas of environmental law, this scheme does not look to maintaining ecological coherence by requiring damage to one site to be compensated—ecologically—by

---

56. M. Day (2001) 3 Env L Rev 163 at 164.

57. The Act also makes provision for the eventual transposition of the 1996 International Convention on Liability and Compensation for Damage in Connection with the Carriage of Hazardous and Noxious Substances by Sea (the 'HNS Convention').

improvements to other areas (see, e.g., p. 832). Also, awards are made based on the lower of the diminution of market value or the cost of repairs (the basic principle behind cars being 'written off' following accidents, where the repair costs would exceed their value). So if an important habitat is badly damaged by a spill, then if the land has a low market value (as land protected by conservation designations often will have, because developing the land will be difficult), it is likely that damage will simply not be repaired. Again, there will be an uncompensated loss of ecological services. For various reasons, therefore, some aspects of environmental damage go uncompensated.

(iii) Environmental Protection Act 1990, s. 73

Section 73(6) of EPA 1990 imposes civil liability for the unlawful deposit of waste (see Box 15.16).

(b) EC developments

A second consideration is the recent adoption of an EC Directive on Environmental Liability (2004/35) and the impact this may have as regards a privately initiated claim to protect the environment. The key features of the Directive (which comes into force in 2007) are:

- Personal injury, damage to private property and economic loss are not covered. There will be liability for 'environmental damage', justified because the unowned environment fares badly under the civil liability regimes of most EC Member States. The Directive does not cover things like noise pollution etc, even though noise control is the subject of numerous EC directives. Environmental damage is restricted to:
  - damage to species and habitats protected under EC conservation legislation (see p. 824);
  - (only if the Member State chooses) sites and species designated under national conservation law such as SSSIs;
  - damage to waters protected by the EC Water Framework Directive (see p. 717); and
  - soil contamination.

This is a narrow view of environmental damage which does not even cover all areas protected under EC law (such as nitrate vulnerable zones) and falls short of what we already have at national level under the contaminated land regime, which extends to more general ecosystem damage (see Chapter 17). It also privileges what might be termed nature conservation biodiversity over agricultural biodiversity, e.g. an organic farm fearing contamination from neighbouring GM crops will not be protected if it lies outside a protected area.

- For environmental damage generally, only certain activities which must be regulated under EC environmental law (e.g. processes subject to IPPC) are covered, though here liability is in principle strict (though see below). However, if the polluter has been at fault or negligent, any operational activity causing damage to species and habitats is covered.

- This approach is notable for differentiating between strict and fault based liability not on the normal grounds that the former is a more appropriate way to internalise the costs of hazardous new technologies or processes. Instead, strict liability appears to be justified because the aim is to improve enforcement of EC environmental law and give polluters incentives to comply with environmental directives, whereas damage to 'national' bio-diversity interests is more a matter for Member State discretion and where to impose strict liability might exceed normal national liability rules.

- In two key situations the strictness of liability is limited. These are where (1) the damage is authorized under a permit issued to comply with the listed EC environmental laws that the directive covers, or (2) 'state of the art' scientific and technical knowledge meant that at the time of the damaging act, environmental damage was not thought likely. These are not complete defences, but their consequence is that the operator may not have to pay the costs of remedial action unless it is shown that they were at fault. (echoing, respectively, the approach in *Allen v Gulf Oil*, and the rules on reasonable foreseeability of damage).

- Many provisions of the Directive bear a strong resemblance to the kinds of statutory pollution prevention and clean-up powers introduced in the UK in the 1990s.[58] There is an obligation on operators to prevent pollution arising where it is imminent, or control and remediate pollution if it has already occurred. In both cases this is backed by powers for competent authorities (such as the Environment Agency or English Nature) to require action or undertake it themselves.[59] In either case it is the polluter who must pay.

- There are detailed provisions about what exactly 'remediation of environmental damage' means. These include, amongst other things, interim ecological compensation and, if there will not be a full ecological recovery of the area damaged, long-term replacement by equivalent natural resources. Some criteria are given, but there is an inevitable vagueness to a lot of what this means.

- A key difference between national rules on pollution prevention and clean up is that the directive gives affected individuals, or bodies like environmental NGOs, the right to press the regulatory authorities to take action. The regulator must give its reasons for either choosing (or declining) to act, and the NGO has the right to question the basis of the regulator's decision (either in a court or another competent and independent and impartial body). This is weaker than earlier drafts of the Directive, which envisaged that NGOs would have standing to bring actions directly if the state had failed to act or to act promptly (akin to what in the US are called 'citizen suits'). Earlier drafts also granted to NGOs, in urgent cases, the right to ask a court to issue an injunction, or be reimbursed for reasonable costs spent in preventing environmental damage. This has also been removed, with the emphasis now being firmly on the regulator acting and imposing liability.

- The emphasis is on remediation of environmental damage: damages awarded would have to be applied to environmental restoration, and to compensatory schemes to cover interim damage and where restoration is not possible.

- Liability would apply only to future damage. But how this is defined is problematic. If a cylinder containing chemicals is dumped and, after some time, begins to leak, it is still not clear whether the incident causing the damage is the date of dumping, or when the

---

58. See, e.g., Water Resources Act 1991, ss. 161 and 161A, discussed at p. 744.

59. Importantly, where the operator cannot be identified ('orphan damage'), or will not act, or is not required to bear the costs, the regulatory body only has a *power*, not a duty, to act itself.

leakage begins. In other words, it remains unclear how the proposals would apply to latent damage.

- Although supported by some Member States, provisions requiring compulsory insurance against environmental damage were not included in the Directive; the issue is to be returned to in a few years time.

These proposals may result in improved protection for the unowned environment. However, the impact on statutory clean up regimes, such as the newly implemented regime for contaminated land under Part IIA of the Environment Act 1990, will be slight. Depending on how any restriction against imposing retrospective liability is interpreted, there would simply be no duplication with the provisions for historic pollution contained in Part IIA of the Environment Act 1990 (see further Chapter 17). Note also that the Directive does not cover liabilities arising from the nuclear sector, or which are covered under international oil pollution conventions. Nor does it cover diffuse pollution unless it is possible to establish a causal link between the damage and the activities of an individual operator.

In essence, the Directive is neither environmental, not does it provide for civil liability. It is little more than an administrative adjunct to EC environmental legislation. This in itself is not a bad thing, but it might be asked whether the tortuous process of agreeing the Directive—which took over 10 years—in order to create a limited liability regime was really worth the effort, or whether it would have been preferable to focus more on ensuring that breaches of EC environmental law are better monitored and punished, and fines or administrative penalties used to pay for environmental clean-up.

CHAPTER SUMMARY

1   There is no overarching principle behind the 'environmental' torts (or torts generally). Private law protects private rights, in the case of tort law by imposing obligations on certain parties not to act in some way that is, broadly, unreasonable.

2   The main torts that might be used to pursue environmentally related interests are private and public nuisance, trespass, negligence and the rule in *Rylands v Fletcher*. These are separate torts[60] with their own particular history and rules.

3   With the exception of negligence and public nuisance, the torts mentioned protect interests in land, i.e. the interests of land owners and those possessing land.

4   The main tort used in environmental cases is private nuisance. This imposes a duty of 'good neighbourliness' between landowners. Whether this is breached depends on a matrix of factors, including the locality, the nature, duration and extent of the nuisance, and the use of the claimant's land. It does not require fault, in the sense of having to show that the defendant acted carelessly.

5   Trespass provides a strict level of protection for property rights against direct interference, but this is of limited use in the context of pollution (which is often spread in an indirect way, e.g. noise or fumes) and may be used to stifle environmental protest.

---

60. Though it has been suggested that the rule in *Rylands* is not a tort based on breaching a duty not to do something harmful, but simply a mechanism for allocating the costs of dangerous behaviour (N. McBride and R. Bagshaw, *Tort Law* (2nd ed. London: Longman, 2005) 32).

6   For isolated escapes of dangerous substances from land, the rule in *Rylands v Fletcher* applies. But the courts have severely limited its practical application by setting a very high hurdle to overcome in showing that an activity is of sufficiently extraordinary risk for the rule to apply. Most such activities will probably be regulated anyway.

7   The main remedies in tort law are injunctions (for continuing harms) and money damages. Where they are available, injunctions should provide a strong degree of protection of property rights, and this may have indirect benefits for wider environmental interests.

8   If a polluting activity is judged to be in the public interest, it may still be a nuisance but damages rather than an injunction might be awarded. Whether compensation adequately protects the environment, or makes the polluter pay, is debatable.

9   In some situations, tort law claims must defer to what Parliament has decided; in other cases where environmental licences have been granted for a polluting activity, the courts are reluctant to see private law claims trumped by regulatory permissions.

10   In recent years, the courts have demonstrated a conservative attitude to developing tort law to fill gaps created by environmental regulation, preferring to leave matters to Parliament. This may make it increasingly difficult for tort to play an important subsidiary role alongside public law controls.

11   Most commentators consider private law to be an inferior environmental protection mechanism compared to public regulation.

12   Environmental litigators must also think about whether there has been any breach of human rights. The European Convention on Human Rights does not expressly secure the right to live in a decent environment free from pollution, or which contains adequate natural resources. A few of the articles of the Convention are now interpreted to protect interests associated with living free from harmful levels of environmental interference (e.g. noise). If human rights have been violated then the court may be asked for remedies in addition to what tort law can provide.

13   There is a very high threshold to establish a human rights violation in environmental cases, and rights violations may be justified on the basis of the wider public interest. Unless the interference is extreme, or wholly unjustified, or has fallen outwith normal regulatory controls, a violation of human rights leading to a claim for damages is highly unlikely.

Some consider that tort law is essentially a mechanism for providing corrective, compensatory justice—of righting wrongs.[61] Tort law may also act as a mild deterrent to harmful behaviour and strategic claims can raise awareness of environmental problems and influencing public policy. But while a tort claim can advance an alternative vision of what 'the public interest' requires, there is little real world evidence to support either of these propositions. While tort law sometimes protects the environment, it is not clear that it should pursue this—or any other—instrumental function. The criticisms of tort made in this chapter are made with this in mind.

---

61. E. Weinrib, *The Idea of Private Law* (Cambridge: Cambridge University Press, 1995). Similarly, see Cane (2001) 13 JEL 3 (arguing that environmental torts are not so special that they should be treated differently *as torts*).

QUESTIONS

1 What private law claims might arise:

   a if GM crops are grown on land neighbouring an organic farm?

   b if a public water supply is contaminated by spills of diesel from a garage forecourt?

   c from road traffic noise?

   d from skyglow (too much artificial lighting of the sky, preventing sight of the stars)?

   What further information would you need?

2 Does tort law make polluters pay? Does it deter environmental pollution? Should it?

3 What values underpin tort law? Could these ever be the basis of a body of private law that better protected the natural environment?

4 Despite fierce local opposition, the Environment Agency and the local planning authority grant the necessary consents for a waste incinerator. After the incinerator begins operation, there are continued fears about its impact on health including concerns that the plant is being run by 'cowboys' who only got planning permission because of very generous community benefits they offered the planning authority. There are also concerns about off-site effects of the incinerator on rare orchids on a nearby nature reserve. Advise the owner of the nature reserve.

5 In 1982 an RAF base was built with all the necessary permissions required at the time. The landing strip is used both by military jets and, on occasion, as an 'overspill' runway by charter airlines when the regional airport is closed due to bad weather. Depending on the prevailing wind, high levels of noise emanate from the base, affecting residents over a wide area. What private law claims, and claims under the Human Rights Act 1998, might be made by:

   a Amy, who has lived in the area since 1969 and who complains that a recent increase in the number of flights has seen the value of her property fall by 20 per cent.

   b Ben, who since 2000 has lived in a rented cottage near the perimeter, whose sleep is disturbed and who is becoming physically ill.

   c The local parish council, which is concerned about the impact of the noise on local wildlife.

 FURTHER READING

General tort texts

If you want to explore English tort law further then excellent introductory texts are P. Giliker and S. Beckwith, *Tort* (2nd ed. London: Sweet and Maxwell, 2004) and S. Hedley, *Tort* (4th ed. London: Butterworths, 2004). Rather more detailed is N. McBride and R. Bagshaw, *Tort Law* (2nd ed. London: Longman, 2005) but it is both very good in thinking through difficult or uncertain areas of the law and offering informed opinion. Alongside these texts we also recommend M. Lee, 'What is Private Nuisance?' (2003) 119 LQR 298 which is an excellent analysis of the way that the law in this area is developing, especially the way in which nuisance is dividing into fault-based, strict liability and 'ordinary' liability (a division we hope is reflected in this chapter).

The function of tort

Although not a traditional textbook, J. Conaghan and W. Mansell, *The Wrongs of Tort* (2nd ed. London: Pluto, 1998) discusses the economic and doctrinal underpinnings to tort law, and has an excellent critique of the limitations of tort law for environmental protection. Against this look at J. Wightman, 'Nuisance—the Environmental Tort?' (1998) 61 MLR 870, a particularly good analysis not just of *Hunter v Canary Wharf* but private nuisance generally. A stronger defence of nuisance law over regulation from a critically economistic perspective is D. Campbell 'Of Coase and Corn: A (Sort of) Defence of Private Nuisance' (2000) Modern Law Review 197. For some, tort law is just a compensation mechanism which, in an age of regulation, should not be relied on to provide socially good things like environmental protection; P. Cane, 'Are environmental harms special?' (2001) 13 JEL 3 argues this in a very readable fashion.

Socio-legal and historical issues

Leading journal articles on the common law and the environment from a broadly socio-legal perspective include J. McLaren, 'Nuisance Law and the Industrial Revolution—Some Lessons from Social History' (1983) Oxford Journal of Legal Studies 155; J. Brenner, 'Nuisance Law and the Industrial Revolution' (1974) Journal of Legal Studies 403; A. Ogus and G. Richardson, 'Economics and the Environment: A Study of Private Nuisance' (1977) Cambridge Law Journal 284, and B. Pontin, 'Tort Law and Victorian Government Growth: The Historiographical Significance of Tort in the Shadow of Chemical Pollution and Factory Safety Regulation' (1998) Oxford Journal of Legal Studies 661.

Private law and public regulation

A good starting point is a strong set of essays assessing the contribution of private law collected together in J. Lowry and R. Edmunds (eds), *Environmental Protection and the Common Law* (Oxford: Hart Publishing, 2000). The interface between private law and public regulation raises legal issues such as the effect of a regulatory licence on a private law claim. But it also raises wider questions about the relative merits of private and public law controls. Discussion of both aspects is contained in J. Steele, 'Private Law and the Environment: Nuisance in Context' (1995) 15 Legal Studies 236 and 'Remedies and Remediation: Foundational Issues in Environmental Liability' (1995) MLR 615. D. McGillivray and J. Wightman, 'Private Rights, Public Interests and the Environment', in T. Hayward and J. O'Neill (eds.), *Justice, Property and the Environment* (Aldershot: Ashgate, 1997) explores the scope for private law to defend alternative, unofficial conceptions of the public interest, a theme developed in M. Stallworthy, 'Environmental liability and the impact of statutory authority' (2003) 15 JEL 3, which also explores the idea of holding regulators liable in civil law for environmental damage caused by their failure to regulate strictly enough (something that earlier versions of the EC liability directive proposed). M. Lee, 'Tort, Regulation and Environmental Liability' (2002) 22 Legal Studies 33 provides a detailed analysis of the public law / private law relationship in the context of the Environmental Liability Directive.

Human rights, property rights and the environment

Many sources in this area are written before the Grand Chamber judgment in *Hatton v UK* in 2003. For a critical view of this decision see D. Hart and M. Wheeler, 'Night Flights and Strasbourg's Retreat from Environmental Rights' (2003) JEL 100, and for more detailed analysis on this case and on *Marcic* an accessible analysis is given in A. Layard, 'Human rights in the balance—Hatton and Marcic' (2004) Env L Rev 196. On more domestic issues see B. Pontin, 'Beyond nuisance: enforcing the right to a healthy environment within the framework of the Human Rights Act 1998' (2002) Environmental Law and Management 305 and M. Wilde, 'Locus standi in environmental torts and the potential influence of human rights jurisprudence' (2003) Review of EC and International Environmental Law 284. Finally, since many of the torts that relate to the environment are property-based, it is fruitful to think more deeply about property and the environment, and an innovative discussion on this theme (with important conclusions to be drawn for environmental regulation) is S. Coyle and K. Morrow, *The Philosophical Foundations of Environmental Law: Property, Rights and Nature* (Oxford: Hart Publishing, 2004).

Other useful sources

Although increasingly out of date, C. Pugh and M. Day, *Pollution and Personal Injury: Toxic Torts 2* (Cameron May, 1994) is still useful on practical issues, and on issues like causation. And C. Rodgers, 'Liability for the release of GMOs into the Environment' (2003) Cambridge Law Journal 371 looks at the range of possible tort actions to this area, including comment on the (then) draft EC civil liability directive. The most comprehensive analysis of liability for damage to natural resources of interest to the general public, including liability via international pollution funds, is E. Brams, *Liability for Damage to Public Natural Resources* (The Hague: Kluwer, 2001).

@ WEB LINKS

There are few web sites of direct relevance to this chapter. Judgments in the cases mentioned can be found through the web sources mentioned in the Online Resources Centre.

PART III

Sectoral coverage

12 Local controls and remedies

 Overview

In Chapter 11 we looked at various private law actions that might be used to curb environmental pollution. And in Chapter 13 we will see that planning law tries to overcome some of the limitations of relying on nuisance law to regulate the harmful consequences of development, for example by taking a strategic approach to deciding 'how much of what goes where'. In this chapter we look at a range of other provisions which, like planning controls, are primarily exercised at the local level by local authorities. The first of these is statutory nuisance, followed by other local controls on noise, local air pollution controls, and controls on traffic. Finally we outline recent laws controlling high hedges. (For some other local controls which we cover elsewhere, or simply cannot cover, see Box 12.1) Before reading this chapter you may want to look again at the outline discussion of local authority functions and decision-making structures at p. 131.

BOX 12.1 Other local controls, responsibilities, duties and powers

Sustainability duties	Local Government Act 2000, s. 2	See p. 132
Contaminated land	EPA 1990, Part IIA	See p. Ch. 17
Waste collection, disposal, recycling, and composting	EPA 1990, ss. 45–49 (as amended by the Household Waste Recycling Act 2003)	See p. 588
Preventing fly-tipping	Control of Pollution (Amendment) Act 1989, ss. 5–7 as amended by Anti-Social Behaviour Act 2003, s. 55	
Litter control	EPA 1990, Part IV as amended by Clean Neighbourhoods and Environment Act 2005 (CNEA 2005), Part 3	
Abandoned vehicles	Refuse Disposal (Amenity) Act 1978, s. 3(1) as amended by CNEA 2005, ss. 10–14	

At the end of this chapter you will:

✔ Understand what statutory nuisance law covers and how it is enforced by local authorities and individuals.

✔ Understand other controls on noise, especially as these are exercised by local councils.

✔ Understand local controls on air pollution (and in conjunction with Chapter 16 appreciate how these work alongside strategic and national controls).

✔ Be able to assess how adequate this range of controls is compared to common law actions, and how these controls operate alongside planning law.

Statutory nuisance

The law of statutory nuisance represents a bridge between the private law of nuisance and the more characteristic statutory mechanisms. Like the various torts considered in Chapter 11, however, statutory nuisance really provides indirect protection for the environment, having developed as a public health mechanism. Nevertheless, there are many ways in which statutory nuisance can be used to combat environmental concerns such as air pollution or the deposit of sewage on beaches, and it is often used to deal with complaints about unacceptable noise levels. The main aim of the statutory nuisance provisions is to provide a quick and easy remedy to abate nuisances with which private law is too slow or too expensive to deal.

History and development of controls

Statutory nuisance law goes back a long way, dating back to public health statutes from 1848, 1855, 1860 and 1875. What underpinned these Acts was a desire to control matters which, although nuisances in the private law sense, were thought to affect sanitation levels and thus public health. It is worth mentioning, however, that before the discovery that diseases like cholera were spread contagiously (mainly through the water supply), the early Victorians laid the blame on foul air, or 'miasms'. Accordingly, this focused attention on things like drainage and the removal of all kinds of refuse (often into the nearest watercourse).

The Victorian legislation was consolidated in the Public Health Act 1936, and updated again, and 'restated', in Part III of the Environmental Protection Act (EPA) 1990 (to which all references in this chapter relate unless otherwise indicated). This lineage means that even very old authorities may still be relevant, and in some cases even determinative (see, e.g. the meaning of 'premises'). It also means, however, that the boundaries of statutory nuisance tend to be fairly well settled; this can make it difficult for statutory nuisance to evolve from its public health background into a more genuinely environmental protection mechanism befitting its place within the EPA 1990. This is not to say that the basic mechanism used in statutory nuisance has not been evolving; indeed, recent controls ranging from contaminated land to problems associated with high hedges draw heavily on the idea of the local authority serving an abatement notice to prevent likely problems arising or stop problems recurring.

The control of statutory nuisances

District councils, London borough councils and unitary authorities are under a duty periodically to inspect their areas for statutory nuisances. In addition, if an individual within an area complains of a statutory nuisance emanating from within that area then a district council is obliged to investigate a more responsive duty (s. 79). The EPA 1990 implies that the level of the local authority's general inspection duty is only to take such steps as are reasonably practicable. Although the duty imposed is only that inspection be periodic, it is clear that if there is strong evidence to suggest that a statutory nuisance exists within an area, and a local authority refuses to inspect, then it is possible that the remedy of judicial review will lie to any aggrieved applicant. It is important, therefore, for any individual wishing to complain to a local authority to ensure that proper evidence is gathered (e.g. dates, times, and length of the nuisance if it has already occurred, or strong evidence to show that the statutory nuisance is about to occur). There are default powers under sch. 3, para. 4 which allow the Secretary of State to take action if local authorities are not carrying out their duty.

The general control of statutory nuisance is contained in section 80. This provides that where a local authority is satisfied that a statutory nuisance exists, or is likely to occur or recur, it is under a mandatory duty to serve an abatement notice on the person responsible for the nuisance or, if that person cannot be found, the owner or occupier of the premises on which the statutory nuisance is present. The nature of this duty was considered in the *Shelley* case (Case box 12.1).

CASE 12.1 *R v Carrick District Council, ex parte Shelley* [1996] Env LR 273

The applicants were two residents of a Cornish village. They complained to the council about sewage which led to sanitary towels, condoms, and weed ending up on the village beach. The applicants asked the council to exercise its powers to deal with statutory nuisances. But the council resolved to do nothing, because the discharges, consented under the Water Resources Act 1991, were being appealed by the sewerage undertaker. The applicants challenged this refusal by judicial review. It was held that the council was under a duty to investigate its area for the existence of statutory nuisances. Once it was found that a statutory nuisance existed, the council was under a duty to serve an abatement notice. So the council could not simply resolve to do nothing pending the appeal. A decision has to be made on the state of affairs which are before the council at any given time and it was not possible to wait for any anticipated improvements before coming to a view on whether a statutory nuisance existed. Following the case, the local authority did in fact find that there was a statutory nuisance and served an abatement notice on the sewerage undertaker requiring screening, which was duly complied with. Note that before the local authority's original resolution, its environmental health officer had originally taken the view that no statutory nuisance existed. If this had been endorsed, then this would only have been challengeable as a matter of fact, not law, leaving the applicants without redress unless the officer's conclusion was one which no reasonable officer could have reached on the evidence.

In some situations, serving an abatement notice might be thought too blunt an instrument to resolve a situation which may have many underlying causes and involve other public bodies exercising their functions (see Case box 12.2).

CASE 12.2 *R v Falmouth and Truro Port Health Authority, ex parte South West Water Ltd* [2000] Env LR 658

Here, the statutory nuisance was sewage effluent being discharged by South West Water, the sewerage undertaker for the area. The undertaker was acting under a discharge consent, and was also under a range of statutory duties concerning the environment and the adequate provision of sewerage services in its area. The wider problem was not one that could be resolved simply by turning the effluent pumps off and might have been thought a situation better resolved by cooperation rather than criminal enforcement. Nevertheless, the abatement notice requiring the nuisance to be abated was upheld. The Court of Appeal also refused to find that the enforcing authority needed to consult on possible abatement action. This might have been desirable as a matter of policy, but was not required as a matter of legal fairness. This decision further emphasises the duties that local authorities have to abate statutory nuisances, and the extent to which the law is intended to allow for a swift response to situations which may have an adverse effect on public health.

The categories of statutory nuisance

There are a number of categories of statutory nuisance contained in section 79. These are supplemented by other statutes which declare specific categories to be a statutory nuisance and thus controlled under the provisions of the Act (s. 79(1)(h)). Much of the language used in section 79 is somewhat antiquated and difficult to reconcile with modern technology. The categories of statutory nuisance are listed in the headings below. The Act lays down certain activities or states of affairs which will amount to a statutory nuisance if 'prejudicial to health or a nuisance'.

'Prejudicial to health or a nuisance'

The main criterion for the existence of a statutory nuisance is that anything complained of must be either 'prejudicial to health or a nuisance'. These are not to be read conjunctively. Showing that something is 'prejudicial to health' is likely to be more difficult; as the House of Lords held in *Birmingham City Council v Oakley* [2001] 1 All ER 385, it is 'something over and above what may be seen as a "nuisance" '.

Prejudicial to health
'Prejudicial to health' means injurious, or likely to cause injury, to health (s. 79(7); and see Case box 12.3).

CASE 12.3 *Coventry City Council v Cartwright* [1975] 1 WLR 845

The Council owned a vacant site within a residential area on which it allowed people to dump all sorts of materials. These included not only normal household refuse, but also building and construction materials. Occasionally, the Council would move household materials. A nearby resident complained of a statutory nuisance under the Public Health Act 1936. The Divisional Court held that, where the accumulation complained of was inert rather than putrescible, the test was whether it was 'an accumulation of something which produces a threat to health in the sense of a threat of disease, vermin or the like'.[1] Note that the test to be used is preventive; it is the *threat* of a public health problem that matters.[2] Although there was a chance that physical injury could be caused to people who walked on the site, that did not amount to being prejudicial to health in the context of public

1. Apocryphal stories tell of a market in dead rats for 'planting' purposes, confirmed by a storyline in the British television soap 'Eastenders'!
2. CIEH guidance is that there must be something which is probably likely, rather than possibly likely, to cause injury to health. Note that in *Shelley* the risk to health there was sufficient.

health legislation. For the same reasons the visual impact of the site was also not a statutory nuisance.

This approach was confirmed in *R v Bristol City Council, ex parte Everett* [1999] Env LR 587, where steep stairs were held not to be prejudicial to the health of a tenant with a back injury. Note, however, that this interpretation of 'prejudicial to health' has arisen in cases involving provisions of Part III which are traced back to the Victorian public health legislation which was concerned with the removal of filth, and may not therefore apply to the provisions applying to noise, which only date back to the Noise Abatement Act 1960 (see p. 420).

Whether something is prejudicial to health must be judged objectively. So in *Cunningham v Birmingham City Council* [1998] Env LR 1 the claims that a property was hazardous to an autistic child failed, since the property was not a statutory nuisance for an 'ordinary' child. As with the common law of nuisance, however, if the state of affairs would be prejudicial to the health of an ordinary person, it is no defence that the person affected is more than usually sensitive, e.g. someone with asthma suffering from dampness and mould (see also *Southwark Borough Council v Simpson* [1999] Env LR 553). In *R (Anne) v Test Valley Borough Council* [2002] Env LR 22 it was held that if spores from a lime tree had given rise to a neighbour's respiratory allergy, the tree would not have been 'prejudicial to health'. This decision purports to apply the objective approach in *Cunningham*. However it fails to recognize that where health problems like allergies etc are actually *caused* by exposure to the thing complained of, and if an ordinary person would be so affected by such exposure, then an objective approach *is* being taken, albeit in two stages. So the *Test Valley* case must be treated with caution; it may not be good authority for saying that any sensitivity to a health problem will rule out a statutory nuisance action (e.g. where asthma has been brought on by dust or fumes etc).

Nuisance

In defining the word 'nuisance', it is generally accepted that the word contained within the EPA 1990 has the same definition as that under the common law. In *National Coal Board v Thorne* [1976] 1 WLR 543, the nuisance complained of amounted to defective guttering and windows within premises. The complainant argued that the physical condition of the building amounted to a nuisance under the Public Health Act. Watkins J said that a 'nuisance coming within the meaning of the Public Health Act 1936 must be either a public or private nuisance as understood by common law'. Thus, when deciding on the point of whether or not a statutory nuisance could arise when it was the inhabitants of premises who were suffering, such a state of affairs could not amount to nuisance because it was not an interference with the use or enjoyment of neighbouring property. Recent cases, however, indicate a relaxation of this requirement, so that there may be a nuisance where there is no emanation from one property affecting others (see *Network Housing Association Ltd v Westminster City Council* [1995] 93 LGR 280 and especially *Carr v London Borough of Hackney* [1995] Env LR 372).

Some cases suggest that the nuisance must involve some kind of personal discomfort, rather than any interference to property or its enjoyment as private nuisance requires (*Salford City Council v McNally* [1976] AC 379). In *Wivenhoe Port Ltd v Colchester Borough*

Council [1985] JPL 175 it was said that dust falling only on a car or a garden would not be a statutory nuisance. Other cases point more decisively to the test being the ordinary common law test (*Godfrey v Conwy County Borough Council* [2001] Env LR 38.[3] *Hounslow LBC v Thames Water Utilities Ltd* (considered below) is important here. Although the decision did not turn on this issue, the court did stress the transfer of the statutory nuisance provisions from the Public Health Acts to the EPA 1990. This may have the more general consequence that what is meant by 'nuisance' should now be given a wider meaning, and that there may be a move away from the stress on public health seen in cases like *Wivenhoe Port Ltd* (this was also discussed, without being decided upon, in the *Shelley* case, p. 405). Finally (and unlike private nuisance) the person affected by an activity which comes within the 'nuisance' limb does not need to have an interest in land for there to be a statutory nuisance. Private nuisance is a tort protecting interests in land, but statutory nuisance is not.

(a) Any premises in such a state as to be prejudicial to health or a nuisance

Section 79(1)(a) provides that where premises are kept in a state which is prejudicial to health or a nuisance then this will amount to a statutory nuisance. 'Premises' includes land and any vessel not powered by steam-reciprocating machinery. The physical extent of the premises must be viewed in context. In *Stevenage Borough Council v Wilson* [1993] Env LR 214, premises extended to the garden of a house where an abatement notice had included only the word 'dwelling'. The provision covers the physical *state* of premises rather than any use to which those premises are put. Therefore, where noise or dust etc. is emitted from those premises from a use, this is not covered by section 79(1)(a). The aim is to prevent situations where there are physical elements which are either prejudicial to health or a nuisance (though since nuisance usually requires some emanation from one plot of land to another, the 'prejudicial to health' limb will invariably be used here.[4] Sewers are not 'premises' under this subsection of the Act (but see Case box 12.4).

Land, or water, in its 'natural' state is unlikely to amount to 'premises', so any nuisance caused simply by a natural build-up of, for example, stagnant water is unlikely to be a statutory nuisance where the category of nuisance must involve premises (although it might well be a nuisance under other heads; see section 79(1)(e) and (h) below).

Until recently the position was that exposure to traffic noise due to a lack of proper sound insulation of council-owned flats might be remedied by a statutory nuisance action (*Southwark London Borough Council v Ince* (1989) 21 HLR 504). But in *London Borough of Haringey v Jowett* [1999] NPC 52 it was held that the changes made under the Noise and Statutory Nuisance Act 1993 (see s. 79(1)(ga), below) not only extended statutory nuisances to include noise from vehicles in the street but at the same time completely excluded traffic noise from being a statutory nuisance. This is a rather surprising outcome, and appears to be heavily influenced by policy factors, especially cost implications for local authorities and the fact that the premises were otherwise of an acceptable standard. It also means that noise

---

3. Note that the test for nuisance in Scots private law is different to that in English law and must be used for statutory nuisance; the leading case is *Robb v Dundee City Council* [2002] Env LR 33; damage to property, or mere discomfort would not amount to a nuisance; note that Part III applies to Scotland since 1996 and therefore the (English) case law applies also, though not in relation to the meaning of nuisance.

4. At least in England; the position in Scotland may be different, see *Robb v Dundee City Council* [2002] Env LR 33.

from railways can still be a statutory nuisance, a distinction that is irrelevant as far as human health or loss of amenity is concerned.

(b) Smoke emitted from premises so as to be prejudicial to health or a nuisance

Section 79(1)(b) replaced the Clean Air Act 1956, s. 16, which previously made separate provision for the control of smoke from premises. If smoke cannot be seen but only smelt, this may still constitute a nuisance (*Griffiths v Pembrokeshire County Council* [2000] Env LR 622). There are exemptions contained within section 79(3) so that the following will not be statutory nuisances:

(i) smoke emitted from a chimney of a private dwelling within a smoke control area;

(ii) dark smoke emitted from a chimney of a building, or a chimney serving the furnace of a boiler or industrial plant attached to a building, or for the time being installed on any land;

(iii) smoke emitted from a railway locomotive steam engine;

(iv) dark smoke emitted, otherwise than as mentioned above, from industrial or trade premises.

Most of these exclusions prevent overlaps with the atmospheric pollution controls in the Clean Air Act 1993 (see below) and with other legal controls.

(c) Fumes or gases emitted from premises so as to be prejudicial to health or a nuisance

Section 79(1)(c) and (4) controls fumes or gases emitted from private dwellings. Fumes are defined as 'any airborne solid matter smaller than dust, gases including vapour and moisture precipitating from vapour' (s. 79(7)). By analogy with *Griffiths v Pembrokeshire County Council* [2000] Env LR 622, smells from fumes or gases may also be covered.

(d) Any dust, steam, smell, or other effluvia arising on industrial, trade, or business premises and being prejudicial to health or a nuisance

The meanings of dust, steam and smell are fairly well established. However, the term 'effluvia' was defined in *Malton Board of Health v Malton Manure Co.* (1879) 4 ExD 302. This case involved the production of manure by the defendant company which produced vapours. It could not be conclusively demonstrated that these vapours were prejudicial to healthy people in the locality, although the Board of Health did demonstrate that it had the effect of making people who were ill more ill. The court held that this effect could amount to effluvia which were prejudicial to health. It is suggested that the meaning of effluvia covers the outflow of harmful or unpleasant substances.

The meaning of 'premises' in this subsection of the Act—s. 79(1)(d)—has recently been considered in a decision with important practical consequences (Case box 12.4).

CASE 12.4 *Hounslow London Borough Council v Thames Water Utilities Ltd* [2004] Env LR 4

The local authority served a notice against a sewerage undertaker (Thames) requiring certain odours at a sewerage works to be abated. Thames objected, claiming that sewage works were not 'premises'. The courts have always been reluctant to characterize sewers as 'premises'. This appears to have been for the policy reasons of not allowing magistrates, in effect, to make decisions relating to very expensive public infrastructure works, or because by their nature sewers may have caused nuisances in the interest of *preventing* the spread of disease (the very objective of the Public Health Acts). This approach, taken in *R v Parlby* (1889) LB 22 QBD 520, had recently been upheld in a case concerning a public sewer (*East Riding of Yorkshire Council v Yorkshire Water Services Ltd* [2000] Env LR 113). However, these cases were under what is now section 79(1)(a) and, remarkably, it had never been decided whether sewerage works fell within premises for section 79(1)(d).

In *Hounslow*, the court decided that the legislative history of what is now section 79 meant that sewerage works were premises for this subsection of the Act. A distinction was drawn between section 79(1)(a)—which related simply to the *state of premises*[5]—and section 79(1)(d) which related to the emission of noxious substances *from premises* (and made no mention of their state). The court also held that any policy considerations in Victorian times that might have justified restricting the scope of statutory nuisance actions against public undertakings no longer applied. Since the court did not cast doubt on the decisions reached in *Parlby* and *East Riding*, however, an anachronistic consequence is that 'premises' now means different things depending on which subsection of the Act is at issue.

The case is important because undesired smells are the subject of increasing numbers of complaints. Many sewage treatment works, originally built on the edge of towns, are now surrounded by new development. Indeed, Government has recognised the problem and is presently consulting on various options ranging from a voluntary code to various kinds of legal control. If the *Hounslow* decision is upheld—and a measure of its importance is that an appeal has 'leapfrogged' directly to the House of Lords—then the courts may have made this decision already. Even if statutory nuisance law does apply to smells etc. from sewerage works, however, note that it will still be a defence to show that the best practicable means of abating the nuisance has been used (see p. 416)

(e) Any accumulation or deposit which is prejudicial to health or a nuisance

To come within the 'prejudicial to health' limb of section 79(1)(e), the accumulation or deposit has to be *capable* of causing disease rather than injury (see *Coventry City Council v Cartwright* [1975] 1 WLR 845, above). The wide range of accumulations or deposits covered by this section have included sheep dung (*Draper v Sperring* (1869) 10 CB 113), cinders which emitted offensive smells (*Bishop Auckland Local Board v Bishop Auckland Iron and Steel Co.* (1882) 10 QBD 138); collections of household and garden waste (*Stanley v London Borough of Ealing* [2000] Env LR D18; *R (Knowsley MBC) v Williams* [2001] Env LR 28); and discharges of sewage on beaches (*R v Carrick District Council, ex parte Shelley* [1996] Env LR 273, above).

The deposit does not need to be caused by human action, and the natural accumulation of a substance can amount to a statutory nuisance, so long as it causes illness; examples include seaweed (*Margate Pier v Town Council of Margate* (1869) 33 JP 437) and pigeon droppings could also be covered. What will be important in these cases is determining by whose 'default or sufferance' there has been the accumulation; will this be the landowner if a public body had a responsibility to prevent, say, the seaweed coming ashore and causing a nuisance?

---

5. *Birmingham City Council v Oakley* [2001] 1 All ER 385.

(f) Any animal kept in such a place or manner as to be prejudicial to health or a nuisance

The keeping of a large number of animals on premises can give rise to a number of different enforcement actions. First, the keeping of a large number of animals may amount to sufficient intensification of a use to give rise to a change of use, which could result in enforcement action under the Town and Country Planning Act 1990 (see *Wallington v Secretary of State for Wales* (1990) 62 P & CR 150). Secondly, there may be common law actions which could be brought for nuisance. Thirdly, there could be action taken by the local authority under by-laws passed under the Public Health Act 1936, s. 81(2), and finally, there could be action taken under the statutory nuisance provisions of section 79(1)(f). Because birds or animals in their natural state are not 'kept', this provision would not apply to things like pigeon droppings (though a public nuisance action might be taken, see *Railtrack v Wandsworth London Borough Council* [2002] Env LR 9). Although (f) applies both to smells and noise, excessively noisy animals are usually dealt with by the following provision.

(g) Noise emitted from premises so as to be prejudicial to health or a nuisance

Noise here includes vibration (problematic issues in relation to quantifying noise nuisance are discussed below). Noise from model aircraft is included; otherwise aircraft noise is excluded (s. 79(6)). The difference between sub-section (g) and section 79(1)(a) is that the focus is on the premises where the noise comes from rather than the premises affected by noise. Also, the 'noise' sub-sections of section 79(1) do not have their origin in the Victorian Public Health Acts; this makes it easier to say that they should not carry a public health meaning and that 'nuisance' here should carry its normal common law meaning (the matter has yet to be ruled on).

Noise that does not exceed background levels may still be a statutory nuisance, as where the noise from a rural recording studio did not produce a measurement on a noise meter because of the background noise of haymaking (*Godfrey v Conwy County Borough Council* [2001] Env LR 38). It has been held (in the Crown Court) that if noise levels fall within advisory standards (e.g. BS 8233) then, despite well-founded complaints, the action was not well founded (*London Borough of Lewisham v Fenner* (1995) 248 ENDS Report 44). There seems to be no principled reason, however, why this should be taken as a general rule, especially in such a subjective area as noise control, and in *Cambridge City Council v Douglas* [2001] Env LR 41 noise which was in compliance with a public entertainments licence was held to be a statutory nuisance; the licence, in other words, could not authorize the nuisance.[6]

(h) Noise that is prejudicial to health or a nuisance and is emitted from or caused by a vehicle, machinery, or equipment in a street

Section 79(1)(ga) was added by the Noise and Statutory Nuisance Act 1993 to deal with certain kinds of street noise. It has been applied to amplified busking in Leicester Square (*Westminster City Council v McDonald* [2003] EWHC 2698). It does not apply to noise made by traffic (see *London Borough of Haringey v Jowett* [1999] NPC 52, discussed above), the

---

6. On the more general issue of the interplay between regulatory permissions and nuisance actions see p. 388.

armed forces or political or other demonstrations. Because it is not concerned with 'premises', slightly different procedures apply to things like identifying the person responsible, and the service of abatement notices.

(i) Smoke, fumes, or gases emitted from any vehicle, machinery, or equipment on a street so as to be prejudicial to health or a nuisance

This provision, which does not apply to any vehicle, machinery or equipment being used for fire brigade purposes, only applies in London boroughs (see s. 79(1)(gb), and the London Local Authorities Act 1996, s. 24). However, a significant exclusion is that it does not apply to smoke, fumes, or gases emitted from vehicle exhaust systems (s. 6B), which are regulated under specific statutory provisions (see p. 658).

(j) Any other matter declared by any enactment to be a statutory nuisance

This provision (s. 79(1)(h)) is to include any statutory nuisance provided for under future statutes. It also includes nuisances from mines, shafts and quarries under the Mines and Quarries Act 1954, s. 151, and various nuisances from the condition of ditches, ponds, etc. and certain watercourses (see further p. 751).

Statutory nuisances and overlapping controls

Many of the exceptions from the definition of statutory nuisance noted above ensure that there is no overlap between statutory nuisance law and more specialist regimes (e.g. local air pollution control). It should also be noted that while in the past statutory nuisance was occasionally used by local authorities in exceptional cases to deal with contaminated land, section 79(1A) excludes 'land in a contaminated state' from being a statutory nuisance. This is because the regime under Part IIA of the EPA 1990—closely modelled on statutory nuisance law—deals with contaminated land (although Part IIA only applies where contamination gives rise to *significant* harm and in trying to ensure that there is clear water between the two regimes the result is that some situations may 'fall between two stools'). Also, if premises are controlled under IPC or IPPC, or LAPC, then the Secretary of State must grant consent before proceedings for statutory nuisance can be instituted (s. 79(10)); again, this is to ensure a degree of consistency between regulatory systems (though the limitation only applies to paragraphs (b), (d), and (e)). In some situations, however, there is no restriction on regulating either under Part III of the EPA or under another environmental law regime; an example is the control of waste deposits, which in addition to being subject to the waste management controls under Part II of the EPA might also be a statutory nuisance under section 79(1)(e).

Under section 215 of the Town and Country Planning Act 1990 a local authority may require steps to be taken to remedy the condition of land which adversely affects the amenity of their area by serving an appropriate notice on the owner or occupier of land. These 'amenity notices' are designed to cover situations where the harm is not severe enough to amount to a statutory nuisance. It is a defence to show that the state of the land has arisen in the ordinary course of events (s. 217(b)), e.g. under a planning permission. Examples of where amenity notices have been served include dilapidated houses, overgrown or squalid gardens, untidy scrap metal yards and land used for the storage of scrap cars.

What is required to satisfy the local authority?

In practice, the local environmental health officer must decide whether or not a statutory nuisance is occurring or is likely to occur. As has been stated, the test is whether or not a statutory nuisance is prejudicial to health or a nuisance. An environmental health officer will visit the premises etc and make an objective decision as to whether or not the state of the premises or anything on those premises amounts to a nuisance. When reverting to the common law for the definition of nuisance, it is up to the environmental health officer to balance the many different factors used when deciding on whether or not a common law nuisance exists. The most important of these factors are:

(a) the nature and the location of the nuisance;

(b) the time and duration of the nuisance; and

(c) the utility of the activity concerned.

Balancing all these factors together is the only way in which an environmental health officer can make an adjudication. If the complaint is about prejudice to health, then the environmental health officer will need to have suitable training in the relation between the conditions of premises and ill health, although this does not mean that a medical qualification is needed (*Southwark Borough Council v Simpson* [1999] Env LR 553). The summary nature of proceedings can also be seen from the fact that technical evidence may not be required. Thus in *Lewisham London Borough Council v Hall* [2003] Env LR 4, a noise nuisance case, acoustic measuring evidence was not required, and the professional judgement of the environmental health officer sufficed. (This might be contrasted with the Noise Act 1996, see p. 424.)

Section 80(1) provides that for a local authority to act, the statutory nuisance must exist or be likely to occur or recur (there is no requirement for the notice to be corroborated by evidence of a particular occupier who has suffered unreasonable interference with the enjoyment of property; *Cooke v Adatia* (1988) 153 JP 129). Although statutory nuisance law has a criminal enforcement mechanism, the local authority must be satisfied only on the balance of probabilities. In the case of anticipated nuisances, however, there must be evidence that the forthcoming activity is likely to give rise to a statutory nuisance, which may be a high hurdle to overcome. However, where these problems can be overcome, such as in the case of a party where there is more than a suggestion that powerful audio equipment will be used, this may well be the only method of prohibiting certain types of nuisances in advance.

Who is the 'person responsible'?

The enforcement of a statutory nuisance is normally against the 'person responsible', which is defined in section 79(7) as being 'the person to whose act, default or sufferance the nuisance is attributable'. This is a particularly wide definition and can include a local authority (see *Rossall v London Borough of Southwark*, unreported), or a landlord who has allowed a tenant to carry on offensive activities, and can include those who fail to abate nuisances which arise naturally (*Margate Pier v Town Council of Margate* (1869) 33 JP 437). It can also include a tenant who has denied access to a landlord who wished to carry out works to abate a nuisance (see *Carr v London Borough of Hackney* [1995] Env LR 372).

However, the courts will look to see whether there has been some failure to meet acceptable standards, e.g. sound insulation standards at the time of construction (see *Salford City Council v McNally* [1976] AC 379; *London Borough of Haringey v Jowett* [1999] NPC 52). This is motivated by policy concerns, especially about resources, which would generally be irrelevant in a common law nuisance claim, unless the nuisance arose from the natural state of the land, see p. 373.

More than one person can be 'the person responsible' (s. 81(1)), though in cases like this it may be that the statutory nuisance arises because of one party's act or default and another party's sufferance (e.g. a child and its parent respectively regarding noise from the child's bedroom).[7] If there are any difficulties in locating the 'person responsible' for the existence of a statutory nuisance, section 80(2)(c) states that the definition of the person responsible can be extended to include the owner or occupier of the premises in question.

The abatement notice

Once the local authority, through its environmental health officers, is satisfied that a statutory nuisance exists, it is under a duty to serve an abatement notice which must require any or all of the following:

(a) the abatement of the nuisance or the prohibiting or restricting of its occurrence or recurrence;

(b) the execution of works or other steps necessary to comply with the notice.

There has been some uncertainty about precisely what this provision means. It has always been clear that there are some kinds of statutory nuisances where the local authority can, in the abatement notice, simply require the cessation of the nuisance. For example, an abatement notice can simply state that the nuisance is 'dogs barking', and leave it to the recipient of the notice to choose the most desirable manner of abatement (*Budd v Colchester Borough Council* [1999] Env LR 739). In noise nuisance cases, e.g. the abatement notice does not need to specify maximum noise levels (see *East Northamptonshire District Council v Fossett* [1994] Env LR 388) and even if it does, this does not necessarily amount to specifying 'steps' which need to be taken (*Sevenoaks District Council v Brands Hatch Leisure Group Ltd* [2001] Env LR 5). On the other hand, it is clear that if works *are* specified in the abatement notice, the requirement must be clear and precise as the recipient needs to know what must be done to comply. This is because criminal sanctions apply if the notice is breached (see *Sterling Homes v Birmingham County Council* [1996] Env LR 121). The notice should specify the time within which compliance is required.

However, certain cases suggested that there could be situations where the notice would have to stipulate the works required. Thus in *Kirklees Metropolitan Council v Field & Others* [1998] Env LR 337, a case about a rock-face and wall which were in imminent danger of collapsing on to a row of cottages, the Court of Appeal held that by not specifying the necessary works the abatement notice was invalid. In contrast to cases like *Budd*, where the nuisance could be abated by some activity being stopped, in *Kirklees* it was obvious that

---

7. In a similar vein, more than one person may 'cause' an environmental pollution offence, see, e.g., p. 734.

major works of a positive nature were necessary, and the Court held that these should have been specified. The same approach was originally taken in *R v Falmouth and Truro Port Health Authority, ex parte South West Water Ltd* [2000] Env LR 658 (see p. 405), where the High Court held that the abatement notice had to say what the sewerage undertaker should do to abate the nuisance because the problem could not be abated simply by turning off the effluent pumps. In the Court of Appeal, however, the *Kirklees* case was overruled and it was held that local authorities could not as a rule be obliged to specify works where work was needed. Instead, as where works did not need to be undertaken, the recipient of the notice should be free to choose their own course of action, so long as in doing so they would comply with the abatement notice.

The Court of Appeal did indicate, however, that there might be extreme cases where this general principle might not be appropriate. The recipient will, of course, always be best placed to choose the method of abatement on grounds of cost and convenience. However, it is at least arguable that where works require considerable technical expertise, then it might be a relevant factor whether the recipient can reasonably be expected to have knowledge of this, or know where to obtain it. In cases like *Kirklees*, therefore, knowledge of what was needed to abate the nuisance might be seen as beyond the reach of the residents of the cottages, and therefore something on which they should properly be advised by the local authority. Thus, it might still be appropriate to distinguish between cases according to the relative degree of awareness and technical expertise as between the local authority and the recipient. But it does not seem that a body acting under statutory duties must be told which steps to take (see the *Falmouth* case, p. 405).

Where an individual has been served with an abatement notice, the contravention of that notice, without reasonable excuse, makes that person guilty of a criminal offence under section 80(4). The criminal nature of statutory nuisance is an obvious contrast with the civil law of private nuisance. It means that the criminal standard of proof applies at the enforcement stage, and also that compensation payments under criminal law may be payable, although they are rarely ordered (but see *Botross v London Borough of Hammersmith and Fulham* [1995] Env LR 217; *Davenport v Walsall Metropolitan Borough Council* [1997] Env LR 24). Once a notice is served it takes effect in perpetuity.

This criminal aspect to statutory nuisance means that Article 7 of the European Convention on Human Rights—one aspect of which is that criminal offences must be formulated sufficiently clearly—is potentially relevant. However, in statutory nuisance cases where an 'abatement', rather than 'works', notice has been served, its relevance has been rejected; see the requirement to abate the noise in *Godfrey v Conwy County Borough Council* [2001] Env LR 38 (above) which was held to be human rights-compliant (see also *Westminster City Council v McDonald* [2003] EWHC 2698). Conceivably, Article 7 might have some application to the very limited cases where a works notice might have to be served, but existing law seems adequately to protect the interests of the nuisance-causer.

'Reasonable excuse'

Part III of the EPA 1990 is somewhat unusual in that having a 'reasonable excuse' for carrying out the activity which results in the contravention is not a *defence* to an offence committed under section 80(4) but rather a component part of the offence itself. If there is a reasonable excuse, the offence is simply not made out. The importance of this is that if the defendant puts forward an excuse, the burden is on the local authority to show, on the criminal standard, that it is not reasonable (see *Polychronakis v Richards and Jerrom Ltd* [1998] Env LR 346).

The test laid down for this would seem to be an objective one, i.e. 'would a reasonable person think that the excuse given was consistent with a reasonable standard of conduct?' The defence is not available where an abatement notice has been contravened deliberately and intentionally in circumstances wholly under the control of the defendant. Thus, a defendant could not argue that because there had been a three-year gap between the service of an abatement notice and its breach and no one had complained about the breach as it was of minimum inconvenience, there was a 'reasonable excuse' (*Wellingborough Borough Council v Gordon* [1993] Env LR 218, where the Court, with some reluctance, effectively held that there does not need be any 'victim' in a statutory nuisance case). It is not sufficient to say that there would be a defence to a private law action in nuisance. Indeed, in *A. Lambert Flat Management Ltd v Lomas* [1981] 1 WLR 898, it was said that COPA 1974, s. 58(4) was designed to provide a defence to a criminal charge where an individual had some reasonable excuse, such as some special difficulty in relation to compliance with the abatement notice. It was not an opportunity to challenge the notice; that should only properly be done on an appeal (see, in relation to the EPA 1990, *AMEC Building Ltd v London Borough of Camden* [1997] Env LR 330).

Defences

The EPA 1990 does contain some defences where there is an offence under section 80(4).

(a) Best practicable means

Where an abatement notice is served on trade or business premises and the nuisance complained of is caused in the course of the trade or business, it is a defence under certain heads of section 79(1) to show that the best practicable means have been used to prevent or counteract the nuisance (s. 80(7)). This does not apply to fumes or gases emitted from premises (s. 79(1)(c)), or the provision under section 79(1)(h) relating to nuisances in other statutes. Although there is not any complete definition contained within the EPA 1990, certain elements must be taken into account under section 79(9). These include local conditions and circumstances, the current state of technical knowledge, the financial implications, and the design, installation, maintenance, manner and periods of operation of plant and machinery.

The defence has to be established on a balance of probabilities, and the burden of proof lies on the defendant to show that it had taken reasonable steps to prevent or counteract the nuisance. Thus, where a defendant had submitted a planning application for noise reducing bunding to counteract a noise nuisance, but failed to answer the local planning authority's request for further information, it failed to discharge the burden of proof that it was using best practicable means to prevent or counteract the nuisance (*Chapman v Gosberton Farm Produce Co. Ltd* [1993] Env LR 191).

BOX 12.2 The best practicable means defence and the duty to serve an abatement notice

Should a 'BPM' defence be taken into consideration before an abatement notice is served? On a strict reading of the Act, and following *Shelley* (see Case box 12.1), it probably should. There is also the practical point that deciding at this stage whether the defence has been made out will delay the serving of notices for weeks or months. On the other hand, even if the defence was made out then the local authority would have to serve another abatement notice, since there would still be a statutory nuisance. There is no authoritative ruling on this point. The answer probably depends partly on what period of time it would be reasonable for the local authority to decide whether BPM applies, and partly on the standard of proof needed (i.e. whether it must be satisfied that BPM applies, or whether the defence is only a possibility). In practice environmental health officers may look to the factors that would justify the defence when they consider whether premises are operating unreasonably in a nuisance sense.

The extent of the defence, and thus a limitation of statutory nuisance, is illustrated in *Manley v New Forest District Council* ([2000] EHLR 113) where an abatement notice was served against kennels following complaints about noise. The best practicable means were already being used at the premises to restrict noise levels, but the Crown Court thought that moving the establishment to a non-residential area could be included within best practicable means. The High Court disagreed, in effect holding that statutory nuisance law is intended to regulate existing trade or business premises, and not to engage in industrial relocation (an approach which reflects the general approach to deciding amenity nuisance cases, see p. 367).

(b) Special defences

There are specific defences available in relation to noise and nuisances on construction sites and in areas where there are registered noise levels under the noise abatement zone procedure (see EPA 1990, s. 80(9) and COPA 1974, ss. 60, 61, and 65–67, discussed further at p. 425).

Appealing against an abatement notice

Where an individual is served with an abatement notice there is a right of appeal against the notice to a magistrates' court. One advantage of the appeal system over a defence to a prosecution under contravention proceedings is that it allows for a far greater range of appeal grounds and therefore provides a greater scope for disputing the nuisance. An appeal normally lies within 21 days of the service of the notice. The grounds of appeal are set down in the Statutory Nuisance (Appeals) Regulations 1995 (SI 1995/2644), made under the EPA 1990. These include that:

(a) the abatement notice is not justified in the terms of section 80;

(b) there has been a substantive or procedural error in the service of the notice;

(c) the authority has unreasonably refused to accept compliance with alternative requirements, or that its requirements are unreasonable or unnecessary;

(d) the period for compliance is unreasonable;

(e) the best practicable means were used to counteract the effect of a nuisance from trade or business premises (see above).

Furthermore, the regulations allow an abatement notice to be suspended pending the Court's decision, unless the local authority overrides the suspension in the abatement notice with a statement to the effect that the notice is to have effect regardless, and that:

(a) the nuisance is prejudicial to health;

(b) suspension would render the notice of no practical effect (e.g. where nuisances are to cease before the action can be heard in court); or

(c) any expenditure incurred before an appeal would not be disproportionate to the public benefit.

Individual action

It is often the case that local authorities' environmental health departments are overworked and understaffed and have neither the resources nor sometimes the inclination to deal with disputes regarding statutory nuisances. Section 82 allows a complaint to be made to a local magistrates' court by any person who is aggrieved by the existence of a statutory nuisance. This procedure allows for any person within an area to bring a more affordable and expeditious proceeding than a private law action. Ironically, complaints are most frequently made *against* local authorities about the poor state of their housing.

BOX 12.3 **Third party rights**

Unlike the person on whom an abatement notice is served (see above), third parties have no right to appeal notices, e.g. if they think that the notice does not go far enough in combating a nuisance. Their remedies are either (i) to seek a judicial review of the notice (expensive); (ii) complain to the Local Government Ombudsman (slow); or (iii) complain under section 82, effectively asking the magistrates' court to serve an abatement order in stronger terms than the original abatement notice served by the local authority. In practice, this cheaper and quicker option is the one most relied upon.

One particular limitation upon this procedure is that the nuisance must be in existence and therefore it cannot be used to anticipate problems. Therefore, a person has no right of action under this section to stop a nuisance which is likely to occur in the future (e.g. loud parties). If the person can satisfy the magistrates that there is an existing nuisance, or that there is likely to be a recurring nuisance, the court must issue an abatement order requiring the defendant to abate the nuisance within a specified time, and to execute any works necessary for that purpose and/or prohibiting a recurrence of the nuisance, and requiring the defendant, within a specified time, to carry out any works necessary to prevent the recurrence. The magistrates may fine a defendant up to £5,000, and £500 per day thereafter, for non-compliance with an order (s. 82(8)).

Section 82(12) provides that if a complaint is brought while the statutory nuisance exists then the person complaining is entitled to the costs of any expenses properly incurred (including the cost of establishing the existence of the nuisance), even if the nuisance is abated by the time of any hearing.

Sentencing powers for contravening an abatement notice

As noted above, contravening an abatement notice is a criminal offence (s. 80(4)). Section 80(5) and (6) provide for the penalties that may be imposed. The matter is triable only in the magistrates' court and, if found guilty, a private offender is liable to a maximum fine of £5,000. If the offence continues after the conviction they are liable to a further maximum fine of £500 for each day the offence continues. The previous levels of fine included under the Public Health Act and Control of Pollution Act indicated that for major industrial uses there were no real disincentives to carry out works to improve premises. Indeed, it was often cost effective to pay fines at a low level in order to ensure that a particular activity could be carried on rather than abated. Section 80(6) closes this particular loophole by imposing a maximum fine of £20,000 on industrial, trade or business offenders (though there is no provision for daily fines on top of this).

In addition to these sanctions, the magistrates have a 'discretion to award compensation' up to a maximum of £5,000. Obviously, if compensation in excess of this amount is being sought, then other remedies may have to be pursued; this may have been behind the decision of the local authority in *Wandsworth LBC v Railtrack* [2002] Env LR 9 to take a case in public and private nuisance, where there is no limit to the amount that a court can award in damages, rather than use its public health and statutory nuisance powers; see pp. 369 and 374).

The use of injunctions and proceedings in the High Court

In many cases the provisions of section 80 would not provide an adequate remedy in terms of either gravity or speed. Under section 81(5), a local authority may take court action to abate, prohibit or restrict any statutory nuisance. It may do this—by seeking an injunction in the High Court—where it considers that proceedings for an offence of contravening an abatement notice would not provide a sufficient remedy, and even where it considers that the abatement notice procedure would not be effective (*Vale of White Horse District Council v Allen & Partners* [1997] Env LR 212). Injunctions are a discretionary remedy and will not be granted lightly. The activity complained of must be of sufficient gravity and/or urgency to justify stopping it; this might include deliberate breaches of the law in the past, or evidence that the nuisance offender will not be deterred by the abatement notice procedure. Injunctions have the practical advantage that breaching an injunction is a contempt of court, for which a two year prison sentence or an unlimited fine may be imposed. This is obviously far in excess of the penalties under the abatement notice procedure.

Local controls on noise

The most frequent use of the law relating to statutory nuisance, discussed above, is to control noise. However, as in other areas of environmental law, noise is controlled by a variety of standards, not just the flexible standards of nuisance law. This section considers some of these other mechanisms—which include a range of product and process controls, as well as controls on noise in particular areas or from particular activities—especially as they are controlled by local authorities. As with statutory nuisance, the legal controls discussed here are often found in controls relating to public health, but in some cases they come from the realm of public order legislation. In this sense they are not tailored environmental controls, but may indirectly regulate ambient noise levels more generally.

Unlike previous editions of this book, we no longer outline in this chapter the whole range of controls on noise.[8] Some of these non-local controls are, however, mentioned below in passing, so that the local controls can be understood in their law and policy context. We also begin this section by considering noise in its wider environmental context.

Noise as environmental pollution

Most of the legal controls described in the following sections approach noise from a narrow anthropocentric perspective. In contrast, our understanding of the impact of noise on broader ecological interests is in its infancy. Although there is evidence of physiological changes, it has proven difficult to show that these give rise to adverse impacts on species. There are instances where noise has had a demonstrable impact on animals leading to successful legal action, as where the noise from a shotgun was maliciously used to interfere with the breeding of mink (*Hollywood Silver Fox Farms v Emmett* [1936] 2 KB 468). There are also examples where the courts have accepted that noise disturbance may affect wildlife. One example is where the High Court considered a challenge to the granting of oil explor-ation licences in the North-East Atlantic on the basis that seismic activity could adversely disturb cetaceans (whales and dolphins) (*R v Secretary of State for Trade and Industry ex parte Greenpeace (No.2)* [2000] Env LR 221; see p. 828). And the European Court of Justice found that Austria had insufficiently protected the corncrake by not controlling various noisy activities associated with a golf course which posed a risk to its habitat (Case C-209/02 *Commission v Austria* [2004] ECR I-1211). But on the whole our understanding of the impact of noise on wildlife is very limited, and precautionary controls have rarely been adopted.

Noise and its perception

Noise is now regarded as a serious object of concern. Complaints about noise nuisance to local authorities in England and Wales have risen dramatically over recent years, from just over 55,370 in 1980 to 310,312 in 2001/02. By far the largest numeric and percentage increases have been in relation to domestic noise. The Chartered Institute of Environmental Health has described this rise as 'apparently inexorable'. These figures relate to complaints

---

8. For a comprehensive overview see C. Penn, *Noise Control* (Crayford: Shaw and Sons, 2002).

made to environmental health officers. However, attitude surveys looking at whether people experience noise, and whether they are affected by it, suggest rather more modest increases, over the 1990s, in the nature of noise as a problematic phenomenon. Moreover, longitudinal research suggests a slight decrease in ambient noise levels over the 1990s.

As an object of regulation, 'noise pollution' poses some particular problems, the most important being as follows:

- Other than in severe cases, the effects of noise are experienced subjectively. The sound of music coming from a neighbouring property may be enjoyed or it may be suffered.

- *Why* noise is generated can be a factor in its perception; for some a wind turbine may be a noisy intrusion in the landscape, or it may be music to the ears of someone more concerned with reducing greenhouse gas emissions.

- What is important about noise levels is the level where the sound is heard, not where it is produced. (Indeed, 'noise' without a hearer is just vibration.) In this sense most noise standards are ambient standards, although some emissions standards regulate the sound made by objects like aircraft and lawnmowers.

- Noise will be experienced differently according to changing lifestyles. For example, as the 'rush hour' lengthens, the burden of noise pollution is increased, even though the area may not change in character and sound insulation levels remain the same. Noise which is normal for the daytime may cause disturbance to those who work at home or at nights. The '24/7 society' undoubtedly creates noise problems.

- It is not simply the level of noise that may cause annoyance. Low whines and repetitive sounds may irritate as much as loud bangs or ill-tempered car horns.

All these features are captured by the non-statutory definition of noise as 'sound which is undesired by the recipient'.[9] It is this inherently subjective nature that means that any statistics about noise pollution must be handled cautiously. For example, in 1995/6 just less than 30 per cent of complaints were confirmed as nuisances, whereas in 2001/02 this percentage had fallen to just under 17 per cent. Bearing in mind the subjective nature of nuisance, it is still revealing that there has been a steady reduction over recent years in the percentage of confirmed nuisances as a fraction of the total number of complaints. As the Chartered Institute of Environmental Health commented: 'Whether this indicates that nuisance is no longer the appropriate standard to use or that the public has unrealistic expectations of the noise climate is unclear',[10] but environmental health officers have reported a steady decline in the last few years about the extent to which higher expectations of quiet are the reason for continued high levels of noise complaints.

Particularly telling is the relative rise in the number of complaints about domestic noise nuisance. In 1983/4 these were roughly equal to the number of complaints about industrial and commercial noise. By 1995/6, noise from domestic sources accounted for more than the number of complaints from all other recognised categories of noise combined. As Fitzpatrick remarks (see further reading), 'It would appear that it is less noise in itself that is the problem, but much more that it is coming from next door, or at least that it is more

---

9. *Final Report of the Parliamentary Committee on the Problem of Noise*, Cmnd 2056, 1963, the 'Wilson Committee'.
10. CIEH, Annual Report (1997), p. 4.

legitimate to complain about it'. The same care must be taken with statistics about the number of noise-related deaths, of which around 20 have been reported in recent years. There is a tendency to report a noise disturbance as the cause of such incidents, rather than as one aspect of much more bitter and tragic neighbour disputes. Finally, there is evidence to suggest that we tend to internalize some costs associated with noise. While we tend to complain to neighbours or the police about noisy neighbours, the response to road traffic and aircraft noise is usually to do nothing or to try to prevent the noise disturbing us, e.g. by double-glazing our houses, using ear plugs, or taking sleeping pills (hence often it is the victim, rather than the polluter, who pays for noise pollution). For a legal challenge to road traffic noise see Murdoch v Glacier Metal Co Ltd [1998] Env LR 732 (Case box 8.1).

Policy approaches

A feature of noise pollution is that it is transient rather than persistent: noise does not accumulate in the environment the way that toxic chemicals do. This has consequences both for the setting and the enforcement of noise controls. Beyond simple tolerance, noise levels can be controlled at two main points:

- where it is produced, through preventive standards. These centre around standards for the decibel levels of manufactured goods; and

- *en route* to the hearer, by some form of barrier. This can be a physical barrier such as sound insulation, or a roadside embankment to muffle traffic noise. Or it may be a spatial barrier such as the separation of the source of the noise from those likely to be affected. This is the realm of planning controls, and planning guidance seeks to separate noise generating and noise sensitive developments.

The after-effects of noise pollution cannot be measured in quite the same way that the consequences of a water pollution incident can be. This also has an impact on the use of strategic mechanisms since, regardless of the subjective experience of noise, it is still much more difficult to categorise any particular area as 'noisy' than, e.g. to categorize a river as of 'poor quality' or land as 'contaminated'. Nevertheless, the general policy approach has been the use of environmental quality standards through nuisance-based controls. In relation to enforcement, this means measuring noise at the time and at the point at which it is experienced, or producing other evidence which attests to the nature of the noise. It also means that, in appropriate situations, emissions standards on machinery or products may be used. These reduce enforcement costs, but the tendency has been to use them selectively. In the last few years, 'noise maps' and the use of action planning has been seen as increasingly important strategic controls (see below). But there remains no national noise policy and tackling ambient noise levels is low on the present government's priorities.

The development of statutory controls

Statutory controls over noise emissions have been relatively late in coming. Noise nuisances were dealt with in some local Acts and in by-laws, but problems tended to be left to individually initiated action. Private law remedies were generally relied on, although in the case of civil aircraft noise these were *removed* quite early on under the Air Navigation Act

1920. The Noise Abatement Act 1960 was the first general Act on noise control, although this only added certain noise nuisances to the range of statutory nuisances controllable under public health law (and now regulated under Part III of the EPA 1990, see above). Following the report of the Scott Committee on *Neighbourhood Noise* in 1971, further controls on noise were introduced in Part III of the Control of Pollution Act 1974, which introduced provisions on street noise, noise from construction sites and noise abatement zone provisions.

Just as there is no national noise policy so there has never been consolidated legislation on noise, no doubt partly because noise controls are often one aspect of wider legislative provisions. This is certainly the case with a number of public order controls under general criminal justice and other 'behaviour control' legislation. But it also applies to quite a wide range of noise provisions in, e.g. the Civil Aviation Act 1978 and the Road Traffic Act 1988 (and to worker safety legislation and entertainment controls, which are outside the scope of this chapter). The impact of EC law has largely been in regulating the free movement of an odd assortment of goods under directives that contain what are in effect noise emission standards. The net result has been an incomplete, incoherent and unprincipled body of law, an 'ugly mosaic of separate legal controls'[11] which makes classification difficult. However, there are moves to integrate the control of noise emissions with other pollutants, such as under the EIA and IPPC Directives.

Domestic controls over noise

In addition to controls under statutory nuisance and under the common law of nuisance, there is a range of other national controls on noise. The approach taken here is to look first at the remaining provisions, other than those contained in the EPA 1990, that are most central to regulating neighbourhood noise, before considering controls on noise from specific sources; preventive and strategic controls; and overlapping controls.

BOX 12.4 **Mediating noise disputes**

Resort to law is not the only way of dealing with noise. Increasingly, local authorities promote (and fund) mediation as an effective way of tackling noise disputes. Mediation can either be through face-to-face meetings of the parties, or indirectly through trained volunteers. Of the 16,000 requests in 2000/01 for the services of Mediation UK (the largest mediation service), 45 per cent related to noise problems, mostly from DIY, noisy children and music. The success rate of mediation—where agreement is reached or there is a substantial improvement in the situation—averages at least 50 per cent.

Further controls on neighbourhood noise

There are a range of statutory provisions which govern neighbourhood noise. While some of these provisions relate to 'neighbour-type' disputes, there is an increasing tendency to regulate noise more generally.

11. F. McManus and T. Burns, 'The Impact of EC Law on Noise Law in the United Kingdom', in J. Holder (ed.) *The Impact of EC Environmental Law in the United Kingdom* (Chichester: Wiley, 1997, p. 185).

(a) Night noise

The stated purpose behind the Noise Act 1996 is to make it easier to take action against night noise disturbances. To this end, a criminal offence is committed if, after a warning, a person is responsible for the emission of noise from a dwelling between 11 p.m. and 7 a.m. and the noise level (in the complainant's dwelling) is above prescribed levels. The test for whether a person is responsible is the same as that used in statutory nuisance. The prescribed levels are set out in Circular 8/97, and provide that the noise level must be at least 35 decibels, if the underlying noise level is 25 decibels or less. Alternatively, if the background noise level is above 25 decibels, then the noise being emitted must be at least 10 decibels above that. To give an indication of how loud this is, the sound of an ordinary bedroom at night is around 25 decibels, and the sound of a library about 40 decibels. An increase of 10 decibels is approximately a doubling of loudness. The offence attracts a fine of up to £1,000, a £100 on-the-spot fixed penalty notice and the summary seizure by the local authority of the sound equipment. There is a defence of proving there is a reasonable excuse for the noise.

There are three key features about the Noise Act 1996. First, it differs from nuisance law in that the determination of whether there is a nuisance is judged according to more or less objective standards. While the locality of the area is taken into account by reference to underlying noise levels, the way in which this is done is much less flexible. Many of the factors taken into account in nuisance law—such as duration and the nature of the activity causing the nuisance—are effectively ignored. Secondly, there is a clear break between an essentially civil (or civil-cum-criminal) law approach and the full use of criminal law sanctions. Third, the 1996 Act originally applied only in areas where the local authority adopted its provisions, with the local authority having an absolute discretion whether to do so. In this respect the Act was reminiscent of many of the early planning and environmental statutory provisions, and notably by 1999 only nine local authorities had adopted the powers. A central reason appeared to be that the 1996 Act really covers little that cannot be regulated under ordinary statutory nuisance law. It is also more draining on local authority budgets, since the duty to investigate complaints must be complied with immediately the complaint is made: authorities cannot wait until the following day when environmental health staff are paid on ordinary rates. Nevertheless, section 42 of the Anti-Social Behaviour Act 2003 now provides that all local authorities in England and Wales *may* use the night-time noise provisions without first having to adopt them. Whether this will see a significant increase in their use remains to be seen; there must be a continuing question mark as to whether environmental health officers are any more enthusiastic about the use of inflexible standards in this area than they were when the 1996 Act was passed.

(b) Housing Act 1996

Part V of the Housing Act 1996 makes it easier for both social and private landlords to evict tenants causing 'nuisance and annoyance' to neighbours. This extends to nuisance arising from a tenant's behaviour anywhere in the locality. As with the Noise Act 1996, a key approach is to amend the relevant procedural requirements. The Housing Act 1996 therefore makes it easier to seize noise-making equipment, and—as with statutory nuisance—

provides for the use of 'professional' local authority witnesses, so that those affected do not need to give evidence.

(c) Anti-social behaviour orders

Under the Crime and Disorder Act 1998 antisocial behaviour orders can be made to combat threatening and disruptive antisocial behaviour which causes, or is likely to cause, harassment, alarm and distress. The orders are ostensibly designed to curb disorder on estates and in communities, rather than to be used in disputes between neighbours. Although they can be used even where one person is affected, strongly worded Home Office guidance counsels against their use in pure neighbour disputes (though this appears not to be followed very rigidly). They may well be sought, however, where there is serious street noise disturbance, since this is not regulated by statutory nuisance provisions.

The orders can be sought by a local authority in consultation with a chief police officer, or vice versa, and are made by the magistrates' courts. To this extent they are civil powers, and civil standards of proof apply when they are being sought, but breach of an order is a criminal offence punishable by up to five years' imprisonment or an unlimited fine. Antisocial behaviour orders, which are now being made with increasing frequency, have been roundly condemned for the inroads they make on civil liberties, their reliance on hearsay evidence and for their rather pernicious blend of civil and criminal provisions. They have been served on harassing 'animal rights' protestors, but it is not clear that they are an appropriate mechanism for striking the right balance between protest and free expression.

Noise from specific sources

There is a patchy collection of provisions that regulate noise from specific sources. These tend to control things like noise from outdoor sources such as construction sites and transport, or be reactions to public order concerns. There is no common approach taken. Controls include 'stop' and notice provisions, licensing, product and specification standards. Noise generally from industrial premises is not regulated as a specific object of control.

(a) Construction noise

There are powers given to local authorities under COPA 1974 for the control of noise from construction and engineering works. Sections 59A, 60, and 61 allow councils to serve notices imposing requirements about the way that work is carried out. These may include quite prescriptive conditions about the type of plant and machinery used, but conditions about the time the noise is emitted and its level are more usually imposed. Although originally aimed at noise from construction sites etc, these provisions are worded widely enough to include noisy DIY works, and are apparently often used in this context.

It is a criminal offence to contravene such a notice without reasonable excuse, but it is a defence that the work was carried out under a consent issued under section 61. Such consents may be applied for in advance of construction work being carried out, which avoids changes to the work being needed because a notice is served after the work has begun. It is a criminal offence to carry out works or knowingly permit works to be carried out which contravene a consent. Such consents are, however, rarely sought, the fear being that stricter standards will be imposed in advance compared with those which might be imposed under notice once the work has begun,[12] an example of the law's reluctance to disturb activities on environmental grounds once wealth generation has begun.

(b) Transport noise

Transport noise, especially from road traffic and from aircraft, has the capacity to cause noise levels which seriously damage quality of life and which are therefore incompatible with sustainable development.[13] Because of their mobile nature, specification and emission standards are often used, as with noise values for cars (generally set at EC level) and aircraft (generally set under international law and transposed into EC legislation). Over the years, these technical standards have seen noise 'emissions' from these sources fall. This is not to say, however, that there has been a concomitant reduction in actual noise levels; e.g. emissions from vehicles are estimated to have fallen by only 1 to 2dB(A) because of factors including the slow replacement of older vehicles, significant growth in traffic and questions over whether the test procedures reflect actual driving conditions. As a general point, then, vehicular or aircraft noise standards have no direct bearing on overall noise levels and can be rendered ineffective through increases in traffic levels.

Other source-based approaches used include things like speed restrictions and curbs on night flights, although a small number of 'barrier' or 'separation' controls are also used. In practice, planning controls are probably as important a mechanism as any in regulating traffic noise, since these are crucial in determining exposure to noise. As a matter of planning policy, however, it appears that there is an emphasis on locating noise-sensitive developments away from noisy areas or activities. The following pages look at transport noise controls exercised at the local level, either by local authorities or highway authorities. We do not cover the numerous controls on specific sources of noise (such as cars or aircraft).

(i) Road traffic noise

Road traffic noise comes mainly from engine noise and from the impact of tyres on the road surface. Noises from these sources are mainly tackled by a mixture of legislatively prescribed design standards and emission limits, often under EC law.

Where increased noise levels are caused by the construction or alteration of a highway, highway authorities must carry our noise insulation works to combat the effect of traffic noise on certain properties. Alternatively, they may provide grants for noise insulation to be fitted, a flexible means of implementing a specification standard rather than the use of economic tools (see the Land Compensation Act 1973, s. 20, and the Noise Insulation Regulations 1975, SI 1975/1763, as amended by SI 1988/2000). There are also powers under the Highways Act 1980 for highways authorities to undertake works to mitigate the adverse effects of constructing or improving highways, e.g. noise bunding (Highways Act 1980, s. 282). A similar scheme applies in relation to noise from railways and tramways.

The composition of the road surface also leads to significant differences in noise levels; for example, porous asphalt surfaces are quieter than conventional concrete surfaces by anything from 4 to 8 dB, although they also have environmental disadvantages such as greater use of quarried aggregates. However, there are so far no statutory controls governing road surfaces, and the composition of public road surfaces is determined only by Depart-

---

12. See *Report of the Noise Review Working Party* (1990).
13. *Transport and the Environment*, RCEP, Eighteenth Report, Cm 2674, 1994, paras. 4.4–4.17.

ment of Transport practice in the case of trunk roads, and otherwise by local authorities. The impact of traffic noise can also be reduced by things like urban bypasses, although not all bypasses reduce traffic movements to the extent intended, as the controversial Newbury bypass illustrates. In any event, such policies have other environmental consequences.

The continuing 'Cinderella' status of noise was emphasised by the low profile of noise issues in the White Paper, *A New Deal for Transport* (Cm 3950, 1998). Indeed, 'noise' as such was not mentioned so much as the need for preserving the 'tranquillity' of the countryside, at least as far as designated 'quiet roads' are concerned (see now s. 268 Transport Act 2000). This suggests both an anti-urban policy focus, as well as an 'enclave' approach to noise control rather than a desire to reduce noise levels generally.

(ii) Aircraft and airport noise

The main control on aircraft noise is under emissions standards which have been set under the framework of the 1944 Chicago Convention, in particular Annex 16. However, increases in the average size of aircraft over the years, and in the number of flights, have reduced the impact of improvements from the significant tightening of standards that has occurred (a phenomenon also experienced in relation to lorry movements). Even with the after-effects of 9/11, and the grounding of Concorde, noise levels around Heathrow still increased in 2001, an illustration of the inadequacy of relying only on emission control standards.

The general legal approach to airport and aerodrome noise is to give the Secretary of State a power to designate certain airports in order to subject them to specific controls on the frequency or time of aircraft movements (Civil Aviation Act 1982, s. 78), the perceived inadequacy of which was the basis for the unsuccessful human rights challenge in *Hatton v UK* (see Case box 11.1).

(iii) Noise from boats

It is briefly worth mentioning section 13(2) of the Countryside Act 1968 which allows a local authority to make by-laws, amongst other things, to prevent excessive noise nuisances in National Parks. Such by-laws may, e.g. regulate noise from boats or vessels by requiring the use of silencers or otherwise regulating noise or vibration levels. By-laws aimed at curbing noise and imposing a 10 mph speed limit on Lake Windermere, effectively ending high-speed power-boating and water-skiing there, come into force in 2005.

(c) Noise controls on other specific sources

There are a number of other disparate provisions which regulate noise from specific sources. Directive 2000/14/EC, a product standard measure, regulates noise from various forms of outdoor equipment, including compressors and even lawnmowers.

At national level, regulations can be made to control noise from plant or machinery under section 68 of COPA 1974, but the policy preference has been to use codes of practice to minimise noise, which have been issued (under s. 71) in relation to various sources such as ice cream van chimes (SI 1981/1828) and model aircraft (SI 1981/1830). Although breach of a code of practice is not itself a criminal offence, codes may be taken into account in legal proceedings, for example in determining whether best practicable means have been employed.

Noise from loudspeakers and audible intruder alarms are regulated separately. It is generally an offence to use a loudspeaker in the street between 9 p.m. and 8 a.m., although exceptions are made for things like the emergency services and mobile grocers (COPA 1974,

s. 62). The Noise and Statutory Nuisance Act 1993 tempered this approach by introducing the right to obtain a consent from the local authority, although only where the local authority has adopted the powers in its area (s. 8 and sch. 2). A similar power to adopt noise control powers under the 1993 Act applies to audible intruder alarms (s. 9 and sch. 3). This power—which as yet is unused—gives local authorities the power to require alarms to comply with prescribed standards, coupled with obligations to notify the police and the local authority. There are also powers for local authorities to turn off alarms, if need be by getting the consent of a justice of the peace and entering by force.

Under the Anti-Social Behaviour Act 2003, the Chief Executive Officer of a local authority has the power, on the spot, to close down licensed premises for up to 24 hours if a public nuisance is being caused, or closure of the premises is necessary to prevent a public nuisance (s. 40). This power can be delegated to environmental health officers (s. 41(2)).

There are other sources of noise where the police are the main enforcement body; these include music from raves (under the Criminal Justice and Public Order Act 1994) and the control of fireworks (the all year round use of which has become the most common source of noise complaint raised by constituents with their MPs, and on which see now the Fireworks Act 2003 and Fireworks Regulations 2003).

General preventive and strategic controls

In addition to regulating specific sources of noise, there are a number of more general preventive and strategic mechanisms which might be used. In practice the town and country planning system has perhaps been the most important, but noise mapping and noise action planning is increasingly becoming a legal requirement.

(a) Noise abatement zones

Under the Control of Pollution Act 1974 a local authority has a discretion to designate all or part of its area as a noise abatement zone (s. 63), although authorities must inspect their areas with the need for designating zones in mind (s. 57). When a noise abatement zone is in operation the local authority records the levels of noise from specified premises (see the Control of Noise (Measurement and Registers) Regulations 1976, SI 1976/37). These are usually trade and business premises, but places such as concert halls could also be covered. Recorded noise levels are then entered in a noise level register, which is open to public inspection. Once noise levels have been registered they can only be exceeded with the local authority's consent, in effect setting a ceiling on noise levels. There is, however, a right for affected premises to request the local authority's consent to exceed a recorded noise level. Consents can be made subject to conditions, and must also be recorded on the register. It is an offence to breach register levels or consent conditions (s. 65(5)). After conviction, the magistrates may make an order requiring works to be done, if the breach is likely to continue or recur. There is a power for the local authority to undertake such works itself and recover expenses from the person convicted (s. 69).

Noise abatement zones are therefore intended to control noise from premises in the long term by preventing an increase in noise levels, but under section 66, noise reductions can be sought if they would secure public benefit and are practicable at reasonable cost. However, a further qualification to this is that for trade and business premises there is still a best practicable means defence to any charge of breaching a noise reduction notice.

Where zones have been designated, relatively small areas such as industrial estates tend to be designated, while some zones govern single noisy industrial premises. However, the noise reduction provisions are generously worded to business, and the main use of zones is to avoid increases in noise levels. Of course, their restriction to premises makes them of little use in combating noise from mobile sources such as traffic, and thus general increases in noise levels. This, coupled with high enforcement costs and the statutory nuisance powers, may explain why, only about 60 zones have been designated in England and Wales.

(b) Other preventive approaches

There is a range of other provisions that aim to control noise arising from states of affairs. Specification standards are used in the case of building design. Under the Building Regulations 1991 (SI 1991/2768) buildings must be constructed to prevent undue noise. The 1991 Regulations only apply to houses in buildings (such as flats) or to semi-detached or terraced properties: detached properties are not covered.

(c) Planning controls

Planning controls will often be the principal, or only, means of regulating noise. This is certainly the case with things like wind turbines, which have no legal standards attached to their noise output. It is also true of general traffic noise from new road developments, where conditions can be imposed relating to things like earth banking, tree screening and proximity from housing. However, the planning system is of little use in regulating an increase in noise due to traffic growth, since this is not 'development'. (No matter how much the noise and traffic intensifies, the land is still a road: there cannot be a material change of use; see further p. 465.) This illustrates the extent to which law is rather better at controlling new activities than regulating existing ones, especially incremental changes to existing uses.

Guidance on 'Planning and Noise' is given in PPG 24. This counsels the use of development plans and the development control system in separating new noise-sensitive developments from major sources of noise. Planning conditions are often used to minimise the impact of noise, e.g. by putting restrictions on the time when noisy activities may take place. A local planning authority can impose a planning condition which is more onerous than restrictions required under an abatement notice served under the statutory nuisance powers of the EPA 1990 (*R v Kennet District Council, ex parte Somerfield Property Co. Ltd* [1999] JPL 361). There is no legal requirement for planning officers and environmental health officers to reach the same decision about what level of noise is acceptable, although this might be thought desirable.

Attempts by the Royal Commission on Environmental Pollution in its Eighteenth Report on *Transport and the Environment* (Cm 2674, 1994) to have general targets for acceptable day and night noise accepted by government were rejected. But PPG 24 goes some way towards introducing these through planning policy. The levels recommended by the RCEP are at the lower end of the noise exposure category which advises that development falling within it should normally be refused planning permission on noise grounds, unless noise reduction measures are taken.

(d) Noise maps

Statistics on noise complaints help understand the extent of noise pollution and its causes, but do not give an overall picture of the noise climate for an area. This is done by noise mapping, a technique which is much more advanced on the continent. Under Directive 2002/49/EC, Member States must complete 'noise maps' for all major conurbations above 250,000 people, roads, railways and airports by 2007. Smaller towns and roads need to be mapped by 2012. The Directive also requires action plans to be produced to reduce high noise levels and protect quiet areas, by 2008 for the major areas and 2013 for the others.

Other environmental controls

With notable exceptions like those relating to aircraft noise, actions under private or public nuisance can still be taken despite the specific statutory provisions discussed above, although if a privately initiated remedy is sought it is more likely that statutory nuisance law will be used if this is possible. A modern example of an attempt to use public nuisance law to combat traffic noise is *Gillingham Borough Council v Medway (Chatham) Dock Co. Ltd* [1993] QB 343 (see p. 388).

As discussed in Chapter 20, noise emissions are not within the remit of integrated pollution control under Part 1 of the EPA 1990, but are a relevant factor in determining the wider concept of BPEO under the IPPC Directive (96/61). Environmental statements for developments requiring assessment under the Environmental Impact Assessment Directive (85/337, as amended) must include estimates of noise emissions. The need for an environmental statement to cover secondary and indirect impact means that noise from increased or altered traffic flows must also be considered.

Local controls on air pollution

In Chapter 16 we describe the legal controls that regulate air pollution and the background to these. As noted there, a key driver has been a number of EC directives, which have set a range of quality standards, emission limits and product standards for things like motor vehicle exhausts. Some of these directives are specifically concerned with air pollution and air quality, while others deal with industrial processes which emit a range of polluting substances. For the more polluting processes the legal controls are mainly the responsibility of the Environment Agency implementing IPC and IPPC, while local authorities control the less polluting processes. These controls, and the strategic context of the National Air Quality Strategy and Local Transport Plans within which they operate, are described in more detail elsewhere. However, there remain a number of national provisions with their origins in public health concerns which continue to apply and which are the responsibility of local authorities. Some of these controls, especially those which control smoke from industrial and domestic premises under the Clean Air Act 1993, are an important part of the National Air Quality Strategy, and are detailed below.

The control of smoke, fumes, dust, and grit under the Clean Air Act 1993

The control of smoke, dust and dirt from industrial and domestic fires was largely ineffective in dealing with the problems associated with such emissions in the early part of the 20th century (see p. 629). Although the Public Health (Smoke Abatement) Act 1926 attempted to control certain categories of industrial smoke, domestic smoke was prohibited only if it amounted to a 'nuisance'. The Clean Air Act 1956, later amended and supplemented by the Clean Air Act 1968, provided a comprehensive control mechanism for the protection of the environment from smoke, dust and fumes. These Acts were consolidated in the Clean Air Act 1993.

This Act constitutes a separate and distinct area of control. Essentially, it controls smoke, dust and grit from all fires and furnaces.

(a) Control of smoke from chimneys

Section 1 of the 1993 Act prohibits the emission of 'dark smoke' from the chimney of any building. Any occupier who breaches section 1 will be guilty of a criminal offence. The section applies to all types of buildings, from domestic houses to industrial premises and crematoria. The mechanism of control specifically applies to chimneys from buildings. Although the definition of the word 'building' covers such structures as a greenhouse, it would have to be a part of a recognized structure (*Clifford v Holt* [1899] 1 Ch 698).

The prohibition applies only to 'dark smoke'; other types of emissions are covered either elsewhere in the Act or under different statutes. In attempting to determine whether smoke is 'dark', enforcement officers must make a visual assessment of the shade of the smoke emission by comparing the darkness of the smoke with a uniform chart known as a 'Ringelmann chart'. The chart contains five shades of grey by cross hatching black lines on a white background from clear (number 0) to black (number 4). The chart is rectangular in shape, measuring some 581 mm × 127 mm. The chart is used in accordance with certain guidelines laid down in British Standard 2742. It is held up by the operator and compared to the smoke from a distance of at least 15 metres and then comparisons are made between the colour of the smoke and the colour on the chart. If the colour of the smoke is as dark as, or darker than, shade 2 on the Ringelmann Scale it then qualifies as dark smoke (s. 3(1)). Where, however, an operator is experienced, section 3(2) allows for an assessment to be made independent of the Ringelmann chart, often by the use of a smaller, more portable smoke chart (129 mm × 69 mm). Some officers rely purely on their experience to assess whether or not the smoke is darker than shade 2 (for an example, see Case box 12.5).

The prohibition also only covers smoke emitted from chimneys. The definition of a chimney can be found in section 64 and is wide enough to cover all structures or openings through which smoke is emitted. Thus, smoke from outdoor fires or, for instance, burning straw or stubble is not covered by section 1.

(b) Strict liability

As in other environmental legislation, liability is strict, therefore prima facie *any* dark smoke emitted from a chimney would give rise to liability under section 1. The Act imposes liability on an occupier of a building from which smoke is emitted, irrespective of responsibility.

(c) Exemptions and defences

Section 1(3) provides for certain exemptions to be made by the Secretary of State. These exemptions are restricted by the duration of emissions. The Dark Smoke (Permitted Periods) Regulations 1958 (SI 1958/498) allows three main exemptions for smoke from chimneys. First, there are time-limits imposed of anything between 10 and 40 minutes during any period of eight hours for emission of dark smoke depending on both the number of furnaces used and whether or not soot is blowing. Secondly, there is a limit of four minutes of continuous emissions of dark smoke where the cause is not owed to burning soot. Lastly, there is a limit of two minutes in each period of 30 minutes where smoke is black (that is, smoke as dark as, or darker than, shade 2 on the Ringelmann chart).

Furthermore, section 1(4) lays down three statutory defences. These defences are not absolute and require certain qualifying steps to be taken to ensure that the defences apply. The section provides that it is a defence to a charge under section 1(1) that the emission was:

(i) solely due to the lighting of a furnace, and that all practicable steps were taken to minimise or prevent emissions;

(ii) solely due to the failure of a furnace, and that the contravention of section 1(1) could not reasonably have been foreseen or provided against and prevented by action taken after the failure;

(iii) solely due to the unavoidable use of the least unsuitable fuel available when suitable fuel was unavailable, and practicable steps were taken to minimise or prevent emissions;

(iv) any combination of (i), (ii), and (iii).

(d) Enforcement and offences

An important prerequisite of bringing a prosecution is that the enforcement authority is under a duty to notify occupiers of the existence of the offence 'as soon as may be'. The relevant enforcement officer will normally give this notification orally. If such oral notification is given, it must be confirmed in writing within four days of the date on which the officer became aware of the offence. In any event, written notice of the offence must be given within that time. If notification is not given, it is a defence to charges under sections 1, 2, or 20 of the Act (s. 51(3)). The offence is only triable in the magistrates' court. There are different maximum levels of fine for emissions from private dwellings (level 3 on the standard scale) and for any other case (level 5 on the standard scale) (s. 1(5)).

(e) Emissions of dark smoke from industrial plants

Section 2 of the Act prohibits the emissions of dark smoke from industrial trade premises other than from a chimney of a building (which is covered under s. 1). 'Premises' include the grounds of factories and open areas such as demolition sites (*Sheffield County Council v ADH Demolition Ltd* (1983) 82 LGR 177). Section 2(2)(b) gives the Secretary of State power to pass regulations giving an exemption to the burning of prescribed matter which emits dark smoke in the open. The Clean Air (Emission of Dark Smoke) (Exemption) Regulations 1969 (SI 1969/1263) exempt certain material such as timber, explosives, tar, and waste from animal or poultry carcases. Section 2(6) provides that industrial or trade premises include premises not used for industrial or trade purposes but on which substances or matter are burnt in connection with such processes. Thus, open areas without any connection to industrial activities would fall within control under this section.

CASE 12.5 *O'Fee v Copeland Borough Council* [1996] Env LR 66

O'Fee lit a bonfire on his farm. An environmental health officer judged that the smoke was 'dark smoke' and O'Fee was prosecuted under section 2 of the 1993 Act. At the trial no evidence was given as to the shade of the smoke when it crossed the boundary of O'Fee's farm 660 metres away. O'Fee appealed on the ground that there was no 'emission from land' (as required by s. 2, because 'premises' includes 'land'). This was rejected. What mattered was that there was an emission into the air, not whether any neighbour's land was affected. This makes practical sense, making enforcement easier. But it also means that the right to pollute the air does not depend on the size of one's property. The decision also shows that the Act is about atmospheric pollution per se, and the rights to the air above one's property are irrelevant.

Section 2(3) refers to the burden of proof required when attempting to show the causation of dark smoke. On trade or business premises, where the burning of material would be likely to give rise to an emission of dark smoke, such an emission can be taken as proved unless the occupier or person accused of the offence can show that no dark smoke was actually emitted. When fires have been extinguished but dark smoke has already been emitted there has often been difficulty in proving the source of the dark smoke. This section allows environmental health officers to act against smoke pollution even though there is no smoke emanating from the premises. The prohibition under section 2 applies not only to occupiers but also to any person who causes or permits the emission of dark smoke from industrial or trade premises.

There is a statutory defence under section 2(4) that the emission of dark smoke was 'inadvertent'. This would suggest that although the offence has an absolute liability, some degree of blameworthiness is necessary for an action to be successful. If the emission was inadvertent, it is also necessary to show that all practicable steps have been taken to prevent or minimise the emission of dark smoke. Practicability is defined in section 64 as meaning reasonably practicable having regard to local conditions and circumstances, to the financial implications and to the current state of technical knowledge. An offence under section 2 is triable only in a magistrates' court, the maximum fine being set at level 5 on the standard scale (s. 2(5)).

(f) The control of grit, dust, and fumes

The Act does not only cover smoke. Emissions from furnaces can also contain particulate matter and the Act extends to cover such particulate matter, ranging from the largest (being grit as defined in the Clean Air (Emission of Grit and Dust from Furnaces) Regulations 1971 (SI 1971/162)), through dust and small solid particles between 1 and 75 Bm in diameter (as defined in BS 3405), to fumes (which are defined as any airborne solid matter smaller than dust) (s. 64). There are proactive measures for preventing smoke, dust, grit, and fumes being emitted from furnaces. Section 4 provides that furnaces over a certain energy value (excluding domestic boilers) should, as far as practicable, be smokeless when using a fuel for which it was designed. This control is implemented by section 4(1), under which anyone wishing to install a furnace has to notify the local authority before doing so. Where the local authority is notified and authorization has been given, then the furnace is deemed to comply with the provision. This, however, does not exempt the furnace from being subject to the prohibition on dark smoke under section 1. Where a furnace is operated without such an approval then the person who installed the furnace will be guilty of an offence (s. 4(4)).

This proactive approach is further strengthened by the requirement for grit and dust arrestment plant to be fitted to furnaces. This power is extended by sections 6 and 7, which control all furnaces partly installed or for which there is an agreement to install after 1 October 1969. Again, details of the type of arrestment plant must be given to the local authority. Prior to 1 October 1969, the only furnaces covered were those in buildings burning pulverised fuel or solid waste or fuel at a rate of 1 tonne or more an hour. After that date, the Clean Air Act 1968 extended the powers to include furnaces in which solid, liquid or gaseous matter is burnt as well as reducing the rate of the use of solid matter to a minimum 100 pounds per hour. The statutory requirements are fleshed out by the Clean Air (Emission of Grit and Dust from Furnaces) Regulations 1971 (SI 1971/162), which contain information as to the quantities of grit and dust which may be emitted by reference to either the heat put out by the furnace or the heat taken in by the furnace.

(g) Exemptions

There are exemptions to the requirement to supply details of plant to the local authority under section 6; section 7 gives two main areas of exemption. First, the Secretary of State can exempt certain furnaces by way of the Clean Air (Arrestment Plant) (Exemption) Regulations 1969 (SI 1969/1262), which exclude mobile or transportable furnaces, and certain other furnaces. Secondly, the local authority may exempt a specific furnace if it is satisfied that the emissions from the furnace will not be prejudicial to health or a nuisance.

(h) Monitoring provisions

To enable the local authority to enforce its responsibilities effectively, section 10 allows the Secretary of State to make regulations which allow the local authority to monitor the emission of grit and dust from furnaces. This provision does not apply to fumes unless they are controlled specifically under other legislation.

The provisions regulating the measurement of grit and dust are contained in the Clean Air (Measurement of Grit and Dust) Regulations 1971 (SI 1971/616) and the Clean Air (Units of Measurement) Regulations 1992 (SI 1992/35). Under these regulations, the local authority has to give occupiers of premises not less than six weeks' notice in writing requiring them to make adaptations to any chimney serving a furnace to allow for plant and machinery to be installed to monitor the dust and grit from the furnace. Thereafter the local authority must give at least 28 days written notice requiring a test to be carried out in accordance with the procedure specified in an otherwise obscure book.[14] Then, after giving at least 48 hours written notice of the date and time of the tests, the occupier must send to the local authority within 14 days the report of the results of the test, results in terms of pounds of grit and dust emitted per hour.

These provisions apply only to a number of specific types of furnace including those that burn pulverised fuel or any other solid matter at a rate of 45 kilograms or more per hour.

---

14. P.G.W. Hawksley, S. Badzioch, and J.H. Blackett, The Measurement of Solids in Flue Gases (Leatherhead: The British Coal Utilization Research Association, 1961).

(i) The control of height of chimneys

As one of the main mechanisms for the control of environmental pollution into the atmosphere was to increase the height of chimneys to disperse the pollutant over a wider area (see p. 629), there is specific legislation to control the height of chimneys. The argument used by many scientists has been that the higher the chimney the higher the emission point, and thus the more diluted any emissions will be when they eventually come back down to the ground.

Under sections 14 and 15, an application for chimney height approval is required to enable the local authority to assess the height required, taking into account the geographical features and the constitution of the emissions, so as to avoid localised pollution. If approval is not obtained, it will only be an offence if the chimney is used once it has been constructed. The application form is prescribed by the Clean Air (Height of Chimneys) (Prescribed Form) Regulations 1969 (SI 1969/412). An application must be made in the following circumstances:

- where a new chimney is erected;
- where the combustion space of a furnace serving an existing chimney is enlarged by adding a new furnace to an existing number of furnaces all serving the same chimney;
- where a furnace is removed, or replaced, but only where a furnace burns pulverised fuel, or burns solid matter at a rate of 100 pounds or more per hour, or burns more than 1.25 million BTU per hour of any liquid or gas.

In addition to these controls, planning permission must also be applied for.

When deciding whether or not to grant chimney height approval, the local authority must be satisfied that the chimney height will be sufficient to prevent, so far as is practicable, the smoke, grit, dust, gases, or fumes emitted from the chimney from being prejudicial to health or a nuisance when taking into account (s. 15(2)):

- the purpose of the chimney;
- the position and descriptions of buildings near it;
- the levels of the neighbouring ground;
- any other matters requiring consideration in the circumstances.

If the local authority decides to grant approval, it can grant it with or without conditions, but these must relate only to the rate and quality of emissions from the chimney (s. 15(3)). If the local authority turns down an application, it must do so giving written reasons and an indication as to what it thinks the lowest acceptable height would be. There is a right of appeal to the Secretary of State (s. 15(6)).

As in other areas of control in the Clean Air Act, the Secretary of State may exempt certain boilers or plants from this control for chimney height approval. These exemptions can be found in the Clean Air (Heights of Chimneys) (Exemption) Regulations 1969 (SI 1969/411). The regulations specifically relate to the need for approval to construct a chimney under section 10 and include mostly temporary or mobile boilers or plant.

The guidelines on assessing chimney heights are contained in the *Third Memorandum on Chimney Heights*, published by HMSO issued with joint Council DoE 25/81, Welsh Office 12/81. This provides specific mathematical calculations which take into account background levels of pollution. Where pollution levels are higher then a chimney must be higher as well. The memorandum indicates that the chimney height required should vary according to the type of area concerned among other factors. It identifies the following types of areas:

- an undeveloped area where development is unlikely;
- a partially developed area with scattered houses;
- a built-up residential area;
- an urban area of mixed industrial and residential development;
- a large city or an urban area of mixed heavy industrial and dense residential development.

By assessing the level of pollution in the atmosphere in these generalized ways, it is hoped to achieve an idea of the required height for a particular chimney. In a large city or urban area it will be a requirement that chimneys should be at their highest.

(j) Miscellaneous controls

Aside from chimneys serving a furnace, section 16 applies similar restrictions on chimneys serving a non-combustion process. There is a much simpler procedure for obtaining approval by submitting building regulation plans. The local authority may reject the plans if the chimney is not adequate to prevent emissions from becoming prejudicial to health or a nuisance. There is a right of appeal against refusal.

The Building Regulations 1991 (SI 1991/2768) apply not only to non-combustible furnace chimneys but also to those controlled by section 15. Building regulation approval is therefore required for all chimneys.

(k) Smoke control areas

To improve conditions over wide areas and to control non-dark smoke, section 18 allows local authorities to designate smoke control areas. As there are difficulties in defining areas in relation to land, two or more authorities are entitled to join together and declare that a larger area than their own area is a smoke control area (s. 61(3)). Most smoke control areas were designated soon after the introduction of the Clean Air Act 1956. Although the process has slowed down since then, the number of smoke control orders continues to rise. By 1990 nearly 10 million premises were subject to control, and the success of the orders was a major factor in achieving compliance with EC Directive 80/779 setting quality standards for smoke and sulphur dioxide.

The effect of designating a smoke control area is to make it an offence for occupiers of premises to allow any smoke emissions from a chimney.

The Act exempts both authorized fuel and certain fireplaces from control. The Smoke Control Areas (Authorized Fuels) Regulations 1991 (SI 1991/1282) include all the types of material which can be burnt without emitting smoke. Fireplaces are exempted under various Smoke Control (Exempted Fireplaces) Orders. Therefore, either authorized fuel can be used per se or unauthorized fuel can be used on exempted fireplaces, and the use of either could amount to a defence to a prosecution under section 20. The burden of proof for showing that such exemptions apply falls upon the occupier.

The local authority may under section 18(2) exempt specified buildings, classes of building or fireplaces from the smoke control area. It may make different provision for different parts of the area or limit their operation to specified classes of buildings in the area, such as factories rather than houses.

The process for making an order designating a smoke control area is contained in schedule 1. There is a requirement for general publicity, which enables the public to make objections. This publicity is effected by placing advertisements in the *London Gazette* in addition to notices being posted around the area. If there are any objections to the order they must be taken into account as material considerations in deciding whether or not to ratify the order. Where an order is made, its operation is delayed for a minimum of six months whilst the authority brings the effect of the order to the notice of the people within the area.

Department of the Environment Circular 11/81 suggests that there should be sufficient supplies of authorised fuel in the area and the operation of the order should be implemented at some time between 1 July and 1 November to ensure that there are adequate provisions of fuel stocks.

Statutory nuisances and the Clean Air Act 1993

Smoke, dust, and other emissions from a chimney (industrial or domestic) are excluded from the definition of a statutory nuisance found in the EPA 1990 (s. 79(7)). In addition, under section 79(10) of the EPA 1990, statutory nuisance actions cannot be taken in respect of emissions which could be the subject of enforcement action under Part I of the EPA 1990. In both cases, the rationale behind these provisions is that there are co-existing provisions which should be used to deal with the problems arising from the emissions (namely, the Clean Air Act 1993 and the air pollution control provisions of the EPA 1990). The provisions of the Clean Air Act 1993 do not apply to processes which are prescribed for control under Part I of the EPA 1990 (Clean Air Act 1993, s. 41).

Local authority controls on traffic pollution

In addition to the strategic management of traffic through Local Transport Plans (see p. 656), there are statutory powers available to control traffic under a number of different statutes. The Road Traffic Reduction Act 1997 places a duty upon local authorities to review the levels of traffic on local roads and to produce targets for reducing numbers. This will be supplemented nationally by the traffic reduction targets produced under the Road Traffic Reduction (National Targets) Act 1999. Under the Road Traffic Regulation Act 1984, local authorities have wide powers to regulate traffic under Traffic Regulation Orders (TROs) which can be used to restrict traffic in certain areas (e.g. pedestrianized areas of city centres) or even single roads. TROs can be made in order to achieve air quality objectives (s. 1(g) of the Road Traffic Regulation Act 1984). Further measures to reduce traffic and contribute to air quality improvements can be made by using traffic calming under the Highways (Traffic Calming) Regulations 1999 (SI 1999/1026) which allow local authorities to create narrow 'gateways' into urban centres. Traffic regulation conditions can now be applied not just to prevent danger to road users or curb congestion, but also to reduce or limit noise or air pollution (Transport Act 1985, s. 7 as amended by Transport Act 2002, s. 142). The Transport Act 2000 also makes provisions for restrictions on workplace parking.

High hedges

A final local authority control that we should mention relates to high hedges. The height that some evergreen hedges can reach, and the speed with which they do so, have been an increasing source of neighbour disputes, because of the amount of light that they block out all year round. The legislative response is Part VIII of the Anti-Social Behaviour Act 2003, which in many ways mirrors Part III of the EPA 1990. A 'high hedge' is defined as two or more evergreens over 2 metres in height, which is a barrier to light or access (unless the hedge has significant gaps in it), and it must adversely affect the reasonable enjoyment of the neighbouring property. The test is an objective one—what would the impact on a prospective occupier be? As with statutory nuisance, the local authority is under a duty to investigate complaints, and under a duty to serve a remedial notice (which it must do so as soon as reasonably practicable), giving reasons.

There are, however, some keys differences which help explain why an initial proposed to add 'high hedges' to the list of prescribed statutory nuisances was not followed through. First, the local authority does not have to serve a remedial notice if it considers that the complainant has not exhausted informal ways of resolving the dispute; secondly, the remedial notice must describe both what initial action is needed *and* what preventive action must be taken (because hedges keep growing); thirdly (because there is not the public health imperative which justifies abatement notices coming into effect immediately), the notice cannot come into effect until the end of a compliance period, which itself can only begin 28 days after the notice is served; fourthly, the fine levels are lower (£1,000), and the court has a discretion not to fine but to re-order that the necessary steps are taken (if this second order is also breached, then a further fine of £1,000, plus £50 per day, is payable); and, finally, both parties to the dispute may appeal the issuing of a notice, or its withdrawal, to the Secretary of State or National Assembly for Wales. Obviously the hedge will not have to be reduced until the appeal is determined, which again distinguishes this area of local authority control from the speed and summary nature which is the essence of statutory nuisance law.

 CHAPTER SUMMARY

1 While many rules of environmental law have evolved from earlier public health law, local authorities continue to play an important role in controlling various forms of local environmental pollution problems such as noise, smoke and smells.

2 Part III of the EPA 1990 covers various listed activities where they are 'prejudicial to health or a nuisance'. Local authorities must investigate their areas for statutory nuisances, and serve an abatement notice where they find such nuisances.

3 As an important fallback, affected individuals can go to a magistrates' court and ask the court to serve an abatement order.

4 Local authorities (or courts) can either require the abatement of the nuisance, or notify the person responsible that certain works must be carried out.

5 Statutory nuisance is intended to be a relatively quick and cheap mechanism, and considerable

discretion is given to local environmental health officers in identifying nuisances and drafting abatement notices.

6   Industry is given a defence of showing that it has used the best practicable means of counteracting the effect of the nuisance.

7   Failure to comply with an abatement notice or order is a criminal offence punishable by a fine. In serious cases an injunction preventing the nuisance might be granted.

8   Statutory nuisance is often used to control excessive noise, but other local controls also do this. Noise control is different from other forms of environmental pollution because of the inherently subjective nature of noise and because it is transient.

9   Local authorities can designate areas as noise abatement zones (although few have been designated) and can control noise from construction sites, noise at night, and neighbour noise disputes. There is an increasing use of the criminal law to control neighbour noise.

10 Air pollution is a global problem, but many disputes are local in nature and local authorities have various control powers under the Clean Air Act 1993.

11 The 1993 Act regulates dark smoke from chimneys and from industrial premises, and grit, dust and fumes from furnaces. It also regulates the height of chimneys in order to disperse atmospheric pollution. Smoke control areas can also be designated.

12 Local authorities also have powers to regulate road traffic in order to improve air quality, and now noise pollution.

13 A recent development is that local authorities now have obligations to curb problems associated with high hedges. The procedure is essentially the same as that for abating statutory nuisances, but there are some notable differences.

Q   QUESTIONS

1   Which of the following might be a statutory nuisance? What further information would you need?
   (i)   A large pile of horse manure in a neighbour's back garden.
   (ii) Security lighting from a neighbouring property.
   (iii) A wind turbine.

2   Gill and Heather occupy adjoining properties. Gill looks after rescue dogs and usually has around seven dogs in her house (although they mostly live in kennels in the garden). As she works shifts, she often does DIY and uses her washing machine very late at night. Heather is bothered by the dogs' noise and smell, and by the noise and vibration of the washing machine. Heather is a part-time car mechanic and her front garden Is littered with car junk. There are also used and unused syringes amongst the rubbish. Occasionally Heather burns car tyres and other refuse at night. Gill complains about the noise from the car repairs and the ash which lands in her garden. As a screen against the sight of Heather's garden, Gill planted a short leylandii hedge which is now 3 metres high. Heather complains that the hedge prevents her growing sun-loving plants. Both Gill and Heather complain to the local authority. Advise the local authority.

3   When dealing with environmental problems, what are the advantages and disadvantages of the various local controls described in this chapter compared to the remedies described in Chapter 11?

FURTHER READING

In relation to statutory nuisance, R. McCracken *et al.*, *Statutory Nuisance* (London: Butterworths, 2001) provides the most detailed discussion, both of the law and of practical issues, and is not shy in offering views on how uncertain areas of the law ought to be resolved. Other comprehensive analyses of the law are R. Malcolm and J. Pointing, *Statutory Nuisance: Law and Practice* (Oxford: Oxford University Press, 2002) and S. Tromans and M. Poustie's annotations to Part III of the EPA 1990 in *Environmental Protection Legislation 1990–2002* (London: Sweet & Maxwell, 2003), the latter including the law in Scotland. There is a good discussion of the wider role of statutory nuisance in Moran, 'Statutory Nuisance and Environmental Protection' (1994) Environmental Policy and Practice 129.

On noise, a good way to get a feel for the area, and trends over time, is to look at the annual surveys produced by the Chartered Institute of Environmental Health. The technical aspects of noise generation and monitoring, as well as a comprehensive survey of the law, is found in C. Penn, *Noise Control: The Law and its Enforcement* (3rd edn Crayford: Shaw & Sons, 2002). Although increasingly out of date on the law, M. Adams and F. McManus, *Noise and Noise Law: A Practical Approach* (Chichester: Wiley Chancery, 1994) is an excellent short introduction to the law and policy. J. Fitz-patrick, 'A Quiet Life: Right or Duty', in I. Pardo (ed.), *The Morals of Legitimacy* (Oxford: Berghahn Books, 2000) is an insightful critique of the creeping use of law to regulate domestic arrangements like neighbour noise disputes.

On local air pollution controls D. Hughes, N. Parpworth, and J. Upson, *Air Pollution Law and Regulation* (Bristol: Jordans, 1998) is a straightforward (but dated) exposition of the statutory materials in the area and covers international, European and domestic sources of law. For a less legal and more policy based approach, the *National Air Quality Strategy for England, Scotland, Wales and Northern Ireland* (Cm 4548, 2000) covers all of the issues in a reader friendly fashion. For sources on the historical background to local air pollution controls see the sources mentioned at the end of Chapter 16.

WEB LINKS

Two good general portals on noise and air quality respectively are <www.air-quality-management.co.uk/noiselinks.htm> and <www.air-quality-management.co.uk/airlinks.htm>. These provide links both to the main government departments and regulatory agencies, as well as to related sites of campaigning organisations such as the National Society for Clean Air and Environmental Protection. (On noise, it is worth noting the increasing reach of the Home Office, and arguably a slight diminution of the importance of Defra.) The web site of the Chartered Institute of Environmental Health <www.cieh.org> includes annual statistics on noise complaints, and comparative statistics are found in the *e-Digest of Environmental Statistics* <www.defra.gov.uk/environment/statistics>. Most local authority websites contain information about how statutory nuisance and noise complaints are handled.

13 Town and country planning

 Overview

The British system of town and country planning is undoubtedly one of the most sophisticated systems of land use control in the world. It is exceptional in incorporating controls over
the use of land as well as over the design and form of the built environment. Accordingly, it
plays a central role in environmental law because of its enormous importance in relation to
locational issues, as well as determining how much of any particular activity (such as house-
building) is allowed where, and the intensity of such development. It is, as stated earlier (see
p. 242), perhaps the pre-eminent example in this country of a proactive, anticipatory system
of control. However, 'town and country planning' is not just about environmental protection. It
has a wider role in organizing economic development, but in balancing economic, political,
social and environmental factors to do with development in a democratic context it ought to
be a key mechanism for making development more sustainable.

Specific aspects of planning law relevant to other chapters within Part III of the book are
summarized at the appropriate place, though some thoughts are offered here on the general
nature of the relationship between town and country planning and environmental protection.
There is also a good deal of overlap between the coverage in this chapter and the next
chapter on environmental assessment. A final introductory point is that this chapter deals
with town and country planning law, rather than the role of planning-type mechanisms in
general. The law now requires various plans relating to the environment, such as the national
strategies for air and waste, and river catchment plans for water quality regulation, while
there are also non-statutory plans like local transport plans and informal plans such as Local
Environment Agency Plans.

At the end of this chapter you will be able to:

✔ Identify and understand the main features and scope of the town and country planning
system.
✔ Appreciate the contribution of planning controls alongside specialist environmental
protection regimes.
✔ Evaluate the strengths and weaknesses of planning law in furthering environmental
protection.

The main features of town and country planning

Because the town and country planning system is not a specialist environmental protection
regime but has wider objectives, it is helpful to set out its main features:

The main features of town and country planning

1   Development is planned and controlled by taking a wide range of factors—social, economic, and environmental—into account. But environmental concerns are becoming increasingly prominent.

2   Individual planning decisions are taken within a framework set by the development plan. Development plans are permissive (i.e. they do not guarantee what is going to happen, or themselves authorize development, but act as guides to future development).

3   All 'development', which includes changes of use as well as physical development, requires planning permission from the local planning authority.

4   Planning permission is deemed to be granted for certain minor developments. Certain changes of use are also excluded from being 'development', where old and new activities have similar land use impacts. In this latter case, planning permission is simply not required.

5   Applications for planning permission involve consultation with other public bodies and some limited public involvement.

6   The local planning authority decides whether to grant permission or refuse it, taking as its starting point the development plan but also recognising central government policies and any other material considerations. Each application must be considered on its merits.

7   If permission is granted, it may (and invariably will) be subject to conditions; some permissions will also be accompanied by planning contributions (contributions by developers to pay for some of the associated infrastructure and environmental costs of the development).

8   The applicant may appeal to the Secretary of State against any refusal or conditions. This is a complete rehearing of the whole matter, including the policy issues, enabling the Secretary of State to exercise a stranglehold on policy by having the final say on it.

9   There is no right of appeal for third parties and no right to appeal against a grant of planning permission.

10 There is a further right of appeal from the decision of the Secretary of State to the High Court on what are essentially the same grounds as for judicial review. The courts thus exercise a supervisory jurisdiction over the procedures and the decisions taken. However, the courts will not intervene on grounds of fact or policy.

11 It is not an offence to develop without permission, but rather an offence to fail to comply with an enforcement notice. Enforcement is discretionary.

12 Planning permission effectively gives a right to develop. Unlike most systems of pollution control, there is no power to vary a planning permission in the future (unless compensation is paid).

13 The role of law and the courts is primarily procedural and supervisory; ensuring that decisions have been reached correctly, rather than interfering with matters of planning policy or judgement.

Town and country planning as a tool of environmental policy

There are three main areas with relevance to environmental law:

- The system of development plans which ensures that environmental protection is considered at the level of policy-making. These plans set the basic ground rules for action on the environment in any particular area, although they must be read in conjunction with central government policy guidance.
- The development control process, in which planning permission is required from the local planning authority for acts of development. This ensures a strict anticipatory control over many activities before they start and normally involves liaison with the specialist environmental regulatory agencies.
- The power to impose conditions, and enter into agreements, relating to environmental protection on a grant of planning permission. These are capable of creating some form of continuing control over activities.

BOX 13.1 **Planning vs Building Controls**

Planning controls are essentially locational, whereas traditionally building control regulations have been to do with ensuring health and safety features of new buildings and building work. But building regulations can now be made for a wide range of environmental reasons, including (specifically) furthering fuel and power conservation, and preventing water wastage or contamination, and (more generally) furthering the protection or enhancement of the environment, or facilitating sustainable development (s. 1 Building Act 1984, as amended by the Sustainable and Secure Buildings Act 2004). These are just permissive, and how far they will in fact contribute to these ends depends upon how strict building standards are made. Historically, UK standards on things like insulation have tended to fall some way short of those in comparable countries.

Planning as a negotiative process

The traditional conflictual model of a regulatory body regulating the applicant by granting or refusing permission is no longer really appropriate here. Modern town planning is best seen as a negotiative process in which consultation between the prospective developer and the local planning authority in advance of the application is the norm, and in which proposals are both made and considered in the light of local and national policies. The local planning authority and the developer often have a community of interest in carrying out a particular development: the developer gets its proposal granted and the local authority obtains the revitalization of the economy of an area, or the creation of jobs, or some other economic benefit. (Indeed, developments by local authorities and developers in partnership with each other are now quite common.) In addition, arrangements between developers and local authorities in which 'planning gain' is bargained for are increasingly used to supplement the regulatory controls (see p. 486).

The scope of planning law

The impact of planning control is in many ways incomplete or inadequate. Planning permission is not required for all environmentally harmful activities, for example for mobile pollutants such as cars, or offshore activities like tidal power schemes (because it governs the development of *land*, which means land out to the mean low water mark), or in relation to most agricultural activities. There are difficulties where some form of continuing control is required, because of the limitations on planning conditions, or where positive management is required, since it is mainly a preventive system. The system also tends to get circumvented in various ways where nationally important development is desired by central government.

Planning law and environmental protection

In 1976 the Royal Commission on Environmental Pollution commented that, 'Our concern is not that pollution is not always given top priority; it is that it is often dealt with inadequately, and sometimes forgotten altogether in the planning process.'[1] C. Wood describes how, in general terms, the town and country planning system was, for a variety of institutional and other reasons, relatively *under*used for environmental protection (e.g. in relation to imposing planning conditions).[2] Now, although planning remains a political process, the concern is not so much that environmental considerations are ignored but that 'a much more comprehensive approach is needed, and . . . new environmental objectives must be integrated into the planning process'.[3]

The planning system is of central importance in many areas of environmental law, especially when used in conjunction with other regulatory controls. This is seen clearly in relation to waste disposal, where planning permission for a waste disposal site is required before a waste management licence can be granted. In other areas, planning control is arguably of greatest importance where the enforcement of pollution control is inadequate, since non-enforcement at the operational end puts increased pressure on initial siting and design issues. But planning controls may also 'trump' specialist environmental or conservation regimes; one example is where acting under a planning permission amounts to a reasonable excuse to damaging a site of special scientific interest (see p. 817).

Town and country planning and some themes of this book

The town and country planning system illustrates a number of the major themes of this book. For instance, it is a good example of a sophisticated anticipatory regulatory mechanism and it emphasizes prevention of harm. That also means that the predominant method of control is through negative, restrictive measures, rather than through positive mechanisms. Local decision-making dominates, although there has been some shift of power towards central government in recent years (see p. 448). It is a highly discretionary system, in which decisions are made on a case-by-case basis. And it is a democratic system in which ultimate political control rests with elected members rather than with officers (on appeal responsibility rests with an elected Secretary of State), although in practice most

---

1. RCEP, Air Pollution Control: An Integrated Approach, 5th Report, Cmnd 6371.
2. C. Wood, *Planning Pollution Prevention* (London: Butterworths, 1989).
3. RCEP, 23rd Report, *Environmental Planning*, Cm 5459, 2002.

decisions are actually taken by officers. It is a fairly open and public system, but with inevitable trade-offs between speed and participation. Enforcement is under-emphasised, being almost exclusively the responsibility of the local planning authority and dependent on political and tactical factors as well as on adequate resources (which in practice are often not available).

But the most important point is that it is a highly political system of decision-making. Local planning authorities and the Secretary of State make discretionary decisions by balancing economic, political, environmental, and social factors. It is therefore just as important to understand the prevailing policy in relation to a particular issue as it is to understand the relevant law.

The role of the law and the courts requires some explanation here. The planning system is one where the law generally exercises a supervisory, or review, function. It is there to define the various concepts used in the planning system (such as what development is, or what types of conditions are legitimate), to ensure that the correct procedures are used and to ensure that discretionary decisions are taken in the proper manner. The law is therefore ultimately about procedures, i.e. about ensuring that decisions are made correctly rather than that the correct decisions are made.

The planning legislation

As Lord Scarman stated in *Pioneer Aggregates (UK) Ltd v Secretary of State for the Environment* [1985] AC 132, 'Planning control is the creature of statute . . . Parliament has provided a comprehensive code of planning control.' Although private law rights can be used for rudimentary development planning and control (see Box 13.2), statutory planning law is not based on common law foundations in the way that, for example, the law of statutory nuisance is. This means that it is a largely self-contained code as far as interpreting planning legislation is concerned.[4]

BOX 13.2 **The shortcomings of private law for planning**

Land development is controlled using private law in one of two main ways. First, nuisance law (a common law land tort) could be used. This prohibits unlawful interference with a person's use or enjoyment of land (e.g. nuisance law can, in theory, control smoke or noise emanating from another property). But nuisance is about actual interference, and is not an effective anticipatory control. Nor, because the courts have generally restricted its scope to damage caused by emanations is it effective in regulating development which does not emit anything harmful, or in protecting things like wildlife or landscapes.

The other mechanism is the restrictive covenant. This can be imposed by an owner on the sale of land, preventing all subsequent owners (not just the purchaser) from developing the land contrary to the covenant. This is a useful anticipatory device, and can regulate

---

4. A point which the courts have had occasion to stress in recent years, see e.g. *R (Reprotech (Pershan) Ltd) v East Sussex County Council* [2002] UKHL 8.

future changes to land uses, but relies on the preferences of individual sellers of land at the time of the sale and is not an effective technique for regulating competing modern uses.

Modern planning legislation is generally traced back to the Housing, Town Planning etc. Act 1909 (see p. 21). The notable features of this Act, with its focus on the urban environment and discretion to implement, characterized much early planning legislation. It was not until the Town and Country Planning Act 1947 that a uniform and mandatory country-wide system of development control—Lord Scarman's 'comprehensive code'—was introduced. One of the most remarkable things about planning is that, whilst there have been numerous detailed additions and amendments to the law, the basic structure of much of this system (apart from that relating to development plans) has remained unchanged since then, although the way in which it is operated has in practice changed quite radically.

The legislation was consolidated in the Town and Country Planning Act 1990. Important changes were made under the Planning and Compensation Act 1991, but inserted into the 1990 Act as amendments or additions. The Planning and Compulsory Purchase Act 2004 makes further important changes to the law; some of these amend the 1990 Act, but some important changes, especially to development planning, have not been consolidated.

Unless otherwise stated, therefore, wherever a section number is given in this chapter without reference to a particular Act, it refers to the 1990 Act. Frequent reference will also be made to subordinate legislation, which fleshes out much of the detail of the law: central here are the:

- Town and Country Planning (General Permitted Development) Order 1995 (SI 1995/418);
- Town and Country Planning (General Development Procedure) Order 1995 (SI 1995/419), and
- Town and Country Planning (Use Classes Order) 1987 (SI 1987/764).

The first two relate to the grant of automatic planning permission for a wide range of activities, while under the latter a significant number of changes in the use of land are declared not to be 'development' and so fall outside the planning system altogether. Much of the actual implementation of the PCPA 2004 will also be left to secondary legislation.

What is town and country planning?

Town planning has been described simply as 'How much of what is put where?'. As befits a political system, the question of what planning covers has, over the years, largely been left to those who make planning decisions. The result has been an expansion of the idea, beyond straightforward amenity, public health and land use issues towards taking into account the economic and social impact of decisions.

This widening of the scope of planning has received the support of the courts. In exercising their supervisory jurisdiction they have often had to ask the question 'What is planning?' in order to decide whether a power has been used legitimately. In doing so they have proved willing to decide that most things are within the scope of planning. The most commonly used legal test is given by Lord Scarman in *Westminster City Council v Great Portland Estates plc* [1985] AC 661 who suggested that town planning covers anything that 'relates to the character of the use of land'.

This general formulation, however, hides fundamental divisions over the legitimate role and scope of planning (see Box 13.3). Until the 1970s town and country planning was a relatively uncontroversial topic in party political terms, with the exception of the questions of compensation for refusal of permission and taxation of profits resulting from a grant of permission (betterment). There was a degree of consensus over what planning should consist of and over the preferred policies. The role of the state as itself a major developer was accepted.

BOX 13.3 **McAuslan's ideologies of planning law**

1　Law exists to protect private property and its institutions (traditional common law approach)

2　Law exists and should be used to advance the public interest, if necessary against 1 (orthodox public administration and planning approach)

3　Law exists and should be used to advance the cause of public participation against both 1 and 2 (radical or populist approach)

(From McAuslan, *The Ideologies of Planning Law* (Oxford: Pergamon Press, 1980))

In the 1980s, there remained agreement that planning should include land use and amenity issues, such as the location and design of new developments, but the extent to which socio-economic issues should be a legitimate part of planning became contested. Some saw planning as one means by which a particular form of social development might be produced. Others wished to see planning restricted as much as possible on the grounds that it interfered unduly with the free market. The second view was effectively the one that was espoused by the Conservative governments of the 1980s, with their firm beliefs in deregulation, a minimalist approach to restrictions on commercial activity, the power of the market as a distributor of resources, and the consequent need for speed and certainty in any system of control. This deregulatory approach included changes to the law, e.g. removing the need for planning permission in many situations, fast-tracking development control in designated areas and centralising decision-making for certain major infrastructure projects under the Transport and Works Act 1992. But it also included important changes to government policy guidance, which emphasized the interests of developers in being granted planning permission and the need to speed up the process of dealing with planning applications. Many of these changes indicated a significant move away from upholding participation as an important objective of the planning system in its own right, a strong theme of the late 1960s and early 1970s (McAuslan's third ideology), and from the more general notion that planning is above all a process through which decisions are made, rather than anything with an absolutely definitive subject matter.

The centrality of planning policy and the Secretary of State

The deregulatory agenda operated both at a procedural and substantive level. There has always been some sort of presumption in favour of granting permission, and the statistics on planning permission show that of the large numbers of applications made each year, approximately 90 per cent are granted. The difference is that in the 1980s this presumption changed in substance from the basic public law requirement that reasons be given for a decision affecting someone's right to develop, to a *policy* in favour of development that may have a great weight attached to it by the decision-maker. This is just one example of the increased importance attached to planning policy in the system, notwithstanding the retention of the basic legal structure of the system outlined above. Increasingly, change was effected by administrative means, particularly by the concerted application of strong central government policy, often on appeal.

In the 1980s, policy guidance sought to increase the role of the free market in generating development. Landmarks in this regard were Circular 22/80, with its overt encouragement of small businesses and private housing, and Circular 14/85 which stated that 'There is always a presumption in favour of allowing applications for development, having regard to all material considerations, unless that development would cause demonstrable harm to interests of acknowledged importance'. Circular 1/85 also played an important role, emphasising that conditions should not be attached unless they could be justified on clear grounds.

Naturally, this pro-development approach was also taken by the Secretary of State on appeal, applying his own policies. Often these would carry so much weight that local planning authorities ignored them at their peril, knowing that developers could exercise their right to appeal. The result was that in the 1980s these explicitly directory circulars grew to have far greater importance than local policies such as development plans. The appeals process was used to support this shift in power from local to central government, and the number of appeals, and successful appeals, rose significantly. A similar story was apparent in relation to appeals against enforcement notices.

In keeping with the policy of doctrinal neutrality on the content of planning policies, the courts did not interfere with these changes, except to preserve the rationality of the decision-making process by insisting that adequate reasons were given for decisions. In this respect it should be recognized that the planning system has always been pro-development to some extent. This stems from the prominence of property-based ideas within it and is evident in, for example, third parties and objectors[5] not being given the same rights to appeal against the grant of planning permission as developers are when permission is refused. The result is that permission will be granted if *either* the local planning authority or the Secretary of State is in favour of it.

---

5. The negative language of 'objectors' is revealing in itself, see A. Davies (2001) 72 TPR 193.

Centralization and decentralization

In the 1980s the planning system became far more centralized, in two main senses: more decisions were taken at a central level and central policy pervaded every decision even at a local level. One effect was to shift power from local government to central government; another to increase the areas of conflict between the two levels. But, interestingly, at the same time the system became in a way *less* centralized. This was because the changes in policy were designed to increase the role of the market at the expense of the State, and to make the system more developer-led. The system moved away from the direct promotion of wider social, economic and environmental objectives; reflecting the shift from public to private development, it became more concerned with resolving a myriad of competing land uses in the wider public interest.

The 1990s also saw a mix of centralizing and decentralizing tendencies. The Secretary of State no longer had to approve all development plans and a presumption in favour of development in accordance with such plans was introduced. But the activity of land use planning became even less contentious politically. There were no longer the same debates about the purposes of planning as there were up to the 1980s, and so less need to impose government policy on appeal. However, the importance of central government rose because planning policy contained ever more prescriptive 'guidance', more in the form of rules for local authorities to follow than best practice to be commended. Increasingly, this prescriptive guidance shaped development plans, although in terms of content the emphasis was on facilitating private development.

In the light of evidence that suggests that in areas of discretion, the main influence on the formulation of local planning officers' judgement is overwhelmingly central government guidance, this can be seen as a further centralizing step. In the 1990s the focus also shifted to the propriety of the planning system,[6] and government guidance effectively put an onus on elected members to justify decisions taken against the advice of officers' written reports.

The role of the courts

A major challenge to the non-interventionist approach of the courts came with the Human Rights Act 1998, which for a short period threatened to upset the traditional approach to planning. In the seminal litigation in *R v Secretary of State for the Environment, Transport and the Regions ex parte Holding and Barnes plc and others* [2001] UKHL 23 (generally known as the '*Alconbury*' case), which related to cases where the decision-maker was the Secretary of State,[7] the Divisional Court had originally objected to the Secretary of State being 'the judge in his own cause where his policy is in play' so that to comply with Article 6 of the Convention (the right to a fair trial, sometimes expressed as including the 'right to a court') 'he cannot be both policy maker and decision-taker'. However, the House of Lords

---

6. The Third Report of the Nolan Committee on *Standards in Public Life* (Cm 3702, 1997) received more complaints about planning than any other activity of local government.

7. Either because the application was 'called in' or an appeal was 'recovered' or for other reasons that meant that the Secretary of State was the decision-maker.

upheld the distinction between the legality of a planning judgment and the merits of a decision, and thought it was misconceived to look on the Secretary of State's role as that of a judge. To have done so would obviously have disturbed the whole scheme of the planning legislation.

The House of Lords has, though, stressed the public law nature of planning (and hence the rejection, for example, of private law concepts like estoppel entering planning law,[8] or the privileging of developer interests in relation to raising challenges to planning decisions).[9] In some ways this is just a continuation of the idea that planning is a comprehensive statutory code, but the decision in *Burkett*—that the time for bringing a challenge to a planning permission runs not from the date that the planning authority resolves to grant permission but from the date that the permission is actually granted—is especially significant, since it represents the courts making a clear choice about the importance of public participation in planning (in effect, elevating McAuslan's third ideology at the expense of the first and second ideologies). According to Lord Slynn:

> I realise that this [decision] may cause some difficulties in practice, both for local authorities and for developers, but for the grant not to be capable of challenge, because the resolution has not been challenged in time, seems to me wrongly to restrict the right of the citizen to protect his interests (on this case see further Box 10.12).

Finally, making planning decisions has become a much more legalistic process. This is especially so in relation to environmental protection where there is an increasing range of legal obligations, some of which arise from EC directives, which must be considered and given due weight in planning decisions (see p. 482). One consequence is that decision-makers, especially on appeal, no longer just take policy guidance and legal obligations into account and apply them; increasingly these sources are *interpreted* in the light of previous decisions and cases. This process of juridification may be seen as a valuable safeguard in ensuring that decisions are reached consistently and in accordance with the 'real meaning' of legal obligations. Alternatively, it may be seen as a threat to the speed and flexibility of response which the modern property market claims to require.

The Planning and Compulsory Purchase Act 2004

Further change to the planning system has come with the Planning and Compulsory Purchase Act 2004. Some indication of the importance of this reform is that its preceding Green Paper[10] received a record number of (mostly highly critical) responses. Some of the Bill's more centralising aspects were eventually removed—the most notable being Government proposals that, in the interests of avoiding drawn out public inquiries like the five-year inquiry into Terminal 5 at Heathrow, the decision in principle on major infrastructure

---

8. *R (Reprotech (Pebsham) Ltd) v East Sussex County Council* [2002] UKHL 8 (a consequence of this was that a decision that converting waste to electricity was ancillary to an existing waste management use was overturned).

9. *R (Burkett) v Hammersmith and Fulham LBC* [2002] UKHL 23.

10. *Planning: Delivering a Fundamental Change* (2001).

projects should be taken by Parliament (see p. 471). But other potentially centralizing measures remain, especially in relation to development planning (see p. 453).

The PCPA 2004, not all of which has yet come into force, is fleshed out by a number of regulations and orders. Perhaps as importantly the Act is just one plank of a planning reform programme which will see the revisions of all existing government policy guidance. In some ways it may be the revisions to policy guidance that will be the most important development, since the stated intention is to simplify this so that guidance concentrates on issues of principle.

However, as a comparison between the Parliamentary debates preceding the 1947 and 2004 Acts shows, concern with social objectives has been replaced by an emphasis on environmental protection and sustainable development (although securing the construction of housing, especially affordable housing, is also an important factor behind many of the reforms, see p. 483). The 2004 Act provides a statutory sustainability objective for the making of development plans (see p. 460), although this may just shift the objectives of at least some aspects of the planning system from the implicitly to the explicitly vague.

A main aspiration behind the reforms was the planning shift from a negative process—a set of constraints to development, which developers have to overcome if they are to get planning permission—to positive management which seeks more active engagement with key stakeholders and the public. The shift towards positive management can be seen in regional spatial strategies, which replace county-level structure plans. The strategies are not restricted to laying down a framework for how land is used and developed, but are intended to have a wider function of coordinating development control with forward-looking mechanisms like transport plans, environmental quality plans and so on. Hence, only certain parts of the spatial strategy will be 'the development plan', with the result, as one commentator has described it, of land use planning 'nesting' within spatial strategies.[11]

However, it is also clear that there will be no return to the post-War vision of the planned national economy; that the private sector will remain the most important driving force behind development; and that—as with its predecessors—the present Labour Government does not see its role as directing development towards less prosperous regions and away from economic hotspots concerned about the impact of new development on the environment. The market economy must 'go ahead at full speed on all engines'.[12]

Whatever the objectives behind the 2004 Act, the tensions between speed and participation, predictability and flexibility, are probably an inescapable feature of planning (as they are with most other regulatory systems).[13] The more streamlined that various parts of the process are made, the more that decisions may be challenged through the courts because stakeholders (and particularly objectors) feel that their views have not been heard or adequately taken into account. For example, the more flexibility is given to decision-makers to relax planning controls at local level—and the 2004 Act allows local planning authorities to make local development orders, in effect a form of local permitted development rights—the more that those with neighbouring land lose certainty about the amenity of their area.

11. M. Tewdwr-Jones [2004] JPL 560.

12. Government Office for the South East, *Regional Planning Guidance for the South East of England: Public Examination May-June 1999—Report of the Panel*, para. 4.9 (Government representation).

13. Whether *in fact* planning acts as a drag on competitiveness may be more myth than reality, see HC ODPM: Housing, Planning, Local Government and the Regions Committee, *Planning, Competitiveness and Productivity*, Fourth Report, 2002–3.

Planning authorities

Most decisions on planning applications are taken by local authorities, which in this context are generically called local planning authorities. There are three main types of local planning authority that deal with most applications: district authorities, single-tier London boroughs and metropolitan districts, and unitary authorities.

Different rules apply to national parks, where development control decisions are taken by the national park authority. (The position is different in Scotland, see p. 864.) In the Broads, the similarly constituted Broads Authority takes all decisions (Norfolk and Suffolk Broads Act 1988). In relation to what are termed 'county matters' such as minerals developments and waste disposal applications, the relevant local authority is the county council. County planning authorities are responsible both for making decisions on planning applications, and for preparing plans relating to these county matters.

Decisions on planning applications take as their starting point the development plan for the area. Development plans have a regional and a local element. Under the PCPA 2004, with the exception of waste and minerals matters, the regional level replaces the county level, county council structure plans being replaced by Regional Spatial Strategies. Keeping RSSs up to date is the responsibility of Regional Planning Bodies, which (in the unlikely event that the English regions ever decide to establish them) will be the elected Regional Assemblies, but for the foreseeable future are an uneasy mix of elected members acting as delegates from local- and county-level planning authorities—at least 60 per cent of the RPB must comprise such members—and unelected members.

The Greater London Authority is not a local planning authority, although it plays a strategic role in relation to development since it must develop a 'spatial development strategy' (see p. 455).

Wales, Scotland, and Northern Ireland

Following devolution, planning in Wales remains subject to the TCPA 1990, but powers in relation to delegated legislation, and powers of the Secretary of State, have passed to the Assembly. Given the extent to which planning law and policy depends on decisions made at this level, there is considerable scope for significant differences to emerge (although as yet none have). Similarly, although the Planning Inspectorate hears most appeals, the Planning Decision Committee of the Assembly has the power to hear cases which have been 'called-in' or where jurisdiction to hear the case has been recovered. However, it is the First Secretary or the Environment and Local Government Secretary who decides whether these cases are referred to the Assembly, and who therefore exercise considerable power, effectively acting as a 'gatekeeper' for decisions on the more complex or controversial cases. Having a smaller panel to decide appeals may meet concerns that giving powers to the full committee would lead to an inconsistent application of policy, although there is some rotation of members to keep the political balance.

In Scotland planning legislation was consolidated in the Town and Country Planning (Scotland) Act 1997, which is broadly similar to the TCPA 1990. Planning cases decided by the House of Lords that have their origins in the Scottish courts are therefore usually equally important elsewhere in Britain, since analogous terms are being interpreted. One difference, though, was that there were often larger differences in the wording of policy guidance, contained in National Planning Policy Guidance notes (NPPG) and Policy Advice Notes, and certainly differences in when guidance came into effect. With devolution, responsibility for town and country planning passed to the Scottish Parliament. Because there is only limited EC involvement in planning law, there is considerable scope for Scottish law and policy to develop in its own direction.

Town and country planning matters in Northern Ireland are also governed by legislation which mirrors the TCPA 1990. This is largely contained in the Planning (Northern Ireland) Order 1991. An important amending order from 2003 (SI 2003/430 (NI8)) brings certain key aspects of the law into line with the rest of the UK, e.g. the legal presumption in favour of the development plan.

The main provisions of the Planning and Compulsory Purchase Act 2004 do not extend to Scotland[14] or Northern Ireland, but it is worth noting that there are already, as a matter of policy, spatial strategies covering each jurisdiction.

Forward planning: development plans

Development plans guide or influence development in the areas they cover. In this country, development plans lay down policies, aims, objectives and goals rather than prescribe what is going to happen in an area. They have no immediate effect other than as a statement of what the local planning authority considers is desirable (see Box 13.4) but they do have a great and growing importance in the decision whether or not to grant planning permission (see p. 476).

BOX 13.4 **Development plans vs zoning ordinances**

In 'zoning' law, plans are *presumptive*. If an area of land is zoned for an activity, and a developer wishes to develop land in accordance with the plan, then the development is authorized (and vice versa). The main area for legal argument is therefore whether the proposed activity conforms to the plan policies. Zoning schemes were used in the UK prior to the TCPA 1947, and are still used in the US and in many European countries (e.g. The Netherlands). This approach usually gives greater weight to the interests of land owners, and an advantage is said to lie in greater certainty for developers.

In the UK, development plans are *permissive*. Plans are the starting point for deciding whether a proposed development will be authorised, but developers must submit a planning application where all the material factors are considered. One consequence is that designating land in a plan will not generally engage rights under Article 6 of the European Convention on Human Rights (see, e.g., *Bovis Homes Ltd v New Forest District Council* [2002] EWHC 483).[15] There are however

---

14. One area where the Act does extend to Scotland is the extension of planning controls to the Crown.

15. Though it might do if it was a protective designation which de facto prevented development (*Oerlemans v Netherlands* (1993) 15 EHRR 561). The contingent nature of development plans has also been considered in relation to the issue of the 'locality' in nuisance claims, see p. 388.

some instances where a zoning-type approach is taken in the UK; examples are enterprise zones, simplified planning zones and local development orders, the essence of which is that desired commercial development should be fast-tracked in certain areas (see p. 469). But experience suggests that these are of limited value, since developers will usually have to engage the planning authority in negotiations anyway, regardless of whether, in principle, the development can proceed.

The system of development plans has been one area within planning law where there seems to have been a constant state of change. There are two main reasons for this. The first is that while the need for some form of forward planning has been recognised since 1947, adopting plans and keeping them up to date has always been a complex and drawn-out affair (made the more so by the recognition in the late 1960s of the need for greater public involvement in plan-making: see the changes introduced by the Town and Country Planning Act 1971). Various changes were made over the years to address this problem, the main one being the introduction of a two-tier system of structure plans and local plans by the Town and Country Planning Act 1968.

The second reason for upheaval is less technical and more political. Development planning was unpopular with the early Thatcher administrations which were unconvinced by the need for strong forward planning and antipathetic to the power of local authorities. Structure plans in particular were downgraded by comparison with local plans by the Local Government, Planning and Land Act 1980, local plan-making was actively discouraged (see Circular 22/84) and plans of all types were accorded ever-decreasing weight in appeal decisions compared with central government policies. This could happen because the law did not stipulate how much weight decision-makers should place on the plan and on other material considerations.

By the early 1990s, however, there was a reversal of fortunes for development plans. The Planning and Compensation Act 1991 strengthened the status of the development plan in decision-making (see p. 477), and in line with this actually extended the scope of development plans. For example, local plans were required to cover the *whole* of the area of a local planning authority (something which few had done in the past, preferring to concentrate their plan-making activities on specific parts of their district) and development plans for the area of a national park became mandatory for the first time, as did a local minerals plan and a waste local plan (the last being intended to complement the waste disposal plan required by the Environmental Protection Act 1990, s. 50).[16] However, in relation to all these types of plan the procedures were streamlined to reduce the delay between initial deposit and final adoption, though the main elements of public participation and consultation were retained.

With the shift towards a plan-led system of development control, however, came a consequent increase in practical and legal importance of the plans. One factor worth mentioning was the increased threat that decisions refusing planning permission which accorded with the development plan would lead to an award of costs against the planning authority (and even the possibility of elected members being personally surcharged). This increase in importance, perhaps inevitably, led to a marked slowdown in the formal

16. See now the National Waste Strategy required under s. 44A EPA 1990, see pp. 571–3.

adoption of development plans—leading to problems similar to those experienced with the original development plans under the 1947 Act. The procedure for adopting local plans (and, for single tier authorities, unitary development plans or UDPs) in particular came under great pressure as developers, local planning authorities and the public recognized the importance of the adopted plan and therefore subjected the proposals within the plan to great scrutiny. Some public inquiries into development plans have lasted for well over a year. The target of achieving complete development plan coverage by the end of 1996 had still not been reached by 2002.

Development planning and the 2004 Act

This permanent revolution has continued with the Planning and Compulsory Purchase Act 2004. The provisions of the 2004 Act relating to development plans, and in particular the replacement of structure plans with regional spatial strategies, are perhaps its most ambitious.

As explained above, prior to 2004 there were two tiers of plan—structure plans and local plans—collectively referred to as 'the development plan' (in metropolitan areas, and in Wales, unitary development plans combined both functions). There was *no* national plan, the nearest equivalent being central government policy set out in Planning Policy Guidance Notes and government circulars. Nor were there formal regional plans, although groupings of local planning authorities did produce general regional strategies, and there was formal regional planning guidance issued by central government, often based on advice from these regional groupings. This was taken a stage further in planning guidance issued in 2000 (PPG 11), which anticipated a strengthened role for regional planning guidance and long-term regional spatial strategies, in line with government policy of establishing regional governance structures (Regional Assemblies). At around the same time, informal spatial strategies began to be adopted in Scotland, Wales and Northern Ireland, while in London the first formal legal recognition of wider spatial planning was provided in the duty on the Mayor to adopt a Spatial Development Strategy (see below).

The 2004 Act, at least for England and Wales, formalizes and strengthens the role of regional spatial strategies by making them the 'upper tier' of development planning, to replace structure plans. To begin with, however, the RSS will be comprised of existing regional planning guidance[17] (although existing structure plan policies have also been saved for three years, i.e. until September 2007). In place of local plans, the 'lower tier' of the development plan is now not one document but a number of discrete Local Development Documents, made under a Local Development Scheme prepared by the local planning authority, including minerals and waste development plan documents adopted by county councils (or, as the case may be, unitary authorities). Again there is a three-year transitional period during which the existing local plan still applies. The Local Development Documents should provide the framework for delivering the spatial strategy for the area.

17. In England see the Town and Country Planning (Initial Regional Spatial Strategy) (England) Regulations 2004 (SI 2004/2206).

Development Plans (England)						
	Upper tier	**Lower tier**				
	Regional spatial strategy*	Local Development Plan Documents (forming part of 'the development plan')			Documents *not* forming part of 'the development plan'	
		Local Development plan documents (general)	Minerals Development plan documents	Waste Development plan documents	Supplementary planning documents	Statement of community involvement
Plan-Making Body	Regional planning body	Local Planning Authority (District Council or UDA)	County Council or UDA	County Council or UDA	District or County Council or UDA	District Council or UDA

Development Plans (Wales)
Local Development Plan (all Welsh authorities are unitary, combining general local planning, waste and minerals functions). Provision is made for a Welsh Spatial Plan, but this is not as yet formally the upper tier

Development Plans (London)	
Spatial Development Strategy	Local Development Plan Documents (all London boroughs are unitary authorities)

* During the three-year transitional period, existing structure and local plans are also included unless, within this period, they are replaced by the draft RSS or, after this period, the Secretary of State directs that they are to continue. Note that RPGs have already replaced structure plans.

As with other areas of the 2004 Act, its provisions relating to development plans require a good deal of fleshing out by regulations (on procedural matters) and guidance.[18]

(a) Regional spatial strategies

These are provided for in Part I of the 2004 Act. Each region must have a spatial strategy which 'must set out the Secretary of State's policies (however expressed) in relation to the development and use of land within the region' (s. 1(1) and (2)). Two related points arise concerning this seemingly straightforward provision.

The first is the enormous width given to the Secretary of State to determine what matters

18. In England see the Town and Country Planning (Regional Planning) (England) Regulations 2004 (SI 2004/2203) and PPS 11, *Regional Spatial Strategies*, and PPS 12, *Local Development Frameworks*.

may be covered by a RSS (and, it would seem, how he can do so). With structure plans, a range of matters (physical, economic, demographic, transport-related) had to be kept under review while, latterly, there were statutory duties to include policies in respect of the conservation of the natural beauty and amenity of the land, the improvement of the physical environment, and the management of traffic. By contrast, a RPB is subject to a much more general duty to keep under review matters which may be expected to affect development in its region and the planning of that development (s. 3(2)). The Act itself contains nothing specifically requiring environmental matters to be included in the RSS; it is only guidance which requires that, amongst other things, 'priorities for the environment', transport and waste management 'should be taken into account' (PPS11, para. 1.3). However, the RSS is not merely to be a negative framework within which decisions on individual planning applications are made (a criticism of structure plans). Spatial strategies are intended to direct development planning towards the *positive management of development* in an integrated, long-term fashion.[19]

The reason for the width discussed above is the second point that can be made about section 1, which is the obvious centrality of the Secretary of State. RSSs are to be vehicles for giving effect to national policy. They stem from national policy guidance, issued mainly by the Secretary of State responsible for planning matters (currently, in England, the Deputy Prime Minister). There is simply no need to circumscribe in law the general subject matter of RSSs. Instead of confining the discretion of county councils over the scope of structure plans, for reasons explained below Part I envisages that disputes over the content of RSSs are as likely to come between government departments (to be thrashed out as matters of politics rather than law).

(b) Local development documents

Local plans have always been more detailed, consisting of written policies and specific land use allocations by reference to a map, so their relevance to individual development control decisions has always been much greater. Thus, while a structure plan would determine the projected number of new houses needed, the local plan would identify specific areas deemed capable of catering for such development.

The same basic approach is retained under the 2004 Act and its guidance. Local Development Plan Documents are adopted by the local planning authority (the district authority or unitary authority), together with waste and minerals development plan documents produced by the county council or unitary authority. Somewhat confusingly, the Local Development Scheme must specify which documents are to be Local Development Documents, and which documents are to be development plan documents, i.e. which documents will form part of 'the development plan' (s. 15(2)). It must be presumed that any documents which are not formally part of the development plan, for the purposes of the presumption in favour of the plan (PCPA 2004, s. 38(6)) will nevertheless be 'material considerations' (and see further below).

In preparing a local development document, regard must be had to various sources, notably central government policy and guidance, the RSS and the community strategy prepared by the authority under section 4 of the Local Government Act 2000 (PCPA 2004,

---

19. See Tewdwr-Jones [2004] JPL 560 and RCEP, 23rd Report, *Environmental Planning*, ch. 10.

s. 19(2)). All development plan documents must be submitted to the Secretary of State for independent examination and anyone making representations regarding changes has a right to be heard (s. 20); any development plan document must be in conformity with the RSS (the formal expression of the two-tier system). There are powers to modify and call-in local development documents (the latter being a power which, under the previous legislation, was very rarely used). As with RSSs, there is no longer any specific legislative requirement to include certain environmental policies in Local Development Plan Documents. Local planning authorities no longer have the right to override an Inspector's recommendations and propose modifications (s. 23). Notably the same restriction does not apply to the Secretary of State in relation to the draft RSS, further illustrating the centralizing nature of the recent reforms.

Non-statutory plans and guidance

Local planning authorities frequently have other policies and drafts that have not gone through the statutory procedures. In practice, a large range of such 'non-statutory' material, ranging from draft local plans to design briefs and technical specifications, is used by local planning authorities in making decisions. But there are obvious problems in this practice, because it may be seen as subverting the statutory public participation requirements, and thus the democratic legitimacy of the planning process.

In *Westminster City Council v Great Portland Estates plc* [1985] AC 661, a distinction was drawn between different types of non-statutory guidance. The House of Lords required that all matters of *policy* should be included in the statutory plan and that only supplementary matters of detail, or those which relate to the implementation of these policies, should be put in non-statutory guidance. However, as long as this non-statutory material is not illegal (i.e. it must relate to the character of the use of land) it is a material consideration under section 70(2) and must be considered alongside the statutory development plan, although perhaps not always accorded the same weight. The weight attached to it will depend on the circumstances in which it was produced.

PPG 12 (2000) indicated that the use of this 'Supplementary Planning Guidance' would be encouraged by central government, which would place 'substantial weight' on it. Local planning authorities have made extensive use of this type of guidance in the last few years, in particular to set out targets for affordable housing and scales of charges towards transport costs associated with new development.

What is now known as Supplementary Planning Documents are not part of 'the development plan'—and so will not be tested by an independent examination—but will be part of the folder of documents making up the Local Development Documents. Since the PCPA 2004 aims to keep the development plan components of Local Development Documents more up to date then has been the case with adopted plans (or even first draft revisions to plans), it may be that in the future less reliance will need to be placed in practice on Supplementary Planning Documents. Nevertheless it may still be tempting to put important policies into supplementary planning documents to avoid a formal examination in public; to a degree, this is checked by rules which require public participation in their making,[20] and by guidance requiring rigorous procedures of community involvement and which also states that they must not be used to avoid policies and proposals which should be included in a

---

20. Town and Country Planning (Local Development) (England) Regulations 2004 (SI 2004/2204).

development plan document being subjected to proper independent scrutiny.[21] At the moment, the courts have taken a fairly generous approach to this kind of guidance, while recognising that it should not be used as a means to bypass public participation in plan-making (*R (JA Pye (Oxford) Ltd and others) v Oxford CC* [2002] EWCA Civ 1116).

(c) Development plans: common issues and themes

The role of the Secretary of State

As explained above, RSSs are an expression of central government policy. Accordingly, the Secretary of State has an important role in overseeing RSSs. In some ways this is merely a continuation of his powers in relation to structure plans, though there are important differences. After 1991, structure plans did not have to be approved by the Secretary of State, although he retained a power to issue directions and, more significantly, to call a plan in and thus was able to exercise ultimate control over policy. Although the power to call in was sparingly used, the threat was ever-present and the power to direct that a plan be modified was used on a number of occasions to force county councils to increase their housing provision (see Box 13.5).

BOX 13.5 Challenging a development plan

Government policy is to meet projections in demand for housing by a significant expansion in numbers of new houses, especially in the South East of England. But doing so requires identifying how many houses each county is to take, and ensuring that development plans provide for this. In *West Sussex County Council v Secretary of State for the Environment, Transport and the Regions* [1999] PLCR 365 the Secretary of State directed the Council to modify its structure plan to provide for an extra 12,800 dwellings. The Council, whose structure plan already provided for 37,900 dwellings, challenged this decision on the grounds that insufficient regard had been given to regional policy guidance (RPG) for the south east which required a consideration of broad planning objectives, economic needs and the local environment.

However, the Court of Appeal held that the statutory provisions relating to development plans in the TCPA 1990 were drafted in wide terms making it clear that the Secretary of State was pre-eminent on issues regarding plan modifications. If he thought that local proposals were unsatisfactory, he could direct their modification, regardless of any consultation and public appraisal processes that the local authority had engaged in, and regardless of government policy guidance (the RPG). The legislation made no provision to appeal such Ministerial decisions, and so the only grounds of challenge were the usual grounds in judicial review. The direction was not wholly irrational and had lawfully been made. This case illustrates where power lies in the planning system. But it also illustrates some of the tensions that were evident between central government and county councils over the allocation of land for house building, and a major driver behind the reforms in Part I of the 2004 Act appears to have been an attempt to end the opposition of county councils to major house building proposals.

---

21. PPS 12, *Local Development Frameworks*, paras 2.41 and 2.44.

In contrast, the 2004 Act once more *requires* the active involvement of the Secretary of State who, as noted above, must be sent draft revisions to the RSS. In all cases, it is the Secretary of State who publishes the final RSS, having considered any Inspector's report and any further representations made. The intention, however, is that elected regional assemblies will take over reviewing, revising and issuing RSSs.[22]

Sustainability

Underpinning the shift towards spatial planning is a duty, in section 39 of the 2004 Act, requiring all plan-making bodies to exercise their functions 'with the objective of contributing to the achievement of sustainable development'. The extent to which this legal duty has any real content or value is debatable (see the similarly worded provision which applies to the Environment Agency in exercising its functions, p. 126). But its drafting indicates a clear desire to insulate individual planning applications from scrutiny through a sustainable development lens (the provision does not apply to Part 4 of the Act dealing with development control). Whether central policy can really be used to *promote* environmentally sustainable developments remains something of a moot point, since there always remains local discretion about whether to permit such development (see, e.g., the case of wind farms, p. 481), and policy guidance on environmentally desirable development is rarely as pro-development as it is with activities deemed to be economically crucial, such as 3G mobile phone masts (see PPG8, *Telecommunications*).

Draft revisions to the RSS (s. 5(4)) and the preparation of local development documents (s. 19(5)) must both be subject to a *sustainability appraisal*. It appears that this appraisal will include the requirements of the regulations implementing the EC Strategic Environmental Assessment Directive (The Assessment of Plans and Programmes Regulations 2004 (SI 2004/1633)). This is subject to guidance, rather than further implementing regulations.[23] It is worth noting concerns that existing RPG has not been adequately appraised, and indeed that the very process of sustainability appraisal has been criticized for marginalizing environmental considerations.[24] On the other hand, the feasibility of meaningfully appraising development plan policies against the checklist mentioned in the SEA Directive has been questioned, the implication being that valuable resources may be channelled to this obligation at the expense of keeping plans up to date and using resources effectively.[25]

Accountability

During the passage of the 2004 Act a major concern with RSSs was the extent to which regional planning bodies might lack a democratic mandate, since there are as yet no elected regional assemblies in England (the Regional Assemblies (Preparation) Act 2003 paves the way for these). This has been addressed, up to a point, by a requirement that at least 60 per cent of the membership of regional planning bodies must be drawn from elected representative planning authorities (district councils, county councils, metropolitan district councils, National Park authorities, or the Broads Authority). Also, in keeping the RSS under

---

22. ODPM, *Draft Regional Assemblies Bill: Policy Statement* (July 2004) para. 50.
23. *Sustainability Appraisal of Regional Spatial Strategies and Local Development Frameworks*, consultation paper, OPDM, Sept. 2004.
24. RCEP 23rd Report, *Environmental Planning* (2002) paras 7.44–7.47.
25. S. Hockman [2003] JPL Supp. 41.

review and monitoring its implementation, the regional planning body must 'seek the advice of' (i.e. consult) any authority exercising 'county-level' planning functions (s. 4). The aim of this is to ensure a continuing involvement for county councils and unitary authorities, although the powers of county councils in development planning are clearly much reduced compared to their role in relation to structure plans (see also Box 13.4). Local development documents remain the responsibility of elected local planning authorities.

Consultation and participation

It is worth noting that, from the late 1990s, some regional planning guidance was made subject to formal scrutiny through an examination in public (a concept explained below). Whenever the RSS is revised, the regional planning body must publish a 'statement of community involvement' (s. 6). This rather open-ended provision is intended to give RPBs some flexibility in consulting on revisions to the RSS, although it is a legal requirement that the statement is complied with and the draft Regulations require that the statement indicates who and how it has consulted, a summary of the main issues raised in the consultation and how these have been addressed in the draft RSS. There are also requirements to consult with a wide range of interested bodies (including the various regulatory agencies with environ-mental responsibilities). Beyond this, much of the detail concerning public involvement—e.g. the level of public involvement in the sustainability appraisal—is yet to be decided (though relevant here will be the Environmental Assessment of Plans and Programmes Regulations 2004).

Once the draft RSS is submitted to the Secretary of State there is further consultation (the minimum requirements being in the draft Regulations). An examination in public into the draft RSS—a limited form of public inquiry at which there is no right to present a case unless invited to do so—*may* be arranged, which might be thought to mark a departure from the previous position under which, unless the Secretary of State directed otherwise, an examination in public had to be held (although in practice this was dispensed with in over half the cases). Curiously, however, draft guidance suggests that only in the exceptional circumstances of a minor revision will an examination in public be unnecessary, which in effect seems to retain something resembling current practice.

For Local Development Documents, the LDS must state that the local planning authority's statement of community involvement is part of the LDD, alongside other components prescribed in regulations. However, the statement of community involve-ment is not a development plan document, i.e. it does not form part of 'the development plan' for the purposes of TCPA 1990 s. 70(2) and PCPA 2004, s. 38(6), but in some respects it is treated as such, notably in that it must be scrutinised by the Secretary of State.

Challenges to development plans

The law here remains basically unchanged following the 2004 Act. A challenge to a revised RSS, or to the adoption of a local development document, can be made by any 'person aggrieved' within six weeks of the decision under section 287 (see PCPA 2004, s. 113). In the interests of speed the aim is to limit legal challenges to this six week 'window', but it is possible for a judicial review application to be made before this period if there has been some error of law, such as a breach of natural justice in the making of representations.[26]

Two grounds of appeal are provided: that the plan is outside the plan-makers' powers, or that there has been some procedural error. In the latter case, any challenge must show that there has been substantial prejudice (which will not be the case where there has been a procedural error but the adopted plan policies would, notwithstanding the error, not have been any different). In practice, the courts have held that these statutory grounds are to be equated with normal grounds for judicial review (see *Warren v Uttlesford DC* [1997] JPL 1130) and there is little difference in judicial review between a person aggrieved and someone with sufficient standing. The leading case remains *Westminster City Council v Great Portland Estates plc* [1985] AC 661. Amongst other things, this emphasizes the need to include *all* land use policies in plans, not least in the interests of public participation.[27] The courts have imposed a stricter duty on local planning authorities to give reasons when their development plan is being adopted than where planning permission is being refused (*Stirk v Bridgnorth DC* [1997] JPL 51). As local planning authorities no longer have the right to override an Inspector's recommendations and propose modifications, this may lead to less challenges being brought.

Developers or prospective developers bring most challenges to structure and local plans, while costs rules force amenity groups to prefer Ministerial lobbying. The same research also reveals the relative lack of challenges that are brought, bearing in mind the legal significance of the development plan after 1991. This may be explained by the fact that plans often simply legitimize national planning policies (which might suggest that we are unlikely to see a significant rise in the number of challenges being brought to the new-style development plans).[28]

Development plans—environmental critique

As far as incorporating environmental considerations is concerned, the record has been somewhat patchy. Despite government guidance,[29] many organizations raised concerns about development plan coverage and content, especially about the lack of mention of nature conservation issues.[30] More detailed research also indicates the priority attached to economic interests. Local authorities may view the environment either as a commodity or service, or in aesthetic terms, with ecological references being largely rhetorical. Integration of the environment with other key sectors like transport may be lacking. Business interests, and elected councillors anxious to create jobs, exercise most power in determining development plan policies. This leads to an inevitable conclusion in those situations where, as is sometimes the case, the development plan indicates that trade-offs between environmental

---

26. See A. Robinson and J. Clement [2003] JPL 1384.

27. A case about supplementary planning guidance. On supplementary planning documents see p. 458 above.

28. M. Purdue [1998] JPL 837.

29. *Policy Appraisal and the Environment*, DoE, 1991; *Environmental Appraisal of Development Plans: A Good Practice Guide*, DoE, 1993.

30. See e.g. CPRE, *Environmental Policy Omissions in Development Plans* (1994).

and non-environmental assets will be handled *through the planning system itself* rather than through any other system of assessing public benefits.[31]

That said, recent years have seen considerable pressure for development plans to serve as vehicles for sustainable development. This was a major theme of PPG 12 on *Development Plans* (2000), which included guidance on sustainability appraisals of development plans, and on the integration of transport and land use policies. However, in its 2002 report on *Environmental Planning*, the RCEP commented that:

Development plans may express admirable sentiments about issues such as energy conservation, but not in a form and context that are likely to change anything in the real world.

It has been held that policies in a development plan which restricted development leading to unacceptable levels of pollution, could be used to justify refusing planning permission to an applicant with previous convictions for pollution offences (*Blake & Sons v Secretary of State for the Environment and Colchester BC* [1998] Env LR 309). This approach neatly side-steps the normal rule that only issues to do with the proposed land use, not the proposed user, are material.

Development control—the meaning of 'development'

'Planning permission is required for the carrying out of any development of land' (s. 57(1), TCPA 1990)

It is in relation to the system of development control that the town and country planning system has its greatest impact on environmental law. Planning permission is required for the carrying out of any development of land. The general approach is to define development very widely so that virtually everything is included initially,[32] and then to relax the need to apply for planning permission, either by:

- *excluding activities from being 'development'*; These include many activities with considerable environmental impacts, such as the use of land for agriculture (see p. 466); or

- by *deeming planning permission to be granted* under some kind of development order or similar provision (see p. 468).

This has the effect of shifting the focus in most practical situations from what is included to what is excluded.

'Development . . . means the carrying out of building, engineering, mining or other operations in, on, over or under land, or the making of any material change in the use of any buildings or other land' (TCPA 1990, s. 55(1))

---

31. S. Davoudi, A. Hull, and P. Healey (1996) 67 Town Planning Review 421.
32. For the avoidance of doubt, some things are specifically stated to constitute development, see s. 55(3)–(5).

This definition of development has effectively remained unchanged since 1947, so past decisions of the courts, which are the ultimate interpreters of the meaning of the Act, are relevant. Decisions of the Secretary of State on appeal are also of importance in understanding the definition. Although these are not binding as legal authority, in practice they can have a prescriptive effect.

The courts have decided that the existence of development is a question of 'fact and degree' in each particular case. It is for the local planning authority (or the Secretary of State on appeal) to apply the relevant law to the facts of each case to decide whether there has been development. The courts limit themselves to supervising and reviewing these decisions under normal judicial review grounds.

There are two limbs to 'development'—operational development and development by a material change of use.

(a) Operational development

This involves building, mining or engineering operations. 'Other operations' is a little discussed (or relied on) catch-all category apparently designed to ensure that matters such as waste disposal and drilling are covered.

- *Building operations.* These are defined very widely in section 336. 'Building' includes any structure or erection, and any part of a building as so defined, but does not include plant or machinery comprised in a building. 'Building operations' include rebuilding operations, structural alterations of or additions to buildings, demolition of buildings, and other operations normally undertaken by a person carrying on business as a builder.

  Any significant works are included, such as rebuilding works, works of alteration, the building of an extension, and the erection of such things as shop canopies, walls, advertising hoardings and large sculptures. In one celebrated example, the erection of a model shark emerging from the roof of a house was held to amount to a building operation (though it ultimately received planning permission: [1993] JPL 194). It is normally considered that very minor alterations, such as the installation of ordinary TV aerials, are not significant enough to amount to development.

- *Engineering operations.* The Act gives little guidance on the meaning of this term. The test used by the courts is whether they are 'operations of the kind usually undertaken by engineers, that is, operations calling for the skills of an engineer' (*Fayrewood Fish Farms v Secretary of State for the Environment* [1984] JPL 267). There are many exceptions for public works in section 55 and the General Permitted Development Order.

- *Mining operations.* These include all forms of extractive operation, such as mining, quarrying and the removal of materials from mineral deposits and waste tips (s. 55(4)). There are additional powers over minerals development, exercised by county planning authorities.

(b) Development by material change of use of land or buildings

The power to control changes in the use of land is virtually exclusive to British town and country planning, and makes it peculiarly able to exercise detailed control over land use. In the debates on the 1947 Act, Lord Reid, then an MP but later a Law Lord, is reported to have said of material change of use, 'Nobody knows what that means.' And very little guidance is given in the Act on the meaning of this rather vague phrase. But over the years the judges have filled in any gaps by the creation of a number of important explanatory concepts.[33] Nevertheless, this remains a somewhat flexible phrase, and flexibility is aided by decisions whether development has taken place in any particular case being a matter for the local planning authority, applying the law to the facts. What is important is that the change must be material in a planning sense, that is it must have:

- a physical impact on the land;
- a substantial impact; and
- an impact that is relevant to town and country planning.

An example of a material change of use relating to environmental pollution would be changing the use of a quarry to a landfill. It is worth noting here that, in 1994, the RCEP recommended that the generation of 'appreciably higher levels of traffic' should always amount to a material land use change (*Transport and the Environment*, Cm 2674, para. 9.66), but this has never been adopted as a legal requirement (although planning policy on transport does require transport assessments alongside planning applications with significant transport implications, see PPG 13).

The unit of land to be considered when ascertaining whether there has been a change of use is called the *planning unit*. This is normally the unit of occupation prior to the change and it is unusual to aggregate together more than one unit of occupation, or to subdivide one, unless 'two or more physically distinct areas are occupied for substantially different and unrelated purposes' (*Burdle v Secretary of State for the Environment* [1972] 1 WLR 1207). Thus a factory is usually treated as one unit, allowing some internal shifting of activities between parts of the site.

The courts have also laid down further tests. Thus, an ancillary use will not normally be of any planning concern (see Box 13.6). But if it becomes a dominant use there has been a material change, such as where 44 dogs were kept in a dwellinghouse. In effect, the house had two main uses: residential and dog-breeding (*Wallington v Secretary of State for Wales* (1990) 62 P&CR 150). And an *intensification* of a use can also be a material change of use: the question the courts often ask is whether the intensified use is so different in nature that it could be given a different name (see *Royal Borough of Kensington and Chelsea v SSE* [1981] JPL 50). This might be the case where someone goes from repairing her own car in her garage to mending several cars on a commercial basis.

---

33. Which might be said to run contrary to the notion that planning is based on a comprehensive legislative code; see p. 445.

> ### BOX 13.6 Changes of use and environmental protection
>
> In *Northavon DC v SSE* (1980) 40 P & CR 332, a farmer wished to improve the drainage of his land, and proposed stripping the topsoil off, putting down a layer of filling including builder's rubble, and then replacing the topsoil. The Court of Appeal held that any deposit of waste that there might be was incidental to the real purpose of the farmer's action, which was to raise the level of his land to improve its drainage. Hence the deposit of waste was not a material change of use. The Court was not swayed by the argument that this would lead to a flytipper's charter.
>
> This line of reasoning has important implications for various multifunctional activities having environmental impact, e.g. a landfill site where the waste gas is tapped off to generate heat. If the purpose of the site is to dispose of waste, then any generation of gas/heat may just be incidental and not a separate use of the land. But the two uses may be impossible to prioritize in this way; an example that the courts have given (in *R (Lowther) v Durham County Council* [2002] Env LR 13, a case decided during the foot and mouth crisis) is the burning of slaughtered animals in power stations. Quite where the dividing line is between these two kinds of cases, however, remains a little cloudy. In the *Lowther*[34] case the Court of Appeal upheld a decision that using secondary liquid fuels as a support fuel at a lime works which had previously only burnt petcoke was not a material change of use: the use remained primarily a lime works, and the argument that any waste disposal or recovery operations would amount to a separate land use in planning terms was rejected. One factor (stressed much more by Pill LJ than Phillips MR) was the existence of extensive regulatory controls over disposal of hazardous waste, and the public concern over this issue did not justify a finding that there was a separate planning use. This suggests that the degree of regulatory control over a use of land may be relevant in deciding whether there has been a material change of use, i.e. controls on the *impacts* of the use may be relevant.

Exemption from the need to apply for planning permission

(a) Activities which do not constitute development

The following operations and uses of land do not constitute development (ss. 55(2)(a)–(g)):

- maintenance, improvement or alterations to a building affecting only its interior, or not materially affecting the external appearance;
- certain works carried out by highway authorities to maintain or improve roads;
- works by local authorities or statutory undertakers for the inspection, repair or renewal of sewers, mains, etc., including breaking open streets;
- the use of any buildings or other land within the curtilage of a dwellinghouse for any purpose incidental to the enjoyment of the dwellinghouse as such;
- a change of use within the same class of the Use Classes Order (see below);
- the use of land for the purposes of agriculture or forestry (including afforestation) and the use for any of those purposes of any building occupied together with land so used (see p. 856);

---

34. The same process was challenged in *R v Environment Agency ex p Gibson* [1999] Env LR 73.

• the demolition of any description of building specified in a direction given by the Secretary of State to local planning authorities generally or to a particular local authority.

(b) The Use Classes Order

The Use Classes Order is used as a way of avoiding the need for planning permission for what are considered to be changes between uses that have a reasonably similar land use impact. For example, the change of use from a post office to a funeral directors would not be development, as both are found in the same Use Class. The current Town and Country Planning (Use Classes) Order 1987 (SI 1987/764) is significantly more liberal than previous Orders, a legacy of the deregulatory strategy followed in the 1980s. More recent widening of the general industrial class (B2) to include what were formerly grouped together as special industrial uses (under SI 1995/297) were justified on the basis that control could be exercised effectively by pollution control agencies. But given the different impacts on amenity that some authorized changes may give rise to—e.g. change from an engineering use to a blood-boiling factory—this might be questioned.

Certain unusual uses (so-called '*sui generis*' uses) are not found in any Class, and neither are concurrent uses where the components are in different Classes. Non-listed uses include petrol stations, scrapyards and mineral storeyards, so a change to these uses always requires planning permission. Some uses of land, such as agricultural uses, are simply not mentioned in the Order, because the use of land for agriculture is not development.

(c) Existing uses

Normally there is a right to carry on the existing use of a site, unless it is in breach of planning control. This is roughly equivalent to a property right attaching to the land and has a distinct value. Of course, when the occupier of land voluntarily changes the use, the existing use right switches from the old to the new use.

Existing use rights may be abandoned by a lengthy period of disuse (*Hartley v Minister of Housing and Local Government* [1970] 1 QB 413). It is also possible to lose their benefit by carrying out works or changes which effect a *radical change* to the site (*Jennings Motors Ltd v Secretary of State for the Environment* [1982] QB 541). This applies whether planning permission is obtained or not. If there is a planning permission, any limitations in it will be operative; if there is no permission, then *any* use of the site will be in breach of planning control. Otherwise, an existing use right can only be removed by a discontinuance order (s. 102), or an order revoking planning permission (ss. 97–100). In both cases compensation is payable.[35]

It is not possible to abandon a planning permission, since it is a public right attaching to the land not the occupier. This is illustrated by *Pioneer Aggregates (UK) Ltd v Secretary of State for the Environment* [1984] 3 WLR 32, where a perpetual permission for quarrying was granted in 1950. Quarrying ceased in 1966 and, when it was recommenced in 1980, the local

---

35. For an example where compensation was not payable, because of the interrelationship between planning and waste management controls, see *R v Secretary of State for the Environment and Havering BC ex parte P F Ahern (London) Ltd* [1998] Env LR 189.

planning authority argued that the use had been abandoned. The House of Lords decided that the planning permission still applied to permit quarrying and any removal of that right would entail payment of compensation.

This position distinguishes planning control from most other areas of environmental control. As a matter of practice, the rules on compensation mean that there is little scope to vary a planning permission once it has been granted, even though variation and revocation are possible in theory (s. 97). Compensation must be paid even where the circumstances have changed radically in a way that was not foreseen at the time the permission was granted. This emphasizes that a grant of planning permission is an irrevocable event, effectively creating rights for the landowner in a way that a consent from a pollution control agency does not. (For an illustration of an environmentally harmful planning permission having to be purchased by English Nature to further nature conservation interests, see Box 21.4.)

In relation to minerals planning permissions, however, the position is rather different, and awareness of the environmental harm that can be caused by permissions granted many decades previously means that old permissions can now have environmental protection conditions attached to them.[36]

'Development' activities for which planning permission is granted by statute

Certain activities are automatically granted planning permission under statute. Some use has always been made of a *general* development order. However, the 1980s saw the use of new ways of deeming planning permission to be granted in *specific* areas, a departure from the previously uniform approach and a key deregulatory mechanism designed to effect the regeneration of the inner cities. The PCPA 2004 provides further ways in which the need to apply for planning permission in the normal way is bypassed.

(a) Development permitted under the General Permitted Development Order

The Town and Country Planning (General Permitted Development) Order 1995 (SI 1995/418) (the GPDO) grants automatic planning permission for 33 classes of development, listed and defined in schedule 1. These are called 'permitted development rights'. The Town and Country Planning (General Development Procedure) Order 1995 (SI 1995/419) (the GDPO) sets out various procedural requirements connected with both permitted development and normal planning applications. Three general types of activity are exempted:

- minor developments;
- developments carried out by a whole range of public services, such as drainage authorities and statutory undertakers; and
- favoured activities, especially agriculture and forestry.

---

36. See Part III of the Act, as amended by the 1991 Act, and generally D. Hughes et al., *Environmental Law* (4th edn, London: Butterworths, 2002), ch. 13.

The GPDO often includes thresholds above which development consent will still be needed. In the case of certain permitted agricultural and forestry buildings, however, local planning authorities have certain powers over their siting and design, and prior notification now also extends to mobile phone masts. And in some cases, permitted development rights are withdrawn for a number of developments including those which require environmental assessment (see the Town and Country Planning (Environmental Assessment) (England and Wales) Regulations 1999 (SI 1999/293); p. 518) or which are likely to have a significant impact upon certain areas of nature conservation value. Certain automatic rights are more restricted in national parks, areas of outstanding national beauty and conservation areas.

Under Article 4 of the GPDO, a local planning authority may restrict automatic rights by serving a direction withdrawing the automatic planning permission, in which case permission must be sought in the ordinary way. The direction may be general to a type of development or specific to a site. Such directions normally require the approval of the Secretary of State, must be made before the development is started and involves the payment of compensation to owners and occupiers, because effectively they take away the right to develop.

(b) Development permitted under a Special Development Order

A more specific version of permitted development is provided under section 59. This process has been used for granting blanket permissions in new towns, urban development areas (a deregulatory product of the Local Government, Planning and Land Act 1980, now in the process of being phased out) and enterprise zones. The Thermal Oxide Reprocessing Plant (THORP) at Sellafield was also permitted in this way by the Town and Country Planning (Windscale and Calder Works) Special Development Order 1978 (SI 1978/523). In this case the Order followed a public inquiry and a Parliamentary debate, but neither is strictly required.

(c) Development in an enterprise zone

Enterprise zones were also introduced by the Local Government, Planning and Land Act 1980 to encourage business activity. The order establishing an enterprise zone, made by the Secretary of State after some limited publicity, grants automatic planning permission for categories of development specified in the enterprise zone scheme (1990 Act, s. 88). However, the local authority draws up the scheme to cover those matters it wishes to permit. Thus, while enterprise zones are formally designated by the Secretary of State, local authorities decide what is to be permitted. They also remain the local planning authority for other development not covered by the scheme.

An enterprise zone normally lasts for 10 years and involves fiscal and administrative advantages for those in it, as well as the planning exemptions. Few new zones are now expected to be made, but development commenced before the expiry of the scheme retains the benefit of the automatic permission.

(d) Development in a simplified planning zone

These were introduced in the Housing and Planning Act 1986. As with an enterprise zone scheme, a simplified planning zone scheme grants automatic planning permission for the matters specified in it, but there are no non-planning effects (1990 Act, s. 82). Despite the streamlining of the designation in 1992 (SI 1992/2414) only a handful of SPZs have been made (10 in England).

The PCPA 2004 (s. 45) limits the discretion enjoyed by local planning authorities whether to make a SPZ and makes them more plan-led. Hence the provisions on SPZs only bite if the need for such a zone is identified in the regional spatial strategy, and must be in conformity with the RSS. Local planning authorities only have a duty to consider whether to impose a SPZ, which they must do if they think this would be desirable, but the Secretary of State may now of his own volition direct that a SPZ is made (so long as the RSS identifies the need for one). A SPZ lasts for up to 10 years (which is more flexible than previously, when they had to be in place for a full ten year period).

Government clearly envisages a small number of SPZs being used to facilitate the development of high-tech business clusters (such as the biotechnology developments around Cambridge), though specific proposals for 'business planning zones' were withdrawn from the Bill preceding the 2004 Act and the provisions on SPZs amended. The value of SPZs, even in their revised form, remains unclear. It is not clear that planning acts as a drag on the economy (see p. 447), requiring the introduction of fast-track measures like SPZs, and in any case the type of development that is anticipated for SPZs will often require environmental impact assessment (the need for which removes it from automatic permission under the SPZ). It is notable that business responses to the government Green Paper preceding the 2004 Act were 2:1 against the proposal for business planning zones as then proposed.

National parks, areas of outstanding natural beauty, conservation areas, sites of special scientific interest, and designated green belt cannot be the subject of a scheme (s. 87). County matters are also excluded, as are matters covered by the need for an environmental impact assessment.

(e) Developments authorized by a government department

If authorization from a government department is needed for a development to be carried out by bodies like local authorities and statutory undertakers, then that authorization also acts as a deemed planning permission (s. 90). This prevents a duplication of effort, but does result in the decision being taken centrally rather than locally. For example, applications for the construction of projects such as major onshore wind farms would be dealt with like this, since permission is also required from the Department of Trade and Industry under the Electricity Act 1989 and operators are classed as statutory undertakers.

(f) Local Development Orders

Section 40 of the PCPA 2004 inserts new provisions into the main Act (as ss. 61A–C) which give local planning authorities the power, by a local development order, to grant planning permission either for a particular development or class of development specified in the order, and to do so for any or all of its area (even a specific site). The main restriction on the use of this enormously wide-ranging power is that orders must implement policies in the local development documents. There is some uncertainty, and concern, about how LDOs might work. One example of concern during the passage of the legislation was that, if the development plan promoted renewable forms of energy, then a LDO might be used to grant blanket planning permission for wind turbines. The major constraint on something like this is that the Secretary of State has a supervisory role in the making of LDOs, and can rein in what he considers any excessive use of them. LDOs are essentially the converse of Article 4 directions (under the GPDO) and can be thought of as a form of local permitted development rights but sharing similarities with the reformed simplified planning zones.

It must be assumed that, in line with the approach taken in the GPDO and with simplified planning zones, development requiring environmental impact assessment will be excluded from the scope of local development orders (though as yet there are no regulations to this effect).

Special cases

Although not cases of 'deemed permission', streamlined procedures apply in the following cases:

• Where local authorities grant themselves planning permission (s. 316 and the Town and Country Planning General Regulations 1992 (SI 1992/1492)). The intention to acquire planning permission must be publicized, and representations taken into account. But any permission the authority resolves to grant itself is deemed to have been granted by the Secretary of State, so there is no right of appeal; it can be challenged only by judicial review. The possible conflicts of interest have led the courts to interpret the procedural requirements strictly (*Steeples v Derbyshire CC* [1985] 1 WLR 256).

• Where use is made of private or hybrid Acts of Parliament. These avoid any of the planning procedures and effectively give the decision to a small Parliamentary joint committee, with limited public scrutiny. An example with a significant environmental effect is the Channel Tunnel Act 1987. Nowadays, the Transport and Works Act 1992 tends to be used, principally for railways and tram projects. There will be a public inquiry and the Secretary of State can (and in practice will) consider granting deemed planning permission at the same time as any Works Order is determined.

• Although for land owned by the Crown and Government Departments (but not nationalized industries) immunity from the need to apply for planning permission has been removed under the PCPA 2004, fast-track provisions allow a Crown body, where development is required as a matter of urgent national importance, to apply directly to the Secretary of State for planning permission (who will treat it as if it has been 'called-in').

Is planning permission required?

There is a fairly simple mechanism for ascertaining whether planning permission is required. Section 192 provides that anyone may apply to the district planning authority for a certificate of lawfulness of proposed use or development, specifying the proposed use or operation. A certificate must be granted if the authority is satisfied that the use or operation—which must be specific rather than hypothetical—would be lawful if subsisting or carried out at the time of the application. This is then conclusive of the legality of the development, as long as circumstances do not change before the development takes place. In other words, a certificate is the equivalent of a planning permission for what it covers. The exact procedures for an application are contained in the GDPO.

Applying for planning permission

Anyone can apply for planning permission. It is not necessary to be the owner or occupier of the property, or even a prospective occupier. An application may even be used as a form of publicity stunt. For example, Friends of the Earth once submitted an application for an oversize replica of the Leaning Tower of Pisa to draw attention to the inadequacy of the UK Atomic Energy Authority's application for a nuclear reprocessing plant at Dounreay.

There are several types of permission the applicant may seek, including full permission or retrospective permission (s. 63(2)), and an application for the renewal of planning permission. In addition, a developer may apply for 'outline permission' only (see s. 92 and GDPO, Art. 3). This allows developers to 'test the water' with the local planning authority to see whether a general type of development would be acceptable. 'Reserved matters' such as design and landscaping need not be submitted at this stage, but must generally be approved within three years (GDPO, Art. 4). Outline permission may also be sought where the nature of the development means that it is difficult to know what it will eventually contain, e.g. retail parks (this has posed problems for developers where environmental impact assessment is needed; see p. 518). Applicants can also ask for a condition of a planning permission to be discharged without putting the rest of the permission at risk (s. 73). This is an important means of removing outdated restrictions and providing a measure of continuing control over development. Attempts to circumvent section 73 through private negotiation or other means will be given hard scrutiny by the courts, since this jeopardises the public's rights in the decision-making process (*Henry Boot Homes Ltd v Bassetlaw District Council* [2002] EWCA Civ 983).

(a) Steps for the applicant to take

The applicant must apply on a standard form provided by the local planning authority. It must also notify owners and tenants of the land and submit a certificate to the authority stating that it has done so. This enables these people to be aware of the application and to make representations that the authority must take into account. It is an offence knowingly to issue a false certificate.

In *Main v Swansea City Council* (1984) 49 P & CR 26, the Court of Appeal decided that failure to carry out such procedures does not necessarily render a subsequent grant of planning permission void: it all depends on whether anyone with standing has been prejudiced as a result (and, of course, whether they bring any challenge without delay).

Fees are payable for all applications for planning permission and deemed applications in connection with an appeal against an enforcement notice. There are fixed charges for different types of applications. At present the fees do not cover the full administrative cost to the local planning authority of processing applications but section 53 of the PCPA 2004 amends section 303 TCPA and gives greater scope for charges or fees including allowing LPAs to set their own (not-for-profit) fees.

(b) Steps for the local planning authority to take

On receipt of an application, the local planning authority will consult with a wide range of public bodies as required for specified situations by the GDPO 1995, Art. 10. These include highways authorities, other local authorities, parish and community councils, the Environment Agency, DEFRA, and the relevant Nature Conservancy Council. There is a code of conduct governing this consultation procedure and those consulted have procedural rights in the event of an appeal. Any representations that are made are material considerations which must be taken into account by the local planning authority before it decides the application. However, it must not slavishly follow the advice of another public body, otherwise the decision will be challengeable for fettering of discretion. The obverse of this is that even where a body like the Environment Agency has a total policy embargo on assenting to certain types of development which may lead to environmental harm, then granting a planning permission against this advice will not be unlawful (see e.g. *Ynys Mon BC v Secretary of State for Wales* [1993] JPL 225).[37]

The local planning authority must also publicize *all* applications (GDPO, Arts. 6 to 8) as follows:

	Local advert	Site notice	Notify neighbours
Major developments, e.g. developments on sites of more than 1 hectare, the building of 10 or more houses, developments involving 1,000 square metres or more of floor space, and mineral and waste applications	✔	Either/or	
Applications requiring EIA, or which do not accord with the provisions of the development plan, or which affect a public right of way	✔	✔	
All other cases		Either/or	

In addition, the Town and Country Planning (Development Plans and Consultation) (Departure) Directions 1999 require that certain applications which do not accord with the

---

37. Discussed in W. Howarth, 'Town and Country Planning and Water Quality Planning' in C. Miller (ed.), *Planning and Environmental Protection* (Oxford: Hart Publishing, 2001).

provisions of the development plan should be referred to the Secretary of State so that a decision can be made whether to call them in.

A failure to comply with these procedures may invalidate a decision, but will not necessarily do so because of the discretionary nature of judicial review. For example, in one case a local planning authority had, in error, failed to notify a neighbour of a planning application but work had begun over two years later. Although the neighbour then promptly sought judicial review, the permission was not quashed despite the seriousness of the procedural error, because of the hardship to the developer (*R (Gavin) v Haringey London Borough Council* [2003] EWHC 2591).

Determining the planning application

The Secretary of State

The Secretary of State has an unfettered power to call in any planning application for determination (s. 77) and, even as a matter of human rights law, does not need to give reasons for any decision not to call in an application (*R (Adlard) v Secretary of State for Transport, Local Government and the Regions* [2002] EWCA Civ 735).[38] This immediately transfers jurisdiction from the local planning authority to the Secretary of State. This power is used sparingly, usually only for matters of national or regional importance or of local controversy, such as significant developments in the Green Belt.[39] There is a right to a public inquiry unless waived by the parties and the Secretary of State and one is normally held. The procedures are virtually the same as for appeals, suitably amended to provide for this being a first determination. There is no formal power to request the Secretary of State to call in an application: objectors should write to the Secretary of State putting their case for this to happen. The Secretary of State also has related powers to make directions to local planning authorities, for example to consult him before deciding an application (GDPO, Art. 10(3)).

A further exception to the local planning authority being the decision-maker is in relation to major infrastructure projects in England.[40] The context behind these specific proposals was concern at the length of time taken to conduct certain high profile inquiries. Government originally proposed that Parliament make the decision in principle, leaving operational matters to a subsequent inquiry, but this was dropped (see p. 446). Section 44 of the PCPA 2004 makes comparatively modest reforms, inserting sections 76A and 76B into the TCPA. These give the Secretary of State a power to call in applications which are of national or regional importance. The difference between these new provisions and the existing call in powers under section 77 is that, in the interests of speed, the Secretary of State may appoint more than one Inspector to hear different aspects of the inquiry. The presumption in favour of the development plan does not apply to such cases.

---

38. This decision has been criticized for being out of step with the more purposive approach to public participation and citizen rights in cases like *Burkett* (see p. 343), which was decided one week after *Adlard* (see [2002] JPL 1379).

39. See ODAM, *The Planning System: General Principles* (2005) para. 26.

40. Originally, Government proposed that Parliament should be given the power to decide in principle whether such developments should go ahead, a proposal that met with fierce criticism but also serious practical problems in terms of Parliamentary procedure.

Regional assemblies

Under the draft Regional Assemblies Bill, elected regional assemblies will be empowered to direct local planning authorities to refuse strategic planning applications which the Assembly considers to contravene the regional spatial strategy. At the time of writing the prospect of elected assemblies is very slim.

The local planning authority

In the usual case, however, a local planning authority has eight weeks in which to decide the application (in accordance with the substantive rules outlined below), after which time the applicant can appeal as if the application were refused (GDPO, Art. 20).[41] It is worth noting that the Best Value reform target—under the Local Government Act 1999—is that authorities should delegate 90 per cent of decisions to officers.

Whether the application is first determined by the LPA or the Secretary of State, the decision-maker may grant planning permission unconditionally, grant permission subject to conditions, or refuse permission. The decision must be in writing and must include reasons for the decision and the imposition of any conditions. These are normally brief and it seems that a failure to provide reasons does not make the decision void. Public registers of all applications and decisions must be maintained (s. 69, and GDPO, Art. 25). These, and the enforcement registers (see p. 495), are an invaluable guide to the planning history of a site, but increasing pressure to accommodate meaningful public participation means that the register now contains much more information on the application itself, including contributions from developers (but see p. 490).

Summary of rights of third parties

Third parties or objectors have limited specific rights under the legislation, although statutory publicity is required for all applications and the Local Government (Access to Information) Act 1985 ensures the right to attend council meetings (see p. 322). Any representations made to the local planning authority must be considered as a material consideration. Furthermore, the local planning authority is now obliged to give a summary of reasons, and relevant plan policies, for *granting* planning permission: this is a human rights requirement, but has been formalized in the Town and Country Planning (General Development Procedure) (England) (Amendment) Order 2003 (amending Art. 22 of the GDPO). (Previously, all that was required was that reasons were given where permission was *refused*, because applicants would need to know this information to judge whether to appeal. Formally developers are still treated more favourably because clear and precise full reasons must be given when permission is refused or—as is invariably the case—conditions are imposed.) There is no right for third parties to address meetings of the local planning authority—though in practice most do allow very brief statements to be made—and no right to insist on a public hearing or inquiry (see p. 491).

Despite a pre-election commitment to give third parties a right to appeal against the grant

41. Even after this period, the LPA may reach a substantive decision, the intention being to prevent appeals going to the Secretary of State if this can be avoided; see PCPA 2004, s. 50, adding TCPA 1990, s. 78A.

of planning permission (as is the case in the Republic of Ireland) this was abandoned by government before the 2001 Planning Green Paper was published. Hence, third parties continue to have no right to appeal against a planning decision,[42] and must apply for judicial review of any adverse decision. The expanded scope of the duty to give reasons when planning permission is granted may prove useful to third parties—developers are often successful in arguing that inadequate reasons have been given. But they still need standing, to act without delay, and be able to afford the large costs involved, and in practice have very little chance of success. Only local planning authority decisions can be subject to judicial review: decisions of the Secretary of State are immune from challenge except under section 288 (see p. 493). If the applicant brings an appeal, third parties have wider procedural rights at that stage.

The local planning authority's discretion

In deciding whether or not to grant permission, the local planning authority 'shall have regard to the provisions of the development plan, so far as material to the application, and to any other material considerations' (s. 70(2) TCPA 1990).

'If, in making any determination under the planning Acts, regard is to be had to the development plan, the determination shall be made in accordance with the development plan unless material considerations indicate otherwise' (s. 38(6) PCPA 2004).

The Secretary of State is subject to the same requirements in relation to decisions where the developer appeals (under s. 78) or which he calls in (under s. 77). It is central to an understanding of planning law to appreciate the scope of the above provisions:

- It gives the local planning authority a wide *discretion* whether or not to grant permission.
- This discretion must be exercised on grounds of *planning policy*, taking the development plan as the starting point.

(a) The role of the Secretary of State and the courts

The principal means of controlling this discretion is through the appeals system. The Secretary of State (usually through an Inspector) considers afresh the whole application, and can form his own opinion on what planning policy requires, effectively exercising a stranglehold over the appeals process. He can consider both legal grounds (e.g. that the objections are not planning objections) and policy grounds (e.g. that too much weight was attached to objections).

By contrast, the courts will only interfere if there has been some illegality in the decision-making process, and ordinary principles of public law are applied (see p. 340). As long as the policies that are applied are lawful (i.e. relevant to planning), the courts do not interfere with their content. This is effectively a principle of non-intervention in policy matters.

---

42. For criticism of this on human rights and Aarhus Convention grounds see M. Grant [2000] JPL 1215 and see generally M. Purdue (2001) 2 Env L Rev 83. Both these pre-dated the HL decision in *Alconbury* (see p. 449).

Accordingly, the *weight* given to any policy is a matter for the decision-maker, unless the decision is perverse. As Lord Hoffmann said in *Tesco Stores Ltd v Secretary of State for the Environment and others* [1995] JPL 581 (discussed in more detail in Case box 13.1):

If there is one principle of planning law more firmly settled than any other, it is that matters of planning judgment are within the exclusive province of the local planning authority or the Secretary of State.

However, it is impermissible to have an absolute policy, or to apply it rigidly, since this would constitute an unlawful fettering of discretion (*Stringer v Minister of Housing and Local Government* [1970] 1 WLR 1281). The courts thus see their role as ensuring that decisions are made rationally in the light of all planning considerations. This is ensured by the requirement that *reasons* must be given for decisions, which now extends to giving reasons for granting as well as refusing planning permission (see p. 475).

As discussed previously, the 1980s saw a strengthening of 'developer-led' planning. This was encouraged by strongly worded policy guidance indicating that the onus was on local planning authorities to show why development could *not* be permitted. Unless specific restraint policies applied, such as in the Green Belt (see PPG 2), the guidance required development to be permitted 'unless the development would cause demonstrable harm to interests of acknowledged importance' (Circular 14/85, repeated in PPG 1 (1988)).

Such explicitly directory planning guidance could be used to great effect because of the Secretary of State's role in the appeals process. But it was also powerful because of the approach of the courts in refusing to prioritize the weight given either to the development plan or to other material considerations. The development plan was an important consideration, but need not be 'slavishly adhered to' (*Enfield London Borough Council v Secretary of State for the Environment* [1975] JPL 155). By stressing the principle of non-intervention in the contents of policies, the courts allowed the government freedom to accord the presumption in favour of development a very high value (see, e.g., *London Residuary Body v Lambeth London Borough Council* [1990] 1 WLR 744).

(b) The presumption in favour of the development plan

This state of affairs has now changed, first, as a result of Ministerial decisions in a number of planning appeals around the start of the 1990s, followed by legislative recognition. The Planning and Compensation Act 1991 inserted section 54A. This section introduced a presumption in favour of following the provisions of the development plan, because it replaced the existing duty to 'have regard to' the plan with a duty to act 'in accordance with' it. Thus, the period of 'market-led' or 'developer-led' planning was replaced by 'plan-led' planning.

The presumption in favour of the plan is now contained in section 38(6) of the 2004 Act, which is essentially worded identically. This might suggest that previous cases on the meaning of section 54A would equally apply to section 38(6), but this may not necessarily be so. The case law on section 54A was influenced by government guidance which referred to the planning system operating 'on the basis that applications for development should be allowed, having regard to the development plan and all material considerations, unless the proposed development would cause demonstrable harm to interests of acknowledged importance'. Thus in *Loup v Secretary of State for the Environment* [1996] JPL 22 the Court of Appeal acknowledged that the whole purpose of the plan-led system was to give certainty to the development plan, which in turn would lead to greater consistency in decision-making. The relative certainty created by the development plan could itself amount to an interest of acknowledged importance.

In what was the leading case on section 54A (and which seems equally applicable to section 38(6) of the 2004 Act), the House of Lords held that the presumption in favour of the plan is neither a 'governing' nor a 'paramount' one (*City of Edinburgh Council v Secretary of State for Scotland* [1998] JPL 224). Nor does a decision-maker have to follow any particular procedure; the plan and the other considerations can, if preferred, be taken together, and the plan need not be considered first in time. The application of the *City of Edinburgh* case to England and Wales was confirmed in *R v Leominster DC ex parte Pothecary* [1998] JPL 335 where it was said that what is important is for it to be apparent how the decision-maker has approached the duty.

Thus, the planning system may be 'plan-led', but this is no guarantee that the plan will always be followed, since the weight to be accorded to the plan remains, ultimately, a matter for the decision-maker. One point that has therefore acquired increased significance is the *interpretation* of development plans. In the past it has often been assumed that this is a matter of law for the courts to decide. This is undoubtedly correct, but it does not solve the question of whether the courts will impose their own interpretation or will be content to adopt the less interventionist method of reviewing whether the decision-maker's interpretation was a reasonable one. This is crucial to the extent to which the courts will interfere with decisions via s. 38(6) of the 2004 Act. Cases such as *ex parte Pothecary*, as well as experience, suggest that the normal, non-interventionist approach will be used, thus reinforcing the view that the real change in planning that was envisaged in the 1990s will result from actual changes in policy rather than from anything the courts require. Or, as Lord Hope put it in *City of Edinburgh*, 'It would be a mistake to think that the effect of [s. 54A] was to increase the power of the court to intervene in decisions about planning control.'

There is guidance on the basic approach that decision-makers ought to employ in determining applications or appeals.[43] However, this does little more than restate section 38(6), and is notably short on fleshing out the policy strength to be given to the plan. For example, previous guidance from 1997 stipulated that if the proposal was in conflict with the plan then the developer would normally have to produce 'convincing reasons' to show why the plan should not have applied, and that the weight to be given to the plan would be strengthened if the Secretary of State has not formally intervened at the plan-making stage. This change of wording may simply be a product of the Government's desire that Planning Policy Statements should be shorter documents. But an alternative view is that, despite the stated commitment to a plan-led system of development management, planning authorities and the Secretary of State will enjoy slightly greater flexibility in their planning decisions.

(c) Other material considerations

The key point as to the meaning of 'other material considerations' is that the Act gives no guidance on this term, which has fallen to the courts to be interpreted. To be material

---

43. ODPM, *The Planning System: General Principles* (2005), para. 10.

a consideration has to be material to planning, and material to the application. Certain matters will always be taken into account: non-statutory plans, government planning guidance such as circulars and PPGs (*Pye Ltd v West Oxfordshire DC* [1982] JPL 577),[44] the results of consultations, and any representations made by third parties or objectors. Any representations made by a regulator like the Environment Agency will be a material consideration which must be weighed alongside other material considerations (but not, as noted at p. 477, slavishly followed), though there are cases which suggest that good reasons must be given for not following such advice.[45] Other matters, such as impacts on amenity, on the local economy, transport and highways considerations, and the balance of land use in the area, will nearly always be material on the facts.

A range of other matters have also been held to be material in certain circumstances: the effect on private rights (*Stringer v Minister of Housing and Local Government* [1970] 1 WLR 1281); the existing use of the site (*Clyde & Co. v Secretary of State for the Environment* [1977] 1 WLR 926); the personal circumstances of the occupier (*Tameside Metropolitan Borough Council v Secretary of State for the Environment* [1984] JPL 180); the precedent effect of a decision (*Collis Radio Ltd v Secretary of State for the Environment* (1975) 29 P & CR 390); and the availability of alternative sites (see Box 13.7).

BOX 13.7 **Alternatives**

The consideration of alternatives is increasingly central to environmental decision-making. Examples include the substitution principle in chemicals regulation (see p. 61) and the status given to considering alternatives in EIA and SEA (see p. 538). In planning law, the general rule developed by the courts is that 'the consideration of alternative sites[46] would only be relevant to a planning application in exceptional circumstances ... such circumstances will particularly arise where the proposed development, although desirable in itself, involves on the site proposed such conspicuous adverse effects that the possibility of an alternative site lacking such drawbacks necessarily itself becomes, in the mind of a reasonable local authority, a relevant planning consideration upon the application in question' (*R (Jones) v North Warwickshire BC* [2001] EWCA Civ 315, emphasis added). Examples which the courts have given include developments such as airports, petro-chemical plants and nuclear power stations (all of which, of course, require EIA), where at most only a very limited number of permissions are likely to be granted. But at the other end of the scale, where alternatives will not need to be considered, are development proposals where the environmental impact is minimal and the planning objections are not especially strong.

In *Jodie Phillips v First Secretary of State and others* [2003] EWHC 2415, the siting of a 3G mobile phone mast was challenged. The development plan provided that where there would be a conflict with environmental objectives it would need to be demonstrated that there was no possibility of sharing existing facilities, no satisfactory alternative sites and no reasonable possibility of using existing structures, which is broadly the position in the relevant policy guidance (PPG8). Richards J held that the test in *Jones* was not exhaustive and that policy

---

44. Note that the meaning of words in policy guidance is a matter of law, but that the courts will only intervene if a planning authority's interpretation is perverse (*R v Derbyshire CC ex parte Woods* [1998] Env LR 277).

45. See, e.g., *Goldfinch (Projects) Ltd v National Assembly for Wales* [2002] EWHC 1275.

46. See further critique of the 'spatial fix' approach at p. 502.

guidance may require alternatives to be considered even where, as here, there was no proven environmental harm; 'the question, it seems to me, is not just "is this an acceptable location" but "is this the best location" '. This resulted in a different approach to *Jones*, which took as the starting point that alternatives would not have to be considered where the development proposed was acceptable in planning terms (an approach which emphasizes the rights of owners to develop their land, rather than the public interest in achieving e.g. the optimum environmental decision). The judge held that the Planning Inspector might have taken a different view on whether there was 'planning harm' if the alternative site put forward by the claimant had been given proper consideration. Put differently, the fears about the siting of the mast—in this case near to a nursery school—might have been given more weight if the alternative site had been properly considered in the decision-making process.

The *Phillips* case illustrates the strength of policy guidance even over the development plan. The implication of this decision is likely to be felt in other areas of planning where a 'sequential test' ranking sites according to their degree of desirability is used, e.g. out of town retail development. The case is also a good example of how public concerns about environmental and health impacts will be material considerations, regardless of the degree to which they might be said to objectively unjustified (see p. 500). But it also shows some difficulties with the concept of 'planning harm'—a concept that is being gradually eroded as planning tries to become more concerned with positive management than negative controls (see PPS1).

The achievement of a separate planning objective of the local planning authority can also be material. Protecting the Royal Opera House by allowing it to raise funds by carrying out office development which would not otherwise have been permitted has been upheld (*R v Westminster City Council, ex parte Monahan* [1988] JPL 557). This principle has been used to fund the conservation of wildlife sites, such as at Barn Elms in West London, by allowing a limited amount of otherwise unacceptable development on the site.

It should be noted that emerging plans (*R v City of London Corporation, ex parte Allan* (1980) 79 LGR 223) and whether the application is premature in the light of such plans (*Arlington Securities Ltd v Secretary of State for the Environment* (1989) 57 P & CR 407) are not 'the development plan' but material considerations to be weighed in the balance. The closer a plan is to being adopted, the more weight it will carry. Equally, supplementary planning documents are not 'the plan' but material considerations. While the need for a development may also be material, it is not the job of the local authority to second-guess the financial viability of a scheme.

Any human rights that are engaged by a planning decision will be a material consideration.[47] Following *Hatton v UK* (2003) 37 EHRR 28 (see p. 358) it may be that acting lawfully under a planning permission would mean, for example, that there has been no 'domestic irregularity' so that substantive Convention rights would not have been breached. If this

---

47. For discussion of how decision-makers should approach human rights concerns, in particular Art. 8 (right to a home) see the (divided) Court of Appeal in *First Secretary of State and others v Chichester District Council* [2004] EWCA Civ 1248.

view were to prevail it might suggest that decision-makers should have an even greater onus to consider the human rights implications of their decisions.

Environmental considerations as material considerations

In relation to environmental matters, it is clear that planning permission may be refused on a number of grounds. An industrial development may be refused because of possible pollution or safety problems (e.g. it is possible to prevent a plant handling dangerous substances, or a waste disposal site, from being sited near to a sensitive watercourse). A housing estate may be refused because of the inadequacy of the existing sewerage provision. The impact of noise or light on neighbouring properties will also be material. Of course environmental considerations will not necessarily point only one way. A good illustration is the Secretary of State's rejection of a bypass around Hastings. The South East Regional Assembly and the county and district councils unanimously supported the bypass, in part to alleviate air pollution problems caused by traffic congestion, but these were outweighed by strong conservation and countryside considerations.

There are also a number of situations in which EC obligations will be material considerations in planning decisions. Often the mechanism used for bringing these to planning authorities' attention is government guidance. For example, PPG 9 gives advice on the extent to which nature conservation interests protected under EC law ought to be taken into account.

However, it must be remembered that these are only some of the matters that must be taken into account. The final decision involves a balancing of all the factors. A clear example of the discretion given to the local planning authority to decide that other factors outweigh environmental ones is *R v Exeter City Council, ex parte J. L. Thomas & Co. Ltd* [1991] 1 QB 471 where a decision to grant planning permission for a development that would be likely to lead to private nuisance claims by the future occupants of the new development was unchallengeable in public law (see also p. 388).[48]

The extent to which environmental risks, 'genuine' or perceived, amount to material considerations is considered in more detail below (see p. 500).

The weight given to environmental considerations

The basic starting point is, as noted elsewhere, that the planning authority can give a material consideration any weight, or no weight at all (see p. 476). The weight accorded to environmental considerations can be seen in *West Coast Wind Farms Ltd v Secretary of State for the Environment and North Devon DC* [1996] JPL 767. An application to construct two wind farms was refused. Although government planning advice (PPG 22) supports energy from wind, it also recognizes the need to protect local environmental quality, and this latter factor was accorded more weight. The Court of Appeal held that there was no policy presumption in favour of such developments, even if they were a policy aim. Although such

---

48. Note that, following *Kane v New Forest District Council (No. 1)* [2001] EWCA Civ 878, which was influenced in part by developments in human rights law, there is no general immunity for local planning authorities from claims in negligence (or, it is submitted, in nuisance) and in principle a LPA might be liable if it insisted on a particular design feature which caused an actionable loss (see A. Samuels [2003] JPL 1514).

sources might be 'needed' in a general sense, each application still had to be decided on its merits. In such situations, of course, refusals can be appealed, and if the policy is genuine it can be enforced appropriately by the Secretary of State. The more difficult situation is where an obviously harmful activity is consented to because each individual contribution to it is minor when looked at in isolation.

An especially difficult issue is how much weight should be given to statutory obligations, especially those emanating from EC environmental directives.[49] In *R (Murray) v Derbyshire County Council* [2002] Env LR 28 it was held that while the waste management objectives in Article 4 of the Waste Framework Directive and its implementing regulations were clearly material considerations in deciding whether to grant planning permission for an extension to a landfill:

an objective . . . is something different from a material consideration . . . An objective which is obligatory must always be kept in mind when making a decision even while the decision maker has regard to other material considerations.

However, the Court of Appeal did not favour creating a hierarchy of material considerations 'whereby the law would require decision makers to give different weight to different considerations'. It did suggest that there may be cases where it was apparent that the objective had been flagrantly disregarded, in which case the obligation would be breached. However, as we discuss elsewhere (Chapter 15), it is not clear that this will necessarily be apparent at the time the decision is made; courts generally place faith in decision makers and problems may only emerge with hindsight. There then becomes a very tricky issue of whether, perhaps some years later, the granting of the permission requires re-examination.[50] In relation to planning and pollution prevention obligations see also *Blewett v Derbyshire County Council* [2004] ECA Civ 1508 (discussed in detail in Case box 15.1).

Planning conditions

Section 70(1) permits the local planning authority (and the Secretary of State on appeal) to impose such conditions 'as it thinks fit'. This wide discretionary power is limited by statutory guidance in sections 72 and 75, judicial control over what is permissible, and central government policy.

Statutory guidance is limited and relatively unimportant. Section 72 states that conditions attached to other land under the control of the applicant, and conditions requiring commencement of the development within a specified time, are permissible. It also allows for temporary permissions, which can be used to grant planning permission on a trial basis. This has been used for fibreglass sharks on roofs (see p. 464), and more seriously for innovative 'low impact developments' such as at Tinker's Bubble in Somerset.

---

49. For a somewhat dated but still useful overview see M. Purdue, 'The Impact of EC Environmental Law on Planning Law in the United Kingdom', in J. Holder (ed.), *The Impact of EC Environmental Law in the United Kingdom* (Chichester: Wiley, 1997)). See also M. Tewdwr-Jones and R. Williams, *The European Dimension of British Planning* (London: Routledge, 2001).

50. Which raises very tricky issues about compensation for the developer, and remedies for any affected individuals.

What are of greater practical importance are the legal tests for the validity of conditions developed over the years by the courts. In contrast with the decisions on material considerations, these have produced some rather restrictive results, possibly because the cases were mainly decided earlier, when a more overt policy of protecting private property rights applied. In the leading case of *Newbury DC v Secretary of State for the Environment* [1981] AC 578, the House of Lords held that to be valid, conditions must:

- be imposed for a planning purpose and not for an ulterior motive;
- fairly and reasonably relate to the development permitted; and
- not be perverse ('so unreasonable that no reasonable authority could have imposed them').

The courts have also held that a condition should not be 'hopelessly uncertain', although they have taken a broad view as to what this must entail so that there may be considerable scope for saying that the terms of a condition are ascertainable (*Alderson v Secretary of State for the Environment* (1984) 49 P&CR 307).

Ground (a) above goes to the nature and limits of planning itself. The courts have done this by concluding that certain matters of a social planning nature do not relate to town and country planning. For example, in *R v Hillingdon London Borough Council, ex parte Royco Homes Ltd* [1974] 2 QB 720, a condition requiring that houses be occupied by people on the local authority housing list, who should then be granted 10 years security of tenure, was held to be illegal. The burden of housing people in need was placed by statute on the housing authority, not private developers. However, the provision of affordable housing has been held to be for a planning purpose, in part because policy guidance has made it so, but also because the stress is on the type of housing rather on the occupiers (*Mitchell v Secretary of State for the Environment* [1994] JPL 916, and see PPG3, Housing)).[51]

Such issues to do with the planning system and social exclusion make it arguable whether the nature and scope of the planning system today is the same as it was in 1974, not least because of the wider policy objectives of using the planning system to achieve sustainability (see PPS1), which necessarily involves going beyond issues of the mere use and character of land. In recent years, the courts have not been asked to rule on the nature of planning, which might be explained by the lack of anyone with sufficient practical interest to do so.

Ground (b) requires that conditions have some geographic and functional link to the site to which the application relates. So a condition requiring works to be carried out on land neither included in the application nor under the control of the applicant is illegal (*Ladbrokes Ltd v Secretary of State* [1981] JPL 427). Thus, a requirement to screen a site by planting trees on neighbouring land will be illegal unless the land is under the applicant's control. But it is possible to make development conditional on the completion of work off-site, such as requiring infrastructure works (roads, sewers, etc) to be satisfactory before development commences (*Grampian Regional Council v Aberdeen District Council* (1983) 47 P&CR 633) ('Grampian conditions').

---

51. Should a developer be required to provide affordable housing when the proposed development would not cause planning harm without it? The answer now seems to be clear, since PPS1 moves away from notions of planning harm to a more positive vision of planning that includes, in the sustainable development equation, social exclusion; see also p. 451.

Finally, a condition can be struck down if it is perverse (ground (c)). This test has normally been used to prevent conditions undermining private property rights without compensation. A prime example is *Hall & Co. Ltd v Shoreham-by-Sea Urban District Council* [1964] 1 WLR 240, where a condition was attached to a permission for industrial development which required an access road to be built on the developer's land at its expense and dedicated to the public. The Court of Appeal held the condition illegal, even though it accepted it was beneficial in planning terms since it created a usable access to otherwise inaccessible land. The position is no different if the developer suggests or accepts such an imposition (*Bradford Metropolitan Council v Secretary of State for the Environment* (1987) 53 P&CR 55). This approach effectively frustrated the use of conditions to secure 'planning gain' for local communities, leading to the rise in the use of planning agreements and obligations for this purpose (see below).

(a) Conditions and policy

On appeal the Secretary of State can add, omit or amend any conditions as part of the total rehearing of the issues. This can be done on legal, factual or policy grounds, so an understanding of the Secretary of State's policy on conditions is essential.

Circular 11/95 requires conditions to be (a) necessary, (b) relevant to planning, (c) relevant to the development permitted, (d) enforceable, (e) precise, and (f) reasonable. In addition, it lays down some very important general policy tests: 'As a matter of policy, a condition ought not to be imposed unless there is a definite need for it'; 'a condition should not be retained unless there are sound and clear cut reasons for doing so'; and a condition 'requires special and precise justification' if planning permission would not be refused if the condition were omitted. The local planning authority should also consider whether the imposition of any conditions may render an otherwise objectionable development acceptable, so as to save the application from being refused.

These are not legal requirements, but a local planning authority ignores these tests at its peril because of the applicant's right of appeal. It also appears from *Times Investments Ltd v Secretary of State for the Environment* [1990] JPL 433 that a failure to have regard to these policies (e.g. not to demonstrate the harm that would be caused by omitting a particular condition) may render the decision illegal for failure to have regard to a material consideration. Once again, therefore, the Secretary of State's guidance imposes significant restrictions on the decisions that may be reached. Circular 11/95 notes types of condition that would normally be illegal and those that require exceptional justification. Appendix A includes a list of model conditions and Appendix B a list of unacceptable ones.

Finally, note that current guidance refers to conditions being imposed if they are 'fair, reasonable and practicable' (para. 21), which seems to dispense with any necessity test.[52]

(b) Planning conditions and environmental protection

From the above it is clear that planning conditions can be used to control a range of environmentally harmful activities, especially where these are not controlled by other regimes. An illustrative example is imposing conditions on new development limiting

---

52. ODPM, *The Planning System: General Principles* (2005), para. 20.

car parking spaces. Conditions may even be imposed where, as part of an enforcement appeal, it is thought better to grant retrospective permission if this will remedy existing environmental problems. This may still fairly and reasonably relate to the development, even though planning conditions are generally aimed at preventing future harm (*Cheshire CC v Secretary of State for the Environment* [1995] Env LR 316).

One particular issue relates to the use of planning conditions to achieve continuing environmental objectives, especially pollution control. There is a slender but marked distinction between the policy tests laid down in PPS 23 (Planning and Pollution Control) and the relevant circulars and the legal tests laid down in *Newbury District Council v Secretary of State for the Environment* [1981] AC 578. One of the important differences is that the legal tests do not suggest that a condition will be unlawful if it duplicates other statutory controls. As long as the matter which is sought to be controlled has a planning purpose (a concept which seems to widen with the passing years), it is lawful.[53]

On the other hand, government policy in PPS 23 (echoing the RCEP in its Fifth Report) makes it clear that planning conditions should not be used to deal with difficulties which are the subject of controls under other legislation. The justification for this approach is that it prevents an unnecessary duplication of control or any argument over the nature of the conditions that are to be imposed. Whether it is desirable in policy terms is another matter and local planning authorities will always be wary of imposing conditions which duplicate other controls as the Secretary of State will, more often than not, amend the condition on appeal.

The problems of overlapping conditions can be significant in pollution control. The Department of the Environment's report on *Planning, Pollution and Waste Management* (1992) found that there were two main circumstances where planning conditions were used in the control of pollution.

First, there were occasions where the only (or in some cases the most straightforward) means of controlling pollution was by imposing planning conditions (e.g. the control of groundwater pollution from direct or indirect sources, such as storage tanks). Secondly, conditions were used to override existing pollution control systems in circumstances where it was argued that planning authorities had little confidence in the pollution control authorities and wished to maintain a degree of control to protect the amenities of the area. Examples included a condition to impose a release limit which would run with the land, rather than be associated with a licence to operate, and a condition to impose a release limit where the planning authority was concerned that the relevant pollution control authority would not enforce its own controls.

These types of conditions were, and still are, clearly contrary to policy but not unlawful. For example, an Inspector imposed an overlapping condition on sulphur dioxide emissions in the planning appeal involving Ferro-Alloys and Metals Smelter in Glossop (see [1990] 2 LMELR 176). There, the planning authority was concerned about the enforcement record of HMIP and by its remarks that it might revise its condition downwards or not enforce it, and this was accepted by the Inspector as good grounds for imposing the condition.

53. If an aspect of the development is governed by another regulatory regime then this might not be the subject of planning conditions, since the planning condition could require action over which the developer has no control, as with the planning condition regulating aircraft flight paths which was unlawful because this is governed by the Civil Aviation Authority under civil aviation legislation: *British Airports Authority v Secretary of State for Scotland* [1980] JPL 260). This elevates the 'enforceability' test to a legal rather than policy test.

Although the powers (and resources) of the Environment Agency have improved since then, the legality of the determination still appears correct. This is because cases such as *Gateshead Metropolitan Borough Council v Secretary of State for the Environment* [1995] JPL 432 (discussed in Case box 20.5) and *R v Bolton Metropolitan Council, ex parte Kirkman* [1998] Env LR 719 go no further than to say that the existence of specialist (and effective) pollution control agencies is no more than a material consideration for the planning authority to weigh in the balance. Unless there are overriding obligations (in *Kirkman*, duties under the EC Waste Framework Directive were important), the courts will not say that the existence of such agencies means that the local planning authority cannot consider matters within their powers, as this would be unduly fettering discretion.[54]

The practical position therefore appears to be that if a planning authority is generally in favour of a development it may be content to leave a wide range of pollution control and environmental protection issues to specialist regulators, deflecting attention away from its own powers. On the other hand, if the development is less central to the local economy, and of a kind which has caused concerns to residents, it may seek to impose conditions to prevent local environmental harm, knowing that such conditions may be overturned on appeal. This would allow it to enforce via, e.g. a breach of condition notice, rather than rely on enforcement by agencies less accountable to the local electorate.[55]

Planning obligations and contributions

The town and country planning legislation has always included powers under which a local planning authority could enter into an agreement relating to the development or use of land. For many years little use was made of these powers, but in the 1970s and 1980s they came to be seen as a mechanism for the provision of some form of 'planning gain' (i.e. some gain to the community that would not necessarily have been obtained without the agreement). However, planning gain may take different forms (a useful model for thinking about the role of this mechanism is given in Box 13.8).

BOX 13.8 **Models of environmental planning gain**[56]

Objective	Example	Comment
Securing implementation	Infrastructure improvements	Minimalist; facilitative
Meeting environmental costs	Habitat replacement	Compensatory
Advancing environmental needs	Securing net habitat gain	Environmentally redistributive

54. Not infrequently, planning controls on noise will be imposed on developments subject to IPPC (which includes noise emissions within the scope of control), see p. 770. See also *Blewett v Derbyshire County Council* [2004] EWCA Civ 1508 regarding the role of the EA and LPAs as regards landfill, p. 572.

55. For examples of the problems faced by local authorities when dealing with odour nuisances see *Tameside Metropolitan Borough Council v Smith Brothers (Hyde) Ltd* [1996] Env LR D4 and *R v Secretary of State for the Environment, ex parte West Wiltshire District Council* [1996] Env LR 312.

56. Adapted from Loughlin (1981) OJLS 61 and P. Healey, M. Purdue, and F. Ennis, *Negotiating Development, Rationales and Practice for Development Obligations and Planning Gain* (Spon, 1995).

The increased importance of agreements—which could be positive or negative in character, and which could require money to be paid to the local planning authority—illustrated the negotiative nature of modern town planning and showed that the concept of planning as a strict system of regulation in which the regulator imposes restrictions on a developer had become rather outdated. But it also gave rise to some concern. There was no need for approval of agreements by the Secretary of State, no provision for publicity or appeal, limited scrutiny of the content of agreements and limited potential for a successful challenge by a third party.[57] As a result, as the Nolan Committee (Cm 3702, 1997) verified, cases arose where LPAs 'sold' planning permission to the highest bidder or the developer effectively offered a bribe in return for favourable treatment.

When the Town and Country Planning Act was consolidated in 1990, the provisions on agreements were included as section 106. However, under the Planning and Compensation Act 1991, developers could give binding unilateral undertakings as well as to enter into agreements. 'Planning obligations' could therefore cover both agreements and undertakings. Although there was no wholesale use of unilateral undertakings as a 'developer's charter', they could be used effectively when the local planning authority was unwilling to agree terms, their greatest advantage to developers being on appeal—a developer could offer an undertaking and the Secretary of State (subject to the tests detailed below) would have to take it into account in deciding whether to allow the appeal.[58]

The law will be further changed under the 2004 Act—although the provisions are not expected to come into force until 2006—the existing law being seen by Government as 'opaque, slow, unfair, complex and reactive'.[59] Although the Government's original intention was to implement a tariff system (e.g. paying a contribution based on the size of a development, and with no element of negotiation), in the end the 2004 Act repeals section 106 and gives the Secretary of State powers, through regulations, to make provision for what are termed 'planning contributions' (s. 46). Section 46 enables developers to pay the local planning authority, in money or quantified benefits in kind or a combination of the two, according to scales which, most likely, will be set out in development plan documents. The central purpose behind planning contributions therefore is to allow developers to pay a pre-determined charge for various services or facilities associated with development, rather than having to negotiate these on a case-by-case basis. For example, contributions towards public transport might be made on this basis (in practice, this was often covered by SPG). Contributions are therefore intended to be less reactive by being planned.[60] However, developers may depart from the pre-determined scales of contribution if they wish, and provision for negotiated agreements is retained (which may be particularly relevant for mitigating environmental harms, where greater flexibility is generally needed).[61]

The creation of a planning contribution does not replace the need to seek planning

57. On the moral dimension to agreements see J. Alder [1990] JPL 880.

58. And the local planning authority has limited discretion to avoid entering into an agreement subsequently, see *R v Warwickshire County Council ex parte Powergen plc* [1997] JPL 843, furthering stressing the influence of the Secretary of State.

59. ODPM, 'Contributing to Sustainable Communities: A New Approach To Planning Obligations' (30 Jan. 2004).

60. For an analysis of how planning obligations subverted the plan-led approach see F. Cornford [2002] JPL 796.

61. Following the Barker reivew on housing, Government appears to favour a form of 'development uplift' to pay for social housing; see <www.odpm.gov>.

permission in the normal way, but the existence of a valid contribution is definitely a material consideration that should be taken into account under section 70(2). The local planning authority will normally link the permission and the contribution by imposing a condition on the permission that implementation depends on the acceptance of a planning contribution. Planning contributions can therefore enable the local planning authority and the developer to supplement a permission by achieving objectives which could not be achieved by planning conditions. Indeed, as the Court of Appeal in *Good v Epping Forest District Council* [1994] JPL 372 remarked about planning obligations, why else would there be provision for them?

Section 46 provides a (very) bare legislative framework and most of the procedural detail concerning planning contributions remains to be fleshed out by regulations. For example, it is unclear whether developers will be able to offer unilateral contributions on appeal (though Government has stated that the new provisions will not be any less flexible). Section 106 contained various rules, for example that planning obligations could only be created by deed and by a person who has an interest in the relevant land; that they were enforceable against successors in title and were local land charges; and rules in relation to enforcement (this could either be by injunction, or by the local planning authority, after giving notice, entering the land, carrying out the appropriate operations and recovering its costs). It must be assumed that similar provisions will be made under the 2004 Act. Obligations made after the Contracts (Rights of Third Parties) Act 1999 came into force may be enforceable by the local residents in whose favour, in a sense, they are made.

Old provisions continue to apply to agreements made before 25 October 1991; in terms of their variation and extinguishment they are governed by the law on restrictive covenants under the Law of Property Act 1925, s. 84. The 2004 Act does not set out any transitional rules regarding planning obligations entered into before section 46 comes into force; these must await the regulations.

(a) The case law

While there is obviously no case law yet on planning contributions, the lawful scope of planning obligations caused difficulties, reflecting the tensions between *legal* tests and *policy* tests discussed above. In *R v Plymouth City Council, ex parte Plymouth and South Devon Co-operative Society Ltd* (1993) 67 P & CR 78 the Court of Appeal had to examine the legality of the offer by two superstore developers of planning gain—including such things as construction of a tourist information centre, provision of a bird-watching hide, a contribution towards a 'Park and Ride' scheme, and up to £1m for infrastructure works at another site. The Court decided that community benefits could be material considerations even where they were not necessary to overcome or alleviate planning objections. A planning obligation had to satisfy the three tests which applied to conditions, i.e. (a) it must have a planning purpose; (b) it must fairly and reasonably relate to the permitted development; and (c) it must not be perverse or grossly unreasonable. The Court decided that the proposed benefits satisfied these tests. The House of Lords subsequently refined this decision in the seminal *Tesco* case (Case box 13.1).

CASE 13.1 *Tesco Stores Ltd v Secretary of State for the Environment* [1995] 1 WLR 759

One superstore developer had entered into a planning obligation offering, in return for being granted planning permission, to fund a new road intended to relieve traffic congestion. The Inspector placed considerable weight on the offer, and recommended permission be granted, but the Secretary of State disagreed and refused permission. In the House of Lords it was argued that the offer of funding was a material consideration and that as the Secretary of State failed to have regard to it his decision was flawed. The House took a different approach from the Court of Appeal in *Plymouth* and distinguished the tests for the legality of conditions and planning obligations. In particular, Lord Hoffmann, in an erudite judgment, held that a planning obligation could be valid even where it would not satisfy the second test set out in *Plymouth* in the sense that the connection to the development had only to be more than *de minimis*. Thus, a planning obligation only has to satisfy tests (a) and (c) above. Whilst it would be unlawful to take into account an obligation which had no connection *whatsoever* with the development, the weight to be attached to the obligation was entirely a matter for the decision-maker (and different decision-makers could take opposing views on the weight to attach to the same obligation). It was not necessary for the obligation to be proportional to the development, nor did it have to be necessary to allow the development to go ahead. All that was required was that the connection between the development and the obligation must be 'material'.

This key decision (see also p. 477) re-emphasizes that the earlier reported cases confused the *legal* question of the legitimacy of obligations with the *policy* test laid down in Circular 16/91 and its predecessors. In particular, the requirement that the development relates to a planning purpose merely reflects the legal requirement to take into account material considerations under section 70(2), TCPA 1990. Moreover, the third test of general reasonableness equates with normal principles of administrative law. On the other hand, the second test set out in *Plymouth* was a test of policy that was specified in Circular 16/91. It remains to be seen whether the regulations implementing section 46 of the 2004 Act will seek to change this position. To do so would require the regulations to specify, for example, that only contributions which were necessary and proportionate would be material considerations. (It is clear that any revised policy guidance that emerges will not, by itself, be able to change the main thrust of the *Tesco* case.) The government has rejected this approach, and although it cautions local authorities not to be swayed by extra inducements it is difficult to see how a keen developer could be prevented from offering them, since it is difficult to envisage contributions which were not material, i.e. which could not be linked to the development in some manner. The *Tesco* case itself, of course, involved the *rejection* of an excessively generous offer by a developer (the contribution of the superstore to traffic on the new road would have been minimal). But the House of Lords showed both a sensitivity towards the great constraints on local government finance (legally, the offer could have been accepted) and a judicial deference to the use of negotiative planning.

(b) Policy and practice

The legal tests are amplified by policy guidance on what is permissible by way of planning gain now set out in Circular 1/97. Given that policy and practice have arguably been more important than law in this area, the terms of the circular are of special significance. They suggest that section 106 should not be used to require a developer to provide more than that which is linked to the development in issue in terms of scale and kind. This appears to mean, for example, that a developer may be asked to provide more sewerage than is needed for the works applied for, but not sewerage for the whole general area. But this limitation seems unenforceable in many cases, since neither the developer nor the local planning authority will wish to challenge an arrangement they have themselves reached. Indeed, such arrangements may be encouraged by the local plan, which was the situation in *Plymouth* (and see also *R v South Northamptonshire DC and others, ex parte Crest Homes plc* [1995] JPL 200).

Moreover, other objectors may well lack either knowledge of the agreement or standing to challenge it. It is significant that the reported cases on planning obligations nearly all concern claims by one developer that a rival is being given preferential treatment as a result of an offer of planning gain that is questionable in terms of law or policy. The low visibility of planning obligations was one aspect of 'planning gain' criticised by the Nolan Committee. Two cases illustrate some of the transparency problems, and how developers are treated more favourably than objectors. In *Daniel Davies and Co. v London Borough of Southwark* [1994] JPL 1116 the Court of Appeal held that if an agreement was merely 'regulatory', determining how premises would be used, then it was not necessary that objectors see the terms of the agreement before it was signed. There could, it was acknowledged, be extreme cases where this rule would not apply, but the Court did not enlarge on what these might be. In *R (Lichfield Securities Ltd) v Lichfield District Council* [2001] EWCA Civ 304, however, it was held that fairness demanded that *other developers* should be able to comment on the terms of planning obligations. This might be the case where major developments such as large retail schemes involved a range of developers or where, as in *Lichfield*, one developer was already contributing towards infrastructure which a neighbouring development would also rely on (since each party would need to know if their financial contribution was fair).

In part such concerns about the openness of the system are addressed by the scale of charges for services being in the publicly available development plan. They have also been addressed by changes to Article 25 of the GDPO which spells out what information must go on Part I of the Planning Register (which contains information about the application).[62] Copies of any planning obligation 'proposed or entered into in connection with the application' must be included. (Obligations *actually* entered into must also be placed on Part II of the Register dealing with permissions granted.) One obvious practical difficulty, however, is in determining when an obligation or contribution has been 'proposed', since this is a negotiative process which might stretch out over many months or even years. (Government guidance is that each main draft should be registered.) Another point worth bearing in mind is that the obligation/contribution actually entered into need not contain the same commitments as earlier proposals, in other words there are practical limitations to public involvement.

Nevertheless, it remains the case that effectively we now have two systems operating concerning planning obligations. Where a planning contribution is being *required* of developers, the Secretary of State ought to apply his necessity policy on appeal (assuming, that is, that this remains government policy, which is not clear—revisions to Circular 1/97 are not expected before 2005). But where the obligation is being *offered* by developers, the decision-makers are likely to give much more latitude to what developers put on the table, and the

---

62. Town and Country Planning (General Development Procedure) (Amendment) (England) Order 2002, SI 2002/828.

courts will intervene only on legal, not policy, grounds. Whether this will remain the case beyond 2005/2006 is unclear, although what can be said is that there is a clear shift in policy underway in line with using contributions to secure positive planning advantages rather than simply mitigating negative effects.

(c) 'Environmental planning gain'

The use of planning contributions to provide for environmental benefits, or at least to prevent net environmental losses, raises important questions about valuation of the environment, perhaps also the 'polluter pays principle' and wider questions about sustainable development in planning. These cannot be explored in depth here. But research suggests that the idea of such 'environmental planning gain' has proved a powerful factor in allowing for greater development of rural land, allowing commodification of nature into a series of discrete environmental assets which could be traded in the interests of maintaining or even enhancing welfare and the environment.[63] However, its significance may rest more in its powerfulness as an idea rather than in practice.

There appears to have been rather limited use of environmental planning gain in practice, although as has been pointed out, what there is tends to be compensatory rather than alleviating or preventing losses caused by the development.[64] However, planning contributions could be used as a means of cleaning up certain contaminated sites. For example, development of a greenfield site could be linked, through a planning obligation, to the clean up of a brownfield site where, for example, the contaminated land was an 'orphan' site for which remediation would otherwise not be possible or paid out of public funds. They could also be used as a way of preventing the generation of additional traffic, for example by requiring the developer of an urban housing development to agree that cars will not be allowed on to the land (though banning car *ownership* would be unlawful since this would not relate to the land).[65]

What is perhaps more important is that planning contributions will still allow decisions about what is in the public interest (including environmental objectives) to be decided in negotiations between developers and planning authorities. The 2004 Act reforms do very little to address this issue.

Planning appeals

Section 78 provides a statutory right of appeal to the Secretary of State (in Wales, to the Planning Decision Committee of the Welsh Assembly) against refusals of permission or the imposition of any conditions, and where the local planning authority has failed to determine an application within eight weeks. Only the applicant can appeal (see p. 475). An appeal amounts to a total rehearing of the application, and the Secretary of State can make any decision originally open to the local planning authority.

---

63. S. Whatmore and S. Boucher (1993) 18 Transactions of the Institute of British Geographers 166.

64. P. Healey et al, *Negotiating Development, Rationales and Practice for Development Obligations and Planning Gain* (Spon, 1995). This approach is clearly sanctioned by *Tesco*.

65. On the possible legality and illegality of 'no car' contributions see A. Samuels [2002] JPL 514.

An appeal is thus not primarily a contest, but a forum in which all relevant information may be produced and tested so that the Inspector may make a rational decision. However, it is clear that, over the years, appeals have come to resemble the confrontational model of court proceedings far more than was originally intended (and the process juridified, see below). There is clear evidence that the appeals process has been politicised, with the opportunity being taken to impose central government policy unless there are strong and clear local policies applicable (e.g. in a local plan), or a clear restraint policy, such as the Green Belt, applies. In recent years around 36 per cent of appeals are successful.

There is also a right to seek judicial review of local planning authority decisions, although as a general principle of public law either any alternative remedies must first be exhausted or it must be shown that they would be inadequate if relied on (see *R v Birmingham City Council, ex parte Ferrero Ltd* [1993] 1 All ER 530; see also *R v Environment Agency, ex parte Petrus Oils Ltd* [1999] Env LR 732). In any event, an appeal to the Secretary of State will encompass policy matters and be cheaper. A decision to grant planning permission, or a refusal to allow an appeal, can only be challenged through judicial review. Such action requires the person initiating the challenge to have standing which is fairly easily satisfied for those with some interest in the case (see *R v Sheffield City Council, ex parte Mansfield* (1978) 37 P&CR 1).

Procedure on appeals

Either party (or the Secretary of State) has a right to a public hearing. In large cases this will be a public inquiry under sections 320 and 321. In an attempt to address some of the criticisms of the public inquiry system, there has been a shift towards the use of informal hearings to resolve planning disputes. Circular 05/00 makes it clear that it is central government policy to use hearings in all suitable cases, and to that end the choice of the hearing procedure is made by the Planning Inspectorate in consultation with the parties. In the vast majority of cases, however, an appeal is dealt with by way of written representations.[66] However, it is clear that it will be very rare for a decision to be quashed because of inadequacies in the procedures actually adopted.

Apart from a very small number of matters of national importance, the decision is normally taken by an Inspector. In the remaining cases, the Inspector's report goes to the Secretary of State, who then makes the final decision in the light of the recommendations. Reasons must be given for the decision. This duty has been supplemented by the courts, which require the reasons to be adequate, intelligible and not self-contradictory. Unlike normal civil litigation where the loser will usually pay all the costs of an action, parties to a planning appeal are normally expected to pay their own costs.

If an inquiry is held it must be public and anyone is entitled to attend. In general, the procedure to be followed is at the discretion of the Inspector, but there are rules set out.[67] However, since the rules are supplemented by the rules of natural justice and human rights protections—as indeed are the written representation procedures—an Inspector

---

66. Town and Country Planning (Appeals) (Written Representations) (England) Regulations 2000 (SI 2000/1628).

67. in the Town and Country Planning (Inquiries Procedure) (England) Rules 2000 (SI 2000/1624) and the Town and Country Planning (Determination by Inspectors) (Inquiries Procedure) Rules 2000 (SI 2000/1625).

normally permits anyone with anything new and relevant to say to put their case properly.

Hearings are not normally imposed by the Planning Inspectorate where third-party evidence is expected, or there are disputed matters of fact, or complex matters of law or policy. As in any decision-making process there is a balance to be struck between speed and informality, and procedural rigour, and in *Dyason v Secretary of State for the Environment and Chiltern District Council* [1998] JPL 778 it was stressed that 'a relaxed hearing is not necessarily a fair hearing'.

The courts have held that even the absence of an oral hearing will usually comply with Article 6 of the ECHR—which provides for a 'fair and public hearing'—so long as there is nothing to suggest that the planning authority has acted unfairly or unreasonably (*R (Adlard) v Secretary of State for the Environment, Transport and the Regions* [2002] EWCA Civ 735). The House of Lords has since held that this is so regardless of whether matters of fact-finding, rather than discretionary judgment, are at issue (*Begum v London Borough of Tower Hamlets* [2003] UKHL 5). Arguably, this is a rather restrictive, and pragmatic, approach based more on not causing chaos to administrative systems like planning—and seeing Article 6 rights not as self-standing but as requiring some other human rights breach to be demonstrated as well[68]—rather than genuinely protecting the interests in particular of third parties.

Challenging the decision of the Secretary of State

The Secretary of State's decision can only be challenged under section 288, owing to section 284 which ousts all other challenges. Section 288 thus provides a statutory appeal: this must be distinguished from judicial review. About 150 cases under section 288 are brought each year. These are the main source of decisions on planning law.

The section 288 grounds approximate to judicial review grounds. A decision can be challenged either if it is not within the powers of the Act, or if substantial prejudice has been caused by a failure to comply with the relevant procedures (e.g. the Inquiries Rules). These will cover bad faith, perverse decisions, failure to take account of relevant factors, taking into account irrelevant factors, mistakes of law, acting on no evidence, giving inadequate reasons, or a want of natural justice.

Under section 288, the High Court is limited to quashing the decision of the Secretary of State and remitting the case. It cannot make the decision for the Secretary of State, but can make some fairly explicit directions as to the relevant law. Thus, even if an appeal under section 288 is successful, there is no guarantee that the redetermination will be any more beneficial. The High Court also has a discretion whether to quash a decision and will refuse to do so if it considers that the defect made no difference to the eventual decision.

Any 'person aggrieved' by the decision can use section 288. This includes all parties who appeared at the inquiry or made representations, as well as the appellant, the local planning authority, and owners and occupiers of the site (see *Turner v Secretary of State for the Environment* (1973) 28 P & CR 123).

---

68. See P. Craig [2003] Public Law 753.

Enforcing planning law

Unlike most pollution control legislation it is not in itself an offence to breach planning law. As discussed elsewhere (see p. 442) the offence consists of failing to comply with a notice served by the planning authority about unauthorised development or breach of a condition. The reason for this is that unauthorised development is not necessarily harmful; it would be wasteful to punish activities that have some social, economic or environmental benefit. There are four types of notices used: planning contravention notices, breaches of condition notices, enforcement notices and stop notices. Of these, planning contravention notices and enforcement notices are used most often (around 4,000 each a year), with around 1250 breach of condition notices and 100 stop notices being served annually. (There has been a slowly decreasing use of all these types of notices in the last few years.) Injunctions can also be sought. All are discretionary mechanisms, in the case of enforcement notices and stop notices it being explicitly provided that they 'may' be sought where the authority considers it 'expedient' to do so.[69] Finally, local planning authorities have wide powers to enter land at any reasonable time to ascertain whether there has been a breach of planning control and what remedial steps may be required (ss. 196A-C).

(a) Planning contravention notices

Where it thinks there may be a breach of planning control, a local planning authority may serve these notices on any owner, occupier or other person who is using or carrying out operations on land, seeking information from them relating to its use or occupation (s. 171C). The authority must have some basis for serving the notice: it cannot be used for a 'fishing trip' (*R v Teignbridge DC, ex parte Teignmouth Quay Co.* [1995] JPL 828). It is a summary offence to ignore such a notice, or knowingly to provide incorrect information (s. 171D). Information about suspected breaches can therefore be gathered, enabling the breach to be remedied co-operatively without recourse to formal enforcement procedures. Clearly, the issuing of such a notice will warn the recipient that the local planning authority will take further action if necessary.

(b) Breach of condition notices

These provide for a simple summary procedure whereby a local planning authority may serve written notice on a person responsible for non-compliance with a condition, or having control over the relevant land, requiring compliance in a period of not less than 28 days (s. 187A). Not complying with such a notice leads to a maximum fine of £1,000. Continuation of the non-compliance constitutes a further offence.

---

69. But note the impact of human rights on this exercise of discretion, p. 498; note also that some instances of non-enforcement may result in a successful complaint being taken up with the Local Government Ombudsman.

(c) Enforcement notices

An enforcement notice under section 172 may be served by a local planning authority in respect of unauthorized development. Notices must be served on all owners and occupiers of the relevant premises, including licensees. The enforcement notice must specify the alleged breach, the steps required to remedy it, the reasons for issuing the notice (including details of development plan policies relevant to the decision to issue the notice), and the relevant land. It also has to specify when it takes effect, which must be at least 28 days from the date of service, and a further period after that for compliance with its requirements. At the end of this compliance period, the owner of the land (or in some cases a person with control of, or an interest in, the land) commits a criminal offence if its requirements have not been met (s. 179). The maximum penalty for these offences is £20,000 on summary conviction, or an unlimited fine on indictment. In determining the fine, the court must have regard to any financial benefit accruing to the convicted person. There is no provision for imprisonment. The local planning authority also has a power to enter the land and remedy a breach at the owner's expense (s. 178). Compliance with an enforcement notice does not discharge it: it attaches permanently to the land (s. 181). However, an enforcement notice is a local land charge, so future purchasers of the land should find out about its existence. Each district planning authority must keep a public register of enforcement notices, stop notices and breach of conditions notices (s. 188).

(d) Stop notices

Enforcement notices cannot require immediate action to remedy breaches of planning law. Accordingly, under section 183, the local planning authority may serve a stop notice on anyone carrying on an unlawful activity. This makes it an offence to continue any activity which is specified in the notice once it has come into force, which may be between 3 and 28 days from service. If it is expedient that the breach is stopped before this date, under section 52 of the 2004 Act (inserting ss. 171E–H) a *temporary* stop notice may be served. This comes into effect as soon as a copy of the notice is displayed on the land and effectively buys the local planning authority time before deciding whether further enforcement action is merited. The penalties for stop notices are the same as for breach of an enforcement notice.

There are limits on the application of stop notices. A stop notice—but not a temporary stop notice—is parasitic on an enforcement notice; that is it must be served together with one or after one has been served, and automatically ceases to have effect if the enforcement notice is withdrawn or successfully appealed. It may not be served to stop use as a dwelling-house, or where an activity has been carried on for more than four years. Most importantly, compensation is payable by the local planning authority if the enforcement notice or the stop notice is withdrawn, or if an enforcement notice appeal is allowed on any other ground than ground (a) of section 174(2)—the policy ground (see p. 498 below). This threat of compensation has meant that stop notices have rarely been used (though it is notable that the rules on compensation for temporary stop notices are less wide). Figures indicate that changes under the Planning and Compensation Act 1991, limiting compensation so that it is not payable if the activity stopped is in breach of planning control, have had no significant impact on the number of notices served.

(e) Injunctions

Section 187B provides a specific power for the local planning authority to seek an injunction from the court if it considers it necessary or expedient to restrain an actual or *potential* breach of planning control. The local planning authority is not required to give a cross-undertaking in damages when seeking injunctions (*Kirklees MBC v Wickes Building Supplies Ltd* [1993] AC 227, a decision which removed a serious practical obstacle that had previously restricted their use).

The penalty for breaching an injunction is potentially far higher than for breaching an enforcement notice, since the developer is in contempt of court and imprisonment is a possibility. An injunction is a discretionary remedy and will not be granted by a court unless the circumstances warrant such a strong solution (see Case box 13.2). This seems in practice to restrict their use to powers of last resort, although there is no requirement that other enforcement methods have been exhausted first.

CASE 13.2 *South Bucks District Council v Porter* [2003] UKHL 26

The local planning authority sought an injunction against a gipsy who, without planning permission, lived in a mobile home on land she owned in the Green Belt. The House of Lords held that the courts have *full jurisdiction* to consider whether to grant an injunction, rather than just a reviewing or supervisory function: 'the court is not obliged to grant an injunction because a local authority considers it necessary or expedient for any actual or apprehended breach of planning control'. This was because the courts are public bodies for Human Rights Act purposes, and because of the need to respect the rights of those people most severely affected by the enforcement action, in particular any right to private life, family life and home (Art. 8, ECHR), a right which applies to a home even if it has been created in breach of planning law. The defendant's personal circumstances and any hardship that an injunction might cause must be taken into account and weighed alongside other factors such as harm to the environment, and any injunction must be proportionate to these objectives. One problem arising from injunction cases is that while the courts should not re-open issues of planning judgment, there is obviously some overlap since some of the considerations relating to injunctions are the same as those relating to whether planning permission should have been granted to begin with. Formally, therefore, these cases do signal a slight shift away from the concern of planning law and the courts being about matters of procedure rather than substance.[70] The reason that human rights have greater impact at the enforcement stage is because the consequences are likely to be more severe.

In a related case, an Inspector had, because of Mrs Porter's chronic ill-health and the lack of alternative sites, granted her a personal planning permission (i.e. once she moved from the site the mobile home was to be removed). The Court of Appeal rejected her claim to having 'very special circumstances', the policy test that would have justified Green Belt development, because she had unlawfully occupied the land in breach of planning law. But this was reversed by the House of Lords which held that, although the breach of planning law was a material consideration, the Inspector had acted within his discretion in placing greater weight on her personal circumstances (*South Bucks DC*

---

70. Though cases such as *Tonbridge and Malling District Council v Davis* [2003] EWHC 1069 suggest a high degree of judicial deference to administrative judgments about what is in the public interest, especially where it is a decision of the Secretary of State.

v Secretary of State for Transport, Local Government and the Regions [2004] UKHL 33 ('*Porter (No.2)*')).[71] The House of Lords also ruled that the Inspector's reasons were adequate, restating the law on this issue (see p. 475).

From an environmental perspective, judicial deference can be seen as a double-edged sword. On the one hand it supports the powers of local planning authorities in upholding planning decisions aimed at protecting areas of land like Green Belts. But equally it seems to reinforce the power of LPAs to take enforcement action *against* development motivated by environmental concerns, if that is their wish. In other words, it is not clear that in practice the law has moved that far from a position where what the decision-maker judges as expedient will be upheld.

(f) Immunity from enforcement under planning law

There are time limits for what is called 'taking enforcement action', which means serving an enforcement notice or breach of condition notice (s. 171A). These provide immunity from the service of such a notice where:

- four years have elapsed from the substantial completion of an operational development (s. 171B(1)), or from a change of use *to* a dwellinghouse (s. 171B(2));
- 10 years have elapsed from any other breach of planning control (s. 171B(3)).

Immunity is also granted where there is a certificate of lawfulness of existing use or development, a certificate of lawfulness of proposed use or development, or an established use certificate granted under earlier legislation relating to the alleged breach (see ss. 191–194). These certificates are conclusive as to the lawfulness of the matters to which they relate. This is the case even where an existing use is in contravention of other environmental legislation, for example where there are ongoing breaches of waste management law. This was the decision of the Court of Appeal in *R (Philcox) v Epping Forest District Council* [2002] Env LR 2, which stressed that it is the legality of the use in *planning* terms that is at issue. The Court of Appeal in *Philcox* denied that this would allow waste operators, for example, to benefit from criminal activity.[72]

While the 2004 Act has repealed the previous rule that planning legislation did not extend to development by, or on behalf of, the Crown on Crown land, section 296A has been inserted which preserves Crown immunity from prosecution for any planning offence (and development which enjoyed Crown immunity will continue to do so even if the land is transferred to a private person). Although a local planning authority may serve an enforcement notice—essentially as a way of indicating steps it would like to see taken—a notice cannot be enforced, either by entering land or applying to the court without the permission of the appropriate authority, i.e. the relevant government or the Crown Estate.

(g) Appeals against notices

The Act has elaborate provisions for appeals to the Secretary of State against enforcement notices. Appeals suspend the enforcement notice until after the Secretary of State's decision.

---

71. Note that there was no issue in *Porter No. 2* of the unlawful development interfering directly with anyone else's human rights, which may have altered the outcome, see the *Antonetto*, Case box 13.3.

72. For a view that this is misguided see M. Cull (2002) 4 Env L Rev 117.

This allows the determined operator scope to delay the final operation of an enforcement notice for a considerable time, although there are provisions which seek to prevent this in blatant cases (see s. 289(4A), (4B), and (5C)).

There are seven grounds of appeal set out in section 174(2):

(a) planning permission ought to be granted, or the relevant condition ought to be discharged;

(b) the alleged breach has not in fact taken place;

(c) the matters alleged in the enforcement notice do not in law constitute a breach of planning control;

(d) the matters alleged in the enforcement notice are immune from enforcement action;

(e) failures to carry out the correct procedures in serving the enforcement notice;

(f) the steps required to remedy the breach are excessive;

(g) the time allowed for compliance with the enforcement notice is unreasonably short.

These grounds are very wide, and cover both policy and legal grounds. Ground (a) is effectively an application for planning permission from the Secretary of State, and the major 'policy' ground. Grounds (b)–(e) are collectively known as the 'legal' grounds because they mix issues of fact and law. Ground (f) is also important. A local planning authority may not 'over-enforce', i.e. put the recipient of an enforcement notice in a worse position than before the breach took place. This relates mainly to ancillary uses; the local planning authority may not require a developer to cease a use which would always have been ancillary (see *Mansi v Elstree Rural District Council* (1964) 16 P & CR 153). The procedure is similar to that for planning appeals. The Secretary of State may uphold an enforcement notice and refuse the appeal, quash it (often this involves granting retrospective planning permission), vary its terms, or amend it.

Challenges beyond grounds (a)–(g) above must be brought through judicial review, e.g. if the notice is hopelessly uncertain or some essential procedural requirement has not been met (see *Miller-Mead v Minister of Housing and Local Government* [1963] 2 QB 196). Because of the detailed appeal mechanisms, the validity of an enforcement notice may not be challenged in a prosecution for breach (*R v Wicks* [1997] 2 All ER 801). By contrast, because there are no rights to appeal against a stop notice or a breach of condition notice, the courts have allowed challenges to their validity when prosecutions for ignoring them have been brought (see *R v Jenner* [1983] 1 WLR 873 and *Dilieto v Ealing BC* [1998] 2 All ER 885 respectively).

(h) Enforcement discretion

Only the local planning authority may serve a notice, although the Secretary of State has a reserve power to serve an enforcement notice (s. 182). A number of studies in the 1980s found that the enforcement of planning law was given a very low profile in many local planning authorities (see, e.g., [1986] JPL 482). Many authorities had no one responsible for enforcement. Monitoring of compliance with conditions and agreements was ad hoc and not guaranteed. And the most common method of discovery of a breach was from a complaint from a member of the public rather than from investigation. When it came to taking action, informal methods of solving the problem were favoured, such as warning letters and requests for details of ownership of the land (an easily recognized threat of more formal enforcement action). Even if an enforcement notice was served, there was no guarantee that it would itself be enforced if ignored, with low fine levels discouraging the bringing of court action.

Concerns such as these prompted the Carnwath report (*Enforcing Planning Law* (DoE, 1989)), from which many of the changes to enforcement made under the Planning and Compensation Act 1991 stem. These provided a welcome broadening of the powers at planning authorities' disposal. The centrality of the planning authority's discretion, however, has largely remained unchecked by the national courts (see M. Lewis [2003] JPL 1109), although the European Court of Human Rights has given a judgment on this issue which may have significant implications for national enforcement practice (see Case box 13.3).

CASE 13.3 *Antonetto v Italy* (2003) 36 EHRR 10

A building was constructed on land adjacent to Antonetto's property but the planning permission had been illegally granted and was quashed. Under Italian law, the planning authority was bound to order demolition but failed to do so. A court then ordered the authority to demolish the building but this too was ignored. The Strasbourg Court held that there had been a breach of Article 6, the right to a fair trial, and also, because of the reduction in the value of Antonetto's land because of loss of light and loss of a view,[73] Article 1 of the First Protocol (right to peaceful enjoyment of possessions).

Although this case does not make 'under-enforcement' unlawful—i.e. not every aspect of the breach must be remedied—a failure to enforce may be challengeable if this leads to an unlawful interference with another's human rights and is not justified by some compelling public interest in the development remaining.[74] (There is some doubt about how strong this conclusion is, however, because of the discretionary nature of enforcement under the TCPA 1990 compared to Italian law, although the Strasbourg Court did find that the actions of the Italian planning authority were per se unlawful, and not just unlawful because it did not follow a national judicial order.) This provides a minimum baseline of protection from unlawful development which is environmentally harmful, but only where the European Convention on Human Rights provides limited protection for the natural environment—as an incident of private property or where serious health impacts arise. So it will be of limited use where e.g. there is unlawful development in the Green Belt not directly affecting any neighbouring property. And, in the case of human rights, note that even where neighbours are affected, there is a very high threshold to overcome, since it would have to shown that any interference was both serious and not justified (see e.g. *Lough v First Secretary of State* [2004] EWHC 23, a case about overshadowing from a high-rise development). In practice, only claims based on procedural grounds are ever likely to succeed

---

Under-enforcement is specifically approved of in official planning guidance on enforcement. And recent years have seen a significant decrease in the numbers of enforcement notices issued under s. 172, and a reduction in the number of enforcement injunctions granted and

---

73. The loss of a view is not per se actionable in tort or property law; see e.g. *Phipps v Pears* [1965] 1 QB 76. The effect of *Antonetto* is probably very limited in relation to landscape conservation, since the focus is the deprivation of private property rights (see also S. Crow [2001] JPL 1349). Note also the similarities between Antonetto and the idea that the planning authority might be liable in tort for authorizing or continuing a nuisance, see p. 363.

74. For more detailed discussion of this case and its implications see J-J. Paradissis [2002] JPL 674.

(in 1997/8) a corresponding increase in the number of injunctions refused. The extent to which economic considerations influence enforcement can be seen by survey evidence that enforcement is more common in South East England than in depressed urban areas.[75] As part of its recent planning reforms Government mooted the possibility of removing local planning authorities enforcement discretion (at least for major breaches), and making breaches of development control law a criminal offence, but these proposals have so far come to nothing.[76]

Powers where there is no breach of planning law

There are some courses of action available to the local planning authority where there is no breach of the planning legislation. Normally these require the payment of compensation for the loss of any rights which have been taken away, so they are little used. But they are of importance as reserve powers where there is something creating an environmental problem that may not be removed or controlled in any other way.

Under section 102 a local planning authority may serve a discontinuance order, which may require that any use be discontinued or that any buildings or works be removed or altered. Under section 97 a local planning authority may revoke or modify a planning permission that has already been granted. In both these cases there are provisions for a public local inquiry to be held and compensation to be paid. The Secretary of State must also confirm these orders before they have effect and has reserve powers to make either type. Indeed, in March 1991, the Secretary of State took the exceptional step of making an order revoking a planning permission which Poole DC had granted to itself for housing on land designated a site of special scientific interest (SSSI) on Canford Heath in Dorset (thus belatedly rendering unnecessary the litigation in *R v Poole Borough Council, ex parte Beebee* [1991] JPL 643).

The local planning authority may also enter into a planning contribution in order to remove an existing building or use, although obviously the owner will require something of benefit in return.

Planning, the environment, and risk

The place of the town and country planning system amongst other tools for environmental protection has already been discussed in outline (see p. 242), as have some more specific issues concerning the relationship between the planning and pollution control regimes (see p. 790). But the planning system also has an important role to play as regards more general issues of environmental risk regulation.

In the first place, planning law helps to shape the way in which environmental harm is conceptualized. Its relative openness and participatory nature, and a number of high profile

---

75. Enforcement may also be compromised by the fact that modern planning, especially for larger developments, is a collaborative process between private developers and planning authorities, see p. 443.

76. DTLR, *Planning: Delivering a Fundamental Change* (2001) para. 5.69; ODPM, *Review of the Planning Enforcement System in England* (2002).

public inquiries such as Sizewell B, have certainly provided valuable opportunities for public expressions of environmental concern.[77] But these features have also contributed to the framing of the public's terms of reference about development and its environmental costs and benefits. This latter role is especially important in recognising public perceptions of risk and uncertainty, regardless of their foundation (see generally Chapter 3).

Secondly, in relation to public fears it is important to distinguish between risks and uncertainties, i.e. between those matters that are feared because of some quantifiable risk, and things which are feared where the odds of something adverse happening are not even known. With the former, there was an indication in *Gateshead MBC v Secretary of State for the Environment* (1995) (see p. 790) that the courts would take a strict line, when Glidewell LJ stated that 'if in the end public concern is not justified, it cannot be conclusive'. But this view was disagreed with by the Court of Appeal in *Newport BC v Secretary of State for Wales and Browning Ferris Ltd* [1998] Env LR 174, which reaffirmed the view that public perception of risk, even where unsubstantiated, could be a material planning consideration, the approach that has been followed in more recent case law.[78] Both cases, however, turned on the policy requirement at the time that 'demonstrable harm' to an important interest must be shown if planning permission was to be refused, a test which has now been slightly diluted (see para. 40, PPG 1, 1997). In any event, one reason why the Secretary of State has the final say in planning matters is precisely to override local opposition if this is deemed to be in the national interest.

What the courts may be more willing to do is hold that a planning authority has illegally ignored the odds in some way and intervene. This was the case in *Envirocor Waste Holdings Ltd v Secretary of State for the Environment, ex parte Humberside CC and British Cocoa Mills (Hull) Ltd* [1996] Env LR 49, a dispute about different calculations of the likely occurrence of a waste transfer station tainting the produce of a nearby factory. In that case, it was possible for the judge to overturn the Inspector's decision, since there were various ways in which the Inspector's calculation of risk could not be sustained. Another case where the courts have overturned an Inspector's risk assessment is *T Mobile (UK) Ltd v First Secretary of State* [2004] EWHC 1713, a challenge to the refusal to grant planning permission for a shared mobile phone mast near to three primary schools. In this case government policy guidance (PPG8) set out how to calculate the odds—in accordance with international standards. Although the emissions from the masts would fall within these limits, the Inspector thought that insufficient reassurances had been given about material harm to living conditions. But the judge held that the policy guidance placed the emphasis on actual risk rather than perceived risk, and the Inspector erred in having regard to the latter.[79]

A general difficulty, however, remains in that it may be difficult to distinguish between risk and uncertainty. There is often a gloss of certainty about some risk calculations, and many assessments of risks are little better than glorified value judgements. Conversely, with some small-scale developments, it may be that what are better seen as quantifiable risks are, because of lack of available data, presented as uncertainties. In cases where there is a regulatory view about the assessment of risk, however, this view may carry considerable

---

77. R. Grove-White (1991) 18 JLS 32.

78. *Trevett v Secretary of State* [2002] EWHC 2696, and see also the *Jodie Phillips* case in Box 13.7.

79. This decision may be subject to an appeal, not just by the local planning authority but also the First Secretary of State (the planning minister).

weight. Indeed, in *R v Tandridge District Council, ex parte al Fayed* [1999] 1 PLR 104 the judge held that 'strong weight' should be given to any such assessment, especially where a particular issue of national policy was at stake such that there was a need for a national consistency of approach to decision-making. An appeal in this case was dismissed (see [2000] Env LR D23), although in the Court of Appeal both sides agreed that objective unjustified fears could be material.

As regards the ultimate response of the planning system to issues of risk and uncertainty, there are essentially three options: ignore the fear, grant permission subject to appropriate conditions, or refuse the application. An uncertainty might conceivably be ignored, but ignoring a risk will make any decision liable to be overturned. The real issue then is whether the risks of environmental harm are managed or avoided. Arguably, PPG1 (1997) took the 'management' approach, advocating the prevention of harm through appropriate decisions about the siting of development and using the planning system to minimise impact.[80] Owens argues that this really combines the more traditional 'technical fix' attitude with a 'spatial fix' approach: if development goes in the least harmful place it is acceptable.[81] This approach obviously runs counter to the notion of environmental carrying capacity in relation to natural environmental resources. It also contributes to the inadequacy of the planning system as an effective mechanism for reversing harmful environmental trends.[82]

Finally, the importance of taking a wider view on risk regulation cannot be avoided. In cases like *Envirocor*, if the waste transfer station was not built, this posed serious regulatory problems for waste management in the area. More broadly, in relation to house building, for example, environmental concerns are not exhausted by the location of the 3.8 million projected new households, but also include concerns about the impact of a doubling of aggregates extraction which may be needed to satisfy such a demand. Regulating this calls for strategic assessment, something which can only really be tackled at a level above that even of development plans (on strategic environmental assessment see p. 549).

Planning and hazardous substances

The storage of hazardous substances was traditionally dealt with under normal planning procedures. There were, however, many occasions when the storage of large amounts of hazardous materials fell outside the scope of existing controls as it was either permitted automatically under the then General Development Order or did not amount to develop-ment at all (under the Use Classes Order or the general definition of development). Thus, it became necessary to control the siting of hazardous materials under a separate but complementary set of controls.

The Planning (Hazardous Substances) Act 1990 requires hazardous substances consent to be obtained if hazardous substances are present on, over or under land in an amount at, or above, a controlled quantity. The Act gives hazardous substances authorities (HSAs), usually the same body as the local planning authority, the opportunity to consider whether the proposed storage or use of the substance is appropriate for the location, having regard to

---

80. See S. Owens (1997) 68 TPR 293.
81. See also the discussion of alternatives when a planning application is being determined in Box 13.7.
82. A broadly similar approach is taken in PPS1.

the risks arising to persons in the surrounding area, the wider implications for the community and other material considerations.

The provisions are not intended to duplicate the effect of other statutory controls. Thus, for example, the Act does not apply to controlled or radioactive wastes. The Planning (Hazardous Substances) Regulations 1992 (SI 1992/656) outline the categories of substances regulated under the Act and the level at which they become subject to its provisions.

The Act operates by requiring any person wishing to store any listed substances at or above prescribed levels to obtain prior consent from the HSA. The conditions attached to any consent granted will be strongly influenced by the opinion of the Health and Safety Executive, which must be sought alongside other statutory consultees (under the GDPO). There is in effect a strong presumption in favour of the HSE's views. Non-compliance with a consent, or acting without a consent, is an offence. There are defences where the defendant took all reasonable precautions and exercised all due diligence to avoid committing the offence, or did not know and had no reason to believe that an offence had been committed.

Amendments to the regime were made to give effect to Directive 96/82 on the control of major-accident hazards involving dangerous substances (the 'Seveso II' Directive). The Planning (Control of Major-Accident Hazards) Regulations 1999 (SI 1999/981) make minor changes to the basic preventive approach already followed, including a requirement that the relevant Nature Conservancy Council is consulted where there is risk to an area of 'particular natural sensitivity or interest'. For guidance see Circular 04/00. The Development Plan Regulations 1999 also include provisions which require development plans to have regard to preventing major-accident hazards.

CHAPTER SUMMARY

The main features of town and country planning have been described at the start of this chapter. These are not repeated here, and the following therefore highlights, and in some cases expands upon, some key themes of the chapter in relation to the nature of planning and its relevance to the environment.

1 Town and country planning law is not a specialised environmental protection regime, but it contributes to environmental protection in increasingly important ways. 'The environment', and now 'sustainable development', have become the dominant narratives of planning (even if this has not been translated into real-world environmental improvements through the planning system).

2 Planning law can control damaging activities which are not generally subject to specific environmental controls (such as noise and light pollution, or the destruction of habitat outside protected areas), or by acting in conjunction with specialist control regimes such as govern waste management or IPPC. But if planning permission is given it can also 'trump' other environmental controls.

3 Planning works mainly through anticipatory controls, though ongoing conditions can be imposed—and ongoing agreements entered into—for environmental reasons.

4 Some activities with potentially harmful environmental consequences are, for historic reasons and because of the complexity involved, not subject to planning controls (the main one being the use of land for agriculture).

5   Even under a plan-led system, planning remains a highly discretionary discipline where individual applications are considered on their merits. This emphasis on discretion, and the centrality of the Secretary of State, are the two most striking features of the British planning system.

6   All plan-making bodies must now exercise their functions 'with the objective of contributing to the achievement of sustainable development'. This duty does not apply to local planning authorities, or to the Secretary of State, when they determine individual planning applications. This is to focus issues about the sustainability of development onto the strategic level of decision-making (e.g. what are the waste management requirements for the county?) rather than on individual planning applications (e.g. is this incinerator 'sustainable'?).

7   Under the 1947 Act, planning had redistributive as well as reconstructive dreams. The former have all but disappeared, and major development and re-development is now generally pursued by private developers in conjunction with planning authorities.

8   The public interest is therefore served by facilitating the market rather than by constraining it. Hence the planning system is always responding to decisions by developers about the most profitable sites to locate new development. The idea that the economy, and its environmental consequences, can be 'planned for' in advance is hopelessly optimistic.

9   There is a constant tension, in making planning decisions, between speed and meaningful public participation. Recent legislative reforms have continued to emphasise the former, while the courts have shown some signs of protecting the latter.

10   Part of the reason why the courts have done so may be an increasing concern with procedural rights, born of a decade of increasingly purposive engagement with the law on environmental impact assessment.

11   As with other areas of environmental criminal law, enforcement tends to be selective but the penalties that may be imposed can be severe (including the removal of buildings built in breach of permission).

12   The 'rights culture' influences both the preceding points; it both provides a major context for upholding participatory rights, but can also operate against strict enforcement of planning controls because of the need to ensure that sanctions which potentially deprive people of their homes are proportionate to the ends being pursued (which may lead to environmental blight).

Q QUESTIONS

1   'Planning law should allow development to proceed unless it will cause harm'. 'Planning law should positively pursue better environmental quality'. To what extent is planning law characterized by either of these statements?

2   In its 23rd Report on *Environmental Planning*, the RCEP proposed that the town and country planning system be given a statutory purpose 'to facilitate the achievement of legitimate economic and social goals while ensuring that the quality of the environment is safeguarded and, wherever appropriate, enhanced' (para. 8.33). What would the advantages and disadvantages of this proposal be?

3   To what extent might 'light pollution' be controlled by planning law? (You might find P. Jewkes [1998] JPL 10 and D. Hughes and M. Taylor (2004) 16 JEL 215 useful here.)

4   What role do economic instruments play in planning? Consider in particular planning obligations and contributions.

5   What is the relationship between planning law and pollution control? Could this be improved upon?

6   The Dobry Report (1975) described enforcement as planning's 'weakest link'. Is this still true? What further reforms might be made?

7   Is the 'possessive individualism' of human rights law a challenge to controlling and managing development in the public interest?

8   (Group exercise). There are proposals to place a mobile phone mast on the roof of a historic church. Divide into groups advising the developer, the local planning authority and nearby residents. What are the key planning issues? What further information would be needed?

 FURTHER READING

There are some excellent texts on planning policy, their value to the law student being that the high policy content of planning law makes them more accessible than normal here. The best general introductory text is B. Cullingworth and V. Nadin, *Town and Country Planning in Britain* (13th edn London: Routledge, 2002), and environmental law students studying planning law in any depth will profit greatly from, at a minimum, chs 1 and 2. Y. Rydin, *Urban and Environmental Planning in the UK* (2nd edn London: Macmillan, 2003) also provides a good overview. C. Miller (ed.), *Planning and Environmental Protection* (Oxford: Hart Publishing, 2001) looks at the role of land use planning in the main areas of environmental law, while stimulating thoughts on how planning might better accommodate more radically environmental development are offered by S. Fairlie, *Low Impact Development* (Jon Carpenter, 1996), coupled with *Defining Rural Sustainability* (available via <www.tlio.org.uk>). The extent of the changes to planning that have occurred since the 1947 Act are captured in B. Cullingworth (ed.), *British Planning: 50 Years of Urban and Regional Policy* (Athlone, 1999), with valuable chapters by Professors Grant and Purdue on compensation issues and the role of the courts respectively.

Still the most useful conceptual framework for thinking about planning law—a framework which is just as valuable when thinking about the important reforms which post-date its publication, notably the impact of human rights law and the 2004 Act—is P. McAuslan, *Ideologies of Planning Law* (Oxford: Pergamon Press, 1980), especially chs 1 and 6. The incorporation of sustainable development concerns are discussed by M. Stallworthy, *Sustainability, Land Use and the Environment* (M. Cavendish, 2002), especially chs 4, 6, and 7. Sustainability issues are also the theoretical focus of S. Owens, ' "Giants in the path": Planning, sustainability and environmental values' (1997) 68 TPR 293, and S. Owens and R. Cowell, *Land and Limits* (London: Routledge, 2001).

In terms of general texts on planning law, J. Cameron Blackhall, *Planning Law and Practice* (2nd edn London: Cavendish, 1999) is a very readable introduction. V. Moore, *A Practical Approach to Planning Law* (9th edn Oxford: Oxford University Press, 2004) also contains useful practical insights but focuses more on the exposition of principle through case-law rather than on policy considerations. Amongst other texts, Duxbury, *Telling and Duxbury's Planning Law and Procedure* (12th edn London: Butterworths, 2002) is readable, but relatively less comprehensive in coverage. Note that any text which predates the Planning and Compulsory Purchase Act 2004 must be treated with caution; it is likely that all the texts mentioned above will soon be revised to take the 2004 Act into account. Until then, useful further reading can be found in House of Commons Transport, Local Government and the Regions Select Committee, *Planning Green Paper*, 13th Report, 2001–2, HC 476-I and II (2002).

For completeness, and to ensure an up to date account of the law, the *Encyclopaedia of Planning Law* (London: Sweet & Maxwell, looseleaf) includes all the relevant statutory and non-statutory material and is updated monthly, with insightful annotations and analysis. Other useful sources for keeping up to date are the *Journal of Planning and Environment Law* (JPL), which contains information on policy documents, Ministerial decisions and case law analysis, and publications like *Planning and the Estates Gazette*. More discursive pieces on policy are contained in the *Town Planning Review* (TPR) and the *Journal of Environmental Planning and Management*.

Various angles on planning and environmental risk regulation are discussed in R. Grove-White, 'Land use law and the environment' [1991] Journal of Law and Society 32; N. Stanley, 'Public concern: the decision-makers' dilemma' [1998] JPL 919 and C. Hilson, 'Planning Law and Public Perceptions of Risk [2004] JPL 1638.

@ WEB LINKS

As well as providing the text of the key primary and secondary legislation (a source such as Westlaw which includes the various amendments to the TCPA is essential) the web is the easiest way to access central government policy guidance and circulars. Familiarization with these— which are in the process of being revised and streamlined—is usually imperative. For England, see <www.odpm.gov.uk>; for the devolved administrations, see <www.scotland.gov.uk>, <www-.wales.gov.uk.>, and <www.doeni.gov.uk>. A very useful portal is <www.planningportal.gov.uk> which is managed by the Planning Inspectorate <www.planning-inspectorate.gov.uk> and which contains information on the planning system, links to on-line development plans (it is worth reading a development plan to get a feel for what they contain), and which allows planning appeals to be tracked.

14 Environmental assessment

→ **Overview**

In the last 30 years or so, environmental assessment (EA) has emerged as one of the key environmental law mechanisms. The essence of EA is that information about likely environmental impacts of things like development projects, and now also plans and programmes, is properly considered before potentially harmful decisions are made. In this sense, it is a preventive tool. But above all it is a procedural technique, which means that damaging development can in theory still proceed. This chapter looks at the international, EC and national laws relating to EA, and the explosion of litigation that has occurred in the last few years.

In looking at environmental assessment, it may be useful to consider various issues and tensions—which we have looked at in Chapters 4, 8 and 10—to inform your reading and understanding of EA. The first of these is the tension between adhering strictly to procedural rules, and pragmatism in reaching decisions that are considered sensible (and doing so in a reasonable time). Beyond this, you might think about the extent to which the value of EA lies in one or more of the following: (1) improving the quality of environmental decisions, e.g. by preventing environmental harm and integrating the environment into decision-making; (2) producing more legitimate environmental decisions; (3) raising public confidence in environmental decisions, and/or (4) giving individuals rights to participate in environmental decision-making. Finally (though related to the previous consideration), is EA used—by developers, decision-makers or the public—in a defensive or a purposive way?

Alongside this chapter helpful companion sources are the Environmental Impact Assessment (EIA) and the Strategic Environmental Assessment (SEA) Directives (you can get these from the European Commission website—see Web links below); the core implementing Regulations for EIA (the Town and Country Planning (Environmental Impact Assessment) (England and Wales) Regulations 1999 (there are similar regulations for Scotland and for Northern Ireland) and, on SEA, the Assessment of Plans and Programmes Regulations 2004 (SI 2004/1633). A further useful source is government guidance (in England, Circular 02/99 on EIA; and (in relation to planning) *SEA: Guidance for Local Planning Authorities* (2003)).

At the end of this chapter you will:

✔ Understand what EA is and how it works.
✔ Appreciate some of the key issues and challenges in using procedural law to protect the environment.
✔ Be able to evaluate how EA is used in practice.
✔ Have gained an insight into the implementation of one of the key EC environmental directives.

What is environmental assessment?

On a simple level, the legal mechanisms of environmental impact assessment (EIA) and strategic environmental assessment (SEA) (which we refer to together as 'environmental assessment') are merely information-gathering exercises enabling decision-makers to understand the environmental effects of certain projects (in the case of EIA) and plans or programmes (SEA) before deciding whether or not to grant consent or approval for that proposal. On this level, however, there is little to distinguish this concept from, say, the normal planning process under which environmental effects are a material consideration in deciding whether or not to grant planning permission. Indeed, prior to specific legislation on environmental assessment there were examples where detailed assessments of the environmental effects of developments had been carried out, for instance in relation to power stations and motorways, and government has been advocating environmental policy appraisal since the early 1990s.

The innovation behind the formal EIA and SEA processes is the systematic use of the best objective sources of information and the emphasis on the use of the best techniques to gather that information. In recent years the importance of allowing meaningful public participation in the decision-making process has also been stressed (see Chapter 10). Thus the ideal EIA, for example, would involve a totally bias-free collation of information about environmental impact, produced in a coherent, sound and complete form, considering impact in an integrated manner. It should then allow the decision-maker and members of the public to scrutinize the proposal, assess the weight of predicted effects and suggest modifications or mitigation (or refusal) where appropriate.

Thus, environmental assessment is both a technique and a process. EIAs and SEAs are inanimate rather than tangible. The key point is that strictly the 'assessment' is undertaken by the decision-maker on the basis of *environmental information* supplied to it. This information consists in part of an *environmental statement* prepared by the developer (or more likely, by hired consultants) which details at least the main environmental impacts of the project and any mitigating measures which are proposed to reduce the significance of those impacts. (With SEA, the equivalent document is termed the *environmental report*.) But just as importantly the environmental information also includes other information supplied by various statutory consultees (e.g. the Environment Agency, English Nature), independent third parties (such as local conservation and amenity groups), members of the public and even the decision-maker itself. So it is worth stressing that the developer does not produce an environmental assessment (a mistake even some judges still make); the decision-maker carries out the assessment on the basis of environmental information supplied.

BOX 14.1 **Key terms**

Environmental Impact Assessment (EIA)

A formal procedure for decision-makers to gather environmental information about projects, and for this information to be taken into account in decision-making.

Strategic Environmental Assessment (SEA)

In EC law, the assessment of plans and programmes in certain sectors where these set a framework for future development consent of projects subject to EIA, or which are required under the EC Habitats Directive. Arguably a procedure of wider use.

Environmental Statement (ES) and Environmental Report

A statement, prepared by the developer, of the main environmental impacts of the project and any proposed mitigating measures to reduce the significance of those impacts (for SEA, the equivalent term is environmental report).

Environmental Information

Information from a range of sources about the environmental impact of the development. Includes the environmental statement or report and information from statutory consultees and the public.

Environmental assessment should also begin as early as possible when projects are being planned, or plans and programmes mooted. A related point is that EIA and SEA should be *iterative* processes, where information that comes to light is fed back into the decision-making process. This has two dimensions: first, a truly iterative process would ensure that the very *design* of the project, plan or programme would be amended in the light of the information gathered. Secondly, and also ideally, it would also involve some kind of monitoring of environmental impact after consent or approval has been given. It may be that for certain activities post-project monitoring is a requirement of international law, but in the EC neither of the main laws in this area—the 1985 EIA Directive and the 2001 SEA Directive—currently require this, though the latter does require an ongoing consideration of environmental information during plan-making. But at present, as a matter of law EA is wholly concerned with likely environmental impacts identified *before* consent or approval is given. (Whether some of the unspecific claims made in environmental statements could be monitored in practice is debatable, but turning this around we could say that statements should not contain claims that cannot be audited.)[1]

Crucially, EIA and SEA are inherently *procedural* mechanisms. Although they are intended to be preventive (and, some would argue, also precautionary), there is nothing that requires the decision-maker to refuse a development project, or amend a development plan, because negative environmental impacts are highlighted by the environment assessment. Nor do EIA or SEA require conditions to be imposed on project consents, or plans to be amended, to mitigate or compensate for any such impact. There is therefore a marked contrast with other legal requirements to carry out assessments which sometimes provide for this. A good example is the duty to undertake an 'appropriate assessment' under

---

1. For figures on the vagueness, or otherwise lack of auditability, of claims see C. Wood, *Environmental Impact Assessment: A Comparative Review* (2nd edn London: Pearson, 2002). This issue might be best dealt with not by a legal obligation on developers, but by institutional change, e.g. by an Environmental Assessment Commission scrutinizing the assessment process, as recommended by the RCEP (*Environmental Planning*, 23rd Report, 2002, para. 7.35).

Article 6 of the EC Habitats Directive, which is coupled with a duty to take certain compensatory or mitigatory measures if this assessment reveals that harm to a protected species or habitat may occur (see p. 830). So, for example, following a valid EIA it will only be by showing that a decision-maker has erred as a matter of general administrative law (e.g. by failing to consider significant impacts raised by the assessment process) that an authorization for a project might be reviewable. By formally imposing no constraints on decision-makers as regards their eventual decisions,[2] therefore, EA is a particularly flexible tool of environmental law. Its importance lies in its ability to elevate attention to environmental impacts in decision-making and induce reflection on the way in which impacts might be reduced. In this sense, EA is one manifestation of the turn towards more reflexive forms of environmental law (see p. 266). In trying to achieve these aims, however, EA imposes strict procedural requirements which contrast sharply with its formal lack of stipulation about eventual outcomes.

Environmental assessment in international law and practice

While most of this chapter is concerned with the environmental assessment regimes at EC and national level, EIA-type requirements are now found in many international agreements, and a number of global and regional organizations—such as the World Bank—now bind themselves by EIA requirements (see Box 14.2). (SEA has recently been the subject of an international convention, the 2003 Kiev Protocol.) EIA is also now firmly established in a wide range of national regimes, to the point where, taking international and national developments together, EIA has arguably reached the status either of a general principle of law or even a requirement of customary international law. Support for this view is found in the numerous references to EIA in Agenda 21 and the World Summit on Sustainable Development's Plan of Implementation, both as a general obligation on states and as a tool to be used in relation to many specific sectors. Perhaps more importantly Principle 17 of the Rio Declaration, in addition to its general advocacy for preventive and participatory measures, states that:

Environmental impact assessment, as a national instrument, shall be undertaken for proposed activities that are likely to have a significant adverse impact on the environment and are subject to a decision of a competent national authority.[3]

BOX 14.2 **The World Bank and EIA**

Any generally accepted international legal requirement for states to conduct an EA applies primarily to development projects with transboundary risks. But at international level,

---

2. Notably, early advocacy of EIA, contained in the 1982 World Charter for Nature, did have this substantive edge.

3. On the status of this Declaration see p. 157 above. Further support came at the 1997 UN General Assembly 'Rio+5' summit, which declared the principle of EIA to be on a par with the polluter pays, precautionary and common but differentiated responsibilities principles.

assessment standards can, in some cases, go beyond dealing with transboundary harms and apply to national development projects that do not generate cross-border risks, e.g. the damming of an internal river for hydro-electricity generation. A leading example of this is the way in which funding from the World Bank is now made subject to EIA. Since 1989, under its Operational Directive (now Operational Policy (OP) 4.01: *Environmental Assessment* (1999)), the World Bank has made the *consideration* of EIA a formal requirement for any of its operations. In particular, Category A projects—those expected to have significant adverse environmental impacts that are sensitive, diverse, or unprecedented—must have a more comprehensive assessment; Category B projects require less scrutiny, and projects below this threshold (projects likely to have minimal or no adverse environmental impact) do not need to be assessed. Although the actual assessment is undertaken by the borrower, at least for Category A projects independent experts must also be involved. Strictly, the Operational Directive is a set of guidelines for World Bank staff, and an aim of this form of EIA is as much capacity building in environmental management in the host country as it is a normative standard.

Nevertheless, experience of this form of EIA shows some of the problems with procedural environmental law in a global setting. In many developing countries without traditions of pluralistic decision-making, for example, expectations of public participation may be low, and there may be limited scope for giving effective voice to those most affected. Indeed, a major criticism of the original 1989 rules was their silence on the provision of information to the public and guaranteed rights for the public to participate in the decision-making process. Now, discussions about the scope of any impact statement are, to encourage NGO involvement, often held in capital cities rather than 'on site'. Evidence suggests that participation requirements have often been overlooked or glossed over, in part because of a lack of receptiveness of World Bank staff to local customary norms, though the guidelines now place greater emphasis on NGO consultation for all Category A or B projects. There is, though, a right to challenge World Bank decisions before an Inspection Panel, and there are examples where the Panel has held that the Operational Directive had not been followed correctly. In one case, for example, funding was withdrawn where there was a failure to complete an EIA before the project was appraised and negotiated, and because the project would commence before necessary institutional structures for monitoring the environmental impacts were in place.

Looking at the EIA of World Bank funding, therefore, shows some of the general challenges for EIA; selecting a means of deciding which projects require EIA (screening), deciding who will carry out the assessment (the proponent of the project, or independent experts), and ensuring that the assessment itself can be followed through into decision-making and subsequent management, while establishing legal rules—about participation and access to justice—that are effective but also sensitive to national legal and administrative traditions, and cultural and political realities.

Source: Kevin R. Gray, 'International Environmental Impact Assessment', Colorado Journal of International Environmental Law and Policy (Winter 2000) 83, and changes to the Operational Policy since then to date.

What 'adverse impact on the environment' means here is not specified, but it would appear to include not merely transboundary environmental harm, but also harm to the global environment (e.g. climate change)[4] and to domestic environments e.g. a decision to

4. Though the Climate Change Convention has a specific provision about EA; see Art. 4(1)(f).

damage a cherished landscape. In this sense, therefore, EIA may represent a sort of common environmental best practice standard in relation to the behaviour of states working towards agreed objectives, since the formulation in the Rio Declaration does not appear to be limited to cases of transboundary harm.[5]

That said, EIA in international law has developed primarily from the obligation on states to cooperate with each other, in good faith, in mitigating transboundary environmental risks, an obligation that rests on prior consultation based on adequate information. (Failure to carry out an EIA may also make it difficult for a state to show that it had exercised 'due diligence' in controlling or preventing foreseeable harm.) As Birnie and Boyle have noted:[6]

Without prior assessment there can be no meaningful notification and consultation in most cases of environmental risk. The duty, in other words, is not merely to notify what is known but to know what needs to be notified.

In response to this line of reasoning, the International Court of Justice has given qualified support for the entrenchment of EIA into international law, at least in relation to transboundary harm. In the *Nuclear Tests II* case (*New Zealand v France* [1995] ICJ Rep. 288), Judge Weeramantry thought that transboundary EIA had 'reached the level of general recognition at which this Court should take notice of it' and his dissenting opinion held that an EIA of French plans to resume underground nuclear tests in the Pacific was required. An indication of the pace with which EIA has become part of international environmental law, however, can be seen from the *Danube Dam* case only two years later (*Case concerning the Gabčíkovo-Nagymaros Project (Hungary/Slovakia)* 37 ILM (1998) 162, see p. 160) where the majority of the ICJ interpreted the Treaty between Hungary and Slovakia as requiring the parties together to 'look afresh' at the environmental effects of the project. This seems to require, as the concurring opinion of Judge Weeramantry expressed it, that there is a duty on states of 'continuous environmental impact assessment'—continual assessment of environmental impact in the light of modern knowledge—and that this is a component of states' procedural obligations in relation to sustainable development (his opinion having argued that sustainable development is a principle of customary international law).

This approach is notable because it goes beyond what is generally required when decisions about consenting harmful activities are being taken. For example, at national level, EIA only needs to be undertaken when the initial application for consent is made (though SEA will require assessment of plans which, in their nature, are likely to be revised every few years). But it is also worth stressing that the ICJ seems to be conceiving of this duty on states to assess environmental impact as being a technical matter, rather than one which involves public participation and the right of the public to have their views taken into account. Whether international EIA law is simply a harmonization of existing state practice is considered in more depth in Box 14.3.

A further example of EIA being required under international law, this time under a specific convention, is Article 206 of the UN Convention on the Law of the Sea which provides that:

When states have reasonable grounds for believing that planned activities under their jurisdiction

---

5. See also Art. 14 of the 1992 Convention on Biological Diversity.
6. *International Law and the Environment* (2nd edn Oxford: Oxford University Press, 2002), 133.

or control may cause substantial pollution of or significant and harmful changes to the marine environment, they shall, as far as practicable, assess the potential effects of such activities on the marine environment.

Again, this is quite a technical—rather than participatory—formulation of EIA. It has been the subject of a dispute between Ireland and the UK over the authorization of a plant to manufacture mixed oxide (MOX) fuel at the Sellafield nuclear complex, the radioactive discharge from which has proven controversial. Ireland argued that the UK had breached Article 206 both because its 1993 assessment did not consider various potential impacts on the Irish Sea and because the assessment had not been updated to take into account developments between 1993 and the authorization of the plant in 2001. When provisional measures were being decided, Judge Mensah (in a separate opinion) took a weak view of EA, seemingly holding that if the UK had violated its procedural obligations then these could be remedied even if the authorisation was not halted in the interim, whereas the minority judge took a stronger view of Article 206 holding that more extensive provisional measures were justified because of the centrality of EIA to what was described as 'the international law of prevention' (see further Boxes 6.5 and 18.2).

What little international case law there is, therefore, indicates that EIA in international law is a procedural requirement that emerges, by inference, from substantive obligations owed between states (but see Box 14.3). But where it is required—and this is perhaps only in cases of transboundary risk to the environment of other states or where provided for under specific treaties as with harm to the marine environment—states may need to undertake a technical assessment (though not necessarily one that involves the wider public), and may have to revisit existing agreements in the light of new knowledge gained from an EIA-type process.

The major difficulty with international EIA law, however, comes in the detail. In specific environmental treaties, as the following example from Article 14(1) of the Biodiversity Convention illustrates, the obligation to carry out EIA may be couched in, depending on one's point of view, either highly flexible or extraordinarily vague terms:

Each Contracting Party, as far as possible and as appropriate, shall: (a) Introduce appropriate procedures requiring environmental impact assessment of its proposed projects that are likely to have significant adverse effects on biological diversity with a view to avoiding or minimizing such effects and, where appropriate, allow for public participation in such procedures.

Formulations like this mean that, as is often the case with customary international environmental law (see p. 152), it may be possible to identify an international principle, but pinning down what it actually requires in real-world situations is difficult. Three problems in particular can be mentioned:

• determining which kinds of activities need to be assessed;

• determining the degree of environmental risk needed to trigger an EIA; and

• determining the procedural requirements for an EIA.

The first of these has two distinct components. First, it might be thought desirable to establish, in advance, the kinds of activities that might be subject to EIA. The regional 1991

UNECE Convention on EIA in a Transboundary Context (the 'Espoo' Convention) does this by listing a range of activities that fall within its remit, such as power stations and nuclear installations. This is backed up by further provisions that allow for projects to fall within its remit if the parties agree, and the Convention sets out criteria (based on size, location and effects) to assist the parties in doing this. But most international environmental treaties, like the Biodiversity Convention, tend not to be so specific, making their application to particular projects uncertain. Secondly, international environmental law is only now embracing strategic environmental assessment (see the 2003 Kiev Protocol to the Espoo Convention), but is generally still wedded to assessing individual activities or projects.

The degree of risk needed to trigger an EIA is especially problematic. The usual formulation, as seen above, is that there must be a likelihood of significant adverse effects on the environment (or some particular aspect of the environment).[7] An obvious difficulty, inherent it must be said to EA law generally, is that the assessment process is there to identify the risks and their significance, so any attempt in advance to set thresholds for when EIA will be required will have a strong element of circularity to it. What is 'significant', therefore, is particularly open-ended, and while instances such as the environmental impact caused by the unilateral damming of the Danube will be fairly clear cut, in many cases there may be uncertainty about how damaging the effects of projects or activities will be.

The actual procedural requirements of EIA in international law are also somewhat vague. For example, what level of information should be provided? And who should be consulted? Only in very limited instances has the type of information that should be generated been spelt out.[8] This has been criticised as falling some way behind accepted national practice (see, e.g., p. 533), but more telling is the criticism that any assessment process which excluded details of impacts, mitigation measures and alternatives would simply fall short of what is required of states to cooperate in good faith on transboundary matters. There has been a tendency to limit consultation requirements to activities near state borders, which seems of limited utility for many projects (the Chernobyl nuclear plant, for instance, is not near an international frontier). Consultation requirements where common space such as the high seas is concerned can also be very limited. There are, though, some signs of improvements; the Espoo Convention requires parties to consider 'more remote proposed activities which could give rise to significant transboundary effects far removed from the site of the development'[9] and the latest proposals by the International Law Commission on transboundary harm require consultation for all activities creating significant transboundary risk wherever situated.[10] The Espoo Convention regime also provides a specific mechanism for resolving any dispute that there might be as to whether EIA is required, by enabling any affected state to submit the issue to a compulsory inquiry commission.

7. Though note that the EC EIA Directive does not require the effects to be adverse, see p. 525.

8. The 1991 Espoo Convention, e.g., requires the state proposing the harmful activity to provide a description of the activity and its likely impact, mitigation measures and practical alternatives, as well as information about any uncertainties in the available knowledge. See also the 1987 UNEP, *Goals and Principles of EIA*.

9. Appendix III, Espoo Convention. On transboundary effects see the impact of the Convention on EC law, at p. 512.

10. Art. 9, 2001 Draft Articles on the Prevention of Transboundary Harm from Hazardous Activities.

BOX 14.3 **'The myth and reality of transboundary environmental impact assessment'**

In this extract, the author (J. Knox (2002) 96 American Journal of International Law 291) considers the rise of EIA in international treaties (mostly, in regional agreements like the Espoo Convention; see p. 514) and questions why—given that the international law obligation is that one state should not cause harm to another—international EIA law has no substantive edge to it.

The dominant story of transboundary environmental impact assessment in international law has the following elements: (1) customary international law prohibits transboundary pollution; (2) according to the classic version of this prohibition, contained in Principle 21 of the 1972 Stockholm Declaration, states must ensure that activities within their territory or under their control do not harm the environment beyond their territory; (3) to ensure that activities within their jurisdiction will not cause transboundary harm, states must assess the potential transboundary effects of the activities; and (4) to that end, states enter into international agreements requiring them to carry out transboundary environmental impact assessment (transboundary EIA) for activities that might cause transboundary harm. Despite its popularity, this story is not true [. . .]

 What, then, is going on? If transboundary EIA agreements are not designed to end transboundary pollution in accordance with Principle 21, what are they designed to do? One clue is that the agreements were not written on a clean slate. Most countries in North America and Western Europe have already enacted domestic EIA laws, which are limited in scope and lacking in substantive prohibitions but do contain detailed procedural obligations and provide important avenues for public participation. In large part, the regional EIA agreements reflect these domestic EIA laws. In fact, the main way that the agreements extend beyond the domestic laws is by ensuring that states apply EIA without extraterritorial discrimination—that they take extraterritorial effects into account just as they take domestic effects into account, and that they enable foreign residents to have access to the domestic EIA procedures to the same extent as local residents.

Knox therefore concludes that customary international EIA law is influenced more by what is known as the principle of nondiscrimination, under which states should apply the same environmental protections to potential harm in other countries that they apply to such harm in their own:

Examined closely, each regional transboundary EIA agreement is an application of the principle of nondiscrimination. The nondiscrimination principle has often been overlooked, cast into shadow by the glow surrounding Principle 21 [. . .].

Note: on Principle 21 of the Stockholm Declaration, and the later reformulation of this in Principle 2 of the Rio Declaration see p. 156.

A final consideration about EIA in an international context is whether an individual or group in one state (i.e. not just the state itself) can challenge a decision to authorize a project in another state where the adequacy of the EIA process is questioned. This dimension to legal standing has two aspects. The first is whether an individual in one state that might be affected by a development project in a neighbouring state has standing to review the EIA process (or lack of one) in the national courts of that neighbouring state, i.e. whether national law provisions can give rights to non-nationals. Here, it is worth mentioning that, in a US case, Canadian nationals affected by oil developments in Alaska were given standing to challenge the adequacy of the EIA carried out under US national legislation (*Wilderness*

Society v Morton 463 F. 2d 1261 (1972)). In the UK, the most that is required, in the EC's EIA Directive, is to allow for consultation with neighbouring states (including the public of the neighbouring state) in relation to transboundary harm, while the provisions of the Espoo Convention apply to non-EC neighbours. But if the potentially affected state does not wish to get involved it is unclear that any individual in that state would have any legal remedy.

The second issue is whether an individual in one state (with EA legislation) can challenge EA defects in relation to projects with impacts in other countries, i.e. whether national EA law applies extra-territorially. Obviously there would need to be some link between the action in the other country and the country with EA law, for example if the country with EA law gave development aid or export credit guarantees that allowed the overseas project to go ahead. For example, could a UK pressure group challenge inadequacies of EIA in relation to dam projects in other countries, if the construction work—to be underwritten by the UK Government—was authorized in breach of that other country's EIA law? The answer would seem to be that this would not be enough, by itself, for a UK court to intervene; the UK court would only be concerned with whether the UK government had complied with its own legal duties, e.g. whether it had followed its own rules and guidance on granting development assistance in the scenario described above.[11] But it is worth noting that there are again US examples where the courts have, under national law, allowed challenges to federal actions— such as spraying herbicide on marijuana plants in Mexico—to be brought in the US courts.

Environmental Impact Assessment in the EC

The EC EIA Directive

International legal developments show that EIA obligations (however vague) have stemmed from general duties of good neighbourliness between states. To some extent, the same is also the case with European Community law, and as noted above there are provisions giving potentially affected Member States the right to be involved in decision-making where projects have transboundary effects.[12] But the origins of Community EIA law lie mainly in two other rationales, one narrow, the other broader. The narrow justification is that Community laws on EA contribute to harmonizing the conditions of competition between Member States. Put simply, the authorization process, say, for a chemical installation in one Member State should be as rigorous, procedurally, as in any other Member State. But this is too formalistic an explanation for the adoption of Community EA legislation. A broader rationale, and better explanation, is that the environment is a matter of common concern across the Community, such that the Member States have collectively relinquished (or pooled) certain aspects of their sovereignty over development decisions likely to have significant effects on the environment, regardless of whether these effects (environmental or economic) are felt across Community frontiers. As Lord Hoffmann said in *R v North Yorkshire CC*,

---

11. As in *R v Secretary of State for Foreign Affairs ex p World Development Movement* [1995] 1 All ER 611.

12. Art. 7, EIA Directive, significantly amended by Directive 97/11 in the light of the Espoo Convention; implemented (eventually) by Regs 27 and 28, 1999 Regulations. The potentially affected Member State has the right to be notified, but then has a discretion whether to get involved in full consultation. This may rule out the possibility that individuals in neighbouring states have rights to be involved in the decision-making process in the other Member State.

ex parte Brown [1998] Env LR 623 (see p. 523): '[the] directive was adopted to protect the environment *throughout* the EU' (emphasis added). In this crucial respect, therefore, EC law goes well beyond accepted international law and practice.

After many years of fierce negotiation,[13] EC Directive 85/337 on the Assessment of the Effects of Certain Private and Public Projects on the Environment (the EIA Directive) was adopted. The EIA Directive established the need to consider information about the effects of a development on the environment as a mandatory component of the decision-making process in relation to certain specified projects.

Directive 85/337, which was amended from 1999 by Directive 97/11, requires Member States to ensure that certain planning decisions likely to have significant environmental effects are taken only after a proper assessment of what those effects are likely to be (see Box 14.4). A distinction is made between projects listed in Annex I to the Directive (where EIA is compulsory) and those listed in Annex II (where EIA is only needed if such significant effects are likely).

BOX 14.4 **The EIA Directive—the general duty**

Member states shall adopt all measures necessary to ensure that, before consent is given, projects likely to have significant effects on the environment by virtue, *inter alia*, of their nature, size or location are made subject to a requirement for development consent and an assessment with regard to their effects. (Article 2(1))

The Directive goes on to set out the detailed requirements for an assessment, which should include direct and indirect effects of a project on a variety of factors, including human beings, fauna, flora, the environment and material assets and the cultural heritage. The developer must submit certain specified information relating to these impacts to the authority dealing with the application (see p. 535). There are also provisions for consultation with the authorities likely to be concerned with the project and with members of the general public, though the detailed arrangements for consultation are left to individual Member States.

Two developments should also be mentioned here. First, the EC Directive on Strategic Environment Assessment (SEA) (Directive 2001/42/EC) came into effect in 2004. This Directive extends the Community's involvement in environmental assessment beyond individual development projects, and takes in the assessment of certain plans and programmes (but not policies) that are prepared for a number of sectors and which set a framework for future development consents of Annex I and II projects. SEA is considered in more detail at the end of this chapter. Secondly, there have recently been further amendments to the EIA Directive in order to align its provisions with those of the Århus Convention on access to information, public participation in decision-making and access to justice in environmental

---

13. On the negotiation of the EIA Directive (and the impact that strongly felt UK and Danish objections had) see N. Haigh (1987) JPL 4; J. Golub (1996) Environmental Politics 700; W. Sheate, *Environmental Impact Assessment: Law and Policy-Making an Impact II* (London: Cameron May, 1996) 18–22.

matters.[14] What is notable about the Aarhus Convention is that it contains much more specific provisions about public participation in decision-making than the EIA Directive, and its implementation may put important limits on the scope for Member States to determine their own procedures (see further Chapter 10).

Implementing the EIA Directive

The original EIA Directive was adopted and implemented in England and Wales by regulations enacted under the European Communities Act 1972.[15] Since then, the Secretary of State has been granted power to make regulations extending, beyond the Directive, the categories of projects that can be subject to assessment.[16] This power has been used once, and in a limited fashion, however, and the extension of the EIA regime to new projects has come about primarily through amendment to the EIA Directive. That said, in the implementation of Directive 97/11 the core Town and Country Planning (Environmental Impact Assessment) (England and Wales) Regulations 1999, which cover projects requiring planning permission and which are listed in the Directive, was made both under the European Communities Act 1972 and under section 71A of the Town and Country Planning Act 1990, so in principle EIA could be required for projects which are not listed in the Directive. But there is an apparent reluctance in practice to extend the scope of EIA beyond that required by EC law.

Projects that do not require planning permission because they are dealt with under separate consent procedures are governed by separate sets of regulations. These include proposals in areas such as afforestation and deforestation, highways, harbour works, marine fish farming, power stations and overhead power-lines, and pipe-lines. These separate regulations all follow the framework of the general planning regulations, but the extraordinary delay in enacting some of these specialist regulations has been striking, and not without environmental cost. For example, failure to implement EIA in relation to certain agricultural operations was considered a possible contributory factor in the serious floods of 2000.[17]

Is the project subject to EIA?

EIA law can be broken down into a number of discrete stages. The first stage is to determine whether or not the project falls within the criteria for the requirement of EIA. As we saw with EIA in international law, there is a central conundrum over which projects should be subject to EIA, because likely effects can really only be known after sort kind of assessment. Logically, therefore, all projects would have to be assessed, but to require formal EIA in relation to every project proposal would be disproportionate to the objectives being sought. One way to address this might be to make a limited initial assessment—in effect a 'mini-EIA'—followed by a more detailed assessment if the potential for significant impact is

---

14. Directive 2003/35/EC. On the Aarhus Convention see p. 317.

15. The main ones were the Town and Country Planning (Assessment of Environmental Effects) Regulations 1988 (SI 1988/1199) (similar regulations applied to areas outside the planning system, and in Scotland).

16. Section 15 Planning and Compensation Act 1991, which inserted s. 71A Town and Country Planning Act 1990.

17. HC Environment, Transport and Regional Affairs Committee, Second Report, Session 2000–01, *Development on, or Affecting, the Flood Plain* (2000), para. 44.

Figure 14.1 Main steps in the EIA process for UK planning decisions.

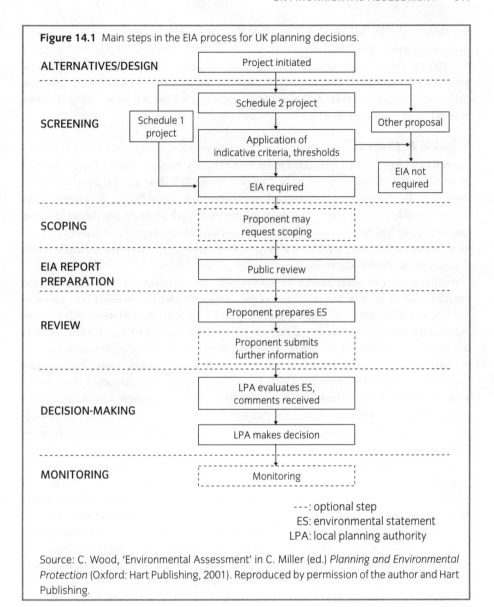

Source: C. Wood, 'Environmental Assessment' in C. Miller (ed.) *Planning and Environmental Protection* (Oxford: Hart Publishing, 2001). Reproduced by permission of the author and Hart Publishing.

revealed.[18] The EIA Directive, however, steers a pragmatic course by assuming that certain projects will give rise to likely effects (those projects listed in Annex I of the Directive) and then, in line with subsidiarity and flexibility, giving Member States more discretion over which projects falling within Annex II of the Directive should be assessed.[19] By implication,

18. An example of this is the provision for Initial Environmental Evaluations in the 1991 Antarctic Environmental Protocol, which are to determine if an activity will have more than a minor or transitory impact. Mini-EIA was recommended by the Commission in its first five-year review of the EIA Directive.

19. A logical consequence is that the decision whether an EIA is needed for a sch. 2 project must be made on the basis of less comprehensive information than would be generated by an EIA, see Case box 14.1.

therefore, under EC law EIA is not required for any project that does not fall within one of the categories of projects listed in Annexes I or II of the Directive. It is worth noting here that the core Town and Country Planning (Environmental Impact Assessment) (England and Wales) Regulations 1999 (the 1999 Regulations) use the terms 'schedule one' and 'schedule two'—rather than Annex I and II—projects; we do the same unless referring expressly to the EIA Directive.

What is a 'project'?

Central to whether an EIA is required is whether there is a 'project', and the related question of whether this project is subject to a 'consent'. In the EIA Directive the term 'project' is defined as the execution of construction works or of other installations or schemes. This equates roughly with the concept of 'development' in English planning law. As noted above, however, many activities listed in the EIA Directive fall outside the range of activities classed as 'development' in planning law, and hence specific regulations have had to be enacted in these areas, e.g. the decommissioning of nuclear power stations.

An illustration of some of the difficulties with the definition of 'project' under the Directive can be seen in the challenge to the congestion charging scheme introduced in inner London in 2003 (*R (Mayor and Citizens of the City of Westminster, Preece and Adamson) v The Mayor of London* [2002] EWHC 2440). It was argued that this amounted to a 'project' but the judge effectively bypassed this question and instead preferred to focus on whether it could fall within one of the categories listed in the Directive. The nearest category was 'urban development project', which the judge thought 'connotes rather more in the nature of building or construction' rather than the traffic management scheme being proposed. What is notable from this case is that whether the scheme was a 'project' or not was really of secondary importance; the main issue was whether it fell within one of the listed categories (see further pp. 524–6).

Two further issues relate to what the 'project' is which might require assessment. EIA might be avoided by breaking up a development project into several small projects, none of which individually require EIA (sometimes known as 'salami-slicing'). More usually, though, the issue is whether decision-makers must consider the cumulative impacts of development projects. An example of this was the decision of the Secretary of State in 1997 not to grant planning permission to UK NIREX Ltd, the government's nuclear waste agency, for a testing facility near Sellafield in Cumbria. NIREX acknowledged that the development was a necessary step in determining the suitability of the site for a nuclear waste repository. The Secretary of State said that any similar application in future would only be considered in the light of the environmental effects of the waste repository.

This practice has now been elevated to the status of formal policy and law. In national guidance, local planning authorities are not just advised to have regard to possible cumulative effects, but where appropriate to consider together more than one application for development to determine whether or not EIA is required (Circular 2/99, para. 46). This follows national case law that has held it appropriate for a planning authority to look beyond what was being applied for if the reality was that the application was part of a more substantial development.[20] The same case, however, decided that the planning authority did

20. *R v Swale Borough Council, ex parte* RSPB [1991] 1 PLR 6 (dredging did not require EIA, but ensuing development on land reclaimed as a consequence might require assessment). See also *R v Secretary of State for Transport, ex parte Surrey County Council*, 1993, unreported (widening of stretches of the M25 motorway).

not need to speculate on what future schemes the present development project would, or could, lead to. This suggests, for example, that whereas the traffic associated with a new development will probably need to be assessed for its impact, new development that may follow from the building of a new road may not be (even though this may be a likely effect). Indeed, the failure of EIA to extend to consequences like those in the latter example is a central reason for the need for strategic environmental assessment of things like transport plans.

The European Court of Justice has yet to pronounce directly on the extent to which competent authorities may or must consider actual or likely projects beyond that under consideration, where the project forms part of a larger project. However, the Advocate-General in one case has made reference to the inclusion of projects within 'current plans' (Case C-396/92 *Bund Naturschutz in Bayern & Others v Freistaat Bayern* [1994] ECR I-3717). The European Court of Justice has, however, pronounced on the issue of cumulative impacts (see Box 14.5)

BOX 14.5 Significant effects—the (ir)relevance of size

Changing rural land uses can have significant environmental impact. Three such uses of land—changing uncultivated land or semi-natural areas to intensive agriculture, initial afforestation, and peat extraction—are Annex II projects. In Case C-392/96 *Commission v Ireland* [1999] ECR I-5901, the Court of Justice held that Ireland had incorrectly transposed the EIA Directive, because very high size thresholds had been used which meant that EIA was not required for every project likely to have significant effects on the environment. The Directive had also been breached because Ireland's transposing law only had regard to the size of projects and did not take their nature or location into account. For example, the rarity and sensitivity of active blanket bogs would, the Court suggested, mean that afforestation would have adverse impact regardless of the size of the planting.

The Court also considered whether the cumulative impacts of individual projects should fall within the scope of the Directive. For example, numerous initial afforestation projects could be undertaken in Ireland without EIA provided they were conducted by different developers each of whom kept within the national threshold used (70ha). The ECJ held that 'not taking account of the cumulative effect of projects means in practice that all projects of a certain type may escape the obligation to carry out an assessment when, taken together, they are likely to have significant effects on the environment'. This suggests that the cumulative impacts of projects may need to be assessed, but probably only where that particular type of project as a whole would otherwise be completely excluded from assessment. That is, simply because one road, for example, falls below a national threshold will not mean that all road projects can be grouped together to take them above the threshold. Or, in other words, the obligation to assess cumulative impacts is different from strategic environmental assessment.

What is a 'consent'?

'Development consent' is defined as the decision of the competent authority that entitles the developer to proceed with the project. There is some difficulty with what 'proceeding with the project' means. This does not necessarily equate with planning permission, as other statutory consents could be required. Many developments such as processes subject to IPPC, for example, may be built under a planning permission but can only be operated with other licences.[21] And there are examples, such as with marine fish farms, where EIA is required when consents are renewed, not just when there is new development. On one interpretation, therefore, it could be argued that the Directive requires the Environment Agency (for example) to request an EIA when considering an application from a landfill site for a waste management licence where the local planning authority had failed to require an assessment. Although this is not the case in UK law we have long argued that it could be since waste disposal installations are Annex II projects and the Directive has direct effect in some situations.[22] There is now some support for this. In *R (Gregan) v Environment Agency* [2003] EWHC 3278, one of the 'ghost ships' cases, in the costs ruling it was found to be at least arguable that substantial modifications to a waste management licence could be a development consent for which EIA was required.

Another tricky issue has been the status of permitted development. Some activities are permitted development for which planning permission is deemed to be granted (see p. 468). These are usually minor developments, or developments in the public interest by statutory undertakers, but until changes to the law were made in 1995 (at the urging of the EC) they effectively fell beyond the reach of EIA.[23] The basic position is that schedule one projects cannot be permitted development, and will always require submission of a planning application and an environmental statement. Schedule two projects will only be permitted development if the decision-maker determines, after screening, that EIA is not required, or if the Secretary of State uses his exceptional powers to direct that the development is exempt from EIA.[24] Otherwise, permitted development rights are withdrawn and a planning application must be submitted together with an environmental statement. Given the often uncontentious nature of much permitted development, it is unlikely that there will be many projects which require EIA, but there may be a few situations where the ability of a planning authority to investigate the impact of a development which would otherwise have automatic permission could prove to be decisive.

Making permitted development subject to environmental assessment went a long way to satisfying the EC that all developments listed in Annexes I and II should be subject to assessment, regardless of the national position in relation to automatic development consent. This interpretation of the Directive was clarified by Directive 97/11, which makes clear that *all* such projects *must* obtain development consent, i.e. that EIA also applies to projects where consent is not needed because the project is not 'development', or the development is permitted by a development order.

Perhaps the most problematic issues with what the 'consent' is arise where the decision-making process is split into stages. Usually, this division is between an initial decision giving

---

21. The RCEP (*Environmental Planning*, 23rd Report, 2002, para. 5.24) called for there to be a common ES when a large industrial plant is seeking both planning permission and an IPPC authorization. That is, narrow legalistic problems can be avoided by a more holistic approach to decision-making.

22. See p. 523. For a more extreme example see the case of offshore wind farms, and the numerous consents needed, G. Plant [2003] JPL 939.

23. The rules on EIA and permitted development are now contained in the 1999 Regulations and in changes to the Town and Country Planning (General Permitted Development) Order 1995. Those developments that are permitted but subject to separate control regimes, such as forestry operations, are covered by separate regulations.

24. Regulation 4(4), 1999 TCPA EIA Regs. On the scope to exempt projects from EIA see p. 534.

the go-ahead in principle for a project, and a later decision fleshing out the details of the permission. An example of how this can give rise to difficulties related to the control of old mining permissions (see Box 14.6). Elsewhere, a similar problem is the particular difficulty in UK planning law deriving from outline planning permission being sought for development and then, if this permission is granted, 'reserved matters' being approved by the local planning authority at a later date. This raises the question as to what stage the developer has to submit the environmental statement. So far, the national courts have held that in these circumstances it is only the outline planning permission that is the 'consent', since at the reserved matters stage the local planning authority cannot raise objections to the principle of the development.[25] Accordingly, in these cases attention has so far focused on the sufficiency of information developers are required to submit in their environmental statements at the outline stage (see Box 14.9).

BOX 14.6 **Old permissions, new conditions—what is 'the consent'?**

Many planning permissions for mineral extraction date back to the 1940s and 1950s when there was little perceived need to consider the environmental impact of mining and quarrying. Quite a few of these permissions however—which were not time limited—are still in force, having been 'banked' for use at a later date. To modernize the law, the Planning and Compensation Act 1991 took the unique approach of attaching conditions to these old permissions to make them more acceptable, especially in terms of their environmental impact. A permission from 1947 for quarrying at Preston-under-Scar in North Yorkshire was registered under changes made by the 1991 Act. Conditions were then attached, but no EIA was required. In *R v North Yorkshire CC, ex parte Brown* [1998] Env LR 623 in the House of Lords, Lord Hoffmann construed the EIA Regulations purposively in the light of the Directive, and held that it was the decision on the new conditions that allowed the quarrying to proceed. The imposition of the conditions was a distinct event from, for example, the attaching of conditions to a planning permission.[26]

Ex parte Brown could therefore be distinguished from a case like *R v Secretary of State for the Environment, ex parte Greenpeace Ltd* [1994] Env LR 401, which concerned the THORP plant at Sellafield. In that case, Potts J rejected an argument that authorisation under the Radioactive Substances Act 1993—without which the plant could not operate—was something for which

---

25. *R v London Borough of Hammersmith and Fulham, ex parte CPRE* [2000] Env LR 549; *R (Barker) v London Borough of Bromley* [2001] EWCA Civ 1766. This latter judgment was despite the Commission having issued a Reasoned Opinion alleging that the failure to assess at 'reserved matters' in these cases breached the EIA Directive. *Barker* suggests that, if significant environmental effects emerge after the grant of outline permission, the remedy is in the planning authority revoking or modifying the original permission (an unhelpful route since the developer would have to be compensated for losses incurred). The matter has now been referred by the House of Lords in *Barker* to the ECJ for a ruling on whether 'consent' has an autonomous meaning. (Quite bizarrely, one week later in *R (Prokopp) v London Underground Ltd* [2003] EWCA Civ 961 the CA rejected this and held it to be *acte clair*).

26. For a similar case involving consent originally granted pre-1988 under a zoning plan, but where a fresh consent procedure was initiated after 1988, see Case C-81/96 *Burgemeester en welthouders van Haarlemmerliede en Spaarnwoude and Others v Gedeputeerde Staten van Noord-Holland* [1998] ECR I-3923.

separate development consent was required. The construction of the plant and its use for disposal of nuclear waste were all part of one project for which consent had been given before the Directive came into force. (The EIA Regulations were subsequently amended in the light of *ex parte Brown*.)[27]

In the subsequent case *R (Wells) v Secretary of State for Transport, Local Government and the Regions* [2004] Env LR 27, a case on similar facts to *Brown*, the European Court of Justice took a similar approach to that taken by Lord Hoffmann:

It would undermine the effectiveness of [the EIA Directive] to regard as mere modifications of an existing consent the adoption of decisions which . . . replace not only the terms but the very substance of a prior consent, such as an old mining permission

The chronology of court judgments here is worth noting. Until fairly recently the UK courts were criticised for not taking a purposive approach to interpreting the EIA Directive, with the main developments coming from the Court of Justice. *Brown* and *Wells* show that this is no longer always the case. (Another example is the issue of horizontality, where *Wells* confirms the purposive approach taken in *ex parte Huddleston* (see p. 223). See further Box 4.1.

Schedule one projects—mandatory EIA

Having considered what, in law, 'projects' and 'consents' are, we turn to look at which types of projects the EIA Directive and the 1999 Regulations cover. As might be expected, the projects falling within schedule 1 to the 1999 Regulations, where EIA is mandatory, include major projects such as crude oil refineries, thermal power stations, integrated chemical installations, motorways and major roads. Following Directive 97/11, the list now also includes such projects as pig and poultry units and groundwater abstraction schemes. The ECJ has held that modifications to Annex I projects may, judged objectively, also fall within Annex I, if the modification itself exceeds the thresholds for Annex I projects (Case C-431/92 *Commission v Germany* [1995] ECR I-2189).

It is worth noting that many of these types of projects have always been subject to thorough scrutiny and are often considered at major public inquiries involving many months of preparation and a vast range of documentation. But it is fair to say that, until the EIA Directive was implemented, the public was largely excluded from the technical debate unless they had the financial resources to instruct experts to act on their behalf. If the EIA process operates satisfactorily in disseminating information in intelligible terms, then the public may be able to play a more effective role in these inquiries.

For most projects falling within schedule 1, the definition of the project is self-explanatory. For some kinds of projects, however, thresholds are used to define the types of project to which mandatory EIA applies. For instance, a thermal power station other than a nuclear power station is subject to mandatory EIA only where it has a heat output of 300 megawatts or more. Where there is any degree of uncertainty over whether or not a project falls within schedule 1, a ruling on the need for an assessment can be obtained from either the Secretary of State or the local planning authority (see p. 532).

---

27. Town and Country Planning (Environmental Assessment) (England and Wales) (Amendment) Regulations 2000, SI 20000/2867, inserting a new Reg. 26A into the 1999 Regulations.

BOX 14.7 **EIA projects—matters of fact or matters of law?**

For many years the English courts took the view that whether a project is of a type that falls within schedule 1 or schedule 2—or indeed neither—was a matter of fact and degree for the planning authority, not a matter of law. This was always a questionable line of authority which dated from a decision from the early years of implementing the EIA Directive (*R v Swale Borough Council ex parte RSPB* [1991] 1 PLR 6 and strong criticism of this decision by M. Grant [1991] JEL 135). This has now been overturned, and it is clear that the courts are sensitive to what the ECJ has described as the 'wide scope and broad purpose' of the Directive (the *Kraaijeveld* case, see p. 528), i.e. that it should not be construed narrowly so that projects which might fall within schedules 1 or 2 are excluded even before their environmental impact is considered (*R (Goodman) v Lewisham London Borough* [2003] Env LR 28). That said, some of the categories of schedule 2 in particular are potentially very wide, e.g. an 'installation for the disposal of waste' could be anything from a compost bin to a landfill site, and decision-makers appear to retain some discretion to decide if, looked at reasonably, an activity could be of the kind that is covered by EIA.

Schedule two projects—EIA only when significant environmental effects are likely

The projects within schedule 2 to the 1999 Regulations are, by and large, the types of development that are less sensitive in nature. Examples include ski-lifts, motorway service areas, metal processing, food manufacture, holiday villages, knackers' yards, golf courses, tanneries, paper manufacture, and urban development projects such as retail parks. The list also includes schedule 1 projects below their thresholds (e.g. a thermal power station with a heat output of less than 300 megawatts), and modifications to schedule 1 and schedule 2 projects.[28] Notably, the significant effects need not be negative; as the judge in one case pointed out, 'benefit, like beauty, is in the eye of the beholder', and there may be disagreement about whether a development project is beneficial or harmful to the environment. A central purpose behind EIA is to give individuals the chance to express their views on such issues.[29] So a waste-water treatment plant, or an urban regeneration project specifically intended to improve the environment, might also need to be assessed.

That a project is of a kind mentioned in schedule 2—which, as discussed above, is not a matter that decision-makers have much discretion over—does not mean that EIA is necessarily required. EIA is only needed when the project is 'likely to have significant effects on the environment by virtue of factors such as its nature, size or location'. Following important changes under Directive 97/11, the 1999 Regulations contain much more explicit guidance on when an EIA will be required. This is through selection (or 'screening') criteria to which the decision-maker must have regard (sch. 3). These are grouped together under general headings of:

---

28. Though a modification to a Schedule 1 project may itself be a Schedule 1 project, see above.

29. *BT plc v Gloucester City Council* [2001] EWHC 1001 paras 64–70. See also *Berkeley (No. 1)*, p. 545 where the trigger for the objection was environmental mitigation work (the river walkway). Note that the usual formulation in international agreements, discussed above, tends to require significant adverse environmental impacts, though there are exceptions (e.g. the Espoo Convention).

- the characteristics of the development;
- the location of the development; and
- the characteristics of the potential impact.

Under the first of these, e.g. the size of the development, its use of natural resources and its waste production must all be considered. (These criteria are basically 'copied out' from Annex III of the Directive.)

Significant effects—the use of thresholds

The 1999 Regulations take advantage of the option under the Directive of using thresholds to 'screen out' from the need for EIA schedule two projects that are unlikely to have significant environmental effects. Rather than determining every application on a case-by-case basis, therefore, relatively low-level 'exclusive' thresholds are used for many schedule 2 developments, their use being to guide planning authorities and lighten the regulatory burden. These thresholds, however, need to be read alongside three general screening factors, contained in DETR Circular 2/99, *Environmental Impact Assessment*, WO Circular 11/99:

- whether the project is of more than local importance in terms of its size and physical scale;
- the sensitivity of the location (e.g. a site of special scientific interest); and
- whether it would give rise to unusually complex and potentially adverse environmental effects (e.g. from a polluting discharge).

These factors flesh out the Secretary of State's interpretation of those situations where the screening criteria will result in an EIA being needed. An Annex to Circular 2/99 also gives guidance on specific projects. For example, any motorway service area in a sensitive area, or above 0.5 hectares, must be screened, but government advice is that EIA is 'more likely' on greenfield sites and if the proposed development would be above five hectares. The guidance also gives further locational factors that might be relevant, such as a Local Biodiversity Action Plan or the effect of the development on places like Air Quality Management Areas and designated bathing waters. Small developments, and even minor modifications, may have major impacts, such as where a small airport runway is extended to accommodate much larger planes.

What limits have the courts placed on the discretion to rule out the need for EIA by the use of thresholds (and, by implication, on the question of 'significance')? The ECJ has held that thresholds cannot be so lax that a Member State can, in advance, effectively exempt whole classes of projects listed in Annex II (Case C-133/94 *Commission v Belgium* [1996] ECR I-2323). Thus in Case C-72/95 *Aanemersbedriff P K Kraaijeveld BV v Gedeputeerde Staten van Zuid-Holland* [1996] ECR I-5403 the applicants challenged the modification of a zoning plan that dealt with the reinforcement of dykes. They argued that the works were subject to EIA under the terms of the Directive. The projects fell within Annex II but the modification fell below the threshold set out in the domestic legislation. Trying to side-step arguments that Annex II was not sufficiently precise to have direct effect (see p. 222), the ECJ held that the Dutch national court was able to consider whether a Member State had exceeded the limits of its discretion in implementing the Directive.[30]

Subsequently, in Case C-435/97 *World Wildlife Fund (WWF) EA and others v Autonome Provinz Bozen and others* [2000] I CMLR 149 the ECJ was asked to consider a challenge to a decision not to require an EIA for redevelopment at Bolzano airport in Italy. The project would have changed the use of the airport from military to civilian and cargo flights, requiring some new development and intensifying effects from things like noise. The Court followed the *Kraaijeveld* case in holding that the key test in relation to Annex II projects was whether such projects were likely to have significant environmental effects because of their size, nature or location. If this was the case, then the relevant authorities had to ensure that the project in question was assessed.

In the *Kraaijeveld* and *Bozen* cases, therefore, what the ECJ has done is hold that the discretion given to the Member States is limited by the overriding need to assess all projects in Annex II if they are likely to give rise to significant environmental effects because of their size, nature, or location.[31] On this basis, therefore, a Member State cannot maintain that an Annex II project will never have significant environmental effects in its territory. Given that the sensitivity of the location is a key factor, this must surely be correct, since, for example, even an innocuous project might have a significant impact if sited in an important wildlife habitat.

Additionally, the European Court has made it clear that *all* the factors—size, nature, and location—must be taken into account in reaching decisions about the need for EIA, and relying exclusively on just one threshold factor (as Ireland did in relying on the size of various damaging rural activities; see Box 14.5) may breach the Directive. The UK approach avoids this pitfall by removing size thresholds where harmful projects are located in 'sensitive areas', which include SSSIs, European sites (under the Conservation (Natural Habitats etc.) Regulations 1994), National Parks, World Heritage sites and AONBs. And exceptionally, projects falling below the relevant 'exclusive' threshold may still require an EIA.[32] But otherwise the UK approach has been criticised for relying heavily (outside sensitive areas) on size factors alone.[33]

The essential point remains, however, that the use of thresholds is circumscribed by the overriding need to ensure that projects with significant environmental effects are assessed. Hence, as a matter of law thresholds can only ever be indicative. This, though, can cut both ways and in theory projects that fall below a threshold might require EIA, while projects that exceed a threshold might not need to be assessed. For example, in *R (Kathro) v Rhondda Cynon Taff BC* [2002] Env LR 15 a community learning centre was proposed by the local authority which, covering 11.5 hectares, was over 20 times in excess of the minimum threshold (0.5 ha) for urban development projects. Following screening, however, no ES was required. The judge held that the local authority had given careful consideration to the likely effects of the development, and that its decision was a 'conclusion reasonably open to it'.

---

30. When the case went back to the Dutch Council of State, the decision not to require EIA for the specific dyke construction works was upheld, emphasizing that a reference to the ECJ simply clarifies a point of law.

31. That is, that the obligation in Art. 4 of the Directive is circumscribed by the general duty to assess projects with significant environmental effects found in Art. 2 of the Directive (see Box 14.5).

32. If the Secretary of State directs, see Reg. 4(8), 1999 Regs. This is a power to direct, not a duty, see *Berkeley v Secretary of State for the Environment, Transport and the Regions (No. 3)* [2002] Env LR 14 (Box 14.12).

33. W. Upton, 'The Continuing Impact of the EIA Regime' UKELA Yearbook 2001.

Conversely, projects which fall below national thresholds may still need to be assessed, although the courts have so far given the Secretary of State a fairly wide discretion in setting thresholds (see Box 14.8).

BOX 14.8 **Minimum thresholds**

Planning permission was granted for a block of flats by the River Thames. EIA had not been required, because the area of the proposed development, at 0.19 hectares, was below the 0.5 hectare threshold for urban development projects and because the development was not in a sensitive area. In *Berkeley v Secretary of State for the Environment, Transport and the Regions (No. 3)* [2002] Env LR 14 the Court of Appeal held that the decision not to require EIA was lawful. In effect, the court upheld the threshold for such projects and decided that, so long as the threshold set by the Secretary of State took into account not just the size per se of the project, then it could lawfully be used to screen out the need for EIA for projects that fell beneath it. *Berkeley (No. 3)*, then, is a good example of the tension between formulating general rules and applying general principles. In the interests of efficient administration the EIA Directive allows thresholds to be used and this must mean that projects below these thresholds are not examined on a detailed case-by-case basis. So the issue becomes whether the thresholds have been set reasonably, and whether the individual project will actually have significant environmental effects is a secondary consideration.

Finally, by implication factors other than size, nature and location should not be taken into account in assessing the significance (or otherwise) of effects; simply because a development proposal is controversial or opposed at local or national level will not per se dictate whether there is an EIA (see Circular 02/99). Although the issue of other factors has not been ruled upon directly, the ECJ has held that the duty in the Habitats Directive to subject projects 'likely to have significant effects' to 'appropriate assessment' does not allow Member States to exempt projects from assessment because of their low cost or their purpose (Case C-256/98 *Commission v France* [2000] ECR I-2487), and it must be likely that the Court would interpret the EIA Directive similarly.

Significant environmental effects—discretion beyond thresholds

From the above it should be clear that thresholds never definitively determine whether EIA is required. So a central question is the extent of discretion that planning authorities have in determining whether a schedule 2 project needs EIA, and the related question of what scope the courts have to overturn a decision that EIA is not required. Neither the Directive not the Regulations explicitly define 'significant environmental effects', but guidance is found in the information that developers must supply in their environmental statements (see Box 14.9). Without repeating this information here, it is worth noting that this includes direct and indirect effects, and effects not just on component parts of the environment such as air and water but also environmental impacts more holistically.

The approach of the national courts has been to give planning authorities a fair degree of discretion in deciding whether a schedule 2 project requires EIA, consistent with the approach taken to questions of discretion generally in planning law.[34] That is, the courts will only intervene if any decision is so unreasonable that no reasonable decision-maker could have reached it. As was said in *R (Malster) v Ipswich Borough Council and Ipswich Town Football Club* [2001] EWHC Admin 711, a case relating to redevelopment of the football ground (and see also *Berkeley (No. 3)*, Box 14.8)

A detailed knowledge of the locality and expertise in assessing the environmental effects of different kinds of development are both essential in answering the question [whether proposed developments will have significant environmental effects], which is pre-eminently a matter of judgement and degree rather than a question of fact. Unlike the local planning authority, the court does not possess such knowledge or expertise.

That said, the courts have imposed a fairly low barrier on challengers to show that a project *might* have fallen within schedule 2, where other procedural defects have been at stake. As Lord Hoffmann said in *Berkeley (No. 1)* (see Box 14.12):

It is arguable that the development was [a schedule 2 development] and the conflicting evidence on the potential effect on the river is enough in itself to show that it was arguably likely to have significant effects on the environment. In those circumstances, individuals affected by the development had a directly enforceable right to have the need for an EIA considered before the grant of planning permission by the Secretary of State and not afterwards by a judge.

This cautious approach can also be seen in relation to applications for outline planning permission. Where outline permission is given for a development and, for example, there is little more than an illustrative plan and nothing to restrict the eventual development to the size or nature indicated, then the courts seem prepared to quash the planning permission for lack of EIA. So in one case where outline permission was sought for an accommodation centre for asylum applicants, the courts in effect said that the likely effects could not be regarded as insignificant because there was nothing in the application which limited the eventual size of the accommodation to a specific number of beds.[35] This, in effect, takes the test used in relation to the sufficiency of the environmental information contained in statements (see p. 536), and applies the same logic to the screening process.

The courts have offered sporadic guidance on the factors that planning authorities need to have regard to in determining whether there might be significant environmental effects. In *R v St Edmundsbury Borough Council, ex parte Walton* [1999] JPL 805[36] a planning officer had recommended that an application by the Greene King brewery be refused planning permission because of impact to, among other things, water meadows. But he had not required an environmental statement to be submitted. On this issue, the decision of the Council not to require EIA was upheld and the case therefore suggests that the mere view

---

34. *R v Swale Borough Council, ex parte RSPB* [1991] 1 PLR 6. See also *R v Metropolitan Borough of Wirral and another, ex parte Gray* [1998] Env LR D13. This contrasts with US law, where a 'hard look' at the likely effects is required and where the courts have in effect placed the onus on the proponent of the project to show that any impacts identified will be insignificant; R. Percivial et al., *Environmental Regulation: Law, Science and Policy* (Little Brown, 1996), 1050–9.

35. *R (Orchard) v First Secretary of State* [2004] Env LR 12. See also *BT plc v Gloucester City Council* [2001] EWHC 1001.

36. Note that the planning permission was quashed because of a procedural defect, see p. 532.

that development should be refused on environmental grounds is not in itself enough to show 'significant' environmental impact such as to require EIA. In addition, in a similar way to the approach of the courts to cases about the planning/pollution interface, the significance of the impact must also be judged assuming that environmental regulators—but including here the action of planning authorities on things like reserved matters—act reasonably competently.[37] This does not mean, however, that significance is to be judged only on the basis of the effects after such authorities have imposed conditions, a matter we consider in more detail below.

It has also been held, in the *Ipswich Town* case, that because the Directive and the Regulations are concerned to protect the environment in the public interest, their purpose is not to protect the amenity of individuals: 'There may be a significant impact upon a particular dwelling or dwellings without there being any likely significant effect on the environment for the purposes of the Regulations.' This raises an important question of scale; within a locality, localised effects may be significant but there is still the issue of the intensity of these effects. The *Ipswich* case points to looking at impacts through a wider lens (as does *ex parte Milne*, see Box 4.10), but neither the Directive nor the implementing Regulations define 'the environment' and a better view would be that consideration must be given both to the nature of the effects and the severity of the impact (the case involved the shadow thrown by a new stand at the football ground, and more intense localised impacts—e.g. the landscape impact of a new football stadium—might perhaps have justified a finding of significance.) The *Ipswich* case also suggests that replacement with a development of similar environmental effects—such as replacing a football stand—will not lead to significant impact, i.e. that in certain cases significance must be judged relative to the status quo.[38]

One possibility is that significance might be linked to the breach of substantive environmental law standards.[39] For example, a road scheme that would result in local air quality standards being exceeded, or even the breach of less formal standards like WHO standards on noise, could be deemed for this reason alone to be likely to give rise to significant environmental effects. So far there is no case law supporting this approach though there is at least one case where the possible breach of conservation law was sufficient for the courts to hold that a 'main effect' of the development project had not been sufficiently explored (see Case box 14.2). Being guided by substantive standards, though, might be thought to go beyond what EC law envisages, since the Directive's screening criteria are expressed in general, qualitative terms—e.g. 'pollution and nuisances'; 'the extent of the impact' etc—and could fairly easily have been linked to exceeding substantive legal standards if this was thought desirable. (It is worth mentioning in this context that in practice the most important factor in identifying impacts for the purposes of screening is professional judgement and experience, which ranks higher than using legal regulations and thresholds as a guide to impacts.)[40]

---

37 *Ex parte Milne* (see Box 14.10) para. 128. *Smith v Secretary of State for the Environment, Transport and the Regions* [2003] EWCA Civ 262 para. 51. On the potential overlap between planning and pollution controls see p. 790.

38. But note that modifications of projects may need to be assessed, see, e.g., p. 522.

39. J. Holder, *Environmental Assessment* (Oxford: Oxford University Press, 2004).

40. J. Becker and G. Wood, *Screening Decision-Making under the Town and Country Planning (EIA) (England and Wales) Regulations 1999* (2003), s 2.3.

Finally, there is the potentially tricky question about the factual basis on which it is argued that a development project is likely—or not—to have significant environmental effects. So far, the scope of the courts in resolving this sort of problem is not yet fully resolved (see Case box 14.1).

CASE 14.1 *R (Jones) v Mansfield DC* [2003] EWHC 7

Planning permission was granted, without EIA, for an industrial estate in open countryside. There were concerns about the impact of the development on golden plover, a bird safeguarded under EC conservation law. To allow for suitable mitigation in due course, the developer had undertaken to survey the site for a year before beginning construction. Richards J held that this element of uncertainty as to the ecological value of the site—and by implication the nature of the impact of the development—was not a strong enough basis on which to say that the development would be likely to give rise to significant environmental effects, and the planning authority's decision could not be overturned. In effect, the court rejected the proposition that at the stage of deciding whether significant effects would be likely the decision-maker should adopt a precautionary approach, stressing that the language used is 'would' give rise to such effects not 'could'.

The *Jones* case is a good illustration of two things. First, it emphasizes that screening must be different from a full assessment (otherwise the practical effect would be that an EIA was needed to decide whether an EIA was needed (!) and the current two schedule approach, and two-stage process of screening followed by full EIA, would be meaningless). Secondly, it shows that the absence of 'full information' is not the barrier at the screening stage that it will be at the stage where an EIA is required; at the screening stage the requirements for public involvement have yet to kick in, whereas at the latter stage they are fully engaged. A useful case to contrast this case with is *R v Cornwell CC ex parte Hardy* [2001] Env LR 25, see Case box 14.2).

Significant effects and mitigating measures

Can mitigating measures be taken into consideration when deciding whether EIA is required? Since the environmental statement must describe any remedial and mitigation measures (see p. 535), a strict approach would suggest that they cannot since mitigating measures could only be a secondary issue. On the other hand, the main aim of EIA is to prevent environmental harm and if this can be designed out before the project is submitted for approval then EIA can be said to have done its job.

The leading case is *Bellway Urban Renewal Southern v Gillespie* [2003] Env LR 30,[41] a case involving the building of 400 houses, and associated facilities, on the contaminated site of an old gasworks. In principle any Schedule 2-type project built on heavily contaminated land would require EIA, since the very act of development, or changing the use of the land, could lead to the risk of exposure to the contaminants. On the other hand, as we describe in Chapter 17 there are now relatively commonplace techniques used—e.g. capping the site or removing the contaminated soil—which if they are carried out correctly will mitigate any likely environmental impacts caused by the contamination. In effect the decision of the

---

41. See also *BT plc v Gloucester City Council* [2001] EWHC 1001 and *R (Lebus) v South Cambridgeshire District Council* [2003] Env LR 17.

Court of Appeal in *Gillespie* is to steer a course between these positions. According to Pill LJ, mitigation measures are not in principle to be ignored for the purposes of screening since that would distort the reality of the project proposal. Notably, then, a purposive construction of the Directive does not always require its provisions to be construed strictly so that EIA is more likely to be required.[42] On the other hand, the mere fact that conditions can take the effects of the development below the threshold of significance are not enough in themselves to rule out the need for EIA. A matrix of factors need to be considered, including the nature of the remedial measures, their complexity and the degree of detail stipulated and, in particular, the prospects that they will be successfully implemented (see paras 39–41 of Pill LJ's judgment in *Gillespie*).

This approach is quite nuanced but it still begs the question whether the EIA process ensures that the *best* advice about mitigating environmental impact emerges (which would be in line with the preventive and participatory nature of the Directive), not simply advice that is standard or sufficient. There are probably many cases where likely significant effects can be mitigated using conventional techniques, e.g. preventing night noise disturbance from factories or clubs by regulating the permitted hours of operation. But as the more forthright judgment of Laws LJ in *Gillespie* suggests, mitigation measures which take a project below the EIA threshold will have to be ones whose 'nature, availability and effectiveness are already plainly established and plainly uncontroversial'. In effect, only mitigation measures like that will not require scrutiny and public consultation, as required by the Directive.

Screening procedures

With the subjectivness of the indicative criteria for schedule 2 projects and the uncertainty of interpreting the definition for schedule 1 projects, there are a number of avenues open to establish whether EIA is required. However, these are open to applicants and not to third parties. Applicants can, at any time prior to making a planning application, seek an opinion from the local planning authority as to whether a proposed development falls within schedule 1 or schedule 2, and whether it exceeds thresholds or is in any other way subject to EIA (a 'screening opinion'; see reg. 5(1), 1999 Regs). Without formal delegation,[43] or at least the involvement of officers with delegated powers,[44] screening opinions cannot be left to planning officers—a measure of the importance attached to EIA, since basic procedures can be delegated informally—and must be made in a publicly available formal statement (interested parties should not have piece together the reasons why screening was or was not required, since this goes against the principle of public participation that pervades the Directive).[45] If the local planning authority either fails to give an opinion within the short period required (three weeks), or finds that the project is subject to EIA, the developer may refer the matter to the Secretary of State for what is

---

42. *World Wildlife Fund v Autonome Provinz Bozen* [1999] ECR I-5613 para. 37 ('actual characteristics').

43. *R v St Edmundsbury Borough Council, ex parte Walton* [1999] JPL 805 (no involvement of officers with delegated powers).

44. *R (Goodman) v Lewisham London Borough* [2003] Env LR 28 (decision taken by officer without delegated powers, but with close involvement of a delegated officer).

45. *R (Lebus) v South Cambridgeshire District Council* [2003] Env LR 17; compare the similar distaste for paper chases taken in relation to environmental statements in *Berkeley (No. 1)*, see Box 14.2.

termed a 'screening direction' (in effect an appeal of the screening opinion; Reg. 5(6)). The Secretary of State can also make a screening direction without a request from a developer, in line with his power to require an ES after an application has been called in or it has gone to appeal (reg. 4(7) and 9).

Any challenge to the failure to require EIA for the development must be made promptly following the screening opinion; challengers cannot wait until planning permission is eventually granted,[46] but nor do they have rights to be involved in the screening process (i.e. there is no obligation on the body doing the screening to publicize that it is going to screen a project and invite comment). For screening opinions, however, developers only need provide minimum information about the proposal, including at least a site plan; a description of the development and its nature and purpose; and its possible effects on the environment. It is therefore possible that following a negative screening opinion, additional material might become available before planning permission is granted—possibly some considerable time later—which might take the development over the EIA threshold.

In *R (Fernback) v Harrow Borough Council* [2002] Env LR 10 the applicant alleged that further information about the traffic impact of a housing development that came to light after a negative screening opinion meant that the local authority should overturn its earlier opinion. The High Court held that the Regulations did not make any provision for revisiting a screening opinion if this had found that EIA was not required, unless the developer sought this. Hence, screening opinions, whether negative or positive, are determinative of whether the project requires EIA, subject to the powers of the Secretary of State to make a screening direction (either at the request of the developer or otherwise). This clearly provides developers with a fair degree of certainty as to whether EIA is required, while giving the Secretary of State a residual, and appellate, function in difficult cases. Although it was open to the local authority to decide, when considering the full planning application, that the proposed development required EIA, the problem in *Fernback* was that the three-week time period for doing so had long since elapsed. The remedy in such cases, it was suggested, was for the Secretary of State to be asked to issue a screening direction, not for the failure to require a further screening opinion to be challenged. (The same approach is taken in the *Ipswich* case.) It was clear, however, that the judge felt the additional impacts that were alleged were fairly minor and there is a suggestion in the decision that, had more substantial new information come to light such that the development would clearly have required EIA, a route might have been found requiring the council to revisit its original screening opinion.

Screening practice

Early research carried out for the DoE showed that 50 per cent of local planning authorities that had not received any environmental statements had applications on their planning registers which were above the relevant thresholds for schedule 2 projects and which could have been suitable for EIA. When questioned further the local planning authorities admitted that a principal cause of these discrepancies was their unfamiliarity with the regulations. Since then the familiarity of planning authorities and other decision-makers with EIA has undoubtedly increased—only 9 per cent of planning authorities have never

---

46. *R (Malster) v Ipswich Borough Council and Ipswich Town Football Club* [2001] EWHC Admin 711. This would seem to be the case even following *Re Burkett* [2002] UKHL 23, discussed in Box 10.12.

screened a schedule 2 project, though only 50 per cent have screened five or more—and research suggests that the strengthening of the screening procedures together with the general impact of the legal rulings considered above and a far less hostile attitude to EIA, have helped create a shift in attitudes.

However, a comprehensive study found that EIA is now more likely to be required by the least experienced planning authorities, while those that screened out the greatest percentage of developments were those authorities with the greatest experience of screening. It would appear that one factor behind this is that the more experienced authorities rely more on their own judgement of the significance of likely effects and place less weight on thresholds, leading some commentators to question whether there is now a problem with some authorities being too formulaic and cautious in requiring EIA where it is not really needed. It is worth noting that the same study found no evidence that factors such as whether the planning authority was urban or rural, or in the north or south of the country, were significant to whether an EIA was required, i.e. there is no evidence to suggest that in practice EIA operates in a discriminating way against developers in more prosperous areas.

Exemptions from EIA

In three defined situations, projects that would otherwise require EIA may be exempted from the normal procedural requirements. First, the Directive does not cover projects serving national defence purposes, although this only exempts projects that mainly serve these purposes and does not apply to projects—like civilian airfields—that might be used accordingly.[47] Secondly, Member States may, in exceptional circumstances, exempt a specific project, in whole or in part, from the Directive's provisions, though the public must be notified of the exemption and the reasons for it, and the Commission must be informed.[48] Finally, the Directive does not apply to projects 'the details of which are adopted by a specific act of national legislation, since the objectives of [the] Directive, including that of supplying information, are achieved through the legislative process'.[49]

This rather curiously worded provision was discussed by the ECJ in relation to a motorway link between Luxembourg and Saarland in Germany (motorways being Annex I projects). The issue in Case C-287/98 *Luxemburg v Linster* [2000] ECR I-6917 was whether the Luxembourg law that authorized compulsory purchase of land to enable construction of the motorway fell within this exemption. The ECJ held in this case that it did not. Although the law had been adopted after public parliamentary debate, the law itself left open various possible routes for the road, and because these had not been explored in the depth required by the Directive for prospective projects, the legislative process did not comply with the Directive. What is notable about the judgment is how the Court interprets this provision to require the legislative process to comply with the purposes behind the Directive, rather than assuming that the legislative process is effectively EIA-compliant. This interpretation means that even where projects are authorized by an Act of Parliament—and the present

---

47. Art. 1(4) EIA Directive and Case C-435/97 *World Wildlife Fund v Autonome Provinz Bozen* [1999] ECR I-5613 paras 65–6.

48. Art. 2(3) EIA Directive; reg. 4(4) TCPA EIA Regs 1999.

49. Art. 1(5) EIA Directive. Parliamentary Standing Orders have been amended in relation to private and hybrid Bills, but not to public general Acts.

Government seemed keen to use Parliament to make the decision in principle on major infrastructure projects such as new airport terminals, before eventually changing its mind (see p. 450)—those affected can raise challenges to the adequacy of the legislative process in EIA terms (which may be a unique example of Parliamentary procedures being open to challenge in the courts).

The environmental statement

A key component of any EIA is the environmental statement (ES). As Lord Bingham put it in *Berkeley (No. 1)*, 'the cornerstone of the regime established by the [EIA] Regulations is provision by the developer of an environmental statement' (*Berkeley v Secretary of State for the Environment, Transport and the Regions* [2001] Env LR 16, para. 4; Box 14.12).

The basic position is that any application that needs EIA must include an ES. If it is not included, then the application is treated as if a screening opinion or direction is being sought (Reg. 7). Where the local planning authority considers that the information given is insufficient to allow for proper consideration of the environmental effects of the development, further information can be requested (Reg. 19). Where the process of consultation has been carried out properly, this should not arise.

There is no statutory provision as to the form of an ES, but it *must* contain at least (reg. 2(1) and Part II, sch. 4):

- a description of the development comprising information on its site, design and size;
- the data required to identify and assess the main effects which the development is likely to have on the environment;
- a description of the measures envisaged in order to avoid, reduce and, if possible, remedy significant adverse effects; and
- an outline of the main alternatives studied by the applicant or appellant and an indication of the main reasons for his choice, taking into account the environmental effects.

In addition, the ES must include certain information as is reasonably required to assess the environmental effects of the development and which the applicant can, having regard in particular to current knowledge and methods of assessment, reasonably be required to compile. In some respects this merely duplicates the categories mentioned above (e.g. mitigation and remediation measures, and the main alternative studied). But beyond this, more detailed information may need to be provided under such heads as mentioned in Box 14.9 (from reg. 2(1) and Part I sch. 4).

BOX 14.9 **The required content of environment statements**

(a) a description of the development, including its physical characteristics and the main characteristics of the production process such as the nature and quantity of the materials used;

(b) an estimate, by type and quantity, of expected residues and emissions;

(c) a description of the aspects of the environment likely to be significantly affected by the development, including population, fauna, flora, soil, water, air, climatic factors, material assets, including the architectural and archaeological heritage, landscape, and the interrelationship between these factors;

(d) a description of the likely significant environmental effects, covering the direct effects and any indirect, secondary, cumulative, short, medium and long-term, permanent and temporary, positive, and negative effects of the development, resulting from:

- the existence of the development;

- the use of natural resources; and

- the emission of pollutants, the creation of nuisances and the elimination of waste, together with a description of the forecasting methods used; and

(d) an indication of any difficulties (technical deficiencies or lack of know-how) encountered by the developer in compiling the required information.

Reference to 'indirect effects' means that, for example, a developer of a brownfield site could refer to the saving of greenfield land. In theory, it would also be open to objectors to refer to negative indirect effects such as effects on climate change, though the ES is not supposed to be a document over which there is specific litigation.[50]

For all of this information, a non-technical summary of any information supplied must also be provided, enabling non-experts to understand its findings. Unfortunately, there have been some decisions suggesting that a very broad-brush approach will be taken to non-technical summaries. A depressing example was the enforcement action brought by the Commission against the UK concerning, amongst other things, the lack of EIA for the controversial routing of the M3 motorway at Twyford Down. The High Court in *Twyford Parish Council v Secretary of State for the Environment* [1993] 3 Env LR 37 would not find that the 322 page Inspector's report could not amount to a non-technical 'summary', and the Commission complaint into this was also dropped on the somewhat extraordinary grounds that the report could amount to the 'equivalent' of such a summary. In the light of more recent case law, especially *Berkeley (No. 1)* (see p. 545), it must be doubted whether the courts would approve of something so inimical to meaningful public participation.

As to the content of statements, an important change made under the 1999 Regulations (following changes to the Directive) was to make much more information mandatory. This was to address concerns that information being supplied was, at worst, framed as little more than a piece of advocacy on behalf of the developer. There are still, however, legal limits on the amount of information that developers must provide in ESs. This is best illustrated by the difficulty, noted above, that surrounds the division between the grant of 'outline' planning permission, and subsequent decisions on 'reserved matters' (see p. 523). Two cases decided by the High Court in relation to planning permission for a large business park in Oldham illustrate current judicial thinking (see Box 14.10).

---

50. Compare the US. For a case where the substance of an ES has formed part of the dispute see *R (Vetterlein) v Hampshire County Council* [2002] Env LR 8.

BOX 14.10 **The Rochdale Cases (or 'The Battle for Kingsway Park')**

The first challenge, 'Tew I',[51] followed the granting of a 'bare outline' planning permission for the business park. The development fell within schedule 2 and an ES had been submitted. But there was only an illustrative plan of the kinds of activities that would eventually be included in the park in 10–15 years time. The permission was quashed because nothing tied the permission to the development shown in the illustrative plan, and hence information about the size and scale of the eventual development (i.e. a proper 'description of the development') could not be given. A further problem with the first application was that the planning permission left many important issues to the reserved matters stage, including some that may have given rise to significant environmental effects. So the likely 'main effects' of the project could not properly be assessed.

Following this decision a revised planning application for outline permission, and an ES, were submitted. Again, there was a challenge but in the second case ('Tew II')[52] the challenge was rejected. The judge stressed that the difficulty of assessing these types of flexible projects was not a reason for frustrating their implementation. What matters is that the ES (and the outline application) must acknowledge the need for details of the project to evolve over a number of years, *within clearly defined parameters*, and consider the likely significant effects of this evolution. But what level of knowledge does this require of developers? Following *Tew II*, the situation appears to be that deciding what information about a project and the likely environmental impacts is primarily a matter for the planning authority as a matter of fact and degree rather than principle. The planning authority does not need to know everything about a project which could have an environmental effect, but it does need to know everything which is likely to have a significant effect, and any mitigation measures, and so to the extent that the ES does not—or cannot—contain this information, any subsequent permission will be unlawful. Hence in *Tew II* it was relevant that the second planning application had been fleshed out, for example, with detail about hectarage of the variety of uses (office, retail, etc) applied for in the park, leaving only design and landscaping matters (which in this case were not of significance) as reserved matters. Using planning conditions so that the eventual development did not stray beyond these bounds made the consent EIA-compliant. The ECJ has yet to rule directly on whether this is the correct approach—and there are currently two cases pending where this is at issue[53]—but there are strong signs from *R (Wells) v Secretary of State for Transport, Local Government and the Regions* [2004] Env LR 27 that it will be.

The *Rochdale* cases nicely illustrate the pragmatic approach of EIA where, like here, the project is intended to evolve over time according to demand. There cannot be 'full knowledge' of the likely effects (as the first recital to the EIA Directive requires) but there are measures that can be taken to ensure that the developer uses its best endeavours to identify

---

51. *R v Rochdale Metropolitan Borough Council, ex parte Tew* [2000] Env LR 1. Similarly see *Elmbridge Borough Council v Secretary of State for the Environment, Transport and the Regions* [2002] Env LR 1.

52. *R v Rochdale MBC, ex parte Milne* [2001] Env LR 22 ('Tew II').

53. Case C-290/03 *R v Bromley LBC v Barker* (a reference from the House of Lords) and *Commission v UK* (arising from the same facts which gave rise to the unsuccessful challenge in *R v Hammersmith and Fulham LBC ex p CPRE* [2000] Env LR 532). See also p. 517 above on the definition of a 'consent'.

the project's significant effects and does not allow the project to develop in such a way that these give rise to significant effects that have not been considered when outline permission is granted. EIA law could, though, go further and require post-project monitoring, i.e. it could look both at projected and actual effects, but as yet this is not required.

A further limitation is the question of alternatives. Only alternatives studied by the developer need to be included in the ES. In theory, therefore, only good practice requires alternatives to be studied as a matter of EIA law. Circular 2/99 states, however, that it would be open to a planning authority to decide that the absence of alternatives, or the known availability of better alternatives, was a material consideration that justified refusal. (These may be material even if the Circular did not mention it.) For example, where the proposal is for a nuclear power station there would be a significant obligation to undertake a thorough search for the best available site. This would unquestionably involve a national investigation. Whether it would require consideration of alternative forms of power generation, or even the scope for increases in energy conservation to offset the need for further power, is unclear (Circular 2/99 only refers to alternative *sites* for projects, not alternatives *to* projects, which is arguably a narrow understanding of what the directive requires). But if the proposal were to establish an intensive pig-rearing unit then clearly there would not be the same degree of obligation. Notwithstanding this, if the unit is large enough there would be an expectation that the site identified for the unit would be the site giving rise to minimal environmental effects.

Scoping: opinions, directions, and good practice

Following Directive 97/11, the 1999 Regulations give developers the chance to ask the local planning authority, before submitting an application, for its opinion on the information to be provided in the ES (see regs 10 and 11). These are known as 'scoping opinions' and must involve consultation bodies (see below) and must be given in writing to developers, usually within five weeks (though a significant number of authorities appear not to do so). Public consultation on scoping opinions is not required; even if carried out (as is good practice), the direction of the scoping opinion rarely changes as a result. Screening and scoping opinions can be requested together. Where the planning authority does not reply in time, there is a right to request a scoping direction from the Secretary of State. But unlike screening opinions there is no right to appeal a scoping opinion. This reflects the extent to which formal scoping is seen as less critical in the UK, which helps explain why the UK has chosen not to require mandatory scoping, as it could do under the Directive. Even where a scoping opinion or direction has been issued, the decision-maker can still request further information at a later date.

Consulting on the environmental statement

As part of the scoping process, in gathering information developers are not only expected to consult local planning authorities; they may also seek views from the statutory consultees and possibly non-statutory consultees.

Ordinarily, the developer will go to the local planning authority first to discuss the project. At that stage the local planning authority may wish to identify the bodies with whom consultations should be undertaken. Such consultees must include, where appropriate, the HSE, the highway authority, English Heritage, English Nature and the Environment Agency (reg. 13), but in practice there may be wider consultation, e.g. with local wildlife trusts. The breadth of consultation depends precisely upon the type of development proposed. In addition English Nature and the Countryside Agency should be consulted if they would not otherwise be consulted as a matter of planning law.

It is the developer's responsibility to approach the statutory consultees. Regulation 12 imposes a duty on the statutory consultees to make available, on request, any information in their possession that is relevant to the preparation of the ES. This does not, however, require the public bodies to obtain information they do not have or to disclose confidential information. The consultees can impose a reasonable charge for making such information available.

The information that it is envisaged would be made available would include specialised information, such as the results of ecological monitoring, which would help the identification and assessment of the environmental effects. Furthermore, there may be non-statutory consultees who could assist with this information. Developers can consult with these bodies where they offer some particular expertise or local insight. This type of non-statutory consultee could include such bodies as the RSPB, The Campaign to Protect Rural England (CPRE), local nature groups, and members of the general public.

The consultation exercise (often extensive) forms the backbone of the whole EIA process and produces a number of advantages. First, quite often in development projects some environmental issues are obvious. The benefit of the consultation exercise, however, is that it identifies those issues that are perhaps not so evident. Secondly, a methodical, even approach to the objective analysis of environmental effects enables alterations to be made to a project at an early stage without great expense or inconvenience. These alterations can mitigate or eliminate adverse effects. Thirdly, where a full and adequate consultation is carried out before a planning application is submitted, the amount of time taken by the local planning authority and other consultees to consider the application when submitted will be greatly reduced. Finally, the consultation process affords the developer the opportunity of communicating with all parties who are likely to have an interest in the project. Misunderstandings can be cleared up on both sides. This then enables the developer and the local planning authority to concentrate on the relevant issues.

Quasi-statements

A developer can simply volunteer an environmental statement and state expressly that the document is to be viewed as being an ES for the purposes of the 1999 Regulations. This in turn means that the local planning authority has to carry out the other information-gathering exercises for the EIA process. This has led to the growth in the submission of quasi-environmental statements. These documents contain the information that would normally be contained within an ES, but are not submitted as formal statements for the purposes of the 1999 Regulations. In such circumstances, if there is any doubt as to the need for EIA the local planning authority can gather the information from one source (i.e. the developer), but is not obliged to go through the whole EIA exercise. One of the consequences of this approach has been that there is a tendency to concentrate on the subjectivity of the developer's assessment of the environmental effects. Thus, the whole purpose and concept of the EIA can be undermined unless this quasi-assessment is carried out thoroughly.

Criticism of environmental statements

Around 700 ESs are submitted every year in the UK, around 75 per cent being made under the main planning regulations. This is nearly double the number of ESs submitted before the 1997 amending directive was implemented, a rise that is accounted for predominantly by the change to the law (rather than by the high level of development in the late 1990s). Considerable attention has focused on the quality of ESs submitted. Early research indicated considerable failings, with most academic studies finding less than half of all statements studied to be of acceptable quality. Most of these deficiencies were to be found in the assessment of the environmental impacts of the project. This was not helped by the lack of formal scoping, and early research showed that as many as 50 per cent of local planning authorities were not consulted at the scoping stage.[54]

A related problem was that few planning officers had any experience of judging the adequacy of ESs, and developers (by using consultants who built up a greater experience of EIA) often possessed an information advantage over the authorities. To some extent this problem is decreasing and many authorities now themselves engage consultants to review the adequacy of statements received. However, it is notable that more than a quarter of local authorities have never issued a scoping opinion and, because of lack of resources, those that have issued opinions spend far less time on them than developers spend on their scoping reports. The overall effect on the quality of ESs, however, is not clear. The issuing of central government guidance, both to developers and to decision-makers,[55] emphasizing the need to differentiate between scientific calculation of impacts and the evaluation of the significance of the impact (for criticism of whether this really happens, see p. 77), has probably helped to improve matters. Some of the worst statements—and worst excesses within ESs—seem to have gone, but problems remain with things like predicting the likely impact of the project. The greater involvement of lawyers in the EIA process has been suggested as one factor in ESs being more conservative about these types of estimates.[56]

A problem was (and remains) that there are no agreed standards for ESs, though academic bodies have developed their own criteria. Calls from influential quarters for an independent 'Council for Environmental Assessment' which would be involved with scoping and quality review—along the lines of the EIA Commission in the Netherlands—have not been taken up in the UK.[57]

Many have argued that improving the quality of ESs is central to improving the quality of the EIA process as a whole. But it is at least arguable that too much attention has been paid

54. Scoping has always formed part of good practice for EIA since the first guidance on EIA was issued in 1995.

55. See *Evaluation of Environmental Information for Planning Projects* (DoE, 1994), and *Preparation of Environmental Statements for Planning Projects that Require Environmental Assessment: A Good Practice Guide* (DoE, 1995).

56. (2003) ENDS Report 340, 29.

57. The RCEP appears to advocate mandatory scoping, see *Environmental Planning* (23rd Report, Cm. 5459 2002), para. 7.31, but this has been rejected by government which sees the existing powers of decision-makers as adequate.

to the adequacy of ESs at the expense of the overall treatment of environmental information. Research suggests that planning officers and consultees generally believe that the results
of the consultation process have a more significant impact on planning decisions than the
content of the ES does.[58]

Determining EIA applications: considering environmental information

Once an ES has been prepared and submitted together with the planning application, there
are further procedural steps that closely follow the standard procedure for planning applications, including the notification of statutory consultees. However, the determination period
for the application is extended to 16 weeks, there are increased publicity requirements,[59] and
a reasonable number of copies should be made available to the public at a reasonable charge
reflecting their printing and distribution costs.[60] The underlying purpose behind these
enhanced procedural requirements is the requirement that the decision on the project takes
'environmental information' into account (reg. 3(2)), and that this information includes
not only the ES but also the views of statutory consultees and any representations made by
other persons about the environmental effects of the development (reg. 2(1)). Any grant of
planning permission that does not take this environmental information into consideration
is invalid.[61]

The importance of the legal right of the public meaningfully to participate in EIA has
nowhere been more clearly expressed than by Lord Hoffmann in *Berkeley (No. 1)* (see
Box 14.12):

> The directly enforceable right of the citizen . . . is not merely a right to a fully informed decision
> on the substantive issue. It must have been adopted on an appropriate basis and that requires
> the inclusive and democratic procedure prescribed . . . in which the public, however misguided
> or wrongheaded its views may be, is given an opportunity to express its opinion on the environ-
> mental issues.

A central aim of EIA is to reduce the amount of uncertainty about decisions over environmentally harmful projects by the gathering, in advance, of environmental information. One
issue that arises is the sufficiency of this information. Here, it is worth mentioning that the
local planning authority may not invalidate an ES because it considers the information
supplied to be inadequate, but must instead use its powers to seek further information.[62]
This provision emphasizes the need to gather information in advance of determining the
application for the project. A different side to this coin can be seen in Case box 14.2.

---

58. Wood and Jones (1997) (see further reading).

59. Reg. 32, 1999 Regulation. The procedures for determining planning applications are described at p. 474.

60. Regs 17 and 18, 1999 Regulations. Note the difference in charging the public for an ES and charging developers
for information to be used in preparing the ES.

61. Reg. 30, 1999 Regulations.

62. Under reg. 19, 1999 Regulations. Where the developer fails to provide further information and the local
planning authority decides to refuse planning permission, or fails to determine the application within the 16-week
period, the developer has the usual right of appeal to the Secretary of State.

CASE 14.2 *R v Cornwall County Council, ex parte Hardy* [2001] Env LR 25

A planning application was submitted to extend an existing landfill site at Redruth. The ES raised a number of concerns, including possible impact on lesser horseshoe bats, a protected species under the EC Habitats Directive (see p. 842). Both English Nature and local wildlife groups advised that the presence of bats needed further study. However, they all thought that any likely impact could be dealt with after permission was granted—but before the development commenced—by appropriately worded planning conditions. The Council had accepted that advice on the basis that the bats or their resting places might be found in the area affected by the development, and were likely to be adversely affected by the development. But in line with the advice of the conservation consultees, the Council only required, through planning conditions, that the applicant undertook further surveys and prepared appropriate mitigation measures.

On a challenge to the planning permission, the High Court held that it was for the local authority to judge the adequacy of the environmental information, subject only to *Wednesbury* irrationality.[63] But Harrison J held that it was an 'inescapable conclusion', because of the protected status of the bats and because the planning conditions effectively conceded that there could be adverse impacts, that this would amount to a 'significant adverse effect' and a 'main effect' of the development. Accordingly, the Council could not have concluded rationally that there were no significant nature conservation effects until it had the survey data. So the Council could not know whether it had the full environmental information it required (by reg. 3) before granting planning permission.

The case is also notable because the judge made it clear that leaving important issues until after the main decision had been taken would prevent the full involvement of consultees and the public when this further information came to light, and hence would conflict with the underlying purpose behind the EIA Directive. This approach follows that taken by the courts to 'bare' outline planning permissions, where meaningful participation on environmental effects is excluded (see p. 523). It is also a good example of the importance of public participation and involvement in EIA, since none of the conservation agencies and groups consulted argued for the strong and purposive approach ultimately taken by the court. Indeed, during the case the Council conceded that 'mitigating for' the impacts on the bats meant that they would have to go.

Following this case, the necessary survey work was undertaken and a revised planning application submitted and approved. If in due course this is acted upon, it is clear that much of the ecological interest on the site will be lost. Indeed, the judgment fails to convey the extent to which environmental harm may arise; in seeking to overturn the initial grant of planning permission counsel for the objector focused on one ground of challenge, to do with the bats and two other species, and other possible grounds were not pursued then. Sullivan J rejected a later challenge, raising some of these further grounds, in part because he thought these issues could and should have been raised earlier. One of these was that the site had not been studied for the presence of nightjar, a European protected species. Amazingly, when this was raised with the European Commission, the response seemed to indicate that as long as any development took place out of the season when nightjar would be at the site, there would not be significant environmental effects!

---

63. See also the opinion of Sullivan J in *ex parte Milne* (Box 14.10).

There is also the question of what obligations there are, if any, on the planning authority if granting planning permission following EIA. The defining characteristic of EIA, it is worth remembering, is its procedural nature. Hence, development projects with significant environmental effects can still proceed even where the EIA process reveals that environmental harm is likely. That said, there are some instances where the hands of planning authorities will effectively be tied. An example is the obligation, in granting outline planning permission, to impose conditions ensuring that the process of evolution of the project keeps within the parameters applied for and assessed at the outline stage, so that the project, as it evolves with the benefit of approvals of reserved matters, remains the same as the project that was assessed (see Box 14.10).

The duty to give reasons

Following Directive 97/11, whether the outcome of an EIA application is to grant or refuse development consent, reasons must be given by the local planning authority to the Secretary of State and to the general public via a newspaper notice and through the planning register. Previously, such reasons were required only where the Member States' legislation so provided. Thus the previous rule in the UK, that reasons need be given only where planning permission is refused, no longer applies where an EIA has been undertaken. Reasons are to include (reg. 21):

- the content of the decision and any conditions attached;
- the main reasons and considerations upon which it is based (on which see the judge's remarks in the *Hardy* case (Case box 14.2)); and
- a description where necessary of the main mitigating and remediation measures employed.

These new provisions, however, do not provide a general duty to give reasons in relation to the *potential need* for EIA. There is, as we have seen, a duty to give clear, precise, and full reasons why EIA is required (reg. 4(6)). But often, information will be sought about the reasons why no EIA was required in the first place. Until recently the UK courts did not recognize any explicit duty to state both the reasons for the decision and the considerations upon which this is based, but this approach may have to be reconsidered in the light of a recent judgment of the European Court of Justice (see Box 14.11).

BOX 14.11 **EIA—screening and reasons**

Can a planning authority simply say that its planning committee has considered the need for EIA but has concluded that the development will not give rise to significant environmental effects and does not therefore require EIA? In a national case involving a Schedule 2 development the Secretary of State did not think that it would give rise to significant environmental effects and so no EIA was required. No further reasons were given. The Court of Appeal, in *R v Secretary of State for the Environment, Transport and the Regions and Parcelforce, ex parte Marson* [1998] JPL 869, held that there was nothing in national or EC law that required more information than had been provided. One rather worrying aspect of the decision is that the Court thought that reasons had been given 'albeit in summary form', when all that the Secretary of State noted was the bare statement that there would not be likely significant effects. To say the least, this is a circular argument that does not give any explicit reason for its own conclusions, and it might be doubted whether it is consistent with the increased emphasis being given to meaningful public participation in environmental decision-making. Indeed, this approach can be contrasted with recent steps to require certain utility regulators to publish reasons when they think that a proposal is important but that an impact assessment of it is *not* required.[64]

Since then the Court of Justice has held that Italy breached the Directive because inadequate reasons were given when a ring road proposal was screened. In Case C-87/02 *Commission v Italy* [2004] nyr the Court traced the decision-making process back to a single engineering report which it was claimed had been relied on, but found that this did not look at the environmental effects of the project, only whether on hydraulic grounds it was appropriate for the road to cross a river. 'Clear and precise reasons' for ruling out EIA had not therefore been given. Underlying this judgment is an obvious concern that the Directive could be a dead letter if the courts could not scrutinize the basis for screening decisions. Grey areas will of course remain, and it is not clear whether the Italy case means only that screening will be inadequate where materials which could not possibly form the basis of a negative screening opinion have been relied on, i.e. how far any duty to give reasons stretches. Nevertheless, the decision does go some way towards giving the interests of 'the environment' a similar degree of procedural protection as those of developers.

What if environmental effects have been considered without EIA?

Even if the courts are prepared to intervene and hold that the development is of a kind for which an environmental statement *should* have been submitted, it does not automatically follow that an EIA will be required. There are two main components to this. The first is whether the procedures used amount to 'substantial compliance' with the Directive; the second is whether any national procedural rules—such as on standing or delay—might prevent EIA being required.

Substantial compliance

For many years the answer to the first issue was that procedures which seemed to generate sufficient information about the project would suffice. In *R v Poole Borough Council, ex parte Beebee* [1991] JPL 643 for example, the Council granted itself planning permission without considering whether or not an EIA was required.[65] Schiemann J took the view that the purpose of an EIA was to draw the decision-maker's attention to any relevant information that would assist in reaching a decision. On the facts, he thought that the local planning

---

64. E.g. s. 5A Utilities Act 2000 (added by s. 6 Sustainable Energy Act 2003).

65. This is not per se incompatible with human rights legislation requiring determination of rights by an independent and impartial tribunal, see *R (Kathro) v Rhondda Cynon Taff County Borough Council* [2002] Env LR 15.

authority had all the relevant information before it and therefore an ES would have been superfluous. All the information that might have been gleaned from a formal statement had already emerged and ensured that the council had not arrived at an irrational decision.

Even on a narrow, technocentric basis, such an approach is questionable. As a central purpose of EIA is to produce a systematic approach to the consideration of environmental effects using best practicable techniques and best available sources of information, it was bold to assert that the local planning authority had all the necessary environmental information for an EIA. Indeed, the transcript of the case suggested that the officers' reports to the decision-making committee had a number of omissions, which would imply that there were deficiencies in the local authority's decision.

The problem with this approach is that the courts would have to prove negatives; that neither more nor better information would come to light if a formal EIA were carried out. It would also mean that the educative value of EIA as a process, and its inclusive, participatory nature, would be diminished. Fortunately, this approach has now been overruled by the House of Lords in a forthright ruling about the sufficiency of the EIA process.

BOX 14.12   **The *Fulham Football Club* case**

The background to this case was that planning permission had been granted without formal EIA for redevelopment of the ground of Fulham Football Club. As well as the ground redevelopment, the proposal involved the building of flats above a riverside walk, and some encroachment onto the River Thames. Mitigation measures were proposed to compensate for potential damage to aquatic habitat caused by the walkway. These satisfied the (then) National Rivers Authority but not the London Ecology Unit. The Secretary of State called in the application, but did not require an EIA and granted the planning permission, albeit subject to various conditions aimed at mitigating the environmental impact. The proposed redevelopment was opposed by a group of local residents.

In a case known as *Berkeley (No. 1)*,[66] the issue was whether the planning permission was lawful, given the failure to undertake an EIA. In the Court of Appeal, the challenge failed because it was held even if a formal ES had been submitted, this would have made no difference to the eventual decision. This was because the planning dispute had dragged on for years, and the decision-makers had an abundance of information before them from various sources including the developer, statutory consultees and local objectors. Before the House of Lords, however, the Secretary of State conceded that this approach was not lawful—the need for EIA could not simply be wished away—but argued instead that there had in fact been *substantial compliance* with the Directive and Regulations because the Secretary of State had before him all the documents he needed to make his decision.[67]

Giving the Regulations and the Directive a very purposive interpretation, however, the House of Lords emphasized the extent to which EIA is a procedural mechanism involving the opportunity

---

66. *Berkeley v Secretary of State for the Environment, Transport and the Regions* [2001] Env LR 16.
67. Case C-431/92 *Commission v Germany* [1995] ECR I-2189 suggested that, if the procedures in the Directive are otherwise complied with, something other than a formal ES might suffice.

for informed public participation. It is not just an information-gathering exercise.[68] Lord Hoffmann, in the leading judgment, held that the available documents provided a mere 'paper chase' which fell short of what was required of a proper ES. It was not sufficient, for example, that interested parties had the opportunity to trace all the relevant documents, if this would require 'a good deal of energy and persistence' on their part. Here, the developer had not provided an ES in a single source, and there was no non-technical summary. So the rights of the public to be involved in the decision-making process were inevitably hindered. This was regardless of how much information was made available for the planning inquiry; of the objector's chance to comment on this and present her own information; and even, it seems, of whether the objector could point to any particular prejudice she had suffered. The House of Lords stressed that when it came to errors of law, especially in cases related to EC law, the courts had little room for discretion.

Two further observations are worth making. First, a depressing feature of the case was that the Secretary of State argued against the value of formal EIA rather than championing it, although his misapplication of the Directive prevented him from recovering all his costs.[69] Secondly, the length of the legal proceedings was such that by the time the case reached the House of Lords the specific proposal had in fact been shelved, and this has been noted by judges in subsequent cases as a reason for limiting the strength of the procedural protections which were granted (see below, and also p. 231). (A revised planning application, which was subjected to EIA, was also challenged unsuccessfully on other grounds).[70]

EIA and national procedural rules

As discussed earlier (see p. 225), one of the problems in bringing cases based on alleged breaches of EC law is the discretion national courts have to decide their own rules of procedure. These include, for example, rules on standing and on whether cases are brought with sufficient speed. When major development projects are at stake, the need to bring challenges quickly is particularly important, since as time passes the developer is likely to be incurring costs at the site, and these costs will be a relevant factor for the court to consider if the case is not brought promptly. Third parties may also be making decisions, e.g. entering into contracts, in reliance on what they think will happen planning-wise. Set against this, however, is Article 10 EC which requires Member States to take 'all appropriate measures' to ensure fulfilment of obligations arising under the EC Treaty.

In EIA cases, a key issue is whether the strictness of the legal duty to assess certain types of projects means that national procedural rules must bend to accommodate this.[71] The starting point now for considering this issue is the decision of the House of Lords in *Berkeley (No. 1)* (Box 14.12). There, the House purposively stressed that breach of the EIA Directive is

---

68. Even after *Berkeley (No. 1)* the attitude that EIA is just about information gathering still persists; for an example where a decision of a local authority not to require EIA was quashed because it had mistakenly thought that it already had enough information see *R (Lebus) v South Cambridgeshire DC* [2003] Env LR 17.

69. *Berkeley v Secretary of State for the Environment (No. 2)*, The Times, 7 Apr. 1998, CA.

70. See *Adlard v Secretary of State for the Environment, Transport and the Regions* [2002] EWHC 7 (Admin) (failed challenge to decision not to call in the application—and hence not to require a public inquiry—following a revised application. A material consideration seems to have been that, by this stage, a valid ES had been submitted and commented on). See further p. 493.

71. Generally on the tension between procedural EC law and national procedural rules in EIA see K-H. Ladeur and R. Prelle (2001) JEL 185.

a serious matter in itself, and hence any discretion not to quash a planning permission on procedural grounds had to be confined to the 'narrowest possible bounds'. However, the national courts have refused to accept that the decisions of the ECJ in *Kraaijeveld* and *Bozen* mean that they must set aside any national rule that would prevent the mandatory obligation to assess projects from being realised. Instead, the courts have had occasion to use legal rules and principles intended to foster good administration to defeat the need for EIA. In *R v North West Leicestershire District Council and East Midlands International Airport Ltd, ex parte Moses (No. 2)* [2000] Env LR 443 a case concerning extension to a runway at the airport, there was a delay of several years in bringing the claim. The applicant invoked the EC principles of legal certainty and proportionality. But the Court of Appeal turned these principles around:

There comes a point, however, when these principles support the rejection rather than the admission of long delayed challenges where third parties have acted in reliance on apparently valid decisions. That point has long since been reached in this case.

Problems with challenging planning permissions at the stage of reserved matters have sometimes meant retracing the steps of the planning process back to the grant of the outline permission, sometimes several years earlier. For example in *ex parte CPRE*[72] there had been a delay of three-and-a-half years since the grant of outline planning permission, while there had been a delay of over a year in *ex parte Barker*[73] where, arguably, the environmental impact of the project was less. In both cases the applications for judicial review were rejected as being out of time. Despite the judgment in *Berkeley (No.1)*, therefore, it appears that the matrix of considerations used by the courts to determine whether there has been undue delay in bringing judicial review apply equally in EIA cases. While non-compliance with the provisions of the Directive will be an important factor in stretching the time for bringing the challenge, this is not the only factor, and other considerations of what the courts deem to be good administration will also be taken into account.[74]

Finally, however, in *Swan v Secretary of State (No. 1)* [1998] Env LR 545 the Scottish courts did establish that a developer can still be required to submit an ES, even though the development to which it relates has begun. In that case, the effects of the afforestation would be continuing, but an EIA was still possible. This decision has particular importance for projects which may not be carried out as soon as permission is granted, e.g. mining and quarrying.

EIA—its impact on decision-making

EIA is widely regarded as a central tool for environmental protection, and the EIA Directive as the most important EC environmental directive. In part this is because it heralded the use of procedural law for environmental protection at EC level. But it is also because the

---

72. *R v London Borough of Hammersmith and Fulham ex parte Trustees of the CPRE* [2000] 81 P&CR 73 (CA). There are ongoing proceedings brought by the Commission before the Court of Justice in relation to the issues raised in this case, see p. 523.

73. *R (Barker) v Bromley London Borough* [2001] Env LR 1 (High Court).

74. *R v Waveney DC ex parte Bell* [2001] Env LR 24 (five-week delay, no prejudice, arguments about delay rejected), and see further p. 225.

Directive was the first to try to integrate environmental concerns into general decision-making—a hallmark of sustainable development. That the Directive has been the subject of more complaints to the Commission about non-implementation than any other EC environmental measure is an indicator of its impact.

Initial fears about the costs to developers appear not to have been realized. Indeed, it is doubtful whether EIA is such a burden that developers should be particularly worried about it being required for their projects, and concerns about costs seem to have receded over the years. As a research study examining the relative costs and benefits associated with implementation of the 1985 Directive in Greece, the Netherlands, Spain, and the UK found, costs in excess of 1 per cent of total capital expenditure were the exception. They also tended to occur in relation to particularly controversial projects in sensitive areas, or where good EIA practice had not been followed. Costs as a proportion of total capital expenditure may be as low as 0.2 per cent, with the EIA component being lowest for the largest projects.[75]

Moreover, the same research recorded a high percentage of respondents (which would appear to be developers and decision-makers only) identifying a number of benefits to them or to the development proposal arising from the conduct of the assessment process. This included a finding that the environmental credibility of the developer had been enhanced in 61 per cent of cases. This is backed up by UK research that suggests that both planning officers (88 per cent) and developers/consultants (76 per cent) felt EIA to have been a net benefit in cases in which they had been involved.[76] Such statistics may be seen as supporting the view of EIA as operating as a developers' charter, 'being used by developers to advance their projects in environmental terms'.[77] The views of consultees and third parties tend to receive less attention, though planning officers tend to take a more positive view of the quality of ESs than researchers and consultees tend to take a more negative view.

As to substantive criticisms, the continued absence of any requirement for post-project monitoring continues to detract from the iterative nature of EIA, arguably detracting from EIA's learning role. And the lack of real powers to prevent biased, or overly cautious, statements still gives cause for concern. But if anything, the centrality of the ES is diminishing, and the *assessment process* elevated. Nowhere is this clearer than in the purposive judgments of the ECJ—and at national level the forceful opinion of the House of Lords in *Berkeley (No. 1)*—emphasizing that EIA gives those affected by development projects rights to be meaningfully involved in the decision-making process. To this extent the national courts in particular have broken out of the confines of early judicial decisions that appeared to struggle with the underlying purpose behind the Directive. These decisions conceptualised EIA within existing parameters of national administrative law and legal traditions, and in particular seemed to be unduly influenced by deferential judicial approaches to national planning law.[78] The approach today is more informed by valuing participation in its own right.

Finally, it is notable that most planning officers feel that EIA probably makes no difference to the decision to permit or refuse any particular application.[79] Of course, this may be

---

75. European Commission, *EIA in Europe: A Study on Costs and Benefits* (1996).

76. C. Jones, C. Wood, and B. Dipper, 'Environmental Assessment in the UK Planning Process: A Review of Practice' (1998) 69 TPR 315.

77. Elworthy and Holder, *Environmental Protection: Text and Materials* (London: Butterworths, 1997), 418.

78. J. Alder, 'Environmental Impact Assessment—the Inadequacies of English Law' (1993) JEL 203.

79. Jones, Wood, and Dipper (1998), op. cit., n. 76.

because greater attention is given to mitigating measures, either agreed early on or eventually required under planning conditions or obligations. On the other hand, it might suggest that the boundaries within which individual decisions are taken leave relatively little scope for a significantly different resolution of the balancing of environmental and other objectives than would otherwise have occurred where environmental impact was considered as a material consideration in town and country planning law. As has been said, 'EIA can be "frozen out" from any real policy or institutional effectiveness if it is not sufficiently linked, formally and informally, to the ways problems are defined, structured and addressed'.[80] Whether formal strategic environmental assessment will sufficiently alter this wider picture remains to be seen.

The Strategic Environmental Assessment Directive

For some years the limitations of project-based assessment have been apparent. Indeed, the National Environmental Protection Act 1969, the US law that inspired the 1985 Directive, covered all major federal *actions* and early drafts of the EIA Directive extended to wider strategic assessment. In 1991, proposals for a draft directive on strategic environmental assessment (SEA) surfaced. Moves to adopt a directive in this area were strengthened by a review of the EIA Directive in 1993, which found that the evaluation of many projects was taking place far too late in the development planning process (see Box 14.13).[81] Initially, the proposals for SEA extended to plans, *policies*, and programmes, but the inclusion of policy assessment in particular was strongly opposed by various Member States. Accordingly, the Directive that was finally adopted, Directive 2001/42/EC, only covers the assessment of the effects of certain plans and programmes on the environment. The SEA Directive, which like the EIA Directive is procedural law, came into force in June 2004.[82] and has been implemented by the Assessment of Plans and Programmes Regulations 2004 (SI 2004/1633).

BOX 14.13 **The limits of EIA and the need for SEA**

Fish farming in Scottish west coast waters expanded rapidly in the 1980s and again in the late 1990s, becoming an important sector of the rural economy but also generating controversy over its environmental impact. Although a Schedule 2 project, during the early years of growth the thresholds were set so high that the sector was effectively excluded from EIA (in the light of subsequent case law on thresholds, a questionable approach at best). However, as one study made clear, even greater use of project-EIA would fail to address the cumulative impacts of proliferation in important coastal habitats, the widespread disturbance to native wildlife caused

---

80. R. Bartlett, 'Ecological Reason in Administration: Environmental Impact Assessment and Administrative Theory' in R. Paehlke and D. Torgerson (eds), *Managing Leviathan: Environmental Politics and the Administrative State* (Peterborough: Broadview Press, 1990), 89.

81. *Report from the Commission on the Implementation of Directive* 85/337/EEC, COM(93)28 final.

82. There is also the Kiev Protocol to the UNECE Espoo Convention on Transboundary EIA which covers SEA.

by operational activities, impacts from the use of chemicals to control disease on fish farms and impacts on wild fish stocks from escapees. Although the EIA Directive requires indirect and cumulative impacts to be included in the ES, none of the impacts mentioned can really be captured by project-based EIA, for which a more strategic approach is needed. If used properly, EIA can address the sources of certain environmental harms, but not its symptoms, which in the case of fish farming include factors like the feeding of wild fish to captive fish, something which is controversial in ecological terms but which only some form of strategic or sustainability appraisal can really address.

Source: S. Thompson et al, (1995) 45 J. of Environmental Management 219.

The plans or programmes for which SEA is required are set out in Figure 14.2.

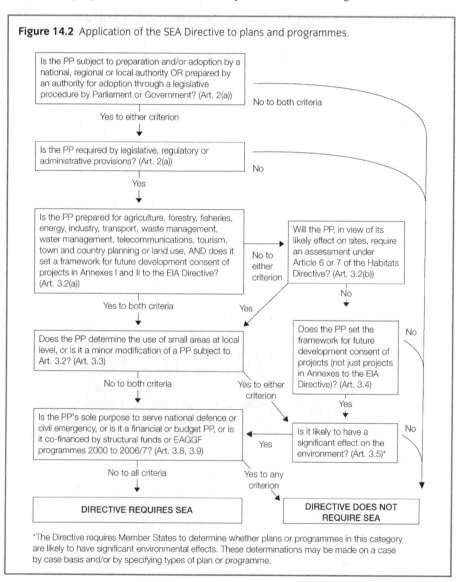

Figure 14.2 Application of the SEA Directive to plans and programmes.

*The Directive requires Member States to determine whether plans or programmes in this category are likely to have significant environmental effects. These determinations may be made on a case by case basis and/or by specifying types of plan or programme.

What is a 'plan' or a 'programme' is not defined either in the Directive or the implementing Regulations. However, guidance from the European Commission[83] suggests that what something is called does not really matter, and it is the substance which must be looked at (e.g. elements of the National Waste Strategy would be covered). The same guidance also notes that 'land use plans setting out how land is to be developed, or laying down rules or guidance as to the kind of development which might be appropriate or permissible in particular areas' could be a plan. This would obviously cover planning policy guidance, but it might also cover governmental policy objectives e.g. on the general location of house-building in the south-east of England.

The plans or programmes must however be 'required by legislative, regulatory or administrative provisions'. This seems intended to limit SEA to public plans and programmes, but the breadth of this phrase is a little unclear. For example, planning policy guidance/statements and circulars are not 'required' in this sense—they are not mentioned in the planning legislation in the way that 'the development plan' is—but as we saw in the previous chapter they are absolutely central to how the whole planning system works. (Note that revisions to a regional spatial strategy will have to be assessed, because it is required under the Planning and Compulsory Purchase Act 2004, whereas the regional policy guidance it replaces has never been 'required' in this sense.) This begs the question whether 'required' should be given a functional interpretation. If the case law of the Court of Justice on the EIA Directive is followed, then this, and a broad, functional reading of what is a 'plan' and a 'programme', is very likely.[84]

Deliberately linking SEA to EIA, as the SEA Directive does, might create problems since, for example, not all aspects of development plans or waste plans will relate to matters governed by EIA. In practice, it must be assumed that the EIA-related aspects of plans and programmes will not be looked at in isolation, and that for convenience (and regulatory coherence) all aspects of these types of plans, for example, the whole of the national waste strategy under the Environment Act 1995 (see p. 571) and perhaps also the air quality strategy under the same Act (see p. 654) will be subject to SEA.

SEA operates in a similar way to project-based assessment. There is a requirement for the proponent to prepare an 'environmental report' setting out information on the assessment of the effects of implementing the plan or programme. This report must include information on, amongst other things:

- existing environmental problems relevant to the plan or programme;

- the environmental characteristics of the area affected;

- environmental obligations imposed to meet international, European, and national objectives and how the plan or programme meets those objectives;

- the likely significant environmental effects which would be brought about by implementing the plan or programme, including consideration of things like cumulative and synergistic effects, and both temporary and long-term effects;

- any envisaged mitigating measures (which must be as full as possible); and

- a non-technical summary.

83. *Implementation of Directive 2001/42 on the Assessment of the Effects of Certain Plans and Programmes on the Environment* (2003).

84. Compare the interpretation of 'projects' in the EIA Directive, see p. 520.

A key feature of the SEA Directive is the attention to the consideration of alternatives. Information about the plan or programme, or the area affected, will always have to consider as well any 'reasonable alternatives' such as alternative types of development or alternative locations for it. There is a watered down version of a requirement to describe the 'do nothing' alternative, and the authority will also have to provide both a statement of how the assessment was conducted and the reasons for not adopting alternatives considered. These clearly go well beyond the provisions relating to alternatives under project-based EIA.

Once the information is provided in an environmental report, there must be consultation with statutory consultees (including relevant environmental NGOs) and with the public in a similar way to EIA. Unlike EIA, however, public authorities have to consult the public on the scope and level of detail of information to be included in the report, effectively providing for mandatory scoping and giving the public two stages in the plan-making process to express their views. A further notable difference is that environmental information must be taken into consideration *during* the plan-making process, rather than simply before adoption; the public must be given an 'early and effective opportunity within appropriate time frames' to comment, although precisely what this means is left to the Member States and it is notable that, regarding participation, the Aarhus Convention requires 'early public involvement, *when all options are open*' (emphasis added). Also, there must be measures for monitoring the implementation of the plan or programme. Both of these go some way towards making SEA a more iterative process than EIA. However, the fact that the same body prepares the environmental report and the assessment may give rise to allegations of bias. Finally, note that just because an SEA has been conducted this does not mean that EIA of projects which are in line with the SEA-ed plan or programme is not needed.

CHAPTER SUMMARY

1 Assessing, in a formal, anticipatory and structured manner, the impact of harmful human activities is increasingly a legal requirement in environmental decision-making. This is taking place at all levels of environmental law, international to national.

2 In international law, EIA duties are now contained in many specific treaties but there is as yet no global EIA treaty. States must carry out an environmental assessment of particularly harmful activities, an obligation that many (but not all) consider flows from general duties to cooperate regarding transboundary harm, but the procedural requirements of this duty are vague.

3 At national level, the environmental impact of development projects has always been a material consideration in making planning decisions, but for many projects the process for assessing environmental impact has now been formalized under EC law.

4 The two main measures are the 1985 Environmental Impact Assessment (EIA) Directive, and the 2001 Strategic Environmental Assessment (SEA) Directive. The former is project-based, while the latter applies to certain plans and programmes. Both share certain common features.

5 Before consent is given, or a plan or programme is adopted, the proponent (e.g. the developer or plan-maker) prepares an environment statement (the term used for EIA) or environmental report (SEA). These documents detail the proposals and their direct and indirect effects on the environment, and any mitigating measures.

6 In both regimes the public and regulatory agencies can comment on the proposals before the decision-maker—who must have regard to all the environmental information (including the views of the public)—undertakes the final assessment.

7 EIA and SEA are essentially procedural tools; they require environmental information to be generated and taken into account by decision-makers, but projects, plans, and programmes having adverse environmental impacts can still proceed.

8 EIA is mandatory for certain kinds of development project, and discretionary for others depending on whether there will be significant environmental effects due to their size, nature or location. The types of project covered by EIA are spelt out in the Directive.

9 SEA applies to plans and programmes in certain sectors where these set a framework for future development consent of projects subject to EIA, or plans and programmes which require an assessment under the EC Habitats Directive, and a significance threshold test also applies.

10 The EIA Directive is implemented by detailed regulations that apply to projects requiring planning permission and by analogous regulations covering activities falling outside the planning system. The SEA Directive has been transposed by a single set of regulations in 2004.

11 With EIA, whether projects require assessment has often been contentious. This can take various forms, including whether something is a 'project' and which stage of its approval is the 'consent'. The latter has proved particularly problematic because of the way that planning permission is usually given for major development projects.

12 Other problem areas are whether projects will have 'significant' environmental effects, the use of legal thresholds, and whether a project should be assessed in isolation or in the light of wider proposals of which it forms a part. These problems may arise where there has not been an EIA, but can also arise in challenges to the adequacy of environmental statements. The SEA Directive goes some way towards considering development projects in their wider context.

13 Another controversial issue has been whether procedures will suffice if they fall short of formal EIA, but nevertheless appear to provide decision-makers with environmental information. The courts have now held that if they frustrate meaningful public participation, then they will not.

14 All these areas of controversy are likely to find equivalents under the SEA Directive.

Q QUESTIONS

1 If EIA is now part of customary international law, what is the exact nature of the obligations on states? And is EIA in international law a matter only for governments and government experts, or does it require public participation?

2 What difficulties are there in ensuring that projects with significant environmental effects are subjected to EIA? Are these legal problems, policy problems or evidential problems?

3 Consider whether EIA should be required for either of the following:
   a Large scale burying and burning of animal carcasses to combat disease.
   b A cement works which starts to burn old car tyres.

4 As things stand, if an ES is thought to be inadequate, the only remedy for the planning authority is to require developers to provide further information. Is this sufficient? Should any other parties be involved in preparing statements? If so, who, and how? And is it problematic that developers prepare environmental statements?

5 How useful a tool does EA seem to be? Should it have a more 'substantive' edge, i.e. if potentially damaging environmental consequences are brought to light should, as a matter of law, the proposal be blocked? Or amended? Or suitable conditions applied? What other options might there be? (You might find it useful to compare EA with the provisions of Article 6 of the EC Habitats Directive, discussed at p. 827.)

6 Bigbucks plc wants to develop the site of a disused steelworks into a multiplex cinema, retail park and 100 houses. It also proposes to set aside one-third of the land as a wetland and actively regenerate this area so that it can host locally rare species. The local planning authority does not require an ES and grants outline planning permission. After three weeks the old steelworks has largely been demolished, but construction has not yet begun. A local amenity group asks you for advice concerning the lack of EIA. Advise them. What further information would you need?

 FURTHER READING

Anyone looking for a thoroughly engaging introduction to the basic issues involved in EIA (and the initial scepticism with which these might be viewed by governments) should look no further than the chapter by Chris Wood, a leading authority on EIA, in C. Miller (ed.) *Planning and Environmental Protection* (Oxford: Hart Publishing, 2001), complete with fictional 'Yes, Minister'-type discussion. Other good introductory accounts of EIA are J. Glasson, R. Therivel, and A. Chadwick, *Introduction to Environmental Impact Assessment* (2nd edn London: UCL Press, 1999) and C. Wood, *Environmental Impact Assessment: A Comparative Review* (2nd edn Pearson, 2002). The journal, *Impact Assessment and Project Appraisal* (formerly *Project Appraisal*) can also be recommended, although much of the good, policy-based research tends to be published together with the general planning literature. Of this, C. Wood and C. Jones, 'The Effect of Environmental Assessment on UK Local Planning Authorities' (1997) 34(8) Urban Studies 1237, and C. Jones, C. Wood, and B. Dipper, 'Environmental Assessment in the UK Planning Process: A Review of Practice' (1998) 69(3) Town Planning Review 315 have been the basis for much of the research data in this chapter, as has a review of recent screening and scoping practice in ENDS Report 340, (May 2003), 29.

Of the more legalistically focused literature, J. Alder, 'Environmental Impact Assessment—The Inadequacies of English Law' [1993] JEL 203, provides not just an excellent and accessible account of some of the early case law and implementation problems, but also an enduring framework through which to think about EIA law and its realization. More recently, J. Holder, *Environmental Assessment* (Oxford: Oxford University Press, 2004) provides the most sophisticated analysis of EA from a socio-legal perspective, focusing on the contested areas of alternatives, prediction and participation. A more practitioner-focused work is S. Tromans and K. Fuller, *Environmental Impact Assessment: Law and Practice* (London: Butterworths, 2003) while judicial developments are the focus of J. Pugh-Smith, 'Environmental impact assessment: the continuing jurisprudence' [2002] JPL 1316. There is, as yet, no specific book-length text on the law of SEA. Useful articles include W. Sheate, H. Byron, and S. Smith 'Implementing the SEA Directive: Sectoral Challenges and Opportunities for the UK and EU' (2003) 14 European Environment 73, while J. Robinson and D. Elvin 'The Assessment of Plans and Programmes' [2004] JPL 1028 provides excellent commentary on what some of the vague phrases in the SEA Directive might mean when applied to the UK.

Although a little dated now, W. Sheate, *Environmental Impact Assessment: Law and Policy-Making an Impact II* (Cameron May, 1996) remains a good discussion of both the policy and legal issues in EIA (and SEA). Useful coverage of the development and status of EIA in international law can be found in

P. Birnie and A. Boyle, *International Law and the Environment* (2nd edn Oxford: Oxford University Press, 2002) and in A. Sands, *Principles of International Environmental Law* (2nd edn Cambridge: Cambridge University Press, 2003). Both consider the status of EIA as a binding norm of international environmental law in more depth than we can here, and the latter also gives a nice account of early objections to EIA by developing countries at the time of the 1972 UN Conference at Stockholm, their concerns being that if EIA required consultation with other states then developed states might use it to block projects in developing countries.

Finally, B. Bryant (ed.), *Twyford Down: Roads, Campaigning and Environmental Law* (London: E & FN Spon, 1996), written by those directly involved, is an entertaining, illuminating and ultimately depressing account of the unsuccessful attempt to save Twyford Down, illustrating very clearly the gap between the aspirations for EIA and actual events.

@ WEB LINKS

At (English) national level the main site is the Office of the Deputy Prime Minister, which now deals with both planning and EIA <www.odpm.gov.uk>. This contains links to the main guidance—which is essential reading for any evaluation of EIA going beyond the material in this chapter—together with fairly user-friendly overviews of EIA and EIA law. The European Commission's EIA Homepage <europa.eu.int/comm/environment/eia/home.htm> has links to all EC legislation and guidance on EIA and SEA, together with useful reports on implementation. The UN Economic Commission for Europe <www.unece.org/env/eia> hosts information about the Espoo Convention on Transboundary EIA and its Kiev Protocol on SEA.

Further information about the World Bank is at <www.worldbank.org>, while the work of the World Bank, including its Inspection Panel decisions, is tracked by the Centre for International Environmental Law <www.ciel.org>. Finally, it is always worth seeing what is available via the EIA Centre at Manchester University <www.art.man.ac.uk/eia/eiac.htm> which for many years has been at the forefront of the evolution and implementation of EIA.

15 Waste management

 Overview

This chapter deals with the legal control of waste. Waste management law is a good example of mixed regulation as a wide range of mechanisms is used to address not only the problems of pollution caused by waste disposal but also positive mechanisms such as producer responsibility which address the causes of waste production. This chapter concentrates on the regulation of the waste chain from initial production to final disposal. This includes the coverage of the difficult question of the definition of waste and an explanation of the waste management licensing system. In addition there is some discussion of the growing number of policies and laws which seek to encourage waste minimisation, recycling and recovery. There is brief coverage of relevant economic instruments such as taxation and tradable permits. In general the chapter looks at national law although the important contribution of EC law and the purposive approach to regulation is also considered. The regulation of international trade in the import and export of hazardous waste is also discussed briefly.

At the end of this chapter you should be able to:

✔ Understand the nature and scale of the problems of managing the production and disposal of waste and some of the main ways they have been addressed at an international, European and national level.
✔ Appreciate the challenge of regulating the management and disposal of waste.
✔ Understand the historical development of waste management law and policy, particularly at national and European levels.
✔ Understand the frameworks of international and European waste management law.
✔ Appreciate some of the main difficulties of defining waste as reflected in the major case law on the topic.
✔ Identify the general definition of waste.
✔ Understand in outline the system of waste management licensing.
✔ Appreciate some of the different approaches to managing waste production including producer responsibility legislation and measures to encourage recycling.
✔ Understand the role of economic instruments in waste management.

The nature and scale of the problem

Managing the production and disposal of waste is one of the most significant environmental challenges the UK faces over the next 20 years. Around 436 million tonnes of waste are produced annually in the UK. This large figure is slightly misleading in that it includes not only waste from households, industry, and commercial sources but also large amounts of waste from construction and demolition sites, farms and spoil from mining and quarrying. Waste from these last three sources amounts to over two-thirds of the total amount of waste. At present large proportions of this are recycled or reused (e.g. inert demolition rubble is reused in new construction projects or road building). Perhaps more critically much of the waste from these categories falls outside present legal controls as it is either not 'waste' for the purposes of waste legislation or it is classified as exempt from many of the controls. Accordingly, most legal controls have been directed at dealing with municipal, industrial and commercial wastes. The amount of municipal waste (mostly from households) is growing at around 3–4 per cent per year which is one of the fastest growth rates in Europe. Unless there are significant changes in the amount of waste produced it is anticipated that the amount of municipal waste will double by 2020.

Not only is the rate of waste production much higher in Britain but waste management methods are much less diversified. Most of the waste disposed of in Britain is deposited in large holes in the ground, such as old quarries. Almost 80 per cent of municipal waste is disposed of in landfill sites and levels of recycling of waste are very low at about 12 per cent. By comparison, on average, other EU Member States send approximately half as much waste to landfill (45 per cent) and recycle more than twice as much waste (26 per cent). In certain countries the figures are even more disparate (see comparisons with other European countries in Figure 15.1). There is a variety of reasons for the comparatively poor per-formance of the UK in comparison to other countries. Much of the reliance on landfill as the preferred option for waste disposal reflects the availability of cheap, old minerals sites with relatively stable geological conditions. The reliance on landfill has, in turn, led to the lack of development of other recycling and recovery options. This abundance of cheap landfill sites has also contributed to an inertia in terms of new laws and policies which encourage alternative waste recycling and recovery options or waste minimisation. For example, there have been few measures to promote waste reduction and many waste producers have little or no incentive to minimise or recycle their waste. This position is in sharp contrast to other European Countries which have made greater use of legal and economic instruments such as bans on the landfilling of certain wastes, extended producer responsibility for waste recycling and recovery, high taxes on landfill and direct charging for the disposal of household waste. A combination of these measures provide incentives to minimise waste production and develop alternative facilities to sort, recover and recycle waste.

This position is in the process of changing with many new initiatives and policies. Partly this is because many existing landfill sites are reaching their full capacity and that the supply of suitable new locations for landfill sites is very limited indeed. In some areas the problem is acute, leading to the need to transport waste long distances. Another driver is the need to implement European legislation which sets waste reduction, recycling, and recovery targets. The main consequence is that although waste production is set to rise, the amount of waste going to landfill will fall dramatically over the next 15 years. On the assumption that this reduction is not met through waste minimization initiatives, there will have to be a huge increase in alternative disposal, recovery and recycling routes. Principally this will be met through an increase in waste incineration capacity with the recovery of the energy produced. Other waste management methods such as composting and recycling will also have to be increased.

Each of these methods of disposal creates its own pollution problems and controversies. As suggested above, landfill sites may give rise to problems of methane emissions and of

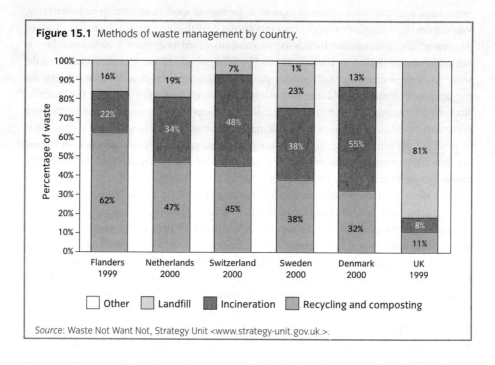

Figure 15.1 Methods of waste management by country.

Source: Waste Not Want Not, Strategy Unit <www.strategy-unit.gov.uk.>.

water pollution as a result of leachate. They also give rise to effects that will be only too obvious to those who live nearby, such as smells, noise, air-borne dust and rubbish, and increased traffic generation. As a result, landfill sites are amongst the uses of land that are most vigorously opposed by local communities. A further factor is that there is a marked tendency for landfill sites to be proposed on 'waste land', which is often precisely that land which is of greatest importance in nature conservation and amenity terms. In relation to incineration, there are obvious problems of air pollution, especially concerning the release of such things as dioxins as a result of incomplete combustion. Even recycling and other waste processing sites are controversial amongst the public.

The challenge of regulating waste management

Waste management provides some different if not unique challenges in comparison with other areas of pollution control. First, the central issue of *what* is controlled, that is to say the definition of waste, is not clear. Most of the problems associated with defining waste adequately stem from the fact that it is not necessarily synonymous with actual pollution or harm. The threat to the environment may arise as a result of the risk of pollution or harm in circumstances where the waste is mishandled or abandoned. Therefore there is a need to regulate the whole waste cycle from the production of the waste through the handling, storing, transportation and treatment of waste up to and including the final disposal, independently of whether there is any actual pollution or harm caused. Consequently, there are many 'grey areas' which can lead to uncertainty and confusion. These include such things as whether something which can be reused but which is discarded should be classified as waste (e.g. electrical equipment which is placed into a dustbin but which functions perfectly); whether something which is not wanted by one person (and is therefore 'got rid of') but is valued by another (which is evidenced by the fact that they will 'buy' it) can be waste; or finally, whether a residue or a by-product from an industrial process which can be used as a replacement for a raw material should be classified as waste.

Secondly, there is the problem of trying to blend different types of legal measures to encourage waste minimization and reuse. There is an inevitable requirement to replace those things which have been discarded and consequently there are issues of resource depletion which can only be tackled through the minimization, reuse and recovery of waste. Traditional forms of regulation are useful when addressing the control of environmental risks (e.g. from the disposal of waste) but in doing so they can often fail to address this issue. In this sense legislative controls over the management of waste have proved to be inadequate as positive mechanisms for environmental improvement. Traditionally, 'command and con-trol' mechanisms have focused on the regulation of activities after the production of the waste. For example, a system which licenses the treatment or disposal of waste is not necessarily efficient when it comes to promoting the reduction of the production of waste or encouraging recycling and recovery.

Finally, and linked closely to the last point, there is the difficult challenge of sustainable waste management. Ultimately, the main indicator of sustainability would be a continuous reduction in the volume of waste arisings. Up until recently, there have been few legal meas-ures introduced to meet this goal. A lack of sufficient information on waste arisings, the use of 'predict and provide' methods which base future growth in waste facilities on extrapolated historic figures and a lack of coordinated waste policies on a national basis have contributed to the failure to address sustainability issues. As with so many other areas, the picture is being changed as a result of European legislation which sets binding targets for the recycling, recovery and reduction of waste (e.g. through the Packaging Waste Directive (94/62/EC) and the Landfill Directive (99/31/EC)). For example, in contrast to the regulation of waste disposal, the introduction of positive instruments such as producer responsibility require-ments makes producers responsible for products throughout their life cycle including designing products for ease of recycling and recovery, imposing an obligation to take back used products and meeting certain recycling and recovery targets for proportions of prod-ucts placed on the market.

History of domestic waste law and policy

An outline of the history of waste regulation is set out in Box 15.1. The key events at both domestic and European levels illustrate the different phases of the development of waste law and policy. This section deals with the history of domestic control, European developments are considered further below. Early domestic laws were not primarily environmental in nature, being aimed at preventing accumulations of waste which might cause public health problems. In addition, the controls were not used to prevent harm but were used to clean up existing problems. Preventative controls were only introduced with the planning system in 1947. This continues to the present day with the existence of some form of planning permission being a prerequisite for waste management licencing. The planning system, however, is not suited to controlling technical or post operational activities on a waste

BOX 15.1 **Waste management—timeline**

Year	Key Events
Pre-1848	Waste production is small as most waste is burned as fuel but 'Rakers' are employed in London to remove household rubbish to be used as compost or dumped on the Essex marshes.
1848	First real controls over waste disposal aimed at protecting human health under Public Health Act 1848.
1875	Public Health Act 1875 imposes duty on local authorities to arrange the removal and disposal of household waste every week. In 1907 this duty extended to include trade waste.
1936	Public Health Act 1936 includes rules governing the accumulation of waste which is a Statutory Nuisance and a framework for the control of landfill sites, which had little practical impact.
1947	The passing of the Town and Country Planning Act 1947 means that new waste sites are subject to anticipatory planning controls under the development control system. Provision for future sites is dealt with in development plans. Pre-existing sites remain relatively uncontrolled.
1971–2	A public outcry over the fly-tipping of drums of cyanide in Nuneaton followed by the publication of RCEP's Second Report which called for the introduction of controls over the tipping of hazardous wastes led to the Deposit of Poisonous Waste Act 1972. The Act is drafted in 10 days and passes through Parliament within a month. It is one of the first controls over the disposal of hazardous waste in the world.
1974	The first comprehensive system controlling the disposal of waste is introduced in the Control of Pollution Act 1974. It is based around a system of licensing for waste disposal activities. Although there are many defects in the system, COPA remains as the centre piece of waste legislation for over 25 years.
1975	The Waste Framework Directive (75/442) (WFD) is the first major piece of European law dealing with waste. The Directive provides for the drawing up of waste management plans and the establishment of systems to authorise waste management installations.
1990	Part II of the Environmental Protection Act 1990 is passed creating a new system of waste management licensing and regulation. In an attempt to address some of the defects of COPA 1974, EPA 1990 separates operational from regulatory functions within local authorities and introduces a duty of care throughout the waste chain. The policy document *This Common Inheritance* sets out a strategy based around waste minimization and recycling. It sets a target of 25 per cent for the recycling of household waste by 2000. No legal measures are proposed as to how this target might be achieved.
1991	The WFD is comprehensively revised under Directive 91/156. The Directive introduces a new definition of waste and sets out certain objectives such as ensuring that waste is recovered and disposed of without endangering human health or harming the environment.
1992	The Duty of Care is implemented and for the first time 'reasonable steps' must be taken to prevent problems caused by waste from production to final disposal.

Year	Key Events
1994	After four years delay, the implementation of the main provisions of Part II, EPA 1990 is accompanied by the Waste Management Licensing Regulations 1994 which transpose the requirements of the WFD such as the definition of Directive waste and the statutory objectives as well as a new system of waste management licensing which applies to waste treatment and storage in addition to disposal. The Packaging Waste Directive (94/62) introduces producer responsibility for packaging waste.
1995	The Environment Act 1995 represents another new era for waste management regulation. The creation of the Environment Agency centralizes regulatory responsibilities transferring them away from local Waste Regulation Authorities. In addition to these institutional changes, the Act contains new powers to produce a National Waste Strategy and to introduce Producer Responsibility for certain types of waste.
1996	The first direct economic instrument dealing with waste, the landfill tax, is introduced in the Finance Act 1996. Initially the tax is set at £7 per tonne on waste going to landfill. The first waste strategy for England and Wales, *Making Waste Work*, is published, re-setting the target of 25 per cent of household waste to be recycled by the year 2000—just as in 1990.
1997	Producer Responsibility for packaging and packaging waste is introduced under the Producer Responsibility Obligations (Packaging Waste) Regulations 1997, requiring businesses to recover and recycle a significant proportion of packaging handled.
1999	The Pollution Prevention and Control Act 1999 implements the Integrated Pollution Prevention and Control Directive. Over 900 landfill sites are made subject to the integrated controls. The Landfill Directive sets specific reduction targets for the amount of municipal waste going to landfill.
2000	A revised waste strategy, *Waste Strategy 2000* revisits the targets for the recycling or composting of household waste. The new targets are set at 25 per cent by 2005, 30 per cent by 2010, and 33 per cent by 2015. The target of 25 per cent recycling of household waste set in *This Common Inheritance* and *Making Waste Work* is missed by over 100 per cent. The End of Life Vehicles Directive introduced imposing producer responsibility on car manufacturers to recover and recycle motor vehicles.
2002	The Landfill (England and Wales) Regulations 2002 transpose the Landfill Directive in relation to the reduction of waste being sent to landfill, banning the disposal of certain wastes and requiring the classification of sites.
2003	The Waste and Emissions Trading Act 2003 sets out a scheme for trading landfill allowances by waste authorities and producer responsibility for motor vehicles is introduced. The Household Waste Recycling Act 2003 requires all English local authorities to provide kerbside collections for all householders for a minimum of two materials by 2010.

management site (e.g. controlling technical specifications of liners or dealing with long-term aftercare of a landfill site).

These weaknesses were only addressed in the 1970s with a phase which can be characterized as concentrating on the regulation of waste disposal. This involved continuing controls over of waste disposal under licencing systems for hazardous waste under the Deposit of Hazardous Wastes Act 1972 and then more generally for most non-hazardous wastes in Part I of the Control of Pollution Act 1974. COPA 1974 introduced a comprehensive system in which a waste disposal licence was required before 'controlled waste' could be finally disposed of either in a landfill site or by incineration. Although the system was not without its flaws it provided a framework which was adopted by other countries, and in particular for the first major European legislation on waste, the Framework Directive (75/442).

Following the implementation of COPA 1974, it became increasingly clear that there were still problems dealing with the management of waste (as compared with its final disposal) and that the scope of the Act was too narrow (see further Box 15.2). Some of the defects should have been obvious at the time the Act was passed whereas others only became clear as time passed.

BOX 15.2 **The defects of COPA 1974**

In 1989, after some 15 years of operation, COPA 1974 was the subject of 'consistent and universal criticism' as part of a House of Commons Environment Committee investigation.[1] The identified defects illustrate some of the challenges of waste regulation and foreshadow some of the changes brought in under EPA 1990:

- COPA sought to control the final deposit of waste rather than its management. Problems arose with the storage, treatment and transportation of waste. For example, where waste had been fly-tipped, it was only possible to prosecute the person who had actually caused or knowingly permitted the deposit of the waste, leaving others further up the chain of waste management free from control notwithstanding the fact that these others may have had a significant degree of responsibility for what had happened.

- There were problems with enforcement. For example, there was no offence of failing to comply with a licence condition. A decision in *Leigh Land Reclamation Ltd v Walsall Metropolitan Borough Council* (1991) 155 JP 547 meant that as long as the deposit of waste was in accordance with the licence conditions, it was irrelevant if other conditions relating to the site were not being complied with. This had the effect of ensuring that many operational and administrative licence conditions were practically unenforceable.

- Once planning permission had been granted for waste disposal operations, there were limited grounds to refuse a grant of a waste disposal licence or to refuse a transfer, or to vary or revoke a licence.

- Licence holders had the right to surrender a disposal licence at any time, in which case any conditions attached to it would automatically cease to have any effect. In practice, this meant that an operator could abandon a site and relinquish any future responsibility for supervision of it.

- There was a lack of strategic guidance on waste management. This failure was at both national and local levels. Only 23 out of a possible 79 waste disposal plans were produced by local waste disposal authorities. National guidance on the application of waste policies in the form of waste management papers were produced very slowly and patchily

- There was a significant overlap in regulatory and operational responsibilities. The regulatory authorities created by COPA 1974, were also the main operators of waste disposal sites. The inherent conflict between these two roles led to an undermining of public confidence in the ability of the regulator to control its own activities.

---

1. House of Commons Environment Select Committee, *Toxic Waste* (Second Report, 1988–9 Session).

Many of these defects were addressed with the introduction of Part II of the Environmental Protection Act (EPA) 1990 which introduced a phase of a greater emphasis on waste *management*. This involved the control of the whole of the waste cycle 'from cradle to grave'. In particular, the EPA 1990 increased controls over waste producers and carriers and restructured the administration of waste regulation. The implementation of Part II (and accompanying secondary legislation) has been piecemeal, mainly as a result of some of the difficult issues it covered. Although some of the provisions were brought into force on 1 April 1992 (e.g. the duty of care) the main bulk of Part II was brought into operation on 1 May 1994 along with the Waste Management Licensing Regulations which transposed the requirements of the amended Waste Framework Directive and provide the bulk of operative waste management licensing provisions.

The most recent phase of waste regulation has addressed the subtler but no less important defects in previous legislation. These include the lack of a consistent approach to strategic waste planning and the failure of 'command and control' regulation to tackle issues of waste prevention, minimisation and recycling. Thus the Environment Act 1995 provided for the production of a National Waste Strategy to articulate specific objectives for waste management. In relation to the encouragement of waste minimisation, the 1995 Act also contained powers to make Producer Responsibility schemes and the Finance Act 1996 introduced a tax on landfill which was designed to reflect the full cost of waste disposal. More recently, the Landfill Regulations 2002 contained specific binding targets for reducing the amount of waste going to landfill.

International law and waste management

Generally, waste regulation has been concerned with controlling the management of waste within the domestic context. There are three main areas in which international environmental law has played a significant part. First, the OECD has played a significant part in harmonising international definitions of waste which in turn is reflected in the European List of Wastes (see below). Secondly, international law has had a major impact on preventing the dumping of waste at sea. UNCLOS provides a general obligation to prevent marine pollution, which covers dumping (Arts 192–4). More particularly, the 1972 London Convention on the Prevention of Marine Pollution by Dumping of Wastes and Other Matter provides a global framework for the control of the deliberate disposal at sea of wastes or other matter with various regional agreements such as the 1998 OSPAR Convention for the Protection of the Marine Environment of the North East Atlantic applying to specific geographical areas (see further Box 3.4 and p. 709).[2]

Thirdly, as waste regulation became tighter in some countries (mainly the US and Europe) the costs of disposal rose and it became common practice to export hazardous wastes to developing countries where it could be disposed of at a lower cost (as a result of lower standards). The control of transboundary movement of hazardous waste is governed at the international level by the Basel Convention on the Control of Transboundary

---

2. W. Howarth and D. McGillivray, *Water Pollution and Water Quality Law* (Crayford: Shaw, 2001), 898.

Movements of Hazardous Waste and their Disposal. The Convention entered into force in May 1992 and was ratified by the UK on 7 February 1994. The Convention establishes a system whereby the exporter of waste must obtain the consent of the regulatory authorities in the importing country prior to shipping that waste. That consent must include a written confirmation that the importer of the waste will deal with the waste in an environmentally sound manner. Where the consignment of waste cannot take place (e.g. where it would not be handled in an 'environmentally sound manner'), the exporter of the waste is bound to take back the waste within 90 days. A subsequent amendment, ratified by the UK in October 1997, prohibits the export of hazardous waste from OECD countries to non-OECD countries. A Protocol adopted in 1999 provides for a liability scheme and compensation for damage resulting from transboundary movements of hazardous wastes.

Whilst the Basel Convention has attempted to regularize the position in relation to the export of hazardous waste to developing countries, it has been argued that the Convention legitimizes the trade in hazardous waste which is open to abuse through the use of vague subjective standards such as managing the transfer in an 'environmentally sound manner' and the lack of effective monitoring and control.[3] The result is that there is a risk that waste is still imported into developing countries either illegally or without proper regard to the risks associated with its recovery.

The EC Regulation on the Supervision and Control of Shipments of Waste within, into and out of the European Community (259/93) gives effect to the Basel Convention throughout the EC. The Regulation subjects the transfer of all waste (not just hazardous) between countries to a system of 'prior informed consent' of the regulatory agencies in the two respective countries. The Regulation has direct effect but the UK subsequently ratified the Basel Convention in 1994 (as required under Council Decision 93/98/EEC) and implemented its requirements under the Transfrontier Shipment of Waste Regulations 1994 (SI 1994/121) and the UK Management Plan for the Imports and Exports of Waste. This management plan sets out the policy behind the regulations. It is advisory and non-binding (although it gains its force through the regulations). The Regulation and the implementing legislation has been shown to be defective in some respects through the saga of the import of the so-called 'US Ghost Ships' (see Box 15.3).

The type of notification which must be given differs depending upon the nature of the waste which is shipped, whether the waste is destined for recovery or disposal and finally whether the waste is transferred between two Member States or out of the EC. Waste which is being transported for disposal is relatively straightforward and must comply with the requirements of the Basel Convention (see above). In the UK the Management Plan for the Imports and Exports of Waste bans all exports of waste for disposal and bans most imports for disposal other than in exceptional cases where wider environmental considerations apply.

Waste transported for recovery is controlled under a more complicated system. The EC Regulation adopts a classification for all wastes (mainly taken from an OECD Council Decision) which divides wastes into three lists: Green, Amber, and Red. The categories are exclusive in the sense that any waste not on the list is treated as being unassigned and Red list waste.

---

3. P. Birnie and A. Boyle *International Law & the Environment* (2nd ed Oxford: Oxford University Press, 2002), 436.

BOX 15.3 **Transfrontier shipments and the 'Ghost Ships'**

The US Maritime administration (MARAD) owned 130 old warships which needed dismantling. The ships were hazardous because of small quantities of hazardous wastes such as PCBs and asbestos within the structures. MARAD approached a British company to carry out the work on 13 of the ships in a dock at Hartlepool. MARAD applied for Transfrontier Shipment consent in June 2003. Under the Regulation, the EA was only allowed 30 days within which consent had to be given or consent was deemed to be granted. Once granted the TFS approval could not be revoked. The EA issued its consent in July 2003. Subsequently, it became clear that there were a number of problems with the proposed recovery processes which were to be carried out on the ships. The planning permission for the site was invalid and the existing waste management licence needed to be modified to cover the proposed recovery operations. As a consequence, the US ships could not be dismantled because the necessary authorizations were not in place. The ships had, however, already set sail for the UK. The EA's attempt to modify the waste management licence breached the Habitats Directive as a result of the failure to assess the potential impact of the dismantling on a nearby nature conservation site. Friends of the Earth overturned the modification in the High Court.

The saga of the 'Ghost Ships' demonstrated that, as in other areas of environmental regulation, the many overlapping powers and responsibilities need to be clearly coordinated. The importation of hazardous waste requires a number of related consents/authorizations in addition to the requirement for TFS approval. The current system does not identify who is to take responsibility for ensuring that adequate coordination takes place. The 30-day period for consent is too short to allow for proper consideration of the overall consequences of importation and there is no formal process of consultation with statutory bodies or the public. In addition, there is presently no power to prevent the importation of hazardous waste when the shipment is destined for recovery. This coupled with the absence of a power to revoke consent presents practical difficulties in circumstances where waste cannot be recovered. Some of these defects are to be addressed in a revision of Regulation 259/93 which will prohibit imports of certain substances by reclassifying shipments of hazardous waste as being for 'disposal' in circumstances which currently would be viewed as 'recovery'.[4]

The Green list can be found in Annex II to the EC Regulation. Shipments of such waste need to be accompanied by basic information such as a description of the waste, quantity shipped, the name and address of the person to whom the waste is consigned and a description of the recovery operation involved. The only other requirement is that the waste should be shipped to a facility licensed in accordance with the Waste Framework Directive. In *R v Environment Agency, ex parte Dockgrange Ltd* [1997] Env LR 575, the High Court held that a policy which treated mixtures of different Green list wastes as unassigned (and therefore treated as Red list waste with the consequent tightening of procedures) was unlawful and that the correct approach was to identify such a shipment as a mixture of assigned wastes which were to be found on the Green list.

4. See *R (Friends of the Earth) v Environment Agency* [2004] Env LR 31, DEFRA, *US Naval Ships: Review of Regulatory Structure* (2003) available at <www.defra.gov.uk> and COM(2003) 379 final: *Proposal for a Regulation on Shipments of Waste*.

Amber list wastes can be found in Annex III to the Regulation. Shipments of Amber waste must be subject to the pre-notification procedures found in the Basel Convention. The notification must contain details of the type, source and quantity of the waste (Art. 6). In addition, Amber list wastes can be shipped under a general notification procedure whereby certain types of shipments going to a particular facility do not have to obtain approval on each occasion (Art. 9).

Red list wastes (and any waste which has not been assigned to one of the lists) are subject to the greatest level of control. The regulatory authority in the exporting country must give notification to the importing regulatory authority prior to export and there is no provision for a general approval as with Amber wastes.

European waste management law and policy

European policy on waste management is based largely upon broad objectives centred around a 'waste hierarchy' (see Box 15.4). One of the weaknesses of the past Action Programmes has, however, been the vagueness of the specific methods of promoting the waste hierarchy. The Sixth Action Programme, *Environment 2010: Our Future, Our Choice* has identified waste and resources as one of the four priority areas for action. The Programme generally follows the waste hierarchy in the setting of objectives in terms of prevention, recycling, and re-use. Various waste streams are identified for specific action and the idea of integrated product policy in reducing waste is emphasized. The general objectives found in the Sixth Action Programme are supplemented by a more specific Thematic Strategy on Waste Prevention which sets out plans to identify priority wastes, measures to ensure their recycling and collection, and instruments to encourage the creation of markets for recycled materials.

BOX 15.4 **The waste heirarchy**

The cornerstone of all waste law is the aim of meeting, as far as possible, a heirarchy of waste with policies and laws designed to promote measures as high up the heirarchy as possible. The heirarchy is:

1 Prevention

The primary aim is to prevent the creation of waste at source through proper design of products and processes. This is linked with such initiatives as the development of integrated product policy, clean technology, eco-labelling and product life cycle analysis.

2 Recycling and reuse

A second aim is to recycle or to reuse waste which is produced, with particular emphasis to be placed on the use of waste as a source of energy, for example through combined heat and power schemes linked to waste incinerators. An obvious example of the EC's role in this area is its development of the Producer Responsibility obligation covering such waste streams as packaging waste, end-of-life vehicles, batteries, electrical and electronic waste.

3 Proper management and disposal

A third aim is that waste should be disposed of safely preferably by incineration with landfill only used as a last resort.

European law on waste management is based around directives which lay down general principles such as the setting up of licensing and inspection systems to ensure that the management of waste does not harm human health and the environment. These general principles can be found in broad framework directives on waste (75/442) and hazardous waste (91/689). These general principles are complemented by more detailed legislation. These cover two main areas. First, there are a number of important directives which address methods of waste treatment including directives on landfill (99/31) incineration (2000/76) and integrated pollution prevention and control (96/61). These directives lay down standards for waste treatment such as emissions of dioxins from incinerators and the type of liner for landfills as well as banning the disposal of certain products in landfills, e.g. liquid wastes and tyres. A combination of these recent directives is expected to have an impact on waste management over the next 20 or so years. The second group of waste directives are more concerned with the management of particular types of waste. Some of these directives address particularly hazardous wastes (e.g. directives dealing with waste PCBs (96/59/EC) and batteries (91/157/EEC)); whereas others seek to reduce the amount of wastes arising in certain waste streams (e.g. packaging, electrical equipment, and vehicles). Many of the directives in the waste management area are relatively new and have a transitional effect. Consequently, the full impact of this recent legislation will only be felt in domestic law and practice over the next 20 years.

(a) The Framework Directive on Waste

The original Waste Framework Directive (75/442) was aimed largely at establishing a common set of principles dealing with the strategic planning and authorization of waste disposal. It was amended in 1991 by Directive 91/156. The central provisions of the Directive are set out in Box 15.5. The Framework Directive as amended was transposed into UK national law by a combination of Part II of EPA 1990 and the Waste Management Licensing Regulations 1994 (SI 1994/1056). Many of the provisions of the Framework Directive have been directly transposed in the Waste Management Licensing Regulations 1994 (sometimes referred to as 'copied out') and therefore the wording and interpretation of the Directive is directly relevant to UK law.

BOX 15.5 **The key provisions of the Waste Framework Directive**

Article 1 sets out the definition of waste as 'any substance or objects in the categories set out in Annex I which the holder discards or intends or is required to discard'.

Article 2 excludes certain wastes from the scope of the Directive. Gaseous effluents are excluded entirely whereas other classes including 'waste waters', waste from mines and quarries and certain classes of agricultural waste are excluded where they are 'already covered by other legislation'.

Article 3 establishes the waste hierarchy by requiring appropriate measures to encourage the prevention or reduction of waste and the recovery of waste by recycling, reuse or reclamation including the conversion of waste to energy through incineration.

Article 4 sets out the 'objectives' for safe waste management requiring Member States to 'take the necessary measures to ensure that waste is recovered or disposed of without endangering human health and without using processes or methods which could harm the environment.

Article 5 sets out a goal of self-sufficiency of waste disposal capacity within the EC with the establishment of a network of disposal installations to deal with waste produced.

Article 7 provides for the need for waste management plans to be drawn up by national authorities (represented in the UK by the National Waste Strategies, waste local plans and waste recycling plans).

Article 8 imposes a duty to ensure that waste is only handled by authorized operators (transposed by the duty of care provisions under EPA 1990, s. 34).

Articles 9–10 provide for the licensing of waste disposal and waste recovery operations (transposed under EPA 1990, ss. 35–42).

Article 14 provides for the keeping of records of the nature of waste, its transport and its treatment (transposed under the transfer note system under the duty of care).

Annex I sets out 16 categories of waste from Q1 to Q16 with Q16 being a catch all category of 'any materials, substances or products which are not contained in the above categories).

Annex IIA lists 15 waste disposal operations from D1 to D15 and Annex IIB lists 13 Waste recovery operations from R1 to R13.

(b) The European List of Wastes

Whilst the Framework Directive sets out objectives and controls over waste generally, there are more specific obligations in relation to categorising waste. Article 1(a) of the Framework Directive along with Art. 1(4) of the Hazardous Waste Directive (91/689) require the drawing up of a list of wastes. Initially this was found in the European Waste Catalogue (see Decision 94/3/EC) which classified waste into one of 20 main groups. The Waste Catalogue was subsequently amended by the European List of Wastes (see Decision 2000/532/EC as amended). This List is used as a way of classifying wastes in many European waste directives and is transposed under the List of Wastes (England) Regulations 2005 (SI 2005/895).

(c) The Hazardous Waste Directive

The Hazardous Waste Directive (91/689 as amended by Directive 94/31), makes provision for the management of certain wastes which are specifically regulated because of their hazardous or toxic properties. Hazardous wastes are subject to the requirements of the Framework Directive in addition to the stricter requirements of the Hazardous Waste Directive. The annexes to the Directive set out the properties which bring wastes within the definition of 'hazardous'. The European List of Wastes has the effect of determining the classes of waste which fall within the definition of 'hazardous'. The List is transposed in domestic law in the List of Wastes (England) Regulations 2005 (SI 2005/895). There are additional provisions in the Directive dealing with licensing, exemptions and the keeping of records in relation to hazardous waste. These requirements have been transposed and are implemented under the Hazardous Waste Regulations 2005 (SI 2005/894).

Waste Treatment Directives

In addition to the general principles laid down in the Framework Directive and in the Hazardous Waste Directive, the second group of European Directives address methods of waste treatment. For example, the Integrated Pollution Prevention and Control Directive regulates waste treatment and encourages waste minimization as part of many significant industrial installations including landfill sites and incinerators (see further Chapter 20). There is an overlap between this Directive and two other important waste treatment Directives on Landfill and Waste Incineration. These latter Directives introduce specific standards for waste treatment (e.g. emission and performance standards) whereas the former Directive applies a general framework of standards and objectives to the waste installation as a whole.

(a) The Waste Incineration Directive

The Waste Incineration Directive 2000/76 replaced and extended two previous Directives on the incineration of municipal (89/369 and 89/429) and hazardous (94/67/EC) waste. The Directive has a general application to both normal incinerators and those plants where the incineration of waste is used primarily as fuel to produce energy or other products (known as co-incineration) (Art. 1). This would include waste to energy plants and such things as cement kilns. All incinerators are required to be subject to authorization (in the UK under the PPC Regulations) and the authorizations/permits must have conditions listing the type and quantities of hazardous and non-hazardous waste which may be treated, the plant's incineration or co-incineration capacity and the sampling and measurement procedures which are to be used (Art. 4). The Directive lays down minimum time and temperatures for waste combustion in order to guarantee complete waste combustion (Art. 5) and there are emission limit values set down for atmospheric emissions of certain substances such as heavy metals, dioxins and furans, and greenhouse gases (Annexes II and V).

(b) The Landfill Directive

The Landfill Directive (99/31) has the main objectives of harmonizing waste disposal standards across Member States with particular emphasis on standards of design, operation, and aftercare for landfill sites. It is also intended to act as the first major stimulant to the recovery and recycling of waste.[5] The main part of the Directive sets out targets for the reduction of the amount of biodegradable municipal waste (i.e. household or similar waste which is capable of decomposition) put into landfills and thereby reduce the amount of methane produced. Thus Article 5 of the directive requires the amount of biodegradable municipal waste which is disposed of in landfills to be reduced in three stages: by 25 per cent, 50 per cent, and 65 per cent of the 1995 levels by 2006, 2009, and 2016 respectively

---

5. See generally H. Cameron (1999) Env L Rev 266.

(these targets were relaxed as a result of lobbying from the UK and other Member States). Even these deadlines can be extended where, as in the case of the UK, more than 80 per cent of biodegradable municipal waste was disposed of in landfills in 1995 (which makes the deadlines 2010, 2013, and 2020 respectively).

Although the new targets are arguably the most significant parts of the Directive, it also:

- Defines different categories of waste (municipal waste, hazardous waste, non-hazardous waste, and inert waste) and landfills (landfills for hazardous waste; for non-hazardous waste; and landfills for inert waste) (Arts 2 and 4).

- Bans the co-disposal of hazardous, non-hazardous and inert wastes in the same landfill and completely bans the landfill of certain hazardous waste, liquid wastes and tyres (Arts 5 and 6).

- Introduces waste acceptance criteria at all sites in order to reduce risks and requires that all waste must be pre-treated before disposal (which includes sorting and compaction of wastes) (Art. 6).

- Requires that an operator makes adequate financial provision for maintenance and after-care (reflecting the polluter pays principle and, to some extent, the approach taken in the UK with the requirement that an operator be a 'fit and proper person') (Art. 10).

- Lays down general standards for all landfills including such things as leachate collection and control, and controls over gas and leachate produced at landfill sites (Annex I). In particular, all landfill gases must be either used to produce energy or flared off; only a minority of current sites do this.

The significance of the Landfill Directive can be assessed against the background of disagreement between Member States which postponed the adoption of the Directive for approximately nine years (with an early version abandoned as a result of the controversy). The Directive has already had a major impact upon current policies and practice and the introduction of landfill quotas, bans on co-disposal and waste acceptance criteria should see a move away from the historical reliance upon landfill in the UK. The Directive is transposed in England and Wales by the Landfill Regulations (England and Wales) 2002 (SI 2002/1559) (see below).

(c) Subject specific waste Directives

The third group of Directives cover a range of specific waste streams. These include:

- A series of Directives imposing Producer Responsibility for certain wastes. These Directives aim to prevent the production of particular types of waste and to encourage its recycling, reuse and recovery. The first of these was a Directive on Packaging and Packaging Waste (94/62) and this has been followed by Directives on the Management of End of Life Vehicles (2000/53) and Waste Electrical and Electronic Equipment (2002/96). Typically these Directives encourage the redesign of products (cars, white goods) to ease recovery and recycling whilst requiring the establishment of waste collection systems and the setting of recovery and recycling targets as percentages of the waste produced.

- Directives on wastes which need regulating in particular ways. These include Waste Oils (75/439), Batteries and Accumulators (91/157), Titanium Dioxide (78/176) and PCBs and polychlorinated triphenyls (PCTs) (96/59). Although the Directives deal with these materials specifically, the transposition of the Directives' requirements is generally through the normal waste management licensing system (with slight variations for batteries and PCBs).

Domestic waste policy

For many years the development of waste policy mirrored that of the law in that the primary aim was to address the environmental risks involved in the disposal of waste. The first steps towards a wider policy base were made with the introduction of the Framework Directive which required Member States not only to control the disposal of waste but to encourage the prevention, recycling, and reuse of waste. The concept of the waste hierarchy was explicitly adopted in the UK in 1990[6] and although these principles provided a good foundation upon which to build waste policy, the growth of detailed policies was largely unstructured, with the effect that the overall objectives were often difficult to discern. In addition, the implementation of waste disposal plans and waste local plans dealing with strategic waste management and planning respectively had been patchy, leading to inconsistent local guidance. In the light of the amendments to the Framework Directive in 1991 (namely the introduction of Art. 7 requiring waste management plans) proposals were made to develop a National Waste Strategy. In 1995 a non-statutory waste strategy was published.[7] In the same year the strategy was given statutory underpinning after the Environment Act 1995 inserted a requirement to produce a national waste strategy under section 44A of the Environmental Protection Act 1990. This gives the Secretary of State power to prepare a statement containing policies in relation to the recovery and disposal of waste. The process of producing the National Waste Strategy was slow and protracted. The House of Commons Environment Select Committee in its Sixth Report in 1998 criticized the 'inertia' which characterized the development of a sustainable waste policy.

The final version of the strategy, *Waste Strategy 2000 for England and Wales*, was published in May 2000.[8] This strategy constitutes the waste management plan for the purposes of the Waste Framework Directive Art. 7, replacing Waste Local Plans under section 50 of the Environmental Protection Act 1990. It also represents the necessary management plans for the purposes of the Hazardous Waste Directive, Packaging Waste Directive and the Landfill Directive.

The strategy must include policies for attaining certain statutory objectives laid down in schedule 2A of the 1990 Act. These objectives reflect Articles 4 and 5 of the Framework Directive (see Box 15.5 above). The overall aim is to make decisions 'in line with' the 'Best Practicable Environmental Option' (BPEO) for particular wastes. This is a flexible concept but incorporates the waste hierarchy, the proximity and self-sufficiency principles, precaution and the polluter pays principle. Unlike other vague statutory objectives the Courts have held that these objectives (along with similar objectives found in schedule 4 of the Waste Management Licensing Regulations) have a special weight (see Case box 15.1).

---

6. *This Common Inheritance* (Cm 1200, 1990).
7. *Making Waste Work: A Strategy for Sustainable Waste Management in England and Wales* (Cm 3040, 1995).
8. Cm 4693, 2000.

CASE 15.1 The role of the National Waste Strategy—*R (on the application of Blewett) v Derbyshire CC* [2005] Env LR 15

The National Waste Strategy plays a special role in the determination of whether to grant consent for waste projects. In addition to the obligation under Article 7 of the Waste Framework Directive mentioned above, Article 8(b) of the Landfill Directive (99/31) places an obligation upon Member States to ensure that any landfill project is 'in line with' the relevant waste management plan—i.e. in the case of the UK, the National Waste Strategy. This requirement applies to the consideration of applications for planning permission for landfill sites in addition to any pollution control permit. The exact nature of this obligation was discussed in *R (on the application of Blewett) v Derbyshire CC*. In that case a local resident applied to quash a decision to grant planning permission to extend a large landfill site on the ground that the local planning authority had failed to carry out an assessment of whether the proposed landfill was the BPEO for waste disposal or whether some other option would be preferable. In the High Court, it was held that the achievement of the BPEO was not a discretionary consideration. Article 8(b) of the Landfill Directive when taken together with the National Waste Strategy 2000 meant that the local planning authority was required to refuse planning permission unless it was 'in line with' the National Waste Strategy. This meant that there was a requirement to assess whether it was the BPEO for this waste stream. As the local authority had failed to do this the decision was quashed.

On appeal, the Court of Appeal agreed that although planning decisions had to be 'in line with' the National Waste Strategy, the policies found in the Strategy were not determinative, i.e. it was not a pre-condition of the grant of planning permission that the BPEO was achieved. This was because whilst the achievement of the BPEO was important it was not overriding (see further on the achievement of the statutory objectives below). The Court of Appeal stressed, however, that the National Waste Strategy was more than just a material consideration. As Auld LJ put it:

One way or another, it can be said that the added focus of waste management calls for particular attention or weight to be given to the objectives of the Waste Framework Directive when considering an application for planning permission for a landfill proposal.

On the facts of the case, the Court of Appeal refused to interfere with the High Court's findings that the local planning authority had failed to demonstrate that they had given sufficient importance or weight to the BPEO policies. It would appear therefore that a planning authority is required to: understand the policies in the National Waste Strategy; attach significant weight to the attainment of those policies; and then consider if there are other more important considerations which outweigh the attainment of the objectives.

The Strategy sets out targets over a 20-year period with reviews every five years. The Strategy sets out specific targets for the reduction of waste. These targets are:

- By 2005 to reduce the amount of industrial and commercial waste going to landfill to 85 per cent of 1998 levels.

- By 2005 to recover 40 per cent of municipal waste with a separate target of recycling 25 per cent of all household waste.

- By 2010 to recover 45 per cent of municipal waste with a separate target of recycling 30 per cent of all household waste.

As the main regulatory controls over waste management found in Part II of the EPA 1990 are not designed to assist with the implementation of these policy goals, economic instruments have been introduced to try and trigger incentives to reduce waste production and increase recycling. Thus the landfill tax, the producer responsibility initiative, the establishment of the setting of and trading landfill quotas (see further below) are seen as the main instruments to provide the incentive to do this. The other main legal instrument which should trigger a move towards these targets will be the implementation of the requirements of the Landfill Directive through the Landfill Regulations (also see below).

The cumulative impact of the Strategy and the legal instruments associated with it is clear, particularly when coupled with the developments in relation to discharges to sewers and controls over incineration. Waste minimization is to be encouraged because the costs of disposal, by whatever route, are likely to increase significantly as the national strategy is implemented. Indeed, the Waste Strategy makes it clear that voluntary initiatives and self-regulation (e.g. best practice programmes for industry sectors) play a vital role in the achievement of the policy targets.

The statutory objectives

The objectives set out in Articles 3–7 of Framework Directive have been transposed into UK law in the Waste Management Licensing Regulations 1994, sch. 4 (see Box 15.6) and through the requirement to incorporate the objectives in the National Waste Strategy under schedule 2A of the EPA 1990. Although the ECJ has held that these objectives do not have 'direct effect' (see *Comitato di Coordianmento per la Difesa della Cava and others v Regione Lombardia and others* [1994] Env LR 281), the Court of Appeal has held that schedule 4 of the Waste Management Licensing Regulations 1994, created a separate self-standing duty upon regulatory authorities to ensure that waste is recovered or disposed of without endangering human health or the environment (*R v Bolton MBC, ex parte Kirkman* [1998] Env LR 719). This duty applies to waste regulatory authorities such as the Environment Agency and local planning authorities exercising waste related functions (the 'competent authorities' identified in schedule 4 para 3 of the 1994 Regulations). In addition to the application to planning authorities, the objectives also apply to the consideration of any waste-related applications. This includes IPPC permits for certain installations. For example, a waste incinerator is both a prescribed installation process for the purpose of the Pollution Prevention and Control Regime and a disposal operation for the purposes of the Waste Framework Directive and the Waste Management Licensing Regulations. In determining any decision to grant an IPPC permit for an incinerator a regulator (i.e. the local authority or the Environment Agency) must consider the Article 4 objectives alongside any other statutory pollution prevention obligations—such as the need to use the Best Available Techniques to prevent pollution—as these objectives are not co-extensive (*R v Environment Agency ex parte Sellars and Petty* [1999] Env LR 73).

BOX 15.6 **The statutory objectives**

The statutory objectives are found in Schedule 4 to the Waste Management Licensing Regulations. The most relevant elements are:

> 2. . . . the competent authorities shall discharge their specified functions, insofar as they relate to the disposal or recovery of waste, with the relevant objectives.
>
> 4. (1) . . . the following objectives are relevant objectives in relation to the disposal or recovery of waste
>
>> (a) ensuring that waste is recovered or disposed of without endangering human health and without using processes or methods which could harm the environment and in particular without:
>>
>>> (i) risk to water, air, soil, plants or animals; or
>>>
>>> (ii) causing nuisance through noise or odours; or
>>>
>>> (iii) adversely affecting the countryside or places of special interest
>
> (2) The following objectives are relevant objectives in relation to the disposal of waste
>
>> (a) establishing an integrated network of waste disposal installations, taking account of best available technology not involving excessive costs; and
>>
>> (b) ensuring that the network referred to at para (a) above enables:
>>
>>> (i) the European Community as a whole to become self sufficient in waste disposal and the Member States individually to move towards that aim, taking into account geographical circumstances or the need for specialised installations for certain types of wastes; and
>>>
>>> (ii) waste to be disposed of in one of the nearest appropriate installations, by means of the most appropriate methods and technologies in order to ensure a high level of protection for the environment and human health.

Whilst transposition of the objectives was relatively simple, implementation has proved to be more of a problem. The objectives are inconsistent, with some aimed at 'ensuring' risk free waste disposal, whereas others are concerned with a high level of environmental protection. 'Ensuring' the avoidance of risk to human health or the prevention of pollution of the environment is a practical impossibility. Most, if not all waste recovery or disposal operations cause some pollution of the environment or, at least, the risk of this. If the 'objectives' in schedule 4, paragraph 1 were interpreted literally in this way they would never be met.

What then do the objectives require? The courts have interpreted the consideration of the objectives in a number of ways. They are mandatory in the sense that they must be considered. Thus in *Sellars and Petty*, the Environment Agency's failure to consider the objectives at all was found to be unlawful. In *Kirkman*, the Court of Appeal considered that the objectives were material considerations which were to be taken into account when determining decisions. This view was adopted in *R v Leicester County Council, Hepworth Building Products Limited and Onyx (UK) Ltd, ex parte Blackfordby and Boothcorpe Action Group Ltd* [2001] Env LR 2 where the High Court held that to meet the objectives a decision maker must consider whether the aim of ensuring that waste is disposed of or recovered without endangering human health or harming the environment would be achieved. The Court of Appeal further clarified the nature of the obligation in *R v Daventry District Council ex parte Thornby Farms Ltd; R (Murray) v Derbyshire County Council* [2002] Env LR 28 where Pill LJ said:

An objective . . . is something different from a material consideration . . . it is an end at which to aim, a goal . . . A material consideration is a factor to be taken into account when making a decision, and the objective to be attained will be such a consideration, but it is more than that. An objective which is obligatory must always be kept in mind when making a decision even while the decision maker has regard to other material considerations.

In practical terms, this means that a decision-maker must state that the objectives have been kept in mind, identify the material considerations which have been taken into account and the extent to which they move towards or away from the aim of the objectives.[9] The decision-maker's discretion is not unlimited however and the Court of Appeal made it clear that there would be circumstances where the considerations produce a result which involves so plain and flagrant a disregard for the objective that there is a breach of obligation under schedule 4. This idea that the objectives are important but not overriding was adopted by the Court of Appeal in *R (on the application of Blewett) v Derbyshire CC* (see Case box 15.1).

Domestic waste law

The statutory framework dealing with the licensing of waste management activities can be largely found in Part II of the Environmental Protection Act 1990. There are other key pieces of legislation and guidance which are summarized in the table below.

Legislation	Main Provisions and related secondary legislation and guidance
Environmental Protection Act 1990	Along with the Waste Management Licensing Regulations 1994 form the main body of waste management licensing law. Includes the definition of waste, the duty of care (with its own set of regulations and Code of Practice) and the institutional and regulatory framework for licensing system.
Control of Pollution (Amendment) Act 1989	Introduced a system of registration for carriers of waste, with strong penalties for operating an unregistered vehicle.
Finance Act 1996	Introduced a tax on waste going to landfill aiming to reduce the amount of waste going to landfill. Supplemented by a series of Landfill Tax Regulations dealing with exempt classes of waste.
Pollution Prevention and Control Act 1999	Controls landfill sites and other waste management sites under the integrated pollution prevention and control system. Actual standards and classification systems for landfills are to be found in the Landfill (England and Wales) Regulations 2002.
Waste and Emissions Trading Act 2003	Introduced a system of allocating quotas of waste going to landfill to waste authorities with the power to trade quotas as between authorities along with penalties for failure.
Household Waste Recycling Act 2003	Private Members Bill requiring waste collection authorities to make arrangements for separate collection of at least two types of waste by 2010.
Clean Neighbourhoods and Environment Act 2005	Makes numerous minor amendments to waste legislation including the introduction of fixed penalty notices for certain waste offences and new clean up powers where a person is convicted of a waste offence.

9. S. Bell (2003) 15 JEL 59.

What is waste?

The definition of waste is multi-faceted. There are general issues such as whether something has the basic characteristic of waste, namely being discarded. Furthermore there are certain categories of waste which are linked to either the properties of the waste itself (e.g. special/ hazardous or inert waste) or the identity of the producer (e.g. household, commercial, or industrial waste) which are used for classification purposes in relation to waste licensing schemes.

The concept of waste has proved to be particularly difficult to define with any certainty. There are a number of reasons for this.[10] First, there is no inherent physical characteristic which can be used to define waste. Unlike other areas of pollution control the idea of waste is not necessarily associated with pollution (although all pollution is associated with waste). The link between waste and environmental harm is that unless waste is managed properly (and therefore regulated accordingly) there is a *potential* for pollution. Secondly, there is the subjective nature of the view which one can take when considering whether the material is waste. In particular, one person's waste can be another person's raw material. This can be closely linked to the third reason, that there is an implicit connection between the concept of waste and a lack of value or worth of an object (i.e. something can only be waste if it is not wanted). There are, however, some categories of objects which have been discarded by the original holder, but which have a value because they can be used either for their original or another purpose (there may be some sort of treatment required prior to reuse). Fourthly, the adoption of the waste management hierarchy simply adds to the problem. Where there is an emphasis placed upon the reuse and recycling of material there is no sense in over regulation by drawing up a very wide definition of waste as this would discourage environmentally beneficial activities which would reduce the amount of raw materials required and consequently the waste produced. On the other hand, many recycling and reclamation processes have the capability of causing harm if left unregulated. In drawing up any definition, the rule maker must seek to strike a balance between these two competing considerations.

BOX 15.7 **Purposive rules vs detailed categories**

In Chapter 4 we discussed the various approaches taken in environmental laws. One of the characteristics of environmental laws is that there is a tendency to combine wide purposive definitions with detailed categories. This approach aims to balance flexibility with certainty. The legislation on the definition of waste is a very good example of this. Note the very wide general definition of waste and contrast this with the detailed categories of waste. The general definition ensures a high level of environmental protection by making the definition of waste contextual (i.e. basing it on the intention of the holder) whilst the detailed categories provide a degree of detail which clarify the general definition.

---

10. I. Cheyne and M. Purdue (1995) 7 JEL 149.

For many years the definition of waste included substances or articles which were scrap or which were required to be disposed of because they were broken, worn out, contaminated or otherwise spoilt (COPA 1974, s. 30 and EPA 1990, s. 75). Under the 1991 amendments to the Framework Directive, however, a common definition of waste was agreed to apply to all Member States. This differed from the previous definition and required amendments to UK legislation. Other amendments have been necessary to ensure full implementation of the Directive. All of the amendments have been incorporated within the Waste Management Licensing Regulations 1994 with subsequent amendments to the EPA 1990. Although the definition of waste and waste management activities is very complex, there are two broad principles which apply. First, the only waste which is regulated under the EPA 1990 is known as 'directive waste' to reflect the description of waste as found in the Directive. Secondly, the activities which are subject to the licensing requirements under Part II of the EPA 1990 are known as directive disposal and directive recovery.

Directive waste

The general definition of directive waste is to be found in Article 1(a) of the Framework Directive (and in reg. 1(3) of the Waste Management Licensing Regulations 1994) which provides the following definition:

'any substance or object in the categories set out in Annex I [to the Framework Directive] which the holder discards or intends or is required to discard.'

The Waste Management Licensing Regs adopts a similar definition and states that 'discard' has the same meaning as in the Directive. Thus the subsequent European case law on the definition of 'discards' is of direct relevance. The starting point for the definition of waste is, therefore, the list of 'categories' which can be found in Annex I of the directive (Part II of sch. 4 to the regulations). There are 16 categories (Q1–Q16) covering a range of descriptions of production residues and contaminated or adulterated materials. Whilst these descriptions are helpful in determining whether something is waste, on closer examination it becomes clear that the description of various categories of waste is illustrative rather than determinative. The first thing to note is that the list sets out substances or objects which are waste *only* when they are discarded. Thus, a substance or object in one of the categories in the list will not necessarily be waste unless it can be demonstrated that it falls within the general definition in Article 1(a). Secondly, there is a totally inclusive category, Q16, which covers all 'materials, substances or products' which are not contained in any of the other categories. This would cover everything which could conceivably exist. The inclusion of this general category suggests that there is a specific purpose in setting out other more detailed categories (otherwise the all-inclusive category would render the others superfluous).

It is clear from the descriptions of the categories that they cover substances or objects which may be presumed to be discarded (or will be discarded in the near future). At best this could set up a rebuttable presumption which could be contradicted by specific evidence of an absence to discard. In addition to these general categories of waste, there is an extensive list of wastes (known as the List of Wastes) prepared by the European Commission (see Decision 2000/532/EC). In common with the Annex I list, this is merely illustrative (as its main purpose is to ensure uniformity in the classification of wastes across Member States) and is not conclusive in determining whether any of the listed substances is actually waste. The practical effect of the general category of waste means that there is a two-stage test which applies to the question of whether a substance, material, or product is directive waste (see Box 15.8).

BOX 15.8 **The two-stage test for determining whether something is directive waste**

---

1   Is it a substance, material or product and does it therefore come within any of the categories set out in the specific definitions in Annex I/Sch. 4? If the answer is yes (and for practical purposes it will almost certainly be the case),

2   Has the substance, material or product been discarded by its holder or is there an intention or requirement to discard it?

It is the second of these two questions which gives the key to the definition of directive waste. As we shall see, the case law on the definition of waste suggests that material is not waste merely because it falls within a class set out in schedule 4, but that the critical question is whether it has been discarded.

In many cases the question of whether something is waste or not will be straightforward. If I throw away perfectly useable top soil by putting it in a skip, my intention to discard it is clear. This is so notwithstanding that the soil might have a commercial value or a useful purpose for a passer-by who might dig it out and then re-use it for landscaping (e.g. see *Kent County Council v Queenborough Rolling Mill Co. Ltd* (1990) 89 LGR 306, Joined Cases C-206/88 and C-207/88 *Vessoso and Zanetti*). There are, however, other situations where the intention to discard is not as clear and it is here that the courts have wrestled with the elusive definition of waste. One of the important factors is whether the substance has been consigned to a waste recovery or disposal operation (as listed in Annex IIA and IIB of the Directive). The definition of 'disposal operations' is relatively straightforward. Annex IIA of the Framework Directive (sch. 4, Part III of the Waste Management Licensing Regulations 1994) lists a series of operations which are standard ways of finally disposing of waste (including varieties of incineration and landfill). By definition when a substance is consigned to a disposal operation (e.g. tipping or incineration) it is clear that there is an intention to discard as the mere fact of final disposal means that it cannot be re-used. One point which should be made, however, is that the list is not exhaustive and there are other types of disposal which are not included (particularly in relation to such things as deliberate discharges of pollutants into the atmosphere) where they are controlled under separate legislation (see p. 583).

The situation with substances consigned to recovery operations is not necessarily as clear as many recovery operations (e.g. use of waste principally as a fuel) are not easily distinguished from industrial processes (i.e. the recovery process is part and parcel of a bigger industrial process).[11] In Case C-304/94 *Euro Tombesi* [1998] Env LR 59, the Advocate

---

11. This problem also is evident in comparing the use of a product (coal) and waste (SLFs), L. Kramer (2003) Env Liab 11(1) 3.

General suggested that the mere consignment of a material to a recovery process listed in Annex IIB of the Framework Directive was sufficient to amount to discarding and therefore identify the substance as waste. This reasoning became known as the 'Tombesi bypass'[12] as it neatly 'bypassed' the question of whether something had been discarded by turning the definition on its head—something consigned to a recovery process has been discarded. The full judgment of the ECJ did not go as far as the Advocate-General, preferring instead to conclude that the consignment of a substance to a recovery process could amount to discarding which would indicate that the substance was a waste.

The general approach taken in *Tombesi* was followed by the ECJ in Case C-126/96 *Inter-Environnement Wallonie v Regione Wallone* [1998] Env LR 625 when the Court concluded that although there was a distinction between industrial processes and recovery operations it would normally be the case that substances subjected to a recovery process would be waste. This reasoning was also adopted in the English Courts in *Mayer Parry Recycling Limited v Environment Agency* [1999] Env LR 489 where it was held that scrap metal which could be reused without being subjected to any recovery operation was not waste.

Problems arise with the *Tombesi* bypass approach where a substance is consigned to a recovery process which can also be a normal industrial process. Take, for example the situation where an industrial by-product is used to partially fuel a cement kiln. This is a recovery operation (the energy 'recovered' from the fuel is used to make cement). It is, however, also a normal industrial process which uses raw materials for fuel (e.g. coal). The decisions in *Tombesi* and *Inter-Environnement Wallonie* did nothing to clarify this distinction. They simply shifted the question from 'has the substance been discarded?' to 'has the substance been consigned to a recovery process?'

One way of differentiating between recovery operations and industrial processes has been the adoption of a separate concept of the 'specialized recovery operation'. There is no specific legislative definition of this phrase but it is described in Circular 11/94 as being intended to cover operations which either reuse substances or objects which are waste because they have fallen out of normal use, or recycle them in a way which eliminates or diminishes sufficiently the threat posed by their original production as waste and produces a raw material which can be used in the same way as raw material or a non-waste compound. In cases where substances are consigned to a specialized recovery operation they will always be waste. Although this approach has been viewed favourably by the ECJ (in *Tombesi*) and the High Court (in *Mayer Parry*), it is still not a legal test and in the light of subsequent decisions discussed below it would seem that it is still a helpful way of determining whether a substance is consigned to a recovery process.

In Case C-418/97 *ARCO Chemie Nederland Ltd v Minister van Volkshuivesting and EPON* ([2003] Env LR 40), the ECJ rejected the interpretation of the Advocate's General's opinion in *Tombesi* concluding that consigning something to a recovery operation did not necessarily mean that it was waste. The only appropriate test was whether the substance had been 'discarded'. This was something which could only be assessed in the light of the circumstances of the case. The court rejected any notion of conclusive tests (such as the *Tombesi* bypass) but concluded that the term 'discard' had to be interpreted generously in the light of the aims of the Waste Framework Directive. Consequently, the decision in *Mayer Parry* that

---

12. G. Van Calster, European Business Law Review [1997] 137.

materials which could be reused without undergoing a recovery operation were not waste was overturned (see Case box 15.2).

CASE 15.2 The closing of the *Tombesi* Bypass—*Attorney-General's Reference (No. 5 of 2000)*

The operators of an animal rendering plant produced a by-product which was collected and spread on farm land. The operators were prosecuted for a breach of the duty of care under s. 34 of the EPA 1990 for failing to prevent the unlawful disposal of waste (the by-product) on land. At the trial, the operators argued that following the decision in *Mayer Parry* the by-product wasn't waste as it was capable of being re-used without being subjected to a recovery process. The trial judge agreed and the operators were acquitted. The Attorney-General referred the matter to the Court of Appeal. The decision in *Arco* had post-dated the decision in *Mayer Parry* and had therefore been doubted in subsequent decisions.[13] The Court of Appeal rejected the decision in *Mayer Parry* and its reliance on the Advocate General's opinion in *Tombesi*. The Court concluded that the by-product was capable of being waste notwithstanding that it had not been subjected to a waste recovery process.[14]

One of the problems with the European case law on the definition of waste is that the ECJ appeared to be very reluctant to lay down specific tests to determine whether something was 'discarded', preferring to leave the judgment of such matters to the national courts. In various cases,[15] certain factors have been identified which might assist in determining whether something has been discarded. These include:

- Meeting the broad aims of the Waste Framework Directive (e.g. to prevent the dangerous disposal of waste).
- Has the substance been consigned to a disposal or recovery operation?
- Is the substance a production residue rather than a product with a subsequent use?
- Is the substance normally regarded as a waste?
- Is there any other use for the substance which could be envisaged other than disposal or recovery?
- What was the degree of likelihood that the substance would be reused without any further reprocessing prior to that use?
- Was there some financial advantage to the holder in reusing the substance?
- Whether any special precautions had to be taken when the substance was reused?

Irrelevant factors have included:

- How and where the substance was stored.

---

13. E.g. see the judgment of Stanley Burnton J in *Castle Cement v Environment Agency and Lowther* [2001] Env LR 45.
14. J. Pike (2002) 14 JEL 197.
15. E.g. Case C-126/96 *Inter Environnement Wallonie*, Case C-418/97 *Arco Chemie*, Case C-9/00 *Palin Granit*.

- Its composition.
- Whether it posed any real risk to human health or the environment.

It should be noted that these are *indicative* not conclusive factors.

CASE 15.3 A broad definition of waste—*Palin Granit Oy* [2002] Env LR 35

An good example of the broad flexible approach to the definition of waste can be seen in Case C-9/00 *Palin Granit Oy v Vehmassaion kansanterveystyon kuntayhtyman hallitus*, Palin Granit stored leftover stone at a granite quarry in Finland. The Finnish waste authorities considered that the leftover stone was waste for the purposes of Finnish Law and that its storage site was a landfill. PG argued that the leftover stone was stored for short periods for subsequent use without the need for any recovery measures and did not pose any risk to human health or the environment. The Finnish waste authority argued that the leftover stone should have been regarded as waste as long as evidence of reuse of the stone had not been provided. The Finnish Court referred to the ECJ the question of whether the leftover stone produced from stone quarrying was capable of being regarded as 'waste'. The ECJ discussed the various factors which had been identified in previous cases and in applying those factors the Court concluded that the leftover stone from quarrying was not the product primarily sought by the operator of a granite quarry and could more properly be described as a 'production residue' and therefore waste. The reuse of the granite was uncertain and only foreseeable in the longer term.

The extensive case law on the definition of waste indicates the complexity of trying to interpret a broad purposive definition within the context of many different factual contexts. The European Court has, after a tentative start, produced successive judgments which have widened the definition of waste considerably. The Court appears to want to avoid trying to produce conclusive principles by pursuing influential, but non-determinative factors which point towards something being discarded. Perhaps the most significant factor is whether the broad aims of the Waste Framework Directive are being met. This promotes a very broad purposive definition of waste which has the advantage of capturing more waste disposal/recovery operations which may give rise to environmental risks.

This purposive approach highlights the fact that the definition of waste is not something which is determined in isolation. It is inherently linked to the management of waste and other objectives of the Waste Framework Directive. In seeking to define waste the courts have in mind the requirement that holders of waste must manage the waste substances in accordance with the requirements of the Framework Directive. These include ensuring that waste should be recovered or disposed of without endangering human health or in ways which could harm the environment (see p. 573) and that there should be a prohibition on the abandonment, dumping and uncontrolled disposal of waste.

Many of the cases brought before the Courts have not really been concerned with the inherent nature of the substances/materials themselves. What was at the heart of many of these disputes was the exact framework under which particular activities should be controlled. Thus *Palin Granit* was primarily concerned with the question of whether a quarry had to be licensed as a landfill site and *Castle Cement* was concerned with the question of whether a cement kiln was regulated as part of an industrial installation or as a separate hazardous waste incinerator. What matters is not whether something is waste but just how it is controlled. This has given rise to the ECJ seeking to expand the definition of waste to include accidental releases of contaminants into soil and groundwater as waste (see Case box 15.4).

CASE 15.4 Extending the concept of 'discarding'—Case C-1/03 *Van de Walle*

In Case C-1/03 *Van der Walle and others* [2005] Env LR 24 the ECJ was asked to consider the question of whether petrol leaking from underground storage tanks at a Texaco filling station was waste. As with the previous case law the key question was whether it could be said that the petrol had been discarded. The ECJ held that accidental leaks and spillages of petrol were substances which the holder did not intend to produce and which were 'discarded' albeit involuntarily at the time of production or distribution. The ECJ also ruled that soils contaminated by the hydrocarbons were waste even where they had not been excavated because the soil could not be recovered or disposed of without some decontamination works. Finally the ECJ considered that Texaco as the petrol supplier was the producer (and therefore holder) of the waste for the purposes of the Framework Directive where the leak was caused (even if only in part) by a 'disregard of contractual obligations' to service and maintain the tanks on the part of Texaco.

In the UK, accidental spillages or leakages of substances have not necessarily been considered to be waste. Thus there are questions about the extent to which the UK has transposed the requirements of the Waste Framework Directive (see further p. 620). The central problem created by the *Van de Walle* decision (and it applies in other Member States in addition to the UK) is that the ECJ has expanded the concept of waste and the application of the Framework Directive into new areas. Whilst that may be necessary to respond to a set of facts in Belgium, the decision cuts across long established statutory controls in other Member States. For example, there are controls to prevent such leaks and to remedy the consequences under various pieces of legislation dealing with, for example, water pollution (e.g. s. 161A, WRA 1991 and the Groundwater Regs 1998, see Chapter 18) and historic pollution (see Chapter 17). It also begs the question about the role and purpose of other EC legislation such as the Water Framework Directive and Environmental Liability Directive which purportedly address such problems.

Taking such a broad all encompassing approach to defining waste raises two main issues. First, a broad definition of waste is a relatively blunt instrument with which to achieve the requirements of the Waste Framework Directive. There is a danger that this approach may lead to over regulation where relatively low-risk sites are subject to onerous waste licensing regulation. In Britain, where the waste licensing system has been aimed at dealing with landfill sites, the application of similar systems of regulation to many recycling sites can act as a disincentive to investment in much needed recycling and recovery operations.

Secondly, the definition of waste becomes so uncertain that it is difficult to carry out activities with materials which might be waste without reference to the Environment Agency. The absence of any formal mechanism for determining the question (unlike for example the case with the definition of development and the need for planning permission see p. 472) means that the resolution of any disputes is complicated and normally only through judicial review or the criminal courts on a prosecution. Although this vagueness of the definition of waste is a practical problem, the courts have held that the definition is sufficiently clear to enable those who are affected to regulate their conduct and therefore there is no breach of Article 7 of the European Convention of Human Rights (see Case box 15.5).

CASE 15.5 The uncertainty of the definition of waste—*R (Rackham) v Swaffham Magistrates Court and the Environment Agency* [2004] EWHC17

The owner of a farm (R) mixed municipal waste with compost and other green waste to make a product. He took the view that the mixed material was not waste. The Environment Agency disagreed and prosecuted. R sought to challenge the prosecution. One of the grounds of challenge was that the definition of waste (as derived from the *Arco Chemie* decision) could not be defined with sufficient certainty to enable R to know what to do to comply with the law. As such the prosecution was a breach of the right no to be punished without law under Article 7 of the European Convention on Human Rights. The High Court dismissed the application, holding that although the decision in *Arco* required the exercise of judgment it was not so uncertain as to amount to a breach of Article 7.

Exceptions—what is not waste

There are various categories of waste which are specifically said to be excluded from the definition of waste and therefore fall outside the waste management licensing system altogether. These should be distinguished from exemptions which are categories of waste which are exempt from statutory control because they fall within set limits laid down in legislation. Regulation 1(3) of the 1994 Regulations excludes anything excluded from the scope of the Directive from the definition of directive waste (and thus controlled waste). These exceptions, known as non-directive waste, only apply where the materials are already covered under 'other' legislation. Six main categories of waste are excepted.

- Gaseous effluent emitted into the atmosphere: controlled under IPPC and the Clean Air Act 1993. Emissions from waste management are, however, covered (e.g. from incineration).

- Radioactive waste: controlled under the Radioactive Substances Act 1993.

- Waste resulting from prospecting, extraction, treatment, and storage of mineral resources and the working of quarries: controlled under the Mines and Quarries (Tips) Act 1969. This also accords with section 75(7) of EPA 1990 which excludes all waste from mines and quarries from the definition of controlled waste.

- Animal carcasses and the following agricultural waste, namely faecal matter and other natural, non-dangerous substances used in farming: controlled under the Animal By-Products Order 1992 (SI 1992/3303). Agricultural waste is excluded from the definition of controlled waste under section 75(7) of EPA 1990.

- Waste waters, with the exception of waste in liquid form: broadly controlled under the Water Resources Act 1991 and Water Industry Act 1991. After much debate the treatment of effluent in treatment plants is not considered to require a waste management licence (see p. 619).

- Decommissioned explosives: controlled under the Explosives Act 1875, the Control of Explosives Regulations 1991 (SI 1991/1531), various regulations under the Health and Safety at Work etc Act 1974 and the Road Traffic (Carriage of Explosives) Regulations 1989 (SI 1989/615).

The key question here is whether, in fact, there is 'other legislation' which applies. For it to qualify as 'other legislation' these alternative controls must result in a level of environmental protection at least equivalent to that aimed at by the Waste Framework Directive notwithstanding the fact that the legislation predates that Directive (Case C-114/01 *Re AvestaPolarit Chrome Oy* [2004] Env LR 44). Particular problems arise in relation to non-agricultural waste from agricultural units generally and non-mineral waste from mines and quarries. Whilst successive Governments have promised to review these exclusions, the European Commission has commenced proceedings against the UK for failure to transpose the requirements of the Waste Framework Directive in respect of agricultural waste; see Case C-62/03 *Commission v UK, The Times*, 6 January 2005.

There is a residual degree of control over non-directive waste. Any person who deposits or who knowingly causes or knowingly permits the deposit of any non-controlled waste commits an offence if the waste has the characteristics of special waste and is not deposited in accordance with a licence or permission of some description (EPA 1990, s. 63(2)). This rather convoluted subsection appears designed to cover such things as the irresponsible disposal of toxic materials. In addition, the Secretary of State may make regulations under section 63(1) applying specified parts of the EPA 1990 to exempt wastes (specifically agricultural and mine wastes), although no such regulations have ever been made.

Controlled waste

The waste management licensing system applies to 'controlled waste' which is defined as 'household, industrial or commercial waste or any such waste' (s. 75(4), EPA 1990). 'Any such waste' does not extend beyond the general categories (*Thanet District Council v Kent County Council* [1993] Env LR 391). Directive waste and controlled waste are effectively synonymous as any substance which is not directive waste cannot be controlled waste (reg. 7A, Controlled Waste Regulations 1992). The categories of household, industrial or commercial waste are still important, however, as the extent of the controls under the waste management licensing system differs depending upon which class waste falls within.

Hazardous waste

There are additional controls over hazardous waste, which for many years has been labelled 'special waste' in the UK. Such waste was primarily controlled under the Special Waste Regulations 1996 (SI 1996/972). These regulations were introduced in order to transpose the Hazardous Waste Directive (91/689) into UK law. The transposition of the requirements of the Directive was inadequate and the Hazardous Waste (England and Wales) Regulations 2005 (SI 2005/894) (along with the List of Wastes (England) Regulations 2005 (SI 2005/895)) are intended to address these defects (see Box 15.9).

BOX 15.9 **Hazardous Waste Proposals**

The Hazardous Waste (England and Wales) Regulations 2005 (SI 2005/894) replace and repeal the Special Waste Regulations 1996 (SI 1996/972). The Regulations came into force over three years after the deadline date for the transposition of the Hazardous Waste Directive. The Regulations have made major changes to the position under the 1996 Regulations and coincided with the introduction of the new 'waste acceptance criteria' at landfill sites (see p. 607). Under the Regulations, the term 'special waste' has been replaced by 'hazardous waste' as defined in the Hazardous Waste Directive and the European List of Wastes.

The Hazardous Waste Regulations, reg. 6, defines hazardous waste as any waste:

- listed as hazardous in the List of Wastes (England) Regulations 2005;
- which is exceptionally classified as hazardous by the Secretary of State or any of the National Executives
- which is declared hazardous by virtue of any regulations under section 62 of the Environmental Protection Act 1990.

There are about 200 types of 'newly hazardous' wastes where the Regulations have redefined certain wastes as 'hazardous' including televisions and fluorescent light bulbs.

Whilst 'domestic' waste may be defined as 'hazardous' if it has hazardous properties, it is excluded from the requirement of the Regulations (reg. 12(2)). Although there is no definition of 'domestic waste' in the regulations, DEFRA has indicated that it comprises waste from accommodation used purely for living purposes (and without commercial gain) and which is disposed of via the normal mixed domestic refuse collection. Asbestos waste and any hazardous waste which is collected separately is not classified as 'domestic waste' regardless of origin. Regulation 19 bans the mixing of hazardous waste with any other non-hazardous wastes or any different category of hazardous wastes unless it is mixed under a waste management licence or IPPC permit. Regulation 20 imposes a duty to separate different categories of Hazardous Waste where technically feasible.

(a) Notification requirements

Regulation 21 requires all premises at which hazardous waste is produced or removed to be notified to the Environment Agency by the producer of the waste or the person who arranges for the removal of the waste (the consignor). The notification requirement is annual (i.e. lasts 12 months). Notification is accompanied by an annual fee. It is an offence to remove hazardous waste from premises which have not been notified, unless they are exempt premises (reg. 22) or the waste has been fly-tipped (reg. 23). The exemptions include a range of residential commercial, educational and medical premises. The exemptions only apply if the premises produce no more than 200kg of hazardous waste in a year. Other than these exemptions, no premises producing hazardous waste, however small the quantity, is exempt from the obligation to notify.

(b) Consignment Notes

The Regulations provide for a system in which movements of hazardous waste must be 'consigned' before transfer (regs. 35–38). Before any hazardous waste can be removed from premises, a consignment note must be completed, and when collected by a Registered Waste Carrier, copies of the note must accompany the load to the place of final disposal or recovery. In many ways the consignment note mirrors the Duty of Care transfer note system (see below) as it records the nature of the waste, the identities of the producer, the carrier and the person responsible for final disposal or recovery. A consignment note is required for every movement of hazardous waste even when the waste is produced from premises which are exempt from the requirement to notify.

(c) Record keeping

The Regulations require producers, holders, carriers, consignors and consignees to keep records of consignment notes (regs. 49–51). These must be kept in the form of a register for a minimum of three years except in the case of carriers where the period is 12 months (regs 49–50). Consignees are required to provide the Environment Agency with a quarterly return setting out the consignments they have received during that period (reg. 53). Consignees are required to send a return to producers or holders who sent waste to them (reg. 54). In addition anyone who deposits hazardous waste in or on any land, or who recovers hazardous waste is required to record the location of each deposit or the nature of the recovery in the form of site records (regs. 47–48). Such records are to be cross-referenced to the register of consignment notes.

(d) Offences

Regulation 65 makes it an offence to fail to comply with the different requirements of the Regulations. For example it would be an offence to fail to notify premises or to remove hazardous waste without a consignment note or to fill out consignment notes incorrectly. It is a defence to prove that the failure to comply was as a result of a grave danger or emergency and that all reasonable steps were taken to minimize any threats to the public and environment and to rectify the failure as soon as reasonably practicable. In non-emergency situations a due diligence defence is available (reg. 66).

The penalties for each offence are a fine of up to £5,000 on summary conviction (i.e. in a magistrates' court) or an unlimited fine and/or up to two years in prison on conviction on indictment (i.e. in the Crown Court). In addition there are offences of knowingly or recklessly making statements which are false or misleading, or intentionally making a false entry in records. In relation to these latter offences, the Environment Agency may issue fixed penalty notices of £300 instead of seeking conviction in relation to such offences.

Waste authorities

The administration of waste management is divided into three and the main functions are set out in the table below. The EPA 1990 separated out the operational functions from the regulatory and the Environment Act 1995 centralised the regulatory function within the Environment Agency. Thus, the main responsibilities fall to the Environment Agency as the main regulatory agency with differing operational functions carried out by Waste Collection Authorities and Waste Disposal Authorities. As the names suggest Collection Authorities are responsible for arranging for waste collection whereas Disposal Authorities must make arrangements for waste disposal in conjunction with private waste disposal contractors.

The Waste and Emissions Trading Act 2003 requires waste authorities in two-tier areas to produce a joint municipal waste strategy by April 2005 (note that there is no such responsibility on single tier authorities). The Waste Disposal Authority must meet landfill reduction targets but must cooperate with Waste Collection Authorities on measures such as recycling and minimisation. In a move to encourage better voluntary performance, authorities with a good record for meeting waste targets will also be exempt from the requirement to prepare such strategies.

Authority	Functions	Main statutory operational provisions
Environment Agency	Waste management licensing	EPA 1990, s. 30
	Supervision, monitoring, and enforcement of licensed activities and waste disposal sites	EPA 1990, ss. 33–42
	Enforcement of Duty of Care	EPA 1990, s. 34
	Registration of exemptions	Waste Management Licensing Regs 1994, Regs 17–18
	Registration of Waste Carriers	Control of Pollution (Amendment) Act 1989
Waste Collection Authorities (District Councils and London Boroughs)	Collect household waste in their areas Collect commercial waste where requested and payment made Collect industrial waste (with consent of Waste Disposal Authority and payment)	EPA 1990, s. 45
	Prepare waste recycling plans	EPA 1990, s. 49
	Making arrangements for the provision of waste bins for household and commercial waste	EPA 1990, ss. 46–7
	Prepare joint municipal waste strategies with responsibility for meeting waste reduction targets	Waste and Emissions Trading Act 2003, s. 32

Authority	Functions	Main statutory operational provisions
Waste Disposal Authorities (County Councils, Metropolitan Authorities and Joint Boards)	Duty to dispose of controlled waste by means of arrangements with private waste disposal contractors	EPA 1990, s. 51
	Duty to provide civic amenity sites where residents can dispose of household rubbish without charge	EPA 1990, s. 51
	Prepare joint municipal waste strategies with responsibility for measures in relation to waste minimization and recycling	Waste and Emissions Trading Act 2003, s. 32

In addition, 'arrangements' must be made between Waste Disposal Authorities and private waste disposal contractors. Originally formed from the operational 'arm' of waste disposal authorities these private companies provide a competitive market for the provision of waste disposal.

Recycling

Although there are administrative and legislative provisions dealing with the promotion of waste recycling, the current emphasis is on voluntary and economic instruments rather than compulsory regulation. As a result, British legislation does not include many formal duties to recycle (with the notable exception of the producer responsibility obligations, see p. 615). This also explains the historical opposition to the introduction of such targets and the difficulties which have been experienced in achieving the targets or in setting up regulatory systems to implement the European legislation.

The authority with the most important role in relation to recycling is the waste collection authority, since it collects most domestic and commercial waste and is able to separate recyclable wastes at an early stage. The authority may require separate receptacles to be used for household wastes that are to be recycled and those which are not (EPA 1990, s. 46(2)). It may buy or acquire waste with a view to recycling it (s. 55) and, if it makes arrangements for recycling waste, it does not have to deliver the waste to the waste disposal authority, as it would otherwise have to do under section 48. It is also under a duty to draw up a waste recycling plan for its area, which involves publicising the arrangements it intends to make to facilitate recycling (s. 49).

Perhaps most significantly in the light of government policy on economic instruments, the waste collection authority is entitled to a recycling credit from the waste disposal authority under section 52 where it recycles waste. The idea behind this provision is that it acts as an incentive to recycle waste by getting the waste disposal authority to pay the waste collection authority the amount of money it saves by not having to dispose of the waste. The amount payable is based on the net saving the waste disposal authority makes as a result of the recycling activities. At present the rate is fixed at half the average cost saving to the waste disposal authority, but the Government has announced that this is to rise to the full amount. The waste disposal authority *may* also make such a payment to anyone else who recycles waste and thus removes it from the waste stream (s. 52(3)).

All of these different incentives provide a framework within which waste authorities *may* undertake recycling. Unfortunately, the British record on recycling is so poor that further measures were required, particularly in light of the statutory obligation to reduce the amount of waste going to landfill required under the Landfill Directive (see p. 607). Thus the *National Waste Strategy 2000* introduced the idea of mandatory recycling targets to be imposed upon local authorities as part of the set of performance indicators known as the 'Best Value' initiative. These statutory targets were formally introduced under the Local Government (Best Value) Performance Indicators and Performance Standards (England) (Order) 2003 (SI 2003/530) which set a general minimum standard increase of between 10 per cent and 33 per cent recycling of waste per council designed to achieve a overall minimum national recycling rate of 17 per cent in 2003 and 25 per cent in 2005/6. These standards are enforced through section 15 of the Local Government Act 1999 which allows the Secretary of State to intervene directly where local authorities are not meeting the 'Best Value' performance indicators.

In addition to these performance standards, the Household Waste Recycling Act 2003 requires all English local authorities to provide kerbside collections for all householders for a minimum of two materials by 2010. The only exceptions to this general duty are where the costs of collection would be 'unreasonably high' (e.g. in rural areas) or where 'alternative arrangements' are made (e.g. aggregated collection points in relation to blocks of flats). Although the Act is one of the first to place specific operational duties upon local authoritative it is unlikely to be very influential given the pre-existing statutory recycling targets. It is these which have caused changes in behaviour and led to greater efforts to segregate wastes at source.

Waste management licensing

Historically, the regulation of waste management, namely the deposit, treating, keeping, or disposing of controlled waste has taken place through the waste management licensing system found in Part II of the EPA 1990. The Integrated Pollution Prevention and Control Directive altered the position so that there are (or will be when IPPC is fully implemented) two parallel systems of control. Any waste installation that is covered under the PPC Regulations 2000 (SI 2000/1973) falls outside the waste management licensing system. This includes large landfill sites and waste incineration plants and certain waste recovery installations (see further Chapter 20). There are, however, a large range of waste activities which fall outside the descriptions found in the PPC Regulations, either because they fall below the threshold for inclusion (e.g. landfill sites with less than 25,000 tonne capacity) or they are not listed as prescribed installations. These activities are controlled under the waste management licensing regime (see Box 15.10).

BOX 15.10 **The main features of waste management licensing**

- Waste management functions; which are split between regulatory and operational functions. The Environment Agency has regulatory control over waste management whilst operational functions are split between the waste collection authorities, waste disposal authorities, and the private sector waste disposal companies.

- A criminal duty of care; which applies to all those who deal with waste and which ensures that waste is properly handled throughout from production through to final disposal.

- An all-embracing criminal offence of treating, keeping or disposing of waste in a manner likely to cause pollution of the environment or harm to human health. This operates independently of the licensing system and effectively imposes minimum standards for the handling of all wastes.

- A comprehensive system of waste management licensing dealing with all aspects of waste management. In particular, there are expanded powers to refuse licences on the ground that the applicant is not a 'fit and proper person', sophisticated powers of enforcement and increased maximum penalties in the event of breach.

- The licensing of directive disposal operations and directive recovery operations.

(a) Applications for a licence

If a waste management licence is required, an application must be made in writing to the EA. There is a standard application form available from the EA and there are penalties for making false statements (s. 44). Where an application form does not provide the requisite information, the Environment Agency is entitled to refuse to proceed with an application and it will not be deemed to have been refused when the statutory period for determination (four months) runs out.

Where the licence relates to the keeping, treating, or disposal of waste in or on land the licence is called a 'site licence', and the application is made to the EA where the site is situated. An application for a licence for mobile plant is made to the EA where the applicant has its principal place of business, thus allowing for a number of pieces of plant to be covered by one licence. Section 35(2) states that only the occupier of the land or the operator of a mobile plant can apply for a licence. There is no definition of an occupier in the Act, but it must be assumed that it relates to the ability to control the waste operation and the use of the land.

The EA must consult with a number of other public bodies if it proposes to issue a licence, and must consider any representations that those bodies make within 21 days. The Health and Safety Executive is a statutory consultee in all cases. In any case where the site is notified as a site of special scientific interest (SSSI), the relevant NCC is also a statutory consultee, reflecting the fact that a number of SSSIs have been lost to waste disposal over the years—though current planning guidance makes it less likely that planning permission will be granted for waste disposal on a SSSI in the future.

The EA must also take into account any central government guidance (s. 35(8)). This will be provided in the form of waste management papers and it is intended that they should produce a situation where a more uniform approach is adopted across the country than has been the case in the past. The most significant paper is Waste Management Paper No. 4, *Licensing of Waste Facilities*, which seeks to provide comprehensive guidance on the criteria for granting a licence, such as the definition of a 'fit and proper person' and on conditions. WMP4 contains a policy that licences should be reviewed annually and fully reconsidered at least every five years. It will also be appropriate to consider the guidance to be found in Circular 11/94.

One feature that is missing is any element of public participation, since the application does not have to be advertised. This situation arises because it is perceived that the grant of a waste management licence is a technical question: the wider question of the appropriateness of the site will have been considered when planning permission was sought.

(b) The powers of the EA

The EA has a discretion to grant or refuse a licence, but this is subject to a number of restrictions. (Similar restrictions apply to the EA's discretion on questions relating to the transfer, modification, suspension or revocation of a licence, though the wording of the relevant sections is usually more restrictive—see below.)

First, an application *must* be refused if planning permission is required for the use of the land and there is no such permission (s. 36(2)). For these purposes, a lawful development certificate granted under the Town and Country Planning Act 1990, s. 191, is treated as a planning permission. An established use certificate granted under earlier legislation will also normally suffice.

Secondly, the EA *must* refuse the licence if there would be direct or indirect discharge of substances in List I of the Groundwater Directive 80/68 which would interfere with the exploitation of groundwater resources (reg. 15 WML). The risk of groundwater pollution is an important consideration in the grant of any licence. There is a strong set of policies for the protection of groundwater, which were formulated by the Environment Agency.[16] There are some doubts over the ability of measures taken to prevent contamination of groundwater from landfill sites. On most sites the preventive measures will involve some form of impermeable membrane to prevent the egress of leachate. Research has shown that over time even the sturdiest membrane can degrade and the groundwater be threatened. The technical decision on the adequacy of any preventive measures is, however, a question of policy and the decision-maker is entitled to rely upon one technical view even if there are competing views (see *R v Vale of Glamorgan Borough Council, ex parte James* [1996] Env LR 102, where a WRA was held to be entitled to rely on the view of the NRA even though another view was put forward).

Interestingly this requirement only applies to applications for licences for waste disposal or 'tipping for the purposes of disposal'. Thus where an application is sought for other waste activities (e.g. keeping or treating waste) such safeguards are not required. Given that the Groundwater Regulations 1998 are specifically said *not* to apply to activities which require a waste management licence (reg. 2(1)(d)), there is a significant gap in the transposing legislation in that activities such as the treating and keeping of waste substances which are listed in the Groundwater Directive are not necessarily regulated under either the Waste

16. See Environment Agency, *Policy and Practice for the Protection of Groundwater*, (1998).

Management Licensing Regulations 1994 or the Groundwater Regulations 1998 in the way which is required by the Directive (e.g. prohibitions on direct or indirect discharges of List I substances, see p. 733). This is a clear case of inadequate transposition of the Groundwater Directive although it should be noted that in practice such restrictions may be placed on conditions of waste management licences—a good example of practical implementation where full legal transposition has not occurred. The danger is, of course, that practical implementation can be variable and is often unenforceable.

Thirdly the EA *may* refuse a licence if it is satisfied that such a step is necessary to prevent pollution of the environment or harm to human health. This gives a fairly wide discretion to the EA, since section 29 defines pollution of the environment to mean pollution due to the release or escape of substances capable of causing harm to any living organism from the land in or on which waste is kept, treated or deposited. Where there is no planning permission in force (i.e. because it was not required—this would cover a site open since before 1948), the EA may refuse a licence if that is necessary to prevent serious detriment to the amenities of the locality (s. 36(3)).

Finally, a licence *may* be refused if the applicant is not a fit and proper person. Relevant considerations include whether:

- the applicant or any other relevant person has committed a relevant offence. A list of relevant offences is contained in the Waste Management Licensing Regulations 1994, reg. 3. Since the list is wide (but by no means exhaustive of environmental offences), the EA can choose to ignore a conviction if it wishes to do so (s. 74(4)). Four factors should be taken into account in exercising the discretion to ignore a conviction. These are: the type of applicant (i.e. individual, partnership or corporate body); whether it is the applicant or another relevant person who has been convicted of the relevant offence; the nature and gravity of the relevant offence(s); and the number of relevant offences which have been committed (Waste Management Paper 4 Ch.3); or

- the management of the site will not be in the hands of a technically competent person. A person is technically competent only if they are the holder of the relevant certificate of technical competence awarded by the Waste Management Industry Training Board (WAMITAB); or

- the applicant cannot make financial provision adequate to discharge the obligations arising under the licence (s. 74(4)). This could be through insurance or some other allocation of funds. Financial provision may be relevant to site acquisition and preparation; site operation; site restoration and landscaping, or aftercare for a new use; and post-closure control and monitoring.

If the EA decides that the applicant is a fit and proper person, it is under a duty to grant a licence (s. 36(3)). This suggests that if the impediment can be avoided by the imposition of appropriate conditions, the licence should be granted with those conditions attached.

(c) Conditions

The EA is given a wide discretion to attach 'appropriate' conditions to a waste management licence (s. 35(3)). This is in sharp contrast to conditions for large landfills which are subject to prescriptive standards laid down in regulations (see p. 607). Applying ordinary public law principles, conditions must relate to the purposes of Part II of the EPA 1990. In *Attorney-*

General's Reference (No. 2 of 1988) [1990] 1 QB 77, the Court of Appeal decided that a condition requiring the site to be operated so as to avoid creating a nuisance was not permissible under COPA 1974, since it did not relate to the purposes of that Act. Even though the purposes of the EPA 1990 are wider than those of COPA 1974 (in that they relate to the protection of the environment as a whole, rather than the protection of water resources), it is still unclear whether such a condition would be acceptable under section 35(3), since it is still arguable that such matters are more appropriately dealt with under the statutory nuisance provisions in Part III of the EPA 1990 (see p. 404).

The EPA 1990 does not provide a list of the types of conditions that are appropriate. In general, appropriate conditions should relate to the operation and management of the site, so as not to duplicate the conditions attached to the planning permission. The range of conditions imposed under the EPA 1990 can be wider than under COPA 1974 in a number of ways. Section 35(3) states that conditions may be imposed which must be complied with before activities begin or after they have ceased. For example, conditions requiring insurance cover to be effected before the site is opened, or the monitoring of a site for methane emissions or for leachate after disposal has finished, are legitimate.

Section 35(4) provides that conditions may require the applicant to carry out works that need the consent of another person (e.g. access to off–site monitoring). This also applies to cases where there is a modification or suspension of an existing licence. There are detailed procedures and arrangements for compensating owners and occupiers which are set out in the Waste Management Licences (Consultation and Compensation) Regulations 1999 (SI 1999/481). Where these powers are exercised, the person whose consent is required must grant any rights in relation to the land that will enable the licence holder to comply with the conditions. For example, this subsection could be used to override landlord and tenant law by allowing a tenant to carry out works that would normally require the landlord's consent.

Regulations may be made prescribing conditions which are or are not to be included (s. 35(6)). In addition, the Secretary of State is given wide powers to direct that specified conditions are, or are not, included in a licence (s. 35). For example, the Waste Management Licensing Regulations stipulate that no conditions designed solely to secure health and safety at work can be imposed (reg. 12), and that, in order to comply with Directive 75/439 on Waste Oils, certain conditions relating to waste oils must be included (reg. 14).

(d) Transfer of a licence

A waste management licence may be transferred by the EA under section 40 if the holder and the proposed transferee make a joint application to the EA. Unless the EA considers that the proposed transferee is not a fit and proper person, it must make the transfer. An application which must be made in writing, must be determined within two months (or longer if agreed). In the absence of any agreement the application is deemed to have been refused.

(e) Surrender of a licence

Under section 39, a site licence cannot be surrendered at will, though a mobile plant licence can. A surrender of a site licence can take place only if the licence holder applies to the EA and it accepts the surrender. Before that happens, the EA must inspect the land and determine whether it is likely or unlikely that the condition of the land will cause pollution of the environment or harm to human health. In making that determination, it must take into account only matters that relate to the keeping, treatment or disposal of waste on the site, and not extraneous factors. The EA must also take into account guidance on the relevant criteria for an application for surrender found in Waste Management papers (s. 35(8)).

If the EA considers that the condition of the land is likely to cause such pollution or harm, it *must* refuse the application (s. 39(6)). But if it is satisfied that the condition of the land is unlikely to cause pollution or harm, it *must* accept the surrender. Where a surrender is accepted, the EA will issue a certificate of completion, and any obligations under the licence (such as to monitor for methane emissions) then come to an end. Since section 39 requires the EA to issue a certificate where pollution or harm is unlikely, it is possible that an operator will be able to surrender a licence even though it has not fully complied with the licence conditions. However, any conditions attached to the planning permission for the site will still apply after surrender: these could cover such things as a requirement to restore the land to its previous use or to landscape it appropriately. Once all the formalities have been complied with, the certificate can be issued and the licence ceases to have effect.

This procedure is of great importance, since until the implementation of the EPA 1990 holders of waste disposal licences could surrender them at will, and thus relinquish any continuing responsibilities for the site. This is no longer possible under the EPA 1990. One side effect of this change was that, in anticipation of the introduction of stricter standards and more rigorous enforcement powers under the EPA 1990, many holders of waste disposal licences under COPA 1974 surrendered them prior to the implementation of the new system, resulting in a significant shake-out of the waste disposal industry.

BOX 15.11 Waste management, insolvency, and the polluter pays principle

The introduction of the surrender provisions when coupled with the requirement for financial provision under the fit and proper person rules (see above) mean that most sites are subject to long term continuing control. There are, however, problems when operators become insolvent.

In *Official Receiver v Environment Agency, Re Celtic Extraction Ltd and Bluestone Chemical Ltd* [2000] Env LR 86, two holders of waste management licences went into compulsory liquidation. The Official Receiver took over responsibility for the licences and asked the Environment Agency to terminate them. The EA refused, relying on the fact that the necessary conditions to allow the surrender of the licences had not been met. The Official Receiver applied to the Court for directions arguing that the licence had become 'onerous property' within the meaning of section 178 of the Insolvency Act 1986. This would allow the Receiver to disclaim the licence on the basis that there were no assets to cover the payment of compliance with the conditions of the licence. The EA argued that to allow the Receiver to disclaim the licence would be directly contrary to the polluter pays principle. The Court of Appeal held that the licence could be disclaimed because the provisions of the EPA 1990 were not sufficiently clear to exclude the operation of section 178 of the 1986 Act. The Court was influenced by the fact that if a licence holder were to die or be dissolved, a licence would terminate and leave a similar situation to the insolvency. In these situations the EA were powerless to stop the termination of the licence.

When a licence is disclaimed (or when termination is brought about by death or dissolution of the holder), an 'orphan' site is created, i.e. no-one is responsible for or can be made to pay to prevent pollution. This would seem to be contrary to the polluter pays principle. The Court of Appeal considered that the principle did not extend to making unsecured creditors of the insolvent company pay. It has also been pointed out that insolvency is more accurately described as the polluter being *unable* to pay.[17] In such circumstances the only way that the site can be cleaned up is under the contaminated land provisions under Part IIA of the EPA 1990 (see Chapter 17). As the original polluter and owner of the land is likely to no longer 'exist' the liabilities are likely to be met by the taxpayer.

One of the obvious ways of avoiding the problems of the insolvent licence holder would be for the EA to require a generous financial provision for long term after care under the 'fit and proper person test' (see above). It is common to require insurance or the establishment of a fund to pay for compliance with long term obligations under a waste management licence as part of any grant of the licence. In *Environment Agency v Hillridge Limited* [2004] Env LR 32, the holders of a waste management licence established such a trust fund. The holders of the licence were placed in liquidation and following the decision in *Re Celtic Extraction* the liquidators disclaimed the licence. The local authority determined that the land was contaminated land for the purposes of Part IIA of the EPA and the Environment Agency sought to use the money in the trust fund to pay for remedial works and aftercare at the site. The High Court dismissed the application holding that neither the liquidators nor the EA were entitled to the money in the fund. When the liquidators disclaimed the licence they also disclaimed the interest in the fund. Likewise, the EA was not entitled to the money because under the terms of the fund it could only be used whilst the licence was still in force. Consequently, no-one owned the money in the fund and it vested in the Crown as bona vacantia. This case underlines the necessity to take care drafting the terms of the trust deed which sets up an aftercare fund. Effectively even though the money had been designated for a specific purpose and was available, it was given to the Crown, hardly a needy recipient. Although such funds may be used for public purposes, the reality is that it would have been most usefully employed in doing what it was intended to do—namely pay for the clean up of a contaminated site.

The provisions on surrender of licences have been supplemented by the closure notice procedure found in the Landfill (England and Wales) Regulations 2002 (see below) in relation to landfills controlled under the Pollution Prevention and Control system.

Exemptions

A lengthy list of exemptions from the need for a waste management licence is set out in regulation 17 and schedule 3. The main types of activity that are covered are as follows:

- activities that are carried on in accordance with the provisions of consents or authorizations granted under other legislation (e.g. a discharge consent granted under the Water Resources Act 1991, or a licence to dump at sea granted under the Food and Environment Protection Act 1985);

17. C. Shelborne (2000) 12 JEL 207.

- the storage of directive waste at its place of production pending its treatment or disposal elsewhere (this will cover such things as storing waste in a skip—there is no time limit as long as the producer can show that it is genuinely going to be collected);
- the storage of special waste at its place of production pending its treatment or disposal elsewhere, as long as certain conditions on quantity and security are met;
- various activities relating to the recovery or reuse of waste, such as sorting waste at the place at which it is produced, baling it, shredding it and compacting it;
- storage or deposit of demolition or construction wastes for the purposes of construction work being undertaken on the land;
- deposit of certain organic matter for the purposes of fertilising or conditioning land;
- in order to encourage recycling, a great variety of recycling activities are exempted, although often subject to detailed restrictions on quantity (e.g. the collection of paper and cardboard, aluminium and steel cans, plastics, glass and textiles for recycling, or the cleaning and washing of packaging or containers so that they can be reused).

These exemptions are not absolute as an activity must also meet the objectives set out in the Waste Framework Directive and schedule 4 of the Waste Management Licensing Regulations (reg. 18 and 17(4)) and see Box 15.6 above). In many of these categories the exemption will not apply if the waste is hazardous waste. The exemptions cannot be varied by letter or conduct (see Case box 15.6).

CASE 15.6 The practicalities of exemptions—*Environment Agency v Newcomb* [2003] Env LR 12

The use of exemptions is a very attractive option for many operators as the full rigours of waste management licences can be avoided. On the other side of the enforcement coin, the Environment Agency does not necessarily want to subject every exempt activity to close scrutiny as this may impose excessive monitoring and inspection requirements. Such a situation occurred in the case of *Environment Agency v Newcomb* where the defendant company was creating a football pitch on waste land using demolition and construction wastes. The Agency wrote to the company saying that biodegradable wastes should not be accepted on the site. Given the practical difficulties of waste segregation, the Agency said it would permit a 5 per cent tolerance. The Agency subsequently prosecuted when it found biodegradable waste on the site. The Magistrates hearing the case concluded that there was less than 5 per cent of biodegradeable waste and that the prosecution had failed to prove the case beyond reasonable doubt. The High Court disagreed with the Magistrates. The fact that the Agency had permitted a 5 per cent latitude was irrelevant to the question of whether the statutory exemption applied. All that was required was for the Agency to prove the facts which took the deposit outside the exemption and the fact that a deposit had been made.

A further requirement is that an exempted activity must be registered with the EA. Under WML, res. 18(1) it is an offence to carry on an exempt activity involving the recovery or disposal of waste without being registered with the appropriate registration authority. The requirement to register covers 'establishments or undertakings'; it does not include private individuals. Registration is effected simply by notifying the EA of the relevant activities, where they are carried on, and the exemption which is being relied on (reg. 18(3)). The EA is required to keep a register of exemptions containing the particulars of the registration (reg. 18(4)). In practice, the requirement to register is administrative in nature as prosecution for the failure to register an exempt activity would only be a last resort. Where serious environmental harm had arisen from exempt activities it would be preferable to rely upon prosecution powers under section 33(1)(c), if possible. Under this section there is a general offence of keeping, treating or disposing of directive waste in a manner likely to cause pollution of the environment or harm to human health will remain applicable in all the above exemptions apart from those in category (a) above which are carried on in accordance with another licence. By contrast, household waste from a private dwelling which is treated, kept or disposed of within the curtilage of the dwelling by, or with the permission of, the occupier, is entirely exempt from section 33 (s. 33(2)).

BOX 15.12 **The use and abuse of waste exemptions—the spreading of waste on land**

The system of exemption from waste management licensing was introduced for activities which were thought to pose minimal risk to the environment or human health. Unfortunately the combination of broad definitions of the categories and minimal monitoring and enforcement of the exemptions has led to a number of areas where problems have arisen. In particular, the spreading of certain wastes on land (e.g. sewage sludge and industrial wastes) has been the subject of criticism. For example, it has been estimated that over 3 million tonnes of industrial wastes are spread on land each year[18] with waste from the paper industry, abbatoirs and the food processing industry contributing substantial proportions. This is a significant amount of waste to dispose of given the relatively light regulatory requirements under the exemption.

The relevant exemption allows up to 250 tonnes of waste to be spread per hectare each year where it results in a 'benefit to agriculture or ecological improvement' (see WML, sch. 3 para. 7). There is a requirement to register the exemption, pre-notify the Environment Agency of the spreading and where repeated spreading takes place submit a six-monthly report to the EA. The system has a number of significant flaws:

- The registration of the exemption is passive. This can be contrasted with licensing systems based upon the authorization of 'fit and proper' operators which takes into account past experience and qualifications. By contrast, anyone can spread exempt waste on land.

- There is a lack of clarity on the definition of such key concepts as 'benefit to agriculture' and 'ecological improvement'.

- There is a lack of clarity about the duties of the occupier of the land to notify the person carrying out any spreading activity in relation to environmental risks such as previous activities and substances which had been spread or the existence of any watercourses which may be polluted.

- There is little monitoring of the activity, the nature of the waste spread and little or no post spreading monitoring.

---

18. (1998) ENDS Report 281, 27.

This general lack of clarity, lax monitoring and supervision and absence of technical competence requirements encourages the illegal disposal of non-exempt waste under the guise of exempt land spreading. Unsurprisingly, there has been a number of significant pollution incidents arising from the land spreading of wastes.[19] In its 19th Report, on the sustainable use of soil, the RCEP criticized the broad nature and abuse of the exemption and called for tighter controls.[20] Although there have been proposals to amend and clarify the exemption in England and Wales no legislation has been made. In Scotland, however, new legislation was introduced in 2003 (see Box 5.1).

The case of land spreading of wastes illustrates broader flaws in the system of exemptions. One of the difficulties with the British waste management licensing system is its 'all or nothing' nature. A non-exempt waste activity which poses a low risk to the environment is required to be licensed in broadly the same way as a complicated landfill site. An exempt waste activity which may pose an environmental risk unless carried out properly falls completely outside the waste management system. A system of risk based regulation would be more flexible yet appropriate to different types of waste activity. Different types of controls are needed for different activities possibly ranging from registered exemptions for the lowest-risk activities through standardised permits to individual licences. Such a waste permitting system has been discussed by DEFRA but no concrete proposals have emerged.

Enforcement powers

It is one of the features of most modern systems of pollution control that the regulatory agencies have strong enforcement powers. These are not limited to bringing prosecutions for breaches of the law, but extend to powers to vary and to revoke licences without compensation. These administrative remedies often represent a greater threat to operators than prosecution because of the potential financial consequences. The EA has a wide range of powers to deal with breaches of waste management licences including powers to modify a licence, to revoke it in whole or in part, to suspend the operation of licensed activities, and to order the carrying out of specified works. In conjunction with these powers, EPA 1990, s. 42 imposes supervisory duties on the EA.

(a) Supervision of a licence

Section 42 puts the EA under a duty to supervise waste management licences. It must take the steps that are needed to ensure that pollution of the environment, harm to human health or serious detriment to the amenities of the locality do not occur. It must also take steps to ensure that licence conditions are complied with. Where there is an emergency, specific powers are given by section 42(3). The EA may carry out necessary works on land or in relation to plant or equipment, and may recover any expenditure from the licence holder.

---

19. See, e.g., a paper sludge disposal operation which caused widespread odour nuisance in Kent, a major illegal land spreading operation in Devon involving food and cesspit wastes and offences relating to land spreading of abattoir and brewery wastes ENDS Report 270, 45.

20. RECP, *Sustainable Use of Soil*, Cm 3165, 196.

(b) Modification of a licence

Powers to modify a licence are of particular importance where circumstances have changed since the initial grant of the licence. The EA may, at its discretion, modify the conditions of a licence where it considers this is desirable and is unlikely to require unreasonable expense on the part of the licence holder (s. 37(1)(a)). But if it considers that in order to ensure that the authorized activities do not cause pollution of the environment or harm to human health, or become seriously detrimental to the amenities of the locality, it is necessary to modify the conditions, it *must* do so to the extent necessary (s. 37(2)). Alternatively, in such circumstances it may decide to revoke the licence under s. 38(1). The consultation requirements apply to an EA proposal to modify a licence in virtually the same way that they apply to an application under s. 36, except that, in an emergency, a reference to a consultee may be postponed. There is a separate right for the licence holder to apply for a modification (s. 37(1)(b)). In each situation any modification made under section 37 must be by notice and must specify when it takes effect (s. 37(4)).

(c) Suspension of a licence

The powers to suspend and to revoke a licence are of great use where licensed activities are giving rise to problems, for example where the site is being inadequately managed or is causing pollution. The grounds for their use are, in general terms, similar to those relating to the refusal of an initial licence application, though they are in fact slightly less wide. They provide an opportunity to police the licence on a continuing basis and may be used in addition to other enforcement mechanisms, such as prosecution or ordering a clean-up.

The EA may suspend a licence by serving a notice on the licence holder. Such a notice must specify when the suspension is to take effect and when it is to cease. This may be on the occurrence either of a specified date or a specified event. A suspension cannot be of the whole of a licence, but can only relate to those parts of the licence that authorize the carrying on of activities. For example, the EA may suspend a licence in so far as it allows certain types of waste to be deposited, whilst retaining in force any conditions that relate to measures the licence holder must take to protect against pollution. Whilst a part of a licence is suspended it does not authorize the licence holder to carry on the activities specified.

The power to suspend is provided for in two separate sections: one where there has been a failure to comply with the licence (s. 42(6)), and another which applies more generally (s. 38(6)).

- Under section 38(6), if the EA considers that the site is no longer in the hands of a technically competent person, it may suspend those parts of the licence that authorize the carrying on of activities. The same power applies if the EA considers that serious pollution of the environment or serious harm to human health has been caused, or is about to be caused, or that the continuation of the activities will cause serious pollution of the environment or serious harm to human health.

- The alternative power is that if, in exercising its supervisory powers under section 42, it appears to the EA that a condition is not being complied with, it may by notice require the licence holder to comply within a specified time. If the licence holder does not do so, the EA may suspend the licence (s. 42(6)). In this situation, the availability of the suspension power acts as an incentive to the proper implementation of conditions.

One limitation on these powers is that, if the Secretary of State determines on appeal that the EA acted unreasonably in suspending a licence, the licence holder can claim compensation for consequential loss from the EA (s. 43(7)). This potential financial liability may act as a brake on the use of suspension notices by the EA.

Whilst a licence is suspended, the EA may require the licence holder to take such measures to deal with or avert pollution or harm as it thinks fit (s. 38(9)). Significantly, this may include matters which fall outside the scope of the original licence conditions. It is an offence to fail to comply with such a requirement (s. 38(10)). The maximum penalty is, on conviction in the magistrates' court, a fine of £5,000 or, on conviction in the Crown Court, two years' imprisonment and/or an unlimited fine. If the waste is hazardous waste, a magistrates' court may imprison for up to six months, and the maximum term of imprisonment on conviction in the Crown Court is five years.

(d) Revocation of a licence

The EA may revoke a licence by serving a notice on the licence holder, specifying when the revocation is to take effect. A revocation may be of the whole of a licence or of part of it—this includes revocation of those parts of the licence that authorize the carrying on of activities, whilst retaining other parts. For example, the EA may revoke a licence in so far as it allows certain waste to be deposited, leaving the rest of the licence in force. Revocation of the whole of the licence is likely to be inappropriate in many cases, since it means that any conditions attached to the licence cease to have effect (s. 35(11)). As these may include conditions requiring the licence holder to carry out works of pollution control, or conditions relating to the restoration and aftercare of a site, revocation would effectively remove most of the licence holder's responsibilities. A licence can be revoked in a number of circumstances.

- Under section 38(1), if the EA considers that the holder of a licence has ceased to be a fit and proper person by reason of being convicted of a relevant offence, it may revoke the licence, wholly or in part. The same power applies if the EA considers that the continuation of the activities authorised by the licence would cause pollution of the environment or harm to human health, or would be seriously detrimental to the amenities of the locality, except that, in such a case, it must also consider that the pollution, harm or detriment cannot be avoided by modifying the conditions of the licence.

- Under section 38(2), if the EA considers that the site is no longer in the hands of a technically competent person, it may revoke those parts of the licence that authorise the carrying out of activities, but not the rest of it.

- The same power of partial revocation applies if the licence holder fails to pay an annual subsistence charge (s. 41(7)).

- As with the power to suspend a licence, if the licence holder fails to comply with a notice served under section 42 requiring compliance with a condition, the EA may revoke the licence, either wholly or in part (s. 42(6)).

(e) Fees and charges

As part of the shift towards transferring funding of the regulation of pollution from the public to polluters, the Environment Act 1995, s. 41, provides for an annual fees and charges scheme (see the Waste Management Licensing (Fees and Charges) Scheme). The scheme is a cost-recovery scheme, meaning that the levels are supposed to be fixed by the Secretary of State so as to cover, in general terms, the cost to the EA of processing an application and supervising a licence.

In order to achieve this objective and to ensure that different operations pay a reasonably fair charge relative to each other, a fairly complex scheme has been implemented. The types of licensable activity are divided into four main classes, although these are then subdivided to take account of such things as whether the waste is being reused, reclaimed or recycled. These classes are: the treatment of controlled waste; the keeping of controlled waste; the disposal of controlled waste; and situations where a site has closed and a certificate of completion is being sought. Having established these general classes, the type of waste which is concerned (e.g. whether it is inert waste, household waste, industrial waste, or hazardous waste), and the amount of waste that the site is licensed to receive annually, are taken into account so that the precise category into which the activity falls can be ascertained. The various fees and charges are then worked out by reference to that category.

There are separate fees for initial applications for a licence, and for applications for transfer, modification and surrender respectively. An annual subsistence charge is also payable, which will normally run into thousands of pounds, depending on the type of facility. The EA has a power to revoke a licence in part if the annual charge is not paid (s. 41(6)).

(f) Public registers

The EA is under a duty to maintain a public register of a wide range of information relating to the waste management licensing system (s. 64, supplemented by the Waste Management Licensing Regulations 1994 reg. 10).

In outline, the registers must contain details of the following: all current or recently current licences and applications, together with any relevant supporting documentation, representations and directions; modification, suspension and revocation notices; matters relating to an application to surrender a licence; reports and monitoring information produced or obtained by the EA in discharging its functions; remedial action taken by the EA; consignment notes and records made for the purposes of the special waste provisions; convictions of licence holders under Part II of the Act; and appeals. A licence is no longer recent 12 months after it ceases to be in force, and an application no longer recent 12 months after its rejection, meaning that the registers are of limited use for historical purposes.

There are powers for the Secretary of State to exclude information from the registers on the ground that its inclusion would be contrary to the interests of national security (s. 65), and for the EA to exclude information on commercial confidentiality grounds (s. 66), though there is an appeal to the Secretary of State if the EA refuses to do so. In relation to exclusions dealt with under section 66, the register will contain an entry indicating the existence of the information.

(g) The powers of the Secretary of State

Apart from the wide-ranging powers to make regulations under the Act and to issue policy guidance, the Secretary of State is provided with very wide powers to give directions to the EA. For example, where an application is made, the Secretary of State may give a binding direction to the EA in relation to the terms and conditions that must, or must not, be included in the licence (s. 35(7)). This power is the equivalent of the call-in powers that exist in other areas of the law. There are similar powers to give binding directions relating to modification (s. 37(3)) and to suspension and revocation (ss. 38(7) and 42(8))—in these cases the Secretary of State can effectively force the EA to take action.

(h) Appeals

There are wide-ranging rights of appeal to the Secretary of State contained in section 43. An appeal can be made where:

- an application for a licence is rejected (or is not determined within four months);
- a licence is subject to conditions;
- the conditions are modified;
- an application for a modification of conditions is rejected (or is not determined within two months);
- a licence is suspended;
- a licence is revoked;
- an application to surrender a licence is rejected (or is not determined within three months);
- an application for a transfer of a licence is rejected (or is not determined within two months).

One exception is where the Secretary of State made the original decision under the various powers of direction. In such a case, an action for judicial review would be the only available option.

There are no specified grounds of appeal. The Waste Management Licensing Regulations 1994 state that an appeal must be brought within six months of the relevant decision (or deemed decision in cases where the appeal is against a non-determination within the required timescale). As is normal in environmental matters the appellant and the EA have a choice as to whether the appeal is in the form of a hearing or by written representations. Unusually, if a hearing is held, section 43(2)(c) states that it is open to the person who hears the appeal to hold it in private, in whole or in part. The appeal will commonly be referred to an inspector or other person, who will normally make the decision on behalf of the Secretary of State.

Modifications and revocations normally have no effect while an appeal is pending or being heard (s. 43(4)). However, the EA may reverse this rule by stating in its notice that this is necessary for the purpose of preventing or minimizing pollution of the environment or harm to human health (s. 43(6)). Suspension notices are not affected by an appeal (s. 43(5)). One limitation on the exercise of the power under section 43(6) is that a licence holder may ask the Secretary of State to determine whether the EA acted unreasonably in activating section 43(6), or in suspending a licence. If the decision goes in favour of the licence holder, it can claim compensation for consequential loss from the EA (s. 43(7)). This may limit the use of suspension notices and of section 43(6).

Offences

Section 33(1) of EPA 1990 and the Waste Management Licensing Regulations 1994, reg. 1(3) and schedule 4, makes it a criminal offence to:

- deposit directive waste in or on land unless it is in accordance with a waste management licence. This applies to any deposit, whether temporary or permanent, and is not restricted to directive disposal and recovery operations;

- treat, keep or dispose of directive waste unless it is under and in accordance with a waste management licence—this offence can be committed either in or on land, or by means of mobile plant. As pointed out above this offence now extends only to directive disposal and recovery operations;

- knowingly cause or knowingly permit either of the above.

These offences are not limited to deposits but extend to keeping, treating or disposing of controlled waste. However, many acts of storage and treatment will in fact be exempted, as the Waste Management Licensing Regulations 1994 show. It is clear that offences in the first two categories above are ones of strict liability, but it should be noted that the last category interposes 'knowingly' in front of both 'cause' and 'permit'.

BOX 15.13 **The meaning of 'deposit'**

The definition of 'deposit' is central to section 33(1)(a) EPA 1990 and the courts have adopted a relatively wide definition. Initially in *Leigh Land Reclamation Ltd v Walsall Metropolitan Borough Council* (1991) 155 JP 547 it was held that waste was deposited at a landfill site only when there was no realistic prospect of further examination or inspection and it had reached its final resting place. This decision caused enormous practical problems for waste regulation authorities as it became difficult to prove that waste had definitely reached its final resting place when defendants argued it was going to be moved on a future occasion. The decision in *Leigh* was overturned by the Divisional Court in *R v Metropolitan Stipendiary Magistrate, ex parte London Waste Regulation Authority* [1993] All ER 113, where it was held that 'deposit' applied to temporary deposits as well as to permanent ones, which seems to reflect both common sense and the wider scope of the EPA 1990 in dealing with waste *management* rather than *disposal*. This definition was widened once again in *Thames Waste Management Ltd v Surrey County Council* [1997] Env LR 148, where it was held that 'deposit' could cover continuing activities where the context of the waste management licence would suggest that it was appropriate to do so. Thus a deposit can continue over a significant period whilst other activities are carried out.

There was some uncertainty over the exact number of offences which could be committed under section 33. Is the treating, keeping or disposing of directive waste a single offence committed in the alternative or are there three separate offences? The practical difficulty which arises as a result of this uncertainty is that if the latter position is correct, any indictment alleging all three in one charge would be duplicitous (as the situation is in relation to causing or knowingly permitting pollution of controlled waters, see p. 733). In *R v Leighton and Town and Country Refuse Collections Ltd* [1997] Env LR 411 the court considered the specific question of whether there are a number of alternative ways of committing the same offence. The court found that although each relevant paragraph of section 33(1) created a separate offence, each of those offences could be committed in any of the ways specified within the paragraph. For example, it was possible to bring a charge of disposing or treating or keeping of controlled waste in a manner likely to cause pollution of the environment or harm to human health contrary to section 33(1)(c) of the EPA 1990. This eases the evidential burden on the prosecution when framing an indictment.

The courts have interpreted the phrase 'knowingly' very strictly. In *Shanks and McEwan (Teesside) Ltd v Environment Agency* [1997] Env LR 305 the defendant was charged with knowingly permitting the deposit of controlled waste in contravention of a licence condition. It was argued that although the defendant knew of the deposit of the waste it did not know it was in breach of condition. The court followed the previous decision in *Ashcroft v Cambro Waste Products Ltd* [1981] 1 WLR 1349 in taking a very strict view of the phrase. The prosecution need only prove knowledge of the deposit of the waste material. It is not necessary to demonstrate knowledge of the breach of the licence condition which gives rise to the offence. Thus, once the prosecution demonstrate that waste had been knowingly permitted to be deposited, the burden then falls on the defence to establish that the deposit was made in accordance with the conditions of the licence (see further Box 9.3).

It is also possible to infer knowledge. In *Kent County Council v Beaney* [1993] Env LR 225 it was held that knowing permission may be inferred from the facts of a case where the deposit of waste was obvious from surrounding events. This concept of constructive knowledge was developed further in the *Shanks and McEwan (Teesside)* decision In that case, Mance J took the view that it was sufficient that the defendant company (including its senior management) knowingly operated and held out its site for the reception and deposit of controlled waste. Once this was established it was not necessary to demonstrate that there was any knowledge of the specific breach of the licence condition. This approach broadens the offence considerably and in effect places the operators of landfill sites under a strict liability for breaches of waste management licence conditions.

As far as the concept of causation is concerned, this has been discussed on a number of occasions in relation to the similar offences under the Water Resources Act 1991 (see p. 736). However, analogies with these cases should be made with care, since they do not consider the situation where 'knowingly' is inserted in front of 'cause'. This appears to suggest that someone who orders another to deposit waste will be guilty under this section only if it is shown that they knew the deposit was to take place unlawfully. One subsection that may help here is section 33(5), which states that where controlled waste is deposited from a motor vehicle, the person who controls the vehicle, or who is in a position to control its use, will be treated as knowingly causing the deposit (see Box Case box 15.7).

CASE 15.7 Vehicle ownership and waste offences—*Environment Agency v Melland* [2002] Env LR 29

The defendant ('M') was prosecuted for offences of fly-tipping waste on an industrial estate. The evidence was that M was the owner of the vehicle which had been seen at the site although M was not the driver. M was acquitted of the offence on the basis that although he owned the vehicle, the element of control required under section 33(5) was not present. On appeal, the High Court held that evidence of ownership of a vehicle was capable of amounting to evidence of control. This is a presumptive test and there will be other occasions where ownership would not indicate control (e.g. if the owner was a hire company).

There is a separate strict liability offence of contravening any condition of a waste management licence (s. 33(6)).

The maximum penalty for these offences is, on conviction in the magistrates' court, six months' imprisonment and/or a fine of £20,000 or, on conviction in the Crown Court, two years' imprisonment and/or an unlimited fine. If the waste is hazardous waste, the maximum term of imprisonment on conviction in the Crown Court is five years. An injunction may also be sought in appropriate cases.

Any director, manager, secretary or other similar officer of a corporate body can be prosecuted personally if the offence is committed with their consent or connivance, or is attributable to their neglect. A 'manager' only covers someone who is part of the 'controlling mind' of the company (see Box 9.4). This liability is additional to the individual liability of the person who carried out, or knowingly caused or knowingly permitted the deposit. Waste management is one area of environmental law where sentences of imprisonment have actually been imposed, though they have been reserved for serious offences and where an offender offends repeatedly.

Defences

There is a defence under section 33(7)(a) where the defendant took all reasonable precautions and exercised all due diligence to avoid the commission of the offence. This is a familiar defence that is included in many pieces of regulatory legislation (although perhaps surprisingly not in relation to water pollution). Essentially, it involves the defendant showing either that it took the appropriate steps on the facts of the case, or that it set up an adequate system. In many ways, the requirements are similar to those laid down by the duty of care. For example, the defence is of great use for receivers of waste (i.e. carriers and waste disposal site operators), who may inadvertently deal with it in an illegal fashion if they are misled by the consignor. However, it does impose quite a high standard on them to take steps to ensure that the consignment contains what it is meant to contain. It is arguable that this defence introduces an element of self-policing into the waste disposal chain in the sense that very specific checks are required to rely on the defence (see Box 15.14).

BOX 15.14 **The due diligence defence**

The nature of the due diligence defence is illustrated in two cases. In *Durham County Council v Peter Connors Industrial Services Ltd* [1993] Env LR 197, a system of operation which relied upon the person disposing of waste regularly collecting a skip which had been filled with waste by another without checking on the contents of the skip every time, was not sufficient to come within an analogous defence under section 3(4) of COPA 1974. It was held that the collector of waste had to take care to inform itself on each occasion that it collected the waste as to the nature of the contents of the skip. The defence required a specific inquiry to be made of any person who knew what the waste was and whether or not the future deposit of that waste would involve a breach of the Act. In *Environment Agency v Short* [1998] Env LR 300, the defendant ('S') left waste timber at a construction site to be burnt after being told incorrectly by the site owner that the site did not require a waste management licence because it was exempt. The High Court held that the onus was on S to make specific inquiries as to whether the exemption extended to the timber.

There are further defences in section 33(7)(b) and (c) relating respectively to employees who act under instructions from their employer and in ignorance of the offence, and to acts carried out in an emergency in order to avoid danger to the public (although not danger to the environment). The onus of proof establishing whether or not an emergency exists rests with the defendant upon the balance of probabilities. In *Waste Incineration Services Ltd v Dudley Metropolitan Borough Council* [1993] Env LR 29 the court viewed the phrase 'emergency' (as used in a condition of a waste disposal licence) objectively and without reference to how the licence holder perceived a given set of facts.

Dangerous disposal of waste

There is a very important further offence created by section 33(1)(c). It is an offence to treat, keep or dispose of controlled waste in a manner likely to cause pollution of the environment or harm to human health. The importance of this paragraph is that it applies irrespective of the need for a waste management licence. In other words, activities which are exempted from the need for a licence are still governed by what is in effect a general requirement to act safely. The paragraph could also be said to supplement the licensing system by acting as a form of residual condition attached to a licence, since in theory it applies even where a licence is being complied with. The offence is drafted remarkably widely, as pollution of the environment is defined in section 29 by reference to harm to *any* living organism. Harm in this context means any harm to the health of living organisms or interference with the ecological systems of which they form a part.

The paragraph is mainly targeted at providing a straightforward offence that can be used in relation to fly-tipping and other forms of irresponsible waste disposal. However, it also covers such things as storage of wastes on the production site—the harm to human health could be a harm to employees. The maximum penalty for breach of section 33(1)(c) is the same as for offences relating to a waste management licence. The section does not, however, apply to activities which are under regulations made under section 33(3). This has only been done in the cases of activities which are adequately controlled under regimes other than waste management.

Clean-up powers

Section 59 gives the EA and waste collection authorities powers to require the removal of controlled waste. They apply whenever controlled waste has been deposited on land in contravention of section 33(1), i.e. the deposit was not in accordance with a waste management licence or it breached section 33(1)(c).

The initial responsibility falls on the occupier of the land. The EA may serve a notice on the occupier requiring the waste to be removed, or steps to be taken to mitigate the consequences of the deposit. The notice must specify a period within which this action should be taken, though it cannot be less than 21 days. There is a right to appeal to the magistrates' court during the 21-day period. Such an appeal must be allowed if the court is satisfied that the appellant neither deposited nor knowingly caused or knowingly permitted the deposit, or if there is a material defect in the notice (s. 59(3)). An appeal suspends the operation of the notice until it is determined (s. 59(4)). It is a summary offence, with a maximum fine of £5,000 to fail to comply with a notice served under section 59 (s. 59(5)). This offence is a continuing one and a further fine of up to £1,000 can be imposed for every day on which the failure to comply continues after conviction. Ultimately, the EA has default powers to carry out the steps specified in the notice itself and to recover any expenses reasonably incurred from the person on whom it was served (s. 59(6)).

Where the occupier did not make or knowingly permit the unlawful deposit, or there is no occupier, the EA may remove the waste or take mitigating steps immediately. This course of action is also available if these steps were immediately necessary to remove or prevent pollution or harm to human health (s. 59(7)). The EA may then recover its costs from any person who deposited the waste, or knowingly caused or knowingly permitted its deposit, unless that person can show that the cost was incurred unnecessarily (s. 59(8)). Ultimate responsibility for unlawfully deposited waste therefore falls on the person who deposited it rather than on the occupier. However, it may not be possible to trace the person responsible, or they may have no money to pay the EA's costs, in which case the position is in practice that the EA has a choice whether to leave the waste where it is or pick up the bill itself. Nevertheless, this is an important power which can be used in addition to a prosecution under section 33, since it tackles directly the problem that faces the EA. The EA's powers under the Water Resources Act 1991, s. 161, should also be considered in this context, since they may be used to deal with deposits of waste that threaten controlled waters (see p. 744).

Landfills

Major landfill sites are controlled under a separate and additional system of control to the waste management licensing system. The Landfill (England and Wales) Regulations 2002 (SI 2002/1559) implemented the requirements of the Landfill Directive 1999/31/EC (see p. 569). The Regulations are a dramatic departure from the discretionary, flexible approach to standards set under the waste management licensing system. The implementation of the operational aspects of the Regulations are carried out under the IPPC regime (see Chapter 20). All landfill sites are controlled under IPPC regime (see p. 788). For landfills, the requirement to impose conditions such as the attainment of the Best Available Technique is derived from these technical conditions found in the Landfill Regulations. The main operational provisions of the Regulations provide for:

- The ending of the UK practice of the co-disposal of hazardous and non-hazardous waste with the classification of landfills into three types: for hazardous, non hazardous or inert waste. Waste from outside the designated class will not be permitted to be disposed of at classified landfills (reg. 7).

- Complete bans on the disposal of certain wastes going to landfill including all liquid wastes; infectious clinical and hospital wastes; tyres; and waste which, in the conditions of landfill, is explosive, corrosive, oxidizing, flammable, or highly flammable (reg. 9)

- Detailed technical requirements for all landfills (schedules 2 and 3). This includes pollution prevention measures and monitoring requirements. This is the first time that detailed standards have been laid down in waste legislation. These standards are prescriptive and apply to all relevant landfills. Landfill operators were required to submit so-called 'conditioning plans' to the Environment Agency that set out how they would meet the relevant standards. Failure to do so meant that the site would be closed. The tightening of standards for hazardous waste sites meant that many operators were forced to undertake significant improvements on certain sites or simply 'switch' to a less onerous class of landfill. It is feared that this might lead to a shortage in the number of sites which are able to accept hazardous waste.

- The requirement to treat most wastes before landfill (reg. 10 and sch. 1).

- Introduction of waste acceptance criteria. The criteria comprise a set of procedures for the characterization of waste and compliance testing, together with a set of leaching and other criteria to define which wastes may be accepted at inert, non-hazardous and hazardous landfills (sch. 1).

- Powers to close landfill sites by means of a 'Closure Notice' procedure with the ability to enforce continuing after care conditions (reg. 15).

- The formal introduction of the European Waste Catalogue descriptions (see above p. 568) The regulations amend the Duty of Care Regulations to require that a Duty of Care transfer note identifies the waste to which it relates by reference to the appropriate codes in the EWC.

- The setting of waste reduction targets for municipal biodegradable waste (discussed above at p. 572).

In the long term, the introduction of the regulations is likely to have a dramatic impact on disposal costs particularly in the case of hazardous wastes. This will result from increased transport costs to fewer sites, and an increase in costs arising from pre-treatment and complying with the waste acceptance criteria. In addition, increased emphasis will be placed on alternatives to landfill including different recovery, treatment and disposal operations as well as incentives to minimize waste production.

CASE 15.8 What is a landfill?—*Blackland Park Exploration Limited v Environment Agency* [2004] Env LR 33

The Landfill Regulations only apply to waste which is disposed of at landfills. A 'landfill' is defined in the Regulations as meaning: 'a waste disposal site for the deposit of waste onto or into land' (reg. 3). This includes any permanent site which is used to store waste for more than one year prior to final disposal but does not include a permanent storage site where waste is stored for a period of less than three years prior to *recovery*. In *Blackland Park Exploration Limited v Environment Agency* [2004] Env LR 33, the Court of Appeal had to consider the question of whether the re-injection of contaminated liquids into groundwater at an on-shore oil production facility was the deposit of waste in a landfill for the purposes of the Regulations. If it was a deposit in a landfill the ban on the disposal of liquid wastes at landfill sites would apply, thereby prohibiting the operation at the site. The operator argued that the re-injection was a discharge to groundwater which should be controlled by means of a discharge consent under the Water Resources Act 1991. The Court of Appeal held that the Directive and the Regulations should be interpreted widely. The fact which was most persuasive to the Court of Appeal was that once the waste was deposited in the groundwater it did not dissipate beyond the site. It was naturally buoyant and constrained by an upper layer of clay. Accordingly the waste was deposited in land and the fact that there was a lot of water present was no different in principle from the presence of water at the bottom of a disused mine. If this reasoning is followed more generally, many other discharges into 'static' waters would be considered to be deposits in landfill.

The Duty of Care

One of the key indicators that the introduction of the Environmental Protection Act 1990 saw a switch from waste disposal to waste management was the introduction of the Duty of Care.[21] Section 34, EPA provides that the duty of care applies to any person who produces, imports, carries, keeps, treats or disposes of controlled waste, or who, as a broker, has control of it. The only exception is that occupiers of domestic premises are not subject to the duty with regard to household waste produced on the property (s. 34(2)). The duty applies only to controlled waste (and therefore does not include such things as agricultural or mining waste). It applies in addition to controls over waste management licensing.

Any person subject to the duty has to take reasonable steps to:

1   Prevent any other person contravening section 33 (i.e. the law relating to the unauthorized deposit, keeping, treatment, or disposal of controlled waste).

This requires steps to be taken to check that waste is dealt with properly by others further down the waste disposal chain. For example, a transferor of waste should know where the waste is going before parting with it, which in turn involves checking that the site where the waste is to be taken is licensed to take it and that the carrier is actually taking it there. The standard of reasonableness is objective in the sense that holders of waste ought to act on signs that something is amiss. However, the standard is also related to the resources and

---

21. A description of the policy background to this change can be found in the RCEP's 11th Report, *Managing Waste: The Duty of Care* (Cmnd. 9675, 1985).

knowledge of the individual, with the result that large firms may be expected to carry out more rigorous investigations than small ones.

2   Prevent the escape of waste.

This requires proper storage and packaging of waste taking into account any hazardous characteristics. The escape of waste does not include deliberate deposits which would fall within the section 33 offences (see Case box 15.9).

3   Ensure that the waste is transferred only to an authorized person.

This would include a waste collection authority, waste management licence holder or registered waste carrier.

4   Ensure that an adequate written description of the waste is given to anyone to whom the waste is transferred.

The Environmental Protection (Duty of Care) Regulations 1991 (SI 1991/2839) require that when controlled waste is transferred there must be a transfer note, though this does not actually have to travel with the waste. The transfer note must identify the waste and state its quantity, the kind of container it is in, the time and place of transfer, and the name, address and other relevant details of the transferor and transferee. The regulations also require that the transferor and transferee sign the transfer note and that the transfer note and the written description are kept for at least two years from the date of transfer. It is permissible for multiple consignments of waste up to one year to be covered by one transfer note, as long as the description of the waste, the identity of the parties and all other details remain the same for each consignment.

There is also a *Code of Practice on the Duty of Care*, produced by the Secretary of State.[22] The Code of practice sets down a guide for what would amount to reasonable steps taken in seeking to fulfil the duty. This is a statutory code, made under section 34(7). Contravention of its provisions is not of itself a criminal offence, but it could be said that contravention gives rise to a presumption that the duty has been breached, since section 34(10) states that it should be taken into account in deciding whether the duty has been complied with and in fixing any penalty. (The Code may also be used as evidence in civil cases and in prosecutions under section 33.)

CASE 15.9 Definition of escape—*Gateway Professional Services (Management) Ltd v Kingston Upon Hull City Council* [2004] Env LR 42

The defendant company deposited a number of black bags containing commercial office waste on land adjoining its site. The company was convicted of the offence of failing to take all reasonable measures to prevent the escape of waste contrary to the Duty of Care. On appeal, the High Court held that a deliberate deposit of waste was not the same as an 'escape'. The deliberate dumping of waste was covered by EPA 1990, s. 33(1)(a).

---

22. *Waste Management, The Duty of Care, A Code of Practice*, (HMSO, 1996).

Everyone in the waste chain is subject to the duty of care. The system should therefore have an element of self-policing. For example, a producer of waste would be well advised not to transfer it to someone they suspect of being a 'cowboy', because if the waste is fly-tipped that could lead the EA to prosecute the producer for breach of the duty of care (and also give rise to possible criminal actions for knowingly permitting the deposit, and to potential liability in civil law, or under clean-up powers). Equally, a waste carrier should not accept improperly labelled or packaged waste, and should make periodic checks on the waste it receives, since it will have responsibility under the duty of care if there is something wrong.

Breach of the duty of care is a criminal offence (s. 34(6)). The maximum penalty is, on conviction in the magistrates' court, a £5,000 fine or, on conviction in the Crown Court, an unlimited fine. It should be noted that the duty of care is broken irrespective of whether harm is caused. It is the failure to take reasonable steps that is the criminal offence, not any damage that results from it. This creates a position where offences will be committed frequently.

The main function of the duty of care is to encourage responsible behaviour and the development of appropriate management systems for the storage, transfer, and monitoring of waste, rather than to punish wrongdoing. Because of the documentation procedures, it also makes waste consignments easier to trace. Some of the reported prosecutions for breaches of the duty illustrate these points. For example, in one case a demolition contractor was fined £800 for failing to ensure that a skip contained only materials described in the transfer note—the infringement came about because employees had not been given sufficient instruction that only certain materials could be put in the skip. When it comes to sentencing for the offence, however, many of the breaches, such as failing to make out a transfer note, are seen by the courts as technical in nature, and thus only small fines are imposed. This seems to underplay the importance of this type of management-based control.

Carriage of waste

Intimately connected with the duty of care is the requirement that all carriers of waste are registered with the EA. The requirements in this respect arise out of the Control of Pollution (Amendment) Act 1989. This was a private member's bill (although it did ultimately have government support) which sought to deal with the growing problem of fly-tipping by providing some powers over carriers. The Act is supplemented by the Controlled Waste (Registration of Carriers and Seizure of Vehicles) Regulations 1991 (SI 1991/1624) as amended by SI 1998/605.

It is an offence under the 1989 Act, s. 1(1), to carry controlled waste without being registered with the EA. The offence is a summary one only, with a maximum fine of £5,000. The defences are very similar to those available for offences under the EPA 1990, s. 33 (see p. 605). It should be remembered that it is normally a separate offence under the duty of care to deal with an unregistered carrier.

Certain bodies such as local authorities, charities and voluntary groups are specifically exempt from the requirement to register by virtue of regulation, 2, which also states that a producer may carry its own wastes without having to seek registration, as long as the waste is not demolition or construction waste. In addition, section 1(1) refers only to carrying waste in the course of a business or with a view to profit, meaning that such things as carrying waste to a local authority waste site on behalf of a neighbour are not covered.

An application for registration must be made to the regional office of the EA where the carrier has its principal place of business (reg. 4). There is only one substantive ground for refusal of registration, which is that the applicant is not a desirable carrier. This fulfils a similar function to the 'fit and proper person' requirement in the waste management licensing system. It has two elements: (i) that the carrier, or someone closely connected with the carrier's business, has been convicted of one of the relevant offences listed in schedule 1 to the regulations; and (ii) that the EA considers it undesirable for the carrier to be authorized to carry controlled waste (reg. 5). There is a power to revoke a registration on these grounds (reg. 10). However, the impact of these provisions is limited somewhat by the Rehabilitation of Offenders Act 1974, which effectively will allow most convictions to become spent after five years. In addition, there is a right to appeal to the Secretary of State against refusal or revocation and, in accordance with the advice in Circular 11/91, a refusal to register was overturned even though the applicant had been convicted of seven waste offences in the past.[23] Unless revoked, a registration lasts for three years, when it must be renewed, though the carrier may surrender a registration at any time. A fee is payable for an application or a renewal (reg. 4(9)). The EA must keep a public register, to be open for inspection free of charge, of firms that are registered in their area (reg. 3).

Enforcement of the Act is mainly in the hands of the EA. Appointed officers (and also police officers) are given powers to stop and search vehicles, as long as they have reasonable grounds for believing that controlled waste is being carried by an unregistered carrier (s. 5(1)). They may also require the carrier to produce its certificate of registration. It is a summary offence intentionally to obstruct an officer exercising these powers, with a maximum penalty of £5,000. Environment Agency officers also have the powers provided under the EPA 1990, s. 71, and the Environment Act 1995, ss. 108 and 109.

In addition, there are separate powers relating to the seizure of vehicles used for unlawful activities (s. 6). If the EA is unable to obtain through its general powers information about the ownership of a vehicle it has reason to believe has been involved in unlawful disposal operations, it may apply for a warrant from a magistrate to seize the vehicle. Once the vehicle has been seized, the EA may take specified publicity measures and, if no one claims it, dispose of it (reg. 23). If the EA does discover who owns the vehicle it can bring a prosecution under the 1989 Act and/or under the EPA 1990, ss. 33 and 34, though in those circumstances it has no power to seize the vehicle.

Waste brokers

There is a growing business in arranging for the disposal or movement of other people's wastes. These people may not require a waste management licence because they never actually handle the waste themselves. The Waste Management Licensing Regulations 1994 control such brokers/dealers in waste. Regulation 20 makes it an offence for any establishment or undertaking to arrange, as a dealer or broker, for the disposal or recovery of directive waste on behalf of another person unless they are registered with the EA.

23. See (1993) 217 ENDS Report 13.

Exemptions apply to those with a waste management licence, or other statutory consents (e.g. a discharge consent), charitable or voluntary registered waste carriers, and bodies with statutory responsibilities for waste management (e.g. waste collection and disposal authorities).

Schedule 5 to the regulations sets out the procedure for registration. Perhaps the most important consideration in determining whether an establishment/undertaking is to be registered is the number of 'relevant offences' committed by the applicant or connected persons. Generally the considerations are the same as the test for 'fit and proper persons' in relation to applications for a waste management licence. A fee is payable on application for registration and the entry in the register is available to the general public. The entry in the register lasts for a maximum of three years unless it is renewed.

Economic instruments and waste management

The use of economic instruments is more common in relation to waste management than in other areas of pollution control. Arguably this is because it is one of the best ways of reflecting the true environmental cost of managing and disposing of waste and can help to provide an incentive to minimize production. The three main instruments (other than the recovery of administration costs through charging schemes) are provisions which encourage producer responsibility for particular wastes, a tax on wastes which are disposed of in landfill sites and a scheme which allows waste disposal authorities to trade in landfill allowances.

(a) The landfill tax

The landfill tax was introduced under the Finance Act 1996. There are various secondary regulations and guidance notes which flesh out the main statutory provisions including the Landfill Tax Regulations 1996, the Landfill Tax (Qualifying Materials) Order 1996 and the Landfill Tax (Contaminated Land) Order 1996. The provisions came into force in October 1996 and have the effect that the vast majority of waste disposed of in landfill sites is subject to a tax at the point of disposal. There are three classes of material, the main class which is subject to the highest rate of tax, a second group of specific 'inactive' materials which is subject to a lower rate of tax and a third class of waste which is exempt from the tax. In 2005 the highest rate of tax was set at £18 per tonne. The intention is to increase this standard rate by £3 per tonne per year up to a long term rate of £35 per tonne.

The definition of 'waste' for the purposes of the tax is found in the Finance Act 1996 s. 64. Although it is similar to the general definition of waste under the EPA 1990 and the WML Regs 1994, it must be borne in mind that the landfill tax legislation has a different statutory purpose as compared to the Waste Framework Directive. Accordingly what might be considered to be waste under the waste framework may not be waste for the purposes of landfill tax legislation (see Box 15.15).

BOX 15.15 **The definition of 'waste' under the landfill tax**

A purposive approach to defining waste can work in more than one way. Although the landfill tax is applied to the disposal of 'waste' this is interpreted in a different way to the definition of waste under the Waste Framework Directive. The aim of the landfill tax is to promote recycling and reduce the amount of waste going to landfill. Thus a purposive approach to the definition is not necessarily constrained by the purposes of the Directive. Landfill tax is only payable on taxable disposals. This includes a disposal of material as waste at a landfill site (s. 40, Finance Act 1996). In *Parkwood Landfill v Customs & Excise Commissioners* [2003] Env LR 19, the Court of Appeal held that materials which had been deposited at a landfill site but which had been subsequently recycled and reused to construct a road and landscaping at the site was not waste for the purposes of determining whether a taxable disposal had been made. Taking a purposive approach to the landfill tax legislation, the Court held that it would be contrary to the promotion of recycling if the use of recycled material at landfill sites would be made subject to the tax. Such material would still, however, be 'waste' for the purposes of the Waste Framework Directive.

The tax is paid by the operators of the landfill sites to the Customs and Excise on a quarterly basis although it is envisaged that this cost will be passed on to the disposers of the waste (and then theoretically to the producers of the waste). Although the main purpose of the tax was to ensure that environmental costs of waste disposal were acknowledged, it is also a source of revenue for central government. Some of the income raised by the tax is used to reduce employers' National Insurance contributions.

At the time the tax was introduced, there was some criticism of the failure to use the revenue for environmental purposes.[24] The Landfill Tax Credit Scheme (LTCS) was introduced to address these concerns. Under the scheme, landfill operators which are subject to the tax can claim a credit against any payment of tax for any contribution which is made to an approved environmental body to pay for a project which is approved under the Landfill Tax Regulations. These cover a wide range of environmental projects including the reclamation and restoration of contaminated land (where it does not benefit the original polluter); the creation of public amenity space or a wildlife habitat; and maintaining historic buildings and churches within the vicinity of a landfill site. The reclaimed credit must not be greater than 20 per cent of the total landfill tax payable and there is a ceiling of 90 per cent credit on each contribution made (i.e. the landfill tax payer must pay at least 10 per cent of the contribution from their own income).

Evidence suggests that the tax has not had a significant impact upon the amount of waste arising.[25] This is largely the result of relatively low rates of tax which were levied at the introduction of the tax. In addition there is some evidence that tax avoidance schemes have exploited loopholes in the waste management legislation (such as using inert waste for landscaping purposes—which is exempt from the waste management licensing system) and that fly-tipping of waste has increased. Although these concerns reflect more than insignificant problems, the landfill tax is becoming an accepted regulatory tool which is to be used in

24. J. Morris and P. Phillips (2000), Env L Rev 150.

25. HC Environment Select Committee, *The Operation of the Landfill Tax* (1999); HM Customs and Excise, *Review of Landfill Tax* (1998); and Coopers and Lybrand, *Landfill Tax—Is it Working?* (1997).

conjunction with other mechanisms to assist in reducing waste arisings and encouraging reuse, recycling and recovery. It is this combined impact of significant rate increases, recycling initiatives and the impact of the requirements of the Landfill Directive which reflects a mixed regulation approach to controlling waste production.

(b) Producer responsibility

Section 93 of the Environment Act 1995 provides for the introduction of regulations to impose obligations on the producers of materials or products to recycle, recover or re-use those products or materials. Three products have been the subject to the producer responsibility legislation, packaging and packaging waste;[26] end of life vehicles; and waste electrical and electronic equipment.

- *Packaging and packaging waste.* The first producer responsibility legislation introduced an obligation to recover and recycle packaging waste in 1997. The Producer Responsibility Obligations (Packaging Waste) Regulations 1997 (SI 1997/648 (as amended)) transposed the requirements of the EC Directive on Packaging and Packaging Waste (94/62/EC). A key feature of the Regulations is the shared approach which spreads the responsibility for meeting the recovery and recycling targets right along the packaging chain from production through to retail.

  Businesses who manufacture raw materials for packaging, convert those raw materials into packaging, fill that packaging with goods or sell the packaging to the final consumer are subject to the three obligations. First, to register with and supply data on annual packaging handled. Secondly, to recover and recycle certain specified percentages of packaging handled in the previous year. Finally, to complete a certificate of compliance which verifies that the company has met the recovery and recycling obligation for the preceding year. An obligated company can choose to meet its obligations individually or join a 'compliance scheme' which takes on the legal responsibility for complying with the regulations on behalf of its members. Where companies join a compliance scheme, they fall outside the operation of the regulations (although in practice the compliance scheme passes on the requirements under the terms of membership). In these cases the compliance scheme is subject to the regulations with the consequent need to comply with the obligations on an aggregate basis on behalf of its members.

  What is most interesting about the scheme of the regulations is the way that a variety of different mechanisms are used to secure the overall objective. The system operates in practice by compelling obligated businesses to purchase evidence of compliance from reprocessors who recover and recycle packaging materials in the form of packaging recovery notes (PRNs). Thus the regulations mix the use of the market in these PRNs (which will fluctuate in price under the normal principles of supply and demand) with the prospect of criminal sanctions for non-compliance to encourage businesses to consider the amount of packaging which they use.[27]

- *End-of-Life Vehicles.* The End-of-Life Vehicles Regulations 2003 (SI 2003/2635) transposed the requirements of the End-of-Life Vehicles Directive (2000/53/EC). The Regulations are intended to promote the recycling and recovery of ELVs but do so in a broader

26. See generally, P. Bailey, *Packaging Law Europe* (Aldershot: Ashgate, 1999).
27. K. Kroepelian (2000) RECIEL 9(2) 165.

fashion than the packaging waste regime.[28] The Directive was transposed over one year late which reflects the complexity and controversy of the proposals. The historic rate of recycling of End-of-Life vehicles (ELVs) is about 75 per cent but the Directive imposes a requirement to recycle 85 per cent of ELVs by weight by 2006, with a further recycling target of 95 per cent by 2015. Manufacturers of vehicles are responsible for the costs of collecting and treating ELVs put on the market after July 2002 where they have a negative value (some ELVs will have a positive value). From 2007, manufacturers will be responsible for the costs of collection and treatment for all ELVs.

The development of the idea of producer responsibility is focused on facilitating recycling and recovery through a number of different methods. For example there are controls over the design of new vehicles which should make them easier to dismantle and therefore recycle. This includes restrictions on the materials which are used in vehicle construction. There is a ban on using certain hazardous substances in the design of new cars and there is a requirement to provide information on the best way to dismantle and recycle ELVs. In addition there are controls over the permitting and standards for the dismantling, recycling and disposal of ELVs by authorized treatment facilities (ATFs). A system using Certificates of Destruction as a condition for de-registering an ELV when it is taken to an ATF has also been introduced.

- *Waste electrical and electronic equipment (WEEE).* The Waste Electrical and Electronic Equipment Directive 2002/96/EC (WEEE) encourages and sets criteria for the collection, treatment, recycling and recovery of all forms of electrical equipment. The Directive adopts the broader approach to producer responsibility taken in the ELV Directive with some focus on the design and manufacture of electrical products to facilitate recycling and recovery. To this end there is a 'sister' Directive which bans the use of certain hazardous substances in electrical equipment (the Restriction on Hazardous Substances Directive 2002/95/EC). The WEEE Directive should have been transposed into national legislation on or before August 13, 2004. On that date only a handful of Member States had officially transposed the directive. This lack of action reflects both the difficult nature of the Directive's obligations and also the broad, direct applicability of the Directive across many small and medium sized businesses.

The legislation applies to all battery or mains operated electrical and electronic equipment falling into one of ten categories set out in the Directive. Under the Regulations *retailers* of electrical equipment must take back consumer WEEE free of charge. *Producers* of electrical equipment will have a number of obligations including:

- provide data on the volumes and types of electrical and electronic equipment placed on the UK market and exported to EU countries and on recycling and recovery of WEEE;
- ensure that products, wherever possible, are designed to enable their reuse and recycling;
- label products with prescribed labels making it clear that products are not to be disposed of in bins;
- pay for recycling and recovery

---

28. M. Lee (2002) 11(4) EELR 114.

The waste facilities which recover and recycle WEEE must use the Best Available Treatment Recovery and Recycling Techniques (BATRRT). Such facilities are also subject to a detailed permitting procedure. The aim is to give priority to the re-use of whole appliances, and then components, sub-assemblies and consumables.

(c) The development of Producer Responsibility

These brief descriptions of the producer responsibility schemes illustrate that producer responsibility legislation has developed over time from a bare requirement to recover and recycle into a more sophisticated approach which uses various methods to facilitate reuse and recycling. This includes banning substances which are difficult to reuse and requiring the use of 'eco-design' principles and increased information on how to recycle waste products as a means of facilitating reuse, recovery and recycling. At the other end of life cycle there are specific controls over the reuse of and recycling of waste products. This approach of trying to influence each stage of the product's life links into the idea of integrated product policy where the whole life cycle of a product is examined in order to minimise environmental impacts (see p. 621).[29]

Waste disposal and town and country planning

The disposal of waste on land presents some difficult questions of a land use nature, indeed the Town and Country Planning Acts were the primary control over waste before COPA 1974 was enacted. The development of land for waste management purposes is controlled under an additional and complementary layer of regulations which has remained largely unchanged through the introduction of waste management licensing legislation. The deposit of waste in land is deemed to be development which requires planning permission (see below). Furthermore, the use of land for waste management purposes other than disposal may require planning permission if it amounts to a material change of use. In most cases, the storage of waste on land will be incidental to the main use (e.g. in the case of an unrelated industrial use) although there may be cases such as the change of fuel in a cement kiln from conventional fuels to waste derived fuels where the boundary is not clearly distinguishable (see Box 20.3).

(a) The administration of waste planning

The main responsibility for waste planning falls to waste planning authorities (normally at a county, metropolitan, or unitary level). Waste planning is addressed at the regional level through the Regional Spatial Strategies (RSS). Under the Planning and Compulsory Purchase Act 2004, the Regional Planning Bodies will be responsible for drawing up RSS which will address regional waste policies and provide a spatial framework for local development frameworks (see p. 455).

(b) Development plans

Waste planning policies have traditionally been considered separately to other policies. Prior to the introduction of the Planning and Compulsory Purchase Act 2004, waste policies were

29. M. Townsend and J. Parry (2002) Env Liab 10(4) 153.

found in Regional Planning Guidance at the regional level and at a more local level in the unitary development plan or a combination of the structure plan and the waste local plan or minerals and waste local plan. Under the 2004 Act, the RSS will replace current Regional Planning Guidance (RPG). All other development plans will be replaced with a Minerals and Waste Development Framework (MWDF). There is a transitional period until September 2007 within which pre-existing development plans are 'saved' and still continue to be operative.

The MWDF is a collection of various Local Development Documents which collectively provide the spatial planning strategy and planning policies for waste (see p. 455). Within the MWDF there are Development Plan Documents which have statutory development status for the purposes of determining planning applications (see p. 457). These include the Minerals and Waste Development Scheme which sets out the policy framework; the Waste Core Strategy which sets out the strategic policies and objectives and a site-specific allocation map. In addition non statutory guidance can form part of the MWDF as Supplementary Plan Documents (SPDs) (see p. 458).

(c) Development control

Section 55(3)(b) of the Town and Country Planning Act 1990 provides that the deposit of refuse or waste materials on land involves the material change in the use of that land if the area of the deposit is extended or the height of the deposit is extended above the original ground level. In addition, depending upon the facts of the case, tipping can amount to an engineering operation (if it involves technical supervision for instance), or even fall within the catch-all definition of an 'other operation'.

A planning application for the use of land, or the carrying out of operations in or on land, for the deposit of refuse or waste materials and/or the erection of any building, plant or machinery designed to be used wholly or mainly for the purposes of treating, storing, processing or disposing of refuse or waste materials is a county matter (see Town and Country Planning Act 1990, sch. 1). The application is made direct to the county planning authority, which is then under a duty to notify the district authority within 14 days as part of the consultation procedure (Art. 12 of the GDPO).

(d) Planning conditions and obligations

The difficulties with using planning conditions to control environmentally sensitive developments have been covered elsewhere (see p. 484). Planning permissions for waste disposal operations require special consideration. The main criterion for conditions on a planning permission for waste disposal is that they be for a planning purpose. Examples of matters which would normally be dealt with by way of conditions on the planning permission include: phasing of operations; the extent of tipping; access to and from the site; the *general* nature of the waste; restoration plans, including site contours, minimum depth of top soil, etc.; and aftercare for a short-term period. To avoid duplicating environmental controls there are certain areas which should not normally be covered as they are more properly dealt with under the waste management regime. These include: the duration of activity; supervision of activities (including site offices and other administrative responsibilities); the specific types of waste to be covered; keeping of records; and associated works. Although it is advisable to separate the two areas of control, it is not unlawful to impose conditions which overlap.

Other overlapping controls

(a) Integrated pollution prevention and control

There is an overlap in European law between the Framework Directive on Waste (75/442) and the Integrated Pollution Prevention and Control (IPPC) Directive (96/61) in that certain waste management installations are covered by both directives (see generally p. 788). In the UK, control over such installations has traditionally fallen within the waste management licensing system. The Pollution Prevention and Control Act 1999 and associated regulations created two parallel systems of control in which many waste disposal installations were taken out of the licensing regime and put into the integrated permitting system All landfills are controlled under PPC permits (see p. 788). There is, however, no explicit overlap between the two regimes. Under the permitting system, waste management installations are excluded from the waste management licensing system and the waste management licensing regime excludes installations which are subject to the permitting system. The PPC regime does overlap with the Landfill Regulations 2002. This includes the use of the technical requirements of the Landfill Regulations which are incorporated into the permitting system via the BAT standard (see further p. 781).

(c) Contaminated land

The deposit or discharge of waste (whether knowingly or otherwise) is a significant cause of contamination and there is a good deal of interaction between the waste management licensing regime and the provisions dealing with the clean up of contaminated land. First, where contamination arises as a result of the illegal deposit of controlled waste, the right to serve a remediation notice under Part IIA is removed (EPA 1990, s. 78YB(3)). This is because there is an equivalent power to remove such waste under EPA 1990, s. 59 (see p. 607). Prior to the decision in Case C-1/04 *Van de Walle* (see Case box 15.4) this would have covered a situation where there was an active deposit of waste (i.e. in the case of an unlicensed landfill) rather than passive leakage of substances (e.g. seeping from an underground tank). The latter would have been controlled under the contaminated land provisions in EPA 1990, Part IIA. Following *Van de Walle*, however, the risk based approach of Part IIA would not be sufficient to implement the provisions of the Waste Framework Directive (see Box 15.3). Secondly, where there is an extant waste management licence in force in relation to a site which is contaminated, the land cannot be identified as contaminated land as there are enforcement powers under the licence to deal with any clean up (EPA 1990, s. 78YB(2)). Finally, where clean-up operations are required under a remediation notice, such operations will require a waste management licence as a disposal or recovery operation.

(d) Water pollution

The treatment of liquid effluent prior to discharge into sewer or into controlled waters is arguably the treatment of waste and there has been some confusion about the extent to which effluent treatment plant fell under the waste management licensing regime. Under the Framework Directive, the physico-chemical or biological treatment of 'waste' is defined as a disposal operation which would be subject to the requirement for licensing. However the

Department of the Environment determined in 1996 that such treatment was excepted from the waste licensing system as it was 'waste in liquid form' which was controlled under other legislation, namely the Urban Waste Water Treatment Directive (91/271) and the corresponding domestic legislation, the Urban Waste Water Treatment (England and Wales) Regulations 1994 (SI 1994/2841) and/or the Water Resources Act 1991.

The landfilling of waste can provide a threat to groundwater quality. In order to implement the Groundwater Directive (80/68), there are provisions which set out requirements in respect of groundwater protection which must be met when determining any waste management licence application. Under the Waste Management Licensing Regulations 1994, reg. 15, a waste management licence can only be granted where there are adequate measures for preventing groundwater pollution by substances listed in List I and II in the Directive. As a result of these controls, activities which are carried out under a waste management licence are exempt from the requirements of the Groundwater Regulations 1998 (see p. 733). There is, however, a gap between the two legislative regimes as the groundwater protection measures under the waste management licensing system only apply to waste disposal. This means that there are other activities which are covered under a waste management licence (e.g. recycling) which may give rise to a risk of groundwater pollution but which are not required to implement the measures found in the Groundwater Directive. This represents an inadequate transposition of the requirements of the Directive (see p. 591).

Civil liability for unlawful disposal of waste

Civil liability is provided for in section 73(6), which is significantly wider than the equivalent provision in COPA 1974, s. 88). This subsection applies where any damage is caused by a deposit of controlled waste in contravention of sections 33(1) or 63(2) (i.e. the deposit was not in accordance with a waste management licence, or it breached section 33(1)(c), or it breached the provision on unlawful disposal of non-controlled waste). Any person who deposited the waste is liable to pay damages for any personal injury or property damage that was caused, except where it was due wholly to the fault of the person who suffered it, or they voluntarily accepted the risk of the damage. Liability also attaches to any person who knowingly caused or knowingly permitted such waste to be deposited, with the result that anyone who orders an unlawful deposit, or who stands by in the knowledge that it is happening, will also be liable. Since liability is linked to the commission of an offence under sections 33 or 63(2), it is strict and fault need not be shown, though the defences available under those sections will also apply. As a result it is likely that an action under section 73(6) will be preferable because it avoids many of the problems associated with proving environmental claims in tort (see p. 382). Thus an action under section 73(6) can be brought in addition to a claim in negligence.

Section 73(6) provides an alternative to the common law causes of action which are explained in Chapter 11. The leading case on waste sites is the Canadian case of *Gertsen v Municipality of Toronto* (1973) 41 DLR (3d) 646, where an occupier of land successfully claimed damages for personal injury. His injuries were the result of an explosion caused by the spark from his car engine when he started it up in his garage, which had filled with high levels of methane escaping from the disused landfill site on which it was built. The action was successful under the rule in *Rylands v Fletcher*, nuisance and negligence, although it must be doubted whether, on the current state of the law, all these causes of action would have succeeded in an English court. Section 73(6) will avoid some of the difficulties associated with the common law actions where there has been an unlawful deposit.

BOX 15.16 Civil liability for dangerous waste management

In practice, section 73(6) appears to be relatively underused. One of the few reported decisions on the issue, *C v Imperial Design* [2001] Env LR 33 illustrates some of the overlap between different types of liability for dangerous waste management.[30] The claimant C, aged 13, found a drum containing waste solvent belonging to the defendant whilst was playing on land near the defendant's factory. C set fire to the solvent and the drum exploded causing severe burns. C brought an action in negligence and breach of the duty in section 73(6). The trial judge found the defendant liable under section 73(6). In doing so, the trial judge sought to rely upon a breach of the duty of care under EPA 1990, s. 34. He considered that by allowing the waste to escape from the factory, the defendant had breached the duty of care and was therefore liable under section 73(6). The Court of Appeal disagreed pointing out that liability under section 73(6) is dependent upon an offence under EPA 1990, s. 33 or 62. Indeed, if an offence has been committed under section 34 it would almost certainly lead to a finding of negligence or vice versa and there would be no reason to create the sort of no fault liability imposed under section 73(6).

On the facts of the case, no criminal conviction had occurred and no finding of fact had been given by the trial judge on whether a criminal offence had been committed. In some cases that would have been fatal to C's claim. Instead the Court relied upon the finding of negligence in relation to the defendant's activities, i.e. the Defendant had failed to take 'reasonable precautions' or 'measures . . . reasonable in the circumstances' to ensure safe waste management. This finding meant that the Court could ignore the statutory claim under section 73(6). This illustrates the point that the only time when it should be necessary to use section 76(3) will be in situations where the strictness of the liability is critical (i.e. when no negligence can be demonstrated).

Future directions—integrated product policy

The existing framework of waste management legislation has been criticised at domestic, European, and international levels.[31] One element of these criticisms is that most waste legislation has been aimed at the last part of a product's life cycle, the 'end of pipe solution' solutions i.e. ensuring that when a product is no longer wanted, it is disposed of safely. Although other environmental controls address 'middle of the pipe' impacts typically arising in the production process (e.g. pollution prevention and waste minimization) there has been little emphasis on the 'front of pipe' impacts, i.e. the research, development and design of products to minimize their overall environmental effects. One response to this

---

30. The case is discussed in detail in M. Lee (2002) 14 JEL 74.

31. See S. Tromans (2001) 13 JEL 13 and E. Tufet-Opi (2002) 14 JEL 3 generally on the inadequacies of waste law and the response of IPP.

dissatisfaction with current approaches has been to consider and reduce environmental impacts over the full life-cycle of a product—from production of raw materials through production, distribution and use to final disposal. There are echoes of this approach in the producer responsibility legislation which promotes reuse and recycling through the use of less hazardous substances in the manufacturing process and through designing products for ease of recycling.

This full life-cycle approach has been developed by the European Commission in its Integrated Product Policy. This started in 2001 with the production of a Green Paper on IPP which outlined the rationale for developing product-related environmental policies, and suggested some possible mechanisms that might be used.[32] Consequently, IPP was identified as one of the primary elements of the 6th Environmental Action Programmes.[33] These ideas were developed further in 2003 with the European Commission's adoption of a Communication on IPP.[34] The Communication is rather heavy on aspirations and light on specific commitments preferring flexibility and stakeholder involvement to prescriptive legislation. The Communication suggests a variety of legal and policy measures which could be used in an IPP depending upon the particular product. To implement its IPP strategy, the Commission has two priorities. First, to establish a basic policy framework which identifies effective instruments to be used across different products. This might include the basis for such things as economic instruments, product or specification standards, eco-labelling, voluntary agreements, green procurement criteria, or standardized life-cycle analysis databases. Secondly, to apply the framework to specific products starting with those products which are considered to be most environmentally damaging.

One of the challenges of IPP is determining the optimal level of regulation (see p. 271). With so many different instruments which could be used within an IPP the difficulty is ensuring that the most effective blend of instruments is selected. Given the direct impact that IPP has upon manufacturers, the effectiveness of any new measures will probably be in proportion to their controversy.

 CHAPTER SUMMARY

1   Managing the production and disposal of waste is one of the most significant environmental challenges the UK faces over the next 20 years.

2   The amount of waste being produced in the UK is increasing. Sustainable waste management should see waste arisings falling which would mean reversing current rising rates of consumption.

3   Traditionally waste management regulation in the UK has concentrated on controlling the disposal on waste in large landfill sites. This is changing partly as a result of dwindling capacity in existing landfill sites and partly because of pressure under European legislation to increase recycling and recovery.

4   Regulating waste is difficult because the concept of waste is difficult to define with any degree of certainty.

32. U. Schleissner (2001) EELR 86.
33. 'Environment 2010: Our future, Our Choice' (2002).
34. Integrated Product Policy: Building on Environmental Life-Cycle Thinking COM(2003) 302.

5   International waste law is largely aimed at controlling transboundary movements of waste and agreeing on the categorization of diferent waste.

6   European waste law is based around a central Waste Framework Directive which lays down a definition of waste, broad objectives for the management of waste and a system of waste regulation.

7   There are other European Directives which address particular waste treatment methods (e.g. incineration and landfill) and particular waste streams (e.g. packaging and batteries).

8   Domestic waste policy is dominated by a national waste strategy for England and Wales which sets out the policy framework and goals for waste regulation. This is formulated by the Secretary of State with full public consultation. The strategy sets out targets for waste management including reduction, recycling, and recovery. The strategy is not legally binding but influences national and local decision-making on waste facilities and licensing.

9   The concept of 'waste' is broadly defined by reference to whether something has been 'discarded'. This covers the disposal, recycling, and recovery of materials although there is a difficult distinction which must be drawn between the use of raw materials in industrial processes (e.g. use of something as a fuel) and the recovery of waste. Within this broad definition there are classes of waste (e.g. household, industrial, and commercial) which are relevant, for example, when considering waste licensing or targets for reduction.

10 Certain wastes known as 'hazardous wastes' are subject to extra controls. Categories of hazardous wastes can be found in detailed lists or the term is defined by reference to general hazardous properties.

11 The management of waste (which includes keeping, treating or disposing) requires a licence or permit from the Environment Agency. Certain activities are exempt from the need for a licence subject to specified limits (e.g. time and quantity limits for the storage of particular wastes).

12 There is a general 'duty of care' which applies to all those who are involved in the waste chain from production to final disposal. Breach of the duty is a criminal offence. Compliance with the duty requires reasonable steps to be taken to ensure that waste is handled safely by an authorized person and that an offence is not committed. There is a Code of Practice which gives some guidance on the types of steps which would be considered to be reasonable.

13 A waste management licence can only be granted where there is a planning permission in force (if planning permission is required); the applicant is a 'fit and proper' person in terms of their technical competence, financial security and absence of criminal conviction; there has been an adequate investigation of whether the activities will lead to the pollution of groundwater; and there will be no pollution of the environment or harm to human health.

14 There is limited consultation on an application and no requirement for public participation (which should have taken place at the planning stage).

15 Licence conditions can relate to any activities which the licence authorizes and can cover matters after the authorized activities have ceased (e.g. monitoring and other aftercare matters) or off-site controls (e.g. leachate management).

16 The EA has a duty to supervise licensed activities and can exercise wide powers including the variation, suspension, or revocation of existing licences.

17 There are controls over the transportation of waste with the registration of waste carriers within domestic legislation.

18 There are economic instruments such as the landfill tax and the producer responsibility legislation which encourage waste minimization and recycling.

19 Integrated Product Policy will make producers consider all the environmental impacts of a product from the design stage to final disposal. It is intended that this will reduce waste production.

Q QUESTIONS

1 In what ways does the law seek to meet the waste hierarchy of the prevention of production of waste; encouraging reuse and recycling; and promoting safe management and disposal?

2 Walter is the inventor of the Inklene ink cleaning and solvent recovery unit. This is a unit which attaches to printing presses and operates a closed loop cleaning system. It cleans the used ink from the presses with non-hazardous solvents. Then, with various filters it cleans the solvents and separates the ink which are then both pumped back to the printing press for reuse on the presses. The unit is connected for 24 hours and then removed elsewhere. At present both the used solvent and ink are thrown away by the printing press owners. The unit will cut down solvent and ink useage by over 95 per cent. The local Environment Agency officer has advised Walter that the Inklene unit requires a waste management licence to operate.

Advise Walter on whether the officer is correct and if so on what steps he must take to obtain a licence.

3 Fred is the owner of a factory. His rubbish is collected once a week from a skip which is placed just inside the factory gates. One week, the waste collection company fails to collect the waste and the skip fills up to overflowing. Fred places his waste in cardboard boxes by the skip. Local youths break into the factory yard at night and play football with the boxes. One of the boxes breaks releasing toxic material which causes severe injuries to one of the youths. The next morning Fred contacts one of his mates and asks him to dispose of the waste. The waste is subsequently found on a nearby playing field.

Advise Fred on the offences he may have committed and the liabilities he may have incurred.

FURTHER READING

General texts

The changes in waste management law over the last 10 years have been rapid and dramatic. Therefore having an up-to-date text is critical because anything before 2000 will fail to cover many of the recent developments in such things as the Landfill Regulations, the definition of waste and new producer responsibility legislation. R. Hawkins and H. Shaw, *The Practical Guide to Waste Management Law* (London: Thomas Telford, 2004) is a superb introduction to the topic. It has the advantage of being up-to-date but it is also highly accessible, with tables and illustrative examples. Be warned though, the commentary is opinionated, controversial, and humorous—this is not a dry academic work. Another recommended text is D. Lawrence, *Waste Regulation Law* (London: Butterworths, 2000) although this is slightly out of date, it is comprehensive in its coverage and is detailed in its evaluation and analysis. A good introduction to some of the problems of European waste legislation can be found in S. Tromans, 'EC Waste Law: A Complete Mess?' [2001] 13 JEL 13. As the title suggests this is an extensive (and devastating) critique of all aspects of European waste management law and covers areas such as the trade in waste which are not covered in this chapter.

Waste policy

The starting point for any research on waste is the *Waste Strategy for England and Wales 2000* (Cm 4693, 2000). This sets the framework for waste management and sets out both the problems and some potential solutions. Like all grand, far reaching strategies the difficulty is in the implementation stage. The seriousness of the problem which the strategy addresses is reflected in the fact that the Prime Minister's Strategy Unit was asked to address the problem and produced a report, *Waste Not: Want Not* (available at <www.number-10.gov.uk/su/waste/report/09.html>) which deals with the implementation of the national waste strategy. It paints a stark picture. To see how far we have come, readers could usefully look at the RCEP's 11th Report, *Managing Waste: The Duty of Care* (Cm 9675, 1985). This Report not only deals with the historical context of waste management law and practice but also provides a damning indictment of past practices.

The definition of waste

There are many articles examining the case law and issues surrounding the definition of waste. Some care should be taken because pre-2000 articles do not necessarily represent the law today. Some of the older articles are still useful however as they discuss some of the problems of coming up with a workable definition of waste. The best articles include: M. Purdue, 'Defining Waste' (1990) 2 JEL 250; J. Smith, 'The Challenges of Environmentally Sound and Efficient Regulation of Waste' (1993) 3 JEL 91; J. Fluck, 'The Term "Waste" in EU Law' [1994] EELR 79; I. Cheyne and M. Purdue, 'Fitting Definition to Purpose: The Search for a Satisfactory Definition of Waste' (1995) 7 JEL 149; M. Purdue and A. van Rossem, 'The Distinction Between Using Secondary Raw Materials and the Recovery of Waste: The Directive Definition of Waste' (1998) 10 JEL 116; G. Van Calster, 'The EC Definition of Waste: The Euro Tombesi Bypass and the Basel Relief Routes' (1997) EBLR 137, I. Cheyne, 'The Definition of Waste in EC Law' (2002) 14 JEL 61, J. Pike, 'Waste Not, Want Not: An (Even) Wider Definition of Waste' (2002) 14 JEL 197 and L. Kramer 'The distinction between Product and Waste in Community Law' (2003) Env Liability 11(1) 3.

Other waste topics

The breadth of this chapter means that there are many other sources which could provide further reading on specialist topics. Works of direct relevance are footnoted. Those listed here are only a selection.

We are in a period in which the impact of waste reduction and recycling targets is becoming more prevalent. The implications of this are discussed in D. Pocklington, 'The Role of Mandatory Targets in Mandatory Waste Management Legislation' (2003) ELM 15(5) 285. There are some areas which have not been covered in this chapter primarily on grounds of space. One of these is the interrelationship between different waste directives. For example the relationship between recycling in the Packaging Waste Directive and the Waste Framework Directive is covered in S. Tromans, 'Defining Recycling' (2004) 16 JEL 80 and M. Lee, 'Resources, Recycling and Waste (2004) Env L Rev 49. An overview of the operational problems in the initial years of the landfill tax can be found in J. Morris and P. Phillips, 'The UK Landfill Tax: An Evaluation of the First Three Years' (2000) Env L Rev 150.

On the question of insolvency and waste management licences see A. Keay and P. de Prez, 'Insolvency and Environmental Principles: A Case Study in a Conflict of Public Interests' (2001) Env L Rev 3(2) 90, C. Shelbourn, 'Can the Insolvent Polluter Pay? Environmental Licences and the Insolvent Company' (2000) 12 JEL 207 and J. Armour, 'Who Pays when Polluters go Bust?' (2000) LQR 200.

F. Nunan, 'Barriers to the Use of Voluntary Agreements: A Case Study of the Development of the Packaging Waste Regulations in the UK', (1999) Euro Env 9(6) 238 provides a good introduction to producer responsibility legislation as compared to alternative methods of addressing the problem. Other articles on producer responsibility include, M. Lee, 'New Generation Regulation? The Case of End of Life Vehicles' (2002) EELR 11(4) 114 and K. Kroepelian, 'Extended Producer Responsibility—New Legal Structures for Improved Ecological Self-Organisation in Europe' (2000) RECIEL 9(2) 165.

Integrated Product Policy is a relatively new initiative but there is some literature which provides the background. Have a look at I. Rose and G. Knighton, 'IPP: A New Approach to Environmental Regulations (1999) EELR 8(10) 266 and U. Schleissner, 'Integrated Product Policy: Where is the EU Heading?' (2001) EELR 10(3) 86.

@ WEB LINKS

The web provides many good information sources for waste. A great gateway into other sites (as well as providing a lot of up-to-date information) can be found at Land Regeneration Network Site at <www.grc.cf.ac.uk/lrn/resources/waste>. A lot of effort has been put into keeping the page up-to-date and there are links to case law, legislation and technical briefing notes on waste-related topics. As with other areas DEFRA's site provides some good resources. <www.defra.gov.uk/environment/waste/intro.htm> is the place where you will find the National Waste Strategy and other policy documents. European resources can be found at <europa.eu.int/comm/environment/waste/index.htm>. There is a lot of information on recycling. <www.letsrecycle.com> and <www.wastewatch.org.uk> provide a lot of information about practical measures which have been taken to increase recovery and recycling. The Waste and Resources Action Programme can be found at <www.wrap.org.uk>. This non-profit making organization was set up to help deliver the targets in the Waste Strategy. It will play an increasingly important role in waste management over the long term. For the industry view, the Environmental Services Association is the trade body for the Waste Industry and provides publications on many waste issues at <www.esauk.org/work/briefings>. On producer responsibility Valpak, the largest compliance scheme can be found at <www.valpak.co.uk>.

16 Air pollution and air quality

Overview

This chapter deals with legal controls over atmospheric emissions and air quality. The complexity of air pollution problems means that many different types of approaches are necessary across a wide range of activities. This can be a little daunting at first as the overlapping of issues such as climate change, ozone depletion, and the effects of air quality on health; sources of pollutants such as transport, energy usage, and industrial pollution; and the technical aspects of things like air quality standards can make it difficult to locate an easy starting point.

Thus the initial coverage focuses on international and European attempts to deal with the big issues of transboundary pollution and climate change. We then consider wider air quality issues and conclude by looking at domestic arrangements. Coverage of certain major elements of domestic air pollution and air quality law is somewhat incomplete in this chapter. For example significant point source emissions of pollutants from many industrial sources fall within the system of integrated pollution prevention and control (see Chapter 20). Furthermore general controls over smoke and fumes are covered in Chapter 12 on Local Controls. The chapter still, however, attempts to provide a degree of coherence by illustrating some of the underlying themes of this book including consideration of the nature of regulatory impact, different types of environmental standards, technocratic approaches to regulatory standard setting and the use of alternative environmental policy instruments such as voluntary agreements and economic instruments.

At the end of this chapter you should be able to:

✔ Understand the nature of air pollution problems and some of the main ways they have been addressed at an international, European and national level.
✔ Understand the historical development of air pollution and air quality law.
✔ Appreciate the use of international law to address transboundary air pollution.
✔ Appreciate the main issues of addressing and managing the impact of climate change through legal means.
✔ Assess the use of a mixed regulatory approach to the control of air pollution.
✔ Assess the use of different types of standards in air quality regulation.

Air pollutants and their sources

The range of problems affecting the atmosphere stretches across the full range of human activities, from highly toxic fumes emitted from a complicated industrial process to such seemingly mundane activities as lighting a fire, driving a car or using spray-on deodorant.

Air pollutants come in many forms, the main ones include:

- *Sulphur dioxide (SO_2).* This is released into the atmosphere as a result of burning fossil fuels which contain sulphur. It is an acidic gas which combines with water vapour to produce acid rain. The most common source of SO_2 is coal fired power stations and other industrial sources although recent research has shown a significant contribution from the burning of marine fuel on container ships and oil tankers.[1] A reduction of the use of coal as an energy source has seen ambient concentrations of SO_2 fall over the last 50 or so years.

- *Various gases produced from combustion processes.* These include carbon monoxide (CO), carbon dioxide (CO_2) and oxides of nitrogen. These are mainly produced from road vehicles. Other major sources include power stations, heating plants and industrial processes. The labelling of carbon dioxide is not without controversy. It is inert, vital food for plants and exhaled by humans. This has led to the US EPA to rule that carbon dioxide is not a pollutant. If pollution is defined as being something which is in excess over that which is desirable, it is clear that, given the acknowledged link between carbon dioxide emissions and climate change, carbon dioxide is capable of being a pollutant.

- *Particulates of lead and other heavy metals.* These arise from various activities including combustion processes in motor vehicles, metal processing industries and waste incineration, particularly waste batteries. The increasing use of unleaded petrol has seen concentrations of lead drop over recent years.

- *PM_{10}.* These are very small airborne particulate matter, the particles of which are <10 μm. They arise from a variety of sources and can vary in physical and chemical characteristics. The principal source of PM_{10} matter is emissions from diesel engines.

- *Various complex pollutants produced by the incomplete combustion of fuels.* These are carcinogenic or highly toxic at very small levels and include: Dioxins, Furans, PAHs (PolyAromatic Hydrocarbons) and PCBs (PolyChlorinated Biphenyls).

- *Volatile Organic Compounds (VOCs).* VOCs are released in vehicle exhaust gases either as unburned fuels or as combustion products, and are also emitted by the evaporation of solvents and motor fuels.

- *Chlorofluorocarbons (CFCs).* These are used in aerosol sprays, solvents, and as refrigerants in fridges, freezers and air conditioning units. CFCs are inert in the lower atmosphere then undergo a significant reaction in the upper atmosphere that destroys stratospheric ozone. This ozone absorbs ultraviolet radiation which would otherwise be harmful to humans, animals and plants.

- *Methane.* This is emitted during the production and transport of coal, natural gas, and oil. Methane emissions also result from the decomposition of organic wastes in landfills and from herds of cattle.

Most of the sources of air pollutants are man made but there are natural sources including soil dust from large areas of land with little or no plant life, dust and sulphur dioxide from

---

1. 'Ships sabotage war on acid rain' *Observer*, 10 Oct. 2004.

volcanic eruptions, smoke from wild fires and methane gas from cattle. Indeed, for some air pollutants (e.g. SO_2) these form the largest sources.

The effects of air pollutants

As with other forms of pollution, the effect of different sources of pollution may differ depending on such things as air temperature, wind speed, the height and velocity of discharge, and the presence of other pollutants including any synergistic effects. The more serious effects are:

- *Acid Rain.* Where sulphur dioxide and nitrogen oxides mix with water vapour (and ammonia from agricultural sources) to form very weak sulphuric acid and nitric acid solutions in rainfall. Acid rain has been linked to the killing of fish, birds, and trees and can cause damage to buildings. Acid rain can be carried for great distances on the wind thereby displacing the source and effect of pollution.

- *Climate Change.* This is thought to be linked largely to the emission of six 'greenhouse gases' namely nitrous oxides, carbon dioxide, PFCs, methane, CFCs, and ground level ozone. These gases trap the infrared radiation emitted by the Earth's surface. This acts like a greenhouse raising the air temperature to create a stable environment. An increase in that air temperature could have dramatic consequences. Some of the predicted changes include the flooding of low-lying land as the polar ice caps melt and increased crop yields.

- *Direct harm to human health.* Many atmospheric pollutants have been linked to harm to human health. These can include respiratory problems (particulates, nitrous oxides and sulphur dioxide), brain damage (lead) and cancer (dioxins). Official estimates suggest that up to 24,000 deaths are brought forward by short-term exposure to certain air pollutants from all sources, including traffic.[2]

Because such a wide range of activities affects the atmosphere, the range of environmental issues is also wide. On the one hand, there have always been difficulties with polluting activities affecting the locality in which they were situated. International difficulties have arisen with the creation of acid rain. In recent years we have seen a realization amongst the international community that individual nations' actions can combine to create truly global difficulties. The destruction of the ozone layer and the issue of global warning have brought home the truly awesome consequences of the combined effect of certain human activities.

History and development of early controls over air pollution

The pollution of the local atmosphere from emissions has traditionally been easy to identify. Such problems date back to the early uses of coal in domestic fires. The production of fumes and particulates from fires caused pulmonary infections and related lung diseases. Thus as far back as the 13th Century bans were placed on the burning of sea coal in parts of South London. With the advent of more complicated processes in the late eighteenth century, the problems of atmospheric pollution grew more severe. The industrial revolution

2. Committee on Medical Effects of Air Pollutants Annual Report (1997/8).

increased the use of coal to drive new machinery and, more importantly, produced very acidic emissions as a consequence of the 'alkali works'. These works used the Leblanc process to produce soda, but the by-product of the chemical process used meant that hydrochloric gas was emitted into the atmosphere which, when mixed with water, created acid rain.

BOX 16.1 Air pollution and air quality—timeline

Year	Key Events
1273	Edward I introduces first controls over smoke in London.
1307	A Royal Proclamation issued prohibiting use of sea-coal in furnaces in parts of London.
1863	Following a Royal Commission investigation into pollution from Alkali works, the Alkali Act 1863 is passed. The Act is consolidated and applied to 'scheduled' industrial processes in Alkali, etc. Works Regulations Act 1906. This requires 95 per cent of the offensive emissions to be arrested by the use of 'best practicable means'.
1866	Sanitary Act 1866 introduced controls to allow sanitary authorities to take action in cases of smoke nuisances.
1875	Public Health Act 1875 introduced further general controls over smoke nuisances. These are extended and amended in future years including the Public Health (Smoke Abatement) Act 1926 and Public Health Act 1936 but form the basis for statutory nuisance controls today.
1940	The *Trail Smelter* arbitration establishes principle of customary international law that no state has the right to use territory in such a manner as to cause injury by fumes in or to the territory of another when the case is of serious consequence and the injury is established by clear and convincing evidence.
1956	Following the Great Smog in London in December 1952, the Beaver Committee on Air Pollution recommended new controls over smoke. This led to the Clean Air Act 1956 which prohibited the emission of dark smoke from chimneys, smoke control areas, and controls over chimney heights. The Act is extended under the Clean Air Act 1968.
1970	First European initiatives on air pollution introduced, based around improved product standards. Directive 70/220/EEC limits emissions of CO and hydrocarbons from petrol engines. Directive 72/306/EEC limits black smoke emissions from diesel engines.
1975	Directive 75/716 is the first in a series of Directives controlling the content of fuels. Limits sulphur content. A further directive 78/611 limits lead content of petrol.
1979	Geneva Convention on Long Range Transboundary Pollution adopted to control the transboundary effects of acid rain and to limit emission of acidifying pollutants. Leads to a number of different protocols restricting emissions of certain substances including sulphur dioxide and NO_x.
1984	Directive 84/360/EEC is a framework directive dealing with air pollution from industrial plant. Required the use of best available technology not entailing excessive costs.
1985	Vienna Convention for the Protection of the Ozone Layer adopted requiring the assessment of causes and effects of ozone depletion. Leads to the adoption of the 1987 Montreal Protocol which sets targets for the reduction and elimination of ozone-depleting substances.

Year	Key Events
1989	The Air Quality Standards Regulations 1989 introduce the first generalized emission limit and guide values for SO_2 and suspended particulates, lead in air and nitrogen dioxide set by EC. The Regulations transpose the requirements of various EC Directives.
1990	The Environmental Protection Act 1990 introduces controls over sources of industrial air pollution under the dual system of Integrated Pollution Control (for more polluting industrial processes) and Air Pollution Control.
1992	The Framework Convention on Climate Change adopted at the Rio Conference aimed at stabilizing greenhouse gases.
1995	The Environment Act 1995 provides a new statutory framework for local air quality management. This includes a National Air Quality Strategy which sets out air quality standards. Local controls include the setting up of local air quality management areas.
1996	Directive 96/62/EC introduces a new framework on ambient air quality and assessment. Sets out a timescale for daughter directives to control sulphur dioxide, nitrogen dioxide, particulate matter, lead and ozone, benzene, carbon monoxide, and other hydrocarbons.
1997	Kyoto Protocol sets down emissions limits and joint implementation mechanisms for the Framework Convention on Climate Change. Publication of the first National Air Quality Strategy sets out alert thresholds (which will trigger further action) and air quality targets. Revisions to the Strategy were published in 1999 and 2000.
1999	Pollution Prevention and Control Act 1999 replaces controls over air pollution under IPC and APC for industrial installations.
2000	Finance Act 2000 introduces the Climate Change Levy which imposes a tax on energy usage for non-domestic users to assist in the reduction of greenhouse gases
2002	The UK emissions trading scheme is introduced. Thirty-one voluntary participants agree to reduce their greenhouse gas emissions against 1998–2000 levels.
2003	Waste and Emissions Trading Act 2003 makes provision for statutory emissions trading.
2005	EU emissions trading scheme begins.

The local effects of acid rain were severe with industrialized areas of the country rendered desolate by very highly acidic moist air, burning trees, shrubs and hedges. One of the centres for the alkali industry, St Helens in Lancashire, was reported as not having a single tree with any foliage on it. This concern led to the setting-up of a Royal Commission to look into the problem of alkali pollution, which subsequently made the recommendations which led to the first Alkali Act, passed in 1863. Under this Act, a new Alkali Inspector was appointed who regulated such alkali processes. Although the Act did not attempt to deal with smoke, it did introduce new stricter controls over the production of acidic emissions. It made the first attempts at restricting the composition of emissions with the introduction of primitive emission standard requirements. Under the Act, there was a requirement that 95 per cent of all noxious emissions should be arrested within the plant, so that only 5 per cent of the previously emitted fumes were allowed into the atmosphere.

Neither of these Acts, nor a consolidation Act of 1906, dealt specifically with the control of smoke from either industrial or commercial premises. Attempts were made to control the emission of smoke through such Acts as the Public Health Act 1875, the Public Health (Smoke Abatement) Act 1926 and the Public Health Act 1936, but these dealt generally with smoke nuisances. These powers could not rid industrial cities of the problems of smoke pollution. The physical evidence of this pollution could be seen on blackened buildings, and by the frequency of smog, which was prevalent from Victorian times. Such smog was caused by fog forming in winter months and combining with smoke particles to produce a compound of gases which could cut visibility to very low levels. Of more concern, however, was the effect that these smogs had upon the dispersion of pollution. With a heavy concentration of smog hanging over a city the air was very still and convection was low. With the onset of these calm conditions, the dispersal of emissions was much more difficult. The effects of these smogs were thought to be minimal until December 1952 when a smog descended upon London which did not clear for five days. Nothing unusual was noticed until prize cattle at the Smithfield Show started to suffer from respiratory problems. The smog got everywhere, even inside the Sadler's Wells Theatre, which resulted in the stoppage of a performance because of the difficulty of seeing the stage. When the smog had lifted it was estimated that at least 4,000 people had lost their lives as a consequence of the smoke and other emissions.[3]

The government immediately responded by setting up the Beaver Committee to report on the difficulties surrounding smoke pollution. The recommendation of the Committee was to introduce legislation to eliminate particulate emissions such as smoke, dust and grit so that such conditions would not arise again. With the introduction of the Clean Air Act 1956, later supplemented by the Clean Air Act 1968, controls were introduced for the first time to restrict the production of smoke, grit and dust from all commercial and industrial activities not covered by the Alkali Acts but also, more importantly, domestic fires as well. The Acts introduced such concepts as smoke control areas and the complete prohibition on 'dark smoke' from chimneys (see further p. 430).

During the 1970s, the problems of the emission of smoke, dirt, dust, and grit lessened and coupled with the new approach to industrial processes a gradual improvement took place in the quality of the atmosphere in the UK. There was a move away from the use of coal as fuel to smokeless substances such as coke and gas. Additionally, the gap left behind with the introduction of clean air zones was met by an increase in the use of electricity for power and heat. The main generator of electricity in Britain, the Central Electricity Generating Board, changed its practices in a direct reaction to the difficulties encountered with local pollution by replacing the short chimneys traditionally used in power stations with larger and taller stacks. The basis of this change was to disperse pollution at a higher level in the hope that any substances would be diluted over greater distances. The consequence would be a reduction in the concentrations of pollutants in the nearby locality. Unfortunately, this reduction in the levels of local pollution only shifted the problems to a different location. Whilst the pollution of the atmosphere declined nationally, the concern internationally rose. The change of policy from short to tall stacks for chimneys saw the creation of the first major transboundary pollution from acid rain. The effects of the transboundary acid rain could be seen not only in disparate parts of the UK but also other countries within Europe where the prevailing winds carried such emissions. In particular, the Scandinavian countries received a

---

3. See generally, D. Davis, *When Smoke Ran Like Water* (New York: Basic Books, 2002), ch. 2.

large percentage of the 'export' of Britain's production of sulphur dioxide and acid rain. It wasn't until the 1980s that international and European efforts were made to address the problem through negotiated treaties and protocols.

BOX 16.2 **Regulatory impact**

One of the historic characteristics of the British approach to environmental regulation has been that it is reactive, responding to known problems rather than proactive in trying to prevent new problems arising. Although there are defects with this approach it has also proved to be an effective means of addressing certain types of environmental harm. The evidence of the history of domestic air quality legislation illustrates that although there has been a recent preference for alternatives (e.g. economic instruments and voluntary measures), the effectiveness of regulation as a mechanism to address environmental problems should not be underestimated. Regulation is a good way of addressing immediate problems and prohibitions on polluting substances or activities can have a dramatic effect. For example, the Alkali Act 1863 and its successors saw a remarkable reduction in the production of acidic emissions from almost 14,000 tonnes to about 45 tonnes. The Clean Air Act 1956 and its successors banned coal fires and provided financial assistance to households to convert to smokeless fuel. As a result sulphur dioxide levels in Manchester city centre fell from 481 $\mu g/m^3$ in 1960 to 58 $\mu g/m^3$ in 1990.

Even in international law which is often characterized as being ineffective because of political constraints and the need to build consensus, there have been clear examples of the effectiveness of regulatory intervention. For example the Montreal Protocol saw a large reduction in the total consumption of the main ozone depleting substances. In 2002 the World Meteorological Organization concluded that the Protocol has been an effective mechanism and that depletion of the ozone layer will begin to ameliorate within the next 10 years or so and will reverse within a further 50 years.

Although regulatory impact can be significant, there are also some obvious flaws in using reactive regulation. First there is the issue of displacement. Where serious problems must be addressed quickly there is always the danger that regulatory measures do not remove the problem completely but merely shift it elsewhere. The construction of tall chimneys to disperse sulphur dioxide simply causes the emissions to fall further away or it may mean that the sulphur dioxide is released high enough into the atmosphere to create acid rain. A further example of displacement is the consequences of the Montreal Protocol which led to a black market in illegal CFCs. Secondly, a reactive approach does not prevent pollution nor does it sit easily with a precautionary approach. This is evidenced by a period of transition from the time when a problem is acknowledged and the implementation and practical effect of the new regulations. Finally, reactive regulation often fails to recognize the complex interconnected nature of environmental problems as it often only addresses one source. Thus, although the Clean Air Acts reduced the amount of sulphur dioxide in the atmosphere it did not eradicate winter smog episodes completely. In the 1990s various UK cities experienced dangerous smog levels. In London in December 1991 levels of nitrogen oxide rose to more than twice the safe level recommended by the World Health Organization and over 160 deaths were attributed to poor air quality. Although regulation had reduced smoke emissions these had been replaced by similar emissions from the increase in the number of motor vehicles in urban areas.

Just as the problem of regional transboundary pollution was being addressed on the international stage in the 1980s, the focus of concern shifted to global threats brought about by air pollution. In the 1980s scientific evidence started to link the release of CFCs and other chlorine based substances with the destruction of the ozone layer. In addition there was evidence that certain 'greenhouse gases' could cause a rise in the earth's temperature leading to climate change. The greenhouse effect, as it was referred to, has arisen because the production of various 'greenhouse' gases have increased in the past century with progressive industrialisation. In the lower atmosphere the production of emissions from power stations, car exhausts and industrial plants have increased by almost 100 per cent. These emissions absorb radiated heat and create a higher ambient temperature level which has led to speculation that there could be shrinking global icecaps and rising water levels.

Additionally, the amount of ozone in the upper atmosphere screens the earth from harmful UV-B radiation. This screen has deteriorated and there have been studies showing a 'hole' above Antarctica and beyond. This depletion of ozone has been linked to the use of chlorofluorocarbons (CFCs). The creation of greenhouse gases and the depletion of the ozone layer are worldwide problems which require international cooperation to solve. The use of international law as a mechanism for environmental protection is relatively unproven (but see the regulatory impact of the Montreal Protocol described in Box 16.2) and there are some limitations to its usefulness. However, the nature of the problems facing the world in terms of these two issues have led to significant steps being taken to prevent any further harm.

The regulatory challenge

Air, unlike other environmental media, is intangible and not capable of being owned. Whilst it is a common resource it is a transient medium which is uncontained and highly mobile. Emissions can diffuse quickly and the immediate impacts can be transferred away from the direct point of discharge. As a result it has often been difficult to identify causal links between particular sources and effects of pollutants. Often a problem has been identified and a regulatory solution proposed when the aggregation of many sources mean that the effects are difficult to reverse. This is true in respect of local, transboundary and truly global problems.

These difficulties of establishing causal links also have the effect of raising the problem of uncertainty, risk and the application of a precautionary approach. Issues such as the effects of acid rain and the existence of climate change have been the subject of intense disagreement between those who believe that a precautionary approach is essential and others who argue that harmful effects have not been sufficiently established, the risks are tentative or unformed and the costs of taking preventative measures too great.

Certain consequences of air pollution have a general impact regardless of the source or how the consequences are created. In this sense they are truly global problems which require co-operation and joint commitment if they are to succeed. Thus political consensus about the nature of the problem, its causes and effects is essential before moving on to consider the specific measures which should be adopted. The whole process can be undermined by countries failing to agree at either level.

A further challenge is that air pollution problems are complex in their causes and solutions. The range of polluters and the sources of pollutant are varied and diverse. This legal, scientific, and economic complexity means that no single regulatory mechanism will have more than a contributory effect. Accordingly, various types of mechanism must be used to deal with different facets of the same problem. Energy production and consumption, different modes of transport, manufacturing and agriculture all have a significant impact upon the atmosphere. Many of these sources are interconnected in the sense that they are strongly associated with industrialization and economic development. Modifying energy production or transport usage raises significant problems for both developed industrialised nations with established consumption patterns and developing nations who wish to encourage future industrialization and economic growth as an objective. This raises questions of fairness as between developed and developing nations where the original cause of global problems such as the depletion of the ozone layer or greenhouse gas emissions is traced to the developed nations' historical pollution, whilst the developed nations seek to impose tighter current controls over those nations who wish to be able to develop in a similar fashion.

International law and air pollution

The influence of international law on the regulation of air pollution has been significant. Perhaps in recognition of the fact that many of the problems caused by air pollution can have impacts across a large geographical area (and in certain circumstances cause truly global effects), there have been a number of areas where international law has helped to shape policies and rules on both a continental and domestic level. In addition, the level of cooperation on such issues is sometimes higher than in other areas as there is a general acceptance that there is a mutual responsibility amongst the nation states of the world.

Transboundary pollution

As the description of the development of the controls over air pollution demonstrates, addressing local problems can often lead to a translocation of the impacts of pollutants over large distances. The problem of transboundary is not a recent phenomenon and air pollution from a Canadian Smelter which destroyed crops and forest over the border in the US saw the creation of a significant principle of customary international law.

CASE 16.1 Transboundary pollution and customary international law—The *Trail Smelter* case: *US v Canada* (3 RIAA 1907 (1941))

A Canadian Mining company operated a large zinc and lead smelter along the Columbia river at Trail, British Columbia. Sulphur dioxide emissions from two large 400-foot chimneys at the smelter had damaged crops (wheat and oats), trees used for logging, and pastures in the US State of Washington about 10 miles south of the smelter. The US government objected to the Canadian government and the dispute went to arbitration on two occasions. The International Joint Commission by the United States and Canada awarded the US government some $428,000 to compensate for damage caused to forests and pastures and imposed emission limits and monitoring requirements on the smelter. In doing so it concluded that:

no state has the right to use or permit the use of its territory in such a manner as to cause injury by fumes in or to the territory of another of the properties or persons therein, when the case is of serious consequence and the injury is established by clear and convincing evidence.

Although the *Trail Smelter* arbitration establishes a clear principle of customary international law, in practice it has been overtaken by negotiated treaties on transboundary air pollution. There are a number of reasons for this. First, there is the evidential difficulty of obtaining 'clear and convincing evidence' of the causal link between source and effects of long range air pollution. The distance of 10 miles and the lack of alternative sources in the *Trail Smelter* case meant that this evidential burden was eased. The Programme for Monitoring and Evaluation of Long-Range Transmission of Air Pollutants in Europe (EMEP) has monitored transboundary pollution since its formation in 1977 and modern monitoring techniques can trace emissions with a degree of accuracy. In many cases, however, the causal link is not necessarily straightforward as most countries 'export' as well as 'import' atmospheric pollution and the problem can be regional in nature rather than bilateral as in *Trail Smelter*. Secondly, the principle is compensatory in nature in that it seeks to pay for serious harm caused rather than prevent future harm. Preventative measures can only be imposed through international agreement on the standards to be employed. The failure to prevent harm is particularly problematic with transboundary pollution where the consequences may not be appreciated until long after damage has been caused. Thirdly, the requirement of 'serious consequences' is problematic in that it is a flexible standard which may be dependent upon the nature of the receiving environment. For example in the *Trail Smelter* case the pollution caused serious damage to economic interests such as agriculture and forestry. If the damage had been caused to an 'unowned' wilderness area it is unlikely that a claim would have been sustained. Fourthly, the complex interconnected nature of transboundary pollution is not something that is easily justiciable in the context of the *Trail Smelter* principle. For example, the eventual negotiation of treaties on transboundary air pollution were slowed down by the reluctance of some countries to accept that there was even a problem. Finally, in cases where the principle is clearly breached, the relaxation of jurisdictional hurdles has increased the ability of private entities to seek redress through national courts.

The 1979 Geneva Convention on Long-Range Transboundary Air Pollution

The Geneva Convention on Long-Range Transboundary Air Pollution, agreed under the UN Economic Commission for Europe (UNECE) in 1979, was the first real attempt to set up a formal framework of controls over air pollution between nations. The Convention was purely preventative in nature and contained no liability provisions. The treaty came into force in 1983 and most of the major industrial European States are signatories along with the United States and Canada. The Convention is a classic example of a political compromise solution to an international problem. It is a framework treaty which sets out various broad principles of cooperation and joint research into the problems of transboundary air pollution. The flexibility in the Treaty is evidenced by the primary obligation which is to endeavour to limit and gradually reduce and prevent air pollution using best available technology where economically feasible (Arts 2 and 6). In this fashion, the treaty is more a statement of intent than a binding legal instrument. In practice the exchanging of information, coordinated research and general collaboration on combating transboundary air pollution has lead to further more specific measures in the shape of five protocols relating to different types of air pollution.

The first protocol on the reduction of sulphur dioxide was originally agreed in 1985 and was eventually replaced by a more prescriptive protocol agreed in Oslo in 1994.[4] The original protocol provided for a flat rate reduction of 30 per cent of sulphur dioxide emissions to be achieved by 1993. Three of the largest producers of sulphur dioxide, including the UK, declined to ratify the protocol on the basis that the flat rate-reduction had not been allocated fairly and the timetable was unrealistic. The 1994 Oslo protocol set different emissions reductions for each party set by reference to actual data on sulphur dioxide sources and effects. The UK signed and ratified the Oslo treaty agreeing to reduce sulphur dioxide emissions to 20 per cent of 1980 levels by 2010. Whilst the original convention was a triumph of political expediency the more rigorous protocols that followed have seen sulphur dioxide levels fall. Implementation of the Convention's requirements have been possible as a result of the so-called 'dash for gas' which has seen polluting coal fired power stations phased out and replaced with more efficient gas fired stations or fitted with expensive desulphurisation abatement equipment.

The second major protocol under the Geneva Convention deals with emissions of NO_X and was concluded in 1988 in Sofia. This protocol required parties to stabilize NOx emissions at 1987 levels by 1994. In a similar fashion to the sulphur dioxide protocol it imposes a requirement to use the best available technology for national emissions standards. Further protocols have been signed in relation to volatile organic compounds, air pollution from persistent organic pollutants and heavy metals. These protocols largely overlap with similar measures agreed within the European Community. Indeed the EC is a signatory of these protocols.

The 1985 Vienna Convention for the Protection of the Ozone Layer

Moves to protect the ozone layer were commenced in 1981 by UNEP. In 1985 the Vienna Convention for the Protection of the Ozone Layer was concluded. This four-year negotiation period reflected the difficulties in achieving a political consensus on the nature of the risks and the measures which were required.[5] Consensus was required because the global impact of ozone depletion could only be addressed effectively through a large number of signatories to the Convention, along with deterrents to prevent the production and consumption of ozone depleting materials by non-signatories. As in the case of the 1979 Geneva Convention on Transboundary Pollution, the Vienna Convention represented a pragmatic solution which sought to recognize the nature of the problem but which took into account the need to ensure cooperation in achieving firm solutions. Thus the Convention was

4. See R. Churchill, G. Kutling, and L. Warren (1994) 6 JEL 169.
5. See R. Benedick, *Ozone Diplomacy* (Cambridge MA: Harvard University Press, 1998).

primarily a framework for future action requiring the assessment of the causes and effects of ozone depletion with cooperation in relation to information and technology transfer. It imposed no specific binding obligations although there was a requirement to take 'appropriate measures' to guard against activities which were modified or were likely to modify the ozone layer.

Notwithstanding the vagueness of the provisions of the Convention it was notable for a number of reasons. It was the first example of international law addressing a *global* environmental problem. Secondly, it was one of the first Conventions which took an explicitly precautionary approach by acknowledging the need to take action against substances which were *likely* to have an impact on the ozone layer even where some parties argued that the causal link between ozone depletion and environmental harm had not been proved. Thirdly, the Convention saw a departure from traditional forms of protection against 'pollution' by referring to 'adverse effects' including climate change. Finally, the fact that consensus could be achieved was significant as it provided the platform for a more substantive response to the problem in the shape of the 1987 Montreal Protocol on Substances that Deplete the Ozone Layer. This set concrete targets for the reduction and eventual phasing out of the production and consumption of substances that depleted the ozone layer. Further amendments in 1991 and 1992 added new substances and brought forward the ban on CFCs and related substances to 1996. Various measures were incorporated into the Protocol to seek to balance the potential problem of the unfairness of phase out on developing nations. These included a ten year derogation from compliance with the phasing out and ban. Alternatively a fund was established to help to smooth the progress of the adoption of alternatives to CFCs. The Protocol also addressed the problem of the production of ozone depleting substances by non-signatories to the Convention by banning trade between parties and non-parties. In order to ensure the effectiveness of the Protocol there are formal non-compliance procedures with various sanctions including loss of financial support from the alternative substances fund and funding from bodies such as the World Bank. The Protocol has proved to be responsive to cases of non-compliance (e.g. Russian exports of CFCs). The evidence suggests that compliance levels are high even with the progressive widening of the controlled substances. The Montreal Protocol is a good example of the effectiveness of international law in addressing environmental problems when the global community is faced with a considerable risk and a relatively straightforward regulatory task of the phasing out and banning of certain substances.

The 1992 Framework Convention on Climate Change

Addressing the problem of climate change has proved to be a much greater challenge than achieving consensus on the problem of ozone depletion. Some countries take a precautionary stance, arguing that climate change poses a risk of serious or irreversible damage and that the lack of full scientific certainty should not be used as an excuse to postpone action. Other countries argue that the risks are controllable and that a precautionary response would have an unjustifiably detrimental impact upon economic development and human welfare.

Climate change is characterized by threats to the global environment, uncertainty in relation to the risks, severity and nature of the impacts and the connection between the sources of greenhouse gases and economic development. Responding to the potential threats of Climate change demands a complex response, addressing areas as diverse as transportation, deforestation, power generation, control over natural resources, and industrial and economic growth which crosses usual sectoral boundaries.

Recognizing the problem of potential global climate change, the World Meteorological Organization (WMO) and the UNEP established the Intergovernmental Panel on Climate Change (IPCC) in 1988. The IPPC's First Report in 1990 provided an assessment of the problem and in 1992 lead to the adoption of the Framework Convention on Climate Change at the Rio Conference. The Convention was ratified by 50 countries (including the EC and the UK) and came into force in March 1994. The Convention is based around the concept of 'common but differentiated responsibility' recognizing the need for global action and the differing levels of obligation placed upon industrialized and developing countries. The Convention was very much a starting position, establishing a process for future action and a framework of principles and objectives which were to be guides to further implementation measures.

The main objective of the Convention was to stabilize greenhouse gas emissions at a level which would not interfere with the climate system or food production but would still allow sustainable economic development (Art. 2). The objective should be met within a timeframe which would allow ecosystems to adapt to any changes. Thus the Convention recognizes the unavoidability of some changes in climate and seeks to achieve the possible by seeking to link it to the ability of nature to adapt to whatever changes occur. Article 3 of the Convention lays down certain guiding principles to follow in seeking to attain the Article 2 objective. These include inter-generational equity; common but differentiated responsibility; the precautionary principle; the right to sustainable development; and the need to cooperate within a supportive and open international economic system. Whilst this comprehensive set of principles does not create any binding obligations, it did set down a template for more specific emissions targets.

Article 4 of the Convention sets out the general commitments applicable to all parties (including the developing nations under Article 4(1)) and more burdensome responsibilities only applicable to the parties listed in Annex I (i.e. the developed nations and economies in transition from Eastern Europe under Article 4(2), (see Box 16.3)). These are general commitments to making national inventories of emissions; the integration of climate change issues across policy making and the adoption of measures to limit emissions of greenhouse gases. There is only one specific aim, applicable to the Annex I parties, of returning emissions to 1990 levels by 2000 (Art. 4(2)(a) and (b)) although the aim was largely superseded on the signing of the Kyoto Protocol.

The need for stronger action was reflected in the setting of binding reduction targets for Annex I parties in the Kyoto Protocol which was adopted in 1997. The Protocol was the subject of tough negotiations primarily as a result of the political difficulties faced by the US in setting significant reduction targets. The Protocol sets out specific reduction targets for different countries in relation to six gases: carbon dioxide, NOx, hydrofluorocarbons (HFCs), perfluorocarbons (PFCs), methane, and ground level ozone. The cuts average out at a 5.2 per cent reduction of 1990 levels of these gases at some time between 2008 and 2012. These different limits reflect the 'common but differentiated responsibility' approach with some countries (e.g. New Zealand and Russia) being required to stabilize emissions and others (e.g. Australia and Norway) permitted an increase.

The Protocol is notable for the joint implementation mechanisms which allow the commitments to be shared amongst parties.

- *Aggregating emissions (Art. 4 of the Protocol).* Two or more Annex I parties can aggregate their combined emissions and provided that the overall limit assigned to the group as a whole is not exceeded it does not matter than individual parties have exceed their own quota. This is useful for regional groupings such as the European Community in giving flexibility over how to meet the overall target.

- *Joint implementation (Art. 6 of the Protocol).* An Annex I party can receive credit for supporting projects which reduce another Annex I party's greenhouse gas emissions. This could include the energy efficiency measures or the transfer of clean technology.

- *Emissions trading systems (Arts 4 and 17 of the Protocol).* This would enable countries with a significant 'surplus' of emissions reduction as a result of exceeding targets, either to sell that surplus to countries which have a 'deficit' (i.e. are having difficulties in meeting their own target) or 'stockpile' it as a safeguard against meeting future reduction targets.

- *The clean development mechanism (Art. 12 of the Protocol).* As the developing nations are not subjected to any reduction targets, there was some concern expressed that there was little incentive for them to adopt measures which would contribute to the overall achievement of the aims of the Climate Change Convention. Thus Annex I Countries can gain credit for assisting the developing countries in the creation of projects which result in certified emission reductions. This could be in relation to sources of greenhouse gases such as 'cleaner' power stations or the reduction overall emission levels. Any reduction achieved can be offset against the Annex I country's own target (as long as the emission reductions achieved are 'additional' to those that would have occurred anyway).

One final notable feature is the use of carbon sinks. Four articles of the protocol allow for generation of carbon sink credits, which permit Annex I countries to reduce their obligation under the Protocol. For every tonne of carbon that is stored in a tree, an equivalent tonne of carbon from fossil fuels can be released into the atmosphere. Thus carbon credits are acquired through afforestation, reforestation, and forest management. The calculation of the actual extent of the reduction is a matter of some controversy as the amount of the reduction in heavily forested countries could be significant in the overall total reduction (e.g. it is estimated that Russia could claim over 25 per cent reduction of its overall target from the use of managed forests).

The progress on agreeing international action to address climate change and its causes has been slow but the process has really only just begun. The Framework Convention and the Kyoto Protocol are the first attempts to set out principles and processes which will assist with the creation of long-term commitments to stabilize and adjust to changes in climate. The Convention takes a pragmatic political approach based upon cooperation, typically characterized by the various joint implementation mechanisms. It is too early to assess the real impact of the measures found in the Convention and the Kyoto Protocol but the ratification of the Treaty by Russia in 2004 and the subsequent coming into force in 2005 was clearly a significant step. Whether the Kyoto Protocol will have a similar regulatory impact as the Montreal Protocol will depend largely upon the position of the world's largest greenhouse gas producer, the US. As one of only four industrialised nations to fail to ratify (Australia, Monaco, and Liechtenstein are the others) the US, with over 36 per cent of the emissions of carbon dioxide at 1990 levels, still has a critical part to play in the success of the Protocol.

Europe and air pollution

The protection of the atmosphere was not seen as a priority by the EC until the mid-1980s. Indeed, relatively few proposals based purely on environmental protection (as opposed to market harmonization) were published before 1984. The reasons for this were twofold. First, a lack of political will and, secondly, a genuine desire to move forward in other areas. As a result of the effects of acid rain, however, the German government pressed for swift action in 1983 and the main framework Directive on emissions from industrial plant (84/360) was introduced nearly 10 years after the framework directives for waste and water pollution.

In policy terms, air pollution and air quality are considered to be a short term priority. The EC's Sixth Environment Action Programme identified air quality standards as falling within 'Environment and Health', one of the four main target areas for action until 2010. The Action Progamme sets the objective of achieving levels of air quality that do not give rise to unacceptable impacts on, and risks to, human health and the environment. This is supplemented by a thematic strategy on air pollution which outlines the environmental objectives for air quality and measures to be taken to achieve the meet these objectives. This thematic strategy is the culmination of the Clean Air for Europe (CAFE) programme (see COM(2001)245) which combined technical analysis and policy development in the area as a basis for a coherent long term strategy—something which has not been evident in the earlier years of European air quality law and policy.

Concern about trans-boundary pollution and wider issues such as climate change and ozone depletion has seen the EC develop a significant role as a party to international negotiations on Conventions and Treaties. The EC has encouraged a number of worldwide initiatives by negotiating in its own right on issues which require global action. Thus, the EC is a signatory to the Vienna Convention for the Protection of the Ozone Layer. This in turn led to the implementation of Regulation 2037/2000 as amended on Substances that Deplete the Ozone Layer—one of the few examples of a European wide ban on specific substances. Other examples include the ratification of the Framework Convention on Climate Change and the Kyoto Protocol. From a relatively slow start the EU has been at the forefront of many of the developments in air quality policy and legislative initiatives.

Europe and climate change

The EC was a key supporter of binding targets and timetables for emissions reduction in the Kyoto Protocol and was responsible for much of the momentum behind the negotiations towards the original Framework Convention. The EC was also highly influential in developing the idea of aggregated emissions quotas which would allow member states to set unified targets. The EC agreed to an aggregated reduction target for greenhouse gases of 8 per cent of 1990 levels by 2008–2012. Box 16.3 sets out the various allocations to member states under aggregated emissions quota. These were used as a basis for the setting of the National Allocation Plan for the purposes of the Emissions Trading Directive (see Annex B of Decision 2002/358/EC).

BOX 16.3 **Allocations of the Kyoto Protocol commitments amongst various Member States**

Member States	Targets as a % of 1990 emissions levels	Actual % change 1990–8	Variance (i.e. difference between Targets and Actual) (%)
Belgium	−7.5	+6.5	+14
Denmark	−21	+9.5	+30.5
Germany	−21	−15.6	+5.4
Greece	+25	+18.1	−6.9
Spain	+15	+21.0	+6
France	0	+0.9	+0.9
Ireland	+13	+19.1	+6.1
Italy	−6.5	+4.4	+10.9
Luxembourg	−28	−24	−4
Netherlands	−6	+8.4	+14.4
Austria	−13	+6.5	+19.5
Portugal	+27	+17.2	−9.8
Finland	0	+1.5	+1.5
Sweden	+4	+6.4	+2.4
United Kingdom	−12.5	−8.3	+4.2

Source: © OECD/IEA, 2002. As modified by the authors. Reproduced with permission.

The EC's response to the Kyoto Protocol was to establish a European Climate Change Programme (ECCP) launched in 2000 (see COM 2000) 88). The approach of the ECCP has been broad and far reaching and is a good example of external integration of environmental considerations into other policy areas as it involves initiatives across the energy, transport and industrial sectors. After an intial planning phase the ECCP has resulted in a broad range of initiatives including:

• A Directive setting up an Emissions Trading Scheme (2003/87/EC).

- A proposal for a Directive to link the joint implementation and clean development mechansims provided for in the Kyoto Protocol with the emissions trading scheme.
- A Directive on the promotion of renewable energy (2001/77/EC) which promotes renewable energy sources thus reducing reliance on fossil fuels which produce greenhouse gases.
- A Directive on the promotion of Biofuels for transport (2003/30/EC) with the aim of making biofuels (ie fuels made from biomass) 5.75 per cent of the transport fuel market by 2011.
- A Directive on the energy perfomance of buildings (2001/91/EC) which sets minimum requirements for the energy performance and certification of energy efficiency for all new buildings.

Other pre-existing measures on air quality will also have an impact upon the reduction of greenhouse gas emissions. Some of these are considered below. For example, the tightening of product standards for motor vehicles and the introduction of IPPC including energy efficiency requirements

Data on greenhouse gas emissions trends show that the EC has already met the commitment under the Framework Convention to stabilize its emissions at 1990 levels by 2000 and in aggregate it has achieved 50 per cent of the emission target set under the Kyoto Protocol. As Box 16.3 shows, the EC is not complacent as many countries are still some way behind the targets and most of the reductions which have been made have arisen as a result of industrial restructuring post German reunification and the switch from coal to gas fired power stations in the UK. The 2nd ECCP report confirmed that in both 2000 and 2001 greenhouse gas emissions rose and that the Kyoto targets would be missed unless further policies and measures were adopted.

The European Emissions Trading System

The idea of a European wide emissions trading system was first found in the 5th EC Environmental Action Programme as an example of a flexible market-based mechanism as a component of environmental policy. This initial idea was developed further in the response to the need for more flexible mechanisms to assist with the emissions reduction target in the Kyoto Protocol (see COM (1998) 353). The final version of the scheme in Directive 2003/87/EC forms a central element of the ECCP and is the first international emissions trading scheme in the world.

The directive applies to the six greenhouse gases found in the Kyoto Protocol (listed in Annex II of the directive) in relation to all combustion installations with a thermal input greater than 20MW, oil refineries, coke ovens, metal production such as iron or works, the pulp and paper industry, and minerals processes such as cement, glass, and brick production (Annex I). This covers over 12,000 installations across the enlarged EU with over 1,000 in the UK. The initial phase of the scheme runs from 2005–7 with a second phase from 2008 to 2012 to link with the emissions reductions target under the Kyoto Protocol. Further 5-year periods are expected subsequently. Each installation subject to the directive must be covered by a permit (Art. 4) which is subject to conditions covering monitoring and reporting of conditions (Arts 6 and 7). In most cases this will be a permit issued under the IPPC legislation (Art. 8).

The scheme works on a 'Cap and Trade' basis. Member States must develop a National

Allocation Plan which sets a national emission allowance for all installations covered by the scheme and specifies how each allowance will be apportioned to individual installations (Art. 9). During the operation of the trading scheme, installations which have emissions levels below their assigned pollution amounts may sell emission rights to other entities that are in danger of exceeding their quotas. An installation must surrender any surplus allowance at the end of any period if it has not used or traded its allowance (Art. 6). It is implemented in the UK through the Greenhouse Gas Emissions Trading Scheme Regulations 2003 (SI 2003/3311) which are described below.

European law and air quality

European law on air quality has developed significantly from the mid-1980s and now can be characterized as taking a mixed regulation approach, i.e. there are a variety of types of mechanism which are used to regulate air quality. These include the traditional use of environmental standards for environmental quality or emissions limit values (for particular installations or substances), product standards (e.g. for fuel or motor vehicles); prohibitions on the production, consumption or use of substances (e.g. CFCs); economic instruments such as emissions trading and information based mechanisms like the European wide pollutant inventory. A general summary of some of the more important air quality and air pollution Directives can be found in the summary table below. One of the problems of this approach has been that there is a degree of overlap and a general lack of coherence although to a certain extent this reflects the complex interrelated nature of problems and solutions.

Summary of main EC legislation on air quality and air pollution

Legislative instrument	Outline of relevant provisions
Directive 1994/63/EC on the control of volatile organic compound (VOC) emissions resulting from the storage of petrol and its distribution from terminals to service stations.	Controls emissions of VOCs at petrol terminals and during distribution at service stations. The Directive uses technical process standards to reduce evaporation of solvents during transport etc.
Directive 1996/61/EC concerning Integrated Pollution Prevention and Control.	Sets down use of Best Available Techniques to prevent or minimize air pollution. Requires efficient use of energy by installations. Also provides basis for European Pollutant Emission Register.
Directive 1996/92/EC on ambient air quality assessment and management.	Framework Directive with the aim of protecting public health and the environment from a range of specified air pollutants, particularly sulphur dioxide, nitrogen dioxide and oxides of nitrogen, and particulates. Daughter Directives followed for these pollutants.
Directive 98/69/EC relating to measures to be taken against air pollution by emissions from motor vehicles.	Latest in a long series of Directives dating back to 1970 restricting emissions of pollutants from light motor vehicles. Similar controls for heavy duty vehicles in Directive 1999/86/EC.

Legislative instrument	Outline of relevant provisions
Directive 1999/13/EC on the limitation of emissions of volatile organic compounds due to the use of organic solvents in certain activities and installations.	Requires certain installations using organic solvents to take steps to reduce emissions of volatile organic compounds to air.
Directive 1999/32/EC relating to the reduction of the sulphur content of certain liquids fuels.	Reduces sulphur content of petrol and diesel fuels.
Directive 2000/76/EC on the incineration of waste.	Sets emission limit values for dust, SO_2, NO_x, and heavy metals. Applies to all waste incinerators.
Directive 2001/80/EC on the limitation of emissions of certain pollutants into the air from large combustion plants.	Controls emissions from large combustion plant to reduce emissions of sulphur dioxide, oxides of nitrogen and particulates.
Directive 2001/81/EC on national emission ceilings for certain atmospheric pollutants.	Sets national emission ceilings for pollutants causing acidification and eutrophication and for ozone precursors.

Environmental quality standards

A Framework Directive on Ambient Air Quality was formally agreed in 1996 (96/62/EC). The Framework Directive uses three types of quality objective: a limit value, a guide value and an alert threshold (which mirrors the approach taken under the national air quality strategy which is discussed below). The Directive identifies 12 pollutants for which limits will be set in subsequent daughter directives. The Framework Directive was followed by daughter directives, which will set the numerical limit values or target values for each of the identified substances. In addition to setting air quality limit and alert thresholds, the daughter directives harmonize information requirements such as monitoring and measuring methods so that standards are comparable throughout the Member States. The first three Daughter Directives covered:

- NOx, SO_2, Pb and PM_{10} (99/30).
- Benzene and carbon monoxide (00/69).
- Ozone (02/03).

The final Daughter Directive will cover arsenic, cadmium, mercury, nickel, and polycyclic aromatic hydrocarbons in ambient air. Member States and their local authorities will need to monitor air quality, provide information to the public, and introduce improvement plans and programmes where air quality fails to meet the specified criteria. These are implemented in the UK through a combination of statutory air quality standards and the air quality management provisions of the Environment Act 1995.

National Emissions Ceilings

In 1997 the European Commission published a proposed acidification strategy which was designed to reduce the emission of sulphur dioxide, oxides of nitrogen and ammonia. Consequently, the National Emissions Ceilings Directive (2001/81/EC) sets upper limits for each member state for the total emissions in 2010 of those four pollutants, but generally leaves the method of implementation to each Member State The Directive obliges Member States to draw up national programmes in order to demonstrate how they are going to meet the national emission ceilings by 2010 and to report each year their national emission inventories and projections for 2010 to the European Commission and the European Environment Agency. These requirements have been implemented in the UK by the National Ceiling Regulations 2002 (SI 2002/3118).

Stationary source emission limits

Various Directives make provision for the control of emissions from stationary point sources (see Box 7.11). The Large Combustion Plants Directive (LCPD) (2001/80/EC) sets out emission limits for SO_2, NO_x and PM_{10} in the case of emissions from power stations with a thermal output of greater than 50 MW (this can also include large industrial power plants in refineries and steelworks). One of the significant aspects of the Directive is that it is retrospective applying to power stations established before the coming into force of the original Large Combustion Plants Directive in July 1987 (although there are derogations for the so-called enlargement states). Under the LCPD 'new' (i.e. post Directive) plant must meet the specified emission limit values for the four substances in the LCPD. For 'existing' plants (i.e. those in operation pre-1987), Member States have an option of complying with the limit values or operating within a 'National Plan' which would set an annual 'emissions bubble' by aggregating a national level of emissions calculated by applying the ELV approach to existing plants.

Process standards

Certain Directives utilize process standards to prevent or minimize atmospheric emissions. For example the IPPC Directive (96/61/EC) does not specify limit values for atmospheric emissions, it specifies general process standards for permitting of specified industrial installations (including some agricultural and waste installations), based on the application of best available techniques (BAT) taking into account local conditions. Community wide emissions limit values *can* be set where a 'need' for Community action is identified through the technical information exchange and the setting of technical guidance found in the BREF standards (see p. 782).

Emissions from motor vehicles

The regulation of transport poses significant challenges in terms of controlling air pollution. The sector is the fastest growing source of CO_2 emissions (e.g. passenger vehicles comprise some 12 per cent of the EU's total emissions). Product standards for vehicles and fuel have been used extensively in the regulation of air pollution. One of the main reasons for this is that, before the amendments to the EC Treaty which permitted environmental protection measures, the introduction of such standards was seen to be justifiable in terms of market harmonization where environmental justifications were not accepted by every Member State.

Vehicle emissions have been controlled under a number of increasingly complex amendments to the original controlling Directive 70/220. Generally, directives have set product standards by fixing emission limits for carbon monoxide, hydrocarbons, nitrogen dioxide and particulates. Various amendments have culminated in Directive 2001/100/EC which sets out limits for cars and light vans. Emissions from larger vans and heavy duty vehicles are controlled under a separate directive (88/77/EC as amended). In addition to the fixed emission limits, there have been a number of directives controlling the roadworthiness of vehicles to ensure that the original product standards are being maintained. Directive 99/52 set out procedures for checking the roadworthiness of private cars. In addition to product standards for vehicles, Directive 98/70/EC (as amended by Directive 2003/17/EC) sets out environmental fuel quality specifications for petrol and diesel. These set specifications for the sulphur content of petrol and diesel and the aromatics content of petrol and are phased in over three stages from 2000 to 2008.

BOX 16.4 **Voluntary instruments—car manufacturers and reducing CO₂ emissions**

The use of voluntary agreements is becoming increasingly popular as part of a mixed regulation approach.[6] In the EC, the 5th Environmental Action Programme promoted their use as a 'flexible mechanism'. Voluntary agreements are thought to offer certain advantages over traditional forms of regulation including a faster more streamlined process of reaching agreement as compared to making legislation; encouraging a responsible and pro-active approach by industry, and allowing a flexible cost-effective approach to environmental problems. There are potential weaknesses in a voluntary approach including a lack of transparency or accountability, the setting of unambitious standards, the absence of technology forcing mechanisms, vague monitoring of compliance and lack of satisfactory enforcement mechanisms. The example of the first European wide environmental agreements bears out some of these criticisms.

In 1996, the European Council of Ministers proposed a long term strategy to reduce CO_2 emissions from passenger cars and improve fuel economy. The strategy aims at achieving an average CO_2 emission figure for new passenger cars of 120g CO_2/km by 2005, and 2010 at the latest. One of three main elements of the strategy was voluntary environmental agreements made between the European Commission and the European, Japanese and Korean car industry associations (ACEA, JAMA, and KAMA respectively). Under these agreements the car manufacturers made a commitment to reduce average CO_2 emissions from new cars to 140 g/km by 2008 (2009 in the case of JAMA and KAMA). The criticisms of the negotiation and final terms of the ACEA agreement were:

• It took some four years to negotiate an agreement which will bite some 10 years after it was concluded. This is hardly a swift alternative to the legislative process which would be expected to finalise a directive which could be transposed and implemented easily within that timetable.

• There was little wider public participation in the negotiation of the agreement which was

---

6. See further COM (1998) 495, COM (1999) 446, Recommendation 1999/125/EC OJ L 40, 13 Feb. 1999, 49–50 and G. Volpi and S. Singer, 'Will voluntary agreements at EU level deliver on environmental objectives? Lessons from the agreement with the automotive industry WWF Discussion Paper' (2000).

largely conducted between the commission and the associations. In addition, compliance data will only be made public on a collective basis across the whole sector meaning that individual manufacturer's performance will not be able to be assessed.

- There were no enforcement mechanisms for non-compliance.

- The targets had become outdated by the foreseeable introduction of existing technologies. In effect the targets represented a 'business as usual' model which would not necessarily stabilize CO_2 emissions from passenger cars at 1999 levels by 2010.

- The targets did not act as a sufficient incentive to develop alternative technologies.

Some of these criticisms go to the heart of the suitability of voluntary agreements as a mechanism to address serious environmental problems. Of course, whether some of these criticisms are valid will depend largely upon the effectiveness of the agreement in terms of reducing CO_2 levels from passenger vehicles. This can only be assessed adequately in 2008. This underlines one of the fundamental flaws of voluntary agreements. If it is proved to be ineffective, there would be little alternative other than to introduce legislative measures which would arguably be akin to shutting the stable door after the horse had bolted.

The European Pollutant Emission Register

A further element in the broad mixed regulation approach to air pollution is the establishment of accurate, publicly available information on air pollution from emissions. Various countries have established national pollutant inventories (e.g. the US Toxic Releases Inventory and the Environment Agency's Pollution Inventory). These registers or inventories aim to encourage transparency, accountability and public participation but can also act as a trigger for pollution prevention programmes.

The European Pollutant Emission Register (EPER) has its origins in the reporting requirement found in Article 15(3) of the IPPC Directive (96/61/EC) and was finally established by Commission Decision 2000/479/EC (see further Box 20.5). It is run jointly by the European Commission and the European Environment Agency. Under the EPER Decision, Member States have to produce a three-yearly report on emissions to air and water at industrial installations which are listed in Annex I of the IPPC Directive. The report covers 50 pollutants in total of which 37 are atmospheric pollutants. These must be included if certain threshold values are exceeded (see Annex AI of the EPER Decision). Reporting of emissions is required for the years 2002, 2004, and 2007 with annual reporting likely to start from 2007 onwards.

The aim of the EPER is to allow direct comparisons of air emissions data across all the Member States. The information is available on the internet at <www.eper.cec.eu.int> and can be searched by country, activity, pollutant, or facility. The web site also has a map search function with a summary of each industrial site and satellite photos. Some care should be taken with the data though as the figures may not necessarily represent an accurate picture of the relative contributions of different Member States. For example, the UK's experience with the setting up and reporting of data for the Pollutant Inventory may mean that it has access to better quality data than other Member States.

Domestic air pollution and air quality law and policy

In the UK, the control of air pollution has been the classic example of the use of reactive legal controls to regulate specific problems as they arise. Policy approaches had hitherto been sparse and incoherent. In the mid-1990s the approach was described as 'the fortuitous sum of a large number of unrelated regulatory decisions and individual choices'.[7] Although the legal controls have been modernized and broadened, it was only recently that a coherent strategy has been developed to deal with the problems of atmospheric pollution. It was not until the introduction of the air quality management system in the Environment Act 1995 that air pollution was addressed in a strategic manner.

The 1995 Act contained a number of framework provisions which enabled the development of various policies on air pollution. A number of factors led to this acceleration of policy- and law-making. First, there was increasing evidence linking health problems with poor air quality, with the increase of the incidence of asthma and other diseases connected with a variety of atmospheric pollutants. There were a number of occasions (particularly in the summer months) when pollution levels rose to dangerous levels in cities. Secondly, the quality of provision of information on air quality was improved with an increase in the number of background monitoring stations. Although air quality standards (AQS) were introduced for a number of pollutants any assessment of measuring improvement depended to a large extent upon the availability of long-term data. Most of England's major cities now have stations to monitor base data in order to assess compliance with standards for the main polluting emissions. It is anticipated that this will increase as the move towards established AQS grows. Thirdly, the link between air pollution and transport, in particular motor transport, had become much more pronounced. The RCEP's Eighteenth Report *Transport and the Environment* (Cm 2674) was published in October 1994. It concentrated on the environmental effects of vehicle emissions proposing a number of objectives and targets for reducing the environmental impacts from transport. as the basis for a transport policy for the UK which will be sustainable well into the next century. It made wide-ranging recommendations about integrating transport policy and land use, increasing the use made of environmentally less damaging forms of transport for passengers and freight, and minimizing the adverse impact of road and rail transport. Finally, and perhaps most importantly, in recent years the most significant air pollution policy and law has been influenced heavily by the need to meet the greenhouse gas reduction targets under the Kyoto Protocol as well as the environmental quality standards laid down under various EC air quality directives. This has seen a shift from the local controls under clean air legislation to a mixed regulatory approach involving detailed national policies on air quality management, product standards, economic instruments voluntary agreements, and public information tools.

---

7. Department of the Environment Consultation Paper, *Improving Air Quality* (DoE, 1994).

The UK and climate change

In recent years the problem of climate change has become a central issue for environmental law and policy in the UK. Although the local and transboundary impacts of air pollutants continues to be subject to legal controls under pollution control and clean air legislation, the size and complexity of challenge of climate change has accelerated the use of new instruments to try and regulate rising greenhouse gas emissions from a variety of sources. The UK's climate change programme launched in 2000 sets out an ambitious programme of measures which are intended to help the UK meet its commitment to reduce greenhouse gas emissions by 12.5 per cent on 1990 levels by 2012 and to meet a self-imposed goal of reducing carbon dioxide emissions by 20 per cent on 1990 levels by 2010. The UK is one of the few countries in the world where greenhouse gas emissions fell in the 1990s, thus complying with the commitments given in the FCCC. Carbon dioxide emissions fell by some 8.7 per cent between 1990 and 2002 and overall greenhouse gas emissions fell by 15.3 per cent over the same period. There is general recognition, however, that these cuts were 'one off' gains brought about from the switch from coal to gas, industrial modernization and a greater reliance on nuclear energy. The gains of greenhouse gases reductions from these sources are projected to level out by 2010 with further emission increases beyond that date.

The regulatory approach adopted in the UK's Climate Change Programme is based upon:

- The reduction of industrial emissions of greenhouse gases through integrated pollution prevention and control permits; this will implement reductions in some greenhouse gases required under the Large Combustion Plants Directive and Emissions Ceilings Directive.

- Energy efficiency measures including alterations to the Building Regulations for new developments (see Box 13.1).

- The promotion of renewable sources of energy including a target to double the UK's energy output from combined heat and power production and a legal obligation to increase supplies of energy from renewable sources by 10.4 per cent by 2010 (see Utilities Act 2000, s. 62).

- Investment in transport measures to reduce pollution caused by traffic congestion.

- The use of relatively blunt economic instruments to reduce the amount and impact of vehicle emissions. These include increases in fuel duties to reflect the environmental cost of vehicle use and promote the benefits of fuel efficiency; the use of fuel duty differentials to encourage, for example, the use of ultra low diesel fuel over normal diesel; the reform of company car taxation; and changes to the road tax.

- The use of two main economic instruments, namely the climate change levy and a national emissions trading scheme as a precursor to the European wide scheme.

Although the range of measures is integrated across a range of sectors including energy production, manufacturing, transport, households, and the public sector, some sectors are excluded from significant action. For example a sizeable proportion of emissions of methane and nitrous oxide come from the agricultural sector (from cattle wastes and fertilizer). Currently, little can be done to reduce such emissions although IPPC controls over large pig and poultry units may have some impact.

Climate Change Levy

The Climate Change Levy (CCL) is a tax upon energy usage and is therefore levied upon users as opposed to a carbon tax which would be levied on the supply of fuel. It was introduced under section 30 and schedule 6 of the Finance Act 2000 and applies to all industrial and public sector users. Domestic use and small businesses who use energy at a 'domestic level' are excluded (paras 9 and 10). Certain fuels are also exempt such as most renewable energy sources (para. 19) and approved combined heat and power schemes (paras 14 and 15).

The introduction of the tax was controversial with many large industrial energy users complaining that it would effect competitiveness in the international marketplace. The CCL has therefore been designed to be revenue neutral to the Government with the money accrued from the tax being used to pay for an across the board 0.3 per cent reduction of employers' national insurance contributions. There is an additional incentive to invest in energy efficiency measures with the companies able to reclaim 100 per cent of the capital allowances for energy efficient products within the first year of expenditure. This also reflects the shift of the burden of taxation from the 'goods' of wealth creation, employment and investment to the 'bads' of resource consumption and pollution.

Users from the most 'energy intensive' sectors are able to obtain an 80 per cent discount from the CCL if they sign up to sectoral climate change agreements (CCA) to reduce carbon emissions or implement energy efficiency measures. An 'energy intensive' sector is defined as one which carries out activities which are listed under Part A1 or A2 headings in Part 1 of schedule 1 to the Pollution Prevention and Control (England and Wales) Regulations 2000 (SI 2000/1973). There are ten major energy intensive sectors (aluminium, cement, ceramics, chemicals, food and drink, foundries, glass, non-ferrous metals, paper, and steel) and over 30 smaller sectors. This includes many (but not all) of the major industrial sectors and intensive pig and poultry units. Plans were announced in the 2004 Budget to extend the CCAs to sectors which passed an energy intensity threshold and a test based upon the effect of the CCL on international competitiveness.

The concluded CCAs set objectives and look at the ends rather than the means of securing reductions or energy efficiency gains. Thus they set reduction targets, monitoring requirements and independent verification of compliance with the agreements. Failure to comply can result in the suspension or withdrawal of the discount. The first two years operation of the CCL showed that the CCA were an effective mechanism for securing emissions reductions.[8]

8. (2003) ENDS Report 339 23.

Emissions trading scheme

The UK emissions trading scheme is a voluntary economic instrument which is aimed at reducing greenhouse gas emissions through a market-based approach that allows participants to buy and sell 'allowances' to produce emissions. The scheme is administered by the Emissions Trading Authority, originally a division within DEFRA but with the intention being that it will become an independent statutory body over time. The UK scheme takes a 'Cap and Trade' approach whereby participants agree to specific reduction targets and receives allowances based upon that 'cap'. The participant can then meet the target in three ways:

- by reducing emissions to the level of the cap;
- by making reductions to below the level of the cap which allows them to bank the surplus or sell the allowance to participants; and
- by meeting the reduction target through the purchase of surplus allowances from others.

There are four ways to participate in the scheme. So-called 'direct participants' accept a voluntary reduction of greenhouse gases in return for a financial incentive (of up to £30 million per year after tax). An auction is used to allocate both the allowance and the financial incentive for reducing emissions. Thus direct participants bid for a share of a fund by specifying the percentage reduction of greenhouse gas emissions taken against a baseline of 1990 emission levels. Although direct participation is voluntary, participants must sign a legally binding contract to meet their reduction targets. If a direct participant does not hold sufficient allowances to meet their target over the period of compliance they must pay a financial penalty per tonne of the shortfall (see Waste and Emissions Trading Act 2003, s. 39).

Secondly, 'agreement participants' agree to meet the reduction targets which are set within the Climate Change Agreements in conjunction with the Climate Change Levy. This allows participants some flexibility in choosing how to meet the CCA targets. The third and fourth classes of participant do not have specific reductions targets but merely trade in the market via credits given for emissions reductions targets or as an interested party irrespective of whether they emit greenhouse gases. In the latter category for example, US NGOs have 'retired' unused allowances to bring about an overall reduction in emissions.

The scheme commenced in 2002 and the first years of operation have illustrated some of the flaws in emissions trading instruments. One of the fundamental problems is that any reduction of greenhouse gases achieved is not necessarily linked to the impact of the trading scheme. In other words the economic rationale of emissions trading in rewarding companies who reduce emissions through efficiency or investment in new technology can be defeated by other factors. One of the most significant arguments is that many participants in the scheme bid for reduction allowances that they were already legally obliged to achieve as a result of pollution control authorization conditions. Other participants gained large reductions through a pre-planned fall in productivity or through loss of capacity as a result of greater competition.[9] The effect of many participants beating their reduction targets was

---

9. See (2002) ENDS Report 326, 25.

that a large surplus of allowances became available to be banked against future increases or traded on the market. Basic economics dictates that when there is a large surplus of supply prices will fall. Consequently it has become cheaper to buy allowances than to invest in abatement technology or energy efficiency measures in order to meet targets. In addition, there is the argument that large sums of public money have been spent in paying some participants to comply with the law.[10]

The introduction of the UK Emissions Trading Scheme in 2002 was a precursor to the EU wide scheme described above under Directive 2003/87/EC. The European system which commenced operation in January 2005 runs concurrently with the UK scheme. The overlap can be confusing but there are some notable distinctions between the two schemes. First the UK system is open to all and not limited to particular sectors like the EU scheme. Secondly, the UK system is voluntary whereas the EC system is based around a permitting system administered by the Environment Agency. Finally, although both schemes cover all greenhouse gases, at present the EU scheme only covers carbon dioxide emissions (although this is likely to be extended to other greenhouse gases in future). In contrast there have been proposals to extend the emissions trading scheme to cover SO_2 and NO_x as a means of assisting with implementation of the Large Combustion Plants Directive and the National Emissions Ceilings Directive.

The EU scheme has statutory backing and has been transposed under the Greenhouse Gas Emissions Trading Scheme Regulations 2003 (SI 2003/3311). These regulations provide the framework for a greenhouse gas emissions trading scheme by identifying those activities that are covered under the scheme (Annex I), making provision for a permitting system for the operation of an installation and the development of the national allocation plan or 'emissions bubble' upon which individual allowances will be based.

BOX 16.5 **Economic instruments and air pollution—an assessment**

The introduction of the Climate Change Levy and the Emissions Trading Scheme is a significant departure from old style command and control regulation in the field of air pollution and air quality law. As a basic taxation instrument the Climate Change Levy attempts to reflect the environmental cost of energy consumption which should incentivize companies to reduce usage and invest in abatement measures. The ultimate aim is to achieve a particular environmental goal, namely the reduction of the emission of greenhouse gases. Environmental taxes have the advantage of being predictable in terms of cost and they can be applied across broad categories of tax-payers. They also have disadvantages in that the aim is to secure an environmental goal but there is a degree of uncertainty about whether this will be done. If a tax is set too low it will not act as an incentive to change behaviour. If set too high it may have a significant impact upon economic development and international competitiveness. Taxes can also be expensive to monitor and enforce. In terms of effectiveness, however, perhaps the biggest disadvantage of the Climate Change Levy is the exemption from the levy for large sources of greenhouse gas emissions, namely the domestic and transport sectors.

The Emissions Trading System has the advantage of being flexible in the sense that it is akin to

---

10. See House of Commons, Committee of Public Accounts, *The UK Emissions Trading Scheme: A New Way to Tackle Climate Change* (2003–4).

a performance standard which encourages technological improvement and fits in with the idea of ecological modernization. The scheme also provides a degree of certainty about the achievement of the environmental goal as the limits are placed on the overall allowances which can be traded. The scheme encourages compliance through efficiency and competitive advantage. It is even possible for there to be wider public participation in the system through the trading of non-target participants. The actual evidence of the system demonstrates some of the disadvantages. Setting the cap is critical. If it is too high the need for efficiency gains is reduced. Too low and the goal becomes unachievable. In addition, care needs to be taken to ensure that reductions are triggered by more than legal obligations under pollution control legislation; reductions in capacity; or 'business as usual' projections. Finally, emissions trading schemes are suitable when there are a relatively small number of participants with large sources of pollutants. Where there are large numbers of small sources (e.g. cars, households, or agriculture) an emission trading scheme would be too cumbersome to operate unless there were operators who could be made responsible for aggregated emissions (e.g. airline operators) (see Box 5.3).

National Air Quality Strategy

Central policy for maintaining and improving air quality is laid down in a National Air Quality Strategy. Under section 80 of the Environment Act 1995, the Secretary of State is under a duty to prepare the Strategy which will enable the UK to meet international and European commitments (most notably on air quality standards and climate change). These standards and objectives provide the foundation for air quality policy and set the context within which detailed legislation must be implemented and enforced. For example, the Environment Agency is to have regard to the Strategy when exercising its pollution control functions (Environment Act 1995, s. 81). The Strategy sets a framework containing air quality standards for certain pollutants which are set centrally and provide overall targets which must not be exceeded. These targets are to be achieved through a variety of mechanisms but principally under pollution control legislation through the setting of emission limits.

The Strategy contains two standards for identified pollutants: a general target standard which forms a long-term objective for policies and legislation; and an alert threshold which triggers the need for specific remedial action when exceeded. The current strategy, the *Air Quality Strategy for England, Scotland, Wales and Northern Ireland* was published in 2000 (Cm 4548). The Strategy covered eight main air pollutants: benzene, 1,3 butadiene, carbon monoxide, lead, nitrogen dioxide, ozone, particulates, and sulphur dioxide. The Strategy is kept under review and some standards were tightened in 2003 whilst new objectives were introduced for polycyclic aromatic hydrocarbons.

The strategy does not, however, have statutory force and imposes no direct obligations upon any regulatory body. Thus, the Environment Act 1995 provides a power to prescribe standards and/or objectives by way of regulation (ss. 87 and 91 of the 1995 Act). These regulations in turn impose certain obligations upon local authorities. The 1995 Act provides for the creation of a system of local air quality management which obliges local authorities to undertake an assessment of air quality in their areas and to take action where statutory objectives are not being met. These statutory objectives have been incorporated into the Air

Quality (England) Regulations 2000 (SI 2000/928) which set down the targets for air quality in each local area for the period between the end of 2003 to the end of 2008. The regulations set down air quality objectives for seven pollutants including sulphur dioxide, nitrogen dioxide, benzene and carbon monoxide. The standards are set in relation to the effect of the pollutant upon human health, although the effect upon the wider environment is also a material consideration.

Air Quality Limit Values Regulations 2003

The obligations under the Strategy and the 2000 Regulations are theoretically separate and distinct from the requirements to transpose and implement the air quality limit values found in the Framework Directive on ambient air quality (96/62/EC) and the various Daughter Directives (e.g. Directive 99/30/EC which sets limit values for sulphur dioxide, nitrogen dioxide and oxides of nitrogen, particulate matter, and lead). The reason for this is that local authorities may have some powers to manage air quality within their areas but this does not apply to all sources of pollutants. For example most major point sources of air pollutants will be regulated and enforced by the Environment Agency under the IPPC regime. Thus in some situations local authorities would be powerless to ensure compliance with the European standards—a position which would clearly be an incomplete trans-position of the Directives' obligations. The strict legal position is that the European stand-ards are transposed and implemented through a stand alone legal duty on the Secretary of State under the Air Quality Limit Values Regulations 2003 (SI 2003/2121). Nevertheless, the Strategy forms the cornerstone of practical implementation in particular because it outlines a range of policy responses that local authorities can use to achieve the national objectives and the actions that would be taken to meet air quality management action plans would also have the effect of meeting the European limit values.

BOX 16.6 **Technocratic regulation—the role of experts in setting air quality standards**

The setting of air quality standards in the National Air Quality Strategy is a good example of a technocratic model of the design of environmental law and policy. Although the emission limit values are laid down in European law, the Strategy sets higher limits in relation to certain pollutants. In drawing the standards in the National Air Quality Strategy, the government places a strong reliance upon the role of independent experts to advise them on the levels of air pollution at which health effects are minimal. Although the government seeks advice from a variety of bodies including the Air Quality Expert Group and the Air Quality Forum, the Expert Panel on Air Quality Standards (EPAQS), made up of both medical and air pollution experts, is seen to have the greatest influence when setting new air quality standards. Thus, EPAQS' recommendations for AQS for ozone, benzene, 1,3-butadiene and carbon monoxide were followed in both the National Air Quality Strategy and its subsequent addendum.

By taking a technocratic approach to policy making, the problem of air pollution is analysed through a scientific assessment of what is an acceptable level of pollutant. There is little or no wider public participation in the process of standard setting (although the National Air Quality

Strategy is the subject of a consultation exercise at a draft stage). Thus the technocratic approach is underpinned by the popular image of scientists determining truths that are unchallengeable.

In recent years the certainty of the scientific assessment of environmental problems and solutions has come under scrutiny precisely because scientific understanding has its own limitations and uncertainties. Of course a scientific assessment of risks, causes, and effects of something as complex as air pollution can never truly represent a single picture of a problem nor the 'right' solution. Setting environmental standards should not be purely a scientific or technocratic matter, it requires a range of factors to be taken into account to determine what is acceptable.

What then should be the role of experts in setting standards such as those found in the National Air Quality Strategy? The RCEP's 21st Report *Setting Environmental Standards* concluded that although experts had a role in informing the policy making process it could not and should not pre-empt it. Science is, however, helpful in presenting a range of possible interpretations of a problem based upon certain assumptions whilst acknowledging the inherent uncertainties. This may (or may not) lead to optional courses of action. The close relationship between science, risk, technology, economics, and public values requires formal procedures which enables each of these elements to be evaluated when selecting the right standard.

The setting of air quality standards is heavily influenced by experts without any real attempt to elicit public values (see Chapter 3). The failure to involve the public in a formal participation process means that the UK was in breach of Directive 2003/35/EC on Public Participation, Art. 2 of which makes detailed provision for public participation in amongst other things the preparation and modification of plans which implement Directive 96/62/EC on ambient air quality assessment and management. For implementation and transposition purposes, the relevant procedures are set out in the Air Quality Limit Values Regulations 2003. Amendments have been made to those regulations by the Air Quality Limit Values (Amendment) Regulations 2004 (SI 2004/2888). These amendments 'copy out' the wording of Article 2 of the Directive. Whether this makes any practical difference to the elicitation of public values in setting standards for air pollution will be a matter for assessment over time.

Meeting the National Air Quality Strategy's objectives

Where any of the statutory objectives are not likely to be met during the specified period, the relevant local authority must designate the area as an Air Quality Management Area (AQMA) and prepare an action plan indicating how the objectives are intended to be met. There are various powers which can be used to assist in meeting the objectives:

- *The use of smoke control powers under the Clean Air Act 1993.* The control of smoke from industrial and domestic premises is an important part of the national air quality strategy. Local authorities have the power to declare a smoke control area (which prohibits the emission of smoke from chimneys and the use of unauthorized fuels) in order to secure objectives contained in an action plan. In practice, however, most of the areas of the country where smoke has been a problem have already been designated as smoke control areas (see further Chapter 12).

- *The use of traffic management and planning powers.* The ability of local authorities to tackle local hotspots of poor air quality which result mainly from vehicles has been enhanced with the introduction of Local Transport Plans (LTPs). A LTP is designed to tackle the adverse effects of traffic including any deterioration of air quality. Under the Transport Act 2000 each local transport authority must produce a LTP which should set out policies for promoting public transport and charging for road users and parking. This could include such things as congestion charging and levies on car parking places. In addition to the strategic management of traffic through LTPs, there are statutory powers available to control traffic under a number of different statutes. The Road Traffic Reduction Act 1997 places a duty upon local authorities to review the levels of traffic on local roads and to produce targets for reducing numbers. This is supplemented nationally by the traffic reduction targets produced under the Road Traffic Reduction (National Targets) Act 1998. Under the Road Traffic Regulation Act 1984, local authorities have wide powers to regulate traffic under Traffic Regulation Orders (TROs) which can be used to restrict traffic in certain areas (e.g. pedestrianized areas of city centres) or even single roads. TROs can be made in order to achieve air quality objectives (s. 1(g) of the Road Traffic Regulation Act 1984). Further measures to reduce traffic and contribute to air quality improvements can be made by using traffic calming under the Highways (Traffic Calming) Regulations 1999 (SI 1999/1026) which allow local authorities to create narrow 'gateways' into urban centres.

• *The use of pollution control measures.* This covers measure such as local authority powers under the Pollution Prevention and Control (PPC) provisions and emissions from PPC installations including controls over both point source emissions and diffuse emissions such as VOCs from the storage and distribution of petrol.

• *The control of land uses under by way of planning controls.* The link between land use planning and air pollution has been recognised explicitly in Planning Policy Guidance Notes 6 and 13. The impact of a development upon air quality in an AQMA would be a material consideration which would be taken into account when considering whether to grant planning permission. In addition the designation of an AQMA would have to be taken into account when drawing up development plan policies in regional and local development plans.

Monitoring of air pollution

The effectiveness of the national air quality strategy can only be assessed with a comprehensive system for measuring pollutants in the atmosphere. Monitoring of smoke, sulphur dioxide, grit, and dust has, in fact, taken place since the early 20th century. This is unsurprising given the major impact that these pollutants have had upon health and the environment and the relatively unsophisticated methods of measurement. In 1961, the establishment of the national survey of air pollution led to a coordinated network of monitoring sites situated throughout the country. These sites concentrated on the accumulation of data on smoke and sulphur dioxide. The network was, however, unwieldy (with approximately 1,200 sites) and unreliable. Over time this network has been replaced and upgraded and the monitoring programme is now organized into 10 different networks made up of automatic and sampler-based monitoring systems.

These monitoring systems are supplemented by emissions inventories on a national and local level. The national atmospheric emissions inventory at <www.naei.org.uk> includes information and emissions estimates for a range of pollutants. The inventory is broken down into information on industry sectors and provides data on trends from 1970 onwards. Local emissions inventories are in operation in certain urban areas where specific air quality problems have been known to occur. These include West Yorkshire, West Midlands, Greater Manchester, London, and Glasgow. The information found in the inventories assists with the identification of problems and cost effective solutions.

There are specific and separate requirements for the monitoring and dissemination of information on ozone levels. The Ozone Monitoring and Information Regulations 1994 (SI 1994/440) implemented the EC Directive on Air Pollution by Ozone (92/72). The Regulations require the establishment of a monitoring network, the dissemination of information, and a system whereby the public are warned when excessive levels of ozone are in the atmosphere. These warnings should be communicated as soon as possible and on a sufficiently wide scale to enable the public to take precautionary measures. The warnings should contain details of the area affected, the length of time that levels are likely to be excessive and precautionary measures which should be taken.

The introduction and expansion of the systems for monitoring and disseminating information on air pollution has been widely welcomed but the quality and accuracy of past monitoring has been criticized strongly. The main criticisms have centred around the selection and quantity of sites. The effectiveness of any monitoring network is primarily dependent upon the location of the monitoring equipment. It has been argued that the monitoring sites are not generally located in areas of high exposure and therefore give a false impression of levels of pollution. Also, although coverage of monitoring sites is spreading there are still large gaps, particularly in some areas of heavy industry and traffic. The introduction of a national air quality strategy based around specific standards and objectives means that the base data provided by the monitoring system has to be credible and sufficiently broad to indicate true levels of improvement.

The control of emissions from motor vehicles

The effect of transport on the environment is varied. There are obvious effects such as emissions, noise, land-take for roads and the use of raw materials (petrol, diesel, in addition to manufacturing materials). Emissions from vehicles are, however, probably the most significant issue which needs to be regulated and controlled.

The problems of pollution from motor vehicles was acknowledged as significant in the RCEP's First Report (Cmnd 4585, 1971) where the Royal Commission warned of the dangers of ignoring the environmental implications of traffic growth. With growth forecasts for road traffic of over 140 per cent between 1988 and 2025 the original warnings have taken on a repetitive nature. In particular, the RCEP's Eighteenth Report on *Transport and the Environment* (Cm 2674, 1994) set out eight key objectives which were intended to make transport policy more sustainable. In relation to atmospheric pollution this included targets for air quality and the reduction of carbon dioxide emissions.

The law in relation to the control of emissions from motor vehicles is under constant review and too detailed to be covered, other than in principle. Most controls target product standards in relation to vehicle-type approval, specified emission limits from vehicles, the content of fuel and maintenance tests. Most limits have their origin within EC legislation (see above).

When a new motor vehicle is produced it must comply with all relevant standards, including EC emission limits. The Motor Vehicles (Type Approval) (Great Britain) Regulations (SI 1994/981) sets out type-approval procedures which are applied to specimen examples of vehicles prior to general sale.

The Road Vehicle (Construction and Use) Regulations, are a series of regulations which set out requirements in reaction to a variety of construction details, including catalytic convertors, the use of unleaded petrol, and emission levels for vehicles in use. In particular, the annual MOT tests (and, more recently, roadside checks) have standards for smoke and carbon monoxide which must not be exceeded.

CHAPTER SUMMARY

1   Controls over air pollution have a long history although the challenges have shifted from local controls to regional issues such as transboundary pollution to global problems such as ozone depletion and climate change.

2   Air pollution problems are complex and require a range of different responses. This means that no single approach will be successful.

3   International problems such as transboundary pollution, climate change, and ozone depletion have been addressed by the international community through various negotiated agreements. The normal pattern for these has been based around an initial framework convention which identifies the problem and calls for cooperation and research, followed by more detailed Protocols which contain specific measures to address the problem.

4   Climate change poses very serious challenges to the international community requiring the balancing of the interests of developed and developing nations. This has been addressed through the adoption of a 'common but differentiated responsibility' approach to the sharing of commitments to reduce greenhouse gas emissions.

5   After a relatively slow start the EC has taken a leading role in negotiating international conventions on behalf of its Member States.

6   The EC is increasingly the most important force in determining new air quality standards nationally. The main driver is a framework strategy on air quality which is supplemented by Daughter Directives which specify air quality limits for particular substances.

7   There are a range of further directives which address emissions from different sources such as industry, power stations and transport.

8   The EC is adopting new innovative policy instruments to address air pollution problems. The use of voluntary agreements with car manufacturers and EU wide emissions trading schemes stand out as the first of their type.

9   The legal duty to comply with European air quality standards rests with the Secretary of State for the Environment, Food and Rural Affairs but in practice responsibility for air pollution rests with a combination of pollution control powers operated by the Environment Agency and local authorities and air quality management powers held by local authorities.

10 Domestic air quality law is dominated by the *National Air Quality Strategy* and associated legislation. The Strategy contains two standards for identified pollutants: a general target standard which forms a long term objective for policies and legislation; and an alert threshold which triggers the need for specific remedial action when exceeded.

11 The strategy is met through a system of local air quality management which obliges local authorities to undertake an assessment of air quality in their areas and to take action where statutory objectives are not being achieved.

12 Local authorities also have control over the emissions of dark smoke and fumes under the Clean Air legislation.

13 The UK has adopted new policy instruments to help reduce greenhouse gas emissions. These include economic instruments such as the Climate Change Levy and the UK Emissions Trading Scheme and voluntary agreements in the form of Climate Change Agreements.

14 Product standards are used to address emissions from transport. These mostly consist of specification standards which are designed to reduced exhaust emission or the content of fuel.

Q QUESTIONS

1 What types of regulatory instruments are used to control air quality and air pollution? Which do you think are most effective and why?

2 What types of standards are used in air quality legislation?

3 What challenges do law and policy makers have to address when faced with the issue of Climate Change? What do you think are the consequences of taking a 'common but differentiated responsibility' to the problem?

4 Albert lives in Acacia Avenue in a major urban area in the South of England. Acacia Avenue is used as a 'rat run' for cars travelling into the city centre. During hot periods during the summer the levels of carbon monoxide, particulates, and sulphur dioxide in the air are much higher than those specified in the national air quality strategy. Albert suffers from bad asthma and has complained to his local authority about the situation. They say that these are peaks and that the standards are only breached during the summer months. The authority has also pointed out that Acacia Avenue has better air quality when compared to other urban areas in the same city and has refused to take any further action. The whole area is in breach of standards laid down in EC Directive 1996/92/EC on ambient air quality assessment and management and the relevant standards laid down in various daughter directives.

Advise Albert on the legal obligations of the local authority and central government in relation to this poor air quality.

FURTHER READING

Historical background and general texts

An interesting overview of the historical background to air pollution in the UK can be found in P. Brimblecombe, *The Big Smoke: History of Air Pollution in London Since Mediaeval Times* (London: Routledge, 1987) which traces legislative developments in the context of social, industrial, and economic change. Another introduction to the issues which also considers the challenges for the future is *The Clean Air Revolution: 1952–2052* (NSCA, 2003). D. Hughes, N. Parpworth, and J. Upson, *Air Pollution Law and Regulation* (Bristol: Jordans, 1998) is now somewhat dated but covers the relevant statutory materials in the area and deals with international, European and domestic sources of law. For a less legal and more policy based approach, the *National Air Quality Strategy for England, Scotland, Wales and Northern Ireland* (Cm 4548, 2000) covers all of the issues in a reader friendly fashion.

International Law

There is a lot of literature on the international aspects of air pollution. Although R. Churchill and D. Freestone (eds), *International Law and Global Climate Change* (The Hague: Kluwer, 1991) is out-of-date, it provides a good introduction to the introduction and agreement of the Climate Change Treaty. If you want to understand the complexity of negotiating an international agreement with insights of the role of governmental and non-governmental actors you should read I. Mintzer and J. Leonard (eds), *Negotiating Climate Change: Inside Story of the Rio Convention* (Cambridge: Cambridge University Press, 2004). This book reveals the extent to which principles are traded and compromise attained. O. Yoshida, *The International Legal Regime for the Protection of the Stratospheric Ozone Layer* (The Hague: Kluwer 2001) is study of the effectiveness of international environmental law in circumstances where there is sufficient political will to achieve specified objectives. P. Okowa, *State Responsibility for Transboundary Air Pollution in International Law*, (Oxford: Oxford University Press, 2000) provides a general overview of the topic. Articles on specific aspects of international law on air pollution can be found in: R. Churchill et al, 'The 1994 UN ECE Sulphur Protocol' (1995) 8 JEL 169; D. French, 'Kyoto Protocol to the 1992 UN Framework Convention on Climate Change' (1997) 9 JEL 227. One of the challenges of international environmental law is the practical implementation of relatively sophisticated instruments across many jurisdictions. There are a number of articles which focus on this aspect. These help to clarify the way in which Treaties work in the real world and flag up some of the problems of ensuring effectiveness. J. Werksman, 'Compliance and the Kyoto Protocol: Building a Backbone into a "Flexible" Regime' (1998) 9 YbIEL 48. P. Lawrence, 'International Legal Regulation for Protection of the Ozone Layer: Some Problems of Implementation' (1990) 2 JEL 17; and P. Lawrence, 'Technology Transfer Funds and the Law: Recent Amendments to the Montreal Protocol on Substances that Deplete the Ozone Layer' (1992) 4 JEL 15.

Other more specialized articles

The broad spread of subject matter in this chapter means that there are a number of articles which whilst not of general interest may be useful if you are looking at a particular topic in depth. These include B. Richardson and K. Chanwai, 'The UK's Climate Change Levy: Is it Working?', (2003) JEL 39, M. Peeters, 'Emissions trading as a new dimension to European environmental law: the political agreement of the European Council on greenhouse gas allowance trading' (2003) ELR 82 and G. Volpi and S. Singer, 'Will voluntary agreements at EU level deliver on environmental objectives? Lessons from the agreement with the automotive industry WWF' Discussion Paper, 2000 available at <www.uneptie.org/outreach/vi/reports/wwf.pdf> provide a good starting point for further research.

@ WEB LINKS

The DEFRA links page gives access to a number of good sources of information on air pollutants, their sources and relevant legislation. The main access point is <www.defra.gov.uk> but there are further links to climate change and air quality pages. In the former you will find the UK's Climate

Change Programme <www.defra.gov.uk/environment/climatechange/index.htm> and in the latter there are links to the National Air Quality Archive (<www.airquality.co.uk/>) which provides air quality statistics and 24-hour forecasts and the National Atmospheric Emissions Inventory (<www.naei.org.uk/a>) which provides aggregated data on emissions from various sources including cars, power stations and industrial plant.

The RCEP's web page at <www.rcep.org.uk> has access to two reports which consider air pollution. The 22nd Report, *Energy—The Changing Climate* is available at <www.rcep.org.uk/new-energy.htm>. This report contains an in-depth study of the links between energy use and climate change. The special report on *The Environment Effects of Civil Aircraft in Flight* highlights a significant threat to air quality from a relatively unregulated source. The full text is available at <www.rcep.org.uk/avreport.htm>. The National Society for Clean Air has a range of links and materials on its web page at <www.nsca.org.uk>.

The European Commission site has detailed information on European legislation on different aspects of air pollution at <europa.eu.int/scadplus/leg/en/s15004.htm>. More general information on European policy initiatives on air quality, pollution and climate change can be found through the relevant links at <europa.eu.int/comm/environment/policy_en.htm>. The home of the European Pollutant Emissions Register can be found at <www.eper.cec.eu.int/eper/>.

The best site for up-to-date information on the international aspects of climate change is the official United Nations site at <www.unfcc.int>. Here you will find the full text of the Treaty and Protocol, information on ratification and resources on the progress made post ratification through the various meetings, Conferences of the Parties (CoPs), National Reports and other technical information. The Inter-Governmental Panel on Climate Change also has a good selection of resources on its web page at <www.ipcc.ch/>. A third potential source of information on climate change is available at <www.undp.org/energy/climate.htm>. Similar sources on the Montreal Protocol can be found at <www.undp.org/seed/eap/montreal/> and the Geneva Convention at <www.unece.org/env/lrtap/welcome.html>.

17 Contaminated land

→ **Overview**

This chapter deals with the clean up of historic sources of pollution. Over recent years there has been a recognition that regulatory intervention is required to deal with the consequences of sources of historic pollution over and above the usual continuing controls over polluting activities. This presents a number of significant challenges such as when should clean up be required, to what level and for what purposes? But probably the most significant of all of these issues is the identification of the party or parties who should pay for the consequences of historic pollution.

Some pre-existing liability systems provide a partial answer to the problem. For example, private law mechanisms such as nuisance and negligence can impose liability for certain heads of damage (see further Chapter 11). In other cases statutory schemes can be used to clean up certain sources of contamination. But the development of liability rules under private law principles has been discouraged whilst other areas of pollution control regulation only address the problem of clean up in a partial and not wholly efficient manner.

As a result we have a patchwork system of liability rules spread across a wide range of areas which address specific problems of contamination and clean up. There was a need to clarify the extent of these powers and to identify any gaps in the legislative patchwork and in this chapter we will be considering the set of laws introduced to do just that. Although the focus of this chapter is relatively narrow (i.e. on the regulation of the clean up of historically contaminated land) it is important to always bear in mind that the basic building blocks of statutory liability for cleaning up pollution can often be found in subject specific legislation which are addressed in different chapters in Part III.

After studying this chapter you should be able to:

✔ Understand and evaluate a key example of statutory environmental liability within the United Kingdom.
✔ Understand the basic framework of the allocation and apportionment of liability for historic contamination under Part IIA of the Environmental Protection Act 1990.
✔ Evaluate one example of the implementation of the 'Polluter Pays' principle.
✔ Understand the definition of 'contaminated land' within the context of Part IIA of the Environmental Protection Act 1990.
✔ Analyse the impact of sustainable development upon the setting of environmental standards.
✔ Assess the role of scientific standard setting in environmental liability regimes.
✔ Distinguish between continuing controls and retrospective liability.
✔ Assess the interaction of various sources of environmental law including primary and secondary legislation with policy and technical guidance.

Introduction

Why does this chapter deal with 'contaminated land' when it would seem consistent with other parts of this book to deal with the laws controlling 'land pollution'? Unlike other areas of pollution control where there is a distinction between 'contamination' which denotes the presence of a foreign substance and 'pollution' which is used to describe harm or threats of harm, land contamination and land pollution are generally considered to be synonymous. Moreover, there is a significant distinction which needs to be drawn between land pollution which is created by existing activities, regulated under pollution control licences and contamination which is the result of historic activity which falls outside present day controls.

The presence of 'contamination' in land does not necessarily lead to harm, whether actual or potential, to the environment or human health. The existence of contamination needs, therefore, to be put into some form of context against which the need to intervene and require clean up can be assessed. Relevant factors include the nature of the polluting substance; the presence and identity of a 'target' which is being affected by the contamination (e.g. humans, nature conservation, or property interests); and the costs and benefits of carrying out clean up works. It is in this sense that the definition of 'contamination' reflects some of the problems with the definition of 'pollution'[1] in that scientific, economic and political factors need to be considered in deciding whether any regulatory control is required. In deciding to take action against contamination, the policy maker and the rule maker must identify the point at which contamination poses an unacceptable risk.

Contaminated land and environmental liability

Liability for environmental harm can take many forms. In some cases, the behaviour which causes contamination is a criminal offence, in others civil liability might arise through nuisance or negligence if damage to a third party were to occur. In some of these situations the law can require the clean up and reinstatement of the environment although the use of voluntary clean up is widespread. Because of this reliance on voluntary action, many of the statutory clean up powers are only used as a fallback position if mandatory action is required. For example, where a criminal offence has been committed, the Environment Agency may negotiate with a polluter in respect of clean up with the threat of compulsory action if necessary. Liability for this type of clean up and reinstatement of contaminated land is a good example of a class of liability which only covers *environmental* harm (as opposed to property damage).

This chapter provides a backdrop to some of the central issues of environmental liability. For example, it is clear that concepts such as the polluter pays principle are not without some difficulty when they are translated into 'real world' rules. Just who is 'the polluter'? What if there is more than one 'polluter', should liability be shared equally, proportionately or should one polluter be made to pay for all? What part should fault play in determining who pays for the consequences of pollution? Should 'polluters' avoid liability if they can

---

1. See W. Howarth [1992] 56 MLR 171.

demonstrate that they were using 'state of the art' pollution prevention systems or were complying with all relevant legislation when the pollution was caused? At what level should 'contamination' be deemed to become 'harmful' enough to require the intervention of law? Just as the decision about what action to take and when to take it is political (with a small 'p'), so is the decision about who should be made to pay for it. Although the polluter pays principle is the foundation of most of the environmental liability systems which deal with land contamination, the characteristics which distinguish particular types of contamination clarify issues about the principle such as whether it is based around fairness or blame.

Current contamination vs historic contamination

(a) Overlapping controls

There are many powers available to prevent and remedy the effect of current contamination. In many cases, 'contamination' is synonymous with pollution and the relevant pollution control regimes apply. For example, where contaminating substances migrate into water, water pollution occurs and the offences and powers of clean up dealing with water pollution are applicable. Box 17.1 sets out the main statutory provisions which deal with contamination which are controlled under existing pollution control regimes. The powers which deal with current contamination do not, however, deal with all forms of contamination. Historic contamination caused before the introduction of comprehensive pollution control regimes falls outside many of the continuing controls set out in Box 17.1 (although some can be used in certain circumstances).

These regimes create a web of liability mechanisms to deal with environmental harm caused by contamination arising out of current activities. These must be placed alongside instruments which create civil liabilities and private law mechanisms such as nuisance and negligence. The breadth of these different mechanisms to deal with 'contamination' reflects one of the recurring themes of this book, that there may be more than one available 'tool' to deal with an environmental problem such as contamination and the key issue is the selection of the most appropriate tool to respond to any given set of circumstances. In some cases, there may be a combination of measures adopted.

(b) The problems of overlapping controls

These overlaps present two different problems. There are difficulties of coordination when there are two concurrent powers available to two different regulators. For example, where pollution of controlled waters is being, or is likely to be, caused from contaminated land, the Environment Agency and the relevant local authority both possess powers to require clean up (under WRA 1991, s. 161A and Part IIA respectively). There is a Memorandum of Understanding which governs how the powers will be used.[2] In summary, where a site is identified as being contaminated land under Part IIA, a remediation notice will normally be most appropriate as it will be the most effective method of ensuring that the 'significant pollution linkage' no longer exists (see below). On the other hand, where the source of

---

2. See *Working Better Together Protocol Series No 5: Land Contamination*, Local Government Association and Environment Agency (2003).

BOX 17.1 **Powers to control current contamination**

Overlapping power	Powers available to deal with contamination	Relevant Statutory Provisions	Who is responsible for clean up?	Can a remediation notice be served?	Is contamination a criminal offence?	Other comments
Integrated Pollution Prevention and Control (IPPC)	Remedy contamination or harm caused by a breach of an IPPC condition (or in some cases Integrated Pollution Control authorizations)	Pollution Prevention and Control Regulations 2000, reg. 26 EPA, s. 27	The holder of the permit or authorization	No (s. 78YB(1))	Yes, where contamination is caused by a breach of a condition of a permit or the implied BATNEEC condition.	A requirement to carry out an investigation into the site conditions to provide a benchmark which can be used to assess clean up requirements when the installation is closed. Additional powers available to vary, and enforce against conditions of permits, see regs 23–26 PPC Regs 2000
Waste Management Licensing	Enforce against breaches of conditions found in a waste management licence	EPA, ss. 35–38	The holder of the waste management licence in question	No (s. 78YB(2))	Yes, where waste is deposited, treated or kept in the absence of or not in accordance with a waste management licence, see s. 33, EPA	The licence has to be current even if the waste disposal activities have ceased. Additional powers/duties to supervise and vary conditions of a waste management licence
Unlawfully deposited waste	Require the removal of illegally deposited waste or to remove waste and remedy harm caused	EPA, s. 59	The occupier of the land on which waste is unlawfully deposited.	No (s. 78YB(3))	Yes, as the waste will have been deposited without a waste management licence, see s. 33, EPA	Arguably this only applies to waste deposited after 1 April 1994 (i.e. the implementation of the waste management licensing regime). The decision in *Van de Walle* suggests that inadvertent deposits of material (e.g. from leaking pipes) is waste and should therefore be cleaned up under this power (see p. 582)

Water Pollution	Powers to serve a works notice prevent or clean up contamination where there is or is likely to be pollution of controlled waters	WRA s. 161–161D	Any person who caused or knowingly permitted the pollution of the controlled waters	Yes	Yes, as it will be causing or knowingly permitting polluting matter to enter controlled waters, see s. 85, WRA	The powers to serve a works notice and a remediation notice are concurrent. Additional powers available to enforce against breaches of and vary existing discharge consents
Statutory Nuisances	Power to abate a statutory nuisance as defined	EPA, ss. 80–81	Any person responsible for the nuisance	Yes	No, only where abatement notice is not complied with within the time limit specified, see s. 80(4), EPA	Where land is in a 'contaminated state' it is excluded from the definition of a statutory nuisance and thus an abatement notice cannot be served
Town and Country Planning	Power to impose planning conditions to clean up contamination prior to carrying out development. Also Breach of condition notice	TCPA, ss. 71(9), 187A	The person responsible for the breach	Yes	Yes, where there has been a breach of a planning condition (e.g. in relation to places of storage). Breach of condition is a criminal offence, see s. 187A, TCPA 1990	The use of conditions to address contamination and the role of the planning system in helping to clean up contaminated sites is dealt with in Circular 2/2000 and PPS 23
Amenity Notices	Power to require steps to be taken to remedy the condition of land which adversely affects the amenity of their area by serving an appropriate notice on the owner or occupier of the land	Town and Country Planning Act 1990, s. 215	Owner/occupier of the land	Yes	No, only where the amenity notice is not complied with, see s. 215 TCP	Tends to be used in respect of visual disamenity.

pollution has completely entered the controlled waters, the works notice powers are likely to be more appropriate as the site cannot be designated as contaminated land under Part IIA.

The second problem is the overlap between the powers to clean up unlawfully deposited waste and the Part IIA powers. The British approach to the problem of contamination from different sources has been to have separate but parallel systems of control. In distinguishing between current and historic sources of contamination, the risk based approach of Part IIA is different from the strict approaches taken to breaches of licences or other pollution caused by current activities. The European case of *Van der Walle and others* (Case C-1/03) has cast some doubt on this British approach. In that case the ECJ held that waste oil and petrol which had leaked unintentionally from underground storage tanks in Belgium were waste for the purposes of the Waste Framework Directive (see further p. 582).

This poses the problem that if accidental contamination is waste, a risk-based approach to clean up is insufficient to transpose the requirements of the Waste Framework Directive. Under Part IIA powers, remediation is only required when there is significant harm and only to the extent necessary to remove that significant harm. This is a much lower standard than that demanded by the Waste Framework Directive which requires the general prevention of pollution and harm. On the other hand, clean up powers under waste management legislation available under section 59 of the EPA 1990 are also inadequate as this power only applies to active deposits or deposits which are knowingly caused or knowingly permitted. In the case of inadvertent leaks or spillages the element of active participation or knowledge may be absent. Consequently, even with a seemingly complex system of overlapping powers to address both current and historic contamination from waste there are apparent defects in the transposition of European waste law. It is worth noting that it is presumed that this gap would only apply to 'waste' deposited after 1 May 1994 when the European definition of waste was transposed into UK law under the Waste Management Licensing Regulations 1994. Arguably historic contamination before that date could be cleaned up on a risk-based approach.

(c) Historic contamination and retrospective liability

One of the distinguishing features of historic contamination as compared to current contamination is the lawfulness of the actions which caused the presence of the contaminative substances. In all cases of current contamination, the actions of the polluter when causing the contamination are unlawful either of themselves or following the administrative action (indeed the unlawfulness of current contamination is axiomatic). In a good proportion of cases of historic contamination, the causal acts will have been lawful. Where contamination arises from acts which were committed lawfully many years ago, any current laws introduced which impose liability (criminal, civil, or statutory) upon the party who caused or permitted the contamination would be retrospective or retroactive in effect.

In many circumstances, retrospective and retroactive can and are used interchangeably. Occasionally, retroactive can be used in a specific sense to mean weakly retrospective. This would include liability rules which were in force at the time of the lawful act but which can apply retrospectively as there has been a change in the *standards* which trigger the liability. For example, there might be legislation which banned the presence of a substance X in water at a certain level. At the time of the act which caused the presence of that substance the level of the substance was below the statutory limit. In five years time, the standard is changed and now the level of X is above the statutory limit. The original legislation may not have had retrospective effect until the standards were changed. In this very specific sense, retroactive liability might be thought of as more legitimate than generally retrospective legislation as the basis for liability existed before the act even if the trigger standard had evolved after the act.

Retrospective laws can be defined as laws that have effect on actions which took place before the law came into force, for example, by imposing sanctions upon conduct that was lawful when it occurred. There are many fundamental objections to the imposition of retrospective legislation. Morally, those that are subject to a law have a legitimate expectation that they will have some notice of the law, so that they can understand the consequences of their actions and exercise their own judgment about what they intend to do in order to comply with the law at any given time. Politically, retrospective legislation can be used as a tool to selectively punish or reward certain identifiable parties. Whilst it is not unknown in modern environmental legislation (e.g. both the End of Life Vehicles Directive and the WEEE Directive require producers to recover and recycle items which were put onto the market before the implementation of the Directive), there is still a requirement to have some strong justification for the imposition of retrospective liability.

By its very nature, historic contamination is the consequence of actions which occurred in the past, sometimes many years distant. In the case of historically contaminated land, the unfairness of retrospective liability is arguably balanced by the need to address the long-term consequences of contamination and the implications for sustainable development should land be left to present environmental problems for many years into the future. The Government has introduced a very complex system for allocating liability (or paying) for the clean up of historically contaminated land. The complexity of the system reflects the Government's attempts to balance the need to introduce a comprehensive and efficient system which is designed to clean up as many historically contaminated sites as possible as against the inherent unfairness of a retrospective liability and retroactive standards (i.e. imposing trigger standards which have increased).

These 'balancing' features include:

- risk based criteria for assessing whether land should be identified as 'contaminated';
- rules which give precedence to liability allocation arrangements between private parties (see further Box 17.13);
- exclusion for certain specified classes of parties;
- exclusion where the allocation of liability would cause hardship.

The European Commission has addressed the unfairness of introducing retrospective legislation by excluding historic contamination from the scope of the Environmental Liability Directive (04/35). Under Article 17 all environmental damage caused by substances released into the environment, or actions carried out, before 30 June 2007, is excluded from the scope of liability under the Directive.

Contaminated land in European and international law

In comparison to other areas of environmental regulation, there have been no significant European initiatives in relation to historically contaminated land.[3] A distinction here should be made between general measures dealing with the clean up of pollution from existing activities and more specific measures designed to address contamination from past uses. Numerous directives contain clean up or environmental restoration provisions. For example, the Groundwater Directive (80/68) is designed to prevent the entry of certain contaminants into groundwater (see p. 733) and breaches of the Drinking Water Directive's quality parameters are used as a trigger for defining more harmful categories of contaminated land in domestic legislation. A further distinction should be made between liability instruments for historic contamination and policy developments in relation to soil protection and the encouragement of 'brownfield' development. On this more general level, the European Commission is moving towards a Soil Strategy as one of seven 'thematic strategies' foreseen under the EU's 6th Environment Action Programme.[4] The strategy is, however, aimed more at current agricultural pollution rather than historic industrial contamination and given the broad nature of the strategy is unlikely to develop into anything other than an information gathering exercise with suggested best practice measures.[5] One consequence of this activity is that there is an increased emphasis on soil protection within domestic policy with the production of the *First Soil Action Plan for England 2004–6*.[6]

At the international level, the 1993 Lugano Convention on Civil Liability for Damage Resulting from Activities Dangerous to the Environment imposes strict liability on 'operators' for environmental harm arising from the operation of certain specified dangerous activities including waste treatment and disposal. The operation of this convention, is, however, limited for two main reasons. First, the Convention does not apply to historic damage (i.e. before the date the Convention came into force) and secondly, neither the UK nor the EC are signatories.

Although there have been few initiatives to address contaminated land at a European or international level, individual countries have fairly sophisticated liability schemes which address the problem of clean up and restoration of contamination.[7] In the United States, the Resource Conservation and Recovery Act 1976 (RCRA) gave the US Environmental Protection Agency (USEPA) the power to recover the costs of cleaning up hazardous waste where there was an imminent and substantial risk to human health or the environment. Under RCRA, liability was strict, retrospective and joint and several although it only applied when a financially responsible operator or owner could be identified. RCRA was augmented by the introduction of the Comprehensive Environmental Response Compensation and Liability Act 1981 (CERCLA) which was itself amended by the Superfund Amendments and Reauthorization Act 1986. CERCLA introduced the idea of the 'Superfund' which was paid for by

---

3. Although see A. Layard, (2004) Env L Rev 97 which suggests a move toward the 'Europeanization' of contaminated land liability.

4. See *Towards a Thematic Strategy for Soil Protection* COM (2002) 179.

5. See G. van Calster (2004) 16 JEL 3.

6. DEFRA, (2004).

7. For a comprehensive survey of such measures see the Comparative Study on Environmental Liability at <europa.eu.int/comm/environment/liability/legalstudy.htm>.

a contribution from polluting industries, mainly the chemical and oil industries, although this was later supplemented by income from general taxes. This Superfund enabled the USEPA to undertake clean up works and to recover the costs of doing so from the polluter after the works had been carried out.

What is contaminated land?

Although the phrase 'contaminated land' has become somewhat of a term of art, it is far from being clear and precise.[8] Contaminated 'land' is often used as shorthand for contamination in land where the presence of that contamination may have a harmful impact on other environmental media including water and even the atmosphere. The presence of contamination poses threats to humans, property and the wider environment (see Box 17.2). The key here is that in the absence of such threats, contamination, i.e. the presence of alien substances in land, is less likely to be the subject of regulatory intervention.

BOX 17.2 The threats posed by contaminated land

Explosions—The Loscoe incident[9]

Methane gas caused by the breakdown of materials in an old landfill migrated into the basement of a house in Loscoe, Derbyshire. When the central heating came on at 6.30 am the flame ignited the gas causing an explosion which destroyed the house and injured three people.

Toxic health effects—Love Canal[10]

In 1892 William T. Love proposed digging a canal to connect the upper and lower parts of the Niagara River near Niagara Falls, New York. The canal was never completed. However, from 1920 to 1953, the canal was used to dump hazardous wastes. In 1953, the canal area was presumed safe, covered with soil, and sold to the Niagara Falls city school board for $1.00 for the purpose of developing a school and houses. During the 1970s residents reported foul smelling sludge and liquids seeping into their basements and gardens. At the same time there were recorded higher levels of miscarriages, birth defects, and illnesses. For example, 56 per cent of children born between 1974 and 1978 suffered birth defects, and there were 300 per cent increases in the rate of urinary tract diseases and miscarriages. Eventually, having determined that there were over 200 hazardous substances dumped in the ground and that the level of these substances in the soil and air were dangerous, officials decided that Love Canal was a health hazard and evacuated the area.

---

8. See, e.g., different definitions of the 'contaminated land' in EPA 1990, s. 78A(2); and the NATO Committee on Challenges to a Modern Society.

9. See House of Commons Environment Select Committee, *Contaminated Land*, First Report, 1989–90 Session.

10. The Love Canal Collection—<www.ublib.buffalo.edu/libraries/projects/lovecanal/>.

Toxic environmental effects—groundwater pollution at Steetley, Hertfordshire

A chemical company operated on a site at Steetley, Hertfordshire until 1980. Contamination from the site was found to be polluting the groundwater with bromates which is a known human carcinogen. The site was cleaned up and developed into a 66-home estate. The local water supplier undertook testing in 2000 and found that the groundwater was polluted with bromate at some 20 times the standard required by statutory drinking water standards. The local borehole used to supply drinking water from groundwaters in the area was taken out of service pending remediation of the contaminated area.[11]

Toxic effects upon property—*Hamilton v Papakura DC and Watercare Limited*

The Hamiltons were Cherry Tomato growers in New Zealand. In 1995, their crop of tomatoes was found dead on the vine. The water supply was sold to the Hamiltons by the District Council who in turn obtained it from Watercare who was the main bulk water supplier for the area. It was alleged that herbicide had found its way into the water supply after Watercare had employed contractors to spray weeds in the area of the lake where the water supply originated. The level of herbicides in the water was high but below the level required for drinking water under New Zealand law. In 2002 the Privy Council held that the District Council and Watercare were not liable for the damage caused by the herbicide contamination as the duty placed upon water suppliers was only to supply water which complied with drinking water standards. Thus establishing a distinction between contamination giving rise to a risk to humans and that giving rise to a risk to property (the latter being deemed to be unforeseeable).[12]

The classification of land as 'contaminated' can have formal significance with legal sanctions. On the other hand, land contamination can have little consequence in terms of environmental harm. The juxtaposition of these two ideas is extremely important as the use of the phrase 'contaminated land' needs to be assessed very carefully. When the phrase occurs, it requires some further investigation, is it being used in a formal sense to indicate a specific legal consequence or is it merely being used as a shorthand for saying 'land in which there may be contamination which may or may not give rise to environmental harm or risk of environmental harm'?

The formal classification of land as 'contaminated' may have detrimental consequences in terms of the effective and productive use of resources. These consequences include the effects of blight and stigma which would cover loss in the value of the land and an inability to sell. These phrases can often be interchanged when used in the context of contamination. They are used here, however, to represent two different facets of the same issue. Where there are areas of land which have been subject to potentially contaminative uses, the risk of contamination is often associated with all of the land in that area regardless of whether it is actually contaminated. This presumption of contamination can have a blighting effect which can sterilize land which would otherwise be brought into effective use.[13]

---

11. (2002) ENDS Report 339, 3.
12. [2002] UKPC 57.
13. See, e.g. M. Lee, (1998) Env Liability 56.

There is a slightly different problem with land which has been identified as being contaminated but has been subjected to clean up works. In such cases the land may continue to be stigmatized with the label of 'contaminated' with the consequence that it too may be sterilized in terms of a productive future use[14]. The main issue here is whether such stigma leads to a recoverable loss or damage, for example, where the sale of land falls through because of past contamination which has subsequently been cleaned up (see e.g. *Blue Circle v Ministry of Defence* [1999] Env LR 22).

BOX 17.3 **Other terminology for 'contaminated land'**

There are many definitions used for land which is contaminated and there is a degree of confusion about the distinctions between the various classes. Note that none of these classes has any legal significance although they are used a great deal in policy documents

Land affected by contamination

This is a much wider term and covers any land which may have contamination but which does not qualify as formal Part IIA land, e.g. land where contamination exists but it has not formally been determined by the local authority under Part IIA, or it has been inspected but a significant pollution linkage does not exist.

Brownfield land

This can also be referred to as 'previously developed' land, which is taken from PPG 3 on Housing which defines such land as:

'Previously developed land is that which is or was occupied by a permanent structure (excluding agricultural or forestry buildings), and associated fixed surface infrastructure.'

Derelict land

Defined by the Department of the Environment in the survey of Derelict Land as 'land that is so damaged by industrial or other development such that it is incapable of beneficial use without treatment'.[15]

Greenfield land

Covers land that has not previously been developed; its current uses are usually for agriculture, forestry, recreation, or nature conservation.[16]

---

14. For a good explanation of the problems with stigma damages see J. Johnson, 15 UCLA J Envtl L & Pol'y 185, 193 and J. Young, 52 SCLR 409.

15. Taken from the National Land Use Database published annually.

16. PPG3, Annex C.

The development of the law dealing with historically contaminated land

The debate about the regulation of historically contaminated land is relatively recent, reflecting the fact that, in contrast to other areas of pollution control, the problems of soil contamination are comparatively well concealed and the legal issues (particularly in respect of liability for historic contamination) arguably more complex and controversial. In the 1970s, during the period of the modernization of pollution control regulation, the issue of soil pollution was only addressed indirectly, i.e. through the introduction of tighter controls to prevent new contamination arising (e.g. see s. 16 under the waste disposal provisions of COPA 1974 which controlled the removal of unlawfully deposited waste). In addition, although there were a number of incidents which were connected to land contamination (see e.g. the incident at Loscoe discussed in Box 17.2), there was no perceived need to introduce reactive legislation to respond to a public outcry or a specific set of circumstances which demanded a quick regulatory response. Finally, the impact of European law in the area of land contamination was relatively subdued (as discussed above). Thus although there were individual attempts to regulate new sources of contamination, it was not until 1990 that there was any serious attempt to introduce a comprehensive system of controls over historically contaminated land in the UK (see Box 17.4).

Since that time there have been a number of unsuccessful steps towards the full implementation of the system but the final 'package' of rules (including regulations and technical guidance) was finally introduced in England in April 2000 with Scotland and Wales slightly later. The rules provide a complicated system for defining and identifying historically contaminated land; for prioritizing action to clean up sites which give rise to the greatest risks; for identifying what works need to be undertaken to deal with those risks; for allocating and apportioning the cost of carrying out the works amongst 'appropriate persons'; and for making those 'appropriate persons' carry out those works where necessary. As such, it provides a very good example of a relatively self contained system for environmental liability.

The statutory framework in Part IIA of the EPA 1990 sets out the structure of the system to deal with contaminated land. There is supplementary secondary legislation in the form of the Contaminated Land (England) Regulations 2000 (SI 2000/227) with corresponding regulations in the devolved countries (the references to regulations in the rest of this chapter refer to the English regulations). These regulations deal with certain aspects of the contaminated land regime including: the definition of 'special sites'; the detailed arrangements for remediation notices including content, service and appeals; and public registers.

In practice, however, the most important elements of the new system are to be found in tertiary rules which can be found in Circular 2/2000, *Contaminated Land: Implementation of Part IIA of the Environmental Protection Act 1990*. The Circular sets out the context for the operation of the rest of the legislation and provides a general description of how the system operates. It provides detailed guidance on risk assessment, the allocation and apportionment of liability and the correct approach to the strategic identification of sites. There are parts of the Circular which are capable of binding the enforcing authorities. In particular, enforcing authorities have to 'act in accordance with' certain aspects of the guidance (this covers the definition and identification of contaminated land and the allocation and apportionment of liability), whilst they must 'have regard to' the remainder (this covers the

BOX 17.4 **Contaminated Land—timeline**

Year	Key Events
1989	The House of Commons Environment Committee produced a Report on 'Contaminated Land' recommending the abolition of the 'buyer beware' rule in relation to the sale and purchase of land so that the seller was under an obligation to inform the buyer of any defects associated with the land (including contamination).
	The governmental response was a consultation paper, *Let the Buyer be Better Informed*, which proposed a register of land which had been used for certain categories of potentially contaminative uses.
1990	Implementation of *Let the Buyer be Better Informed* found in the setting up of a statutory register of historical contaminative uses s. 143 of the Environmental Protection Act 1990. Two consultation exercises followed dealing with the details.
1991–1992	The consultation exercises raised a number of fundamental objections to the system of registers.
1993	The proposals to set up the register of contaminative uses were abandoned. A review was announced which would deal with such things as the allocation of liabilities and cost recovery.
1994	Consultation Paper: *Paying for Our Past* was issued in March 1994 dealing with seven broad topics including: government policy objectives; the statutory framework; the relationship with the common law; the extension of strict liability; and the identity of the person liable for clean-up.
	In November 1994 the government published *The Framework for Contaminated Land*, which set out the broad future strategy for dealing with contaminated land.
1995	The outline of the new statutory scheme was introduced in the Environment Act 1995 which set out the statutory framework as inserted into the EPA 1990 as a new Part IIA.
2000	The Contaminated Land (England) Regulations 2000 dealing with the procedural matters and definition of Special Sites. DETR Circular 2/2000 is published setting out statutory guidance.
	Legislative Scheme comes into force in England on 1 April 2000
	First site designated as contaminated land and remediation notice served in relation to loose asbestos on footpath blowing dust onto neighbouring properties. The remediation notice has since been rescinded
2001	In England, a mere 23 sites had been identified as 'Contaminated Land' under Part IIA. 33% of Local Authorities missed the deadline for the publication of a strategy
2005	In May 2005, all but one of the 353 Part IIA authorities in England had formally adopted a strategy with the one recalcitrant having published a draft. 304 sites had been determined by local authorities and 22 Special Sites determined by the Environment Agency. The local authority figure is misleading as some sites have multiple determinations (e.g. different residential properties). True figure suggests an average of 15 determinations per year.

remediation requirements and the recovery of the costs of remediation). and the allocation and apportionment of liability), whilst they must 'have regard to' the remainder (this covers the remediation requirements and the recovery of the costs of remediation).

The contaminated land regime—an introduction

Part IIA is concerned with:

- identifying land which needs cleaning up;
- deciding how to clean it up; and
- determining who is going to do this (or pay for it being done by the regulators).

There are some other important aspects, such as the provision of public information through registers, and compensation for the exercise of powers to require entry onto land to effect clean up. One important point is that the intention is not to significantly increase the level of expenditure on clean up and restoration, but rather to target it more effectively. As the timeline indicates, the powers have not been used to a great extent but the intention is that clean up should be voluntary where possible and through the redevelopment and recycling of land where desirable—so that any development may provide some funds for remediation.

Box 17.5 sets out the main procedures which are laid down by Part IIA. Although the list conveys a linear process, in reality it is much more complex with difficult decisions and assessments at almost every stage.

BOX 17.5 **The main features of the controls over historically contaminated land**

1 The local authority has the primary role in inspecting land within its area and identifying land which is deemed to be 'contaminated' for the purposes of Part IIA.

2 The definition of 'contaminated land' is narrow for the purposes of Part IIA and only covers situations where the contamination gives rise to significant harm, significant risk of significant harm or pollution of controlled waters.

3 Once 'contaminated land' has been identified, responsibility is divided, with the Environment Agency taking control over sites where the risks from the contamination are perceived to be higher (known as 'special sites') and all other sites remaining within the control of the local authorities.

4 In the absence of an emergency, the appropriate enforcing authority is under a duty to ascertain the person or persons who is/are responsible for cleaning up the land.

5 In cases where there is an emergency, the enforcing authority can carry out the clean up works and seek to recover the costs of doing so from the person or persons who would otherwise have had to carry out the works.

6 In cases where there is no emergency, the enforcing authority must identify all persons who might be affected by any requirement to carry out clean up works. This includes owners, occupiers and those responsible for the contamination.

7 The enforcing authority must come up with a scheme for the clean up of the land. Any scheme must take into account the costs and benefits of carrying out the works.

8 After the scheme has been drawn up, the enforcing authority must consult the potentially affected parties. Where voluntary works are agreed, no further action can be taken by the enforcing authority.

9 Responsibility for clean up works rests primarily with the original polluters (although this relatively simple phrase conceals a number of complex issues) and in cases where the original polluter cannot be found, responsibility is transferred to the owners or occupiers of the land. After identifying the person or persons who should pay for the clean up, the enforcing authorities must exclude less blameworthy persons in accordance with various tests set down in statutory guidance (known as 'exclusion tests'). After these exclusion tests have been applied, the costs of carrying out the clean up works must be apportioned between the remaining responsible persons.

10 The enforcing authority is under a *duty* to serve a notice setting out the details of the clean up scheme requiring the recipient of the notice to comply with the notice (known as a remediation notice) if it is able to do so. It cannot serve a remediation notice in certain circumstances (e.g. if any person would suffer 'hardship' if the costs of carrying out the works would be recovered from them or where the responsible person agrees to carry out clean up works voluntarily). If the enforcing authority cannot serve a remediation notice, there is a *power* to carry out the works and to seek to recover all or any part of the costs of doing so.

11 There are rights of appeal against the service of a remediation notice. Appeals are made to the magistrates' court or the Secretary of State (in relation to special sites only). A notice is suspended until the appeal is finally determined or withdrawn.

12 It is an offence to fail to comply with the requirements of a remediation notice without reasonable excuse.

13 Each enforcing authority is required to maintain a system of public registers which should contain details of remediation notices and areas of contaminated land for which that authority is responsible.

The definition of contaminated land

The definition of contaminated land is central to the operation of Part IIA as it is the trigger for all other procedures to commence. It also reflects the distinction in the liability imposed in relation to historic contamination as distinguished from current sources. Box 17.6 sets out the definition found in section 78(2). The section distinguishes between contamination which is present in, on or under land and contamination which, although present in land is entering or likely to enter into controlled waters. The two categories of contaminated land are defined to reflect the policy of only requiring clean up when the contamination is causing unacceptable risks to the environment or human health. Although this definition provides the trigger for the operation of Part IIA, the statutory phrases are deliberately vague. It should therefore be noted that the statutory definition is meaningless without the backing of the statutory guidance. The importance of the guidance definition is emphasised by the fact that the enforcing authorities are to 'act in accordance with' the guidance on the definition of contaminated land (s. 78R(2)).

BOX 17.6 The definition of contaminated land

Section 78A(2), EPA 1990 (as amended) provides that for the purposes of Part IIA (and those purposes alone) contaminated land is:

'any land which appears to the local authority in whose area it is situated to be in such a condition, by reason of substances in, on or under land, that:

(a) significant harm is being caused or there is a significant possibility of such harm being caused; or

(b) significant pollution of controlled waters is being caused or there is a significant possibility of such pollution being caused

Section 78(4) defines harm as meaning:

'harm to the health of living organisms or other interference with the ecological systems of which they form part and, in the case of man, includes harm to his property.'

The definition can be broken down into smaller sub-definitions.

(a) The existence of a pollutant linkage

The guidance fleshes out the statutory definition of 'significant harm and significant possibility' by introducing the concept of the 'pollutant linkage'. A pollutant linkage is formed when there is a linkage between a contaminant (a pollutant) and a receptor or target (e.g. humans or property) by means of a pathway. If any one aspect is missing, no linkage is formed. For example where there is contamination but it is self contained in the ground with no route into the wider environment, there is no pathway and the linkage cannot be formed. Where such a linkage is present, it must be 'significant' (forming what is known as a 'significant pollutant linkage' (SPL)) for the land to come within the definition of 'contaminated land'. Significance is assessed in relation to the types of targets which are being harmed by the contamination; the degree or nature of that harm; and the possibility of the harm being caused.

(b) The types of receptor/target

The guidance narrowly defines the types of receptors or targets which can form part of the SPL. These are: human beings; nature conservation sites (which includes all of the sites which are protected under nature conservation laws); buildings; and other property (which covers crops and animals which are subject to property rights such as livestock). Anything which is a target which falls outside these categories (e.g. wild animals, nature conservation sites which are not protected under nature conservation laws or personal property such as cars) does not fall within Part IIA.

(c) The nature of the harm

The guidance provides that in assessing the significance of the harm the local authority needs to consider whether the harm caused to the specified receptors falls within specified categories in relation to each of those receptors. For example, in relation to humans this includes serious injury, birth defects, and impairment of reproductive functions. In relation to nature conservation sites it includes any harm which results in an irreversible or substantial adverse change to the functioning of the ecosystems which form a substantial part of the site. In relation to property it includes substantial loss in crop value or substantial damage to buildings.

(d) The possibility of significant harm being caused

In the absence of actual significant harm, the local authority must assess whether there is a significant possibility of significant harm being caused. The guidance explains that this should be based on an assessment of the risks involved with the contamination and in particular the 'magnitude or consequences' of the different types of significant harm being caused. This is a complicated exercise which should take account of the nature and degree of the harm (e.g. an explosion of methane gas or toxic effects on the growth of crops); the susceptibility of the receptors (e.g. a nearby school or a building with concrete foundations); and the timescale within which the harm might occur (imminent or over a period of 50 to 100 years). Putting all the factors together it might be found that the possibility of a methane gas explosion on a site next to a school which could occur imminently would have more significance than a site which was leaching corrosive chemical which might destroy the foundations of a building over a 100-year period. When considering the statistical assessment of the possibility of significant harm, the guidance provides that in all cases other than harm to human health this is assessed on the balance of probabilities (i.e. is it more likely than not to cause significant harm). In cases of harm to human health the relevant standard is that the risk must be medically 'unacceptable'.

(e) Pollution of controlled waters

The second limb of the statutory definition of contaminated land covers situations where poisonous, noxious, or polluting matter is entering or is likely to enter controlled waters from the land in question (s. 78A(9)). The statutory guidance provides that the likelihood of the entry of the contaminant is to be assessed on the balance of probabilities. It should be noted that this definition excludes substances which have entered controlled waters at some time in the past and the entry has now ceased and is unlikely to recur (e.g. contamination which is caused by past leaks from underground storage tanks which are currently empty). Unlike the other limb of 'contaminated land', the statutory definition was not originally risk based nor fleshed out in guidance and potentially small amounts of contamination could have triggered the requirement for expensive clean up. In order to clarify the situation, section 86 of the Water Act 2003 amended the definition of 'contaminated land' by requiring that such water pollution was 'significant' with further guidance on what triggers this level of contamination.

The identification of contaminated land

Local authorities are under a duty to inspect their areas from time to time for the purposes of identifying:

- contaminated land;
- special sites (s. 78B(1)).

In undertaking this duty local authorities must 'act in accordance' with the statutory guidance. When identifying contaminated land, a local authority is entitled to take into account the cumulative impact of two or more separate sites when assessing whether there is 'significant harm' or 'pollution of controlled waters'. This will be important where the 'cocktail' effect of a number of contaminated sites causes significant harm whereas any individual site will not give rise to any notable pollution (s. 78X(2)). In seeking to identify contaminated land, local authorities may rely upon information from a number of sources including the owners or occupiers in question (who may have carried out a voluntary investigation of their own land). Where pollution of controlled waters is being caused or the contamination is harming a nature conservation site, the local authority must consult the EA and English Nature respectively and have regard to any comments which they make before making the determination as to whether the land should be designated as 'contaminated land'. In cases where this information is not sufficient to enable the local authority to identify the land as contaminated, it can carry out an inspection of the land where there is a 'reasonable possibility' that there is a pollutant linkage on the land. For the purposes of the identification duty, local authorities have the same powers of inspection and entry as the EA has under s. 108 (see p. 293).

Special sites

When contaminated land has been identified, local authorities must consider whether the site falls within one of the categories of special sites as defined under the regulations. Special sites are regulated directly by the EA. The general criteria for special sites are the seriousness of the harm or water pollution which would be (or is being) caused and whether the EA is more likely to have the expertise to act on those particular sites. For special sites to be designated, the local authority must first formally identify the land as contaminated for the purposes of Part IIA. In practice, however, the Environment Agency has a role to play in the identification of special sites either in conjunction with the local authority (by carrying out any investigation on behalf of the authority) or on its own account. Where the authority considers that the land should be designated as a special site it is under a duty to notify the EA (after seeking its advice), the owner/occupier, and any person who might be responsible for paying the costs of remediation (s. 78C(1)–(3)). The EA has inspection and entry powers in relation to special sites (s. 78Q). The EA also has the power to terminate the designation of a special site where it appears to the EA that it is no longer suitable for designation (s. 78Q(4)), although the land will continue to remain 'contaminated land' as identified by the local authority).

BOX 17.7 **What is a special site?**

The Contaminated Land (England) Regulations 2000 provide the classification of special sites (sch. 1). These include land:

- subject to IPPC under the PPCA 1999;
- contaminated by waste acid tars;
- occupied for defence purposes;

- used for petroleum refining, or the manufacture of explosives;
- used for the manufacture or disposal of weapons;
- within a nuclear site;
- designated under section 1(1) of the Atomic Weapons Establishment Act 1991;
- adjoining the above which is contaminated by substances escaping from special sites;
- contaminated by listed defined chemicals which are now affecting certain groundwaters;
- with a major impact on drinking waters;
- affecting certain controlled waters by reason of its contamination.

Notification and consultation

Once land has been identified as being contaminated, the local authority is under a duty to notify this fact to all owners, occupiers, people who appear to the local authority to be liable to pay the clean up costs and the Environment Agency (s. 78B(3)). In practice, many of those people will already be aware of the potential designation as a result of supplying information as part of the identification process. The notification to the EA enables it to consider whether the site should be designated as a special site and whether there is any need for site specific guidance on the level or nature of the clean up work.

After notification, there follows a period of consultation with the notified parties (s. 78H(1)). This duty does not apply in cases of where it appears to the authority that there is an imminent danger of serious harm or pollution of controlled waters (ss. 78G(4), 78H(4)). There is a minimum period of three months for consultation (before the service of a remediation notice) and the government has expressed the desire that this period be used at best to achieve agreement between the enforcing authorities and the persons who are carrying out the remediation and at worst to narrow the areas of disagreement. Indeed, the emphasis on the voluntary nature of this process is formalized with the preclusion of any further formal action (i.e. the service of a remediation notice) where a person has undertaken to carry out voluntary remediation works. Where such agreement is reached, the person must describe the works in a Remediation Statement which is published on the public register (s. 78H(7)).

The second main purpose of the consultation period is to discuss the works which are necessary and in particular whether they should be phased or whether a single action could deal with a number of SPLs (e.g. digging out contaminated soil and disposing of it might deal with a number of different contaminants which have been caused by different people). Alternatively, the enforcing authority may consider that remediation would not be reasonable bearing in mind the costs and the benefits (e.g. where there were very low levels of water pollution). In such circumstances, the enforcing authority must publish a remediation declaration explaining that no remediation is required notwithstanding the formal identification of the land as contaminated under Part IIA (s. 78H(6)).

Remediation standards

The two clean-up levels which are most commonly adopted when cleaning up historic contamination refer to the use to which the land is put and the level of clean up which is required to put the land to such a use without any of the risks associated with the original contamination. The so-called 'multifunctional' approach requires land to be cleaned up to a level so that it is fit for any possible use including ecological uses. On the other hand, the 'suitable for use' standard is assessed against the current use or during the determination of any permission which is required for a future use (e.g. the land is cleaned up prior to the commencement of development to a standard which is suitable for the future use). This approach ensures that the action is proportionate and does not have to address possible unknown future risks.

These standards which underpin the legal framework dealing with the clean up of historically contaminated land need to be viewed in the wider context of the extensive impacts which such contamination has upon sustainable development. For example, identifying the appropriate level for clean-up standards for contaminated land involves questions of policy, science, and economics which are closely linked to differing interpretations of sustainable development (see Box 17.8).

Although the 'suitable for use' approach is used to deal with historic contamination, there is an exception where contamination has been caused as a result of activities which are covered by an extant statutory authorisation or licence. Where the relevant statutory provisions provide for a power to order clean up, the requisite standard is to a reinstatement level (i.e. to remove the contamination completely). Of course, in addition to these two general approaches to standard setting there is the problem of setting the specific levels of contaminants which apply in particular cases.

BOX 17.8 **Standard setting for contaminated land and sustainable development**

In addition to the direct threats to the environment and human health caused by harmful contamination, there are significant consequences in terms of resource depletion. This arises out of the inability to re-use previously developed land and the supplementary increase in pressure to develop green field sites. This has to be balanced against the high cost of cleaning up contamination with its knock-on economic effects on an individual, local, regional, and even national scale. What standard should be adopted—multi-functional, 'suitable for use' or some other alternative?

The suitable for use standard has been criticized mainly on the ground that there is little account taken of the effect that any contaminants may have upon future development. In its 19th Report, the RCEP took the view that the standard had 'serious limitations' in particular the way in which a 'cheap' clean up of land so that it was suitable for open space could leave contaminants in the ground which might sterilize the land for other more sensitive uses and increase the pressure to develop 'greenfield' sites.[17]

Under the 'multifunctional' approach unnecessary work may be required which can have

---

17. See 19th Report, *Sustainable Use of Soil*, (1996) Cm 3165.

significant financial consequences without any proportionate environmental benefits. This reflects some of the experience in the Netherlands which introduced a multi-functional standard under their Soil Protection Act 1987. At the outset, it was estimated that there were 2,000 sites which would need to be cleaned up at a cost of $500 million—a target which was achievable within a generation. There were, however, approximately 100,000 contaminated sites with an estimated total clean up bill of $50 billion. The soaring cost of meeting the multi-functional standard was largely met by the Dutch Government. In the face of such cost, the multi-functional approach was abandoned in 1997.[18]

The RCEP suggested an alternative approach which would adopt the advantages of the two existing standards.[19] In considering both remediation standards and future use of the site, it was suggested that the test of the Best Practicable Environmental option be adopted as a goal. Once established, the highest remediation standards that could be reached without excessive cost should be used regardless of the use immediately intended after clean up.

All of these standards reflect some of the central issues of sustainable development. The suitable for use approach reflects a weak version of sustainable development. There is a trade off between the recycling of 'brown land' as a sustainable resource and the level of costs required to recycle that resource. On the other hand, the multifunctional and BPEO approaches provide slightly 'stronger' versions of sustainable development in the sense that they aim to maximize environmental improvement with costs less of a factor. In the final analysis, however, all clean up standards reflect a strongly anthropocentric version of sustainable development with the emphasis on economic development. For example, a survey of 367 remediation projects carried out between 1996 and 1999 revealed that the vast majority of sites were cleaned up because of the threat to human health and to enable redevelopment as opposed to ecological reasons or simply to manage pollution.[20]

The nature of remediation works

When determining the most appropriate works required to meet the suitable for use standard, the enforcing authority must apply the best practicable technique for the pollution linkage in question both to the elimination of any significant pollution linkage and also to the remedying of any harm caused. Where elimination is not possible, the standard becomes one of best practicable technique of reducing the harm and remedying its impact, or at least minimising its effect. The work may be spread over years to take into account technical or financial considerations. Indeed it may be the case that a certain technological solution is impossible/unaffordable at the present time and can only be implemented at a later date.

The remediation methods will only be assessed as against the facts of any individual situation but assessment and ongoing monitoring can be included as 'remediation' along-side preventative and restorative works. In comparing remediation methods the costs and the benefits of each method must be assessed. This can include environmental as well as financial costs (e.g. it would be appropriate to consider the environmental costs of dumping

18. See *Dutch in Policy Retreat on Contaminated Land* (1997) ENDS Report, 269, 46.

19. See RCEP, 19th Report op. cit., n. 17.

20. See Environment Agency, R & D Technical Report P401, *Survey of remedial techniques for land contamination in England and Wales.*

contaminated soils in a landfill site as against the financial cost of maintaining *in situ* remediation over a long period). Remediation can include assessment processes to establish the presence of a pollution linkage and actions to eliminate or minimize its impact by removing or treating the pollutant, interrupting the pathway or protecting the receptor. It is necessary to measure the total costs against the benefits of intervention, and this itself involves weighing seriousness of harm or pollution and the remedial or minimizing effects of the works. Seriousness is judged by considering a number of factors relating mainly to the receptor. These include the size of the receptors, their nature and importance (taking into account their existing state), the impact upon them and whether it would be lasting. Similar factors apply where the receptor is water.

Section 78E(4) requires action on the part of the enforcing authority to be reasonable, and the guidance requires this also in relation to the cost of the remediation. The test for reasonableness of costs is that there is no alternative remediation scheme that would achieve the same standard for lower costs. Authorities must also take into account whether harm is already being caused (and if not its probability) and any wider environmental risks.

The duty to serve a remediation notice

Once land has been identified as contaminated, consultation has taken place between the enforcing authority and the relevant persons and the relevant remediation works identified, the authority must serve a remediation notice (s. 78E). Although this duty is similar to the duty to serve an abatement notice under the statutory nuisance regime (see p. 405 and the discussion of *ex parte Shelley*) there are limits to the mandatory nature of the duty. There are a number of situations, however, where an enforcing authority is precluded from serving a remediation notice (see Box 17.9).

If the enforcing authority is precluded from serving a remediation notice, it has a *power* to carry out the works itself and to seek to recover the costs of doing so (if that is possible)

BOX 17.9 **When is a remediation notice not allowed to be served?**

The enforcing authority is specifically precluded from serving a remediation notice in certain circumstances. These include:

- where there are other statutory powers which can be used to enforce a clean up of the land (s. 78YB). The justification for the primacy of these other statutory provisions is that the introduction of Part IIA was not intended to add to the pre-existing regulatory burden: the policy aim was merely to clarify the law on contamination rather then introduce new liabilities;

- where any requirement to carry out remediation would be unreasonable (s. 78H(5)(a)). For example because the costs outweighed the benefits or where the statutory guidance suggests that particular works would be unreasonable. In such cases a remediation declaration is required (s. 78H(6));

- where the appropriate person has agreed to undertake voluntary remediation (s. 78H(5)(b);

- where one of the persons who would be served with a remediation notice would suffer 'hardship' if they were required to pay for their share of any of the costs of remediation (s. 78N(3)(e)). 'Hardship' is undefined in Part IIA and the guidance suggests that it should be determined on a case-by-case basis and having regard to the statutory guidance on the issue (Chapter E of the Statutory Guidance). In such cases, the enforcing authority is precluded from serving the notice on *any* of the parties who would have been served with the notice (where there is more than one party responsible (s. 78H(5)(d));

- where the enforcing authority is itself the appropriate person (e.g. as a result of owning a contaminated site or by being the original polluter (s. 78H(5)(c));

- where it is considered that there is imminent danger of serious harm or pollution (s. 78N(3)(a));

- where there is pollution of controlled waters and the only appropriate persons who can be found are owners/occupiers (s. 78J);

- where, after reasonable inquiry, no appropriate person can be found (s. 78N(3)(f).

from the appropriate persons. The importance of these exceptions cannot be under-estimated as they are wide (particularly in the case of hardship) and shift the regulatory focus from mandatory duties to discretionary powers.

The remediation notice is to be served on the 'appropriate person' and is required to set out what must be done and the time period for carrying out the specified steps (s. 7E(1)). In specifying the steps required under a remediation notice the authority is under a duty to have regard to the statutory guidance and to balance the costs of carrying out the work with the seriousness of the harm/pollution caused (s. 78E(4)). The statutory guidance makes it clear that environmental benefits should be considered in addition to any financial benefits.

Remediation notices

Once the enforcing authority has allocated and apportioned liability it must serve the remediation notice. Section 78E(1) and reg. 4 make provision for the details which must be included in the notice. Although there are certain prescribed pieces of information which must be included, the government is hoping to avoid some of the legalistic issues which have been raised in relation to abatement notices (see p. 414). The notice should give the recipients a clear picture of the nature of the work; who is required to carry it out; where there is more than one appropriate person, what proportion of the costs of the work must be borne by each of them; by when the work must be carried out; the identity of the other appropriate persons; the reasons for serving the notice; the rights of appeal and any other information which can help to clarify any uncertainty.

Appeals

Any person who is the recipient of a remediation notice has the right of appeal within 21 days of the service of the notice (s. 78L(1)). Where the notice was served by a local authority the appeal is made to the magistrates' court; in relation to special sites, the right of appeal is to the Secretary of State. Regulation 7 sets out the 19 main grounds of appeal. In summary these cover such things as: whether the land is 'contaminated land' for the purposes of Part IIA; whether the appellant is an appropriate person; whether the appellant should have been excluded form the relevant liability group; whether the enforcing authority was precluded from serving a remediation notice; whether the requirements of the notice were reasonable; and whether the enforcing authority has acted in accordance with the statutory guidance.

An appeal suspends the operation of the notice until the determination or withdrawal of the appeal (reg. 15). The distinction between the appeal procedure in relation to special sites and other contaminated land is significant in a number of ways. First, the Secretary of State may hold a public inquiry (reg. 11(1)(b)) where third parties are able to make representations. Secondly, the Secretary of State may delegate the decision to the Planning Inspectorate (indeed it is anticipated that most appeals will be determined in this way). Inspectors appointed may be technically qualified and may be assisted by assessors with experience in contaminated land issues. On the other hand, 'contaminated land' appeals are to be allocated to stipendiary magistrates who are not necessarily equipped to deal with the complicated technical issues involved.[21] Finally, 'just and reasonable' costs are normally awarded against the unsuccessful party in the magistrates' court, whereas costs in relation to special site appeals will not be awarded in written representation appeals and in other cases (i.e. hearings and inquiries) except where there has been unreasonable behaviour on behalf of one of the parties which has led to unnecessary expense. Whilst this division of responsibility is understandable (with the division reflecting procedures for statutory nuisance appeals and pollution control appeals respectively), there would not appear to be any coherent justification for this.

Compliance with a remediation notice

After 21 days from the date of service of the notice, there are two possible outcomes. First, the notice is complied with. In such circumstances, it may be necessary to serve an additional remediation notice if it becomes clear as a result of complying with the original notice that further or different works are required. Alternatively, the works may be sufficient to address the risks brought about by the SPL. Although there is no formal procedure for declassifying the land as 'contaminated', the enforcing authority must enter the details of the remediation carried out on the public register (see below) and it may confirm that no further enforcement action is anticipated.

Non-compliance with a remediation notice

The second possible outcome after the service of a remediation notice is that it is either not complied with or partially complied with. It is an offence to fail to comply with a remediation notice without reasonable excuse (s. 78M). There are, however, relatively minor

---

21. Note that the Clean Neighbourhood and Environment Act 2005, s.104 provides for the transfer of *all* appeals to be heard by the Secretary of State.

penalties which undermines the deterrence factor. The offence can only be tried in the magistrates' court. Where the contaminated land is currently industrial, trade or business premises the maximum penalty is a fine of £20,000 with a further daily fine of up to £2,000 for every day before the enforcing authority has carried out any remediation (s. 78M(4)). In cases of other contaminated land the maximum fine is £5,000 with a maximum daily fine of £500 (10 per cent of Level 5)(s. 78M(3)).

The relevant authority has the power to carry out remediation works where the recipient of the remediation has failed to comply either with or without the appropriate person's agreement (s. 78N). The Agency has the power to recover all or part of its reasonable costs (s. 78P). In recovering costs regard must be had to any hardship which the cost-recovery might impose. In England and Wales the relevant authority also has the power to serve a charging notice on the owner which will constitute a charge on the premises which consist of or include the contaminated land in question. The costs of any charge may be paid by installments over a maximum 30-year period. A person served with the charging notice has a right of appeal which must be made to the county court within 21 days of the receipt of the notice (s. 78P(8)).

Registers

Each enforcing authority is required to keep a public register of information in relation to Part IIA (s. 78R). Schedule 3 to the regulations sets out the details of the information which is to be kept on the register. These include: particulars of remediation statements, declarations and notices; appeals; convictions; notices in relation to special sites; and information about remediation work notified to the authority although there is no official guarantee of compliance with remediation notices (s. 78R(3)).

The allocation of liability—who is liable?

(a) The 'appropriate person'

The issue of the identity of the 'appropriate person' on whom the remediation notice is served is, together with the definition of contaminated land, one of the central elements of Part IIA.[22] The question of 'who pays?' in a liability regime which imposes costs on a retrospective basis for something as complicated as historic contamination was always going to require the resolution of difficult issues. In accordance with the 'polluter pays' principle the appropriate person is defined as the person, or any of the persons, who caused or knowingly permitted the substances, or any of the substances, which have been the cause of the contamination to be in or under the land (s. 78F(2)). On some interpretations of this section, however, it could be argued that the 'polluter pays' principle is given a wide meaning which would cover a person who brought potentially polluting substances onto land regardless of whether the substances polluted whilst under their control. In addition to contamination on the site where it was originally present, the appropriate

22. For an excellent overview of the issues see D. Lawrence and R. Lee (2003) 66 MLR 261.

person can also be responsible for contamination which has escaped onto other land (s. 78K). Within the statutory guidance those appropriate persons who have caused or knowingly permitted the presence of the substances are known as 'Class A persons'. The phrase 'caused or knowingly permitted' is familiar in the context of environmental offences (particularly in relation to water pollution), however, great care must be taken in extrapolating the principles in those cases and applying them in the contaminated land context (see Box 17.10).

BOX 17.10 **Who is the polluter?—the polluter pays principle in action**

Under the provisions concerning liabilities, responsibility for paying for remediation will, where feasible, follow the 'polluter pays' principle. In the first instance, any persons who caused or knowingly permitted the contaminating substances to be in, on or under the land will be the appropriate person(s) to undertake the remediation and meet its costs. However, if it is not possible to find any such person, responsibility will pass to the current owner or occupier of the land.

DETR Circular 2/2000, Annex 1: para. 38

Who should pay for the clean up of contaminated land? In accordance with accepted principles, the Government suggests that, where 'feasible', it should be the 'polluter' who pays. But who is the 'polluter'? Under Part IIA, the assertion of the 'polluter pays principle' is nothing more than shorthand for a complex system of detailed regulatory tests.

The 'polluter pays principle' is much wider than the idea that those with a direct responsibility for a polluting action should pay for the consequences of that pollution. The principle is a system designed to address the consequences of pollution through economic measures. Its basis lies within economic theory which suggests that pollution is an unacknowledged cost, that is the destruction of a collective good, which should be met by those who benefit from the fact that cost has not been accounted for. This can be most easily understood by the idea of the 'unowned' environment which is a good which is for the benefit of all. In legal terms, the corollary of the 'unowned' environment is any harm caused is 'uncompensatable'. The polluter pays principle seeks to attach a value to such common goods and extract compensation for any harm caused.

When examining the concept by reference to the system of allocating liability for historic contamination we see that the statutory definition of the 'polluter' found within Part IIA and which is referred to above illustrates a number of points about the identity of the 'polluter'. First, the polluter is not defined narrowly by reference to either intention, blame, or reason behind the pollution. Generally, when identifying a 'polluter' we might look to direct links between intention and/or a direct link to the pollution. The guidance suggests that strict liability will apply. Going further, the test of 'knowing permission' may include the most peripheral of 'polluters', for example a landowner who has turned a blind eye to pollution caused by someone else.

In addition, the identification of the 'polluter' is not linked to any explicit idea of punishment. There are criminal sanctions for illegally disposing of waste or of polluting groundwater. Why not simply punish the historic polluter? This is because the polluter pays principle is not concerned with explicit punishment. If this were the case, there were be many 'polluters' under the Contaminated Land regime who would justifiably feel hard done to as their 'punishment' arises out of retroactive legislation.

The key to the pure application of the polluter pays principle is that it is fair and just to apply the principle when the pollution/contamination is a necessary consequence of an activity even if it was not an intended goal. Thus intention and even foreseeability play no part in the application of the principle.

It should also be borne in mind that where the 'polluter pays principle' breaks down, i.e. where the actual polluter can no longer be found, the artificiality of the definition is revealed. In such circumstances, an innocent owner or occupier of the land becomes the 'polluter' for the purposes of allocating liability.

(b) 'Caused'

Whether a person has 'caused' the presence of contamination should be viewed as a question of fact in each case. Following the existing case law, liability is strict (i.e. fault, negligence, or knowledge are not required). There might be arguments which could be put forward to justify a distinction between the strictness of the liability for causing environmental criminal offences (where the strictness is mitigated by varying the punishment to reflect the blameworthiness of the defendant) and causing historic contamination (where the financial 'penalty' is fixed and potentially much more significant than any fine). The counter to these arguments would be that the statutory regime has other mechanisms for promoting fairness (e.g. the exclusion tests and the 'hardship' exemption) and that the policy aims behind the legislation would be defeated should 'innocent' parties be allowed to escape liability on basis of their lack of fault. In particular, the government rejected a suggestion that there should be a 'state of the art' defence (i.e. liability would not attach to a person who could demonstrate that they had adopted 'state of the art' practices at the time the original contamination arose).

The government has suggested that, in line with the water pollution cases on the issue,

---

BOX 17.11 **Causing contamination**

The differing circumstances in which contamination arises gives some indication of the challenges faced when applying the polluter pays principle. These different situations reveal the difficulty in applying the Polluter Pays Principle across different factual scenarios.

Accidents

Company A operates a industrial process under an Integrated Pollution Prevention and Control Permit. Company B delivers chemicals which Company A uses in the process. During one delivery, the self employed driver of Company B's Lorry fails to connect the pipe to the delivery vehicle causing the chemical to escape into the ground. The chemical pollutes the groundwater over a large area.

Long-term spillages

Company A stores chemicals on site in drums. Over time, some of the drums become slightly corroded allowing the chemicals to escape into the ground and into the groundwater. This is in breach of the IPPC permit. Company A employs a contractor to check the drums on a regular basis.

> **Deliberate action**
>
> Company C owns land situated in the middle of the open countryside. The land has been used by various developers and builders to dump waste including asbestos. Company C turned a blind eye to this dumping.
>
> **Permitted behaviour**
>
> Company D owned and operated at a site from 1937–1972. During that time it had used part of the land as a waste tip for its hazardous waste. The Company has never broken any relevant environmental laws. The waste materials are now being linked to symptoms of ill health in the area.

causation would be established where the person concerned was involved in some active operation to which the presence of the contaminating substance was attributable although a failure to act could amount to causation in certain circumstances (see p. 736). In practice, in most cases where contamination is found on a site, there would be a rebuttable presumption (i.e. assumed unless the contrary could be proved) that the operator/occupier of the site at the time of the contamination had caused the presence of the pollutant. The presumption would be particularly strong where it could be demonstrated that the operator/occupier had generated or used the substances in question.

Causation could be direct (e.g. the person was responsible for placing pollutants in the ground) or indirect (e.g. through leaks from equipment). In addition, more than one person could be said to have 'caused' the presence of the contaminant (e.g. a contractor dumping the operator's waste contaminants on the operator's site—both parties would be appropriate persons).

(c) 'Knowingly permitted'

The definition of 'knowingly permitted' raises more complex issues than under the 'caused' limb. When the Environment Act 1995 was passing through Parliament, a ministerial statement suggested that the government's view of the phrase was that it required both knowledge that the substances were in, on or under the land and the existence of a power to prevent that presence. This does not deal with all of the issues with the phrase. Other matters which are subject to argument include the following.

- *The extent of the required knowledge.* There is an important distinction between knowing that a substance is present in, on or under land and knowing that it has the potential to be present in such a way as to render the land as contaminated for the purposes of Part IIA. For example, land could be transferred through a number of ownerships with each owner knowing that a substance had been stored on the land some time in the past (e.g. in underground storage tanks). On the former interpretation, the date on which the substances left the storage tank and entered into the land would be irrelevant, the determining factor would be the presence of the substance, regardless of whether it was safely contained in the storage tank. On the latter interpretation only knowledge of the escape of the substance into the land and the knowledge of the requisite standard of harm would give rise to a potential liability (with the date of escape being the trigger date).
- *The standard of the knowledge.* This point is connected to the extent of the knowledge

in the sense that the word 'knowingly' could be narrowly construed to mean actual knowledge of the presence of the substance. Alternatively, and the view which would accord most readily with other areas of environmental regulation,[23] knowledge can be implied from the factual circumstances. This would include constructive knowledge (i.e. a reasonable person would have known given the circumstances) and wilful blindness (i.e. shutting one's mind to the obvious). Thus, buying a site where an operator had carried on an operation using hazardous substances might be sufficient to raise the presumption of knowledge in the absence of actual information.

- '*Permitting*'. Although there is case law on the definition of 'permitting' in relation to regulatory matters, most of it relates to one-off incidents (e.g. permitting the entry of polluting matter into controlled waters). Permission in this context is generally a positive act in the sense that involves some form of explicit or implied consent for the thing to be done. The *presence* of substances, on the other hand, is a continuing state of affairs where permission may be assumed from a failure to address the presence of the pollutant. As in the example above, this could arise from ownership of land and knowledge of the presence of substances, regardless of a positive permission. Aggregating these three issues above, it would be possible to argue that owning land for even a short period with the knowledge that substances are stored on the land (which could be constructive i.e. there are storage tanks on or in the land) may be sufficient for the owner to become a 'knowing permitter' even in the absence of the escape of the pollutant. On this interpretation, the only way to avoid this classification would be to ensure that the substance was no longer present on the land (i.e. in this case to empty the storage tanks).

(d) Owners and occupiers

Where the owner or the occupier of the land is not a Class A person, they can only be the appropriate person where no Class A person can be 'found' after reasonable inquiry (s. 78F(4)). In these circumstances, owners and occupiers are known as Class B persons for the purposes of the statutory guidance. 'Found' in this context would not include people who had died or companies which had ceased to exist. There are situations where owners/occupiers could fall within both Class A and Class B where they are responsible for the presence of some but not all of the substances on the land (as a Class A person) and the parties who are responsible for the residual contamination cannot be found (as a Class B person). One final important point to note is that Class B persons cannot be served with a remediation notice in respect of works relating to pollution of controlled waters or in respect of contamination which has escaped from other land onto their land other than remediation in respect of land or water which they own or occupy (ss. 78J and 78K(3)), (4) respectively).

'Owner' is defined in section 78A as being the person entitled to receive a market rent (as opposed to a token or peppercorn rent) for the property. It specifically excludes mortgagees not in possession which means that lenders can receive remediation notices where they are mortgagees in possession. Insolvency practitioners are also protected from personal liability

---

23. E.g. water pollution, see *Schulmans Incorporated Limited v NRA* [1993] Env LR D1 and waste management, see *Kent CC v Beaney* [1993] Env LR 225.

unless the contamination is attributable to their own negligence (s. 78X(3)). 'Occupier' is not defined.

(e) Practical issues

Although these provisions in respect of responsibility for contamination provide a complicated hierarchy of liability, the practical difficulties of establishing responsibility must not be overlooked. Unfortunately contamination does not necessarily carry clear identification of responsibility. In particular in areas where there has been a long history of industrial activity, distinguishing between different polluters will present evidential hurdles which will have to be overcome before a remediation notice can be served. The rules provide a framework for the allocation of liability but the evidential problems of linking individuals or companies with particular pollutant linkages will undoubtedly provide the enforcing authorities with an extremely difficult task. The standard of proof in relation to these issues is the balance of probabilities.

Allocation of liability

The identification of the potential appropriate persons is an integral part of the notification of the identification of contaminated land under Part IIA. This is, however, only one stage of the process of allocating liability for the clean up of historically contaminated land. The other significant stages in the process include the following.

(a) Forming liability groups

First, the enforcing authority must identify the numbers of SPLs on the land (i.e. the number of different pollutants which are giving rise to significant harm etc. via a pollutant linkage). This could be a single pollutant (with one SPL) or a number of different pollutants (with corresponding numbers of SPLs). The enforcing authorities must then identify each Class A person who is linked to each SPL (i.e. those parties who caused or knowingly permitted the presence of the contaminant). This group is referred to as the Class A liability group in relation to each SPL. Alternatively, in the absence of Class A persons in relation to any SPL, the owners/occupiers of the land form what is known as the Class B liability group in relation to that SPL. Thus, areas of contaminated land might have different substances which form different SPLs where either some or all of the persons who caused or knowingly permitted the presence of the substance can be found (forming Class A liability groups) or in cases where none of the Class A persons can be found, the owners and occupiers of the land on which the SPL is found form the Class B liability group.

(b) Applying the exclusion tests

Where a liability group has two or more members, the enforcing authority is obliged to apply a series of 'exclusion tests'. These tests exclude appropriate persons from liability. The tests are applied in a specific order and seek to exclude what might be perceived to be categories of appropriate persons who might appear to be less blameworthy. Thus where there are large liability groups the tests seek to differentiate between different causers and permitters. The rationale behind the exclusion tests would seem to be to mitigate any unfairness inherent in a system based upon strict and retrospective liability. The main flaw in this rationale is that the tests might, in certain circumstances, operate to increase the unfairness where liability groups are small.

There are six main tests for excluding Class A liability group members which can be grouped under three headings. The first test (Test 1—'Excluded activities') excludes all those persons who have Class A liability solely by reason of carrying out certain specified activities including: providing financial assistance, such as lending money; underwriting insurance; being a landlord where the tenant has caused the pollution; and providing technical, legal or scientific advice. The second group of tests excludes parties who have transferred the responsibility for the contamination either by reducing the price of the land in question to reflect the condition of the land (Test 2—'Payments made for remediation') or by selling the land with information on the condition of the land such that it is reasonable to expect that the purchaser of the land should pay for the clean up of the land (Test 3—'Sold with information'). The last group of tests excludes parties who are less blameworthy as a result of a change in circumstances from the date when the substance was originally in, on or under the land. These include: harmful changes to the original substance brought about by the unforeseeable introduction of later substances (Test 4—'Changes to substances'); new activities which have caused the substances to escape from the original land (Test 5— 'Escaped substances'); and the introduction of new developments which cause the creation of a SPL (Test 6—'Introduction of pathways or receptors'). The details of the Exclusion Tests are set out in Box 17.12.

BOX 17.12 **The Exclusion Tests**

CLASS A PARTIES

Name	Who is excluded?	What does the Test apply to?	Other comments
Test 1 'Excluded activities'	Person carrying out the 'excluded activity'	Excluded activities include: • lending to; insuring; advising; licensing; consenting to the activities of; or leasing land to another Class A party; • consigning waste to another person (whether or not that person can be found) where that other person took a contractual responsibility for disposing of the waste or the management of the site on which it was disposed; • being employed as a contractor where any actions or omissions which led to the presence of the contaminative substance were carried out in accordance with the contract	Exclusion applies only where person caused or knowingly permitted the presence of the contaminative substance solely by reason of performing the excluded activity

CLASS A PARTIES			
Name	**Who is excluded?**	**What does the Test apply to?**	**Other comments**
Test 2 'Payments made for remediation'	Any person making a 'payment for remediation'	Where a payment is made for remediation to be carried out and that remediation has not been carried out. A payment can be made: • voluntarily in response to a claim for the costs of remediation; • to meet a contractual obligation to pay; • to settle a legal claim; • to meet a Court Order; • as part of a sale of land even where the 'payment' is a reduction of the price to reflect the cost of remediation as long as the contract reflects this explicitly	Exclusion only applies where excluded person has no further control over the land in question (e.g. by retaining a contractual right to supervise works or a reversion after the expiry of a long lease)
Test 3 'Sold with information'	Seller of Land where Buyer is made aware of any pollutant which forms a SPL	Where: • prior to the sale becoming binding; • there is an 'arms length' sale of land to another Liability Group Member (the Buyer); • the Buyer has sufficient information that would reasonably allow that particular person to be aware of the 'broad measure' of a pollutant in any SPL; • the Seller did nothing to misrepresent the implications of the presence	Only applies to the sale of the freehold or long leases (>21 years). Seller must not retain any interest or rights over the land. Since 1990 where the buyer is a large commercial organisation or public body permission from Seller to allow Buyer to undertake investigations is normally sufficient to indicate that Buyer has information
Test 4 'Changes to Substances'	Class A Person where the presence of the substance has only created an SPL because of interaction with another substance introduced by another person at a later date	Where a substance has become 'significant' by reason of a change (physical, chemical, biological or other) brought about by the introduction of a later substance	It was not reasonably foreseeable that: • later substance would be introduced or that the change would occur; and that reasonable precautions were taken to prevent the introduction of the later substances.

CLASS A PARTIES			
Name	**Who is excluded?**	**What does the Test apply to?**	**Other comments**
			Once the change has occurred, the Class A person must not: • allow any more of the original substance to enter the land; do anything to contribute to the change; or fail to take reasonable steps to prevent the change happening.
Test 5 'Escaped Substances'	Class A Person where land has become contaminated as a result of the escape of substances from other land	Where the escape is the responsibility of another Liability Group Member	
Test 6 'Introduction of Pathways or Receptors'	Class A Person where SPL formed solely because of a subsequent introduction of a new pathway or receptor	Where a substance is made into a SPL solely because of the effect of actions subsequent to the introduction of the substance which introduce new receptors/targets	Only applies to 'development' for the purposes of Town and Country Planning legislation; or failure to take a step to prevent the creation of a receptor/pathway; or unreasonable failure to maintain/operate risk management system used to prevent creation of new SPL
CLASS B PARTIES			
	Occupiers and tenants who pay a full market rent for the land		Excludes all of those who do not have a capital interest in the land in question i.e. those who could not recover the costs of remediation in the enhanced value of the land on sale

Class B exclusion is much simpler excluding occupiers and tenants paying a market rent. These parties are excluded on the basis that they have no interest in the long-term value of the land and therefore will not benefit from any increase in the value should it be cleaned up.

There are a number of general rules which apply to all of the tests. First, the rules cannot exclude parties if the result would be to exclude all of the liability group. Secondly, exclusion is only referable to the specified liability group and not across all liability groups (i.e. an appropriate person may be excluded from one group but not necessarily from another). Thirdly, the tests must be applied in numerical order. Fourthly, where members of liability groups have reached a private agreement on the basis upon which liability should be allocated between them, and a copy of the agreement has been provided to the enforcing authority, the authority must allocate and apportion any liability on the basis of that agreement, in relation to the parties to the agreement alone. For example a buyer of land might agree to pay for any future liabilities which would be allocated to the seller of the land in return for a slightly reduced price. Any liabilities allocated to other appropriate persons would not fall within this agreement. A private agreement can be disregarded if it would have the effect of transferring liabilities to a person who would suffer hardship (on the basis that in these circumstances, the enforcing authority would be precluded from serving a remediation notice and private agreements could be drafted as a liability avoidance mechanism). Fifthly, the financial circumstances of the parties are disregarded when carrying out the exclusion tests (avoiding the problems of the so called 'deep pockets' discrimination where the enforcing authority targets only those who can afford to pay). Finally, where two or more of the persons within the liability group are part of the same group of companies, they are treated as a single person.

BOX 17.13　**The privatization of environmental liability**

One of the interesting features of the exclusion tests is the way in which, by use of policy and statutory guidance, the Government has effectively privatized large elements of environmental liability. Most statutory liability schemes identify clearly the polluter who is liable to pay. Contractual provisions (known as indemnities) agreed between private parties (such as the buyer and seller of companies or land) can seek to allocate sums of money to pay for any environmental liabilities imposed by statute as between the parties. That agreement, does not, however, affect the primary liability, as the statutory enforcing authority seek to recover costs from the polluter identified within the statute.[24]

In the case of Part IIA, the enforcing authority are obliged to give effect to private agreements and/or to exclude parties under various tests that are not necessarily clear or straightforward.[25] In effect, a private agreement made between a buyer and seller of contaminated land changes the definition of 'polluter' for the purposes of the statutory definition. The rationale for privatising the liability system through giving effect to private agreements and applying exclusion tests is that it is allowing the market to negotiate the transfer of liability at a cost, normally reflected in the reduced value of contaminated land. This is designed to mitigate the inherent unfairness of the statutory scheme by allowing private parties to agree to allocate and apportion the liabilities

---

24. For a good example of this see *Eastern Counties Leather plc v Eastern Counties Leather Group Limited* [2003] Env LR 13.

25. eg Test 2 and 3 deal with transfers of liability as arranged by private organizations (see Box 17.12).

between themselves. It is also designed to introduce a degree of certainty into the allocation of liability so that the parties may share out the potential risk within the transaction itself.

Whilst such a system is interesting for lawyers and no doubt creates a vehicle for sharing liability so that the market can have a degree of confidence in the application of the liability model, it has the disadvantage of creating a system of rules within rules which make the whole system incredibly complex. Complex legislation is not, of itself, a bad thing. Many of the issues which had to be addressed in Part IIA are not without difficulty and simplistic regulation would merely have caused greater problems than it solved. Accordingly, the combination of a scheme which imposes retrospective liability for historic pollution needs to be carefully drafted in order to avoid injustice. In addition, the science and economics of land remediation are not necessarily straightforward and no amount of legislative language can spell out the detail required to address these sort of issues. On the other hand there are large parts of the statutory guidance which appear to have been drafted in order to complicate and obfuscate. Whilst certainty in environmental legislation is always desirable, there are always going to be some 'unknowables' and the layering of complex rules such as in the case of contaminated land legislation merely serves to identify different and equally complicated issues.

Apportionment of liability

Once the exclusion tests have been carried out and the liability groups finalized, the enforcing authority must determine how much of the costs of carrying out the remedial works should be apportioned to each appropriate person. In general terms, the starting point is that liability should be apportioned on the basis of relative responsibility of each of the group members for creating or continuing the risk caused by the SPL. This might be related to the extent of time of occupation of the land or the use of a substance. In the absence of reasonable information upon which to base such an assessment of responsibility, the enforcing authority should apportion the costs equally between the group members.

Contaminated Land and the market

In all of the complexity of Part IIA and the accompanying regulations and guidance it is sometimes easy to forget that the aim of the new legislation is relatively simple to understand. Where there are unacceptable risks to human health or the environment there is an associated cost of clean up which is required to minimise or remove that risk. That cost has to be met by somebody whether it be the original polluter, the owner of the land or by the taxpayer. In the alternative the cost is met by those living in close proximity to the land and the habitats and resources which are affected by the contamination.

In many cases of contaminated land the real focus is not on the operation of cumbersome rules of liability allocation and apportionment but on creative ways of financing the cost of clean up. The lengthy periods of consultation and critically the ban on the service of a remediation notice where voluntary action has been offered illustrate the point that the whole philosophy underpinning the new regime is that remedial action should generally be voluntary. In this sense, the role of the property market is paramount as voluntary remediation is likely to take place where there are financial incentives, typically arising from the redevelopment of the land. Thus the planning system is to be at the forefront of tackling land contamination issues, with the Part IIA powers kept in reserve for when the voluntary/development-led approach has failed.

Accordingly, the Planning system is intended to complement the contaminated land regime under Part IIA of the Environmental Protection Act 1990. As stated above, Part IIA only covers the existing use of land and so issues regarding contamination in relation to future uses of land will generally fall to the planning system to resolve, because the remediation of contaminated land will be promoted through the planning system, even where the site is identified as 'contaminated land' under the EPA Part IIA. With regard to the operation of Part IIA, the 'Suitable for Use' policy uses the development control context to set the boundaries for liability. The other side of this, of course, is that development unlocks new potential liabilities, by changing the context for the Suitable for Use assessment. For example any harm which may arise in respect of a site may be satisfactorily dealt with where the use is as a car-park, but redevelopment for a residential use may introduce new pathways and receptors, so that new remediation requirements and liabilities may arise. Although planning conditions or obligations might deal with this, the new regime could operate to impose new liabilities on the original polluters, and even if not used directly, is likely to play a significant background role. Finally, one aim of Part IIA is to support the wider policy objective of recycling previously developed (though not necessarily contaminated) land, i.e. the national target for 60 per cent of new development to take place on brownfield sites.

 CHAPTER SUMMARY

1 Contamination is not synonymous with environmental harm. The key issues in designing laws to clean up contaminated land are the level at which 'contamination' is deemed to become harmful enough to require the intervention of law and who should be required to clean it up.

2 A distinction can be made between contamination arising out of current activities (regulated or otherwise) and historic activities. Care needs to be taken when regulating the latter type of contamination because the imposition of retrospective legislation is inherently unfair.

3 Contaminated land has a very specific meaning in relation to historic activities. This is based around the presence of substances in, on, or under land which are giving rise to significant harm or the significant risk of significant harm.

4 The legislation dealing with the clean up of historically contaminated land is found in Part IIA of the EPA 1990. This, along with secondary legislation and statutory guidance, sets out how contaminated land is to be identified, how it will be cleaned up and who will pay for it. The legislation is complex and evidence suggests that it has been used sparingly in practice.

5 The allocation of liability for historically contaminated land is said to be based upon the Polluter Pays Principle i.e. the person who caused or knowingly permitted the presence of the contaminating substances. In practice, however, the 'polluter' can be many different people including the innocent owner or occupier of the land.

6 There are various methods by which the inherent unfairness of the retrospective liability of the contaminated land provisions are mitigated. The most significant of these is that voluntary action to clean up land will preclude the operation of the provisions. In addition, certain tests operate to exclude parties who are less blameworthy.

7 Voluntary remediation is most likely to take place where there are financial incentives, typically arising from the redevelopment of contaminated land. Thus the planning system plays an

important role in addressing contamination with the Part IIA powers kept in reserve for cases where the voluntary/development-led approach fails.

Q QUESTIONS

1   Do you think that the implementation of Part IIA of the Environmental Protection Act was an effective method of dealing with historically contaminated land? What elements do you think are more effective and which are less?

2   What type of regulatory instrument(s) can be found under the system of liability under Part IIA? What other regulatory instruments could be used?

3   How does the planning system operate as a market mechanism to deal with the costs of cleaning up contaminated land?

4   A site which has recently been designated as Contaminated Land under Part IIA of the Environmental Protection Act 1990 was first developed as an Engineering Factory in the late 1950s. It was owned and operated by Hobblers Limited until 1978. At that time Hobblers were bought by Acme Engineering. In 1982 Acme went bust and the site was run by a Receiver for a six month period. Subsequently, the land was sold by the Receiver to a Chemical Company called Truchem. In 1989, Truchem undertook a survey of the land prior to sale.

The site was eventually sold in 1994 to Polluto. When Truchem sold to Polluto they did not say anything about the survey of the land carried out in 1989. They did however stress that the transaction was to be viewed as 'sold as seen' and they reduced the price below the market value to reflect the fact that it was polluted to some extent. Polluto did not carry out any survey of the property. Polluto sold the site to Green Inc six months ago. Subsequently Polluto have got into financial trouble and are on the verge of closing their operations in the UK.

Recent investigations have revealed that chemicals have been leaking from faulty underground storage tanks which were negligently installed by Fix-It Limited employed as contractors in 1969. These tanks were used by each occupier of the site up to and including Polluto. Green Inc have not used the tanks.

Who can be served with a remediation notice?

📖 FURTHER READING

Contaminated Land is a specialist area and this is reflected in the relative paucity of the academic writing on the subject. The starting point for any understanding of the contaminated land regime is the DETR's Circular 2/2000 which provides as clear a picture as possible (given the complexity of the provisions) of the way in which the law should work in practice. On wider issues related to contaminated land, there is one work which stands head and shoulders above the rest. S. Tromans and R. Turrell-Clarke, *Contaminated Land* (London: Sweet & Maxwell, 1994), together with its first supplement (London: Sweet & Maxwell, 1998) provides a comprehensive coverage of the pre-Part IIA law including precedents and practical matters such as commercial and property considerations. Post implementation rules are covered in S. Tromans and R. Turrell-Clarke *Contaminated Land: The New Regime* (London: Sweet & Maxwell, 2000).

Other than these general works, the articles tend to concentrate on particular aspects of the Contaminated Land Regime. There is an excellent overview of the problems of allocating liability for contaminated land in D. Lawrence and R. Lee, 'Permitting Uncertainty: Owners, Occupiers and

Responsibility for Remediation' (2003) 66 MLR 261. Other articles focus on other elements of the regime ranging from the definition of contaminated land in risk assessment in R. Kimblin, 'Risk, Jurisprudence and the Environment' (2000) JPL 359 to a general overview in D. Woolley, 'Contaminated Land—The real world' (2002) JPL 5. Although there is not much coverage of European initiatives on contaminated land in this chapter (for reasons that are spelt out in the relevant section) there are some moves towards developing European policy. A. Layard 'The Europeanisation of Contaminated Land' (2004) Env L Rev 97 summarizes the position and S. Christie and R. Teeuw 'Policy and Administration of Contaminated Land within the EU' (2000) Eur Env 24 gives a comparative perspective.

There have been a number of articles which discuss the impact of the rules on the practice of environmental law and in the sale and purchase of contaminated land. This is a real issue as can be seen in S. Payne, 'Clean Up and Indemnity: A Postscript to *Cambridge Water*' (2003) 15 JEL 202 which analyses a case dealing with the contractual allocation of liability for contamination arising out of the *Cambridge Water* decision. Other articles are a little specialist, dealing with the drafting of warranties and indemnities to transfer or limit liability post sale. If that is what you are interested in then have a look at any one of the following: B. Adams, 'Contaminated Land—The new clean-up regime takes hold' (2000) 11 PLC 29; V. Fogelman, 'Transferring remediation liabilities in commercial transactions' (2001) 13 Env Law Mgmt 83; A. Thomson, 'Environmental Indemnities—Controlling exposure' (2002) 13 PLC 43.

For a stimulating examination of the problems of trying to regulate the clean up of contaminated land whilst taking note of market effects (the stumbling block for the ill-fated Contaminative Uses Register) see J. Steele, 'Remedies and Remediation: Issues in Environmental Liability' (1995) 58 MLR 615.

If you are interested in a comparative approach you may wish to analyze the operation of the Superfund legislation in the US. This legislation has been the subject of much criticism but it does illustrate a different way of approaching the problem. A good set of essays on the topic is found in R. Revesz and R B Stewart (eds), *Analyzing Superfund: Economics, Science and Law* (Resources for the Future, 1995). There is also a lot of literature in US Journals on the topic. A few which may be of interest and which can be sourced through one of the electronic databases (e.g. Westlaw) are J. Lyons, 'Deep Pockets and CERCLA: Should Superfund be Abolished?' (1987) Stanford Environmental Law Journal 6, 271; C. Meyer, 'Does Minimizing Expenditures for CERCLA Site Remediation Increase the Future Public Abatement Costs?' (1993) Journal of Natural Resources and Environmental Law 9, 381; E. James, 'An American Werewolf in London: Applying the Lessons of Superfund to Great Britain' (1994) 19 Yale Journal of International Law 349.

@ WEB LINKS

The recent development of the contaminated land regime means that there is good web-based access to may of the primary materials. DEFRA's web site at <www.defra.gov.uk/environment/land/index.htm> has links to the Regulations and relevant statutory and technical guidance on contaminated land as well as material on soil protection. The Land Registration Network has extensive resources on contaminated land generally and Part IIA in particular. The site can be found at <www.grc.cf.ac.uk/lrn/resources/land/index.php>. A good source of European materials including a number of comparative studies of contaminated land legislation across the world can be found at <europa.eu.int/comm/environment/liability/>. Finally, if you're interested in the technical aspects of contaminated land have a look at <www.clarinet.at/> which provides an excellent database of materials and other resources dealing with the approaches taken across Europe to address contaminated land.

Water pollution and water quality

This chapter is about the quality of the water environment. This is a big topic, because there are well-developed bodies of law at national, EC and international level, all covering different ground. In the interests of space, therefore, we focus on the control of pollution of inland and coastal waters and do not cover in any detail wider issues about water resource management such as land drainage or flood defence, while the abstraction of water from the natural environment—which is becoming more tightly regulated, see, e.g., Part I Water Act 2003—is only discussed insofar as this has an impact on water quality. Discharges to sewers, which have as much in common with waste disposal as with water pollution and which have their own, more basic, regulatory system operated by sewerage undertakers, are dealt with in following chapter.

Before reading this chapter, you will find it useful if you already have an appreciation of EC environmental law, especially the legal status of directives and their implementation and enforcement (Chapter 7); the role of the Environment Agency (Chapter 5); differing regulatory approaches and techniques, especially the contrast between emission and target standards (Chapter 8); and civil and criminal liability (Chapters 11 and 9).

At the end of this chapter you will:

✔ Know about the state of the water environment and the main sources of water pollution.
✔ Understand in outline the regulation of the water industry and the role of the Environment Agency, and appreciate how improvements to water quality are funded.
✔ Understand how water pollution is defined and controlled and know about standards for water quality.
✔ Appreciate the scope of the main criminal offences for water pollution, and the main responses to the challenge of diffuse water pollution.
✔ Be able to evaluate the importance of EC law to the water environment.
✔ Appreciate in outline how international law affects national water law.

Water pollutants and their sources

Water pollutants come in many forms, including:

- deoxygenating materials, for example, sewage and other organic wastes, such as silage, farm wastes and wastes from a number of heavily polluting industrial processes (e.g. food processing and the production of smokeless fuel, textiles, paper, and dairy products);

- nutrient enrichment by such things as fertilizers, which may give rise to eutrophication, causing an accelerated growth of plants and algae and leading to a decline in water quality;

- solids, such as silt, which may impede flows, or block out light for growth;

- toxic materials: some materials, such as heavy metals, pesticides, or nitrate, are toxic to humans, animals, plants, or all three, often depending on the level of the dose received;

- materials which cause an impact on amenity, such as car tyres or shopping trolleys in rivers or canals;

- disease-carrying agents, such as bacteria;

- heat, which may affect biological conditions and also deoxygenates water.

The effect of any potential pollutant varies according to the size, temperature, rate of flow, and oxygen content of the receiving waters, as well as the local geology and the presence of other pollutants and any resulting synergistic (i.e. 'cocktail') effects. The use made of a stream is also of enormous importance in deciding whether it can be said to be polluted, and this factor has a large impact on the attitude of the regulatory bodies towards the setting of standards and their enforcement. It is not sufficient to look only at pollution of surface waters, since 30 per cent of the public water supply is taken from ground waters. As a result the control of water pollution encompasses the control of liquid discharges to land, or from land such as landfill sites (see further p. 607).

The sources of pollution are also varied. For example:

- There are around 75,000 discharges where there is a consent for discharge to waters. Many of these involve toxic materials or organic pollutants.

- Most consents (around 62,000) relate to sewage works, where the organic content of the discharge makes it highly polluting. Sewage pollution currently gives rise to the most number of serious water pollution incidents, and regulating sewage pollution has been a central concern in the history of water pollution.

- Agricultural pollution is problematic, giving rise both to a significant number of pollution incidents annually, as well as the more diffuse entry of pollutants from pesticide and fertiliser run-off. Groundwater contamination from pollutants like sheep dips is also a major regulatory problem. The Policy Commission on the Future of Farming and Food (2002) noted that 'Agriculture is the number one polluter of water in the country' (as it appears to be across Europe).[1]

- Spills of oils and fuels are a frequent source of water pollution incident.

- Accidents often cause pollution, particularly from the storage and transport of hazardous substances.

- Leachate from waste sites, including disused ones, are often highly contaminated.

Natural events can also influence water quality: heavy rainfall may lead to greater pollution from farm run-off, while drought—or over-abstraction—will tend to concentrate pollu-

---

1. Farming and Food: A Sustainable Future (2002), p. 68.

tants. Also, the more the environment is already under some form of 'stress', the more severe pollution incidents will tend to be.

The state of the water environment

The general state of inland water quality is measured by the Environment Agency (EA) using the General Quality Assessment (GQA) scheme. This has four separate elements, covering chemical and biological quality, nutrient status, and aesthetic quality.

Taking 1990 as a baseline, the GQA shows a marked improvement overall in *chemical quality*, the indicator of general organic pollution. In 2002, 94 per cent of rivers were of good or fair quality, with (net) 42 per cent of rivers improving their quality classification over this period (although this improvement is now levelling off). The general improvement is largely attributed to better treatment of effluent by sewerage undertakers, following significant investment by the water industry after privatization in 1989. The upward trend in chemical quality, however, was punctuated in the mid-1990s partly because of dry weather and partly due to water abstraction, emphasizing the importance of proper regulation over water quantity if water quality is to be improved.

By also including *biological assessment* (based on small water fauna), however, the GQA provides a better picture of the overall effect of all pollutants on the health of river ecosystems, although the grading of waters in this way is rather imprecise and biological quality depends on factors other than the quality of discharges. Currently, 95 per cent of rivers are of good or fair biological quality. Taking a baseline of 1990, figures indicate a net improvement in biological water quality of around 28 per cent, though again there has been some levelling off in recent years.

In 2002, 54 per cent of rivers had high concentrations of phosphate, and 29 per cent of nitrate—these being the major factors affecting the *nutrient status* of waters. Improvements here have been more modest than with organic pollutants, indicating the relative difficulty of controlling the input of pollutants like fertilisers from diffuse sources. A survey of frequently visited sites in 2000 revealed that around two-thirds were of *aesthetically* good or fair quality.

Taken together, the GQA and the EA's recording of water pollution incidents show some significant results in combating pollution from discrete discharge points (known as 'point sources'), but also the increasing challenge of combating diffuse sources of water pollution. However, differences in quality between areas and regions still persist and the quality of some stretches of river can still decline between surveys. What is undeniable, however, is that water quality is far removed from the 19th century when a letter could be written with river water[2] and the lower reaches of the River Thames were little more than an open sewer.

The regulatory challenges

As the chapter title suggests, the central regulatory and environmental issue here is not simply preventing or controlling unwanted substances from entering the natural water environment. Indeed, the traditional British approach to water quality regulation has been

2. Royal Commission on Rivers Pollution, Third Report, *Pollution Arising from the Woollen Manufacture* (1871), vol. 1, 12.

to defend the view that it makes no sense to start by asking 'what dangerous substances should we prevent from entering water?' since many substances can have a damaging impact on water quality in sufficient quantities. For example, there has been a successful water pollution prosecution following a spill of carbonated apple juice, and milk has a polluting effect around 300 times that of sewage (see also Case box 9.1). This illustrates that, in part, water quality regulation is about controlling the discharge of substances which are not inherently toxic or harmful, but which may have negative impacts depending on how much is discharged and where such substances are discharged.

The counterpart of this is that there is usually 'water pollution' only where waters are rendered unfit for some desirable use such as drinking water supply or supporting fish life.[3] The law therefore tends to aim to ensure a particular quality of water for various purposes, rather than just preventing or minimizing the entry of 'pollutants' (although some standards are clearly set to eliminate certain substances being present in certain waters, even where there is little evidence of actual harm being likely: the pesticides standards in the Directive on Drinking Water are fairly clear examples of this). This also allows for natural differences in the composition of water, and things like the rate and amount of flow, to be taken into account.

In legal terms, this is reflected in a preference for target standards based on the character of the receiving environment rather than the adoption of emission standards reducing certain harmful substances from the water environment. (This preferred approach has, with one or two notable exceptions, basically been followed in EC water directives.) It is also reflected in the particular approach taken to regulating individual discharges, which is that official permission is not strictly needed before substances are discharged. Rather, the purpose of a discharge consent, issued by the EA, is to act as a defence to any charge of polluting water.

This peculiar legal nature of discharge consents has some important implications. Most notable is that in the setting of consents, the adoption of process-based standards such as best available techniques to minimize pollution has not generally been required. (There was a defence for companies under the Rivers Pollution Prevention Act 1876 to use 'best practicable means'.) In the context of quality standards, such an approach could lead to over-regulation and inefficiencies, although another way of looking at this is to emphasize that, as a result, discharge consents do not necessarily encourage a progressive tightening up of standards. On the other hand, however, strict water quality objectives have never been favoured. Instead, consents have tended to be set (and enforced) on an individualized basis, having general regard to the quality of the river and its catchment, and to particular things like the location of abstraction points for public supply.

Many of the more obvious sources of pollution are being brought under control. This is focusing attention on the release of substances into the environment which have an uncertain impact, such as the impact of hormone disrupting substances (so-called 'gender-bender' chemicals) which appear to feminise male fish like roach, leading to concerns over their impact on humans. But perhaps the most important regulatory problem is the increasing contribution of diffuse sources, such as agricultural run-off and pollution from urban development and vehicle emissions, to reductions in water quality. Such non-point

---

3. Although the main water pollution offence of causing polluting matter to enter controlled waters does not require actual harm, see p. 734.

sources of water pollution cannot really be controlled by consents, and instead need an imaginative mix of policy and legal mechanisms (see p. 748).

Two final issues relate to reaching fair decisions about who should pay for improving water quality and who should be given rights to pollute. The first of these is illustrated by looking at who pays for nitrate and pesticide removal. At present, this is mainly done by the water companies using expensive technology, which is ultimately paid for by water customers. But there is a strong argument for saying that farmers—the main users of these pollutants, which do not just affect water for drinking—should pay, with the cost filtering down to food consumers.

The second issue is that, as with certain air pollution limits, once it is decided that a certain overall level of pollution is to be tolerated, it must be decided how 'rights' to pollute are divided up, and on what basis. This is something determined in the day-to-day setting and revision of consents, but it illustrates the more profound issues the consent regime raises than simply protecting individual dischargers from criminal liability. The consent system, as well as other mechanisms to prevent or reduce water pollution, must be transparent, participatory and accountable if it is to operate with any legitimacy.

History of the water sector and controls on water quality

Over the years, the law on water pollution has tended to be the most developed of the systems of pollution control. It has also had the greatest degree of coherence, both in terms of the institutional arrangements and in terms of substantive law. These institutional arrangements have changed markedly over time, and must be appreciated alongside changes to the structure of the water sector (see Timeline).

The water sector and regulatory water pollution controls—timeline	
Rivers Pollution Prevention Act 1876 River Boards Act 1948	Absolute prohibition on pollution, but broad defences for industry and almost totally unworkable Previously water supply and sewage disposal functions exercised by municipal authorities. Public health matters also dealt with on a local authority basis. This Act created 32 river boards on a catchment area basis with certain regulatory functions
Rivers (Prevention of Pollution) Act 1951	River board consent required for new industrial or sewage discharges into most inland waters (controls extended to tidal and estuarial waters under the Clean Rivers (Estuaries and Tidal Waters) Act 1960)
Rivers (Prevention of Pollution) Act 1961	Existing discharges (pre-1951) brought under control
Water Resources Act 1963	Controls extended to discharges to certain underground waters. River boards converted into 27 river authorities, with various regulatory functions, including pollution control and the new system of licensing water abstraction. Water supply and sewage disposal remained essentially a local authority function (157 water supply undertakings and no less than 1,393 sewage authorities)

Water Act 1973	10 regional water authorities established, responsible for all water related functions within river basin areas, i.e. both operational and regulatory.[4] System generally seen as ineffective, mainly because of under-funding for sewage treatment and because the regional water authorities were both poacher and gamekeeper regarding water pollution. A general decline in standards
Control of Pollution Act 1974	Pollution controls extended out to three miles offshore. Limited public participation provisions (re)introduced (public registers, private prosecutions). Stronger preventive and remedial measures. Main measures not brought into force until the mid-1980s because of cost concerns. Certain provisions never implemented.
Water Act 1989	Water supply and sewerage functions privatised. Water and sewerage companies subject to economic regulation (under OFWAT) and environmental regulation (under the National Rivers Authority (NRA)). Operation/regulation split. Provision for statutory water quality objectives. Charging for trade and sewage discharges introduced. Improvements to preventive and remedial powers.
Environmental Protection Act 1990	Gave responsibility for discharges to water from the most polluting processes to HMIP
Environment Act 1995	NRA subsumed within the Environment Agency
Water Resources Act 1991	Consolidation of water law. The Water Resources Act 1991 deals with quality and quantity; the Water Industry Act 1991 deals with the water and sewerage industries
Environment Act 1995	Creation of Environment Agency unites main enforcement bodies (NRA and HMIP)[5]
Water Act 2003	OFWAT will become a Regulation Authority (a panel of regulators rather than a single Director) in 2006

Note that alongside these national level changes, since the 1970s there have been important EC directives and international agreements which have greatly shaped national water pollution law.

As the timeline above suggests, the water industry has historically been dominated by water collection, treatment and supply, and the provision of sewers, sewage works and sewage disposal. However, historically the water industry also encompassed a range of additional concerns including:

- water pollution control;
- the regulation of bodies providing water services;
- fisheries;
- navigation;

4 The only real exception was the retention of 29 private water companies responsible for water supply in defined areas.

5. Note that the Drinking Water Inspectorate remains outside the EA, and there are some areas of uncertainty about the role of local authorities in relation to discharges to water under the integrated permitting system in the Pollution Prevention and Control Act 1999.

- flood defence and land drainage;
- recreational activities; and
- conservation responsibilities.

From this list it is clear that in reality this is a set of activities, connected in the sense that they all relate to the water cycle, but separate in their objectives. Pollution control was only one function of the water industry prior to privatisation in 1989, but its place in relation to these other activities needs to be understood.

(a) Legal controls on water quality

Some of the difficulties of relying on the common law of nuisance or of riparian rights to control water pollution are expanded in Box 2.1, while the limitations of the Rivers Pollution Prevention Act 1876 are outlined in Box 2.2. However, even with the advent in 1951 of the discharge consent regime, the emphasis was always on flexible standards, with most consents being set on an individualised basis by reference to the effect of a discharge on the receiving waters. Particular emphasis has been placed on biochemical oxygen demand (BOD) and the level of suspended solids, rather than on such things as metals and toxic substances, especially in relation to sewage discharges. In a sense, the setting of consents could almost be described as a 'rule of thumb' method. This approach is, however, changing in response to EC directives and as a result of creating a more uniform system of control nationwide, begun under the NRA.

(b) Water quality policy style and techniques

Until 1989 it was difficult to identify a coherent national water quality policy. The Department of the Environment had overall responsibility for all water matters, but most policy decisions were left to the regional water authorities, with the DoE appearing more preoccupied with financial matters than with water quality. Of course, there were often unspoken aims, such as that of getting treatable wastes into the sewerage system if possible, and cleaning up waters for economic reasons, since the public water supply was increasingly taken from them. In addition, EC standards effectively laid down a set of priorities, leading to such things as a policy to minimize the discharge of dangerous substances and if possible to cut them out entirely—effectively a precautionary policy.

The establishment of the NRA meant that the opportunity could be taken to establish a truly national policy on water quality—or at least one applicable to England and Wales. Key elements of this policy included increased attention to prevention of harm in such areas as farm pollution and pollution from abandoned mines, and a more rigorous enforcement policy involving greater use of prosecution. The NRA also established a national strategy for reviewing all existing consents on a catchment area basis and harmonizing consenting procedures and levels of consents; this included bringing sewage works consents into line with industrial consents. However, it remains the case that consents are mainly set on an individualized basis, with the main determinant being the effect on the receiving waters. The general approach adopted by the NRA (and continued by the EA) was that river catchments should be managed on an integrated basis. This process is a good example of aspects of environmental policy being set by a body other than central government. However, the government also has an important role to play here. *River Quality: The Government's*

Proposals (DoE, 1992) set out a general strategy for water quality which is still being followed. This made it quite clear that the cost-effectiveness of environmental improvements— and the question of who should pay for them—was a major factor in government policy, hence the slow progress that is being made on such things as statutory water quality objectives. More recently—at least for England[6]—DEFRA re-stated its vision of 'further improvements in water quality standards wherever the costs are proportionate to the benefits and risks'. The need for increased action on tackling diffuse agricultural and urban pollution (see p. 748), and for improving integration between water and other policies and between different aspects of water policy, were also stressed.

(c) Scotland, Wales, and Northern Ireland

The position in the devolved administrations is slightly different. In Scotland, the water industry has not been privatized, and water supply and sewerage services are provided by Scottish Water, a public sector body accountable to the Scottish Parliament but run on the lines of a private company. The Water Act 1989 did not make any institutional changes, but in schedule 23 it did amend the Control of Pollution Act 1974, which still remains in force in Scotland. Unfortunately, this has meant that there are slightly different wordings for some sections on each side of the border. Whilst water pollution law is thus very similar in Scotland, it cannot always be guaranteed that it is exactly the same. Regulations which are likely to be made under the Water Environment and Water Services Act (Scotland) 2003, enacted in part to allow implementation of the EC Water Framework Directive (2000/60/EC), may see a greater divergence of regulatory approach north and south of the border.

The Environment Act 1995 established the Scottish Environment Protection Agency (SEPA), which replaced the river purification boards and Her Majesty's Industrial Pollution Inspectorate (HMIPI) and thus brought together all water pollution functions in one body (although SEPA does not have functions in relation to general water management such as flood control or fisheries). Following the Scotland Act 1998, water pollution is a matter for the Scottish Parliament, although importantly the negotiation of EC directives remains with the UK government.

Under the Government of Wales Act 1998, responsibility for water pollution is a matter for the National Assembly for Wales although the Assembly cannot amend primary legislation such as the Water Resources Act 1991. As with Scotland there is also the significant limitation that matters concerning EC water law and policy remain the responsibility of central government. General references below to 'the Secretary of State' or 'the Minister' should be read as including the Welsh Assembly where appropriate.

Water quality matters in Northern Ireland are the responsibility of the Environment and Heritage Service of the Department of the Environment (Northern Ireland). Water legislation was overhauled by the Water (Northern Ireland) Order 1999 (SI 1999/662) (NI.6) which brought the controls on discharge consents more into line with practice elsewhere in the UK and gave more powers to the DoE (NI) to make pollution prevention regulations.

---

6. DEFRA, *Directing the Flow: Priorities for Future Water Policy* (2002).

International law and water quality

(a) Marine pollution and the quality of the marine environment

Not surprisingly, international law has mostly been concerned with marine waters rather than water quality at national level, although it is the nature of the water cycle that there is no clear divide between the two.

Roughly, it has been estimated that around 77 per cent of marine pollution globally results from discharges from land. Of this, around 60 per cent originates from run-off, either through direct discharges into coastal water or into fresh water passing into the sea through river estuaries, with the remainder coming via the atmosphere. Hence much of the contamination entering the marine environment (around 56 per cent), is regulated, at the point of origin of the contaminants, by the regime that governs the quality of inland waters (described in detail below). It is worth stressing that much of the marine pollution which derives from atmospheric deposits is not regulated with specific regard to the eventual impact on the marine environment (e.g. vehicle emissions).

(b) Policy approaches

In international conventions on marine pollution a target standard approach in the sense of using water quality objectives (binding or otherwise) is not generally taken. But in some respects the approach is difficult to classify as an emission control approach, since apart from controlling things like major oil spills the objective is as much to do with preventing the release of oil and other substances per se regardless of impact. For example, most of the offences relating to discharging oil—which originate in international treaties—are committed even in the absence of any polluting impact.

(c) The impact of international conventions

Compared with EC law, the impact of international conventions has been less dramatic, although there are instances where EC standards and policy originate in hard and soft international law (see e.g. Box 2.7). One of the key provisions of the EC Water Framework Directive has its origins in a regional marine convention (see Box 18.1).

BOX 18.1 International and EC law and hazardous substances in the water environment

For what are intrinsically hazardous substances, the EC Water Framework Directive (2000/60/EC, see p. 714) requires measures which must be aimed at progressively reducing and, for priority hazardous substances, at ceasing or phasing out discharges, emissions and losses (Art. 16(1)). The background to this wording lies in a Declaration of the International North Sea Conference, and the Hazardous Substances Strategy under the 1992 OSPAR Convention, under which parties are bound to make every endeavour to move towards the target of cessation of discharges, emissions and losses of hazardous substances by 2020. During the late stages of negotiating the Water Framework Directive the European Parliament sought to incorporate the water quality strategy taken under the OSPAR Convention. Additionally, parties to the OSPAR

Convention have agreed to achieve continuous reductions in releases of hazardous substances with the ultimate aim of achieving concentrations in the environment near background levels for naturally occurring substances and close to zero for man-made synthetic substances. However, the wording of the Framework Directive requires a progressive (rather than 'continuous') reduction in hazardous substances and only applies the phasing out obligation to 'priority hazardous substances' (currently, 11 substances out of the initial 33 substances identified as hazardous). However, the Framework Directive also defines the 'close to zero' and 'background levels' requirements as part of what 'high ecological status' entails, and the baseline requirement to achieve 'good ecological status' (under Art. 4) does not therefore include these specific obligations which are now the cornerstone of regional international marine pollution law under OSPAR.

Decisions taken by the International Conferences for the Protection of the North Sea have also influenced the development of the precautionary principle and, in line with this, banning the disposal of sewage sludge at sea, a measure now contained in the EC Urban Waste Water Treatment Directive (91/271). The impact of this on national disposal practices, such as greater spreading of sludge on land, as well as similar bans on the dumping and incineration of industrial waste, and coastal dumping of colliery spoil and power station ash, illustrates the way in which measures to protect the marine environment may have direct consequences at national level, to say nothing of the significant costs involved.

This impact of international law on national practices is also seen with the various international provisions aimed at preventing marine pollution from ships, notably the 1973/78 'MARPOL' Convention, which regulates deliberate, operational discharges of oil and, through Protocols, certain other substances (e.g. noxious liquid substances and sewage) from vessels. These provisions must be enforced both by flag states and against foreign vessels by port states, and apply to the territorial sea as well as (in some situations) the exclusive economic zone. The Convention also regulates design, construction and maintenance standards for oil tankers, although it originally contained rather generous provisions for existing vessels which, because of the life span of tankers, limited its effectiveness. This was addressed in amendments to the Convention adopted in 1992, which both strengthened the inspection procedures for older vessels and added a requirement to retrofit double hulls or an equivalent to tankers of 25 years of age and older.

The MARPOL Convention regime therefore takes a preventive approach to marine oil pollution. This is in contrast to other international agreements in this area. These include the 1969 Intervention Convention, which allows for intervention on the high seas in the case of accidental oil spills from vessels in distress (introduced following the *Torrey Canyon* incident in 1967). They also include measures regulating liability and compensation for oil pollution damage under the 1992 Conventions on Civil Liability for Oil Pollution Damage and Establishment of an International Fund for Compensation for Oil Pollution Damage (discussed in more detail in Box 11.1).

By contrast with what are quite tightly defined obligations in relation to oil and other noxious substances, there are more general provisions in the 1982 UN Convention on the Law of the Sea on preventing, reducing and controlling pollution of the marine environment from land based sources (Art. 207) and similar obligations for pollution from things like oil rigs and sea bed mining (Art. 208). There are also rules about pollution from dumping (Art. 210), though as with many provisions of UNCLOS in this area, states are encouraged to seek regional solutions and the 1992 Paris Convention dealing with the North Sea and North East Atlantic area (the 'OSPAR' Convention) is important, at least in relation to the development of policy. Specifically, following the *Brent Spar* affair (see Box 3.4), the parties to OSPAR agreed in 1998 to a ban on the disposal of redundant steel oil and gas platforms at sea, which will have knock-on consequences for waste disposal on land (although concrete platforms can still be dumped). The parties also agreed to reduce to 'close to zero' by 2020 concentrations of artificial radioactive substances.

BOX 18.2 **Sellafield and international water pollution law**

Under Article 206 of UNCLOS, 'when states have reasonable grounds for believing that planned activities under their jurisdiction or control may cause substantial pollution of or significant and harmful changes to the marine environment, they shall, as far as practicable, assess the potential effects of such activities on the marine environment'. This obligation is similar to that imposed by EC and national law on environmental impact assessment (see Chapter 14). In 2001, Ireland brought proceedings against the UK alleging that the UK had breached Art 206 because it had authorized a mixed oxide (MOX) fuel plant at Sellafield in reliance on an Environmental Impact Statement from 1993 which had not considered the impact of the plant on the marine environment of the Irish Sea. The majority of the International Tribunal on the Law of the Sea (ITLOS) declined to suspend the plant's operation pending a full hearing on its merits. However, the Tribunal did order the parties to cooperate and exchange information on possible environmental consequences of the plant being commissioned, and to devise measures to prevent pollution of the marine environment which might result from the plant's operation. This ruling, which Sands[7] notes has 'a certain precautionary character', was based on considerations of 'prudence and caution'. It is worth noting, though, that part of Ireland's claim relates to the possible impact of the transportation of nuclear waste to Sellafield. Although this claim is made in the context of harm to the Irish Sea, any tightening of controls that it may lead to will probably have an indirect effect on parts of the marine environment that fall outside national jurisdiction.

A final point is that the Tribunal rejected the UK's claim that ITLOS could not rule on the case because other treaties (OSPAR, and the EC and Euratom Treaties) also governed the plant's impact. This issue of jurisdiction is important, because Member States of the EC (and Euratom) have a general duty to resolve their disputes through European law. The European Court of Justice has been asked to rule on this issue—and may reach a different conclusion—which shows the unsettled hierarchy of laws in areas like international water pollution law (see Box 6.5).

Taken together, these developments seem to mark a continuing move away from a 'dilute and disperse' approach in the waters around the UK. However, it is also interesting that, in the case of oil rig decommissioning, the use of individual BPEO assessments has also now

---

7. P. Sands, *Principles of International Environmental Law* (2nd ed. Cambridge: Cambridge University Press (2003), 276.

been rejected in favour of a more prescriptive policy approach. This suggests a subtle shift towards an emission standards approach based on the political unacceptability of some high profile entries to the water environment. Notwithstanding the reactive steps that are being taken to combat high profile incidents like this—and like major tanker spills—the overall global picture remains pessimistic. The global ocean remains a dumping ground for land-based and atmospheric pollution, and on the whole international law has yet to find adequate, proactive ways of dealing with this.

The EC and water quality

The EC has had an enormous impact on water pollution law and policy over the years. The First Action Programme on the Environment in 1973 picked out water pollution as a priority matter, and there has been a steady stream of directives since. These have tackled such diverse topics as the reduction of pollution from dangerous substances, the improvement of the quality of bathing waters, nitrates in water and the progressive introduction of adequate sewage treatment systems. The gradual implementation of the Water Framework Directive will mean that all pollutants in all waters will be covered by EC law.

EC water directives follow three basic models as regards standard setting:

- those which adopt emission standards, which are mainly used for reducing dangerous substances;

- those which impose quality objectives on waters that are mainly set according to the use that is to be made of those waters;

- those which regulate particular polluting processes.

There are also isolated cases where directives take different approaches to control, focusing on particular kinds of pollutants. Directive 73/404 on Detergents sets a product standard by prohibiting the marketing of detergents with average biodegradability of less than 90 per cent. Directive 78/176 on Titanium Dioxide sets standards in relation to a specific industry (the paint industry.

(a) Emission standard approaches

One of the first major water directives was 76/464 on Dangerous Substances in Water. This is a framework directive passed with the aim of reducing or eliminating certain dangerous substances from water. It covers essentially the same waters as those controlled by the EA and has led to very tight controls over certain dangerous substances in discharge consents. Most of the Directive is still in force, but it will be fully repealed by the Water Framework Directive (see p. 717) in 2013. The Directive lays down two lists of substances:

- List I (the 'black list'); and

- List II (the 'grey list').

In relation to black list substances, the Directive seeks the elimination of pollution. Any discharge of a black list substance must be subject to some form of authorization granted by a competent national authority. Such an authorization must conform to very strict requirements. It must *either* set an emission standard which does not exceed the appropriate EC limit value, or the emission standard must be set so that the EC environmental quality standard for the receiving waters is kept to at all times. Only Britain adopted the second approach (see below), the competent authority being the EA, which operates the discharge consent systems so as to ensure that the EC environmental quality standards are met at all times.

However, implementation of this part of the Directive proceeded very slowly. The Directive itself identifies potential black list substances in general terms only—they are those which are highly toxic, persistent, carcinogenic, or liable to bio-accumulate—but only a few 'daughter directives' providing specific standards for substances like cadmium and mercury were ever adopted. Under the Water Framework Directive the black list has, from 2000, been replaced by the list of priority hazardous substances. Where a daughter directive is not agreed for a potential black list substance, the substance is treated as on the grey list (see below).

For grey list substances, the Directive again lays down a fairly general list. This includes a range of metals (such as zinc, copper, tin, nickel, and chromium), biocides, cyanides, fluorides, ammonia, and nitrites. The objective is that pollution by these substances should be reduced. Accordingly, if any such substance has a deleterious effect on the aquatic environment, Member States must develop a national environmental quality standard and ensure that it is met in the receiving waters. These standards are set at a national, rather than at an EC, level. The Member State must also introduce a reduction programme for grey list substances and must control discharges by setting standards in discharge consents which enable the environmental quality standards to be achieved.

It was Directive 76/464 which first demonstrated the differences between Britain and the rest of the EC over standard setting. Britain's system of a decentralized setting of non-uniform consents by reference to the quality of the receiving waters was seen to be directly contradictory to the desire of other Member States for uniform (i.e. minimum), centrally set emission standards for dangerous substances. After much argument, this led to the agreement of the alternative approaches for 'black list' substances in the Directive explained above.

Directive 76/464 has had an enormous impact on British pollution control. Having claimed that it set its consents by reference to quality objectives for the receiving waters, the British government was forced to introduce such a system on a formal basis, and water quality objectives were introduced for the first time in the late 1970s, at first by administrative action. This was insufficient for compliance with EC law and sections relating to *statutory* water quality objectives were first introduced in the Water Act 1989.

The Directive also led to specific changes in relation to controls over dangerous substances. For example, whilst many existing discharges were given deemed consent when COPA 1974 was finally brought into force, those involving dangerous substances were subject to specified emission standards. In general, significant discharges of 'black list' and 'grey list' substances are subject to integrated pollution control. The rules providing for control by the EA of prescribed substances discharged to sewers are also a result of this directive.

A similar story attaches to Directive 80/68 on Groundwater, except in this case List I substances are to be prevented from entering ground waters, whilst discharges of List II substances should be limited, in both cases by a consent system.

One problem with the emission standards approach is that it does not work well for pollution from non-point (i.e. diffuse) sources, nor where there are multiple polluters in one catchment area (although it may have to deal with what are effectively diffuse discharges; see Case C-231/97 *van Rooij* [1999] ECR I-6355). Directive 86/280 attempts to tackle this issue by requiring all *sources* of 'black list' substances to be monitored.

(b) Quality objective approaches

For the quality approach there are a number of stages:

(a) water with particular uses must first be identified (this is usually left to the discretion of the Member States but must be done on objective grounds);

(b) the EC must establish a number of parameters: these are normally expressed either as Imperative (I) values, which must be kept to, or Guide (G) values, which Member States must try to achieve;

(c) environmental quality objectives must be set for the waters, having regard to the parameters;

(d) a competent national authority must be established for monitoring purposes and uniform sampling techniques are set by EC directives (e.g. 79/ 869 on Sampling Surface Water for Drinking);

(e) procedures are established for updating the I and G values in the light of new knowledge.

Directives which have adopted this approach include those on Surface Water for Drinking 75/440, Shellfish Waters 79/923, Water Standards for Freshwater Fish 78/659, Bathing Waters 76/160. The Drinking Water Directive (98/83/EC) also applies this approach, although in this case it is the quality of water at the tap that is regulated (see p. 721).

The water quality approach is best illustrated by the Bathing Waters Directive. This lays down 19 parameters (mainly bacteriological) with which all 'traditional' bathing waters must comply, within specified percentile compliance rates. It covers fresh and marine waters although the Directive is very vague as to precisely which waters are covered. The British response was unenthusiastic: identification of the relevant waters was left to the regional water authorities and only 27 were initially identified—fewer than, for example, land-locked Luxembourg. (In addition, no inland bathing waters were identified until nine sites were selected in 1998—a bemusing approach.) No doubt the reason was the fear of the cost of cleaning up discharges of sewage effluent. In consequence of a reasoned opinion on non-implementation from the EC Commission, and intense EC and public pressure, the number of designated beaches in England and Wales is now 483. Nevertheless, Britain was taken to the European Court of Justice over non-implementation of the Directive and in July 1993 was found to be in breach in relation to standards on Blackpool and Southport beaches (see Case C-56/90 *Commission v United Kingdom* [1993] ECR I-4109). This case, where proceedings were stalled by the Commission so that the decision of the ECJ was given after the 1992 UK general election, confirmed the decision in Case C-337/89 *Commission v United Kingdom* [1992] ECR I-6103 relating to the Drinking Water Directive, which had made clear that the duty to comply with the standards laid down in the Directive is absolute, rather than simply to take all practicable steps to comply (see Case box 7.3). Some further considerations showing the nature of the duty to achieve water quality standards can be seen in Case box 18.1.

CASE 18.1 Case C-92/96 *Commission v Spain* [1998] ECR I-505

The Commission alleged that Spain was not complying with the Bathing Water Directive at a number of freshwater bathing waters. Spain raised four grounds to justify non-compliance, namely that:

(a) an abnormal drought, lasting five years, amounted to 'abnormal weather conditions';

(b) Commission proposals to revise the Directive (see below), as well as (at the time) proposals for a Water Framework Directive made the Bathing Water Directive obsolete;

(c) the main factor behind poor bathing water quality was urban waste water, which was the subject of the Urban Waste Water Treatment Directive, the provisions of which, and the timetable for compliance in which, should be taken into consideration; and

(d) that many of the bathing areas inspected were no longer used as a result of a change in social habits.

In relation to all but the first justification, the Court of Justice held that neither the envisaged amendments to the Directive, nor that Member States are allowed a longer period in which to comply with certain provisions of the Urban Waste Water Treatment Directive, nor the change in social habits said to have resulted in bathers abandoning a large number of bathing areas, forms part of the derogations provided for in the Directive. Hence those considerations could not justify a failure to fulfil the water quality obligation imposed by the Directive. The Court did, however, recognize that drought could amount to 'abnormal weather conditions', but dismissed this contention because Spain had not produced any specific evidence.

This case formed the first breach of EC law which subsequently led to Spain being fined a hefty annual penalty payment for not complying with this judgment (see Case box 7.5)

In the last few years, UK compliance with the Directive has significantly improved, and by 2003 98.8 per cent of designated beaches complied with the standards.

There are ongoing proposals to revise the Directive, which has always been controversial, in the light of new scientific knowledge and the subsidiarity principle. These proposals would also see compliance with the Directive being assessed on a rolling three-year average, rather than the present position where a single year of poor quality can in theory result in infringement proceedings and the possibility of individual enforcement and liability actions. The threat of fines (see the fine against Spain relating the Directive, discussed above) may be one reason why a practice has recently emerged of declassifying contaminated bathing sites, or banning bathing at sites, rather than cleaning them up (this is not required by the present Directive, although the ECJ has held that bathing *must* be banned if not doing so would be a health hazard; Case C-307/98 *Commission v Belgium* [2000] ECR I-3933).[8]

---

8. There is an instructive comparison with 'suitable for use' in relation to contaminated land—see Chapter 17.

(c) Directives regulating particular polluting activities

There are two directives from 1991 which regulate particular polluting activities. The Directive on Urban Waste Water Treatment (91/271) is potentially the most significant in terms of compliance costs. It lays down minimum standards for the treatment of urban waste waters (i.e. domestic sewage and industrial waste waters). These treatment standards, and the time-scales within which they must be met, vary according to the population of the area concerned, but the basic idea is that some form of biological treatment ('secondary treatment') should be usual for domestic wastes. For example, a secondary or equivalent system of sewage treatment is required by the end of 2000 for a town with a population equivalent of more than 15,000. Stricter standards are required in sensitive areas and lower standards are permitted in less-sensitive areas. The Directive also required all Member States to cease dumping sewage sludge at sea by the end of 1998. The Directive therefore grafts an emissions standard approach on to a quality standards framework, and is fairly unusual in that water quality is not protected because of any immediate use value.

The Directive has had a particular impact on Britain, the only Member State which carried out sewage sludge dumping and which traditionally employed a 'dilute and disperse' policy of discharging virtually untreated sewage into the sea via outfalls. The Directive was implemented by the Urban Waste Water Treatment (England and Wales) Regulations 1994 (SI 1994/2841). These regulations largely adopt the wording of the directive, except that instead of 'less sensitive areas' the regulations refer to 'high natural dispersion areas'. In 1994, 33 sensitive areas and 58 high natural dispersion areas were initially identified. One area of controversy, however, was the classification of a number of estuarial waters as coastal for the purposes of the regulations, thus allowing lower levels of treatment to be applied.

CASE 18.2 *R v Secretary of State for the Environment, ex parte Kingston upon Hull City Council* [1996] Env LR 248

The Secretary of State had drawn the boundaries of the estuary for the Humber and Severn rivers at the Humber and Severn road bridges, thus ensuring lower (and therefore cheaper) levels of treatment for treatment works alongside the rivers. His decision was successfully challenged on the grounds that costs should not have been taken into account, and that the correct way of drawing the boundaries was to carry out a genuine and rational assessment of what actually constituted the estuary. (Subsequently, the estuaries were redefined as a line between the two furthest points of land on each side of the river.) The case illustrates the need for an objective approach to area designations (the ECJ has reached the same conclusion for a range of water quality and area-related directives). But it is also a good example of a successful challenge to the implementation of an EC directive, and notable because issues of direct effect were not raised. It was enough that the local authorities could show that there had been an error in interpreting the Directive, without issues of individual rights being raised.

Further sensitive areas were designated in 1998 and 2002. As important have been increases to funding under which the amount of sewage outfalls receiving secondary treatment is now well above the 2 per cent level it stood at before the Directive.

The Agricultural Nitrates Directive (91/676) also regulates a particular polluting activity, requiring Member States to designate 'nitrate vulnerable zones' and implement action programmes in these areas. The Directive therefore takes a largely quality objective approach, but like Directive 91/271 is distinct in regulating water quality through the control of a particularly polluting activity. For more detail on the Directive and its implementation see p. 747.

(d) Summary of the impact of EC law

The EC has thus had a great impact on British water pollution practice. Whilst there have been many arguments about technical matters, such as the levels laid down for nitrate in drinking water and the need for a Bathing Waters Directive at all, most of the standards required have been introduced in one way or another, although normally belatedly. A formal system of water quality classifications and objectives, statutory regulations on drinking water quality, the introduction of specific standards for dangerous substances, and a dramatic shift in relation to the discharge of sewage effluent to the sea can all be attributed to EC initiatives. The general approach to pollution control has also been altered significantly.

Perhaps the greatest impact, however, has been the great publicity that has been engendered by having specific standards set at EC level against which government action can be measured. This has certainly contributed to the intensity of the debate over nitrate. EC requirements also had an impact on the proposals for the privatisation of the water industry. It became clear that the EC would not accept a private pollution regulator as a 'competent authority' for the purposes of directives, and this was one reason for the creation of the NRA (and also a separate Drinking Water Inspectorate). Finally, when combined with this greater specificity, the public health nature of most water directives may help direct legal challenges to non-implementation (although individual rights do not need to be infringed for there to be a remedy in flagrant cases of breach, see p. 224).

(e) The Water Framework Directive

EC water pollution policy is presently undergoing fundamental change following the adoption of the Water Framework Directive (2000/60/EC), an ambitious attempt at comprehensively overhauling EC water policy. This followed a general recognition that much of the Community's existing water legislation was outdated, and in particular insufficiently holistic, in its approach to pollution control. The Directive is being phased in over a period of years, and by 2013 a number of existing directives will have been repealed because of the scope of the Framework Directive; the main ones are the Dangerous Substances Directive (76/464), the Groundwater Directive (80/68), the Fish Waters Directive (78/659), and the Shellfish Water Directive (79/923). (It is worth noting that some key water directives will not be repealed; the main ones being the Bathing Water Directive (76/160), the Drinking Water Quality Directive (98/83), the Agricultural Nitrates Directive (91/676), and the Urban Waste Water Treatment Directive (91/271).) Unlike previous water legislation, the Framework Directive covers surface water and groundwater together, as well as estuaries and coastal waters. Its main purposes are:

• to prevent further deterioration in, and to protect and enhance, the status of aquatic ecosystems;

• to promote sustainable water consumption based on the long-term protection of available water resources;

- progressively to reduce discharges, emissions and losses of priority substances;
- for priority hazardous substances, their cessation or phasing out with the ultimate aim that concentrations in the marine environment are near background levels for naturally occurring substances and close to zero for man-made synthetic substances;
- the progressive reduction of groundwater pollution and to prevent further pollution;
- to contribute to the provision of good quality surface and groundwaters needed for sustainable, balanced and equitable water use.

The Directive's overriding requirement is that Member States *aim to achieve* good surface water status (meaning both good chemical status and good ecological status), good eco-logical potential (for artificial or heavily modified waters), and good groundwater status in all waters by the end of 2015. For groundwater, good status is measured in terms of both quantity and chemical purity (i.e. abstractions and alterations to the natural rate of recharge are sustainable in the long term without leading to loss of ecological quality); for surface waters ecological quality is an additional criterion (i.e. in addition to ensuring that con-centrations of certain 'black list' substances—now termed priority hazardous substances—do not exceed relevant environmental quality standards and other Community legislation setting such standards, 'good ecological status' means that a body of water which is demonstrated to be significantly influenced by human activity, nevertheless has a rich, balanced and sustainable ecosystem). Although the definition of good status is rudimentary, in many cases it will require Member States to improve on the present situation.

One of the Framework Directive's innovations is that rivers and lakes must be managed by river basin—the natural hydrological unit—instead of according to administrative or political boundaries. With each river basin the directive makes provision for the preparation of a strategic plan, a 'river basin management plan'; these must be published first by 2009 and updated every six years. The purpose of the plan will be to establish a programme of measures to ensure that all waters in the river basin achieve the objective of good water status. Although institutionally a catchment approach is taken in the UK, the programme of measures requires integrated catchment management, which the UK has yet to adopt (see, e.g., the current approach to nutrients, which still tends to focus on water companies' removing nitrates and pesticides rather than requiring farmers to reduce their inputs). Indeed, the Directive is as much about land use generally as it is about water management. The Directive also requires that the public have the opportunity to be involved in the formulation of these plans (which marks a departure from the UK's approach which has been more technocratic).

The Directive avoids some of the problems of adopting a singular approach to environ-mental standards. Indeed it recognizes the strengths of arguments in favour of both approaches which were put forward at the time of the 1976 Dangerous Substances Directive (see pp. 250 and 712). It takes a 'combined approach' requiring Member States to set down in their programmes of measures both limit values to control emissions from individual point sources and environmental quality standards to limit the cumulative impact of such emissions. For listed hazardous substances, however, as noted above (see Box 18.1) the Directive requires that these be phased out.

The Framework Directive is also the first piece of EC water legislation to address the issue of water *quantity*, which is important in part because of the links between water quantity and water quality (see p. 702). One consequence of this is that 'full cost recovery' pricing for water use is required by 2010. This will include costs of water use in terms of environmental damage as well as adverse effects caused by over-abstraction (though the details of this obligation are contested, e.g. the water companies argue that it requires that the cost of removing diffuse pollutants from water are not subsidized by water consumers).

There is no doubting that the Framework Directive requires a fundamental change in existing law—both European and domestic. There remains, however, much uncertainty—and scepticism—about how the Directive will work in practice. For example, 'high eco-logical status' is defined in terms of what a pristine water environment would be, and 'good ecological status' is defined in terms of a slight distortion or deviation from pristine conditions due to human activities. Since there are no truly pristine water environments in the UK, this means that defining 'good ecological status' means defining the legally required standard against a contestable baseline (for a useful exchange on what this will require see [2003] ENDS Report 347, 23). Secondly, the Directive gives scope to Member States to decide whether waters have been 'heavily modified' by human action. Effectively this enables the human benefits of existing water uses (such as flood protection) to be taken into account, and the costs of improving the quality of these waters to be proportionate and not unduly expensive for the water quality improvements that might be made. Also, as an exception to the general aim of achieving good status, less stringent environmental objectives can be established where the natural condition of waters have been so affected by human activity that the necessary improvements would be unfeasible or disproportionately expensive and, in effect, the proposed improvement measures are the least worst option for the water environment. In these and other cases, it is clear that the Directive marks a profound shift away from common standards that apply across the EC. Whereas under most existing water directives the difficulty with, and cost of, implementation is irrelevant, under the Framework Directive factors like these are likely to be central.

The idea of 'full cost recovery pricing' also begs a number of questions about the methodology of calculating the cost of 'environmental harm' (although if some form of pricing can be agreed which is generally applicable, it may provide a firm basis for valuing the environment as a commodity in other areas). Finally, a key issue is what 'the aim of achieving' good status actually means. The terminology used is clearly different from *requiring*, as an *objective*, good status (in the way that the ECJ has interpreted previous water directives such as the Bathing Water and Drinking Water Directives as requiring obligations of result; see p. 188). This may lead to difficulties for individuals or groups trying to enforce the Directive, although it might be possible to point to provisions of the Directive which list exceptional cases—where failing to achieve good status will be condoned—as supporting the view that the good status requirement is an obligation of result and not just of means. The uncertainties about what the Directive actually requires means that estimating the cost of implementation is impossible, although it will undoubtedly run to billions of pounds. What is easier to predict is that the inherently flexible nature of the Directive, and its regard to costs and notions of proportionality, will make enforcement much less straightforward and give to EC water law some of the less satisfactory qualities seen in the past in the UK.

As regards implementation, there is as yet only really framework implementing provisions (see the Water Environment (Water Framework Directive) (England and Wales) Regulations 2003 (SI 2003/3242), and for Scotland see p. 708).[9]

---

9. A good summary of implementation developments at the time of writing is [2003] ENDS Report 343, 45.

Water supply and water industry finance

Strictly speaking, the provision of a clean water supply is a consumer protection rather than an environmental protection measure. However, there is an intimate relationship between water supply and pollution control. The public water supply is abstracted from inland and ground waters, so pollution of those waters will lead to a reduction in the available source and to an increase in the cost of treatment of the water that is abstracted. To this end, it is an offence to pollute any 'waterworks' likely to be used for human consumption, which covers pollution of springs, wells, boreholes, and service reservoirs (Water Industry Act 1991, s. 72). In addition, Directive 75/440 on Surface Water for Drinking (which will be repealed under the Water Framework Directive by 22 December 2007) imposes, indirectly, controls on the quality of inland waters.

There is also a more indirect link which is tied up with the highly charged political question of who should pay for the cost of environmental protection, and which requires some understanding of how the water industry as a whole is regulated and paid for. As pointed out earlier in the chapter, the water industry was massively underfunded when it was in public control prior to 1989, with the result that sewage works were major sources of pollution, and the quality of the public water supply was questionable. Since 1989, the public water supply and sewerage services have been provided by the privatized water undertakers under the regulatory oversight of the Director General of Water Services (OFWAT) (and, from April 2006, the Water Services Regulatory Authority, a Board rather than a single regulator), and the Secretary of State. Water bills have risen considerably above inflation and, compared with the position prior to 1989, the way in which consumers pay for water and sewerage services is more explicit, since the full amount is paid in charges rather than a proportion being hidden in general taxation.

However, the water companies' overall charges for water and sewerage services are regulated by the Director General under the Water Industry Act 1991. This is achieved by reference to a formula, known as RPI + K, under which the weighted average charge is allowed to increase by the retail price index plus a company-specific factor set by the Director General (known as the K factor). The Director General has to take water companies' costs, including the cost of 'environmental' improvements such as upgrading of sewage works and improvements in drinking water quality, into account when setting the K factor. Once the K factor is set, the water companies have to operate within it. This means that the trade-offs between environmental improvements by the water companies (for example, improved performance from sewage works, improved water quality from the public water supply and reduced losses from leakage), improvements in levels of service, efficiency savings and increased company profits and directors' pay, are very clear.

K factors are set every five years. It is clear that, in determining K, binding obligations under EC directives cannot be avoided, despite the costs to consumers. This is not to say that price reviews have always ensured that compliance with mandatory standards have been achieved; for example neither the 1989 or 1994 reviews aimed at ensuring sufficient compliance with the Bathing Water Directive. Where there is clear discretion is in the extent to which the water companies should finance desirable but non-mandatory environmental improvements, such as 'guide values' in EC water directives (see p. 714) or where river SSSIs

Figure 18.1 Distribution of the number of environmental improvements schemes by the water industry from 1995 to 2005. Figures up to 2001–02 represent completed schemes; figures for 2002–03 represent projects scheduled for that year that were nearing completion; and figures for 2003–04 onwards represent scheduled schemes

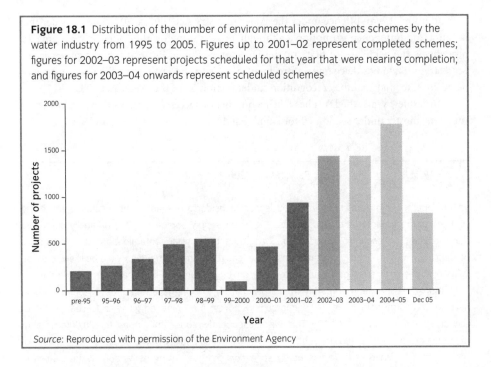

Source: Reproduced with permission of the Environment Agency

are affected. Given the increased levels of discretion that Member States will have under the Water Framework Directive, it is likely that decisions of the economic regulator will become even more critical in determining both policy choices and legal obligations.

Drinking water quality

As far as the quality of the public water supply is concerned, under the Water Industry Act 1991, s. 67, domestic water must be 'wholesome'. This term is defined in legislation in the Water Supply (Water Quality) Regulations 2000 (SI 2000/3184)—which implement the revised Drinking Water Quality Directive (98/83/EC)—which lay down a large number of specific criteria with which water must comply if supplied for domestic or food production purposes. The revised directive demonstrates signs of the impact of the subsidiarity principle being applied, in that the number of parameters is reduced and parameters without a health impact are set only for monitoring and remediation purposes. The regulations require that information on water quality must be made available to the public.

Enforcement of section 67 is through enforcement orders issued by the Secretary of State. The use of these has proven controversial and, although upheld by the domestic courts, has fallen foul of EC law and required changes to national legislation (on which see Box 7.12).[10] There is at present no scope for direct criminal liability, but under the Water Act 2003 the Secretary of State and the Drinking Water Inspectorate (DWI) will, probably from 2005, have the power to fine water companies for supplying water which is not wholesome.

---

10. The statutory mechanism of enforcement orders has also been central to determining whether there is civil liability for things like sewage flooding, see *Marcic v Thames Water Utilities plc* [2004] Env LR 25, see p. 374.

In addition, it is an offence under the Water Industry Act 1991, s. 70 to supply water that is 'unfit for human consumption', although prosecution for this offence may only be brought by the Secretary of State or the Director of Public Prosecutions. In practice, the Secretary of State has delegated enforcement powers to the DWI, with the Chief Inspector being given formal statutory recognition under section 57 of the Water Act 2003.

In the last few years, the DWI has taken a number of successful prosecutions against water suppliers, mostly under section 70 for supplying discoloured water (see Case box 18.3).

CASE 18.3 *R v Yorkshire Water Services Ltd* [2002] Env LR 18

Various operational failures resulted in four separate incidents of visibly contaminated water being supplied to large numbers of households. The water supply company (YWS) originally contested that this breached section 70, since there was no bacteriological contamination. At a preliminary hearing in the Crown Court, it was held that water could be 'unfit' either if it would be likely to cause injury or if, due to its smell or appearance, a 'reasonable customer of firm character' would refuse to drink it or reject its use in preparing food. This challenge having failed (had it succeeded it would have blown a large hole in the DWI's enforcement policy), YWS pleaded guilty to 17 charges under section 70 and was fined £119,000. This was subsequently reduced on appeal to £80,000. Notably, the Court of Appeal stressed the centrality of the overall culpability of the defendant and nature of the breach. The charges were essentially specimen charges, taking at random various affected households, and the blameworthiness of YWS had to be determined in the round, and then apportioned amongst the charges on the indictment. Otherwise, potentially vast fines could be imposed where a relatively minor contamination incident affected a large number of households. In more serious cases, however, the fine may not be the greater cost. In 1995, following a contamination incident in Worcestershire that did in fact result in thousands of householders suffering vomiting and diarrhoea, the water supplier was fined £45,000 but paid out £875,000 under Ofwat's Guaranteed Standards Scheme (which compensates for interruptions to supply but does not compensate for poor water quality per se).

A failed prosecution following a cryptosporidium outbreak because of evidential problems (see [1997] Water Law 161), however, meant the introduction of stringent monitoring and prevention provisions at supply works which in practice amount to the use of a process standard. The general enforcement approach, however, remains cooperative (see p. 294). There is the possibility of an action at common law for breach of statutory duty or negligence (see *Read v Croydon Corporation* [1938] 4 All ER 631, where a ratepayer successfully sued in negligence for water supplied to his household which caused his daughter to contract typhoid). Widespread incidents, such as at Camelford in 1988, may give rise to an action in public nuisance (*R v South West Water Authority* [1991] LMELR 65).

The scope for an action in negligence and in contract was recently considered by the Privy Council in *Hamilton v Papakura District Council* [2002] UKPC 57 a case brought by farmers in New Zealand who grew tomatoes hydroponically and whose water supply was contaminated with a herbicide which, while not affecting the quality of the water for normal drinking water purposes, affected their crop. The Privy Council unanimously rejected the claim in negligence, essentially because the farmers were not owed a duty of care to provide them with water of this exceptionally high quality. (Claims in nuisance and under the rule in *Rylands v Fletcher* were rejected on the grounds of lack of foreseeability of damage.) The nature of supplying water to the public was central to this decision; if the water had to meet this high standard for the tomato growers then in practice it would have to be of this quality for all the council's water customers (which would put too onerous a burden on the council). (See also Box 17.2.) The action in contract was more finely balanced, but by a 3–2 majority was rejected. Whether an action in contract for supplying poor quality water could get off the ground in the UK, however, is a matter of dispute; the traditional view is that the relationship between water companies and their customers is statutory, and the respective rights and duties of the parties is contained in the water industry legislation.

Standard setting, water quality, and consents for the discharge of trade or sewage effluent

As noted previously, most pollution loading comes from discharges where there is a consent in order to avoid liability for a water pollution offence. It is therefore important to think of the consent system and of how consents are set within the context of the principal water pollution offences. Although water quality objectives are discussed at the end of this section, this does not mean they are a final consideration for the EA when determining a consent application. Rather, because of the emphasis on environmental quality standards, they are likely to be central. But even where there are mandatory EC quality standards to be achieved, there will usually be some flexibility in the system when individual consents are set.

A consent is required from the EA for:

- any discharge of trade or sewage effluent into 'controlled waters';
- any discharge of trade or sewage effluent through a pipe from land into the sea outside the limits of 'controlled waters';
- any discharge where a prohibition is in force.

It is an offence under the Water Resources Act 1991, s. 85 to 'cause or knowingly permit' such a discharge, although there is a defence if it is carried out in accordance with a consent. This means it is also an offence to breach any conditions attached to a consent, a point made explicit by section 85(6). There is no need to show that the discharge has polluted the receiving waters because the offence consists of discharging otherwise than in accordance with the consent.

'Trade effluent' is defined in section 221 and includes any effluent from trade premises (these include agricultural, fish farming and research establishments), other than domestic sewage or surface water. 'Sewage effluent', also defined in section 221, includes any effluent, other than surface water, from a sewerage works. The discharge must be of effluent, so it seems that if trade materials, such as fuel oil, escape they are covered by the general pollution offence (see p. 734). But there is some doubt here since effluent is defined in section 221 to mean 'any liquid' and is not specifically limited to wastes.

A further problem relates to the interpretation of the word 'discharge'. This word is not defined in the Act. It is capable of carrying either an active meaning (i.e. that the release of materials has to be part of a deliberate trade or sewage process) or a passive meaning (as in the discharge of blood from a wound). It is suggested that it carries an active meaning, because otherwise potential dischargers would be in the impossible position of having to apply for a consent for something that was not meant to happen. The effect of this reasoning is that accidental and non-routine emissions of trade or sewage effluent do not require a consent and are covered by the general water pollution offence (see p. 734).

On the other hand, the ECJ has now held that 'discharge' for the purposes of the Dangerous Substances in Water Directive (76/464) can include discharges of listed substances (PAHs) found in wood preservative with which wooden posts used for shoring up riverbanks had been treated (Case C-232/97 *Nederhoff* [1999] ECR I-6385) and discharges of polluted steam precipitating into watercourses (*van Rooij*, p. 714). This is clearly a more expansive understanding of what 'discharge' means, and while it clearly applies to discharges regulated under this Directive, it remains to be seen whether the EA will insist on consents for similar discharges regulated solely as a matter of national law (and, if it does, how).

The prohibition is a device first introduced by the Water Act 1989. It is designed to cover those cases where the type of discharge is not necessarily harmful and thus the blanket requirement of a consent is not justified. By prohibiting discharges on a selective basis, control can be exercised over just those situations where it is required (see s. 86, Water Resources Act 1991).

There are three situations where a prohibition may apply:

• Where the EA by notice prohibits a discharge of trade or sewage effluent from a building or fixed plant to any land or land-locked waters outside the definition of controlled waters. This includes such situations as soakaways from trade premises and some agricultural activities.

• Where it prohibits a discharge of matter other than trade or sewage effluent from a drain or sewer. Trade and sewage effluent are automatically covered by the need for a consent, so the intention here is to restrict such things as discharges of dangerous substances from a storm drain.

• In addition, any such discharges involving substances prescribed by regulations *automatically* invoke the prohibition.

In relation to the first two categories, the prohibition can only come into force three months after notice to the discharger, unless the EA is satisfied that there is an emergency.

Controlled waters

The discharge consent system, and the water pollution offences, apply to 'controlled waters'. 'Controlled waters' are defined in section 104 and include virtually all inland and coastal waters. Controlled waters are made up of four sub-categories:

• relevant territorial waters (i.e. the sea within a line three miles out from the baselines from which the territorial sea is measured, despite the extension of the territorial limit to 12 miles in the Territorial Sea Act 1987);

• coastal waters (i.e. the sea within those baselines up to the line of the highest tide, and tidal waters up to the fresh water limit as defined by the Secretary of State on maps produced for that purpose);

• inland waters (i.e. rivers, streams, underground streams, canals, lakes, and reservoirs, including those that are temporarily dry); and

• groundwaters (i.e. any waters contained in underground strata or in wells or boreholes).

In addition, the courts have held that a river bed can form part of 'controlled waters' (see *National Rivers Authority v Biffa Waste* [1996] Env LR 227), as can a man-made ditch, if it drains into controlled waters (*Environment Agency v Brock plc* [1998] Env LR 607). Because section 104 refers to 'waters *of* any watercourse' rather than waters *in* any watercourse, the definition extends to streams that have diverted from their normal course (*R v Dovermoss Ltd* [1995] Env LR 258). Water supply mains and pipes, and sewers and drains (where separate controls on discharges apply) are excluded from the definition of controlled waters.

The consent system

The system for acquiring a consent is set out in the Water Resources Act 1991, sch. 10, and the Control of Pollution (Applications, Appeals and Registers) Regulations 1996 (SI 1996/2971), and it involves a higher degree of public involvement than many other licensing-type systems.

Each discharge requires a consent, so if a factory has three discharge pipes it needs a consent for each one. The applicant applies to the EA, which has a discretion as to the details required. Normally the applicant will have to state the place, nature, quantity, rate of flow, composition, and temperature of the proposed discharge. It is an offence under section 206 to give incorrect information.

The applicant must publicise the application in a local newspaper and in the *London Gazette* and notify any relevant local authorities and water undertakers. However, this publicity may be dispensed with if the EA considers that the discharge will have 'no appreciable effect' on the receiving waters. Great use was made of this dispensation by the regional water authorities in the past, so that an estimated 90 per cent of all applications were exempted from publicity in this way. Guidance on this vague and subjective discretion is given in the EA's *Discharge Consents Manual* which suggests a complex set of tests to be considered, the main one being that a change is not to be considered appreciable if there is less than a 10 per cent increase on all relevant parameters, unless some significant environmental amenity is affected. This is a good example of the use of administrative methods to define a legal requirement. It is objectionable that the operation of such an important publicity procedure rests on a rather restrictive interpretation given in a departmental circular. The EA must take into account timely written representations. It has the power to grant consent, either unconditionally or subject to conditions, or to refuse consent.

A fee for making an application for a new or revised consent was introduced from 1 October 1990. The intention is that the EA should recover the overall costs incurred in processing applications. A standard charge is payable for each new or revised consent. There is a reduced charge for certain minor discharges of sewage effluent or cooling waters and for those surface water discharges which require consent (see *Scheme of Charges in Respect of Applications and Consents for Discharges to Controlled Waters*).

(a) Conditions

The EA may attach 'such conditions as it may think fit' and schedule 10, paragraph 2(5) includes a non-exhaustive list. This includes such things as the quality, quantity, nature, composition, and temperature of the discharge, the siting and design of the outlet, the provision of meters for measuring these matters, the taking and recording of samples by the discharger, and the provision of information to the EA. Frequently, the most significant conditions will relate to biochemical oxygen demand, levels of toxic or dangerous materials, and suspended solids, although the EA is presently considering the introduction of a more sophisticated test based on the toxicity of the discharge to aquatic life. For industrial discharges it is normal to attach absolute numerical limits for the various parameters covered in the consent, with the result that any excess amounts to a breach of the consent.

Conditions requiring a specified treatment process are legal, but are not generally imposed, since in the past it has been government policy to require compliance with environmental standards whilst giving a discharger a choice of methods to achieve the standard. For some discharges, however, the effect of the Urban Waste Water Treatment Directive (91/271) may be that specific treatment methods are required (e.g. biological treatment), although generally the Directive requires quality standards to be met. It is permissible for conditions to be staggered so that they get progressively stricter.

There is also a procedure for granting a retrospective consent which enables the EA to formalise the legal position in relation to a discharge and also to attach conditions to an existing discharge.

A significant problem under COPA 1974 was the position of new pollutants. This phrase covers substances which the discharger introduces into the discharge after the consent has been obtained, or new substances unknown at the time the consent was set, or substances which were only later traceable or later considered to be polluting. Such substances would not be mentioned in the consent, and it appeared that discharging them may not have been in breach of the consent, since there was a breach only if the conditions were not met. It seems that this possible loophole has been avoided by the Water Resources Act 1991, which requires that the discharge must be 'under and in accordance with' the consent in order for the defence in section 88 to apply. Following a number of discharge consent appeals brought by sewerage undertakers, however, the Minister has decided that the EA's policy of including a general condition excluding the discharge of any substance not specified in the consent should be qualified so that it usually applies only where it is 'reasonably practicable' for the undertaker to do so (see below).

(b) Sewage discharge consents

Sewage discharges have always caused regulatory problems, both because of their potent polluting power and because of the previous conflict of interest between regulator and regulated when the water authorities were responsible for operating treatment works and policing discharges from such works (see p. 27). However, the same conflict also existed when the local authorities ran the sewage works, since they also provided members for the river authorities and thus exercised an influence on their decisions.

Under the Water Resources Act 1991, there is no conflict of interest. Sewerage undertakers are treated similarly to other dischargers in requiring a consent from the EA. One slight difference relates to the offences under section 85. Because sewerage undertakers treat wastes discharged by other people, and thus have limited control over what is actually put into the sewers, they have a special defence under section 87(2). This operates if the contravention of their discharge consent was due to an unconsented discharge made into the sewer by another person which they could not reasonably have prevented (see *National Rivers Authority v Yorkshire Water Services Ltd* [1995] 1 AC 444, discussed at p. 737).

A more significant difference is that sewage works have in the past had their consents set on different terms from other dischargers. Before privatization, the relative lack of control over the quality of sewage effluent or its containment was comparatively unimportant, since the poacher/gamekeeper relationship meant that there was considerable scope for selective enforcement. With privatization pending, however, consents were relaxed so that instead of containing absolute numerical limits, with the result that any breach of the limit amounted to a criminal offence, consents were set by reference to 'look-up' tables intended to ensure a 95 per cent compliance rate over a rolling 12-month period. Only in exceptional cases, where a generous maximum (or 'upper tier') limit was exceeded would there be liability for a one-off sewage pollution incident.

These relaxations, which have been described as 'a sort of environmental betrayal'[11] in order to reduce the undertakers' potential liabilities and make privatisation more attractive, were not however the first time sewage discharge consents had been relaxed. In the late 1970s, the National Water Council commenced a review of consents that led to some relaxations, although the review was never completed and the results never published. Consents were also relaxed in the 1980s in anticipation of the implementation of COPA 1974 and the consequent availability of a right to bring private prosecutions.

Under first the NRA and now the EA, these 'percentile' consents are being replaced by absolute limits when consents come up for review. This has led to a significant rise in the number of prosecutions brought against sewerage undertakers, since only a single sample is now needed rather than a series of samples from a 12-month period. It has also had a knock-on effect on trade effluent consents granted by the sewerage undertakers under the Water Industry Act 1991 (see Chapter 19). But the Secretary of State has decided that some leeway must still be given to take account of events beyond the control of the sewerage undertakers, and revised consents give some protection to sewerage undertakers where they can show that they have operated the works reasonably practicably so as to minimize polluting effects, for example, where a sewage system overflows during heavy rainfall.[12]

A final issue is the impact of the Urban Waste Water Treatment Directive (91/271), discussed above. This imposes various restrictions on sewage discharges, although the general tenor of the Directive is purposive rather than standard-setting, that is it seeks to achieve specific goals depending on the area and population concerned rather than mandating that compliance with specific parameters or treatment methods should be met by all sewage works. Some new and revised consents require, in general terms, compliance with the Directive as a consent condition. Taken on its own, such a condition is probably meaningless, and likely to be void for uncertainty.

(c) Revocation and variation

Under schedule 10, paragraph 7, the EA has a discretion to review consents from time to time. A variation or a revocation can be made simply by notifying the discharger.

---

11. D. Kinnersley, *Coming Clean* (Harmondsworth: Penguin, 1994), 49.
12. The key clauses are reproduced in S. Payne [1998] Water Law 13.

Alternatively the Secretary of State may direct that a variation take place (sch. 10, para. 9). No compensation is payable except in one case considered below. There is no provision for public participation in relation to a variation or revocation. This power to make variations or revocations is a wide one which reflects the need to cater for new circumstances, such as a new polluter in the catchment area, or a newly perceived pollution threat, or a change in EC or international obligations. It also reasserts the position that no one has a right to pollute.

However, there are limits on when a variation or revocation can be made. A period will be stipulated in the original consent. This cannot be less than four years and a variation or revocation cannot take place within that period (measured from the setting of the original consent or the last variation), except with the permission of the discharger. In practice, there seems to be considerable variation between EA regions when it comes to reviewing consents after the four year period; figures from 2001 showed that some regions reviewed 18–19 per cent of consents, while in other regions the figure was 1–2 per cent. Exceptionally, the Secretary of State may direct a modification within the period in order to give effect to an EC or international obligation, or to protect public health, or flora and fauna dependent on an aquatic environment. There is no right to vary early solely because the discharger has been in breach of the consent, or in order to cater for a new pollutant: both are situations where such a right would be desirable. Arguably, this four year period will lead to difficulties in taking a targeted approach to implementing the Water Framework Directive through revising consents. The EA will have to pay compensation to the discharger if a direction is made on the public health or protection of flora and fauna ground within the period.

Discharge consent charges and paying for water pollution

The EA may make annual charges for discharge consents under the general charging provisions of sections 41 and 42 of the Environment Act 1995, although any scheme requires the approval of the Secretary of State and the consent of the Treasury (see p. 129).

The basic philosophy underpinning the charging scheme is cost-recovery, i.e. that the EA should recover from dischargers the actual cost of its activities connected with discharges. This includes the sampling of discharges, inspection of discharges, discharge-related impact monitoring, work on the review of consents, laboratory services, and direct administration connected to these matters. Expenditure on general water quality monitoring, general administration and pollution incidents is not recovered by these charges, but will come from the general budget of the EA.

Further principles are that the charges are uniform throughout the country and are not to vary locally; that they relate to what is consented to rather than to the actual discharge; and that they are set according to a formula which has three separate elements—the volume of the discharge, its content, and the nature of the receiving waters. For each of these three elements broad bands have been devised, each being accorded a weighted value (i.e. a number of units). For volume, there are eight broad bands, with larger volume discharges having a higher value than lower ones. There are exceptions for emergency discharges, intermittent discharges and rainwater drains. For content, there are seven bands, reflecting the relative complexity and cost of monitoring the discharge. For receiving waters, there are four bands, with estuarine waters having a higher weighting than inland watercourses, which in turn are weighted more highly than discharges to coastal waters or to groundwaters.

Each discharge thus has three separate values, which are multiplied together to give a final figure in terms of a number of units. This final figure is then multiplied by a national financial factor, so that all dischargers know in advance what their charge is going to be. This financial factor is varied annually. It can be expected that most dischargers will face a significant annual bill for their discharges.

While the Environment Act 1995 limits charges to the recovery of administrative costs, the charging system does give partial effect to the 'polluter pays' principle. The possibility of going further and introducing charges reflecting the full environmental costs of discharges has been on the political agenda since 1990[13] and in 1992 was taken further by the RCEP.[14] The Labour Government consulted on this issue as part of a wider look at using economic instruments to control water pollution,[15] but appeared to conclude that the difficulties in full cost recovery outweighed any likely benefits. Part of the reason for this was no doubt because of the complex relationships between the various parties involved (dischargers and sewage undertakers) and the impact of extraneous factors such as water flows on pollution levels. In short, calculating the cost of water pollution per cubic metre of discharge is simply much harder than, say, putting a price on the emission of a tonne of carbon dioxide. The 1997 Consultation also looked at the possible use of tradable permits, but this has not been followed up (no doubt in part because there are very few stretches of river where there are enough dischargers for there to be meaningful competition).

The role of the Secretary of State

The Secretary of State has a general, and very wide, power under section 40 of the Environment Act 1995 to issue directions of a general or specific nature to the EA in relation to pollution control, amongst other matters. The supplementary powers of the Secretary of State to require information from the EA in section 202 should also be noted. The reason for the width of this power is the fact that large policy-making powers have effectively been delegated to the EA, making some mechanism for central control desirable. The use of directions to achieve this should be compared with the use of Circular guidance in other areas of environmental law, since they fulfil similar purposes. Directions are often used in relation to EC directives, supplementing implementing regulations (see also p. 115). At any stage the Secretary of State may call in an application for decision (sch. 10, para. 5). This is an unfettered discretion and ousts the jurisdiction of the EA to consider the consent. It is rarely exercised.

Appeals

The applicant or discharger has a right to appeal to the Secretary of State against a refusal of consent, the attachment of unreasonable conditions, any adverse variation or revocation of a consent, or the setting of the period in which a consent cannot be varied (s. 91). The procedures for called in applications and for appeals are set out in the Control of Pollution (Applications, Appeals, and Registers) Regulations 1996 (SI 1996/2971).

---

13. HM Government, *This Common Inheritance* (Cm 1200, 1990).
14. RCEP, Sixteenth Report, *Freshwater Quality* (Cm 1966, 1992).
15. DETR, *Economic Instruments for Water Pollution* (1997).

An appeal is a general rehearing of the matter in issue and the Secretary of State has the same powers as the EA originally had. As with planning appeals, in practice appeals are heard by the Planning Inspectorate, although the Secretary of State retains the final decision in more important cases. Compared with the system of planning appeals, which accords enormous opportunities for argument on policy, this appeal right is far less commonly used. This may be because there is little perceived difference in policy between the Secretary of State and the EA. However, because of the length of time it takes for appeals to be decided, an understanding of the principles to be applied on appeal is only building up slowly, although the decisions on sewerage undertakers' liability for unseen pollutants (see p. 726) are a good indication of thinking.

How are consents set?

The EA, or the Secretary of State on appeal, has a wide discretion in setting the consent and it will be set by reference to a variety of factors. Although schedule 10 is silent as to the factors which must be taken into account, applying ordinary public law principles the EA must have regard to all material considerations. In addition, certain requirements appear from other sections of the Act, especially section 84, and from EC law.

As stated before, it is important to grasp the individualized and flexible nature of these consents, although uniformity and consistency is now being sought by the EA. Relevant matters include:

- The water quality objectives and standards set for the receiving waters under section 83 (see below). This emphasises that one of the crucial elements in fixing a consent is the effect on the receiving waters. This in turn depends on the use that is intended for those receiving waters.

- Any other effects on the receiving waters, such as on a fishery or downstream user. In particular, regard will be had to whether the waters are used for abstraction for water supply or irrigation.

- Any relevant EC standards for the discharge concerned or for the quality of the receiving waters.

- Any 'cocktail' effect of the discharge. The EA will consider not only the immediate effect of the discharge but also any impact the discharge will have in combination with the current contents of the waters and any potential future discharges.

- The desirability of minimizing discharges of hazardous substances as far as possible in accordance with Directive 76/464.

- The EA's environmental duties laid out in the Environment Act 1995, s. 6 (see p. 126).

- The specific duty in relation to sites of special scientific interest set out in section 8 of the 1995 Act (see p. 127).

- Any relevant objections and representations made and the results of any consultation carried out.

- Certain informal standard tests for particular types of discharge. For example, 'normal' standards for sewage works were suggested by the Eighth Report of the Royal

> Commission on Sewage Disposal in 1912 and these were applied for many years. The EA is now seeking to establish some uniformity of standards across the country for all types of discharge.
>
> • Any other material considerations.

There would be scope for having general binding rules applying across an industrial sector but so far there appears to be little enthusiasm for these. In other Member States, their use has been criticized by the regulators for making it harder to establish and maintain a co-operative relationship with dischargers.[16]

Water quality objectives

Although the British approach to the control of water pollution has tended over the years to concentrate on the environmental impact of pollutants, the development of *statutory* water quality objectives owes a great deal to the EC. In the 1970s, in debates on EC directives such as 76/464 on Dangerous Substances in Water, the British government argued that its system of water pollution control was different from the systems operated by other EC Member States in that it was based on individualized consent standards set by reference to local environmental quality objectives, rather than on uniform emission standards or limit values which did not take the environmental effects fully into account. At the time, however, there were no formally set quality objectives, so in order to show that this was indeed how the system worked, the government was forced to introduce more explicit objectives.

(a) Classification schemes

In 1978, the National Water Council developed a water quality classification.[17] This had five basic classes of river waters (there was a similar but separate classification for estuaries):

1A High quality waters suitable for all abstraction purposes with only modest treatment. Capable of supporting game or other high class fisheries. High amenity value.

1B Good quality waters usable for substantially the same purposes as 1A though not as high quality.

2 Fair quality waters viable as coarse fisheries and capable of use for drinking water provided advanced treatment is given. Moderate amenity value.

3 Poor waters polluted to the extent that fish are absent or only sporadically present. Suitable only for low grade industrial abstractions.

4 Bad quality waters which are grossly polluted and likely to cause a nuisance.

This classification was adopted by the regional water authorities in setting informal river quality objectives over the next few years. It was also used for the five-yearly national survey of water quality. However, as an administrative method of implementing EC directives, it was clearly insufficient to satisfy EC law (see p. 217) so it became inevitable that a statutory system would be adopted.

The Water Act 1989 introduced statutory water quality classifications and objectives for

---

16. See [1998] Water Law 195.
17. *River Water Quality: The Next Stage* (National Water Council, 1978).

the first time. The provisions are now reproduced in the Water Resources Act 1991, ss. 82–84. When fully operational (which will not be for many years), statutory water quality objectives will make the system more open and will be an important element in the general process of establishing a rationally planned, transparent and properly accountable system of water resources management.

The essential features are that, over the next few years, classification regulations should (in theory) be made which set the standards that waters must reach in order to come within a certain classification. This will be done under section 82. The Secretary of State will then establish (under s. 83) a water quality *objective* for each stretch of controlled waters. This will set specified classifications as an objective, and will accordingly incorporate the relevant water quality *standards*. These will then act as explicit policy goals for the EA, which will be under a legal duty under section 84 to exercise its functions, including the granting of discharge consents, so as to achieve and maintain the statutory water quality objective at all times, at least as far as it is practicable to do so. There are thus three different processes involved, although these are intertwined.

The first process is the setting of classification systems for waters under section 82. In order to comply with certain EC directives, a number of regulations have been made. To give one example, the Bathing Waters (Classification) Regulations 1991 (SI 1991/1157) establish a classification that reflects the mandatory (but not the guide) standards laid down in the EC Bathing Waters Directive.

To comply with EC law, these classifications have also been issued as initial water quality objectives under section 83 (see below). This has been done by the Secretary of State under the power to make directions (see p. 729). In doing so the publicity and consultation requirements set out in section 83(4) are now always dispensed with.

The Surface Waters (River Ecosystem) (Classification) Regulations 1994 (SI 1994/1057) is the only classification that has been made for purely national reasons, which may explain why there is no obligation imposed under the regulations requiring their use as water quality objectives for particular waters under section 83. Although there are no specific biological parameters there is a link here with the biological GQA (see p. 703), but the regulations do not seem to have been used as the basis for any water quality objective yet imposed.

(b) Classifying individual waters

The second process is that water quality objectives for individual stretches of controlled waters may be set by the Secretary of State (s. 83). The choice of an objective by the Secretary of State would mean that the appropriate standards laid down for that objective in the classification regulations would apply to the stretch of water. In addition, appropriate EC standards laid down for that objective in the classification regulations would apply to the stretch of water. In addition, appropriate EC standards laid down in directives would be incorporated where relevant (e.g. if the waters were bathing waters designated under Directive 76/160).

Because of the mandatory nature of EC quality standards, as noted above the publicity and consultation obligations are now always overridden, effectively integrating the classification and designation stages, at least for objectives based on EC law.

(c) The effects of classification

The third process is that, as stated above, under section 84 the EA and Secretary of State must exercise their powers under the Act so as to achieve statutory water quality objectives at all times, so far as it is practicable to do so. It does not follow that the EA is in breach of section 84 simply by failing to achieve the appropriate standards. But it does mean that its powers in relation to the setting and variation of consents, remedial and enforcement action, and preventive controls should be exercised to achieve the standards if practicable, since a judicial review action could conceivably be brought to ensure the enforcement of the duty (although a more fruitful avenue would probably be to press the Secretary of State to use her powers under section 40 to issue a direction to the EA). Under the EPA 1990, s. 7(2)(c), a similar duty is placed on the EA to try to achieve statutory water quality objectives when considering authorisations for integrated pollution control. The PPC Regs 2000 also require stricter emission limits values if these are required by an environmental quality standard, though only if the EQS is under an EC directive (under sch 1, para 3 of the PPCA 1999 the Minister can direct that national quality objectives are adhered to). These must be used regardless of whether they are 'available' (and so cost considerations seem to be irrelevant; see regs 12(6) and (7)).

(d) Criticisms of the system of quality objectives

One of the criticisms of the system of statutory water quality objectives when they were first passed was that no timetable was set for their introduction. It is now clear that full implementation will take many years. There is still some work to be done on the development of precise classification criteria. After that, the process of setting individual objectives will, in the Conservative government's words, extend 'over a number of years', starting with a very limited number of selected river catchments. Even then, the current proposals relate only to rivers: statutory water quality objectives for estuaries, coastal waters, groundwaters, canals, and lakes are clearly many years off. The existing informal river quality objectives will remain in force until superseded by the statutory objectives. There is plainly little enthusiasm for the costs involved in setting statutory water quality objectives, despite the great benefits they would produce in terms of a rational and transparent system of pollution control.

Groundwater pollution

Different provisions apply to certain activities that may lead to black or grey list substances contaminating groundwater. Particularly risky activities here include manufacturing leaks and spills, the disposal of agricultural pesticides including sheep dips, and underground storage tanks.

The Groundwater Regulations 1998 (SI 1998/2746) belatedly implemented the 1980 EC Groundwater Directive (80/68) (although the Directive's provisions were implemented in relation to waste disposal by the Waste Management Licensing Regulations 1994). The Regulations require the discharge consent system to prevent the entry of black list substances, and pollution from grey lists substances. But the regulations also use consent-type provisions to regulate indirect discharges such as might arise from the disposal and tipping of listed substances, at least where these are not regulated by waste management provisions (reg. 18, and see reg. 15 of the Waste Management Licensing Regulations 1994, discussed at p. 591). They also provide for a 'notice' provision similar to prohibition notices in relation to activities on or in the ground (such as underground storage tanks), although only where pollution might arise (reg. 19). The EA has discretion whether to serve such a notice, and must take account of any Code of Practice issued. There are very limited publicity requirements for these authorizations and notices. In practice, notices seem to be used as a last resort, where negotiation and persuasion have failed.

A significant difference is that the Groundwater Regulations 1998 also create a specific offence of discharging listed substances where there is a *risk* of *indirect* groundwater pollution, by amending the wording of section 85 of the Water Resources Act 1991 specifically to cover this situation. What is unique about this is not that the risk of pollution is covered (see below) but that what amounts to a pollution offence is defined in the Water Resources Act 1991 and that no actual entry or discharge into water is required.

Water pollution offences

Turning from the consent system, it is important to remember that a key purpose of this system is to guard against criminal liability for polluting controlled waters. The water pollution offences in the Water Resources Act 1991 which are described below[18] are therefore important in that they provide the context for the consent system (it should be stressed again that the discharge consent system does not require dischargers to be 'licensed' or to meet general process-based standards, as is the case, for example, with industrial operators under the IPC or IPPC systems, although in practice the difference is not that great). However, the water pollution offences are also the key means of imposing criminal liability on those who discharge without a consent, e.g. where substances are illicitly dumped into a river or there is a pollution spill after an incident. The offences below are in addition to the offence of breaching any condition of a discharge consent, which of course only applies to consent holders (s. 85(6)).

(a) General pollution offence

There is a general offence under section 85(1) of causing or knowingly permitting any poisonous, noxious or polluting matter or any solid waste to enter controlled waters. As is common within the flexible definitions of British pollution control, the words 'poisonous, noxious or polluting' are not defined. However, the wording is very wide (see Box 18.3).

BOX 18.3 'Poisonous, noxious or polluting'

In *R v Dovermoss Ltd* [1995] Env LR 258, slurry had been spread on farmland. A stream had become blocked and changed its course so that it ran over the field, causing the slurry to contaminate spring water with levels of ammonia in excess of the levels prescribed under EC drinking water legislation. The Court of Appeal held that 'polluting' requires simply that a likelihood or *capability* of causing harm to animals, plants or those who use the water could be demonstrated. Actual harm is not necessary. Even mere discolouration may be sufficient, at least for the matter to be 'polluting'.[19] The case illustrates how the main water pollution offences are

---

18. Less commonly used offences are contained *inter alia* in Salmon and Freshwater Fisheries Act 1975, s. 4 (relating only to waters containing fish) and in specific regulatory provisions prohibiting the supply of certain polluting substances, e.g. anglers' lead weights, PCBs and tri-organotin compounds.

19. See also *Express Ltd v Environment Agency* [2005] Env LR 7. For discussion of this issue see W. Howarth (1993) MLR 171.

not focused on pollution, but rather on the discharge or entry of polluting matter. One reason for this is because the actual effect of the polluting matter may depend on subsequent factors. As was held in an earlier case, 'If the act would be criminal in fair weather when a river was low, it does not become innocent because rainfall causes a flood' (R v Justices of Antrim (1906) 2 IR 298). It also illustrates how, despite increasing attention being paid to ecological effects, the law also protects more mundane human interests such as the aesthetic look of a river.[20]

This general offence complements the more specific offence of discharging trade or sewage effluent without consent (s. 85(3)). Obviously it covers any entry of polluting matter which is not trade or sewage effluent. But, unlike COPA 1974, where the general and the specific offences were made exclusive of each other by section 31(2)(e), under later Acts this exclusivity has been removed, so an illegal discharge of trade or sewage effluent also amounts to an offence under the general offence if it causes pollution.

The general offence also covers accidental and non-routine escapes of trade or sewage effluent because, whilst the specific offence requires a 'discharge', the general offence only requires an entry. In addition, non-point discharges, such as agricultural run-off, are potentially covered by the general offence.

There is a further offence in section 85(5) of substantially aggravating pollution by impeding the proper flow of inland, non-tidal waters.

(b) Defences

A number of defences to these water pollution offences are set out in section 88. A discharge or entry made in accordance with any of the following is a defence:

- a discharge consent from the EA (or earlier equivalents);
- an IPC authorisation or an IPPC permit (see Chapter 20);
- a waste management licence or a waste disposal licence (except where the offence is of discharging trade or sewage effluent or where a prohibition is in force);
- a 'dumping at sea' licence granted by DEFRA under the Food and Environment Protection Act 1985;
- an Act of Parliament;
- any statutory order (such as a drought order).

Amongst a miscellany of other defences, section 89 provides a defence if the entry or discharge was made in an emergency in order to avoid danger to life or health: in such a case the discharger must inform the EA as soon as reasonably practicable and take reasonable steps to minimize any pollution. This defence was successfully relied on in *Express Ltd (t/a Express Dairies Distribution) v Environment Agency* [2003] Env LR 29 where, following a tyre blow out, the driver of a milk tanker pulled over onto the hard shoulder of a motorway and the milk entered a brook via roadside drains. The Court accepted that the defence applied even though it also held that the chain of causation in relation to the water pollution

---

20. For another case on this same issue in a different context (the EC Agricultural Nitrates Directive) see the broad interpretation given to 'eutrophication', as including visual disamenity as well as adverse ecological effects, in Case C-280/02 *Commission v France* [2004] ECR nyr.

offence had not been broken (see below). What mattered was not that the operation which caused the polluting matter to enter the controlled water was done in an emergency, but rather that the entry was caused in order to avoid danger to life or health. It appears that only a danger to human life or health would suffice.

There are some complex provisions in section 87 relating to responsibility for discharges from sewerage works. In addition to the impact of the wide interpretation given to the concept of 'causing' on sewerage undertakers (see below), section 87(1) deems sewerage undertakers to have caused a discharge of sewage effluent if they were bound to receive into the sewer or works matter included in the discharge. In other words, they are responsible for all discharges from sewers or works unless the pollution is caused by an illegal (i.e. unconsented) discharge into the sewer. However, section 87(2) provides a defence where a contravention of section 85 is attributable to an unconsented discharge into the sewerage system by a third party which the sewerage undertaker could not reasonably have been expected to prevent. In *National Rivers Authority v Yorkshire Water Services Ltd* [1995] 1 AC 444, the House of Lords decided that, notwithstanding the precise wording of section 87(2), the defence applies to all the offences in section 85. It should be noted that the defence covers the situation where the sewerage undertaker could not reasonably have prevented the discharge *into* the sewer, rather than *from* the sewer, but that the original discharger into the sewer can be prosecuted under section 85 for causing pollution of controlled waters as well as under the Water Industry Act 1991, s. 118, for the illegal discharge to the sewer (see Chapter 19).

Although farmers no longer have a defence of acting in accordance with good agricultural practice there is non-binding guidance (*The Water Code Revised* 1998, issued under SI 1998/3084) which will affect any decision whether to prosecute and the level of any fine imposed. Conformity may also influence any decision about whether the actions of a farmer are judged reasonable for the purposes of a nuisance action (see *Savage v Fairclough* [2000] Env LR 183).

(c) The meaning of 'cause or knowingly permit'

The offences under section 85 require that the defendant 'cause or knowingly permit' the relevant discharge or entry. It is clear that there are two separate offences, 'causing' and 'knowingly permitting', and that the former lays down an offence of strict liability because it is not conditioned by any requirement of knowledge.

Until recently, the leading case in this area was the *Alphacell* case, where the House of Lords provided reasonably clear guidance as to what 'causing' required.

CASE 18.4 *Alphacell Ltd v Woodward* [1972] AC 824

Settling tanks at a paper factory overflowed into a river. The biochemical oxygen demand (BOD) of the discharge was well above the level permitted in the consent. Although the magistrates did not find that the firm had been negligent (a strange decision since pumps which should have stopped the flow were blocked by brambles and ferns), the House of Lords held that there was no need to prove negligence or fault. Alphacell was guilty of the general offence of causing pollution simply by carrying on the activity that gave rise to the pollution. As long as its activities were themselves intentional all that needed to be shown was a causal link between them and the discharge. The directness of the entry was also irrelevant: in this case the entry was via a channel into a river. For further discussion of strict liability in environmental crime see p. 283.

This test was reiterated in many cases. For example, in *F.J.H. Wrothwell Ltd v Yorkshire Water Authority* [1984] Crim LR 43, a company director who had poured herbicide into what he thought was a drain leading to the public sewer, but which in fact led to a nearby stream, was guilty of causing pollution, despite the unintended result of his action. In *National Rivers Authority v Yorkshire Water Services Ltd* [1995] 1 AC 444, an industrial solvent had been discharged illegally into the sewers by an unidentified industrial firm. The solvent had travelled through the sewers and, as a result of the design of the sewage works, into controlled waters, in a virtually undiluted condition. The House of Lords, reaffirming *Alphacell*, stated that there was ample evidence on which to find that the sewerage under-taker had caused the discharge from the sewage works (although in fact the conviction was quashed because the undertaker could take advantage of the special defence in section 87(2), see above).

Two further cases illustrate the scope of liability. In *CPC (UK) Ltd v National Rivers Authority* [1995] Env LR 131, a factory operator was held to have caused polluting matter to enter controlled waters when a pipe carrying cleaning fluid fractured, allowing the fluid to flow into a river via a storm drain. The conviction was upheld even though the cause of the fracture was defective work carried out by subcontractors for the previous owner, a defect which a rigorous environmental audit of the premises before it was bought by the current owners had failed to detect. The current owners caused the pollution because they were operating it at the time of the polluting incident: this was enough to satisfy the test laid down by Lord Wilberforce in *Alphacell* that causing 'must involve some active operation or chain of operations involving as a result the pollution of the stream'. And in *Attorney-General's Reference (No. 1 of 1994)* [1995] 1 WLR 599, a sewerage undertaker was held to have caused a water pollution incident by running a sewerage system in an unmaintained state. Although it was argued that this was an omission, the court reformulated the issue by pointing out that the active operation was running a sewage disposal system in an unmain-tained state. The court also added that it was possible for more than one person to be liable for causing one pollution incident—the offence simply required that the defendant caused the discharge or entry, not that it was the sole, or even the principal, cause. (Thus in the *CPC* case, an action could also have been brought against the subcontractors, or in the *Yorkshire Water Services* case also against the original discharger into the sewer, had they been identi-fied. Indeed, in one case involving pollution from a landfill site, three separate parties—the landfill operator, the contractor and a firm of consultants brought in to advise on certain works—were successfully prosecuted; see [2001] ENDS Report 319, 53).

There was a line of cases, however, where the courts held that the defendant had been passive rather than active, and therefore not liable for causing pollution. These began with *Price v Cromack* [1975] 1 WLR 988, where a farmer had a contract permitting an animal firm to discharge waste into lagoons on his land. One lagoon wall failed and the resulting escape severely polluted a river. The farmer was acquitted of causing pollution on the ground that he had only permitted the accumulation and had not caused the pollution. *Price v Cromack* was followed in *Wychavon District Council v National Rivers Authority* [1993] 1 WLR 125 and *National Rivers Authority v Welsh Development Agency* [1993] Env

LR 407. In the *Wychavon* case, raw sewage escaped from a sewer under the control of the Council acting as agent of the water company in maintaining and repairing the sewerage system. The immediate cause was a blockage in the sewer. The Divisional Court held that the Council was not guilty of the causing offence since it had merely remained inactive. In the *Welsh Development Agency* case, the court decided that the landlord of an industrial estate did not cause a discharge of trade effluent from the estate's surface water drains when the effluent originated from one of the units on the estate. These two cases both purported to follow *Alphacell*, but appeared to ignore that in *Alphacell* it was the underlying operation, not the immediate cause of the pollution, that must be active. (In *Alphacell*, the active operation was identified as a complex one that involved the carrying on of a paper factory with an effluent treatment plant situated next to a river and which had an overflow channel that led directly to a river: it was inevitable that if something went wrong, polluting matter would enter the river.)

In its decision in the *Empress Car* case, however, this suspect line of cases was reviewed by the House of Lords.

CASE 18.5 *Empress Car Company (Abertillery) Ltd v National Rivers Authority* [1998] Env LR 396

An oil tank had a protective bund, but to make it easier to use the oil, the tank was connected via a pipe to a smaller drum outside the bund. The outlet from the tank had an unlocked tap, which was vandalized. The drum overfilled, leading to pollution of a river via a storm drain. Following *Alphacell*, Lord Hoffmann held that the defendant must have 'done something', but this something need not be the immediate act which led to the pollution. Maintaining a diesel tank was 'doing something': so was maintaining lagoons or operating sewerage systems. The *Wychavon* and *Welsh Development Authority* cases were therefore strongly disapproved of as being too restrictive, and an attempt was made to restore the meaning of 'active operation' laid down in *Alphacell*. This case continues the purposive approach to interpreting 'cause' in water pollution offences, without which it is generally considered that the legislation would be ineffective.

A further point here is that WRA 1991, s. 217(3) makes it an offence if a breach of any of the water pollution offences is due to the act or default of some other person. If this is the case, then that person can be charged with an offence regardless of whether proceedings are taken against the person who was directly responsible. This provision of concurrent liability was probably intended to apply where, for example, someone who caused pollution was 'acting under orders'. Since, as noted above, more than one person can cause water pollution under section 85 it is not clear that this provision is of much practical use. However, it has been successfully relied on in *Express Ltd v Environment Agency* [2005] Env LR 7 to prosecute a dairy owner who allowed its premises to be used to transfer cream from an outside supplier to one of its customers, and some of the cream ended up, via surface drains, in a brook. The Divisional Court held that the method of transferring the cream was unsafe and had not been subject to an adequate risk assessment, which would have been required if the dairy owner was to be immune from liability under section 217(3) (see also Case box 9.1).

(d) Third parties, natural forces, and other intervening 'causes'

Despite the apparent strictness of *Alphacell*, there was a line of cases where the courts imposed limits to the wide interpretation of the concept of causing pollution where a third party or other intervening act was thought to interrupt the chain of causation. In *Impress (Worcester) Ltd v Rees* [1971] 2 All ER 357, fuel oil from a tank was released into the River Severn. The defendant successfully pleaded that this was the act of a trespasser. In *National Rivers Authority v Wright Engineering Co. Ltd* [1994] 4 All ER 281, vandals had interfered with an oil storage tank, which then leaked into controlled waters. Once again, the company was held not to have caused the polluting entry, although it was accepted that the forseeability of the vandalism would be a relevant factor in deciding who caused the pollution incident. In *Alphacell*, however, the presence of leaves and other debris that blocked the overflow channel were to be expected in autumn. Similarly, in *Southern Water Authority v Pegrum* (1989) 153 JP 581, the heavy rain which filled up slurry lagoons so that they overflowed and polluted a river was not so out of the ordinary as to break the chain of causation.

In *Empress Car*, Lord Hoffmann reaffirmed what had really already been laid down in *Alphacell* concerning causation, namely that once it was established that something had been done to cause pollution, the only question that needs to be asked is whether the defendant caused the pollution. But he then stated a general test as to when the chain of causation will be broken. He did so by trying to avoid questions of whether the specific intervention was foreseeable (the approach that had been taken in *Wright Engineering*).

The true common sense distinction is, in my view, between acts and events which, although necessarily foreseeable in the particular case, are in the generality a normal and familiar fact of life, and acts or events which are abnormal and extraordinary.

In his view, vandalism is foreseeable, whereas a terrorist attack is not. This approach may make it easier for magistrates to determine whether or not the defendant caused the pollution, but does not wholly remove scope for argument. For example, terrorist attacks may be extraordinary, but they are planned against by water companies. On the other hand, incidents of vandalism may be rare in some rural settings. Ultimately, though, the new test does leave some room for arguments that, in individual cases, an event is extraordinary. In *Environment Agency v Brock plc* [1998] Env LR 607, a case involving pollution following a fracture to a pipe with a latent defect, however, the Divisional Court seemed to imply that any such defect would always be an 'ordinary fact of life', suggesting that this was a matter of law rather than fact.

The ambit of this approach to causation was further explored in the *Express Ltd* case (see p. 735). The tanker owners argued that the series of events from the tyre blow out to the milk entering the brook (the blown-out tyre damaged the mud flap which then dislodged the side under run protection rail which then became detached and sheered the outlet valve for the milk) was so extraordinary, being unheard of to them, that the chain of causation had been broken. But this was rejected on the grounds that blow outs are ordinary events and nothing extraordinary, in the sense of an action by a third party or natural event, had happened between the blow out and the eventual spill. This confirms the strict approach to criminal liability that will be taken by the courts under section 85, but might be considered to lead to harsh consequences where a quite unforeseeable chain of events not involving ultroneous causes follows an initially ordinary event.

(e) 'Knowingly permitting'

The offence of 'knowingly permitting' has given rise to fewer cases and is clearly more limited than the 'causing' offence because of the knowledge requirement. However, it may be of use in situations where a person is passive even after knowing of the polluting incident. For example, in *Price v Cromack* the judge suggested the farmer could well have been charged with knowingly permitting the pollution; and in the *Wychavon* case it is fairly clear that the local authority could have been charged with knowingly permitting the pollution once it had been drawn to its attention (on the facts it had delayed for some time before taking steps to remedy the situation). One issue of great importance to the 'knowingly permitting' offence is the level of knowledge required. In *Schulmans Incorporated Ltd v National Rivers Authority* [1993] Env LR D1 the judge held that constructive knowledge was sufficient, although he did not go on to elaborate the point.[21]

(f) Liability of companies and consent holders

Two final cases are of importance for the section 85 offences. In *Taylor Woodrow Property Management Ltd v National Rivers Authority* (1994) 158 JP 1101, a property company held a discharge consent relating to an outfall from an industrial estate. Even though it did not itself actually make any discharge, it was held liable under section 85(6) for contravening the conditions of the consent. It thus appears that the holder of a consent is always capable of being prosecuted for breach of positive conditions attached to the consent. It can also be noted that this is a very neat way of avoiding any argument concerning whether the defendant has carried out an active operation, but only where there is a consent.

Company directors and other senior managers can be guilty of a water pollution offence in addition to any charge brought against the company, if there is consent or connivance on that person's part, or some form of neglect (s. 217(1)) although this has never been used. And in *National Rivers Authority v Alfred McAlpine Homes East Ltd* [1994] 4 All ER 286, the company was held to be vicariously liable for acts of its employees, irrespective of whether those employees exercised 'the controlling mind' of the company. This appears to be a straightforward application of the principle of vicarious liability, but it does illustrate the need for companies to establish proper environmental management systems.

(g) Summary of judicial attitudes to the general water pollution offences

It is quite clear, from comments in the cases referred to above, that the judges have been prepared to adopt a fairly purposive view of the legislation in order to further the aim of environmental protection. One result has been that the section 85 offences have been given a very wide interpretation. This has had a number of implications. First, a wide range of accidental occurrences are offences. Secondly, any excess over the requirements of a numerical consent amounts to a criminal offence, no matter how small it is. Thirdly, firms are given a clear incentive to adopt an appropriate environmental management system so that accidents and breaches of consent do not occur. Fourthly, when a prosecution is brought there is a very high success rate (it is currently around 95 per cent). However, the EA has a discretion whether to prosecute and has adopted a policy which means that a prosecution will not be brought in every case (see Chapter 9 and p. 741 below).

---

21. See D. Wilkinson [1993] Water Law 25 for discussion.

The courts also have a discretion in sentencing, which may mitigate perceived injustices: in the *CPC* case, the defendants were eventually given an absolute discharge. This discretion on prosecuting and on sentencing, however, means that it would be dangerous for the courts to import the interpretation of 'causing' given in *Empress Car* into other provisions such as those in relation to contaminated land (see p. 689) or water pollution clean up powers (see p. 744), where there is less discretion to mitigate the strictness of liability.

Sampling and enforcement powers

Environment Agency officers have wide rights of entry to property under section 108 of the Environment Act 1995. These include a right to take samples of water or effluent or to install monitoring equipment. In practice, some form of monitoring requirement, typically self-monitoring, is now included in most discharge consents, and section 111 states simply that information provided or obtained as a result of a licence condition is admissible, including where it is provided by means of an apparatus (i.e. some form of measuring device). There is a rebuttable presumption that such an apparatus is accurate. Hence the results of self-monitoring can be used for enforcement purposes, at least where required under a consent. In practice, most consents which require self-monitoring will also make it a condition to pass on information gathered, so that failure to do will also be an offence.

There is also a potential problem relating to the admissibility of the public registers, since it is fairly clearly hearsay evidence. It appears that samples taken by the EA are admissible under the Criminal Justice Act 1988, s. 24. This section also seems to avoid any problem relating to self-incrimination where the discharger's own voluntarily taken data are used, as that data will count as a confession (see the Police and Criminal Evidence Act 1984, ss. 76 and 82). Although it is arguable that the decision in *Saunders v United Kingdom* (1997) 23 EHRR 313 changes this, the decision in *R v Hertfordshire County Council, ex parte Green Environmental Industries Ltd* [2000] 1 All ER 773 indicates that information placed on the registers can be relied on, because it is not sought as part of a specific criminal investigation. In the unlikely event that information supplied under self-monitoring was held by the courts to be inadmissible, the Environment Agency might have to use remote monitoring, for example, using telemetry (a costly option which might be thought excessive). But it is worth stressing that there would remain sound regulatory reasons to require self-monitoring; good environmental management practice demands that firms gather information about their environmental impact and use this to improve performance over time.

Enforcement policy and penalties

A central issue relating to water pollution, and indeed of this whole book, is whether the rules are actually enforced by the regulators (see generally Chapter 9). The NRA established a national prosecution policy and it became clear that the traditional recipe of a conciliatory approach to enforcement with very low prosecution rates was rapidly reformulated.

Prosecution policy is governed by the EA's revised *Enforcement and Prosecution Policy* and associated *Functional Guidelines* (see p. 301). Statistics on water pollution incidents are

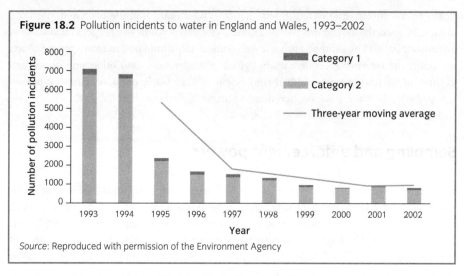

Figure 18.2 Pollution incidents to water in England and Wales, 1993–2002

Source: Reproduced with permission of the Environment Agency

given in annual reports by the EA (though finding statistics on prosecutions is increasingly difficult as the EA now prefers to highlight the worst offenders on a sector-by-sector basis). As Figure 18.2 illustrates, the long-term steady decrease in incidents since the mid-1990s has begun to level off. Under the EA's policy, the Category 1 incidents are likely to result in prosecution, making around 100 water pollution prosecutions a year.

One difficulty with the annual published statistics is that they do not include breaches of discharge consents, and it remains the case that most prosecutions are for accidental or other unusual incidents rather than for consistent breaches of consent. This has led to complaints from environmental groups that the NRA (and now the EA) has not taken action against persistent polluters with significant rigour. This seems to be borne out by compliance statistics, which indicate that only around a dozen or so prosecutions are taken annually for breach of consent conditions. These statistics also show, however, that *monitoring* of consents for breaches is very variable; on average, only two-thirds of consents are monitored annually, and those regions where monitoring is lowest have (perhaps unsurprisingly) the lowest levels of prosecutions for consent breaches (see [2001] 321 ENDS Report 37).

In this regard, the scope to bring a private prosecution under the Water Resources Act 1991 is important. While little used, its availability remains a threat to dischargers, particularly in the light of the information on the public registers, and it may also be used by environmental groups as a means of registering their disquiet over official inaction over certain discharges. This was the case, for example, when Greenpeace successfully prosecuted Albright & Wilson in 1991, and the threat of a private prosecution following the *Sea Empress* spill may have galvanized the EA into prosecuting (see p. 294; see also the use of a private prosecution in Case box 18.6).

Owing to the strict liability nature of water pollution offences most prosecutions (over 90 per cent) are successful. And the Agency is increasingly willing to bring prosecutions in the Crown Court, where fines may be unlimited. But it is difficult to predict what level of fine will be imposed. The level of fines has undoubtedly increased from the late 1980s (when the average fine was estimated to be around £250) and the highest fine imposed for a water pollution offence was £4 million against the Milford Haven Port Authority following the spillage of oil from the *Sea Empress* in 1996 (reduced to £750,000 on appeal). The courts are, however, clearly hostile to the use of tariffs and continue to insist that sentences are imposed on a case-by-case basis. As discussed in more detail elsewhere (see Box 9.14) the main factors appear to be the culpability of the defender, and the environmental and economic damage done. The courts seem to regard water pollution as a serious environmental offence, and that industry ought to have preventive systems in place when accidents occur, but they are mindful of a range of further factors.

CASE 18.6 *R v Anglian Water Services* [2004] Env LR 10

Following an operational failure at a sewage treatment works, 200 tonnes of sewage entered a river, causing catastrophic damage to fish and other wildlife. A local resident considered that the Agency was dragging its heels and brought a private prosecution, and a fine of £200,000 was imposed. The Court of Appeal reduced the fine to £60,000 (see Box 9.14). Previous incidents at other of its treatment works suggested that the company had not sufficiently improved its management practice, but rather than look to management failures on the part of the company as a whole the court considered that its 65 previous convictions had to be seen in the context of the extensive area covered by the company. The seriousness of the offence was mitigated by its prompt action in limiting the extent of the damage, and by its guilty plea. Finally, 'the fine must be at a level to make some impact on the company and overcome any suggestion that it is cheaper to pay the fines than undertake the work that is necessary to prevent the offence in the first place'. Quite why £200,000 was 'manifestly excessive' for a company which is part of a group which made £166 million profit in the financial year 2003 was, however, unsatisfactorily dealt with, and the conclusion may be that the court was influenced by what it perceived might be the impact of large fines on sewerage undertakers operating a large number of often outdated treatment works under prescribed funding formulae (as discussed at p. 720).

In contrast to waste management offences, scant use has been made of custodial sentences (a magistrates court can impose a three-month sentence, and a Crown Court a two-year sentence): so far, only one two-month sentence has been imposed for a water pollution offence following an agricultural oil pollution incident (see [1998] Water Law 66).

Access to information

For the first time, the Control of Pollution Act 1974 provided for public registers of a range of environmental information relating to water pollution, although these provisions were not implemented until 1985. Prior to that the system tended to be operated with a fair degree of secrecy about consents and samples taken. The relevant provisions are repeated in the Water Resources Act 1991 with some amendments.

Under section 190, a public register must be kept by the EA of all applications for consent, consents actually granted, any conditions attached to a consent, and notices of water quality objectives made under section 83. Prescribed details of authorizations granted for the purposes of integrated pollution control must also be recorded on the water registers. In addition, the results of *any* samples of the receiving waters or of effluent (which includes samples taken by a discharger as a condition of consent) and any information produced by analysis of them, must be registered.

Registers must be open for inspection by any member of the public free of charge at all reasonable times, with reasonable facilities for taking copies afforded on payment of a reasonable fee. The Control of Pollution (Applications, Appeals and Registers) Regulations 1996 (SI 1996/2971) specify the detailed shape of the registers. Details of any sample must be entered on the register within two months of the date of the sample.

The public register provides an invaluable database for groups and individuals wishing to monitor water quality. It can be used to mount a private prosecution (as in *Wales v Thames Water Authority* (1987) 1(3) Environmental Law 3, where the water authority was successfully prosecuted for pollution from a sewage works in reliance on the information which it had itself recorded on the register), or to provide evidence for a civil claim, but its use in providing general information on the state of the water environment is rather limited. The admissibility of the registers as evidence seems quite clear now that they are kept by the EA (see p. 741).

Preventative and remedial powers

In common with other areas of pollution control, the regulatory system which controls water pollution has a range of powers in relation to the prevention of harm. The exercise of these powers is undoubtedly aided by the presence of water quality objectives against which action may be judged. These powers can be used both for consented discharges (where 'enforcement notices' are used) and for activities which are unconsented but where water pollution may need to be prevented (where the EA can either recover the costs of preventing or remedying harm or serve a notice on the responsible person to do so).

(a) Anti-pollution works and enforcement notices

Under section 161, the EA has widely drafted powers to prevent pollution incidents where there is a threat of water pollution, to clean up after them and to carry out remedial or restorative works. For example, section 161 covers such things as diverting a potential pollutant spilt in an accident in order to prevent it from entering a watercourse, cleaning up the effects of a spillage, restocking a river with fish, and investigations into pollution incidents. The main problem with section 161 is that it requires the EA itself to undertake works or operations before recovering the costs, thus adding to uncertainty over the prospect of cost-recovery which, in turn, means that the power to carry out works is often not exercised. Accordingly, under section 161A-D, the EA can now serve a works notice on the appropriate responsible person requiring that person to prevent or clean up pollution. Only where it is necessary for the EA to carry out works 'forthwith' or if the polluter cannot be found, can the EA act. Failure to comply with a works notice is an offence (procedural issues are dealt with in the Anti-Pollution Works Regulations 1999, SI 1999/1006). Where there is an overlap with the contaminated land regime, Part IIA of the EPA 1990 should be used, since this is a mandatory provision. (This also has the benefit that the contaminated land provisions ought to remediate harm caused to other parts of the environment.)

Where the EA has acted, it can recover the costs incurred in these works, operations or investigations from anyone who has caused or knowingly permitted the pollutant to be present in controlled waters, or who has caused or knowingly permitted the pollutant to be a threat to controlled waters. There is a degree of overlap between these powers and the power to clean up contaminated sites. There is published guidance on the manner in which each of these powers should be exercised (see p. 665). The one exception is that these powers cannot be exercised so as to impede or prevent the making of a discharge in pursuance of a consent. In this case the EA is limited to considering whether the consent should be varied, although there is no power to override the period of immunity against variation merely on the grounds that a discharger has committed a breach or an act of pollution.

During the 1990s the record of the NRA and then the EA in recovering costs was criticised, not least because it failed to meet the stated policy objective that polluters should pay for the consequences of their actions. Now, however, section 161 is routinely used by the EA for recovering both investigation and remediation costs following significant pollution incidents. A further change is that section 161 is now used *before* prosecution is brought, and indeed there may be circumstances where *only* the powers in section 161 are used and there is no prosecution (the legality of this can be seen in *Bruton v Clarke* [1994] Water Law 145). This suggests that cost-recovery is no longer seen as a supplement to prosecution but an important regulatory device in its own right (and is a good example of the EA prioritising environmental quality over sanctioning criminal acts, see Chapter 9). Section 161 is particularly useful because the potential cost may act as a greater deterrent than the threat of prosecution. In most cases the costs of a clean-up operation are likely to be higher than the potential fine. For example, in *National Rivers Authority v Shell (UK)* [1990] Water Law 40, Shell was fined £1m for a major leak of oil into the River Mersey (a fine level that, in the light of the recent cases noted above, would perhaps not be repeated), but it was reported as having paid over £6m in clean-up costs. In the *Bruton* case, a county court case concerning damage to a fishery, the approach to valuing a claim under section 161 is shown, with the judge limiting the NRA to costs necessarily incurred as a result of the pollution incident and not allowing costs incurred in *improving* the fishery.

Where there has been or is likely to be a breach of a discharge consent condition, the EA may serve an *enforcement notice* under WRA 1991, s. 90B. This must identify the breach (or likely breach), the steps required to remedy the breach and the time within which these must be carried out. Failure to comply with an enforcement notice is an offence and there are the normal rights of appeal (see above). Enforcement notices give the EA another option other than prosecution when faced with a pollution incident. They are also useful in preventing pollution from non-accidental sources and requiring improvements in situations where there is an 'accident waiting to happen'.

(b) Other preventive and precautionary tools

There are also other mechanisms which can be used against activities which cannot be consented because they do not generally 'discharge' (e.g. slurry tanks) and which do not necessarily give rise to an immediate risk of harm. Hence, some of the measures described below might be said to be precautionary rather than merely preventive controls, in that they include measures which, for example, seek to create what in effect are 'buffer zones' between water pollutants like oil or (in some areas) chemical stores, and controlled waters.

(i) Precautions against pollution

Under section 92, the Secretary of State may make regulations concerning precautions to be taken in relation to any poisonous, noxious, or polluting matter to prevent it from entering controlled waters. Such regulations may prevent anyone having custody or control of poisonous, noxious or polluting matter unless the steps required in the regulations or specified by the EA are carried out. These regulations may create additional criminal offences and administrative remedies in relation to breaches, although these may not have penalties higher than for the pollution offences under section 85.

The Control of Pollution (Silage, Slurry and Agricultural Fuel Oil) Regulations 1991 (SI 1991/324, as amended by SI 1997/547) were the first regulations made under section 92. They introduced precautionary controls over the design and operation of some potentially very polluting activities by imposing specific controls over silage making operations, slurry stores and agricultural fuel oil stores. All new or substantially altered facilities are covered (many of which are performance standards rather than strict design requirements), though it is possible for the EA to bring existing activities under control if it is satisfied there is a significant risk of pollution to controlled waters. These regulations complement the planning system in preventing pollution problems arising. However, control is exercisable over operational details in a more specific way than is possible through the planning system; oversight and monitoring is carried out by a more specialist body; and the controls relate to agricultural matters not normally covered by planning powers. The legislative approach, however, is clearly limited to the adequacy of containment facilities and has been criticized for not addressing the eventual disposal of farm wastes more generally, e.g. through farm waste management plans.

Further regulations govern industrial fuel oil stores more generally, though only in England (Control of Pollution (Oil Storage) (England) Regulations 2001 (SI 2001/2954)). They aim to tackle the fact that oil spills are one of the most common sources of pollution incident. As with the earlier regulations, they require preventive measures such as adequate bunds around oil tanks; failure to adhere to these requirements is a criminal offence. The Regulations do not in practice extend to single private dwellings, nor do they apply to underground tanks (which are covered by the Groundwater Regulations 1998), though they do apply to all kinds of oil (except waste oils), not just fuel oil. For existing tanks the Regulations are effective from 1 September 2005, though the EA may serve a notice before then if there is a significant risk of pollution.

(ii) Water protection zones

Under section 93, the Secretary of State may designate water protection zones. Such an order may effectively establish a system of local law within the zone with regard to water pollution. Orders under this section may either prohibit or restrict specified activities within the designated zone with a view to preventing or controlling the entry of poisonous, noxious, or polluting matter into controlled waters, or provide for a system whereby the EA determine prohibited or restricted activities. It is not possible to require the carrying out of positive works. An order may also include provisions relating to procedures for obtaining consent for such restricted activities from the EA, with criminal sanctions being available for breaches.

Similar provisions were included in COPA 1974 but never used. The first water protection zone—of only two so far—was eventually designated in 1999, covering most of the River

Dee catchment (Water Protection Zone (River Dee Catchment) Designation Order 1999, SI 1999/915). The order effectively provides for a specialist consent regime within the zone to regulate the storage and use of certain controlled substances by industrial and other processes, although construction sites, retail premises, farms, and sites covered by integrated pollution control are excluded. Consents are determined following a risk assessment, and BATNEEC principles apply where there is an appreciable risk of pollution (see the Water Protection Zone (River Dee Catchment) (Procedural and Other Provisions) Regulations 1999, SI 1999/916). It is thought that there will be such a risk in relation to about 100 of the 300 to 500 sites affected. Undertaking activities without a consent or in breach of its conditions is an offence, although by contrast with the strictness of the main water pollution offences there is a 'due diligence' defence, and also rather generous defences of showing genuine lack of knowledge that the activity was being carried on or an excessive amount of substances being kept or used. There were also transitional provisions which effectively deemed consent to be given to any ongoing activity. This consent could not be varied within two years, unless there were changes in circumstances. While generous in places to industry, these provisions should contribute to protecting the catchment from accidental and diffuse discharges at least cost overall. They also make explicit provision for precautionary consent conditions to apply. It is notable that water protection zones have only been used as a response to industrial point source hotspots rather than, for example, diffuse pollution from agriculture.

One limitation, in section 93(3), is that a water protection zone should not concern itself with nitrate from agricultural sources. This is because protection against nitrate is provided for in section 94, a section which was hurriedly written into the legislation during its passage in response to public worries about nitrate in groundwaters used for water supply and the action against the UK government in the European Court of Justice for non-compliance with EC Directive 80/778 on Drinking Water (see p. 714). From a legal point of view it is difficult to see why the nitrate problem could not have been tackled through the designation of water protection zones, and it is hard to avoid the conclusion that specific nitrate sensitive area provisions were something of a political gesture.

(iii) Nitrate vulnerable zones

As noted above, in response to legal action by the European Commission relating to the 1980 Drinking Water Quality Directive, a national scheme for nitrate sensitive areas was established. Although the Nitrate Sensitive Areas Regulations 1994 (as amended) represented a fairly sophisticated response to nitrate pollution in designated areas, they are insufficient to comply with the Agricultural Nitrates Directive (91/676), which has more programmatic objectives (on complying with these generally see Box 7.11). As a result, the Protection of Water against Agricultural and Nitrate Pollution (England and Wales) Regulations 1996 (SI 1996/888) were introduced.

The regulations designate Nitrate Vulnerable Zones (NVZs) in specific areas where there are excessive levels of nitrate pollution from agricultural sources (all nitrate sensitive areas are now in NVZs). The Secretary of State must then draw up action plans for each NVZ which are designed to reduce and prevent water pollution from nitrates and agricultural sources (see Action Programmes for Nitrate Vulnerable Zones (England and Wales) Regulations 1998, SI 1998/1202). These plans include fairly detailed rules about things like when fertilizers can be applied.

Unlike nitrate sensitive areas, NVZs are always mandatory, and there is no prospect of compensation payments for farmers in NVZs. This helps explain the concerns raised by many farmers to the designations, which culminated in a legal challenge brought by two farmers, supported by the NFU. In Case C-293/97 *R v Secretary of State for the Environment and Minister of Agriculture, Fisheries and Food, ex parte Standley* [1999] Env LR 801, the main ground of challenge was that the UK Government, when drawing up its initial list of NVZs, had failed to consider whether the excessive nitrate levels were caused by non-agricultural sources. The farmers argued that this failure discriminated against agricultural users in the NVZ as the cost of reducing the nitrate concentrations to an acceptable level was to be borne wholly by the farmers when there were other users which may have been responsible for the nitrate pollution. The case was referred to the European Court of Justice, which upheld the approach of the Government in identifying waters where agricultural sources made a 'sufficient contribution' to excessive nitrate levels, in line with a purposive interpretation of the Directive. Indeed, the Court hinted that something rather less than a significant contribution might have been enough, showing the amount of freedom that Member States enjoy. This flexibility is also seen in the Court's rejection of an argument that the UK violated the 'polluter pays' principle (see now Art. 174(2), EC Treaty), since the Directive had sufficient room to ensure that action programmes targeted the contribution of farmers proportionate to those of other polluters.

The Directive says little about how such other sources are to be regulated, although other sources like sewage treatment works will probably be subject to duties to reduce nitrate pollution under measures like the Urban Waste Water Treatment Directive, under which a small number of sensitive areas were designated in 1997 and again in 2002 because of risks from nitrate.

One danger with flexibility here, though, is that it might be used to implement the Directive minimally. Originally, 68 NVZs were designated on the basis that nitrate levels in surface or groundwater used for drinking water abstraction were above the Drinking Water Directive limit of 50 mg/l. However, in Case C-69/99 *Commission v UK* [2000] ECR I-10979 the Government conceded that it ought also to have designated *all* surface water and groundwater where nitrate levels exceeded this limit, i.e. it should not have interpreted the Agricultural Nitrates Directive as a directive concerned only with improving drinking water quality. As a result of this decision, around 55 per cent of land area in England is now covered by NVZ designations. By contrast, the whole of the Netherlands, Denmark, and Germany have been designated.

BOX 18.4 **Diffuse water pollution and the law**

The increasing need to tackle water pollution from diffuse sources such as agriculture and urban run-off has already been noted (see pp. 702 and 704). Cases like *Standley* illustrate some of the difficulties that the law faces. Whereas point sources are under the control of dischargers, diffuse pollutants may accumulate as they are washed from one area of land to another, making it difficult to attribute the input of pollutants such as nitrates and phosphates to particular individuals. Pollution is also caused by seemingly innocuous activities; phosphorous may be lost by ploughing or even overgrazing and tractor tramlines compacting the soil and making pollutants run off the land. And some pollutants may take several years before they eventually contaminate a river or a borehole, so there is a problem of regulating a moving target and apportioning the costs of diffuse pollution fairly, potentially over decades. All of this requires a mix of legal and other responses designed to change agricultural land management practices to prevent or min-imize inputs e.g. by controlling inputs of fertilizers (perhaps through voluntary action, or by some form of taxation, see below), or by using mechanisms like cross-compliance under which farmers will only receive support payments where their land is kept in good agricultural and environ-mental condition (see further p. 867). There is some use of 'thou shalt not' forms of law, for example in addition to the action programme rules for NVZs there is a notice provision under the Groundwater Regulations 1998 under which the Environment Agency can effectively put restric-tions on the use of sheep dips and petrol stations. But it is not clear that there exists the political desire to micro-manage activities like agriculture through the use command-style regulation, with the criminal responsibilities which would attach to this.

(iv) Economic instruments

Finally, brief mention should be made of the use of economic tools to combat water pollu-tion. Two proposals deserve mention. First, in 1998 DETR issued a consultation paper on *Economic Instruments for Water Pollution*. This suggested that point source dischargers could be made to pay a charge reflecting either the value of improved water quality or the marginal cost of pollution abatement. These proposals, however, received little support, not least because they appeared to envisage that pollution charges could reduce administrative regu-lation (something the Royal Commission on Environmental Pollution in its 1992 Report on *Freshwater Quality* had rejected as being unrealistic). Aside from potential problems with 'hotspots' where pollution might become concentrated (which would clearly be a problem in complying with statutory or EC-driven water quality objectives), the proposals have so far come to nothing. This is because the existing consent systems already take environmental impact into account when charges for trade effluent consents and discharge consents are set; the EA must already take costs and benefits into account when determining consents (see p. 128); and because it is not clear why a discharger should be required to improve the quality of effluent if it is not harmful to the environment (a point which goes back to one of the general themes of this chapter about the nature of water pollution).

Although new forms of environmental charges may have limited utility in relation to point sources, the need for innovative regulatory approaches to combat diffuse water pollu-tion means that there is more likelihood that we will see developments here. One particular proposal has been the introduction of a pesticide tax, which might go some way to reducing the UK's relatively high usage of pesticides compared to other EC countries. This was first mooted in 1998 but rejected by government in 2000 when, in the midst of a crisis, the farming industry put forward alternative proposals of a voluntary nature to reduce pesticide use. There are signs, however, that if these voluntary initiatives fail then a pesticide tax is still within present government thinking.

Overlapping controls

(a) Land use planning controls

Local planning authorities have the ability to make important decisions relating to water pollution through the town and country planning system. However, it is clearly recommended in central government guidance, such as Circular 11/95 on planning conditions and Planning Policy Guidance Note 23, *Planning and Pollution Control*, that planning powers should be used mainly for locational and siting decisions and that matters about the regulation of pollution should be left to the specialist regulators to control through the specialist consent systems.

It is clear that potential water pollution arising from a proposed development is a material consideration in any planning decision, and the EA is a statutory consultee under the General Development Procedure Order in relation to many applications for planning permission. This is of great importance in relation to groundwaters, since the NRA published a set of very strong policy statements on the protection of groundwater,[22] and through the planning system the EA may be notified of potentially harmful activities which it can then seek to control using its own powers. In addition, planning permission may be refused because of inadequate sewerage in the area. Of course, the EA will also have an important role to play in the making of development plans. The generous exemptions for agricultural activities and buildings may be of significance in the context of increasing evidence of water pollution by agriculture.

It is notable that there are specific regulations governing certain abstractions of water which may have significantly harmful environmental effects, and that for these the Environment Agency is the competent authority (these were made under the revised EIA Directive). However, there is nothing comparable as regards water quality, with the result that in relation to environmental impact assessment and water quality matters, the EA is only ever a consultee in the assessment process.

(b) Integrated pollution control

There are separate controls for those processes prescribed for Part I of the Environmental Protection Act 1990 (i.e. those processes subject to integrated pollution control) and processes for which an IPPC permit is required. Acting in accordance with an IPC authorisation or IPPC permit will be a defence to the water pollution offences under section 85 of the Water Resources Act 1991 (see generally Chapter 20).

(c) Waste management

Some of the overlaps, and gaps, between waste management licensing and water pollution controls are discussed at p. 619. It is worth mentioning though that a waste management licence can only be granted where, amongst other things, the applicant is a 'fit and proper' person, a test which includes an absence of criminal convictions, which could include convictions for water pollution offences.

---

22. NRA, *Policy and Practice for the Protection of Groundwater* (1992).

(d) Radioactive discharges

Under the Control of Pollution (Radioactive Waste) Regulations 1989 (SI 1989/1158), the radioactivity of a discharge is to be ignored for the purposes of the Water Resources Act 1991. In other words, the non-radioactive elements of a discharge or entry are dealt with under the Water Resources Act 1991 and the radioactive elements under the Radioactive Substances Act 1993 by the EA.

(d) Statutory nuisances

In addition to the statutory nuisances listed in Part III of the EPA 1990 (see p. 406), two further statutory nuisances are provided for in the Public Health Act 1936. Section 259(1)(a) provides that any pool, pond, ditch, gutter, or watercourse which is in a state that is prejudicial to health or a nuisance is a statutory nuisance. This will cover small ponds and ditches which are not within the consent system, as well as controlled waters although not estuarial or coastal waters (*R v Falmouth and Truro Port Health Authority, ex parte South West Water Ltd* [2000] NPC 36). Section 259(1)(b) covers any watercourse which is silted up or choked so as to obstruct the proper flow of water and thus causing a nuisance or which is prejudicial to health. This is limited to watercourses which are not normally navigated. The normal procedures for statutory nuisance apply to these situations, thus creating an alternative course of action for a local authority or individual wishing to clean up a grossly polluted watercourse.

(e) Nature conservation

Under the EC Habitats Directive (92/43), discharge consents can only be granted, and must be reviewed, in light of their potential impact upon European sites (see p. 838).

(f) Contaminated land

Historically contaminated land may be contaminating controlled waters, or pose the risk of such contamination. In such cases Part IIA of the Environmental Protection Act 1990 will apply (see Chapter 17). It is worth noting that the inconsistency caused by defining contaminated land by reference to significant environmental harm or to the pollution of controlled waters has been addressed in section 86 of the Water Act 2003, which now requires there to be *significant* pollution of controlled waters (hence disapplying Part IIA in cases of minor water pollution).

Water pollution and private law controls

Private law controls still play a significant role in the control of water pollution. Indeed, for various technical reasons they are probably of greater use for water pollution than for other forms of pollution and may be used to produce, directly or indirectly, environmental improvements although they have at best a limited strategic role.

One right which has already been mentioned is the right of private prosecution for breaches of the criminal law. This has been available for many water pollution offences since 1985 as a result of the removal by COPA 1974 of the restrictions on it. More significant, however, are the various civil law claims that may be brought. For example, the Anglers'

Conservation Association is estimated to have been involved in over 1,000 cases involving water pollution since the Second World War. The two main remedies available are damages to compensate an owner of the river bed, the river banks, or a fishery for any losses caused, and an injunction to restrain future breaches of the law.

It is important to note that acting within the terms of a discharge consent does not act as a defence to a civil action, since the private law system operates separately from the public regulatory mechanisms. This is made explicit in the Water Resources Act 1991, s. 100(b), but it can also be implied from the important decision in *Wheeler v J.J. Saunders Ltd* [1996] Ch 19, which decided that a planning permission cannot license what is otherwise a nuisance (see p. 389).

There are a number of reasons why water pollution cases, at least from point sources, have proved easier to bring than e.g. air pollution cases:

- Causation is easier to show because of the defined channels in which water normally flows.

- Apart from tidal waters, water only flows one way, so there is not the same 'give and take' involved between the polluter and the polluted. Hence the substantive legal rules tend to be more protective of the polluted.

- Many rural landowners have the money to bring an action: indeed, pollution to fisheries will often justify an action in commercial terms.

- There are a number of campaigning and amenity bodies concerned with water problems, far more than are concerned with air (or noise) pollution.

- Acquiring evidence is more straightforward, particularly since the advent of the public registers, which may provide evidence relating to the quality of the receiving waters before and after an incident and also relating to discharges.

(a) Riparian rights

The usefulness of the civil law in this area stems mainly from the nature of riparian rights. Owners of land adjoining a watercourse (including estuaries), termed riparian owners, normally own the river bed, but not the water itself. However, as a natural incident of the soil itself, they have the right to receive the water in its natural state, subject only to reasonable usage by an upstream owner for ordinary purposes (*Chasemore v Richards* (1859) 7 HL Cas 349). Owners of other property rights such as fisheries have the same right.

The most authoritative statement of this principle was given by Lord Macnaghten in *John Young & Co. v Bankier Distillery Co.* [1893] AC 691. He stated, at p. 698:

A riparian proprietor is entitled to have the water of the stream, on the bank of which his property lies, flow down as it has been accustomed to flow down to his property, subject to the ordinary use of the flowing water by upper proprietors, and to such further use, if any, on their part in connection with their property as may be reasonable in the circumstances. Every riparian owner is thus entitled to the water of his stream, in its natural flow, without sensible diminution or increase, and without sensible alteration in its character or quality.

This means that any unreasonable interference with the natural quantity or quality of the water is an actionable nuisance. The strictness of this test was shown in *John Young & Co. v Bankier Distillery Co.* An upstream mineowner discharged water into a stream from a mine.

This altered the chemistry of the water from soft to hard and thus altered the quality of the downstream distillery's whisky. The water had not been made impure, but the distillery obtained an injunction because the nature of the water had been changed. The case illustrates the relative nature of the definition of water pollution and indeed emphasizes that the common law does not lay down any absolute standards in relation to water quality. It is worth noting, however, that this test only applies where the upstream usage is not ordinary; a good example of the balancing process the law of nuisance tries to carry out.

Some of the technical difficulties relating to the law of nuisance, such as the causation question and the locality doctrine, have been neatly answered in the water pollution cases. It appears from the reasoning in *Bankier Distillery Co.* that an invasion of the natural right to water is treated as equivalent to damage to land, thus circumventing the locality doctrine. It is also clear that actual harm need not be shown, merely a 'sensible alteration', a position that is supported by *Nicholls v Ely Beet Sugar Factory Ltd* [1936] Ch 343, where the claim of interference with riparian rights was held to be analogous to trespass. It follows that an action can be brought against any upstream polluter, even if only one of many and responsible for only a part of the whole pollution. All that needs to be shown is that the polluter is contributing to the pollution (*Crossley and Sons Ltd v Lightowler* (1867) LR 2 Ch App 478).

As can be seen, however, many of the leading cases on riparian rights are of some antiquity, and it is an open question whether a court would give the same strict level of protection today. For example, the rise of extensive regulatory controls over the 20th century, and the general trend of incorporating negligence considerations like foreseeability into the land torts, might justify the higher courts in diluting the strictness of protection that the law on riparian rights affords (it is worth pointing out, however, that by requiring the actions of the upstream owner to be 'unreasonable' there is a certain element of built-in flexibility to the law here).

(b) Pollution of groundwater

Liability may also arise in nuisance for polluting percolating groundwaters, as long as causation can be shown. This was first established in *Ballard v Tomlinson* (1885) 29 ChD 115, where a brewery successfully sued for the contamination of its well caused by a neighbour who used his own well for the disposal of sewage. However, the extent of this liability was clarified in *Cambridge Water Co. v Eastern Counties Leather plc* [1994] 2 AC 264, a case discussed in detail on p. 364. As explained there, the House of Lords took the opportunity to move the law of nuisance and the law under the rule in *Rylands v Fletcher* towards negligence, by requiring the defendant to show that the type of damage that occurred was foreseeable. *Ballard v Tomlinson*, where foreseeability did not arise, was distinguished. This decision satisfied those whose primary concern was with avoiding the prospect of retrospective civil liability, but disappointed those commentators who argued for the primacy of strict liability in the civil law of water pollution as a reflection of the polluter pays principle.

The decision also casts great doubt on whether there is anything particularly strict about liability for groundwater pollution law any more, at least as far as liability for past activities is concerned. However, it does not necessarily restrict the recovery of damages, or the imposition of an injunction, in cases where polluting activities currently cause damage to groundwaters or, indeed, where the cause of the pollution was recent. It must be pointed out that liability in nuisance is personal in the sense that, even if the original polluter is liable for pollution damage, it does not follow that a subsequent purchaser of the site would also be liable. But purchasers of potentially contaminated land must bear in mind the possible implications of cases such as *Goldman v Hargrave* [1967] 1 AC 645, which establish that there is liability for 'adopting' a natural nuisance in certain circumstances (see p. 373).

(c) Other claims

Other common law claims may also be available. In *Jones v Llanrwst Urban District Council* [1911] 1 Ch 393, the owner of a river bed claimed successfully in trespass for deposits of solid wastes. In restricted cases, a claim in negligence might also be upheld (see further p. 371). Following the Camelford aluminium poisoning incident in 1988 a successful criminal action in public nuisance was also taken: see *R v South West Water Authority* [1991] 3 LMELR 65 (as a criminal matter this would now be dealt with under section 70 of the Water Industry Act 1991, see p. 721), and private claims were settled out of court on the basis of an admitted breach of the statutory duty to supply wholesome water.

In the context of water pollution, the High Court has struck out a claim under breach of statutory duty following damage to shellfish beds which the claimant alleged were attributed to unlawful acts of a sewerage undertaker, holding that such claims had to be pursued in public law (*Bowden v South West Water Services Ltd* [1998] Env LR 445). In a follow up to this case (reported at [1999] Env LR 438), however, the Court of Appeal allowed the claimant to pursue a claim based on liability against the state (a '*Francovich*' claim; see p. 224) because of the extent to which the Directive on Shellfish Waters (79/923) might be said to confer rights on individual shellfishermen. However, similar claims under the Urban Waste Treatment Waters Directive (91/271) and the Bathing Waters Directive (76/160) were rejected because the claimant could not say that he derived individual rights under them. This decision gives a good indication of the extent to which the need to prove an individual right to take a state liability claim may, in practice, mean showing that an individual economic interest might be infringed, rather than appealing to any wider environmental interests, limiting such claims to quite narrow classes of claimants.

Lastly, it is often stated that a prescriptive right to acquire an easement to pollute can be acquired. Whilst this remains true as a matter of principle, such an occurrence will be rare because it is not possible to acquire a prescriptive right where the act relied upon to gain the right is illegal. In most water pollution cases the polluting activity will be illegal.

(d) Remedies

Damages will be recoverable for any loss to the person whose rights have been infringed. This will include such things as any clean-up costs, the cost of restocking the water with fish, any loss of profits from subscriptions for such things as fishing rights and, in some circumstances, loss of amenity (see *Bruton v Clarke* [1994] Water Law 145).

Injunctions are also available for water pollution, though they will normally be suspended to allow the defendants time to correct matters. For example, in *Pride of Derby and Derbyshire Angling Association Ltd v British Celanese Ltd* [1953] Ch 149, injunctions and damages were obtained against British Celanese Ltd (for industrial effluent), Derby Corporation (for untreated sewage), and the British Electricity Authority (for thermal pollution from a power station), but suspended for two years.

CHAPTER SUMMARY

1   Water pollution law is the most developed of the systems of pollution control. It has also had the greatest degree of institutional and legal coherence.

2   The body with general responsibility for water quality in England and Wales is the Environment Agency (EA), usually acting under the Water Resources Act 1991.

3   There is no overall statutory national strategy comparable to those found in the air quality and waste management sectors. For England, DEFRA published *Directing the Flow: Priorities for Future Water Policy* (2002) but this is not a document which required public participation and consultation before adoption.

4   The addition of any substance into inland or coastal waters is not generally prejudged as being harmful; it is only harmful if it interferes with some desirable use for the water.

5   Accordingly, environmental quality standards are generally preferred, though for the more hazardous polluting substances, which may not break down quickly or which bioaccumulate, emission standards are used.

6   This policy approach does not mean that precedence is given to binding objectives for water quality. At national level, such objectives tend to be non-binding, although the impact of EC directives has changed this in relation to certain waters such as bathing waters. Otherwise, quality objectives act to guide the EA in setting discharge consents.

7   EC law is increasingly the most important force in determining new water quality standards, and in driving up the costs of compliance. The introduction of more precise standards has also contributed enormously to raising public debate about water quality, and increased the scope for legal challenges to poor water quality.

8   For the future, the EC Water Framework Directive will have a significant impact on all aspects of water pollution control and water quality management. But some of the key legal requirements in the Directive, such as 'good ecological status' and the aim of achieving good status of waters, remain vague.

9   Under national law, it is an offence to 'cause or knowingly permit' the discharge or entry of polluting matter, but acting in accordance with a discharge consent acts as a defence.

10   What amounts to 'polluting matter' is very wide, extending to substances *capable* of causing harm to humans or the water environment and not just those which cause *actual* harm.

11   Accordingly, much of the focus of case law has been on what will amount to 'causing' water pollution. The courts have interpreted this very purposively.

12   Only the most serious incidents are likely to result in prosecution by the EA. Selective enforcement and sensitive sentencing generally temper the wide interpretation given to causing water pollution.

13   The EA has powers to require polluters to clean up water pollution or, as a last resort, undertake works itself and charge the polluter. Clean-up costs often exceed fines.

14   Pollution from diffuse sources such as agricultural run-off is not consented, because there are no specific discharge points that can be monitored. Pollution from these types of sources must therefore be controlled using other methods, and integrative solutions.

15 The methods most commonly used to control diffuse discharges are specification standards, such as apply to the storage of oil or farm slurry, or area-based controls over sites designated because of, for example, high nitrate levels. A programmatic approach to reduction may also be taken, such as under the EC Agricultural Nitrates Directive.

16 Financial controls are increasingly used. The charges levied by the EA for discharge consents go some way towards making the polluter pay, while subsidies are sometimes (controversially) used to encourage farmers in certain areas to reduce their nitrate loading. The future may see full cost recovery charges introduced for all discharges, tradable discharge consents and specialist taxes, e.g. for pesticides, though none of these are imminent.

17 International law has tended to affect national standard-setting only indirectly. In recent years, the international treaty regime concerning the North Sea has become more influential.

Q QUESTIONS

1 Alfie stores silage in a store which has recently been constructed for him by a reputable contractor. Following exceptionally unseasonable weather, the local river bursts its banks and, because of a latent defect, the store is flooded. Silage ends up in the river, where fish and wildlife are harmed. The Environment Agency is alerted, and incur costs in removing the silage and restocking the river. Advise Alfie about any legal action that might be taken by the Environment Agency and by the local angling club, which claims it has been adversely affected, and how he should respond.

2 What legal difficulties might there be in implementing and enforcing the Water Framework Directive? (You might want to treat this as a research question, since over the coming years the shape of the implementing measures will become clearer.)

3 What legal measures might be passed to combat diffuse water pollution? What practical, policy and legal difficulties might there be?

 FURTHER READING

Good starting points for understanding water quality regulation, and the recent development of policy, are D. Kinnersley, *Coming Clean: The Politics of Water and the Environment* (Harmondsworth: Penguin, 1994), a refreshingly polemical account and, more academically and historically, W. Maloney and J. Richardson, *Managing Policy Change in Britain: The Politics of Water* (Edinburgh: Edinburgh University Press, 1995). Current water quality policy, or at least an agenda for a future policy, is found in DEFRA, *Directing the Flow: Priorities for Future Water Policy* (2002).

Comprehensive surveys of the law relating to water quality, including EC and international law, are J. Bates, *Water and Drainage Law* (London: Sweet & Maxwell, looseleaf) and W. Howarth and D. McGillivray, *Water Pollution and Water Quality Law* (Clayford: Shaw & Sons, 2001). The latter has chapter-by-chapter bibliographies which may serve as a useful springboard to further research, as may the *Journal of Water Law*, which contains both current awareness and articles. S. Elworthy, 'Finding the Causes of Events or Preventing a "State of Affairs"?: Designation of Nitrate Vulnerable Zones' [1998] JEL 92 is an excellent analysis of the problems of regulating pollution from diffuse sources and of what making the water polluter pays means.

For an up to date account of EC policy and law a key source is, as ever, N. Haigh, *Manual of European Environmental Policy* (Leeds: Maney Publishing, looseleaf, updated), which considers all the Directives mentioned here. Implementation deficits are discussed in M. Stallworthy, 'Water Quality: the Capacity of the European Community to Deliver' [1998] Water Law 127. Some of the policy issues in the negotiation of the 'second generation' of EC water directives are discussed in A. Jordan, 'European Community Water Policy Standards: Locked in or Watered Down?' (1999) 37(1) JCMS 13, while the views of the Director General of OFWAT on balancing environmental and economic interests are nicely outlined in I. Byatt, 'The Impact of EC Water Directives on Water Customers in England and Wales' (1996) 3(4) JEPP 665.

Recommended writings on water quality law at national level are R. Macrory, 'The Privatisation and Regulation of the Water Industry' [1990] MLR 78; W. Howarth, 'Poisonous, Noxious or Polluting' [1993] MLR 171 (which explores the laws reluctance to define water pollution); W. Howarth, 'Self-Monitoring, Self-Policing, Self-Incrimination and Pollution Law' [1997] MLR 200; C. Ryan, 'Unforesee-able but not Unusual: The Validity of the Empress Test' [1998] JEL 345; N. Stanley, 'The Empress Decision and Causing Water Pollution' [1999] Water Law 37, and D. Wilkinson 'Definition of a Break in the Chain of Causation' [2003] Journal of Water Law 96, the titles of which are fairly self-explanatory. As can be seen, the specialist Journal of Water Law (six issues per year, Lawtext publishing) is the principal periodical in this area, and covers all levels of water law developments (including interesting comparative analyses).

@ WEB LINKS

The Environment Agency <www.environment-agency.gov.uk> has the latest facts and figures about river quality and pollution incidents, though little prosecution and sentencing data. DEFRA and its devolved counterparts hold useful information, especially on current policy reforms and on the implementation of EC directives, of which the ongoing implementation of the Water Framework Directive during the currency of this issue should be kept abreast of (see e.g. <www.defra.gov.uk/environment/water/quality/index.htm>). The web sites of Ofwat <www.ofwat.gov.uk> and the Drinking Water Inspectorate <www.dwi.gov.uk> are usefully browsed when looking at water supply and financing issues. On EC water quality law and policy see <europa.eu.int/comm/environment/index_en.htm>. Relating to the international agreements considered above, see the OSPAR Convention <www.ospar.org>, the latest International North Sea Conference <www.dep.no/md/nsc> and the International Tribunal for the Law of the Sea <www.itlos.org>.

19 Disposal of waste to sewers

→ **Overview**

We continue to deal with disposals of waste to the sewerage system in a self-contained chapter. The reasons for this are because they are a separate form of waste disposal with their own particular and unique regulatory regime (and to keep the preceding chapter from being longer than it already is). The treatment of wastes at sewage works is an integral part of general policies on waste disposal and protection of the natural environment. The alternative to such disposal (waste minimization apart) is often some form of direct discharge to the environment, so sewage treatment offers an important weapon in the search for the best practicable environmental option (BPEO).

Before reading this chapter, you should be aware of the regulation of water pollution and water quality (Chapter 18), the general roles of the Environment Agency and Ofwat, and the functions of sewerage undertakers (Chapter 5), and in particular the specific provisions in the Water Resources Act 1991 which govern discharges of sewage effluent (pp. 726–7).

At the end of this chapter you will understand:

✔ The respective roles of the Environment Agency and the economic regulators.
✔ How discharges to sewers are controlled and paid for.
✔ How EC water quality law affects sewerage undertakers.

Sewage disposal and environmental protection

In addition to the introductory points made above, there are other links with environmental protection that justify detailed consideration of sewage disposal. Sewage treatment is only an intermediate step in the ultimate disposal of waste and the operators of sewers and sewage works must dispose of their own wastes. This will often (though not always) be after a treatment process and will involve a combination of liquid discharges into watercourses or the sea, the dumping of sludge on land and incineration. Indeed, sewage works have been responsible for the low quality of many of our inland and coastal waters. The Government announced a commitment to phase out the dumping of sewage sludge at sea by 1998 at the Third International Conference for the Protection of the North Sea in March 1990 (an obligation later contained in the Urban Waste Water Treatment Directive (91/271): see Box 2.7) which has meant that greater attention has had to be paid to treating sewage effluent and disposing of it safely on land or in inland watercourses.

Sewerage and sewage treatment have always been closely related with the water industry and most books have tended to treat discharges to sewers as a part of the law on water pollution. This can be explained on the grounds that discharges to sewers are liquid and that most sewage works themselves discharge into watercourses, but it also relates to the historical institutional connections. Sewerage, public water supply, and the prevention of water pollution have often been carried out by the same bodies, most notably between 1974 and 1989 when the 10 regional water authorities in England and Wales carried out all functions in relation to water and sewage on an integrated basis. This included regulating discharges both to the sewers and to surface waters.

Since 1 September 1989 there has been a reversion to a system of split responsibilities for liquid effluent. Private sewerage undertakers own and operate the sewerage network and the sewage works, as well as regulating discharges to sewers, whilst the EA (originally the NRA) regulates discharges to the natural environment and has responsibility for combating surface water pollution.

Trade effluent discharges

The sewerage undertaker plays its most important environmental protection role in the regulation of trade effluent discharges, although since 1989 certain dangerous discharges have been regulated by HMIP and now the EA (see below). Measured in terms of pollutant load, a far greater quantity of industrial effluent is discharged into the sewers than directly into surface waters or by any other disposal route.

The regulatory regime relating to discharges to sewers is an old and somewhat rudimentary one, though there have been periodic developments designed to bring it more up-to-date. It involves a rather basic system of individualised consents set by the operators of the sewers, involving little input from other bodies or from the public at any of the various stages of policy-making, standard-setting, consent-setting, or enforcement. The legislation is contained in the Water Industry Act 1991, to which all section numbers refer.

It is a criminal offence to discharge any trade effluent from trade premises into sewers unless a trade effluent consent is obtained from the sewerage undertaker (s. 118). 'Trade effluent' and 'trade premises' are defined widely in section 141 to include all liquid discharges from industry, shops, research establishments, launderettes and agriculture, except for domestic sewage. Under section 88 of the Water Act 2003, the Secretary of State now has a power in effect either to widen or narrow the definitions of 'trade effluent' and 'trade premises' so that certain discharges can, by order, either be included or excluded where there is reason to do so.

It is also an offence to breach the terms of a consent. This is a unique system of control in that it is the only example in this country of a private body exercising regulatory functions with regard to environmental protection.

Applying for a trade effluent consent

The discharger applies for a trade effluent consent by serving a trade effluent notice on the sewerage undertaker at least two months prior to the commencement of the discharge. This notice is effectively an application and must state the nature and composition of the proposed effluent, the maximum daily volume and the maximum rate of discharge in order to enable the sewerage undertaker to establish its likely effect. Under changes contained in section 89 of the Water Act 2003, the notice must now also set out the steps that the discharger proposes to take, for example, by pre-treatment, to minimize the polluting effects of the discharge both on any controlled waters, and on sewerage services.

The sewerage undertaker then has a discretion whether to grant or refuse consent, though if the sewerage system can cope with the discharge, it is normal for consent to be granted subject to conditions. The scope of these conditions is laid down in section 121. They may include such matters as the place of discharge, the nature, temperature, and composition of the discharge (including requirements as to the elimination or maximum concentration of any specified constituent), the rate and timing of discharges, and ancillary matters such as the fixing of meters to register the volume of the discharge, the monitoring of the nature and volume of the discharge, and the keeping of records. Most importantly, conditions on the payment of effluent charges will also be included. Conditions must be imposed to meet the requirements of schedule 4 to the Urban Waste Water Treatment (England and Wales) Regulations 1994 (SI 1994/2841), although it appears in practice that there is little discretion in doing so (see p. 726). In line with the changes made to the application procedure (see above), mitigation measures may also be included as consent conditions.

It is not usual to attach conditions which require the fitting of specified treatment plant. The normal practice has been to specify the effluent standards that must be met and to leave it to the discharger to determine how to meet those standards, albeit often with advice from the sewerage undertaker. One reason for this has been a widespread belief that most effluent is better and more efficiently treated at the sewage works than at each factory, but it also reflects the policy of preserving some element of choice for producers. The changes made under the Water Act 2003 (see above), while they may in a reflexive way encourage dischargers to undertake more pre-treatment, do not fundamentally change this practice. An impact of the Urban Waste Water Treatment Directive, however, is that the increased cost of treating effluent to the higher standards required is being reflected in much higher trade effluent charges; as a result, many more firms are likely to do more pre-treatment work at their sites to lower their costs.

How are consents set?

Since discharges to sewers are distinct from other discharges in being to an artificial environment, the matters that are taken into account in setting a consent differ from other consents and licences. In particular, environmental protection is only one factor.

The objectives of trade effluent control are set out clearly in a booklet produced by the Water Authorities Association in September 1986 entitled *Trade Effluent Discharged to the Sewer*. They are that the system of control seeks:

(a) to protect the sewerage system and the personnel who work in it;

(b) to protect the sewage works and their efficient operation (for example, most sewage works operate by a biological process and care has to be taken not to neutralise that process);

(c) to protect the environment generally from the residues of the sewage treatment process or from direct discharges from parts of the system such as storm drains; and

(d) to ensure that dischargers pay a reasonable charge for the cost of the treatment.

In addition, the booklet stresses that it is important for correct information on discharges to be kept, so that dischargers can know how to improve their trade effluent control and sewerage undertakers can plan for future sewerage provision and operate the treatment process efficiently.

With these factors in mind, the consent will in general be set by reference to the receiving capabilities of the sewer and sewage works. If the works are already overburdened, the consent may be refused or subject to tight limits, whereas if there is spare capacity at the works, the limits will be much more generous. Certain pollutants, such as heavy metals or persistent chemicals, may be unsuitable for sewage treatment and may be banned from the discharge. The discharger may then have to pre-treat the effluent to remove these constituents, or find an alternative method of disposal. Other relevant matters are taken into account, such as the sewerage undertaker's own potential liability for discharges from the works under the Water Resources Act 1991 and the requirements of EC law.

The sewerage undertaker has a power to vary a consent unilaterally by giving two months' notice to the discharger (s. 124). This enables it to take steps to meet the terms of the consent for the sewage works set by the EA. Since 1989, variation has been a common occurrence, as sewerage undertakers have renegotiated consents inherited from the regional water authorities and established a more uniform system for their areas and also as, formerly, the NRA and now the EA tightened consents relating to discharges from sewage works. It should be noted, however, that there is no power for the sewerage undertaker to revoke a consent.

Variation of a consent is, however, possible only after two years have elapsed from the grant of the consent or the last variation. Exceptionally, a variation may be made within this period if it is necessary to provide proper protection for people likely to be affected by the discharge. In this situation, compensation will be payable to the discharger unless the variation was necessary as a result of a change of circumstances unforeseeable at the time of the grant of the consent or its last variation (s. 125). A variation can be made on environmental grounds to comply with the Urban Waste Water Treatment Regulations 1994 (SI 1994/2841, reg. 7(6)). In this case, no compensation is payable.

The discharger has a right of appeal to the Director General of Water Services (i.e. to Ofwat and, from 2006, the Regulation Authority) against a refusal or variation of consent or the imposition of conditions, except that there is no appeal against trade effluent charges (ss. 122, 126). An appeal against a deemed refusal may also be brought if no decision is given on the trade effluent notice within two months. (It used to be the case that such a failure to determine an application led to an automatic consent, but that rule was removed by the Water Act 1989.) As with planning appeals, an appeal is effectively a rehearing and the Director General may make any decision that the sewerage undertaker could have made. There is a further right of appeal to the High Court on a matter of law. The right of appeal being to the economic regulator emphasizes the essentially commercial nature of the arrangement. The vast majority of appeals are facilitated without formal resolution.

An alternative to seeking a consent is for the discharger and the sewerage undertaker to reach an agreement for the reception or disposal of trade effluent under section 129. Such an agreement may provide for the discharger to pay for works necessary to treat the wastes, such as an extension to a sewage works.

Trade effluent charges

Trade effluent charges are levied for discharges to sewers and a charges scheme may be made under the Water Industry Act 1991, s. 143. (Under their terms of appointment, sewerage undertakers must always have such a scheme in force.) All the sewerage undertakers currently use a similar formula based on the so-called 'Mogden Formula', in which charges are calculated according to the volume and strength of the effluent, as measured by the chemical oxygen demand (COD) and the solids content. Dischargers are therefore advised to consider whether their processes can be changed so as to minimise wastes, and thus costs. No extra charges are currently levied by the sewerage undertakers in relation to metals or other hazardous items: undesirable levels of these are controlled by the consent limits rather than by charging mechanisms. However, levels of charges are rising fast as a consequence of the fact that sewerage undertakers are themselves liable for charges for their own discharges from sewage works. The charging system thus operates in tandem with the consent system to reduce discharges. To a limited extent it encourages the reduction of pollution, although it does not make dischargers fully responsible for the environmental costs of their discharges. It remains to be seen whether a system of incentive charging will be introduced in this area: that would require legislation.

Public participation

Public rights in relation to the trade effluent system are very limited. There is no right for a member of the public to be informed of an application for a trade effluent consent and no right to participate in the decision whether to grant one, or in any appeal. Under the Water Industry Act 1991, s. 196, all consents, variations, agreements and directions by the sewerage undertaker or the Director General, and all decisions by the Secretary of State (effectively the EA in this context) must be placed on a public register.

However, this is a limited right, since there is no public right to information on any samples taken. Indeed, it is a criminal offence under section 206 for an employee of the sewerage undertaker to disclose information furnished under the Act. There is also no right of private prosecution for breach of a consent, except by a 'person aggrieved' or with the consent of the Attorney-General.

The Environmental Information Regulations 2004 regime clarifies the point that private bodies like sewerage undertakers are subject to disclosure rules when they are engaged in public functions. However, the Regulations continue to use a rather imprecise definition of 'environmental information' which does not lend itself to finding any clear answer to whether they apply to the sewers.

'Red List' substances

In order to ensure compliance with EC directives, such as 76/464 on Dangerous Substances in Water, an additional control has been introduced for specified dangerous substances. The Secretary of State is empowered to prescribe certain substances or processes for which the EA is effectively made the consenting body. Currently 24 such substances are listed in schedule 1 to the Trade Effluents (Prescribed Processes and Substances) Regulations 1989 (SI 1989/1156, as amended by SI 1990/1629), and five processes involving asbestos or chloroform are listed in schedule 2. The 24 prescribed substances consist of the 'Red List' (a dangerous substance list similar to the EC 'black list'—see p. 712—but with origins in the OSPAR treaty regime), plus carbon tetrachloride.

All discharges where any of these substances is present in more than background concentration, or where a prescribed process is carried on (often known collectively as 'special category effluent'), must be referred to the EA, which may then issue a direction (against which there is no appeal) to the sewerage undertaker on whether to grant a consent and on any conditions it might impose. Before deciding an application, the EA must provide the sewerage undertaker and the applicant with an opportunity to make representations. The same procedures apply where more than 30 kg per year of trichloroethylene or perchloroethylene is discharged (Trade Effluent (Prescribed Processes and Substances) Regulations 1992 (SI 1992/339)).

Existing discharges covered by the regulations are also reviewable by the EA. As with ordinary trade effluent discharges, a review may not normally be made within two years of the previous review. However, review is possible within two years if there has been a contravention of a consent or agreement, to give effect to an international or EC obligation, or to protect public health or aquatic flora and fauna. Compensation is payable in some of these circumstances, unless the review resulted from a change of circumstances unforeseeable at the time of the setting of the consent or the previous review.

Any process discharging significant amounts of 'Red List' substances will normally be a prescribed process for the purposes of integrated pollution control under Part I of the EPA 1990 and therefore require an authorization from the EA. This is in addition to the trade effluent consent that will also be required. In relation to further processes regulated under the IPPC Directive (96/61), the Pollution Prevention and Controls Regulations 2000 take the same general approach as under IPC which is that a release into water includes a release into a sewer, but the effect of a waste water treatment plant may be taken into account when determining the emission limit values applying in relation to indirect releases into water from a Part A process (PPC Regs 2000, regs 2(3)(a) and 12(5)).

Enforcement

The penalty for the offence of discharging into a sewer without consent, or in breach of a condition, is, on summary conviction, a fine not exceeding £5,000, and on conviction on indictment, an unlimited fine (ss. 118 and 121). It is possible for the same unlawful event to lead both to this offence, and to a water pollution offence under the Water Resources Act 1991. But only the actual occupier of the premises can be found guilty of the former.

CASE 19.1 *National Rivers Authority v Hickson & Welch Ltd* (1996, unreported)

A large quantity of nitrotoluene was spilt at the defendant's industrial premises. The chemical passed into the sewerage system at the premises and was transmitted by sewers to a treatment works, operated by a sewerage undertaker, Yorkshire Water Services Ltd, resulting in the contamination of settlement tanks. The contamination severely reduced the capacity of the sewage treatment works to deal with effluent; consequently, discharges to controlled waters breached the discharge consent for the treatment works. The undertaker brought proceedings against the defendant for the discharge of matter into a public sewer likely to affect prejudicially the treatment and disposal of its contents (under. s. 111(1)(a)), which resulted in a £35,000 fine. The Agency brought proceedings against the defendant for the offence of causing polluting matter to enter controlled waters (under WRA 1991, s. 85(1)), which resulted in a £2,500 fine.

There are no 'enforcement notice'-type provisions here. Enforcement of the legislation is by the sewerage undertaker so this would mean one company dictating operational matters to another company. In the past this has led to a conciliatory approach to enforcement, since officials have seen themselves as problem-solvers rather than as police officers. One of the main surveys of enforcement attitudes was a survey of trade effluent control officers.[1]

Discharges from sewage works

Under the Water Resources Act 1991, sewerage undertakers have consents set for their own discharges into controlled waters and may be prosecuted by the EA or any individual if they breach them. They are responsible for all discharges from their sewers or works, subject only to a defence that the breach was caused by an illegal discharge to the sewer and that they could not reasonably have been expected to prevent the entry of the unlawful discharge into the sewage works (Water Resources Act 1991, s. 87(2) and *National Rivers Authority v Yorkshire Water Services Ltd* [1995] 1 AC 444). This means that sewerage undertakers are ultimately responsible if they are unable to treat adequately discharges they have permitted. They thus have an incentive to restrict discharges to those which are treatable.

Domestic sewage discharges

Some discharges are prohibited entirely by the Water Industry Act 1991, s. 111 (although a trade effluent consent is a defence). These are discharges of anything liable to damage the sewer, or to stop its flow, or to prejudice the sewage works treatment; any chemicals, or any liquids over 110 °F, which will be dangerous or a nuisance; and any petroleum spirit, including motor oils. For example, drainage of used car oils is an offence under this section. The maximum penalties are, on summary conviction, a fine of up to £5,000, and, on conviction on indictment, an unlimited fine and/or up to two years' imprisonment.

---

1. G. Richardson, A. Ogus, and P. Burrows, *Policing Pollution* (Oxford: Clarendon Press, 1983).

Otherwise, there is no restriction on discharges of domestic sewage. There is a right of connection to the public sewer conferred on owners and occupiers by the Water Industry Act 1991, s. 106, with very limited powers of refusal. These do not include the potential overloading of the system: as Upjohn J stated in *Smeaton v Ilford Corporation* [1954] Ch 450, 'they [i.e. the sewerage undertakers] are bound to permit occupiers of premises to make connections to the sewer and to discharge their sewage therein'. Indeed, the duty has been held to require connections notwithstanding that the sewer is already overloaded, with obvious consequences (*Tayside Regional Council v Secretary of State for Scotland* [1996] SLT 473, concerning near identical provisions to section 106 in the Sewerage (Scotland) Act 1968, s. 12). The counterpart of this duty is the restriction on criminal liability for water pollution caused by sewage which the undertaker must accept (see above, and p. 735). Powers to requisition new sewers for domestic purposes are set out in the Water Industry Act 1991, s. 98.

However, it is permissible for the local planning authority to refuse planning permission on the ground that the local sewage works are overburdened or inadequate, since that is a material consideration. Alternatively, it could seek some planning gain in relation to the provision of sewers by the use of conditions or planning obligations under the Town and Country Planning Act 1990 (see pp. 486–91 for the limitations on this course of action).

In *Marcic v Thames Water Utilities Ltd* [2004] Env LR 25, it was held that, in a case where serious sewage flooding arose from an overburdened sewer, the sewerage undertaker was not liable in nuisance, nor under the Human Rights Act 1998, to the affected property owner. In respect of both claims, the House of Lords stressed the statutory framework under which the sewerage undertaker operated, both in terms of its communication duty and the funding formula under which it received money from government to upgrade sewerage infrastructure. These placed it both outside the normal rules governing the measured duty of care owed between neighbouring landowners for naturally occurring hazards, and beyond the protections provided by the Human Rights Act (see further Case box 11.8).

Q QUESTIONS

1 Are the sewers part of 'the environment'? In what ways does it matter?

2 How is the public involved in setting trade effluent consents? Should there be greater public involvement in the setting of consents?

3 Should the defence given to sewerage undertakers be reformulated so that what matters is whether the undertaker could reasonably have prevented an unlawful discharge from *leaving* a treatment works rather than entering the works? For example, would the defence apply where a sewerage undertaker does not take decisive action against a trader who persistently breaches the terms of his trade effluent consent, and who subsequently discharges a highly toxic liquid into the sewers which passes through the treatment works and pollutes a river?

FURTHER READING

Chapter 11 of W. Howarth and D. McGillivray, *Water Pollution and Water Quality Law* (Crayford: Shaw and Sons, 2001) contains more detail than provided here, especially on the cases cited, as does J. Bates, *Water and Drainage Law* (London: *Sweet & Maxwell*, looseleaf).

@ WEB LINKS

See the sources at the end of Chapter 18. The 'Mogden Formula' can be found at <www.ofwat.gov.uk>.

20 Integrated pollution prevention and control

→ **Overview**

This chapter covers a relatively new type of regulation which seeks to control a wide range of environmental impacts from industrial installations. The system, known as integrated pollution prevention and control (IPPC), is the central system of industrial pollution regulation in the UK. IPPC has been developed as a response to the perceived weaknesses in the traditional, sectoral approaches to pollution control which concentrated on 'end of pipe' emissions. At the heart of the legal controls is the idea that the environmental impacts of industrial installations need to be considered as a whole, as opposed to individual controls over emissions to different environmental media. Thus, IPPC controls emissions to air, discharges to water (including sewers) and disposal on land, in addition to a variety of other environmental impacts. All of these emissions and impacts are considered together as part of a single permitting procedure. The grant of a permit is subject to the setting of conditions which are designed to achieve a high level of environmental protection as a whole. The basis for these conditions is a process standard known as the Best Available Techniques (BAT), which aims to balance the costs of preventing or minimizing environmental impacts against the benefits to the environment.

As such IPPC represents the use of technological solutions to pollution problems by encouraging technical innovation in addressing environmental impacts. Typically this would be through the use of new abatement technologies but could be through the use of different raw materials or energy efficiency and waste minimization measures. This is coupled with a progressive approach which requires the monitoring, review and improvement of the use of BAT throughout the life of the installation. At the end of operations IPPC takes the integrated approach further by requiring the clean-up of any contamination caused by the operator of the installation, thus restoring the site to the state it was in prior to occupation.

You may find it useful to re-read the material on environmental standards and in particular the definitions of different types of standard such as emissions, process and environmental quality standards. The interrelationship between these types of standards lies at the heart of the system of integrated pollution prevention and control.

At the end of this chapter you will:

✔ Understand the main legal provisions dealing with the system of integrated pollution prevention and control.

✔ Appreciate the application of different types of environmental standards within an applied context of pollution control regulation.

✔ Be able to evaluate the benefits of an integrated system of pollution control.

✔ Appreciate in outline the idea of ecological modernization within the context of industrial pollution control.

✔ Understand the role of pollution prevention rules in a system of industrial environmental regulation.

The development of integrated pollution prevention and control

From the earliest days, the evolution of pollution control legislation can be characterized as being reactive and piecemeal responding to particular problems as and when they arose (see further Chapter 2). As new environmental issues emerged, legislation was introduced which often resulted in a number of disparate laws and regulatory agencies being responsible for discrete areas.[1] As a consequence, there was no unified concept of environmental protection. Each individual medium was seen as a separate area of control and no consideration was given to the possible consequences of imposing control on one sector in relation to others. For instance, where strict controls were placed upon the levels of effluent discharge into water, a simple alteration to the production process may shift the disposal of the effluent to another sector, such as by incineration (air) or landfill. In addition, the large number of regulatory agencies often led to administrative inefficiency, differing approaches to such things as enforcement or standard setting and a general lack of transparency and accountability.

BOX 20.1 Integrated pollution prevention and control—timeline

Year	Key Events
1862	House of Lords Select Committee under Lord Derby reports on the problems caused by 'noxious vapours evolved in certain manufacturing processes' recommending the legal control of such processes which lead to the passing of the Alkali Act in the following year.
1863	The Alkali Act created the Alkali Inspectorate, the first agency to have powers to deal with pollution from factories. The Act required a 95 per cent reduction of hydrochloric acid emissions from the chemical industry—primarily through the use of 'best practicable means'.
1906	The Alkali, &c, Works Regulation Act is passed, expanding the powers of the Alkali Inspectorate to include many different sources of air pollution.
1958	Following the recommendations of the Beaver Committee in 1954, the number of industrial works which are subject to the control by the Alkali Inspectorate is raised from 872 to 2,160.
1972	Following the recommendations of the Robens Committee Report on health and safety and welfare at work, the Alkali and Clean Air Inspectorate (as it had become known) is incorporated within the Health and Safety Executive (HSE).
1976	The Royal Commission on Environmental Pollution's Fifth Report identifies many problems connected to taking a fragmented approach to industrial pollution control. It recommended the creation of a unified regulator and system which controlled all environmental impacts from industrial installations.

---

1. See N. Haigh and F. Irwin (eds), *Integrated Pollution Control in Europe and North America* (Washington D.C.: The Conservation Foundation and the Institute for European Environmental Policy, 1990).

Year	Key Events
1982	In Pollution Paper No. 18, the Government finally rejects the RCEP's recommendations. The Alkali and Clean Air Inspectorate changes its name to the Industrial Air Pollution Inspectorate (IAPI).
1987	Her Majesty's Inspectorate of Pollution (HMIP) is created from IAPI, the Hazardous Waste Inspectorate and water pollution staff within the Department of the Environment. Overall responsibility for the new organisation is transferred away from the HSE and back into the Department of the Environment.
1988	Government issues the first consultation paper proposing a single system of 'integrated pollution control' for certain industrial processes.
1990	The Environmental Protection Act 1990 introduces integrated pollution control for prescribed industrial processes. HMIP regulates all environmental emissions based upon the use of the Best Available Techniques Not Entailing Excessive Cost (BATNEEC). The system was phased in from 1991 to 1996.
1993	The European Commission publishes its Fifth Environmental Action Programme which makes integrated pollution control and prevention of waste a priority.
1996	The Integrated Pollution Prevention and Control Directive (96/61/EC) is published which requires significant amendments to the existing integrated pollution control system under the EPA 1990.
1999	The Pollution Prevention and Control Act 1999 transposes the general requirements of the IPPC Directive. As from October 1999, IPPC applies to all *new* installations, as well as significant changes to existing installations. Other *existing* installations are to be phased in over an 8 year period.
2001	The First Technical Guidance on the use of 'Best Available Techniques' for controlling environmental impacts is issued in BREF documents.
2007	Final group of existing installations brought within IPPC.

It was not until the 1960s the idea that environmental problems required broader, more integrated solutions was first proposed.[2] Since that time various attempts have been made to provide integrated solutions to pollution problems.[3] In 1976 the Royal Commission on Environmental Pollution recognized that the control of air pollution in isolation was likely to lead to a less than optimum solution of the total pollution control problems posed by industrial installations since that approach failed to take account of the fact that the reduction of pollution in one form may well lead to an increase of pollution of other forms.[4] In particular, the RCEP argued that the existing standard of best practicable means be replaced by the use of the 'best practicable environmental option' (BPEO) which could be used to assess the aggregated pollution works emitted by an industrial operation and then to arrive at a balance in terms of disposals to land, emissions to air and discharges to water. The

2. L. Caldwell (1963) 23 Public Administration Review 138.
3. J. Krier and M Brownstein (1991) Environmental Law 119.
4. Fifth Report: *Air Pollution Control: An Integrated Approach*, (Cmnd 6731, 1976).

idea of a BPEO was followed up in the RCEP's 10th Report, *Tackling Pollution—Experience and Prospects* (Cmnd 9149, 1988) and the 11th Report, *Managing Waste: The Duty of Care* (Cmnd 9675, 1985), before detailed consideration in the 12th Report *Best Practicable Environmental Option* (Cm 310, 1988). In addition, the RCEP suggested that before integrated solutions could be attempted, a single unified regulatory agency was required. The move towards a unified regulatory agency was partially secured with the introduction of Her Majesty's Inspectorate of Pollution (HMIP) in 1987 although the division of responsibility for particular areas of pollution control continued beyond the creation of the National Rivers Authority in 1989. It was only with the creation of the Environment Agency in 1996 that true integration of many of the pollution control functions took place.

With the creation of HMIP in 1987, the way was open for the introduction of an integrated system of pollution control which took account of the requirements of assessing impacts upon the environment as a whole. The introduction of IPC in Part I of the EPA 1990 established two systems of control with one dealing with emissions to all media and the other, containing the same principal mechanisms of control, dealing with atmospheric emissions alone (thereby replacing antiquated provisions on air pollution under the Health and Safety at Work Act 1974 and the Alkali, &c. Works Regulations Act 1906). Much of the case law which is referred to in this chapter relates to processes controlled under Part I of the EPA 1990, either under IPC or Local Authority Air Pollution Control. The relevance of these cases is that the principles discussed and interpreted such as the meaning of the process standard BATNEEC are directly applicable to the IPPC system.

At the same time as the IPC provisions were being implemented in Britain, the European Commission was putting forward its proposals on 'integrated permitting' for industrial processes. This proposal developed into a directive on integrated pollution control which met considerable resistance from some Member States who objected to the concept of a single permit for all environmental releases.[5] Subsequently the proposal metamorphosed into the Directive on Integrated Pollution Prevention and Control (96/61/EC) which placed an emphasis on the preventive nature of the control mechanism rather than the integration of the permitting system.

In many ways, the Directive echoed the existing IPC system in the UK although there was a shift from control over environmental emissions to wider environmental impacts and from isolated industrial processes to a wider definition of activities and installations. The UK was in the forefront of the argument in favour of bringing forward the requirements of this Directive for existing operations, primarily as a result of its experience with the system of IPC and the desire to ensure that the affected industrial sectors in other Member States did not gain any competitive advantage during the implementation period. Thus the introduction of one of the first comprehensive systems of integrated pollution control in Part I of the EPA 1990 means that the UK is an acknowledged leader, at least in European terms, in this integrated approach.[6] This is backed by the European Commission's own report on the Directive which suggested that four years after the IPPC Directive was to have been transposed, only the UK had complied fully with all aspects of the Directive.[7]

---

5. M. Doppelhammer (2000) EELR 199.
6. J. Zottl (2000) 12(3) 281.

IPPC and EC law

In Europe, an integrated approach to pollution prevention and control was first put forward in the Fifth Environmental Action Programme which identified IPPC as one of the priority areas for action. Subsequently, the European Commission drew heavily from the UK's experience with IPC when putting forward a proposal for an IPPC Directive. The proposed Directive relied heavily upon meeting locally set environmental quality standards rather than centrally set emission standards, thus reflecting the UK's approach to setting pollution control standards (see p. 250). This approach was the subject of criticism from some Member States. In particular, Germany argued uniform emission standards were vital in order to implement a harmonized system of integrated controls across all Members States, to meet the precautionary principle and to avoid distortions of competition.[8] The concern was that by allowing the setting of conditions which took into account local conditions, there would not be a 'level playing field' and standards would differ from Member State to Member State. Indeed, the Commission accepted that although each Member State would be controlled under the same regime, different countries and sectors might have different targets. These targets would be set by reference to varying factors such as the quality of the local environment and economic viability of the installation.[9] There was, however, a degree of compromise in the final Directive (96/61/EC) which allowed for the setting of Community wide emission standards if a 'need' for Community action could be identified (Art. 18).

In its final form, the Integrated Pollution Prevention and Control Directive reflects the newer, more flexible approach to environmental directives adopted towards the end of the 1990s. It is less prescriptive than previous environmental directives, with the main provisions being based upon the application of broad principles and procedures rather than specified standards. The Directive sets out the types of installations which are covered (in terms of thresholds and industry sectors—Art. 1 and Annex I of the Directive), the obligations which apply to operators (Art. 3), the conditions which should be imposed in permits (critically the use of the BAT standard and its interrelationship with emissions standards and environmental quality standards, see Arts 9 and 10) and various procedural matters in relation to the integrated permit system (Arts 4–9). Critically, in terms of environmental standards it is silent in terms of specific environmental limits or even targets. This is in contrast to earlier pollution control directives which set out such limits explicitly (e.g. the Dangerous Substances in Water Directive 76/464). The main coordination of European wide standards comes through the exchange of information between the Commission and industry on BAT through the production of a BAT Reference (BREF) document for each of the industrial sectors covered under the Directive (Art. 16). Member States are required to take the BREF Documents into account when setting permit conditions but do not have to apply the guidance for every installation. Another way in which the Directive provides for some consistency between Member States is through the setting of Community wide

7. COM(2003) 354.
8. M. Doppelhammer (2000) EELR 199.
9. A. Gouldson and J. Murphy: *Regulatory Realities: The Implementation and Impact of Industrial Environmental Regulation* (London: Earthscan, 1998), 47.

emissions limit values (Art. 18(1)). Where a 'need' for Community action is identified (in particular through the information exchange and BREF process) standard emissions lint values can be set across all Members States and individual permits conditions must reflect these ELVS. This combination of flexibility to set permit conditions by reference to local conditions combined with the 'back-stop' measures such as the information exchange and the ability to set Community wide ELVs ties in with the principle of subsidiarity but with an institutional safeguard to prevent distortions as between Member States.[10]

IPPC and UK Law

The requirements of the IPPC Directive were transposed under the Pollution Prevention and Control (England and Wales) Regulations 2000 which were made under the Pollution Prevention and Control Act 1999 (SI 2000/1973). There are very similar regulations in Scotland (SSI 2000/323), Northern Ireland (Statutory Rule 2003/46) and in relation to off-shore installations (SI 2001/1091). These regulations will replace the system of integrated pollution control found under Part I of the EPA 1990. The main features of IPPC are set out in Box 20.2.

BOX 20.2 The main features of integrated pollution prevention and control

- The system of Integrated Pollution Prevention and Control does not have a general application. It only applies to activities carried out at certain prescribed industrial installations.

- The vast majority of the IPPC system is administered centrally by the Environment Agency (these are known as Part A(1) installations). There is a relatively small number of less polluting installations controlled under IPPC by local authorities (either for all environmental impacts, known as Part A(2) installations or just atmospheric emissions, known as Part B installations).

- The aim of IPPC is to provide an integrated approach to pollution control by achieving a high level of protection of the environment taken as a whole by first preventing or, if that is not practicable reducing emissions and other environmental impacts. This aim is met through the imposition of permit conditions which are based on the use of the Best Available Techniques (BAT).

- IPPC utilizes a combination of process standards, emission limit values, and environmental quality standards to control emissions and environmental impacts. These process standards are aimed at ensuring that emissions or environmental impacts are minimised particularly by using the best available techniques (BAT) to prevent pollution. Guidance on what constitutes BAT is found in guidance notes. The use of BAT requires a balancing of the costs of using particular techniques and benefits to the environment of doing so.

---

10. M. Doppelhammer, op cit, n. 16

- IPPC controls apply to a wide range of environmental impacts over and above environmental emissions. These include energy efficiency, waste minimisation, noise production, accident prevention and site restoration after an installation has been closed.

(a) The scope of IPPC

In total there are approximately 6,500 installations covered under IPPC.[11] The list of controlled installations is found in schedule 1 to the Regulations and is divided into six chapters of industrial activity including the energy industry; the chemicals industry; the production and processing of metals; the minerals industry; waste management; and a generic category referred to as 'other activities'. It is interesting to note what is not included in the list. Some of the most significant polluting installations such as sewage works, fish farming and intensive agricultural activities (other than poultry or pig farms) and nuclear installations all fall outside the IPPC system for varying reasons. Although it should be noted that, with the exception of the intensive agricultural units, controls under other pollution control legislation would apply. For example sewage works are controlled under the Water Resources Act 1991. Such controls do not, however, encourage innovation nor take into account wider environmental impacts.

Each chapter is sub-divided into more specific definitions of particular groups of activities in that industrial sector. These groups are further subdivided into categories for the purposes of allocating to a regulatory agency, Part A(1) to the control of the Environment Agency, and Part A(2) and B activities to the relevant local authority. Part B activities represent a continuation of the Local Authority Air Pollution Control regime under Part I of the EPA 1990. Although it is similar to the IPPC system in terms of procedure, it is substantively different in that the installations covered are not included in the IPPC Directive and only emissions to air are controlled.

Many of these industrial sectors were regulated under Part I of the EPA either under integrated pollution control or local authority air pollution control. As such, the change in regulation under the IPPC system is somewhat incremental rather than dramatic. The most significant changes in the types of activities controlled are as a result of the 'extra' activities which are regulated for the first time. These fall into several broad groups. First, waste management installations (including landfill sites) which were previously controlled under the waste management licensing system under Part II, EPA 1990. Their inclusion means that the IPPC system has had to incorporate aspects of the waste management licensing regime (e.g. the 'fit and proper person' test). Secondly, those activities which were controlled under differing regimes (e.g. local authority air pollution control, discharge consents and/or trade effluent consents) which come within the classes of activities prescribed for IPPC under the directive (e.g. food and drink manufacturing). Finally, those activities which were not specifically controlled under any regime or alternatively were not comprehensively controlled (e.g. intensive agricultural units).

'Installation' is defined as any stationary technical unit (thus excluding mobile plant) where a prescribed activity is carried out and any other directly associated activities carried out on the same site which have a technical connection with the prescribed activities and

---

11. UK Article 16(3) Report to 31 December 2002 (DEFRA, 2003).

which could have an effect on pollution (reg. 2). Thus, the crucial test appears to be whether or not the activity in question is directly associated with, or has a technical connection with, or could have an effect on emissions and pollution from the installation. Examples would include a power station with an area for the storage of coal, or a chemical plant served by a separate effluent treatment works on the same site. All installations listed in Annex I must be subject to the requirement to seek a permit. Thus, there are no exemptions under the IPPC legislation. An 'operator' is defined as the person who has control over an installation (reg. 2(1)).

(b) The Regulators

There is split regulatory control over IPPC installations. In England and Wales, the Environment Agency regulates all Part A(1) installations which comprise about 85 per cent of all IPPC installations. All other installations under Part A(2) and B are regulated by the relevant local authority, either the district, metropolitan borough or London council in England and the county or borough council in Wales. In certain areas, both the Agency and Local Authority will provide expert support to the other in determining applications (e.g. in relation to noise impacts from A(1) installations where the local authority has expertise through the regulation of noise nuisances and in relation to water impacts from A(2) installations where the Agency has greater expertise). Both the Environment Agency and local authorities are statutory consultees in relation to installations over which they do not have control (sch. 4, para. 1). In Scotland and Northern Ireland there is sole control under the Scottish Environment Protection Agency and the Northern Ireland Environment and Heritage Service respectively.

(c) Transitional arrangements

All operators must apply for an IPPC permit for any 'new' installation. New installations include those commencing operations on or after 31 October 1999 other than an existing installation (sch. 3, para. 6). In addition, existing installations carrying out activities which undergo a 'substantial change' after that date also require a permit. Installations operating before 31 October 1999 must apply for a permit within three-month 'application windows' set for each of the six industrial sectors over a period from June 2001 to March 2007. Pipeline installations operating on or after 31 October 1999 and before 31 October 2000 are also considered to be 'existing if a relevant authorization was applied for or granted before 31 October 1999' (see *Furness and Guildford BC v Environment Agency* [2002] Env LR 659).

This transitional period is not required by the Directive but was intended to ensure that regulators and industry could get to grips with the new procedures over time and thereby avoid an short implementation period. The difficulties of the new process are apparent. In the first year after the introduction of IPPC, fewer than a third of permits applied for had been granted.[12] In many cases, the delay is not necessarily problematic as there will be continuing controls under the IPC system and there is no breach of the requirements of the Directive until the final implementation date in 2007.

---

12. (2002) ENDS Report 332, 5–6.

Application procedure

An application for IPPC permit has to made before the installation and activities are brought into operation (reg. 9). Thus it is possible for operators to commence construction of a new installation before seeking a permit. The onus falls upon the operator to demonstrate the achievement of BAT for any particular installation. Applications are generally determined on a site-by-site basis rather than by reference to prescriptive principles or rules; the exception is where generally binding rules are adopted.

An application for a permit must contain a wide variety of information including: information on the condition of the site (and any associated pollution risks) on which the installation is situated (which is used as a baseline study for comparative purposes when the installation is closed); the raw materials and energy used in the carrying out of the activity; waste minimisation and prevention measures; the foreseeable emissions and environmental effects of the activity; information on the technology and other techniques used for reducing emissions and other environmental impacts; and arrangements for monitoring impacts (see regs 7, 10, and sch. 4). In addition, the application must be accompanied by a non-technical summary (in an echo of the requirements under the EIA legislation). Each application must be accompanied by the payment of the appropriate fee.

(a) Public participation and other consultation procedures

There are extensive provisions for public participation in the application procedure along-side other appointed statutory consultees (sch. 4 which also covers all the provisions outlined below). There are circumstances where the Environment Agency has adopted enhanced consultation procedures in situations where there is public concern such as in the case of burning substitute liquid fuels in cement kilns (see Box 20.3). These procedures are extra statutory and whilst they would give rise to a legitimate expectation that they would be followed they have no formal status. There is an obligation on every applicant to advertise all applications for authorization and all variations involving a substantial change. The advertisement must be placed in a local newspaper circulating in the area in which the activity is to be carried out and in the case of Part A activities it must be advertised in the *London Gazette*. The advertisement must contain details of the name and address of the applicant and the installation where the activity is to be carried out; a brief description of the activities; reference to the availability of information about the application on public registers; and an invitation to make representations within 28 days of the date of the advertisement. Regulators are required to maintain public registers containing information about applications, decision and the results of monitoring as required under any permit condition (reg. 29).

Other statutory consultees are given the right to make representations. The list of consultees reflects the varied nature of the impacts caused by an activity in terms not only of the environment but also the workplace. The bodies entitled to be consulted include: the Health and Safety Executive; the health authority in whose area the installation will be situated; the relevant Nature Conservancy Council where a potential emission might affect an SSSI; and the water services company or any other sewerage undertaker, in relation to release to a sewer. In addition there is to be close liaison between local authorities and the EA on all

Part A applications (see further below). Where an operation at an installation involves a waste management activity the relevant planning authority must be consulted. There is also provision for transboundary consultation (in practice this is likely only to be an issue in relation to installations based in Northern Ireland where impacts may be felt in the Republic of Ireland). Where the Secretary of State is 'aware' that an activity is likely to have significant negative effects on another member state, he is under a duty to notify that other Member State of the application so that 'consultation' may take place within a framework of bilateral relations.

All of these consultees are entitled to notification within 14 days of receipt of an application for a permit or variation. They are then given 28 days in which to make representations (although in practice this period can be extended). These representations are to be taken into account as a material consideration in addition to any further information which has been obtained under any environmental assessment which has been carried out (e.g. where planning permission was required for the commencement of the activity). In normal circumstances, the time period for determining an application for a permit is four months from the date of receipt or any longer period which has been agreed between the applicant and the regulatory body. The exceptions to this rule are where the application has been 'called in' by the Secretary of State and where the application has been notified to another Member State and bilateral consultation is taking place. When an application is called in, the Secretary of State has no power to grant the authorization, but instead must direct the enforcing authority as to whether to grant the application and, if so, as to the conditions which are to be attached. Where the regulator requests further information from the applicant and no information is supplied within the specified time period, the agency is entitled to notify the applicant that the application is deemed to have been withdrawn.

(b) Commercial confidentiality and national security

In normal circumstances, the public is allowed free access to information regarding an application for a permit and associated matters (regs 28–29). There are, however, exceptions to this on the ground of commercial confidentiality and in relation to issues affecting national security (regs 30–31). Where an applicant believes that any information contained within an application should be restricted, then an application may be made to exclude such information from the public registers. This application is included along with the information relating to the permit, and the regulatory agency has to determine whether or not such information is commercially confidential. In the case of information affecting national security, the only criterion is that the Secretary of State has to be of the opinion that the inclusion in the register of that information would be contrary to the interests of national security.

On commercial confidentiality grounds the regulatory agency has 14 days in which to determine whether the information is not commercially confidential, if it is undetermined within that period it is deemed to be treated as such. Where the enforcing authority determines that the information is not commercially confidential, it must not enter such information on the register for 21 days so as to allow an applicant time to appeal against the decision to the Secretary of State. Pending any appeal the information is also excluded from the register.

(c) Substantial changes

Where a 'substantial change' is made to an existing installation an application for an IPPC permit must be made even if the site is already regulated (e.g. under an IPC authorization). Substantial change is defined as meaning a change in the operation which may have significant negative effects on human beings or the environment (reg. 2(1)). The question of whether a change is 'significant' or not is assessed against a range of factors (including the extent, magnitude, duration, and complexity of any impact),[13] with the aim of identifying whether there would be any justification for requiring the operator to submit proposals to consultation both with the public and statutory consultees. Whether a change is substantial or not can have significant practical consequences in terms of the manner in which the change is publicised and monitored and most critically whether it is subject to the rigours of the application procedure. Some of the problems in dealing with significant changes can be seen in the issue of burning substitute liquid fuels (SLF, which can also be used to mean Secondary Liquid Fuels) in cement kilns (see Box 20.3).

BOX 20.3 **SLF and 'substantial change'**

Cement manufacture is a prescribed installation under the IPPC legislation and was controlled under IPC authorizations prior to this. In the early 1990s, as a cost saving exercise, the cement, industry sought to use fuels, other than the traditional coal, to heat the kilns used in the manufacturing process. In 1992, Castle Cement, one of the main manufacturers of cement, introduced a new fuel, Cemfuel, at its Clitheroe works. Cemfuel was made up of waste chlorinated solvents from processes such as paint manufacture and printing.

The local community surrounding the plant was concerned about the health effects of the burning of Cemfuel. At the outset HMIP (as it was then) accepted that the change of fuel type from coal to Cemfuel did not constitute a 'substantial change' for the purposes of IPC. Cemfuel was used for over a year before Castle Cement applied for an IPC authorisation. After substantial objections from members of the public and other criticisms, HMIP decided to vary the IPC authorisation to limit the time to a trial period. By this time other operators such as Blue Circle were conducting lengthy 'trial runs' of SLF as substitute fuels in cement kilns.

Subsequently, the Environment Agency (as it had become) was heavily criticized by the Environment Select Committee which characterized the Agency's regulation of the cement industry as including a 'failure to command public confidence' a 'lack of openness', 'lax regulation', and 'inadequate monitoring'. The Report went on to recommend that further use of SLF should not be allowed unless it was treated as a 'substantial change' under IPC with all of the consequences in terms of public consultation and monitoring that this required.

In order to meet these criticisms, the Environment Agency adopted a special Protocol which would be followed when dealing with the introduction of SLFs as fuels in cement kilns. This Protocol sets out procedural guidance including enhanced public consultation before decisions to allow not only where trials of burning SLF are proposed but also before any decisions to allow continuous burning of SLF. The requirements for consultation under the Protocol go far beyond that required for normal applications and include public meetings, 'surgeries' with local Agency

---

13. *Integrated Pollution Prevention and Control: A Practical Guide: Edition 2*, Annex II (DEFRA).

staff, attendance at local parish council meetings, exhibitions, and letters to residents. The Agency has also extended the list of organizations it consults with beyond statutory consultees to include County Councils, local health authorities, parish councils in the relevant area, and local liaison committees.

The determination of the application

The determination of an application for an IPPC permit is a technical judgment with relatively few obvious policy considerations. As such any decision to grant a permit is difficult to challenge.

CASE 20.1 *Levy v Environment Agency* [2003] Env LR 11

Mr Levy lived near a Cement Works which was regulated under an IPC authorization. In August 2001 the Environment Agency granted a variation of the authorization to permit the permanent use of scrap tyres as a substitute fuel for the works. Mr Levy applied for a judicial review of the decision to grant the variation. Amongst the different grounds for making the application Mr Levy argued that the Environment Agency had approached the determination of the application in an unlawful manner by failing to require the use of BATNEEC.

In holding that the Agency had approached the determination of application lawfully, Silber J effectively narrowed the potential for challenging determination processes involving technical questions such as in the case of IPPC applications. He held that the Courts would be unlikely to intervene in the EA's discretion to determine technical questions (e.g. the adequacy of pollution prevention techniques). He took the view that in determining what was BATNEEC, the Agency had to 'use very sophisticated specialized scientific and environmental knowledge and expertise' and that this was only available to relatively few people. The technical nature of the decision meant that the Courts should be 'very slow to interfere'. Accordingly the Agency should be given a wider margin of appreciation than in other examples of administrative decision-making.

Of course this does not mean that such decisions are not capable of being challenged as there may be procedural or substantive irregularities in the decision-making process. It does, however, mean that it is more likely that questions which are based upon technical matters, for example the use of one technique as opposed to another, will fall under the sole decision of the Environment Agency. As Silber J put it, 'it is not for the court to second-guess the judgment of a specialized tribunal'.

In determining a permit application, the regulator must either grant the permit subject to conditions or refuse the application (reg. 6). Note that there is no power to grant an unconditional permit. There is a duty to refuse the permit in certain circumstances. First, where the regulator is unable to reasonable grant the permit subject to the conditions required or authorized to be imposed. This might be because the environmental impacts from the installation would be unacceptable due to the sensitivity of the local environment or the inadequacy of the techniques used (reg. 10(2). Alternatively it may be because the operator has failed to provide sufficient information for the regulator to determine what conditions should be imposed (e.g. in relation to BAT). Secondly, the regulator must refuse a permit application where it is considered that the applicant will not operate the installation concerned so as to comply with the conditions which would be included in the permit (reg. 10(3)). In *R v Secretary of State for the Environment and RJ Compton and Sons ex parte West Wiltshire District Council* [1996] Env LR 312, this duty has been interpreted as being a practical test of determining whether an applicant would be able to comply with all of the conditions which would be imposed. In asking this question it would be relevant to consider the previous history of the applicant and the extent to which there had been compliance or non-compliance with conditions (see Case box 20.2). Finally, in the case of waste management installations and activities there are certain pre-requisites such as the grant of planning permission and the 'fit and proper person' requirement which must be met before a permit can be granted.

CASE 20.2 *R v Secretary of State for the Environment and RJ Compton and Sons ex parte West Wiltshire District Council* [1996] Env LR 312

RJ Compton and Sons operated an animal rendering business. There was evidence of operational failures such as bad housekeeping, unauthorized emissions and poor storage of waste which suggested that significant operational improvements were required. RJ Compton applied for an authorisation under Part I of the Environmental Protection Act 1990. The Local Authority refused the application and the company appealed.

One of the issues at the appeal was the track record of the company and whether it would be able to achieve the required environmental standards. The Inspector hearing the appeal thought that the company would not be able to comply with the BATNEEC standard and recommended that the appeal be dismissed. The Secretary of State disagreed and directed that the authorisation be granted. The Secretary of State considered that the issue was whether it was *possible* that the applicant would carry on the operations in compliance with conditions. This was a theoretical approach which is relatively easy to demonstrate. This view was justified by the Secretary of State on the basis that the regulator had enforcement options available to it to use as and when the operator failed to comply with the conditions.

The High Court disagreed with the Secretary of State's view holding that he had failed to apply the test properly. The test should have been whether the applicant was *able* to comply with the conditions which was a more *practical* test. On this basis, a history of non-compliance or environmental offences might be relevant in determining whether to refuse an application.

There are certain matters that the regulator is obliged to consider in determining the type of conditions which should be imposed (reg. 12). The most important of these is the imposition of Emission Limit Values (ELVs) in relation to polluting substances. Certain substances, listed in schedule 5 in respect of emissions to air and water, are considered to be suitable for stricter ELVs by virtue of their impact on the receiving environment. The specific ELV will be set by reference to the Best Available Techniques in addition to the individual circumstances of the installation and the local environment. This site specific approach ensures that permitting is flexible, taking account of the techniques employed at the installation concerned, the local environment and its location. There are two exceptions to this general approach. The first is where General Binding Rules (GBRs) are applied for certain classes of installation (reg. 14). No GBRs were introduced in the first three years of

IPPC. These GBRs apply homogenous conditions across all installations which share similar characteristics. The regulators have a discretion to ignore the application of GBRs if it is decided that they would be inappropriate (e.g. if the site was situated near to a sensitive environmental receptor such as a sensitive aquifer or a special area of conservation). The second is where Community wide ELVs have been set (under Art. 18). No Community wide ELVs have yet been set, but the Commission has made it clear that where ELVs are being set at a low level which is not based on BAT, such limits will be used.[14]

There are other general principles which must be taken into account when imposing conditions (reg. 11). These include the need to take all preventative measures to prevent pollution of the environment as a whole, in particular through the application of BAT. BAT is a process standard which in theory is designed to prevent environmental emissions or in the alternative reduce them to zero. How this is done is set out by way of technological methods of achieving ELVs set out in guidance notes. These give guideline values to establish a level of performance which should be achieved for that particular installation. The danger is that the setting out of ELVs in guidance notes can replace BAT as the real standard, causing regulators to focus the achievement of ELVs to the exclusion of BAT. Such an approach was criticised in the case of *Thornby Farms Ltd v Daventry District Council* (see Case box 20.3). Although this decision concerned the application of BATNEEC, which is slightly different to BAT, it represents a relevant analysis of the question of what is meant by the application of the preventative principle in the context of industrial pollution control.

CASE 20.3 *Thornby Farms v Daventry District Council* [2002] Env LR 28[15]

Thornby Farms ('TF') owned farmland next to two pet incinerators. TF challenged the grant of an IPC authorisation by Daventry District Council to operate the incinerators on the basis that the emission levels specified in the conditions were higher than could be achieved in practice. TF's primary concern was that the conditions had been set for ease of compliance rather than the objective of preventing pollution. TF argued that the District Council had to apply the preventative principles laid down in the statute. These would not be met by conditions which permitted levels of emissions higher than the levels which the incinerator was capable of achieving.

The Court of Appeal dismissed the application on the basis that the ELVs did not represent BATNEEC and the ELVs specified in the guidance were minimum levels which were not to be exceeded and not necessarily the best which could be achieved. The District Council had a discretion to decide the most appropriate method of achieving the pollution prevention objective but that did not weaken the obligation to ensure that BATNEEC would be used.

The BAT standard under IPPC closely reflects the BATNEEC standard under IPC. The use of BAT is aimed at ensuring environmental impacts from an installation as a whole are be prevented or minimised. The decision in *Thornby Farms* indicates that BAT can only be translated as requiring the 'best that can be achieved' bearing in mind the general obligation to reduce emissions and environmental impacts.[15]

---

14. COM(2003) 354.
15. S. Bell (2003) 15 JEL 59.

Other specific issues which must be considered when imposing conditions include: long distance/transboundary pollution, protection of soil and groundwater, post closure restoration of the installation and the requirement to monitor emissions (reg. 12).

(a) BAT

At the heart of the IPPC system is the idea that operators must use the Best Available Techniques (BATs) in order to ensure a high level of protection of the environment when taken as a whole. The application of the BAT principle is made in the context of local conditions which includes such things as the local environment and economic factors. Emissions limit values (ELVS) are then set by reference to both BAT and local conditions. Environmental Quality Standards (EQS) are considered once the ELVs have been set. In circumstances where an EQS set under European or National standards would be breached, it is possible to set conditions which would be stricter than BAT or to refuse the permit. The directives which include relevant EQS include most of the water quality directives, e.g. surface water, drinking water, bathing waters, groundwater, and air quality standards found in such directives as the waste incineration directive. For discussion of the imposition of stricter conditions and/or refusal see *R v Secretary of State for the Environment and RJ Compton and Sons ex parte West Wiltshire District Council* Case box 20.2 above). In this sense EQS represent a minimum threshold for the imposition of ELVs with BAT meeting a higher standard of prevention and/or reduction over and above the EQS.

(b) 'Best available techniques'

The phrase 'best available techniques' is further broken down in the regulations. 'Best' is defined in relation to the effectiveness of the techniques in achieving a high level of protection of the environment as a whole (reg. 3(1)). 'Best' is not an absolute term and there may be a number of different techniques which would fall within this definition. 'Available' techniques are those which have been developed on a scale which allows implementation by the relevant industrial sector under economically and technically viable conditions, taking into consideration the costs and advantages, whether or not the techniques are used or produced inside the UK, as long as they are accessible to the operator. This should exclude experimental techniques or techniques which have only been tested under conditions which are peculiar to other countries. 'Techniques' includes both the technology used and the way in which the installation is designed, built, maintained and decommissioned. In relation to costs, any determination of BAT takes into account two broad criteria: the economic and environmental costs and benefits of particular techniques of pollution control; and the affordability of such techniques in the sector of industry concerned.

The statutory terms are vague which allows the regulatory agencies some discretion in determining applications on a case-by-case basis. There is, however, some supplementary guidance to be found in sector guidance notes and the BREF documents. The guidance notes are supposed to provide a coherent context in which decisions can be made in relation to permit conditions. The national statutory guidance notes are based upon the BREF documents. The IPPC notes are non-prescriptive, providing indicative standards for both new and existing installations with clear timetables for upgrading in the case of existing plant. Each application is, however, considered individually, and variations from the guidance note standard may be acceptable in certain circumstances.

BOX 20.4 The 'Sevilla Process' and the production of BREF Documents—technocratic participatory standard setting

In practice the determination of BAT and ELVs which are to be used in IPPC permits are set by reference to European and national guidance. The IPPC Directive Article 16(2) requires the European Commission to establish an exchange of information between Member States and the industries which are controlled under IPPC in order to establish what is meant by BAT. This exchange of information is often referred to as the 'Sevilla Process' because the body responsible for coordinating the BREF documents is based in Seville in Spain. The technical guidance is known as a BAT Reference (BREF) document and this is taken into account when determining BAT either for a sector or for an installation. However, individual circumstances will also be taken into account and the BAT reference document will not set down uniform emission limits. Where the BAT reference document is widely accepted across all of the Member States, it may form the basis for sectoral daughter directives to the main IPPC Directive.

The process of agreeing the BREF documents is a classic example of technocratic participatory standard setting. In many cases standards are set 'top down' by Government bodies or regulators (e.g. the Expert Panel on Air Quality Standards (EPAQS) gives guidance on air quality standards but is appointed by the Secretary of State and made up of mainly academic researchers, see further Box 16.6). This type of technocratic standard setting is often a source of criticism of traditional command and control regulation. This criticism is that in order to regulate effectively, the regulator needs to understand the workings of industrial sectors. Thus there is a 'clear imbalance' between the industrial participants and others involved in the standard setting process.[16] The correction of this imbalance involves lengthy information gathering exercises in order to establish the standard. The 'Sevilla Process' seeks to address some of these problems by taking a more participatory approach to standard setting.[17] A technical working group has been set up for each BREF document. This group consists of industry representatives, regulators, research institutes and NGOs. The Directive makes provision for most of these groups to participate. NGOs were not included but were the special invitees of DG Environment in an attempt to widen participation. The working group then spends a considerable amount of time negotiating over the exact terms of BAT (experience suggests that between 2 and 3 years is the average).[18] Empirical research showed that a wide range of factors were taken into account when setting standards including political and legal issues. The establishment of BAT was as much concerned with pragmatism as it was technological and scientific matters.[19] Under the Directive BAT was to be identified by reference to two criteria only, the costs and benefits of using particular techniques and the effectiveness of the techniques in ensuring the protection of the environment as a whole. In the 'real world' however, the discussion of BAT was not necessarily as clear cut as this because there was little data available on cross media impacts nor any methodology to determine the trade offs between environmental impacts across different media.

---

16. N. Gunningham and P. Grabosky, *Smart Regulation: Designing Environment Policy* (Oxford: Clarendon Press, 1998), 44
17. B. Lange (2002) European Law Journal, 246.
18. COM(2003) 354.
19. B. Lange (2002) European Law Journal, 246.

(c) IPPC and wider environmental impacts

In addition to the imposition of ELVs shaped by the application of BAT, permits also must contain conditions relating to other environmental impacts of an activity. After an installation has closed it must be returned to a satisfactory state and pollution risks arising as a result of the permitted activities should be avoided (reg. 11(3)). Every Part A application must include an installation site condition report which should set out the pre-commencement site conditions. If the report includes information on pre-existing contamination this could form the trigger for remedial action under other statutory controls over clean up of contaminated land (e.g. WRA 1991, s. 161A and EPA 1990, Part IIA). Special consideration must also be given to a list of matters found in the regulations. These include raw material usage, energy efficiency, noise and vibration, and accident prevention.

(d) Transfer of permits

A permit is personal to an applicant/operator. It is, however, possible to transfer a permit from one operator to another (reg. 18). Therefore if a business has been sold, it is possible to transfer an existing permit to the new owner/operator. An operator wishing to transfer a permit to someone else must make a joint application and pay a fee. There are provisions for partial transfer in cases where part of the installation will remain within the control of the original operator. The only grounds for refusal to transfer are that the regulator considers that the proposed transferee would not comply with the conditions of the transferred permit or, in the case of waste management installations, that the proposed transferee would not be a 'fit and proper person'. There is a two-month time limit for determination of a transfer. If no determination has been made or no extension of the time period agreed between the parties, the permit is deemed to have been transferred. Otherwise, the transfer is effected on a date which is agreed between the parties.

(e) Surrender of permits

As IPPC regulates the cleanup of pollution which has been caused by permitted activities, there is a need to regulate the cessation of activities by the operator so that an assessment of the condition of the site can be made and remedial works undertaken (reg. 11(3)). Indeed, the risks associated with surrender and other decommissioning of the installation must be taken into account when determining whether the installation meets the requirement of BAT at the design stage. Site restoration is controlled in a number of different ways. First, the operator must submit a site condition report as part of the permit application. Secondly, conditions can be imposed upon the permit setting out various steps which must be taken prior to, during and after cessation of activities of the installation. Thirdly, an operator has to submit an application to surrender a Part A permit (reg. 19). An application to surrender can be made for all of the activities covered under the permit or just parts of the operation of the installation (known as a partial surrender). The application must be accompanied by certain information including the name and address of the operator; a plan identifying the part of the site which is the subject of the surrender; a site report describing the condition of the site which identifies any changes in condition of the site; and a description of the steps taken to avoid any pollution risk or to return the site to a satisfactory state.

It is presumed that the operator is responsible for any material difference between the condition of the site as contained in the original base line report which was submitted with the application and the conditions contained in any report submitted with an application for surrender. This presumption would appear to be irrefutable as the regulator must be satisfied that there is no pollution risk and that no further steps need to be taken to return the site to a satisfactory state, irrespective of the cause of that pollution risk, before accepting the surrender of the permit. Naturally this emphasizes the importance of ensuring that the original site report submitted with the application must be as comprehensive as possible, so that pre-commencement liabilities which are attributable to other causes/parties do not appear in the pre-surrender report, as they will not be distinguishable from the contamination caused by the operation of the installation. Where pollution is caused prior to cessation, the regulator has the power to serve an enforcement notice to remedy any harm caused.

The regulator must issue a notice of determination on the application for surrender within three months or longer if agreed between the parties and where the regulator has requested further information from the applicant which has not been supplied. If no determination is made within that period the application is deemed to have been refused if the operator notifies the regulator of this in writing.

(f) Reviewing permits

The regulator is under a duty to review periodically the conditions of permits but is also given a discretion to review at any time (reg. 17). Such reviews are intended to capture changes in circumstances such as environmental impacts, available techniques or Community wide ELVs.[20] There is no prescribed period within which reviews must be undertaken and the recommended period will be set down in any sectoral guidance, which in turn will be informed by the BREF process. Reviews are *required* when there is such significant pollution that the ELVs must be changed; BAT has changed and it would not involve excessive costs to upgrade; or there are safety reasons for switching to new techniques (reg. 15(2)). This review process is a key factor in ensuring the efficiency of a technology forcing process standard such as BAT.[21]

Enforcement powers

There are a wide range of enforcement options to deal with operational breaches of permits including the power to serve enforcement notices, to suspend permitted activities, to revoke a permit and to vary the conditions of a permit (regs 23–5). This flexibility ensures that the regulator has enforcement discretion when dealing with regulatory breaches.

The regulators have an overriding duty to supervise the operation of permitted installations (reg. 23). There is, however, an emphasis on self monitoring and regulators must impose appropriate conditions requiring self monitoring and reporting on breaches.[22] Failure to report a breach of a condition will normally constitute a further breach. The regulator must take any steps needed for the purpose of ensuring that the conditions of the permit are complied with. The mandatory nature of this duty means that where breaches

---

20. IPPC—A Practical Guide, para. 13.1.
21. G. Lubbe-Wolff (2001) 13 JEL 84.
22. See e.g. W. Howarth (1997) MLR 200.

of permit are occurring or likely to occur, the regulator cannot ignore it. It does *not* mean that the regulator is required to take formal enforcement action against that breach. The duty simply means that necessary steps must be taken to ensure compliance with conditions.

(a) Variation notices

The ability to vary a permit is not strictly an enforcement power when compared with, for example, enforcement, suspension or revocation notices as there is no explicit sanction for non-compliance (other than general powers for breach of condition). The effect of a variation may, however, be such that an operator would view it as having no practical distinction from an enforcement notice. The distinctive character of a variation notice relates more to a proactive approach of minimizing environmental impacts than punishing for breaches of existing conditions. A regulator may vary permit conditions at any time (reg. 17). Normally variation would be required as a result of a permit review, new considerations such as changes in materials or intensification of processes, or the introduction of new EQS. The variation procedure requires the consultation and publicity where the change is 'significant' and at the discretion of the regulator (see Box 20.3).

Operators must notify the regulator of all changes to the installation which might have environmental consequences (see the definition of 'change in operations' discussed under 'significant change' above). Such a change may fall into one of two categories, either a *notification* of a proposed change which is not likely to require a variation of permit conditions (reg. 16) or an *application* for a proposed change which would require a variation in conditions (reg. 17). In the case of notifications there is a 14-day period within which the regulator can act to stop prevent the alteration through the use of enforcement actions if necessary.

(b) Revocation notices

The regulator has the power to revoke a permit either in part or in whole at any time by serving a revocation notice on the operator (reg. 21). The power to revoke a permit is general in nature and is not restricted. It is somewhat of an extreme measure and will normally only be appropriate when other enforcement options are inappropriate (e.g. where activities on an installation have ceased and are not to be recommenced) or have been exhausted. In such circumstances, revocation might apply to the activities on the site whilst leaving the site closure conditions to be enforced against.

Although the power to serve a revocation notice would appear to be draconian, it is subject to the right of appeal and subsequently from challenge by way of judicial review. The need to resolve any dispute by way of administrative appeal prior to any judicial review can be seen in *R v Environment Agency, ex parte Petrus Oils* (see Case box 20.4). A revocation notice can be withdrawn at any time before it takes effect.

CASE 20.4 *R v Environment Agency ex parte Petrus Oils Ltd* [1999] Env LR 732

Petrus Oils operated a waste oil refinery which was controlled under an IPC authorization. There were many complaints from neighbours about the smells from the operation. The Agency issued a revocation notice. Petrus appealed against the revocation notice and applied for a judicial review of the Agency's decision to revoke the authorization. The High Court held that Petrus should have pursued the revocation notice through the appeals process rather than by arguing that it was unlawful. It was only in exceptional cases that a court would give leave to apply for judicial review where Parliament had provided for a statutory right of appeal against the decision which was sought to be challenged by way of judicial review. The real issue in dispute was whether the revocation was required in order to protect the environment. That involved questions of fact which were more appropriately dealt with by an Inspector on appeal.

(c) Enforcement notices

Where the regulator is of the opinion that the operator of an installation has contravened, is contravening, or is likely to contravene any condition of the permit, the regulator has a discretionary power to serve an enforcement notice (reg. 24). The notice has to specify the steps required to remedy the problem and the timescale within which the steps must be taken.

(d) Suspension notices

If the regulator is of the opinion that the operation of an installation involves an imminent risk of serious pollution, the regulator is under a duty to serve a suspension notice (reg. 25). The only exception to this mandatory duty is where the regulator intends to take action itself in relation to the risk. This duty to serve a suspension notice is independent of any breach of a permit. The effect of a suspension notice is dramatic. Any permit ceases to have effect either partially or totally. When the steps required in the notice have been taken, the notice can be withdrawn.

Offences and remedies

The regulations provide a long list of offences in relation to the IPPC system (reg. 32). The most serious offences relate to operational breaches such as operating a prescribed installation without a permit, or in breach of a permit conditions, or failing to comply with a statutory notice. Less serious offences are committed in relation providing false information. Finally, the least serious category of offences relate to the obstruction of a regulator in the exercise of their duties or failing to comply with the regulator's requirements. All of these offences are punishable in the Magistrates' Court with a maximum fine of £20,000 in the case of the most serious offences and £5,000 for the lesser two categories.[23] The first two categories of offence are also triable in the Crown Court with an unlimited fine and/or imprisonment for a term of up to two years.

In any trial the onus of proof falls upon the operator to show that there was no better available technique which could be employed for that particular installation. It is open to any court in sentencing an offender for failure to comply with an enforcement or suspension notice to order that the effects of the offence be remedied. This allows for cleanup and compensation costs to come directly out of the offender's pocket. In many instances, these costs will far outstrip any reasonable fine that could be imposed. Perhaps even more importantly, where an installation has been operated without any permit or has not been in compliance with a condition of a permit, the regulatory agency can arrange for reasonable

---

23. The Clean Neighbourhoods and Environment Act 2005 raises the former limit to £50,000.

steps to be taken towards remedying any harm caused as a consequence and recover the costs of taking such steps from any person committing the offence. Before doing so, however, the regulatory agency must obtain the Secretary of State's approval in writing. Thus, even where a court is not willing to impose the high financial burden of cleanup costs on an offender, it will be open to the agency to remedy such harm. There are further remedies available to the regulatory agency in the High Court. The regulator can seek an injunction where the enforcement of the criminal law is not securing adequate compliance. It must, however, exhaust other remedies before seeking an injunction (see *Tameside MBC v Smith Bros (Hyde) Ltd* [1996] Env LR 312).

Appeals

There is a right of appeal against the refusal to grant or vary a permit; revocation, variation, enforcement, and suspension notices; and the imposition of unreasonable conditions upon a permit. Furthermore, there is a right of appeal where the regulatory agency has notified an operator that information contained within a permit, or application for permit, is not commercially confidential.

Generally, the time limit for appeals is similar to that in the planning system, being six months from the date of refusal, or deemed refusal to grant a permit. Where there is an appeal against an enforcement, suspension or variation notice, the time limit is two months from the date of the notice. Where the regulatory agency is seeking to revoke a permit, the appeal must be made before the date on which the notice takes effect. Finally, where there is an appeal concerning commercial confidentiality, it must be submitted within 21 days from the date of refusal.

A revocation notice will not take effect pending the hearing of an appeal. In all other cases (i.e. enforcement, suspension or variation) there is no suspension of the notice pending an appeal. Thus an operator cannot gain an economic advantage where there is a rush order by appealing against a notice so as to stop the enforcement process, continuing to pollute until the order is completed, and then stopping the process before the appeal is heard. An appeal must be made in writing to the Secretary of State. The appeal has to be accompanied by any relevant information including any application, permit, correspondence or decision and a statement as to how the appellant wishes the appeal to be determined.

An appeal can be heard in one of two ways: either by written representations or by a hearing. If either party to the appeal requests that it be heard by hearing, the Secretary of State must hold a hearing although there is a discretion as to whether the hearing is held in public. The Secretary of State also has a power to direct that a hearing be held.

Overlapping controls

Although the introduction of IPPC has seen a simplification of the administration and control of many environmental impacts from industrial processes, there is still a degree of overlap between different systems of pollution control.

(a) Waste management

There is a significant overlap between the IPPC system and waste management regulation. The IPPC Directive applies to certain landfills (those receiving more than ten tonnes a day or with a total capacity exceeding 25,000 tonnes excluding those that only receive inert waste). The PPC Regulations were amended by the Landfill Regulations 2002 so that *all* landfills are controlled under PPC permits. Other waste management activities including waste disposal (other than landfill sites), incineration and certain recovery operations also fall within the PPC Regulations. When considering an application for a PPC permit for any specified waste management activity, the regulator must consider whether certain pre-requisites have been met including whether the operator is a 'fit and proper person' and whether there is a planning permission in force. In addition, in determining an application the regulator must seek to achieve the relevant 'objectives' set out in Schedule 4 of the Waste Framework Directive including implementing the requirements of the National Waste Strategy 2000 and other strategic waste management plans (For a fuller discussion of meeting the relevant objectives of the Waste Framework Directive see p. 572 and *R (on the application of Blewett) v Derbyshire CC* [2005] Env LR 15).

The Landfill Regulations overlap with the PPC Regulations in a number of ways. First, the application for a PPC permit for a landfill installation takes as a base the conditioning plan which was submitted under the Landfill Regulations. Secondly, the BAT standard for landfills is only taken from the requirements of the Landfill Directive. Thus, when granting a permit, the regulator must impose conditions to achieve BAT but not the general or specific conditions required for other installations. The Landfill (England and Wales) Regulations 2002 set out the required conditions (these include conditions specifying the types and quantity of the waste to be deposited in the site; the nature of prohibited wastes; monitoring; site closure; and aftercare' and any other conditions which relate activities on a landfill site may be included (e.g. off and on site odour management).

Waste management licensing under EPA Part II does not apply to waste activities controlled under the PPC Regulations (Waste Management Licensing Regulations 1994, reg. 16). The Duty of Care under section 34, does, however, continue to apply to PPC permitted activities (EPA 1990, s. 34(1)(aa)). There are, however, still many waste management activities which fall under Part II either because they are not listed in the PPC Regulations or they fall underneath the quantitative thresholds set down in the Regulations.

(b) Water pollution

The key overlap in respect of water pollution can be found in the case of Part A(2) installations which are controlled by local authorities. Traditionally, discharge consents have been regulated by specialised public bodies and local authorities have not developed any expertise in dealing with water quality issues and the imposition of conditions. Dealing with this aspect of permits was considered to be a major challenge for local authorities. The Environment Agency, with the greatest expertise in this area, has been given an overriding supervisory role in the setting of conditions for discharges to water for all Part A(2) installations. In the case of a Part A(2) installation, the Environment Agency has the power to give notice to the relevant local authority specifying the minimum conditions controlling discharges to water (reg. 13). There is a discretion to impose more onerous conditions but there would have to be some specific justification based around site specific circumstances. Under section

88 of the Water Resources Act 1991, discharges made in accordance with an IPPC permit are not an offence under section 85 of that Act (i.e. causing or knowingly permitting the pollution of controlled waters).

(c) Discharge of trade effluent into sewers

The discharge of trade effluent into sewers can be controlled under IPPC permits. Indirect discharges to water (i.e. via sewers/treatment plant) are taken into account when setting permit conditions. The effect of any pre-treatment prior to discharge into water will be taken into account when determining emissions limit values for particular pollutants provided that there would not be any increase in levels of pollution as a result of the treatment (reg. 12(5)). There continues to be an overlap of controls, however, as all discharges to sewers require consent from the sewerage undertaker (WRA 1991, s. 118). Such a consent may set limits on the volume, composition and temperature of the discharge in addition to setting out the charges for the consent.

(d) Statutory nuisances and noise

As an IPPC permit is designed to address all environmental impacts from an installation, a permit should include controls over impacts which could give rise to statutory nuisances. Thus, where there are powers to take enforcement action for breaches of an IPPC permit, the relevant local authority can only serve an abatement notice with the consent of the Secretary of State (EPA 1990, s. 79(10)). In circumstances where there is no power to take enforcement action under IPPC legislation (e.g. because the nuisance does not arise from the installation or regulated activities, such as in the case of burglar alarms), the power to take action against the nuisance is still available. In addition, the right of a private individual to bring a complaint under section 82 of the EPA 1990 is still unaffected by IPPC legislation although compliance with permit conditions may create a presumption that such a nuisance does not exist or that the defence of Best Practicable Means is available.

(e) Contaminated land

In theory, there is no overlap between the IPPC legislation and the controls over the clean up of historically contaminated land under Part IIA of the EPA 1990. Where contamination arises as a result of activities permitted under IPPC legislation, the power to clean up arises after site closure. On the other hand, contamination which is in existence prior to the application for an IPPC permit should be dealt with under controls to be found in concurrent legislation or under the provisions dealing with historic contamination under Part IIA. In practice, however, the information on site contamination which is a necessary part of the application for an IPPC permit will give local authorities and the Environment Agency (as regulators under Part IIA) the opportunity of identifying those sites which might be historically contaminated and therefore be potentially designated sites under the contaminated land regime. The dilemma for operators is that they will have to balance a desire to portray the site in its 'warts and all' state prior to commencement of IPPC activities in order to establish a 'dirty' comparator when it comes to site closure, against the inevitable investigations and enforcement under other legislation (including Part IIA) where the site condition report discloses heavy contamination. One important technical distinction between the use of clean up powers under Part IIA and the post-closure IPPC requirements is that the standard of clean up under IPPC legislation is much higher than under the contaminated land regime. Under IPPC, the land must be cleaned up to a standard based upon the site conditions before the permitted activity was commenced (i.e. before the date of issue of the permit). Under Part IIA the clean up must be to a 'suitable for use' standard.

(f) Town and country planning and environment assessment

Unlike some of the other pollution control regimes, there is no legislative reference to any connection between the planning system and IPPC (the one exception is in the case of specified waste management activities where one of the pre-requisites for the grant of a PPC permit is that planning permission, if required, is in force). There is no obligation to obtain a planning permission for any development associated with a new or altered installation prior to obtaining a permit under the IPPC legislation (the reverse is also true). However, as a wide range of environmental impacts are material considerations in applications for permits, there is a practical link between environmental scrutiny under the planning regime and under IPPC legislation. Many of the installations which require a permit to operate will also be subject to the need for environmental assessment under the relevant legislation. In these cases, much of the information included within an environmental statement would form the basis of the information submitted with an IPPC application. The IPPC Directive and the EIA Directive allow for information produced for the purposes of one directive to be recycled for the purposes of the other. In practice therefore it would be appropriate to submit an environmental statement with both applications (although the IPPC application would need to concentrate on additional technical matters such as emission limit values and BAT).

Another important practical overlap is in the decision-making process. When dealing with a planning application, local authorities are advised to consider only the land-use implications of the development. This leads to inevitable questions about the nature of 'land-use' implications. The courts have examined the nature of the overlap between planning and pollution control in relation to the IPC system (which for the purposes of the discussion is the same as the IPPC system) in *Gateshead Metropolitan Borough Council v Secretary of State for the Environment* (see Case box 20.5).

CASE 20.5 Planning and Pollution Control—*Gateshead Metropolitan Borough Council v Secretary of State for the Environment* [1995] Env LR 37

The Secretary of State granted planning permission for a clinical waste incinerator in Gateshead. The inspector appointed to hear the appeal recommended that permission be refused. One of the issues which was taken into account by the inspector was the public fear that pollution from the site would be unacceptable. The Secretary of State concluded that the issue could be satisfactorily addressed as part of the IPC application and granted planning permission. That decision was challenged by the local planning authority on the basis that the two systems were so closely inter-linked that it was unreasonable to grant planning permission without knowing if emissions could be adequately controlled under the IPC system.

In the High Court, Sullivan J decided that although the two statutory regimes overlapped, the extent of the overlap would vary on each occasion. It was envisaged that there would be a range of cases, from those where environmental considerations could be dealt with adequately under the pollution control system to those where environmental considerations could not be incorporated satisfactorily into an IPC authorization. The correct legal test was whether or not it was reasonable in the *Wednesbury* sense to arrive at the decision reached by the decision-maker.

On appeal, the Court of Appeal affirmed this decision with only a slight variation of judgment. The issue of whether there was an unacceptable risk was, in the Court's view, a matter for the pollution control authority and the fact that the public had expressed concern about the issue was not conclusive. The Court went on to say, however, that the fact that planning permission had been granted should not have been viewed as a restriction on the pollution control authority's discretion to refuse the pollution control application if it thought it fit to do so.

Thus, there is no definite dividing line between planning and pollution control and each decision-maker is entitled to arrive at different conclusions if it exercises its discretion reasonably. Although this decision would apply to the overlap between IPPC and the planning system, the dividing line will be much more blurred as the consideration of environmental impacts in each system will be largely similar. Therefore it would be unusual (but seemingly not unlawful) if one regulatory body arrived at a different conclusion from another even with the same information supporting the application (or in the case of the Part A(2) installations, if the same regulatory body arrived at two different conclusions).

(g) IPC and IPPC

For 'existing' installations which were controlled under the IPC system under EPA Part I, there is a transitional overlap between IPPC and IPC. When an application for an IPPC permit is ultimately determined (on appeal if necessary), the IPC authorization for existing processes will cease to apply (Pollution Prevention and Control Act 1999, sch. 3). There are, however, many practical overlaps between the two systems. For example, there is unlikely to be a significant shift in the process standards which are used during the initial transitional period. Where BREF documents are unavailable at the time when a sector is scheduled to come within IPPC, the existing IPC process guidance notes will be adapted for use to guide decisions on granting IPPC permits. In addition there will be a degree in continuity in the approach to decision-making and enforcement under IPPC. One of the advantages of having implemented an integrated system of pollution control is that many of the teething problems which are associated with introducing an integrated permitting system (e.g. setting conditions, assessing environmental impacts, upgrading existing processes to new standards, cost–benefit analysis) have been addressed under the system of IPC.

Is IPPC a better way of approaching pollution?

IPPC represents a significant departure from traditional forms of environmental regulation. In many ways it echoes the 'British' approach to pollution control. It is flexible, pragmatic, and tailored to individual circumstances. Yet it is principled, progressive, and based upon pollution prevention. After some four years of experience with transposing and implementing the requirements of the IPPC Directive, it is difficult to draw any real conclusions on the question of whether IPPC is actually a better way of dealing with pollution from industrial sources than previous techniques. In economic terms the use of a standard which encourages technological innovation is more 'efficient' than one which prescribes a uniform standard as flexible standards allow operators to develop individual responses to meet the pollution prevention targets set for them. By contrast uniform standards are perceived to be economically inefficient because there may be no incentive to reduce pollution below the uniform standard even if it could be done at a lower cost.[23]

The use of process based preventative standards also ties in with the ideas of ecological modernization and the weak view of sustainable development. The use of BAT adopts a positive view of pollution and suggests that technology can and will address environmental impacts. It identifies a move away from control technologies based around end of pipe abatement to 'clean technologies' used in overall processes and based around integrated environmental solutions such as energy efficiency, resource usage and waste minimization. Perhaps most significantly it indicates an emphasis on continual technological improvements and therefore enhanced environmental performance.

There are some weaknesses in the IPPC system. First the scope of activities covered is still relatively narrow. Many major sources of pollutant (e.g. greenhouse gas emissions from transport) are excluded. Secondly, the controls are aimed at the largest industrial operators and therefore exclude many small- and medium-sized enterprises which could benefit from pollution prevention technology. Thirdly, there is the problem of maintaining a 'level playing field', i.e., the difficulties of benchmarking the achievement and performance of BAT in different Member States. Although the information exchange is designed to address this potential problem, the process is too slow, the individual monitoring too weak and the enforcement too lax to ensure that all Member States are implementing the provisions in the same manner.

These potential disadvantages of IPPC reflect the negative side of ecological modernization, i.e. that it is based around technical solutions proposed and agreed by technical people. The whole idea of 'sustainable production' is based around a model of economic growth which is unacceptable to some.[24] This technocratic approach has a knock on effect that the public tend to be more excluded from the decision-making processes than in other areas (e.g. Planning) because of the technical nature of the debate. This is evidenced by the problems associated with the burning of SLF in Cement Kilns (see Box 20.3).

In addition the parameters of the debate are often constrained by decisions made at European level as to appropriate BAT or ELVs which promote even less public involvement (at least on a general level). The idea that levels of public participation in the permitting system is low reflected in the creation of extended rights for the public as seen in the Aarhus Convention and proposed changes to the IPPC Directive.[25] Other initiatives to increase transparency and accountability include the establishment of the European Pollutant Register.

BOX 20.5 **The European Pollutant Emission Register**

The European Pollutant Emission Register (EPER) is an aggregated database of information on emission from individual IPPC installations across Europe.[26] Member States are required to report

---

23. J. Simila (2002) 14 JEL 143 and N. Gunningham and P. Grabosky, *Smart Regulation: Designing Environmental Policy*, (Oxford: Clarendon Press, 1999).

24. D. Wilkinson, *Environment and Law* (London: Routledge, 2002), 249

25. See COM(2003) 354.

26. Commission Decision 2000/479/EC on the implementation of a European Pollutant Register, and Guidance Document at <europa.eu.int/comm./environment/ippc/eper/index.htm>.

emissions of 50 pollutants to water and air from individual facilities every three years. This information is intended to provide 'like-for-like' comparisons between Member States whilst at the same time providing objective evidence as to the effective implementation of IPPC across each country. This comparative analysis is critical as it will be able to benchmark the effects of the flexible use of BAT across different Member States. If significant discrepancies can be found there may be need for fixed standards such as Community wide ELVs. The Register is available on the internet.[27] The initial report indicates that there is some problems with data collection because there were significant differences in the quality and quantity of reporting on emissions in different Member States.[28] Even if some of these problems can be ironed out, the EPER is likely to be replaced within the next ten years with the introduction of a 'Pollutant Release and Transfer Registry' (PRTR). The PRTR, introduced as part of the implementation of the Aarhus Convention broadens the scope of the existing EPER to cover more activities as well as releases to land, off-site transfers of waste and the collection of data on diffuse pollution sources. The driving force behind these initiatives is the desire to increase transparency in an area which has been traditionally dominated by technical experts.

The final point which can be made is that the integrated nature of IPPC is something which still has some scope to be developed. The term integrated pollution prevention and control is used in this chapter to convey a set of rules with relatively narrow application. As such it represents one of the latest developments of traditional 'command and control' regulation. There is, however, a much broader, general (and as yet theoretical) meaning which covers pollution prevention and control over much wider areas such as transport, aggregated resource depletion, etc. This is a future challenge but one which would be impossible to meet without the implementation of IPPC.[29]

CHAPTER SUMMARY

1   The historical approach of addressing pollution problems from industrial operations by way of controls on emissions to individual media has been replaced by an integrated system of control over all environmental impacts, known as Integrated Pollution Prevention and Control (IPPC).

2   IPPC derives from a European Directive 96/61/EC which in turn was based upon the UK's system of Integrated Pollution Control found in the Environmental Protection Act 1990. The IPPC Directive takes a flexible approach to regulation and is based upon Member States applying broad principles and procedures rather than specific numerical standards.

3   An integrated approach to pollution problems is achieved through considering emissions to air, water and land, along with a range of other environmental impacts and by setting permit conditions so as to achieve a high level of protection for the environment as a whole.

4   An IPPC permit is based upon the use of the 'Best Available Techniques' (BAT), a flexible process standard, which takes into account local circumstances and balances costs against

27. <www.eper.cec.eu.int>.
28. (2004) 349 ENDS Report, 22.
29. See N. Haigh and N. Emmott (1996) 8 JEL 301.

environmental benefits. Emission standards (ELVs) are then set by reference to the BAT for a particular installation. Environmental Quality Standards are taken into account in setting ELVs above those related to BAT where the quality standards represent national or European standards or where local conditions require it.

5 IPPC applies only to activities carried out at the most polluting industrial installations. The vast majority of IPPC installations are controlled by the Environment Agency with a small residual number controlled by Local Authorities. It applies to both new and existing installations. It is being phased for existing industrial installations from 1999 until 2007.

6 There are standard application procedures. In certain sensitive installations such as burning substitute liquid fuels in cement kilns, greater public participation, and more rigorous consultation requirements have been adopted to meet public concerns about the transparency of certain application procedures.

7 The strengths of IPPC include the way in which it promotes technological innovation in an economically efficient manner; encourages the regulation of industrial sources by considering all environmental impacts as a whole; shifts the focus of industrial pollution control from end of pipe solutions to clean technology; and the practical workings of the idea of ecological modernisation.

8 The weaknesses of IPPC could include: the relatively small scope of application; the bias in favour of technological solutions which exclude greater public participation; the promotion of weaker forms of 'sustainable development' which do nothing to address underlying issues of resource depletion and over consumption; and the lack of true integration of controls over all sources of pollution.

Q QUESTIONS

1 What are the advantages of taking an integrated approach to pollution problems as seen in the Integrated Pollution Prevention and Control system under Directive 96/61 and domestic law? Are there any disadvantages?

2 How 'integrated' is IPPC?

3 What is meant by the use of the environmental standard 'Best Available Techniques' to prevent or reduce pollution? How does the use of BAT relate to the use of other environmental standards such as emission and environmental quality standards in the system of Integrated Pollution Prevention and Control?

4 What is meant by a 'substantial change' in activities controlled under an IPPC permit? Why has this proved to be so controversial in the context of the burning of Substitute Liquid Fuels? What does this controversy say about the application procedures under IPPC?

5 Megawaste operates an waste incineration business. They are presently trying to commence operations at a new site in Blackoldton. Waste incineration is a Part A(1) installation under the Pollution Prevention and Control Regulations 2000. The Environment Agency reject the application for an IPPC permit on the ground that Megawaste cannot demonstrate the use of BAT. The Agency consider that other technologies are more suitable. In particular microwaving waste should be preferred to incineration. There are no microwave waste disposal units operating in the UK although they are used successfully in Denmark and the USA. Secondly, although the incinerator can meet the ELVs set out in the existing BREF document it does not meet those set

in a recently published European Directive on incineration which sets much lower limits. The Directive, however, only requires these limits to be met within the next four years. Finally, the EA argue that even if the ELVs could be met, the aggregated effects of this plant would be that it would be harmful. The plant is situated in an area with a lot of motorways and atmospheric conditions are close to breaching European and national air quality standards for certain substances.

Advise Megawaste on the legal validity of these grounds of refusal.

 FURTHER READING

IPPC is a relatively 'dry' topic which appears to be dominated by procedural and technical matters. One of the ways of trying to bring it to life would be to study the SLF saga. Although this deals with the IPC regime, many of the issues are the same. For further reading on this see: The House of Commons Environment Select Committee Session 1994/5, 2nd Report, *The Burning of Secondary Liquid Fuels in Cement Kilns*, The House of Commons Environment Select Committee, Session 1996/ 7, 3rd Report, *The Environmental Impact of Cement Manufacture* and the associated case law *R v Environment Agency ex parte Gibson and Leam* [1999] Env LR 73, *R v Durham County Council ex parte Lowther* [2002] Env LR 13 and *Levy v Environment Agency* [2003] Env LR 11. Also see the Environment Agency's response on the *Substitute Fuels Protocol for use on Cement and Lime Installations* at <www.environment-agency.gov.uk>.

Another way of finding good relevant further reading in this area is to identify works which contextualize the detailed provisions in a general way. A. Gouldson and J. Murphy, *Regulatory Realities* (London: Earthscan, 1998) puts a lot of the technical detail into context by examining the regulatory impacts of IPPC, IPC and the voluntary system of environmental management standards under EMAS. Written by non-lawyers, the book does not cover the detail of the law but provides a good illustration of the use of different legal mechanisms used to bring about environmental improvement. See especially, chapters 3 and 5.

For a clear understanding of the workings of IPPC there is no better place to start than the Government's own *Integrated Pollution Prevention and Control: A Practical Guide* (3rd edn) which is available on DEFRA's web page. This guide puts a complicated system into plain(ish) English in a structured and understandable fashion. Another useful guide is J. Farthing, B. Marshall, and P. Kellett, *Pollution Prevention and Control The New Regime* (London: Lexis Nexis UK, 2003).

Neither of these guides provide any analytical or comparative context but much can be found elsewhere for that. For example, C. Backes and G. Betlem (eds), *Integrated Pollution Prevention and Control: The EEC Directive from a Comparative Legal and Economic Perspective* (The Hague: Kluwer, 1999) provides a comparative context by examining the position in three Member States (Germany, the UK, and the Netherlands). Different perspectives on the IPPC Directive can be found in N. Emmott and N. Haigh, 'Integrated Pollution Prevention and Control: UK and EC Approaches and Possible Next Steps' [1996] JEL 301, M. Doppelhammer, 'More Difficult than Finding The Way Round Chinatown? The IPPC Directive and its Implementation' (2000) EELR 199, M. Faure and J. Lefevre, 'The Draft Directive on Integrated Pollution Prevention and Control: An economic perspective' [1996] EELR 112 and M. Pallemaerts, 'The Proposed IPPC Drective: Re-regulations or De-Regulation?' [1996] EELR 174. There is a study of the background to the Sevilla Process and the writing of BREF documents in B. Lange, 'From Boundary Drawing to Transitions: the Creation of Normativity under the EU Directive on Integrated Pollution Prevention and Control' (2002) 8(2) European Law Journal 246.

Background reading on the concept of integrating pollution controls can be found in J. Krier and M. Brownstein, 'On Integrated Pollution Control' (1991) Environmental Law 119 and N. Haigh and F. Irwin (eds), *Integrated Pollution Control in Europe and North America* (Institute for European Environmental Policy and the Conservation Foundation, 1990).

For historical interest there are a few articles on the system of IPC which are worth looking at. A. Mehta and K. Hawkins, 'IPC and its Impact: Perspectives from Industry' (1998) 10 JEL 61 is an empirical study of the effect of the regime upon industry. A similar approach (although with a greater focus on enforcement practice) is taken in C. Lovat, 'Regulating IPC in Scotland', (2004) 16 JEL 48. Finally M. Purdue, 'Integrated Pollution Control and the Environmental Protection Act 1990: A Coming of Age for Environmental Law?' [1991] 54 MLR 534 deals with the significance of the introduction of the IPC system in terms of its impact upon environmental standard setting.

@ WEB LINKS

The starting point for any web-based research of IPPC should probably be the European Commission's web page at <europa.eu.int/comm/environment/ippc/index.htm>. The European IPPC Bureau's web site at <eippcb.jrc.es> is a good source of technical information about the IPPC Directive and BREF documents. On a national level, both the Environment Agency at <www.environment-agency.gov.uk/business> and DEFRA at <www.defra.gov.uk/environment/ppc> are good starting points for technical, legal and policy documents.

21 The conservation of nature

→ **Overview**

This chapter looks at the laws that aim specifically to protect plants, animals, and natural habitats. This has become a popular subject in recent years, for a variety of reasons. These include increasing interest in all things connected with wildlife, and alarm at the appalling rate of decline in and loss of the natural environment. Using the law to conserve nature, however, involves finding solutions to some complex policy issues. Finding space for species and habitats to be conserved often clashes with other legitimate social interests like economic development and respect for private property. These tensions—which mean that nature conservation law can be a controversial policy area[1]—are the central theme of this chapter.

In looking at laws that have as their primary focus the conservation of species and their habitats, we distinguish between laws that are justified as a matter of straight wildlife conservation, and those that relate to matters of amenity and landscape (which are dealt with in the following chapter). It must be recognized, however, that in many ways the law now pursues both these objectives together. This is especially true of the use of economic instruments in furthering nature conservation, landscape and recreational interests in an integrated way and as we will see a major challenge is the integration of nature conservation into general decision-making (e.g. as regards agriculture or the control of development). Little coverage, though, is given to international conservation law, and reference to the works mentioned at the end of the chapter is recommended. Partly this is because international laws are often effectively subsumed within more enforceable regimes at national level (this is basically the case with the protection given to sites designated under the 1971 Ramsar Convention on wetlands). But largely it is because the central themes of this chapter can be more than adequately explored by looking at national and EC law.[2]

Finally, it must be stressed that the effective conservation of species and habitats depends as much on the responses to other environmental threats—especially climate change,[3] pollution, and inappropriate land uses—as on the specific methods of protecting species and habitats mentioned here, which would undoubtedly be useless if applied in isolation.

---

1. E.g. the contentious passage of the Wildlife and Countryside Act 1981, described in P. Lowe et al, *Countryside Conflicts* (London: Gower, 1986), ch. 6.

2. This means that certain mechanisms to secure the sustainable and equitable use of the components of biodiversity—such as intellectual property rights, farmers' rights and differentiated responsibilities as between 'northern' and 'southern' countries—are not covered.

3. Climate change may not of course be a threat to some habitats and species, which may prosper, yet even in the medium term some habitats and species may be lost completely from the UK.

Before reading this chapter you may find it useful to have looked at competing perspectives on how the natural environment can be valued and how wildlife interests are treated from a sustainable development perspective (see p. 67); the legal status of EC directives (there are two key directives in this area); and the use of a range of regulatory approaches, especially economic tools.

At the end of this chapter you will be able to:

✔ Appreciate a range of reasons for conserving nature.

✔ Understand the main regulatory challenges in nature conservation, especially the drawbacks of using a 'do not' approach to conserving habitats and finding the right balance between the costs of nature conservation falling on landowners or the general public.

✔ Evaluate how the law weighs conservation interests against other valued interests like economic development.

✔ Assess some of the approaches to, and challenges of, integrating nature conservation into decision-making.

Why conserve?

'Conscious of the intrinsic value of biological diversity and of the ecological, genetic, social, economic, scientific, educational, cultural, recreational and aesthetic values of biological diversity and its components

Conscious also of the importance of biological diversity for evolution and for maintaining life sustaining systems of the biosphere'

[Preamble, 1992 Convention on Biological Diversity]

There are many reasons why species and habitats are valued. One reason for conserving nature is scientific study. The seminal 1947 Huxley Report advocated designating protected areas for their educative value as 'living laboratories',[4] and it is notable that the main national habitat designation dating from this period is the Site of Special *Scientific* Interest (SSSI). Nature might also be conserved on aesthetic or cultural, or even spiritual, grounds. An example of this is the Convention on the International Trade in Endangered Species, Appendix III of which restricts the trade in species which are not strictly endangered, but which nevertheless have a special place in the life of a country, e.g. as emblematic of the nation.

Of course, species may be valued for the economic and social benefits they now provide, such as food, and early hunting laws essentially protected game species to ensure their continued exploitation. Nature can also be valued for the benefits that it might provide in the future—e.g. new strains of crops or new pharmaceutical products—for which a diversity of genetic material is probably needed, while diversity may also be needed to maintain the functioning of resilient biological systems that all humans and animals depend on (e.g. by protecting against events like pest infestation or disease that might reduce the diversity of

---

4. *Conservation of Nature in England and Wales*, Wildlife Conservation Special Committee (the 'Huxley Committee'), Cmd 7122.

species). Nature can also be seen as having considerable economic value, though this value is not always appreciated sufficiently by decision-makers because it is often not very well captured in the market place. Addressing the unprecedented rate of species extinctions by conserving biological diversity (or 'biodiversity')—i.e. the richness of life on earth—can be justified as a form of long term insurance for human health and welfare.

In practice, though, most protected areas in Britain are designated on the basis of the rarity of relatively large and well-known organisms such as birds, plants, and larger invertebrates like molluscs. It is difficult to say, therefore, that the laws considered in this chapter have as their focus the conservation of biological diversity in the sense that this is defined, in Article 2 of the Biodiversity Convention, as including diversity within species, between species and of ecosystems.

As well as some of the temporal considerations mentioned above—e.g. the rights or interests of future generations—there are also spatial dimensions to valuing nature which influence conservation policy. Although there are obviously examples of distant species being highly valued (e.g. whales), the greatest value placed on plants, animals, and habitats is generally at the local level.[5] But similarly, the value of potentially damaging activities like economic development or agricultural improvements are also of greatest importance locally. In different ways, therefore, often the value of plants and animals *and* the potential economic benefits from developing their habitats are felt most strongly at the local level, while the wider public benefits (either for economic and social development or for biodiversity conservation) are either more abstract or more diffusely appreciated.

The reasons for valuing nature conservation outlined above are utilitarian and essentially anthropocentric. Even statutes aimed at protecting wild animals from cruelty can be justified on the grounds of civilizing human behaviour. There have been some soft law moves in the direction of justifying conservation laws on the basis that, as the UN World Charter for Nature (1982) put it 'all life warrants respect regardless of its usefulness to Man', but binding legal texts tend to retreat from this point of view. Thus, despite the 1992 Convention on Biological Diversity speaking of the 'intrinsic value' of biodiversity, its real focus is the sustainable use of nature, i.e. making biodiversity pay its way.

Three final points are worth making here. The first is that there are obviously values that compete with those of nature conservation. These, of course, may include development which can only be achieved at the expense of wildlife and habitat. But it can also include other values. For example, in *R (Greenpeace) v Secretary of State for the Environment, Food and Rural Affairs* [2003] Env LR 9, a case involving an import of Brazilian mahogany, the majority of the Court of Appeal stressed that exporters should be able to rely on documents which on their face authorized the shipment. In doing so they placed greater value on the importance of commercial certainty than they did on nature conservation, which (as Laws LJ in the minority clearly wished) could have been more highly valued if the circumstances surrounding the grant of the export permit were given more weight.

Secondly, as many of the above justifications show there are good reasons to take a precautionary approach to conservation. Yet there is a considerable degree of uncertainty about what to conserve. The most species? Or higher taxonomic categories? Or the breadth

---

5. Which in practice often influences how resources are devoted, when compared to losses at higher spatial scales.

of these categories? Or the evolutionary distance between species?[6] This is something that there is no real consensus about. There is also the key issue of how damaging or destroying natural assets is conceived in terms of pursuing sustainable development, in particular whether 'strong' or 'weak' formulations of this concept—which (partly for reasons of risk perception) place different emphases on the substitutability of natural resources like species and habitats—should be taken (see p. 67). In law, this is often played out in the resolution of disputes between conservation and other land-use interests; for example, what degree of damage to a particular habitat or habitat type can be authorized, and the form of compensatory measures (if any) that should be taken.

The history and development of controls

Landmarks in the modern evolution of nature conservation law

Year	UK	EC	International
1947	Huxley Report		
1949	National Parks and Access to the Countryside Act		
1973	Nature Conservancy Council		CITES treaty
1979		Wild Birds Directive	Berne and Bonn Conventions
1981	Wildlife and Countryside Act		
1982			UN World Charter for Nature
1990	NCC split		
1992		Habitats Directive	Biological Diversity Convention
1994	UK Biodiversity Action Plan; Conservation (Natural Habitats etc) Regulations		
2000	Countryside and Rights of Way Act		

A brief history of nature conservation helps explain the current structure of the law. Until the 19th century, the need to protect wildlife was normally perceived solely in human terms, such as the desirability of preserving game and quarry species and protected areas in which to hunt them. There is little doubt that an incidental benefit of this human-centred approach was the protection of other animals and plants and the preservation of whole areas

6. See C. Stone (1995) 68 S Cal L Rev 577 at 614.

(for example the New Forest) in a fairly undeveloped state, but there were few laws designed specifically to protect wildlife.

Early controls

From Victorian times, the tendency was to enact legislation outlawing unwelcome activities in response to particular problems as they were identified. The rationale for this piecemeal intervention was as much based on concern about cruelty as on any positive desire to conserve nature for its own sake. Some good examples are the Sea Birds Protection Acts of 1869, 1872, and 1880, passed to combat the slaughter of birds at places such as Flamborough Head, and various pieces of legislation intended to restrict the international trade in feathers for clothing and hats. However, there was no grand design underlying these restrictions. The weight of conservation fell on voluntary organisations—indeed Britain had the world's first developed conservation movement—and no official bodies were established to monitor or enforce the legislation that did exist.

These voluntary organisations gradually developed a strategy that became, and remains, the typical approach to nature conservation. This is the designation of selected areas or sites that are specially protected. The first modern uses of this technique related to the protection of common lands for recreational purposes, but it was soon used for the development of nature reserves, even though at this time they were seen as a somewhat peripheral interest of the nature conservation movement. For example, the National Trust acquired parts of Wicken Fen in 1899, the Norfolk Naturalists Trust was founded to buy Cley Marshes in 1926 and the Royal Society for the Protection of Birds bought its first nature reserve (on Romney Marsh) in 1929. However, in the absence of any legislative protection for such sites, their safety lay in the exercise of ordinary property rights. After all, the property owner's freedom to exclude others and to use the land for any purposes is one mechanism for controlling land use in limited areas. But the limitations of this approach are well illustrated by the RSPB's first reserve, which had to be abandoned when drainage activities on neighbouring land destroyed its natural interest.

The post-war period

After 1945, the site designation approach was adopted as a matter of national policy. The beginning of the modern age of nature conservation can be traced to that time in the publication of two influential reports, the Huxley and Ritchie Reports,[7] many of whose recommendations were accepted and acted upon.

A specialist national nature conservation body—the Nature Conservancy—was established and one of its main roles was to create a series of protected sites across the nation, rather than the somewhat random series produced by private acquisition. The two main habitat protection measures, the national nature reserve (NNR) and the site of special scientific interest (SSSI), both date from this period. The scientific basis of nature conservation was emphasised and it was linked firmly to education and research on the natural environment. Nature conservation was also split from amenity, recreation and

7. The 'Huxley Committee' report, Cmd 7122 (see p. 795); *Nature Reserves in Scotland*, Scottish Wild Life Conservation Committee (the 'Ritchie Committee'), Cmd 7184.

landscape matters, which were given their own separate institutions and laws, and it is worth reflecting that the powers for nature conservation at that time were both stronger and met with far less opposition than those for recreation in the countryside. However, nature conservation law was intimately bound up with two key Acts from this period dealing with the promotion of agriculture (the Agriculture Act 1947) and with development control (the Town and Country Planning Act 1947, which excluded agricultural land use from the meaning of 'development') (see p. 857). Together, they reflected the view that the main threat to nature was from urbanization, rather than from changing agricultural practices, and set the scene for the decades ahead.

Current policy

Many of the features of this structure remain, but the climate in which they operate has changed radically, with the result that many of the similarities the current system has with that structure are illusory. There have been devastating changes in both the urban and rural environments and these have altered the role of site designation dramatically from an educational to a safeguarding one. One result has been the expansion of the NNR and SSSI system way beyond that envisaged, or indeed considered necessary, by the Huxley and Ritchie Committees, in order to ensure that at least a basic pool of key sites is protected. Conceiving of nature conservation interests as a 'common heritage' or 'common concern' amongst states has also emerged, and so for many sites and species the main body of rules now stem from the implementation of EC directives or international conventions.

Another result is that general environmental awareness has now shifted the focus of policy away from the designation and protection of certain key sites towards the protection of the wider countryside. It is now accepted that there is little future in having isolated areas of protected wildlife in an otherwise barren landscape, and so nature conservation is increasingly seen as a factor to weigh in the balance when considering policy everywhere. This adds to the political dimension which nature conservation has rapidly acquired. It also leads nature conservation law into a potential head-on collision with traditional views of property and personal rights, and the clash of values this entails.

In addition, the enjoyment of nature has emerged as a major leisure pursuit, blurring the distinction in the public mind and in policy between nature conservation as a scientifically justified discipline and as a recreation. There has been an undreamt-of increase in voluntary activity in relation to the countryside, resulting in large numbers of reserves and sites protected by voluntary bodies and non-statutory designations.

Future directions and challenges

There is now a greater appreciation of the dynamic qualities of nature, and of the major challenges to conservation that climate change in particular will bring. Nature conservation interests cannot be frozen in time, since they are constantly evolving and adapting to changing environmental circumstances. This sits uneasily with the current approach to conservation that looks to preserve existing species and habitats for the future. Instead of just trying to preserve the best of what we presently have, we may need more imaginative thinking about the sort of natural heritage we want, or need, to meet future circumstances. This may involve the promotion of much larger protected areas (which are more robust in conservation terms) than we have at present, and taking a more relaxed view of things like non-native species (e.g. Britain may need to host species struggling to maintain a presence in their original habitat).

Types of legal protection and the conservation law toolbox

From this brief survey it can be seen that the protections and safeguards offered by the law can be divided into four rough categories, in each of which different legal mechanisms tend to be relied upon.[8]

Habitat conservation by designating key sites

This has been a favoured technique, and a bewildering array of legislative designations has built up, the special rules and protections differing for each one.[9] There is quite a degree of overlap here and many designations are cumulative. The main issue in site designation is whether, because of its conservation importance, the statutory conservation agencies (or a sympathetic wildlife organisation) already own the land. If they do, then designation empowers those seeking to conserve the site; if they do not, then designation may clash with the way the landowner wishes to see the land used. The main point to stress here is that straight criminal offences are rarely invoked to protect natural habitats from damage or destruction, and other methods have traditionally been preferred. These have involved, for example, getting local authorities to recognise the value of conservation interests when making land-use planning decisions, or giving landowners financial incentives to manage their land in ways that are sympathetic to nature conservation. Recent reforms, however, have heralded a greater willingness to criminalize behaviour that damages valued habitats (see e.g. p. 814).

Protecting individual animals and plants

While protecting animals and plants within their natural habitats is central to nature conservation, certain species are also protected regardless of whether they are within designated areas. This type of protection is done on a somewhat ad hoc basis, though a degree of coherence is provided by the Wildlife and Countryside Act 1981 and laws implementing key EC Directives, both of which contain various criminal offences and licensing regimes. Nature conservation is not the only aim being pursued: there is still a large element of protection against cruelty, and there are important exceptions relating to game and quarry species. Criminal offences and licensing are also the main legal tools used to control (with varying degrees of success) potentially harmful movements of animals and plants, whether through wildlife trafficking, where import and export permits are used (as under the

---

8. Since biodiversity is a public good, in some measure its component species have a value that cannot be captured by markets.

9. Strictly, habitat protection is a narrower category than site protection, since the former relates to protecting habitats of valued species or valued habitat types per se, whereas the latter may be used to protect and conserve a wider range of interests, but the terms are used synonymously here.

measures implementing the 1973 CITES convention), or, more problematic ecologically, the import of invasive non-native species (see WCA 1981, s. 14 and sch. 9) (space prevents further discussion of these topics here).

Integrating nature conservation

The realization that the protection of species and of isolated sites is insufficient, both in scientific terms and in terms of the expectations of people who are interested in nature, has led to the search for general policies conducive to nature conservation, especially as part of agriculture and forestry policy (see p. 867). Grants and incentives are often used to meet these policy objectives. This is all part of the general trend towards integrating environmental considerations into decision-making, for example by placing conservation duties on public bodies, through impact assessment or by requiring decision-makers to act in ways that achieve conservation objectives.

Incidental protection

It remains clear that nature conservation interests are often served by taking advantage of legal powers that were not designed with nature conservation in mind. The best example is the purchase of private nature reserves by voluntary bodies, thus taking advantage of ordinary property rights, but another good example is the nature conservation value of the large tracts of land used for Ministry of Defence training grounds.

The conservation law toolbox: conclusions

A striking feature of nature conservation law is that very little 'do not'-type regulation is used, certainly when compared to many other areas of environmental law. There are three main explanations for this.

One lies in the importance of human influence for nature conservation. Many bird species, for example, prosper in areas of lowland heath kept free from the invasion of scrub and trees, while the interest of chalk downland depends on grazing. Indeed, safeguarding most species and habitats requires active land management—grazing, harvesting, water-level management, etc—rather than restrictions designed to prevent things happening. This is reflected in recent reforms, under which there are now enforceable powers to compel landowners to manage their land in the interests of conservation (see p. 813).

A second, related, reason is that habitats and species are subject to certain population dynamics (reflected, e.g. in how they respond to changing pressures) which means that containing them within designated parcels of land requires a greater degree of active land management than would allowing habitats or populations of species to move around in response to natural environmental changes (i.e. the very nature of protected area controls, especially in small areas like those designated in the UK, requires more interventionist management).

A third reason is that nature conservation laws may conflict with the core private law right of landowners to determine the use of their property. Although much circumscribed in practice, the *idea* of this right has always exercised a powerful influence over nature conservation law. Respect for private property rights lies at the heart of the historic approach of the law in prioritizing the pro-development planning system over nature conservation interests, and in seeking voluntary agreement with landowners (through financial incentives or compensation) rather than imposing prescriptive regulatory controls.

The nature conservation agencies

The administration of nature conservation, which was once the responsibility of the Nature Conservancy Council (a Great Britain-wide body), is presently divided between national agencies. Under the EPA 1990, there is:

- English Nature.
- Countryside Council for Wales.
- Scottish Natural Heritage.

While English Nature's statutory remit remains solely nature conservation, the Scottish and Welsh agencies combine the functions of the NCC and the (then) Countryside Commission in their countries, and thus combine nature conservation with amenity and recreational matters (EPA 1990, s. 130; Natural Heritage (Scotland) Act 1991). The three national bodies inherited most of the responsibilities of the NCC within the appropriate geographical area and thus have very similar powers and duties relating to nature conservation. For ease of explanation, we use 'NCC' throughout this book to refer to the relevant national body in its own area. (In Northern Ireland, nature conservation is a matter for the Environment and Heritage Service of the Department of the Environment.)

Each of the three national bodies is established on a similar basis. Council members are appointed by government, and they are the government's statutory advisers on nature conservation issues, with specific responsibilities for advising on species and habitat protection, the dissemination of knowledge about nature conservation, the support and conduct of research into nature conservation, and the safeguarding of protected sites (EPA 1990, s. 132). In particular, they are responsible for selecting and managing NNRs and for the designation and oversight of SSSIs. They are also statutory consultees in relation to a large number of decisions made by other public bodies, including decisions on applications for planning permission and for pollution consents. In one sense, therefore, the three bodies are classic quangos and could be said to be largely unaccountable for many of their decisions. But they could also be said to be accountable to the interests of wildlife and ecology, though like the EA whether this extends merely to implementing and enforcing the law as it is, or going beyond this to 'champion' the cause of nature conservation, has proven contentious.[10]

The splitting up of the NCC was undoubtedly the most controversial part of the EPA 1990, many feeling that the main motivation was the political desirability of reducing the NCC's power in Scotland, where it had been active in opposing such things as the inappropriate afforestation of the unique Flow Country of Caithness and Sutherland. The controversy led to the establishment in the EPA 1990 of a further GB-wide body, the Joint Nature Conservation Committee (JNCC) (see EPA 1990, sch. 7). The JNCC has few executive functions, but carries out important roles in relation to the international responsibilities of the old NCC (e.g. under the Ramsar Convention and other international agree-

---

10. HC Environment, Transport and Regional Affairs Committee, *English Nature* (1998).

ments), matters affecting Great Britain as a whole, and the retention of common standards throughout Great Britain (for example, common criteria for the designation of SSSIs).

Despite specialist nature conservation agencies, a final point of note mirrors those made above about integrating conservation into all aspects of policy. It is important that all bodies whose activities impact on the natural environment should have to consider the impact of their decisions on nature conservation. A small step in this direction is recent legislation that places a general duty on all public bodies to further and enhance nature conservation, though only in relation to certain designated sites (see pp. 821 and 838). Yet in practice the process of integrating conservation policies into environmental decision-making can prove to be challenging. The Environment Agency, which within certain constraints has a duty to further conservation, has been criticized for insufficiently integrating nature conservation concerns into its core functions.[11]

At the time of writing, it has been announced that an integrated agency (to be called Natural England) is to be established, bringing together English Nature, certain functions (mainly related to landscape conservation) of the Countryside Agency, and most of the functions of the Rural Development Service, to begin in 2006/7.

Habitat conservation—national law

Although there is a rapidly growing number of protective designations for areas of habitat, the main domestic ones remain the interrelated categories of NNR and SSSI.[12] The increasingly important EC designations are discussed later in this chapter. Both NNRs and SSSIs were originally introduced in the National Parks and Access to the Countryside Act 1949 on the recommendation of the Huxley and Ritchie Committees. The NNR powers remain essentially those enacted in 1949, but the SSSI provisions have been significantly altered and strengthened, first by Part II of the Wildlife and Countryside Act 1981 (WCA 1981), and more recently by amendments in England and Wales to the 1981 Act made under Part III of the Countryside and Rights of Way Act 2000 (CROWA 2000). (In Scotland, the 1981 Act has been strengthened, along broadly similar lines, by the Nature Conservation (Scotland) Act 2004.)[13]

The difference between NNRs and SSSIs can best be explained by saying that NNRs are actively controlled and managed by the NCC, whereas in SSSIs the occupier of the land retains control subject to a number of restrictions on use decided by the NCC. Since all NNRs are notified as SSSIs and benefit from the restrictions on them, however, it is more useful if the legal protections for SSSIs are explained in detail. Focusing on SSSIs also makes practical sense, since generally the nature conservation interest has to co-exist with other land uses like agricultural or economic development. By contrast, the intention in the

---

11. HC Environment, Transport and the Regions Committee, *The Environment Agency* (2000), paras 137–9.

12. There is also separate provision for limestone pavements, see WCA 1981, s. 34. Most if not all significant areas of this unique habitat (and geological feature) are covered by limestone pavement orders. Limestone pavements are also listed in Annex I of the EC Habitats Directive (see p. 825).

13. However, greater emphasis is placed on involving a wider range of bodies, and the public, in site designation and management, albeit in the context of sites still being designated on scientific grounds.

Huxley report (p. 13) was that NNRs should be selected where the land was 'for one reason or another beyond the margin of economic development' and, because the study and conservation of nature is the predominant use of the land, the conservation condition of NNRs is generally much better than SSSIs.

National nature reserves (NNRs)

NNRs are areas managed for study or research into flora, fauna or geological or physiographical interest, or for preserving such features that are of special interest (NPACA 1949, s. 15).[14] There were 352 NNRs in Great Britain as at August 2003, covering over 226,000 hectares. Designation is simple: the NCC merely declares that an area is one. But to do this it has to have control of the site so that it can manage it. Control is achieved either by buying the land, leasing it, or entering into a nature reserve agreement with the owner, so NNRs are not necessarily the very best sites and private property rights are central to their conservation. About a third of NNRs are now declared on nationally important land managed by an approved body (e.g. a Wildlife Trust),[15] a useful device that has allowed the NCC to expand the number of NNRs without incurring the costs associated with acquiring land. Since byelaws can now be made for any SSSI, however, there are now no additional statutory restrictions on the use of an NNR other than those imposed on all SSSIs. There are no NNRs in Northern Ireland, though there are 47 nature reserves, declared by Government, of equivalent status.

BOX 21.1 Marine nature reserves (MNRs)

MNRs are the counterparts to NNRs in tidal and coastal waters and may be designated for any area of land or water from the high tide mark to a line three miles from the baselines established for measuring the territorial sea.[16] They may be designated on the same grounds of conservation and study as NNRs (WCA 1981, s. 36), and are actively managed by the NCC. There are a number of differences from NNRs. Some stem from the absence of property rights over most of the potential area of MNRs, others are a consequence of the limited vision of MNRs in the 1981 Act. Designation is by the Secretary of State on the application of the NCC, but there are significant obstacles: the procedure is lengthy (WCA 1981, sch. 12), and the main control is the power for the NCC to make by-laws which, though, cannot restrict any lawful right of passage by vessels other than pleasure boats (s. 37). Only three small MNRs have ever been designated, though this may reflect the NCC's priorities lying elsewhere in the 1980s. There are a few voluntary marine reserves, and in Scotland a number of non-statutory marine consultation areas have been designated (mostly on the west coast), as a flag to other decision-makers about the quality and sensitivity of the marine environment.

---

14. At local level, local authorities may designate and manage local nature reserves along broadly similar lines, see NPACA 1949, s. 21. Mostly they have been designated to promote conservation education in urban areas.

15. WCA 1981, s. 35. Strictly, only these latter sites are NNRs; those designated under s. 15 of the 1949 Act are strictly 'nature reserves', but they have always been referred to as national nature reserves.

16. See the Territorial Sea Act 1987.

The inadequate conservation of the marine environment has long been a source of concern. In 2004 a major *Review of Marine Nature Conservation* (DEFRA) confirmed the need for significant, integrated reforms. Although a Marine Wildlife Conservation Bill was blocked in the House of Lords in 2002, it may be that another attempt at enacting legislation in a future Parliamentary session will be more successful. Such a Bill is likely to use many of the mechanisms of the law on SSSIs discussed below, such as a duty to designate sites on scientific grounds, the use of management schemes, and general conservation duties on all public authorities. If enacted, national law on marine conservation would be strengthened, though it would still lag some way behind the level of protection given to marine species and habitats under EC law (see p. 839).

Sites of Special Scientific Interest (SSSIs)

SSSIs are a representative sample of British habitats, each site being seen as 'an integral part of a national series' established with the aim of 'maintaining the present diversity of wild animals and plants in Great Britain'. Site selection is on scientific grounds rather than to enhance amenity or provide recreation. For biological sites, the best examples of various habitat types (including natural, semi-natural, and man-made landscapes) are chosen, determined on the basis of 'naturalness, diversity, typicalness and size', along with sites catering for rare habitats and species. A geographical spread is ensured by selecting typical sites within sub-regional areas.[17] Geological SSSIs are treated differently, the intention being to 'conserve those localities essential to the continued conduct of research and education in the earth sciences', again in the context of a national representative series.[18]

By the end of March 2003 (May 2003 for Wales), throughout Great Britain there were 6,581 SSSIs notified under the 1981 Act (4,112 in England, 1,018 in Wales, and 1,451 in Scotland). Together they covered 2,322,737 hectares—over 7 per cent of the land area—though the proportion is far higher in some areas, notably Scotland (12.8 per cent). The size of individual SSSIs ranges from The Wash, covering 66,050 hectares, to many sites of less than half a hectare. Also included are a number of linear sites, such as rivers.

Conservation law and policy and SSSIs

A few preliminary points need to be made about the evolution of the law relating to SSSIs. These require an appreciation both of changing threats to SSSIs since 1949, as well as significant, even radical, changes to law and policy.

Under the 1949 Act, the idea was that the main focus of the NCC's work would centre on the acquisition and management of NNRs. By contrast, SSSIs were to be protected only through notification to local planning authorities which, under their newly acquired planning functions, were to include SSSIs in development plans and hence protect them from (mainly urban) development through planning controls. Consistent with this approach—but remarkable nonetheless—there was no duty to notify landowners of SSSIs. Hence the NCC played a fairly limited role in relation to SSSIs, and at best an information-based approach was preferred. With the advent of new pressures on nature conservation,

17. See, in general, *Guidelines for Selection of Biological SSSIs* (NCC, 1989).
18. *Geological Conservation Review* (NCC 43 (Volume series from 1977 onwards)).

however, the limitations of this approach became clear, evidenced for example by NCC statistics released at the time the 1981 Act was being debated showing that between 10 and 15 per cent of SSSIs had suffered significant damage or loss in 1980 alone—the majority of which was caused by agriculture rather than urban development.

The 1981 Act, however, took only very limited strides towards overcoming the short-comings in relation to SSSIs, which by then had become the dominant site designation. Despite some strengthening, there was a continued preference for a policy of voluntariness (which might have been expected from the Conservative Government of the day). This is the view that compulsory controls should only be used as a last resort, because they will only serve to antagonise landowners, who are seen as having the main responsibility for site protection. Pursuant to this policy, the favoured mechanism of control was the management agreement: many damaging activities were either unregulated or could proceed with planning permission, and so the Act forced the NCC into seeking to enter into agreements with landowners to protect the site, with compensation being paid for losses incurred by owners. To do this, many of the legal requirements focused on a duty to notify the NCC of threats to sites.

Despite an ever-increasing number of management agreements, by the late 1990s a momentum had built up for further reform. Figures from a 1994 study by the National Audit Office reported that over one-fifth of SSSIs in England suffered loss and damage between 1987 and 1993.[19] And the annual reports of English Nature between 1996/97 and 2000/01 charted a significant decline in the percentage of sites whose condition was favour-able or improving, and corresponding increases in those identified as unfavourable, declining or destroyed. These official reports also highlighted the changing threats to SSSIs, a point reinforced by a number of independent analyses.[20] Some threats, such as those arising from agriculture or development, had always been deliberately excluded from control. But other damaging activities were of more recent origin: these included the neglect of land, which creates difficult issues of management and control; activities by statutory undertakers; and recreational activities such as quad biking.

In England and Wales the CROWA 2000 has addressed some of these problems, and in doing so has shifted the policy of the law from voluntarism to regulated site management (see the guidance in *SSSIs: Encouraging Positive Partnerships* (DEFRA, 2003)). As explained below, the NCC now has much greater powers to ban adverse activities and to require positive management, and for this reason the whole process of safeguarding SSSIs is more regulatory and increasingly legalistic. But the policy of the law has not shifted to one of 'command and control'. What lies behind the new law is a model, as the DEFRA guidance puts it, of 'constructive dialogue and partnership', albeit a partnership where the bargaining position of the NCC has been significantly strengthened.

Government has imposed a Public Service Agreement (PSA) target that, by 2010, 95 per cent of all land in SSSIs should either be in favourable condition or, if unfavourable, recovering. By September 2004, only 64.16 per cent of land in SSSIs had met this target. (The comparable figure for NNRs is 80.25 per cent.)

19. *Protecting and Managing Sites of Special Scientific Interest* (National Audit Office, 1994).
20. Rowell, *SSSIs: A Health Check* (Wildlife Link, 1991); WWF-UK, *A Muzzled Watchdog? Is English Nature Protecting Wildlife* (WWF-UK, 1997). The position in Scotland may be even worse.

Notifying SSSIs

> Where the Nature Conservancy Council are of the opinion that any area of land is of special interest by reason of any of its flora, fauna, or geological or physiographical features, it shall be the duty of the Council to notify that fact—
>
> (a)   to the local planning authority in whose area the land is situated;
>
> (b)   to every owner and occupier of any of that land;[21] and
>
> (c)   to the Secretary of State.[22]
>
> WCA 1981, s. 28(1)

As can be seen, the NCC is given a wide discretion both to formulate reasonable criteria for notification and to carry out the task of individual selection.

An important feature of section 28(1) is that the NCC has a *duty* to notify the people and bodies listed.[23] With the stronger regulatory measures introduced under the CROWA 2000, the consequences of notification are that much greater, arguably making the largely unaccountable nature of the notifying agencies more problematic (on which see Box 21.2). Notifications must specify the special features of the site, and also list operations that the NCC considers likely to damage the site (see Box 21.3). Since a valid criticism of the 1981 Act was that landowners perceived notification as negative in nature, in line with the recognised need for active site management the CROWA 2000 now requires that notifications also contain a statement of the NCC's views about the management of the land, including any views about the conservation and enhancement of flora or fauna or other notified features (s. 28(4)). Management statements for all existing SSSIs must be made by the end of January 2006.

The nature of the duty to notify was discussed in *R v Nature Conservancy Council, ex parte London Brick Co. Ltd* [1996] Env LR 1, which concerned a challenge to the notification of a SSSI relating to old clay pits on a brickworks in Peterborough. May J discussed the procedures for establishing a SSSI and decided that there were, in fact, two steps involved.

(a) Under s. 28(1), a *duty* is imposed on the NCC to notify a site that fulfils the appropriate scientific criteria. This notification has provisional effect, but a period of three months is provided during which representations or objections can be made.

(b) The NCC must consider these representations or objections and then has a *discretion* whether to confirm the notification (with or without modifications). If confirmation is not made within nine months of the date when the notification was served, the notification lapses.[24]

---

21. Including commoners—see *SSSIs: Encouraging Positive Partnerships* (DEFRA, 2003), para. 15 (a provision originally in the Bill). See also the discussion of public bodies duties at p. 818.

22. Since CROWA 2000, the general public is now also notified through advertising, see p. 809. The Nature Conservation (Scotland) Act 2004 requires a much wider range of bodies and interested parties to be notified.

23. Notably, the Secretary of State has no power of direction over the NCC regarding SSSI notifications, see EPA 1990, ss. 131(4) and 132(1)(a).

24. Under WCA 1981, s. 28(4A), now WCA 1981, s. 28(5) (as amended by CROWA 2000).

In *Fisher v English Nature* [2004] Env LR 7, however, Lightman J took a different approach. Although section 28 states that the site 'may' be confirmed, the judge noted that if the NCC continues to believe that the criteria for listing are satisfied, then it can only exercise its discretion one way, i.e. to confirm. If it did not, then even if the site were not confirmed as an SSSI it would still satisfy the criteria for notification and the NCC would have to notify again, and Lightman J clearly thought it would absurd if this was required. Hence 'Section 28(1) affords scope for judgement; it affords no scope for discretion.' This approach was essentially approved of by the Court of Appeal ([2005] Env LR 10), although the court stressed that confirmation 'is to be exercised in accordance with the conclusion reached as a result of the outcome of a genuine, open-minded consultation/investigation process' between notification and confirmation.

In *London Brick*, May J accepted that English Nature's policy normally to confirm a notification unless the site is unavoidably going to be destroyed[25] is a reasonable policy, and he upheld the confirmation. And in *Fisher*, Lightman J held that the NCC could not refuse to confirm simply because the species or habitat might be better conserved through other means e.g. voluntary agreements (or even under EC conservation law!).[26] In the interests of natural justice, however, confirmation must be on the same basis as notification,[27] and following CROWA 2000 a confirmation cannot add to the list of potentially damaging operations or extend the area to which the designation applies (s. 28(7)).

The implications of the decisions in *London Brick* and in *Fisher* are significant, since they both strongly suggest that it would be illegal for the NCC to refuse to notify on political or tactical grounds (although it must exercise its 'opinion', not rigidly apply rules, and it could arguably refuse to confirm a notification if, as a matter of expert judgement, the conservation interest on the site was doomed). So it may well be possible for an environmental group to succeed in an action to compel the NCC to notify—and if *Fisher* is followed, confirm—a site. Conversely, it will be difficult to mount a successful challenge against an unwelcome notification where the requisite special interest can be shown.

A further effect of this definition is that the list is not unchanging. New SSSIs will be notified as new information about sites—or about species ecology—is acquired, and as the importance of safeguarding certain habitats increases.[28] It must also be understood that, in an age when sites are being damaged and destroyed, one site may become of greater importance simply because of the loss of another site. The NCC now has formal power to denotify a site where its special interest has been lost and cannot reasonably or practicably be recovered,[29] although in doing so the Environment Agency and certain statutory undertakers—as well as the original parties notified—are effectively given up to nine months to make representations before the denotification is confirmed. This breathing space mirrors the two-stage process to notification in sections 28(1) and (5).

25. But see comment on the *Aggregate Industries* case in Box 21.2
26. *Fisher v English Nature* [2004] Env LR 7 para. 20.
27. *R v Nature Conservancy Council, ex parte Bolton Metropolitan Borough Council* [1995] Env LR 237.
28. See on this *Aggregate Industries*, Box 21.2, paras 110–18.
29. Although there was no express power to do so, between 1981 and 1991, 579 SSSIs (around 15 per cent of the total) were denotified because they had lost the features making them 'special'.

BOX 21.2 Notifying SSSIs and human rights law

In many ways, the legal rules under which sites are notified as SSSIs seem outdated in modern regulatory terms. Officers of the NCC normally make the notification, and there is no scope formally for the landowner or the general public to comment until the start of the nine-month confirmation period. Thereafter, the eventual decision to confirm is taken by the Council of the NCC—a classic quango—from which there is no right to appeal. (In Scotland, there is an independent review body that advises Scottish Natural Heritage when the scientific basis for notification is challenged.) This procedure reflects the extent to which identifying SSSIs has always been presented as one where experts make judgements and take decisions on the basis of specialist knowledge.

   R (Aggregate Industries Ltd) v English Nature [2003] Env LR 3, the facts of which are mentioned elsewhere (see p. 810), raised the compatibility of this process with the 'due process' protections under Article 6 of the ECHR (see p. 493). It was argued that because the Council of English Nature confirm decisions made by its officers, this could not be done independently and impartially.[30] The High Court held that, because of the impact on landowners' rights to use their land, SSSI designation did involve Article 6 rights, and rejected arguments that landowners are only affected if and when they apply for consent for a potentially damaging operation.[31] However, while the dispute was effectively between English Nature's officers and the landowner, the role of the Council of English Nature in confirming the SSSI notification was held to be human rights compliant. This was because of various procedural safeguards for landowners such as the right to make informed representations, to appeal a refusal to consent to an activity, and to ask for the notification to be varied or revoked. But the position of English Nature as an expert conservation body, exercising its judgement on difficult questions of scientific policy, was also important. Where such expert bodies take decisions, then the ordinary right to seek judicial review may be enough for the process as a whole to conform to human rights law.[32] What is notable from this decision, then, is that the human rights issues are being decided in the light of the entire body of rules governing the designation and control of SSSIs. But the decision also confirms the status of the NCC as an expert agency whose decisions about the conservation value of land will only rarely be challengeable in the courts.

   In *Aggregate Industries* s. 28 was not challenged as violating the right to property contained in Article 1 of the First Protocol to the Convention. This has been raised in subsequent cases, but so far this argument has been rejected: see *Fisher v English Nature* [2005] Env LR 10 and *Trailer and Marina (Leven) Ltd v Secretary of State for the Environment, Food and Rural Affairs* [2004] EWCA Civ 1580 (see p. 820).

---

   30. A second challenge under Art. 6 was that the procedures under the 1981 Act were not fair and public, but since 2001 meetings of the Council are held in public and landowners are given the chance to make written and oral representations, and this argument was rejected. Note that the same grounds had been successfully argued in *William Sinclair Holdings Ltd v English Nature* [2002] Env LR 4 but not on the basis of a full hearing and fully argued determination.

   31. *Oerlemans v The Netherlands* (1991) 15 EHRR 561.

   32. See now *Runa Begum v Tower Hamlets LBC* [2003] UKHL 5.

It is up to the NCC to define the exact boundaries of the SSSI. In the *Aggregate Industries* case (see Box 21.2), it was held that the whole of a large tract of afforested land could be notified, even though the rotational plantation and management of the site meant that at any one time only certain areas would in fact provide suitable habitat (a mix of open and overgrown land) for the bird species that the NCC was aiming to conserve (especially woodlark and nightjar). This is a variant of the principle that emerged from *Sweet v Secretary of State and Nature Conservancy Council* [1989] JEL 245 where it appeared permissible for land of lesser intrinsic scientific interest to be notified if it is part of the same environmental unit as land which is of interest, but it avoids any doubt (s. 28B). The new provision, however, makes no mention of what might be described as surrounding 'buffer lands' and it must now be doubted whether they may be notified.[33] One geographical limitation, though, is that while inland waters are included within the definition of 'land' in the Act, SSSIs cannot be notified for waters below the low water mark (thus excluding many estuaries). In the absence of effective specialist designations for the marine environment, marine nature conservation therefore continues to be afforded secondary legal status at national level (see further Box 21.1).

There is also the question whether land should be notified where the species it hosts are only there temporarily. The Act does not say anything about this, but it is English Nature's policy to notify sites even if they are just of temporary significance for internationally important species (this might be the case where, as in the SSSI at the centre of the *Aggregate Industries* case, afforested land only provides suitable habitat until the tree crop closes over).[34] It is not clear whether in practice the NCC will also apply this policy to SSSIs that are only of national importance, but it would appear to be defendable because the presence of any species on a site is, to some extent, temporary, and the more temporary the occupation, the less that there will be any adverse consequences to the landowner in the longer term (since the site can be denotified).

A final point of note here is that until the CROWA 2000 the NCC had no power to enter land to decide whether it should be notified as an SSSI. This absurd situation has now been corrected, and the NCC may enter any land to determine whether it should be designated (these powers of entry also extend to entering land to check its condition and to investigate whether any criminal offences have been committed, a necessary power in light of the strengthening to the law discussed below).

Duties on owners and occupiers

Once SSSIs have been notified, the previous position was that owners and occupiers were placed under a reciprocal duty. They had to notify the NCC in writing before carrying out any operation likely to damage an SSSI (see Box 21.3). However, four months after this

---

33. The NCC now has a power to designate 'extra land' (WCA 1981, s. 28B), but this can only be done after notification of the SSSI and is probably a provision intended to allow the boundaries of large SSSIs to be corrected without having to re-notify the whole site, rather than to allow for buffer land to be designated (though S. Payne [2001] ELM 239 takes a different view). The 'sub-heading' in the legislation speaks of 'enlargement'.

34. See also *Fisher v English Nature* [2004] Env LR 7 where the confirmation as an SSSI of a large tract of cultivated land was upheld despite the migratory stone curlews only occupying the habitat from March to October and changing their sites annually with the rotation of the crops (upheld [2005] Env LR 10).

notification, or earlier if the written consent of the NCC was obtained, the operation could go ahead unimpeded—unless it required and failed to get planning permission. It was an offence 'without reasonable excuse' to carry out a potentially damaging operation either without notifying the NCC, or within the four-month period, but the maximum penalty was only a £2,500 fine.

Until the CROWA 2000, then, the restrictive effect of designation as an SSSI was therefore only to impose a four-month ban on potentially damaging operations. These provisions illustrate the voluntary mechanism that, until recently, was the favoured policy approach. The whole purpose of the law was to give the NCC an opportunity to persuade the owner or occupier not to act in a harmful manner, if necessary by negotiating a management agreement. As the figures mentioned above about the declining condition of SSSIs showed, however, this approach left a lot to be desired. As Lord Mustill observed in *Southern Water Authority v Nature Conservancy Council* [1992] 1 WLR 775 (at p. 778):

It needs only a moment to see that this regime is toothless, for it demands no more from the owner or occupier of an SSSI than a little patience . . . In truth the Act does no more in the great majority of cases than give the council a breathing space within which to apply moral pressure, with a view to persuading the owner or occupier to make a voluntary agreement.

Under section 29 of the WCA 1981, slightly stronger powers were available for areas subject to a nature conservation order. These were mainly used to protect sites imminently threatened with destruction and, for awkward landowners, provided a longer period to agree a management agreement and carried with it the threat of compulsorily purchase. But these powers were sparingly used; there was no duty to make orders—only about 40 were ever made—and the NCC never used these compulsory purchase powers as a result of a dispute over conservation.

Following the CROWA 2000, the ability to impose obligations on landowners and occupiers has increased significantly, with the result that nature conservation orders have been abolished (since all SSSIs now receive greater protection than sites designated under WCA 1981, s. 29). A dual approach is taken, depending on whether the threat to the SSSI is prospective or ongoing.

(a) Prospective threats

Where a potentially damaging operation is to be carried out, the NCC must still be notified, but the major change is that it may now refuse consent indefinitely (s. 28E). Failure to respond to the request for consent is taken to be a deemed refusal, closing completely the former 'waiting period' approach. Harmful activities can only be carried out, therefore, if the NCC consents, or if the work is carried out under a management agreement or management scheme (see below), and it is an offence, subject to a fine of up to £20,000 in the magistrates' court or an unlimited fine in the Crown Court, to cause or permit a potentially damaging operation to be carried out (s. 28P(1)). In setting fine levels, courts must have regard to any actual or potential financial benefit that accrues to the offender (s. 28P(9)). When compared to other environmental law offences, however, and especially species conservation offences (see p. 847), the absence of even limited custodial sanctions for this and other offences relating to habitat conservation is remarkable.

BOX 21.3 **Operations likely to damage SSSIs**

Where the threat to an SSSI is from future activities, the NCC must specify the features of the land that are of special interest (see above) but must also specify any operations that are likely to damage those features. What, then, are 'operations likely to damage' (often referred to as a 'potentially damaging operations')?

The courts have made it clear that 'operation' can include virtually anything that has an impact on the site and 'operations' is not limited to its meaning under town and country planning legislation. In *Sweet* (see p. 813), it was held to include:

cultivation, including ploughing, rotavation, harrowing and reseeding; grazing; mowing or other methods of cutting vegetation; application of manure, fertilisers and lime; burning; the release into the site of any wild feral or domestic animal, reptile, amphibian, bird, fish or invertebrate, or any plant or seed; the storage of materials; the use of materials; the use of vehicles or craft likely to damage or disturb features of interest.

Such things as drainage, building operations and the application of pesticides are clearly covered. Because it is impossible to predict all the threats to an SSSI, or the amount of damage a particular activity will do, the listed activities on any SSSI—which are modified from a national template—is necessarily lengthy and general. One consequence of this is that the vast majority of requests for consent to undertake a potentially damaging operation are granted, since they will relate to listed activities at the innocuous end of the spectrum (e.g. taking down a dangerous tree on an SSSI where tree management is a listed operation).

One thing that is not an 'operation', however, is doing nothing, and on many sites neglect, as much as wilful damage, will be detrimental to the conservation interest. A good example of this is the species of water beetle threatened in the *London Brick* case (see p. 810) following the decision to stop pumping out the pits. For this reason, the CROWA 2000 uses a different mechanism—the management scheme—to combat this type of conservation problem (see p. 816).

Finally, what does 'likely' mean? In the Scottish case of *North Uist Fisheries Ltd v Secretary of State for Scotland* 1992 SLT 333 the judge suggested that 'likely' required any potential damage to be probable rather than a bare possibility. If this interpretation (which was strictly *obiter*) is correct, it would undermine the whole of the legislation on SSSIs. It is submitted that the judge's reasoning should not be followed, since it seems to be based on an entirely incorrect understanding of the context of the legislation.

Consents may be made subject to conditions and may be time-limited. Consents can also be modified or withdrawn at any time, though only if the NCC compensates for losses incurred (s. 28M). In practice, most consents are granted. Figures for 2002/3 show that, out of 1,836 requests to carry out a potentially damaging operation, English Nature refused nine and made 138 subject to conditions.

To balance the restrictions imposed by this new approach, however, in cases of conflict landowners and occupiers may appeal to the Secretary of State or Welsh Assembly.[35] A hearing or public inquiry must be held if this is requested either by the landowner/occupier or the NCC, and in effect the Secretary of State determines the request for consent afresh

---

35. In 2002/03, no appeals were lodged against English Nature; *Annual Report* (2003), 11.

(s. 28F). The right to appeal is a significant factor in the courts holding the notification process to be human rights compliant (see Box 21.2 above), but there is little scope for other interested parties to voice their opinions, not least because landowners need only notify the NCC of their proposals, the NCC need not publicise these, and hearings may be in private. Guidance recommends the use of mediation.

As things stand, under the CROWA 2000 the only legal criteria against which the NCC must decide whether to allow or refuse a potentially damaging operation, or which guide the Minister when hearing an appeal, is the general duty that both have (along with all other public bodies) to further the conservation and enhancement of the features that justified notification of the land as an SSSI (see p. 821). Unlike other public bodies, however, which will usually be subject to conflicting duties (e.g. the Forestry Commission's duty to provide timber), it may be possible to bring an action in judicial review against the NCC if it were to consent to activities which did not further an SSSI's conservation and enhancement.[36] It is notable that in Scotland there is a right to appeal to the Scottish Land Court on the merits, not simply to seek a judicial review of the legality of the restriction.[37]

(b) Ongoing problems

In the case of ongoing problems with an SSSI, such as might arise from neglect or poor management, positive regulation can be required. The NCC may propose a 'management scheme' (s. 28J) for the conservation or restoration of an SSSI and must, after at least three months consultation, serve this on every owner and occupier. From the time that the proposals are first served, the NCC has nine months to decide whether the scheme will take effect. Modifications to the scheme can be made, but not if the final scheme would be more onerous on the landowner or occupier. In effect, therefore, the consultation period may only be used to ameliorate the strictness of any obligations being proposed (though it is open to the NCC at any time to propose a new management scheme with more stringent conditions).

A twin-track approach is taken to securing compliance with management schemes. First, the NCC must try to agree a reasonable management agreement with the landowner, so this remains the preferred policy approach. But if it cannot reach agreement, management schemes can be enforced by serving 'management notices' (s. 28K). Management notices allow the NCC to require reasonable measures to ensure that the land is managed in accordance with the management scheme. For example, in order to conserve bird habitat, the NCC might serve a management notice that scrub be cleared. If the notice is not complied with, the NCC can enter the site and carry out the works itself, including restoration works, charging to the owner or occupier any reasonable costs incurred. There may be cases, though, where it will simply not be feasible for the NCC to undertake the work itself (e.g. if the problem was under-grazing, the NCC might be reluctant to add extra

---

36. Though under s. 37 of the Countryside Act 1968 the NCC must also have due regard to the needs of agriculture and forestry and to the economic and social interests of rural areas.

37. It had been proposed that this appeal would have to consider whether SNH acted reasonably and proportionately, an alternative course of action would not damage the SSSI, and social or economic benefits of national importance outweigh the adverse effects on the SSSI. These steps have some similarities with those required in relation to 'European sites' under EC law (see p. 830), but also some important differences. For example, there is no mention of a requirement to undertake action to compensate for damage that is consented.

livestock itself). In these situations, the only available sanction will be to seek a fine against the landowner for not complying with the management notice.

Management notices may be appealed along similar lines to appeals relating to consents. One notable difference, though, is that landowners can appeal on the grounds that another owner or occupier of the SSSI is responsible for its conservation or restoration. This might apply, for example, where there are multiple owners and occupiers of an SSSI (as might be the case, for example, with common land) and there is a dispute about where responsibility for the site's inadequate conservation or restoration lies. In this situation, the Secretary of State must engage in a balancing exercise deciding, as between the various landowners and occupiers, on whose shoulders responsibility under the management notice should lie. This is done according to a matrix of factors that try to ensure that responsibility is imposed equitably: the relative interests of landowners and occupiers in the land, their relative responsibility for the unfavourable state of the SSSI, and the relative degree of benefit to be derived from carrying out the requirements of the management notice.

The provision for management notices is a considerable advance from the old law, under which restoration of an SSSI could only be required where a nature conservation order was breached. Because of the requirement to try to agree a reasonable management agreement, however—and because policy guidance suggests that notices will only be used in exceptional circumstances—these new measures may only go a limited way towards shifting the financial burden of addressing environmental damage or degradation from the public purse to the landowner (though they should strengthen the hand of the NCC in negotiating management agreements).

Defences

Taken together, these new obligations on landowners and occupiers clearly strike at the heart of the voluntary principle. But they do not completely circumscribe landowners' and occupiers' control of their land. This is because the CROWA 2000 continues the previous policy of the law in, first, exempting operations carried out in an emergency, but also, and much more importantly, making it a reasonable excuse to carry out a potentially damaging operation if the local planning authority has granted planning permission. This does not include an automatic planning permission,[38] but it does mean that a planning permission considered on its merits still trumps any controls that the NCC may impose on an SSSI (see further below).

A further defence arises where an activity has been carried out in accordance with a consent from any public body (e.g. a drainage authority). This new provision is in line with changes made under the CROWA 2000, under which public bodies must engage in a dialogue with the NCC before granting authorizations (see p. 821).

Planning permission

In addition to any controls specific to SSSIs, planning permission is required for operations and material changes of use that fall within the definition of 'development' (see p. 463).

---

38. I.e. one granted by the General Permitted Development Order, see WCA 1981, s. 28P(4).

Where the application relates to an SSSI or is likely to affect an SSSI, or relates to development within a 2-km 'consultation area' around an SSSI, the local planning authority must consult with the NCC before making a decision.[39] The objective is the familiar one of informing the NCC in advance of a potential threat to the site, so it may give advice or offer a management agreement. Prior to the 1981 Act, this was the *only* legal protection for SSSIs.

These requirements are very limited in practice. Many activities likely to damage SSSIs, such as those relating to agriculture, forestry and works carried out by statutory undertakers, are not covered by the need for planning permission, either because they are not development or because they are granted exemption. In any case, the local planning authority is not bound by the NCC's advice—it is just one material consideration to be taken into account. The economic and other arguments in favour of the development may well outweigh the need to protect the SSSI. For example, in 1990 Havering DC granted outline planning permission for a large theme park on Rainham Marshes, the largest SSSI in Greater London. The Secretary of State refused to call the application in, even though this would have been the largest ever loss of SSSI land to a development with planning permission. In another example, Poole BC granted itself planning permission for housing on Canford Heath, an SSSI within the town's boundaries. After an unsuccessful High Court challenge (*R v Poole Borough Council, ex parte Beebee* [1991] JPL 643) the Secretary of State took the almost unprecedented step of revoking the planning permission.

English policy on planning and nature conservation is currently set out in Planning Policy Guidance Note 9, *Nature Conservation* (PPG 9, October 1994).[40] As well as explaining the various statutory and international protections, PPG 9 emphasizes that the nature conservation interest of a site, and the importance of the site in national and international terms, is clearly a material consideration when it comes to a decision whether to grant planning permission, although it does refer to the potential use of conditions or planning obligations to avoid damaging impacts. In particular, PPG 9 includes some especially strong policies in relation to international sites ('European sites' and Ramsar sites), including that environmental impact assessment will normally be required where such a site (including a proposed site) could be affected.

However, there is a difficulty here concerning the relationship between safeguarding sites through the planning machinery and the formal designation of SSSIs. If a formal policy against granting planning permission on internationally important sites were to be adopted, it might be argued that the procedures for designation of those sites need to be upgraded so as to include rights of objection, the possibility of a public inquiry and so on, since such a restraint policy would effectively take away any real chance of realizing the development value of the land (see Box 21.2). But it is highly unlikely that such a policy would ever be implemented; even on internationally important sites nature conservation interests co-exist with some form of human activity and it is important to remember that these sites are not designated for their 'wilderness' qualities.

If planning permission is granted for development, then as noted above it acts as a defence to a prosecution for damaging an SSSI (s. 28(8)). This does not just apply to new permissions. It also exempts existing mineral and peat extraction permissions over SSSIs

39. Town and Country Planning (General Development Procedure) Order 1995, art. 10.
40. This guidance is due to be revised in the light of CROWA 2000, and the reforms to the planning system under the Planning and Compulsory Purchase Act 2004.

from the 1981 Act. These are on sites that tend not to have been identified as of importance when the permission was originally granted. The NCC's options are limited and all involve the payment of potentially large sums of money since:

- revocation of the planning permission entails a liability to pay compensation;
- a management agreement would probably have to compensate for lost profits; and
- compulsory purchase will normally be at the market price (see Box 21.4).

BOX 21.4 Buying out conservation interests

The raised mires at Thorne and Hatfield Moors in Yorkshire are important for their species richness and as a paleoenvironmental resource. For these reasons some of the Moors is owned and managed by English Nature as a NNR, while this and other areas are SSSIs. But the Moors are also a rich source of peat extracted under long-standing planning permissions. These, of course, 'trump' the SSSI designations (see above). The Moors became something of a conservation *cause celebre* in the 1990s when English Nature suggested that they might be denotified (though in the end SSSI status was maintained). For many the visible removal of much of the conservation interest by lawful peat stripping seemed to embody key inadequacies of the WCA 1981, and peat-winning machinery at Thorne Moor was damaged by the protest group EarthFirst!

The identification of much of this land (and land at Wedholme Flow in Cumbria) as a proposed special area of conservation under the EC Habitats Directive, however, meant that these planning permissions needed to be reviewed for their compatibility with EC conservation law (see p. 833). This led the main stakeholders—the peat extractors (Scotts), English Nature and the Government—to review the sites' prospects. The outcome was that, for over £18 million, English Nature essentially bought Scott's freehold or leasehold interests in the land, as well as its interests in the peat itself. Although in time English Nature will manage the sites, it also paid Scott's to undertake initial restoration work. (A more detailed summary of the agreement can be found via English Nature's web site.)

The buy-out of these peat moors is a good illustration of the continuing need, despite the shift in approach taken by CROWA 2000, to pay certain landowners not to damage conservation interests. When the damaging activity has planning permission the only real course of action for the NCC is to compensate the owner for the loss of income which the permission would have generated. In other words, the planning permission gives the landowner a legitimate expectation about future profits which, if it is to be lost, the law must compensate (see below). But compare farming: this does not require planning permission, so there is nothing equivalent that the State has given and hence nothing to be compensated. At best, farmers receive public money to encourage particular activities and—as the recent changes to the CAP indicate—this can be redirected towards different objectives (or, in theory, simply removed) (see p. 868).

A final point is to consider the impact of a new SSSI designation on land such as peat moors. So long as the peat removal is carried out under a valid planning permission, the extractor will not suffer any loss directly from the designation; in principle removal can continue. But the extractor may suffer losses because of pressure on consumers not to buy peat taken from designated conservation areas. If so, the law will not compensate for the loss of market share, since this arises not because of any taking of rights by the state but because of the actions of retailers and individual consumers.

Management agreements

Management agreements are effectively contracts in which owners or occupiers of land agree to manage it in the interests of nature conservation in return for payment from the NCC.[41] They normally provide for positive management of the site as well as for restrictions, but it appears that only restrictive arrangements in the agreement will be binding on successors in title (s. 15(4)). As will already be clear, the possibility of a management agreement underpinned the voluntary approach to nature conservation favoured by successive administrations until the CROWA 2000 (though they were little used before the WCA 1981, and even after 1981 the great majority of potentially damaging operations notices were resolved without using agreements). The NCC can now enter into management agreements not just with owners and occupiers of SSSIs but, so long as this benefits the SSSI, with *anyone* with an interest in any other land (Countryside Act 1968, s.15, as amended by CROWA 2000, s. 75(3)), unlike the previous position which limited agreements to those with interests in adjacent land. This is in line with the current policy preference for securing agreements that cover whole farm units rather than just individual parcels of protected areas.

Historically, a valid criticism of management agreements was that—because as a matter of government policy they were based on assessing the net profits foregone or the difference in capital values with or without the restriction, which includes such things as lost agricultural grants or lost revenues had the land been converted to a more profitable use[42]—they compensated landowners for *not* doing something desirable, in this case positive management, which is both inefficient and poor conservation policy.[43] There was even the suggestion that, in order to claim for 'lost profits', some enterprising landowners threatened works they never really intended to undertake, putting the NCC in the invidious position of having to decide whether to call the landowners bluff.[44] Even prior to CROWA, however, such compensatory agreements were in practice being replaced by agreements under which positive management was encouraged,[45] and it is these types of payments that now predominate.

The changes to management agreement policy that were already taking place have now been formalized in guidance that makes it clear that, for *new* operations, payment will not be made unless there is some positive conservation benefit.[46] As Ouseley J said in *Trailer and Marina (Leven) Ltd v Secretary of State for the Environment, Food and Rural Affairs* [2004] EWHC 153 (Admin), an unsuccessful challenge that the decision not to continue compensating a canal owner for lost profits breached their property rights under Article 1 of

---

41. A contractual approach also lies behind the use of planning obligations to secure nature conservation gain, see p. 487 above. Land of outstanding scientific interest may also qualify for tax relief (see *Capital Taxation and Nature Conservation*, (English Nature, 1992)).

42. See the Appendix to DoE Circular 4/83.

43. Probably the worst example of how the former guidelines worked is *Cameron v Nature Conservancy Council* 1991 SLT (Lands Tribunal) 85. The system was nicely captured in the unofficial acronym CUCU ('cough up and clear off').

44. In most cases, proprietors brought forward proposals that they had only been tentatively been thinking about, see J. Rowan-Robinson et al, *Management Agreements for Nature Conservation in Scotland* (Univ. of Aberdeen, 1990).

45. In England, the Wildlife Enhancement Scheme; in Wales, Tir Gofal (the latter being a 'whole farm' scheme which has always extended beyond land notified as an SSSI, and which integrates environmentally sensitive area payments.) See C. Rodgers and J. Bishop, *Management Agreements for Nature Conservation* (RICS, 1998).

46. *Guidelines on Management Agreement Payments and Other Related Matters* (DETR, 2001).

the First Protocol to the European Convention on Human Rights, '[t]he restriction on compensation reflects a changing view over time as to the relationship between an owner's rights and the a public interest, the importance of which has grown significantly' (para. 94).[47]

However, agreements will still compensate for income foregone (though this will be assessed in the light of payments received for positive land management), and payment is *required* if an existing consent is modified or withdrawn and the owner or occupier suffers loss, or if a stop notice is issued (CROWA 2000, s. 28M(1), and sch. 11, paras 9 and 17, respectively). But it is not merely the guidance that has changed. The whole context within which management agreements were once negotiated has now changed and, unless a potentially damaging operation will be undertaken under a planning permission (see e.g. Box 21.3), the NCC's bargaining position has been strengthened considerably. Even where seeking a management agreement remains the policy of the law, as with management schemes, the context is different, since although the law requires the NCC to enter into 'reasonable' agreements, management notices (that government guidance indicates are to be used exceptionally) still exist as a theoretical further tier of controls. And there are also revised powers to compulsorily purchase sites where either the NCC:

(a) cannot conclude, on reasonable terms, a management agreement; or

(b) has entered into an agreement, but it is being breached in such a way that the land is not being managed satisfactorily.[48]

As with the pre-CROWA position, however, it must be unlikely that these powers will be greatly used, because of the expense involved and because it is rarely an effective use of the NCC's resources.[49]

Duties on public bodies

A further limitation of the original 1981 Act was that, while criminal liability for carrying out a potentially damaging operation within the four-month 'waiting' period was strict, it could only be committed by owners and occupiers of the SSSI. (Owners and occupiers know about the designation of a site, either because they are notified, or because it is a local land charge: s. 28(9).)

This restriction was given a narrow meaning by the courts. In *Southern Water Authority v Nature Conservancy Council* [1992] 1 WLR 775 the House of Lords decided that for the purposes of section 28 someone is an occupier if they have some form of stable relationship with the land. As a result, a water authority that carried out drainage works whilst temporarily on an SSSI did not commit an offence under section 28, even though it knew that these were potentially damaging operations and that they would cause significant harm to the SSSI (pointedly, the House of Lords referred to its actions as 'ecological vandalism').

---

47. Upheld on appeal—see [2004] EWCA Civ 1580.
48. WCA 1981, s. 28N, and see also CROWA 2000, s. 75(4).
49. An interesting contrast is Danish law, where compensation is provided 'in kind' by the State buying good farming land and exchanging it for high nature conservation land held by farmers. The NCC cannot do this because it has no power to purchase land which is not designated as an SSSI, unless it is subject to a management agreement, see CROWA 2000, s. 28N and s. 75(4).

A partial remedy to this kind of problem was provided by placing specific duties in relation to SSSIs on water and sewerage undertakers under the Water Industry Act 1991, s. 4, and on the Environment Agency in the Environment Act 1995, s. 8. The essence of these duties is to bring potential problems to the attention of the NCC so that it may give advice (it does not normally offer a management agreement to public bodies, considering that their general environmental duties should suffice to make them act in a responsible fashion).

The CROWA 2000 has strengthened the law in relation to a wide range of public bodies and privatized utilities (in effect superceding the above-mentioned duties), though it is significant that it has done so essentially using a beefed-up version of the advice-based approach described above. New duties are now imposed on all public bodies, including:

- government ministers and departments;
- the National Assembly for Wales;
- local authorities, e.g. local planning authorities;
- statutory undertakers including private utilities.

These public bodies are placed under a duty—similar to the general conservation duties on the EA other than in relation to its pollution control functions (see p. 126)—to take reasonable steps, consistent with the proper exercise of their functions, to further the conservation and enhancement of the features that justified notification of the land as an SSSI. For environmental law, this is quite a strongly worded provision, though it is probably enforceable (by judicial review) in only the most flagrant of cases. Public bodies must also give at least 28 days' notice of any operations likely to harm any feature of special interest within an SSSI. This duty applies regardless of whether the operations are to take place within the SSSI. After notice is given, the NCC can either assent to the works (with or without conditions) or it may refuse to assent. If no assent is given, or it is made conditional, then the public authority must not carry out the works without giving written notice of how it has taken into account the NCC's advice, and giving at least a further 28 days' notice before carrying the works.

These provisions, then, are not intended to prevent harmful activities using licensing-type powers but, in line with the general policy approach, try to create a dialogue between the public authority and the NCC and guidance requires the advice of the NCC to be given due weight and less damaging alternatives to be considered.[50] They mean, though, that an undertaker that is also an owner or occupier is subject to less stringent duties than other owners and occupiers, which as a matter of principle does not seem justified.[51] However, the CROWA 2000 also requires public authorities to minimize damage caused by their operations and, as far as is reasonably practicable, restore any damaged features, which provides a regulatory 'bottom-line' to this advice-focused approach. Breach of these provisions makes a public authority liable to a fine, in the magistrates court, of up to £20,000 or, in the Crown Court, an unlimited fine, and as with offences carried out by owners and occupiers, fines must be set with regard to any benefit accruing.

---

50. *Sites of Special Scientific Interest: Encouraging Positive Partnerships* (DEFRA, 2003), para. 75. On reflexive environmental regulation see Chapter 8 above.

51. That is, the CROWA 2000 has not reversed the *Southern Water Authority* case by deeming undertakers to be 'occupiers'. A pragmatic factor behind this may be the difficulty of notifying undertakers *qua* occupiers.

Similar provisions to these apply to works which, though not undertaken by public authorities, are authorised by them (see p. 817). These provisions would apply, for example, to impacts on an SSSI like increased run-off from a housing development granted planning permission by a local planning authority. However, there is no criminal sanction against any public authority that authorizes works in breach of the Act (though the matter might be referred to Ministers, and there is the option of judicial review).

A notable contrast north and south of the border is that, under section 1 of the Nature Conservation (Scotland) Act 2004, all public bodies must, in exercising their functions, further the conservation of biodiversity consistent with the proper exercise of these functions. In doing so, regard must be had to the Scottish Biodiversity Strategy, which is provided for in section 2. The main point to note here is that this duty is not limited to SSSIs or to any other protected area.

Duties on the general public

A further implication of the restriction in the WCA 1981 to activities by owners and occupiers was that members of the general public were not placed under any legal obliga-tions in relation to SSSIs.[52] This was understandable in policy terms when the main threats were seen as coming from development and adverse land management, but became increas-ingly untenable the more that new threats to SSSIs emerged from activities carried out by outsiders (e.g. bait digging or off-road motorcycling).

The CROWA 2000 now makes it an offence where *any* person intentionally or recklessly destroys or damages an SSSI, or intentionally or recklessly disturbs a site's fauna. However, the person must know that what is destroyed, damaged or disturbed is within an SSSI (which explains why notifications must now also be advertised). It is notable that the offence only extends to the special interest of the land, and does not extend to *any* damage to an SSSI. However, it is clear that the extent of knowledge that needs to be shown is only that the land is an SSSI; members of the public need not know of the specific conservation importance and management requirements of the features of the site that are damaged.

The penalties are similar to those on public bodies. However, an exception is made where the damaging activity is done under planning permission (and other statutory consent if this is needed and validly obtained) or is done in an emergency. One implication of this is that an offence will be committed if a non-owner or occupier does something which a public body has consented but where the public body has not itself complied with the Act, though it must be doubted whether the NCC would ever prosecute in such circumstances.

National habitat law—conclusions

It is wise not to overstate the recent reforms to the law on SSSIs. The policy of the law, it is true, is no longer voluntaristic and there is a more legalistic edge to the legislative scheme. But following CROWA 2000 the main mechanism will remain the use of financial incentives rather than negative controls. The main difference is probably that in reaching agreements, the hand of the NCC has been strengthened by its power to refuse to give its consent to

52. Anyone could commit an offence on a site where a nature conservation order had been made under WCA 1981, s. 29, a position justified by the publicity given to such orders. These were little used.

activities, whereas previously its ultimate sanction was compulsory purchase and the whole context of the law was hostile to this approach. CROWA 2000 has therefore responded to some of the specific, day to day, problems encountered under the previous legislation, and for the first time actually seems intended—and able—to protect sites, but it does not appear to herald a radical change in realigning the balance between the interests of private land-owners and of the public in conserving nature.

Habitat conservation—EC law

In terms of their direct impact on UK conservation law, two EC Directives have had the greatest influence and will continue to be of paramount importance in the future:

- Directive 79/409 on the Conservation of Wild Birds (the 1979 Wild Birds Directive); and
- Directive 92/43/EC on the Conservation of Natural Habitats and of Wild Fauna and Flora (the 1992 Habitats Directive).

Together these contain some important provisions on the protection of individual animals and plants (which we discuss below) but arguably their greatest impact is in relation to habitat conservation. As with sites protected under national law, the key to understanding the law in this area is to keep a clear distinction between the law relating to the designation of sites, and the laws governing the level of protection of these sites.[53] As with SSSIs, the latter are usually weaker and more flexible than the former, especially when it comes to taking economic interests into account.

EC habitat conservation law and policy

A central aim of EC law is to designate a Community-wide network of sites (known as 'Natura 2000') that are important for their conservation importance. These sites are designated, and conserved, under Community law, and the legal tool used is the directive, giving member states like the UK a certain flexibility about the way in which the directives' binding obligations are achieved. The UK approach to implementation—and some of the shortcomings of this—is discussed below, but at this point it is worth emphasizing that habitat conservation law is one of the more contentious areas of Community environmental law.[54] For example, the Habitats Directive was only adopted after many years of argument within the EC, and has been beset by implementation problems. A central reason for this is that, as with environmental impact assessment, EC habitat conservation laws necessarily restrict the extent to which Member States can determine how parts of their territory are used, e.g. for development, a central aspect of state sovereignty. Weighed against this, how-ever, is the view, found in the Habitats Directive, that 'the threatened habitats and species

---

53. The Habitats Directive also includes some more general duties, including a requirement that Member States monitor the conservation status of *all* habitats and species (Art. 11) and a general duty relating to the management of certain important landscape features (Art. 10).

54. E.g. over 50 per cent of EC environmental infringement cases in the last decade related to the Wild Birds and Habitats Directives, see H. Neal, 'Enforcing Biodiversity: A UK and EU Perspective' in J. Boswell and R. Lee (eds) *Economics, Ethics and the Environment* (Cavendish, 2002), p. 56, while historically conservation law has generated more ECJ case law than any other area of environmental law (see, e.g. W. Wils [1994] JEL 222).

form part of the Community's natural heritage',[55] a perspective which justifies both a common degree of restraint amongst the Member States, and common responsibilities,[56] in the interests of nature conservation in the EC.

Designating Natura 2000 sites

A central feature of the Habitats Directive is that it provides for the creation of a coherent ecological network known as Natura 2000. The network will consist of special areas of conservation (SACs), that is sites containing the natural habitat types listed in Annex I of the Directive (e.g. raised bogs) and sites containing the habitats of the species listed in Annex II of the Directive. It will also incorporate, however, the special protection areas classified under the Wild Birds Directive. Hence, Natura 2000 is made up of sites designated under two separate directives with different rules about designation.

(a) Special protection areas

Under the Wild Birds Directive, Member States are required in general terms to take measures, including the creation of protected areas, to maintain a sufficient diversity of habitats for *all* European bird species (Arts. 1, 2, and 3). They must also take special conservation measures to conserve the habitats of the rare or vulnerable species listed in Annex I and of all regularly occurring migratory species (Art. 4). These special measures should include the designation of special protection areas (SPAs) for such birds.

In Case C-355/90 *Commission v Spain* [1993] ECR I-4221 the European Court of Justice held that the Spanish government was in breach of Article 4 by failing to designate an important wetland area, the Marismas de Santoña (or 'Santoña Marshes'), as an SPA. The case established that a Member State is effectively under a duty to designate an area as a SPA (and thus to protect it) if it fulfils the objective ornithological criteria laid down in the directive. Subsequent decisions of the European Court of Justice have followed this strict approach to the duty of Member States to designate SPAs (see Case box 21.1).[57]

CASE 21.1 The *Lappel Bank* case

In Case C-44/95 *R v Secretary of State for the Environment, ex parte Royal Society for the Protection of Birds* [1997] QB 206, the RSPB challenged the failure of the Government to exclude an area known as 'Lappel Bank' from an SPA on the Medway Estuary and Marshes in Kent. The area did not itself host Annex I or migratory species, but its loss would likely affect the overall integrity of the ecosystem.[58] The UK Government argued that economic considerations were relevant, since these

---

55. Preamble. See also the 'Lappel Bank' case, para. 23 (Case box 21.1) and Case C-339/87 *Commission v Netherlands* [1990] ECR I-851 in which the Court speaks of 'common heritage' in relation to the Wild Birds Directive.

56. Common responsibility is seen in relation to the most endangered, or 'priority', habitats and species where, because they are unevenly distributed and are often numerous in less economically wealthy states, the Directive provides for EC co-financing as an exception to the 'polluter pays principle'.

57. Other factors which the ECJ has rejected for not designating SPAs includes the effect of the Common Agriculture Policy (Case C-96/98 *Commission v France* [2000] 2 CMLR 681); waiting for public consultation, and the fact that the land is State owned (Case C-166/97 *Commission v France* [1999] Env LR 781).

58. By holding that the area should have been designated, therefore, the case is a good example of the ECJ in practice taking a precautionary approach to adjudication.

are mentioned in the Directive's preamble and the reason for not designating the area was to allow for economic development of the Port of Sheerness. The RSPB relied on the ECJ decision in the *Santoña Marshes* case to argue that at the designation stage only ornithological criteria were relevant. The ECJ essentially took the latter view of the Directive, holding that the duty to designate sites was an obligation on Member States that was unaffected by economic considerations. Regrettably, however, the House of Lords had refused interim relief pending the ECJ's decision (see [1997] Env LR 431), and the RSPB was unable to make the necessary financial undertaking to the developers (essentially setting compensation money aside) should the ECJ have decided differently. Consequently, the habitat was destroyed by the building of a 22-hectare car park.

In Case C-3/96 *Commission v Netherlands* [1999] Env LR 147 the issue for the ECJ was not the failure to designate a particular site, or part of a site, but rather whether the Netherlands had breached its obligations under the Directive by not designating a *sufficient* number (and total area) of sites. A study in 1989 for the Commission had suggested that 70 sites (covering 797,920 hectares) should have been designated, but in fact only 23 sites (covering 327,602 hectares) had been designated. In finding against the Netherlands, the Court held that the Member States' discretion extended only to the application of objective ornithological criteria in identifying the most suitable territories for the conservation of Annex I species. The Netherlands had not put forward any evidence to suggest that the 1989 study was not a valid indication of how many sites should have been designated, nor could it argue that other conservation methods were being used on undesignated sites. But where there is evidence that the 1989 study is no longer authoritative, then any listing of a site in it cannot be determinative (*Bown v Secretary of State for Transport* [2004] Env LR 26).

(b) Special areas of conservation

Under the Habitats Directive, the procedure for producing the list of SACs is more prescriptive. Member States must send the Commission a list of candidate sites, drawn up by reference to the criteria laid down in Annex III (Stage 1) of the Habitats Directive (e.g. representivity and area). The Commission must then draw up a draft list of 'sites of Community importance', taking account of the criteria set out in Annex III (Stage 2). The Commission adopts a final list thereafter in the light of scientific advice from a committee of independent experts. The Commission will produce a separate list of those sites which host one or more of the *priority* habitat types or species that are identified in Annexes I and II (termed 'priority sites'). There are provisions for a bilateral consultation process between the Commission and a Member State where the Commission considers that a priority site has been left off a Member State's list, with ultimate recourse to the EC Council (Art. 5). Once the Commission has adopted the list of sites of Community importance, Member States are under a duty to designate any site on the list as a special area of conservation. As the table on p. 828 indicates, however, in practice the timetable for each of these stages is running well behind schedule, due mainly to member states' tardiness in submitting adequate lists of candidate SACs.

While case law had made clear that only ornithological criteria were relevant in designating SPAs under the Wild Birds Directive, the Habitats Directive contains a general provision stating that 'measures taken pursuant to [the] Directive shall take account of economic, social and cultural requirements and regional and local characteristics' (Art. 2(3)). Whether this allowed economic considerations to influence the designation of candidate SACs was the subject of a referral from the English High Court to the ECJ (see Box 21.5). In a subsequent case—mirroring its approach to SPAs under the Wild Birds Directive—the ECJ has held that a Member State can breach its obligations under the Habitats Directives if it submits a list of candidate SACs that is manifestly inadequate (Case C-71/99 *Commission v Germany* [2001] ECR I-5811). From an enforcement perspective, taking action against a Member State on these grounds is clearly preferable to taking numerous separate actions, but the Court has not spelt out with any clarity the parameters of 'manifest inadequacy', and important evidential issues remain.

BOX 21.5 **Economic considerations and special areas of conservation**

First Corporate Shipping Ltd ('FCS') is the statutory port authority at Bristol. The Secretary of State was minded to propose the Severn Estuary as a candidate SAC. FCS judicially reviewed this decision and the High Court referred the matter to the ECJ. The question for the ECJ was whether, as FCS argued, economic and other non-ecological considerations mentioned in Article 2(3) of the Habitats Directive were relevant to the designation of candidate SACs. In Case C-371/98 *R v Secretary of State for the Environment, Transport and the Regions, ex parte First Corporate Shipping Limited* [2001] ECR I-9235, however, the ECJ held that Member States may not take economic considerations into account when submitting candidate SACs. The selection criteria laid down in the Directive were exclusively ecological. Moreover, taking non-ecological criteria into account at this stage would frustrate the scheme of the Directive since it would prevent the Commission from drawing up the draft list of sites of Community importance solely on the basis of sites' ecological importance.

Although this was the only point the ECJ was asked to rule on, the Advocate General also considered subsequent stages of the designation process. He noted that under guidance issued in 1996, the Commission must also be sent information about 'impacts and activities in and around the site', which 'may have an influence, either positive and negative, on the conservation and management of the site'. The guidance suggests that, for habitat types, relevant factors 'may include the human activities, both in the site or in its neighbouring areas, that are likely to influence the conservation status of the habitat type, the ownership of the land, the existing legal status of the site . . .' This might suggest, for example, that land owned by a conservation NGO might be preferred to land in multiple profit-making ownership. But the central point should, in principle, be that such activities are material to the designation process only because they are likely to influence the conservation status of the habitat type, not because the activity per se justifies the exclusion of sites *merely because of the economic impact of including them*.[59] The difficulty with the Advocate General's approach is that he refers to economic 'requirements'. This seems to suggest that it is economic *needs*, not *effects*, that are relevant. The ECJ has yet to pronounce on this guidance; if it were to follow the Advocate General's approach on this issue the danger would be that important sites would not be designated because of economic needs, which seems to contradict other provisions of the Directive that require existing consents etc which affect European sites to be reviewed.

---

59. For a comparison see p. 811 on the non-notification of SSSIs where the conservation interest is 'doomed'.

A further issue is the geographic extent of SPAs and SACs. Although the view of the UK Government was that the Habitats Directive, which applies to the 'European territory of the Member States', did not extend beyond the 12-mile territorial limit, the High Court has held that the Directive applies as far as the continental shelf. In a purposive decision in *R v Secretary of State for Trade and Industry, ex parte Greenpeace (No. 2)* [2000] Env LR 221, a challenge to the awarding of oil exploration licences, the Court took into account, among other things, that some distant water species are listed in the Directive.[60]

(c) UK law and policy on site designation

By July 2002, 243 SPAs covering 1,454,500 hectares had been designated in the UK[61] and only a small number of additional sites are designated annually. Following the government's view that the Wild Birds Directive also applies beyond territorial limits, and promised legislation to this effect, there is likely to be an expansion in the number of SPAs in the marine environment.

More problematic has been the designation of candidate SACs. By June 1999, 340 sites in the UK had been submitted to the Commission, with the Government indicating that this marked the end of this stage. Just before a meeting with the Commission and with other Member States in the Atlantic bioregion of the EC, however, the UK agreed to review its selection of SACs and as at July 2002, 571 sites covering 2,389,228 hectares had been submitted.[62] Further candidate SACs have been designated since then (there were 608 by September 2004) and there is the prospect that more sites will eventually be selected, not least in the marine environment, although there is a practical difficulty in designating candidate SACs for species like seals, dolphins and porpoises which range widely.

Designating SACs

Stages in designation	Required by	UK Practice / Comments
Stage 1. UK to submit candidate SACs to the Commission	June 1995	Still being submitted (32 tranches by July 2004).
Stage 2. Commission to identify draft list of sites of Community importance (SCIs)		The Commission's scrutiny of candidate lists for their adequacy means that Stages 1 and 2 have effectively been merged.
Stage 3. Commission identifies final list of SCIs	June 1998	Atlantic Bioregion list (which includes the UK) agreed in December 2004 (excluding marine sites).
Stage 4. UK designates SACs	June 2004 (or earlier if possible)	Timescale uncertain

60. A view criticized by J. Jans (2000) JEL 385. See now the Offshore Petroleum Activities (Conservation of Habitats) Regulations 2001 (SI 2001/1754). There are draft regulations which would extend the Wild Birds and Habitats Directives *generally* to the outer limit.

61. The selection guidelines are available at <www.jncc.gov.uk>.

62. On selection criteria and implementation see JNCC, *The Habitats Directive: Selection of Special Areas of Conservation in the UK*, at <www.jncc.gov.uk/SACselection>.

Designation under the Habitats Directive has been considered on at least three occasions by the UK courts (including the *ex parte Greenpeace (No. 2)* case, referred to above).

In *R v Secretary of State for Transport, ex parte Berkshire, Buckinghamshire and Oxfordshire Naturalists Trust* [1997] Env LR 80 an application for judicial review of the construction of the Newbury bypass was rejected. It was argued that the decision to proceed with the bypass necessarily frustrated any future decision to submit the site as a candidate SAC due to the presence of terrestrial pulmonate snails which, given the importance of the site for the snail, would have been likely. A significant reason why the site was not a candidate SAC was because the government takes the view that all terrestrial sites must first be SSSIs, an approach to implementation of the Directive which has no basis in law and which, as here, has presented problems for a significant minority of sites.[63] But Sedley J could not find any basis for striking down the Government's approach, partly because of efforts by English Nature and the Highways Agency to translocate the snail population off the site. However, he did reach his decision with regret, noting that 'one can appreciate the force of the view that if the protection of the natural environment keeps coming second we shall end up by destroying our own habitat'.

Most recently in *World Wildlife Fund-UK Ltd and Royal Society for the Protection of Birds v Secretary of State for Scotland and others* [1999] Env 632 WWF and RSPB sought judicial review in the Scottish courts of various decisions connected with the exclusion of areas of Cairngorm from a candidate SAC. The area excluded was to be used for a funicular railway to take skiers up the mountain. However, it was held that although choosing sites and drawing boundaries was all part of one exercise, there was room for discretion in the drawing of boundaries so long as the discretion was exercised only on ornithological grounds. But these did not need to be so objective that a court could rule on them. The Scottish Office and its advisers had taken one view, the objectors another. It was not for the judge to say that the official line was wrong. An interesting feature of the case, however, is that the area was excluded from the candidate site in part because it was already developed. This begs questions about the extent to which the presence of existing development can justify not designating areas of otherwise important sites.

The practical implication of this case is that decisions on the drawing of boundaries around sites, unless the boundaries are wholly irrational, are unlikely to be interfered with by the courts, which may lessen the impact of any decision about taking economic considerations into account on designation. Reasoning from the case law of the ECJ on site designation not being manifestly inadequate,[64] the prospect is that the government may, if it chooses, implement a minimalist designations policy involving designating a 'not insufficient' number of sites, and then draw the boundaries around such sites as tightly as the courts hostility to reviewing such decisions as being irrational allows. Needless to say, such an approach would hardly fall within the spirit of the Directive.

63. This is no longer Scottish policy, and some candidates SACs there are not 'underpinned' by SSSI notification. For an interesting (though ultimately unsuccessful) attempt to argue that selection as an SSSI was unnecessary for designation as an SPA see *Fisher v English Nature* [2004] Env LR 7, a case which suggests that in some cases having land designated as an SSSI may now be considered more onerous to the landowner than designation as a European site.

64. Case C-3/96 *Commission v Netherlands* [1999] Env LR 147, and Case C-71/99 *Commission v Germany* [2001] ECR I-5811, discussed above.

Conserving and managing Natura 2000 sites

As originally adopted in 1979, under the Wild Birds Directive once an SPA has been designated, Member States had to take appropriate steps to avoid significant pollution or deterioration of the habitat or disturbance of the birds within it (Art. 4(4)). The meaning of this rather curtly worded provision was considered by the ECJ in Case C-57/89 *Commission v Germany* [1991] ECR I-883, a case about an area known as the 'Leybucht Dykes'. This established that reducing the area of a SPA was only justified on very limited grounds, such as where the works were necessary for reasons of public health or public safety (which was actually the situation in the case itself), and that works could not be permitted for economic or recreational reasons, thus creating a strong presumption against development in such an area. This point was reinforced by the *Santoña Marshes* case, which applied the same test to the deterioration of a site as a result of pollution or other works.

The effect of these rulings, however, was very quickly mitigated by the Habitats Directive. As far as maintaining the conservation status of sites is concerned, this brought the Wild Birds Directive into line with a new regime laid down in Article 6 of the Habitats Directive.[65] (As a matter of national law, the UK also applies these tests to candidate SACs, and as a matter of policy to proposed SPAs, see below.) The details of the new regime are set out in Box 21.6.

BOX 21.6 Conservation of Natura 2000 sites—Article 6 of the Habitats Directive

The protection provided by the Habitats Directive divides between general measures that apply at all times, and measures that apply to specific, future activities

General provisions	Applies to:
Adopt 'necessary conservation measures' such as management plans, and 'appropriate statutory, administrative or contractual measures' (Art. 6(1)) (i.e. the focus is proactive).	SACs only (the only provision that does not apply to SPAs, but there are analogous provisions in Art. 4(1) and (2) Wild Birds Directive)
Take appropriate steps to avoid the deterioration of the sites and significant disturbance of the species for which the areas have been designated (Art. 6(2)).[66]	SACs Sites of Community Importance (SCIs) SPAs Sites subject to the Art. 5 consultation procedure

---

65. A curious effect is that sites which *should* have been designated as SPAs continue to be subject to the old provisions of Art. 4(4), since the less restrictive provisions of the Habitats Directive only apply to areas actually classified as SPAs, see Case C-374/98 *Commission v France* [2000] ECR I-10799. Because, as discussed below, Art. 4(4) has been held to be directly effective, this gives Member States a certain incentive to designate SPAs.

66. Member States must therefore adopt conservation plans *and* ensure that they are implemented. So in Case C-117/00 *Commission v Ireland* [2002] ECR I-5335 the ECJ held that Ireland had in fact to ensure that sheep densities were reduced on heath and bog land to conserve the red grouse.

General provisions	Applies to:
Provisions regarding specific plans and projects	
Subject any plan or project[67] not directly connected with the management of the site, but which is likely to have a significant effect on it, to an 'appropriate assessment' of the implications.[68] The competent national authorities can then agree to the plan or project only if it will not 'adversely affect the integrity of the site concerned' (Art. 6(3)).[69]	SACs SCIs SPAs
If there is no alternative solution, a plan or project may be carried out if there are 'imperative reasons of overriding public interest, including those of a social or economic nature' (Art. 6(4)). But the Member State must take compensatory measures to ensure the overall coherence of Natura 2000.	SACs SCIs SPAs

(a) Significant disturbance

In *Royal Society for the Protection of Birds v Secretary of State for Scotland* [2001] Env LR 19 the granting of licences to shoot barnacle geese, to prevent crop damage, was held to breach Article 6(2) of the Directive. The shooting was to be on an SPA on Islay designated for the conservation of the geese. But on appeal the court held that the Directive's obligation to avoid significant disturbance to the species meant assessing this in relation to the individual Natura 2000 site in question and not, as had been done, their whole area of distribution in the EC.

This important decision illustrates a key feature of nature conservation; that the cumulative impact of decisions with relatively minor impact is as significant as more major interventions, and must be judged accordingly. The prospect of a species or habitat 'dying by a thousand cuts' is thereby reduced. Nevertheless, there are still tricky questions of scale to be considered, and it is not clear that the impact on individual sites will always be determinative. Take the example of 'managed retreat', the policy of not defending the whole coastline from the sea but in certain areas allowing nature to take its course. This policy will mean that in some areas saltmarsh and mudflat habitats (Annex I habitats) will be lost but overall there may in fact be a net gain of these habitats. Reasoning from the *Islay Geese* case above, implementing this policy would be difficult since it might be arguable that each area of habitat lost would violate Article 6(2).[70] Insofar as Article 6(2) is directed at general

---

67. On the meaning of plan or project see Case C-127/02 *Landelijke Vereniging tot Behoud van de Waddenzee, Nederlandse Vereniging tot Bescherming van Vogels v Staatssecretaris van Landbouw, Natuurbeheer en Visserij*, ECJ, 7 Sept. 2004, which relied on the interpretation of 'project' in the EIA Directive (see p. 520).

68. This is not an EIA under the EIA Directive, but shares many similarities. In principle an 'appropriate assessment' is a technocratic assessment focusing on the integrity of the site, unlike an EIA which is a much wider procedure involving mandatory public consultation. But a properly conducted EIA should suffice. There must be a 'probability or a risk' of significant effects, in line with the precautionary principle, see Case C-127/02 above.

69. There must be 'no reasonable scientific doubt' remaining about the absence of such effects, Case C-127/02.

70. Since the law offers no protection to property owners from the consequences of managed retreat (i.e. the law does not require decision-makers to avoid losses to property or property values) this example is often held up by the anti-conservation lobby to illustrate how law favours the interests of 'nature' over human interests. Colloquially it is said here that the 'rights' of nature take precedence over human rights.

conservation policy rather than consented activities on specific sites, however, a distinction might be drawn if the overall purposes of the Directive are achieved.

(b) Alternatives

As with other areas of environmental law, there is provision in the Habitats Directive for justifying harmful activities on the grounds that there is no alternative. Commission guidance suggests that this might involve alternative locations (or, in the case of linear developments, different routes), different scales or designs of development, or alternative processes, while the alternative of doing nothing should also be considered (see Box 21.3). It is also conceivable that a court might demand that the proponent of a project show that the development proposed is the only way to create jobs in an area, and that the expansion of other sectors might not achieve this (it is notable that the Directive does not refer to 'reasonable alternatives'). The main issue, though, probably lies in the quality and quantity of evidence a decision-maker should have in reaching decisions on alternatives. In a case where, on safety grounds, a proposal to re-route a road through a candidate SAC was at stake, the German courts held that, first, the authorities should have shown that it was impossible to make the existing road safer (e.g. by road junctions or adjusted speed limits), and secondly, that the authorities should have presented evidence that the new road would in fact lead to fewer casualties.[71] And a challenge to the exclusion from consideration of expansion at Gatwick airport—because in 1979 the government had concluded an agreement with West Sussex County Council that no further runways would be constructed there before 2019—was successful because the effect of this would mean that a proposal to construct a runway at an SPA in Kent could not consider expansion at Gatwick as an alternative solution, and therefore whether the site in Kent was needed because of imperative reasons of overriding public interest (*R (Medway Council) v Secretary of State for Transport* [2002] EWHC 2516).

(c) Compensatory measures

Even if imperative economic or social reasons justify developing a European site, compensatory measures must be taken to ensure the overall coherence of Natura 2000. But what does compensatory mean in this context? Some examples given by the Commission that might amount to valid compensatory measures are:[72]

- recreating a habitat on a new or enlarged site, to be incorporated into Natura 2000;
- improving a habitat on part of the site or on another Natura 2000 site, proportional to the loss due to the project;
- in exceptional cases, proposing a new site under the Habitats Directive (this is clearly problematic, since the total stock of possible sites will have been diminished).

Also, the result of compensatory measures must normally be operational at the time when the damage occurs on the Natura 2000 site (i.e. there should be no 'time gap').

The idea of compensation is found in other environmental law contexts, e.g. the use of contributions in planning law (see p. 486). The difference here is that compensation must ensure the overall coherence of Natura 2000, so it must go beyond mere mitigation, and

---

71. Federal Administrative Court [2000] 22 *Natur und Recht* 8, 448–53.
72. *Managing Natura 2000 sites: the provisions of Article 6 of the 'Habitats' Directive* 92/43/EEC (2000).

other things that might improve human welfare—like health care or recreational facilities—will not compensate for conservation interests.[73] There has been little case law on this aspect of the Directive, but the approach of the European Commission to the Cardiff Bay barrage scheme (Box 21.7), and of the Secretary of State to the proposed contained port at Dibden Bay (Box 21.8) are instructive.

BOX 21.7 **The Cardiff Bay Barrage**

To promote development, the Cardiff Bay Development Corporation proposed a barrage across the mouth of the Taff and Ely rivers in order to create a large 'freshwater' lake. The barrage, however, would destroy inter-tidal mudflats that hosted internationally important numbers of wintering dunlin and redshank. On economic grounds, the Government excluded the area from the Lower Severn SPA,[74] but it was recognized that under the Habitats Directive there was a need to compensate for the area lost and eventually, following compulsory purchase of farm land, a new wetland reserve on the Gwent Levels was constructed. This, however, was as part of a wider compensation package, a noticeable feature of which was that it did not directly compensate for the loss of habitat for the dunlin and redshank. Instead, two species of ducks were selected for achieving nationally important numbers on the new site, while compensation for the dunlin and redshank took the form of general UK monitoring of their population and undertaking an accelerated programme of designating large numbers of significant estuarine sites for their conservation. Since the habitat loss will be permanent, there is also the problem of ensuring that the compensatory measures can, through adequate funding, continue in perpetuity. It is important to emphasize that the compensatory measures were never subject to judicial scrutiny.[75] Nevertheless, as one commentator put it (R. Cowell [2000] J. Env. Planning and Management 689),

the detailed involvement of the EC added weight to the requirement for environmental compensation but also facilitated the negotiation of loss, by allowing nature to be constructed in substitutable terms, in which 'coherence' and site 'integrity' became defined in terms of what is quantifiable, manageable and creatable.

Balanced against this, however, is the reality that the new site will be actively managed for conservation, unlike the site that was lost.

BOX 21.8 **Dibden Bay**

Associated British Ports sought permission for a deep-water container port at Dibden Bay on Southampton Water. The proposed development would have harmed an SPA, and two candidate SACs. At the public inquiry, English Nature advised that the proposed compensatory measures would not be adequate to off-set the detriment to these sites. The Secretary of State for Transport agreed, and permission was refused. The Secretary of State also followed the Commission's

---

73. Under Electricity Act 1989, sch. 9, reasonable mitigation measures must be provided for, which is obviously a weaker formulation of an ecological compensation duty.

74. In the light of subsequent case law, this was clearly unlawful, see p. 825.

75. Though a public inquiry was held in relation to the compulsory purchase of the farmland.

guidance on alternatives in deciding that these had to go beyond simply considering alternative local sites for the development, and might extend to considering alternative solutions located in other regions or even other countries.

In other jurisdictions, compensatory measures have included the creation of habitat and species 'banks'. For example, under the 1973 US Endangered Species Act, if a landowner hosts specimens of a species in excess of a determined minimum, then these can be banked and either used to off-set damaging development on other parts of their land or even 'sold' to other landowners to off-set their requirements. One reason behind this is that at the margins it is more economic for an existing landowner to conserve than require, say, a landowner which hosts a small number of rare species to establish new habitat for them. As such it is a good example of the use of economic instruments in nature conservation, although there are obviously some differences from, e.g. carbon trading, since the environmental effects of one tonne of carbon being emitted are not locationally specific whereas the ecological value of one hectare of habitat may vary enormously.

(d) Priority sites

When compared with the position set out in the *Leybucht Dykes* case the exception in Article 6(4) lessens the protection that is offered. However, for priority sites Article 6(4) limits the exception to considerations relating to human health or public safety, situations where the impact is beneficial to the environment, and where the Commission has accepted that there are reasons of overriding public interest. It is relevant, therefore, that there are no priority bird species, and thus the stronger controls applicable to priority sites cannot apply to SPAs designated under the Wild Birds Directive.

It was originally thought that the effect of this was to retain the *Leybucht Dykes* position for priority sites. From the handful of opinions that the Commission has given, however, all that it seems to do is use the criteria that apply to non-priority sites (are there alternatives? is the ecological compensation appropriate?) and apply these, albeit rigorously. In other words, economic considerations are reintroduced into the derogations procedure.[76] This seems contrary to the intention of Article 6(4).

(e) Article 6 and direct effect

There are some important issues relating to whether the above habitat conservation provisions are directly effective in national courts (on direct effect see p. 220). In the *Santoña Marshes* case (see p. 825) the ECJ suggested that Article 4(4) of the Wild Birds Directive had direct effect, so the scheme for conserving SPAs would apply to sites that should have been designated. Paragraphs (2)–(4) of Article 6 of the Habitats Directive are in very similar terms, in that they lay down clear requirements, so it is arguable that they are also directly effective. There is a difficulty, however, in that designating SPAs is a matter only for the Member States, whereas the process of designating SACs is more complex and involves the Commission in making a judgment, on the basis of the lists submitted, about which sites to select as sites of Community importance. This will involve discretion, so arguably the provisions for designating SACs are insufficiently precise and unconditional for direct effect. There is

76. P. Nollkaemper [1997] JEL 271; J. Lowther [2003] Env. Liability 155.

also the point that a Member State can, in law, hold out against the designation of a priority site on its territory, since any decision by the Commission to put forward such a site needs a unanimous vote in the Council.

In *ex parte Greenpeace*, the High Court held that 'the [Habitats] Directive does have direct effect', but the reasons for reaching this blunt conclusion are obscure. Elsewhere in the Community, at least some national courts have found Article 6 of the Habitats Directive to be directly effective. The highest administrative court in the Netherlands, for example, has used the purposive route of stating that, although the Commission had not yet published its list of sites, Member States must nevertheless adhere to Article 6 because of Article 10 of the EC Treaty which requires Member States to abstain from measures that could jeopardize the attainment of the objectives of the EC Treaty.[77] On this persuasive reasoning, both the general and specific provisions of Article 6 could be directly effective (in the sense of needing to have useful effect, see p. 222), since Member States and their competent author-ities must not act in a way that would prevent the Habitats Directive achieving its ultimate objectives. This interpretation, which has now been upheld by the Court of Justice,[78] seems to have influenced UK policy, see below.

A final point that can be made here is that an individual or organization might be able to assert that a species protection provision of the Wild Birds or Habitats Directives has been breached. These are described below, but essentially for certain species they provide a level of protection against disturbance and deterioration of breeding and resting places regardless of whether these areas have been designated (see p. 842). This line of argument would avoid having to show that a particular site should, in law, have been designated.

(f) UK implementation

In Britain, the preferred approach to implementing both the Wild Birds and Habitats Directives was initially to provide protection through the town planning and SSSI systems. But there are problems with this approach; first, this did not impose any additional domestic requirements on owners or occupiers to those applicable to all SSSIs; secondly, parts of many SPAs (and also many Ramsar sites) are below low-water mark—where SSSIs cannot be notified—and many estuarine sites in particular are of Community importance. In the light of the *Leybucht Dykes* and *Santoña Marshes* cases it became clear that this approach would be inadequate in legal terms, especially to implement the more detailed requirements of the Habitats Directive. As a result, the Conservation (Natural Habitats etc.) Regulations 1994 (SI 1994/2716) were enacted. The Habitats Regulations apply to 'European sites' and it is important to note what is covered by this definition (see Box 21.9). However, it should also be borne in mind that government has accepted, as a matter of planning policy, that all sites that meet the criteria for designation as an SPA (termed 'potential SPAs') should be treated as if they had been formally designated. For example, in July 1992 the Secretary of State refused planning permission for a number of major developments in North Kent, giving the need to protect a potential SPA as one of the main reasons (see [1993] Water Law 89). This policy—which extends to possible SACs (i.e. sites being considered as candidate SACs but not yet submitted to the Commission)—is now enshrined in planning guidance.[79]

77. *Korenburgerveen* [2002] 29 Milieu en Recht 3, 95–9.
78. Case C-127/02, op. cit., n. 67.
79. PPG9, *Nature Conservation* (1994); *Habitats and Birds Directive: June 2000* (Scottish Executive).

BOX 21.9 **European sites**

The 1994 Habitats Regulations apply additional protections to 'European sites', which are defined as:

- a special area of conservation (once finally designated by government);

- a site adopted by the Commission as a site of Community importance;

- a special protection area designated under the Wild Birds Directive;

- a site subject to consultation under Article 5 of the Habitats Directive (although here the protection is limited, as under the directive, to the obligations under Article 6(2)); and

- candidate SACs submitted to the Commission (until such sites are either adopted as SACs or fail to make the final list).[80]

The Secretary of State draws up a public register of European sites (reg. 11) and notifies them to the NCC (reg. 12), which then notifies local planning authorities, owners and occupiers and anyone else the Secretary of State may direct (reg. 13).

In enacting the Habitats Regulations, rather than remodel the law on nature conservation entirely, a minimalist approach was adopted, and the Regulations simply engrafted onto the existing SSSI and town planning mechanisms the additional protections required by the Directive, and then only where absolutely necessary.[81] The central features of the Habitats Regulations are that:

- if it appears to the NCC that a plan or project is likely to have a significant effect on the site, it must carry out an appropriate assessment and may only give consent for a potentially damaging operation if the plan or project will not affect the site's integrity;

- if the NCC considers that there is a risk that the operation will be carried out without consent, it must notify the Secretary of State, who has the power to make a special nature conservation order. Where such an order is in force, the NCC must carry out an appropriate assessment and *must* refuse consent, unless it is satisfied that the plan or project will not affect the integrity of the site. The owner or occupier may refer the refusal to the Secretary of State, who is given a power to direct the NCC to grant consent. But this power of direction can be used only if: (i) there is no alternative solution; and (ii) the plan or project must be carried out 'for imperative reasons of overriding public interest' (which is defined as in Art. 6(4) of the Directive and includes the more restrictive test for priority sites).[82] If consent is granted, appropriate compensatory measures must be carried out;

- existing consents must be reviewed by the NCC and may be withdrawn or modified without compensation; and

---

80. Added by SI 2000/192, which gives legal force to the policy (since 1994) of treating candidate SACs as European sites.

81. See S. Ball, 'Reforming the Law of Habitat Protection', in C. Rodgers (ed.) *Nature Conservation and Countryside Law*, ed. Rodgers (University of Wales Press, 1996), and C. Rodgers [2001] JPL 265.

82. The UK hosts a number of priority habitat types (such as Caledonian Scot's pine forests and limestone pavements) but only one priority plant species—the liverwort Western rustwort.

- by-laws may be made for terrestrial European sites (and over surrounding or adjoining sites) as if they were national nature reserves.

It is notable that the British position is that whether there are 'imperative reasons of over-riding public importance' will depend on the following guiding principles:

- a need to address a serious risk to human health and public safety;
- the interests of national security and defence;
- provision of a clear and demonstrable direct environmental benefit on a national or international scale;
- a vital contribution to strategic economic development or regeneration;
- where failure to proceed would have unacceptable social and/or economic consequences.[83]

It is also stated that issues of scale will be important in any calculation, i.e. nationally important projects are more likely to pass the threshold than projects of local significance. (On the 'overriding public interest' test see further p. 834.)

The power to make a special nature conservation order is the central feature of the Habitats Regulations, since it provides a form of absolute protection by introducing a mechanism through which a damaging activity may be prevented permanently. However, the success of the whole Regulations (at least in terms of whether the Directive is properly implemented in practice) depends on the willingness of the Secretary of State to make such orders and then to refuse consent where appropriate. Only a handful of orders have been made, however, and it is clear from the whole scheme of protection that the government envisaged special nature conservation orders as instruments of last resort to be used only when absolutely necessary. As with SSSIs, the main mechanism that has been used is the management agreement, and around half of all sums paid out by the NCC has been in relation to European sites. Set against that, reg. 3(2) requires the Secretary of State and the nature conservation bodies to exercise their nature conservation functions 'so as to secure compliance' with the Directive.

The ability to impose permanent bans on operations was a radical departure for UK nature conservation law. With the changes to the law made under the CROWA 2000, however, similar powers are now available for all SSSIs, and the same is also true of many of the other provisions that were once specific to European sites (e.g. the power to make by-laws). Moreover, in certain respects the protection given to nationally important sites is now greater than that enjoyed by European sites, and at the time of writing there are proposals to strengthen the Habitats Regulations in line with the level of protection given to all SSSIs. Amongst other things these would remove the power to make special nature conservation orders, since in effect these would now be redundant.

Some differences would still remain. As noted above, when it comes to considering plans or projects that might harm sites, the law on SSSIs is still not structured in the staged, risk assessment way that the law governing European sites is, and there are no specific legislative objectives that guide decision-making in the way that the concept of 'favourable conserva-tion status' is central to the Habitats Regulations. Also, designation of sites will remain with Ministers rather than the NCC.

83. <www.defra.gov.uk/wildlife-countryside/ewd>; and see *Habitats and Birds Directive: June 2000* (Scottish Executive).

(g) European sites, public bodies, and other regulatory systems

A feature of the Habitats Directive is that, because it places a general obligation on Member States to secure the favourable conservation status of Natura 2000 sites and European protected species, the Habitats Regulations:

- place general duties on all public bodies to have regard to the Directive's requirements;

- (more strongly) specifically require environment and agriculture ministers and the NCC to exercise their nature conservation functions so as to secure compliance with the Directive; and

- also make important amendments to a number of other regulatory systems.

Hence, where a plan or project is likely to have a significant effect on a European site, before granting such things as planning permission or a pollution authorization, the relevant regulatory agency must consult with the NCC and carry out an appropriate assessment of the implications of the plan or project for the site (reg. 48). The agency must agree to the plan or project only if it will not adversely affect the integrity of the site, unless the provisions of regs. 49 and 53 are satisfied (these repeat the exceptions laid down in Art. 6(4) of the Directive). The Secretary of State is also given powers to prohibit the plan or project, either temporarily or permanently. In addition, *existing* permissions, consents and authorizations must be reviewed as soon as reasonably practicable (reg. 50). If the integrity of the site is adversely affected, the agency should use its normal powers of revocation or modification, paying compensation if that would be the usual position. There are also restrictions on a developer taking advantage of a development order in order to carry out development on a European site (regs. 60–64). By way of example, the Environment Agency has issued detailed policy guidance on how it will comply with these duties when making decisions on new or existing EA permissions (such as discharge consents). It is notable that the timetable agreed between the EA and central government for reviewing existing consents envisages that the review process will be completed by 2010, though there will be prioritization within this period.[84]

An example of how these provisions work was the first such action of its kind under the Habitats Regulations. In November 1998 the Secretary of State confirmed the revocation of a planning permission which would have resulted in the loss of 82 hectares of grazing marsh in the Medway Estuary by the disposal of river dredgings. The planning permission pre-dated the classification in 1993 of the Medway Estuary and Marshes as a special protection area.[85] The Minister accepted that there were alternatives to the disposal of the dredged material on the Marshes that would be less damaging to wildlife, and judged that cost factors were irrelevant in reaching this decision.

Under anticipated revisions to the Habitats Regulations, the general duties on public bodies in sections 28G, H and I of the WCA 1981 will co-exist with general obligations and obligations re other consents.

---

84. The guidance, which is divided between a number of documents, is at <www.environment-agency.gov.uk/business>.

85. The same area formed the wider background to the *Lappel Bank* litigation, see Case box. 21.1.

European marine sites

As far as European sites that are marine or tidal are concerned (on the marine limits see p. 828), the Habitats Regulations are at present far more loosely worded. Every public body having functions relevant to marine conservation must exercise these so as to secure compliance with the requirements of the Directive (reg. 3(3)). In addition, more specific powers and duties are laid down (regs 33–36). The NCC must advise other relevant authorities (a term which includes local authorities, the Environment Agency, water and sewerage undertakers, internal drainage boards, navigation authorities, harbour authorities, and fisheries committees) about the conservation objectives for the site and any potentially damaging operations. Any relevant authority *may* then establish a management scheme for the site and the NCC *may* make by-laws under the Wildlife and Countryside Act 1981, s. 37 as if the site were a marine nature reserve. The relevant Minister is given a wide power to make directions to the relevant authorities concerning management schemes. Guidance was published by the Department of the Environment, Transport and the Regions and the Welsh Office in 1998, but it must be doubted whether these vague arrangements, which in the absence of town planning and SSSI controls are the only real powers available below the low-water mark, are adequate to ensure the proper implementation of the Habitats Directive. (At the time of writing there are draft regulations which will extend both the Wild Birds and the Habitats Directives generally to the wider marine environment.) Having said that, marine habitats and species are poorly represented in the Directive itself, which has an almost exclusive focus on territorial and coastal habitats.

EC habitat law: conclusions

In many ways EC law has provided a more rigorous legislative scheme for conserving valued sites and habitats than previously existed. By requiring staged risk assessment when potentially damaging plans or projects are proposed, and by doing so against specific conservation objectives (site integrity, favourable conservation status, etc.), it has undoubtedly raised the status of conservation interests beyond simply being a 'material consideration' in decision-making that can be trumped by competing interests like economic development. This is not to say, however, that nature conservation is elevated above other interests, and the overturning of the *Leybucht* decision by the Habitats Directive is testimony to the Community's desire for a flexible conservation law that will not completely emasculate important national interests especially economic interests.

As a final point about habitat conservation (which applies equally to SSSIs) one commentator[86] has advanced four priorities, summarized as: (1) protect the best; (2) restore the rest; (3) recreate some of what we have lost; and (4) create new habitats for new circumstances. Together with the reforms to the law on SSSIs, EC law has formally strengthened the first of these—protecting the existing 'jewels in the crown' of nature conservation—but comparable legal strides have not been taken in the other areas that need action, in particular to plan ahead to meet future challenges like the effects of climate change. In reality, the challenge of going beyond 'freezing in time' the present pattern of habitat and species distribution is probably beyond the reach of regulatory legal rules, and demands more facilitative responses.

86. M. Avery (2001) ECOS 3.

The protection of individual animals and plants

The common law is generally unsympathetic to wild creatures, according them no rights of their own. However, property rights may usefully be exercised in order to protect them. Wild animals are subject to the qualified ownership of the landowner whose land they are on while, in property law terms, wild plants are part of the land itself. As a result, wild animals and plants have no common law protection against the landowner. But anyone else who kills or injures a wild animal or picks a wild plant commits the torts of trespass and interference with property. Whilst the normal remedy would be damages for the value of the item taken (and thus is of little practical use), it would be possible to seek an injunction to restrain continued breaches. An owner of a nature reserve could in theory use these property rights to protect against threats to the wildlife on it. In addition, a person who uproots plants may commit the crimes of theft and criminal damage, though there is an exception in the Theft Act 1968, s. 4(3) for picking flowers, fruit, foliage, and fungi.

As a consequence of the limitations of the common law, the main protection for wild creatures is statutory. Part I of the WCA 1981 contains the bulk of the law in this area, although the Habitat Regulations 1994 have made some important changes to ensure compliance with the species conservation provisions of the Habitats Directive.[87] Some important changes to Part I of the 1981 Act have been made in England and Wales by the CROWA 2000, and in Scotland by the Nature Conservation (Scotland) Act 2004.

Furthering conservation or preventing cruelty?

The main national legislation (the Wildlife and Countryside Act 1981) combines nature conservation and welfare-oriented provisions and provisions outlawing collecting. But other wildlife statutes, while in various respects furthering conservation, are better seen as primarily concerned with preventing cruelty or unnecessary suffering.[88] The EC, on the other hand, has an ambiguous attitude to adopting legislation aimed at protecting wildlife from cruelty. While there is legislation relating to cruelty to non-Community species such as seal pups,[89] the EC has generally been unsympathetic to adopting welfare-based legislation for wild species within the Community (see Box 21.10) though it has signed up to certain international agreements that contain significant welfare obligations.[90]

---

87. See Arts 12–16, Habitats Directive. There are also numerous pieces of legislation relating to hunted species, such as deer, game birds, wildfowl, rabbits, and of course fish, though in all these Acts protection of individual animals is incidental. Reference to specialist books is recommended.

88. See many provisions of the Conservation of Seals Act 1970 and the Protection of Badgers Act 1992, and the Wild Mammals (Protection) Act 1996.

89. See, e.g., a number of relatively early measures relating to things like restricting the import of pelts from animals caught by leghold traps (reg. 3254/91), and banning certain imports of seal skins (Directive 83/129) and whale products (reg. 348/81).

90. E.g. the 1973 CITES Treaty and agreements in relation to fur traps, discussed in Nollkaemper (1996) JEL 237; S. Harrop and D. Bowles [1998] JIWLP 64; S. Harrop (2000) JEL 333.

BOX 21.10 **The EC and wildlife cruelty—the case of zoo animals**

EC proposals dating back to the early 1990s advocated a Directive alleviating cruelty to wild animals in zoos. In 1999, however, the Directive eventually adopted—after a complete change of position by the UK—was concerned with the contribution of zoos to public education about biodiversity conservation, implementing in part the 1992 Biodiversity Convention. This is in line with the 1997 Amsterdam Treaty, which—under Protocol 33 and Declaration No. 24—limits the EU's regard to animal welfare to agriculture policy, transport, internal market, and research. The exclusion of EC environmental policy indicates that this provision applies only to farm, not wild, animals. Thus, while many of the provisions of EC wildlife law may in practice prevent suffering to endangered species, it is clear that, as things stand, preventing animal cruelty is only an incidental consequence of EC conservation law.

Species conservation offences—national law

Although they have differing or overlapping rationales, the chosen method of control under statute for both conservation and cruelty-based provisions has traditionally been to establish criminal offences of interfering with specified wildlife.

The strongest provisions relate to **wild birds** (a legacy of the historical influence of the voluntary bodies here, but also a result of the Wild Birds Directive, which requires certain legislative protections) in the sense that they are reverse listed—i.e. the 1981 Act applies unless the birds are exempted in the Schedules covering pest and quarry species. Specifically, it is an offence (ss. 1(1) and (2)):

- intentionally to kill, injure or take any wild bird;
- intentionally to take, damage or destroy a nest whilst it is in use or being built;
- intentionally to take or destroy eggs;
- to be in possession of a wild bird or egg (live or dead).

There are also offences—both for reasons of avoiding cruelty and preventing over-exploitation—relating to indiscriminate methods of killing or taking wild birds and the sale or advertising for sale of wild birds (ss. 5 and 6). For these purposes a bird is presumed to be wild unless proved otherwise. It is notable that birds are divided into two categories, with rarer birds being listed in Schedule 1 to the Act and receiving slightly greater protection. Thus, intentionally or recklessly disturbing a Schedule 1 bird on or near its nest, or disturbing its dependent young, is an offence (WCA 1981, s. 1(5) as amended by CROWA 2000, s. 81, sch. 12, para. 1).

Animals and plants, on the other hand, are covered only if specifically listed in other Schedules. Regarding animals, schedule 5 to the 1981 Act includes all bats, reptiles and amphibians, but only the rarest mammals (e.g. otters and red squirrels), fish, butterflies, and other forms of life. For those animals that are protected, there is a range of offences similar to those for wild birds. It is an offence intentionally to kill, injure, or take any scheduled wild animal, or to possess any such animal, live or dead, or any part of one. Additional offences relate to the sale or advertisement for sale of wild animals, illegal methods of killing or taking any wild animal, and illegal methods of killing or taking those animals listed in sch. 6

(see respectively WCA 1981, ss. 9(1), (2), and 5 and 11(1) and (2)). There is also an offence of intentionally or recklessly damaging, destroying, or obstructing any structure or place used for shelter or protection by a schedule 5 animal, or disturbing such an animal whilst it is occupying such a structure (s. 9(4)). For species that habitually return to the same breeding site, such as bats, this criminalizes damage or destruction even if the site is not presently occupied. For dolphins, whales, and basking sharks, which do not have a 'shelter' as such, the CROWA 2000 now makes their intentional or reckless disturbance an offence, the intention being that this will apply to inappropriate use of things like motorboats and jet skis (see Box 21.12) (s. 9(4A)).

For **plants**, it is an offence for anyone other than the owner, occupier, or other authorised person intentionally to uproot any wild plant. In addition, it is an offence for anyone (i.e. including the landowner) intentionally (but not, it must be noted, recklessly) to pick, uproot or destroy any of the numerous species of rare wild plants listed in schedule 8. The sale or advertisement for sale of schedule 8 plants is also an offence (s. 13). In some cases a plant can be subject only to these latter provisions on sale rather than the full protection of schedule 8 listing; a current example is the bluebell.

Species conservation offences—EC law

In addition to the above, the Habitats Regulations create some further offences in relation to the animals and plants defined as 'European protected species', which are listed in schedules 2 and 4 to the regulations respectively (see Box 21.11).

BOX 21.11 **European protected species**

Animals	Plants
Bats, Horseshoe (all species)	Creeping Marshwort
Bats, Typical (all species)	Early Gentian
Common Otter	Fen Orchid
Dolphins, porpoises and whales (all species)	Floating-leaved water Plantain
Dormouse	Killarney Fern
Great Crested Newt (or warty)	Lady's Slipper
Large Blue Butterfly	Shore Dock
Marine Turtles	Slender Naiad
Natterjack Toad	Yellow Marsh Saxifrage
Sand Lizard	
Smooth Snake	
Sturgeon	
Wild Cat	

To ensure compliance with the EC Habitats Directive, the Government chose to set out the requirements of the Directive in full, rather than amend the existing legislation. The result is that the regulations cover similar ground to the WCA 1981, but with some occasional subtle changes in wording to make the offences wider than normal. The key provisions make it an offence:

- deliberately to capture or kill any wild animal of a European protected species;
- deliberately to disturb any such animal;
- deliberately to take or destroy eggs from the wild of such an animal;
- to damage or destroy a breeding site or resting place of such an animal;[91]
- deliberately to pick, collect, cut, uproot or destroy a wild plant of a European protected species;
- to keep, transport or sell such a plant, or animal, whether live or dead.

Compared with the WCA 1981, some features of the Habitats Regulations are worth highlighting, including the general preference for prohibiting 'deliberate' rather than 'intentional' acts, which may mean that criminal intent (i.e. *mens rea*) need not be shown. There is also much greater protection given to breeding and resting sites because (subject to any licence that is given, on which see below) the prohibition in the Habitats Regulations is not qualified and is therefore a strict liability provision, whereas in the WCA 1981 any interference with a place of shelter or protection must be intentional or reckless for it to be unlawful. Also, the only prohibition relating to species habitats in Part I of the WCA that does not need the action to be 'intentional' or 'reckless' relates to disturbing a listed animal species whilst it is *occupying* a place of structure or protection, whereas the Habitats Regulations cover damage or destruction of breeding or resting places *at any time*.

BOX 21.12 **Do not disturb**

Birds, animals and plants can be harmed in many ways from the accidental to the intentional. One of the offences that is commonly provided for covers disturbing a species, whether intentionally, deliberately, or recklessly, or simply without qualification. For example, bats roosting in such typical places as attics, outbuildings, caves, and belfries cannot be disturbed by rebuilding or timber treatment unless the NCC is notified in advance and allowed to offer advice.[92] On the other hand, laws often provide defences to these offences where the harm that is caused is incidental to some other lawful activity. What, then, is unlawful disturbance?

In Case C-103/00 *Commission v Hellenic Republic* [2002] ECR I-1147 Greece was held to have failed to prevent deliberate disturbance to the endangered loggerhead turtle. The breach was both a failure to enact suitable legislation and a breach in fact. Although areas had been designated for strict protection, mopeds, pedalos, and small boats were being used on or close to key breeding beaches. Clearly any disturbance to the turtles was unintentional but incidental to

---

91. The Directive refers to 'deterioration or destruction' (Art. 12(1)(d)). There are draft proposals to add the carrying out of an act which results in the deterioration of these places.

92. For all these offences the maximum penalty is £5,000. In WCA 1981, ss. 10 and 16 there are similar provisions relating to defences and licences to those available for wild birds.

tourist activity. But the Court of Justice held that Greece had failed to prevent acts of deliberate disturbance, though only because they were prohibited and because there were notices at the beaches referring to the area being protected. So if these actions had been lawful, e.g. authorized development rather than the illegal buildings on some of the beaches (which was found to breach the Directive's provisions on deterioration and destruction of breeding sites, which do not need to be done deliberately) the Court may not have held that the disturbance was deliberate. The Court also seemed to stress that Greece had failed to prevent *repeated* breaches of its rules, suggesting that a one-off incident might not amount to disturbance. That the number of loggerhead turtle nests had not decreased over the previous 15 years was irrelevant to these findings, a good example of how securing implementation involves attention to long-term legal and institutional structures as well as to results. This case is also an excellent example of the shortcomings of international conservation law. Since its inception the parties to the 1979 Berne Wildlife Convention had discussed this problem, but moral pressure had failed and the file was eventually closed when the European Commission took action under the Habitats Directive.

This interpretation of the Directive focuses on the illegality of the harmful action, and mirrors the approach taken in the national courts. In *R v Secretary of State for Trade and Industry and others ex parte Greenpeace Ltd* [2000] Env LR 221 Greenpeace argued that granting oil exploration licences would breach the Directive because of the impact on whales, dolphins and porpoises, and that this disturbance would be 'deliberate' because it was foreseeable. The High Court, however, interpreted 'deliberate' as the opposite of 'incidental', and held that exempting the incidental results of lawful operations like authorized oil exploration, as the Habitats Regulations do, was allowable. This approach is somewhat questionable. First, the Directive sets out an exhaustive set of criteria for judging when Article 12 can be derogated from and the Habitats Regulations require any balancing of conservation and other interests to be done by the NCC or agriculture Ministers. Secondly, as a matter of policy should it not be for conservation agencies to determine what is acceptable incidental interference, rather than effectively leave this to other bodies that authorise potentially harmful activities? Finally, the view of DEFRA at least is that lawful activities will not give rise to deliberate disturbance unless such disturbance was known to be the inevitable consequence. This clearly is a much softer line than that taken in the High Court in *ex parte Greenpeace*.

Two further points are worth making. First, 'disturbing' a species is not controlled just by species conservation offences but also by habitat conservation provisions (see p. 831), hence there may be more than one way to address harmful disturbance. Secondly, in ecological terms species disturbance (in the sense that species are exposed to stresses that induce evolutionary responses) is seen as an important factor in population dynamics, so while the law prevents unlawful *human* disturbance, there may be value in 'natural' disturbances such as forest fires.

Exceptions, defences, and licensing

A feature of species conservation offences is the numerous exceptions and defences for acceptable activities, many of which require permission or a licence from an official body. For example, game birds (i.e. pheasant, partridge, grouse, and ptarmigan) are excluded from the protection provided by the WCA 1981, apart from anti-cruelty measures relating to illegal methods of killing or taking them (s. 27). A long list of further exceptions also applies if a licence has been obtained from the appropriate official authority. It includes such things as the carrying out of research, educational activities, conservation work, and ringing of birds (s. 16), and most licences are granted for these relatively uncontentious activities which are aimed at benefiting species conservation.

The most problematic issue, however, is the extent to which species may be killed or harmed if this is done to further some legitimate social objective like agriculture or development (or even the conservation of other species). There are two dimensions to this.

(a) Species licensing

The first relates to those situations where a licence is sought from the appropriate authority either to control a so-called 'pest' species, or to facilitate development. Historically, the law has always allowed for the destruction of species considered to be pests, and in early times even *required* landowners to do so (e.g. in Scotland, the law required wolf hunts, which clearly proved successful). Under the WCA 1981, it is a defence for any owner or occupier or other authorized person to show that killing or injuring is necessary for things like crop protection, disease prevention or the protection of public health and safety, and prior permission is not needed (s. 4—birds; s. 10(4)—animals listed in sch. 5). For listed animal species, however, the defence does not apply if, beforehand, it was apparent that the harmful action would be necessary and a licence was not applied for or had yet to be determined.[93]

This policy preference for licensing—and away from blanket criminal offences and defences—is typical of the recent approach of the law, in part as a response to the Wild Birds and Habitats Directives. Hence the WCA 1981 no longer lists any bird species that owners, occupiers or authorized persons may, without further permission, kill, take, or destroy their nests or eggs (s. 2(2) and sch. 2 Part II). Instead, listed pest species of birds may be interfered with under general licences issued by environment and agriculture ministers, but only for the reasons given in the licence (e.g. public health, crop protection, etc).[94] The policy approach, therefore, is a more administrative one. Indeed, virtually any prohibited activity affecting wild birds may be licensed, but only if there is no other satisfactory solution (s. 1A(a)).

For European protected species, a licence can be granted for preventing serious damage to crops etc. from such species and, more generally, can also be granted for imperative reasons of overriding public interest, including those of a social or economic nature (Habitats Regulations, reg. 44).[95] But it must be shown that there is no satisfactory alternative and that the authorized action will not be detrimental to maintaining the favourable conservation status of the species in its natural range. This is an important legal baseline notable by its absence in the WCA 1981, but exactly what it means is unclear. Until 1999, where development impacted on a European protected species the practice was to issue licences under reg. 44(2)(c) i.e. 'conservation' licences, thus allowing for development to go ahead if the species was in some way conserved (e.g. translocated off-site, an approach which is often used where great created newts are found on development sites) but following a reasoned opinion from

---

93. A circuitous way of saying, in effect, that these provisions are obsolete.

94. *RSPCA v Cundey* [2002] Env LR 17 (a good example of a voluntary body prosecuting wildlife crime).

95. See *Newsum v Welsh Assembly* [2004] EWHC 50, and analysis by J. Holder at (2004) 16 JEL 377. See now Newsum v Welsh Assembly [2005] Env LR 16 (Court of Appeal).

the Commission, since 2000 the 'overriding public interest' derogation must now be used. Because of the policy judgements to be made in situations involving development, central government is now the licensing authority (though the NCC advises on the impact on favourable conservation status).[96] This way of proceeding was challenged by the European Commission in an action against the UK on the grounds that the practice for potentially harmful development—under which the decision to grant planning permission is taken first, followed by the application for a licence being considered by government—suggested that 'licences seem to be issued as a formality after development consent for a construction or infrastructure project has already been given, and do not appear to involve a careful weighing of the arguments for and against allowing damage to occur'. However, in Case C-434/01 *Commission v UK* [2003] ECR I-13239 the Court of Justice rejected the Commission's complaint because the licence issuing authority is formally required to consider strictly the conditions contained in regulation 44, and that this was sufficient performance of the Directive's provisions. The mere suggestion that licences were being issued with, in effect, one hand tied behind the decision-maker's back, was not enough (a good example of law looking to matters of form over substance).

Nevertheless, guidance in Scotland and Wales seeks to tighten this by requiring planning authorities to consider the derogations in Article 16 of the Directive, that is, coupling the decisions on planning permissions and on licensing (which will put an added strain on local authority resources) but formally the position in England is as yet unchanged.

(b) 'Incidental result of a lawful operation'

The second main dimension to the conflict between species conservation and other activities is that, under the WCA 1981, it is a defence where the action is an 'incidental result of a lawful operation and could not reasonably have been avoided'.[97] This type of defence would clearly apply to such events as unavoidable road accidents (a serious problem for otter conservation) but its application to activities where damage to a species is knowable in advance and yet still authorised is more problematic. This is because the defence does not require that harmful activities are reasonably avoided but simply that, in carrying out any lawful operation, the consequence is one that cannot reasonably be avoided. This, obviously, is a rather different matter but if, say, bats were discovered on a site after planning permission had been granted but the NCC was not consulted there would be a strong case to say that the developer was not protected by this defence (unless it could be shown that the NCC's advice could not have prevented the bats from inevitable harm). Controversially, the defence has found its way into the Habitats Regulations in relation to European protected species (see Box 21.11). This creates a potential loophole to the strictness of the species conservation provisions found in the Habitats Directive, since it seems to bypass the key safeguards there, and it must be doubted whether relying on this defence would be lawful if, aware of the presence of a European protected species, activities compromised a species' favourable conservation status in its natural range.

---

96. In Scotland, licensing had always been handled by central government.

97. WCA 1981, ss. 4(2)(c) (birds), 10(3)(c) (sch. 5 animals), 13(2) (plants). Similarly see Protection of Badgers Act 1992, s. 6(c).

Enforcing wildlife crime

As the above indicates, the piecemeal approach to species conservation in Part I of the WCA 1981, and the relevant provisions in the Habitats Regulations, contain numerous criminal offences. The specific penalties for these cannot be covered exhaustively, but some general observations may be made. First, the previous distinction that the WCA 1981 made between ordinary penalties, and 'special' penalties in relation to offences involving schedule 1 bird species, has largely been removed with the higher penalties applying to most offences. Secondly, following the CROWA 2000 most of the offences in Part I of the WCA 1981 can now be punished both by fines (of up to £5,000) and by the possibility of six months imprisonment.[98] This brings the WCA 1981 into line with other conservation and cruelty laws like the Protection of Badgers Act 1992 and the Wild Mammals (Protection) Act 1996 which have always been enforceable through custodial sentences. It also moves species conservation law into line with other conservation and environmental crimes, though maximum fines relating to habitat conservation laws are significantly higher. Thirdly, however, there have as yet been no changes to the penalty provisions of the Habitats Regulations, with the paradoxical result that offences involving European protected species presently attract lesser penalties than under the WCA 1981. (There is greater consistency re sentencing powers, and higher fines generally, in Scotland.)

Increasing the penalties for species offences goes some way to elevating the status of these sorts of crimes. But there are many practical and legal problems with enforcing wildlife crime. First, many offences are simply very difficult to detect, especially if they take place in remote locations. Secondly, despite most police forces having wildlife liaison officers, wildlife crimes are not recordable crimes. This means that solving them will not appear in the headline crime statistics, so police forces may be disinclined to devote appropriate resources to tackling them. For this and other reasons, the favoured policy approach is to try to share the burden of enforcing wildlife crime between the police, the NCC and organizations like the RSPB and the RSPCA, showing a continuing reliance being placed on voluntary bodies in species conservation (see also Box 9.6).[99]

Integrative approaches

At one level, current policy tends to isolate conservation from the pressures of the wider economy, without doing anything to lessen the forces creating those pressures. This is reflected in the conservation 'stamp collecting' approach of designating protected sites. Yet the most apparent trend in modern conservation law and policy has been integration. This is reflected in provisions like Article 10 of the 1992 Biological Diversity Convention, which require the integration of biodiversity conservation into national decision-making. While this is a largely exhortatory provision, there are a number of ways in which an integrative approach to nature conservation can be taken, for example, integrating nature conservation objectives into other fields such as agriculture policy through financial incentive schemes, which we discuss elsewhere (see p. 868), and even the limited approach

---

98. Recent cases are at <www.defra.gov.uk/paw/prosecutions>.
99. See the Partnership for Action Against Wildlife Crime, <www.defra.gov.uk/paw>.

of placing obligations on a wide range of public decision-makers[100] can be considered a (limited) integrative measure.

Biodiversity action plans

The 1992 Convention on Biological Diversity aims to conserve biological diversity through a variety of means including species and habitat conservation. Under Article 6 of the Convention the contracting parties must, in accordance with their particular conditions and capabilities, develop or adapt national strategies, plans and programmes for biodiversity conservation, and integrate the conservation and sustainable use of biological diversity into relevant sectoral or cross-sectoral plans, programmes and policies. This is one of the few provisions of the Convention that does not require action only 'as far as possible and as appropriate', a general feature of the Convention that clearly weakens its effectiveness. Nevertheless, it goes beyond a protected area approach to conservation, and in the UK has given considerable impetus to the development of wider conservation initiatives.

Under Article 6, the UK Biodiversity Action Plan 1994 was produced, an important document guiding subsequent policy in this area. This in turn has led to the development of action plans for, to date, 391 species of plants and animals and 45 habitats. The scheme is intended to increase public awareness and involvement, but also to develop costed targets for key species and integration between public sector agencies. An important tool used is to seek 'champions' for species, especially from the voluntary and private sectors, as well as government funding, but where these have come forward they have tended, understandably, to be interested in sponsoring charismatic species like otters and butterflies. Alongside the changes to SSSI law in the CROWA 2000, these plans are the most important development in national conservation policy since the 1981 Act, though they are not immune to charges of being overly bureaucratic and species-centred (and have not yet actually rescued a single species).

Biodiversity action plans have in effect been given legal recognition by section 74 of the CROWA 2000 which now places general duties on government Ministers and departments to have regard to the purpose of biodiversity conservation in accordance with the provisions of the Biodiversity Convention, and requires the Secretary of State to list species and habitats of principal importance for biodiversity conservation (e.g. red squirrel, otter, corncrake) and take reasonably practicable steps to further their conservation or promote this by others. Implementing the species and habitats action plans will be one means of fulfilling this duty, but their listing under section 74(2), while giving biodiversity action plans a legal underpinning, does not confer statutory status on the plans themselves. Moreover, it is not obvious how such an general obligation on the Secretary of State will be enforced, if at all, but its very existence may alleviate some of the funding problems the NCC experienced in implementing biodiversity action plans.

CHAPTER SUMMARY

1   Nature is valued for a wide range of reasons, but a central policy choice lies in deciding which species and habitats should be conserved and at what cost.

100. See p. 821 (duties on public bodies regarding SSSIs), and compare the duties on government and other public bodies to implement the Habitats Regulations 1994 (p. 838).

2   The administration of nature conservation law is primarily the responsibility of specialist agencies with a scientific focus. These bodies have greater legitimacy in identifying species and habitats for special protection than they do in making trade-offs between conservation and other socially valued interests, which has more of a political dimension.

3   Nature conservation laws often divide into the use of criminal offences to conserve protected species, and administrative and fiscal controls to conserve habitats. In both respects, however, licensing regimes are increasingly subject to overriding conservation objectives.

4   There are species conservation offences not just about direct interference (e.g. unlawful killing) but also about disturbing habitat, so it is difficult to draw a bright line between laws about conserving species and conserving their habitats. Often both will apply to an activity such as potentially damaging development.

5   The most important protected area designations are found at national and EC level. At national level, the law governing sites of special scientific interest (SSSIs) has recently been strengthened under the CROWA 2000, shifting policy from voluntarism to regulated site management, backed by binding prohibitions. But there remains an emphasis on voluntary agreement being reached between the NCC and landowners, facilitated by the use of financial incentives for positive conservation benefits.

6   There remains no overarching objective for the legislation on SSSIs. By contrast, EC law is directed towards maintaining or restoring important habitat types and habitats of species at a favourable status. This requires stability of a species or habitat's range over the long term, but adverse affects on individual sites cannot be marginalized because of lack of harm to a species' conservation as a whole.

7   At national level, there is a lot of flexibility in striking the balance between conservation and other interests. When activities damaging to a species are being licensed, there is a modest requirement that no other satisfactory solution exists. Habitat damage can be consented by the NCC, subject only to its general statutory duties, but if planning permission is required then damage may be authorized subject to government guidance. This requires conservation impact to be a material planning consideration but falls some way short of a strong presumption against development.

8   Under the Habitats Directive, striking the balance on Natura 2000 sites between nature and other interests is a more tightly defined process based on a staged risk assessment and the provision of (environmental) compensation. For the most endangered species and habitats, economic reasons cannot justify damaging activities.

9   A key challenge for nature conservation law and policy is integration. This can range from long-standing practices (such as notifying planning authorities of SSSIs in their area) to more modern approaches such as placing general conservation obligations on public bodies or requiring action plans for key species and habitats to be drawn up.

Q   QUESTIONS

1   What should the objective of what we call nature conservation law be? To protect animals, plants and habitats? To conserve them? To restore them? To enhance them? What are the implications (for regulators, landowners and others) of taking each of these approaches?

2   Should the law focus so much on the endangered and the rare (in comparison most pollution controls apply to the whole of an environmental media, or even the environment as a whole)?

3 Who should pay for conserving nature? Is the 'polluter pays' principle applicable to nature conservation?

4 Does the law on SSSIs now steer the right course between seeking cooperation with landowners through financial incentives, and preventing damaging activities?

5 Compare and contrast the law relating to SSSIs with that relating to 'European sites'. You might consider here:

a any legal purposes or objectives (or otherwise);

b the designation of sites;

c conserving such sites.

Does either regime strike the right balance between nature conservation and economic interests? (You may find that competing theories of sustainable development (see p. 65) provide a useful framework here.) Consider both the terrestrial and marine environments.

6 The Habitats Regulations impose a very heavy administrative burden on the NCC and the various regulatory agencies which are required to review consents. There is evidence that the extra attention paid to European sites means that, in practice, the resources available to protect other sites like SSSIs is being downgraded.[101] Advise Government on what to do.

7 A ferry operator is planning to expand operations. On the land to be developed—which is in an area of regionally high unemployment—there are a number of otter holts. Some of the land is an SSSI (though not because of the otters), but none of the land has been designated as a European site. The local planning authority grants planning permission for the development, subject to a condition requiring artificial otter holts to be built on another site and the otters translocated. A local wildlife organization seeks to review the grant of planning permission on the grounds that, under the EC Habitats Directive:

a the land should have been designated as a European site;

b the planning authority should not have authorised development that would adversely affect the otter holts on the site;

c the 'compensation' measures fell short of what was required, because the general state of the habitat surrounding the new holts was not as favourable for otters; and

d the planning authority did not have regard to the otter being a priority species.

Advise the wildlife organization. What further information would you need?

 FURTHER READING

There are many more provisions aimed at conserving species and habitats, at national EC and international level, than the illustrative selections in this chapter. For these, C. Reid, *Nature Conservation Law* (2nd edn, Edinburgh: W. Green, 2002) provides the best (and most up to date) overview (with far greater coverage of Scots law, though not the 2004 Act). Useful articles include K. Last, 'The Wildlife and Countryside Act 1981: Has it Made a Difference?' (1999) JEL 15 and D. Brock, 'Is nature taking over?' [2003] JPL Supp 50, the latter questioning whether the balance in the legal protection of conservation interests has now tipped too far towards 'nature' at the expense of humans. A really excellent article which critiques wildlife law for focusing too much on what are really welfare con-

---

101. Some accounts for the NCC seem to bear this out, see e.g. Countryside Council for Wales, *Annual Report 2000–01*, 31.

cerns at the expense of more ecological approaches, and which criticises the failure to conserve the 'commonplace' in biodiversity is S. Harrop, 'Conservation regulation: a backward step for bio-diversity?' (1999) 8 Biodiversity and Conservation 679.

International Conservation Law

Our omission of international conservation law can be rectified by the relevant chapters of Birnie and Boyle, *International Law and the Environment* (2nd edn, Oxford: Oxford University Press, 2002), which also contain a useful account of the development of scientific thinking and policy at international level (and how the law has often lagged far behind these), or P. Sands, *Principles of International Environmental Law* (2nd edn, Cambridge: Cambridge University Press, 2003). Other useful sources are M. Bowman and C. Redgewell (eds) *International Law and the Conservation of Biological Diversity* (The Hague: Kluwer, 1996) and L. Guruswamy and J. McNeely (eds) *Protection of Global Biodiversity: Converging Strategies* (Durham: Duke University Press, 1998), the latter contain-ing an excellent essay by M. Sagoff arguing that intrinsic worth is the most compelling reason to value nature. The wide-ranging Convention on Biological Diversity is very clearly explained, article by article, in the *Handbook on the Convention on Biological Diversity* (London: Earthscan, 2001), pro-duced by the Convention's secretariat, which also comments on further agreements between the contracting parties. There is also a special issue of the Review of EC and International Environmental Law (11(1) (2002)) concerned with biodiversity. Finally, for many years S. Lyster's *International Wild-life Law* was the leading work in this area, and a new edition of this, by Bowman, Davies, and Redgewell, is keenly awaited.

Conservation policy

On conservation generally, M. Jeffries, *Biodiversity and Conservation* (London: Routledge, 1997) is a very useful and concise introduction to the area. A stimulating book with a specific focus on the UK, written by a former Chief Scientist at the NCC who had a special involvement in the drawing up of the current SSSI criteria, is N. Moore, *Bird of Time: The Science and Politics of Nature Conservation* (Cambridge: Cambridge University Press, 1987) although the definitive insiders account is now P. Marren, *Nature Conservation: A Review of the Conservation of Wildlife in Britain, 1950–2001* (HarperCollins, 2002), a forthright book which gives colour to most of the legal provisions, and many of the legal cases, considered here. Of many other good books (which often consider landscape and countryside issues as well) D. Evans, *A History of Nature Conservation in Britain* (2nd edn London: Routledge, 1997), nicely captures the development of the conservation movement, while W.M. Adams, *Future Nature* (rev. ed. London: Earthscan, 2003) is a hugely engaging attempt to think critically about what conservation means in the modern world. Useful book chapters on conservation policy include S. Young, 'Running Up the Down Escalator: Developments in British Wildlife Policies after Mrs Thatcher's 1988 Speeches' in T. Gray (ed.), *UK Environmental Policy in the 1990s* (London: Macmillan, 1996) and J. Dixon, 'Nature Conservation' in P. Lowe and S. Ward (eds), *British Environ-mental Policy and Europe* (London: Routledge, 1998).

M. Shoard, *The Theft of the Countryside* (London: Temple Smith, 1980), is a book which caused enormous controversy when it first appeared in the run-up to the Wildlife and Countryside Act 1981, and it provides a polemical view of what was (and arguably still is) happening in the countryside. G. Harvey, *The Killing of the Countryside* (London: Jonathan Cape, 1997) examines wider issues of countryside destruction and attacks the Common Agricultural Policy as one of the primary causes of excessive farming and loss of biodiversity. Because of the close links between conserving the natural and cultural heritage, reference should also be made to the further reading to Chapter 13.

WEB LINKS

Law and guidance at national level can be found via DEFRA <www.defra.gov.uk>—in particular the pages of the wildlife and countryside division—and its devolved counterparts. Information on nature conservation policy, and some of the differences across Britain, can be found through the web sites of the national agencies: <www.english-nature.org.uk>, <www.ccw.gov.uk>, <www.snh.org.uk>, and <www.ehsni.gov.uk>, and of the Joint Nature Conservation Committee <www.jncc.gov.uk>, the latter now containing a lot of information about how Natura 2000 sites are selected in the UK and also, at <www.jncc.gov.uk/idt/>, the first UK report on implementation of the Habitats Directive. The European Commission maintains a site that has both the main directives and key policy guidance, such as on implementation of the Habitats Directive <europa.eu.int/comm/environment/nature>, while the leading international conservation treaties are gathered together at <www.biodiv.org/rioconv/websites.html>.

Voluntary organizations play an important role in developing and enforcing nature conservation law. Special mention should be made of WWF and of Friends of the Earth, both of whom were instrumental in campaigning for reform to the laws on SSSIs, and the 'wildplaces' section of <www.foe.co.uk> has information about the location of SSSIs according to postcode (something that English Nature has been advised by Ministers to do).

Landscape management

This chapter looks at the legal protection and management of various features of the British countryside: its landscape, trees, forests, and hedgerows. (We do not consider specific protections of human artefacts such as archaeological sites.) This involves applying some controls you have already looked at, in particular town and country planning law. Sometimes this gives added levels of protection, but many activities which shape the countryside are not covered by planning law. Nature conservation designations are also important here, since what humans see as landscape features may also be the habitat of protected species of plants and animals. But effective landscape management relies heavily on using economic instruments, especially grants and subsidies to landowners. For all these reasons, you will get most from this chapter if you have already looked at Chapters 8, 13, and 21, and if you bear in mind that this topic demands that you think about the full scope of the regulatory toolbox.

At the end of this chapter you will:

✔ Appreciate the particular legal challenges in managing natural landscapes.
✔ Understand the main landscape designations and how they work in practice.
✔ Understand the main ways that positive assistance is given to promote landscape management.
✔ Know how traditional legal approaches are used to protect forests, trees and hedgerows.

Introduction

Effective landscape management involves a number of different things. As regards landscape there is the restriction of urban expansion and urban development in the countryside; the preservation of the particular rural character of an area; and the protection of distinctive landscapes or landscape types. With trees, forests, and hedgerows the focus is generally on smaller, sometimes individual, environmental features, the key problem for the law being in grappling with two familiar and related difficulties—controlling destructive, rather than constructive, acts and establishing adequate control over natural things. In both cases, however, protection and management pose some difficult problems. The two main reasons are that, first, the shape of most of what is to be protected is the result of hundreds of years of human intervention. Secondly, landscape management is inherently subjective, which makes it difficult to decide what exactly to preserve and why (see Box 22.1). Some of the difficulties here can be seen in the statement of the (then) Countryside Commission that future generations must be passed a national inheritance 'with all its richness intact'.[1] However obscure this objective, it must surely be preferable to the view, expressed by 90 per cent of respondents to a survey in 2003 by the Countryside Agency, that it is important 'to keep the English countryside the way it is now', which fails to recognise the changing nature and perception of the countryside, and changing priorities. Landscape plays a role in constructing cultural identity, and this is a key motivation behind the Council of Europe European Landscape Convention (see below). This might form one part of a more 'bioregional' approach to decision-making, in which nature conservation would also play an important part. As discussed briefly in Chapter 21, nature conservation and landscape issues are increasingly being integrated, following many decades of relative isolation.

BOX 22.1 Landscape, values and communities—the case of wind farms

Wind farms are an increasingly common feature of the countryside. They are often located in exposed areas of high landscape value. This has led to conflict between those who stress the contribution of wind energy in reducing greenhouse emissions, and those who place greater weight on the importance of not 'spoiling' the landscape. But this clash of opinion is complicated by various factors. Wind farms are a further change to land continuously altered by humans over the centuries, and it is a subjective judgement to say that a wind turbine is less appropriate in a national park, or less beautiful than, a poorly insulated 'chocolate box' cottage. Also, those who object to wind turbines may do so on grounds unrelated to landscape, e.g. that energy efficiency or reduced demand for electricity would be preferable, or even that the need to address climate change is so acute that only more drastic steps like a revival of nuclear energy will be effective.

We saw in Chapter 3 the role that values play in this kind of decision-making, and in particular how possible clashes between individual and collective perspectives (NIMBY-ism, or 'not in my back yard') may colour attitudes to polluting or obtrusive development. There is survey evidence, however, indicating that wind farms are viewed in a relatively positive light by local residents. In a 2003 poll of residents near to the larger wind farms in Scotland,[2] 20 per cent of respondents said that their local wind farm had a broadly positive impact on the area, compared with 7 per cent who said it had a negative impact, while most respondents said that the impact was neutral. Those living closest to the wind farms were even more positive about their impact. And while 27 per cent thought that there *would* be landscape problems, only 12 per cent said that the landscape had *actually* been spoiled. A majority of respondents (54 per cent), and an even higher percentage of those living closest supported significant expansion of the wind farm. This is a good illustration of the extent to which environmental values are not static but change, not just through debate but also experience. Note that, partly for planning reasons, much development is likely to take place offshore.

---

1. *Protecting our Finest Countryside: Advice to Government* (1998).
2. MORI Scotland, *Public Attitude to Windfarms* (Scottish Executive Social Research, 2003).

Regulatory mechanisms

Three main methods of control may be discerned:

(a) One is to rely on the town and country planning legislation to control developments in the countryside in the same way they are controlled in towns.

(b) A second is to impose special protections in designated areas, or in relation to designated features such as hedgerows. In practice, these added protections often tend to stem from the town and country planning system as well, though there are some that do not.

(c) A third main mechanism is to utilise grants and other incentives to ensure the proper care of the countryside or natural features, again with special schemes available in selected areas. Economic tools are widely used in the promotion of desirable objectives such as tree planting and hedge laying.

A particular feature of the third mechanism is the reliance on voluntary controls, rather than on compulsion. Since most countryside land is privately owned it is perhaps inevitable that positive action, as much as restrictive controls, will be used.

The international and EC dimension

Compared with most other topics covered in this book, international and EC law has had relatively little direct impact on national law and policy relating to landscape management. This is undoubtedly because of the often local and subjective nature of this topic, although some conventions have in recent years included landscape features within a general definition of 'the environment', as is the case with the 1991 Espoo Convention on Environmental Impact Assessment in a Transboundary Context and the 1992 Transboundary Watercourses Convention. Attempts to conclude a global convention on forests have so far been unsuccessful, and only a Non-binding Statement of Forest Principles was agreed at the Earth Summit in 1992, although there are emerging signs that a global treaty may now be more acceptable to countries such as Indonesia which strongly resisted such a development at Rio, and in 2000 the United Nations Forum on Forests was created.

The 1972 World Heritage Convention, however, is a notable example of an attempt to use international law to protect national features of global significance. As well as cultural treasures, the treaty aims to protect natural heritage of 'outstanding universal value' for aesthetic or scientific reasons. The treaty is unusual since states are obliged not only to protect sites which are eventually accepted onto a 'World Heritage List', but are also under general obligations to protect any areas worthy of inclusion on such a list. States must keep under review heritage covered by the treaty, and protect it even if it is not accepted on to the list, although it is unlikely that any decision about an area forming part of the world heritage would be reviewable by the courts (for an Australian example see *Queensland* v *Commonwealth* (1989) 167 CLR 232). The added protection of being listed is that sites are eligible for assistance from the World Heritage Fund, run by UNESCO. The list is currently biased in favour of cultural heritage, and the 25 sites for which the UK is responsible are also mostly built heritage, e.g. Canterbury Cathedral.

At the European level, there is no EC legislation relating directly to landscape. The Environmental Impact Assessment Directive (85/337) does require information about the

---

CASE 22.1 *Coal Contractors v Secretary of State for the Environment* [1995] JPL 421

Planning permission was applied for an open cast coal mine very near to Hadrian's Wall, a World Heritage Site (WHS). Although there is no planning policy on WHSs, there is a Ministerial statement to the effect that inappropriate development should be avoided at such sites. Applying his own policy, the Minister decided that to grant planning permission would adversely affect the wider setting of the WHS, even though the effect on the landscape was—for topographical reasons—not adverse. Permission was therefore refused. WHS designation can therefore provide extended landscape protection in and around such sites, but notably WHS designation added an extra dimension to the decision beyond just the landscape impact of the development. Note also that the Secretary of State found that there 'was no complete embargo on any particular form of development within a WHS'. Ultimately, it was a matter of political judgement and discretion whether the development was approved, and if the decision had been to grant planning permission this decision, while it might have been politically (and even diplomatically) unpopular would almost certainly have been unchallengeable.

---

effects of projects on landscape and cultural heritage to be assessed, but the impact of the EC is most closely felt through the Common Agricultural Policy (note that forestry is not included in this) and from EC Regulations aimed at integrating agricultural and environmental objectives (see below). Under the Habitats Directive (92/43), Member States must encourage in their land-use planning and development policies the conservation of linear landscape features, such as hedgerows, which play an important part in biodiversity conservation. This obligation marks an important break from a pure protected areas approach to conservation (on which see generally Chapter 21) and emphasizes the links between nature conservation and landscape management that are increasingly being made.

In 2004 a Council of Europe European Landscape Convention entered into force. This has more general application than the World Heritage Convention, going beyond protecting the 'jewels in the crown' but, depending on one's perspective, either puts rather too general, or too wide-ranging, obligations on the parties. The UK has not signed the Convention.

Town and country planning

The starting point for protecting the countryside has always been the development control system. But it has never proved particularly successful because, despite its name, it has always had an urban bias. There have been very few adaptations of the basic structure to cope with countryside matters. Indeed, it is commonly referred to as the 'town planning' system, the countryside aspect being forgotten.

There are a number of reasons for this. A major one is the history of the system, which had a consequent effect on the nature of the legal mechanisms that were adopted. The town and country planning system developed in 1947 was specifically designed to meet predominantly urban problems, such as community layout and design, industrial location, post-war reconstruction, public health and overcrowding, and transportation changes. As far as the rural environment was concerned, the main policy was the protection of the countryside against urban creep and expansion. The legal mechanisms that were adopted were thus mainly negative, such as the need for planning permission, and did not reflect the need for positive management in the countryside.

In addition, in 1947 there was perceived to be little need to control developments in the countryside, since it was generally considered that landowners and farmers had done a good job in shaping the landscape, and in any case agriculture itself required protection after the rural depression of the 1930s and the Atlantic Blockade of the Second World War. Agriculture and forestry, the two main activities likely to have an impact on the landscape, were granted generous exemptions in the legislation which, despite some minor changes, still remain today.

As a result there are distinct limitations on the use of development control in the countryside, and its most important role is in controlling new buildings and structures:

- Many rural activities which have a significant impact on the landscape do not constitute development. For example, afforestation or deforestation, hedgerow or stone wall removal, ploughing, and the cultivation of new crops (such as oil seed rape) are all entirely excluded from the development control system.

- The Town and Country Planning Act 1990, s. 55(2)(e), provides that a change of use to agriculture or forestry is not development. Whilst it is obvious that this covers a change from an urban to a rural use, in landscape terms it is more significant that this paragraph excludes from development control a change from unused land (often of high nature conservation or landscape value) to agriculture or forestry, or from agriculture to forestry, or from forestry to agriculture, or from one type of agriculture or forestry to another. 'Agriculture' is defined very widely in the Town and Country Planning Act 1990, s. 336, to include such diverse things as intensive livestock production, fish farming, horticulture and extensive grazing.

- Further exemptions are set out in the Town and Country Planning (General Permitted Development) Order 1995 (SI 1995/418) (the GPDO) sch. 2, under which blanket automatic planning permissions (permitted development rights) are granted. For example, the GPDO exempts the construction of fences and walls up to two metres in height, and temporary uses up to 28 days per year (although not war games, motor sports and clay pigeon shooting within SSSIs).

- The GPDO, sch. 2, parts 6 and 7 provide permitted development rights for a wide range of agricultural and forestry operations, such as new roads, buildings, drainage works and excavations, subject to some generous limitations on size and height (e.g. each building may be up to 465 square metres in area and 12 metres in height). There are other, more technical limitations, such as that the erection or alteration of structures for the accommodation of livestock, or for storing slurry or sewage sludge, within 400 metres of non-agricultural dwellings or other buildings is not permitted under the GPDO.

- A final limitation on the usefulness of the development control system in the countryside is that this is a political system. Decisions are made by local planning authorities and are likely to reflect the economic needs and policy preferences of local residents, although reference must always be made to Planning Policy Statement 7, *Sustainable Development in Rural Areas*, which sets out general government planning policies towards the country-side. Local authorities may also underestimate the importance of a local area in national terms.[3]

BOX 22.2 **Landscape and spatial planning**

As noted in Chapter 13, a central aim of the reforms under the Planning and Compulsory Purchase Act 2004 was to make planning more integrative. In relation to landscape, some steps towards this aim were already provided for by placing statutory duties on public bodies to have regard to the main landscape designations (see pp. 861 and 865). This is fleshed out by planning guidance under which, in the revision of regional spatial strategies, regional planning bodies are expected to demonstrate how they have taken the statutory purposes of the National Parks and AONBs into account, including significant indirect effect on a National Park or the Broads (but not AONBs) on the landscape setting (PPS11, para. 2.9). Regional spatial strategies should also take into account agriculture (but not, for some reason, forestry) (PPS11, para. 1.3). The 2004 Act does not therefore bring agriculture and forestry within the planning system in the sense of requiring planning permission, but it does go some way towards integrating them into the wider planning of development. Whether these concerns will be integrated in practice remains to be seen; in its 23rd Report on *Environmental Planning* (Cm 5459 2002) the RCEP was critical of how effective local planning authorities have been in doing so.

Extra protections under planning law

In some circumstances, there are extra protections provided by the town and country planning system in the countryside:

- The extent of development permitted under the GPDO is limited in national parks, the Norfolk and Suffolk Broads, areas of outstanding natural beauty, conservation areas and any area specified by DEFRA under the Wildlife and Countryside Act 1981, s. 41(3) (collectively these areas are known as Art. 1(5) land). Whilst the limitations are not great, this does mean that stricter controls apply to such things as extensions to houses and other buildings.

- A system of prior notification applies to farm or forestry developments otherwise permitted by the GPDO, sch. 2, parts 6 and 7. This means that 28 days' prior notification of the proposed development must be submitted to the local planning authority, which may then impose conditions relating to the siting, design and external appearance of the development in the light of the likely effects on the surroundings. In making this decision, the local planning authority must take into account not only the visual aspects of the development, but also the desirability of preserving ancient monuments and their set-

---

3. These same limitations explain why the network of SSSIs is not protected properly by controls dependent on the town and country planning system (see p. 817).

tings, archaeological sites, the setting of listed buildings and sites of recognised nature conservation value. Since 1999, prior notification procedures now also apply to mobile phone masts, although only ground-based masts (as opposed to antenna and masts on buildings) require publicity, which—along with the sums of money offered—helped explain the preference for masts on buildings like schools and churches (until the Stewart Report in 2000 stressed the need for caution in relation to the impacts on children, from which point no new masts have been erected on schools).

- As a matter of policy, the local planning authority may impose restrictive conditions on activities requiring permission. For example, specific design criteria are commonly imposed where there is a local style. It may also make non-statutory designations of such things as sites of high landscape value in its development plan.

- An Article 4 direction may be imposed under the GPDO, requiring planning permission to be sought for something that would otherwise be granted automatic permission (see p. 469). For example, this mechanism was used on Halvergate Marsh in the Norfolk grazing marshes in 1984 to prevent agricultural drainage and ploughing damaging the landscape importance of the area, though in confirming the direction, the DoE stressed that the main purpose was to compel the farmer involved to accept a management agreement on the land. Since Article 4 directions entail the payment of compensation by the local planning authority if planning permission is then refused, their use is rare (even though the cost is sometimes grant-aided by central government agencies).

It is important to note that green belts, creatures of planning policy but never planning law, are primarily intended to act as a brake on suburban growth. There is a policy presumption against major development in green belts, unless 'very special circumstances' dictate otherwise (see Planning Policy Guidance Note 2, *Green Belts* (1995)), which around many urban areas entrenches the divide between urban and rural. While green belts are not designated on nature conservation or landscape grounds, they undoubtedly contribute indirectly to these objectives.

The Countryside Agency

In England, landscape matters were for many years the responsibility of the Countryside Commission, originally created in 1949 as the National Parks Commission. In April 1999, a new Countryside Agency was formed by changing the name of the Countryside Commission to the Countryside Agency, and then transferring certain functions of the Rural Development Commission (RDC) to the new Agency (see SI 1999/416). The result is that the functions of the Countryside Agency are still found in sections 1 and 2 of the Countryside Act 1968, which provide that the Agency has responsibilities for the conservation and enhancement of natural beauty in England and the provision of recreational activities. These amenity functions distinguish it from English Nature. Constitutional matters and funding are governed by schedule 13 to the Wildlife and Countryside Act 1981, which provides that its members are appointed by the Secretary of State and its finance is provided by central government grant aid. The Agency has few operational powers, apart from the designation of national parks and areas of outstanding natural beauty, but it has an important role in providing advice and finance in relation to its objectives. It is important to note that the creation of the Countryside Agency is bound up with the establishment of Regional Development Agencies in England, under the Regional Development Agencies Act 1998, which have inherited rural regeneration functions from the RDC. Equivalent responsibilities to those of the Countryside Agency are carried out in Scotland by Scottish Natural Heritage and in Wales by the Countryside Council for Wales, although neither body has assumed the rural development remit of the former RDC.

All the landscape agencies, and all Ministers, government departments and public bodies, must have regard to the desirability of conserving the 'natural beauty and amenity' (in Scotland, the 'natural heritage'; see Countryside (Scotland) Act 1967, s. 66) of the countryside (Countryside Act 1968, s. 11). These are broad-ranging duties, applying to the functions of these bodies under any enactment, but their usefulness is limited by the weakness of their formulation.

Under the Natural Environment and Rural Communities Bill, an integrated agency (to be called Natural England) is to be established, bringing together English Nature, certain functions (mainly related to landscape conservation) of the Countryside Agency, and most of the functions of the Rural Development Service, to begin in 2007.[4] The rest of the Countryside Agency will become the Commission for Rural Communities which will have more of a rural advocacy function.

Landscape designations

Apart from the limited protection accorded to landscapes by planning law, there are a number of designations of land that may be made. However, these depend ultimately either on the town planning system, or on voluntary powers. There are few, if any, compulsory powers to support landscape protection.

In line with this voluntary philosophy, there is a power for any local planning authority to enter into a management agreement with any owner of land for conserving or enhancing its natural beauty or amenity, or for promoting its enjoyment by the public (Wildlife and Countryside Act 1981, s. 39). Such an agreement is grant aided by the Countryside Agency, but under the Countryside and Rights of Way Act 2000, the Countryside Agency and CCW also have powers under this section to enter into management agreements, and a conservation board for an area of outstanding natural beauty (see below) may do so for land in its area (WCA 1981, s. 39(5), as amended). Unlike the position for agreements made in relation to SSSIs, the financial guidelines laid down in the Wildlife and Countryside Act 1981, s. 50 do not apply to agreements made under section 39 (see p. 820 on these guidelines). In practice, local authorities have been reluctant to use these powers, because of concerns that they may impose on them uncertain long-term burdens, and a good illustration of their weakness was the reluctance of local authorities to enter into management agreements offered by the Forestry Commission when the policy of the time was to sell off Forestry Commission land.

---

4. In practice, the constituent bodies are already working together in partnership in anticipation of this change.

BOX 22.3 **Countryside designations: benefit or burden?**

A feature of key landscape designations is that they may actually *increase* pressure on the land designated. Particularly with national parks, it is at least debatable whether the designation increases some of the adverse effects associated with high tourist demand, or simply reflects already existing demands, but what is clear is that many visitors are drawn to areas in part because of their designation. There is a clear contrast here with nature conservation designations, which generally do not have this potentially damaging 'honey pot' effect. On the other hand, nature conservation designations tend to depress the value of land, whereas land values inside national parks tend to be higher than those immediately outside the park. One historic consequence of the depressed land value of nature conservation sites was, paradoxically, to expose them to particular development pressures. A designation such as an SSSI could prevent planning permission being granted to the landowner for a profitable development, but this would not prevent permission being granted by local or central government for public developments like infrastructure projects. In these cases, the public interest would weigh more heavily, and designated land would have the advantage that the cost of compensating affected landowners was relatively low (because landowners would only receive compensation for the value of their land in its undeveloped state).

National parks

National parks in Britain do not equate to the concept of a national park used in most other countries. Instead of being wilderness areas with few, if any, inhabitants, they contain land on which large numbers of people live. They are effectively working environments. The aim of national park designation is to plan and manage the area so as to create a balance between recreation, amenity, wildlife, and economic development. Land ownership is unaffected by designation, although various public bodies are given powers to purchase land, and in practice much of some parks is in the ownership of a public body, or of the National Trust.

(a) General objectives and duties

National parks were first provided for in the National Parks and Access to the Countryside Act 1949. This Act still provides the basic structure of the legislation on national parks, although it has been much amended, especially by the Countryside Act 1968 and the Environment Act 1995, Part III. The purposes of national parks were originally stated in the Hobhouse Report (*National Parks in England and Wales*, 1947), and set out in the National Parks and Access to the Countryside Act 1949, s. 5, in terms of two general objectives: the preservation and enhancement of the natural beauty of the areas; and the promotion of their enjoyment by the public. In recognition of the way that attitudes towards the national parks have changed since 1949, the Environment Act 1995, s. 61 substitutes a new section 5 which sets out somewhat wider purposes:

   (a) conserving and enhancing the natural beauty, wildlife and cultural heritage of the areas . . .; and

(b) ... promoting opportunities for the understanding and enjoyment of the special qualities of those areas by the public.

BOX 22.4 **The separation (and integration?) of landscape**

The historian TC Smout has written that 'Every age constructs nature in a different way. In the seventeenth century, use and delight were very difficult to separate. By the end of the eighteenth, they occupied different spheres in the mind. By the twentieth, they were in frequent conflict.'[5] This nicely captures the way in which, historically, landscape (and nature conservation) emerged as discrete concerns. This came from a separation in how the countryside was seen from, initially, a place where work and leisure were inextricably bound together, to a position where the aesthetic and leisure interests of one section of society often clashed with the economic interests of other groups. In thinking about the objectives of national parks (and also AONBs, see below), and how these are prioritized, it is worth reflecting on this historical development.

A new section 11A(2) of the 1949 Act also gives statutory effect to the so-called 'Sandford principle', which is that where there is a conflict between purposes (a) and (b), then greater weight should be attached to purpose (a). The balance between environmental, amenity and economic factors is also made explicit in a new section 11A(1), which requires national park authorities to seek to foster the economic and social well-being of local communities within the national park, albeit in the context of pursuing the purposes set out in section 5.

The impact of the changed purposes is reinforced by section 11A(2) which also requires all public bodies and statutory undertakers to have regard to the new purposes when exercising or performing any functions affecting land in a national park. A review in 2002 by DEFRA of National Park Authorities, however, suggests that these provisions are not adequately applied in practice, because of a lack of awareness, understanding and compliance, both on the ground and at departmental level.[6]

The criteria for designation mirror the twin statutory objectives. Responsibility for proposing and designating a national park originally lay with the National Parks Commission, which designated the 10 existing parks in the 1950s. This responsibility has now devolved to the Countryside Agency and the Countryside Council for Wales.

Currently there are 10 national parks in England and Wales, covering 9 per cent of the land area and with almost 250,000 permanent residents. The parks are the Peak District, the Lake District, the Yorkshire Dales, the North York Moors, Northumberland, Snowdonia, the Brecon Beacons, the Pembrokeshire Coast, Exmoor, and Dartmoor. In addition, the Broads Authority was established by the Norfolk and Suffolk Broads Act 1988. This has a similar constitution and powers to the national parks, with the inclusion of powers over navigation and water space. For the purposes of most legal protections it is treated as a national park.

Latterly, the Countryside Commission/Agency had taken the view that further designations of national parks in England would devalue the concept (although in 1998 they

---

5. T.C. Smart, Nature Contested (Edinburgh: Edinburgh University Press), p. 18.
6. *Review of English National Park Authorities* (DEFRA, 2002), para. 18, see [2002] JPL 1334.

eventually supported designation of the New Forest). In September 1999 the Government announced that it was asking the Countryside Agency to consider designating national parks in the South Downs and the New Forest. The latter is now a national park, and designation of the former is at an advanced stage. What is interesting about the recent development is that, despite responsibility for proposing and designating parks resting with the Countryside Agency, what has happened is that central government, whose confirmation and funding is needed, has been able to initiate the designation process by political direction. The rationale for these new parks appears to be slightly different from the existing parks. For example, there was already a New Forest Heritage Area in which, as a matter of government policy, the same planning principles that govern development in national parks were applied. Proposals for these parks have required extensive publicity and consultation and public inquiries, after which the designation will be confirmed by the Secretary of State.

Until recently there were no national parks in Scotland, although there were designations with a roughly similar impact. This has now changed with the National Parks (Scotland) Act 2000, which enables the Scottish Parliament to propose and designate national parks.[7] The procedure for designation is somewhat different. In addition to being satisfied about the outstanding national importance of the area's natural heritage, or natural and cultural heritage combined, Ministers must be satisfied that the area has a distinctive character and coherent identity, and that designation would meet the special needs of the area and would be the best means of ensuring that the aims of the National Park are achieved in a co-ordinated way. (Proposing a National Park is a power, not a duty.)

The statutory objectives of Scottish National Parks are similar to those in England and Wales in that they include conservation of the natural and cultural heritage, and public understanding, enjoyment and recreation. But they also include the promotion of the sustainable use of the natural resources of the area, and the promotion of sustainable social and economic development of the communities of the area. As with the 1949 Act, there is a version of the 'Sandford principle' in that where there is a conflict of aims, it is the conservation aim which must be given greater weight. So far, Loch Lomond and the Trossachs, and the Cairngorms, have been designated, following advice from Scottish Natural Heritage.

(b) Administrative responsibilities

The national parks are the only areas where a new institutional structure has been created in an attempt to protect the countryside. However, control remains essentially local, since the Countryside Agency and the Countryside Council for Wales have no executive functions. Under section 63 of the Environment Act 1995, the Secretary of State has power to establish by order a national park authority in the form set out in schedule 7. This has altered the previous arrangements whereby each national park was administered by an authority run by a committee of the relevant county council or a separate, autonomous board. This has had the effect of creating autonomous local authorities for national parks with primary responsibility for planning functions.

The national park authorities were formally established on 1 April 1997. Schedule 7 provides that a national park authority is subject to most legislative provisions affecting local authorities, including those on access to meetings, and the jurisdiction of the

---

7. Notably, the DEFRA review (note 6 above) contains many proposals which would adapt policy and governance in line with the approach taken in Scotland.

Commissioner for Local Administration (the Ombudsman). Following a late amendment to the 1995 Act, for national parks in England the balance between the various appointees to the authorities was altered, a change that led to accusations from some quarters that national park authorities will be turned into centralized quangos. (In Wales, half the members are appointed by the National Assembly, after consultation with the Countryside Council for Wales, and half appointed by the constituent local authorities.) One half plus one of the members are appointed by the constituent county and district councils, with the remainder appointed by the Secretary of State, after consultation with the Countryside Agency. Of those Secretary of State appointees, half minus one must be members of parish councils in the national park. The total number on the authority and the exact number of appointees from each local authority is set out in the specific order establishing each national park authority. The authority then elects its own chair and deputy chair. The position in Scotland is slightly different; there is an equal division between appointees nominated by the Scottish Parliament and the relevant local authorities, but only after at least 20 per cent of each governing board has been directly elected at local level.

In England and Wales, under section 66 of the Environment Act 1995 national park authorities must prepare a national park management plan, though they may adopt existing management plans (made under the Local Government Act 1972). There are provisions for regular review (Environment Act 1995, s. 66). The management plan performs a different strategic function from the purely planning-based development plan, covering wider management policy issues. In Scotland, there is a similar duty on National Park Authorities to produce plans which, following consultation, are approved by Ministers (National Parks (Scotland) Act 2000, s. 12). Unlike in England and Wales, a more explicitly integrative approach is taken, and a plan must set out and coordinate 'the functions of other public bodies and office-holders so far as affecting the National Park' (s. 11), and all public bodies must have regard to these plans in exercising their functions as these affect national parks (s. 14). This puts on public bodies a more specific obligation than the general duty on public bodies in section 11A(2) of the 1949 Act.

There are powers to provide funding for the national park authorities. Under the Environment Act 1995, s. 72, the relevant Secretary of State has a wide discretion to make grants to a national park authority, whilst section 71 empowers the authorities to issue levies to the constituent local authorities. 75 per cent of funding comes from central government. Grants from the Countryside Agency and the Countryside Council for Wales for works and schemes are normally payable at a higher rate in a national park than they are outside.

(c) Controls on development

Protection of the parks has always been strongly tied to the town and country planning system. The national park authority is designated the sole local planning authority for its area. One exception concerns tree preservation orders, where the district council retains concurrent jurisdiction with the national park authority. Strategic planning in national parks centres around the national park development plan that was first required by the Planning and Compensation Act 1991 (as with all plan-making in national parks, this requires consultation with the Countryside Agency or the Countryside Council for Wales).

In Scotland, planning functions are not automatically transferred to National Park Authorities, and decisions are taken on a park-by-park basis. In Loch Lomond and the Trossachs, all development planning and development control functions (and TPO functions) have been transferred to the National Park Authority with the exception of structure plan functions. For these functions, responsibility continues to be exercised by local authorities, in consultation with the National Park Authority. In the Cairngorms, however, the major difference is that development control functions have not been transferred, although the National Park Authority has the power to call in, for its own determination, planning applications which raise a planning issue of general significance to the National Park aims. In both parks, however, where responsibilities have been transferred to a National Park Authority, these are exercised by a committee which must have a majority of members who are either directly elected, or who are members of a local authority. These provisions are aimed at addressing concerns—voiced in England and Wales—that planning functions in national parks lack a sufficient local democratic mandate, and a consequential tension between local authorities and national park authorities.

As far as the substantive detail of planning law is concerned, apart from the limited restrictions referred to above, the main protection lies in the formulation and application of sensitive policies for the protection of the park through the planning process. But national parks are certainly not inviolable, as the siting of Fylingdales Early Warning Station, Milford Haven Oil Terminal, and numerous quarries in the Peak District illustrate.

BOX 22.5 **Planning policy, national parks, and AONBs, and low-impact living**

Until recently policy guidance stated that 'major development should not take place in the National Parks . . . save in exceptional circumstances', and that it must demonstrably be in the public interest. The public interest was to be assessed by considering the national need for the development; the impact on the local economy of permitting or refusing consent; the cost of alternatives; and detrimental environmental effects (para. 4.5, PPG 7).

An illustration of exceptional circumstances justifying development is *Dartmoor National Park Authority v Secretary of State for Transport, Local Government and the Regions* [2003] EWHC 236. The National Park Authority opposed a planning application for what the applicants described as 'low impact sustainable development'. This involved the erection in woodland of a number of 'benders', mostly for living in. The Inspector thought the proposed development would seriously harm the character of the woodland, contrary to the development plan. However, strong material considerations amounting to exceptional circumstances justified granting planning permission. Key factors were the experimental, and temporary, nature of the development ('The principles of sustainability behind the experiment are central to Government policy and it is therefore of importance that they are tried and tested in a practical way'); the need to live in the woodland—which is normally resisted—being central to the applicants' philosophy; and the positive management of the wood that would result (including replacing non-native species with indigenous trees, to make the woodland more in keeping in landscape terms). A challenge to this decision in the High Court was rejected.

Since 2000, following an answer to a Parliamentary question, the same guidance was applied to major developments in AONBs (and is now found in para. 22, PPS 7 (2004), which repeats the tests mentioned above), another example of the many and varied ways in which rules of environmental law emerge.

Areas of outstanding natural beauty

Areas of outstanding natural beauty (AONBs), first provided for under the 1949 Act, are now designated, under the Countryside and Rights of Way Act 2000, s. 82, solely for their natural beauty, with the objective of conserving and enhancing these features. Even though in landscape terms they are meant to be the equivalent of national parks, by comparison with the parks they are little known and understood. Unlike national parks, there is no duty to consider their designation and many of the powers available within them are optional for the local planning authority. Indeed, writing in 1980, Marion Shoard described them as the 'Cinderellas of the landscape designation system'.[8]

AONBs have a number of similarities with national parks, and since the changes made under the Countryside and Rights of Way Act 2000 the similarities in regulatory approach are even stronger. For example, there are now general duties on all public bodies as there are with national parks (s. 85). AONBs tend to be extensive areas: 41 have been designated, covering over 14 per cent of England and Wales. (The designation does not extend to Scotland, where there are National Scenic Areas.) They are designated in the same way as national parks, i.e. the Countryside Agency makes a proposal for designation which requires confirmation by the Secretary of State, normally after extensive consultation (in only one case has there also been a public inquiry). They rely on town planning procedures for their legal protection and the town planning powers are essentially the same as in national parks, including the duty to consult with the Countryside Agency over the making of development plans. Since the CROWA 2000 there are also duties to prepare management plans for all AONBs and keep these under review (s. 89) and relevant authorities (i.e. public bodies) must have regard to the statutory purposes of AONBs (s. 85). This duty to prepare management plans falls either on local authorities in the area or, if one has been established by the Secretary of State (under s. 86 and Sch. 13) a conservation board. Conservation boards build on non-statutory partnerships between local authorities and other key actors in AONBs, which were encouraged in the 1990s and proved to be generally successful. In practice, conservation boards are likely to be established only for larger AONBs.

However, there are significant differences too. AONBs do not have a statutory role as far as recreation is concerned (although under s. 87(1) conservation boards (only) must have regard to protecting beauty *and* its enjoyment). Nor is extra finance specifically provided for AONBs, although the establishment of the Countryside Agency brought with it some increased funding (and power to make grants to conservation boards, s. 91). But perhaps the major difference from national parks is that the local planning authority generally remains unchanged. This is the case even where a conservation board has been established. Although certain planning functions may be transferred to conservation boards, this does not extend to functions relating to development planning, development control, or planning enforcement.

8. M. Shoard, The Theft of the Countryside (London: Temple Smith, 1980), 144.

Other landscape protections

A further type of designation is *heritage coast*. Areas are selected by the Countryside Agency and the local planning authority acting together and are subject to protective policies within the planning process. Forty-four areas covering 1,493 km of coast have been designated although there have been no new designations since 1991. It should also be noted that a fairly strong Planning Policy Guidance Note No. 20, *Coastal Planning*, establishes a number of restraint policies on coastal development. Balanced against this, however, is the general policy of 'managed retreat', meaning that in certain cases coastal land is allowed to erode naturally, because stemming the erosion would not be useful.

There is a power for the Secretary of State and the Minister of Agriculture to make moorland conservation orders by Statutory Instrument (Wildlife and Countryside Act 1981, s. 42). These orders impose a notification requirement similar to that applied to SSSIs, with the intention that the national park authority may offer a management agreement. It is accordingly a criminal offence to plough or convert any moor or heath subject to an order which has not been agricultural land within the preceding 20 years, unless the national park authority has been notified in advance. This section is distinctly limited. Orders can only be made in a national park and only provide for a temporary ban on operations, and works can go ahead after 12 months even if the national park authority refuses consent for them. It does not appear that any such orders were ever made. With the strengthening of the law on the protection of SSSIs under the Countryside and Rights of Way Act 2000 (see Chapter 21) the policy approach now appears outmoded, and even as a procedural protection such orders have been superseded by the EIA Regulations covering primary conversion of uncultivated land and semi-natural areas, which are not limited to national parks but apply to all such land (see p. 871 below).

Landscape protection orders were recommended by the House of Commons Select Committee on the Environment in 1985. Despite support from the Countryside Commission, this proposal produced a very limited response from the government, which envisaged their use only as a stopgap power pending the making of a management agreement, and the proposals have never been acted upon.

Finally, there is a conditional exemption from inheritance tax if owners agree to maintain land, preserve its character and provide reasonable public access to it. This is an economic instrument which plays a role in conserving landscapes, albeit on a haphazard basis. If these measures are not undertaken, then the exemption is removed and tax is payable. Currently 319 estates and properties enjoy the exemption.

Agriculture and landscape

There is insufficient space in this book to trace the history of agricultural grants and their relationship with damage to the countryside, but in the past their availability has often been held responsible for a great number of damaging changes (see, for example, the works by Shoard and Harvey in the Further Reading section, below). The nature of agricultural grants and, indeed, of the whole shape of agriculture has changed dramatically in recent years, as farm incomes have fallen, the EC has sought to reform the Common Agriculture Policy and farmers are increasingly paid to produce landscapes and habitats. In the last 10 years, the sums of money paid in the UK under agri-environment schemes has increased from £32 million to £247 million, and now accounts for 10 per cent of total spending on agriculture.

BOX 22.6 **The changing nature of agricultural support**

One of the main criticisms levelled against the EC's Common Agriculture Policy is that it has historically subsidized farmers according to their productivity, giving farmers incentives to intensify production, bring marginal land into productivity and put excessive numbers of farm animals on their land. Some of the downsides of these payments include the removal of hedgerows and overgrazing, which is a problem both for nature conservation reasons and landscape management (and contributes to other problems, such as flooding). Recent reforms[9] have sought to change this, so that farmers are subsidized according to how much land they farm ('area payments' or 'single payments') and there will be a 'decoupling' between pro-duction and subsidy. In the UK, decoupling will come into force in 2005. One factor behind decoupling is to move agricultural support into what is known as the 'Green Box' for World Trade Organization purposes, which would signify that it has minimal or non-trade distorting impact, rather than the present CAP which is more trade distorting (and categorized in the 'Amber Box').

The impacts of decoupling may be mixed: pressures on soils, air, and water resources may reduce, but impacts on landscape and biodiversity could be damaging. To counter this, single payments will be linked to requirements to meet specific EC legislation on the environment (e.g. the Wild Birds and Habitats Directives, and Nitrates Directive),[10] and to keep farmland in good agricultural and environmental condition. This is known as cross-compliance; farmers must comply with these obligations or lose their entitlement to payments.[11] But the exact content of it remains unclear, because directives like the Habitats Directive are addressed to the Member States, not to individuals such as farmers, and because Member States will have a certain amount of discretion to determine what, e.g., 'good environmental condition' entails (at the time of writing it is envisaged that cross-compliance will be used to support the enforcement of various landscape and conservation protections, but may go beyond this to cover landscape features that are currently unprotected, such as hedgerow trees). The new support arrangements may, however, make agri-environmental schemes (see below) more attractive because they are not competing with much higher payments based on productivity.

There are three protective procedures which have an important impact on the protection of the landscape and deserve greater attention:

---

9. Under, in particular, EC Regulation 1782/2003.

10. For an example of cross-compliance being used to implement the Nitrates Directive see Box 18.4.

11. Only with intentional non-compliance is there likely to be scope for full withholding of payment; negligent non-compliance is treated differently. See the Common Agricultural Policy Single Payment and Support Schemes Regulations 2005 (SI 2005/219).

(a) Prior notification

Since 1980 there has been a scheme in which farmers in national parks and the Broads should give advance notification to the national park authority of their intention to seek agricultural grants. (A similar scheme applies in relation to SSSIs, requiring prior notification of the relevant NCC.) The scheme is non-statutory and therefore is not backed up by any legal sanctions, but it has had a high success rate in preventing objectionable proposals from being carried out.[12] The then Countryside Commission recommended that the scheme be extended to cover AONBs.

The scheme works as follows. The farmer should notify the national park authority of an intention to seek agricultural grant. If no objection is received, the work may go ahead. If there is an objection, discussions follow between the two parties, and the Rural Development Service within DEFRA is able to mediate at this stage. If a satisfactory arrangement cannot be reached informally, one solution is for a management agreement to be concluded under the Wildlife and Countryside Act 1981, s. 39.

If no agreement can be reached, the farmer may seek a decision on the grant from the Minister of Agriculture, who may approve or refuse it. The possibilities for damaging development are thus either that (a) the Minister approves the grant against the opposition of the national park authority; or (b) the farmer goes ahead with the works without grant.

In making the decision, the Minister is under a duty to seek to achieve a reasonable balance between the interests of agriculture and of conservation of the natural beauty of the countryside (Agriculture Act 1986, s. 17), and this may be given as the reason for a refusal. However, the Minister may give as the reason for the refusal of grant the objection by the national park authority, in which case the authority is under a duty to offer a management agreement, to which the financial guidelines made under the Wildlife and Countryside Act 1981, s. 50 will apply (see the 1981 Act, s. 41(4)), although it does not appear that this procedure has ever been used.

(b) Environmentally sensitive areas (ESAs)

These designations formally date from EC Regulation 797/85 on Improving the Efficiency of Agricultural Structures, which permitted Member States to give special aid to farmers in environmentally sensitive areas. However, the current powers are modelled on an experimental scheme established earlier in the Broads to solve the problems experienced in Halvergate Marsh as a result of proposals to plough part of the Marsh.[13] Effect was given to the EC Regulation in Britain by the Agriculture Act 1986, s. 18, which allows DEFRA to designate an ESA after consultation with the Countryside Agency and English Nature, or with the Countryside Council for Wales, with the aim of conserving landscape and wildlife. Twenty-two ESAs covering 1.1m hectares have been designated in England. There are six ESAs in Wales covering 165,000 hectares, but the scheme there is now closed to new applicants (see the discussion of Tir Gofal below). Overall in the UK, around 15 per cent of agricultural land area is subject to an ESA.

Within these ESAs standard rates of annual payment are made by DEFRA to farmers in return for their agreeing to farm in accordance with specified practices. The order establishing each ESA includes a list of practices (and of grant rates) specially tailored for that ESA,

12. *Farm Grant Notifications in National Parks* (Countryside Commission, 1987).
13. See the Broads Grazing Marshes Conservation Scheme 1985–8.

but the exact terms of each agreement are a matter for the management agreement between the farmer and DEFRA. One important point about these protections, apart from the fact that they rely wholly on the voluntary agreement of the farmer, is that payment is made by DEFRA rather than by the conservation bodies. Another is that, by providing for standard rates of payment for standard practices, the system is administratively far simpler than the one established for SSSIs, where each management agreement has to be negotiated individually (although this has not prevented strong criticism by the Public Accounts Committee about high administrative costs). As a result, the take-up rate for the ESA scheme is far higher, and in England continues to rise steadily.

(c) Countryside Stewardship/Tir Gofal

The Countryside Stewardship scheme was originally established in 1991 on a pilot basis by the Countryside Commission in England as a means of wider countryside conservation outside of ESAs. The Scheme is now run by DEFRA, although unlike ESAs the scheme is not restricted to farm businesses. The revised scheme aims to protect, restore and re-create targeted landscapes, their wildlife habitats and historical features. There are therefore both nature conservation and landscape management objectives.

A slightly extended range of landscape types are now eligible, including chalk and limestone grassland; lowland heath; waterside land; uplands; old meadows and pastures; and field boundaries. As with ESAs the scheme is entirely voluntary on both sides, and applicants enter into agreements, usually for 10 years, to undertake specified conservation works. One criterion used to determine which applications are successful is opportunity for public access. By 2000 around 10,000 agreements had been entered into in England, and a recent review of the Scheme indicates considerable success in achieving additional environmental improvements beyond what might have been achieved in the absence of the Scheme.

In Wales the pilot Tir Cymen scheme has been replaced by Tir Gofal, which incorporates features not merely of ESAs and Countryside Stewardship, but also incorporates nature conservation management agreements. As with Countryside Stewardship the scheme extends to whole farms, and has no explicit statutory basis.

It is anticipated that, from 2005, a new scheme in England—the Environmental Stewardship Scheme—will be established, the twin aims of which are to broaden the scope of using positive assistance and provide for more targeted payments where these are needed. A two-tier payment scheme will therefore be established. The main innovation lies in the lower tier—the 'Entry Level Scheme'—which will not be restricted to specific features, habitats, or landscape types, making it open to most farmers. Modest support for limited commitments from landowners will be available, but it does seek to incentivise landscape and nature conservation into wider countryside management and move beyond an 'enclave' approach. The higher tier will be more targeted, and will be more akin to that in ESAs and under CSS (and existing agreements under these schemes would be transferred).

(d) The EC Rural Development Regulation (1257/99)

As an adjunct to the Common Agriculture Policy, the EC has since 1992 operated an agri-environment policy intended to support farmers to merely as food producers but also as custodians of nature conservation and landscape interests. The 1992 Agri-Environment Regulation was replaced, as from 1 January 2000, by Chapter VI of the EC

Rural Development Regulation (1257/99). This allowed for financial support to be given for 'agricultural production methods designed to protect the environment and to maintain the countryside' (Art. 22). Farmers have to commit for at least five years, though the Member States are given a lot of room to decide what practices must be undertaken (or avoided) to get the money. The Countryside Stewardship Scheme is one way in which the Rural Development Regulation is implemented. (In Scotland, note the Rural Stewardship Scheme (under SSI 2001/300)). As the name suggests, the main aim of the Regulation is in keeping farmers on the land, especially in more marginal areas.

Finally, under the Environment Act 1995, s. 98, DEFRA and the Welsh Assembly may make grants for any purposes conducive to the conservation or enhancement of the natural beauty or amenity of the countryside (including its flora and fauna), or the promotion of the enjoyment of the countryside by the public.

Agriculture, landscape, and EIA

Projects for the use of uncultivated land or semi-natural areas for intensive agricultural purposes have always been listed in Annex II of the EC Environmental Impact Assessment Directive. However, their inclusion in schedule 2 to the general implementing regulations covering town and country planning was always meaningless, since these activities fall outside the town and country planning system. This gap was (very belatedly) plugged by the Environmental Impact Assessment (Uncultivated Land and Semi-Natural Areas) (England) Regulations 2001 (SI 2001/3966). The particular importance of these regulations lies in the fact that a consent procedure is—for the first time—established, because projects must be screened for the significance of their environmental impact and, if they are likely to give rise to significant environmental effects, then an Environmental Statement must be submitted to DEFRA and the consent of the Secretary of State given. Guidelines indicate a range of landscape designations and considerations (and other factors, such as designated conservation areas) that the Secretary of State will take into account (Defra Guidelines, 2002). A particular feature of these regulations, therefore, is that they provide for criminal liability if uncultivated land is brought into more intensive production without EIA, and there have been successful prosecutions under this provision (see (2004) ENDS Report 353, p. 162). It is unclear whether 'intensive' is an objective or a relative term.

Trees, woodland, and hedgerows

The rest of this chapter looks at the protection afforded to trees, woodlands, and hedgerows. What we see is a development from early, mainly negative, controls such as the use of tree preservation orders (TPOs), which have existed in town and country planning law since 1932, towards a more varied approach, encompassing the use of economic instruments and consumer information. We also see a slight shift in emphasis from pure amenity considerations (which have always been to the fore with TPOs) towards wider environmental considerations. A good example of these are the limited environmental duties to which the Forestry Commission is subject when granting felling licences, although the primary focus of forestry legislation with trees as commercial items means that this general area is covered only briefly. The conservation of some trees can, of course, be safeguarded through protective designations or agreements of the kind discussed in Chapter 21.

In theory, the use of negative restrictions is particularly unsuitable for the proper management of natural resources such as trees that require positive management. Although some lessons have been learnt, the Hedgerows Regulations 1997 are arguably a throwback to 'command and control' measures, a central weakness of which is the inability to address mismanagement or neglect, now the major threat to hedgerow conservation. But there are also environmental consequences from tree or hedge *planting* (see, e.g. the concerns raised in *Kincardine and Deeside District Council v Forestry Commissioners* [1993] Env LR 151). For larger projects this is dealt with through environmental impact assessment (see the Environmental Impact Assessment (Forestry) (England and Wales) Regulations 1999, SI 1999/2228).

Tree planting on a smaller scale is unlikely to be legally regulated, falling outside the town and country planning system and being unlikely to give rise to any private law remedy, since there is neither a general right to a view (*Hunter v Canary Wharf* [1997] 2 WLR 684, and see Box 11.5) nor to light (other than light to buildings). Under Part VIII of the Anti-Social Behaviour Act 2003, local authorities now have obligations to deal with complaints about high evergreen hedges, and powers to reduce such hedges to a reasonable height. These provisions, though, are best seen as a measure to tackle neighbour disputes; they apply when the reasonable enjoyment of a neighbour's property is affected, and are not a landscape conservation provision in any wider sense. They are considered in more detail at p. 438.

Trees and planning permission

Ordinary town planning rules have a limited impact on tree protection. Planning permission is not required for the planting or cutting down of trees or woodland, because trees, being natural, are not structures or buildings for the purposes of the development control system. Section 55(2)(e) also excludes from the definition of development any change of use of land to forestry or woodland. But specific protective measures are found in sections 197–214 of the Town and Country Planning Act 1990, which deal with Tree Preservation Orders (TPOs). All references to section numbers in relation to TPOs refer to this Act.

Section 197 imposes a general duty on local planning authorities to make adequate provision for trees when planning permission is granted. This may involve attaching conditions relating to trees to the permission (e.g. that certain trees should be retained or replaced by others, or that new trees should be planted as part of the landscaping of the site). It also involves considering whether to impose a TPO on any existing trees. A further possibility is to refuse permission on the grounds that existing trees or woodland should be retained. Full advice on trees and the planning system is given in *Tree Preservation Orders: A Guide to the Law and Good Practice* (DETR, 2000).

Tree preservation orders (TPOs)

A TPO is a means by which individual trees, groups of trees or woodlands may be protected against damage. A woodland TPO is arguably the most restrictive, since it includes trees which take root after the order is made. A TPO may be imposed on specified trees 'if it appears to a local planning authority that it is expedient in the interests of amenity' (s. 198). Since the section refers explicitly to amenity, it does not seem that a tree could be protected for nature conservation purposes. Most TPOs are made in urban areas, though rural woodland may also be protected. The DETR Guidance suggests that TPOs will not normally be made on trees under good arboricultural or silvicultural management.

(a) TPO offences

Any person who, in contravention of a TPO, '(a) cuts down, uproots or wilfully destroys a tree, or (b) wilfully damages, tops or lops a tree in such a manner as to be likely to destroy it', commits an offence, unless consent has been obtained from the local planning authority (s. 210(1)). On summary conviction the maximum fine is £20,000. On conviction on indictment the level of the fine is unlimited. In determining the amount of any fine, the court must have regard to the financial benefit accruing, or likely to accrue, to the convicted person in consequence of the offence. This is a significant provision, since many offences against TPOs are committed by developers who stand to make a substantial gain on the development value of their land (see, for example, the £50,000 fine imposed on a property company for deliberately felling 25 trees after designation, reported at [1991] JPL 101). There is a further offence of contravening the provisions of a TPO (s. 210(4)), for which the maximum fine is £2,500. This will cover such things as ignoring conditions imposed on works permitted by a TPO. If no other enforcement action works, an injunction to stop contravention of a TPO is available (s. 214A), though courts will be reluctant to exercise their discretion to issue an injunction except in clear cases. One notorious persistent offender (a Kent farmer) was, however, imprisoned for failing to comply with the terms of an injunction.

These offences may be committed by any person, not just the owner or occupier of the property. They are offences of strict liability (see generally p. 283). Thus, in *Maidstone Borough Council v Mortimer* [1980] 3 All ER 552, a contractor was guilty of an offence even though the owner of the site had assured him that consent for the works had been given. (It seems that the owner would also commit an offence in such a situation, because the contractor is acting as an agent.) This strict position is justified by the fact that a TPO is a public document (it is a local land charge), so anyone can check the position before carrying out works.[14]

Part of the offence requires that it be committed 'wilfully'. This has been interpreted to mean that it is the act of damaging or destroying the tree that must be wilful (i.e. deliberate), not the contravention of the TPO. *Barnet London Borough Council v Eastern Electricity Board* [1973] 1 WLR 430 illustrates that this may include a negligent act. In that case, contractors negligently damaged the roots of six trees subject to a TPO, shortening their life expectancy.

---

14. Compare the justifications for the strictness of felling licences (see Case box 22.4).

The Divisional Court held that this amounted to a wilful destruction. The case also illustrates that the concept of destruction includes something less than immediate death to the tree, e.g. ring-barking.

(b) Making a TPO

The local planning authority has responsibility for making TPOs. This normally means the district planning authority, or the national park authority in a national park.[15] The authority which imposes the TPO is then the relevant local authority for all procedures for consent and for enforcement purposes. The Secretary of State has a reserve power to make a TPO under section 202, although this is unlikely to be used much.

The procedures for making a TPO are set out in the Town and Country Planning (Trees) Regulations 1999 (SI 1999/1892). The local planning authority produces a draft TPO, which is placed on public deposit, and all owners, occupiers and those with felling rights are notified. At least 28 days are then allowed for objections, which must be considered before the local planning authority itself confirms the TPO (prior to 1980 a TPO required confirmation by the Secretary of State). There is no appeal against the making of a TPO, though there is a right to challenge its validity in the High Court under section 288. In practice, arguments about the desirability of protecting the tree are considered at the stage of seeking consent to fell.

Normally a TPO does not have effect until it is confirmed. But under section 201 a provisional (or interim) TPO may be made by the local planning authority. This is done simply by stating that section 201 applies and the TPO will then have immediate effect, though it will lapse if not confirmed within six months. Such a provisional TPO is of obvious use where there is an imminent threat of felling.

Each TPO is separately drafted and accompanied by a map. This position allows for flexibility (e.g. conditions specific to that TPO may be attached, or permitted woodland management operations may be established for a coppiced woodland), but it does make the making of a TPO quite a cumbersome process—certainly more cumbersome than those protective designations where all that is required is that standard rules or restrictions apply to the designated land. However, there is a standard form, which is set out in the Schedule to the 1999 Regulations, and most TPOs will be substantially in the form set out in the schedule. The normal position is therefore that TPOs include a list of permitted operations and of prohibited operations, some of which are especially tailored for that site.

BOX 22.7 **What is a tree?**

In *Kent County Council v Batchelor* (1976) 33 P & CR 185, Lord Denning MR somewhat arbitrarily suggested that a diameter of 7–8 inches at least was needed before something could be said to be a tree. However, this was expressly not accepted by Phillips J in *Bullock v Secretary of State for the Environment* (1980) 40 P & CR 246, who thought that anything ordinarily called a tree could

---

15. A county planning authority has jurisdiction over its own land and where it grants planning permission (e.g. on waste disposal or minerals applications).

be covered by a TPO. In that case he accepted expressly that a coppiced woodland could be covered, a position which seems sensible, since from an ecological point of view a coppice is effectively a single entity and not a collection of unconnected trees. Phillips J's view is to be preferred and is supported by section 206(4). This states that a TPO will attach to any tree planted as a replacement for one subject to a TPO. Such a replacement will often be a sapling or smaller tree. However, although the dividing line is imprecise, some things cannot be the subject of a TPO, e.g. hedges, bushes and shrubs. It appears to be accepted that a stump of a tree is capable of remaining a tree if it is still alive. So a TPO can continue to apply to felled trees but not uprooted trees.

A further issue relates to whether local authorities actually have the resources to make TPOs. It appears that a number of local authorities have adopted a policy of not making any further TPOs because of the time and expense involved. The legality of such a policy must be questioned, as it appears to amount to an effective fettering of discretion.

(c) Defences to TPO offences

There are a number of exceptions to these offences:

- Some works are permitted in the TPO itself. For example, the standard form of TPO exempts works on cultivated fruit trees, and now also any pruning of a fruit tree if this is in accordance with 'good horticultural practice'. Also exempt are the 'cutting down, topping, lopping or uprooting of a tree' where needed to implement a planning permission. There has, though, been some narrowing in relation to development permitted under the GPDO. This is only exempted if carried out by a statutory undertaker or body like the Environment Agency.

- It is possible to seek consent from the local planning authority (see below).

- It is an exception to cut down, uproot, top or lop trees which are dead, dying or dangerous, or 'so far as may be necessary for the prevention or abatement of a nuisance' (s. 198(6)). The nuisance exception relates to the position where a tree is a civil nuisance. It is potentially a very wide exception, because it may be a civil nuisance for a tree to affect a neighbour's foundations or access,[16] but presumably if measures short of cutting down or uprooting could abate the nuisance then the exception would not apply to more drastic action. However, it is not a nuisance to deprive a neighbour of the right to a view or the right to light to his land (see p. 872), so this section would not justify interference with protected trees on these grounds (though the 'high hedges' provisions of the Anti-Social Behaviour Act 2003 might be used, see p. 438).

- There are further exceptions where the Forestry Commission is already effectively controlling forestry activities on the land through a forestry dedication covenant, or a grant or loan made under the Forestry Acts (s. 200).

---

16. On which see the important decision in *Delaware Mansions v Westminster City Council* [2001] UKHL 55.

CASE 22.2 *Elliott v Islington London Borough Council* [1991] 1 EGLR 167

This case illustrates the potential for conflict between public and private rights when dealing with private nuisance. Mr Elliott obtained a mandatory injunction against Islington LBC requiring that a horse chestnut tree, which was in an adjoining park and was damaging his garden wall, be removed. (The tree was not actually subject to a TPO because it was the council's practice not to designate trees on its own land, but this does not affect the point being made.) It is believed that the injunction was in fact never enforced following a later compromise agreed between the parties, but in the Court of Appeal Lord Donaldson MR showed the primacy accorded to private rights over the public interest when he stated, 'It is not generally appropriate to refuse to enforce specific private rights on the basis that that would cause hardship to the public: the court would be legislating to deprive people of their rights.'

(d) Consent

It is possible to apply to the local planning authority for consent to carry out any works which are prohibited by a TPO. Any consent which is granted may be subject to conditions, such as the planting of replacement trees. There are no publicity requirements for an application for consent, though Circular 36/78 encourages it and notification of neighbours and the placing of site notices are common. There is an appeal to the Secretary of State[17] against a refusal of consent, and the procedures and powers on an appeal are similar to those for an appeal against refusal of planning permission, although they give effect to recent proposals on streamlining (see p. 492). There are now powers to vary or revoke a TPO (reg. 9), which would fulfil the same purpose.

CASE 22.3 *Robinson v East Riding of Yorkshire Council* [2003] JPL 894

Robinson wanted to use some of his extensive grounds for touring caravans, which would involve felling a number of trees. As a matter of urgency, and following a brief inspection, the council made a TPO covering all the grounds (including areas without trees). The Court observed that, depending on the circumstances, protecting landowners' rights might mean that more specific orders rather than one 'blanket' TPO may be needed, at least in the long run. But the law relating to TPOs was inevitably anticipatory in character, and there are safeguards to protect landowners' interests. Although a TPO cannot be appealed, the same result is achieved by seeking consent from the local authority to carry out works on a tree, and an appeal to the Secretary of State thereafter (see above). Hence 'The making of a tree preservation order is . . . the beginning of the road and not the end of it'. The appeal was dismissed.

(e) Replacement trees

The replacement of trees covered by a TPO may be required by the terms of the TPO itself (e.g. in return for permitted works), by a condition attached to a planning permission, by

---

17. Inevitably, Inspectors who will visit the site will hear appeals. The scope for the Secretary of State, on the basis of papers and photographs only, to reach a different decision to the Inspector will be limited; see *Richmond upon Thames LBC v Secretary of State for the Environment, Transport and the Regions (Tree Preservation Order)* [2002] JPL 33.

the terms of a consent, or by section 206. Section 206 provides that, if a tree is removed or destroyed in contravention of a TPO, or because it was dead, dying or dangerous, a replacement tree of appropriate size and species must be planted at the same place as soon as reasonably possible. The owner may ask the local planning authority for this requirement to be lifted. The TPO attaches to the replacement tree.

Special provisions apply to woodlands. There is no need to replace a dead, dying or dangerous tree, and the obligation is to replace the same number of trees on or near those removed, or as agreed by the local planning authority. Flexibility has been provided in such a case because it will often be impossible to determine exactly how many trees were removed and from where (reg. 8).

(f) Enforcement notices

Since contravening a TPO is itself a criminal offence, there is less need for an enforcement notice requirement than for ordinary breaches of development control. But there is a power for the local planning authority to serve an enforcement notice where a replanting obligation is not complied with. Such a notice must be served within four years of the failure and may require such replanting as is specified by the authority (s. 207). There is a right of appeal against an enforcement notice to the Secretary of State, who may uphold, modify, or quash it (s. 208).

Failure to comply with an enforcement notice is not a criminal offence but the local planning authority may enter the relevant land, carry out the replanting as required, and recover the cost from the owner (s. 209).

Conservation areas

All trees in a designated conservation area are subject to a statutory restriction (effectively a statutory TPO) which prohibits the cutting down, lopping, topping, uprooting, wilful damage or wilful destruction of the tree (s. 211). This is more limited than most individual TPOs. In addition, regulations may be made by the Secretary of State that exempt specified works (s. 212).

There is one crucial difference between these statutory TPOs and ordinary ones: prohibited acts may go ahead six weeks after notification of an intention to do them has been given to the local planning authority. The purpose of this section is to enable the local planning authority to have prior notification of potentially damaging works to trees in conservation areas. (A similar form of control is applied for the protection of SSSIs—see p. 813.) It then has six weeks in which to decide whether to impose a TPO: if it does not the works may go ahead. It is an offence to do any of the prohibited acts without notifying the local planning authority and waiting six weeks, unless consent is given earlier. The penalties for this offence, and the replanting and enforcement provisions, are the same as for ordinary TPOs.

Compensation

No compensation is payable for the imposition of a TPO, but it is payable where loss or damage is caused by a refusal of consent (including revocation or modification) or by a conditional consent (s. 203).

Originally it was thought that this compensation was payable to compensate for the value of cut timber forgone, but this assumption was shown to be unwarranted by *Bell v Canterbury City Council* [1989] 1 JEL 90. In this case the Court of Appeal confirmed that the level of compensation payable was for the loss in value of the land. Accordingly, it awarded compensation at £1,000 per acre to a farmer who was prevented from converting a coppiced woodland to beef or sheep farming. Such large amounts of compensation would obviously limit the use of TPOs by local authorities, especially on woodlands which may have potential for agricultural or urban development.

An immediate response was to alter the existing regulations, namely the TPO Regulations 1969. It had always been possible for the local planning authority to certify that refusal was in the interests of good forestry or that the trees were of outstanding or special amenity value: in such a case no compensation would be payable. This certificate was originally available for individual trees, but the 1969 Regulations were amended (in SI 1988/963) to apply the procedure to woodlands. However, a more significant response was to alter the practice of the Forestry Commission in relation to woodland TPOs. In woodland, the volume of timber being cut will normally require a felling licence from the Forestry Commission (see below). Normally, the Commission would refer any application relating to trees subject to a TPO to the local planning authority. However, a change of practice consequent to *Bell v Canterbury CC* was that the Commission agreed to refuse a felling licence if TPO consent would be refused. The effect is that the Commission pays compensation, but at the level set out in the Forestry Act 1967, which relates to the value of the timber. The 1999 Regulations give statutory effect to this position by limiting compensation to loss in value of the timber, and then applying this valuation method to trees covered by felling licences. Losses under £500 cannot be recovered.

Proposals for change

The 1999 Regulations give effect to some of the changes suggested as far back as 1990 when the Conservative Government issued a consultation paper entitled *Review of Tree Preservation Policies and Legislation*, and later in a further review of the legislation in 1994. Many of the proposals made there, however, would require primary legislation, including amending section 201 so that all TPOs have immediate effect and proposals to give local authorities positive powers to demand works on protected trees. This has not been forthcoming.

Forests

There are legal controls on afforestation and deforestation, involving economic incentives and other voluntary schemes, licensing powers, and the utilization of private property rights.

BOX 22.8 **Forests—lessons from history, satellites, and trade**

The word 'forest' has legal origins, originally being used to mark out land for deer—and not necessarily for trees—and delineating land where specific Forest Law and Forest courts operated.

The legal Forest was nearly always much wider than the physical forest, to cover deer when they strayed beyond the trees. This, as Oliver Rackham notes, led scholars to make the double error of assuming that land described as forest represented physical forest, and that all these areas were wooded. 'Hence the pseudo-historical belief that medieval England was very wooded.' Today, there are twice as many trees as there were a century ago, probably more than at any time since the Middle Ages, a resurgence almost entirely due to planting. Much of this planting, however—which until recently tended to be monocultures of fast-growing spruce—has been considered unfavourable, both in landscape and nature conservation terms. And, notably, despite this increase the UK is one of the world's largest importers of wood products, importing around 85 per cent of its timber needs.

Afforestation

Outside of any requirement for environmental impact assessment, the main tool used to regulate afforestation is incentive payments, of which there are two main schemes. The removal in the 1988 Budget of the notorious tax breaks relating to forestry was, it appears, effected to ensure that no significant afforestation would occur without the official approval which grant aid effectively provides. This duly happened, although a dramatic reduction in new planting followed. The Woodland Grant Scheme, dating from 1990, marks a clear departure from the previous overriding policy objective of timber production (which led, by 1984, to 98 per cent of Forestry Commission plantings being non-native conifers, mainly the much-despised Sitka spruce).

The scheme has several purposes, which include the pursuit of landscape, conservation and amenity objectives. This multi-purpose approach is restated in *Our Forests—The Way Ahead: Enterprise, Environment, Access* (Cm 2644, 1994). To be eligible for funding, projects must have regard to landscape considerations, and must include a diversity of tree species. Higher sums are paid for broadleaved woods, reflecting in part their greater landscape and nature conservation importance, and the majority of new planting is now broadleaved. There is also the Farm Woodland Premium Scheme (SI 1992/905) which, as its name suggests, is designed to encourage the creation of new woodlands on farms, the underlying purpose being to take land out of agricultural production. Payments under this scheme—approvals being made under the EC Rural Development Regulation (1257/1999)—reflect agricultural revenues forgone.

Felling licences

By contrast with the minimal legal controls over afforestation, under section 9(2) of the Forestry Act 1967, a felling licence is required from the Forestry Commission for the felling of trees over 8 cm in diameter (15 cm in coppices) measured 1.3m from the ground. It is an offence to fell without a licence, which again may be committed by anyone (see *Forestry Commission v Frost* (1989) 154 JP 14). Fines either of up to £2,000 or twice the value of the trees when they were felled can be imposed, but in practice the development value of the land without the trees may far exceed this. However, that the sanctions are so low, and non-custodial, does have a bearing on whether criminal liability can be imposed without mens rea (i.e. whether the Act gives rise to strict liability criminal offences; see Case box 22.4).

CASE 22.4 *R (Grundy & Co Excavations Ltd) v Halton Division Magistrates Court* [2003] EWHC Admin 272

How do the courts view tree-felling offences? Here, the claimants had felled 86 trees without a licence, but they had done so in agreement with the landowner. Clearly the landowner was guilty of an offence, but were the contractors? This is obviously an important practical issue, because land-owners will rarely undertake large-scale felling personally. The answer turned on whether the offence was one of strict liability, or whether *mens rea* (criminal intent) was needed. With environmental crimes like water pollution offences we have seen that the courts have dispensed with the need for *mens rea* because the regulatory system would otherwise be unworkable, although the price of doing so has been to label such crimes as quasi-criminal and not 'true' crimes (see p. 285 above). Here, the Court of Appeal thought that the offence of unlicensed tree felling was:

plainly on the 'quasi-criminal' and not the 'truly criminal' side of the line. . . . The offence involves only a monetary penalty and carries no real social disgrace or infamy and no moral stigma or obloquy. It is a classic regulatory offence designed not . . . to protect segments of the public such as employees, common consumers and motorists, but to protect the nation's trees . . . comparatively little weight should be attached to the presumption that *mens rea* is required before a person can be held guilty of a criminal offence and that the presumption is displaced here because it was clearly or by necessary implication the intention of the statute. The statute is concerned with an issue of public concern, namely the preservation of the country's natural heritage and, to my mind the creation of strict liability is likely to promote these objects.

Felling controls are based on commercial factors, rather than on amenity factors. However, the Forestry Commission is under a duty to endeavour to achieve a balance between the management of forests and the conservation of landscape and nature (Forestry Act 1967, s. 1(3A), inserted by the Wildlife and Countryside (Amendment) Act 1985, s. 4). A felling licence is not required for fruit trees, trees in gardens, orchards, churchyards, or public open space, topping or lopping of trees, operations under a forestry dedication scheme, thinning trees less than 10cm in diameter, or harvesting less than 5 cubic metres of timber per quarter. Nor is a licence required where felling is immediately required for development authorized under the town and country planning system, or where the felling is necessary for preventing danger or preventing or abating a nuisance. The onus is on the defendant to prove that he can rely on one of these exceptions. Because, for example, the defendant is best placed to say what the diameter of a tree was, and the licensing system would be unworkable otherwise, this onus is not incompatible with human rights law (*Grundy*, Case box 22.4).

To avoid duplication of effort, if a felling licence is required and there is a TPO in force, the following procedure applies. The application goes to the Forestry Commission, which has three choices: it may refer the matter to the local planning authority, in which case the TPO legislation applies; it may refuse the licence, in which case it will pay compensation under the Forestry Act 1967; or it may grant a licence. A felling licence is the equivalent of a TPO consent, but before the Commission grants a licence it must consult with the local planning authority. If the authority objects to a proposed grant of a licence, the matter is referred to the Secretary of State for decision. If a licence is granted there is an obligation to restock the land, unless the Commission waives it (see the Forestry Act 1986).

LANDSCAPE MANAGEMENT • **881**

Consultation on felling and afforestation

There are no formal requirements for the Forestry Commission (or in the case of the Farm Woodland Premium Scheme, DEFRA) to consult on applications for felling licences or grant applications. However, it is Forestry Commission policy to consult local authorities and bodies such as the Countryside Agency and English Nature about grant applications, and all applications for new planting are placed on a public register. In both cases there is an appeal, ultimately to the Minister.

Community forests and the National Forest

There is a 'Forests for the Community' programme run as a joint venture between the Countryside Agency and Forestry Commission, together with local authorities. The aim is to promote the creation, regeneration and multi-purpose use of well-wooded landscapes around major towns and cities. Community forests are non-statutory designations, and their establishment is facilitated in part through planning policy guidance under which development plans should play a facilitative role and provide that any development proposals within them respect the woodland setting. Their establishment therefore relies heavily on the exercise of private rights by the Forestry Commission. To date there are 12 Community Forest areas in England, together with the National Forest in the Midlands, the establishment of which is being facilitated in a similar way.

Consumer information and certification schemes

One consequence to emerge from the Forest Principles and from Agenda 21, both agreed at the 1992 Rio Earth Summit (see p. 157), has been the emergence of forest management certification and ecolabelling as a preferred policy approach both of producers and of wider civil society (such as environmental NGOs). At national level, we now have the UK Woodland Assurance Scheme,[18] which aims to assure purchasers of wood products in the scheme that the timber has come from sustainably managed sources. The voluntary scheme is notable for being a partnership between the public and private sectors, and environmental organizations, and operates through a combination of auditing of producers by a certification body, and subsequent use of an ecolabel.

Hedgerows

There has been an enormous loss of hedgerows since 1945, mainly as a result of agricultural intensification. However, hedges have never had the same protection as trees, because the definition of a tree means that the TPO legislation does not apply to hedges, though it is capable of applying to trees in hedgerows. Numerous promises were made in relation to hedgerow protection until finally the Environment Act 1995, s. 97, made provision for the protection of special categories of hedgerows (but only in England and Wales). Under this

18. And now also the Forest Stewardship Council (FSC) UK Standard.

section, the Secretary of State has the power to make regulations prohibiting the removal, damage or destruction of 'important hedgerows'. The Hedgerows Regulations 1997 (SI 1997/1160) generally apply to a wide class of hedgerows (in particular to hedgerows which are 20 metres or more long or which meet another hedgerow at each end and which, in each case, are on or adjacent to land used for certain specified purposes). Domestic hedgerows are excluded.

The protection is basic, to say the least. An owner (or in certain cases a relevant utility operator) must notify the local planning authority before removing any hedgerow, or stretch of hedgerow. The local planning authority has 42 days in which to serve a retention notice, failing which consent is deemed to have been given. Consent can only be refused if the hedgerow is important. The 'unimportant' hedgerows can be removed after that period. To qualify as an important hedgerow the hedge must be not less than 30 years old and must comply with certain detailed criteria laid down within the regulations relating to such matters as the number and type of species contained in the hedgerow. Thus, the range of hedgerows which can actually be protected is relatively narrow.

The accompanying Guidance emphasises cooperation with farmers rather than confrontation, thus continuing the tradition of voluntariness found in other areas pre-CROWA. Where an offence is committed, however, fines can be imposed on defaulters (as with TPOs, the courts are directed to take account of any financial benefit accruing from the removal) and the courts can also order replanting.

CASE 22.5 *Conwy County Borough Council v Lloyd* [2003] Env LR 264

In this case a landowner served a removal notice on the local authority, but before the 42-day period expired he removed the whole hedgerow. He was prosecuted, but successfully argued that what he had done was permitted under the Regulations as being for the 'proper management of the hedgerow' (reg. 6(1)(j)) since it was claimed the hedge was at risk of collapse and dangerous to livestock and machinery. On appeal the local authority argued that proper management could not mean the removal of the whole hedgerow, particularly a hedgerow of some 100 metres length. But the Court held that the 'very structure of the Regulations themselves . . . contemplate the possibility of removal without notice'. Whether removal constituted 'proper management' was a question of fact. While this approach may be correct in law, the danger is that unscrupulous landowners may be encouraged to remove a hedgerow—on 'proper management' grounds—in order to make it harder for the local authority to determine whether the hedge was important. The position is not helped by the absence of any requirement to replant hedges which have been removed for management reasons (a requirement which would seem to be justified in cases like this where it is the *condition* of the hedge that was the alleged problem).

The Hedgerow Regulations have been criticized for placing too much emphasis on the need for objectively verifiable indicators of importance, and thus restricting their ambit to a small category of hedges (around 20 per cent) of historic importance. For Holder, this is a consequence of seeing the importance of hedgerows as 'little more than the sum of their parts', rather than trying to give weight to matters of cultural and local importance ([1999] MLR 100). This is also evidenced in the absence of public consultation built into the regulations.

A government review of the Hedgerow Regulations in 1998 merely observed that giving greater powers to local authorities to determine local importance would reduce the consistency, and commercial certainty, currently provided for. However, the review went on to recommend various reforms which would allow for local distinctiveness to be a factor in assessing 'importance' (e.g. beech hedges in Exmoor), although this still falls some way short of local recognition of local importance. The review also suggested that the presence of priority species in the UK Biodiversity Action Plan could also be an indicator of 'importance', which would go some way towards the Hedgerow Regulations making more of a contribution to nature conservation. Nevertheless, loss of natural and cultural features through neglect, which has now overtaken uprooting as the greatest threat to hedgerows, would still not be addressed in law.

In the absence of control under the regulations, other legal remedies may be possible. These include individual enforcement of the provisions of enclosure Acts, such as in *Seymour v Flamborough Parish Council, The Times*, 3 January 1997, where Cracknell J ordered the Council to preserve what was an 'undistinguished, badly maintained, straggly and unkempt' hawthorn hedge because it was still bound by the Flamborough Enclosure Act 1765 which required the parish council to maintain the hedge forever, a somewhat ironic note on which to end a book on 21st century environmental regulation.

CHAPTER SUMMARY

1 Landscape management ranges from the protection of wide areas of land for their scenic value, down to much smaller objects like trees and hedgerows.

2 The challenge for the law is that this often involves controlling destructive, rather than constructive, acts and establishing adequate control over natural things. What is a valued landscape, tree etc is a subjective judgement.

3 Protecting the most prized areas for their landscape value involves land designations, but on designated land the controls used are either slightly stronger planning laws than would normally apply, or the use of positive assistance.

4 Prized landscapes do not have the same kind or degree of legal protection that important habitats enjoy. They remain working environments rather than wildlife havens and are not immune from development.

5 Increasingly, nature conservation and landscape management goals are pursued together, e.g. through management planning or financial incentives.

6 In the wider countryside, economic instruments are the policy tool of choice, because the aim is positive protection of the countryside. Traditional legal tools are almost never used.

7 Financial assistance can be given by a countryside agency under an agreement, or it can be given as a condition of an agricultural subsidy (cross-compliance). There is a clear shift towards paying farmers to conserve or establish landscape and wildlife.

8 Local authorities can require tree planting when planning permission is granted, but otherwise town and country planning law does not generally cover tree planting and felling.

9 The main exception to this is when a local planning authority makes a tree preservation order. These can protect anything from an individual tree to a woodland from destruction.

10 Commercial afforestation is generally steered by the use of grants, which now encourage the planting of native trees and with much greater emphasis on landscape and conservation.

11 Commercial tree felling must be done under licence.

12 Local authorities can conserve important hedgerows by serving retention notices, but this power is quite limited in scope.

Q QUESTIONS

1 Are there 'standards' for landscape conservation?

2 Sam and Tina flee the rat-race and buy a small farm in a national park. They aim to farm the land as an experiment in sustainable agriculture; this will involve re-roofing their house with photo-voltaic cells and setting up a mini 'Eden Project' in a natural dip in the land. To help pay the bills, they intend to allow paying visitors into the glass houses. Some local residents are concerned about the impact of the project, including the loss of a stand of trees and a section of hedgerow if the development goes ahead. Advise the local authority.

3 (Assuming prior knowledge of Chapter 21) How do the legal controls on landscape differ from those that are used to conserve nature? Think about:

   a any different policy issues

   b the legal force of their respective objectives

   c the tools used to achieve these objectives.

   Does the level of protection for landscape and landscape features seem adequate?

4 Look at the Council of Europe European Landscape Convention <www.coe.int>. Advise Ministers whether, in your view, the UK ought to sign and ratify.

FURTHER READING

Greater detail than we can provide here can be found in J. Garner and B. Jones, *Countryside Law*, (3rd edn Crayford: Shaw & Sons, 1997) and in J. Rowan-Robinson and D. McKenzie Skene (eds) *Countryside Law in Scotland* (Edinburgh: T and T Clark, 2000) and—in relation to the latter sections of this chapter—C. Mynors, *The Law of Trees, Forests and Hedgerows* (London: Sweet & Maxwell, 2002).

Many books on planning law include a brief chapter on tree preservation. C. Willmore, 'What's in a Name? The Role of "National Park" Designation' [2002] JPL 1325 looks at whether national parks really live up to expectations about their level of protection, while J. Holder, 'Law and Landscape: The Legal Construction and Protection of Hedgerows' [1999] MLR 100 considers the Hedgerows Regulations 1997 against a backdrop of reflections on legal constructions of landscape.

On policy questions, M. Shoard, *The Theft of the Countryside* (London: Temple Smith, 1980) puts the case for extending planning controls to agriculture and forestry, and G. Harvey, *The Killing of the Countryside* (London: Jonathan Cape, 1997) focuses on the negative effects of the Common Agricultural Policy. A more optimistic version of conservation (and landscape amenity) in the wider countryside is B. Green, *Countryside Conservation* (London: E & FN Spon, 1996), which examines the range of policy options in this area, in particular whether to make agriculture generally less extensive, or to allow further intensification on the best farmland and use the remaining land primarily for its amenity and conservation value.

Beyond the legal literature, we must mention some outstanding works which give a rounded appreciation of nature and landscape, especially Oliver Rackham's superlative works *The History of the Countryside* (London: Orion Publications, 2000) and *Trees and Woodlands in the British Landscape* (Abingdon: Routledge, 1996), and K. Thomas, *Man and the Natural World* (London: Penguin, 1984). More recently, the role that values and perceptions play in our understanding of the countryside, and the conflicts that arise, has been the subject of two outstanding and engaging works: T. Smout, *Nature Contested* (Edinburgh: Edinburgh University Press, 2000) and P. Macnaghten and J. Urry, *Contested Natures* (London: Sage, 1998).

@ WEB LINKS

An excellent general starting point for web research is Naturenet <www.naturenet.net>, which has comprehensive links to numerous official (and unofficial) sites, as well as brief information about countryside law. In terms of official policy and information the main starting points are the national countryside agencies—the Countryside Agency <www.countryside.gov.uk>, the Countryside Council for Wales <www.ccw.gov.uk> and Scottish Natural Heritage <www.snh.org.uk>—and central government <www.defra.gov.uk>; <www.scotland.gov.uk>, and <www.wales.gov.uk>. The web sites of the national agencies usually contain reports to government on the state of the countryside, and now have postcode searching to establish whether land is within an ESA etc. The Association of National Parks <www.anpa.gov.uk> and the Association of AONBs <www.aonb.org.uk> provide helpful information about these areas. For forestry issues, start with the Forestry Commission <www.forestry.gov.uk>.